was transformed into one of the finest palaces in the world.

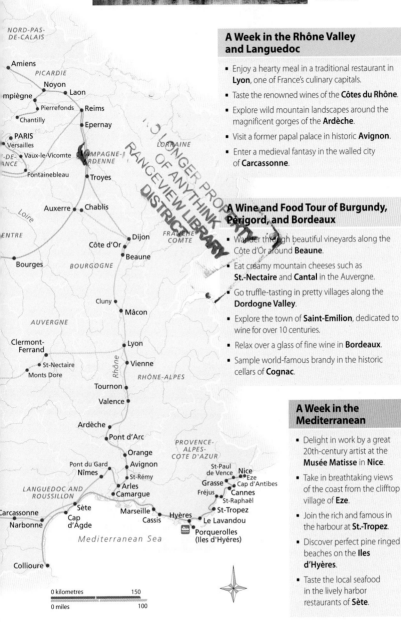

## A Week in the Rhône Valley and Languedoc

- Enjoy a hearty meal in a traditional restaurant in **Lyon**, one of France's culinary capitals.
- Taste the renowned wines of the **Côtes du Rhône**.
- Explore wild mountain landscapes around the magnificent gorges of the **Ardèche**.
- Visit a former papal palace in historic **Avignon**.
- Enter a medieval fantasy in the walled city of **Carcassonne**.

## A Wine and Food Tour of Burgundy, Périgord, and Bordeaux

- Wander through beautiful vineyards along the Côte d'Or around **Beaune**.
- Eat creamy mountain cheeses such as **St.-Nectaire** and **Cantal** in the Auvergne.
- Go truffle-tasting in pretty villages along the **Dordogne Valley**.
- Explore the town of **Saint-Emilion**, dedicated to wine for over 10 centuries.
- Relax over a glass of fine wine in **Bordeaux**.
- Sample world-famous brandy in the historic cellars of **Cognac**.

## A Week in the Mediterranean

- Delight in work by a great 20th-century artist at the **Musée Matisse** in **Nice**.
- Take in breathtaking views of the coast from the clifftop village of **Eze**.
- Join the rich and famous in the harbour at **St.-Tropez**.
- Discover perfect pine ringed beaches on the **Iles d'Hyères**.
- Taste the local seafood in the lively harbor restaurants of **Sète**.

The great glass pyramid entrance to the Musée du Louvre, viewed from across the fountain pool

## Two Days in Paris

*With its great art, glorious architecture, chic shopping, gourmet food, and unique street life, the French capital offers an array of attractions.*

- **Arriving** Charles-de-Gaulle international airport is about 18 miles (30 km) from the city. RER Line B trains run frequently to central Paris (40 mins). International trains arrive at seven Paris stations, all with connections to the city Métro network.

- **Booking ahead** It is wise to book tickets for the Eiffel Tower in advance.

### Day 1

**Morning** There is so much to see and do in Paris that a two-day visit can only be a taster, but for a first dose of Parisian atmosphere begin with a café breakfast on the riverside docks of **Ile St.-Louis** *(p89)*, for a fabulous view of the Seine and the buttresses of **Notre-Dame cathedral** *(pp90–91)*. Then stroll across to the Ile de la Cité to visit the cathedral itself and see the Gothic jewel of **Sainte-Chapelle** *(p88)*. Cross to the Left Bank on the **Pont Neuf** *(p87)* and walk along the docks to the **Musée d'Orsay** *(pp124–5)*. Allow about 2 hours, and don't miss the Impressionist masterpieces and stunning paintings by van Gogh and Toulouse Lautrec. Then cross back to the Right Bank for a rest and lunch in one of the **Louvre**'s courtyard restaurants.

**Afternoon** Give at least 2 to 3 hours to the **Musée du Louvre** *(p104–7)*. The display of historic art is vast and awe-inspiring. Be sure to see the *Mona Lisa* and the Greek and Roman sculptures. Then take a break in the **Jardin des Tuileries** *(pp102–3)* and wander up to **Place de la Concorde** *(p102)* for majestic vistas. From there, take a taxi or bus along the **Champs-Elysées** *(pp110–12)* to the **Arc de Triomphe** *(p111)*, and go to the top to watch the chaotic traffic below. Return to the center for dinner, stopping to browse the chic fashion stores on **rue St.-Honoré** and irresistible food stores in **Place de la Madeleine** *(p101)*.

### Day 2

**Morning** Explore the bohemian Left Bank, beginning at the **Panthéon** *(p129)* and **La Sorbonne** *(p127)* in the

The iconic Eiffel Tower, from across the River Seine

old **Latin Quarter** *(pp128–9)*. Wander through the district toward the river, perhaps with a stop at **Musée de Cluny** *(pp126–7)* for Roman baths and medieval art, then head west to **St.-Germain-des-Prés** *(p126)*, past lively rue de Buci with its street market. Stop for coffee in one of the classic intellectual cafés, Café de Flore or the Deux Magots. Then cross the Seine through the Ile de la Cité and head right to enter the **Marais** *(pp92–3)* district for lunch on **place des Vosges** *(p95)*, arguably Paris's most attractive square.

**Afternoon** Stroll around the 17th-century streets of the Marais, with their trendy stores, cafés, and historic Jewish Quarter. Return to modern Paris at the **Centre Pompidou** *(pp96–7)*; (2 hours), to see works by Picasso, Matisse, and other 20th-century masters, and the views from the tube-like escalators. Then take the Métro or a cab – or walk part of the way along the river – to the **Eiffel Tower** *(p117)*, and get to the top in time for the views at sunset. Dine in one of the Tower restaurants, or, for less view but more Parisian color, head to boulevard du Montparnasse to eat in one of its classic 1920s brasseries.

> **To extend your trip...**
> Spend a day in the **Luxembourg Quarter** *(pp130–31)* and window-shop on **rue du Faubourg-St-Honoré**.

## A One-Week Tour of Great Architectural Sites

*Within a short distance of Paris, discover an extraordinary range of famous buildings – Gothic, Renaissance, and Baroque.*

- **Airports** Arrive and depart from Paris.
- **Transportation** A rental car is essential for the full route, but many places can be visited by train on day trips from Paris.
- **Booking ahead** Advisable at Versailles in July and August.

### Day 1: Versailles, Vaux-le-Vicomte, Fontainebleau
Louis XIV's palace of **Versailles** *(pp178–81)* is the epitome of regal grandeur. Take time to walk through the equally magnificent gardens to the Trianon palaces and Marie Antoinette's village. Rest for lunch, then drive south to more discreet **Vaux-le-Vicomte** *(pp182–3)*, model of French 17th-century mansion style, and Napoleon's favorite palace at **Fontainebleau** *(pp184–5)*. Relax after châteaux-visiting in the lovely surrounding forest.

### Day 2: Chartres to the Loire Valley
Head west to **Chartres** *(p310)* to the most intact of all medieval **cathedrals** *(p312–15)*. The stories and images in its stunning

stained glass are fascinating to trace. Move on to Renaissance architecture at **Blois** *(pp308–9)*, one of the first royal châteaux. Explore the old town before a short hop east to François I's vast palace at **Chambord** *(pp306–7)*, surrounded by a delightful wooded park.

### Day 3: The Loire: Amboise to Chinon
Looming over the tiny town, the royal château of **Amboise** *(p305)* has a dramatic history, and a few streets away is the Clos-Lucé mansion, where Leonardo da Vinci lived just before his death. Nearby, **Chenonceau** *(pp302–3)* and its gardens typify the grand life of the Loire Valley châteaux. For one of the loveliest French gardens, stop at **Château de Villandry** *(p300)*. A very different château is **Chinon** *(pp298–9)*, a 12th-century fortress built for Henry II of England, in a medieval town known for fine wines.

### Day 4: Fontevraud to Bourges
The Benedictine **Abbaye Royale de Fontevraud** *(p298)* reflects the deep spirituality of the Middle Ages. To the east, the rugged ruined keep at **Loches** *(p304)* is one of the oldest Loire castles, set in an exquisite walled town. Nearby is idyllic **Montrésor** *(p305)* with its 15th-century castle. In the afternoon head to **Bourges** *(p317)*, a little-known gem with a giant cathedral and

Stained-glass window at Chartres Cathedral in the Loire Valley

a Gothic merchant mansion, the Palais Jacques Coeur.

### Day 5: Into Champagne
Northeast from Bourges, in Burgundy, **Auxerre** *(pp334–5)* is famed for the cathedral and its fine stained glass. Champagne and Picardy contain several great Gothic monuments. Ancient **Troyes** *(p220)* has a wonderful old center of Gothic churches and half-timbered houses. Carry on north through green hills and vineyards to **Epernay** *(p215)*, home of Champagne, and visit at least one cellar for a tasting.

### Day 6: Reims to Amiens
Explore **Reims** *(pp214–15)* and its magnificent **cathedral** *(pp216–17)*, site of the coronations of French kings. To the northeast in Picardy are a number of astonishing Gothic cathedrals: **Laon** *(p209)*, with its curious carvings; harmonious **Noyon** *(p205)*; and glorious **Amiens** *(p204)*, with a facade that has been called "the Bible in stone."

### Day 7: Royal Compiègne and Chantilly
The château and forest at **Compiègne** *(p205)* were a royal hunting estate for centuries. Napoleon III's own Neo-Gothic castle, **Château de Pierrefonds** *(p205)*, is nearby. To the south, visit the Musée Conde inside the **Château de Chantilly** *(pp208–9)*. Don't miss the *Très Riches Heures du Duc de Berry*, one of the world's finest medieval manuscripts.

Champagne vineyards at Ville-Dommange, near Reims

## A Week in Northern France

- **Airports** Arrive and depart from Paris.
- **Transportation** A rental car is essential for the full route, but many places can be visited by train on separate trips from Paris.
- **Booking ahead** Advisable at Champagne cellars on weekends.

### Day 1: Giverny, Rouen, and Honfleur

Travel to **Giverny** *(p270)* in time for the 9:30am opening of Monet's house (Apr–Oct only), and enjoy the stunning colors of the artist's garden with the fewest crowds. In the afternoon, continue down the Seine Valley to lively **Rouen** *(pp268–9)* and its three great Gothic jewels: the churches of St.-Ouen and St.-Maclou, and the magnificent cathedral, painted many times by Monet. Finish the day with dinner beside the quaint harbor at **Honfleur** *(p266)*.

### Day 2: Heart of Normandy

Living up to its name, the **Côte Fleurie** (Flowery Coast); *(p259)*, west of Honfleur, contains attractive beach resorts including the bohemian Trouville and elegant Deauville. Just inland is Normandy's most exuberantly lush green countryside, in the cider farms of the **Pays d'Auge** *(p259)*. Linger there, or go on to

**Caen** *(pp257–8)* to visit the two great abbeys built by William the Conqueror and his queen. From there it's a short drive to **Bayeux** *(pp256–7)*, where the unmissable tapestry portrays the vivid details of William's invasion of England. Bayeux is also an ideal base for visiting the coast nearby at Arromanches and **Omaha Beach** *(p255)*, which witnessed the dramatic events of the June 1944 Allied invasion.

### Day 3: Mont-St.-Michel and St.-Malo

Soaring up out of the sea, **Mont-St.-Michel** *(pp260–65)* is one of France's greatest sights, a magical monument to medieval ambition. It dominates the view as you continue west around the giant bay, past charming **Cancale** *(p287)*, toward **St.-Malo** *(p286)* and its fascinating walled city. Relax on the city's beaches or across the river at **Dinard** *(p285)*, a classic Breton beach resort.

### Day 4: Rennes to Tours

Turn inland to visit Brittany's capital, **Rennes** *(pp288–9)*, with its half-timbered houses, and on the way west don't miss **Vitré** *(p289)*, a picture-book medieval walled town. Stop for lunch in **Le Mans** *(p295)*, famed for motor racing but also for its fascinating ancient city and Roman walls. Join the Loire Valley at **Tours** *(pp300–1)* and visit the soaring Gothic cathedral and atmospheric riverside old quarter.

### Day 5: Loire Valley Highlights

The Loire is famously studded with magnificent mansions. Be sure to see luxurious **Chenonceau** *(pp302–3)*, regal **Amboise** *(p305)*, and majestic **Chambord** *(pp306–7)*. Then cross the river north to **Chartres** *(pp311–15)*, and stay in the town to enjoy the spectacular light show around the cathedral (mid-Apr–mid-Sep only).

The imposing facade of the cathedral at Reims

### Day 6: Reims and Champagne Country

Start early and drive east around Paris on the outer-ring roads to **Reims** *(pp216–17)* and its sumptuous cathedral. Relax after the drive by visiting some of the famous Champagne houses in Reims and in the soft green countryside toward **Epernay** *(p215)*. Continue on to **Troyes** *(pp220–21)*, with another fine Gothic cathedral and a delightfully preserved old city.

### Day 7: Into Burgundy

Burgundy's capital **Dijon** *(pp344–6)* has a particular grandeur inherited from the days when the region's dukes were a great power in the medieval world. To the south, some of the world's most celebrated vineyards, many open to visitors, extend along the **Côte d'Or** *(p348)* down to the delightful old wine town of **Beaune** *(p348)*, with its superb **Hôtel-Dieu** *(pp350–51)*.

> **To extend your trip…**
> Continue through the southern Côte d'Or to **Lyon** *(pp382–5)* or head east to **Besançon** *(p354)*.

Normandy's Mont-St.-Michel, one of the most enchanting sights in France

*For practical information on traveling around France, see pp632–41*

The famous medieval fortified town of Carcassonne

## A Week in the Rhône Valley and Languedoc

- **Airports** Arrive at Lyon and depart from Toulouse airport, or arrive and depart from Paris and take trains to Lyon (2 hours) and back from Toulouse (5 and a half hours).
- **Transportation** A rental car is essential to tour the route after Vienne.

### Day 1: Lyon
France's sophisticated second city, **Lyon** (pp382–5) has an array of attractions, from Roman amphitheaters and a lovely old quarter to trendy stores and a variety of museums. It's also one of France's culinary capitals, so be sure to sample *cuisine lyonnaise* in a *bouchon* or traditional restaurant.

### Day 2: Vienne and the Côtes du Rhône
Take the train or rent a car and make the short journey south to **Vienne** (p386), a charming town with an extraordinary concentration of Roman relics as well as a Gothic cathedral. In the afternoon, drive down the Rhône Valley to **Valence** (p388), with detours east near **Tournon-sur-Rhône** (p388) to taste robust red Côtes du Rhône wines in the village of Tain l'Hermitage.

### Day 3: The Ardèche
The rugged rocky hills west of the Rhône contain dramatic scenery around the spectacular gorges of the fast-flowing **Ardèche** (pp388–9) river. Make a detour to wander among captivating hill villages and enjoy stunning views, ending up at the fabulous natural bridge Pont d'Arc, near Vallon-Pont d'Arc.

### Day 4: Orange and Avignon
Return to the Rhône and head for **Orange** (p506), with its Roman theater and Arc de Triomphe. Nearby, the vineyards of **Châteauneuf-du-Pape** (pp506–7) are famed for their powerful red wines. **Avignon** (pp507–9) is perhaps the archetypal southern French city, with its golden stone walls, relaxing squares, and warm sunlight, plus the 14th-century **Palais des Papes** (pp508–9), 12th-century bridge, and vibrant summer arts festival.

### Day 5: Arles to the Camargue
Little **St.-Rémy-de-Provence** (p511) is where Vincent van Gogh produced many of his famous paintings. He is also associated with **Arles** (pp512–13), where many places he painted are easy to recognize. Don't miss the Roman amphitheater. The misty

Diners in Lyon enjoying traditional cuisine at a small bistro known as a *bouchon*

flat landscape of the **Camargue** (pp514–15) also begins just outside town. Head back north to the astonishing Roman aqueduct **Pont du Gard** (pp498–9) before arriving in Nîmes for the night.

### Day 6: Nîmes to Narbonne
Ancient **Nîmes** (pp500–1) has France's most complete Roman monuments in the Maison Carrée, the giant Arènes amphitheater, and more. Spend much of the day there, or head southwest along the coast for lunch in the great Mediterranean port of **Sète** (p496). Take a walk along the harbor and then continue to **Narbonne** (pp490–91). See the Gothic cathedral and cloisters, before ending the day in Carcassonne.

### Day 7: Carcassonne and Toulouse
**Carcassonne** (pp492–3), a carefully restored medieval city of stone walls and winding alleys, stuns everyone who sees it. Visitors who stay overnight can explore before the crowds arrive toward noon. From there it's a short distance to **Toulouse** (pp450–51), with, at its heart, a charming old town and historic buildings such as the Jacobins church and Musée des Augustins, housed around an exquisite Gothic cloister.

### To extend your trip...
Drive west from Toulouse to the university town of **Pau** (p462); (2 hours) or to the Atlantic surf beaches around **Biarritz** (p456); (3 hours).

The River Dordogne, viewed from the village of Trémolat, near Sarlat

## A Wine and Food Tour of Burgundy, Périgord, and Bordeaux

*This tour takes you to some of France's classic regions for fine wines and food, focusing on local specialties along the way.*

- **Airports** Arrive at Paris, and depart from there or Bordeaux. Rent a car in Paris or take trains to Auxerre (2 hours) and back from Bordeaux (just over 3 hours).
- **Transportation** A rental car is essential.
- **Booking ahead** Required at larger Burgundy vineyards and the châteaux wine estates near Bordeaux.

### Day 1: Chablis to the Côte d'Or
Burgundy's northernmost wine district is found just east of **Auxerre** *(pp334–5)* around the pleasant village of **Chablis** *(p335)*, famed for delicious whites. Make a brief stop in **Dijon** *(pp344–6)* before reaching one of the most famous and beautiful wine regions in the world along the **Côte d'Or** *(p348)*. The roads here are lined with village names magnetic to any wine lover – Nuits-St.-Georges, Gevrey-Chambertin – and there are plenty of great opportunities for tasting. End the day in lovely **Beaune** *(p348)*, which has a wine museum in a Gothic palace as well as the famous Hôtel-Dieu hospital.

### Day 2: Beaune to Beaujolais
Continue down the southern half of the Côte d'Or, and for a change from wines stop to visit the impressive ruins of **Cluny Abbey** *(p349)*. In the afternoon, leave the main routes south of Mâcon to explore the charming villages and vineyards of the **Beaujolais** *(p381)* district. Stay the night in **Lyon** *(pp382–5)*, and enjoy some of the city's famous cuisine.

### Day 3: The Auvergne
To the west, beyond Clermont-Ferrand and the extinct volcanoes the **Monts Dore** *(p366)*, the mountains of the Auvergne are known for fine soft cheeses such as **Cantal** *(p367)* and **St.-Nectaire** *(p364)*. Driving westward through rugged landscapes, be sure to explore the enticing displays of local produce in village stores and markets, reaching the borders of Périgord in the evening.

Vineyards and fields in the wine district around Chablis

### Day 4: Périgord and the Dordogne
The Périgord region and Dordogne Valley are equally famed for beautiful scenery and delicious foods. Window-shop and learn about truffles in the capital **Périgueux** *(p435)*, and be sure to catch the spectacular market in **Sarlat** *(pp436–7)*. Try the Périgord's famed specialties – truffles, duck, *foie gras* – in the restaurants of the many pretty villages along the Dordogne, notably **Domme** *(p439)*.

### Day 5: Saint-Emilion to Bordeaux
**Saint-Emilion** *(pp426–7)* has been producing wine since Roman times, and its winding streets are full of historic buildings and early medieval churches. Visit famous estates in the village of **Figeac** *(p427)*, and in nearby Libourne and Pomerol. Then head into Bordeaux to end the day with a relaxing drink in the city's Maison du Vin wine center.

### Day 6: Bordeaux and Graves
The center of **Bordeaux** *(pp424–7)* retains its 18th-century grandeur. Admire the huge Neo-classical **Grand Théâtre** *(p426)*, and stroll along the docks beside the River Garonne. Later, explore the southern areas of Bordeaux's wine region around Graves and Sauternes, known for sweet dessert wines, or, if you have time, head south to **Mont-de-Marsan** *(p429)*, home of Armagnac.

### Day 7: Médoc and Cognac
The grandest Bordeaux wines – Château Mouton-Rothschild, Château Latour – all come from the Médoc district north of the city around **Pauillac** *(p427)*, from estates presided over by grand châteaux that provide a luxurious setting for tasting. If there's time, return to Bordeaux and head north to **Cognac** *(pp422–3)* for a sample of its famous brandy.

> **To extend your trip...**
> Relax on the beaches and sample seafood at **La Rochelle** *(p420)* and the **Ile d'Oléron** *(p421)*.

## A Week in the Mediterranean

*This tour visits some of the finest beaches and beauty spots of France's celebrated south coast.*

- **Airports** Arrive and depart from Nice, Toulouse, or Paris. Return to Nice (6 and a half hours) or Paris (5–6 hours) by train from Perpignan.
- **Transportation** Several parts of the trip can be made by train, but for others a car is essential.
- **Booking ahead** Pre-book boat trips from Cassis to the Calanques in July and August.

Bright sun and Mediterranean colors seen from the perched village of Eze

### Day 1: Nice
Capital of the Côte d'Azur, **Nice** *(pp530–31)* has superb restaurants and an elegant seafront. Don't miss the Musée Matisse, with stunning works by the painter who celebrated Mediterranean colors more than any other artist. In the afternoon, rent a car to visit the exquisite coastline east of the city, at **Cap Ferrat** *(p532)* and especially the clifftop village of **Eze** *(p533)*, for unforgettable views over the Riviera.

### Day 2: St.-Paul de Vence to Cannes
Take a car and drive inland to **St.-Paul de Vence** *(pp528–9)*, an artists' mecca full of echoes of Picasso and Chagall, and the perfume capital of **Grasse** *(p521)*, ringed by fields of lavender and jasmine. Drop down to the sea again for a look at the

opulent **Cap d'Antibes** *(p525)* before ending the day in ever-fashionable **Cannes** *(p524)*.

### Day 3: West to St.-Tropez
All along the winding coast road west from Cannes there are magnificent views and seascapes. The road runs into **St.-Raphaël** *(p521)* and **Fréjus** *(p521)*, two pleasant, relaxed resorts with long beaches. Farther west again, **St.-Tropez** *(p520)* has been the chicest spot on the Riviera since Brigitte Bardot arrived in the 1950s. Watch the fashion parade around the harbor, and count the luxury yachts.

### Day 4: Island Beaches
The coast road west through Le Lavandou to the charming harbor of **Hyères** *(p518)* is one of the loveliest on the Côte d'Azur, but there is also a faster inland road. From Hyères take a boat to Porquerolles, the largest of the **Iles d'Hyères** *(p519)*, with turquoise seas and perfect beaches that are easily explored by rented bicycle. Return to Hyères to stay for the night.

> **To extend your trip…**
> Stay overnight to enjoy Porquerolles' beaches to the full, or spend a day exploring **Marseille** *(pp516–17)*.

### Day 5: Cassis and the Calanques
**Cassis** *(p517)* is one of the most vibrant small towns on the Provençal coast, with a lively

café-lined fishing harbor. The surrounding coast is magnificently wild and rocky, and boats run regularly to the **Calanques** *(p517)*, jagged inlets accessible only by sea that are fabulous for swimming and known for an abundance of birds and wildflowers.

### Day 6: Sète and Cap d'Agde
Leave your car in Marseille and take an early train to **Sète** *(p496)*; (2 hours) to transfer to a very different Mediterranean coast, in Languedoc. Sète is an atmospheric old port town, with superb, no-frills seafood restaurants along its canalside docks. Walk or take a train or bus beside the endless sandy beaches south toward **Cap d'Agde** *(p491)*, and watch the colorful sails running in the wind at one of Europe's foremost windsurfing and kitesurfing locations.

### Day 7: Collioure
Take another train down the coast to **Collioure** *(p487)*, a classic small Mediterranean harbor loved by artists such as Matisse and Derain. Explore the old port and medieval Catalan castle, then lie back on the beaches with a superb view of the town's imposing stone church.

> **To extend your trip…**
> Catch a boat or plane to **Corsica** *(pp536–47)* for some of France's purest Mediterranean beaches.

Rocky coastline and the narrow inlet of Calanque d'En-Vau near the Bouches-du-Rhône

# Putting France on the Map

France, one of the largest countries in Europe, has airline connections with most cities in the world. Paris is the major transportation hub, with two international airports; others include Bordeaux, Lille, Lyon, Nice, and Toulouse. There are good, high-speed train links with the rest of Europe, and a network of efficient highways. A number of ferry routes cross the Mediterranean to Corsica and beyond. Cross-Channel ferries serve several ports, with the Channel Tunnel providing an alternative link by train.

UNITED KINGDOM

Harwich

London
Reading
Ramsgate
Oostende
Dover
Portsmouth
Newhaven
Calais
Dunke
Lil
Do
M3
M20
A16
A26

*English Channel*

Abbeville
Amiens
Dieppe
A1

Cherbourg
Le Havre
Rouen

*Plymouth, Weymouth*
Caen
A13
A28
A13
PARIS
*See inset map above*

Roscoff
St-Malo
Brest
N12
Alençon
Chartres
A5
N165
Rennes
A81
Le Mans
A11
A19

Lorient
Orléans
*Loire*

0 kilometers    100
0 miles    100

St-Nazaire
Nantes
A11
Angers
*Loire*
Tours
Bourges

A85
A10

F R

*Spain*
A83
N137
Poitiers
A20
A71

Les Sables-
d'Olonne
La Rochelle

N10
Limoges
Clermont-
Ferrand
A10

A89

Brive-la-
Gaillarde

Bordeaux
A89
*Dordogne*

A63
*Garonne*
A20
Rodez
N88
Millau

N10
A65
A62
Albi

Biarritz
Toulouse
Béziers
Pau
A64
Tarbes
Carcassonne
A61

AP68
A1
A15
Perpignan
Vitoria
Gasteiz
Pamplona
Andorra
ANDORRA

AP15
S P A I N
Huesca
AP7

Soria
AP68
*Ebro*
A22
Giro

Zaragoza
Lleida
Barcelona
A2
AP2

## Europe

NORWAY
FINLAND
SWEDEN
ESTONIA
*North
Sea*
DENMARK
LATVIA
LITHUANIA
UNITED
KINGDOM
REP. OF
IRELAND
NETHERLANDS
BELARUS
POLAND
BELGIUM
GERMANY
CZECH
REP.
UKRAINE
SLOVAKIA
FRANCE
SWITZ.
AUSTRIA
HUNGARY
SLOV.
CROATIA
ROMANIA
*Atlantic
Ocean*
BOSNIA
HERZ.
SERBIA
ITALY
MONTEN.
KOS.
BULGARIA
MAC.
ALBANIA
SPAIN
GREECE
PORTUGAL
MOROCCO
ALGERIA
TUNISIA

## Key

═══ Freeway

═ ═ Freeway under construction

──── Highway

──── Train line

▬▬▬ International border

- - - Ferry route

**For keys to symbols** *see back flap*

# Regional France

France has a population of around 66 million, and receives over 85 million visitors a year. It covers an area of 210,025 sq miles (543,965 sq km). Paris is the largest city, followed by Lyon, Marseille, and the conurbation of Lille-Lens-Valenciennes. The Loire, Seine, Garonne, and Rhône are the longest of France's many rivers. This book divides the country into 15 regions, plus a separate section for Paris and Ile-de-France, although officially France comprises 13 *régions*.

**Key**

- ▭▭ Freeway
- ▭ ▭ Freeway under construction
- ▭▭ Highway
- ▭▭▭ Minor road

0 kilometers      100

0 miles      100

**For keys to symbols** *see back flap*

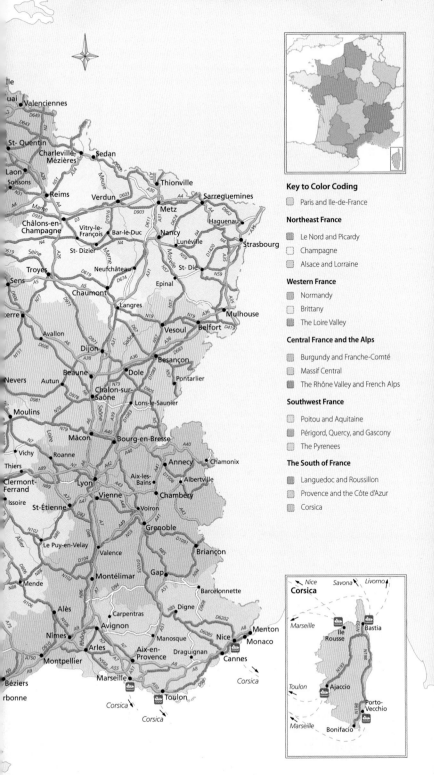

**Key to Color Coding**

Paris and Ile-de-France

**Northeast France**

Le Nord and Picardy

Champagne

Alsace and Lorraine

**Western France**

Normandy

Brittany

The Loire Valley

**Central France and the Alps**

Burgundy and Franche-Comté

Massif Central

The Rhône Valley and French Alps

**Southwest France**

Poitou and Aquitaine

Périgord, Quercy, and Gascony

The Pyrenees

**The South of France**

Languedoc and Roussillon

Provence and the Côte d'Azur

Corsica

# A PORTRAIT OF FRANCE

The French are convinced that their way of life is best, and that their country is the most civilized on earth. Many millions of visitors agree with them. The food and wine are justly celebrated. French culture, literature, art, cinema and architecture can be both profound and provocative. Whether cerebral, sensual or sportive, France is a country where anyone might feel at home.

France's landscape ranges from mountain plateaux to lush farmland, traditional villages to chic boulevards. Its regional identities are equally diverse. The country belongs to both northern and southern Europe, and encompasses Brittany with its Celtic maritime heritage, the Mediterranean sunbelt, Germanic Alsace-Lorraine, and the hardy mountain regions of the Auvergne and the Pyrenees. Paris remains the lynchpin, with its famously brusque citizens and intense tempo. Other cities range from the industrial conglomeration of Lille in the north, to Marseille, the biggest port on the Mediterranean. The differences between north and south, country and city are well-entrenched, indeed cherished. The TGV (high-speed train), internet and mobile phone technology have reduced distance (both physical and emotional) yet have simultaneously provoked an opposite reaction: as life in France becomes more city-based and industrialized, so the desire grows to safeguard the old, traditional ways and to value rural life.

The idea of life in the country – *douceur de vivre* (the good life) is as seductive as ever for residents and visitors alike. Nevertheless, the rural way of life has been changing. Whereas in 1945 one person in three worked in farming, today it is only one in 35. France's main exports used to be luxury goods such as perfumes and Cognac; these have largely been overtaken by cars, aircraft, nuclear power stations and telecommunications equipment.

Château de Saumur, one of the Loire's most romantic and complete castles

◀ Glass pyramid entrance to the Musée du Louvre, Paris

People remain firmly committed to their roots, and often retain a place in the country for holidays or retirement. On average, more French people have second homes than any other nationality; and in many areas, such as Provence, dying villages have found new life as chic summer residences for Parisians. Many artists and artisans now live and work in the country, and entrepreneurs have set up factory workshops there.

The ever-popular scooter

The decline in the influence of the Catholic Church has resulted in social changes. Today only 5 per cent of people attend Mass regularly. Many couples live together before marriage, and are allowed the same tax status as married couples. Abortion is now legal, and, since 2013, same-sex couples can legally marry.

Feminism in France has quite a different look than in Anglo-Saxon countries. French feminists are unwilling to condemn frivolous sex appeal. As EU citizens, women in France have legal equality with men, but French attitudes remain traditional. It may have seemed like a milestone in 1991, when Edith Cresson became France's first woman prime minister, but her unpopularity and the 1999 corruption case against her arguably held back women's equality in French politics. Ségolène Royal re-established a prominent political role for women when she won 47 per cent of the vote in the 2007 presidential elections, as did Martine Aubry in 2008, when she became head of the French Socialist Party.

Another female role model is Christine Lagarde, who in 2011 became the first woman to lead the International Monetary Fund (IMF). Anne Hidalgo, the first female mayor of Paris, has been pushing a progressive, eco-friendly agenda since her election in 2014.

## Social Customs and Politics

French social life, except between close friends, has always been marked by formality – hand-shaking, the use of titles, the preference for the formal *vous* rather than the intimate *tu*. However, this is changing among the younger generation, who now tend to call you by your first name. Known for their stylishness, the French have been influenced by globalisation and evolving trends. Fashion is much more functional than before, with young fashionistas making a simple pair of jeans and tee shirt look chic.

Formality lingers on, however, and France remains very legalistic – whether you are buying a house or exporting an

The May 1968 disturbances, a catalyst for profound change in France

Farming in Alsace-Lorraine

antique. But the French are insouciant about their famous red tape. Rules and laws are there to be ingeniously evaded, twisted or made more human. This sport of avoiding cumbersome bureaucracy has a name of its own, *le système D*, to be accompanied with a shrug and a smile.

After the end of the Cold War, the sharp Left/ Right divisions in French society were replaced by pragmatic centrism. For 14 years, President François Mitterrand – elected in 1981 as head of a Socialist–Communist coalition – steadily moved towards a more central-focused political agenda. In 1995, he was replaced by Jacques Chirac, who promised right-wing policies; he too moved to the centre. By 2002, immigration and security fears, broken electoral promises and political corruption had caused widespread disenchantment and a swing to the Front National. The result was the elimination of Socialist Lionel Jospin in the first round of the presidential elections and the election of Chirac by default in the second round. Further electoral discontent was revealed by the rejection of the European Constitution in 2005.

Charles de Gaulle

In 2007, Chirac's Deputy Prime Minister, Nicolas Sarkozy, won the presidency by addressing public fears and promising an end to corruption. He forged a closer relationship with the US, re-engaged France in the European Union and opened up his government to ministers from the Left. But his popularity waned in 2010, after his plans to raise the retirement age provoked strikes, and deportation of gypsies drew criticism from other European states.

In 2012, François Hollande was elected France's second Socialist president. Early reforms included increasing the income tax rate on high earnings (this was later rejected) and supporting same-sex marriage. He also sent French troops to curtail Islamic extremists in Mali. However, with a rise in unemployment figures and a slump in economic growth, Hollande's presidency reached historic levels of unpopularity. France dealt with particularly troubling times with the terrorist attacks by Islamic extremists in 2015 and 2016. With the election of centrist president Emmanuel Macron in 2017, the country hopes to move forward to understand its role in this ever-changing world.

Traditional Breton costumes, worn for festivals and *pardons*

## Culture and the Arts

Culture is taken seriously in France, and writers, intellectuals, artists, and fashion designers are held in high social esteem. As a result, the state finances a large network of provincial arts centers and has traditionally given subsidies that allow experimentation in art and design. The French remain justly proud of their own cinematic tradition and are determined to defend it against pressures from Hollywood. Other activities – from the music industry to the French language itself – are subject to the same protectionist attitudes.

Avant-garde art and literature and modern architecture all enjoy strong patronage in France. Some of the more exciting architectural projects range from the striking modern buildings in Paris – the Fondation Louis Vuitton and the Philarmonie de Paris – to the Post-Modern housing developments of Nîmes, Montpellier, and Marseille in the south.

## Modern Life

While one half of the French were heralding the new millennium in true Gallic style, the other half were plunged into darkness caused by some of the worst storms ever to hit Europe. This is an extreme illustration of French ambivalence toward modernism. France's agro-business is one of the most advanced in the world, but the peasant farmer is deeply revered. France hankers after a leading role in the world, yet the country effectively closes down for the whole of August, when the French take to the roads and coastal resorts of France. However, two factors have forced a change of pace: the internet, which France embraced keenly, and the euro, which, in one fell swoop, swept away Europe's oldest decimalized currency, the franc.

The French are enthusiastic, discerning consumers. Even small towns have stylish

The ultra-modern Philarmonie de Paris

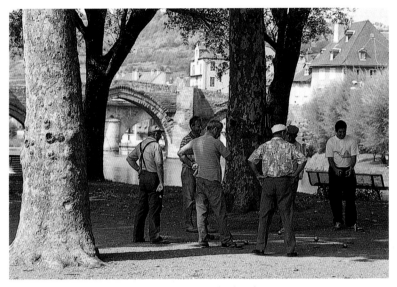

The traditional game of *boules* or *pétanque,* still extremely popular – especially in the south

clothing stores and street markets with the best of local produce. France also has Europe's largest hypermarkets, which have

Southern produce: melons, peaches, and apricots

been steadily ousting the local grocery or convenience store. These are remarkably French in what they sell: a long delicatessen counter may display 100 or so French cheeses and types of *charcuterie,* while the range of fresh vegetables and fruit is a tribute to their role in French cuisine.

However, modern pressures have been changing eating habits in a curious way. The French used to eat well daily as a matter of course. Today many are in a hurry, and for most, meals during the working week are simple – either a quick steak or pasta dish at home, or a snack in town (hence the wave of fast-food places that have sprung up, in defiance of French tradition). But meals still remain an important part of French culture – not just for the food and wines, but also for the pleasure of lengthy meals and good conversation around a table with family or friends. They will reserve their gastronomy for the once- or-twice-a-week special occasion, or the big family Sunday lunch, an important French ritual. It is at these times that the French zest for life really comes into its own.

Remote farm – a nostalgic reminder of rural life

# Areas of Natural Beauty

France has some of the most memorable and diverse landscapes in Europe. While often pushed to the background in favor of fairytale towns or majestic castles, the natural landscape is hardly less impressive. Two dramatically different coastlines feature in the north and south, with prominent mountain ranges towering in the east, south, and west. In between there are lush marshes, plunging gorges, and ancient volcanos. Mix in a diverse range of flora and fauna, and France is a nature-lover's haven. Every region has some natural wonder to discover.

**Etretat Cliffs**
These famous cliffs in Normandy overlook the English Channel where the coastline draws summer crowds.

**Côte de Granit Rose**
The north of France along the English Channel has its share of beautiful locations. These pink-hued beaches in Brittany are not least among them.

**Loire Valley**
Most travelers come here for the châteaux, but the Loire Valley is also known for the wildlife that royalty used to hunt here. Today, the paths lining the river are popular with cyclists.

**Marais Poitevin**
The "Green Venice" of France includes miles of canals through the marshland carved by monks centuries ago, and is populated with a rich variety of wildlife.

Amiens
Le Havre
Rouen
Caen
Paris
Rennes
Le Mans
Orléans
Nantes
Tours
Poitiers
La Rochelle
Limoges
Bordeaux
Toulouse
Pau

**Cirque de Gavarnie (The Pyrenees)**
In the southwest of France, this soaring natural amphitheater is part of the natural wonders hewn through the mountains and hills by glaciers over the past millennium.

**Auvergne**
The most wilderness-like region of France, complete with former volcanoes, the Auvergne attracts hikers, nature lovers, and sports enthusiasts to its Massif Central.

**Burgundy**
Rolling vineyards and stone formations make up the landscapes that get even better with a few glasses of the local wine.

0 kms 100
0 miles 100

Lille

Reims

Nancy

Strasbourg

Troyes

Dijon

urges

Lyon

St-Etienne

Briançon

Montpellier

Nice

Aix-en-Provence

**Trois Vallées**
These stunning mountains and valleys are best known for their wintertime skiing, when France's elite hit the slopes, but summertime hiking reveals equally beautiful views through the mountain passes.

**Gorges du Verdon**
Cut by the Verdon River millions of years ago, this breathtaking gorge is today a popular route for kayakers who paddle through the limestone structures.

**Corsica**
The Scandola Nature Reserve surrounding the Golfe de Porto is just one of seemingly endless natural wonders to explore on the island of Corsica, which boasts 620 miles (1000 km) of pristine coastline.

**The Camargue**
Sandy beaches and marshland are home to flocks of rosy flamingoes that share the landscape with white horses and black bulls in this Mediterranean marvel.

**Calanques**
The Calanques, stunning cliffs and islets surrounded by the blue Mediterranean, are best explored by boat while visiting Marseille or Cassis.

# The Wines of France

Winemaking in France dates back to pre-Roman times, although it was the Romans who disseminated the culture of the vine and the practise of winemaking throughout the country. The range, quality, and reputation of the fine wines of Bordeaux, Burgundy, the Rhône, and Champagne in particular have made them role models the world over. France's everyday wines can be highly enjoyable too, with plenty of good-value ones now emerging from the southern regions.

Traditional vineyard cultivation

## Wine Regions

Each of the ten principal wine-producing regions has its own identity, based on grape varieties, climate, and *terroir* (soil). *Appellation d'Origine Protégée* laws guarantee a wine's origins and production methods.

**Key**

- ▢ Bordeaux
- ▢ Burgundy
- ▢ Champagne
- ▢ Alsace
- ▢ Loire
- ▢ Provence
- ▢ Jura and Savoie
- ▢ The Southwest
- ▢ Languedoc and Roussillon
- ▢ Rhône

## How to Read a Wine Label

Even the simplest label will identify the wine and provide a key to its quality. It will bear the name of the wine and its producer, its vintage, if there is one, and whether it comes from a strictly defined area (*Appellation d'Origine Protégée*), or is a more general *IGP* (*Indication Géographique Protégée*) wine or *vin de France*. It may also have a regional grading, as with the *crus classés* in Bordeaux. The shape and color of the bottle is also a guide to the kind of wine it contains. Green glass is often used, since this helps to protect the wine from light.

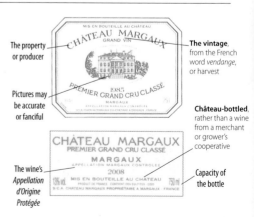

The property or producer

The vintage, from the French word *vendange*, or harvest

Pictures may be accurate or fanciful

Château-bottled, rather than a wine from a merchant or grower's cooperative

The wine's *Appellation d'Origine Protégée*

Capacity of the bottle

## How Wine is Made

Wine is the product of the juice of freshly picked grapes, after natural or cultured yeasts have converted the grape sugars into alcohol during the fermentation process. The yeasts, or lees, are normally filtered out before bottling.

Old wine press

### White Wine     Red Wine

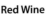

**Newly harvested grapes**, whether red or white, are first lightly crushed to bring the sugar-rich juices into contact with the yeasts in the grape skins "bloom."

**Red wine** gets its backbone from tannins present in red grape skins. The stems also contain tannins, but of a harsher kind; most winemakers de-stem most or all of their red grapes before they crush them.

Tanks for maceration

Crusher and de-stemmer

**For young** white wines and some reds (eg simple Beaujolais) that do not gain complexity from ageing, the crushed grape juice may be steeped, or macerated, with the grape skins for a few hours to add aroma and flavor.

**Pressing** comes at a different stage for white and red grapes. White wine uses only free-run or lightly pressed juice for the freshest, fruitiest flavors. For red wine, the grapes are pressed after fermentation; this *vin de presse*, rich in tannins and other flavors, can be blended back into the wine as needed.

Press

**Fermentation** is a natural process, but can be unpredictable; nowadays, many growers use cultured yeasts and hygienic, temperature-controlled stainless-steel tanks to control fermentation and ensure consistent results.

**Early drinking wines** may be filtered straight into their bottles, but barrels are used to age many finer wines. The flavors imparted by the oak are an integral part of many wines' identities – for example, the tobaccoey "wood-shavings" character of red Bordeaux.

Fermentation vat

Oak casks

Different shades of glass identify the wine regions

Bottle shapes typical of red Bordeaux (left) and Burgundy

# Artists in France

Artists have always been inspired by France, especially since landscape became a legitimate subject for art in the 19th century. Art and tourism have been closely linked for over a century, when the establishment of artists' colonies in the forest of Fontainebleau, Brittany, and the south of France did much to make these areas attractive to visitors. Today, one of the pleasures of touring the countryside is the recognition of landscapes made famous in paintings.

**A few months** before his tragic death in July 1890, Vincent van Gogh painted *The Church at Auvers*. He noted that the building "appears to have a violet-hued blue color; pure cobalt."

**Gustave Courbet,** socialist and leader of the Realist School of painting, captured this famous coastal town in *The Cliffs at Etretat after a Storm* (1870).

**Emile Bernard** was fascinated by the wild, almost primitive character of the Breton landscape and the individuality of its inhabitants. He was one of the community of artists based in Pont Aven. His *La Ronde Bretonne* (1892) portrays local Celtic customs.

**In his** *Eiffel Tower* (1926) Robert Delaunay investigated the abstract qualities of color. His wife, artist Sonia Delaunay, said, "The Eiffel Tower and the Universe were one and the same to him."

**Neo-Impressionist** artist and exponent of Pointillism, Paul Signac indulged his love of maritime subjects on the coasts of France. *Entrance to the Port at La Rochelle* (1921) shows his use of myriad dots of color to represent nature.

Amiens

Le Havre

Rouen

Caen

Paris

Rennes

Le Mans

Orleans

Tours

Nantes

Poitiers

La Rochelle

Limoges

Bordeaux

Toulouse

Pau

| 0 kilometers | 100 |
| 0 miles | 100 |

**Follower of** the French Classical tradition of landscape painting, Jean-Baptiste-Camille Corot recorded *The Belfry of Douai* (1871).

**Scenes from** everyday life were realistically rendered by Gustave Courbet, as here in *Young Ladies of the Village Giving Alms to a Cow Girl in a Valley near Ornans* (1851–2).

ile

**Maurice Utrillo** painted this village scene, *The Church of St. Bernard, Ain, in Summer* (1924), while staying at his mother's home. The sombre tone and emptiness reflect his unhappy life.

Reims

Nancy

Strasbourg

Troyes

Dijon

Bourges

Lyon

St-Etienne

Briançon

Aix-en-Provence

Nice

Montpellier

**Théodore Rousseau,** the leading light of the Barbizon School *(see p185)* of landscape painters, visited the Auvergne in 1830. It was here that he began to paint "en plein air" (in the open air). The results are seen in this sensitively observed scene, *Sunset, Auvergne* (around 1830).

**The French Riviera** attracted many artists *(see pp476–7)*. Raoul Dufy particularly appreciated its pleasures, seen in this typical scene of blue skies and palm trees, *The Pier and Promenade at Nice* (1924).

*Landscape at Collioure* (1905) depicts the vivid colors of this little Catalan fishing village. It was here that Henri Matisse founded the art movement of the Fauves, or "Wild Beasts," who used exceptionally bright, expressive colors.

# Writers in France

Writers and intellectuals traditionally enjoy high prestige in France. One of the most august of French institutions is the Académie Française, whose 40 members, most of them writers, have pronounced on national events and, on occasion, held public office.

The work of many French novelists is deeply rooted in their native area, ranging from the Normandy of Gustave Flaubert to Jean Giono's Provence. In addition to their literary merit, these novels provide a unique guide to France's regional identities.

Colette's house in Burgundy

## The Novel

The farmland of the Beauce, where Zola based his novel, *La Terre*

The most renowned Renaissance writer in France was Rabelais, in the 16th century, a boisterous, life-affirming satirist *(see p299)*. Many writers in the Age of Enlightenment that followed emphasized the tradition of reason, clarity, and objectivity in their work. The

Marcel Proust, author of *Remembrance of Things Past*

19th century was the golden age of the French humanist novel, producing Balzac, with his vast fresco of contemporary society; Stendhal, a critic of the frailties of ambition in *Scarlet and Black*; and Victor Hugo, known for epics such as *Les Misérables*. George Sand broke ground with her novels such as *The Devil's Pool*, which depicted peasant life, albeit in an idealized way. In the same century, Flaubert produced his masterwork *Madame Bovary*, a study of provincialism and misplaced romanticism. In contrast, Zola wrote *Germinal*, *La Terre*, and other studies of lower-class life.

Marcel Proust combined a poetic evocation of his boyhood with a portrait of high society in his epic novel, *Remembrance of Things Past*. Others have also written poetically about their childhood, such as Alain-Fournier

in *Le Grand Meaulnes* and Colette in *My Mother's House*.

A new kind of novel emerged after World War I. Jean Giono's *Joy of Man's Desiring*, and François Mauriac's masterly *Thérèse Desqueyroux*, explored the impact of landscape upon human character. Mauriac, and also George Bernanos in his *Diary of a Country Priest*, used lone spiritual struggle as a theme. The free thinker André Gide was another leading writer of the inter-war years with his *Strait is the Gate* and the autobiographical *If it Die*.

In the 1960s Alain Robbe-Grillet and others experimented with Nouveau Roman, which subordinated character and plot to detailed physical description. Critics held it in part responsible for the decline of the novel. Acclaimed best-selling contemporary writers include Michel Houllebecq and Catherine Cusset, while Mark Levy's many novels include *If Only It Were True*, which was made into a Steven Spielberg movie in 2005.

Hugo's novel *Les Misérables*, made into a musical in the 1980s

## Theater

The three classic playwrights of French literature, Racine, Molière, and Corneille, lived in the 17th century. Molière's comedies satirized the vanities and foibles of human nature. Corneille and Racine wrote noble verse tragedies. They were followed in the 18th century by Marivaux, writer of romantic comedies, and Beaumarchais, whose *Barber of Seville* and *Marriage of Figaro* later became operas. Victor Hugo's dramas were the most vigorous product of the 19th century. The exceptional dramatists of the 20th century range from Jean Anouilh, author of urbane philosophical comedies, to Jean Genet, ex-convict critic of the establishment. In the 1960s, Eugéne Ionesco from Romania and Samuel Beckett from Ireland were among the pioneers of a new genre, the "theater of the absurd." Since then, no major playwrights have emerged, but experimental work flourishes in state-subsidized theater companies.

Molière, the 17th-century dramatist

## Poetry

The greatest of early French poets was Ronsard, who wrote sonnets about nature and love in the 16th century. Lamartine, a major poet of the early 19th century, also took nature as one of his themes (his poem *Le Lac* laments a lost love). Later the same century, Baudelaire *(Les Fleurs du mal)* and Rimbaud *(Le Bateau Ivre)* were judged to be provocative in their day. Nobel prizewinner in 1904, Frédéric Mistral wrote in his native Provençal tongue. The greatest poet of the 20th century is considered to be Paul Valéry, whose work is profoundly philosophical.

## Philosophy

France has produced a large number of major philosophers in the European humanist tradition. One of the first was Montaigne, in the 16th

Novels by Albert Camus, who won the Nobel Prize in 1957

Sartre and de Beauvoir in La Coupole restaurant in Paris, 1969

century, an inspired moralist. Then came Descartes, the master of logic, and Pascal. The 18th century produced Voltaire, the supreme liberal, and Rousseau, who preached the harmonizing influence of living close to nature.

In the 20th century, Sartre, de Beauvoir, and Camus used the novel as a philosophical vehicle. Sartre led the existentialist movement in Paris in the early 1940s with his novel *Nausea* and his treatise *Being and Nothingness*. Camus's novel, *The Outsider,* was equally influential.

The 1970s and 1980s brought the structuralists, such as Foucault and Barthes, with their radical ideas. Post-structuralism took this rationalist approach into the 1990s, with Derrida, Kristeva, Deleuze, and Lyotard. At the start of the 21st century, Alain Badiou, known for his political ideas, is considered to be one of France's key philosophers.

### Foreign Writers

Many foreign writers have visited and been inspired by France, from Petrarch in 14th-century Avignon to Goethe in Alsace in 1770–71. In the 20th century the Riviera attracted novelists Somerset Maugham, Katherine Mansfield, Ernest Hemingway, and Graham Greene. In 1919 the American Sylvia Beach opened Paris's first Shakespeare and Company bookstore, which became a cultural center for expatriate writers. In 1922 she was the first to publish James Joyce's masterwork, *Ulysses*.

Hemingway with Sylvia Beach and friends, Paris 1923

# Romanesque and Gothic Architecture in France

France is rich in medieval architecture, ranging from small Romanesque churches to great Gothic cathedrals. As the country emerged from the Dark Ages in the 11th century, there was a surge in Romanesque building, based on the Roman model of thick walls, round arches, and heavy vaults. French architects improved this basic structure, leading to the flowering of Gothic in the 13th century. Pointed arches and flying buttresses were the key inventions that allowed for much taller buildings with larger windows.

**Locator Map**
① *Romanesque abbeys and churches*
⑬ *Gothic cathedrals*

## Romanesque Features

**The plan of Angoulême** shows the cross shape and the rounded eastern apse typical of Romanesque architecture.

**A section of Le Puy** reveals a high barrel-vaulted nave with round arches and low side aisles. Light could enter through windows in the side aisles and the central lantern tower.

**The massive walls** of the nave bays of St.-Etienne support a three-story structure of arcades, a gallery, and clerestory.

## Gothic Features

**The plan of Amiens** shows the nave and apse flanked by a continuous row of chapels.

**A section of Beauvais** shows how the nave could be raised to staggering heights thanks to exterior support from flying buttresses.

**Pointed arches** withstood greater stress, permitting larger windows, as in the nave at Reims.

## Where to find Romanesque Architecture

① St.-Etienne, Caen *p258*
② Mont-St-Michel, Normandy *pp260–63*
③ St.-Pierre, Angoulême *p423*
④ Notre-Dame, Le Puy *p369*
⑤ St.-Pierre, Moissac *pp446–7*
⑥ St.-Sernin, Toulouse *p451*
⑦ Ste.-Foy, Conques *pp372–3*
⑧ Sacré-Coeur, Paray-le-Monial *p349*
⑨ St.-Philibert, Tournus *pp348–9*
⑩ St.-Etienne, Nevers *p342*
⑪ Ste.-Madeleine, Vézelay *pp340–41*
⑫ Marmoutier, Saverne *p237*

## Where to find Gothic Architecture

⑬ Notre-Dame, Strasbourg *p234*
⑭ Notre-Dame, Reims *pp216–17*
⑮ Notre-Dame, Laon *p209*
⑯ Notre-Dame, Amiens *pp206–7*
⑰ St.-Pierre, Beauvais *p204*
⑱ St.-Denis, Ile-de-France *pp176–7*
⑲ Sainte-Chapelle, Paris *pp88–9*
⑳ Notre-Dame, Paris *pp90–91*
㉑ Notre-Dame, Chartres *pp312–15*
㉒ St.-Etienne, Bourges *p317*

## Terms used in this Guide

**Basilica:** Early church with two aisles and nave lit from above by clerestory windows.
**Clerestory:** A row of windows illuminating the nave from above the aisle roof.

**Rose:** Circular window, often stained glass.
**Buttress:** Mass of masonry built to support a wall.

**Flying buttress:** An arched support transmitting thrust of the weight downward.
**Portal:** Monumental entrance to a building, often decorated.

**Tympanum:** Decorated space, often carved, over a door or window lintel.
**Vault:** Arched stone ceiling.
**Transept:** Two wings of a cruciform church at right angles to the nave.
**Crossing:** Center of cruciform, where transept crosses nave.
**Lantern:** Turret with windows to illuminate the interior, often with cupola (domed ceiling).
**Triforium:** Middle story between arcades and the clerestory.
**Apse:** Termination of the church, often rounded.
**Ambulatory:** Aisle running around the east end, passing behind the sanctuary.
**Arcade:** Set of arches and supporting columns.
**Rib vault:** Vault supported by projecting ribs of stone.

**Gargoyle:** Carved grotesque figure, often a water spout.
**Tracery:** Ornamental carved stone pattern within Gothic window.
**Flamboyant Gothic:** Carved stone tracery resembling flames.

**Capital:** The top of a column, usually carved.

**The west facade of Marmoutier Abbey** with its towers, narrow windows, and small portal give it a fortified appearance.

**The east end of Nevers** has a rounded apse surrounded by a semi-circular ambulatory and radiating chapels. The chapels were added to provide space for altars.

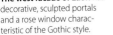

**The west facade of Laon** has decorative, sculpted portals and a rose window characteristic of the Gothic style.

**The east end of Beauvais**, with its delicate buttresses topped by pinnacles, is the culmination of High Gothic.

# Rural Architecture

French farmhouses are entirely products of the soil, built of stone, clay, or wood, depending on what materials are found locally. As the topography changes, so does the architecture, from the steeply sloped roofs covered in flat tiles in the north to the broad canal-tiled roofs of the south.

Despite this rich regional diversity, French farmhouses fall into three basic categories: the *maison bloc,* where house and outbuildings share the same roof; the high house, with living quarters upstairs and livestock or wine cellar below; and courtyard farmsteads, with their buildings set around a central court.

Shuttered window in Alsace

Symmetrical facade

Wood from local forests

**The chalet** is typical of the Jura, Alps, and Vosges mountains. The *maison bloc* housed both family and livestock throughout the winter. Gaps between the gable planks allowed air to circulate around crops stored in the loft, and an earth ramp behind gave wagons access. Many lofts also had a threshing floor.

**Half-timbered houses** are typical of Normandy, Alsace, Champagne, Picardy, the Landes, and Basque country. The filling between the timbers was wattle and daub or in some cases brick, but it is the arrangement of the smaller posts, different in each region, that best expresses the local style.

Normandy wood structure

Flat-tiled roof

Dovecote with flat tiles

Raised stone foundations

Steps to front door

Animals or wine housed here

**The high house** is most prominent in the southeast, and is normally built of stone with an exterior stone staircase and upstairs porch. Wine growers' barrels could be stored on the ground floor without hoisting, or livestock could be stabled there. High houses in the Lot Valley often boast a dovecote.

**The longhouse** is the oldest form of *maison bloc*, with family and livestock at opposite ends of the building – originally one room. In this Breton version, separate doorways lead to house and stable. A dividing wall only became common in the 19th century.

Local stone

Slate roof

Entrance to lodging

Stable entrance

Dovecote with canal tiles

Ocher and beige colors of the south

Rendered facade

**The word** *"mas"* generally refers to any Provençal farmhouse. In the Camargue and the Crau, it is a farmstead for large-scale sheep farming built in an "agglomerated" style: the outbuildings, although attached to one another, are of different heights. Often, a dovecote is included.

## Walls

Limestone, granite, sandstone, and pebbles were all used for building walls. But if no stone was available, clay was dug for infilling half-timbered houses, as wattle and daub. The alternative was to use a cob mixture *(pisé)*, pressed into blocks in a process called *banchange*. Adobe (sun-dried brick) was also used but fired brick was fairly rare as it was expensive to bake. However, brick was sometimes used as trim or combined with chalk or pebbles in a "composite" walling. Walls were generally rendered with mortar.

Pebble-and-brick wall

Half-timber and brick

Compressed cob: *pisé*

Sun-dried adobe bricks

Pebbles in lime mortar

Brick, flint, and chalk

## Roofing

Two roof styles distinguish the north and south. Northern roofs are steeply pitched, so that any rainwater runs off easily. In the south, roofs are covered with canal clay tiles, and more gently sloped to prevent the tiles sliding off.

Flat terracotta tiles in colors of local sand

Pantiles, used in Flanders and Picardy

Canal clay tiles typical of the south

# FRANCE THROUGH THE YEAR

The French, with their farming roots, are deeply aware of the changing seasons, and the mild climate means that they can celebrate outdoors most of the year. History and tradition are honored with *fêtes*, such as Bastille Day (July 14). For culture lovers, thousands of arts festivals are held throughout France, ranging from the huge Avignon Theatre Festival down to small village affairs. Large national sports events, such as the Tour de France cycle race, are a key feature in the calendar. Throughout the year, festivals take place celebrating every kind of food and wine. In high summer, the cities empty, and French and foreign visitors flock to the beaches and countryside.

## Spring

France's outdoor life resumes in spring, terrace-cafés filling up in the sunshine. Easter is a time of Catholic processions and concerts of sacred music. The Cannes Film Festival in May is the best known of the season's many conventions and trade fairs.

### March

**International Half Marathon, Paris**, beginning and ending at Château de Vincennes.

**Six Nations Rugby Tournament**, Stade de France, Paris.

**Tinta' Mars** *(2 weeks)*, Langres. Cabaret and musical evenings at various venues.

**Babel Med Music, Marseille** *(mid-Mar)*. Three-day international music festival.

**Europa Jazz Festival** *(mid-Mar–mid-May)*, Le Mans. International jazz festival.

Formula One racing at the Monaco Grand Prix

La Bravade procession honoring St. Torpès (the resort's namesake) in St.-Tropez

**Banlieues Bleues Jazz Festival** *(late Mar–early Apr)*, St.-Denis. Jazz music.

**Les Détours de Babel** *(late Mar–early Apr)*, Grenoble. Festival of contemporary world music.

### April

**Festival de Pâques** *(2 weeks)*, Deauville. Chamber music.

**Feria Pascale** *(Easter week)*, Arles. Start of the bullfighting season *(see pp512–13)*.

**Lourdes Pilgrimage** *(Palm Sun to Oct, see pp462–3)*.

**Floréal Musical d'Epinal** *(early Apr–mid-May)*, Epinal. Multi-genre music festival.

**Bourges Spring Festival** *(end Apr/early May, see p317)*. Modern music.

**Joan of Arc Festival** *(end Apr–early May)* Orléans. Pageant and cathedral service *(see p316)*.

**Paris International Marathon** Competitors run 26 miles (42 km) through the city, from place de la Concorde to avenue Foch.

### May

**Asparagus harvest**, notably in the Loire.

**International Grand Prix de Monaco** *(Ascension weekend, see p534)*.

**International Sailing Week** (first half of May), La Rochelle.
**La Bravade** (May 16–18), St.-Tropez (see p520).
**Cannes Film Festival** (second and third week, see p524).
**Gypsy Pilgrimage** (late May), Stes.-Maries-de-la-Mer (see p514).
**Fête de la Transhumance** (end May). Herds are taken up to summer pastures.
**International Garden Festival** (May–mid-Oct), Chaumont sur Loire.
**Nîmes Feria** (Pentecost). Bullfights and street music (see pp500–1).
**Grandes Eaux Musicales** (Apr–Oct: Sat & Sun; mid-May–Jun: Tue), Versailles. Fountain jets set

Traditional transhumance of animals to summer pastures

to classical music on the grounds of the château.
**Puy du Fou Pageant** (May–Sep). Actors, audio guides, and horse stunts make

a "living pageant", which evokes local life through the ages (see p294).
**Football Cup Final** (second week), Stade de France, Paris.

## Summer

The French vacation season begins mid-July, with the return to work and school (la rentrée) in early September. Beaches, marinas, and campgrounds are all full to bursting. Each village has its fête and there are festivals, sporting events, and flea markets.

### June

**French Tennis Open** (last week May–first week Jun), Stade Roland Garros, Paris.
**Le Mans 24-Hour Automobile Race** (second or third weekend, see p295). The world's oldest endurance sports car race.
**Fête de la Musique** (Jun 21). Numerous music events are held all over France.
**La Marche des Fiertés**

**Lesbiennes, Gaies, Bi, et Trans** (late June/early Jul). LGBT parade in Paris.
**Fête de St.-Jean** (24 Jun). Music and fireworks all over France.
**Le Printemps des Arts** (late Jun), Nantes area. Baroque dance and music.
**Des Rives et Des Notes** (1 week late Jun), Oloron-Ste.-Marie (near Pau). Jazz festival.
**Tarasque Festival** (last weekend), Tarascon (see p511).

### July

**Festival d'Art Lyrique** (Jun–Jul), Aix-en-Provence. International classical music festival.
**Avignon Theatre Festival** (all month, see p507).
**Troménie** (Sun Jul), Locronan. Penitents' procession (see p277).

Bullfighting in Mont-de-Marsan

**Tombées de la Nuit** (first week), Rennes. Arts festival.
**Jazz Vienne** (first 2 weeks), Vienne (see p386).
**Tour de France cycle race** (first 3 weeks). The grand finale takes place on the Champs-Elysées, Paris.
**Francofolies** (mid-Jul). Music festival at La Rochelle.
**Paris-Plage** (mid-Jul–mid-Aug). Paris and other cities get an annual temporary beach.
**Mont-de-Marsan Feria** (third or fourth weekend). Bullfights and music (see p429).
**International Jazz Festival** (second half), Antibes and Juan-les-Pins (see p525).
**Nice Jazz Festival** (late Jul).
**Comminges Music Festival** (Jul–end Aug, see p466).
**Pablo Casals Festival** (end Jul–mid-Aug), Prades (see p484).

Cyclists competing in the famous Tour de France cycle race

Vacationers on a crowded beach in Cannes on the Côte d'Azur

### August
**Mimos** (first week), Périgueux. World-famous international mime festival.
**Fête du Jasmin** (first weekend), Grasse. Floats, music and dancing in town.
**Foire aux Sorciers** (first Sun), Bué (near Bourges). Costumed witch and wizard festival and folk groups.

**Parade of Lavender Floats** (first or second weekend), Digne (see p521).
**Fête de la Véraison** (first or second weekend), Châteauneuf-du-Pape (see pp506–7). Medieval celebration of thanks-giving for the fruit harvest.
**Interceltic Festival** (second week), Lorient. Celtic arts and music.

**Feria – Bullfight** (mid-Aug), Dax (see p429).
**St.-Jean-Pied-de-Port-Basque Fête** (mid-Aug, see p458). Celebration of Basque culture with music and dancing.
**Fête de St.-Louis** (around Aug 25), Sète (see p496).
**Les Rendezvous de l'Erdre** (last weekend), Nantes. Jazz and riverboats.

### Autumn

In wine regions, the grape harvest is the occasion for much jollity, and every wine village has its wine festival. When the new wine is ready in November, there are more festivities. The hunting season begins – everywhere there is game shooting. In the southwest, migrating birds are trapped.

### September
**Deauville American Film Festival** (first two weeks).
**Le Puy "Roi de l'Oiseau"**, (second week). Renaissance-style festival (see pp368–9).
**Grape harvest**, wine regions throughout France.
**Biennale de Lyon** (mid-Sep–Dec). Dance festival and art festival alternate years.
**Journées du Patrimoine**, (third weekend). Over 14,000 historical buildings can be visited, many not normally open.
**Musica** (late Sep–early Oct), Strasbourg. International music festival.

Ceremony for the Induction of new Chevaliers at the Hospice de Beaune at the Wine Auctions

### October
**Dinard British Film Festival** (first week,).
**Prix de l'Arc de Triomphe** (first Sun), Horse racing at Longchamp, Paris.
**Jazz Pulsations** (mid-Oct), Nancy. International jazz fest.
**Espelette Pepper Festival** (last weekend, see p457).
**Festival de Lanvellec and Trégor** (mid-Oct). Baroque music festival.

**Les Castagnades** (Oct–Nov). Chestnut festival throughout the Ardéche.

### November
**Dijon International Food and Wine Festival** (first 2 weeks). Traditional gastronomic fair.
**Wine Auctions and Les Trois Glorieuses** (third weekend), Beaune (see p350).
**Truffle season** (until Mar), Périgord, Quercy, and Provence.

## Winter

At Christmas, traditional nativity plays are held in churches and there are fairs and markets throughout France. In the Alps and the Pyrenees, and even the Vosges and Massif Central, the ski slopes are crowded. In Flanders and Nice, carnivals take place before Lent.

### December

**Feast of St. Nicolas** *(weekend in early Dec)*, Nancy. A celebration with parades, concerts, floats, and a fireworks display.
**Critérium International de la Première Neige** *(early Dec)*, Val d'Isère. First skiing competition of the season.
**Festival of Lights** *(early Dec)*, Lyon. The city's architecture – buildings, streets, squares, and parks – provides the backdrop for a contemporary light show.

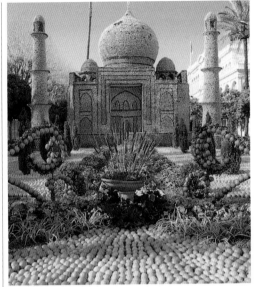

The Taj Mahal re-created at the Lemon Festival in Menton

**Habits de Lumière** *(weekend in mid-Dec)*, Epernay. This three-day event along the famous avenue de Champagne offers street theater, concerts, and exhibitions, plus Champagne tastings and a vintage car parade.

### January

**Monte-Carlo Rally** *(usually mid-Jan, see p534)*.
**Limoux Carnival** *(until Mar)*. Street festival held since the Middle Ages.
**Fashion shows**, Paris. Summer collections.

**Festival du Cirque** *(end)*, Monaco. International event.
**Festival de la Bande Dessinée** *(last weekend)*. International strip cartoon festival, Angoulême.

### February

**Lemon Festival** *(mid-Feb–Mar)*, Menton *(see p533)*.
**Nice Carnival and the Battle of Flowers** *(late Feb–early Mar, see p530)*.
**Paris Carnaval**, *(date varies, check)*, Quartier St.-Fargeau.
**Fête de Mimosa**, *(third Sun)*, Bormes-les-Mimosas.

Downhill skier on the slopes in the French Alps

Bastille Day parade past the Arc de Triomphe

## Public Holidays

**New Year's Day** (Jan 1)
**Easter Sunday and Monday**
**Ascension Day** (sixth Thursday after Easter)
**Whit Monday** (second Monday after Ascension)
**Labour Day** (May 1)
**VE Day** (May 8)
**Bastille Day** (Jul 14)
**Assumption Day** (Aug 15)
**All Saints' Day** (Nov 1)
**Remembrance Day** (Nov 11)
**Christmas Day** (Dec 25)

# The Climate of France

Set on Europe's western edge, France has a varied, temperate climate. An Atlantic influence prevails in the northwest, with westerly sea winds bringing humidity and warm winters. The east experiences Continental temperature extremes with frosty, clear winters and often stormy summers. The south enjoys a Mediterranean climate with hot, dry summers and mild winters, punctuated by violent winds.

### PARIS AND ILE-DE-FRANCE

Average monthly maximum temperature
Average monthly minimum temperature
Average daily hours of sunshine
Average monthly rainfall

| °F | Apr | Jul | Oct | Jan |
|---|---|---|---|---|
| max | 58 | 75 | 61 | 44 |
| min | 44 | 59 | 49 | 36 |
| sunshine | 6 hrs | 8 hrs | 4.5 hrs | 2 hrs |
| rainfall | 2 in | 2.3 in | 2.2 in | 2.2 in |
| month | Apr | Jul | Oct | Jan |

### NORMANDY

| °F | Apr | Jul | Oct | Jan |
|---|---|---|---|---|
| max | 55 | 71 | 61 | 46 |
| min | 41 | 55 | 46 | 36 |
| sunshine | 5.5 hrs | 7 hrs | 4 hrs | 2 hrs |
| rainfall | 1.8 in | 1.9 in | 2.7 in | 2.5 in |
| month | Apr | Jul | Oct | Jan |

### LOIRE VALLEY

| °F | Apr | Jul | Oct | Jan |
|---|---|---|---|---|
| max | 59 | 76 | 64 | 47 |
| min | 43 | 57 | 48 | 37 |
| sunshine | 6 hrs | 8.5 hrs | 4.5 hrs | 2.5 hrs |
| rainfall | 2 in | 1.8 in | 3.1 in | 3.4 in |
| month | Apr | Jul | Oct | Jan |

### BRITTANY

| °F | Apr | Jul | Oct | Jan |
|---|---|---|---|---|
| max | 58 | 75 | 63 | 46 |
| min | 42 | 55 | 47 | 36 |
| sunshine | 6 hrs | 8 hrs | 4.5 hrs | 2 hrs |
| rainfall | 1.7 in | 1.5 in | 2.4 in | 2.5 in |
| month | Apr | Jul | Oct | Jan |

### POITOU AND AQUITAINE

| °F | Apr | Jul | Oct | Jan |
|---|---|---|---|---|
| max | 62 | 79 | 66 | 49 |
| min | 44 | 58 | 48 | 37 |
| sunshine | 6.5 hrs | 9 hrs | 5.5 hrs | 2.5 hrs |
| rainfall | 2.8 in | 1.9 in | 3.5 in | 3.9 in |
| month | Apr | Jul | Oct | Jan |

### PYRENEES

| °F | Apr | Jul | Oct | Jan |
|---|---|---|---|---|
| max | 59 | 77 | 66 | 50 |
| min | 41 | 56 | 46 | 33 |
| sunshine | 5 hrs | 7.5 hrs | 5.5 hrs | 3.5 hrs |
| rainfall | 3.9 in | 2.4 in | 3.1 in | 3.7 in |
| month | Apr | Jul | Oct | Jan |

### PERIGORD, QUERCY, AND GASCONY

| °F | Apr | Jul | Oct | Jan |
|---|---|---|---|---|
| max | 62 | 81 | 66 | 47 |
| min | 43 | 58 | 48 | 36 |
| sunshine | 6 hrs | 9 hrs | 4.5 hrs | 2.5 hrs |
| rainfall | 2.4 in | 2 in | 2.2 in | 2.6 in |
| month | Apr | Jul | Oct | Jan |

Le Havre
Par
Rennes
Tours
Nantes
Bordeaux
Montauban
Biarritz

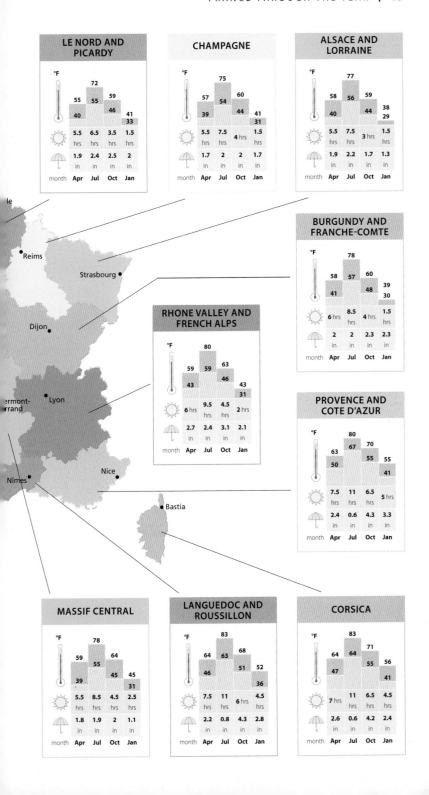

## LE NORD AND PICARDY

| °F | | | |
|---|---|---|---|
| 55 | 72 | 59 | |
| 40 | 55 | 46 | 41 |
| | | | 33 |

| month | Apr | Jul | Oct | Jan |
|---|---|---|---|---|
| ☀ | 5.5 hrs | 6.5 hrs | 3.5 hrs | 1.5 hrs |
| ☂ | 1.9 in | 2.4 in | 2.5 in | 2 in |

## CHAMPAGNE

| °F | | | |
|---|---|---|---|
| 57 | 75 | 60 | |
| 39 | 54 | 44 | 41 |
| | | | 31 |

| month | Apr | Jul | Oct | Jan |
|---|---|---|---|---|
| ☀ | 5.5 hrs | 7.5 hrs | 4 hrs | 1.5 hrs |
| ☂ | 1.7 in | 2 in | 2 in | 1.7 in |

## ALSACE AND LORRAINE

| °F | | | |
|---|---|---|---|
| 58 | 77 | 59 | |
| 40 | 56 | 44 | 38 |
| | | | 29 |

| month | Apr | Jul | Oct | Jan |
|---|---|---|---|---|
| ☀ | 5.5 hrs | 7.5 hrs | 3 hrs | 1.5 hrs |
| ☂ | 1.9 in | 2.2 in | 1.7 in | 1.3 in |

## BURGUNDY AND FRANCHE-COMTE

| °F | | | |
|---|---|---|---|
| 58 | 78 | 60 | |
| 41 | 57 | 48 | 39 |
| | | | 30 |

| month | Apr | Jul | Oct | Jan |
|---|---|---|---|---|
| ☀ | 6 hrs | 8.5 hrs | 4 hrs | 1.5 hrs |
| ☂ | 2 in | 2 in | 2.3 in | 2.3 in |

## RHONE VALLEY AND FRENCH ALPS

| °F | | | |
|---|---|---|---|
| 59 | 80 | 63 | |
| 43 | 59 | 46 | 43 |
| | | | 31 |

| month | Apr | Jul | Oct | Jan |
|---|---|---|---|---|
| ☀ | 6 hrs | 9.5 hrs | 4.5 hrs | 2 hrs |
| ☂ | 2.7 in | 2.4 in | 3.1 in | 2.1 in |

## PROVENCE AND COTE D'AZUR

| °F | | | |
|---|---|---|---|
| 63 | 80 | 70 | |
| 50 | 67 | 55 | 55 |
| | | | 41 |

| month | Apr | Jul | Oct | Jan |
|---|---|---|---|---|
| ☀ | 7.5 hrs | 11 hrs | 6.5 hrs | 5 hrs |
| ☂ | 2.4 in | 0.6 in | 4.3 in | 3.3 in |

## MASSIF CENTRAL

| °F | | | |
|---|---|---|---|
| 59 | 78 | 64 | |
| 39 | 55 | 45 | 45 |
| | | | 31 |

| month | Apr | Jul | Oct | Jan |
|---|---|---|---|---|
| ☀ | 5.5 hrs | 8.5 hrs | 4.5 hrs | 2.5 hrs |
| ☂ | 1.8 in | 1.9 in | 2 in | 1.1 in |

## LANGUEDOC AND ROUSSILLON

| °F | | | |
|---|---|---|---|
| 64 | 83 | 68 | |
| 46 | 63 | 51 | 52 |
| | | | 36 |

| month | Apr | Jul | Oct | Jan |
|---|---|---|---|---|
| ☀ | 7.5 hrs | 11 hrs | 6 hrs | 4.5 hrs |
| ☂ | 2.2 in | 0.8 in | 4.3 in | 2.8 in |

## CORSICA

| °F | | | |
|---|---|---|---|
| 64 | 83 | 71 | |
| 47 | 64 | 55 | 56 |
| | | | 41 |

| month | Apr | Jul | Oct | Jan |
|---|---|---|---|---|
| ☀ | 7 hrs | 11 hrs | 6.5 hrs | 4.5 hrs |
| ☂ | 2.6 in | 0.6 in | 4.2 in | 2.4 in |

le

Reims

Strasbourg

Dijon

Lyon

ermont-
rrand

Nimes

Nice

Bastia

# THE HISTORY OF FRANCE

The only European country facing both the North Sea and the Mediterranean, France has been subject to a particularly rich variety of cultural influences. Though famous for the rootedness of its peasant population, it has also been a European melting pot, even before the arrival of the Celtic Gauls in the centuries before Christ, through to the Mediterranean immigrations of the 20th century. Roman conquest by Julius Caesar had an enduring impact, but from the 4th and 5th centuries AD, waves of Barbarian invaders destroyed much of the Roman legacy. The Germanic Franks provided political leadership in the following centuries, but when their line died out in the late 10th century, France was socially and politically fragmented.

### The Formation of France

The Capetian dynasty gradually pieced France together over the Middle Ages, a period of great economic prosperity and cultural vitality. The Black Death and the Hundred Years' War brought setbacks, and the dynasty's power was seriously threatened by the rival Burgundian dukes. France recovered and despite the wars of religion flourished during the Renaissance, followed by the grandeur of Louis XIV's reign. During the Enlightenment, in the 18th century, French culture was the envy of Europe.

The Revolution of 1789 ended the absolute monarchy and introduced major social and institutional reforms, many of which were endorsed and consolidated by Napoleon. Yet the Revolution also inaugurated the instability that remained a hallmark of French politics until de Gaulle and the Fifth Republic: since 1789, France has known five republics, two empires, and three brands of royal power, plus the Vichy government in World War II.

Modernization in the 19th and 20th centuries proved a slow process. Railroads, the military service, and radical educational reforms were crucial in forming a sense of French identity among the citizens.

Rivalry with Germany dominated French politics for most of the late 19th and early 20th century. The population losses in World War I were traumatic for France, while during 1940–44 the country was occupied by Germany. Yet, today, together with Germany, France forms the backbone of the European Union.

Inlaid marble table top showing the map of France in 1684

◀ *La République*, painted by Charles Landelle in 1848

# Kings and Emperors of France

Following the break-up of the Roman Empire, the Frankish king Clovis consolidated the Merovingian dynasty. It was followed by the Carolingians, and from the 10th century by Capetian rulers. The Capetians established royal power, which passed to the Valois branch in the 14th century, and then to the Bourbons in the late 16th century, following the Wars of Religion. The Revolution of 1789 seemed to end the Bourbon dynasty, but it made a brief comeback in 1814–30. The 19th century was dominated by the Bonapartes, Napoleon I and Napoleon III. Since the overthrow of Napoleon III in 1870, France has been a republic.

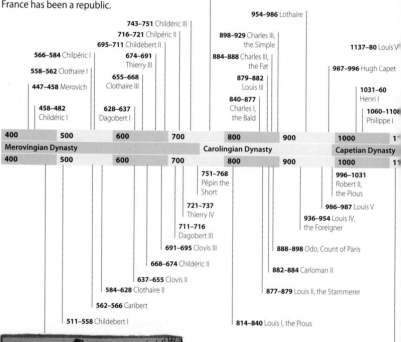

**768–814** Charlemagne

**954–986** Lothaire

**743–751** Childéric III
**716–721** Chilpéric II
**695–711** Childebert II

**898–929** Charles III, the Simple

**884–888** Charles III, the Fat

**1137–80** Louis V

**566–584** Chilpéric I

**674–691** Thierry III

**879–882** Louis III

**987–996** Hugh Capet

**558–562** Clothaire I

**655–668** Clothaire III

**840–877** Charles I, the Bald

**1031–60** Henri I

**447–458** Merovich

**458–482** Childéric I

**628–637** Dagobert I

**1060–1108** Philippe I

| 400 | 500 | 600 | 700 | 800 | 900 | 1000 | 1 |
|-----|-----|-----|-----|-----|-----|------|---|
| **Merovingian Dynasty** | | | | **Carolingian Dynasty** | | **Capetian Dynasty** | |
| 400 | 500 | 600 | 700 | 800 | 900 | 1000 | 1 |

**751–768** Pépin the Short

**996–1031** Robert II, the Pious

**721–737** Thierry IV

**986–987** Louis V

**711–716** Dagobert III

**936–954** Louis IV, the Foreigner

**691–695** Clovis III

**888–898** Odo, Count of Paris

**668–674** Childéric II

**882–884** Carloman II

**637–655** Clovis II

**584–628** Clothaire II

**877–879** Louis II, the Stammerer

**562–566** Caribert

**511–558** Childebert I

**814–840** Louis I, the Pious

**1108–37** Louis VI, the Fat

**482–511** Clovis I

**1226–70** Louis IX (St. Louis)

**1515–47** François I

**1498–1515** Louis XII, Father of his People

**1483–98** Charles VIII

**1774–92** Louis XVI

**1422–61** Charles VII, the Victorious

**1270–85** Philippe III

**1285–1314** Philippe IV, the Fair

**1316–22** Philippe V

**1328–50** Philippe VI

**1547–59** Henri II

**1559–60** François II

**1610–43** Louis XIII

**1643–1715** Louis XIV, the Sun King

**1804–14** Napoleon I

| 1200 | 1300 | 1400 | 1500 | 1600 | 1700 | 1800 |
|------|------|------|------|------|------|------|

**Valois Dynasty**

**Bourbon Dynasty**

| 1200 | 1300 | 1400 | 1500 | 1600 | 1700 | 1800 |
|------|------|------|------|------|------|------|

**1314–16** Louis X

**1322–28** Charles IV, the Fair

**1380–1422** Charles VI, the Beloved

**1364–80** Charles V, the Wise

**1350–64** Jean II, the Good

**1560–74** Charles IX

**1574–89** Henri III

**1589–1610** Henri IV

**1814–24** Louis XVIII

**1824–30** Charles X

**1830–48** Louis-Philippe I

**1852–70** Napoleon III

**1223–6** Louis VIII

**1180–1223** Philip Augustus

**1461–83** Louis XI, the Spider

**1715–74** Louis XV

# Prehistoric France

The earliest traces of human life in France date back to around 2 million BC. From around 40,000 BC, *Homo sapiens* lived an itinerant existence as hunters and gatherers. Around 6000 BC, following the end of the Ice Age, a major shift in lifestyle occurred, as people settled down to herd animals and cultivate crops. The advent of metal working allowed more effective tools and weapons to be developed. The Iron Age is associated particularly with the Celts, who arrived from the east during the first millennium BC. A more complex social hierarchy developed, consisting of warriors, farmers, artisans, and druids (Celtic priests).

**France in 8000 BC**

- Former coastline
- Present-day land mass

**These carvings** of horses' heads were found in the Pyrenees and date from around 9000 BC.

**Carnac Stone Alignments** (4500–4000 BC)
The purpose of the extensive networks of megaliths around Carnac *(see pp282–3)* remains obscure. They possibly served in pagan rituals or as an astronomical calendar.

**The mammoth**, here carved from animal bone, was a thick-coated giant who died out after the end of the Ice Age.

**Cro-Magnon Man**
This skull, dating to around 28,000 BC, was discovered at Cro-Magnon in the Dordogne in 1868. In comparison with most of his predecessors, Cro-Magnon man was tall, robust, and had a large head. He differed only marginally from us.

## Prehistoric Art

*The rich deposits of cave art in France have only been recognized as authentic for just over a century. They include wall paintings and daubings but also various engraved objects. Venus figurines, carved with flint tools, probably had ritual and religious rather than erotic purposes.*

Painting of bulls in Lascaux

**2,000,000 BC** Early hominid societies

**Around 30,000** Cro-Magnon man

| 2,000,000 BC | 30,000 | 25,000 | 20,000 |

Primitive stone tool

**400,000** Discovery of fire by *Homo erectus*

**28,000** The first Venus sculptures, possibly representing fertility goddesses

**Doorway, Roquepertuse**
Religion was an important part of Celtic life. The Celts made a cult of severed heads – presumably of their enemies – as seen in this sanctuary doorway dating from the 3rd century BC.

**The prehistoric** hunter's quarry is here represented by a flock of chamois carved on a piece of bone.

**This carved bone**, found in Laugerie-Basse in the Dordogne, shows a bison chased by a man with a spear.

**This highly stylized** female figure, a Venus figurine found in southwest France, was carved from mammoth tusk in around 20,000 BC.

## Where to See Prehistoric France

The Lascaux cave paintings in Périgord (*see p438*) are among the best in the world. More cave decoration is found around Les Eyzies (*pp438–9*), at the Vallée des Merveilles near Tendes in the Alpes-Maritimes (*p533*), and in the Grotte du Pech Merle in the Lot Valley (*p442*). The intriguing menhirs at Filitosa in Corsica (*pp546–7*) are about 4,000 years old.

**The Lascaux** cave paintings, dating from 16,000–14,000 BC, include images of bulls and mammoths.

**Copper Axe** (around 2000 BC)
Copper tools preceded the arrival of the stronger and more malleable bronze alloy. Iron was to prove the toughest and most useful metal of all.

**Bronze Armor**
Bronze and Iron Age people were highly warlike. The Celtic Gauls were feared even by Romans. Their protective armor, such as this breastplate dating from 750–475 BC, was light but reasonably effective.

**15,000** Hunters live on wandering herds of mammoth, rhinoceros, and reindeer. Art includes the Lascaux caves and Val Camonica/Mont Bego engravings

**7000–4500** Neolithic revolution: farming, megaliths, and menhir stone sculptures

**600** Greek colony at Marseille. Mediterranean luxury goods exchanged for tin, copper, iron, and slaves. Early urban development

|15,000|10,000|5,000|
|---|---|---|

**10,000** End of Ice Age. More regions become inhabitable

**10,000–6000** Mammoth herds disappear, and hunters must rely on animals of the forest, including wild boar and aurochs

*Celtic helmet*

**1200–700** Arrival of the Celts during the Bronze and Iron Ages

**500** Celtic nobles bury their dead with riches such as the Vix treasure (*see p338*)

# Roman Gaul

The Romans had annexed the southern fringe of France by 125–121 BC. Julius Caesar brought the rest of Gaul under Roman control in the Gallic Wars (58–51 BC). The province of Gaul prospered: it developed good communications, a network of cities crammed with public buildings and leisure amenities such as baths and amphitheaters, while in the countryside large villas were established. By the 3rd century AD, however, barbarian raids from Germany were causing increasing havoc. From the 5th century barbarians began to settle throughout Gaul.

**France in 58 BC**
☐ Roman Gaul

**Emperor Augustus**, who was considered a living God, was worshiped at this altar.

**Roman Dolce Vita**
The Romans brought material comfort and luxury, and wine-growing became widespread. This 19th-century painting by Couture conveys a contemporary view of Roman decadence.

**Vercingetorix**
The Celtic chieftain Vercingetorix was Julius Caesar's greatest military opponent. This bronze statue is at Alise-Ste.-Reine *(see p338)*, the Gauls' final stand in 51 BC.

**La Turbie**
*This impressive monument near Monaco was erected in 6 BC by the Roman Senate. It celebrates Augustus's victory over the Alpine tribes in 14–13 BC. Badly pillaged for its stone, restoration only began in the 1920s.*

**125–121 BC** Roman colonization of Southern Gaul

**31 BC** Frontiers of the Three Gauls (*Gallia Celtica, Gallia Aquitania,* and *Gallia Belgica*) established by Augustus

*Augustus*

| 200 BC | 100 | 0 | AD 100 |
|---|---|---|---|

**58–51 BC** Julius Caesar's Gallic Wars result in establishment of Roman Gaul

**16 BC** Maison Carrée built in Nîmes (*see pp500–1*)

**AD 43** Lugdunum (Lyon) established as capital of the Three Gauls

**52–51 BC** Vercingetorix revolt

*Julius Caesar*

### Dancing Girl
Celtic art continued uninfluenced by Roman naturalistic ideals. This bronze statuette of a young woman dates from the 1st–2nd century AD.

**A statue** of Augustus was placed at the top of the original monument.

### Enameled Brooch
This decorative Gallo-Roman brooch dates from the second half of the 1st century BC.

### Where to See Gallo-Roman France

Gallo-Roman remains are to be found all over France, many of them in Provence. In addition to La Turbie (see p533), there is the Roman amphitheater in Arles (p512–13), and the theater and triumphal arch in Orange (p506). Elsewhere, there are ruins at Autun in Burgundy (p343), the Temple d'Auguste et Livie in Vienne (p386), Les Arènes in Nîmes (pp500–1), and fragments of Vesunna in Périgueux (p435).

**Les Arènes in Nîmes**, built at the end of the 1st century AD, is still in use today.

### The Claudian Tables
In AD 48, Emperor Claudius persuaded the Senate to allow Gauls full Roman citizenship. The grateful Gauls recorded the event on stone tables found at Lyon.

**The 44 tribes** subjugated by Augustus are listed on an inscription, with a dedication to the emperor.

### Emperor Augustus
Augustus, the first Roman Emperor (27 BC–AD 14), upheld the Pax Romana, an enforced peace that allowed the Gauls to concentrate on culture rather than war.

**AD 177** First execution of Christian martyrs, Lyon. St. Blandine is thrown to the lions, who refuse to harm her

*St. Blandine*

**360** Julian, prefect of Gaul, proclaimed Roman emperor. Lutetia changes name to Paris

| 200 | 300 | 400 |
|---|---|---|

**275** First Barbarian raids

**313** Christianity officially recognized as religion under the rule of Constantine, the first Christian emperor

**406** Barbarian invasion from the east. Settlement of the Franks and Germanic tribes

**476** Overthrow of the last Roman emperor leads to end of the western Roman Empire

# The Monastic Realm

The collapse of the Roman Empire led to a period of instability and invasions. Both the Frankish Merovingian dynasty (486–751) and the Carolingians (751–987) were unable to bring more than spasmodic periods of political calm. Throughout this turbulent period, the Church provided an element of continuity. As centers for Christian scholars and artists, the monasteries helped to restore the values of the ancient world. They also developed farming and viticulture and some became extremely powerful, dominating the country economically as well as spiritually.

**France in 751**

☐ Carolingian Empire

Stable with lay brethren's quarters above

**Charlemagne** (742–814)
The greatest of Carolingian rulers, Charlemagne created an empire based on strictly autocratic rule. Powerful and charismatic, he could neither read nor write.

Bakery

**The great infirmary hall**
could accommodate about 100 patients. It was flanked by the Lady Chapel.

## Cluny Monastery

*The Benedictine abbey of Cluny (see p349) was founded in 910 with the aim of major monastic reforms. This major religious center, here shown as a reconstruction (after Conant), had great influence over hundreds of monasteries throughout Europe.*

**St. Benedict**
This Italian-born saint established the Benedictine rule: monks were to divide their time between work and prayer.

---

**482** Clovis the Frank becomes first Merovingian king

**508** Paris made capital of the Frankish kingdom

**c.590** St. Colombanus introduces Irish monasticism to France

**732** Battle of Poitiers: Charles Martel repulses Arab invasion

| **500** | **600** | **700** |
|---|---|---|

**496** Conversion of Clovis, king of the Franks, to Christianity

**629–37** Dagobert I, the last effective ruler of the Merovingian dynasty, brings temporary unity to the Frankish kingdom

*Dagobert I*

**751** Pepin becomes first king of the Carolingian dynasty

**Baptism of Clovis**
The Frankish chieftain Clovis was the first barbarian ruler to convert to Christianity. He was baptized in Reims in 496.

## Where to See Monastic France

The monastic realm has survived in austere Cistercian abbeys in Burgundy, such as Fontenay (see pp336–7). Little remains of Cluny, but some of the superb capitals can still be admired (p349). The best way to experience monastic France might be to retrace the steps of medieval pilgrims and visit the monastic centers on the route to Santiago de Compostela (pp404–5), such as Vézelay (pp340–41), Le Puy (pp368–9), Conques (pp372–3), Moissac (pp446–7), and St.-Sernin in Toulouse (pp450–51).

Cluny capitals

**The abbey church**, begun in 1088, was the largest church in Europe before St. Peter's was built in Rome in the 16th century.

Cemetery chapel

**Monastic Arts**
In scriptoriums, talented artists dedicated their time to the meticulous art of illuminating and copying manuscripts for the libraries.

**Monastic Labor**
Monks of the Cistercian rule were renowned for their commitment to manual labor such as cultivating the land and producing wine and liqueurs.

Carolingian soldiers

**1096** First Crusade

**1066** Conquest of England by the Normans

**987** Hugh Capet, first Capetian ruler

| 800 | 900 | 1000 |
|---|---|---|

**800** Coronation of Charlemagne as Holy Roman Emperor

**843** Treaty of Verdun: division of the Carolingian Empire into three parts including West Francia

**910** Foundation of the Benedictine monastery of Cluny

**1077** Bayeux tapestry

*William the Conqueror steering his ship on the Bayeux tapestry*

# Gothic France

The Gothic style, epitomized by soaring cathedrals *(see pp36–7)*, emerged in the 12th century at a time of growing prosperity and scholarship, crusades, and an increasingly dominant monarchy. The rival French and Burgundian courts *(see p347)* became models of fashion and etiquette for all of Europe. *Chansons de gestes* (epic poems) performed by troubadours celebrated the code of chivalry.

**France in 1270**

- Royal territory
- Other fiefs

### Ciborium of Alpais
Alpais, a renowned 12th-century goldsmith in Limoges, made this superb ciborium used to hold wafers for the Holy Communion.

Winch to lift up stone sections

### Courtly Love
According to the code of chivalry, knights dedicated their service to an ideal but unapproachable lady. Courtesy and romance were introduced in art and music.

**The king** supervised the building of the cathedral, accompanied by the architect.

### Draper's Window
The textile trade benefited from the era of urban prosperity. This stained-glass window in a church in Semur-en-Auxois *(see p339)* shows wool-washers at work.

**c.1100** First edition of the epic poem *Chanson de Roland*

**1117** Secret marriage of the scholar Abelard and his student Héloise. Her uncle, canon Filibert, does not approve and forces him to become a monk, while she retires as a nun

**1154** Angevin Empire created by Anglo-Norman dynasty starting with Henry Plantagenet, count of Anjou and king of England (as Henry II)

**1100**  **1125**  **1150**  **1175**

**1115** St. Bernard founds the Cistercian abbey at Clairvaux

**1120** Rebuilding of the abbey of St.-Denis; birth of the Gothic style

*King Philip Augustus, who adopted the fleur-de-lys emblem*

**1180–1223** Reign of Philip Augustus

## The Crusades

In an attempt to win back the Holy Land from the Turks, Philip Augustus set out on the Third Crusade (1189) alongside England's Richard the Lionheart and Holy Roman Emperor Frederick Barbarossa.

**Lace-like sculpture** adorned the facades of the Gothic cathedrals.

**Stonemasons** cut stones on site.

## Eleanor of Aquitaine

Strong-willed and vivacious Eleanor, duchess of independent Aquitaine, contributed to the conflict between France and England. In 1137 she married the pious Louis VII of France. Returning from a Crusade, Louis found that their marriage had broken down. After the annulment in 1152, Eleanor married Henry of Anjou, taking her duchy with her. Two years later Henry successfully claimed the throne of England. Aquitaine came under English rule, and thus the Angevin Empire began.

**Eleanor of Aquitaine** and Henry II are buried in Fontevraud (*p298*).

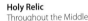

**St. Bernard** (1090–1153) Key figure of the Cistercian rule and counsellor to the pope, St. Bernard preached rigorous simplicity of life.

### Holy Relic

Throughout the Middle Ages most churches could boast at least one saint's relic. The cult of relics brought pilgrims and more riches.

## The Building of a Cathedral

*In affluent, mercantile towns, skilled masons constructed towering Gothic cathedrals of revolutionary design, such as Chartres (see pp312–15) and Amiens (pp206–7). With their improbable height and lightness, these buildings were a testimony to both faith and prosperity.*

*Louis IX on his deathbed*

**1226** Louis IX crowned king

**1270** Death of Louis IX at Tunis in the Eighth Crusade

**1305** Papacy established in Avignon

| 1200 | 1225 | 1250 | 1275 | 1300 |
|------|------|------|------|------|

**1214** Battle of Bouvines. Philip Augustus begins to drive the English out of France

**1259** Normandy, Maine, Anjou, and Poitou acquired from England

**1285** Philip the Fair crowned

**1297** Louis IX is canonized, becoming St. Louis

# The Hundred Years' War

The Hundred Years' War (1337–1453), pitting England against France for control of French land, had devastating effects. The damage of warfare was amplified by frequent famines and the ravages of bubonic plague in the wake of the Black Death in 1348. France came close to being permanently partitioned by the king of England and the duke of Burgundy. In 1429–30 the young Joan of Arc helped rally France's fortunes, and within a generation the English had been driven out of France.

**France in 1429**
- France
- Anglo-Burgundy

**Angels** with trumpets announce the Last Judgment.

**Men of War**
One of the reasons men enlisted as soldiers was hope for plunder. Both the French and English armies lived off the land, at the expense of the peasantry.

**The elect**, springing resurrected from their graves, are ushered into Heaven.

**The Black Death**
The plague of 1348–52 caused 4–5 million deaths, about 25 percent of the French population. For want of medicines, people had to put their faith in prayers and holy processions.

*14th-century flame-throw*

**1346** Battle of Crécy: French defeated by English

**1328** Philip VI, first Valois monarch

**1356** French defeat at the Battle of Poitiers

**1325**

**1350**

**1375**

**1337** Start of the Hundred Years' War

*Plague victims*

**1348–52** The Black Death

**1358** Bourgeois uprising in Paris led by Etienne Marcel. The Jacquerie peasant uprising in Northern France

**Medieval Medicine**
The state of the heavens was widely held to influence earthly conditions, such as health, and a diagnosis based on the zodiac was considered reliable. The standby cure for all sorts of ailments was blood-letting.

**English Longbow**
The king's troops fought against England, but the individual French duchies supported whichever side seemed more favorable. In the confused battles, English bowmen excelled. Their longbows caused chaos among the hordes of mounted French cavalry.

**Christ as Supreme Judge** is flanked by angels bearing the instruments of the Passion.

**Archangel Michael**, resplendent with peacock wings, holds the judgment scales. The weight of sinners outbalances the elect.

**John the Baptist** is accompanied by the 12 apostles and the Virgin Mary, dressed in blue.

**The damned,** with hideously twisted faces, fall into Hell.

**The Last Judgment**

*With war, plague, and famine as constant visitors, many people feared that the end of the world was nigh. Religious paintings, such as the great 15th-century altar screen by Rogier van der Weyden in the Hôtel-Dieu in Beaune (see pp350–51), reflected the moral fervor of the time.*

**Attack on Heresy**
The general anxiety spilled over into anti-Semitic pogroms and attacks on alleged heretics, who were burned at the stake.

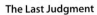

**1415** Battle of Agincourt. French defeat by Henry V of England

**1429** Intervention of Joan of Arc: Charles VII crowned king

**1453** End of the Hundred Years' War. Only Calais remains in English hands

**1400**

**1425**

**1450**

**1411** *Les Très Riches Heures du Duc du Berry* prayer book, by Paul and Jean de Limbourg *(see pp208–9)*

**1419** Charles VI of France makes Henry V of England his heir

**1431** Joan of Arc burned at stake as witch by the English

*Joan of Arc*

# Renaissance France

As a result of the French invasion of Italy in 1494, the ideals and aesthetic of the Italian Renaissance spread to France, reaching their height during the reign of François I. Known as a true Renaissance prince, he was skilled in letters and art as well as sports and war. He invited Italian artists, such as Leonardo and Cellini, to his court and enjoyed Rabelais's bawdy stories. Another highly influential Italian was Catherine de' Medici (1519–89). Widow of Henri II, she virtually ruled France through her sons, François II, Charles IX, and Henri III. She was also one of the major players in the Wars of Religion (1562–93) between Catholics and Protestants, which divided the nobility and tore the country to pieces.

**France in 1527**
- Royal territory
- Other fiefs

**Galerie François I, Fontainebleau**
The artists of the School of Fontainebleau blended late Italian Renaissance style with French elements.

**The corner towers** are a Gothic feature transformed by Italian lightness of touch into pure decoration.

**Power Behind the Throne**
Catherine de' Medici dominated French politics from 1559 to 1589.

## Azay-le-Rideau

*One of the loveliest of the Loire châteaux, Azay was begun in 1518 (see p300). Italian influences are visible, and it is clear that this is a dwelling meant for pleasure rather than defence.*

**1470** First printing presses established in France

*Prototype tank by Leonardo da Vinci*

**1519** Leonardo da Vinci dies in the arms of François I at the French court in Amboise

**1536** Calvin's *Institutes of the Christian Religion* leads to a new form of Protestantism

| 1470 | 1480 | 1490 | 1500 | 1510 | 1520 | 1530 |

**1477** Final defeat of the dukes of Burgundy, who sought to establish a middle kingdom between France and Germany

**1494–1559** France and Austria fight over Italian territories in the Italian Wars

**1515** Reign of François I begins

*Golden coin showing the fleur-de-lys and the salamander of François I*

**Gold Pomander**
Pomanders containing sweet-smelling herbs such as amber and cinnamon were carried in time of plague to ward off the bad air held responsible for contagion.

**Ballroom with Flemish tapestries**

**The staircase** was in the new Italian fashion with double flights of steps rather than a spiral.

The Red Room

**New France**
French expansion and quest for colonies started with Cartier's expedition to Canada in 1534 (see p286).

## Where to See Renaissance France

In Paris, many churches and the impressive place des Vosges (see p95) date from the Renaissance. There are countless 16th-century châteaux in the Loire and Burgundy. Among the finest are Chenonceau (pp302–3) and Tanlay (p335). Salers (p367) is a virtually intact Renaissance town. The historic center of Toulouse (pp450–51) has many elegant Renaissance palaces.

**This fireplace** stands in François I's room in the Château de Chenonceau.

**François I and the Italian Influence**
François I, here receiving Raphael's painting *The Holy Family* in 1518, collected Italian art at Fontainebleau. Among the favored painters were Michelangelo, Leonardo, and Titian.

**1539** Edict of Villers Cotterets makes French the official language of state

**1559** Treaty of Cateau–Cambrésis ends the Italian Wars

**1562** Wars of Religion between Catholics and Protestants start

**1572** Massacre of Protestants on St. Bartholomew's Eve in Paris

**1589** Henry III murdered. The Huguenot Henry IV becomes first Bourbon king of France

**1593** Henry IV converts to Catholicism and ends the Wars of Religion

**1598** Edict of Nantes: tolerance for Protestantism

**1608** Foundation of Quebec

| 1540 | 1550 | 1560 | 1570 | 1580 | 1590 | 1600 |

*St. Bartholomew's Day Massacre*

# The Grand Siècle

The end of the Religious Wars heralded a period of exceptional French influence and power. The cardinal ministers Richelieu and Mazarin paved the way for Louis XIV's absolute monarchy. Political development was matched by artistic styles of unprecedented brilliance: enormous Baroque edifices, the drama of Molière and Racine, and the music of Lully. Versailles *(see pp178–81)*, built under the supervision of Louis's capable finance minister Colbert, was the glory of Europe, but its cost and Louis XIV's endless wars proved expensive for the French state and led to widespread misery by the end of his reign.

**France in 1661**

- Royal territory
- Avignon (papal enclave)

**Molière** (1622–73)
Actor-playwright Molière performed many plays for Louis XIV and his court, though some of his satires were banned. After his death, his company became the basis of the French state theater, the Comédie Française.

Madame (married to Monsieur) as Flora

Monsieur, the king's brother

**Madame de Maintenon**
In 1683, following the death of his first wife Marie-Thérèse, Louis secretly married his mistress Madame Maintenon, then aged 49.

### The Sun King and his Family
*Claiming to be monarch by divine right, Louis XIV commanded court painter Jean Nocret to devise this allegorical scene in 1665. Surrounded by his family, the king appears as the sun god Apollo.*

**1610–17** Marie de' Medici acts as Regent for Louis XIII

*Cardinal Richelieu*

**1624** Cardinal Richelieu becomes principal minister

**1635** Foundation of the literary society Académie Française

**1642–3** Death of Louis XIII and Cardinal Richelieu. Accession of Louis XIV with Mazarin as principal minister

| 1610 | 1620 | 1630 | 1640 | 1650 |
|---|---|---|---|---|

**1617** Louis XIII accedes at the age of 17

**1631** Foundation of *La Gazette*, France's first newspaper

**1637** Descartes's *Discourse on Method*

**1635** Richelieu actively involves France in the Thirty Years' War

**1648–52** The Fronde: French civil wars

**Louis XIV's Book of Hours**
After a lively and libertine youth, Louis became increasingly religious. His *Book of Hours* (1688–93) is in Musée Condé *(see p209)*.

**Royal Wedding**
Louis XIII and Anne of Austria were married in 1615. After his death, Anne became regent for the young Louis XIV with Cardinal Mazarin as minister.

**Baroque Figurine**
The royal glory was reflected in the arts. This objet d'art features Christ made of jasper on a pedestal decorated with gilded cherubs and rich enameling.

Louis XIV
as Apollo

Anne of Austria
as Cybele

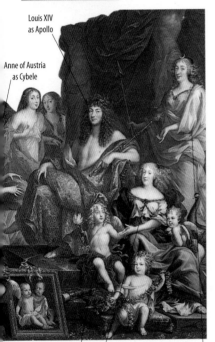

Grande Mademoiselle, the
king's cousin, as Diana

The dauphin
(the king's son)

Queen Marie-Thérèse
as Juno

## Where to See Architecture of the Grand Siècle

Paris boasts many imposing Grand Siècle buildings, such as the Hôtel des Invalides *(see p118)*, the Dôme church *(p119)*, and the Palais du Luxembourg *(pp130–31)*, but the Château de Versailles *(pp178–81)* is the ultimate example of the flamboyance of the period. Reminders of this glory include the sumptuous Palais Lascaris in Nice *(p530)* and the Corderie Royale in Rochefort *(p421)*. At the same time, military architect Vauban constructed mighty citadels, such as Neuf-Brisach *(see pp230–31)*.

**Versailles's** interior is a typical example of the gilded Baroque style.

---

*Playwright Jean Racine
(1639–99)*

**1661** Death of Mazarin: Louis XIV becomes his own principal minister

**1680** Creation of the theater Comédie Française

**1685** Revocation of the Edict of Nantes of 1598: Protestantism banned

**1709** Last great famine in French history

| 1660 | 1670 | 1680 | 1690 | 1700 |
|---|---|---|---|---|

**1662** Colbert, finance minister, reforms finances and the economy

**1682** Royal court moves to Versailles

**1689** Major wars of Louis XIV begin

**1686** Opening of the Café Procope (first coffee house in Paris)

*17th-century cannon*

# Enlightenment and Revolution

In the 18th century, Enlightenment philosophers such as Voltaire and Rousseau redefined man's place within a framework of natural principles, thus challenging the old aristocratic order. Their essays were read across Europe and even in the American colonies. But although France exported worldly items as well as ideas, the state's increasing debts brought social turmoil, triggering the 1789 Revolution. Under the motto "Liberty, Equality, Fraternity", the new Republic and its reforms had a far-reaching impact on the rest of Europe.

**France in 1789**
- Royal France
- Avignon (papal enclave)

**Voltaire** (1694–1778)
A master of satire, Voltaire wrote numerous essays and the novel *Candide*. His fierce critiques sometimes forced him into exile abroad.

Jacobin Club

National Assembly

**The Guillotine**
This infamous invention was introduced in 1792 as a humane alternative to other forms of capital punishment, which had usually involved torture.

**Place de la Révolution** *(see p102)* is where Louis XVI's execution took place in 1793.

The Tuileries

**Café Le Procope** was the haunt of Voltaire and Rousseau.

**Palais Royal**
The private residence of the Duke of Orléans, the Palais Royal *(see p103)* became a center of revolutionary agitation from 1789. It was also the site of several printing presses.

**1715** Death of Louis XIV, accession of Louis XV

**1743–64** Madame de Pompadour, Louis XV's favorite, uses her influence to support artists and philosophers during her time at court

*Madame de Pompadour*

| 1715 | 1725 | 1735 | 1745 | 1755 |

**1720** Last outbreak of plague in France: population of Marseille decimated

*Physician's protective costume worn during the plague*

**1751** Publication of the first volume of Diderot's *Encyclopaedia*

**1756–63** Seven Years' War: France loses Canada and other colonial possessions

### Revolutionary Symbols
The motifs of the Revolution such as the blue, white, and red of the *Tricolor* even appeared on wallpaper in the 1790s.

### Queen Marie Antoinette
Marie Antoinette's frivolous behavior helped to discredit the monarchy. She was held in the Conciergerie and brought to the guillotine in 1793.

**The Marais**, earlier an aristocratic area, fell into decay as a result of the Revolution.

Bastille

### Revolutionary Paris
*From 1789, Paris housed numerous political clubs, such as the left-wing Jacobins, and many revolutionary newspapers. The war tune* La Marseillaise, *introduced by volunteers from the south, was soon heard everywhere.*

### Where to See 18th-Century France

The Palais de l'Elysée, built in 1718 (*see p112*), is an outstanding example of 18th-century Parisian architecture. Examples across France include the curious Saline Royale in Arc-et-Senans (*p354*), the Grand Théâtre in Bordeaux (*p426*), the elegant mansions in Condom (*p444*) and the merchants' houses in Ciboure (*p457*). The Château de Laàs in Sauveterre de Béarn is a feast of 18th-century art and furniture (*p458*).

**The Grand Théâtre** in Bordeaux is an excellent example of elegant 18th-century architecture.

### Revolutionary Calendar
A new calendar was introduced, the months named after seasonal events. This engraving shows Messidor, the month of harvest.

---

**1768** Annexation of Corsica

**1789** Storming of the Bastille, and establishment of constitutional monarchy: abolition of feudal laws

**1783** First balloon ascent, by the Montgolfier brothers

**1793** Execution of Louis XVI and Marie Antoinette at the guillotine

| 1765 | 1775 | 1785 | 1795 |

**1774** Accession of Louis XVI

**1762** Rousseau's *Emile* and the *Social Contract*

**1778–83** France aids the 13 colonies in the War of American Independence

Electors' card for the Convention of 1792

**1794** Overthrow of Robespierre and end of the Terror

**1792** Overthrow of Louis XVI: establishment of First Republic

# Napoleonic France

Two generations of Napoleons dominated France from 1800 to 1870. Napoleon Bonaparte took the title of Emperor Napoleon I. He extended his empire throughout most of Western Europe, placing his brothers and sisters on the thrones of conquered countries. Defeated in 1814 and replaced by the restored Bourbon dynasty, followed by the 1830 Revolution and the so-called July Monarchy, the Napoleonic clan made a comeback after 1848. Napoleon I's nephew, Louis Napoleon, became President of the Second Republic, then made himself emperor as Napoleon III. During his reign Paris was modernized, and the industrial transformation of France began.

**Europe in 1812**
- Napoleonic rule
- Dependent states

The Laurel, crown of the Roman emperors

**Napoleon**, as First Consul, is crowned by Chronos, the God of Time.

**Musée du Louvre**
The museum had opened in 1792, but it flourished during Napoleon's reign. He took a personal interest in both the acquisitions and organization.

**The revolutionary** tricolor flag was kept throughout the empire.

**Imperial Insignia**
Napoleon I created a new titled aristocracy, who were allowed coats of arms. Only his, however, was permitted a crown. The eagle symbol was adopted in 1800, an evocation of Imperial Rome.

Légion d'Honneur medal

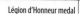

---

**1804** Napoleon crowned as Emperor. Napoleonic Civil Code established

**1800** Establishment of the Bank of France

*Josephine's bed at Malmaison*

**1809** Josephine and Napoleon divorce. She retains the Château de Malmaison (see p177)

**1814** Defeat of Napoleon by the Allies (England, Russia, Austria, and Prussia). Napoleon exiled to Elba

**1800**

**1810**

**1820**

**1802** Treaty of Amiens brings temporary peace to Europe

**1802** Establishment of the Légion d'Honneur

**1806** Arc de Triomphe commissioned

**1803** Resumption of wars to create the Napoleonic Empire

**1815** The "Hundred Days": Napoleon returns from Elba, is defeated at Waterloo, and exiled to St. Helena

**July Revolution**
Three days of street fighting in July 1830 ended unpopular Bourbon rule.

**The Napoleons**
This imaginary group portrait depicts Napoleon I (seated), his son "Napoleon II" *(right)* – who never ruled – Napoleon's nephew Louis Napoleon (Napoleon III), and the latter's infant son.

**The Civil Code,** created by Napoleon, is here shown as a tablet.

**Napoleon on Campaign**
A dashing general in the late 1790s, Napoleon remained a remarkable military commander throughout his reign.

## Empire Fashion

Greek and Roman ideals were evident in architecture, furniture, design, and fashion. Women wore light, classical tunics, the most daring with one shoulder or more bare. David and Gérard were the most fashionable portraitists, while Delacroix and Géricault created many Romantic masterpieces.

**Madame Récamier** held a popular salon and was renowned for her beauty and wit. David painted her in 1800.

### Napoleonic Glory

*Though professing himself a true revolutionary, Napoleon developed a taste for imperial pomp. However, he also achieved some long-lasting reforms such as the Civil Code, the new school system, and the Bank of France.*

**1832** Cholera epidemics begin

**1838** Daguerre experiments with photography

**1848** Revolution of 1848: end of the July Monarchy and establishment of the Second Republic

**1851** Coup d'état by Louis Napoleon

**1852** Louis Napoleon is crowned as Emperor Napoleon III

**1830**

**1840**

**1850**

**1860**

**1830** Revolution of 1830: Bourbon Charles X replaced by the July Monarchy of King Louis-Philippe

**1840** Large-scale railroad building

*Train on the Paris–St.-Germain line*

**1853** Modernization of Paris by Haussmann

**1857** Baudelaire (*Les Fleurs du Mal*) and Flaubert (*Mme Bovary*) prosecuted for public immorality

**1859–60** Annexation of Nice and Savoy

# The Belle Epoque

The decades before World War I became the *belle époque* for the French, remembered as a golden era forever past. Nevertheless, this was a politically turbulent time, with working-class militancy, organized socialist movements, and the Dreyfus Affair polarizing the country between Left and anti-Semitic Right. New inventions such as electricity and vaccination against disease made life easier at all social levels. The cultural scene thrived and took new forms with Impressionism and Art Nouveau, the Realist novels of Gustave Flaubert and Emile Zola, cabaret and cancan, and, in 1895, the birth of the movie industry.

**France in 1871**
- ⬜ Under Third Republic
- ▨ Alsace and Lorraine

Statue of Apollo by Aimé Millet

Copper-green roofed cupola

Stage

**Universal Exhibition**
The 1889 Paris exhibition was attended by 3.2 million people. Engineer Eiffel's breathtaking iron structure dominated the exhibition and caused great controversy at the time.

Backstage area

**Peugeot Car** (1899)
The car and bicycle brought new freedom, becoming a part of people's leisure time. Peugeot, Renault, and Citroën were all founded before World War I.

**The auditorium**, in gold and purple, seated over 2,000 people.

*Woman on the barricades in 1871*

**1869** Opening of the Suez Canal, built by Ferdinand de Lesseps

**1871** The Paris Commune leads to the Third Republic

**1880s** Scramble for colonies in Africa and Asia begins

**1889** Universal Exhibition in Paris; Eiffel Tower built

| 1865 | 1870 | 1875 | 1880 | 1885 | 189 |
|---|---|---|---|---|---|

**1870–71** Franco-Prussian War: defeat and overthrow of Napoleon III; France cedes Alsace and Lorraine to Germany

**1881–6** Reforms in education by Jules Ferry

**1874** Impressionist Movement begins

**1885** Pasteur produces vaccine for rabies, the first tested on a human

**1890** Peugeot constructs one of the earliest automobiles

### Poster Art
The poster was revolutionized by Art Nouveau, with designs by Alphonse Mucha particularly popular. This one from 1897 is for beer, the beverage of the lost Alsace and Lorraine, which became a "patriotic" drink.

### Staircase at the Opera
The grand staircase had colored marble columns and a frescoed ceiling. As this painting by Béroud from 1877 shows, it soon became a showcase for high society.

Emperor's pavilion

Grand Foyer with balconies and lavishly decorated ceiling

Grand staircase

### Where to See the Belle Epoque

*Belle époque* buildings include the Negresco Hotel, Nice *(see p530)*, the Grand Casino in Monte-Carlo *(p534)*, and the Palais Hotel in Biarritz *(p456)*. The Musée d'Orsay in Paris *(pp124–5)* exhibits Art Nouveau objects and furniture.

**Guimard's** Métro entrance is a typical example of the elegant, swirling lines of Art Nouveau.

### Opéra National Garnier
*Founded by Napoleon III in 1862, the new opera was opened to great public acclaim in 1875 and became a focus of belle époque social life. Designed by Charles Garnier, its extravagant exterior was matched by its sumptuous interior decor.*

### The Divine Sarah
Actress Sarah Bernhardt (1844–1923) worked in all theatrical genres, dominating the Paris stage.

Caricature of Zola

**1894–1906** The alleged treason of Dreyfus sparks the Dreyfus Affair, involving the author Zola among others

**1905** Official separation of Church and State

**1909** Blériot flies the Channel

**1917** Mutinies in the army suppressed by Pétain

**1916** Battle of Verdun

**1918** Germany asks for armistice to end war

| **1895** | **1900** | **1905** | **1910** | **1915** |
|---|---|---|---|---|

**1895** First public movie by the Lumière brothers

**1898** Marie and Pierre Curie discover radium

**1913** Publication of Proust's first volume of *Remembrance of Things Past*

**1914** World War I breaks out

*French recruit, 1916*

**1919** Treaty of Versailles

# Avant-Garde France

Despite the devastation wrought by two world wars, France retained its international renown as a center for the avant garde. Paris in particular was a magnet for experimental writers, artists, and musicians. The cafés were full of American authors and jazz musicians, French Surrealists, and movie-makers. The French Riviera also attracted colonies of artists and writers, from Matisse and Picasso to Hemingway and F. Scott Fitzgerald, along with the wealthy industrialists and aristocrats arriving in automobiles or by the famous Train Bleu. And from 1936 paid vacations meant the working classes could also enjoy the new fashion for sunbathing.

**France in 1919**
☐ French territory

African Gods of Creation

**Art Deco 1925**
The International Exhibition in Paris in 1925 launched the Art Deco style: characterized by geometrical shapes and utilitarian designs, adapted for mass production.

Dancers in heavy cardboard costumes

**The Jazz Age**
Paris welcomed American jazz musicians, such as Sidney Bechet in 1925 and Dizzy Gillespie *(left)*, co-founder of bebop in the 1940s.

**Citroën Goddess** (1956)
This elegant model became an icon of the new French consumerism evident in the 1950s and 1960s.

**The costumes**
and scenery by the Cubist Léger were striking and made to look partly mechanical.

Air France aircraft, 1937

**1920** French Communist Party founded. Publication of Tristan Tzara's Dada Manifesto

**1928** Premiere of *Un Chien Andalou* by Luis Buñuel and Salvador Dalí

**1933** Air France begins operation

**1937** Premiere of *La Grande Illusion* by Jean Renoir

**1920**

**1930**

**1924** Olympic Games in Paris. André Breton publishes the *Surrealist Manifesto*

*Poster for the 1924 Olympics*

**1936–38** The "Popular Front": radical social program introduced, including paid vacationss

**1929–39** The Depression

**1938** Munich Conference: height of appeasement

**Coco Chanel** (1883–1971)
Chanel, photographed here by Man Ray, revolutionized fashion in the 1920s with her elegant but comfortable clothes.

**Par Avion**
France pioneered the use of airmail, starting in 1927.

First Man and Woman

## World War II

Following the collapse of the Third Republic in 1940, Paris and the north and west parts of France were occupied by the Germans until the Liberation in 1944. South-east France formed the collabora-tionist Vichy state, led by Marshal Pétain and Pierre Laval. Meanwhile, the Free French movement was led by Charles de Gaulle, with Jean Moulin coordinating the operations of the many different Resistance factions.

**German soldiers** liked to pose in front of the Eiffel Tower during the occupation of Paris.

LA REVUE DES
**FOLIES-BERGERE**
1926-1927

## La Création du Monde (1923)

*Artistic experimentation thrived in the early 20th century. La Création du Monde by Les Ballets Suédois had costumes by Léger and music by Milhaud. Diaghilev's Ballets Russes also competed for avant-garde artists including Picabia, Cocteau, Satie, and Sonia Delaunay.*

**The African** theme was based on text by Blaise Cendrars.

**Josephine Baker** (1906–75)
The music hall flourished in the 1920s with Mistinguett and Josephine Baker as its undisputed queens.

**1940** The Fall of France. Vichy government led by Pétain. De Gaulle fights on from London

**1942** The whole of France controlled by Germany

**1949** Establishment of NATO. Founding of the Council of Europe

**1958** Fifth Republic begins under President de Gaulle

**1956** Late in her career, Edith Piaf crowns her success at Carnegie Hall, New York

**1940**

**1950**

Edith Piaf

**1944** D-Day: Allied landings in Normandy (June). Liberation of Paris (August)

**1946** Sartre establishes *Les Temps Modernes.* First Cannes Film Festival

**1954** France withdraws from Indochina after Battle of Dien Bien Phu. Start of Algerian insurrection

**1939** Declaration of World War II

**1945** End of the war. Fourth Republic begins. Votes for women

# Modern France

After the 1950s, the traditional foundations of French society changed: the number of peasant farmers plummeted, old industries decayed, and jobs in the service sector and high-technology industries grew dramatically. High-profile projects, such as Concorde, TGV, La Défense, and the Centre Pompidou, brought international acclaim. Prestigious building projects in the 21st century include the Tour D2 at La Défense, Fondation Louis Vuitton, and Philarmonie de Paris. The turn of the century brought more social change as France legalized same-sex marriage and emerged as a leader in environmental issues.

**France Today**
- France
- European Union

**Centre Pompidou** (1977)
The Centre Pompidou's controversial building changed the aspect of the historic quarter of Beaubourg. A major arts center, it has revitalized the formerly rundown area (*see pp96–7*).

**Gleaming white "sails"** composed of glass panels encase the building, giving it an appearance of a sailboat or a huge bird.

**21st-Century Film**
Among the successes of 21st-century movies are *Amélie* (2001) and *The Artist* (2011), which won acclaim for their heartwarming stories.

**Fondation Louis Vuitton**
*Opened in 2014 in the Bois de Boulogne, Frank Gehry structure is one of France's most daring architectural feats. It features 11 exhibition spaces housing contemporary art and temporary exhibitions, but the building is enough of a draw in itself.*

| | | | | | |
|---|---|---|---|---|---|
| **1960** First French atomic bomb. Decolonization of black Africa | **1967** Common Agricultural Policy, subsidizing Europe's farmers | **1973** Extension of the Common Market (EU) from six to nine states | **1974** Giscard d'Estaing elected president | | **1989** Bicentenni celebratic of the Frenc Revolutic |
| | | | **1980** Giverny, Monet's garden, opens to the public (*see p270*) | **1981** Socialist Mitterrand becomes president for 14 years | |

**1960**     **1970**     **1980**

| | | | | |
|---|---|---|---|---|
| **1963** First French nuclear power station | **1969** Pompidou replaces de Gaulle as president | **1976** Concorde's first commercial flight | **1977** Jacques Chirac first mayor of Paris since 1871. Opening of the Centre Pompidou | **1987** Mitterrand and Thatcher sign agreement for Channel Tunnel. Trial in Lyon of ex-SS Officer Klaus Barbie |
| **1968** May student riots | | | | |
| **1962** Evian agreements lead to Algerian independence | | *The Concorde's maiden take-off* | | *François Mitterra* |

**EU Flag**
France has been one of the leading forces in the European Union ever since the move toward closer European collaboration began in the 1950s.

**TGV**
The TGV (*Train à Grande Vitesse*) is one of the world's fastest trains (*see pp632–3*). It typifies the French government's commitment to high technology and improved communications.

**Fashion by Saint Laurent**
Despite less demand for haute couture, Paris is still a major fashion center. The designs shown on the catwalk, here by Saint Laurent, remain proof of the world-renowned skills of French labels and designers.

## Charlie Hebdo

Following the terrorist attacks at the satirical magazine *Charlie Hebdo* in 2015, the world showed solidarity with the French people and journalistic freedom through the social media hashtag #jesuischarlie. The paper continues today despite losing many of its prominent contributors and cartoonists, defying those who challenge the right to free speech in France.

**A stepped water fountain** is located under the building.

**Charlie Hebdo**, a French weekly satirical magazine, featuring cartoons, reports and jokes

Prince Albert II

**1994** Channel Tunnel opens

**2002** National Front defeat Socialists in first round of presidential campaign. France re-elects Jacques Chirac

**2010** The head of France's King Henry IV is found after it was lost in 1793

**2012** Socialist candidate François Hollande is elected as president

**2013** Legalization of same-sex marriage

**2000**

**2010**

**2020**

**91** Edith Cresson is made France's first woman Prime minister

**2002** Euro replaces franc as legal tender

**1995** Jacques Chirac is elected president

**2005** Prince Rainier III of Monaco dies and is succeeded by his only son, Prince Albert II

**2008** Jean-Marie Gustave Le Clézio wins the Nobel Prize for literature

**2007** Center-right Nicolas Sarkozy is elected president

**2017** Emmanuel Macron becomes the youngest president in French history

# PARIS AND ILE-DE-FRANCE

Introducing Paris and
  Ile-de-France                    76–77

A River View of Paris              78–83

Ile de la Cité, Marais,
  and Beaubourg                    84–97

Tuileries and Opera               98–107

Champs-Elysées
  and Invalides                   108–119

The Left Bank                     120–131

Farther Afield                    132–143

Stores and Markets                144–153

Entertainment in Paris            154–157

Paris Street Finder               158–173

Ile-de-France                     174–185

# Introducing Paris and Ile-de-France

The French capital is rich in museums, art galleries, and monuments. The Louvre, Eiffel Tower, and Centre Pompidou are among the most popular sights.

Surrounding Paris, the Ile-de-France takes in 4,600 sq miles (12,000 sq km) of busy suburbs and commuter towns punctuated by châteaux, the most celebrated being Versailles. Farther out, suburbia gives way to farmland, forests, and the magnificent palace of Fontainebleau.

Arc de Triomphe
*(see p111)*

Opéra National
Garnier *(see p101)*

AVENUE FOCH

PLACE
CHARLES
DE GAULLE

BOULEVARD HAUSSMANN

AVENUE D'IENA

AVENUE DES CHAMPS-ELYSEES

CHAMPS-ELYSEES
AND INVALIDES
(See pp108–19)

PLACE
DE LA
MADELEINE

COURS ALBERT 1er

PLACE
DE LA
CONCORDE

RUE

*La Seine*

QUAI D'ORSAY

AVENUE DE LA BOURDONNAIS

RUE DE BABYLONE

**The Musée d'Orsay,** opened in 1986, was created from a late 19th-century train terminus *(see pp124–5)*. Its magnificent collection of 19th- and early 20th-century art (notably Impressionist works) includes Jean-Baptiste Carpeaux's *Four Quarters of the World* (1872).

**The Eiffel Tower**, designed for the Universal Exhibition of 1889, scandalized contemporary critics but is now the capital's most famous landmark *(see p117)*.

◄ The iconic Eiffel Tower, viewed from below

**Ile-de-France**
*Pages 174–85*

Cergy
St-Denis
Meaux
Mantes-la-Jolie
Nanterre
PARIS
*(See main map)*
Colomiers
Versailles
Créteil
Rambouillet
Évry
Nangis
Ponthierry
Provins
Fontainebleau
Nemours

0 kilometers 25
0 miles 25

Louvre
*(see pp104–7)*

HAUSSMANN

Château de
Versailles
*(see pp178–81)*

TUILERIES
AND OPERA
*(see pp98–107)*

RUE REAUMUR

PLACE
DE LA
RÉPUBLIQUE

RUE DU LOUVRE

BLVD DE SEBASTOPOL

ILE DE LA CITE,
MARAIS, AND
BEAUBOURG
*(See pp84–97)*

BLVD BEAUMARCHAIS

RIVOLI

La Seine

RUE DE RIVOLI

PLACE
DE LA
BASTILLE

GERMAIN

THE LEFT BANK
*(See pp120–31)*

BOULEVARD ST- MICHEL

D'ASSAS

**The Centre Pompidou**
(1977) is as famous for its
novel inside-out design as
it is for masterpieces by
Picasso, Matisse, and
Miró *(see pp96–7).*

**Notre-Dame**, a stunning example of Gothic architecture
begun in 1163, took two centuries and armies of medieval
workers to complete *(see pp90–91)*. Architect Viollet-le-Duc
designed the spire in the 19th century.

0 kilometers 1
0 miles 0.5

# A RIVER VIEW OF PARIS

The remarkable French music-hall star Mistinguett described the Seine as a "pretty blonde with laughing eyes." The river most certainly has a beguiling quality, but the relationship that exists between it and the city of Paris is far more than one of flirtation.

No other European city defines itself by its river in the same way as Paris. The Seine is the essential point of reference to the city: distances are measured from it, street numbers determined by it, and it divides the capital into two distinct areas: the Right Bank on the north side of the river and the Left Bank on the south side. These are as well defined as any of the official boundaries. The city is also divided historically: the east is linked to the city's ancient roots and the west to the 19th–20th centuries. Many of the most notable buildings in Paris are either along the riverbank or within a stone's throw of it. The docks are lined by bourgeois apartments, magnificent town houses, world-renowned museums, and striking monuments.

Above all, the river is very much alive. For centuries, fleets of small boats used it. Today, the river is busy with commercial barges and massive *Bâteaux-Mouches* (pleasure boats) carrying sightseers. Initiatives have been put in place to restrict motorized traffic along the Seine and both riverbanks in the city center are largely traffic-free.

**The Berges de Seine** is a river promenade on the Left Bank running from the Musée d'Orsay to Pont de l'Alma. It has sport and leisure amenities along with numerous cafés.

see pp80–81

CHAMPS-ELYSEES AND INVALIDES

see pp82–3

TUILERIES AND OPERA

ILE DE LA CITE, MARAIS AND BEAUBOURG

Seine

CHAMPS-ELYSEES AND INVALIDES

Seine

THE LEFT BANK

**This map** shows the sections of the river depicted on the following pages.

**Les Bouquinistes**, the bookstands on the riverbanks, are treasure troves of secondhand books and prints, and perfect for an afternoon's browsing.

0 kilometers    2
0 miles    1

**Key**

Illustrated area

◄ River view of Paris from the height of the Eiffel Tower

# From Pont de Grenelle to Pont de la Concorde

The grand monuments along this stretch of the river are remnants of the Napoleonic era and the Industrial Revolution. The elegance of the Eiffel Tower, the Petit Palais, and the Grand Palais is matched by more recent buildings, such as the Palais de Chaillot and the Musée du Quai Branly.

**Palais de Chaillot**
Built for the 1937 Exhibition, the spectacular colonnaded wings house several museums and a theater *(pp114–15)*.

**The Palais de Tokyo**
Bourdelle's statues adorn the facades *(p114)*.

**The Pont Bir-Hakeim** has a dynamic statue by Wederkinch rising at its north end.

Bateaux Parisiens
Tour Eiffel
Vedettes de Paris
Ile-de-France

Trocadéro **M**

Pont d'Iéna

Passerelle Debilly

Musée du Quai Branly

**Maison de Radio France**
is an imposing circular building, inaugurated in 1963. It houses studios as well as a radio museum.

Passy **M**

Pont de Bir-Hakeim

**Eiffel Tower**
This is Paris's most identifiable landmark *(p117)*.

Champ de Mars Tour Eiffel **RER**

Prés. Kennedy
Radio France
**RER**

**M**
Bir-Hakeim

**The *Statue of Liberty***
was given to the city in 1885. It faces west, toward the original Liberty in New York.

Pont de Grenelle

## Key

**M** Métro station

**RER** RER station

**O** Batobus stop

 River trip boarding point

**Grand Palais**
Major exhibitions and a science museum are based here (p113).

**Petit Palais**
Now the Paris museum of fine arts, this was first designed as a companion to the Grand Palais (pp112–13).

Champs-Elysées Clemenceau Ⓜ

Pont des Invalides

Pont Alexandre III

Pont de la Concorde

Alma Marceau Ⓜ

Pont de l'Alma

RER Pont de l'Alma

Ⓜ RER Invalides

Bateaux-Mouches

La Tour Maubourg Ⓜ

**The Zouave**, a statue on the Pont de l'Alma, is a useful gauge for checking flood levels.

**The Liberty Flame** is a memorial to the fighters of the French Resistance during World War II.

**The Assemblée Nationale Palais-Bourbon** was originally built for Louis XIV's daughter. It has accommodated the lower house of the French Parliament since 1830.

**Dôme des Invalides**
The majestic dome (p119), now used as a burial site for many of France's war heroes, is here seen from Pont Alexandre III. Napoleon's tomb is in the crypt.

**Pont Alexandre III**
Flamboyant statuary decorates Paris's most ornate bridge (p113).

# From Pont de la Concorde to Pont de Sully

The historic heart of Paris lies on
the banks and islands of the east
river. At its center is the Ile de la
Cité, a natural stepping stone
across the Seine and the cultural
core of medieval Paris. Today it
is still vital to Parisian life.

**Jardin des Tuileries**
These are laid out in the
formal style (pp102–3).

**Musée du Louvre**
Before becoming the world's greatest
museum and home to the *Mona Lisa*,
this was Europe's largest royal palace
(pp104–7).

**Musée de l'Orangerie**
An important collection of
19th-century paintings is on
display here (p102).

**Musée d'Orsay**
This converted railway station houses
Paris's outstanding collection of
Impressionist art (pp124–5).

**Vedettes du
Pont-Neuf**

**Monnaie de Paris,**
the Mint, built in 1778,
has an extensive coin and
medallion collection in its
old milling halls and
features a restaurant by
famed chef Guy Savoy.

## Batobus cruises

The boarding points are: **Eiffel Tower. Map** 6 D3.
Ⓜ Bir-Hakeim. **Champs-Elysées. Map** 7 B1.
Ⓜ Champs-Elysées-Clemenceau or Concorde.
**Musée d'Orsay. Map** 8 D2. Ⓜ Assemblée
Nationale. **Louvre. Map** 8 E2. Ⓜ Palais Royal-Musée
du Louvre. **Hôtel de Ville. Map** 9 B4. Ⓜ Hôtel de
Ville. **Notre-Dame. Map** 9 B4. Ⓜ St-Michel or
Maubert-Mutualité. **St.-Germain-des-Prés. Map** 8
E4. Ⓜ St-Germain des Prés. **Jardin des Plantes.
Map** 13 C1. Ⓜ Jussieu or Cardinal-Lemoines.
***Departures*** early Sep–early Apr: 10am–7pm (every
25 mins); early Apr–early Sep: 10am–9:30pm (every
20 mins). **Tel** 08 25 05 01 01. 🖳 **batobus.com**

**Passerelle des Arts**
This steel reconstruction
of Paris's first cast-iron
bridge (1804) was
inaugurated in 1984.

*For hotels and restaurants in this region see pp554–5 and pp576–9*

Concorde Ⓜ

Pont de la Concorde

Assemblée
Nationale Ⓜ

Passerelle Solférino

Musée d'Orsay RER

Pont Royal

Pont du Carrousel

Passerelle des Arts

## How to Take a Seine Cruise

### Vedettes du Pont-Neuf

Boarding point: **Square du Vert-Galant** (Pont Neuf). **Map** 8 F3. **Tel** 01 46 33 98 38. Ⓜ Pont Neuf. ⓇⒺⓇ Châtelet/St.-Michel. 🚌 27, 58, 67, 70, 72, 74, 75. **Departures** Mar 15–Oct 31: 10:30 am, 11:15am, noon, 1:30–10:30pm (every 30 mins) daily; Nov–Mar 14: 10:30am, 11:15am, noon, 2–6:30pm (every 45 mins), 8pm, 10pm Mon–Thu, 10:30am, 11:15am, noon, 2–6:30pm (every 30 mins), 8pm, 9pm, 10pm Fri–Sun. **Duration** 1 hr. Snacks available. Ⓦ **vedettesdupontneuf.com**

### Bateaux-Mouches

Boarding point: **Pont de l'Alma. Map** 6 E2. **Tel** 01 76 64 79 12 Ⓜ Alma-Marceau. ⓇⒺⓇ Pont de l'Alma. 🚌 28, 42, 63, 72, 80, 81, 92. **Departures** Apr–Sep: 10:15am–10:30pm daily (every 20–45 mins); Oct–Mar: 11am–9:20pm Mon–Fri, 10:15am–9:20pm Sat & Sun (every 30–60 mins). **Duration** 1hr 10 mins. **Lunch cruise** 1pm Sat, Sun, bank hols (boards 12:15pm). **Dinner cruise** 8:30pm daily (boards 7:30–8:15pm). **Duration** 2 hrs 15 mins. Jacket and tie. Ⓦ **bateaux-mouches.fr**

### Vedettes de Paris Ile-de-France

Boarding point: **Port du Suffren. Map** 6 D3. **Tel** 01 44 18 19 50. Ⓜ Trocadéro, Bir-Hakeim. ⓇⒺⓇ Champ-de-Mars–Tour Eiffel. 🚌 22, 30, 32, 42, 44, 63, 69, 72, 82, 87. **Departures** mid-Feb–Oct 10:30am–9pm (Apr–Sep: to 11pm; Oct: 10pm) (every 45 mins); Nov–mid-Feb: 11:15am–9pm Mon–Fri, 10:30am–10pm Sat & Sun (every 20–45 mins). **Duration** 1hr. **Champagne cruise** 6pm Thu–Sat (May–Aug: 6:30pm daily). **Duration** 1hr. **Dinner cruise** 9:15pm daily. **Duration** 2 hrs 30 mins. Ⓦ **vedettesdeparis.com**

### Bateaux Parisiens Tour Eiffel

Boarding point: **Port de la Bordonnais** (foot of Eiffel Tower). **Map** 6 D2. **Tel** 08 25 01 01 01. Ⓜ Trocadéro, Bir-Hakeim. ⓇⒺⓇ Champ-de-Mars–Tour Eiffel. 🚌 42, 82. **Departures** Apr–Sep: 10am–10:30pm (Jun–Aug: to 11pm); Oct–Mar: 10:30am–10pm (every 30 mins). **Duration** 1 hr. **Lunch cruise** 12:30pm daily (duration 2 hrs). **Dinner cruises** 6pm (boards 5–6pm, duration 1 hr, 30 mins) & 8:30pm (boards 7:15–8:15pm, duration 2 hrs, 30 mins) daily. Jacket and tie. Ⓦ **bateauxparisiens.com**

### Ile de la Cité
This tiny island on the Seine was first inhabited around 200 BC by a Celtic tribe known as the Parisii (pp86–7).

### Notre-Dame
This towering cathedral surveys the river (pp90–91).

**The Ile St.-Louis** has been a desirable address since the 17th century, when its elegant houses were built (p89).

### Conciergerie
During the Revolution this building, with its distinctive towers, became notorious as a prison (p87).

# ILE DE LA CITE, MARAIS, AND BEAUBOURG

The Right Bank is dominated by the modernistic Forum des Halles and Centre Pompidou in the Beaubourg. These are Paris's most thriving public areas, with millions of tourists, shoppers, and students flowing between them. Parisians look for the latest street fashions and designer boutiques in the underground shopping complex at Les Halles, with its huge undulating glass-and-steel roof known as "The Canopy." All roads from here appear to lead to the Centre Pompidou, an avant-garde assembly of pipes, ducts, and cables housing the Musée National d'Art Moderne. The smaller streets around the center are full of art galleries housed in crooked, gabled buildings. The neighboring Marais was abandoned by its royal residents during the 1789 Revolution, and it descended into an architectural wasteland before being rescued in the 1960s. It has since become a very fashionable address, peppered with boutiques, hip restaurants, small cafés, and artisan bakeries.

Notre-Dame cathedral, the Palais de Justice, and Sainte-Chapelle draw tourists to the Ile de la Cité. At the eastern end, a bridge connects with the Ile St-Louis, a former swampy pastureland transformed into a residential area with pretty, tree-lined quays and mansions.

## Sights at a Glance

### Islands and Squares
- ❼ Ile St.-Louis
- ❽ Forum des Halles
- ❿ Place des Vosges
- ㉑ Place de la Bastille

### Churches
- ❹ Sainte-Chapelle
- ❻ Notre-Dame pp90–91
- ❾ St-Gervais–St-Protais
- ⓬ St.-Eustache

### Historic Buildings
- ❷ Conciergerie
- ❸ Palais de Justice
- ❿ Hôtel de Ville
- ⓫ Tour St.-Jacques

### Museums and Galleries
- ❺ Crypte Archéologique
- ❽ Hôtel des Archeveques de Sens
- ⓮ Centre Pompidou pp96–7

- ⓯ Musée d'Art et d'Histoire du Judaïsme
- ⓰ Hôtel de Soubise
- ⓱ Musée Picasso
- ⓲ Musée Carnavalet
- ⓴ Maison de Victor Hugo

### Bridges
- ❶ Pont Neuf

See also Street Finder maps 8, 9, 10

0 meters 500
0 yards 500

# Street by Street: Ile de la Cité

The origins of Paris are on the Ile de la Cité, the boat-shaped island on the Seine first inhabited by Celtic tribes in the 3rd century BC. One tribe, the Parisii, eventually gave its name to the city. The island offered a convenient river crossing on the route between northern and southern Gaul and was easily defended. In later centuries the settlement was expanded by the Romans, the Franks, and the Capetian kings to form the nucleus of today's city.

Remains of the first buildings can still be seen today in the archeological crypt of the great medieval cathedral of Notre-Dame. At the other end of the island is Sainte-Chapelle, another Gothic masterpiece.

❷ ★ **Conciergerie**
This sinister-looking building was the country's chief prison during the Revolution.

**The Marché aux Fleurs et Oiseaux** in place Louis-Lépine is one of the largest flower markets in Paris, with birds for sale on Sundays.

Métro Cité

To Pont Neuf

QUAI DES ORFÈVRES

PONT AU CHANGE

QUAI DE LA CORSE

RUE DE LUTECE

BLVD DU PALAIS

PONT ST-MICHEL

QUAI DU MARCHE-NEUF

RUE DE LA CITÉ

PETIT PONT

PALAIS DU PARVIS NOTRE DAME

❸ **Palais de Justice**
With a history spanning over 16 centuries, the old palace is today a massive complex of law courts.

❹ ★ **Sainte-Chapelle**
A jewel of Gothic architecture, Sainte-Chapelle is famous for its magnificent stained-glass windows.

CRYPTE DU PARVIS

**Point Zéro** marks the spot from which all road distances are measured in France.

To Latin Quarter

❺ **Crypte Archéologique**
Deep under the square lie remnants of houses dating back 2,000 years.

**Key**

— Suggested route

*For hotels and restaurants in this region see pp554–5 and pp576–9*

**Hôtel Dieu**, the oldest hospital in Paris, was founded in AD 651 by St. Landry, Bishop of Paris.

**Locator Map**
*See Street Finder maps 9, 10*

**6 ★ Notre-Dame**
This cathedral, with its magnificent south-facing rose window and impressive array of gargoyles, is one of the finest examples of French Gothic architecture.

**Square Jean-XXIII**, a formal garden with a Neo-Gothic fountain opened in 1844, is an ideal spot from which to view the east end of the cathedral.

0 meters 100
0 yards 100

Pont Neuf, the city's oldest bridge

**❶ Pont Neuf**

75001. **Map** 8 F3. Ⓜ Pont Neuf, Cité.

Despite its name (New Bridge), this bridge is the oldest in Paris and has been immortalized by major literary and artistic figures. The first stone was laid by Henri III in 1578, but it was Henri IV (whose statue stands at the center) who inaugurated it and gave it its name in 1607.

**❷ Conciergerie**

2 bd du Palais 75001. **Map** 9 A3. **Tel** 01 53 40 60 80. Ⓜ Cité. **Open** 9:30am–6pm daily; last adm: 30 mins before closing). **Closed** Jan 1, May 1, Dec 25. Combined ticket with Sainte-Chapelle *(see p88)* available. phone to check. **w conciergerie. monuments-nationaux.fr**

Forming part of the huge Palais de Justice, the historic Conciergerie served as a prison from 1391 to 1914. Henri IV's assassin, François Ravaillac, was imprisoned and tortured here in 1610.

During the Revolution the building was packed with over 4,000 prisoners. Its most celebrated inmate was Marie Antoinette, who was held in a tiny cell until her execution in 1793. Others included Charlotte Corday, who stabbed Revolutionary leader Marat.

The Conciergerie has a superb four-aisled Gothic hall, where guards of the royal household once lived. Renovated during the 19th century, the building retains its 11th-century torture chamber and 14th-century clock tower.

A sculptured relief on the Palais de Justice

## ❸ Palais de Justice

4 bd du Palais (entrance at 8 bd du Palais) 75001. **Map** 9 A3. **Tel** 01 44 32 52 52. Ⓜ Cité. **Open** 8:30am–6pm Mon–Fri. **Closed** public hols & Aug recess. Ⓦ ca-paris.justice.fr

This huge block of buildings making up the law courts of Paris stretches the entire width of the Ile de la Cité. It is a splendid sight with its Gothic towers lining the docks. The site has been occupied since Roman times, when it was the governors' residence. It was the seat of royal power, until Charles V moved the court to the Marais following a bloody revolt in 1358. In April 1793 the notorious Revolutionary Tribunal began dispensing justice from the Première Chambre Civile, or first civil chamber. Today the site embodies Napoleon's great legacy – the French judicial system.

## ❹ Sainte-Chapelle

8 bd du Palais 75001. **Map** 9 A3. **Tel** 01 53 40 60 80. Ⓜ Cité. **Open** Apr–mid-May and mid-Sep–end Sep: 9am–7pm; mid-May–mid-Sep: 9am–9:30pm; Oct–Mar: 9am–5pm. **Closed** Jan 1, May 1, Dec 25. 🎟 Combined ticket with Conciergerie (see p87) available. No sharp objects permitted. 📷 📹 Ⓦ sainte-chapelle.fr

Ethereal and magical, Sainte-Chapelle has been hailed as one of the greatest architectural masterpieces of the Western world. In the Middle Ages the devout likened this church to "a gateway to heaven." Today no visitor can fail to be transported by the blaze of light created by the 15 magnificent stained-glass windows, separated by pencil-like columns soaring 50 ft (15 m) to the star-studded roof. The windows portray more than 1,000 biblical scenes in a kaleidoscope of red, gold, green, and blue. Starting from the left near the entrance and proceeding clockwise, you can trace the scriptures from Genesis through to the Cruci-fixion and the Apocalypse.

The chapel was completed in 1248 by Louis IX to house what was believed to be Christ's Crown of Thorns and fragments of the True Cross (now in the treasury at Notre-Dame). The king, who was canonized for his good works, purchased the relics from the Emperor of Constantinople, paying three times more for them than for the entire construction of Sainte-Chapelle.

The building actually consists of two separate chapels. The somber lower chapel was used by servants and lower court officials, while the exquisite upper chapel, reached via a narrow spiral stair-case, was reserved for the royal family and its courtiers. A discreetly placed window enabled the king to take part in the celebrations unobserved.

## ❺ Crypte Archéologique

Parvis Notre-Dame–7 pl Jean-Paul II 75004. **Map** 9 A4. **Tel** 01 55 42 50 10. Ⓜ Cité. **Open** 10am–6pm Tue–Sun (last adm: 30 mins before closing). **Closed** Jan 1, May 1 & 8, Aug 15, Dec 25 & religious hols. 🎟 📷 Ⓦ crypte.paris.fr

Located beneath the *parvis* (main square) of Notre-Dame and stretching 393 ft (120 m) underground, the crypt was opened in 1980.

There are Gallo-Roman streets and houses with an underground heating system, sections of Lutetia's 3rd-century-BC wall, and remains of the cathedral. Models explain the development of Paris from a settlement of the Parisii, the Celtic tribe who inhabited the island 2,000 years ago.

## ❻ Notre-Dame

*See pp90–91.*

During the Revolution the building was badly damaged and became a warehouse. It was renovated a century later by Félix Duban and Jean-Baptiste Lassus.

Today, evening concerts of classical music are held regularly in the chapel, taking advantage of its superb acoustics.

The magnificent interior of Sainte-Chapelle

## ❼ Ile St.-Louis

75004. **Map** 9 C4. Ⓜ Pont Marie, Sully Morland. St.-Louis-en-l'Ile: 19 rue St.-Louis en l'Ile. **Tel** 01 46 34 11 60. **Open** 9:30am–1pm & 2–7:30pm daily (7pm Sun & public hols). ✝ 6:45pm Mon–Fri, 6:30pm Sat, 11am Sun. Concerts 🔲 **saintlouisenlile. catholique.fr**

Across Pont St.-Louis from Ile de la Cité, Ile St.-Louis is a little haven of quiet streets and riverside docks. The luxurious restaurants and stores include famous ice-cream maker Berthillon. Almost everything on the Ile was built in Classical style in the 17th century. The church of **St.-Louis-en-l'Ile**, with its marble-and-gilt Baroque interior, was completed in 1726 from plans by royal architect Louis de Vau. Note the 1741 iron clock at the church entrance, the pierced iron spire, and a plaque given in 1926 by St. Louis, Missouri. The church is twinned with Carthage Cathedral in Tunisia, where St. Louis is buried.

The interior of St.-Louis-en-l'Ile

## ❽ Hôtel des Archeveques de Sens

1 rue du Figuier 75004. **Map** 9 C4. **Tel** 01 42 78 14 60. Ⓜ Pont-Marie. **Open** 10am–7:30pm Wed, Thu (from 1pm Tue, Fri, Sat). **Closed** public hols. 📷

One of only a handful of medieval buildings still standing in Paris, the Hôtel de Sens is home to the Forney arts library. During the period of the Catholic League

in the 16th century, it was turned into a fortified mansion and occupied by the Bourbons, the Guises, and Cardinal de Pellevé.

## ❾ St.-Gervais–St.-Protais

Pl St.-Gervais 75004. **Map** 9 B3. **Tel** 01 48 87 32 02. Ⓜ Hôtel de Ville. **Open** 5:30am–9pm daily. Organ concerts.

Named after Gervase and Protase, two Roman soldiers martyred by the Emperor Nero, this church has magnificent origins, which go back to the 6th century. It boasts the earliest Classical facade in Paris, dating from 1621, with a triple-tiered arrangement of Doric, Ionic, and Corinthian columns.

Behind the facade lies a late Gothic church renowned for its association with religious music. François Couperin (1668–1733) composed his two Masses for this church's organ.

---

## Upper Chapel Windows

1 Genesis
2 Exodus
3 Numbers
4 Deuteronomy: Joshua
5 Judges
6 *left* Isaiah *right* Rod of Jesse
7 *left* St. John the Evangelist *right* Childhood of Christ
8 Christ's Passion
9 *left* St. John the Baptist *right* Story of Daniel
10 Ezekiel
11 *left* Jeremiah *right* Tobias
12 Judith and Job
13 Esther
14 Book of Kings
15 Story of the Relics
16 Rose Window: The Apocalypse

**The spire** rises 245 ft (75 m) into the air.

**The stained-glass windows** of the upper chapel constitute a vast illustrated Bible.

**The upper chapel** was reserved for the royal family and its entourage.

**The Crown of Thorns** adorns the chapel's pinnacle.

**The Rose Window** tells the biblical story of the Apocalypse in 86 panels of stained glass.

Main portals

**The lower chapel** was used by servants and commoners.

# ❻ Notre-Dame

No other building epitomizes the history of Paris more than Notre-Dame. Built on the site of a Roman temple, the cathedral was commissioned by Bishop de Sully in 1159. The first stone was laid in 1163, marking the start of two centuries of toil by armies of Gothic architects and medieval craftsmen. It has been witness to great events of French history, including the coronations of Henry VI in 1422 and Napoleon Bonaparte in 1804. During the Revolution it was desecrated and rechristened the Temple of Reason. Extensive renovations (including the addition of the spire and gargoyles) were carried out in the 19th century by architect Viollet-le-Duc (1814–79). Notre-Dame received a new set of bells in 2012 to celebrate its 850th anniversary.

★ **West Facade**
The beautifully proportioned west facade is a masterpiece of French Gothic architecture.

★ **Galerie des Chimères**
The cathedral's legendary gargoyles (chimères) gaze menacingly from the cathedral's ledge.

## KEY

① **The Kings' Gallery** features 28 stone images of the kings of Judah.

② **West Rose Window** depicts the Virgin in a medallion of rich reds and blues.

③ **Some 387 steps** lead to the top of the south tower, where the famous Emmanuel bell is housed.

④ **The spire**, designed by Viollet-le-Duc, soars to a height of 315 ft (96 m).

⑤ **The treasury** houses the cathedral's religious treasures, including ancient manuscripts and reliquaries.

⑥ **The transept** was built at the start of Philippe-Auguste's reign, in the 13th century.

**Portal of the Virgin**
The Virgin surrounded by saints and kings is a fine composition of 13th-century statues.

★ **Flying Buttresses**
Jean Ravy's spectacular flying buttresses at the east end of the cathedral have a span of 50 ft (15 m).

## VISITORS' CHECKLIST

### Practical Information
6 Parvis Notre-Dame–pl Jean-Paul II. **Map** 9 B4. **Tel** 01 42 34 56 10. **Open** 8am–6:45pm (7:15pm Sat, Sun). Towers: **Open** 10am–5:30pm (6:30pm Apr–Sep). **Closed** Jan 1, May 1, Dec 25. 🛐 8am, 9am, noon, & 6:15pm Mon–Fri; 8am, 9am, & 6:30pm Sat; 8:30am, 10am, 11:30am, 12:45, & 6:30pm Sun. 🗐 🖵 🖩 notredamedeparis.fr

### Transportation
Ⓜ Cité. 🚌 21, 27, 38, 47, 85, 96. ⓇNotre-Dame. 🅿 pl Parvis.

**The Interior**
The view from the main entrance takes in the high-vaulted central nave, choir, and high altar.

★ **South Rose Window**
This south facade window, with its central depiction of Christ, is an impressive 43 ft (13 m) high.

**The "Mays" Paintings**
These religious paintings, by Charles Le Brun and Le Sueur among others, were presented by the Paris guilds every May 1 from 1630 to 1707.

# Street by Street: The Marais

Once an area of marshland (*marais* means "swamp"), the Marais grew steadily in importance from the 14th century, by virtue of its proximity to the Louvre, the preferred residence of Charles V. Its heyday was in the 17th century, when it became a fashionable area for the monied classes, many of whose grand mansions (*hôtels*) have now been restored as museums. Once again fashionable, chic designer boutiques alternate with small restaurants and stores.

RUE BARBETTE

RUE ELZEVIR

RUE DU PARC R

RUE PAYENNE

RUE DES HOSPITALIERES-ST-GERVAIS

To the Centre Pompidou

RUE DES

FRANCS

RUE DES ROSIERS

RUE MALHER

RUE PAVEE

**⑰ ★ Musée Picasso**
The palatial home of a 17th-century salt-tax collector houses the most extensive collection of Picassos in the world.

**Rue des Francs-Bourgeois**, built in 1334, was named after the *francs* – almshouses for the poor at Nos. 34 and 36.

**Musée Cognacq-Jay** contains an exquisite collection of 18th-century paintings and furniture.

**Hôtel de Lamoignon** was built in 1584 and houses Paris's historical library.

**Rue des Rosiers**, heart of the city's oldest Jewish quarter, is lined with 18th-century houses, stores, and cafés serving dishes such as hot pastrami and borscht.

**Key**

— Suggested route

| 0 meters | 100 |
| 0 yards | 100 |

**⑱ ★ Musée Carnavalet**
Occupying two large mansions, this museum covers the history of Paris from Prehistoric and Gallo-Roman times.

**🔞 ★ Place des Vosges**
This enchanting square is an oasis of peace and tranquillity.

**Locator Map**
*See Street Finder maps 9, 10*

**🔞 Maison de Victor Hugo**
Author of *Les Misérables*, Victor Hugo lived at 6 place des Vosges, now a museum of his life and work.

RUE DE BEARN

TURENNE

RGEOIS

RUE DE

RUE DE BIRAGUE

To Métro Sully Morland

Hôtel de Sully, with its orangery and courtyard, is an elegant Renaissance mansion.

## 🔟 Hôtel de Ville

Pl de l'Hôtel de Ville, 29 rue de Rivoli 75004. **Map** 9 B3. **Tel** 01 42 76 40 40. Ⓜ Hôtel-de-Ville. **Open** Groups: phone 2 months in advance (01 42 76 54 04). Individuals: days/hours vary, phone to reserve (01 42 76 43 43). **Closed** public hols, and for official functions (phone to check). ♿

The home of the city council is a 19th-century reconstruction of the 17th-century town hall burned down by insurgents of the Paris Commune in 1871. It is a highly ornate example of Third Republic architecture, with elaborate turrets and statues overlooking a pedestrianized square.

The 16th-century Tour St.-Jacques

## 🔟 Tour St.-Jacques

Sq de la Tour St.-Jacques 75004. **Map** 9 A3. Ⓜ Châtelet. **Open** Jun–late Oct: 10am–5pm Fri–Sun (01 83 96 15 05). Gardens open year-round. ♿ Ⓦ desmotsetdesarts.com

This imposing late Gothic tower, dating from 1523, is all that remains of a church used as a rendezvous by pilgrims setting out for Compostela in Spain. The building was destroyed by revolutionaries in 1797.

Earlier, Blaise Pascal, 17th-century philosopher, mathematician, physicist, and writer, used the tower for barometric experiments. His statue stands at the base of the tower, now used as a meteorological station.

## ⑫ St.-Eustache

2 impasse St.-Eustache 75001. **Map** 9 A1. **Tel** 01 42 36 31 05. Ⓜ Les Halles. Ⓡ Châtelet-Les-Halles. **Open** 9:30am–7pm Mon–Fri, 10am–7pm Sat, 9am–7pm Sun. 🕆 12:30pm Mon–Fri, 6pm Sat, 11am, 6pm Sun. Concerts. Ⓦ **saint-eustache.org**

With its Gothic plan and Renaissance decoration, St.-Eustache is one of Paris's most beautiful churches. Its massive interior is modeled on Notre-Dame, with five naves and side and radial chapels. The 105 years (1532–1637) it took to complete the church saw the flowering of the Renaissance style, which is evident in the magnificent arches, pillars, and columns.

St.-Eustache has hosted many ceremonial events, including the baptisms of Cardinal Richelieu and Madame de Pompadour, and the funerals of fabulist La Fontaine, Colbert (prime minister to Louis XIV), 17th-century dramatist Molière, and the revolutionary orator Mirabeau. It was here that Berlioz first performed his *Te Deum* in 1855. Today talented choir groups perform regularly, and organ recitals are often held here.

## ⑬ Forum des Halles

101 Porte Bergère 75001. **Map** 13 A2. **Tel** 01 44 76 87 08. Ⓜ Les Halles. Ⓡ Châtelet-Les-Halles. **Open** 10am–8pm Mon–Sat, 11am–7pm Sun (movie theaters/restaurants: 9:30am–11pm). Le Forum des Images: 2 rue du Cinéma. **Tel** 01 44 76 63 00. **Open** 12:30–9pm Tue–Fri, 2–9pm Sat & Sun. Ⓦ **forumdeshalles.com** Ⓦ **forumdesimages.fr**

Known simply as Les Halles and built amid controversy on the site of a famous fruit-and-vegetable market, the large underground complex is covered by an undulating glass-and-steel roof, known as "The Canopy", unveiled in 2016. Stores and restaurants abound, and there are two multiplex movie theaters, a movie resource center (the **Forum des Images**), and a gym and swimming pool. Above ground are gardens, pergolas, and mini-pavilions.

St.-Eustache and sculptured head, *L'Ecoute*, by Henri de Miller

## ⑭ Centre Pompidou

*See pp96–7.*

## ⑮ Musée d'Art et d'Histoire du Judaïsme

Hôtel de St.-Aignan, 71 rue du Temple 75003. **Map** 9 C2. **Tel** 01 53 01 86 60. Ⓜ Rambuteau. **Open** 11am–6pm Mon–Fri, 10am–6pm Sun. **Closed** Jewish hols. 🅿 ♿ 💻 📷 Ⓦ **mahj.org**

This museum in a Marais mansion, the elegant Hôtel de St.-Aignan, brings together collections formerly scattered around the city, and commemorates the culture of French Jewry from medieval times to the present. Visitors learn that there has been a sizable Jewish community in France since Roman times, and some of the world's greatest Jewish scholars – Rashi, Rabenu Tam, the Tosafists – were French. Much exquisite craftsmanship is displayed, with elaborate silverware, Torah covers, fabrics, and items of fine Judaica and religious objects for use both in the synagogue and in the home. There are also photographs, paintings, and cartoons and historical documents, including some on the anti-Semitic Dreyfus Affair around the turn of the 20th century.

## ⑯ Hôtel de Soubise

60 rue des Francs-Bourgeois 75003. **Map** 9 C2. **Tel** 01 40 27 60 96 (guided tours: 01 40 27 60 29). Ⓜ Rambuteau. **Open** 10am–5:30pm Mon, Wed–Fri, 2–5:30pm Sat & Sun. **Closed** public hols. 🅿 📷 1st Sat of month.

This imposing mansion, built from 1705 to 1709 for the Princesse de Rohan, houses the Musée des Archives Nationales. It boasts a majestic courtyard and 18th-century interior decoration by some of the best-known artists of the time.

Notable items held here include Natoire's *rocaille* work in the princess's bedchamber and Napoleon's will. Some of the rooms are accessible only to researchers, by appointment. Concerts and special events also take place here.

## ⑰ Musée Picasso

Hôtel Salé, 5 rue de Thorigny 75003. **Map** 10 D2. **Tel** 01 85 56 00 36. Ⓜ St.-Sébastien Froissart. **Open** 11:30am–6pm Tue–Fri (from 9:30am Sat, Sun & hols; to 9pm 3rd Fri of month). **Closed** Jan 1, May 1, Dec 25. 🅿 ♿ 📷 groups by appointment only. 📷 💻 Ⓦ **museepicassoparis.fr**

On the death of the Spanish-born artist Pablo Picasso (1881–1973), who lived most of his life in France, the French State inherited one quarter of his works in lieu of death duties. In 1986, it used them to create

*Woman Reading* (1932) by Pablo Picasso

the Musée Picasso in the beautifully restored Hôtel Salé, one of the loveliest buildings in the Marais. It was built in 1656 for Aubert de Fontenay, collector of the dreaded salt tax (salé means "salty").

Comprising 5,000 works, including over 200 paintings, 158 sculptures, 88 ceramic works, and some 3,000 sketches and engravings, this unique collection shows the enormous range and variety of Picasso's work, including examples from his Blue, Pink, and Cubist periods.

Highlights include his Blue period Self-portrait, painted at age 20; Still Life with Caned Chair, which introduced collage to Cubism; the Neo-Classical Pipes of Pan; and The Crucifixion.

The museum frequently loans canvases for special exhibitions elsewhere, so some works will be on show in other galleries.

# ⑱ Musée Carnavalet

16 rue des Francs-Bourgeois 75003. **Map** 10 D3. **Tel** 01 44 59 58 58. Ⓜ St-Paul, Chemin Vert. **Closed** for major renovations until 2020. 📷 ⓦ **carnavalet.paris.fr**

Devoted to the history of Paris since prehistoric times, this vast museum in two adjoining mansions is currently closed for major renovations until 2020. The interiors include entire decorated rooms with gilded paneling, furniture, and objets d'art; many works of art, such as paintings and sculptures of prominent personalities; and engravings showing Paris being built.

The main building is the Hôtel Carnavalet, which was built as a town house in 1548 by Nicolas Dupuis. The literary hostess Madame de Sévigné lived here between 1677 and 1696, entertaining the intelligentsia of the day and writing her celebrated Lettres. Many of her possessions are in the first-floor exhibition covering the Louis XIV era.

The 17th-century Hôtel le Peletier, opened in 1989,

Magnificent 17th-century ceiling painting by Charles Le Brun, Musée Carnavalet

features reonstructions of early 20th-century interiors and artifacts from the Revolution and Napoleonic era. The Orangery houses a section devoted to Prehistory and Gallo-Roman Paris. The collection includes pirogues discovered in 1992, during an archaeological dig in the Parc de Bercy, which unearthed a Neolitich village.

# ⑲ Place des Vosges

75003, 75004. **Map** 10 D3. Ⓜ Bastille, St-Paul.

This perfectly symmetrical square, laid out in 1605 by Henri IV, is considered among the most beautiful in the world. Thirty-six houses, nine on each side, are built over arcades that today accommodate antiques shops and fashionable cafés. The square has been the scene of many historical events over the centuries, including a three-day tournament in celebration of the marriage of Louis XIII to Anne of Austria in 1615.

# ⑳ Maison de Victor Hugo

6 pl des Vosges 75004. **Map** 10 D3. **Tel** 01 42 72 10 16. Ⓜ Bastille. **Open** 10am–6pm Tue–Sun. **Closed** public hols. 📷 Library ⓦ **maisonvictorhugo.paris.fr**

The French poet, dramatist and novelist lived on the second floor of the former Hôtel de Rohan-Guéménée, the largest house on the square,

from 1832 to 1848. It was here that he wrote most of Les Misérables. On display are reconstructions of some of the rooms in which he lived, complete with his desk, his drawings, and mementos from key periods of his life, from his childhood to his exile between 1852 and 1870. There are also regular temporary exhibitions.

# ㉑ Place de la Bastille

75004. **Map** 10 E4. Ⓜ Bastille.

Nothing remains of the infamous prison stormed by the revolutionary mob on July 14 1789, the event that sparked the French Revolution.

The 164-ft (50-m) Colonne de Juillet stands in the middle of the traffic-clogged square to honor the victims of the July Revolution of 1830. On the south side of the square (at 120 rue de Lyon) is the 2,700-seat **Opéra National de Paris Bastille**, completed in 1989, the bicentennial of the French Revolution.

To the south of the square is **Bassin de l'Arsenal** marina, with pleasure boats, bars, restaurants, and art galleries, and the small **Jardin de l'Arsenal**. Just east of the Opéra Bastille is the start of the **Promenade Plantée**, a 2.8-mile (4.5-km) elevated walking trail along a disused railroad.

The "genius of liberty" statue on top of the Colonne de Juillet, Place de la Bastille

# ⓮ Centre Pompidou

The Centre Pompidou is like a building turned inside out: escalators, elevators, air and water ducts, and even the massive steel struts that make up the building's skeleton are all on the outside. This allowed the architects, Richard Rogers, Renzo Piano, and Gianfranco Franchini, to create a flexible exhibition space. Among the artists featured in the Musée National d'Art Moderne (MNAM) inside are Matisse, Picasso, Miró, and Pollock, representing such schools as Fauvism, Cubism, and Surrealism. The Centre Pompidou also keeps abreast of the Paris art scene with frequently changing temporary exhibitions. Outside in the piazza, crowds gather to watch street performers.

**Key**

☐ Exhibition space
▨ Nonexhibition space

**This riotous jumble** of glass and steel, known as Beaubourg, is Paris's top tourist attraction, built in 1977 and drawing over 7 million visitors a year.

**Mobile on Two Planes** (1955)
The 20th-century American artist Alexander Calder introduced the mobile as an art form.

To the Atelier Brancusi ↗

## Gallery Guide

*The permanent collections are on the fourth, fifth, and sixth levels: works from 1905 to 1960 are on the former, contemporary art on the latter. The first and sixth levels also host temporary exhibitions; the second and third house a library. The lower levels make up "The Forum," the focal public area, with a performance center, a movie theater, stores, and a children's workshop.*

**Sorrow of the King** (1952)
This collage was created by Matisse using gouache-painted paper cutouts.

**Portrait of the Journalist Sylvia von Harden** (1926)
The surgical precision of Otto Dix's style makes this a harsh caricature.

**Le Duo** (1937)
Georges Braque, like Picasso, developed the Cubist technique of representing different views of a subject in a single picture.

Basin and Sculpture Terrace

**With the Black Arc** (1912)
The transition to Abstraction, one of the major art forms of the 20th century, can be seen in the works of Wassily Kandinsky.

**Stravinsky Fountain**
This fountain, which was inaugurated in 1983, is in the place Igor Stravinsky near the Centre Pompidou. It was designed by sculptors Jean Tinguely and Niki de Saint Phalle, both of whom are represented in the Centre Pompidou.

## Brancusi Workshop

The Atelier Brancusi, on the rue Rambuteau side of the piazza, is a reconstruction of the workshop of the Romanian-born artist Constantin Brancusi (1876–1957), who lived and worked in Paris. He bequeathed his entire collection of works to the French state on condition that his workshop be rebuilt as it was. The collection includes over 200 sculptures and plinths, 1,600 photographs, exhibited in rotation, and tools that Brancusi used to create his works. Also featured are some of his more personal items, such as documents, pieces of furniture, and his book collection.

Interior of the Brancusi workshop, designed by Renzo Piano

# TUILERIES AND OPERA

The 19th-century grandeur of Baron Haussmann's *grands boulevards* offsets the bustle of bankers, theatergoers, sightseers, and shoppers who frequent the area around the Opéra. A profusion of shops and department stores, ranging from the exclusively expensive to the popular, draws the crowds. Much of the area's older character is found in the early 19th-century shopping arcades, with elaborate steel-and-glass roofs. They are known as *galeries* or *passages*, and were restored to their former glory in the 1970s. Galerie Vivienne, which is the smartest, has an elaborate, patterned mosaic floor. The passage des Panoramas, passage Verdeau, and tiny passage des Princes are more old-style Parisian. These streets abound with curious stores of all kinds, from mouthwatering food stores to antiquarian bookstores and stamp collectors' havens.

The Tuileries area lies between the Opéra and the river, bounded by the vast place de la Concorde in the west and the Louvre to the east. The Louvre palace combines one of the world's greatest art collections with I. M. Pei's avant-garde glass pyramid. Elegant squares and formal gardens give the area its special character. Monuments to monarchy and the arts coexist with modern luxury at its most ostentatious. Place Vendôme, home to exquisite jewelry stores and the luxurious Ritz Hotel, is a heady mix of the wealthy and the chic. Parallel to the Jardin des Tuileries are two of Paris's foremost shopping streets, rue de Rivoli and rue St.-Honoré, full of expensive boutiques, bookstores, and deluxe hotels.

## Sights at a Glance

### Museums and Galleries
❸ Musée Grévin
❻ Galerie Nationale du Jeu de Paume
❽ Musée de l'Orangerie
⓫ Musée des Arts Décoratifs
⓮ *Musée du Louvre pp104–7*

### Squares, Parks, and Gardens
❺ Place Vendôme
❼ Place de la Concorde
❾ Jardin des Tuileries

### Monuments
⓬ Arc de Triomphe du Carrousel

### Historic Buildings
❷ Opéra National de Paris Garnier
⓭ Palais Royal

### Churches
❶ La Madeleine
❿ St.-Roch

### Shops
❹ Les Passages

*See also Street Finder maps 3, 4, 7, 8*

# Street by Street: Opéra Quarter

It has been said that the whole world will pass you by if you sit for long enough at the Café de la Paix (opposite the Opéra National de Paris Garnier). During the day, the area is a center of commerce, tourism, and shopping, with mammoth department stores lining the adjacent *grands boulevards*. In the evening, the clubs and theaters in this area attract a totally different crowd, and the cafés along boulevard des Capucines throb with life.

**❷ ★ Opéra National de Paris Garnier**
Dating from 1875, the grandiose opera house has come to symbolize the opulence of the Second Empire.

Statue by Gumery on the Opéra

**No. 26 place de la Madeleine** is home to Fauchon, the most exclusive gourmet food store in Paris.

Métro Madeleine

**❶ ★ La Madeleine**
The original model of the Madeleine can be seen at the Musée Carnavalet (*see p95*).

**Boulevard des Capucines**
(No. 14) is where the Lumière brothers staged the first public screening of a movie on December 28, 1895.

**Locator Map**
*See Street Finder maps 3, 4*

**Bibliothèque and Musée de l'Opéra** contains the scores of every ballet and opera performed at the Opéra, and memorabilia, from Nijinsky's dancing shoes to Pavlova's tiara.

**PL DIAGHILEV**

Opéra National de Paris Garnier

PL DE L'OPERA

Métro Opéra

RUE DAUNOU

**Place de l'Opéra** was designed by Baron Haussmann and is one of Paris's busiest intersections.

**Key**

— Suggested route

| 0 meters | 100 |
| 0 yards | 100 |

Marochetti's *Mary Magdalene Ascending to Heaven* in La Madeleine

## ❶ La Madeleine

Pl de la Madeleine 75008. **Map** 3 C5. **Tel** 01 44 51 69 00. Ⓜ Madeleine. **Open** 9:30am–7pm daily. ✝ 12:30pm Mon–Fri, 6:30pm Tue–Fri, 6pm Sat, 9:30am, 11am, 6pm Sun. 🎵 Concerts Ⓦ eglise-lamadeleine.com

Modeled after a Greek temple, La Madeleine was begun in 1764 but not consecrated until 1845. Before that, there were proposals to turn it into a stock exchange, a bank, or a theater.

Corinthian columns encircle the building, supporting a sculptured frieze. Three ceiling domes crown the inside, which is richly decorated with sculptures, rose marble, and gilt.

## ❷ Opéra National de Paris Garnier

Pl de l'Opéra 75009. **Map** 4 E4. **Tel** 08 92 89 90 90 or 01 75 25 24 23 (from abroad); 08 25 05 44 05 (bookings). Ⓜ Opéra. **Open** 10am–4:30pm daily (until 5:30pm mid-Jul–late Aug). **Closed** Jan 1, May 1 & special events. 🎵 (Wed, Sat & Sun in English). Ⓦ visitpalaisgarnier.fr

Sometimes compared to a giant wedding cake, this lavish building was designed by Charles Garnier for Napoleon III in 1862. The Prussian War and the 1871 uprising delayed the opening until 1875.

The interior is famous for its Grand Staircase made of white Carrara marble, topped by a huge chandelier, as well as for its auditorium bedecked in red velvet and gold, with a false ceiling painted by Chagall in 1964. It is primarily used for dance, but shares operatic productions with the Opéra National de Paris Bastille *(see p157)*.

## ❸ Musée Grévin

10 bd Montmartre 75009. **Map** 4 F4. **Tel** 01 47 70 85 05. Ⓜ Grands Boulevards. **Open** 10am–6pm Mon–Fri, 9:30am–7pm Sat, Sun & school vacations. 📷 🎵 Ⓦ grevin.com

Sign outside the Grévin

Founded in 1882, this is a Paris landmark, on a par with Madame Tussauds. The historical scenes include Louis XIV at Versailles and the arrest of Louis XVI. Notable figures from the worlds of art, politics, film, and sport are also on display. On the first floor is a holography museum devoted to optical tricks. The museum also houses a 320-seat theater.

## ❹ Les Passages

75002. **Map** 4 F5. Ⓜ Bourse.

The early 19th-century glass-roofed shopping arcades (known as *galeries* or *passages*) are to be found mainly between boulevard Montmartre and rue St.-Marc. They house an eclectic mixture of small stores selling anything from designer jewelry to rare books and art supplies. One of the most charming is the Galerie Vivienne (off rue Vivienne or rue des Petits Champs) with its mosaic floor and excellent wine bar.

## ❺ Place Vendôme

75001. **Map** 8 D1. Ⓜ Tuileries.

Perhaps the best example of 18th-century elegance in the city, the architect Jules Hardouin-Mansart's royal square was begun in 1698. The original plan was to house academies and embassies behind its arcaded façades, but instead bankers moved in and created sumptuous mansions for themselves. The square's most famous residents include Frédéric Chopin, who died here in 1849 at No. 12, and César Ritz, who established his famous hotel at No. 15 in 1898.

## ❻ Galerie Nationale du Jeu de Paume

Jardin des Tuileries, 1 place de la Concorde 75008. **Map** 7 C1. **Tel** 01 47 03 12 50. Ⓜ Concorde. **Open** 11am–9pm Tue, 11am–7pm Wed–Sun. **Closed** Jan 1, May 1, Dec 25. 🄯 ♿ 🄯 🄯 🄿 Ⓦ jeudepaume.org

The Jeu de Paume – literally "game of the palm" – was built as two royal tennis courts by Napoleon III in 1851 on the north side of the Tuileries Gardens. The courts were later converted into an art gallery and exhibition space. The Jeu de Paume now has rotating exhibitions of photography, video, and film.

## ❼ Place de la Concorde

75008. **Map** 7 C1. Ⓜ Concorde.

One of Europe's most magnificent and historic squares, the place de la Concorde was a swamp until the mid-18th century. It became the place Louis XV in 1775, when royal architect Jacques-Ange Gabriel was asked by the Louis XV to design a suitable setting for an equestrian statue of himself.

The monument, which lasted here less than 20 years, was replaced by the guillotine (the Black Widow, as it came to be known), and the square was renamed place de la Révolution. On January 21, 1793 Louis XVI was beheaded, followed by over 1,300 other victims, including Marie Antoinette, Madame du Barry, Charlotte Corday (Marat's assassin), and revolutionary leaders Danton and Robespierre.

The blood-soaked square was optimistically renamed place de la Concorde, after the Reign of Terror finally came to an end in 1794. In the 19th century a 3,300-year-old Luxor obelisk was presented to King Louis-Philippe as a gift from the viceroy of Egypt (who also donated Cleopatra's Needle in London), and two fountains and eight statues personifying French cities were added to the square.

Flanking rue Royale on the north side of the square are two of Gabriel's Neoclassical mansions, the Hôtel de la Marine and the exclusive Hôtel Crillon.

Monet's *Waterlilies (Nymphéas)* on display in the Musée de l'Orangerie

## ❽ Musée de l'Orangerie

Jardin des Tuileries, place de la Concorde 75001. **Map** 7 C1. **Tel** 01 44 77 80 07. Ⓜ Concorde. **Open** 9am–6pm Wed–Mon. **Closed** May 1, Dec 25. 🄯 🄯 🄿 by appt. 🄯 Ⓦ musee-orangerie.fr

Paintings from Claude Monet's crowning work, representing part of his waterlily series, fill the two oval upper floor rooms. Known as the *Nymphéas*, most of the canvases were painted between 1899 and 1921.

This superb work is complemented by the Walter-Guillaume collection, including 27 Renoirs, notably *Young Girls at the Piano*, works by Soutine, and 14 Cézannes, including *The Red Rock*. Picasso is represented by works including *The Female Bathers*, and Rousseau by nine paintings, notably *The Wedding*. Other works are by Matisse, Derain, Utrillo, and Modigliani.

## ❾ Jardin des Tuileries

75001. **Map** 8 D1. Ⓜ Tuileries, Concorde. **Open** Apr–May and Sep: 7am–9pm; Jun–Aug: 7am–11pm; Oct–Mar: 7:30am–7:30pm.

These Neoclassical gardens once belonged to the Palais des Tuileries, which the Communards razed to the ground in 1871. They were laid out in the 17th century

The 3,300-year-old obelisk from Luxor

by André Le Nôtre, who created the broad central avenue and geometric topiary. Ongoing restoration has created a new garden with lime and chestnut trees, and modern sculptures.

## ❿ St.-Roch

296 rue St.-Honoré 75001. **Map** 8 E1. **Tel** 01 42 44 13 20. Ⓜ Tuileries, Pyramides. **Open** 8:30am–7pm daily. **Closed** non-religious public hols. ✝ 12:30pm, 6:30pm Mon, Wed–Fri, 6:30pm Tue & Sat, 11am, 12:15pm, 6:30pm Sun. Concerts.

This huge church was designed by Jacques Lemercier, architect of the Louvre, and its foundation stone was laid by Louis XIV in 1653. It is a treasure house of religious art, much of it from now-vanished churches and monasteries, and contains the tombs of the playwright Pierre Corneille, the royal gardener André Le Nôtre, and the philosopher Denis Diderot.

Vien's *St. Denis Preaching to the Gauls* (1767) in St.-Roch

## ⓫ Musée des Arts Décoratifs

Palais du Louvre, 107–111 rue de Rivoli 75001. **Map** 8 E2. **Tel** 01 44 55 57 50. Ⓜ Palais Royal, Tuileries. **Open** 11am–6pm Tue–Sun (to 9pm Thu). **Closed** public hols. Library: **Tel** 01 44 55 59 36. **Open** 1–7pm Mon, 10am–7pm Tue, 10am–6pm Wed–Fri. **Closed** public hols. ♿ Ⓦ lesartsdecoratifs.fr

Occupying the northwest wing of the Palais du Louvre (along with the Musée de la Publicité

and the Musée de la Mode et du Textile), this museum offers an eclectic mix of decorative art and domestic design from the Middle Ages to the present day. The Art Nouveau and Art Deco rooms include a reconstruction of the home of couturier Jeanne Lanvin. Other floors show Louis XIV, XV, and XVI styles of decoration and furniture. Contemporary designers are also represented. The restaurant has breathtaking views over the Tuileries Gardens.

## ⓬ Arc de Triomphe du Carrousel

Pl du Carrousel 75001. **Map** 8 E2. Ⓜ Palais Royal.

This rose-marble arch was built by Napoleon to celebrate various military triumphs, notably the Battle of Austerlitz in 1805. The crowning statues, added in 1828, are copies of the famous Horses of St. Mark's, which Napoleon had stolen from Venice and was subsequently forced to return after his defeat at Waterloo in 1815.

The Buren Columns in the main courtyard of the Palais Royal

## ⓭ Palais Royal

Pl du Palais Royal 75001. Gardens: 6 rue de Montpensier. **Map** 8 E1. **Tel** 01 47 03 92 16. Ⓜ Palais Royal. Gardens and court: **Open** Apr–Sep: 8am–10:30pm daily; Oct–Mar: 8am–8:30pm daily. Ⓦ **palais-royal. monuments-nationaux.fr**

This former royal palace, built by Cardinal Richelieu in the early 17th century, passed to the Crown on his death and became the childhood home of Louis XIV. Under the 18th-century royal dukes of Orléans, it became the epicenter of brilliant gatherings, interspersed with periods of gambling and debauchery. It was from here that the clarion call to revolution roused the mobs to storm the Bastille on July 14 1789.

Today the south section of the building houses the Councils of State and the Ministry of Culture. Just to the west is the Comédie Française, established by Louis XIV in 1680. At the back of the palace are luxury stores where artists such as Colette and Cocteau once lived.

The Arc de Triomphe du Carrousel crowned by Victory riding a chariot

# ⑭ Musée du Louvre

The Musée du Louvre, containing one of the most important art collections in the world, has a history dating back to medieval times. First built as a fortress in 1190 by King Philippe-Auguste to protect Paris against Viking raids, it lost its keep in the reign of François I, who replaced it with a Renaissance-style building. Thereafter, four centuries of kings and emperors improved and enlarged it. Visitors should request a schedule of room closures from the information point, as not all rooms are open on any given day.

The Louvre's east facade, facing St.-Germain l'Auxerrois

**The Jardin du Carrousel** was once the grand approach to the Tuileries Palace, which was set ablaze in 1871 by insurgents of the Paris Commune.

Pyramid entrance

## KEY

① **Denon Wing**

② **The Carrousel du Louvre**, an underground visitors' complex (1993), with galleries, gift shops, restrooms, parking, and an information desk, lies beneath the Arc de Triomphe du Carrousel.

③ **An inverted glass pyramid** brings light to the subterranean complex, echoing the museum's main entrance on the Cour Napoléon.

④ **Cour Marly** is the glass-roofed courtyard that now houses the *Marly Horses* (see p107).

⑤ **Richelieu Wing**

⑥ **Cour Puget**

⑦ **Cour Khorsabad**

⑧ **Cour Carrée**

⑨ **The Salle des Caryatides** is named after the four monumental statues created by Jean Goujon in 1550 to support the upper gallery. Built for Henri II, it is the oldest room in the palace.

⑩ **Sully Wing**

⑪ **Cour Napoléon**

⑫ **Hall Napoléon** is located under the pyramid.

⑬ **Cour Visconti** houses Islamic art: over 3,000 objects from the 7th to the 19th centuries.

★ **Arc de Triomphe du Carrousel**
This triumphal arch was built to celebrate Napoleon's military victories in 1805.

## The Glass Pyramid

Plans for the modernization and expansion of the Louvre were first conceived in 1981. They included the transfer of the Ministry of Finance from the Richelieu Wing of the Louvre to new offices elsewhere, as well as a new main entrance designed by architect I. M. Pei in 1989. Made of metal and glass, the pyramid enables visitors to see the buildings around the palace, while allowing light down into the underground visitors' reception area.

### VISITORS' CHECKLIST

**Practical Information**
Main entrance: 99 rue de Rivoli, Pyramid Cours Napoléon. **Map** 8 E2. **P** Carrousel du Louvre (entrance via av du Général Lemonnier); pl du Louvre. **Open** 9am–6pm Wed–Mon (9:45pm Wed & Fri). **Closed** Jan 1, May 1, Dec 25. 🖼 (free 1st Sun of month, but with some restrictions Oct–Mar, for under-18s & 18- to 26-year-old EU nationals). ♿ 🎧 🎫 Switchboard 01 40 20 50 50, reception 01 40 20 53 17. 📷 📷 📷
**W louvre.fr** Advance bookings:
**W ticketweb.com W fnac.com**

**Transportation**
Ⓜ Palais Royal, Musée du Louvre. 🚌 21, 24, 27, 39, 48, 68, 69, 72, 81, 95. 🚆 Châtelet-Les-Halles. 🚤 Louvre.

**The Louvre of Charles V**
In about 1360, Charles V transformed Philippe-Auguste's old fortress, with its distinctive tower and keep, into a royal residence.

**★ Perrault's Colonnade**
The east facade, with its majestic rows of columns, was built by Claude Perrault, who worked on the Louvre with Louis Le Vau in the mid-17th century.

## Building the Louvre

Over many centuries the Louvre was enlarged by royalty, leaders, and architects, shown below with their dates.

### Major Alterations

- Reign of François I (1515–47)
- Catherine de' Medici (about 1560)
- Reign of Henri IV (1589–1610)
- Reign of Louis XIII (1610–43)
- Reign of Louis XIV (1643–1715)
- Reign of Napoleon I (1804–15)
- Reign of Napoleon III (1852–70)
- I. M. Pei (1989) (architect)

**★ Medieval Moats**
The base of the twin towers and the drawbridge support of Philippe-Auguste's fortress can be seen in the excavated area.

# Exploring the Louvre's Collection

Owing to the vast size of the Louvre's collection, it is useful to set a few viewing priorities before starting out. The collection of European paintings (1200–1848) is comprehensive, with over half the works by French artists. The departments of Oriental, Egyptian, Greek, Etruscan, and Roman antiquities feature numerous acquisitions and rare treasures. The varied display of objets d'art includes furniture and jewelry.

*The Raft of the Medusa* (1819) by Théodore Géricault

## European Painting: 1200 to 1848

Painting from northern Europe (Flemish, Dutch, German, and English) is well covered. One of the earliest Flemish works is Jan van Eyck's *Madonna of the Chancellor Rolin* (about 1435), showing the Chancellor of Burgundy kneeling in prayer before the Virgin and Child. Hieronymus Bosch's *Ship of Fools* (around 1500) is a satirical account of the futility of human existence. In the fine Dutch collection, Rembrandt's *Self-*

*Mona Lisa* (around 1503–19) by Leonardo da Vinci

*Portrait*, his *Disciples at Emmaus* (1648), and *Bathsheba* (1654) are examples of the artist's genius.

The three major German painters of the 15th and 16th centuries are represented by important works. There is a youthful *Self-Portrait* (1493) by Albrecht Dürer, a *Venus* (1529) by Lucas Cranach, and a portrait of the great humanist scholar Erasmus by Hans Holbein.

The impressive collection of Italian paintings is arranged in chronological order from 1200 to 1800. The father figures of the early Renaissance, Cimabue and Giotto, are here, as is Fra Angelico, with his *Coronation of the Virgin* (1430–32), and Raphaël, with his stately portrait of Count Baldassare Castiglione (1514–15). Several paintings by Leonardo da Vinci are on display; for instance, the *Virgin with the Infant Jesus and St Anne*, which is as enchanting as his *Mona Lisa*.

The Louvre's fine collection of French painting ranges from the 14th century to 1848. Paintings after this

date are housed in the Musée d'Orsay *(see pp124–5)*. Outstanding is Jean Fouquet's portrait of Charles VII (1450–55). The great 18th-century painter of melancholy, J. A. Watteau, is represented, as is J. H. Fragonard, master of the Rococo, whose delightfully frivolous subjects are evident in *The Bathers* from 1770.

## European Sculpture: 1100 to 1848

Early Flemish and German sculpture in the collection has many masterpieces such as Tilman Riemenschneider's *Virgin of the Annunciation* from the end of the 15th century, and a life-size nude figure of the penitent Mary Magdalene by Gregor Erhart (early 16th century). An important work of Flemish sculpture is Adrian de Vries's long-limbed *Mercury and Psyche* (1593), which was originally made for the court of Rudolph II in Prague.

The French section opens with early Romanesque works, such as the figure of Christ by a 12th-century Burgundian sculptor, and a head of St. Peter. With its eight black-hooded mourners, the late 15th-century tomb of Philippe Pot (a high-ranking official in Burgundy) is one of the more unusual pieces. Diane de Poitiers, Henri II's mistress, had a large figure of her namesake Diana, goddess of the hunt, installed in the courtyard of her castle west of Paris. It is now in the Louvre.

The tomb of Philippe Pot (late 15th century) by Antoine le Moiturier

The celebrated *Marly Horses* (1745) by Guillaume Coustou

The works of French sculptor Pierre Puget (1620–94) have been assembled in the Cour Puget. They include a figure of Milo of Crotona, the Greek athlete who got his hands caught in the cleft of a tree stump and was eaten by a lion. The wild horses of Marly now stand in the Cour Marly, surrounded by other masterpieces of French sculpture, including Jean-Antoine Houdon's early 19th-century busts of luminaries including Diderot and Voltaire.

The collection of Italian sculpture includes such splendid exhibits as Michelangelo's *Slaves* and Benvenuto Cellini's Fontainebleau *Nymph*.

## Oriental, Egyptian, Greek, Etruscan, and Roman Antiquities

The Louvre's collection of antiquities ranges from the Neolithic period to the fall of the Roman Empire. Among the exhibits are Greek and Roman glassware dating from the 6th century BC. Important works of Mesopotamian art include one of the world's oldest legal documents, a basalt block bearing the code of the Babylonian King Hammurabi, dating from about 1700 BC.

The warlike Assyrians are represented by delicate carvings and a spectacular reconstruction of part of Sargon II's (722–705 BC) palace with its winged bulls. A fine example of Persian art is the enameled brickwork depicting the king of Persia's personal guard of archers (5th century BC). Most Egyptian art was made for the dead, who were provided with the things they would need for the afterlife. Examples include the lifelike funeral portraits, such as the *Squatting Scribe* and several sculptures of married couples.

The departments of Greek, Roman, and Etruscan antiquities contain a vast array of fragments, among them some exceptional pieces. There is a geometric head from the Cyclades (2700 BC) and an elegant swan-necked bowl hammered out of a gold sheet (2500 BC). The two most famous Greek marble statues, the *Winged Victory of Samothrace* and the *Venus de Milo*, both belong to the Hellenistic period (late 3rd to 2nd century BC), when more natural-looking human forms were produced.

The undisputed star of the Etruscan collection is the terracotta sarcophagus of a married couple, who look as though they are attending an eternal banquet, while the highlight of the Roman section is a 2nd-century bronze head of the Emperor Hadrian.

*Venus de Milo* (Greece, late 3rd–early 2nd century BC)

*Squatting Scribe* (around 2500 BC), a lifelike Egyptian funeral sculpture

## Objets d'Art

The catch-all term objets d'art (art objects) covers a vast range of items: jewelry, furniture, clocks, watches, sundials, tapestries, miniatures, silver and glassware, cutlery, Byzantine and Parisian carved ivory, Limoges enamels, porcelain, French and Italian stoneware, rugs, snuffboxes, scientific instruments, and armor. The Louvre has well over 8,000 pieces, from many ages and regions.

Many of these precious objects came from the Abbey of St.-Denis, where the kings of France were crowned. The treasures include a serpentine stone plate from the 1st century AD with a 9th-century border of gold and precious stones, a porphyry vase that Suger, Abbot of St.-Denis, had mounted in gold in the shape of an eagle, and the golden sceptre made for King Charles V in about 1380.

The French crown jewels include the coronation crowns of Louis XV and Napoleon, scepters, swords, and other accessories of the coronation ceremonies. On view also is the Regent, one of the purest diamonds in the world, which Louis XV wore at his coronation in 1722.

One whole room is taken up with a series of tapestries called the *Hunts of Maximilian*, originally executed for Emperor Charles V in 1530. The large collection of French furniture ranges from the 16th to the 19th centuries. The 18th-century furniture rooms are assembled by period, from Louis XIV to Marie Antoinette. On display are pieces by such prominent furniture-makers as André-Charles Boulle, Louis XIV's cabinet-maker, who worked at the Louvre in the late 17th to mid-18th centuries.

# CHAMPS-ELYSEES AND INVALIDES

The River Seine bisects this area, much of which is built on a monumental scale, from the imposing 18th-century buildings of Les Invalides to the Art Nouveau avenues surrounding the Eiffel Tower. Two of Paris's grandest avenues dominate the neighborhood to the north of the Seine: the Champs-Elysées has many smart hotels and stores but today is more mainstream,

while the more chic rue du Faubourg St.-Honoré has the heavily guarded Palais de l'Elysée. The village of Chaillot was absorbed into the city in the 19th century, and many of its opulent Second Empire mansions are now embassies or company headquarters. Streets around place du Trocadéro and Palais de Chaillot are packed full of museums and elegant cafés.

## Sights at a Glance

### Historic Buildings and Streets

2 Avenue des Champs-Elysées
3 Palais de l'Elysée
14 Les Egouts
17 No. 29 Avenue Rapp
18 Parc du Champ-de-Mars
19 Ecole Militaire
21 Hôtel des Invalides

### Museums and Galleries

4 Petit Palais
5 Grand Palais
7 Musée d'Art Moderne de la Ville de Paris
8 Palais Galliera
9 Musée National des Arts Asiatiques Guimet

10 Cité de l'Architecture et du Patrimoine
11 Musée Dapper
13 Palais de Chaillot
15 Musée du Quai Branly
22 Musée de l'Armée
25 Musée Rodin
27 Musée Maillol

### Churches

23 Cathedral of St.-Louis-des-Invalides
24 Eglise du Dôme
26 Sainte-Clotilde

### Monuments and Fountains

1 Arc de Triomphe
16 Eiffel Tower p117

### Modern Architecture

20 UNESCO

### Gardens

12 Jardins du Trocadéro

### Bridges

6 Pont Alexandre III

See also Street Finder maps 1, 2, 3, 5, 6, 7, 8

0 meters 500
0 yards 500

◄ The Parc du Champ-de-Mars leading up to the magnificent Ecole Militaire

For keys to symbols see back flap -

# Street by Street: Champs-Elysées

The formal gardens that line the Champs-Elysées from place de la Concorde to the Rond-Point have changed little since they were laid out by the architect Jacques Hittorff in 1838. The gardens were used as the setting for the World Fair of 1855, which included the Palais de l'Industrie, Paris's response to London's Crystal Palace. The Palais was later replaced by the Grand Palais and by the Petit Palais, which was created as a showpiece of the Third Republic for the Universal Exhibition of 1900. They sit on either side of an impressive vista that stretches from the place Clémenceau across the elegant curve of the Pont Alexandre III, with its four strong anchoring columns, to the Invalides.

**Théâtre du Rond Point**, an original Champs-Elysées building, presents the work of active authors.

To Arc de Triomphe

Ⓜ Métro Franklin D. Roosevelt

**❷ ★ Avenue des Champs-Elysées**
This was the setting for the victory parades following the two World Wars.

**❺ ★ Grand Palais**
Designed by Charles Girault, and built between 1897 and 1900, this elaborate exhibition hall with its splendid glass dome is frequently used for major exhibitions.

**The Lasserre** restaurant is decorated in the style of a luxury ocean liner dating from the 1930s.

**Palais de la Découverte**, a museum of scientific discovery, was originally opened in the Grand Palais for the World Fair of 1937.

RUE JEAN GOUJON

RUE FRANÇOIS TER

AVE FRANKLIN D ROOSEVELT

AVE GL EISENHOWER

PL DU CANADA

COURS LA REINE

PONT DES INVALIDES

0 metres    100
0 yards     100

**Key**

— Suggested route

**The Jardins des Champs-Elysées**, with their fountains, flowerbeds, and pleasure pavilions, have been a popular spot since the 19th century.

**Locator Map**
*See Street Finder maps 3, 7*

CHAMPS-ELYSEES AND INVALIDES

Métro Champs-Elysées-Clémenceau

To place de la Concorde

**❹ ★ Petit Palais**
The art collections of the city of Paris are housed here. They contain 19th-century works from objets d'art to paintings by the Barbizon School.

**Pont Alexandre III**
This ornate, single-span structure symbolizes the optimism of the *belle époque* at the turn of the 20th century.

The east facade of the Arc de Triomphe

# ❶ Arc de Triomphe

Place Charles de Gaulle 75008. **Map** 2 D4. Ⓜ Charles de Gaulle-Etoile. **Tel** 01 55 37 73 77. **Open** Apr–Sep: 10am–11pm daily; Oct–Mar: 10am–10.30pm daily (last adm: 30 mins earlier); May 8, Jul 14, Nov 11: am only (last adm: 45 mins before closing). **Closed** Jan 1, May 1, Dec 25. ♿ 🖼 🅦 arc-de-triomphe. monuments-nationaux.fr

After his greatest victory, the Battle of Austerlitz in 1805, Napoleon promised his men they would "go home beneath triumphal arches." The first stone of the world's most famous triumphal arch was laid in 1806, but disruptions to architect Jean Chalgrin's plans and the demise of Napoleonic power delayed completion. Standing 164 ft (50 m) high, the Arc is encrusted with reliefs, sculptures and shields, and offers splendid views.

The body of the Unknown Soldier was placed beneath the arch in 1921 to commemorate the dead of World War I. The tomb's eternal flame is lit every evening at 6:30pm.

High relief by J. P. Corot, celebrating the Triumph of Napoleon

## Baron Haussmann

A lawyer by training and civil servant by profession, Georges-Eugène Haussmann (1809–91) was appointed Prefect of the Seine in 1853 by Napoleon III. For 17 years Haussmann was responsible for the urban modernization of Paris. With a team of the best architects and engineers of the day, he demolished the crowded, insanitary streets of the medieval city and created a well-ventilated and ordered capital within a geometrical grid. The new scheme involved redesigning the area at one end of the Champs-Elysées and creating a star of 12 avenues, which were centered on the new Arc de Triomphe.

Arc de Triomphe

Two avenues forming a star (*étoile*)

Place de l'Etoile

AVE DES CHAMPS-ELYSEES
AVE DE FRIEDLAND
AVE HOCHE
AVE DE WAGRAM
AVE MAC-MAHON
AVE CARNOT
AVE DE LA GRANDE ARMEE
AVE FOCH
AVE VICTOR-HUGO
AVE KLEBER
AVE D'IENA
AVE MARCEAU
Place de l'Etoile

## ❷ Avenue des Champs-Elysées

75008. **Map** 3 A5. Ⓜ Charles de Gaulle-Etoile, George V, Franklin D. Roosevelt, Champs-Elysées-Clemenceau, Concorde.

The majestic tree-lined avenue "of the Elysian Fields" (the mythical Greek heaven for heroes), first laid out in the 1660s by the landscape designer André Le Nôtre, forms a 2-mile (3-km) straight line from the huge place de la Concorde to the Arc de Triomphe. The 19th century saw it transformed into an elegant boulevard lined with cafés and restaurants. The Champs-Elysées keeps a special place in the French heart. National parades are held here, the finish of the annual Tour de France cycle race is always on the Champs-Elysées, and it is the site of the city's largest Christmas market. Above all, ever since the homecoming of Napoleon's body from St. Helena in 1840, it has been the place where Parisians congregate at times of major national celebration.

## ❸ Palais de l'Elysée

55 rue du Faubourg-St.-Honoré 75008. **Map** 3 B5. Ⓜ St-Philippe-du-Roule. **Closed** to the public.

Built in 1718 amid splendid gardens, the Elysée Palace has been the official residence of the French President since 1848. Several occupants left their mark. Louis XV's mistress, Madame de Pompadour, had the whole site enlarged. After the Revolution, it became a dance hall. In the 19th century, it was home to Napoleon's sister, Caroline Murat, and his wife Empress Josephine. The President's Apartments are today on the first floor.

### Grand Palais

## ❹ Petit Palais

Av Winston Churchill 75008. **Map** 7 B1. **Tel** 01 53 43 40 00. Ⓜ Champs-Elysées-Clemenceau. **Open** 10am–6pm Tue–Sun (to 9pm Fri for temporary exhibitions). **Closed** public hols. 🅿 🖼 for exhibitions. ♿ 🖥 🆆 petitpalais.paris.fr

Built for the Universal Exhibition in 1900, this jewel of a building houses the **Musée des Beaux-Arts de la Ville de Paris**. The architect, Charles Girault, arranged the palace around a semicircular courtyard and garden. Permanent exhibits, housed on the Champs-Elysées side, include the Dutuit Collection

Exhibition space

Iron supports

Pont Alexandre III, built 1896–1900 and inaugurated at the Universal Exhibition

of medieval and Renaissance objets d'art, paintings, and drawings; the Tuck Collection of 18th-century furniture and objets d'art; and the City of Paris collection, with work by Ingres, Delacroix, and Courbet, and the landscape painters of the Barbizon School. Temporary exhibitions are housed in the Cours de la Reine wing.

Entrance to the Petit Palais

## ❺ Grand Palais

Porte A, 3 av Général Eisenhower 75008. **Map** 7 A1. **Tel** 01 44 13 17 17. Ⓜ Champs-Elysées-Clemenceau. Galeries Nationales: pl Clemenceau; sq Jean Perrin, Champs-Elysées; av Winston Churchill. **Open** for temporary exhibitions only; usually 10am–10pm Wed–Mon (to 8pm Sun & Mon). **Closed** May 1, Dec 25. 🖾 🖾 🖳 🖳 🖳 🖳 🖳 🖳 **grandpalais.fr** Palais de la Decouverte: av Franklin D. Roosevelt 75008. **Tel** 01 44 43 20 20. Ⓜ Franklin D. Roosevelt. **Open** 9:30am–6pm Tue–Sat, 10am–7pm Sun. **Closed** Jan 1, May 1, Jul 14, Dec 25. 🖾 🖳 🖳 🖳 **palais-decouverte.fr**

Built at the same time as the Petit Palais opposite, this huge, glass-roofed palace housing the Galeries Nationales has a fine Classical facade adorned with statuary and Art Nouveau ironwork. Bronze flying horses and chariots stand at the four corners. The Great Hall and the glass cupola can be admired during the palace's superb exhibitions. The **Palais de la Découverte**, on the west side of the building, is an imaginative child-oriented science museum.

## ❻ Pont Alexandre III

75008. **Map** 7 A1. Ⓜ Champs-Elysées-Clemenceau.

This is Paris's prettiest bridge, with exuberant Art Nouveau decoration of gilt and bronze lamps, cupids and cherubs, nymphs, and winged horses at either end. It was built between 1896 and 1900 to commemorate the 1892 French–Russian alliance, and in time for the Universal Exhibition of 1900. Pont Alexandre III was named after Tsar Alexander III (father of Nicholas II), who laid the foundation stone in October 1896.

The style of the bridge reflects that of the Grand Palais, to which it leads on the Right Bank. The construction of the bridge is a marvel of 19th-century engineering. It consists of an 18-ft- (6-m-) high single-span steel arch across the Seine. The design was subject to strict controls that prevented the bridge from obscuring the view of the Champs-Elysées or the Invalides, so today you can still enjoy the magnificent views from here.

Great Hall

Glass cupola

*Quadriga* (chariot and four horses) by Récipon

## ❼ Musée d'Art Moderne de la Ville de Paris

Palais de Tokyo, 11 av du Président-Wilson 75016. **Map** 6 E1. **Tel** 01 53 67 40 00. Ⓜ Iéna, Alma-Marceau. **Open** 10am–6pm Tue–Sun (until 10pm Thu for temporary exhibitions). **Closed** public hols. 🎨 for temporary exhibitions. ♿ 🎁 📷 🏛 Ⓦ **mam.paris.fr**

This museum covers trends in 20th-century art and is located in the east wing of the Palais de Tokyo. The Fauves and Cubists are well represented here. Highlights include Raoul Dufy's gigantic mural, *The Electricity Fairy* (created for the 1937 World Fair), and Matisse's *The Dance* (1931–3). There is also a collection of Art Deco furniture.

## ❽ Palais Galliera

10 av Pierre 1er de Serbie 75116. **Map** 6 D1. **Tel** 01 56 52 86 00. Ⓜ Iéna, Alma-Marceau. **Open** 10am–6pm Tue–Sun (to 9pm Thu). **Closed** some public hols (check website). 🎨 Children's Room. Ⓦ **galliera.paris.fr**

Devoted to the evolution of fashion, this museum, also known as the Musée de la Mode de la Ville de Paris, is housed in the Renaissance-style palace built for the Duchesse Maria de Ferrari Galliera in 1892. The collection includes more than 250,000 outfits, fashion accessories, items of underwear, drawings, and prints, from the 18th century to the present day. Donations have been made by such fashion icons as Baronne Hélène de Rothschild and Princess Grace of Monaco. Eminent couturiers such as Balmain and Balenciaga have donated their designs.

Due to their fragility, the collections are not on permanent display. Pieces are shown in two or three temporary major exhibitions each year. The museum is closed between exhibitions.

Trocadéro fountains in front of the Palais de Chaillot

## ⓫ Musée Dapper

35bis rue Paul-Valéry, 75016. **Map** 1 B5. **Tel** 01 45 00 91 75. Ⓜ Victor-Hugo. **Open** 11am–7pm Wed, Fri–Mon. 🎨 Ⓦ **dapper.com.fr**

A world-class ethnographic research center, this is one of France's premier showcases of African and Caribbean art and culture. Located in an attractive building with an "African" garden, it is a treasure house of color and powerful, evocative work. The focus is on precolonial folk arts, with sculpture, carvings, and tribal work, but there is later art on display, too. The highlight is tribal masks, with a dazzling array of richly carved religious, ritual, and funerary masks, as well as theatrical ones used for comic, magical, or symbolic performances.

## ⓬ Jardins du Trocadéro

75016. **Map** 6 D2. Ⓜ Trocadéro. Cinéaqua: **Tel** 01 40 69 23 23. **Open** 24 hours daily. **Closed** Jul 14. 🎨

The centerpiece of these beautiful gardens is a long rectangular ornamental pool, bordered by stone and bronze-gilt statues, and it looks spectacular at night, when the fountains are illuminated. The statues include *Woman* by Georges Braque and *Horse* by Georges Lucien Guyot. On either side of the pool, the slopes of the Chaillot hill lead gently down to the Seine and the Pont d'Iéna. Cinéaqua, the high-tech aquarium here, has over 25 sharks and a petting pool for children.

## ⓭ Palais de Chaillot

Pl du Trocadéro 75016. **Map** 5 C2. Ⓜ Trocadéro. Théâtre National de Chaillot: **Tel** 01 53 65 30 00. Ⓦ **theatre-chaillot.fr** Musée de l'Homme: **Tel** 01 44 05 72 72. **Open** 10am–6pm Wed–Mon. Ⓦ **museedelhomme.fr** Musée National de la Marine: **Tel** 01 53 65 69 53. **Closed** for renovation until 2021. Ⓦ **musee-marine.fr**

The Palais, with its huge, curved, colonnaded wings each culminating in a vast pavilion, has three museums and a theater. Designed in Neoclassical style for the 1937 Paris Exhibition by Azéma, Louis-Auguste Boileau, and Jacques Carlu, it is adorned with sculptures and bas-reliefs; inside, the gold inscriptions on the walls were written by the poet and essayist Paul Valéry.

Buddha head from the Musée Guimet

## ❾ Musée National des Arts Asiatiques Guimet

6 pl d'Iéna 75016. **Map** 6 D1. **Tel** 01 56 52 53 00. **M** Iéna. **Open** 10am–6pm Wed–Mon. 🅿 🚻 🛗 Panthéon Bouddhique, 19 av d'Iéna. **Tel** 01 40 73 88 00. **Open** 10am– 5:45pm Wed–Mon (phone ahead), garden to 5pm. **Closed** Jan 1, May 1, Dec 25. **W** guimet.fr

One of the world's leading museums of Asian art, the Guimet has a fine collection of Cambodian (Khmer) art. It was set up in Lyon in 1889 by Emile Guimet, and later moved to Paris. It includes a comprehensive Asian research center.

## ❿ Cité de l'Architecture et du Patrimoine

Palais de Chaillot, pl du Trocadéro 75016. **Map** 5 C2. **Tel** 01 58 51 52 00. **M** Trocadéro. **Open** 11am–7pm Wed–Sun (until 9pm Thu). **Closed** Jan 1, May 1, Dec 25. 🅿 🚫 📷 **W** citechaillot.fr

This museum charts French architecture through the ages and includes models of great French cathedrals, such as Chartres (see pp311–15). There is also a reconstruction of an apartment designed by Le Corbusier.

## Palais de Chaillot

Théâtre National de Chaillot

Place du Trocadéro

Musée National de la Marine

Musée de l'Homme

AVE DU PRESIDENT WILSON

PL DU TROCADERO

AVE ALBERT DE MUN

AVE DES NATIONS UNIES

NEW YORK

PL J MARTI

AVE PAUL DOUMER

RUE FRANKLIN

Cinéaqua

PL DE VARSOVIE

PONT D'IENA

AVE DES NATIONS UNIES

Cité de l'Architecture et du Patrimoine

Palais de Chaillot

BLVD DELESSERT

RUE LE NOTRE

AVE DE

Jardins du Trocadéro

Trocadéro Fountains

The square (parvis) between the pavilions has bronze sculptures, ornamental pools, and fountains. Steps lead down from the terrace to the **Théâtre National de Chaillot**, offering an experimental approach to all genres.

The **Musée de l'Homme**, in the west wing, is an anthropological and ethnographic museum that traces the history of human evolution. Next door is the **Musée National de la Marine**, devoted to French naval history and aspects of the modern-day navy. This is closed due to extensive renovations until 2021. The east wing of the palais contains the vast **Cité de l'Architecture et du Patrimoine** (see above).

# ⓮ Les Egouts

Pont d'Álma, opposite 93 quai d'Orsay 75007. **Map** 6 F2. **Tel** 01 53 68 27 81 (in English). Ⓜ Alma-Marceau. RER Pont-de-l'Alma. **Open** 11am–5pm (6pm in summer) Sat–Wed. **Closed** last 2 wks Jan. 🏛 📷 🎦

One of Baron Haussmann's finest achievements, most of Paris's sewers (*égouts*) date from the Second Empire. If laid end to end, the 1,490 miles (2,400 km) of sewers would stretch from Paris to Istanbul. One-hour walking tours of this attraction have been limited to an area around the quai d'Orsay entrance. Visiting the sewers without a guide can be dangerous, and is against the law. Visitors can discover the mysteries of underground Paris in the sewer museum and learn how the machinery used has changed over the years.

# ⓯ Musée du Quai Branly

37 quai Branly 75007, or 206/218 rue de l'Université. **Map** 6 E2. **Tel** 01 56 61 70 00. Ⓜ Alma-Marceau. RER Pont-de-l'Alma. **Open** 11am–7pm Tue, Wed, Sun, 11am–9pm Thu–Sat. **Closed** May 1, Dec 25. 🎦 free 1st Sun of month & for 18–25s after 6pm Sat. 🏛 🎦 Exhibitions, theater, movie, library. W **quaibranly.fr**

Built to give the arts of Africa, Asia, Oceania, and the Americas a platform as shining as that for Western art in the city, this museum has a massive collection of

**Aztec mask, Musée du Quai Branly**

more than 300,000 objects. It is particularly strong on Africa, with stone, wooden, and ivory masks, as well as ceremonial tools. The Jean-Nouvel-designed building, which is raised on stilts, is a worthwhile sight in itself, while the ingenious use of glass in its construction allows the surrounding greenery to act as a natural backdrop.

# ⓰ Eiffel Tower

See p117.

Original Art Nouveau doorway at No. 29 avenue Rapp

# ⓱ No. 29 Avenue Rapp

75005. **Map** 6 E3. Ⓜ Alma-Marceau. RER Pont-de-l'Alma.

A prime example of Art Nouveau architecture, No. 29 avenue Rapp won its designer, Jules Lavirotte, first prize at the Concours des Façades de la Ville de Paris in 1901. Its ceramics and brickwork are decorated with animal and flower motifs intermingling with female figures. These are superimposed on a multicolored sandstone base to produce a facade that is deliberately erotic, and was certainly subversive in its day. Also worth visiting nearby is No. 3 square Rapp, an apartment building, complete with watchtower.

# ⓲ Parc du Champ-de-Mars

75007. **Map** 6 E3. Ⓜ Ecole-Militaire. RER Champ-de-Mars–Tour-Eiffel.

The vast gardens stretching from the Eiffel Tower to the Ecole Militaire (Military School) were originally a parade ground for young officer cadets. The area has since been used for horseracing, balloon ascents, and mass ceremonies to celebrate the anniversary of the

Revolution on July 14. The first ceremony was held in 1790, in the presence of a glum, captive, Louis XVI.

Mammoth exhibitions were held here in the late 19th century, among them the 1889 World Fair for which the Eiffel Tower was erected.

Today, this is a popular park, with playgrounds and a café.

# ⓳ Ecole Militaire

1/21 pl Joffre 75007. **Map** 6 F4. **Tel** 01 80 50 14 00. Ⓜ Ecole-Militaire. Open: to the public during European Heritage Days in Sep.

The Royal Military Academy of Louis XV was founded in 1751 to educate 500 sons of impoverished officers. Louis XV and Madame de Pompadour commissioned architect Jacques-Ange Gabriel to design a building that would rival Louis XIV's Hôtel des Invalides. Financing the building became a problem, so a lottery was authorized and a tax was raised on playing cards. One of the main features is the central pavilion – a magnificent example of the French Classical style, with ten Corinthian columns and a quadrangular dome. Four figures adorn the entablature frieze, symbolizing France, Victory, Force, and Peace.

An early cadet at the academy was Napoleon, whose passing-out report stated "he could go far if the circumstances are right."

A 1751 engraving showing the planning of the Ecole Militaire

# ⓰ Eiffel Tower

Built for the Universal Exhibition of 1889, and to commemorate the centennial of the Revolution, the 1,063-ft (324-m) Eiffel Tower (Tour Eiffel) was meant to be a temporary addition to Paris's skyline. Designed by Gustave Eiffel, and fiercely decried by 19th-century aesthetes, it was the world's tallest building until 1930, when New York's Chrysler Building was completed. The Eiffel Tower draws as many as 7 million visitors a year, and its first level houses a modern, fully accessible visitor center.

## Daring Feats

The tower has always inspired crazy stunts. In 1912, Reichelt, a Parisian tailor, attempted to fly from the parapet with only a cape for wings. He plunged to his death in front of a large crowd.

Stuntman Reichelt

**The double-decker elevators** have a limited capacity, and there can be long waits. Lining-up for the elevators requires patience and a good head for heights. Book your tickets online ahead of your visit.

**Pavillon Ferié**
Multimedia displays and touch screens illustrate the history of the tower.

**★ Eiffel Bust**
The achievement of Eiffel (1832–1923) was honored by Antoine Bourdelle, who placed this bust under the tower in 1929.

**The third level**, 905 ft (276 m) above the ground, can hold 400 people at a time. Gustave Eiffel's office is located here, plus a champagne bar.

**★ Viewing Gallery**
On a clear day it is possible to see for 45 miles (72 km), including a distant view of Chartres Cathedral.

**The second level** is at 380 ft (115 m), separated from the first level by 359 steps or a few minutes in the elevator. Food outlets and souvenir shops can be found here.

**The Jules Verne restaurant** is rated highly in Paris, offering not only superb food, but a breathtaking panoramic view.

**The first level**, 187 ft (57 m) high, is reached by elevator or by 345 steps. The glass floor allows visitors to see right down to the ground.

## Les Invalides

Musée de l'Armée

Hôtel des Invalides

Cour d'Honneur

Musée de l'Ordre de la Libération

Eglise du Dôme

St.-Louis-des-Invalides

Musée des Plans-Reliefs

in 1670 for his wounded and homeless veterans. Designed by Libéral Bruand, it was completed in 1676 by Jules Hardouin-Mansart. He later incorporated the Eglise du Dôme, with its golden roof, which was built as Louis XIV's private chapel. Nearly 6,000 soldiers once lived here. Today there are fewer than 100.

The harmonious Classical facade is one of the most impressive sights in Paris. The building houses the Musée de l'Armée and the Musée de l'Ordre de la Libération, set up to honor feats of heroism during World War II under the leadership of Charles de Gaulle. The story is told using film, photographs, and mementos. The Musée des Plans-Reliefs also houses a large collection of military models of French forts.

### ❷ UNESCO

7 pl de Fontenoy 75007. **Map** 6 F5. **Tel** 01 45 68 10 00. M Ségur, Cambronne. **Open** for guided tours only: 10am & 3pm Tue–Fri (reservations essential, email visits@unesco.org). **Closed** public hols. ♿ 📷 🚭 📷 W **unesco.org**

This is the headquarters of the United Nations Educational, Scientific, and Cultural Organization (UNESCO). Its aim is to contribute to international peace through education, science, and culture.

UNESCO is a treasure trove of modern art, including an enormous mural by Picasso, ceramics by Joan Miró, and sculptures by Henry Moore, and the calm Japanese garden by Noguchi. Exhibitions and movies are also hosted here.

### ❷ Hôtel des Invalides

6 bd des Invalides 75007. **Map** 7 A3. **Tel** 08 10 11 33 99. M La Tour Maubourg, Invalides, Varenne. **Open** 7:30am–7pm daily (Apr–Sep: to 9pm Tue). **Closed** Jan 1, May 1, Dec 25. 🚭 good for admission to all attractions. 📷 book ahead online. W **musee-armee.fr**

This imposing building, from which the area takes its name, was commissioned by Louis XIV

### ❷ Musée de l'Armée

129 rue Grenelle 75007 (also 6 bd des Invalides). **Map** 7 A3. **Tel** 08 10 11 33 99. M Varenne, La Tour Maubourg, Invalides. RER Invalides. **Open** 10am–6pm daily (to 9pm Tue; to 5pm Nov–Mar; to 5:30pm school hols). **Closed** 1st Mon of month Oct–Jun, Jan1, May 1, Dec 25. 🚭 for admission to all attractions. ♿ 📷 📷 📷 W **musee-armee.fr**

One of the most comprehensive museums of military history in the world is housed in two galleries on either side of the magnificent courtyard of the Hôtel des Invalides. The "Priests' Wing" holds the World War II galleries.

A major exhibit of France's victories and defeats, dedicated mainly to the Napoleonic era, includes the emperor's death mask and stuffed horse, Vizier. Also on display are François I's ivory hunting horns and a model of the 1944 Normandy landing.

The facade of the Musée de l'Armée

Altar of St-Louis-des-Invalides with banners seized in battle

## ㉓ Cathedral of St-Louis-des-Invalides

6 bd des Invalides, Hôtel des Invalides 75007. **Map** 7 A3. M Invalides, La Tour Maubourg, Varenne. **Tel** 08 10 11 33 99. **Open** 10am–6pm daily (Jul–Aug: to 7pm; Apr–Sep: to 9pm Tue). W **musee-armee.fr**

Also known as the "soldiers' church," this is the chapel of the Hôtel des Invalides. It was built from 1679 to 1708 by Jules Hardouin-Mansart, to Bruand's design. The stark Neoclassical interior is well proportioned, designed in the shape of a Greek cross.

There is a fine 17th-century organ, on which the first performance of Berlioz's *Requiem* was given on December 5 1837, with more than 200 musicians and choristers participating.

## ㉔ Eglise du Dôme

6 bd des Invalides, Hôtel des Invalides, 129 rue de Grenelle, 75007. **Map** 7 A4. **Tel** 08 10 11 33 99. M La Tour Maubourg, Varenne, Invalides. ▤ 82, 92 to Les Invalides. ▤ Invalides. ▢ Tour Eiffel. **Open** 10am–6pm daily (Apr–Sep: to 9pm Tue; Jul–Aug: to 7pm). **Closed** 1st Mon of month, Jan 1, May 1, Dec 25. ▨ ♿ restaurant. ▤ ▢ ▨ W **musee-armee.fr**

Jules Hardouin-Mansart was asked in 1676 by the Sun King, Louis XIV, to build the Eglise du Dôme to complement the existing buildings of the Invalides military refuge, designed by Libéral Bruand. The Dôme was to be reserved for the exclusive use of the Sun King and as the location of royal tombs.

The resulting masterpiece is one of the greatest examples of 17th-century French architecture, the period known as the *grand siècle*. After Louis XIV's death, plans to bury the royal family in the church were abandoned.

The main attraction is the tomb of Napoleon; 20 years after his death on the island of St. Helena, his body was returned to France and installed in this magnificent crypt, encased in six coffins in a vast red porphyry sarcophagus.

Eglise du Dôme with cupola, first gilded in 1715

## ㉕ Musée Rodin

79 rue de Varenne 75007. **Map** 7 B3. **Tel** 01 44 18 61 10. M Varenne. **Open** 10am–5:45pm Tue–Sun (to 8:45pm Wed). **Closed** Jan 1, May 1, Dec 25. ▨ free 1st Sun of month & for 18–25s after 6pm Sat. ♿ restricted. ▢ ▨ W **musee-rodin.fr**

Auguste Rodin (1840–1917), regarded as one of the greatest French sculptors, lived and worked in the Hôtel Biron, an elegant 18th-century mansion, from 1908 until his death. In return for a state-owned apartment and studio, Rodin left his work to the nation, and it is now exhibited here. Some of his most celebrated sculptures are on display in the garden: *The Burghers of Calais, The Thinker, The Gates of Hell (see p124)*, and *Balzac*.

The indoor exhibits are arranged in chronological order, spanning the whole of Rodin's career. Highlights include *The Kiss* and *Eve*.

## ㉖ Sainte-Clotilde

23bis rue Las Cases 75007. **Map** 7 B3. **Tel** 01 44 18 62 60. M Solférino, Varenne, Invalides. **Open** 9am–7:30pm Mon–Fri, 10am–8pm Sat & Sun (to 7pm daily in summer). **Closed** Mon (Aug), non-religious public hols. Concerts.

Designed by the German-born architect Franz Christian Gau and built in 1846–56, this Neo-Gothic church was inspired by the 19th-century enthusiasm for the Middle Ages, popularized by such writers as Victor Hugo.

Inside are wall paintings by James Pradier and stained-glass windows with scenes relating to the patron saint of the church. The composer César Franck was organist here from 1858 to 1890.

## ㉗ Musée Maillol

61 rue de Grenelle 75007. **Map** 7 C4. **Tel** 01 42 22 59 58. M Rue du Bac, Sèvres-Babylone. **Open** 10:30am–6:30pm daily during exhibitions (to 9:30pm Fri). ♿ ▢ ▨ W **museemaillol.com**

This museum was created by Dina Vierny, muse to Aristide Maillol. His work is exhibited here in all its diverse forms: drawings, engravings, paintings, sculpture, and decorative objects. The museum also plays host to two major temporary exhibitions a year. Allegorical figures of the city of Paris and the four seasons adorn Bouchardon's fountain outside.

Rodin's *The Thinker* in museum garden

# THE LEFT BANK

The Left Bank has long been associated with poets, philosophers, artists, and radical thinkers of all kinds. It still has its share of bohemian street life and pavement cafés, but the smart set has moved in, patronizing Yves Saint-Laurent and the exclusive interior design stores on rue Jacob.

The Latin Quarter is the ancient area lying between the Seine and the Luxembourg Gardens, and is today filled with bookstores, art galleries ,and cafés. Boulevard St.-Michel, bordering the Latin Quarter and St.-Germain-des-Prés, has slowly given way to commerce,

and is full of fast-food outlets and bargain stores. The surrounding maze of narrow, cobblestone streets has retained its character, with ethnic stores and avant-garde theaters dominated by the facade of the Sorbonne, France's first university, built in 1253. Many Parisians dream of living near the Luxembourg Gardens, a quiet area of charming old streets, gateways, and elaborate gardens full of paths, lawns, and tree-lined avenues. Students come here to chat, and on warm days Parisian men still meet underneath the chestnut trees to play chess or the traditional French game of *boules*.

## Sights at a Glance

### Churches
**5** St.-Germain-des-Prés
**9** St.-Séverin
**10** St.-Julien-le-Pauvre
**12** St.-Etienne-du-Mont
**13** Panthéon
**15** St.-Sulpice
**17** Val-de-Grâce

### Museums and Galleries
**1** Musée d'Orsay pp124–5
**6** Musée Eugène Delacroix
**8** Musée de Cluny
**16** Fontaine de l'Observatoire

### Historic Buildings and Streets
**2** Boulevard St.-Germain
**3** Quai Voltaire
**4** Ecole Nationale Supérieure des Beaux-Arts

**7** Rue de l'Odéon
**11** La Sorbonne
**14** Palais du Luxembourg

### Fountains
**16** Fontaine de l'Observatoire

See also Street Finder maps 7, 8, 9, 12, 13

▲ La Fontaine de l'Observatoire, in the Luxembourg Gardens

For keys to symbols *see back flap*

# Street by Street: St.-Germain-des-Prés

After World War II, St.-Germain des-Prés became synonymous with intellectual life centered on bars and cafés. Philosophers, writers, actors, and musicians mingled in the cellar nightspots and brasseries, where existentialist philosophy coexisted with American jazz. The area is now smarter than in the heyday of Jean-Paul Sartre and Simone de Beauvoir, the enigmatic singer Juliette Greco and the New Wave movie-makers. However, the writers are still around, enjoying the pleasures of sitting in Les Deux Magots, Café de Flore, and other haunts. The 17th-century buildings have survived, but signs of change are evident in the affluent stores dealing in antiques, books, and fashion.

**Les Deux Magots** became a focus of bohemian and literary activity in the 1920s.

**Café de Flore**, the former favorite haunt of Jean-Paul Sartre, Simone de Beauvoir, and other French intellectuals, still has a classic Art-Deco interior.

RUE BONAPARTE

RUE DU DRAGON

RUE DU SABOT

RUE DE RENNES

RUE BONAPARTE

BLVD ST-G

RUE DU FOUR

Métro St.-Germain-des-Prés

**Brasserie Lipp**, decorated with colorful ceramics, is a renowned brasserie frequented by politicians.

**❺ ★ St.-Germain-des-Prés**
The philosopher René Descartes is among the notables buried here in Paris's oldest church.

**❷ ★ Boulevard St.-Germain**
Café terraces, boutiques, movie theaters, restaurants, and bookstores characterize the central section of the Left Bank's main street.

**Key**

— Suggested route

TUILERIES
ILE DE LA CITE,
MARAIS AND
BEAUBOURG
INVALIDES
THE LEFT BANK

**Locator Map**
*See Street Finder map 8*

# ❶ Musée d'Orsay

*See pp124–5.*

# ❷ Boulevard St.-Germain

75006, 75007. **Map** 8 D3. Ⓜ Solférino, Rue du Bac, St-Germain-des-Prés, Mabillon, Odéon, Cluny-La Sorbonne, Maubert-Mutualité.

The Left Bank's most celebrated thoroughfare slinks across three districts from the Ile St.-Louis to the Pont de la Concorde. The architecture is homogeneous, because the boulevard was another of Baron Haussmann's bold strokes of urban planning, but it encompasses a wide range of different lifestyles, from bohemian to bourgeois.

Starting from the east, it passes the Musée de Cluny and the Sorbonne. It is most lively from boulevard St.-Michel to St.-Germain-des-Prés, with its café culture.

# ❸ Quai Voltaire

75006, 75007. **Map** 8 D3. Ⓜ Rue du Bac. Ⓡ Museé d'Orsay.

The quai Voltaire is now home to some of the most important antiques dealers in Paris. Many famous people have lived in the attractive 18th-century houses; among others, Voltaire at No. 27 and Richard Wagner, Jean Sibelius, and Oscar Wilde (separately) at No. 19.

❻ ★ **Musée Eugène Delacroix**
The home of the Romantic painter Eugène Delacroix (1798–1863) is now a museum devoted to his art.

**Palais Abbatial de St.-Germain-des-Prés**
was the residence of abbots from 1586 till the 1789 Revolution.

**Rue de Buci** was for centuries an important street and the site of some real tennis courts. It now holds a lively market.

RUE BOURBON LE CHATEAU
RUE DE BUCI
RUE MAZARINE
RUE DE SEINE
RUE DE L'ANCIENNE-COMEDIE
RUE DE MONTFAUCON
RUE FELIBIEN
RUE MABILLON
CARREFOUR DE L'ODEON

Ⓜ Métro Mabillon

Ⓜ Métro Odéon

0 metres        100
0 yards         100

Plaque marking the house in quai Voltaire where Voltaire died in 1778

# ❶ Musée d'Orsay

In 1986, 47 years after it had closed as a mainline train station, Victor Laloux's turn-of-the-century building reopened as the Musée d'Orsay. Built as the Orléans railroad terminal in the heart of Paris, it narrowly avoided demolition in the 1970s. In the conversion to a museum, much of the original architecture was retained. The museum presents the rich diversity of visual arts from 1848 to 1914, featuring mainly the Impressionist, Postimpressionist, and Art Nouveau movements, and explains the social and technological context in which the works were created. Exhibits include paintings, sculptures, furniture, and decorative objects. The museum also has a program of classical music concerts. Exhibits are subject to change.

**The Gates of Hell** (1880–1917)
Rodin included figures that he had already created, such as *The Thinker* and *The Kiss*, in this famous gateway.

**Dance at the Moulin de la Galette** (1876)
Renoir painted this picture outside to capture the light as it filtered through the trees.

**The Dance** (1865–9)
Carpeaux's dynamic sculpture caused a scandal when it was first unveiled in 1869.

### Key to Floorplan

- Architecture and Decorative Arts
- Sculpture
- Painting before 1870
- Impressionism
- Neoimpressionism and Postimpressionism
- Naturalism and Symbolism
- Art Nouveau
- Temporary exhibitions
- Nonexhibition space

**Doctor Paul Gachet** (1890)
This portrait by van Gogh is one of three and was painted the same year that the artist died.

## Gallery Guide

*The ground floor has works from the mid- to late 19th century. The middle level features Art Nouveau, decorative art, and late 19th- to early 20th-century paintings and sculptures. The upper level showcases the celebrated Impressionists, as well as temporary exhibitions.*

Upper level

Middle level

Entrance

Ground floor

Shop entrance

## VISITORS' CHECKLIST

### Practical Information
Quai A France/rue de la Légion d'Honneur 75007. **Map** 8 D2. **Tel** 01 40 49 48 14. 🚗 **P** Carrousel du Louvre/Bac Montalembert. **Open** 9:30am–6pm Tue–Sun (to 9:45pm Thu; last entry 1 hr before closing). **Closed** Jan 1, May 1, Dec 25. 🚗 ♿ 📷 🎫 Events: call 01 53 63 04 63. **W** musee-orsay.fr

### Transportation
Ⓜ Solférino. 🚌 24, 68, 69, 84 to quai A France; 73 to rue de la Légion d'Honneur; 63, 83, 84, 94 to bd St-Germain. Ⓡ Ⓒ Musée d'Orsay.

## Exploring the Musée d'Orsay

Many of the paintings in the Musée d'Orsay came from the Louvre and the Impressionist collection once in the Jeu de Paume. Paintings from before 1870 are on the ground floor, presided over by Thomas Couture's massive *Romans of the Decadence*. Neoclassical masterpieces, such as Ingres's *La Source*, hang near Romantic works including Delacroix's turbulent *Tiger Hunt*. These exotic visions contrast with Realist works by artists such as Courbet and early canvases by Degas and Manet, including the latter's famous *Olympia*.

The museum's central aisle overflows with sculpture, from Daumier's satirical busts of members of parliament to Carpeaux's exuberant *The Dance* and Rodin's *The Gates of Hell*. Decorative arts and archi-tecture are on the middle level, where there is also a display of Art Nouveau –

*Blue Waterlilies* (1916–19) by Claude Monet

sinuous lines characterize Lalique's jewelry and glassware and the designs of Hector Guimard, who produced the characteristic curvy entrances of the Paris Métro.

Among the many highlights of the Impressionist rooms are Monet's *Rouen Cathedral* series *(see p271)* and Renoir's joyful *Dance at the Moulin de la Galette*. The Postimpressionist collection on the middle level includes the *Eglise d'Auvers* by van Gogh, Seurat's Pointillist compositions such as *Le Cirque*, Gauguin's highly colored Symbolist works, and Toulouse-Lautrec's depictions of Parisian night-life. Among the highlights of the post-1900 display is Matisse's *Luxe, Calme et Volupté*.

*Le Déjeuner sur l'Herbe* (1863) by Edouard Manet

The facade of the Ecole Nationale Supérieure des Beaux-Arts

## ❹ Ecole Nationale Supérieure des Beaux-Arts

14 rue Bonaparte 75006. **Map** 8 E3. **Tel** 01 47 03 50 00. M St.-Germain-des-Prés. **Open** from 10am Mon–Fri for guided visits only (01 42 46 92 02 to book). 🅿 📖 Library.
W **beauxartsparis.com**

The main French school of fine arts has an enviable position at the corner of rue Bonaparte and the riverside quai Malaquais. It is housed in several buildings, the most imposing being the 19th-century Palais des Etudes. A host of budding French and foreign painters and architects have crossed the courtyard, which contains a 17th-century chapel, to learn in the ateliers of the school. Many American architects have studied here.

## ❺ St.-Germain-des-Prés

3 pl St-Germain-des-Prés 75006. **Map** 8 E4. **Tel** 01 55 42 81 10. M St.-Germain-des-Prés. **Open** 8am–7:45pm Mon–Sat, 9am–8pm Sun. 🅿 3pm Tue, Thu & 3rd Sun of month (call 01 55 42 81 18). Concerts: 8pm (usually Thu & Fri).
W **eglise-sgp.org**

The oldest church in Paris originated in 542 as a basilica to house holy relics. It became a powerful Benedictine abbey, rebuilt in the 11th century, but most of it was destroyed by fire in 1794. Major restoration took place in the 1800s. One of the three original towers survives, housing one of France's oldest belfries. The interior is a mix of styles, with 6th-century marble columns, Gothic vaulting, Romanesque arches, and 19th-century frescos. Famous tombs include that of 17th- century philosopher René Descartes.

## ❻ Musée Eugène Delacroix

6 rue de Fürstenberg 75006. **Map** 8 E4. **Tel** 01 44 41 86 50. M St.-Germain-des-Prés. **Open** 9:30am–5:30pm Wed–Mon. **Closed** Jan 1, May 1, Dec 25. 🅿 free 1st Sun of month & for 18–25s (EU residents). 📷 W **musee-delacroix.fr**

The leading Romantic painter Eugène Delacroix lived and worked here from 1857 until his death in 1863. Here he painted *The Entombment of Christ* and *The Way to Calvary* (which hang in the museum). He also created murals for the Chapel of the Holy Angels in the nearby St.-Sulpice church (see p131).
The apartment and studio has a portrait of George Sand and Delacroix self-portraits.

*Jacob Wrestling with the Angel* by Delacroix, in St.-Sulpice (see p131)

## ❼ Rue de l'Odéon

75006. **Map** 8 F5. M Odéon.

Opened in 1779 to improve access to the Odéon theater, this was the first street in Paris to have sidewalks with gutters, and it still has many 18th-century houses.
Sylvia Beach's bookstore, the original Shakespeare & Company, stood at No. 12 from 1921 to 1940. It was a magnet for writers such as James Joyce, Ezra Pound, and Hemingway.

## ❽ Musée de Cluny

6 pl Paul-Painlevé 75005. **Map** 9 A5. **Tel** 01 53 73 78 16/00. M St.-Michel, Odéon, Cluny. 🚇 St.-Michel. **Open** 9:15am–5:45pm Wed–Mon. **Closed** Jan 1, May 1, Dec 25. 🅿 📷 Concerts: W **musee-moyenage.fr**

The museum (officially the Musée National du Moyen Age) is a unique combination of Gallo-Roman ruins, incorporated

Stone heads of the Kings of Judah carved around 1220

## ❾ St.-Séverin

1 rue-des-Prêtres-St.-Séverin 75005. **Map** 9 A4. **Tel** 01 42 34 93 50. M St.-Michel. **Open** 11am–7:30pm Mon–Sat, 9am–8:30pm Sun. 📷 W **saint-severin.com**

St.-Séverin, one of the finest churches in Paris, is named after a 6th-century hermit who lived locally. It is a perfect example of the Flamboyant Gothic style. Begun in the 13th century and finished in the early 16th, it includes a double aisle encircling the chancel. In the garden is the church's medieval gable-roofed charnel house.

Gargoyles adorning the gables of the Flamboyant Gothic St.-Séverin

*The School* woodcarving (English, early 16th century)

## Lady with the Unicorn Tapestries

These six outstanding tapestries are fine examples of the *millefleurs* style. Developed in the 15th and early 16th centuries, the style is noted for its graceful depiction of animals and people, and its fresh and harmonious colors.

The poetic elegance of a unicorn on the sixth tapestry

into a medieval mansion (in newly created medieval gardens), and one of the world's finest collections of medieval art and crafts. Its name comes from Pierre de Chalus, Abbot of Cluny, who bought the ruins in 1330. The present building dates from 1485–98. Among the star exhibits are the tapestries, remarkable for their quality, age,

and state of preservation. The highlight of the sculpture section is the Gallery of the Kings, while one of Cluny's most precious items, the Golden Rose of Basel from 1330, is found in the collection of jewelry and metalwork. Other treasures include stained glass, woodcarvings, and books of hours.

## ❿ St.-Julien-le-Pauvre

79 rue Galande 75005. **Map** 9 A4. **Tel** 01 43 54 52 16. Ⓜ St.-Michel. **Open** 9:30am–1pm, 3–6:30pm daily. ✝ 12:15pm Tue & Thu; 10am, 11am & 6pm Sun. Concerts. 🆆 sjlpmelkites.fr

The church is one of the oldest in Paris, dating from between 1165 and 1220. The university held its official meetings in the church until 1524, when a student protest created so much damage that they were barred from the church by parliament. It has belonged to the Melchite sect of the Greek Orthodox Church since 1889 and is now the setting for classical and religious concerts.

## ⓫ La Sorbonne

1 rue Victor Cousin 75005. **Map** 9 A5. **Tel** 01 40 46 22 11. Ⓜ Cluny-La Sorbonne, Maubert-Mutualité. 🗓 Mon–Fri & 1 Sat a month, by appt. Email visites.sorbonnes@ac-paris.fr. 🆆 paris-sorbonne.fr

The Sorbonne, one of the oldest universities in the world, was established in 1253 by Robert de Sorbon, confessor to Louis IX, for 16 poor scholars to study theology. It went on to become

the center of scholastic theology. In 1469, three printing presses were brought from Mainz, and the first printing house in France was founded. The college's opposition to liberal 18th-century philosophical ideas led to its suppression during the Revolution. It was re-established by Napoleon in 1806, and the 17th-century buildings replaced in 1969, the Sorbonne split into 13 separate universities, but the building still holds some lectures.

## ⓬ St.-Etienne-du-Mont

Pl Ste.-Geneviève 75005. **Map** 13 A1. **Tel** 01 43 54 11 79. Ⓜ Cardinal Lemoine. **Open** 6:30pm–7:30pm Mon, 8:45am–7:45pm Tue–Thu (to 10pm Wed), 8:45am–noon & 2–7:45pm Sat & Sun. ✝ 6:45pm daily, plus 12:15pm Tue–Fri, 11am Sat, 9 & 11am Sun. 📷 🗓 monthly. 🆆 saintetienne dumont.fr

Part Gothic and part Renaissance, this church houses the shrine of Paris's patron saint, Geneviève, and remains of literary figures Racine and Pascal.

**St.-Etienne-du-Mont**

16th-century belfry tower

Rood screen

Medieval window

# Street by Street: Latin Quarter

Since the Middle Ages this riverside quarter has been dominated by the Sorbonne, and acquired its name from the early Latin-speaking students. It dates back to the Roman town across from the Ile de la Cité; at that time rue St.-Jacques was one of the main roads out of Paris. The area is generally associated with artists, intellectuals, and a bohemian way of life; it also has a history of political unrest. In 1871, place St.-Michel became the center of the Paris Commune, and in May 1968 it was a site of student uprisings. Today the eastern half has become sufficiently chic, however, to house members of the Establishment.

**❾ ★ St.-Séverin**
Begun in the 13th century, this church took three centuries to build and is a fine example of the Flamboyant Gothic style.

Métro St.-Michel

St.-Michel Notre-Dame

**Boulevard St.-Michel**, or Boul'Mich, as it is affectionately known by locals, is a lively melange of cafés and book and clothing stores, with nightclubs and experimental movie theaters nearby.

Métro Cluny La Sorbonne

QUAI ST MICHEL
RUE DE LA HARPE
RUE DE LA HUCHETTE
RUE DU PETIT
RUE GA
BLVD ST.-MICHEL
RUE ST.-JACQUES
BLVD ST.-GERM
RUE THE NARD
RUE DES ECOLES

**❽ ★ Musée de Cluny**
One of the finest collections of medieval art in the world is kept here in a superb late 15th-century building, incorporating the ruins of Gallo-Roman baths.

**Locator Map**
*See Street Finder maps 8, 9*

**⑩ ★ St.-Julien-le-Pauvre**
Rebuilt in the 17th century, this church was used to store animal feed during the Revolution.

Métro Maubert
Mutualité

| 0 meters | 100 |
|---|---|
| 0 yards | 100 |

**Key**

— Suggested route

## ⑬ Panthéon

Pl du Panthéon 75005. **Map** 13 A1. **Tel** 01 44 32 18 00. **Ⓜ** Maubert-Mutualité, Cardinal-Lemoine. **ⓡ** Luxembourg. **Open** Apr–Sep: 10am–6:30pm daily; Oct–Mar: 10am–6pm daily (last adm: 45 mins before closing). **Closed** Jan 1, May 1, Dec 25. 🅿 🄲 🅆 **pantheon. monuments-nationaux.fr**

When Louis XV recovered from illness in 1744, he was so grateful that he conceived a magnificent church to honor Ste. Geneviève, the patron saint of Paris. The French architect Jacques-Germain Soufflot planned the church in Neoclassical style. Work began in 1764 and was completed in 1790 under the control of Guillaume Rondelet. But with the Revolution underway, the church was soon turned into a pantheon – a monument housing the tombs of France's great heroes. Napoleon returned it to the Church in 1806, but it was secularized and then desecularized once more, before finally being made a civic building in 1885.

The facade, inspired by the Rome Pantheon, has a pediment relief depicting the mother country granting laurels to her great men. Those resting here include Voltaire, Rousseau, and Zola, and the ashes of Pierre and Marie Curie, and André Malraux.

**The Panthéon Interior**
The interior has four aisles arranged in the shape of a Greek cross, from the center of which the great dome rises.

**Iron-Framed Dome**
The fresco in the dome's stone cupola represents the *Glorification of Sainte Geneviève*, commissioned by Napoleon in 1811.

The dome lantern

The dome galleries

Entrance

**Crypt**
Under the building, the vast crypt divides into galleries flanked by Doric columns. Many French notables rest here, including Voltaire and Emile Zola.

# Street by Street: Luxembourg Quarter

Located only a few steps from the bustle of St.-Germain-des-Prés, this graceful and historic area offers a peaceful haven in the heart of a modern city. The Jardin du Luxembourg and Palais du Luxembourg dominate the surroundings. The gardens became fully open to the public in the 19th century under the ownership of the Comte de Provence (later to become Louis XVIII), when for a small fee visitors could come in and feast on fruit from the orchard. Today the gardens, palace, and old houses on the streets to the north remain unspoiled and attract many visitors.

**Place St.-Sulpice**, ringed by flowering chestnut trees, was begun in 1754.

To St.-Germain-des-Prés

**⓯ ★ St.-Sulpice**
This huge Neoclassical church, by six different architects, took more than a century to build. Highlights include murals by Delacroix.

RUE HENRI DE JOUVENEL  RUE FEROU

RUE SERVANDONI

RUE GARANCIERE

RUE DE TOURNON

**The Jardin du Luxembourg** is a popular garden where people come to relax, sunbathe, sail boats on the pond, or admire the many beautiful statues erected in the 19th century.

RUE DE VAUGIRARD

| 0 meters | | 100 |
| 0 yards | | 100 |

**⓮ ★ Palais du Luxembourg**
First built as a royal residence, the palace has been used for various purposes from prison to Luftwaffe headquarters. This garden facade was added in 1841.

**Key**

— Suggested route

*For hotels and restaurants in this region see pp554–5 and pp576–9*

**Locator Map**
*See Street Finder maps 8, 12*

**Fontaine Médicis** is a 17th-century fountain in the style of an Italian grotto. It is thought to have been designed by Salomon de Brosse.

**Ste. Geneviève**, patron saint of Paris, whose prayers saved Paris from the Huns in AD 451, is honored by this statue by Michel-Louis Victor in 1845.

# ⓮ Palais du Luxembourg

15 rue de Vaugirard 75006. **Map** 8 E5. **Tel** 01 42 34 20 00. Ⓜ Odéon. Ⓡ Luxembourg. 📷 groups: Mon, Fri, Sat (apply 3 months in advance: 01 42 34 20 60); indiv: email visites@senat.fr for sponsorship.. ✉ 🌐 **senat.fr/visite** Museum: **Tel** 01 40 13 62 00. **Open** 10am–7pm (to 10pm Mon) daily during exhibitions. ⚟ **Closed** May 1. 🌐 **museeduluxembourg.fr**

Now home to the French Senate, this palace was built to remind Marie de' Medici, widow of Henri IV, of her native Florence. It was designed by Salomon de Brosse in the style of Florence's Pitti Palace. By the time it was finished (1631), Marie had been banished from Paris, but it remained a royal palace until the Revolution. In World War II it became the Luft-waffe headquarters. The Musée du Luxembourg in the east gallery hosts art exhibitions.

# ⓯ St.-Sulpice

2 rue Palatine, pl St.-Sulpice 75006. **Map** 8 E5. **Tel** 01 42 34 59 98. Ⓜ St.-Sulpice. **Open** 7:30am–7:30pm daily. 📷 call 01 43 25 03 10; for tours of the crypt (3:30pm, 2nd & 4th Sun of month), 01 42 34 59 98. Concerts. 🌐 **paroisse-saint-sulpice-paris.org**

This imposing church, started in 1646, took more than 100 years to finish. Its simple facade has two tiers of elegant columns and two mismatched towers at the ends. Large windows fill the interior with light. The side chapel to the right has murals by Eugène Delacroix, including *Jacob Wrestling with the Angel (see p126)*.

The Classical two-storey west front of St.-Sulpice with its two towers

Carpeaux's fountain sculpture

# ⓰ Fontaine de l'Observatoire

Pl Ernest Denis, av de l'Observatoire 75006. **Map** 12 E2. Ⓡ Port Royal.

Located at the southern tip of the Jardin du Luxembourg, this is one of the finest fountains in Paris. The central sculpture, by Jean-Baptiste Carpeaux, was erected in 1873. Made of bronze, it has four women holding aloft a globe representing four continents – the fifth, Oceania, was left out for reasons of symmetry. There are some subsidiary figures, including dolphins, horses, and a turtle.

# ⓱ Val-de-Grâce

1 pl Alphonse-Laveran 75005. **Map** 12 F2. **Tel** 01 40 51 51 92. Ⓜ Gobelins. Ⓡ Port Royal. **Open** 2–6pm Tue–Thu, noon–6pm Sat & Sun. **Closed** Aug. ✝ 11am Sun. 📷 📷 except for nave. 🌐 **valdegrace.org**

This is one of the most beautiful churches in France, and forms part of a military hospital complex. Built for Anne of Austria (wife of Louis XIII) in gratitude for the birth of her son, young Louis XIV himself laid the first stone in 1645.

The church is noted for its dome. In the cupola is Pierre Mignard's enormous fresco, with over 200 triple-life-size figures. The six huge marble columns framing the altar are similar to ones in St. Peter's in Rome.

# FARTHER AFIELD

Many of Paris's famous sights are slightly out of the city center. Montmartre, long a mecca for artists and writers, still retains much of its bohemian atmosphere, and Montparnasse is full of bustling cafés and theater crowds. The famous Cimetière du Père Lachaise numbers Chopin, Oscar Wilde, and Jim Morrison among its dead and, along with the parks and gardens, provides a tranquil escape from sightseeing. Modern architecture can be seen at Fondation Louis Vuitton, Fondation Le Corbusier, and La Défense, and there is a huge selection of museums to visit. To the northeast, the science museum at La Villette provides an educational family day out.

## Sights at a Glance

### Museums and Galleries
**3** Fondation Louis Vuitton
**6** Musée Marmottan Monet
**9** Musée Gustave Moreau
**16** Cité des Sciences et de l'Industrie pp140–41
**21** Cité Nationale de l'Histoire de l'Immigration
**25** Musée National d'Histoire Naturelle

### Churches and Mosques
**7** St.-Alexandre-Nevsky
**11** Sacré-Coeur
**28** Grande Mosquée de Paris

### Parks and Gardens
**2** Bois de Boulogne
**8** Parc Monceau
**18** Parc des Buttes-Chaumont
**24** Parc Montsouris
**26** Jardin des Plantes
**29** Parc André Citroën

### Cemeteries
**13** Cimetière de Montmartre
**19** Cimetière du Père-Lachaise
**31** Cimetière du Montparnasse

### Historic Districts
**10** Montmartre pp136–7
**17** Canal St.-Martin
**30** Montparnasse

### Historic Buildings and Streets
**5** Rue La Fontaine
**12** Moulin Rouge
**22** Château de Vincennes
**32** Catacombes

### Modern Architecture
**1** La Défense
**4** Fondation Le Corbusier
**20** Bercy
**23** Bibliothèque Nationale de France
**27** Institut du Monde Arabe

### Markets
**14** Marché aux Puces de St.-Ouen

### Key
▓ Main sightseeing area
═ Freeway
▬ Highway
═ Other road
— Railroad

0 kilometers   4
0 miles   2

◀ La Grande Arche at La Défense

# West of the City

## ❶ La Défense

La Grande Arche. **Tel** 01 49 07 27 55.
🚇 La Défense. **Open** 10am–7pm daily
(to 8pm Apr–Aug). Rooftop: **Closed** for
renovation; call for information. 🅿 ♿
📷 🎫 🅦 grandearche.com

This skyscraper business city on
the western edge of Paris is the
largest office development in
Europe. La Grande Arche is an
enormous hollow cube large
enough to contain Notre-Dame
cathedral. Designed by Danish
architect Otto von Spreckelsen
in the late 1980s, the arch
houses a gallery, conference
center, computer museum, and
video-game museum and has
superb views.

La Grande Arche in La Défense

## ❷ Bois de Boulogne

75016. 🚇 Porte Maillot, Porte
Dauphine, Porte d'Auteuil, Sablons.
**Open** 24 hrs daily. 🅿 to specialty
gardens and museum. ♿

The 3.3-sq-mile (8.5-sq-km) Bois
de Boulogne, located between
the western edges of Paris and
the River Seine, offers a vast belt
of greenery for strolling, cycling,
riding, boating, picnicking, or
spending a day at the races.
The Bois de Boulogne was once
part of the immense Forêt du
Rouvre. In the mid-19th century
Napoleon III had the Bois
designed and landscaped by
Baron Haussmann, along the
lines of Hyde Park in London.
Several self-contained parks
within the forest include the
Jardin d'Acclimatation, which
has a theme park and activities
for children, Pré Catalan, and the

Rose garden in the Bois de Boulogne

Bagatelle gardens with
architectural follies and an
18th-century villa famous for its
rose garden. The villa was built
in just 64 days after a bet
between the Comte d'Artois
and Marie Antoinette.

By day the Bois is busy with
families, joggers, and walkers,
but after dark it is notoriously
seedy – and best avoided.

## ❸ Fondation Louis Vuitton

8 av du Mahatma Gandhi, Bois de
Boulogne, 75116. **Open** hours vary
according to exhibitions. 🅿
🅦 fondationlouisvuitton.fr

Located close to the Jardin
d'Acclimatation in the Bois de
Boulogne, Frank Gehry's dramatic
glass structure consisting of
12 glass "sails" is a thrilling
example of modern architecture.
It contains a gallery hosting
contemporary art exhibitions
and events. A shuttle to the arts
center leaves Place Charles de
Gaulle every 15 minutes.

## ❹ Fondation Le Corbusier

8–10 sq du Docteur-Blanche 75016.
Villa La Roche: **Tel** 01 42 88 75 72.
🚇 Jasmin. **Open** 1:30–6pm Mon,
10am–6pm Tue–Sat. **Closed** public
hols. 🎫 in English 2pm Tue (and Fri
during summer). 🅿 Films, videos.
Maison Jeanneret: **Tel** 01 42 88 41 53.
🅦 fondationlecorbusier.fr

In a quiet corner of Auteuil
stand the villas La Roche and

Jeanneret, the first two Parisian
houses built by the influential
20th-century architect Charles-
Edouard Jeanneret, better
known as Le Corbusier. Built at
the start of the 1920s, they
demonstrate his revolutionary
use of white concrete in Cubist
forms. Rooms flow into each
other, allowing maximum light
and volume, and the houses
stand on stilts with windows
along their entire length.

Today, the villas host lectures
on Le Corbusier and his work.

## ❺ Rue la Fontaine

75016. **Map** 5 A4. 🚇 Michel-Ange-
Auteuil, Jasmin. 🚇 Radio-France.

Rue la Fontaine and the
surrounding streets act as a
showcase for some of the most
exciting early 20th-century Art
Nouveau architecture, featuring
sinuous decorative detail. At
No. 14 stands the Castel

An Art Nouveau window in rue
la Fontaine

Béranger, a stunning apartment building made from cheap building materials to keep costs low, yet featuring stained glass, convoluted ironwork, balconies, and mosaics. It established the reputation of architect Hector Guimard, who went on to design the city's Art Nouveau Métro entrances. Other examples of his work can be seen farther along the street, such as the Hôtel Mezzara at No. 60.

## ❻ Musée Marmottan Monet

2 rue Louis Boilly 75016. **Tel** 01 44 96 50 33. Ⓜ Muette. **Open** 10am–6pm Tue–Sun (to 9pm Thu). **Closed** Jan 1, May 1, Dec. 25 🖼 ♿ 📷
Ⓦ **marmottan.fr**

This museum was created in the 19th-century mansion of the famous art historian Paul Marmottan, in 1932. He bequeathed his house, plus his Renaissance, Consular, and First Empire paintings and furniture, to the Institut de France.

In 1966 the museum acquired a fabulous collection of work by Impressionist painter Claude Monet, the bequest of his son, Michel. Some of Monet's most famous paintings are here, including *Impression – Sunrise* (hence the term "Impressionist"), a painting of Rouen Cathedral (*see p271*), and the *Waterlilies* series (*see p102*). Also here is the work painted at Giverny during the last years of Monet's life. This includes *The Japanese Bridge* and *The Weeping Willow*. The iridescent colors and daring brushstrokes make these some of the museum's most powerful works.

Part of Monet's personal art collection was passed on to the museum, including work by fellow Impressionists Camille Pissarro, Pierre-Auguste Renoir, Edgar Degas, Paul Gauguin, and Alfred Sisley. The museum also displays medieval illuminated manuscripts and 16th-century Burgundian tapestries. Piano and chamber music concerts are occasionally held here.

Colonnade beside the *naumachia* basin in Parc Monceau

# North of the City

St.-Alexandre-Nevsky Cathedral

## ❼ St.-Alexandre-Nevsky

12 rue Daru 75008. **Map** 2 F3. **Tel** 01 42 27 37 34. Ⓜ Courcelles, Ternes. **Open** 3–5pm Tue, Fri, Sun. 📷 by appt, call 03 86 91 97 88. ✝ 6pm Sat, 10:30am Sun.

This imposing Russian Orthodox cathedral with its five golden-copper domes signals the presence of a large Russian community in Paris. Designed by members of the St. Petersburg Fine Arts Academy and financed jointly by Tsar Alexander II and the local Russian community, it was completed in 1861.

Inside, a wall of icons divides the church in two. The Greek-cross plan and the rich mosaics and frescoes decorating the interior are Neo-Byzantine, while the exterior and gilt domes are traditional Russian Orthodox.

## ❽ Parc Monceau

Bd de Courcelles 75017. **Map** 3 A3. **Tel** 01 42 27 08 64. Ⓜ Monceau. **Open** 7am–8pm daily (10pm summer). 📷 by appt.

This green haven dates back to 1778, when the Duc de Chartres commissioned the painter-writer and amateur landscape designer Louis Carmontelle to create a magnificent garden. The result was an exotic landscape full of architectural follies in the English and German styles.

In 1852 the garden became a chic public park. A few original features remain, among them the *naumachia* basin – an ornamental version of a Roman pool that was used for simulating naval battles.

## ❾ Musée Gustave Moreau

14 rue de la Rochefoucauld 75009. **Map** 4 E3. **Tel** 01 48 74 38 50. Ⓜ Trinité. **Open** 10am–5:15pm Wed–Mon. **Closed** 12:45–2pm Mon, Wed,& Thu. 🖼 📷
Ⓦ **musee-moreau.fr**

The Symbolist painter Gustave Moreau (1826–98), known for his symbolic works depicting biblical and mythological fantasies, lived and worked in this handsome town house. *Jupiter and Semele*, one of the artist's outstanding works, is displayed here, along with other major paintings, and some of the collection's 7,000 drawings and 1,000 oils and watercolours.

# ⑩ Montmartre

The steep *butte* (hill) of Montmartre has been associated with artists for 200 years. Théodore Géricault and Camille Corot came here at the start of the 19th century, and in the 20th century Maurice Utrillo immortalized the streets in his works. Today, street artists thrive predominantly on the tourist trade, but much of the area still preserves its rather louche, villagey prewar atmosphere.

The name of the area is ascribed to martyrs who were tortured and killed in the area around AD 250, hence *mons martyrium*.

**Clos Montmartre**
This is one of the last Parisian vineyards. The harvest is celebrated on the first Saturday in October.

Métro Lamarck Caulaincourt

**Au Lapin Agile**
"The Agile Rabbit" is a famous cabaret that was popular with artists and poets such as Picasso, Renoir, Apollinaire, and Paul Verlaine.

RUE DE L'ABREUVOIR
RUE DES SAULES
RUE COR
RUE
ST VIN
RUE
NORVIN
RUE ST.
RUE LEPIC
PL JB CLEMENT
RUE POULBOT
RUE DE LA MIRE
RAVIGNAN
PL E GOUDEAU
RUE BERTHE
RUE DES TROIS FRERES
RUE

**Musée de Montmartre**
Changing Montmartre-related exhibitions usually include works by artists who lived here, such as this *Portrait of a Woman* (1918) by Amedeo Modigliani.

**Espace Dalí Paris**
Some 330 works by the Surrealist painter and sculptor are on display here.

**Place du Tertre**
The tourist center of Montmartre is full of portraitists. Artists first exhibited in the square in the 19th century.

**Key**

— Suggested route

| 0 meters | | 100 |
|---|---|---|
| 0 yards | | 100 |

**La Mère Catherine**
This was a favorite French restaurant of Russian cossacks. They would shout "Bistro!" (meaning "quick") – which gave the bistro its name.

**Locator Map**
*See Street Finder map 4*

**⓫ Sacré-Coeur**
This Neo-Romanesque church, started in the 1870s and completed in 1914, contains many treasures, such as this figure of the *Virgin Mary and Child* (1896) by P. Brunet.

**St.-Pierre de Montmartre**
This is an early Parisian church with origins dating back to the 6th century.

**The *funiculaire*,** or cable railroad, at the end of rue Foyatier takes you to the foot of the basilica of the Sacré-Coeur. Métro tickets are valid for it.

**Square Willette** lies below the forecourt of the Sacré-Coeur. It is laid out on the side of the hill in a series of descending terraces with lawns, shrubs, trees, and flowerbeds.

**Musée de la Halle Saint Pierre**
Exhibitions here showcase Outsider Art and Art Brut, such as this piece by S. Feleggakis.

# ⓫ Sacré-Coeur

33–35 rue du Chevalier-de-la-Barre 75018. **Map** 4 F1. **Tel** 01 53 41 89 00. Ⓜ Abbesses (then *funiculaire* to steps of Sacré-Coeur), Anvers, Jules Joffrin, Pigalle. 🚌 30, 31, 80, 85. Basilica: **Open** 6am–10:30pm daily. Dome: **Open** 9am–6pm daily. 🅿 ✝ 3–4 times a day (call for hours). Vespers 4pm Sun. Ⓦ **sacre-coeur-montmartre.com**

The Sacré-Coeur basilica, dedicated to the Sacred Heart of Christ and consecrated in 1919, was built as a result of a private religious vow made at the outbreak of the Franco-Prussian war. Two Catholic businessmen, Alexandre Legentil and Hubert Rohault de Fleury, promised to finance the basilica should France be spared from assault. Despite the war and the Siege of Paris, invasion was averted and work began in 1875 to Paul Abadie's designs. Never considered very graceful, the basilica is vast and impressive, and one of France's most important Roman Catholic buildings.

**The stained-glass gallery** affords a view of the whole interior.

**The great *Mosaic of Christ*** (1912–22), by Luc Olivier Merson, dominates the chancel vault.

**The ovoid dome** is the second-highest point in Paris, after the Eiffel Tower.

**Bronze doors** in the portico show the Last Supper and other biblical scenes.

**The crypt vaults** house a chapel containing Alexandre Legentil's heart in a stone urn.

# ⓬ Moulin Rouge

82 bd de Clichy 75018. **Map** 4 E1. **Tel** 01 53 09 82 82. Ⓜ Blanche. Dinner: 7pm. Shows: 9pm & 11pm daily. 🅿 Ⓦ **moulinrouge.com**

Built in 1885, the Moulin Rouge was turned into a dance hall as early as 1900. Henri de Toulouse-Lautrec immortalized the wild and colorful cancan shows here in his posters and drawings of famous dancers such as Jane Avril. The high-kicking routines continue today in glitzy, Las-Vegas-style revues.

# ⓭ Cimetière de Montmartre

20 av Rachel 75018. **Map** 4 D1. **Tel** 01 53 42 36 30. Ⓜ Place de Clichy. **Open** 8am–6pm Mon–Fri (from 8:30am Sat, from 9am Sun). ♿

This has been the resting place for many luminaries of the creative arts since the beginning of the 19th century.

The composers Hector Berlioz and Jacques Offenbach (who wrote the renowned cancan tune), Russian dancer Vaslav Nijinsky and film director François Truffaut are just a few of the famous people who have been buried here over the years.

There is also a Montmartre cemetery near square Roland-Dorgelès, known as the St.-Vincent cemetery. This is where the French painter Maurice Utrillo is buried.

African stand in the Marché aux Puces de St.-Ouen

# ⓮ Marché aux Puces de St.-Ouen

Rue des Rosiers, St.-Ouen 93406. Ⓜ Porte-de-Clignancourt, Garibaldi. **Open** 9am–6pm Sat, 10am–6pm Sun, 10am–5pm Mon (reduced hours in summer). *See Markets p153.* Ⓦ **marcheauxpuces-saintouen.com**

The oldest and largest Paris flea market spans 15 acres (6 ha) near the Porte de Clignancourt. In the 19th century, rag merchants and tramps would gather outside the fortifications that marked the city limits and offer their wares for sale. Today the area is divided into separate markets, and is well-known for its heavy Second Empire furniture and ornaments.

# ⓯ Parc de la Villette

211 av Jean Jaurés, 75109. **Tel** 01 40 03 75 75. **Open** daily. Ⓜ Porte de la Villette, Porte de Pantin.

Straddling the canal in the city's northeast corner, this park houses the Cité des Sciences et de l'Industrie, as well as a popular children's outdoor playground. It's also home to Jean Nouvel's Philharmonie de Paris, a shimmering modern concert hall inaugurated in 2015.

## ⑯ Cité des Sciences et de l'Industrie

*See pp140–41.*

## ⑰ Canal St.-Martin

Ⓜ Jaurès, J. Bonsergent, Goncourt.

A walk along the docks on either side of the Canal St.-Martin gives a glimpse of how this thriving, industrial, working-class area of the city looked at the end of the 19th century. The 3-mile (5-km) canal, opened in 1825, provided a shortcut for river traffic between loops of the Seine. A smattering of brick-and-iron factories and warehouses survive from this time along quai de Jemmapes. Here, too, is the legendary Hôtel du Nord, from Marcel Carné's 1930s film of the same name. Around it are tree-lined docks with quirky stores and cafés, iron footbridges, and public gardens. At Jaurès, it meets the Canal de l'Ourcq, which offers a pleasant stroll to Parc de la Villette *(see p140)*.

## ⑱ Parc des Buttes-Chaumont

Pl Armand Carrel 75019. No phone. Ⓜ Botzaris, Buttes-Chaumont. **Open** May–Sep: 7am–10pm daily; Oct–Apr: 7am–8pm daily.

Urban planner Baron Haussmann converted the hilly site from a garbage dump and quarry with gallows at the foot, to English-style gardens in the 1860s. His colleague was landscape architect Adolphe Alphand, who was responsible for a vast 1860s program to provide new sidewalk-lined Parisian avenues *(see p112)* with benches, street-lights, kiosks, and urinals.
     Others involved in the creation of this highly praised park were

Boats moored at Port de l'Arsenal

the engineer Darcel and the landscape gardener Barillet-Deschamps. They created a lake, made an island with real and artificial rocks, gave it a Roman-style temple, and added a waterfall, streams, and footbridges leading to the island. Today, in summer, visitors will also find donkey rides and a puppet *(guignol)* theater for the kids, and beautiful lawns.

# East of the City

## ⑲ Cimetière du Père-Lachaise

16 rue du Repos 75020. **Tel** 01 55 25 82 10. Ⓜ Père Lachaise, A. Dumas. 🚌 60, 69, 102 to pl Gambetta. 🅿 Pl Gambetta. **Open** 8am–5:30pm daily (to 6pm Apr–Nov; from 8:30am Sat, from 9am Sun & hols). 🗺

Paris's most prestigious cemetery is set on a wooded hill over-looking the city. The land was once owned by Père de la Chaise, Louis XIV's confessor, but it was

bought by order of Napoleon in 1803. The cemetery became so popular that the boundaries were extended six times in the 19th century. Here are buried celebrities such as writer Honoré de Balzac and composer Frédéric Chopin, singer Jim Morrison, and actors Yves Montand and Simone Signoret.

## ⑳ Bercy

75012. Ⓜ Bercy, Cour St.-Emilion. 🚌 24, 64, 87. Cinémathèque Française: 51 rue de Bercy. **Tel** 01 71 19 33 33. Museum: **Open** noon–7pm Wed–Mon (Library: till 8pm). 🗺

This former wine-trading quarter just east of the city center, with its riverside warehouses and pavilions, has been transformed into an ultramodern district. An automatic Métro line (Line 14) links it to the heart of the city.
     The centerpiece is the AccorHotels Arena, which is the city center's principal concert venue, as well as its premier sports stadium. The vast pyramidal structure, its sides clad with real lawns, has become a landmark for the eastern part of central Paris.
     Other architecturally adventurous buildings dominate the skyline, notably Chemetov's Ministry of Finance building, and Frank Gehry's American Center, which houses the **Cinémathèque Française**, a movie museum with screenings, a library, and retrospectives on directors.
     At the foot of these structures, the Parc de Bercy provides a welcome green space.

Cinématique Française (former American Center), designed by Frank Gehry, Bercy

# ⑯ Cité des Sciences et de l'Industrie

This hugely popular science and technology museum occupies the largest of the old Villette slaughterhouses, which now form part of a massive urban park. Architect Adrien Fainsilber has created an imaginative interplay of light, vegetation, and water in the high-tech, five-story building, which soars 133 ft (40 m) high. At the museum's heart is the Explora exhibit, a fascinating guide to the worlds of science and technology. Visitors can play computer games on themes of space, the earth and ocean, computers, and sound. On other levels there are a children's science city, movie theaters, a science newsroom, a library, and stores.

**Planetarium**
In this 260-seat auditorium you can watch eclipses and fly over Martian landscapes, thanks to their 3-D video system.

**Le Nautile**
This full-scale model of the *Nautile*, France's technologically advanced exploration submarine, represents one of the most sophisticated machines in the world.

## KEY

① **The moat** was designed by Fainsilber, so that natural light could penetrate into the lower levels of the building.

② **The main hall** is vast, with a soaring network of shafts, bridges, escalators, and balconies, and has a cathedral-like atmosphere.

③ **The greenhouse** is a square hothouse, 105 ft (32 m) high and wide.

400-seat auditorium

Hemispheric screen

Main lobby

## La Géode

This giant entertainment sphere houses a huge hemispherical movie screen, 11,000 sq ft (1,000 sq m), showing IMAX movies on nature, travel, history, and space.

★ **The Story of the Universe**
An exploration of the birth of the universe, this exhibit takes you back 13.7 billion years to the creation of the first atom.

**Cupolas**
The two glazed domes, 56 ft (17 m) in diameter, filter the flow of natural light into the main hall.

③

**Mirage Aircraft**
A full-size model of the French-built jet fighter is one of the exhibits illustrating advances in technology.

To La Géode ↘

★ **Children's City**
In this lively, extensive area, children can experiment and play with machines that show how scientific principles work.

**Walkways**
The walkways cross the encircling moat to link the various floors of the museum to the Géode and the park.

Bibliothèque Nationale de France

## ㉑ Cité Nationale de l'Histoire de l'Immigration

293 av Daumesnil 75012. **Tel** 01 53 59 58 60. Ⓜ Porte Dorée. **Open** 10am–5:30pm Tue–Fri (7pm Sat & Sun). **Closed** Jan 1, May 1, Jul 14, Dec 25. 🅿 ♿ restricted. 📷 🆆 **histoire-immigration.fr**

Housed in the Palais de la Porte Dorée, this museum is devoted to immigration in France. The palace is an Art Deco building designed by Albert Laprade and Léon Jaussely for the city's grand colonial exhibition in 1931.

The cellar also contains tropical fish collections, along with tortoises and crocodiles.

## ㉒ Château de Vincennes

Av de Paris 94300 Vincennes. **Tel** 01 48 08 31 20. Ⓜ Château de Vincennes. 🆁🆁 Vincennes. **Open** 10am–5pm daily (6pm mid-May–Sep). **Closed** Jan 1, May 1, Nov 1 & 11, Dec 25. 📷 Chapel & donjon: **Tel** 01 40 74 19 12. 🅿 📷 🆆 **chateau-vincennes.fr**

The Château de Vincennes was the permanent royal residence until the 17th century, before the court moved to Versailles. The donjon, the tallest fortified medieval building in Europe, the Gothic chapel, 17th-century pavilions, and moat are all worth seeing.

Beyond lies the Bois de Vincennes. Once a royal hunting ground, it is now a landscaped forest with ornamental lakes and a racetrack.

## ㉓ Bibliothèque Nationale de France

Quai François-Mauriac 75013. **Tel** 01 53 79 59 59. Ⓜ Bibliothèque François-Mitterrand. **Open** 10am–8pm Tue–Sat, 1–7pm Sun. **Closed** public hols, 1 week Sep. 🅿 ♿ 📷 🆆 **bnf.fr**

These four great book-shaped towers house 10 million volumes. The libraries offer more than 400,000 titles. Other resources include digitized illustrations and sound archives. There are also frequent temporary exhibitions.

# South of the City

## ㉔ Parc Montsouris

2 rue Gazan, bd Jourdan 75014. **Tel** 01 40 71 75 60. Ⓜ Pte d'Orléans. 🆁🆁 Cité Universitaire, Glacière. **Open** 9am–9:30pm (to 5:30pm in winter) daily, but times vary, so call ahead. 📷 ♿

This English-style park, the second largest in Paris, was laid out by Adolphe Alphand from 1865 to 1878. Its restaurant, lawns, and lake – home to a variety of birds – are enduringly popular.

Skull of the reptile dimetrodon

## ㉕ Musée National d'Histoire Naturelle

36 rue Geoffroy Saint-Hilaire 75006. **Map** 13 C2. **Tel** 01 40 79 54 79/56. Ⓜ Jussieu, Austerlitz. **Open** 10am–6pm Wed–Mon. **Closed** May 1. 🅿 📷 ♿ 📷 📷 Library. 🆆 **mnhn.fr**

The highlight of the museum is the Grande Galerie de l'Évolution. There are also four other departments: palaeontology, featuring skeletons, casts of various animals and an exhibition showing the evolution of the vertebrate skeleton; palaeobotany, devoted to plant fossils; mineralogy, including gemstones; and entomology, with some of the oldest fossilized insects on earth. The bookstore is in the house that was occupied by the naturalist Buffon, from 1772 until his death in 1788.

## ㉖ Jardin des Plantes

57 rue Cuvier 75005. **Map** 13 C1. **Tel** 01 40 79 56 01 or 01 40 79 54 79. Ⓜ Jussieu, Austerlitz. **Open** 7:30am–8pm daily (8am–5:30pm winter). 🆆 **jardindesplantes.net** Parc Zoologique: av Daumesnil & rt de la Ceinture du Lac. **Tel** 08 11 22 41 22. **Open** daily. 🆆 **parczoologiquedeparis.fr**

The botanical gardens were established in 1626, when Jean Hérouard and Guy de la Brosse, Louis XIII's physicians, founded a royal medicinal herb garden. A school of botany, natural history, and pharmacy followed. The garden, which opened to the public in 1640, houses a natural history museum, botanical school, and zoo.

As well as vistas and walkways flanked by ancient statues, the park has an alpine garden with plants from Corsica, Morocco, the Alps, and the Himalayas, and an unrivalled display of herbaceous and wild plants. The Cedar of Lebanon here, originally from Britain's Kew Gardens, was the first to be planted in France.

Rue Mouffetard, one of several markets near the Jardin des Plantes

## ㉗ Institut du Monde Arabe

1 rue des Fossés St.-Bernard, pl Mohammed V 75005. **Map** 9 C5. **Tel** 01 40 51 38 38. Ⓜ Jussieu, Cardinal-Lemoine. Museum & temp exhibs: **Open** 10am–6pm Tue–Sun (to 7pm Sat & Sun). **Closed** May 1. 🖼 📷 ♿ 🖥 ♻ 🅦 imarabe.org

This magnificent contemporary building was designed by French architect Jean Nouvel, and cleverly combines high-tech details with the spirit of traditional Arab architecture. From the fourth to seventh floors there is a comprehensive display of Islamic art from the 9th to 19th centuries, including glassware, ceramics, and sculpture. The museum's highlight is its collection of astrolabes, the much-prized tool used by ancient Arab astronomers.

## ㉘ Grande Mosquée de Paris

2 bis pl du Puits de l'Ermite 75005. **Tel** 01 45 35 97 33. Ⓜ Place Monge. **Open** 9am–noon, 2–6pm Sat–Thu (till 7pm in summer). **Closed** Muslim hols. 🖼 📷 🖥 ♻ Library. 🅦 mosqueedeparis.net

Built in the 1920s in the Hispano-Moorish style, these buildings are the center for Paris's Muslim community. Once used solely by scholars, the mosque has expanded over the years and now houses some rather salubrious but fun Turkish baths, a fine restaurant, and a beautiful *salon de thé*.

Tour Montparnasse

Institut du Monde Arabe, covered with photosensitive lightscreens

## ㉙ Parc André Citroën

2 rue Cauchy, Quai André Citroën 75015. **Tel** 01 40 71 75 60. Ⓜ Balard. **Open** May–Sep: 8am–8:30 pm daily; Oct–Apr: 8am–7pm daily (from 9am Sat & Sun). ♿

This park, built on the site of a former automobile manufacturing plant, is a fascinating blend of styles, ranging from wild-flower meadow in the north to monochrome mineral and sculpture gardens in the southern section. Modern water sculptures dot the park, and there is also a chance to take a hot-air balloon ride.

## ㉚ Montparnasse

75014 & 75015. **Map** 11 & 12. Ⓜ Montparnasse, Vavin, Raspail, Edgar Quinet. Tour Montparnasse: 33 av du Maine. **Tel** 01 45 38 52 56. **Open** Apr–Sep: 9:30am–11:30pm; Oct–Mar: 9:30am–10:30pm (to 11pm Fri, Sat & hols). 🅦 tourmontparnasse56.com

The name Montparnasse was first used ironically, when 17th-century arts students performed on a "mount" of rubble left over from quarrying. In ancient Greece, Mount Parnassus was dedicated to poetry and music. By the 19th century, crowds were drawn to the local cabarets and bars by duty-free prices. The mixture of art and high living was especially potent in the 1920s and 1930s, when Hemingway, Picasso, Cocteau, Giacometti, Matisse, and Modigliani were residents here. The modern *quartier* is dominated by the much-hated **Tour Montparnasse**, although the view from the top (the 56th floor) is spectacular.

## ㉛ Cimetière du Montparnasse

3 bd Edgar Quinet 75014. **Map** 12 D3. **Tel** 01 44 10 86 50. Ⓜ Edgar Quinet. **Open** mid-Mar–Nov: 8am–6pm Mon–Fri, 8:30am–6pm Sat, 9am–6pm Sun; Dec–mid-Mar: closes 5:30pm. 📷 01 40 33 85 85

Montparnasse cemetery opened in 1824. Among those buried here are Serge Gainsbourg, Charles Baudelaire, Jean-Paul Sartre and Simone de Beauvoir, and Guy de Maupassant.

Skulls and bones stored in the Catacombes

## ㉜ Catacombes

1 av du Colonel Henri Rol-Tanguy 75014. **Map** 12 E4. **Tel** 01 43 22 47 63. Ⓜ Denfert-Rochereau. **Open** 10am–8:30pm Tue–Sun (ticket office closes 7:30pm). **Closed** public hols. 🖼 📷 🅦 catacombes.paris.fr

A long series of quarry tunnels built in the 13th century, the catacombs are lined with ancient bones and skulls. Thousands of rotting corpses were transported here in the 1780s to absorb the excess from the insanitary Les Halles cemetery.

# STORES AND MARKETS

For many people, Paris epitomizes luxury and good living. Exquisitely dressed men and women sip wine by the banks of the Seine against the backdrop of splendid French architecture, or browse at small specialist stores. The least expensive way of joining the chic set is to create French style with accessories or fashion jewelry. Alternatively, try shopping in the January or July sales. If your budget allows, take the opportunity to buy world-famous Paris fashions, or feast on the wonderful gourmet delicacies displayed with consummate artistry. Parisian shopping streets and markets are the ideal place to indulge in the French custom of strolling for the express purpose of seeing and being seen. For up-to-the-minute high fashion, rue du Faubourg-St.-Honoré, with its exquisite couture window displays, is hard to beat. Browsing around the bookstands along the Seine is another favorite French pastime. A survey of some of the best and most famous places to shop follows.

Shopping on avenue Montaigne

## Opening Hours

Shops are usually open from 10am to 7pm, Monday to Saturday, but hours can vary. Many department stores stay open late on Thursdays, while boutiques may shut for an hour or two at midday. Markets and local neighborhood stores usually close on Mondays. Large department stores, supermarkets, and many stores in the main shopping areas are open on Sundays. Some places shut for the summer, usually in August.

## Payment and VAT

Cash is readily available from the ATMs in most banks, which accept both credit and bank debit cards. Visa and MasterCard are the most widely accepted credit cards.

A sales tax (TVA) from 5.5 to 20 percent is imposed on most goods and services in EU countries. Non-EU residents shopping in France are entitled to a refund of this if they spend a minimum of €175 in one store in one day. You must have been resident in France for less than six months and either carry the goods with you out of the country within three months of purchase, or get the store to forward them to you. Larger stores will generally supply a form (bordereau de détaxe or bordereau de vente) and help you to fill it out. When you leave France or the EU you present the form to Customs, who either permit you to be reimbursed straight away, or forward your claim to the place where you purchased the merchandise; the store eventually sends you a refund.

The Chanel logo, recognized worldwide

## Sales

The main sales (soldes) are held in January and July, although more and more you can find good deals throughout the year. If you see goods labeled Stock, it means that they are stock items that have been reduced for clearance. Dégriffé means designer labels, (with the label cut out) marked down, frequently from the previous year's collections. Fripes indicates that the clothes are secondhand.

### The Center of Paris Couture

The couture houses are concentrated on the Right Bank, around rue du Faubourg-St.-Honoré and avenue Montaigne.

## Department Stores

Much of the pleasure of shopping in Paris is derived from going to the small specialist stores. But if time is short, try the *grands magasins* (department stores) or the mall at **Beaugrenelle**, which offers a wide range of stores at all price levels, including a FNAC and a Marks & Spencer, plus a movie theater and a food court. Some stores still operate a ticket system for selling goods. The store clerk writes up a ticket for goods from their own boutique. You take the ticket to one of the cashiers, and then return with the validated ticket to pick up your purchase. This can be time-consuming, so go early in the morning and don't shop on Saturdays, unless you enjoy a crush. The French do not pay much attention to lines, so be assertive! One peculiarity of a visit is that the security guards may ask to inspect your bags as you leave. These are random checks and should not be taken as an implication of theft.

All department stores have places to eat, although the stores themselves tend to have different emphases. **Au Printemps** is noted for its exciting and innovative household goods section, vast cosmetic range, and large menswear store. The clothing departments for women and children are well stocked. Fashion shows are held at 10am on Tuesdays (and each

The 1865 facade of Au Printemps department store

Kenzo designerwear in place des Victoires

Friday from April to October: by invitation only). The lovely domed restaurant in the cupola often hosts chic afterhours parties, which are private, but a visit to the restaurant during shopping hours is worthwhile.

**BHV** (Le Bazar de l'Hôtel de Ville) is a DIY enthusiast's paradise, and sells a host of other items, such as designer decor. The Left Bank's **Le Bon Marché** was Paris's first department store and today is its chicest. The designer clothing sections are well sourced, the high-end accessories are excellent, and the own-brand linen has a good quality-to-price ratio. The prepared food and gourmet grocery sections serve restaurant-quality fare to take away.

**Galeries Lafayette** is perhaps the best-known department store and has a wide range of clothing available at all price levels. Its first-floor trends section plays host to lots of innovative designers. Galeries Lafayette Gourmet, the food court, sells a range of French and international delicacies. Across the road is the store's homeware building, which stocks a good selection of kitchenware.

**FNAC** specializes in CDs, books (foreign editions can be found at Les Halles), and electronic equipment, while **FNAC Beaugrenelle** sells a wide range of the latest technological equipment. **Gibert Joseph** has an impressive selection of books, CDs, and DVDs.

## DIRECTORY

### Department Stores

**Au Printemps**
64 bd Haussmann 75009.
Map 4 D4.
Tel 01 42 82 50 00.
W printemps.com

**Beaugrenelle**
12 rue Linois 75015.
Map 5 B5.
Tel 01 53 95 24 00.
W beaugrenelle-paris.com

**BHV**
52 rue de Rivoli 75004.
Map 9 B3.
Tel 09 77 40 14 00.
W bhv.fr

**Le Bon Marché**
24 rue de Sèvres 75007.
Map 7 C5.
Tel 01 44 39 80 00.
W lebonmarche.com

**FNAC**
Forum des Halles, 1/7 rue Pierre Lescot 75001.
Map 9 A2.
Tel 0825 020 020.
W fnac.com

**FNAC Beaugrenelle**
5 rue Linois 75015.
Map 5 B5.
Tel 0825 020 020.
W fnac.com

**Galeries Lafayette**
40 bd Haussmann 75009.
Map 4 E4.
Tel 01 42 82 34 56.
W galerieslafayette.com

**Gibert Joseph**
5 rue Pierre Sarrazin 75006.
Map 8 F5.
Tel 01 44 41 88 88.
W gibertjoseph.com

# Clothing and Accessories

For many people Paris is synonymous with fashion, and Parisian style is the ultimate in chic. More than anywhere else in the world, women in Paris seem to be in tune with current trends and when a new season arrives appear, as one, to don the look. Though less trend-conscious generally, Parisian men are aware of style, and mix and match patterns and colors with *élan*. Finding the right clothes at the right price means knowing where to shop. For every luxury boutique on the avenue Montaigne, there are ten young designers' stores waiting to become the next Jean-Paul Gaultier – and hundreds more selling imitations.

## Haute Couture

Paris is the home of haute couture. The original couture garments, as opposed to the imitations and adaptations, are one-off creations, designed by one of the nine haute couture houses listed with the Fédération Française de la Couture. The rules for being classified are fairly strict, and many of the top designers are not included. Astronomical prices put haute couture beyond the reach of all but a few immensely deep pockets, but it is still the lifeblood of the fashion industry providing inspiration for the mass market.

## Women's Clothes

Most *couture* houses are found on or near the rue du Faubourg St.-Honoré and avenue Montaigne: **Christian Dior**, **Pierre Cardin**, **Chanel**, **Christian Lacroix**, **Versace**, **Givenchy**, **Nina Ricci**, **Giorgio Armani** and **Yves Saint Laurent**.

**Hermès** has classic country chic. **MaxMara**'s Italian elegance is popular in France, and no one can resist a Giorgio Armani suit. The legendary **Prada** store has stuck to the Right Bank, but many fashion houses prefer the Left Bank.

Many designers have a Left Bank branch in addition to their Right Bank bastions, and most have ready-to-wear stores here. For sheer quality there's **Georges Rech** and **Jil Sander** for exquisite tailoring. Try **Sonia Rykiel** for knitwear, and **Barbara Bui** for soft, feminine clothes. **Comptoir des Cotonniers** and

**Anne Fontaine** have branches throughout Paris and stock excellent basics, and **Vanessa Bruno** is extremely popular for feminine flair.

For ready-to-wear, head to Japanese designers **Kenzo** and **Comme des Garçons**, with quirky fashion for both sexes. In nearby rue du Jour, find the timeless elegance of **Agnès B**.

The Marais is a haven for up-and-coming designers. One of the best streets is rue des Rosiers, which includes the wonderful **L'Eclaireur**. Daring designer **Azzedine Alaïa** is just around the corner.

The Bastille area has trendy boutiques, as well as established names, including **Paul and Jo** and high-street stores such as **Petit Bateau**. **Isabel Marant**'s boutique is renowned for original designs.

Young designers' creations are found at **Stella Cadente** and **Zadig & Voltaire**.

## Children's Clothes

Lots of options for children exist in various styles and many price ranges. Many top designers of adult clothing also have boutiques for children. These include **Kenzo**, **Baby Dior**, and **Agnès B**. Ready-to-wear stores such as **Jacadi** and **Du Pareil au Même** are serviceable and wide ranging, and **Tartine et Chocolat**'s best-selling garments are coveralls. **Bonpoint** stocks adorably chic clothing for mini-Parisians. **Petit Bateau** is coveted as

much by adults as it is by children. The inevitable has finally happened – children now have their own concept store in **Bonton**.

For little feet, **Froment-Leroyer** probably offers the best all-round classics.

## Men's Clothes

Paris has plenty of clothing stores that cater to style-conscious men. On the Right Bank, there's **Giorgio Armani**, **Pierre Cardin**, and **Lanvin** (also good for accessories). On the Left Bank, **Yves Saint Laurent** and **Michel Axel** are known for their ties. **Francesco Smalto**'s elegant creations are worn by some of the world's leading movie stars. Yohji Yamamoto's clothes in **Y3 No. 42** are for those who are intent on making a serious fashion statement, while **Gianni Versace** is classic, suave, and Italian in style. **Sauver le Monde des Hommes** has stylish shirts, jeans, T-shirts, and accessories.

The ultimate in Parisian elegance for men, however, is a suit, custom-made shirt, or silk tie from **Charvet**.

## Vintage and Secondhand Stores

The vintage craze hit Paris some time back, and there are some wonderful stores to plunder for a retro look. The best of the bunch is **Didier Ludot**, where an Aladdin's cave of chic haute couture is elegantly displayed. The **Depôt-Vente de Buci-Bourbon** is another good place to bargain-hunt. A cheaper option is to head for one of the secondhand consignment stores. Chic Parisians discard their outfits with the seasons, so it is very easy to pick up some quality items, often in top condition, from places such as **Réciproque** in Passy or **Emmaus Alternatives** in the Marais.

A budget option for sample pieces and sale stock can be found at **Le Mouton à Cinq Pattes**.

## Jewelry

The *couture* houses probably stock some of the best jewelry and scarves. **Chanel**'s jewels are classics and those of **Christian Lacroix**'are fun. Boutique YSL is a great place for accessories.

Among the main expensive Paris jewelry outlets are **Boucheron**, **Mauboussin**, and **Poiray**. They are for the serious jewelry buyer. Other top retailers include **Harry Winston** and **Cartier**. **Dinh Van** has some quirky pieces, while **Mikimoto** is a must for pearls, and **H. Stern** has some innovative designs using semi-precious and precious stones. For a range of more unusual jewelry and accessories,

try the **Swarovski Boutique**, which is owned by the Swarovksi crystal family.

## Shoes and Bags

For both classic and wild footwear designs, you can't beat **Miu Miu**. **Rodolphe Ménudier** and **Christian Louboutin** are mainstays for sexy stilettos. **Carel** stocks smart basics, and **Jonak** is a must for good imitations of designer footwear.

For ladies' purses, nothing beats **Chanel** or Dior at the top end of the scale, although **Goyard** comes close. Mid-range purses from **Furla** are a great compromise. Fabric bags from **Jamin Puech** or **Vanessa Bruno**

are a feature in every chic Parisian closet. For those with tighter purse strings, cheap, cheerful, and stylish bags can be found at **Lollipops**.

## Lingerie

For modern lingerie go to **Fifi Chachnil**, whose store is filled with colorful underwear. **La Boîte à Bas** sells fine French stockings, whereas **Princesse Tam Tam** offers quality items at reasonable prices, and divine designer underwear can be found at cult store **Sabbia Rosa**. The ultimate in Parisian lingerie can be bought off the peg or made to order at **Cadolle**, the store that invented the bra.

# DIRECTORY

## Women's Clothes

**Agnès B.**
6 rue du Jour 75001.
Map 9 A1. Tel 01 45 08 56 56. W agnesb.fr
One of several branches.

**Anne Fontaine**
24 rue Boissy d'Anglas 75008. Map 3 C5.
Tel 01 42 68 04 95.
W annefontaine.fr
One of several branches.

**Azzedine Alaïa**
7 rue de Moussy 75004.
Map 9 C3. Tel 01 42 72 30 69. W alaia.fr

**Barbara Bui**
62 rue du Faubourg St.-Honoré 75008. Map 3 B5.
Tel 01 42 66 05 87.
W barbarabui.com
One of several branches.

**Chanel**
51 av Montaigne 75008.
Map 3 A5. Tel 01 44 50 73 00. W chanel.com
One of several branches.

**Christian Dior**
30 av Montaigne 75008.
Map 6 F1. Tel 01 40 73 73 73. W dior.com

**Christian Lacroix**
2–4, Pl St.-Sulpice 75006.
Map 8 E4.
Tel 01 46 33 48 95.
W christian-lacroix.fr

**Comme des Garçons**
54 rue du Faubourg St.-Honoré 75008. Map 2 E3.
Tel 01 53 30 27 27.

**Comptoir des Cotonniers**
12 pl St.-Sulpice 75006. Map 8 E4.
Tel 01 46 33 42 37.

**L'Eclaireur**
40 rue de Sévigné 75003.
Map 10 D3. Tel 01 48 87 10 22. W leclaireur.com

**Georges Rech**
190 blvd St.-Germain 75006. Map 8 D4.
Tel 01 45 44 36 26.
W georges-rech.fr
One of several branches.

**Giorgio Armani**
2 av Montaigne 75008.
Map 6 F1. Tel 01 56 62 12 16. W armani.com

**Givenchy**
36 av Montaigne 75008.
Map 6 F1. Tel 01 44 43 99 90. W givenchy.com

**Hermès**
24 rue du Faubourg St.-Honoré 75008. Map 3 C5.
Tel 01 40 17 46 00.
W hermes.com
One of several branches.

**Isabel Marant**
16 rue de Charonne 75011. Map 10 F4.
Tel 01 49 29 71 55.
W isabelmarant.com

**Jil Sander**
56 av Montaigne 75008.
Map 6 F1. Tel 01 44 95 06 70. W jilsander.com

**Kenzo**
51 rue George V 75008.
Map 2 E5. Tel 01 47 23 33 49. W kenzo.com
One of several branches.

**MaxMara**
31 av Montaigne 75008.
Map 6 F1. Tel 01 47 20 61 13. W maxmara.com
One of several branches.

**Nina Ricci**
39 av Montaigne 75008.
Map 6 F1. Tel 01 83 97 72 12. W ninaricci.fr

**Paul and Jo**
64–66 rue des Saints Pères 75007.
Map 8 D4.
Tel 01 42 22 47 01.
W paulandjo.com

**Pierre Cardin**
59 Faubourg St.-Honoré 75008. Map 3 B5.
Tel 01 42 66 92 25.
W pierrecardin.com

**Prada**
10 av Montaigne 75008.
Map 6 F1. Tel 01 53 23 99 40. W prada.com

**Sonia Rykiel**
175 bd St-Germain 75006. Map 8 D4.
Tel 01 49 54 60 60.
W soniarykiel.com
One of several branches.

**Stella Cadente**
6 rue Alfred Roll 75017.
Map 2 E1.
Tel 09 51 26 06 38.
W stella-cadente.com

**Vanessa Bruno**
25 rue St.-Sulpice 75006. Map 8 E5.
Tel 01 43 54 41 04.
W vanessabruno.com

**Versace**
45 av Montaigne 75008. Map 3 A5.
Tel 01 47 42 88 02.
W versace.com

**Yves Saint Laurent**
38 rue du Faubourg St.-Honoré 75008. Map 3 C5.
Tel 01 42 65 74 59.
W ysl.com
One of several branches.

**Zadig & Voltaire**
9 rue du 29 Juillet 75001. Map 8 D1.
Tel 01 42 92 00 61.
W zadig-et-voltaire.com
One of several branches.

# DIRECTORY

## Children's Clothes

**Bonpoint**
320 rue St-Honoré 75001.
**Map** 9 A2.
**Tel** 01 49 27 94 82.
W bonpoint.com

**Bonton**
82 rue de Grenelle 75007.
**Map** 6 F3.
**Tel** 01 44 39 09 20.
W bonton.fr

**Du Pareil au Même**
1 rue St-Denis 75001.
**Map** 9 B3.
**Tel** 01 42 36 07 57.
W dpam.com

**Froment-Leroyer**
7 rue Vavin 75006.
**Map** 12 E1.
**Tel** 01 43 54 33 15.
W froment-leroyer.fr

**Jacadi**
17 rue Tronchet 75008.
**Map** 3 C5.
**Tel** 01 42 65 84 98.
W jacadi.com

**Petit Bateau**
116 av des Champs-
Elysées 75008. **Map** 2 E4.
**Tel** 01 40 74 02 03.
W petit-bateau.com

**Tartine et Chocolat**
84 rue du Faubourg
St-Honoré 75008.
**Map** 3 B5.
**Tel** 01 45 62 44 04.
W tartine-et-chocolat.fr

## Men's Clothes

**Charvet**
28 pl Vendôme 75001.
**Map** 4 D5.
**Tel** 01 42 60 30 70.
W charvet.com

**Francesco Smalto**
44 rue François 1er 75008.
**Map** 2 F5.
**Tel** 01 47 20 70 63.
W smalto.com

**Gianni Versace**
45 av Montaigne 75008.
**Map** 6 F1.
**Tel** 01 47 42 88 02.
W versace.com

**Giorgio Armani**
18 av Montaigne 75008.
**Map** 6 F1.
W armani.com

**Kenzo**
(see p147).

**Lanvin**
22 rue du Faubourg St.-
Honoré 75008. **Map** 10 F4.
**Tel** 01 44 71 33 33.
W lanvin.com

**Michel Axel**
44 rue du Dragon 75006.
**Map** 8 E4.
**Tel** 01 42 84 13 86.
W michelaxel.com

**Pierre Cardin**
(see p147).

**Sauver le Monde des
Hommes**
8 rue Beaurepaire 75010.
**Map** 10 E2. **Tel** 09 83 84
60 88.

**Y3 (No. 42)**
42 rue de Sevigné 75003.
**Map** 10 D3. **Tel** 01 44 61
78 11. W y-3.com

**Yves Saint Laurent**
6 pl St.-Sulpice 75006.
**Map** 8 E5. **Tel** 01 43 29
43 00. W ysl.com

## Vintage and Secondhand Stores

**Depôt-Vente de Buci-
Bourbon**
4–6 rue de Bourbon-le-
Château 75006. **Map** 8 E4.
**Tel** 01 46 34 28 28.

**Didier Ludot**
24 Galerie de Montpensier
75001. **Map** 8 E1.
**Tel** 01 42 96 06 56.
W didierludot.fr

**Emmaus Alternatives**
35 rue Quincampoix
75004. **Map** 9 B2.
**Tel** 01 44 61 69 19.

**Le Mouton à
Cinq Pattes**
8/18 rue St.-Placide 75006.
**Map** 8 D5. **Tel** 01 45 48
86 26 or 01 42 84 25 11.
W moutonacinq
pattesparis.com

**Réciproque**
89–101 rue de la Pompe
75016. **Map** 5 A1.
**Tel** 01 47 04 30 28.
W reciproque.fr

## Jewelry

**Boucheron**
26 pl Vendôme 75001.
**Map** 4 D5. **Tel** 01 42 61 58
16. W boucheron.com

**Cartier**
13 rue de la Paix 75002.
**Map** 4 D5. **Tel** 01 58 18 23
00. W cartier.fr

**Dinh Van**
16 rue de la Paix 75002.
**Map** 4 D5. **Tel** 01 42 61
74 49. W dinhvan.com

**H. Stern**
3 rue Castiglione 75001.
**Map** 8 D1. **Tel** 01 42 60
22 27. W hstern.net

**Harry Winston**
29 av Montaigne 75008.
**Map** 6 F1. **Tel** 01 47 20 03
09. W harrywinston.com

**Mauboussin**
15 rue de la Paix 75002.
**Map** 4 D5. **Tel** 01 80 18
15 90. W mauboussin.fr

**Mikimoto**
8 pl Vendôme 75001.
**Map** 4 D5. **Tel** 01 42 60
33 55. W mikimoto.fr

**Poiray**
17 rue de la Paix 75002.
**Map** 4 D5. **Tel** 01 40 41 94
91. W poiray.com

**Swarovski Boutique**
146 av des Champs-
Elysées 75008. **Map** 2 E4.
**Tel** 01 45 61 13 80.
W swarovski.com

## Shoes and Bags

**Carel**
2 rue Tronchet 75008.
**Map** 4 D4. **Tel** 01 42 66
21 58. W carel.fr

**Christian Louboutin**
38–40 rue de Grenelle
75007. **Map** 6 F3.
**Tel** 08 00 94 58 04.
W christianlouboutin.
com

**Furla**
74 av des Champs-Elysées
75008. **Map** 2 F5. **Tel** 01
40 75 02 40. W furla.com

**Goyard**
233 rue St.-Honoré 75001.
**Map** 8 D1. **Tel** 01 42 60
57 04. W goyard.com

**Jamin Puech**
43 rue Madame 75006.
**Map** 8 E5.
**Tel** 01 45 48 14 85.
W jamin-puech.com

**Jonak**
70 rue de Rennes 75006.
**Map** 12 D1.
**Tel** 01 45 48 27 11.
W jonak.fr

**Lollipops**
Les Halles, 1 rue Pierre
Lescot 75001.
**Map** 9 A2.
**Tel** 01 40 26 32 95.
W lollipopsparis.fr

**Miu Miu**
219 rue St.-Honoré 75001.
**Map** 8 D1.
**Tel** 01 58 62 53 20.
W miumiu.com

**Rodolphe Ménudier**
14 rue de Castiglione
75001. **Map** 8 D1.
**Tel** 06 07 02 81 91.
W rodolphmenudier.
com

**Vanessa Bruno**
(see p147).

## Lingerie

**La Boîte à Bas**
27 rue Boissy-d'Anglas
75008. **Map** 3 C5.
**Tel** 01 42 66 26 85.

**Cadolle**
4 rue Cambon 75001.
**Map** 4 D5.
**Tel** 01 42 60 94 22.
W cadolle.com

**Fifi Chachnil**
231 rue St.-Honoré 75001.
**Map** 8 D1.
**Tel** 01 42 61 21 83.
W fifichachnil.com

**Princesse Tam Tam**
52 bd St-Michel 75006.
**Map** 8 F5.
**Tel** 01 40 51 72 99.
W princessetamtam.
com

**Sabbia Rosa**
73 rue des Sts-Pères
75006. **Map** 8 D4.
**Tel** 01 45 48 88 37.

# Gifts and Souvenirs

Paris has a wealth of stylish gift options, from designer accessories to Eiffel Tower paperweights. Stores on rue de Rivoli and around major tourist attractions offer a range of cheap holiday paraphernalia, or for something more quirky go to one of the specialty stores such as **Les Drapeaux de France.**

## Perfume

Many stores advertise discounted perfume. They include **Eiffel Shopping** near the Eiffel Tower. The **Sephora** chain has a big selection, or try the department stores for a range of beauty brands that are hard to find elsewhere.

**Parfums Caron** has many scents created at the turn of the 19th century, and unavailable elsewhere. Beautifully packaged perfumes made from natural essences are available from **Annick Goutal. Guerlain** has the ultimate in beauty care, while the elegant stores of **L'Artisan Parfumeur** specialize in exquisitely packaged scents evoking specific memories.

## Household Goods

It is difficult to ignore some of the world's most elegant tableware. Luxury homeware stores line rue Royale. **Lalique**'s Art Nouveau and Art Deco glass sculptures are collected all over the world. Impeccable silverware comes from **Christofle**.

For beautiful porcelain tableware and crystal, go to French specialists **Villeroy & Boch** or **Baccarat**.

**La Chaise Longue** has a selection of fun gift ideas to suit most tastes, while **BoConcept** has an extensive range of contemporary goods to add a new lease on life to any home.

## Books

Some department stores sell books, and there are several English-language bookstores such as **W. H. Smith** and **Brentano's. Shakespeare and Company** and **Librairie Galignani** (the first English bookstores in Continental Europe) are good for convivial browsing among expats. French-language bookstores include **La Hune**, specializing in art, cinema, fashion, and photography, and **Gibert Joseph**, for academic books.

## Specialty Stores

**A La Civette** is perhaps Paris's most beautiful tobacconist, stocking a vast range of cigars. **La Boîte à Joujoux** is one of the largest dollhouse boutiques in Paris, while the name **Cassegrain** is synonymous with high-quality stationery and paper products. **Les Drapeaux de France** sells miniatures and toy tin soldiers.

## DIRECTORY

### Perfume

**Annick Goutal**
16 rue de Bellechasse 75007. **Map** 7 C3.
**Tel** 01 45 51 36 13.
W annickgoutal.com

**L'Artisan Parfumeur**
24 bd Raspail 75007.
**Map** 12 D1.
**Tel** 01 42 22 23 32.
W artisanparfumeur.com
One of several branches.

**Eiffel Shopping**
9 av de Suffren 75007.
**Map** 6 D3.
**Tel** 01 45 66 55 30.

**Guerlain**
68 av des Champs-Elysées 75008. **Map** 2 F5.
**Tel** 01 45 62 52 57.
W guerlain.com

**Parfums Caron**
34 av Montaigne 75008.
**Map** 6 F1.
**Tel** 01 47 23 40 82.
W parfumscaron.com

**Sephora**
70–72 av des Champs-Elysées 75008. **Map** 7 B1.
**Tel** 01 53 93 22 50.
W sephora.fr

### Household Goods

**Baccarat**
11 pl des Etats-Unis 75116.
**Map** 2 D5. **Tel** 01 40 22 11 22. W baccarat.fr

**BoConcept**
8 bd de Sebastopol 75004.
**Map** 9 A3. **Tel** 01 42 78 66 66. W boconcept.fr

**La Chaise Longue**
30 rue Croix-des-Petits-Champs 75001. **Map** 8 F1.
**Tel** 01 42 96 32 14.
W lachaiselongue.fr

**Christofle**
24 rue de la Paix 75002.
**Map** 4 D5. **Tel** 01 42 65 62 43. W christofle.com

**Lalique**
11 rue Royale 75008. **Map** 3 C5. **Tel** 01 53 05 12 81.
W lalique.com

**Villeroy & Boch**
94 bd de Montparnasse 75014. **Map** 12 D2.
**Tel** 01 56 54 10 00.
W villeroy-boch.fr

### Books

**Brentano's**
37 av de l'Opéra 75002.
**Map** 4 E5.
**Tel** 01 42 60 87 37.

**Gibert Joseph**
26–34 bd St.-Michel 75006.
**Map** 8 F5. **Tel** 01 44 41 88 88. W gibertjoseph.com

**La Hune**
16–18 rue de l'Abbaye 75006. **Map** 8 D4.
**Tel** 01 42 01 43 55.

**Librairie Galignani**
224 rue de Rivoli 75001.
**Tel** 01 42 60 76 07.
W galignani.com

**Shakespeare and Company**
37 rue de la Bûcherie 75005. **Map** 9 A4. **Tel** 01 43 25 40 93. W shakespeareandcompany.com

**W. H. Smith**
248 rue de Rivoli 75001.
**Map** 7 C1.
**Tel** 01 44 77 88 99.
W whsmith.fr

### Specialty Stores

**A La Civette**
157 rue St.-Honoré 75001. **Map** 8 F2.
**Tel** 01 42 96 04 99.

**La Boîte à Joujoux**
41–43 passage Jouffroy 75009.
**Tel** 01 48 24 58 37.
W joujoux.com

**Cassegrain**
109 bd Haussman 75008. **Map** 3 B4.
**Tel** 01 42 60 20 08.
W cassegrain.fr

**Les Drapeaux de France**
1 pl Colette 75001.
**Map** 8 E1.
**Tel** 01 40 20 00 11.
W lesdrapeauxdefrance.com

# Food and Drink

Paris is arguably more famous for food than for fashion. Gastronomic treats include *foie gras*, cold meats from the *charcuterie*, cheese, and wine. Certain streets are so overflowing with food stores that you can put together a picnic for 20 in no time: try rue Montorgueil *(see Map 9 A1)*. Rue Rambuteau, running on either side of the Centre Pompidou, has a marvelous row of fishmongers and delicatessens.

## Bread and Cakes

There is a vast range of breads and pastries in France's capital. The *baguette* is often translated as "French bread," a *bâtard* is similar but thicker, while a *ficelle* is thinner. A *fougasse* is a crusty, flat loaf often filled with onions, cheese, herbs, or spices.

Croissants can be bought *ordinaire* or *au beurre* – the latter is flakier and more buttery. *Pain au chocolat* is a chocolate-filled pastry eaten for breakfast, and *chausson aux pommes* is filled with apples. There are also pear, plum, and rhubarb variations. A *pain aux raisins* is a bread-like wheel filled with custard and raisins.

**Poilâne** sells perhaps the only bread in Paris known by the name of its baker (the late Lionel, brother of Max), and his hearty wholewheat loaves are tremendously popular.

Many think **Ganachaud** bakes the best bread in Paris. Thirty different kinds, with ingredients such as walnuts and fruit, are made in the old-fashioned ovens.

**Maison Kayser**, a high-end chain bakery, produces a variety of artisan breads including *pain aux céréales* (multigrain bread) and *pain d'amande* (almond bread), the owner's favorite.

The Jewish delicatessens have the best ryes and the only pumpernickels in town. One of the best is **Sacha Finkelsztajn**.

**Le Moulin de la Vierge** uses a wood fire to bake organic breads and rich pound cakes. **Boulanger et Pâtisserie Secco** is known for madeleines and "Paris–Brest" (*choux* pastry filled with hazelnut praline buttercream, in honor of the famous bicycle race).

**Pierre Hermé** is to cakes what Chanel is to fashion, while **Ladurée**'s macaroons are legendary.

## Chocolate

Like all food in France, chocolate is to be savored. **Un Dimanche à Paris** is a concept store dedicated to cocoa. The chocolate theme continues in the adjacent restaurant. **Dalloyau** makes all types of chocolate and is not too expensive (it is also known for its pâtisserie and cold meats). **Fauchon** is world-famous for its luxury food products. Its chocolates are excellent, as is the pâtisserie. Robert Linxe at **La Maison du Chocolat** is constantly inventing fresh, rich chocolates with mouthwatering exotic ingredients. **Edwart** offers an array of ganaches and pralines with fragrant flavors from all over the world.

## Cheese

Although Camembert is undoubtedly a favorite, there is an overwhelming range of cheeses available and a friendly *fromager* will always help you choose. **Marie-Anne Cantin** is one of the leading figures in the fight to protect traditional production methods, and her fine cheeses are available from the store that she inherited from her father. Some say that **Alléosse** is the best cheese delicatessen in Paris – all the cheeses are made according to traditional methods. **Fromagerie Quatrehomme** sells farm-made cheeses, many of which are in danger of becoming extinct. These include a rare and delicious truffle Brie (when in season). **Le Jardin Fromager** is one of the best stores in Paris for all types of cheese – the *chèvre* (goat's cheese) is particularly good, as are the *camemberts au lait cru* (cheese made with unpasteurized milk), which ooze over the plate. **Laurent Dubois**, medaled cheese maker in the boulevard St.-Germain, is known for his marinated goat's cheese.

**Androuët** is a Parisian institution with several branches across the city. Try a pungent Munster or a really ripe Brie. A charming cheese store, **La Fermette** offers a dazzling array of dairy products, which the staff will encase in plastic for the journey home – imperative when bringing cheese through customs.

Well-heeled locals line up down the street to buy oozing *livarot* and sharp *chèvre* from **La Fromagerie d'Auteuil**.

## Other Gourmet Foods

*Charcuteries* often sell cheese, snails, truffles, smoked salmon, caviar, and wine as well as cold meats. **Fauchon** has a good grocery, as does the department store **Le Bon Marché – La Grande Epicerie de Paris**. **Hédiard** is a luxury store similar to Fauchon, and **Maison de la Truffe** sells *foie gras* and sausages as well as truffles. For Beluga caviar, Georgian tea, and Russian vodka, go to **Petrossian**.

Award-winning *charcutier* **Gilles Verot**'s delicacies are internationally renowned. His stores are a feast for the eyes as well as the stomach. **Maison Pou** is a sparklingly clean and popular store selling *pâté en croute* (pâté baked in pastry), *boudins* (blood and white puddings), Lyonnais sausages, ham, and *foie gras*. Just off the Champs-Elysées, **Vignon** has superb *foie gras* and Lyonnais sausages as well as popular prepared food.

Together with truffles and caviar, *foie gras* is the ultimate in gourmet food. Though most specialty food stores sell *foie gras*, you can be sure of quality at **Comtesse du Barry**, which has six locations in Paris. **Divay** is relatively inexpensive and will ship overseas. **Lafitte** has a wide range of *foie gras* and wines, including gift boxes suitable for giving as presents.

## Wine

The chain store that has practically cornered the everyday tippling market is **Nicolas** – there is a branch in every neighborhood that can provide a range of wines to suit all pockets. As a rule, the salespeople at Nicolas are knowledgeable and helpful. Try the charming **Legrand Filles et Fils** for a carefully chosen selection of high-end champagnes. **Caves Taillevent** on rue du Faubourg St.-Honoré is well worth a sightseeing tour. It is an enormous, overwhelming cellar with some of the most expensive wine available.

**Cave Péret** on rue Daguerre has a vast selection of wines, and staff can offer personal advice to help you with your purchase. The beautiful **Ryst-Dupeyron**, in the St.-Germain quarter, displays whiskies, wines, ports, and Monsieur Ryst's own Armagnac. On request, he will even personalize a bottle for that special occasion.

Other great wine stores in Paris include **Lavinia**, which is the largest in Europe. The staff at **Les Caves Augé** is also very knowledgeable and friendly.

## DIRECTORY

### Bread and Cakes

**Boulangerie Flute Gana by Ganachaud**
226 rue des Pyrénées 75020. **Tel** 01 43 58 42 62. W gana.fr

**Boulangerie et Pâtisserie Secco**
75 bd de Grenelle 75015. **Map** 6 D5.

**Ladurée**
75 av des Champs-Elysées 75008. **Map** 2 F5. **Tel** 01 40 75 08 75. W laduree.fr

**Maison Kayser**
8 rue Monge 75005. **Map** 9 B5. **Tel** 01 44 07 01 42. W maison-kayser.com

**Le Moulin de la Vierge**
105 rue Vercingétorix 75014. **Map** 11 A4. **Tel** 01 45 43 09 84. W lavierge.com

**Pierre Hermé**
72 rue Bonaparte 75006. **Map** 8 E4. **Tel** 01 43 54 47 77. W pierreherme.com

**Poilâne**
8 rue du Cherche-Midi 75006. **Map** 8 D4. **Tel** 01 45 48 42 59. W poilane.com

**Sacha Finkelsztajn**
27 rue des Rosiers 75004. **Map** 9 C3. **Tel** 01 42 72 78 91. W finkelsztajn.com

### Chocolate

**Dalloyau**
101 rue du Faubourg St.-Honoré 75008. **Map** 3 B5. **Tel** 01 42 99 90 00. W dalloyau.fr

**Edwart**
17 rue Vieille du Temple 75004. **Map** 10 D2. **Tel** 01 42 78 48 92. W edwart.fr

**Fauchon**
24–26, 30 pl de la Madeleine 75008. **Map** 3 C5. **Tel** 01 70 39 38 00/02. W fauchon.fr

**La Maison du Chocolat**
225 rue du Faubourg St-Honoré 75008. **Map** 2 E3. **Tel** 01 42 27 39 44. W lamaisondu chocolat.com

**Un Dimanche à Paris**
4-6-8 Cour du Commerce Saint André. **Map** 8 F4. **Tel** 01 56 81 18 18.

### Cheese

**Alléosse**
13 rue Poncelet 75017. **Map** 2 E3. **Tel** 01 46 22 50 45. W fromage-alleosse.com

**Androuët**
134 rue Mouffetard 75005. **Map** 13 B1. **Tel** 01 45 87 85 05. W androuet.com

**La Fermette**
86 rue Montorgueil 75002. **Map** 9 A1. **Tel** 01 42 36 70 96.

**La Fromagerie d'Auteuil**
58 rue d'Auteuil 75016. **Map** 5 A5. **Tel** 01 45 25 07 10. W lafromagerie dauteuil.fr

**Fromagerie Quatrehomme**
62 rue de Sèvres 75007. **Map** 7 C5. **Tel** 01 47 34 33 45. W quatrehomme.fr

**Le Jardin Fromager**
53 rue Oberkampf 75011. **Map** 10 E1. **Tel** 01 48 05 19 96.

**Laurent Dubois**
47 ter bd St-Germain 75007. **Map** 9 A5. **Tel** 01 43 54 50 93. W fromages laurentdubois.fr

**Marie-Anne Cantin**
12 rue du Champ-de-Mars 75007. **Map** 6 F3. **Tel** 01 45 50 43 94. W cantin.fr

### Other Gourmet Foods

**Le Bon Marché – La Grande Epicerie de Paris**
24 rue de Sèvres 75007. **Map** 7 C5. **Tel** 01 44 39 80 00. W lagrande epicerie.com

**Comtesse du Barry**
1 rue de Sèvres 75006. **Map** 8 D4. **Tel** 01 45 48 32 04. W comtessedu barry.com

**Divay**
4 rue Bayen 75017. **Map** 2 D2. **Tel** 01 43 80 16 97. W foie-gras-divay.com

**Gilles Verot**
7 rue Lecourbe 75015. **Map** 11 1A. **Tel** 01 47 34 01 03. W verot-charcuterie.fr

**Hédiard**
21 pl de la Madeleine 75008. **Map** 3 C5. **Tel** 01 43 12 88 88. W hediard.com

**Lafitte**
Ile St.-Louis, 8 rue Jean du Bellay 75004. **Map** 9 B4. **Tel** 01 43 26 08 63. W lafitte.fr

**Maison de la Truffe**
19 pl de la Madeleine 75008. **Map** 3 C5. **Tel** 01 42 65 53 22. W maison-de-la-truffe.com

**Maison Pou**
16 av des Ternes 75017. **Map** 2 D3. **Tel** 01 43 80 19 24. W maisonpou.com

**Petrossian**
18 bd de la Tour-Maubourg 75007. **Map** 7 A2. **Tel** 01 44 11 32 22. W petrossian.fr

**Vignon**
13 rue Clément-Marot 75008. **Map** 2 E5. **Tel** 01 47 20 10 01.

### Wine

**Cave Péret**
6 rue Daguerre 75014. **Map** 12 D4. **Tel** 01 43 22 57 05. W maisonperet.com

**Les Caves Augé**
116 bd Haussman 75008. **Map** 3 C4. **Tel** 01 45 22 16 97. W cavesauge.com

**Caves Taillevent**
228 rue du Faubourg St.-Honoré 75008. **Map** 2 F3. **Tel** 01 45 61 14 09. W taillevent.com

**Lavinia**
3–5 bd de la Madeleine 75008. **Map** 4 D5. **Tel** 01 42 97 20 20. W lavinia.fr

**Legrand Filles et Fils**
1 rue de la Banque 75002. **Map** 8 F1. **Tel** 01 42 60 07 12. W caves-legrand.com

**Nicolas**
35 bd Malesherbes 75008. **Map** 3 C5. **Tel** 01 42 65 00 85. W nicolas.com

**Ryst-Dupeyron**
79 rue du Bac 75007. **Map** 8 D3. **Tel** 09 54 39 72 78. W vintageandco.com

# Art and Antiques

In Paris you can buy art and antiques either from stores and galleries with established reputations, or from flea markets and avant-garde galleries. Many of the prestigious antiques shops and galleries are located around rue du Faubourg St.-Honoré and are worth a visit even if you can't afford to buy. On the Left Bank is Le Carré Rive Gauche, an organization of 30 antiques dealers.

## Exporting

Objets d'art over 50 years old, worth more than a given amount, will require a *Certificat pour un bien culturel* to be exported (provided by the vendor), plus a *licence d'exportation* for non-EU countries. Seek professional advice from the large antiques shops. The **Centre des Renseignements des Douanes** has a booklet, *Bulletin Officiel des Douanes*, with all the details.

## Antiques

If you wish to buy antiques, you might like to stroll around the areas that boast the most galleries – in Le Carré Rive Gauche around quai Malaquais, try **L'Arc en Seine** and **Anne-Sophie Duval** for Art Nouveau and Art Deco. Rue Jacob is still one of the best places to seek beautiful objects, antique or modern. Close to the Louvre,

the **Louvre des Antiquaires** comprises 250 shops selling mainly expensive, quality furniture. Many of the prestigious antiques shops are near rue du Faubourg St.-Honoré, including **Didier Aaron**, expert on furniture from the 17th and 18th centuries. **Village St.-Paul** is the most charming group of antiques shops and is also open on Sundays. In the south of the city, **Le Village Suisse** also groups many art and antiques dealers.

## Art Galleries

Most established art galleries are located on or around avenue Montaigne. However, the **Fondation Cartier** can be found in the 14th *arrondissement*. Set in a glass building, it houses modern exhibits in a range of media, from sculpture to performance art.

On the Left Bank **Galerie Maeght** has a tremendous stock of paintings at prices to suit most

budgets; it also publishes fine art books. Under the Eiffel Tower is **Millésime Gallery**, which displays works by new artists.

Rue Louise-Weiss, known as Scène Est, has become the area for cutting-edge creativity and innovation. The **Air de Paris** gallery is popular.

In the Marais try **Yvon Lambert** and **Galerie du Jour Agnès B.**; in the Bastille, try **Arts Factory**, also a fashionable place to buy catalogs on new artists, if not their works.

## Auction Houses

The great Paris auction center, in operation since 1858, is **Drouot**. Bidding can be intimidating, since most of it is done by dealers. Beware of the auctioneer's high-speed patter. *La Gazette Drouot* tells you what auctions are coming up when. Drouot also has its own auction catalog. The house only accepts cash and French checks, but there is an exchange desk in house. A 10–15 percent commission to the house is charged, so remember to add it on to any price you hear. You may view from 11am to 6pm on the day before the sale, and from 11am to noon on the morning of the sale.

---

## DIRECTORY

### Exporting

**Centre des Renseignements des Douanes**
Tel 08 11 20 44 44
or 01 72 40 78 40.
W douane.gouv.fr

### Antiques

**Anne-Sophie Duval**
5 quai Malaquais 75006.
Map 8 E3. Tel 01 43 54 51 16. W annesophie duval.com

**L'Arc en Seine**
31 rue de Seine 75006.
Map 8 E3. Tel 01 43 29 11 02. W arcenseine.com

**Didier Aaron**
152 bd Haussmann 75008. Map 3 A4.
Tel 01 47 42 47 34.
W didieraaron.com

**Louvre des Antiquaires**
2 pl du Palais Royal 75001. Map 8 E2. Tel 01 42 97 27 27. W louvre-antiquaires.com

**Village St.-Paul**
Between rues St.-Paul, Ava Maria, Charlemagne, and Jardins St.-Paul 75004.
Map 9 C4. W levillage saintpaul.com

**Le Village Suisse**
78 av de Suffren 75015.
Map 6 E4. Tel 01 73 79 15 41. W villagesuisse.com

### Art Galleries

**Air de Paris**
32 rue Louise-Weiss 75013.
Map 14 E4. Tel 01 44 23 02 77. W airdeparis.com

**Arts Factory**
27 rue de Charonne 75011.
Map 10 F4. Tel 06 22 85 35 86. W artsfactory.net

**Fondation Cartier**
261 bd Raspail 75014.
Map 12 E3. Tel 01 42 18 56 50. W fondation. cartier.com

**Galerie du Jour Agnès B.**
44 rue Quincampoix 75004.
Map 9 B2. Tel 01 44 54 55 90. W galeriedujour.com

**Galerie Maeght**
42 rue du Bac 75007. Map 8 D3. Tel 01 45 48 45 15.
W maeght.com/galeries

**Millésime Gallery**
41 av de la Bourdonnais 75007. Map 6 E3.
Tel 06 82 55 57 96. W millesime-gallery.com

**Yvon Lambert**
108 rue Vieille-du-Temple 75003. Map 10 D2.
Tel 01 42 71 89 05.
W yvon-lambert.com

### Auction Houses

**Drouot**
9 rue Drouot 75009.
Map 4 F4. Tel 01 48 00 20 20. W drouot.fr

# Markets

For eye-catching displays of wonderful food, or a lively shopping atmosphere, there is no better place than a Paris market. There are large covered food markets, markets where stands change regularly, and permanent street markets. Some of the more famous venues, with approximate opening times, follow. While you are enjoying browsing round the stands, remember to keep an eye on your valuables and be prepared to bargain.

## Food Markets

The French still shop daily, hence food markets are always packed. Most fruit-and-vegetable markets are open from around 8am to 1pm and from 4 to 7pm Tuesday to Saturday, and from 9am to 1pm Sunday. Watch out for rotten goods – buy produce loose, not in boxes. A little language is useful for specifying *pas trop mûr* (not too ripe), or *pour manger ce soir* (to be eaten tonight).

### Marché d'Aligre

Pl d'Aligre 75012. **Map** 10 F5. Ⓜ *Ledru-Rollin*. **Open** 9am–1pm, 4–7:30pm Tue–Sat, 9am–1:30pm Sun. Ⓦ **marchedaligre.free.fr**

Reminiscent of a Moroccan bazaar, this must be the city's cheapest and liveliest market. Ingredients include North African olives, peanuts, and hot peppers, and there are even a few halal butchers. Stands on the square sell mostly secondhand clothes and bric-a-brac. This is a less affluent area, with few tourists and many Parisians.

### Marché des Enfants Rouges

39 rue de Bretagne 75003. **Map** 10 D2. Ⓜ *Temple, Filles-du-Calvaire*. **Open** 8:30am–1pm, 4–7:30pm Tue–Sat, 8:30am–2pm Sun.

This part-covered fruit-and-vegetable market is the oldest covered market in Paris and dates from 1620. Famous for the freshness of its produce, on Sunday mornings street singers and accordionists enliven the proceedings.

### Marché Raspail

Between blvd Raspail, rue Cherche-Midi and rue de Rennes, 75006. **Map** 8 D4. Ⓜ *Rennes*. **Open** 7am–2:30pm Tue & Fri, 9am–2pm Sun.

Conveniently sited between Montparnasse and St.-Germain, this market sells fresh produce during the week and organic-only produce on Sundays.

### Marché St.-Germain

4–86 rue Lobineau 75006. **Map** 8 E4. Ⓜ *Mabillon*. **Open** 8am–1pm, 4–8pm Mon–Sat, 8am–1:30pm Sun.

St.-Germain is one of the few covered markets left in Paris. Here you can buy Italian, Mexican, Greek, Asian, and organic produce.

### Rue Montorgueil

75001 & 75002. **Map** 9 A1. Ⓜ *Les Halles*. **Open** 10am–6pm Mon–Sat, Sun am only (subject to change).

The paved rue Montorgueil is what remains of the old Les Halles market. Here you can buy exotic fruit and vegetables, from green bananas to yams, or sample offerings from the delicatessens. Expect high prices.

### Rue Mouffetard

75005. **Map** 13 B2. Ⓜ *Pl Monge*. **Open** 8am–1pm Tue–Sun.

This is one of the oldest market streets in Paris, and, although it has become touristy, it is still a charming winding street full of quality fresh food.

### Rue Poncelet

75017. **Map** 2 E3. Ⓜ *Ternes*. **Open** 8am–1pm, 3–7:30pm Tue–Sat, 8am–1pm Sun.

Situated away from the main tourist areas, this market street is worth visiting for its authentic French atmosphere. Choose from many bakeries, patisseries, and *charcuteries*.

## Flea Markets

It is often said that you can no longer find bargains at the Paris flea markets. Though this may be true, it is still worth going to one for the sheer fun of browsing. Whether you pick up any real bargains has as much to do with luck as with judgment. Often the sellers themselves have little or no idea of the true value of their goods – which can work either for or against you. The biggest and most famous market,

incorporating several smaller ones, is the Marché aux Puces de St.-Ouen. Keep an eye on your wallet, as pickpockets frequent these markets.

### Marché aux Puces de la Porte de Vanves

Av Georges-Lafenestre & av Marc-Sangnier 75014. Ⓜ *Porte-de-Vanves*. **Open** 7am–2 or 5pm Sat & Sun. Ⓦ **pucesdevanves.fr**

Porte de Vanves is a small market selling good-quality bric-a-brac and junk, as well as some secondhand furniture. It's best to get to the market early on Saturday morning for the best choice of wares. Artists exhibit nearby.

### Marché aux Puces de Montreuil

Porte de Montreuil, 93 Montreuil 75020. Ⓜ *Porte-de-Montreuil*. **Open** 7am–7:30pm Sat–Mon.

Go early to the Porte de Montreuil flea market for a better chance of picking up a bargain. The substantial secondhand clothes section attracts many young people. Stands sell everything from used bicycles to bric-a-brac and exotic spices.

### Marché aux Puces de St.-Ouen

(See p138).

This is the most well-known, the most crowded, and the most expensive of all the flea markets. Here you'll find a range of markets, locals dealing from their car trunks, and large buildings packed with stands. Some of them are very upscale; others sell junk. *A Guide des Puces* (guide to the flea markets) can be obtained from the information kiosk in the Marché Biron on rue des Rosiers.

### Marché Couvert Saint Quentin

85 bis, Blvd Magenta 75010. **Open** 8am–8pm Tue–Sat, 8am–1:30pm Sun. **Tel** 01 48 85 93 30.

Located steps from the Gare du Nord, this 19th-century covered market is the perfect place to stock up on last-minute cheese and charcuterie before leaving Paris. The dozens of vendors also sell flowers, local beers, breads, and pastries, and a variety of other delicacies.

# ENTERTAINMENT IN PARIS

Whether your preference is for classical drama, avant-garde theater, ballet, opera, jazz, cinema, or dancing the night away, Paris has it all. There is plenty of free entertainment, too, from the street performers outside the Centre Pompidou to musicians busking all over town and in the Métro.

Parisians themselves like nothing better than strolling along the boulevards or sitting at a sidewalk café nursing a drink as they watch the world go by. If, however, you're looking for the ultimate "Oh la-la!" experience, you can take in any of the celebrated nightclubs.

For fans of spectator sports there is tennis, the Tour de France, or horse racing. Recreation centers and gyms cater to the more active. And for those disposed to more leisurely pursuits, there is always a quiet game of *boules* to be played in the park.

The glass facade of the Bastille Opéra

## Booking Tickets

Depending on the event, tickets can be bought at the door, but for popular events it is wiser to check online for availability and purchase tickets in advance at one of the **FNAC** stores or at **Carrefour Spectacles**. Theater box offices open daily from about 11am to 7pm. Credit cards are accepted for bookings online or by telephone.

## Theater

From the grandeur of the **Comédie Française** to slapstick farce and avant-garde drama, theater is flourishing, both in Paris and in its suburbs. Founded in 1680 by royal decree, the Comédie Française is the bastion of French theater, aiming to keep classical drama in the public eye and to perform works by the best modern playwrights. Formerly the second theater of the Comédie Française, the **Odéon Théâtre de l'Europe** now specializes in plays from other countries, performed in their original languages. In an underground auditorium in the Art Deco Palais de Chaillot, the **Théâtre National de Chaillot** is famed for staging some very lively productions of European classics. The **Théâtre National de la Colline** specializes in contemporary drama.

Among the most important of the serious independents is the **Comédie des Champs-Elysées**, while for over 100 years the **Théâtre du Palais Royal** has been known as the temple of risqué farce. The café theaters such as **Théâtre d'Edgar** and **Le Point Virgule** are always good venues for seeing the best of the emerging new talent. In the summer, street theater thrives in tourist areas such as the Centre Pompidou, Les Halles, and St.-Germain-des-Prés. Open-air performances of Shakespeare and classic French plays are given at the Shakespeare Garden in the Bois de Boulogne.

## Classical Music

Paris has many first-class venues with an excellent range of opera, classical, and contemporary music productions. Opened in 1989, the stylish, 2,700-seat **Opéra National de Paris Bastille** stages classic and modern operas. The beautifully renovated **Opéra National de Paris Garnier** stages mostly ballets and some operas.

The **Philharmonie de Paris** in the Cité de la Musique – Parc de la Villette is Paris's principal concert hall and one of its most vibrant. It houses the Orchestre de Paris and Radio France's Philharmonic Orchestra. The venue is renowned for its eclectic music programs and workshops, while the museum charts the history of music and exhibits over 4,000 instruments. Both the **Théâtre des Champs-**

### Listings Magazines

*Pariscope* and *L'Officiel des Spectacles* are the best listings magazines in Paris. Published every Wednesday, you can pick them up at any newsstand. *Le Figaro* also has a good listings section on Wednesdays. *Time Out Paris* online or *Premier* online are also handy websites for up-to-date events listings.

The famous silhouette of the Moulin Rouge nightclub

Elysées and the **Théâtre du Châtelet** (closed till 2019) are recommended for their varied high-quality programs. Venues for chamber music include the **Salle Gaveau** and the **Théâtre de la Ville**.

## Dance

The opulent **Opéra National de Paris Garnier** has space for 450 artists and is home to the Ballet de l'Opéra de Paris, which has earned a reputation as one of the best classical ballet companies in the world. Government support has helped the **Théâtre de la Ville** to become Paris's most important modern dance venue, with subsidies keeping ticket costs relatively low.

The **Maison des Arts de Créteil** stages famous overseas companies, as well as its own much-praised productions.

## Clubs and Cabaret

Music in Paris clubs tends to follow the trends set in the US and Britain. Only a few

clubs such as **Balajo**, once frequented by Edith Piaf, and the ultra-hip **Showcase**, under the Alexandre III bridge, are genuinely up-to-the-minute with their music.

**Manko Cabaret** is a trendy nightspot, attracting people from the fashion world and showbusiness. For comedy in English, try **La Java**. The stage of this club, where Edith Piaf once performed, now showcases British and American comedians.

When it comes to picking a cabaret, the rule of thumb is

simple: the better-known places are best. The **Folies-Bergère** is the oldest music hall in Paris and probably the most famous in the world. It is closely rivaled by the **Lido** and the **Moulin Rouge**, birthplace of the cancan. **Paradis Latin** is the most "French" cabaret in the city. It shows variety acts with sketches enlivened by remarkable special effects and scenery.

## Rock, Jazz, and World Music

The top international acts are usually to be found at the enormous arenas such as the **AccorHotels Arena** or the **Zénith**. The Art Deco **Salle Pleyel**, which formerly hosted classical music, is now a venue for rock, pop, and jazz concerts. For a more intimate atmosphere, the legendary **Olympia** has assigned seating and good acoustics. To hear indigenous rock groups such as Les Négresses Vertes and Mano Negra, go to **La Cigale** or **Elysée-Montmartre** in the Pigalle area.

Jazz-crazy Paris has innumerable packed clubs, where the best talent in the world can be heard on any evening. All the great jazz musicians have performed at **New Morning**, which also hosts African, Brazilian, and other sounds. For Dixieland, go to **Le Petit Journal St.-Michel**.

World music and jazz lovers alike can see top acts and dance until dawn at the excellent **Chapelle des Lombards**.

The spectacular facade of the Opéra National de Paris Garnier

## Movies

Paris is the world's capital of film appreciation. It was the cradle of the cinematograph in the 1890s. Then in the late 1950s and early 1960s the city nurtured that very Parisian vanguard movement, the New Wave, when movie directors such as François Truffaut and Jean-Luc Godard revolutionized the way movies were made and perceived.

There are now more than 370 screens within the city limits, distributed among over 100 movie theaters. Most are concentrated in movie theater belts, which enjoy the added appeal of nearby restaurants and stores. The Champs-Elysées has the densest movie theater strip in town, where you can see the latest Hollywood smash or French *auteur* triumph, as well as some classic reissues.

In the vicinity of the Opéra de Paris Garnier, the movie theaters on the Grands Boulevards in-clude two notable landmarks: the 2,800-seat **Le Grand Rex**, with its Baroque decor, and the **Max Linder Panorama**, which was completely refurbished in the 1980s. Place de Clichy is the last Parisian stronghold of Pathé, while the hub of Right Bank movie theaters is in the Forum des Halles mall. France's largest screen is at **La Géode**.

On the Left Bank, Odéon-St.-Germain-des-Prés has taken over from the Latin Quarter as the city's heartland for art and repertory movie theaters. The huge, **MK2 Bibliothèque** points to the future with its collection of 14 screens, a bar, shops, and exhibition space.

The dome of the 2,800-seat Le Grand Rex movie theater

## Sport

Paris, is host to some of the foremost sports events in the world. Citywide frenzy sweeps Paris when the Tour de France bicycle race finishes there in July. From late May to mid-June Parisians live and breathe tennis during the **Roland Garros** national tennis championship. The Prix de l'Arc de Triomphe, held at the **Hippodrome de Longchamp** on the first Sunday in October, provides the opportunity to see the wealthy in all their finery, as well as first-class flat racing.

The **AccorHotels Arena** is the venue for a vast range of events, including the Paris tennis open and rock concerts, as is the new **Stade de France** at St.-Denis. **Parc des Princes** is home to Paris's top soccer team, Paris St.-Germain.

## The Celebrated Cafés of Paris

One of the most enduring images of Paris is the Left Bank café scene, where great artists, writers, and eminent intellectuals consorted. Before World War I, hordes of Russian revolutionaries, including Lenin and Trotsky, whiled away their days in the Rotonde and the Dôme in Montparnasse. In the 1920s, Surrealists dominated café life. Later came the American writers led by Ernest Hemingway and F. Scott Fitzgerald, whose haunts included La Coupole. After World War II, Jean-Paul Sartre and other Existentialists shifted the cultural scene slightly northward to St.-Germain.

Newspaper reading remains a typical café pastime

# DIRECTORY

## Booking Tickets

**Carrefour Spectacles**
29 rue du Pont Neuf 75001.
**Map** 9 A2. **w** carrefour.fr

**FNAC**
26–30 av des Ternes
75017. **Map** 2 D3. **Tel** 0825
020 020. Forum Les Halles,
1 rue Pierre Lescot 75001.
**Map** 9 A2. **Tel** 0825 020
020. **w** fnac.com

## Theater

**Comédie des
Champs-Elysées**
15 av Montaigne 75008.
**Map** 6 F1. **Tel** 01 53 23
99 19. **w** comedie
deschampselysees

**Comédie Française**
1 pl Colette 75001. **Map** 8
E1. **Tel** 08 25 10 16 80.
**w** comedie-francaise.fr

**Odéon Théâtre de
l'Europe**
Place de l'Odéon 75006.
**Map** 12 F5. **Tel** 01 44 85 40
40. **w** theatre-odeon.eu

**Le Point Virgule**
7 rue Ste.-Croix de la
Bretonnerie 75004. **Map** 9
C3. **Tel** 01 42 78 67 03.
**w** lepointvirgule.com

**Théâtre d'Edgar**
58 bd Edgar-Quinet
75014. **Map** 12 D2.
**Tel** 01 42 79 97 97.
**w** theatre-edgar.com

**Théâtre National
de Chaillot**
Pl du Trocadéro 75016.
**Map** 5 C2. **Tel** 01 53 65 30
00. **w** theatre-chaillot.fr

**Théâtre National
de la Colline**
15 rue Malte-Brun 75020.
**Tel** 01 44 62 52 52.
**w** colline.fr

**Théâtre du Palais
Royal**
38 rue Montpensier 75001.
**Map** 8 E1. **Tel** 01 42 97
40 00. **w** theatrepalais
royal.com

## Classical Music

**Cité de la Musique**
221 av Jean-Jaurès 75019.
**Tel** 01 44 84 44 84.
**w** citedelamusique.fr

**Opéra National de
Paris Bastille**
Pl de la Bastille,
120 rue de Lyon 75012.
**Map** 10 E4. **Tel** 08 92 89
90 90. **w** operadeparis.fr

**Opéra National de
Paris Garnier**
Pl de l'Opera 75009.
**Map** 4 E4. **Tel** 08 92 89 90
90. **w** operadeparis.fr

**Philharmonie de Paris**
Cité de la Musique, 221 av
Jean-Jaurès 75019.
**w** philharmoniede
paris.fr

**Salle Gaveau**
45–47 rue la Boétie 75008.
**Map** 3 B4. **Tel** 01 49 53 05
07. **w** sallegaveau.com

**Théâtre des Champs-
Elysées**
15 av Montaigne 75008.
**Map** 6 F1. **Tel** 01 49 52 50
50. **w** theatrechamps
elysees.fr

**Théâtre du Châtelet**
2 rue Edouard Colonne
75001. **Map** 9 A3.
**Tel** 01 40 28 28 40.
**w** chatelet-theatre.
com

**Théâtre de la Ville**
2 pl du Châtelet 75004.
**Map** 9 A3. **Tel** 01 42 74
22 77. **w** theatredela
ville-paris.com

## Dance

**Maison des Arts de
Créteil**
Pl Salvador Allende 94000
Créteil. **Tel** 01 45 13 19 19.
**w** maccreteil.com

**Opéra National de
Paris Garnier**
*(See Classical Music.)*

**Théâtre de la Ville**
*(See Classical Music.)*

## Clubs and
Cabaret

**Balajo**
9 rue de Lappe 75011.
**Map** 10 E4. **Tel** 01 47 00
07 87. **w** balajo.fr

**Folies-Bergère**
32 rue Richer 75009.
**Tel** 08 92 68 16 50.
**w** foliesbergere.com

**La Java**
105 rue du Faubourg-du-
Temple 75010. **Tel** 01 42
02 20 52. **w** la-java.fr

**Lido**
116bis av des Champs-
Elysées 75008. **Map** 2 E4.
**Tel** 01 40 76 56 10.
**w** lido.fr

**Manko Cabaret**
15 av Montaigne 75008.
**Map** 6 F1. **Tel** 01 49 07 20
54. **w** manko-paris.com

**Moulin Rouge**
82 bd de Clichy 75018.
**Map** 4 E1. **Tel** 01 53 09 82
82. **w** moulinrouge.fr

**Paradis Latin**
28 rue du Cardinal-
Lemoine 75008.
**Map** 9 B5. **Tel** 01 43 25 28
28. **w** paradislatin.com

**Showcase**
Under Pont Alexandre III.
Porte des Champs-Elysées
75008. **Map** 7 A1. **Tel** 01 45
61 25 43. **w** showcase.fr

## Rock, Jazz, and
World Music

**AccorHotels Arena**
8 bd de Bercy 75012.
**Map** 14 F2. **Tel** 01 75 44
04 00. **w** accorhotels
arena.com

**Chapelle des
Lombards**
19 rue de Lappe 75011.
**Map** 10 F4. **Tel** 01 43 57
24 24. **w** la-chapelle-
des-lombards.com

**La Cigale**
120 bd de Rochechouart
75018. **Map** 4 F2. **Tel** 01 49
25 89 99. **w** lacigale.fr

**Elysée-Montmartre**
72 bd Rochechouart
75018. **Map** 4 F2.
**Tel** 01 44 92 78 00.

**New Morning**
7–9 rue des Petites-Ecuries
75010. **Tel** 01 45 23 51 41.
**w** newmorning.com

**Olympia**
28 bd des Capucines
75009. **Map** 4 D5.
**Tel** 08 92 68 33 68.
**w** olympiahall.com

**Le Petit Journal
St.-Michel**
71 bd St-Michel 75005.
**Map** 12 F1. **Tel** 01 43 26
28 59. **w** petitjournal
saintmichel.fr

**Salle Pleyel**
252 rue du Faubourg St.-
Honoré 75008. **Map** 2 E3.
**Tel** 01 42 56 13 13.
**w** sallepleyel.fr

**Zénith**
Parc de Villette, 211 av de
Jean-Jaurès 75019.
**Tel** 01 44 52 54 56.
**w** zenith-paris.com

## Movies

**La Géode**
26 av Corentin-Cariou
75019. **Tel** 08 92 68 45 40.
**w** lageode.fr

**Le Grand Rex**
1 bd Poissonnière
75002. **Tel** 01 45 08 93 89.
**w** legrandrex.com

**Max Linder
Panorama**
24 bd Poissonnière
75009. **Tel** 01 48 00 90 24.
**w** maxlinder.cine.
allucine

**MK2 Bibliothèque**
128–162 av de France
75013. **Tel** 08 92 69 84 84.
**w** mk2.com

## Sport

**AccorHotels Arena**
*(See Rock section.)*

**Hippodrome de
Longchamp**
Rte des Tribunes 75016.
**Tel** 01 44 30 75 00.

**Parc des Princes**
20 av du Parc des Princes
75016. **Tel** 3275.
**w** leparcdesprinces.fr

**Stade de France**
St.-Denis 93216.
**Tel** 01 55 93 00 00.
**w** stadefrance.com

**Stade Roland
Garros**
2 av Gordon-Bennett
75016. **Tel** 01 47 43 51 11.
**w** rolandgarros.com

# PARIS STREET FINDER

The map references given with sights, stores, and entertainment venues described in the Paris section of the guide refer to the maps on the following pages. Map references are also given for Paris hotels *(see pp554–5)* and restaurants *(pp576–9)*, and for useful addresses in the *Travelers' Needs* and *Survival Guide* sections at the back of the book. The maps include not only the main sightseeing areas but also the most important districts for hotels, restaurants, shopping, and entertainment venues. The key map below shows the area of Paris covered by the *Street Finder*, with the *arrondissement* numbers for the various districts shown in green. The symbols used for sights and other features on the *Street Finder* maps are listed opposite.

**Paris** is divided into 20 *arrondissements*, outlined in green and numbered on this map.

0 km   1
0 miles  0.5

17

18

1

2

3

4

9

8

10

5

16

6

7

Tuileries and Opéra

8

9

Champs Elysées and Invalides

1

Ile de la Cité, Marais and Beaubourg

3

7

6

The Left Bank

4

11

12

13

5

15

14

13

**Key**

-- *Arrondissement* boundary

# How the Map References Work

**The first figure** tells you which *Street Finder* map to turn to.

## ❿ Hôtel de Ville

Pl de l'Hôtel-de-Ville 75004.
**Map** 9 B3. **Tel** 01 42 76 40 40. Ⓜ Hôtel-de-Ville. **Open** to groups: phone to arrange (01 42 76 54 04). **Closed** public hols and for official functions (phone to check). ♿

**The letter and number** give the grid reference. Letters go across the map's top and bottom; figures, on its sides.

**The map** continues on page 13 of the Street Finder.

## Key to Street Finder

- Major sight
- Other sight
- Other building
- 🚊 Train station
- Ⓜ Métro station
- RER RER station
- 🚌 Main bus stop
- Riverboat boarding point
- ◎ Batobus boarding point
- ℹ Tourist information
- ➕ Hospital with emergency room
- Police station
- ✝ Church
- ✡ Synagogue
- Train line
- Highway
- Traffic-free street
- «130 House number (main street)

## Scale of Map Pages

0 meters      200
0 yards      200    1:12,000

# ILE-DE-FRANCE

Set at the heart of France, with Paris as its hub, the Ile-de-France extends well beyond the densely populated suburbs of the city. Its rich countryside incorporates a historic royal region of monumental splendor central to *"la gloire de la France".*

The region became a favorite with French royalty after François I transformed Fontainebleau into a Renaissance palace in 1528. Louis XIV kept the Ile-de-France as the political axis of the country when he started building Versailles in 1661. This neoclassical château, created by the combined genius of Le Nôtre, Le Vau, Le Brun, and Jules Hardouin-Mansart, is France's most visited sight. It stands as a monument to the power of the Sun King and is still used for state occasions. Rambouillet, closely linked with Louis XVI, is now the summer residence of the French president, while Malmaison was the favorite home of Empress Josephine. To the north, the Musée National de la Renaissance in the Château d'Ecouen offers a showcase of Renaissance life and to the south Vaux-le-Vicomte boasts some of the loveliest formal gardens in France.

Nourished by the Seine and Marne rivers, the Ile-de-France is a patchwork of chalky plains, wheatfields, and forests. The serene, poplar-lined avenues and rustic charm of the region have been an inspiration to painters such as Corot, Rousseau, Pissarro, and Cézanne.

## Sights at a Glance

**Châteaux and Museums**

❷ Musée National de la Renaissance
❺ Château de Malmaison
❻ Château de Versailles *pp178–81*
❼ Château de Sceaux
❽ Sèvres: Cité de la Céramique
❾ Château de Rambouillet
⓫ Château de Vaux-le-Vicomte
⓭ Château de Fontainebleau *pp184–5*

**Towns**

❹ St-Germain-en-Laye
⓬ Provins

**Abbeys and Churches**

❶ Abbaye de Royaumont
❸ Basilique St.-Denis

**Theme Parks**

❿ Disneyland® Resort Paris

**Key**

Greater Paris
Central Paris
═══ Freeway
▬▬▬ Highway
═══ Minor road

0 kilometers        20
0 miles        10

◀ Stunning formal gardens at the Château de Fontainebleau

For keys to symbols *see back flap*

The vaulted Gothic refectory of the Abbaye de Royaumont

# ❶ Abbaye de Royaumont

Fondation Royaumont, Asnières-sur-Oise, Val-d'Oise. **Tel** 01 30 35 59 00. **Open** 10am–6pm daily (Nov–Feb: to 5:30pm) 🅿 ♿ 🗎 🎦 Concerts. 🆆 royaumont.com

Set among woods 22 miles (35 km) north of Paris, Royaumont is the finest Cistercian abbey in the Ile-de-France. Chosen for its remoteness, the abbey has stark stonework and a simplicity of line that reflect the austere teachings of St-Bernard. However, unlike his Burgundian abbeys, Royaumont was founded in 1228 by Louis IX and his mother, Blanche de Castille. "St-Louis" showered the abbey with riches and chose it as a royal burial site.

The abbey retained its royal links until the Revolution, when much of it was destroyed. It was then a textiles mill and orphanage, until its revival as a cultural center. The original pillars still remain, along with a gravity-defying corner tower and the largest Cistercian cloisters in France, which enclose a charming Classical garden. The monastic quarters border one side of the cloisters.

The Château de Royaumont, erected as the abbot's palace on the eve of the Revolution, is set apart and resembles an Italianate villa. On the grounds are monks' workshops, woods, ponds, and Cistercian canals.

In summer, concerts are held in the abbey on weekends (01 34 68 05 50 for details; www.3emeacte.com for tickets).

# ❷ Musée National de la Renaissance

Rue Jean Bulant, Château d'Ecouen, Val-d'Oise. **Tel** 01 34 38 38 52. **Open** 9:30am–12:45pm & 2–5:15pm Wed–Mon (mid-Apr–Sep: to 5:45pm). **Closed** Jan 1, May 1, Dec 25. Park: no animals. 🅿 museum only. ♿ 🗎 🆆 musee-renaissance.fr

The imposing, moated Château d'Ecouen, now a Renaissance museum, provides an authentic setting for an impressive collection of paintings, stained glass, jewelry, tapestries, coffers, carved doors, and staircases salvaged from this and other 16th-century châteaux.

Ecouen was built in 1538 for Anne de Montmorency, adviser to François I and Commander-in-Chief of his armies. As the second most powerful person in the kingdom, he employed Ecole de Fontainebleau artists and craftsmen to adorn his palace. Their influence is apparent in the painted fireplaces, depicting biblical and Classical themes in mysterious landscapes. The most striking room is the chapel, containing a gallery and vaulted ceilings painted with the Montmorency coat of arms.

Upstairs is one of the finest series of 16th-century tapestries in France. Equally compelling are the princely apartments, the library of illuminated manuscripts, vivid ceramics from Lyon, Nevers, Venice, Faenza, and Iznik, and a display of historical mathematical instruments. There are also 16th- and 17th-century engravings from France, Italy, and Germany. The castle is set within beautiful formal gardens.

# ❸ Basilique St.-Denis

1 rue de la Légion d'Honneur, St.-Denis, Seine-St.-Denis. **Tel** 01 48 09 83 54. Ⓜ Line 13 Basilique de St.-Denis. **Open** 10am–6:15pm Mon–Sat, noon–6:15pm Sun (Oct–Mar: 10am–5pm Mon–Sat, noon–5:15pm Sun). **Closed** Jan 1, May 1, Dec 25. 🅿 ♿ 🗎 ✝ 8:30am & 10am Sun. 🆆 saint-denis.monuments-nationaux.fr

According to legend, St.-Denis struggled here clutching his decapitated head, and an abbey was erected to commemorate him. Following the burial of Dagobert I in the basilica in 638, a royal link with St.-Denis began that was to span 12 centuries. Most French kings were entombed in St.-Denis, and all the queens of France were crowned here.

The elegant, early Gothic basilica rests on Carolingian and Romanesque crypts. Of the medieval effigies, the most impressive are of Charles V (1364) and a 12th-century

Statue of Louis XVI at St.-Denis

The west wing of Musée National de la Renaissance

The Renaissance tomb of Louis XII and Anne de Bretagne in St.-Denis

likeness in enameled copper of Blanche de France with her dog. The masklike serenity of these effigies contrasts with the graphically realistic Renaissance portrayal of agony present in the grotesque mausoleum of Louis XII and Anne de Bretagne. Both are represented as naked figures, their faces eerily captured at the moment of death. Above the mausoleum, effigies of the finely dressed royal couple contemplate their own nakedness.

## ❹ St.-Germain-en-Laye

Yvelines. 🚈 41,000. 🚉 🚌 🛈 Maison Claude Debussy, 38 rue au Pain. **Tel** 01 30 87 20 63. **Open** Oct–Apr: Tue–Sat; May–Sep: daily. 🖥 Tue, Wed, Fri–Sun. 🗺 ot-saintgermainenlaye.fr

Dominating place Général de Gaulle in this chic suburb is the legendary Château de St.-Germain, birthplace of Louis XIV. Louis VI built the original

stronghold in 1122, but only the keep and St.-Louis chapel remain. Under François I and Henri II, the medieval upper tiers were demolished, leaving a moated pentagon. Henri IV built the pavilion and terraces that run down to the Seine, and Louis XIV had Le Nôtre landscape the gardens before leaving for Versailles in 1682.

Today the château houses the **Musée d'Archéologie Nationale**, which exhibits archeological finds from prehistory to the Middle Ages. Created by Napoleon III, the collection includes a 22,000-year-old carved female, a megalithic tomb, a bronze helmet from the 3rd century BC, and Celtic jewelry. The finest treasure is the Gallo-Roman mosaic pavement.

🏛 **Musée d'Archéologie Nationale**
Château de St.-Germain-en-Laye, pl Charles de Gaulle. **Tel** 01 39 10 13 00. **Open** 10am–5pm Wed–Mon. **Closed** Dec 25, Jan1. 🗺 📷 🖥 📷
🗺 musee-archeologienationale.fr

## ❺ Château de Malmaison

Rueil-Malmaison, Hauts-de-Seine, av du Château de Malmaison. **Tel** 01 41 29 05 55. **Open** 10am–12:30pm & 1:30–5:15pm daily (to 5:45pm Apr–Sep and weekends year-round). **Closed** Jan 1, Dec 25. 🗺 🖥
🗺 chateau-malmaison.fr

Located 9 miles (15 km) west of Paris, this 17th-century estate is best known for its Napoleonic associations. Bought by Josephine as a retreat from the formality of the Emperor's residences at the Tuileries and Fontainebleau, it has charming rural grounds. While Josephine loved this country manor, Napoleon scorned its entrance as fit only for servants, and so he had a curious drawbridge built at the back of the château.

The finest rooms are the frescoed and vaulted library, the canopied campaign room, and the sunny Salon de Musique. Napoleon's restrained, yellow canopied bedroom contrasts with the bedchamber in which Josephine died, a magnificent indulgence bedecked in red. Many of the rooms overlook the romantic "English" gardens and the rose garden that Josephine cultivated after her divorce.

Memorabilia abounds, from imperial eagles to David's moody portrait of Napoleon, or Gérard's painting of the languid Josephine reclining on a chaise-longue.

The Nearby Château Bois Préau, set on the wooded grounds, houses a museum dedicated to Napoleon's exile and death.

Empress Josephine's bed at the Château de Malmaison

# ❻ Château de Versailles

The present palace, started by Louis XIV in 1668, grew around Louis XIII's original hunting lodge. Architect Louis Le Vau built the first section, which expanded into an enlarged courtyard. From 1678, Jules Hardouin-Mansart added north and south wings, and the Hall of Mirrors. He also designed the chapel, completed in 1710. The Opera House (L'Opéra) was added by Louis XV in 1770. André Le Nôtre enlarged the gardens and broke the monotony of the symmetrical layout with expanses of water and creative use of uneven ground. Opposite the château is the Académie du Spectacle Equestre, where you can watch dressage shows.

**★ Formal Gardens**
Geometric paths and shrubberies are features of the gardens.

**★ Château**
Under Louis XIV, Versailles became the center of political power in France.

**Fountain of Latona**
Four marble basins rise to Balthazar Marsy's statue of the goddess Latona.

## KEY

① **Fountain of Neptune** sculptures spray spectacular jets of water in Le Nôtre's 17th-century garden.

② **Ornamental Pools (Parterre d'Eau)**

③ **The Orangery** was built beneath the Parterre du Midi to house exotic plants in winter.

④ **The king's garden** features a mirror pool in the 19th-century garden created by Louis XVIII.

⑤ **Colonnade** is a series of marble arches designed by Mansart in 1685.

**Dragon Fountain**
The fountain's centerpiece is a winged monster.

**The Grand Canal** was the setting for Louis XIV's boating parties.

**Petit Trianon**
Built in 1762 as a retreat for Louis XV, this small château became a favorite with Marie Antoinette.

Interior of the chapel at Versailles

**★ Grand Trianon**
Louis XIV built this small palace of stone and pink marble in 1687 to escape the rigors of court life, and to enjoy the company of Madame de Maintenon.

# Inside the Château de Versailles

The sumptuous main apartments are on the first floor of this vast château complex. Around the Marble Courtyard are the private apartments of the king and queen. The apartments of the *dauphin* (the heir) and the *mesdames* (the daughters of Louis XV), on the ground floor, are also open to visitors. On the garden side are the state apartments, where official court life took place. These were richly decorated by Charles Le Brun with marble, stone and woodcarvings, murals, velvet, silver, and gilded furniture. Beginning with the Salon d'Hercule, each state room is dedicated to an Olympian deity. The climax is the Hall of Mirrors, where 17 vast mirrors face tall arched windows. Not all rooms are open at the same time, so check on arrival.

**★ Queen's Bedroom**
In this room the queens of France gave birth to the royal children in public view.

**The Salle du Sacre**
is adorned with huge paintings of Napoleon by Jacques-Louis David, including his vast, celebrated *The Coronation of Napoleon (Le Sacre du Napoléon)*, of 1807.

Entrance

Entrance

**The Marble Courtyard** is overlooked by a gilded balcony.

Stairs to ground-floor reception area

**★ Chapelle Royale**
The chapel's first floor was reserved for the royal family and the ground floor for the court. The beautiful interior is lavishly decorated with Corinthian columns and white marble, gilding and Baroque murals.

**Key to Floorplan**

- South wing
- Coronation room
- Madame de Maintenon's apartments
- Queen's apartments and private suite
- State apartments
- King's apartments and private suite
- North wing

**★ Hall of Mirrors**
Great state occasions were held in this room stretching 233 ft (70 m) along the west facade. Here, in 1919, the Treaty of Versailles was ratified, ending World War I.

Salon de Oeil-de-Boeuf

**The King's Bedroom**
is where Louis XIV died in 1715.

**The Cabinet du Conseil**
was used by the king to receive his ministers and family.

**Salon de la Guerre**
The room's theme of war is reinforced by Antoine Coysevox's stuccoed relief of Louis XIV riding to victory.

**Louis XVI's library**
features Neoclassical paneling and the king's terrestrial globe.

**★ Salon de Vénus**
A statue of Louis XIV stands amid the rich marble decor of this room.

**Salon d'Apollon**
Designed by Le Brun and dedicated to the god Apollo, this was Louis XIV's throne room. A copy of Hyacinthe Rigaud's famous portrait of the king (1701) hangs here.

Salon d'Hercule

*Louis XV*

| 1650 | 1700 | 1750 | 1800 | 1850 | 1900 |
|---|---|---|---|---|---|

**1667** Grand Canal begun

**1668** Construction of new château by Le Vau

**1671** Interior decoration by Le Brun begun

**1661** Louis XIV enlarges château

**1722** 12-year-old Louis XV occupies Versailles

**1715** Death of Louis XIV. Versailles abandoned by court

**1682** Louis XIV and Marie-Thérèse move to Versailles

**1793** Louis XVI and Marie Antoinette executed

**1837** Inauguration of the museum of the Château de Versailles

**1789** King and Queen forced to leave Versailles for Paris

**1774** Louis XVI and Marie Antoinette live at Versailles

**1919** Treaty of Versailles signed on 28 June

## ❼ Château de Sceaux

Domaine de Sceaux, Hauts-de-Seine. **Tel** 01 41 87 29 50. **Open** Apr–Oct: 10am–6pm Wed–Mon (to 6:30pm Sun); Nov–Mar: 10am–5pm Wed–Mon. **Closed** public hols & lunchtimes. **domaine-de-sceaux.hauts-de-seine.net**

The Parc de Sceaux, bounded by elegant villas, is an appealing mixture of formal gardens, woods and water. The gardens, designed by Le Nôtre, use water to great effect, with tiered waterfalls and fountains presenting a moving staircase that cascades into an octagonal basin. This feeds into the Grand Canal and offers a poplar-lined view to the Pavillon de Hanovre. This elegant pavilion is one of several that adorn the park, which also contains Mansart's Classical Orangerie. Today it hosts exhibitions and music concerts.

Built for Colbert in 1670, the original château was demolished and rebuilt in Louis XIII style in 1856. The stylish reconstruction contains the Musée de l'Ile-de-France, which celebrates the landscapes and châteaux of the region with paintings, furniture, and sculpture.

## ❽ Sèvres: Cité de la Céramique

Place de la Manufacture, 92310 Sèvres. **Tel** 01 46 29 22 00. **Open** 10am–5pm daily. **Closed** Tue. **sevresciteceramique.fr**

With over 50,000 objects on display, this fascinating museum traces the history of porcelain around the world from antiquity onward. The building was erected in 1756 as a royal factory under Louis XV and has remained under state ownership ever since. In 1824 it became home to the world's first ceramics museum. The collections include the latest pieces by 21st-century designers. Visitors can explore objects from America, Japan, and all across Europe as they discover how techniques for making and decorating porcelain and ceramics have changed over the centuries.

Château de Rambouillet

## ❾ Château de Rambouillet

Rambouillet, Yvelines. **Tel** 01 34 83 00 25. **Open** 9:50am–6pm Wed–Mon (Oct–Mar: to 5pm). **chateau-rambouillet.fr**

Bordering the deep Forêt de Rambouillet, once the favorite royal hunting ground, this ivy-covered red-brick château, flanked by five stone towers, is beautiful. Adopted as a feudal castle, country estate, royal palace, and Imperial residence, it reflects a composite of French royal history. Since 1897, it has been the president's official summer residence.

Inside, oak-paneled rooms are adorned with Empire-style furnishings and Aubusson tapestries. The main facade overlooks Classical parterres. Nearby is the Queen's Dairy, given by Louis XVI to Marie Antoinette, so that she could play milkmaid.

**Environs**
About 27 km (17 miles) north on the D11, the **Château de Thoiry** has a safari park and an innovative play area for children.

## ❿ Disneyland® Resort Paris

Marne-la-Vallée, Seine-et-Marne. **Tel** 08 25 30 05 00. **Open** hours vary according to season – check website. Marne-la-Vallée-Chessy. TGV from Lille or Lyon. from both airports. **disneylandparis.com**

Disneyland® Resort Paris has two theme parks, seven hotels, facilities for shopping and dining, and convention centers. Most interesting are the Parks – the first with its five themed Lands, offering magic dominated by Sleeping Beauty Castle, and Walt Disney Studios®.

Minnie Mouse

## ⓫ Château de Vaux-le-Vicomte

Maincy, Seine-et-Marne. **Tel** 01 64 14 41 90. shuttle from Melun train station (runs Apr–mid-Nov: weekends & hols). late Mar–early Nov: 10am–7pm (May 6–Oct 7: to midnight Sat); late Nov–early Jan: 11am–7pm. **Closed** 2 wks in Nov. **vaux-le-vicomte.com**

Set north of Melun, not far from Fontainebleau, the château enjoys a peaceful rural location.

### Sèvres Porcelain

In 1756 Madame de Pompadour and Louis XV opened a porcelain factory near Versailles at Sèvres to supply the royal residences with tableware and objets d'art. Thus began the production of exquisite dinner services, statuettes, Etruscan-style vases, romantic cameos and porcelain paintings, depicting grand châteaux or mythological scenes. Sèvres porcelain is typified by its translucence, durability and narrow palette of colors.

*Le Pugilat* (1832), one of a pair of vases from Sèvres

### André Le Nôtre

As the greatest French landscape gardener, Le Nôtre (1613–1700) created masterpieces in château gardens all over France. His Classical vision shaped many gardens in the Ile-de-France, such as those at Dampierre, Sceaux, and Vaux-le-Vicomte. At Vaux he perfected the concept of the *jardin à la française*: avenues framed by statues and box hedges; water gardens with fountains and ornate pools; graceful terraces and geometrical parterres "embroidered" with motifs. His genius lay in architectural orchestration and a sense of symmetry, typified by the sweeping vistas of Versailles, his greatest triumph.

Nicolas Fouquet, a powerful court financier to Louis XIV, challenged the architect Le Vau and the decorator Le Brun to create the most sumptuous palace of the day. The result is one of the greatest 17th-century French châteaux. However, it also led to his downfall. Louis and his ministers were so enraged – because its luxury cast the royal palaces into the shade – that they arrested Fouquet.

The interior is a gilded banquet of frescoes, stucco, caryatids, and giant busts. The Salon des Muses boasts Le Brun's magnificent frescoed ceiling of dancing nymphs and poetic sphinxes. La Grande Chambre Carrée is decorated in Louis XIII style with paneled walls and an impressive triumphal frieze, evoking Rome. However, its many rooms feel intimate and the scale is not overwhelming.

Yet Vaux-le-Vicomte's continuing fame is due to André Le Nôtre's stunning gardens. The landscape designer's early training as a painter is evident in the magnificent succession of terraces, ornamental lakes, and fountains, which descend to a formal canal. On Saturday evenings from May to October, the castle is lit with over 2,000 candles, and classical music is played in the lounge bar in the gardens.

## ⑫ Provins

Seine-et-Marne. 🚐 12,500. 🚉 🚌 ⓘ Chemin de Villecran 77482 (01 64 60 26 26). 🚹 Sat. **W** **provins.net**

As a Roman outpost, Provins commanded the border of Ile-de-France and Champagne. Today, it offers a coherent vision of the medieval world. Ville Haute, the upper town, is clustered within 12th-century ramparts, complete with crenellations and defensive ditches. The ramparts to the west are the best preserved. Here, between the fortified gateways of Porte de Jouy and Porte St.-Jean, the fortifications are dotted with square, round, and rectangular towers.

The town is dominated by Tour César, a keep with four corner turrets and a pyramid shaped roof. The moat and fortifications were added by the English during the Hundred Years' War. A guardroom leads to a gallery and views over place du Chatel, a busy square of medieval gabled houses, and over the wheatfields beyond.

Provins is proud of its crimson roses. In addition to a daily medieval show, a floral celebration is held in the riverside rose garden every June, an event marked by a medieval festival with falconry and jousting.

Aerial view of the splendid Château de Vaux-le-Vicomte, with its gardens designed by Le Nôtre

# ⑬ Château de Fontainebleau

Fontainebleau is not the product of a single vision but is a bewildering cluster of styles from different periods. Louis VII built an abbey here, which was consecrated by Thomas Becket in 1169. A medieval tower survives, but the present château harks back to François I. Originally drawn by the local hunting, the Renaissance king created a decorative château modeled on Florentine and Roman styles.

Fontainebleau's abiding charm comes from its relative informality and spectacular forest setting. The *grands appartements* provide a sumptuous introduction to this royal palace.

Ground floor

**Jardin de Diane**
Now more romantic than Classical, the garden features a bronze fountain of Diana as huntress.

**★ Escalier du Fer-à-Cheval**
This imposing horseshoe-shaped staircase, built in 1634, by Jean Androuet du Cerceau, lies at the end of Cour du Cheval Blanc. Its ingenious design allowed carriages to pass beneath the two arches.

## KEY

① **The Cour du Cheval Blanc** was once a simple enclosed courtyard. It was transformed by Napoleon I into the main approach to the château.

② **Chapelle de la Sainte Trinité** was designed by Henri II in 1550. The chapel acquired its vaulted and frescoed ceiling under Henri IV and was completed by Louis XIII.

③ **Cour Oval**

④ **Cour de la Fontaine**

⑤ **The Appartements de Napoléon I** house his grandiose throne in the Emperor's Salle du Trône, formerly the Chambre du Roi.

⑥ **The Jardin Anglais** is a romantic "English" garden, planted with cypress and plantain trees. It was redesigned in the 19th century by Maximilien-Joseph Hurtault.

Museum entrance

**Key to Floorplan**

    Petits Appartements

    Galerie des Cerfs

    Musée Chinois

    Musée Napoléon

    Grands Appartements

    Salle Renaissance

    Appartements de Madame de Maintenon

    Grands Appartements des Souverains

    Escalier de la Reine/ Appartements des Chasses

### Porte Dorée
Originally a feudal gatehouse, this was transformed into the entrance pavilion to the forest by Gilles Le Breton for François I.

First floor

## VISITORS' CHECKLIST

**Practical Information**
Seine-et-Marne. **Tel** 01 60 71 50 70. **Open** 9:30am–5pm Wed–Mon (6pm Apr–Sep). 🅿 ♿ 📷 🎫 Gardens: **Open** 9am–5pm daily (6pm Mar–Apr & Oct, 7pm May–Sep). **Closed** Jan 1, May 1, Dec 25. 🆆 **musee-chateau-fontainebleau.fr**

#### ★ Salle de Bal
The Renaissance ballroom, designed by Primaticcio (1552), was finished under Henri II. His emblems adorn the walnut coffered ceiling, forming a pattern reflected in the parquet floor.

#### ★ Galerie François I
This gilded gallery is a tribute to the Italian artists in the Ecole de Fontainebleau. Rosso Fiorentino's allegorical frescoes pay homage to the king's wish to create "a second Rome".

## The Barbizon School

Artists have been drawn to the glades of Fontainebleau since the 1840s, when a group of landscape painters, determined to paint only from nature, formed around Théodore Rousseau and Millet. They settled in the nearby hamlet of Barbizon, where the Auberge Ganne, a museum dedicated to the Ecole de Barbizon, is located.

*Spring at Barbizon*, painted by Jean-François Millet (1814–75)

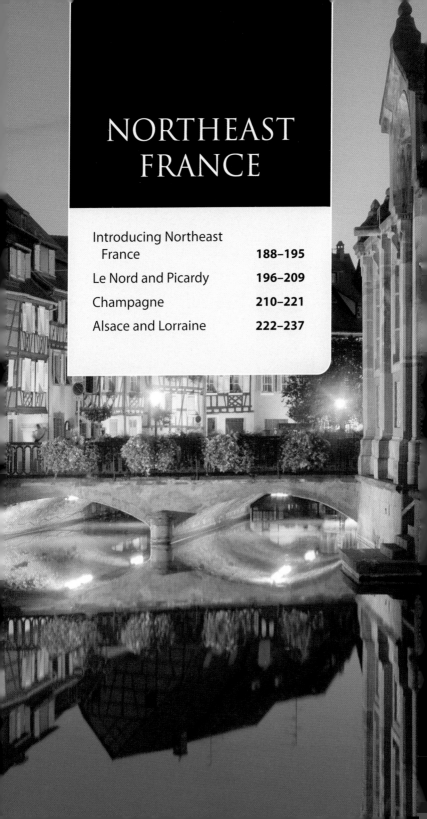

# NORTHEAST FRANCE

Introducing Northeast
    France                        188–195

Le Nord and Picardy              196–209

Champagne                        210–221

Alsace and Lorraine              222–237

# Introducing Northeast France

The rolling plains of Northern France run from the English Channel to the wooded Ardennes hills and the Vosges mountains of Alsace. Aside from somber battle memorials, the area has France's finest Gothic cathedrals – and a long tradition of brewing good-quality beers. There is fine wine, too, in Champagne and Alsace. The old heavy industry has gone, while Lille's growth as a transportation hub has brought new prosperity. This map shows some of the most notable sights.

Dunkerque
Calais
St-Omer
Boulogne-sur-Mer
Lille
Béthune
Lens
Hesdin
Valencienne
Douai
Arras
Maubeuge
Abbeville
Cambrai

**LE NORD AND PICARDY**
*(See pp196–209)*

La Capelle-en-Thiérache

Amiens
St-Quentin
Breteuil
Noyon
Laon
Beauvais
Compiègne
Clermont
Reir
Chantilly
Château-Thierry
Épernay

Compiègne
*(see p205)*

Reims Cathedral
*(see pp216–17)*
Sézar
Romi sur-S

Tr

Chaour

**Amiens Cathedral** is renowned for its fine woodcarvings and its nave, the highest in France *(see pp206–7)*.

**The pride of Beauvais** is its Gothic cathedral and astronomical clock *(see p204)*, which escaped heavy bombing during World War II.

◀ River Lauch by night, Colmar

**Half-timbered houses** and Renaissance mansions line the streets and alleys of Troyes' Old Town *(see p220)*, rebuilt after the great fire in 1524. Its cathedral has remarkable stained-glass windows.

**The legacy of World War I** is strong in this area of former battlefields. The Douaumont Memorial outside Verdun *(see p226)*, with its 15,000 graves, is only one of many memorials and cemeteries here.

Porte Chaussée, Verdun *(see p226)*

**Haut-Koenigsbourg**, a castle painstakingly rebuilt by Kaiser Wilhelm II when Alsace-Lorraine was under German rule, is one of Alsace's most popular attractions *(see p232)*.

**Strasbourg**, seat of the Council of Europe, has a fine Gothic cathedral *(see pp234–5)*, built using the red-pink sandstone from the Vosges.

crol

Charleville-Mézières

Sedan

Longwy

Thionville

Verdun

Metz

Sarreguemines

ons-en-pagne

ALSACE AND LORRAINE
*(See pp222–37)*

Saverne

Haguenau

e-is

St-Dizier

Toul

Nancy

Lunéville

Strasbourg

Joinville

CHAMPAGNE
*(See pp210–21)*

Neufchâteau

St-Dié

Sélestat

Epinal

Colmar

Chaumont

Langres

Place Stanislas, Nancy
*(see p228)*

Mulhouse

0 kilometers    50

0 miles    50

# The Flavors of Northeast France

The cuisine of northeast France is robust and warming, with rich beef stews, suckling pig, sausages and hams, dumplings, and sauerkraut dishes, many of them closely related to German or Flemish staples. There is good fish from the Atlantic and from freshwater lakes and rivers. Vegetables and fruit are produced in abundance, and often served in a variety of savory and sweet tarts, of which *quiche lorraine*, with bacon, eggs, and cream, is the best known. Rich cakes are popular, especially *kougelhopf*, a ring-shaped cake of raisins and almonds soaked in kirsch, and madeleine sponge cakes.

Leeks from a local market

Golden mirabelle plums alongside the more usual variety

## Le Nord and Picardy

The northern coast offers a wide variety of fish and shellfish dishes, the most popular being steamed mussels served with fries. Herrings are pickled, soused, grilled, or smoked and North Sea shrimp are fried and eaten whole. Chicken may be cooked in beer, duck is made into pies and terrines, and eel is served smoked as an appetizer. The market gardens *(hortillons)* of Picardy are famous for their vegetables, often made into delicious soups. Leeks or chicory, braised or in gratins, accompany many dishes. Strong, washed-rind cheeses, such as Maroilles, are typical of the region.

Beer is often drunk with meals in the northeast, where traditional methods and small breweries thrive.

## Champagne

Champagne encompasses arable plains and wooded uplands as well as vineyards, and produces game, *charcuterie* and delicious freshwater fish. Nothing, however, can compete with its main claim to fame, Champagne itself, which is often used as a luxury cooking ingredient as well as, of course, being enjoyed in its own right.

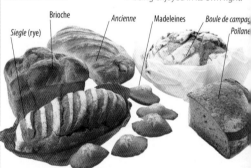
*Siegle* (rye)   *Brioche*   *Ancienne*   Madeleines   *Boule de campagne*   *Poilâne*

Selection of typical regional breads and patisserie

## Regional Dishes and Specialties

The classic dish of the region is *choucroute garni*, a platter of pickled cabbage, flavored with juniper berries, and cooked with white wine, ham hock, and smoked pork belly. Smoked Montbeliard and Strasbourg sausages are added toward the end of cooking. Sausages come in many variations, from *saucisses de Strasbourg* to *bratwurst*, made from veal and pork, *lewerzurscht* (liver sausage), *andouillettes* (spicy chitterling sausages), *boudin noir* (black pudding of pork and pig's blood), and *boudin blanc* (white meat without blood). There are also smoked hams, cooked hams, and many different terrines, such as *presskopf* (pig's brawn in jelly) and the jellied white meat terrine, *potjevleesch*. *Langue lucullus* is smoked ox tongue studded with *foie gras*, a specialty of Valenciennes.

Beetroot

**Ficelle picardie** Pancakes are filled with mushrooms and ham in a crème fraîche sauce, and baked with grated cheese.

Display of traditional northern French *charcuterie*

Wild boar, deer, rabbit, hare, quail, partridge, and woodcock are all found in the Ardennes, made into game pâtés and terrines as well as roasts and stews. The Ardennes is also noted for its fine-quality smoked ham, while *jambon de Reims* is cooked ham with mustard, Champagne, and Reims vinegar. Troyes is famous for its *andouillettes*, usually served with onions or baked in a creamy mustard sauce. Fish come from the small lakes east of Troyes, and trout are abundant in the clear streams of the Ardennes. The two best cheeses of Champagne are Chaource and Langres.

## Alsace and Lorraine

Rolling pastures, orchards, pine forests, and rivers produce the ingredients of Alsatian cooking. Meat is important, particularly pork, roasted or made into hams and sausages. In winter, game stews abound. There is a strong tradition of raising geese; after all, *foie gras* production originated in Strasbourg. The rivers are a

Shopping at the fish market in the port of Boulogne

good source of pike, trout, crayfish, and carp, often cooked in beer and served on festive occasions. Locally grown vegetables include cabbage, potatoes, and turnips, and fruit includes bilberries, quince, redcurrants, and the golden mirabelle plums of Lorraine, the latter prized for both jam and *eau de vie* (fruit brandy). The best-known cheese is Münster, a soft cow's milk cheese.

The white wines of Alsace range from steely, bone-dry Riesling (the region's finest variety) to aromatic Muscat and Gerwurztraminer. For more on the wines of Alsace, *see pp236–7.*

### ON THE MENU

**Anguille au vert** Eel baked with green herbs and potatoes.

**Cassolette de petits gris** Snails in Champagne sauce.

**Flamiche aux poireaux** Leek tart.

**Flammekueche** Pizza-style tart topped with bacon, crème fraîche, and onions.

**Marcassin à l'Ardennaise** Wild boar with celeriac.

**Potée champenoise** Pork, ham, sausage, beans, and vegetable stew.

**Potée Lorraine** Casserole of salt pork with vegetables.

**Zewelwai** A rich onion tart.

**Truite à l'Ardennaise** Trout is stuffed with breadcrumbs and finely chopped Ardennes ham, then baked.

**Carbonnade de boeuf** Steak and caramelized onions are covered with beer and cooked for 3 hours.

**Babas au rhum** These are dry yeast cakes of raisins, eggs, and butter, doused in rum and served with cream.

# France's Wine Regions: Champagne

Since its fabled "invention" by the monk Dom Pérignon in the 17th century, no other wine has rivaled Champagne as the symbol of luxury and celebration. Only wines made in this region by the *Méthode Champenoise* can be called Champagne *(see p214)*. Most Champagne is non-vintage: the skill of the blenders, using reserves of older wines, creates consistency and excellence year on year. The "big names" (*grandes marques*) command the prestige and prices, but many small growers and cooperatives also produce excellent-value wines well worth seeking out.

**Locator Map**

▨ Champagne wine region

### Wine Regions

*Champagne is a compact wine region, largely in the French département of the Marne. Certain areas within it are particularly identified with certain styles of wine. The Aube produces 25 percent of all Champagne as well as the exclusive Rosé des Riceys.*

Grapes going for pressing, Montagne de Reims

**PICARDI**

N2

Vailly-sur Aisne

Soissons

Fère-e Tardeno

Neuilly-Saint-Front

Château-Thierry

La Ferté-sous-Jouarre

Charly-sur-Marne

A4

Montn

Est

Courgivaux

Nogent-su Sein

## Key Facts about Champagne

**Location and Climate**
The cool, marginal climate creates the finesse that other sparkling wines strive for, but seldom achieve. Chalky soils and east- and north-facing aspects help produce the relatively high acidity that Champagne needs.

**Grape Varieties**

Three varieties are grown, red **Pinot Noir** and **Pinot Meunier**, and white **Chardonnay**. Most Champagne is a blend of all three, though Blanc de Blancs is 100 percent Chardonnay and Blanc de Noirs, although white, is made only from red grapes.

**Good Producers**
*Grandes Marques:* Bollinger, Gosset, Krug, Möet et Chandon, Joseph Perrier, Louis Roederer, Pol Roger, Billecart-Salmon, Veuve Clicquot, Taittinger, Ruinart, Laurent Perrier, Mumm, Lanson, and Pommery.
*Négociants, cooperatives and growers:* Boizel, M. Arnould, Cattier, Bricout, Drappier, Ployez-Jacquemart, H. Blin, Gimmonet, André Jacquart, Chartogne-Taillet, Vilmart, Alfred Gratien, Emile Hamm, B. Paillard, P. Gerbais.

**Good Vintages**
2015, 2012, 2009, 2008, 2005, 2003.

**BOLLINGER**
*Spécial Cuvée*
BRUT
*Champagne* *Ay France*

**From a name** famous even to non-wine lovers, this is in the classic *brut* (dry) style; only *brut non dosage* or *brut sauvage* is drier.

**Key**

▨ Vallée de la Marne district
▨ Montagne de Reims district
▨ Côte de Sézanne district
▨ Côte des Blancs district
▨ Aube district

0 kilometers 15

0 miles 15

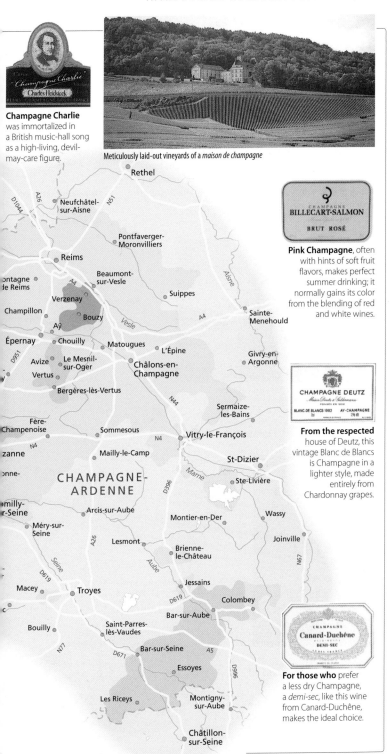

**Champagne Charlie** was immortalized in a British music-hall song as a high-living, devil-may-care figure.

*Meticulously laid-out vineyards of a maison de champagne*

**Pink Champagne**, often with hints of soft fruit flavors, makes perfect summer drinking; it normally gains its color from the blending of red and white wines.

**From the respected** house of Deutz, this vintage Blanc de Blancs is Champagne in a lighter style, made entirely from Chardonnay grapes.

**For those who** prefer a less dry Champagne, a *demi-sec*, like this wine from Canard-Duchêne, makes the ideal choice.

# The Battle of the Somme

The many cemeteries that cover the Somme region serve as a poignant reminder of the mass slaughter that took place on the Western Front in World War I (which ended with the Armistice on November 11, 1918). Between July 1 and November 21, 1916, the Allied forces lost more than 600,000 men and the Germans at least 465,000. The Battle of the Somme, a series of campaigns conducted by British and French armies against fortified positions held by the Germans, relieved the hard-pressed French at Verdun; but hopes of a breakthrough never materialized, and the Allies only managed to advance 10 miles (16 km).

**Locator Map**

▨ Somme battlefield

**Beaumont Hamel Memorial Park**, a tribute to the Royal Newfoundland Regiment, has a huge bronze caribou.

• Serre

D50

Beaumont•

Hamel•   Ancre

Courcelette •

• Thiepval

Pozières •

Ovillers•

• La Boisselle

D938   D929

Albert •

• Mar

D93

D329

• Bray-sur-

**Thiepval Memorial** was designed by Sir Edwin Lutyens. It dominates the landscape of Thiepval, one of the most hard-fought areas of the battle, appropriately chosen as a memorial to the 73,367 British soldiers with no known graves.

**Albert** was the site of heavy bombardment by German artillery in 1916. Today, the town is a convenient center for visiting the battlefields. The Albert Basilique, with its leaning Virgin statue, was damaged but is now restored. It was a landmark for thousands of troops.

**Lochnager Mine Crater**, formed by the largest of the British mines exploded on July 1, 1916, lies on the ridge by La Boisselle.

**The British Tank Memorial**, on the main road from Albert to Bapaume, commemorates the first use of tanks in warfare on September 15, 1916. The attack was a limited success; the tanks of World War I were too few before 1918 to transform warfare dominated by artillery, machine guns, and barbed wire.

**Propaganda in World War I** was employed by both sides to maintain support at home. This French postcard has a popular image for civilian consumption. It shows a dying soldier kissing the flag, under the tender gaze of a ministering nurse, affirming his faith in the cause with his last breath.

**Delville Wood** South African Memorial and Museum show the importance of Commonwealth forces in the Somme.

• Flers

Morval •

nchy •

• Maurepas

ourt

• Péronne

## VISITORS' CHECKLIST

### Practical Information
D929, D938 from Albert.
📍 30 pl de la République,
80800 Corbie. **Tel** 03 22 96 95 76.
**W** somme-tourisme.com
Albert Basilique, Beaumont
Hamel Memorial Park, La Boissele,
Thiepval, & Pozières memorials:
**Open** daily. Ulster Tower: **Tel** 03 22
74 81 11. **Open** Feb–Mar: Tue–
Sun; Apr–Nov: daily. South African
Memorial, Delville Wood,
Longueval. **Tel** 03 22 85 02 17.
**Open** Feb–Nov: Tue–Sun.
**Closed** hols. Historial de Péronne:
**Tel** 03 22 83 14 18. **Open** Apr–
Sep: daily; Oct–Mar: Tue–Sun.
**Closed** mid-Dec–mid-Jan. 🚫 ♿
🎧 💻 🎦 **W** historial.org

**Poppies** were one of the few plants to grow on the battlefield. Genghis Khan brought the first white poppy from China and, according to legend, it turned red after battle. Today poppies are a symbol of remembrance.

0 kilometers          5

0 miles          5

### Key

▨ Allied forces

▢ German forces

▨ Front Line before July 1, 1916

▨ Front Line progress
   July–September 1916

▨ Front Line progress
   September–November 1916

**The Front Line trenches** stretched from the North Sea to the Swiss frontier; only by keeping underground could men survive the terrible conditions. Trenches remain in a few areas, including the Beaumont Hamel Memorial Park.

# LE NORD AND PICARDY

*Pas de Calais · Nord · Somme · Oise · Aisne*

Beneath the modern skin of France's northernmost region, the sights and monuments bear witness to the triumphs and turbulence of its past: soaring Gothic cathedrals, stately châteaux, and the battlefields and memorials of World War I.

The Channel ports of Dunkerque, Calais, and Boulogne, and the refined resort of Le Touquet, are the focal points along a busy coastline that stretches from the Somme estuary to the Belgian frontier. Boulogne has a genuine maritime flavor, and the white cliffs running from here to Calais provide the most dramatic scenery along the Côte d'Opale.

Flemish culture holds sway along the border with Belgium: an unfamiliar France of windmills and canals, where the local taste is for beer, hotpots, and festivals with gallivanting giants. Lille is the dominant city here, a sprawling modern metropolis with a lively historic heart and an excellent art museum. To the southwest, the grace of Flemish architecture is handsomely displayed in the central squares of Arras, the capital of Artois. From here to the Somme Valley, the legacy of World War I, with its memorial cemeteries and poppy-strewn battlefields, makes compelling viewing.

Cathedrals are the main appeal of Picardy. In Amiens, its capital, Cathédrale Notre-Dame is a pinnacle of the Gothic style – its magnificence echoed by the dizzying achievements at Beauvais farther south. Splendid cathedrals at Noyon, Senlis, and the delightful hilltop town of Laon chart the evolution of the Gothic. Closer to Paris, two châteaux command attention. Chantilly, the epicenter of French equestrianism, boasts gardens by Le Nôtre and a 19th-century château housing copious art treasures. Compiègne, bordered by a large and inviting forest, plays host to a lavish royal palace favored by French rulers from Louis XV to Napoleon III.

Memorial cemetery in the Vallée de la Somme, an area still haunted by the memory of World War I

◀ Château de Pierrefonds, overlooking the Forêt de Compiègne

# Exploring Le Nord and Picardy

As the gateway to England and Belgium, this northern corner of France is buzzing with business and industries, with the large, Euro-oriented city of Lille offering great culture as well as a modern high-tech district. Yet peace and quiet are never far away. The coast between the historic port of Boulogne-sur-Mer and the Vallée de la Somme has a rich birdlife and is perfect for a relaxing beach break. Inland, the many Gothic cathedrals such as Amiens and Beauvais make an impressive tour, and the World War I battlefields and memorials provide an important insight into 20th-century history. Farther south, the grand châteaux at Compiègne and Chantilly – which has the fascinating Musée Condé – are easily visited en route to or from Paris.

**Key**

- ▭▭ Freeway
- ▭▭ Highway
- ▬ Secondary road
- ▭▭ Minor road
- ▬ Scenic route
- ▬▬ Main railroad
- ---- Minor railroad
- ▬▬ International border
- ▬▬ Regional border

Lively outdoor café in the historic Grand'Place in the heart of Arras

## Sights at a Glance

① Le Touquet
② Boulogne-sur-Mer
③ Calais
④ Dunkerque
⑤ St-Omer
⑥ Flandre Maritime
⑦ Lille
⑧ Arras
⑨ Vallée de la Somme
⑩ Amiens
⑪ Beauvais
⑫ Noyon
⑬ Compiègne
⑭ Château de Pierrefonds
⑮ Senlis
⑯ Chantilly
⑰ Parc Astérix
⑱ Laon

The meandering waters in the Vallée de la Somme

## Getting Around

The main entry point into the region is Calais (and the Channel Tunnel terminal 2 miles/3 km south). From here, *autoroutes* A16 and A26/A1, several major N and D roads, and mainline train services run directly to Paris. In addition, TGVs serve Calais-Frethun, Lille, and Paris. There is a dense road network throughout the region. With their many local bus and train connections, Lille and Amiens make good bases. The A26 (or *Autoroute des Anglais*) crosses the whole region from Calais to Troyes, via Arras and Laon, giving easy access to eastern Picardy. It's also a useful route if you're heading south and want to avoid Paris. Finally, the airport at Beauvais is a convenient entry point.

Poppies, the symbol of World War I battlefields, in the Vallée de la Somme

Le Touquet beach at low tide

# ❶ Le Touquet

Pas de Calais. 🗺 5,500. 🚌 🚢 🅸
Palais du Congrès, pl de l'Hermitage (03
21 06 72 00). 🅰 Thu & Sat (Jun–mid-
Sep: also Mon). 🅦 letouquet.com

Properly known as Le Touquet
Paris-Plage, this resort was
created in the 19th century and
became fashionable with the
rich and famous between the
two world wars. A vast pine
forest, planted in 1855, spreads
around the town sheltering
stately villas. To the west, a grid of
smart hotels, vacation homes,
and sophisticated stores and
restaurants borders a long,
sandy beach. A racetrack and
two casinos are complemented
by beach amusements and
sport amenities, including two
excellent golf courses, horseback
riding, and land yachting.

Farther inland, the hilltop
town of **Montreuil** has lime
washed 17th-century houses,
abundant restaurants, and a
tree-shaded rampart walk.

# ❷ Boulogne-sur-Mer

Pas de Calais. 🗺 45,000. 🚌 🚢
🅸 Parvis de Nausicaa (03 21 10 88
10). 🅰 Wed & Sat (pl Dalton), Sun
(pl Vignon & pl Gambetta).
🅦 tourisme-boulognesurmer.com

An important fishing port and
busy marina, Boulogne rewards
its visitors well. Its attractions
come neatly boxed in a walled
Haute Ville, with the Porte des
Dunes opening onto a 17th- to

19th-century ensemble of
Palais de Justice, Bibliothèque,
and Hôtel de Ville in **place de
la Résistance**.

The 19th-century **Basilique
Notre-Dame** is capped by a
dome visible for miles. Inside,
a bejeweled wooden statue
represents Boulogne's patroness,
Notre-Dame de Boulogne. She
is wearing a *soleil*, a headdress
also worn by women during the
*Grande Procession* held annually
in her honor. Nearby, the
powerful moated 13th-century
**Château**, built for the Counts
of Boulogne, is now a well-
organized historical museum.

In the center of town, stores,
hotels, and fish restaurants line
quai Gambetta on the east
bank of the River Liane. To the
north lie Boulogne's beach and
**Nausicaa**, a vast, spectacular,
and innovative aquarium and
Sea Center.

North of the town, the
**Colonne de la Grande Armée**
was erected in 1841 as a monument to Napoleon I's planned
invasion of England in 1803–5.
From the top there is a
panoramic view along the coast
toward Calais. This is the most
scenic stretch of the Côte
d'Opale (Opal Coast), with the
windblown headlands of **Cap**
**Gris-Nez** and **Cap Blanc-Nez**
offering breathtakingly extensive
views across the Channel.

🏠 **Château**
Rue de Bernet. **Tel** 03 21 10 02 20.
**Open** Wed–Mon. **Closed** May 1,
Dec 25, 1st wk Jan. 🅿

🐟 **Aquarium Nausicaa**
Bd Sainte-Beuve. **Tel** 03 21 30 98 98.
**Open** daily. **Closed** 3 wks Jan, Dec 25.
🅿 🅰 🅦 nausicaa.fr

# ❸ Calais

Pas de Calais. 🗺 76,000. 🚌 🚢 🚆
🅸 12 bd Clémenceau (03 21 96 62
40). 🅰 Wed, Thu & Sat. 🅦 calais-
cotedopale.com

Calais is a busy Channel port with
a sandy beach to the west.
Clumsily rebuilt after World War II,
it seems to have little to offer at
first sight. Many visitors get no
closer than the huge Cité Europe
shopping mall by the Eurotunnel.

The **Musée des Beaux Arts**,
however, has works by the Dutch
and Flemish Schools. Also on
show are studies for Auguste
Rodin's famous statue *The
Burghers of Calais* (1895). The
statue stands outside the Hôtel
de Ville, and celebrates an event
during Edward III's siege of Calais
in 1347, when six burghers

The windswept Cap Blanc-Nez on the Côte d'Opale

*The Burghers of Calais by Auguste Rodin (1895)*

offered their lives to save the rest of the town.

The **Cité de la Dentelle et de la Mode** recalls the town's lace-making industry. **Musée Mémoire 1939–1945**, housed in a battle-scarred German blockhouse, presents a detailed account of local events during World War II.

**🏛 Musée des Beaux-Arts**
25 rue Richelieu. **Tel** 03 21 46 48 40. **Open** Tue–Sun pms. 🅿 🛗

**🏛 Cité de la Dentelle et de la Mode**
Quai du Commerce. **Tel** 03 21 00 42 30. **Open** Wed–Mon. **Closed** first 2 wks Jan, May 1, Dec 25. 🅿 🛗
**w** cite-dentelle.fr

**🏛 Musée Mémoire 1939–1945**
Parc St.-Pierre. **Tel** 03 21 34 21 57. **Open** Mon & Wed–Sat (May–Sep): daily. **Closed** Jan & Dec. 🅿 🛗

## ❹ Dunkerque

Nord. 🅰 375,000. 🚂 🚌 ⛴ **i** Le Beffroi, rue Amiral Ronarc'h (03 28 66 79 21). ⛴ Wed, Sat. **w** ot-dunkerque.fr

Though a major industrial port, Dunkerque has much Flemish character. Start a tour from place du Minck, with its fresh fish stands. Nearby **Musée Portuaire** celebrates the town's maritime history. In the old center, a statue commemorates local hero Jean Bart, a 17th-century corsair, who lies in **Eglise St.-Eloi**. Its belfry (1440) offers fine views.

**Le Mémorial du Souvenir** has an exhibition of the dramatic evacuation of 350,000 British

and French troops in 1940. The **Lieu d'Art et d'Action Contemporaine (LAAC)** features ceramics and glassware.

**🏛 Musée Portuaire**
9 quai de la Citadelle. **Tel** 03 28 63 33 39. **Open** Wed–Mon (Jul & Aug: daily). **Closed** Jan 1, May 1, Dec 25. 🅿 🛗

*The port at Dunkerque*

**🏛 Le Memorial du Souvenir**
Rue des Chantiers de France. **Tel** 03 28 66 79 21. **Open** Apr–Sep: daily. 🅿 📷 🛗 ground floor only.

**🏛 Lieu d'Art et d'Action Contemporaine**
Jardin des Sculptures. **Tel** 03 28 29 56 00. **Open** Tue–Sun. **Closed** public hols. 🅿 🛗

## ❺ St.-Omer

Pas de Calais. 🅰 15,000. 🚂 🚌 **i** 7 pl Victor Hugo (03 21 98 08 51). ⛴ Sat. **w** tourisme-saintomer.com

With its cobblestone streets and 17th- and 18th-century buildings, St.-Omer appears untouched. The **Hôtel Sandelin** houses a fine and decorative arts museum, while the cathedral boasts 13th-century tiles and a huge organ. The **Bibliothèque d'Agglomération** contains rare manuscripts from the Abbaye St-Bertin, a ruined 15th-century abbey nearby. Three miles (5 km) from St.-Omer, **La Coupole** is a World War II museum inside a converted bunker.

**🏛 Hôtel Sandelin**
14 rue Carnot. **Tel** 03 21 38 00 94. **Open** Wed–Sun. 🅿 🛗 ground floor.

**🏛 Bibliothèque d'Agglomération**
40 rue Gambetta. **Tel** 03 21 38 35 08. **Open** Tue, Wed, Fri & Sat. **Closed** public hols. 🛗

**🏛 La Coupole**
Rue Clabaux, 62570 Helfaut. **Tel** 03 21 12 27 27. **Open** daily. **Closed** 2 wks in Jan, Dec 24 & 25. 🅿 🛗

### Channel Crossings

Calais is only 22 miles (35 km) southeast of the English coast, and crossing the waters of the Channel – which the French know as *la Manche* (the Sleeve) – has inspired many intrepid exploits. The first crossing by balloon was in 1785 by Jean-Pierre Blanchard; Captain M. Webb made the first swim in 1875; and Louis Blériot's pioneering flight followed in 1909. Plans for an undersea tunnel, first laid as early as 1751, were finally achieved in 1994 with the opening of a railroad link between Fréthun and Folkestone.

*Children watching Louis Blériot taking off, 1909*

## ❻ Flandre Maritime

Nord. 🚗 5,000. ✈ Lille. 🚂 Bergues.
🚌 Dunkerque. 🛈 Bergues, Le Beffroi,
pl Henri Billiaert (03 28 68 71 06).
W bergues-tourisme.fr

South of Dunkerque lies a flat, agricultural plain with narrow waterways and expansive skies – an archetypal Flemish landscape with canals, cyclists, and ancient windmills. The **Noordmeulen**, built just north of Hondschoote in 1127, is thought to be the oldest windmill in Europe.

From Hondschoote the D3 follows the Canal de la Basse Colme west to Bergues, a fortified wool town with fine 16th- to 17th-century Flemish works in its **Musée Municipal**. Farther south, the hilltop town of **Cassel** has a cobblestone Grande Place with 16th- to 18th-century buildings, and views across Flanders and Belgium from its Jardin Public.

### 🏛 Musée Municipal
1 rue du Mont de Piété, Bergues.
**Tel** 03 28 68 13 30. **Open** Thu–Mon pms. **Closed** Nov–Apr. 🗒

## ❼ Lille

Nord. 🚗 230,000. ✈ 🚉 🚌
🛈 1 rue du Palais Rihour (08 91 56 20 04). 🚃 Tue–Sun. W lilletourism.com

Lille has excellent stores and markets and a powerful sense of its historic Flemish identity – the Flemish name, Rijssel, is still used, and some of the area's one million residents speak a Franco-

Flower stands in the arcades of the Vieille Bourse in Lille

Flemish patois. With heavy industry declining, the city has turned to high tech. A modern commercial quarter, including the ultramodern Euralille shopping complex, adjoins Lille Europe station, the TGV/Eurostar/Thalys train interchange. The "Métro," VAL, is a driverless automatic train.

However, the city's charm lies in its historic center, Vieux Lille – a mass of cobblestone squares and narrow streets packed with stylish stores, cafés, and restaurants. Place du Général de Gaulle forms its hub, with facades including the 17th-century **Vieille Bourse** (Old Exchange). Adjacent stand the **Nouvelle Bourse** and the **Opéra**, both built in the early 20th century. The moated five-point brick Citadel by Vauban is also worth a look.

### 🏛 Musée de l'Hospice Comtesse
32 rue de la Monnaie. **Tel** 03 28 36 84 00. **Open** Wed–Sun, Mon pm. 🗒🛗
A hospital was founded here in 1237. Now its 15th- and 17th-century buildings house exhibitions. The Sick Room has a barrel-vaulted ceiling; the

Place du General de Gaulle in Lille's historic center

Community Wing has a Delft kitchen. There is also a collection of ancient instruments.

### 🏛 Palais des Beaux-Arts
Pl de la République. **Tel** 03 20 06 78 00. **Open** Wed–Sun, Mon pm. **Closed** Jan 1, May 1, Jul 14, Nov 1, Dec 25. 🗒🖭🛗

One of the best art collections outside Paris, the museum is strong on Flemish works, including Rubens and Van Dyck. Other highlights are *Paradise and Hell* by Dirk Bouts, van Goyen's *The Skaters*, Goya's *The Letter*, Delacroix's *Médée*, as well as works by Courbet and Impressionist paintings.

### 🏛 Musée d'Art Moderne, d'Art Contemporain et d'Art Brut (LaM)
1 Allée du Musée, 59650 Villeneuve-d'Ascq. **Tel** 03 20 19 68 68. **Open** Tue–Sun. **Closed** Jan 1, May 1, Dec 25 🗒🛗

Lille's contemporary art museum and sculpture park focuses on 20th- and 21st-century art. The collection showcases works by Picasso, Modigliani, Miró, Braque, and Léger. It also boasts the largest permanent collection of outsider (brut) art in France.

# ❽ Arras

Pas de Calais. 🏔 45,000. 🚆 🚌
ℹ Hôtel de Ville, pl des Héros (03 21 51 26 95). 🗓 Wed, Thu, Sat, Sun.
ⓦ explorearras.com

The center of Arras, capital of the Artois region, is graced by two picturesque cobblestone squares enclosed by 155 houses with 17th-century Flemish-style facades. A triumph of postwar reconstruction, each residence in the **Grand'Place** and the smaller place des Héros has a slightly varying design, with some original store signs still visible.

A monumental **Hôtel de Ville** rebuilt in the Flamboyant Gothic style stands at the west end of place des Héros – in the lobby are four giants, Colas, Dédé, Ami Bidasse, and Jacqueline, who swagger round the town during local festivals. From the basement you can take an elevator up to the belfry for superb views, or take a guided tour into the labyrinth of underground passages below Arras. These were cut in the lime-stone in the 10th century. They have often served as shelter, during World War I, notably, as a sub-terranean army camp.

The huge Abbaye St.-Vaast includes an 18th- to 19th-century Neoclassical cathedral and the **Musée des Beaux-Arts**, which contains fine examples of medieval sculpture, including a pair of beautiful 13th-century angels. Among other exhibits are a local *arras* (tapestry) and 19th-century works by the School of Arras, Realist landscape painters.

🏛 **Hôtel de Ville**
Pl des Héros. **Tel** 03 21 51 26 95.
**Open** Jul–Aug: Sun pm, Mon–Fri.
Tunnels: **Open** Feb–Dec: daily. Belfry:
**Open** daily. **Closed** Jan 1, Dec 25,
📷 obligatory for tunnels. 🚫

🏛 **Musée des Beaux-Arts**
22 rue Paul Doumer. **Tel** 03 21 71 26 43.
**Open** Wed–Mon. **Closed** pub hols. 🚫

# ❾ Vallée de la Somme

Somme. ✈ 🚆 🚌 Amiens. ℹ 16 pl André Audinot, Péronne (03 22 84 42 38). ⓦ somme-tourisme.com

The name of the Somme is synonymous with the slaughter and horror of trench warfare during World War I *(see pp194–5)*. Yet the Somme Valley also means pretty countryside, a vast estuary wetland, and abundant wildlife. Lakes and woods alongside provide enjoyable camping, walking, and fishing. Battlefields lie along the river and its tributaries north and northeast of Amiens, and extend north to Arras. Neat World War I Commonwealth cemeteries cover the area. The **Historial de la Grande Guerre** at Péronne gives a thoughtful introduction.

Roadside shrine, Somme Valley

Boating on the River Somme

Parc Mémorial Beaumont-Hamel, near Albert, is a real battlefield being allowed to disappear in its own time. Travel to Vimy Ridge Canadian Memorial, near Arras, to see a bloodbath battle site preserved as it was, and to Notre-Dame de Lorette, the landmark French National Cemetery.

West of Amiens, **Samara** – Amiens' Gallo-Roman name – is France's largest archeological park, with reconstructions of prehistoric dwellings, and exhibitions explaining early crafts such as flint-cutting and corn-grinding. Farther downstream, Eglise St.-Vulfran at Abbeville is noted for its Flamboyant Gothic west front with beautifully carved 16th-century door panels.

St.-Valéry-sur-Somme is a charming harbor resort with a historic upper town and a tree-lined promenade looking across the estuary. William departed for England from here in 1066. Birders should visit the Maison de la Baie de Somme et de l'Oiseau nearby at Lanchéres, or the Parc Ornithologique de Marquenterre on the far shore near delightful Le Crotoy. In summer, a little train links the two sides, passing through dunes and marshes.

🏛 **Historial de la Grande Guerre**
Château de Péronne. **Tel** 03 22 83 14 18. **Open** Apr–Sep: daily; Oct–Mar: Thu–Tue. **Closed** mid-Dec–mid-Jan.
🚫 ♿ 📷 ⓦ historial.org

🏛 **Samara**
La Chaussée-Tirancourt. **Tel** 03 22 51 82 83. **Open** Apr–Oct: daily. 🚫 ♿
ⓦ samara.fr

The 16th-century carvings on Eglise St.-Vulfran in Abbeville, Somme Valley

# ❿ Amiens

Somme. 🏛 130,000. 🚉 🚌 ℹ 23 pl
Notre Dame (03 22 71 60 50). 🛍 Wed
& Sat. 🌐 amiens-tourisme.com

There is more to Amiens, the
capital of Picardy, than its
**Cathédrale Notre-Dame** *(see
pp206–7)*. The picturesque St.-
Leu quarter is a traffic-free
area of low houses and flower-
lined canals with waterside
restaurants and artisans' shops.
Farther east are the colorful
**Les Hortillonnages**, a
patchwork of marshland market
gardens, once tended by
farmers using punts that now
ferry visitors around the
protected natural site.

The **Musée de Picardie** has
many fine medieval and
19th-century sculptures and
16th- to 20th-century paintings,
including a set of 16th-century
group portraits, commissioned
as offerings to the cathedral.
To the south is the Cirque
d'Hiver, which Jules Verne
(1828–1905) inaugurated in
1889. **Maison de Jules Verne**
has over 700 objects spread
over four floors relating to the
famous author, who lived here
from 1882 until 1900.

🏛 **Musée de Picardie**
48 rue de la République. **Tel** 03 22
97 14 00. **Closed** for renovation
until 2019. 🚫 ♿ 📷

🏛 **Maison de Jules Verne**
2 rue Charles Dubois. **Tel** 03 22 45
45 75. **Open** Wed–Mon & Tue pm
(mid-Oct–Easter: Mon & Wed–Fri;
Sat & Sun pms). 📷

**The clock** depicts
Christ surrounded
by the 12 apostles.

Solstice
indicator

**Mechanical figures**
perform scenes from
the Last Judgment.

Clock showing
the age of
the world

Astronomical clock in Beauvais Cathedral

# ⓫ Beauvais

Oise. 🏛 61,000. ✈ 🚉 🚌
ℹ 1 rue Beauregard (03 44 15 30 30).
🛍 Mon, Wed, Thurs, Sat.
🌐 visitbeauvais.fr

Heavily bombed in World War II,
Beauvais is now a modern town
with one outstanding jewel.
Though never completed,
**Cathédrale St.-Pierre** is a
poignant, neck-cricking finale
to the vaulting ambition that
created the great Gothic
cathedrals. In 1227, work began
on a building designed to soar
above all predecessors, but the
roof of the chancel caved in
twice from lack of support
before its completion in the
early 14th century. Delayed by
wars and inadequate funds, the
transept was not completed
until 1550. In 1573 its crossing
collapsed after a tower and
spire were added.

What remains today is
nevertheless a masterpiece,
rising 157 ft (48 m) high. In the
transept much of the original
16th-century stained glass survives, while near the north door
is a 90,000-part astronomical
clock assembled in the 1860s.
Displays take place daily at
30 minutes past the hour (€5).
What would have been the nave
is still occupied by the remnants
of a 10th-century church known
as the Basse-Oeuvre.

The former Bishop's Palace
is now home to **Le MUDO –
Musée de l'Oise**. The collection
includes archaeological finds,
medieval sculpture, tapestries,
and local ceramics. Beauvais
has a long tradition of tapestry

## Viollet-le-Duc

The renowned architectural theorist Viollet-le-Duc (1814–79)
was the first to fully appreciate Gothic architecture. His 1854
dictionary of architecture celebrated medieval building

techniques, showing that the
arches and tracery of Gothic
cathedrals were solutions
to architectural problems,
not mere decoration. His
restoration work included
Château de Pierrefonds,
Notre-Dame in Paris
*(see pp90–91)*, and
Carcassonne *(see pp492–3)*.

Medieval architects, as drawn
by Viollet-le-Duc

production. The tourist office organizes visits to the local **Manufacture Nationale de la Tapisserie** factory at Beauvais.

🏛 **Le MUDO – Musée de l'Oise**
Ancien Palais Episcopal, 1 rue du Musée. **Tel** 03 44 10 40 50. **Open** Wed–Mon. **Closed** Jan 1, Easter, May 1, Jun 9, Nov 1, Dec 25.

🏛 **Manufacture Nationale de la Tapisserie**
24 rue Henri-Brispot. Contact tourist office for reservations. 📷 Jul & Aug: Wed pm. 📷

The rib-vaulted nave of Cathédrale de Notre-Dame, Noyon

## ⑫ Noyon

Oise. 🗺 15,000. 🚉 ℹ pl Bertrand Labarre (03 44 44 21 88). 🛒 Wed & Sat, first Tue of each month.
🅦 noyon-tourisme.com

Noyon has long been a religious center. The **Cathédrale de Notre-Dame**, dating from 1150, is the fifth to be built on this site and was completed by 1290. It provides a harmonious example of the transition from Romanesque to Gothic style.

A local history museum, the **Musée du Noyonnais**, occupies part of the former Bishop's Palace, and at the cathedral's east end is a rare half-timbered chapter library built in 1506.

Jean Calvin, the Protestant theologian and one of the leaders of the Reformation, was born here in 1509 and is commemorated in the small **Musée Jean Calvin.**

🏛 **Musée du Noyonnais**
Ancien Palais Episcopal, 7 rue de l'Evêché. **Tel** 03 44 09 43 41. **Open** Tue–Sun. **Closed** Jan 1, Nov 11, Dec 24–Jan 2. 📷

## ⑬ Compiègne

Oise. 🗺 70,000. 🚉 🚌 ℹ pl de l'Hôtel de Ville (03 44 40 01 00). 🛒 Tue–Sat.
🅦 compiegne-tourisme.fr

Compiègne is where Joan of Arc was captured by the Burgundians in 1430. A 16th-century Hôtel de Ville with a towering belfry rules over the centere, but the town is most famous for its royal **Château**.

Designed as a summer residence for Louis XV, the château was completed by Louis XVI, restored by Napoleon and later became a residence of Napoleon III and Empress Eugénie. Tours of the Imperial Apartments take in private chambers, such as the sumptuous bedrooms of Napoleon I and Marie-Louise.

Within the Château, the Musée du Second Empire and Musée de l'Impératrice display furniture, memorabilia, and portraits, while the Musée de la Voiture is an assembly of historic carriages, bicycles, and early motor cars.

South and east of the town, the old hunting grounds of the **Forêt de Compiègne** spread as far as Pierrefonds, with ample space for walks and picnics beneath its oaks and beeches. East of the D130, Les Beaux Monts provide majestic views back to the château.

The Clairière de l'Armistice, north of the N31, marks the spot where the armistice of World War I was signed on November 11, 1918. The small **Musée Wagon de l'Armistice** has a replica of the railroad car where the ceremony took place, which was used again in World War II by Hitler as a humiliating venue for the signing of the French surrender on 22 June 1940.

🏰 **Château de Compiègne**
Pl du Général de Gaulle. **Tel** 03 44 38 47 00. **Open** Wed–Mon. **Closed** Jan 1, May 1, Dec 25. 📷 🅦 palais-decompiegne.fr

🏛 **Musée Wagon de l'Armistice**
Clairière de l'Armistice. **Tel** 03 44 85 14 18. **Open** Wed–Mon (Apr–mid-Sep: daily). **Closed** Jan 1, Dec 25. 📷

## ⑭ Château de Pierrefonds

Oise. **Tel** 03 44 42 72 72. **Open** daily. **Closed** Jan 1, May 1, Dec 25. 📷 📷 🎵 Concerts. 🅦 chateau-pierrefonds.fr

The immense Château de Pierrefonds dominates the small village below. A mighty castle was constructed here by Louis d'Orléans in the 14th century, but by 1813 it had become a picturesque ruin, which Napoleon I purchased for less than 3,000 francs.

In 1857, Napoleon III commissioned the architect Viollet-le-Duc to restore it, and in 1884 Pierrefonds was reborn as a museum of fortification. The exterior, with its moat, drawbridge, towers, and double sentry walks, is a diligent reconstruction of medieval military architecture. The interior, by contrast, is enlivened by romantic fancies. There are guided tours and a historical exhibition.

Path through the Forêt de Compiègne

# Amiens Cathedral

Work on France's largest cathedral started around 1220. It was built to house the head of St. John the Baptist, brought back from the Crusades in 1206 and is still displayed here. Within 50 years, Notre-Dame was complete, a masterpiece of engineering – Gothic architecture carried to a bold extreme. Restored in the 1850s by Viollet-le-Duc *(see p204)*, and having miraculously survived two world wars, the cathedral is famous for its statues and reliefs, which inspired John Ruskin's *The Bible of Amiens* in 1884. The La Cathédrale en Couleurs sound-and-light show recreates the original colors of the statuary around the west door.

**★ West Front**
The King's Gallery, a row of 22 colossal statues representing the kings of France, spans the west front. The statues are also thought to symbolize the Kings of Judah.

**Weeping Angel**
Sculpted by Nicolas Blasset in 1628, this sentimental statue in the ambulatory became a popular image during World War I.

## KEY

① **The Calendar** shows signs from the zodiac, with the corresponding monthly labors below. It depicts everyday life in the 13th century.

② **St. Firmin Portal** is decorated with figures and scenes from the life of St. Firmin, the martyr who brought Christianity to Picardy and became the first bishop of Amiens.

③ **The Flamboyant tracery** of the rose window was created in the 16th century.

④ **A double row** comprising 22 elegant flying buttresses supports the construction.

⑤ **The flooring** was laid down in 1288 and reassembled in the late 19th century. The faithful followed its labyrinthine shape on their knees.

**Central Portal**
Scenes from the Last Judgment adorn the tympanum, with the *Beau Dieu*, a statue of Christ, between the doors.

**Towers**
Two towers of unequal height frame the west front. The south tower was completed in 1366; the north in 1402. The spire was replaced twice, in 1627 and 1887.

## VISITORS' CHECKLIST

**Practical Information**
Pl Notre-Dame. **Tel** 03 22 80 03 41.
**Open** 8:30am–6:15pm (Oct–Mar: to 5:15pm). La Cathédrale en Couleurs light show: Jun–Sep & Christmas hols (nightly).
Towers: **Open** Mon, Wed–Sat, & Sun pm. 🔒 **Closed** Jan 1, last Sun Sep. ✝ 9am daily; 9am, 10:30am Sun. 🅿 📷
🅦 **amiens-cathedrale.fr**

★ **Nave**
Soaring 138 ft (42 m) high, with support from 126 slender pillars, the brightly illuminated interior of Notre-Dame is a hymn to the vertical.

★ **Choir Stalls**
The 110 oak choir stalls (1508–19) are delicately carved with over 4,000 biblical, mythical, and real-life figures.

★ **Choir Screens**
Vivid scenes from the lives of St. Firmin and St. John, carved in the 15th- to the 16th centuries, adorn the ambulatory.

## ⑮ Senlis

Oise. [population] 17,000. [icons] [i] pl du Parvis Notre-Dame (03 44 53 06 40). [icon] Tue & Fri. [W] senlis-tourisme.fr

Senlis, 6 miles (10 km) east of Chantilly, is worth visiting for its Gothic cathedral and the well-preserved historic streets that surround it. **Cathédrale Notre-Dame** was constructed during the 12th century, and the sculpted central doorway of its west front, depicting the Assumption of the Virgin, influenced later cathedrals such as Amiens (see pp206–7). The south tower's spire dates from the 13th century, while the Flamboyant south transept, built in the mid-16th century, makes an ornate contrast with the austerity of earlier years. Opposite the west front, a gateway leads to the ruins of the Château Royal and its gardens. Here the **Musée de la Vénerie**, housed in a former priory, celebrates hunting through paintings, old weapons, and trophies.

The **Musée d'Art** recalls the town's Gallo-Roman past, and also has an excellent collection of early Gothic sculpture.

**🏛 Musée de la Vénerie**
Château Royal, pl du Parvis Notre-Dame. **Tel** 03 44 29 49 93. **Open** Wed–Sun. **Closed** Jan 1, May 1, Dec 25. [icon] [icon] obligatory for upper floor rooms, pms only.

**🏛 Musée d'Art et d'Archéologie**
Ancien Evêché, 2 pl Notre-Dame. **Tel** 03 44 24 86 72. **Open** Wed–Sun. [icon]

*Les Très Riches Heures du Duc de Berry*, on show in Chantilly

## ⑯ Chantilly

Oise. [population] 11,000. [icons] [i] 73 rue du Connétable (03 44 67 37 37). [icon] Wed & Sat. [W] chantilly-tourisme.com

The horseracing capital of France, Chantilly offers a classy combination of château, park, and forest that has long made it a popular excursion. With origins in Gallo-Roman times, the château of today started to take shape in 1528, when Anne de Montmorency, Constable of France, had the old fortress replaced and added the Petit Château. During the time of the Great Prince of Condé (1621–86), renovation work continued and André Le Nôtre created a park and fountains that made even Louis XIV jealous. Destroyed in the Revolution, the Grand Château was again

### Chantilly Horseracing

Chantilly is the capital of thoroughbred racing in France, a shrine to the long-standing love affair between the French upper classes and the world of horses. It was the firm belief of Prince Louis-Henri de Bourbon, creator of Chantilly's monumental Grandes Ecuries, that he would one day be reincarnated as a horse. Horseracing was introduced from England around 1830 and soon became very popular. The first official race meeting was held here in 1834 and today around 3,000 horses are trained in the surrounding forests and countryside. Every June, Chantilly becomes the focus of the social and flat racing season when top riders and their thoroughbreds compete for its two historic trophies, the Prix du Jockey-Club and Prix de Diane-Hermès.

Prix de Diane-Hermès, one of many prestigious races at Chantilly rebuilt, and its receptions and hunting parties became crowded by the fashionable high society of the 1820s and 1830s. It was finally replaced by a Renaissance-style château in the late 19th century.

Today the Grand Château and the Petit Château form the **Musée Condé**, displaying art treasures collected by its last private owner, the Duke of Aumale. These include work by Raphael, Botticelli, Poussin, and Ingres, and an entertaining gallery of 16th-century portraits by the Clouet brothers. Among the most precious items is the famous 15th-century illuminated manuscript *Les Très Riches Heures du Duc de Berry*, reproductions of which are on view. You can also tour the stately apartments, with decorative conceits ranging from frolicking monkeys to triumphant battles.

Both châteaux are somewhat upstaged by the magnificent stables (Grandes Ecuries), an equestrian palace designed by Jean Aubert in 1719 to accommodate 240 horses and 500 dogs. It is occupied by the **Musée du Cheval**, presenting various breeds of horses and ponies, and horseback riding displays.

**Musée Condé**
Château de Chantilly. **Tel** 03 44 62 62 62. **Open** daily (Dec–Mar: Wed–Mon).

**Musée du Cheval**
Grandes Ecuries du Prince de Condé, Chantilly. **Tel** 03 44 27 31 80. **Open** daily (Dec–Mar: Wed–Mon). domainedechantilly.com

## ❼ Parc Astérix

Plailly. **Tel** 08 26 46 26 26. **Open** Apr–early Nov (times vary, check website. parcasterix.fr

Near Charles de Gaulle airport a small fortified Gaulish village has its own customs controls, currency, and radio station (Menhir FM). One of the most

popular theme parks in France, it is dedicated to Asterix the Gaul and all the other characters in Goscinny and Uderzo's famous cartoon strip: Getafix, Obelix, Cacofonix, et al. The Romans are driven crazy as they try to subdue these larger-than-life Gauls, who dodge patrolling Roman centurions. Hilarious battles take place.

The Parc is as much about French history as about the cartoons. Via Antiqua and the Roman City are lighthearted but still genuinely educational. Rue de Paris shows Paris through the centuries, including the construction of Notre-Dame cathedral. There are nonhistorical attractions too, such as a dolphinarium and Zeus' Thunder high-speed rollercoaster. Check out the latest rides – there's usually something new every year.

Asterix with friends, Parc Astérix

## ❽ Laon

Aisne. ⛪ 27,000. 🚉 🛈 Hôtel-Dieu, pl du Parvis Gauthier de Montagne (03 23 20 28 62). 🕐 Tue–Sat. 🌐 **tourisme-paysdelaon.com**

The capital of the Aisne *département*, Laon occupies a dramatic site on top of a long,

The traffic-free rue Châtelaine, a main shopping street in Laon

Rose window in the 13th-century Cathédrale de Notre-Dame, Laon

narrow ridge surrounded by wide plains. The old town, on top of the mount, is best approached by Poma, an automated cablecar that swings up from the train station to the place du Général Leclerc.

The traffic-free rue Châtelaine leads to Laon's splendid **Cathédrale de Notre-Dame**. Completed in 1235, the cathedral lost two of its original seven towers in the Revolution but remains an impressive monument to the early Gothic style.

Details include the deep porches of the west facade, the four-story nave, and the carved Renaissance screens enclosing its side chapels. The immense 13th-century rose window in the apse represents the Glorification of the Church. Protruding from the cathedral's western towers are statues paying tribute to the oxen that were used to haul up stone for its construction.

The rest of medieval Laon rewards casual strolling: a promenade rings the 16th-century **Citadelle** farther east, while to the south you can follow the ramparts past the Porte d'Ardon and Porte des Chenizelles to **Eglise St.-Martin**, with views of the cathedral from rue Thibesard.

South of Laon is Chemin des Dames, named after Louis XV's daughters, who used to take this route, but more often remembered as a World War I battlefield and lined with cemeteries and memorials.

# CHAMPAGNE

*Marne · Ardennes · Aube · Haute-Marne*

Champagne is a name of great resonance, conjuring up images of celebration and the world-famous cathedral at Reims. Yet beyond the glamor lies an unspoiled rural idyll of two strikingly contrasting landscapes: the rolling plains of Champagne, giving way to lakes and water meadows to the south, and the dense forests and hills of the Ardennes in the north.

The so-called "sacred triangle of Champagne," linking Epernay, Reims, and Châlons-en-Champagne, is like a magnet for wine lovers. Here, the experience of drinking fine Champagne is enhanced by gourmet meals of stuffed trout, Ardennes ham, and the famous tripe sausages called *andouillettes*.

The signposted *route touristique du champagne* wends its way through vineyards toward endless cereal plains stretching southward to the "lake district," an area of oak forests, water meadows, and streams.

On the border between France and Belgium lies the Ardennes, named after the Celtic word for "deep forest." This wild borderland of dramatic valleys, deciduous forests, and hills is cut by the meanderings of the River Meuse. Border fortifications include the vast citadel of Sedan and the star-shaped town and fortress of Rocroi, as well as the Maginot Line outposts built before World War II. The Ardennes may offer appealing countryside, but Champagne is culturally superior, with impressive towns that have painstakingly restored historic centers. It has some striking churches, from the Gothic majesty of Reims Cathedral to the rustic charm of its typical half-timbered *champenoises* churches. These feature vivid stained-glass windows by the famous School of Troyes, whose subtle craftsmanship seems to typify the appeal of this quiet region.

Timber-framed *champenoise* church at Lac du Der-Chantecoq

◀ Interior of Cathédrale Notre-Dame, Reims

# Exploring Champagne

Champagne's fizz draws wine lovers to the sacred triangle between Reims, Epernay, and Châlons-en-Champagne, but the region also attracts culture lovers to its great churches, notably Reims Cathedral. Reims abounds in gastronomic restaurants, but Troyes, the former capital of Champagne, makes the most delightful base. Much of Champagne is flat or gently undulating, and the wild and wooded Ardennes to the north attracts walkers and nature lovers. North of Reims, the Ardennes canal can be explored by barge or pleasure boat from Rethel; to the south, watersports are popular on the lakes to the east of Troyes.

Fishing by a canal in Montier-en-Der near Lac du Der-Chantecoq

## Getting Around

The region's main *autoroute* is the A26, which gives access to Reims in under 3 hours from Calais, and also provides easy connection to most of the region all the way down to Troyes and Langres (via the A5). The A4 highway also links Reims to Paris and Alsace. Paris–Reims by the TGV high-speed train takes 45 minutes. Train transportation within the region is reasonably good, and so are the roads. To explore the wine-growing region, follow the signposted roads marked "Route de Champagne."

Windmill at Verzenay, Parc Naturel de la Montagne de Reims

**For keys to symbols** *see back flap*

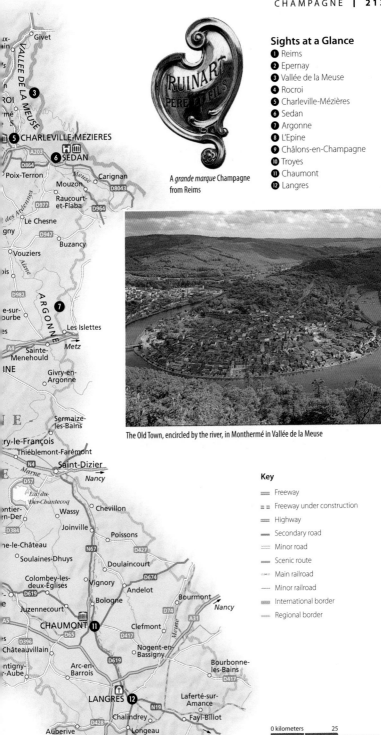

A *grande marque* Champagne from Reims

## Sights at a Glance

1 Reims
2 Epernay
3 Vallée de la Meuse
4 Rocroi
5 Charleville-Mézières
6 Sedan
7 Argonne
8 L'Epine
9 Châlons-en-Champagne
10 Troyes
11 Chaumont
12 Langres

The Old Town, encircled by the river, in Monthermé in Vallée de la Meuse

## Key

═══ Freeway
═ ═ Freeway under construction
═══ Highway
─── Secondary road
═══ Minor road
─── Scenic route
▬▬▬ Main railroad
─── Minor railroad
▬▬▬ International border
─── Regional border

0 kilometers       25

0 miles       25

Interior of Basilique St.-Remi, Reims

# ❶ Reims

Marne. 🗺 185,000. ✈ 🚊 🚌
ℹ 6 rue Rockefeller (03 26 77 45 00).
🏛 daily. 🌐 reims-tourisme.com

Reims is home to some of the best-known *grandes marques* in Champagne, and several are grouped around the Basilique St.-Remi. But the city has another, much earlier, claim to fame: since the 11th century, all the kings of France have come here to be crowned in the city's remarkable Gothic **Cathédrale Notre-Dame** *(see pp216–17)*.

Although World War II bombing destroyed much of Reims's architectural coherence, there are some remarkable monuments here. The **Cryptoportique**, part of the forum, and Porte Mars, a triumphal Augustan arch, recall the Roman past. The **Musée des Beaux-Arts** (open Wed–Thu) houses a fine collection of 15th- and 16th-century canvases depicting biblical scenes, portraits by the Cranachs, *The Death of Marat* by David, and landscapes by Corot. Also here are the Barbizons, Impressionists, and modern masters.

In 1996 Reims celebrated the 1,500-year anniversary of the baptism of Clovis, first king of the Franks, in its cathedral.

## 🏛 Musée de la Reddition

12 rue F. Roosevelt. **Tel** 03 26 47 84 19. **Open** Wed–Mon. **Closed** Jan 1, May 1, Jul 14, Nov 1 & 11, Dec 24, 25 & 31. 📷 (free 1st Sun of month).

In 1945, the German surrender was signed here, Eisenhower's French HQ during World War II.

## 🏛 Musée Hôtel le Vergeur

36 pl du Forum. **Tel** 03 26 47 20 75.
📷 📹 🌐 museelevergeur.com

This early Renaissance townhouse was bought by traveler and photographer Hugues Krafft in 1910. He dedicated his time and fortune to restoring the mansion after it was badly damaged in World War I. An avid collector, he filled the rooms with Renaissance and Neo-Gothic furniture, 16th- to 20th-century works of art, and photographs and objects from his travels in Asia. Many of the artifacts and works of art illustrate the history of Reims. The highlight of the collection is a set of original prints of *Apocalypse* and the *Large Passion* by Albrecht Dürer (1471–1528).

## 🏛 Basilique St.-Remi

Pl St.-Rémi. **Open** daily. ♿

This Benedictine abbey church, the oldest church in Reims, began as a Carolingian basilica dedicated to St. Remi (440–533). Inside, an Early Gothic choir and radiating chapels can be seen, as well as sculpted Romanesque capitals in the north transept.

Porte Mars, a reminder of Reims in Roman times

## Méthode Champenoise

To produce its characteristic bubbles, Champagne has to undergo a process of double fermentation. **First fermentation:** The base wine, made from rather acidic grapes, is fermented at 68–72 °F (20–22 °C) in either stainless-steel tanks or, occasionally, in oak barrels. It is then siphoned off from the sediment and kept at colder temperatures to clear completely, before being drawn off and blended with wines from other areas and years (except in the case of vintage Champagne). The wine is bottled and the *liqueur de tirage* (sugar, wine, and yeast) is added. **Second fermentation:** The bottles are stored for a year or more in cool, chalky cellars. The yeast converts the sugar to alcohol and carbon dioxide, which produces the sparkle, and the yeast cells die leaving a deposit. To remove this, the inverted bottles are turned and tapped daily *(remuage)* to shift the deposits into the neck of the bottle. Finally, the deposits are expelled by the process known as *dégorgement*, and a bit of sugar syrup *(liqueur d'expédition)* is added to adjust the sweetness before the final cork is inserted.

Champagne Mumm of Reims

### 🏛 Musée St.-Remi

53 rue Simon. **Tel** 03 26 35 36 90.
**Open** daily pm only. **Closed** Jan 1,
May 1, Jul 14, Nov 1 & 11, Dec 25.

Set in the former abbey, the
adjoining museum encloses
the original Gothic chapterhouse
within its cloistered 17th-century
shell. On display are archeological artifacts, 15th-century
tapestries depicting the life of
St. Remi, and a collection
of weapons dating from the
16th–19th centuries.

### 🚻 Fort de la Pompelle

5 miles (8 km) southeast of Reims.
**Tel** 03 26 49 11 85. **Open** Tue–Sun.
**Closed** May 1, Jul 14, Nov 1, mid-Dec–
mid-Jan.

Built to protect Reims after the
Franco-Prussian War, this fort
houses a museum of German
Imperial military headgear.

## ❷ Epernay

Marne. 🏔 25,000. 🚉 ℹ 7 av de
Champagne (03 26 53 33 00). 🛒 Wed,
Thu, Sat, & Sun. 🆆 ot-epernay.fr

The main reason for visiting
Epernay is to burrow into the
chalky *caves* and taste the
Champagne. The town lives
off the fruits of its profitable
Champagne industry. As proof,
the avenue de Champagne

Statue of Dom Perignon at Moët

quarter abounds in mock-
Renaissance mansions. **Moët &
Chandon**, dating back to 1743,
is the largest and slickest
*maison*, the star of the Moët-
Hennessy stable. Its cellars
stretch some 18 miles (28 km)
underground.

The group also owns other
Champagne houses, such as
Mercier, Krug, Veuve Clicquot,
and Ruinart. There is little to
choose between a visit to the
cellars of Moët & Chandon or

Mercier – both are on avenue
de Champagne. Mercier has
the distinction of displaying
a giant tun (cask) created for
the 1889 Paris Exhibition, and
takes you through the *caves*
on an electric train.

**De Castellane** offers a more
personalized tour, accompanied
by a heady *dégustation*.

### 🚻 Moët & Chandon

20 av de Champagne. **Tel** 03 26 51 20
20. **Open** by appt only. Apr–mid-Nov:
daily; mid-Nov–Dec & Feb–Mar: Mon–
Fri. 🗓 🎫 only. 🆆 moet.com

### 🚻 Mercier

70 av de Champagne. **Tel** 03 26 51 22
22. **Open** Apr–mid-Nov: daily; mid-
Nov–mid-Dec & mid-Feb–Mar: Thu–
Mon. 🗓 ♿ 🎫 obligatory.
🆆 champagnemercier.fr

### 🚻 De Castellane

57 rue de Verdun. **Tel** 03 26 51 19 19.
**Open** mid-Mar–Dec: daily. 🗓 ♿ restr.
🎫 obligatory. 🆆 castellane.com

***Dégorgement*** is the final
removal of the yeast deposits
from the bottle. The neck of the
bottle is plunged in freezing brine
and the frozen block of sediment
is then removed.

**Seductive marketing** of Champagne since the
19th century has ensured its continuing success.

**The bubbles in Champagne** are produced during the second
fermentation. Champagnes, especially vintage ones, improve
with ageing.

# Reims Cathedral

The magnificent Gothic Cathédrale Notre-Dame at Reims is noted for its monumentality. A cathedral has stood on this site since 401, but the present building was begun in 1211. Reims has been the backdrop for coronations from medieval times till 1825, when Charles X was crowned. The coronation of Charles VII here in 1429 was attended by Joan of Arc.

During the Revolution, the rood screen and windows were destroyed, but the stonework survived. World War I damage was fully restored in 1996, to coincide with the 1,500th anniversary of the baptism of Clovis, King of the Franks, at Reims – considered the first coronation of a French king.

**★ Great Rose Window**
Best seen at sunset, the 13th-century window shows the Virgin surrounded by the apostles and angel musicians. It is set within a larger window, a feature common in 13th-century architecture.

**The Nave**
Compared with the nave at Chartres (see pp312–15), Reims is taller. Its elegant capitals are decorated with naturalistic floral motifs such as ivy and berries.

WEST FACADE

SOUTH FACADE

## KEY

① **South transept**

② **The clerestory windows** pioneered Gothic tracery by dividing the lights with slender bars of stone, creating a decorative, intersecting pattern.

③ **The radiating chapels** of the apse are supported by flying buttresses and adorned with octagonal pinnacles.

④ **Pinnacles** on the flying buttresses shelter guardian angels, symbolic protectors of the cathedral.

**★ Smiling Angel**
Rich in statuary, Reims is often called "the cathedral of angels." Located above the left (north) portal, this enigmatic angel with unfurled wings is the most celebrated of the many that grace the building.

**★ Gallery of the Kings**
The harmonious west facade, decorated with over 2,300 statues, is the most notable feature at Reims. Fifty-six stone effigies of French kings form the Gallery of the Kings.

## Palais du Tau

The archbishop's palace adjoining the cathedral is named after its T-shaped design, based on early episcopal crosses. (*Tau* is Greek for "T.") The palace, built in 1690 by Mansart and Robert de Cotte, encloses a Gothic Chapel and the 15th-century Salle du Tau, rooms associated with French coronations. On the eve of a coronation, the future king would spend the night in the palace. After being crowned in the cathedral, he held a magnificent banquet in the palace. The Salle du Tau, or banqueting hall, is the finest room in the palace, with a magnificent barrel-vaulted

ceiling and walls hung with 15th-century Arras tapestries. The palace now houses a museum of statuary and tapestries from the cathedral, including a 15th-century tapestry of the baptism of Clovis, the first French Christian king.

Salle du Tau – the banqueting hall

APSE

SIDE SECTION

**Apse Gallery**
The restored *claire-voie* (open work) gallery on the apse is crowned by statues of mythological beasts.

**Chagall Window**
The windows in the axial chapel were designed by the 20th-century artist Marc Chagall and made by local craftsmen. This one depicts the Crucifixion and the Sacrifice of Isaac.

The *sentier touristique*, a walk along the ramparts of Rocroi

# ❸ Vallée de la Meuse

Ardennes. 🚍 9,000. 🚆 Monthermé. 🛈 Rue Jean Baptiste Clément, Monthermé (03 24 54 46 73). 🌐 **tourisme-meuse.com**

The Meuse meanders through the Ardennes among spectacular scenery of wild gorges, woods, and warped rock formations of granite or schist.

Dramatically set on a double meander of the Meuse, **Revin** is a rather unremarkable town in an exceptional site, its Vieille Ville enfolded in the north bend. From the dock, you can see wooded **Mont Malgré Tout** and a route dotted with observation points and steep trails. Just south is **Dames de la Meuse**, a rocky outcrop over the river gorge.

**Monthermé** lies on two banks, with the Vieille Ville clustered on the charming left bank. The rocky gorges around **Roche à Sept Heures** on the far bank entice climbers and hikers. The jagged crest of **Rocher des Quatre Fils d'Aymon** suggests the silhouette of four legendary local horsemen.

# ❹ Rocroi

Ardennes. 🚍 2,400. 🚌 🚆 Monthermé. 🛈 1ter rue du Pavillon (03 24 54 20 06). 🕑 Tue & first Mon of month. 🌐 **otrocroi.com**

Set on the Ardennes plateau, the star-shaped citadel of Rocroi was originally built under Henri II in 1555, and later made impregnable by Vauban in 1675 (*see p226*). The main attraction is the walk along the ramparts from the southern gateway. The nature preserve at Rièzes is home to orchids and carnivorous plants.

# ❺ Charleville-Mézières

Ardennes. 🚍 58,000. 🚆 🚌 🛈 4 pl Ducale (03 24 55 69 90). 🕑 Tue, Thu & Sat. 🌐 **charleville-tourisme.com**

This riverside ford was originally two towns. The medieval citadel of Mézières only merged with the neat Classical town of Charleville in 1966. Mézières has irregular slate-covered houses curving around a bend in the Meuse. Battered fortifications and gateways are visible from avenue de St.-Julien. Tucked into the ramparts is the much remodeled Gothic **Notre-Dame de l'Espérance**.

The centerpiece of Charleville is **place Ducale**, a model of Louis XIII urban planning, echoing place des Vosges in Paris (*see p93*). The poet Arthur Rimbaud was born nearby in 1854. His modest birthplace at No. 12 rue Bérégovoy is still there, along with his childhood home on the Meuse at what is now 7 quai Arthur Rimbaud.

Just along the dockside is the Vieux Moulin, the town house whose view inspired "Le Bateau Ivre," Rimbaud's greatest poem. Inside is the **Musée Rimbaud**, with manuscripts and photographs by the poet.

🏛 **Musée Rimbaud**
Quai Arthur Rimbaud. **Tel** 03 24 32 44 65. **Open** Tue–Sun. **Closed** Jan 1, May 1, Dec 25. 🎟 (free 1st Sun of month).

# ❻ Sedan

Ardennes. 🚍 20,000. 🚆 🚌 🛈 32 rue du Menil (03 24 27 73 73). 🕑 Wed & Sat. 🌐 **tourisme-sedan.fr**

Just to the east of Charleville is the **Château de Sedan**, the largest fortified castle in Europe. There has been a bastion on these slopes since the 11th century, but each Ardennes conflict has spelled a new tier of defences for Sedan.

In 1870, during the Franco-Prussian War, with 700 Prussian cannons turned on Sedan, Napoleon III surrendered, and 83,000 French prisoners were deported to Prussia. In May 1940, after capturing Sedan, German forces reached the French coast a week later.

The seven-storey bastion contains sections dating from medieval times to the 1500s.

The poet Rimbaud, whose birthplace was Charleville, painted by Jef Rosman (1873)

Highlights include the ramparts, the 16th-century fortifications and the magnificent 15th-century eaves in one tower. The **Musée du Château** has a fine collection of armor, brought here by Napoleon Bonaparte. There are also tableaux of wax figures illustrating medieval life.

The bastion is surrounded by 17th-century slate-roofed houses, which hug the banks of the Meuse. These reflect the city's earlier prosperity as a Huguenot stronghold.

🏛 **Musée du Château**
1 pl du Château. **Tel** 03 24 29 98 80.
**Open** daily. 🖼

**Environs**
Farther south is **Fort de Villy-la-Ferté**, one of the few forts on the Maginot Line to have been captured in devastating combat with the enemy in 1940.

Courtyard inside the heavily fortified Château de Sedan

Gargoyle on the Basilique de Notre-Dame de L'Epine

## ❼ Argonne

Ardennes & Meuse. ▦ Châlons.
🚉 Ste.-Menehould. 🛈 5 pl du
Général Leclerc, Ste.-Menehould
(03 26 60 85 83). 🌐 **argonne.fr**

East of Reims, the Argonne is a compact region of picturesque valleys and forests, dotted with priories, trenches, and war cemeteries.

As a wooded border between the rival bishoprics of Champagne and Lorraine, the Argonne was home to abbeys and priories. Now ruined, the Benedictine abbey of **Beaulieu-en-Argonne** boasts a 13th-century wine press and has forest views. Just north is **Les Islettes**, known for its faïence pottery and tiles. The hilly terrain here was a battleground during the Franco-Prussian War and World War I. The disputed territory of **Butte de Vauquois**, north of Les Islettes, bears a war memorial.

## ❽ L'Epine

Marne. ▦ 650. 🚉 Châlons. ▦
🛈 3 quai des Arts, Châlons en
Champagne (03 26 65 17 89).

L'Epine is worth visiting if only for a glimpse of the **Basilique de Notre-Dame de l'Epine**, surrounded by wheatfields. Designed on the scale of a cathedral, this 15th-century Flamboyant Gothic church has been a pilgrimage site since medieval times. Even French kings have come here to venerate a "miraculous" statue of the Virgin.

On the facade, three gabled portals are offset by floating tracery, a gauzy effect reminiscent of Reims Cathedral. All around are gruesome gargoyles, symbolizing evil spirits and deadly sins, chased out by the holy presence within. Unfortunately, the most risqué sculptures were destroyed, judged obscene by 19th-century puritans. The subdued Gothic interior contains a 15th-century rood screen and the venerated statue of the Virgin.

### Champagne Timber Churches

Skirting Lac du Der-Chantecoq lies a region of woodland and water meadows, containing 12 Romanesque and Renaissance half-timbered churches with curious pointed gables and *caquetoirs*, rickety wooden porches. They have intimate and often beautifully carved interiors with stained-glass windows designed in the vivid colors of the School of Troyes. Rural roads link churches at Bailly-le-Franc, Châtillon-sur-Broué, Lentilles, Vignory, Outines, Chavanges, and Montier-en-Der.

The 16th-century timber church in Lentilles

# ⑨ Châlons-en-Champagne

Marne. 🖼 48,000. 🚉 🚌 *i* 3 quai des Arts (03 26 65 17 89). 🔄 Wed, Fri am, Sat, Sun am. 🔲 **chalons-tourisme.com**

Encircled by the River Marne and minor canals, Châlons has a sleepy bourgeois charm thanks to its half-timbered houses and gardens mirrored in canals. Nearby are vineyards producing Blanc de Blancs.

From quai de Notre-Dame there are views of old bridges and the Romanesque towers of **Notre-Dame-en-Vaux**, a masterpiece of Romanesque Gothic. Behind the church is a well-restored medieval quarter and the **Musée du Cloître**, containing the original Romanesque cloisters.

**Cathédrale St.-Etienne**, by the canal, is a cool Gothic affair with a Baroque portal, Romanesque crypt and vivid medieval windows. Beyond is **Le Petit Jard**, riverside gardens overlooking the Château du Marché, and a turreted tollgate built by Henri IV. Excellent river tours of the city are available from the tourist office.

### 🏛 Musée du Cloître de Notre-Dame-en-Vaux
Rue Nicolas Durand. **Tel** 03 26 69 38 53. **Open** Wed–Mon. **Closed** Jan 1, May 1, Nov 1 & 11, Dec 25. 🗟 🗟

# ⑩ Troyes

Aube. 🖼 63,000. 🚉 🚌 *i* 16 rue Aristide Briand (08 92 22 46 09). 🔄 daily. 🔲 **tourisme-troyes.com**

Troyes is a delight, a city of magnificent Gothic churches and charming 16th-century half-timbered houses, in a historical center shaped like a champagne cork. The city is famous for its stained glass and sausages (*andouillettes*), and its hosiery industry and factory outlets.

The battered Flamboyant Gothic west front of the **Cathédrale St.-Pierre-et- St.-Paul** opens on to a splendid vaulted interior. The nave is bathed in mauvish-red rays from

Statuary in the Cathédrale St.-Pierre-et-St.-Paul, Troyes

the 16th-century rose window, complemented by the discreet turquoise of the Tree of Jesse window and the intense blue of the medieval windows of the apse.

Nearby, **Eglise St.-Nizier** glitters in the faded quarter behind the cathedral with its shimmering tiled Burgundian roof. Inside, it is lit by windows in a range of warm mauves and soothing blues.

The Gothic **Basilique St.-Urbain** boasts grand flying buttresses and fine 13th-century windows. **Eglise Ste.-Madeleine** is noted for its elaborate 16th-century rood screen resembling lacy foliage, grapes, and figs. Beyond is a wall of windows in browns, reds, and blues. The quaint ruelle des Chats, a covered passageway, connects rue Charbonnet and rue Champeaux.

Set in one of the best-preserved quarters is the **Eglise**

Rue Larivey, a typical street with half-timbered houses, in Troyes

**St.-Pantaléon**. Its Gothic and Renaissance interior houses an imposing collection of 16th-century statuary and severe *grisaille* windows. The 17th-century **Hôtel de Vauluisant** contains the Musée d'Art Champenois (Regional Art Museum) and the Musée de la Bonneterie, dedicated to hosiery.

### 🏛 Musée d'Art Moderne
14 pl St.-Pierre. **Tel** 03 25 76 26 80. **Open** Tue–Sun. **Closed** public hols. 🗟 🗟

Beside the cathedral, the former episcopal palace is now a museum of modern art, with a sculpture by Rodin and an especially fine collection of Fauvist paintings, as well as other modern art.

### 🏛 Cité du Vitrail
1 rue Roger-Salengro. **Tel** 03 25 42 52 87. **Open** Tue–Sun. **Closed** Jan 1, May 1, Nov 11, Dec 25 & 26.

A short walk from the cathedral, this museum in the 18th-century Hôtel-Dieu presents a collection of stained glass from the Middle Ages to the present day.

### 🏛 Hôtel du Petit Louvre
Rue de la Montée St.-Pierre. Courtyard only **Open** daily.

Set off quai Dampierre, this well-restored *hôtel particulier* boasts a fish-scale roof, medieval tower, Renaissance courtyard, staircase, and well. The highlight is a facade adorned with quizzical multicolored faces.

## Environs
The city's green playground, **Lac et Forêt d'Orient**, is 24 km (15 miles) east of Troyes. The forest is dotted with marshes, nature preserves, and smaller lakes. Lac d'Orient, the largest artificial lake in Europe, is popular for sailing, with water-skiing on Lac Amance and fishing at Lac du Temple.

## ⓫ Chaumont
Haute-Marne. 🗺 26,000. 🚆 🚌 7 av du Général de Gaulle (03 25 03 80 80). 🛒 Wed & Sat. 🌐 **tourisme-chaumont-champagne.com**

As the former residence of the Counts of Champagne, this feudal town enjoyed great prestige in the 13th century. On the far side of a ravine, the old town is on a rocky spur, with the Palais de Justice and the medieval castle keep dominating.

The keep is a reminder that this quiet administrative center had a formidable past. This impression is confirmed by the Renaissance town houses, which are bulging with *tourelles d'escaliers*, turreted staircases.

**Basilique St.-Jean-Baptiste**, a grey-stone Champenois church, is the most remarkable monument in Chaumont. The interior is enlivened by a spider's web of vaulting, a striking turreted staircase and Renaissance galleries. Near the entrance is a tiny chapel containing an unsettling *Mise au Tombeau* (1471), an intense multicolored stone group of ten mourners gathered around Christ laid out on a shroud in his tomb. In the left transept is a bizarre but beguiling *Tree of Jesse*. On this ill-lit Renaissance stone relief, a family tree sprouts from the sleeping Jesus.

## Environs
Twenty-three kilometres (14 miles) northwest of Chaumont, **Colombey-les-Deux-Eglises** will forever be associated with General Charles de Gaulle (1890–1970). The de Gaulles bought their home, **La Boisserie**, in 1933, but had to

**Cathédrale St.-Mammès in Langres**

abandon it during the war, when it was badly damaged. After its restoration, de Gaulle would return to La Boisserie from Paris on the weekends to write his memoirs. He died here on November 9, 1970. The house is now a museum.

In the village churchyard, the General lies in a simple tomb, but a giant granite cross of Lorraine, erected in 1972, dominates the skyline. At its foot is the **Mémorial**, a museum dedicated to de Gaulle's life.

### 🏛 La Boisserie
Colombey-les-Deux-Eglises. **Tel** 03 25 01 52 52. **Open** daily (Oct–Mar: Wed–Mon). **Closed** mid-Dec–Jan. 🖼 ♿

### 🏛 Mémorial Charles de Gaulle
**Tel** 03 25 30 90 80. **Open** Oct–Apr: Wed–Mon. **Closed** Jan, Dec 24, 25, & 31. 🖼
🌐 **memorial-charlesdegaulle.fr**

## ⓬ Langres
Haute-Marne. 🗺 9,000. 🚆 🚌 🎫 square Olivier Lahalle (03 25 87 67 67). 🛒 Fri. 🌐 **tourisme-langres.com**

Set on a rocky spur, Langres lies beyond Chaumont, in the backwaters of southern Champagne. This ancient bishopric was one of the gateways to Burgundy and the birthplace of the encyclopedist Denis Diderot (1713–84). Langres promotes itself as a land of springs, claiming that its proximity to the sources of the Seine and Marne grant it mystical powers.

Virtually the whole town is enclosed by medieval ramparts, Langres's undoubted attraction. A succession of towers and parapets provide glimpses of romantic town gates and sculpted Renaissance mansions, with panoramic views of the Marne Valley, the Langres plateau, the Vosges, and, on a clear day, even Mont Blanc.

Near Porte Henri IV is the much-remodeled **Cathédrale St.-Mammès**. The gloomy vaulted interior, in Burgundian Romanesque style, is redeemed by the sculpted capitals in the apse, reputedly taken from a temple of Jupiter. The town's Musée d'Art et d'Histoire has some interesting collections.

Langres's lively summer season includes historical re-enactments, theater and fireworks.

**Memorial to General de Gaulle at Colombey-les-Deux-Eglises**

# ALSACE AND LORRAINE

*Meuse · Meurthe-et-Moselle · Moselle · Vosges · Haut-Rhin · Bas-Rhin*

As border regions, Alsace and Lorraine have been fought over for centuries by France, Austria, and Germany, their beleaguered past recalled by many a military stronghold and cemetery. Today, the region presents only a peaceful aspect with pastel-painted villages, fortified towns, and sleepy vineyards.

At the northeast frontier of France, bordered by the Rhine, Alsace forms a fertile watershed between the mountains of the Vosges and the Black Forest in Germany. Lorraine, with its rolling landscape on the other side of the mountains, is the poorer cousin but is more overtly French in character.

## Embattled Territory

Caught in the wars between France and Germany, Alsace and part of Lorraine have changed nationality four times since 1871. Centuries of strife have made border citadels of Metz, Toul, and Verdun in Lorraine, while Alsace abounds with castles, from the faithfully reconstructed Haut-Koenigsbourg to

Saverne's ruined fortress, built to guard a strategic pass in the Vosges. However, the area has a strong identity of its own, taking pride in local costumes, traditions, and dialects. In Alsace, Route des Vins vineyards nudge pretty villages in the Vosges foothills. Strasbourg, the capital, is a cosmopolitan city with a 16th-century center, while Nancy, Lorraine's historical capital, represents elegant 18th-century architecture.

Much of the attraction of this region lies in its cuisine. Lorraine offers beer and quiche lorraine. In Alsace, cozy *winstubs*, or wine cellars, serve sauerkraut and flowery white wines, such as Riesling and Gewurztraminer. There are also fine restaurants here.

Villagers enjoying the view from their window in Hunspach, north of Strasbourg, in the northern Vosges

◄ Half-timbered houses lining the canals of Petite Venise, Colmar

# Exploring Alsace and Lorraine

Visitors seeking art and architecture will be amply rewarded by the charming medieval towns and excellent city museums of the region. Undiscovered Lorraine is the place to clamber over military citadels, walk in unspoiled countryside, and unwind at relaxing spas. By contrast, Alsace offers magnificent forests, rugged mountain drives in the Vosges, quaint villages, and rich wines. The Route des Vins *(see pp236–7)* is one of the region's many scenic routes. It is particularly popular during the wine harvest festivities but is worth visiting in any season.

## Sights at a Glance

1. Verdun
2. Toul
3. Metz
4. Nancy
5. Gérardmer
6. Mulhouse
7. Guebwiller
8. Neuf-Brisach
9. Eguisheim
10. Colmar
11. Riquewihr
12. Ribeauvillé
13. Château du Haut-Koenigsbourg
14. Sélestat
15. Obernai
16. Strasbourg
17. Saverne
18. Betschdorf

Field of sunflowers just outside the village of Turckheim

0 kilometers   20

0 miles   10

**For keys to symbols** *see back flap*

The picturesque village of Riquewihr on the Route des Vins

## Getting Around

There are good roads and train links between Strasbourg, Colmar, Metz, and Nancy, and on to Switzerland and Germany. The main highways to and through the regions are the N4, A31, A35, A4 to Paris and N59, and the tunnel under the Vosges. The spectacular journey over the Vosges and along the Route des Vins is best made by car or on organized trips from Colmar or Strasbourg. The TGV link to the region from Paris takes 2 hours 20 minutes.

### Key

— Freeway
— Highway
— Secondary road
— Minor road
— Scenic route
—— Main railroad
--- Minor railroad
▬▬ International border
— Regional border
△ Summit

The Ossuaire de Douaumont, a sentinel for the regiments of crosses on the battlefields of Verdun

# ❶ Verdun

Meuse. 🚊 21,000. 🚌 🚏 *i* pl de la Nation (03 29 86 14 18). 🕑 Fri.
**w** verdun-tourisme.com

Verdun will be forever remembered for the horrors of the 1916 Battle of Verdun, when about a million men died in almost a whole year of continuous bloodshed that is considered the worst single battle of the Great War. The Germans intended to strike a blow at French morale by destroying the forts of Douaumont and Vaux (which had been built to prevent a repeat of the humiliating French defeat of the Franco-Prussian War of 1870) and capture Verdun, France's northeastern stronghold. The French fought simply to prevent the town being taken. The stalemate and the killing continued here right up to the end of the war, and not until 1918 did the Germans draw back from their positions just 3 miles (5 km) from the town.

Several poignant museums, memorials, battle sites, and cemeteries can be visited in the hills just outside Verdun on the north side. In this devastated region, nine villages were obliterated without trace. The **Musée-Memorial de Fleury** tells their story. Nearby, the **Ossuaire de Douaumont** contains the unidentified bones of over 130,000 French and German dead. One of the most striking monuments to the Battle of Verdun is Rodin's memorial in Verdun itself. It depicts the winged figure of

Victory unable to soar triumphant because she has become caught in the remains of a dead soldier.

The town of Verdun was heavily fortified over the centuries. The crenellated **Porte Chaussée**, a medieval river gateway, still guards the eastern entrance to the town and is the most impressive of the remaining fortifications.

Although battered by war damage, the **Citadelle de Verdun** retains its 12th-century tower, the only relic from the original abbey that Vauban incorporated into his new military design. Now a war museum, the **Citadelle Souterraine**, it recreates Verdun's role in World War I. The citadel casemates come to life as grim trenches, and the presentation ends by showing how the "Unknown Soldier" was chosen for the symbolic tomb under the Arc de Triomphe in Paris *(see p111)*.

The town center is dominated by the cathedral, where Romanesque elements were rediscovered after the 1916 bombardments.

The 16th-century cloisters of Eglise St.-Gengoult in Toul

🏛 **Citadelle Souterraine**
Ave du Soldat Inconnu **Tel** 03 29 84 84 42. **Open** daily. **Closed** Dec 24–late Jan. 🚫 ♿

# ❷ Toul

Meurthe-et-Moselle. 🚊 17,000.
🚌 🚏 *i* 1 pl Charles de Gaulle (03 83 64 90 60). 🕑 Wed, Fri & Sat.
**w** lepredenancy.fr

Lying within dark forests west of Nancy, the octagonal fortress city of Toul is encircled by the Moselle and the Canal de la Marne. Along with Verdun and Metz, Toul was one of the 4th-century bishoprics. In the early 18th century, Vauban built the citadel, from which the ring of defensive waterways, the octagonal city ramparts, and the **Porte de Metz** remain.

The **Cathédrale St.-Etienne**, begun in the 13th century, took over 300 years to build. It suffered damage in World War II but the purity of the Champenois style has survived, notably in the arched, high-galleried interior. The imposing Flamboyant Gothic facade is flanked by octagonal towers. Rue du Général-Gengoult, behind the Gothic **Eglise St.-Gengoult**, contains a clutch of sculpted Renaissance houses. North of the city the local "gray" Côtes de Toul wines are produced.

**Environs**
South of Toul, near the town of Neufchâteau, is the birthplace of Joan of Arc at Domrémy-La-Pucelle. Next door to the house where she was born

is an exhibition about her remarkable life.

The vast **Parc Régional de Lorraine** takes in red-tiled cottages, vineyards, forests, cropland, *chaumes* (high pasture-land), marshes, and lakes. Inns in the area are especially noted for their quiche lorraine and *potée lorraine*, a bacon casserole.

*Jupiter Slaying a Monster* on the Column of Merten in La Cour d'Or

## ❸ Metz

Moselle. 🚂 125,000. ✈ 🚊 🚌 *i* pl d'Armes (03 87 39 00 00). 🛒 Tue, Thu & Sat. 🖥 tourisme.metz.fr

An austere yet appealing city, Metz sits at the confluence of the Moselle and the Seille. Twenty bridges crisscross the rivers and canals, and there are pleasant walks along the banks. This Gallo-Roman city, now the capital of Lorraine, has always been a pawn in the game of border chess – annexed by Germany in 1871, regained by France in 1918.

Set on a hill above the Moselle, the **Cathédrale St.-Etienne** overlooks the historic center. Inside, there are stained-glass windows, including some by Marc Chagall.

To the northwest of the cathedral, a narrow wooden bridge leads across to the island of Petit Saulcy, site of the oldest French theater still in use. Located on the other side of the cathedral, the **Porte des Allemands**, spanning a river, resembles a medieval castle because of its bridge, defensive towers, and 13th-century gate with pepper-pot towers.

In the Vieille Ville, the delightful place St.-Louis is bordered by arcaded 14th-century mansions. **Eglise St.-Pierre-aux-Nonnains** claims to be one of France's oldest churches. The external walls and facade date from Roman times, while much of the rest belongs to the 7th century. Nearby is the 13th-century **Chapelle des Templiers**, built by the Knights Templar; it can be visited by guided tour.

### 🏛 Centre Pompidou Metz
1 parvis des Droits de l'Homme. **Tel** 03 87 15 39 39. **Open** Wed–Mon. **Closed** May 1. 🖼 🛗 🖊 📷

This museum is an annex to the Centre Pompidou in Paris *(see pp96–7)*. Modern European art is displayed inside an unusual hexagonal building.

### 🏛 Musée de la Cour d'Or
2 rue du Haut-Poirier. **Tel** 03 87 20 13 20. **Open** Wed–Mon. **Closed** public hols. 📷

Also known as the Musée d'Art et d'Histoire, this is set in the Petits-Carmes, a deconsecrated 17th-century monastery incorporating Gallo-Roman baths and a medieval barn. On display are Merovingian stone carvings; Gothic painted ceilings, and a variety of German, Flemish, and French paintings.

### White Storks

The white stork, traditionally a symbol of good fortune in Alsace, used to be a frequent sight in northeast France. White storks spend the winter in Africa but migrate north to breed. However, the gradual draining of marshy ground, pesticides, and electric cables have threatened their survival here. A program to reintroduce them to the area has set up breeding centers, as at Molsheim and Turckheim, which means that these striking birds can once again be seen in Alsace-Lorraine.

The 13th-century Chapelle des Templiers, with restored frescoes, in Metz

Place Stanislas in Nancy, with statue of Stanislas Leczinski, Duke of Lorraine and father-in-law of Louis XV

# ❹ Nancy

Meurthe-et-Moselle. 🗺 105,000. ✈
🚉 🚌 🚶 14 pl Stanislas (03 83 35 22 41). 🏛 Tue–Sat. 🌐 nancy-tourisme.fr

Lorraine's historic capital backs on to the Canal du Marne and the River Meurthe. In the 18th century, Stanislas Leczinski, Duke of Lorraine (*see p306*), transformed the city, making it a model of 18th-century town planning.

Nancy's second golden age was the turn of the 20th century, when glassmaker Emile Gallé founded the Ecole de Nancy, a forerunner of the Art Nouveau Movement in France.

Nancy's principal and most renowned landmark is **place Stanislas**. Laid out in the 1750s, this elegantly proportioned square is enclosed by highly ornate gilded wrought-iron gates and railings, which have been beautifully restored. Lining the square are fine *hôtels particuliers* (town houses) and chic restaurants.

An Arc de Triomphe leads to Place de la Carrière, a gracious, tree-lined square. At the far end, flanked by semicircular arcades, is the Gothic **Palais du Gouvernement**. Next door in the Parc de la Pépinière is Rodin's statue of Claude Lorrain, the landscape painter, born near Nancy.

Grande Rue provides a glimpse of medieval Nancy. Of the original fortifications the only remaining one is the Porte de la Craffe, which was used as a prison after the Revolution.

## 🏛 Eglise et Couvent des Cordeliers et Musée Régional des Arts et Traditions Populaires

64 & 66 Grande Rue. **Tel** 03 83 32 18 74. **Open** Tue–Sun. **Closed** Jan 1, Easter Sun, May 1, Jul 14, Nov 1, Dec 25. 🖼

The dukes of Lorraine are buried in the crypt, and the adjoining converted monastery contains the Musée Régional des Arts et Traditions Populaires, covering folklore, furniture, costumes, and crafts.

## 🏛 Musée des Beaux-Arts

3 pl Stanislas. **Tel** 03 83 85 30 72. **Open** Wed–Mon. **Closed** some public hols. 🖼♿🅿

A renovation and modern extension have enabled 40 percent more of the museum's remarkable collection of 14th- to 20th-century European art to be seen, including works by Delacroix, Manet, Monet, Utrillo, and Modigliani. The Daum glassware is stunning.

## 🏛 Musée Historique Lorraine

Palais Ducal, 64 Grande Rue. **Tel** 03 83 32 18 74. **Closed** for renovation until 2020. 🖼

The Museum of the History of Lorraine has a rich collection of archeological finds, sculptures, and paintings, including two by Georges de la Tour.

## 🏛 Musée de l'Ecole de Nancy

36–38 rue de Sergent Blandan. **Tel** 03 83 40 14 86. **Open** Wed–Sun. **Closed** Jan 1, May 1, July 14, Nov 1, Dec 25. 🖼🅿

Exhibits in reconstructed Art Nouveau settings include furniture, fabrics, and jewelry, as well as the fanciful glassware of Emile Gallé, founder of the Ecole de Nancy.

Arc de Triomphe in place Stanislas, leading to place de la Carrière

Vosges landscape seen from the Route des Crêtes

## The Route des Crêtes

This strategic mountain road, 52 miles (83 km) long, connects the Vosges valleys from Col du Bonhomme to Cernay, east of Thann, often through woodland. Hugging the western side of the Vosges, the Route des Crêtes was created during World War I to prevent the Germans from observing French troop movements. When not shrouded in mist, there are breathtaking views over Lorraine from its many "ridges" (*crêtes*).

*For hotels and restaurants in this region see pp558 and pp582–3*

# ❺ Gérardmer

Vosges. 🚇 10,000. 🚌 🚠 𝒊 4 pl
des Déportés (03 29 27 27 27). 🛍 Thu
& Sat. 🆆 **gerardmer.net**

Nestling on the Lorraine side
of the Vosges, on the shore of a
magnificent lake stretching out
before it, Gérardmer is a setting
rather than a city. In November
1944, just before its liberation,
Gérardmer was razed by the
Nazi scorched-earth policy, but
has since been reconstructed.
Sawmills and woodcarving
remain local trades, though
tourism is fast replacing the
textile industry.

Gérardmer is now a popular
vacation destination. In winter,
the steep slopes of the Vosges
Cristallines around the town
turn it into a ski resort, while
the lake is used for watersports
in summer. The town's
attractions also include
lakeside walks and boat trips,
as well as Géromée cheese,
similar to the more famous
Munster, from just over the
Alsatian border. Gérardmer
also boasts the oldest tourist
information office in the
country, dating from 1875.

The scenic drives and
mountain hikes in the Vosges
attract adventurous visitors.
Most leave the lakeside bowl
to head for the Alsatian border
and the magnificent **Route
des Crêtes**, which can be
joined at the mountain pass
of Col de la Schlucht.

Recreating village crafts in the Ecomusée d'Alsace in Ungersheim

# ❻ Mulhouse

Haut-Rhin. 🚇 115,000. ✈ 🚆 🚌
𝒊 1 av Robert Schuman (03 89 35
48 48). 🛍 Tue, Thu & Sat.
🆆 **tourisme-mulhouse.com**

Close to the Swiss border,
Mulhouse is an industrial city,
which was badly damaged in
World War II. However, there
are technical museums and
shopping galleries, as well as
Alsatian taverns and Swiss wine
bars. Most visitors use the city as
a base for exploring the rolling
hills of the Sundgau on the
Swiss border.

Of the museums, **Musée
de l'Impression sur Etoffes**, at
14 rue Jean-Jacques Henner, is
devoted to textiles and fabric
painting, while **Musée Français
du Chemin de Fer**, at 2 rue

Alfred Glehn, has a collection of
steam and electric locomotives.
A revamped **Cité de l'Automobile**, at 15 rue de l'Epée,
boasts over 100 Bugattis, a
clutch of Mercedes and Ferraris,
and Charlie Chaplin's Rolls-
Royce. In the Renaissance
former town hall, on place
de la République, is
the **Musée Historique**.

Alsatian black pig in the Ecomusée d'Alsace
in Ungersheim

### Environs

At Ungersheim, north of
Mulhouse, the **Ecomusée
d'Alsace** displays and preserves
the region's rural heritage. The
12th-century fortified house from
Mulhouse is a dramatic building,
complete with Gothic garden.
Farms are run along traditional
lines, with livestock such as the
Alsatian black pig. Rural crafts can
be seen in their original settings.

🏛 **Ecomusée d'Alsace**
Chemin du Grosswald. **Tel** 03 89 74
44 74. **Open** Tue–Sun (Jun–Aug: daily).
**Closed** Jan, Mar, Dec. 🅿 ♿ 📷
🆆 **ecomusee.alsace**

The lake at Gérardmer, offering sport and leisure activities

# ❼ Guebwiller

Haut-Rhin. 🗺 12,000. 🚌 ℹ️ 71 rue de la République (03 89 76 10 63). 🗓 Tue & Fri. 🌐 **tourisme-guebwiller.fr**

Surrounded by vineyards and flower-filled valleys, Guebwiller is known as "the gateway to the valley of flowers." However, as an industrial town producing textiles and machine tools, it feels cut off from this rural setting. The *caves* and churches make it worth a visit.

Set on a pretty square, **Eglise Notre-Dame** combines Baroque theatricality with Neoclassical elegance, while **Eglise des Dominicains** boasts Gothic frescoes and a fine rood screen. **Eglise St.-Léger**, the richly decorated Romanesque church, is the most rewarding, especially the facade, triple porch, and portal.

Eglise St.-Léger in Guebwiller

**Environs**

The scenic Lauch valley, northwest of Guebwiller, is known as "Le Florival" because of its floral aspect. **Lautenbach** is used as a starting point for hikes through this recognized *zone de tranquillité*. The village has a pink Romanesque church, with a portal depicting human passion and the battle between Good and Evil. The square leads to the river, a small weir, *lavoir* (public washing place), and houses overhanging the water.

# ❽ Neuf-Brisach

Haut-Rhin. 🗺 2,100. 🚌 ℹ️ Palais du Gouverneur, 6 pl d'Armes (03 89 72 56 66). 🗓 Sat. 🌐 **tourisme-paysrhin brisach.com**

Located near the German border, this octagonal citadel is the military strategist Vauban's masterpiece. Built between 1698 and 1707, the citadel forms a typical star-shaped pattern, with symmetrical towers enclosing 48 equal squares. In the center, from where straight streets radiate for ease of defense, is

## The Citadel of Neuf-Brisach

**The outer ring** of defenses was built around two moats.

Porte de Bâle

**Place d'Armes**, once the parade ground, provided the innermost refuge.

**Porte de Strasbourg** was originally protected by a drawbridge.

Bastion

**The fortress** is divided into 48 *ilôts* or squares.

**The Porte de Belfort** houses the Musée Vauban. A walk links Porte de Belfort with Porte de Colmar.

**The fortress walls** are 30 ft (9 m) high and 14.5 ft (4.5 m) wide at their base.

Porte de Colmar

The celebrated Issenheim altarpiece by Matthias Grünewald in Colmar

place d'Armes and the Eglise St.-Louis, which was added in 1731–6. This was the usual homage to Louis XV, implying that the church was dedicated to the king, rather than the saint.

The Porte de Belfort houses the **Musée Vauban**, which includes a model of the town, showing the outlying defenses, now concealed by woodland. They represent Vauban's barrier to the fortress, and it is to his credit that the citadel was never taken.

🏛 **Musée Vauban**
Pl Porte de Belfort. **Tel** 03 89 72 03 93.
**Open** May–Sep: Wed–Mon; Oct–Apr: groups only, by appt.

## 🔵 Eguisheim

Haut-Rhin. 🚹 1,600. 🚌
ℹ 22a Grand'Rue (03 89 23 40 33).
🌐 ot-eguisheim.fr

Eguisheim is an exquisite small town, laid out within three concentric rings of 13th-century ramparts. The ensemble of austere fortifications and elegance within makes for a surprisingly harmonious whole.

In the center of town is the octagonal feudal **castle** of the Counts of Eguisheim. A Renaissance fountain in front has the statue of Bruno Eguisheim, born here in 1002. He became Pope Léon IX and was later canonized.

The Grand'Rue is lined with half-timbered houses. Close to the castle is the **Marbacherhof**, a monastic tithe barn and corn hall. On a neighboring square,

the modern parish church retains the original Romanesque sculpted tympanum.

The rest of the town has its share of Hansel-and-Gretel atmosphere, while inviting courtyards offer tastings of *grands crus*. From rue de Hautvilliers, outside the ramparts, a marked path leads through scenic vineyards.

## 🔟 Colmar

Haut-Rhin. 🚹 68,000. 🚉 🚌
ℹ Rue Unterlinden (03 89 20 68 92).
🗓 Mon, Wed, Thu & Sat.
🌐 **tourisme-colmar.com**

Colmar is the best-preserved city in Alsace. As a trading post and river port, it had its heyday in the 16th century, when wine merchants shipped their wine along the waterways running through the picturesque canal quarter, now known as **Petite Venise**. "Little Venice" is best seen on a leisurely boat trip that takes you from the tanners' quarter to

rue des Tanneurs. The adjoining place de l'Alsacienne Douane is dominated by the **Koifhüs**, a galleried customs house with a Burgundian tiled roof, overlooking half-timbered pastel houses sporting sculpted pillars.

Nearby, place de la Cathédrale quarter is full of 16th-century houses. **Eglise St.-Martin**, essentially Gothic, has a noted south portal. To the west, the place des Dominicains, with busy cafés, is dwarfed by the Gothic **Eglise Dominicaine**. Inside is *La Vierge au Buisson de Roses* (1473), the red-and-gold "Virgin of the Rosebush" by Martin Schongauer, a renowned painter and native son of Colmar.

Place d'Unterlinden, the adjoining square, has the **Musée d'Unterlinden**. In a Dominican monastery, it displays early Rhenish paintings. The highlight is the Issenheim altarpiece. A masterpiece of emotional intensity, it is part of an early 16th-century Alsatian panel painting by Matthias Grünewald. A three-storey wing houses modern and contemporary art.

In the historic center, the quaint rue des Têtes has the former wine exchange, a Renaissance townhouse known as the Maison des Têtes because of the grimacing heads on the gabled facade. And in rue Mercière, **Maison Pfister**, with its slender stair turret and galleried flower-decked facade, has come to typify the city.

The **Musée Bartholdi**, on rue des Marchands, is devoted to Colmar-born Frédéric-Auguste Bartholdi, designer of the Statue of Liberty.

Along Quai de la Poissonnerie in the Petite Venise area of Colmar

## ⓫ Riquewihr

Haut-Rhin. 🏘 1,300. 🚌 ℹ️ 2 rue de la 1ère Armée (03 89 73 23 23). 🗓 Fri.
🌐 ribeauville-riquewihr.com

Vineyards run right up to the ramparts of Riquewihr, the prettiest village on the Route des Vins *(see pp236–7)*. Deeply pragmatic, Riquewihr winemakers plant roses at the end of each row of vines – both for their pretty effect and as early detectors of parasites. The village belonged to the counts of Wurttemberg until the Revolution and has grown rich on wine, from Tokay and Pinot Gris to Gewurztraminer and Riesling. Virtually an open-air museum, Riquewihr abounds in cobblestone alleys, geranium-clad balconies, galleried courtyards, romantic double ramparts, and watchtowers.

From the Hôtel de Ville, **rue du Général de Gaulle** climbs gently past medieval and Renaissance houses, half-timbered, stone-clad, or corbelled. Oriel windows vie with sculpted portals and medieval sign boards. On the right lies the idyllic **place des Trois Eglises**. A passageway leads through the ramparts to the vineyards on the hill. Farther up lies the **Dolder**, a 13th-century belfry, followed by the **Tour des Voleurs** (both are museums, the latter with a medieval torture chamber), marking the second tier of ramparts. Beyond the gateway is the **Cour des Bergers**, gardens laid out around the 16th-century ramparts. Visitors outnumber the locals in summer or during the superb Christmas market.

The pretty – and popular – village of Riquewihr, set among vineyards

## ⓬ Ribeauvillé

Haut-Rhin. 🏘 5,000. 🚗 🚌
ℹ️ 1 Grand'Rue (03 89 73 23 23).
🗓 Fri & Sat. 🌐 ribeauville-riquewihr.com

Overlooked by three ruined castles, Ribeauvillé is stiflingly prettified, as may be expected from a favored town on the Route des Vins. This status is partly due to healthy sales of the celebrated *grands crus* of Alsace, especially Riesling. There are ample opportunities for tastings, particularly near the park, in the lower part of town *(see p236)*.

On Grand'Rue (No. 14) is the **Pfifferhüs**, the minstrels' house. As locals declare, Ribeauvillé is the capital of the *kougelhopf*, the almond-flavored Alsatian cake.

Tortuous alleys wind past steep-roofed artisans' and *vignerons'* houses in the upper part of the town. Beyond are Renaissance fountains, painted facades, and **St.-Grégoire-le-Grand**, the Gothic parish church. A marked path, which begins in this part of town, leads into the vineyards.

## ⓭ Château du Haut-Koenigsbourg

Orschwiller, Bas-Rhin. **Tel** 03 69 33 25 00. **Open** daily. **Closed** Jan 1, May 1, Dec 25. 🚫 📷 ♿ 🏛 🚭
🌐 haut-koenigsbourg.fr

Looming above the pretty village of St.-Hippolyte, this castle is the most popular attraction in Alsace. In 1114, the Swabian Emperor, Frederick of Hohenstaufen, built the first Teutonic castle here, which was destroyed in 1462. Rebuilt and added to under the Habsburgs, it burned down in 1633. At the end of the 19th century, Kaiser Wilhelm II commissioned Berlin architect Bodo Ebhardt to restore the castle. The result of his painstaking work was a precise reconstruction of the original building.

With a drawbridge, fierce keep, and rings of fortifications, this warm sandstone hybrid is a sophisticated feudal château.

The Cour d'Honneur is a breathtaking recreation, with a pointed corner turret and creaky arcaded galleries. Inside are gloomy "Gothic" chambers and "Renaissance" rooms. La Grande Salle is the most far-fetched, with a Neo-Gothic gallery and ornate paneling. From the battlements, almost 2,500 ft (760 m) above the Alsace plain, stretches a Rhineland panorama, bordered by the Black Forest and the Alps. On the other side are views from the high Vosges to villages and vineyards below.

Upper garden

West bastion

West wing

Outer walls

Chapelle St.-Sébastien outside Dambach-la-Ville, along the Route des Vins

## ⓮ Sélestat

Bas-Rhin. 🚉 17,000. 🚉 🚌 ℹ️ Commanderie Saint Jean, bd du Général Leclerc (03 88 58 87 20). 🏛 Tue, Sat. W selestat-haut-koenigsbourg.com

During the Renaissance, Sélestat was the intellectual center of Alsace, with a tradition of humanism fostered by Beatus Rhenanus, a friend of Erasmus. The **Bibliothèque Humaniste** has a collection of editions of some of the earliest printed books, including the first book to name America, in 1507. Nearby are the Cour des Prélats, a turreted ivy-covered mansion, and the Tour de l'Horloge, a clocktower. **Eglise Ste.-Foy** is 12th century, with an octagonal bell tower. Opposite is **Eglise St.-Georges**, glittering with green and red "Burgundian tiles."

### 🏛 Bibliothèque Humaniste

1 rue de la Bibliothèque.
**Tel** 03 88 58 07 20.
**Closed** until mid-2018 due to major reconstructiion.
🗺 W bibliotheque-humaniste.eu

## Environs

Medieval **Dambach-la-Ville**, another pretty town, is linked to Andlau and red-tiled Itterswiller by a delightful rural road through vineyards.

**Ebersmunster**, a picturesque hamlet, has an onion-domed abbey church, with a Baroque interior that is a sumptuous display of gilded stucco.

## ⓯ Obernai

Bas-Rhin. 🚉 11,000. 🚉 🚌 ℹ️ pl du Beffroi (03 88 95 64 13). 🏛 Thu.
W tourisme-obernai.fr

At the north end of the Route des Vins, Obernai retains a flavor of authentic Alsace: Alsatian is spoken, at festivities women wear traditional dress, and church services are well attended in the cavernous Neo-Gothic **Eglise St.-Pierre-et-St.-Paul**. Place du Marché is well preserved and features the gabled

Young *Alsaciens* in traditional costume

**Halle aux Blés**, a 16th-century corn hall (now a restaurant) above a former butcher's shop, with a facade adorned with cows' and dragons' heads. Place de la Chapelle, the adjoining square, has a Renaissance fountain and the 16th-century **Hôtel de Ville** and the **Kapellturm**, the galleried Gothic belfry. Side streets have Renaissance and medieval timber-framed houses. A stroll past the cafés on rue du Marché ends in a pleasant park by the ramparts.

## Environs

Odile, Alsace's 7th-century patron saint, was born in Obernai, but she is venerated on **Mont Sainte-Odile**, to the west.

**Molsheim**, a former bishopric and fortified market town 6 miles (10 km) north, is noted for its Metzig, a Renaissance-style butchers' guildhall.

**Le Mémorial de l'Alsace-Moselle** at Schirmeck commemorates the 10,000 who died at the Struthof concentration camp across the valley.

North wing, with kitchens

South wing, with chapel

Entrance ramp to upper castle

Hostelry

Outer walls

Guardroom

Entrance

Well tower

Drawbridge within the walls of Château du Haut-Koenigsbourg

# ⑯ Strasbourg

Halfway between Paris and Prague, Strasbourg is not surprisingly often known as "the crossroads of Europe". The city wears its European cosmopolitanism with ease – after all, its famous cathedral has catered to both Catholic and Protestant congregations – and as one of the capitals of the European Union has sensibly located the futuristic European Parliament building some way from the historic center. One of the ways to see this, along with the more traditional city sights, is to take a boat trip along the waterways encircling the Old Town. On the way you will take in the Ponts-Couverts, covered bridges linked by medieval watchtowers that provide an observation point for the four Ill canals, and the scenic Petite France, once the tanners' district, dotted with mills and crisscrossed by bridges.

Pont-Couvert, linked by medieval watchtowers

The central portal of the west facade of the cathedral

### ⬆ Cathédrale Notre-Dame

A masterpiece of stone lacework, the sandstone cathedral "rises like a most sublime, wide-arching tree of God", as Goethe marveled. Though construction began in the late 11th century (the choir is Romanesque, the nave is Gothic), it ended only in 1439, with the completion of the west facade, begun in 1277. The three portals are ornamented with statues. But the crowning glory is the rose window. The south portal leads to the Gothic Pillar of Angels

(around 1230), set beside the Astronomical Clock: mechanical figures appear accompanied by chimes at 12:31pm. There are wonderful views over the city from the viewing platform, and on some summer evenings there are organ concerts.

In place de la Cathédrale, **Maison Kammerzell**, now a popular restaurant, was once a rich merchant's mansion, its highly elaborate, carved facade, dating from the mid-15th to late-16th centuries.

### 🏛 Palais Rohan

2 pl du Château. **Tel** 03 68 98 51 60. **Open** Wed–Mon. **Closed** Jan 1, Good Fri, May 1, Nov 1 & 11, Dec 25. 📷 ♿ Ⓦ musees.strasbourg.eu

Designed by the king's architect, Robert de Cotte, in 1730, this grand Classical palace was intended for the prince-bishops of Strasbourg. It houses three museums: the Musée des Beaux-Arts; the Musée Archéologique; and the Musée des Arts Décoratifs, which contains the sumptuous State Apartments and one of the finest collections of ceramics in France.

*For hotels and restaurants in this region see p558 and pp582–3*

The Musée d'Art Moderne et Contemporain on Strasbourg's waterfront

### Strasbourg City Center

① Cathédrale Notre-Dame
② Maison Kammerzell
③ Palais Rohan
④ Musée Historique
⑤ Musée Alsacien
⑥ Musée de l'Oeuvre Notre-Dame
⑦ Musée d'Art Moderne et Contemporain

0 meters 250
0 yards 250

### 🏛 Musée de l'Oeuvre Notre-Dame

3 pl du Château. **Tel** 03 68 98 51 60.
**Open** Tue–Sun. **Closed** Jan 1, Good Fri, May 1, Nov 1, Dec 25. 🔲 ground fl.

The cathedral's impressive museum contains much of its original sculpture, as well as magnificent 11th-century stained glass. This somber gabled house also displays a collection of Medieval and Renaissance Alsatian art.

### 🏛 Musée d'Art Moderne et Contemporain

1 pl Hans-Jean Arp. **Tel** 03 68 98 51 55. **Open** Tue–Sun. **Closed** Jan 1, Good Fri, May 1, Nov 1 & 11, Dec 25.

Adrien Fainsilber's cultural flagship for the 21st century is a marvel of glass and light (particularly at night, when it appears to float on the river). Its superb collections run from 1860 to 1950 (modern) and from 1950 onward (contemporary). The Art Café is a welcome respite for art-weary feet.

### 🏛 Musée Historique

2 rue du Vieux-Marché-aux-Poissons. **Tel** 03 68 98 51 60. **Open** Tue–Sun. **Closed** Jan 1, Good Fri, May 1, Nov 1 & 11, Dec 25.

The museum occupies the 16th-century city abattoir and focuses on Strasbourg's political and military history.

### 🏛 Musée Alsacien

23 quai St.-Nicolas. **Tel** 03 68 98 51 52. **Open** Wed–Mon. **Closed** Jan 1, Good Fri, May 1, Nov 1, Dec 25.

Housed in a series of inter-connecting Renaissance buildings, the museum has fascinating exhibits on local traditions and popular arts and crafts.

### 🏛 MM Park Museum

4 rue Gutenberg, La Wantzenau 67610. **Tel** 03 88 59 25 43. **Open** daily. **Closed** Jan 1, Dec 25.

The largest private collection of World War II artifacts in Europe is housed here, 7.5 miles (12 km) north of Strasbourg. The collection includes around 120 vehicles, about 400 male and female uniforms, and numerous weapons. A highlight are the objects and documents from the 1944 Sussex Plan to spy on Nazi troops before and after the D-Day landings.

**For keys to symbols** *see back flap*

# The Alsace Route des Vins

Meandering over 110 miles (180 km) from Marlenheim to Thann, the picturesque wine route takes in historic towns with cobble-stone streets, medieval timber-framed houses, and Renaissance fountains. Romantically appointed *winstubs,* or cellars, offer traditional *choucroute garnie* and flowery white Alsatian wines. Dedicated wine lovers could spend two or three days covering the route at leisure, or may want to make shorter trips in either direction to or from Colmar. For a refreshing contrast from the unremitting charm of the towns and villages, escape occasionally into *sentiers viticoles* – lovely paths through the vineyards themselves.

Harvesting grapes in Alsace

① **Molsheim** Renaissance build and Riesling viney vie for attention w Bugatti motor mu

② **Obernai** The galleried Kapellturm in place du Marché dates from the 13th to 16th centuries.

③ **Dambach-la-Ville** Vintne carts now serve as decoration in this pretty medieval town, which is renowned for its *gra cru* Frankstein.

④ **Ribeauvillé** Famed for its Riesling, the town celebrates Pipers' Day, the first Sunday in September, with a fountain spouting free wine.

⑤ **Riquewihr** A showcase of medieval and Renaissance houses, this is one of France's most-visited towns.

⑥ **Turckheim** Ancient buildings encircle place Turenne in this Renaissan town, which is famous for Brand wine.

⑦ **Eguisheim** This ancient town ringed by medieval houses produces two *grands crus,* Eichberg (Oak Hill) and Pfersigberg (Peach Hill).

⑧ **Guebwiller** Eglise St.-Léger dates from the Middle Ages, when Guebwiller grew rich on wine. Today it is a busy textile town.

**Key**

▬ Wine route

═ Other roads

0 kilometers 5
0 miles 5

## ce Wine

e wines are usually aromatic,
nd full-bodied. All are white
ot Pinot Noir, used for light reds.

-harvested Alsatian classic

## y Facts

**Location and climate**
Protected by the Vosges, Alsace has a
rm climate and France's lowest
ual rainfall.

**Grape varieties**
Alsace wines are known simply by
their grape variety.
*wurztraminer*, with its exotic
e-petal character, is most
ically Alsatian, although the
*sling* is arguably the finest.
*scat* is another aromatic
iety. Spicy but less assertive
n Gewurztraminer, *Pinot Gris*
d the crisper, dry *Pinot Blanc*
well with food. *Pinot Noir* is
only red variety.
usciously rich, sweet,
-harvested wines are an
ace specialty.

**st producers**

Albert Boxler,
Marcel Deiss, Rolly
Gassmann, Beyer, Meyer-
Fonne, Kuentz-Bas,
Domaine Weinbach,
Dopff & Irion, Olivier
d-Humbrecht, Charles
léret, Domaines Schlumberger,
maine Ostertag, Domaine
mbach, Hugel & Fils, Cave de
ckheim.

**Good vintages**
2015, 2012, 2010, 2008,
2004, 2001, 1998, 1996.

The 12th-century chapel of the Château du Haut-Barr, near Saverne

## 🔟 Saverne

Bas-Rhin. 🏘 12,000. 🚊 🚌 🛈 37
Grand'Rue (03 88 91 80 47). 🗓 Tue &
Thu. 🌐 tourisme-saverne.fr

Framed by hills, and located on the River Zorn and the Marne–Rhine canal, Saverne is a pretty sight. The town was a fief of the prince-bishops of Strasbourg, and its sandstone Château des Rohan was a favorite summer residence. Today, it houses the **Musée du Château de Rohan-Pontivy**, with a collection tracing Saverne's past. On the far side of the château, the Grand'Rue is studded with restaurants and timber-framed Renaissance houses.

### 🏛 Musée du Château de Rohan-Pontivy

Château des Rohan. **Tel** 03 88 71 63 95. **Open** Jan–mid-Jun & mid-Sep–Dec: Mon–Fri pm, 10am–6pm Sat & Sun; mid-Jun–mid-Sep: 10am–noon & 2–6pm daily. **Closed** Tue. 🎟 ♿ restricted.

### Environs
To the southwest, perched on a rocky spur, the ruined **Château du Haut-Barr** – the "Eye of Alsace" – once commanded the pass of Col de Saverne. In **Marmoutier**, 4 miles (6 km) south, is an abbey church with a Romanesque-Lombard facade and octagonal towers.

## 1️⃣8️⃣ Betschdorf

Bas-Rhin. 🏘 4,000. 🛈 1 rue des Francs, La Mairie (03 88 54 48 00).
🌐 betschdorf.com

The vibrant village of Betschdorf borders the Forêt de Haguenau, 28 miles (45 km) north of Strasbourg. Many residents occupy timber-framed houses dating from the 18th century, when pottery made the village prosperous. Generations of potters have passed down the knowledge of the characteristic blue-gray glaze to their sons, while the women have been entrusted with decorating it in cobalt blue. A pottery museum, with a workshop attached, displays rural ceramics. Betschdorf

Betschdorf pottery

is a good place to try *tartes flambées* – hot, crispy bases topped with cheese or fruit.

### Environs
Another pottery village, **Soufflenheim**, lies 6 miles (10 km) southeast. Its earth-colored pottery is usually painted with bold flowers. To the north, close to the German border, the picturesque town of **Wissembourg** has many half-timbered houses and the second-largest church in Alsace after Strasbourg Cathedral, Eglise St.-Pierre et St.-Paul.

*For hotels and restaurants in this region see pp558 and pp582–3*

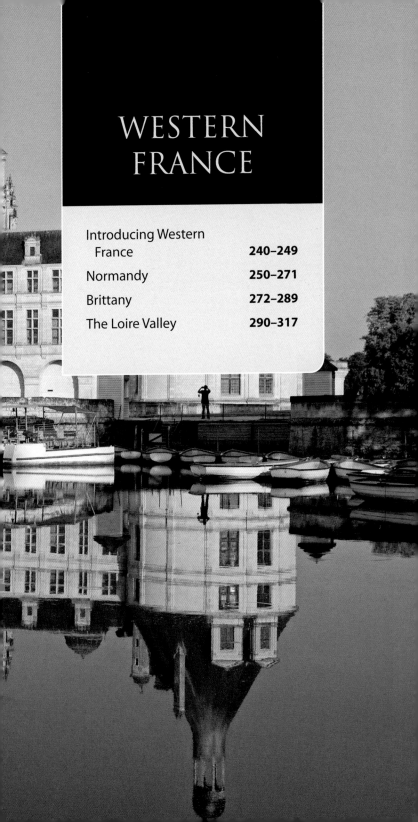

# WESTERN FRANCE

Introducing Western
  France                         **240–249**

Normandy                   **250–271**

Brittany                      **272–289**

The Loire Valley        **290–317**

# Introducing Western France

The western regions of France have played very different historical roles, from the royal heartland of the Loire Valley to separatist Celtic Brittany. These are mainly rich farming regions, with fishing important along the coasts. Heavy industry and oil refineries are concentrated around Rouen and Le Havre. Visitors come for the wonderful beaches, quiet rural byways, and the sumptuous Loire châteaux. This map shows some of the region's most celebrated sights.

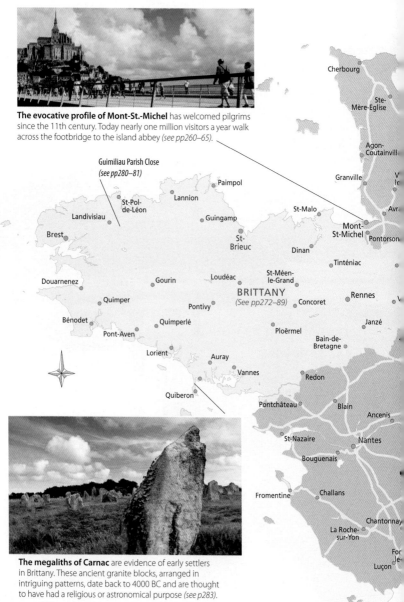

**The evocative profile of Mont-St.-Michel** has welcomed pilgrims since the 11th century. Today nearly one million visitors a year walk across the footbridge to the island abbey *(see pp260–65).*

Guimiliau Parish Close
*(see pp280–81)*

Cherbourg

Ste-Mère-Eglise

Agon-Coutainvill

Granville

V le

Paimpol

Lannion

St-Pol-de-Léon

St-Malo

Avr

Landivisiau

Guingamp

St-Brieuc

Mont-St-Michel

Pontorson

Brest

Dinan

Tinténiac

Douarnenez

Gourin

Loudéac

St-Méen-le-Grand

BRITTANY
*(See pp272–89)*

Concoret

Rennes

Quimper

Pontivy

Bénodet

Quimperlé

Janzé

Pont-Aven

Ploërmel

Bain-de-Bretagne

Lorient

Auray

Vannes

Redon

Quiberon

Pontchâteau

Blain

Ancenis

St-Nazaire

Nantes

Bouguenais

Fromentine

Challans

Chantonnay

La Roche-sur-Yon

For le-

Luçon

**The megaliths of Carnac** are evidence of early settlers in Brittany. These ancient granite blocks, arranged in intriguing patterns, date back to 4000 BC and are thought to have had a religious or astronomical purpose *(see p283).*

◄ Château de Chambord, reflected in the River Cossan

**The Bayeux Tapestry** (see pp256–7) shows William the Conqueror's invasion of England from the French point of view. Among its 58 scenes, key events such as the Battle of Hastings in 1066 are depicted with great vigor and finesse. Here, two of William's messengers are shown hurrying to meet him.

Le Tréport

Rouen Cathedral
(see pp268–9)

Dieppe

St-Valery-
en-Caux

Tôtes

Etretat

Yvetot

Harfleur

Rouen

Honfleur

Elbeuf

ux

Ouistreham

Caen

Lisieux

Bernay

Vernon

Évreux

Falaise

NORMANDY
(See pp250–71)

L'Aigle

Chartres Cathedral
(see pp312–15)

Verneuil-
sur-Avre

Dreux

front

Sées

Mortagne-
au-Perche

Chartres

Alençon

yenne

Evron

La Ferté-
Bernard

Pithiviers

Châteaudun

Montargis

Le Mans

St-Calais

Orléans

Ecommoy

Beaugency

La Flèche

Château-
Renault

THE LOIRE VALLEY
(See pp290–317)  Briare

Cheverny

Tours

Saumur

Loches

Vierzon

La Charité

Le Mans Cathedral
(see p295)

Châtillon-sur-
Indre

Issoudun

Bourges

Château de Villandry
(see p300)

Châteauroux

St-Amand-
Mont-Rond

Château de Chenonceau
(see pp302–3)

Argenton-
sur-Creuse

**Château de Chambord** is the largest and most extravagant of the Loire châteaux (see pp306–7). François I transformed the original hunting lodge into a luxurious moated castle in 1519. Its splendor was completed by Louis XIV in 1685. Inside the 440 rooms are François's salamander emblem and 365 fireplaces, one for every day of the year.

0 kilometers          50

0 miles          50

# The Flavors of Western France

The Atlantic coast, the rich agricultural hinterland of dairy farms, orchards, and vegetable fields, and the rivers of the Loire Valley combine to produce some of France's best-loved food. Vegetables are grown in abundance in Brittany and the alluvial soils of the Loire, and the orchards of Normandy are bountiful. Fish from the windswept coast of Brittany or the channel ports of Normandy play a key role in the cuisine. Hearty meat dishes range from the celebrated Rouen duck to rabbit and game of the Sologne in the Loire. Fine cheeses are made here, and butter is the favored cooking medium.

Normandy apples

Norman cheese producer displaying his wares

## Normandy

Normandy's lush green pastures, dotted with brown-and-white cows, and orchards heavy with apples, make it a great source of veal, milk, cheese, cream, butter, apples, and pears. Duck is a specialty, as is *pre-salé* lamb from the salt-rich marshes around Mont-St.-Michel. Many vegetables are grown, and wild mushrooms thrive in the damp meadows and woodlands in autumn. Fish is important, with catches of sole, plaice and mackerel, skate and herrings, and 80 percent of France's scallops, plus a great variety of shellfish.

Camembert is Normandy's most famous cheese; others include Pont l'Evêque, the pungent-smelling Livarot, rich Brillat-Savarin and Petit-Suisse, a small, fresh white cheese eaten with sugar. Apples symbolize Normandy above all, and cider is traditionally drunk with food, while Calvados, the fiery apple brandy, is served with meals as *le trou normand*.

## Brittany

Thousands of miles of coastline yield an abundance of fish and shellfish. Oysters are highly prized, as are mussels, harvested

Artichokes    Asparagus    Watercress    Shallots    Broccoli    Radishes
Some of the favorite vegetables of western France

## Regional Dishes and Specialties

Fish dominates the menus here, most spectacularly in the *plateau de fruits de mer*, featuring oysters, crabs, langoustines, shrimps, cockles, and clams, piled on a bed of ice. Oysters are served simply with lemon or shallot vinegar, but can also come stuffed, gratinéed, or wrapped in pastry. Fresh fish may be grilled, baked in sea salt (*sel de Guérande* is the best), braised in cider or served with *beurre blanc* ("white butter" sauce with shallots, wine vinegar, and cream). Lobster is often served *à l'armoricaine*. Cotriade, the Breton fish stew, combines a selection of the catch of the day with onions and potatoes. *Moules marinières* (mussels steamed in white wine with shallots and butter) is the popular classic. As a change from fish, look for *gigot de sept heures* – lamb slowly pot-roasted for seven hours.

Pears

**Homard à l'armoricaine**
Lobster, served in a herby tomato-and-onion sauce, enriched with brandy.

Superb Breton oysters for sale at a regional fish market

both wild and cultivated. Other fish caught include monkfish, tuna, sardines, scallops, and lobster. Pig-rearing is important, so expect roast pork, smoked sausages, hams, and *boudin noir* (blood sausage), delicious served with apples. A great delicacy is the *pre-salé* lamb from Ile de Ouessant, served with haricot beans. Artichokes are the symbol of Brittany, an indication of the importance of vegetables, especially winter produce such as cauliflower, onions, and potatoes.

*Crêpes* (pancakes), both sweet and savory, are a key element of the Breton diet. They come as buckwheat *galettes* with savory fillings such as ham, cheese, spinach, or mushrooms, or as lacy, light dessert versions with sweet fillings and known as *crêpes dentelles* (*dentelle* meaning "lace").

## The Loire Valley

This huge region takes pride in a truly diverse range of specialties. Grass-fed cattle are raised in Anjou, and sheep are bred in the Berry region. Excellent free-range chickens, *poulet fermier*

Cheese and charcuterie at Loches market in the Loire Valley

*Loué*, are raised in Touraine and the Orléanais. The forests and lakes of the Sologne yield deer, wild boar, pheasant, partridge, hare, and duck. *Charcuterie* includes *rillettes* (shredded and potted pork) and ham from the Vendée. The Atlantic coast produces a variety of fish and the Loire itself is a source of pike, shad, tench, salmon, eels, and lampreys. Mushrooms are cultivated in the limestone caves around Saumur, but of the many vegetables grown, the best of all is Sologne asparagus. Superb goat's cheeses include Sainte-Maure de Touraine, ash-coated Valençay, and the little Crottins de Chavignol.

### ON THE MENU

**Alose à l'oseille** Shad in a sorrel sauce.

**Côte de veau vallée d'Auge** Veal in mushrooms, cream, and cider or Calvados.

**Far aux pruneaux** Egg batter pudding baked with prunes.

**Kig ha farz** Meat-and-vegetable hotpot with buckwheat dumpling.

**Marmite Dieppoise** Assorted fish stewed in cider or white wine with cream.

**Tergeule** Creamy baked rice pudding with cinnamon.

**Tripes à la Mode de Caen** Tripe with calves' feet, onions or leeks, herbs, and cider.

**Sole Normande** Baked sole in sauce of egg and cream, garnished with mussels, oysters, mushrooms, and shrimps.

**Canard á la rouennaise** Duclair duck, part-roasted then finished in a rich sauce of duck liver and shallots.

**Tarte Tatin** Caramelized upside-down apple tart, originally made at the Hotel Tatin in the Loire Valley.

# France's Wine Regions: the Loire

With a few exceptions, the Loire is a region of good rather than great wines. The fertile agricultural soils of the meandering flatlands of the "Garden of France" are fine for fruit and vegetables, less so for the production of great wines. The cool, northern, Atlantic-influenced climate nonetheless produces refreshing reds and summer rosés, both dry and lusciously sweet white wines, and attractively bracing sparkling wines. Very much in the majority here, and usually intended for early consumption, are the dry white wines, so vintages in the Loire tend to matter less than in the classic red wine regions.

**Locator Map**

▦ Loire wine region

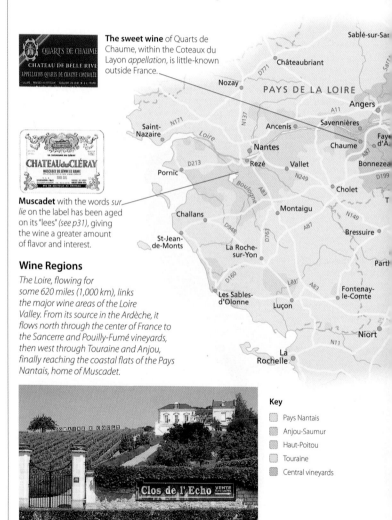

**The sweet wine** of Quarts de Chaume, within the Coteaux du Layon *appellation*, is little-known outside France.

**Muscadet** with the words *sur lie* on the label has been aged on its "lees" *(see p31)*, giving the wine a greater amount of flavor and interest.

## Wine Regions

*The Loire, flowing for some 620 miles (1,000 km), links the major wine areas of the Loire Valley. From its source in the Ardèche, it flows north through the center of France to the Sancerre and Pouilly-Fumé vineyards, then west through Touraine and Anjou, finally reaching the coastal flats of the Pays Nantais, home of Muscadet.*

Map labels: Sablé-sur-Sar, Châteaubriant, Nozay, PAYS DE LA LOIRE, Angers, Saint-Nazaire, Ancenis, Savennières, Faye d'A., Chaume, Nantes, Rezé, Vallet, Bonnezea, Pornic, Cholet, Challans, Montaigu, Bressuire, St-Jean-de-Monts, La Roche-sur-Yon, Parth, Les Sables-d'Olonne, Fontenay-le-Comte, Luçon, Niort, La Rochelle

**Key**

▦ Pays Nantais

▦ Anjou-Saumur

▦ Haut-Poitou

▢ Touraine

▦ Central vineyards

Clos de l'Echo, Chinon, producer of fine, herbaceous red wine

0 kilometers 15

0 miles 15

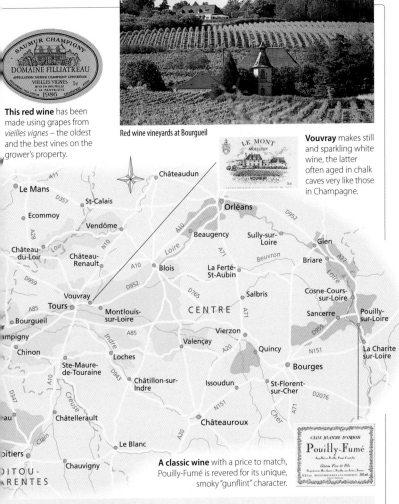

**This red wine** has been made using grapes from *vieilles vignes* – the oldest and the best vines on the grower's property.

Red wine vineyards at Bourgueil

**Vouvray** makes still and sparkling white wine, the latter often aged in chalk caves very like those in Champagne.

**A classic wine** with a price to match, Pouilly-Fumé is revered for its unique, smoky "gunflint" character.

## Key Facts About Loire Wines

**Location and Climate**
Fertile agricultural soils support fruit, vegetables, and cereals; the poorer soils support grapes. The climate is cool, influenced by the Atlantic, giving the wines a refreshing acidity.

**Grape Varieties**
The *Melon de Bourgogne* makes simple, dry white wines. The *Sauvignon* makes gooseberryish, flinty dry whites, finest in Sancerre and Pouilly-Fumé but also good in Touraine. The *Chenin Blanc* makes dry and medium Anjou, Savennières, Vouvray, Montlouis, and Saumur, sparkling Vouvray and Saumur, and the famous sweet whites, Bonnezeaux,

Vouvray, and Quarts de Chaume. Summery reds are made from the *Gamay* and the fruity, herbaceous *Cabernet Franc*.

**Good Producers**
*Muscadet*: Sauvion, Guy Bossard, Michel Brégeon. *Anjou, Savennières, Vouvray*: Richou, Ogereau, Nicolas Joly, Huet, Domaine des Aubuissières, Bourillon Dorléans, Jacky Blot, François Pinon. *Touraine (white)*: Pibaleau. *Saumur-Champigny (red)*: Filliatreau, Château du Hureau. *Chinon, Bourgueil*: Couly-Dutheil, Frédéric Mabileau. *Sancerre, Pouilly-Fumé, Ménétou-Salon*: François Cotat, Vacheron, Mellot, Vincent Pinard.

# From Defense to Decoration

The great châteaux of the Loire Valley gradually evolved from purely defensive structures to decorative palaces. With the introduction of firearms, castles lost their defensive function and comfort and taste predominated. Defensive elements such as towers, battlements, moats, and gatehouses were retained largely as symbols of rank and ancestry. Renaissance additions, from galleries to dormer windows, added elegance.

Salamander emblem of François I

Slate and stone walls

**Angers** *(see p295)*, a fortress built from 1230 to 1240 by Louis IX, stands on a rocky hill in the town center. In 1585, Henri III removed the pepper-pot-shaped towers from 17 fortifications which were formerly 98 ft (30 m) high.

Fortifications with pepper-pot towers removed

Circular tower, formerly defensive

Corbeled walkways, once useful in battle

**Chaumont** *(see p310)* was rebuilt in 1445–1510 in Renaissance style by the Amboise family. Although it has a defensive appearance, with circular towers, corbeled walkways, and a gatehouse, these are mainly decorative. It was restored after around 1833.

Decorated turret

**Azay-le-Rideau** *(see p300)*, regarded as one of the most elegant and well-designed Renaissance châteaux, was built from 1518 to 1527 by finance minister Gilles Berthelot and his wife Philippa Lesbahy. It is a mixture of traditional turrets with Renaissance pilasters and pinnacles. Most dramatic is the interior staircase with its three stories of twin bays and an intricately decorated pediment.

Renaissance carved windows

Pilasters (columns)

Dormer windows

Cylindrical tower

**Ussé** *(see p299)* was built in 1462 by Jean de Bueil as a fortress with parapets containing openings for missiles, battlements, and gunloops. The Espinay family, chamberlains to both Louis XI and Charles VIII, bought the château and changed the walls overlooking the main courtyard to Renaissance style with dormer windows and pilasters. In the 17th century the north wing was demolished to create palatial terraces.

# Breton Traditions

Brittany was christened Breiz Izel (Little Britain) by the Welsh and Cornish migrants who fled here in the 5th and 6th centuries AD and imposed their customs, language, and religion on the local Gauls. Brittany resisted Charlemagne, the Vikings, the Normans, English alliances, and even French rule until 1532. Today, Breton is taught in some schools, and a busy calendar keeps Brittany in touch with its past and with other Celtic regions.

**Breton music** has strong Celtic links. Instruments including the *biniou*, similar to the bagpipes, and the oboe-like *bombarde*, are often heard at local festivals.

Bigouden lace headdresses

A **pardon** is an annual religious festival honoring a local saint. The name derives from the granting of indulgences to pardon the sins of the past year. Some *pardons*, such as those at Ste.-Anne d'Auray and Ste.-Anne-la-Palud, still attract thousands of pilgrims, who carry banners and holy relics through the streets. Most *pardons* take place between April and September.

Lace *coiffe*

Embroidered apron

Small headdress

Baggy Breton trousers

Felt hat

**Breton costumes**, still seen at *pardons* and weddings, varied, as each area had distinctive headdresses or *coiffes*. Artists such as Gauguin often painted the costumes. There are good museum collections in Quimper *(see p278)* and Pont l'Abbé in Pays Bigouden *(see p277)*.

# Brittany's Coastal Wildlife

With its granite cliffs, sweeping bays, rias, and deep estuaries, the Brittany coastline contains a wealth of varied wildlife habitats. Parts of the coast have a tidal range of more than 150 ft (50 m), the highest in France, and this great variation in sea level divides marine life into several distinct zones. Most of the region's famous shellfish, including mussels, clams, and oysters, live on the lower shore, either on rocks or in muddy sand, where they are submerged for most of the day. Higher zones are the preserve of limpets and barnacles, and several kinds of seaweed, which can survive out of the water for long periods. Above the sea, towering cliffs offer a nursery for seabirds and a foothold for many kinds of wild flowers.

Cliffs at the Pointe du Raz, Brittany

The Ile de Bréhat at low tide

## Features of the Coast

This scene shows some of the wildlife habitats found on the Brittany coastline. When exploring the shore, make a note of the tide times, particularly if you plan to walk along the foot of the cliffs.

**Dunes**, where marram grass grows, stabilize the sand.

**Mud and sand** is inhabited by clams and cockles, which filter food from the water.

**Rock stacks** provide secure nurseries for nesting seabirds.

**Salt-marsh** flowers are a their best in late summer

## Oyster Beds

Like most marine molluscs, oysters begin their lives as tiny floating larvae. The first step in *ostréiculture*, or oyster cultivation, consists of providing the larvae with somewhere to settle, which is usually a stack of submerged tiles. The developing oysters are later transferred to beds and left to mature before being collected for the market.

Oyster beds at Cancale

**Clifftop turf** often contains a narrow band of wild flowers sandwiched between fields and the sea.

**Rock pools** are flooded twice daily by the tide. They are inhabited by fish, molluscs, sea anemones, and sponges.

## Coastal Wildlife

The structure of this shore determines the wildlife that lives on it. In a world beset by wind and waves, rocks provide solid anchorage for plants and a secure habitat for many small animals. Muddy sand is rich in nutrients, and has a greater abundance of life – although most of this is concealed beneath the surface.

### Cliffs

**The rock dove** is a cliff-dwelling ancestor of the well-known city pigeon.

**Thrift** is a common spring flower, found on exposed ledges near the sea.

### Rocks and Rock Pools

**Seaweed** of many different varieties is exposed each day by the falling tide.

**The limpet**, a slow-moving creature, scrapes tiny plants from the rock surface.

**The goby**, with its sharp eyesight, dashes for cover at the first sign of movement above.

### Mud and Sand

**Crabs** live at many different water depths. Some species are extremely good swimmers.

**Cockles** live in large numbers just beneath the surface of muddy sand.

**The curlew** has a forceps-like curved beak for extracting shell-fish from mud and sand.

# NORMANDY

*Manche · Calvados · Orne · Seine-Maritime · Eure*

The quintessential image of Normandy is of a lush, pastoral region of apple orchards, contented cows, cider, and pungent cheeses – but the region also spans the windswept beaches of the Cotentin and the wooded banks of the Seine Valley. Highlights include the great abbey churches of Caen, the mighty island of Mont-St.-Michel, and Monet's garden at Giverny.

Normandy gets its name from the Viking Norsemen who sailed up the River Seine in the 9th century. Pillagers-turned-settlers, they made their capital at Rouen – today a cultured cathedral city that commands the east of the region. Here the Seine meanders seaward past ancient abbeys at Jumièges and St.-Wandrille to a coast that became an open-air studio for Impressionist painters during the mid- and late 19th century.

North of Rouen are the chalky cliffs of the Côte d'Albâtre. The mood softens at the port of Honfleur and the elegant resorts of the Côte Fleurie to the west. Inland lies the Pays d'Auge, with its half-timbered manor houses and patch-eyed cows. The western half of Normandy is predominantly rural, a *bocage* countryside of small,

high-hedged fields with windbreaks composed of beech trees.

The modern city of Caen is worth visiting for its two great 11th-century abbey churches built by William the Conqueror and his queen, Matilda. Close by, in Bayeux, the story of William's invasion of England is told in detail by the town's famous tapestry. Memories of another invasion, the D-Day landings of 1944, still linger along the Côte de Nacre and the Cotentin Peninsula. Thousands of Allied troops poured ashore on to these magnificent beaches in the closing stages of World War II. The Cotentin Peninsula is capped by the port of Cherbourg, still a strategic naval base. At its western foot stands one of France's greatest attractions: the monastery island of Mont-St.-Michel.

Half-timbered manor house in the village of Beuvron-en-Auge, near Lisieux

◀ The harbor at Honfleur, Calvados

# Exploring Normandy

Normandy's rich historical sights and diverse landscape make it ideal for touring by car or bicycle. Rewarding coastal drives and good beaches can be found along the windswept Côte d'Albâtre and the Cotentin Peninsula. Farther south is one of France's most celebrated sights, Mont-St.-Michel. Inland, follow the meanders of the Seine Valley, passing cider orchards and half-timbered houses along the way, to visit historic Rouen and Monet's garden at Giverny.

Apple trees in blossom in the Pays d'Aug

**Key**

══ Freeway

── Highway

── Secondary road

┄┄ Minor road

── Scenic route

┅┅ Main railroad

── Minor railroad

══ Regional border

The Côte d'Albâtre coastline

## Sights at a Glance

❶ Cotentin
❷ Cherbourg
❸ Coutances
❹ Granville
❺ Avranches
❻ Mont-St.-Michel
   (see pp260–65)
❼ Côte de Nacre
❽ Bayeux
❾ Caen
❿ Suisse Normande
⓫ Parc Naturel Régional
   de Normandie-Maine
⓬ Côte Fleurie
⓭ Pays d'Auge
⓮ Honfleur
⓯ Le Havre
⓰ Côte d'Albâtre
⓱ Dieppe
⓲ Basse-Seine
⓳ Rouen
⓴ Haute-Seine
㉑ Giverny
㉒ Evreux

**For keys to symbols** *see back flap*

## Getting Around

Access to and through the region from Calais is quick and direct on the A16, which links up with the A28–A29 and A13 freeways to Paris, and runs west to Caen, and beyond on the A84. There are also highway and rail links to the cross-Channel ports of Dieppe, Le Havre, Caen (Ouistreham), and Cherbourg. Travel by public transportation beyond these arteries is limited. The region is threaded with minor roads, particularly delightful in the Pays d'Auge and Cotentin Peninsula. The main airports are at Rouen, Le Havre, and Caen.

Le Tréport

Calais

Biville-sur-Mer

Gamaches

DIEPPE 17

A28

Offranville

Londinières

Saint-Valery-en-Caux

16

D925

Béthune

Longueville-sur-Scie

Aumale

COTE D'ALBATRE

Fécamp

D20

Doudeville

N27

A29

CHANNEL

Etretat

D926

Fauville-en-Caux

Yerville

Totes

Neufchâtel-en-Bray

D915

Goderville

D929

A28

Buchy

Bolbec

Yvetot

Clères

A29

Harfleur

Caudebec-en-Caux

Pavilly

Gournay-en-Bray

HAVRE 15

A131

BASSE-SEINE

18

A151

A150

N31

HONFLEUR

14

Jumièges

19 ROUEN

Reims

FLEURIE

St-Martin-de-Boscherville

Lyons-la-Forêt

Trouville-sur-Mer

A13

Boos

12

Deauville

HAUTE

20

Étrépagny

Houlgate

Pont-l'Évêque

Pont-Audemer

HAUTE-SEINE

D6014

Gisors

Beuvron-en-Auge

Cormeilles

Elbeuf

NORMANDIE

Les Andelys

Lisieux

Brionne

Louviers

Seine

13

D613

PAYS D'AUGE

Bernay

Le Neubourg

A28

N154

A13

cœur

Saint-Pierre-sur-Dives

D438

D840

D613

Vernon

21 GIVERNY

Paris

Livarot

Orbec

Broglie

ÉVREUX 22

N13

Pacy-sur-Eure

Vimoutiers

Conches-en-Ouche

Saint-André-de-l'Eure

D916

La Neuve-Lyre

Eure

Gacé

D830

D840

N154

Ivry-la-Bataille

Argentan

L'Aigle

Nonancourt

Paris

Le Merlerault

D926

Verneuil-sur-Avre

N12

D958

Château d'O

Moulins-la-Marche

Paris

Mortrée

Courtomer

Tourouvre

MANDIE-MAINE

Sées

Mortagne-au-Perche

acelle

N12

Le Mêle-sur-Sarthe

Rémalard

N12

Alençon

A28

Mamers

Bellême

D338

Le Mans

| 0 kilometers | 25 |
| 0 miles | 25 |

The town of Les Andelys, shrouded in mist

Rugged cliffs on the Cotentin Peninsula

# ❶ Cotentin

Manche. ✈ 🚉 🚌 ⛴ Cherbourg.
🛈 2 quai Alexandre III, Cherbourg
(02 33 93 52 02).
Ⓦ **manchetourisme.com**

Thrusting into the English
Channel, the Cotentin Peninsula
has a landscape similar to
Brittany's. Its long sandy beaches
have wild and windblown headlands around Cap de la Hague and
Nez de Jobourg. The latter is
popular among birdwatchers –
gannets and shearwaters fly by
in large numbers. Along the east
coast stretches Utah Beach, where
American troops landed as part
of the Allied invasion on June 6,
1944. Inland, Ste.-Mère-Eglise
commemorates these events with
its **Musée Airborne** (Airborne
Troops Museum). Just outside Ste.-
Mère-Eglise, the **Ferme-Musée du
Cotentin** has farm animals and
activities, which give an insight
into rural life in the early 1900s,
while farther north, in the market
town of Valognes, the **Musée
Régional du Cidre et du Calvados**
celebrates the thriving local talent
for making cider and Calvados.

Two fishing ports command
the Peninsula's northeast corner:
Barfleur and St.-Vaast-la-
Hougue, the latter famous for
oysters and a base for boat trips
to the Ile de Tatihou. The Val de
Saire is ideal for a scenic drive,
with a viewpoint at La Pernelle,
the best place to survey the
coast. On the west side of the
Peninsula, warmed by the Gulf
Stream, the resort of Barneville-
Carteret offers sandy beaches
and summer boat trips to the
Channel Islands. The low-lying,
marshy landscape east of

Carentan forms the heart of
the Parc Régional des Marais
du Potentin et du Bessin.

🏛 **Musée Airborne**
14 rue Eisenhower, Ste.-Mère-Eglise.
**Tel** 02 33 41 41 35. **Open** Feb–Nov:
daily. **Closed** Jan & Dec. 🅿 ♿
Ⓦ **airborne-museum.org**

🏛 **Ferme-Musée du Cotentin**
Rte de Beauvais, Ste.-Mère-Eglise. **Tel**
02 33 95 40 20. **Open** Jul–Aug: daily;
Apr–Jun, Easter & Nov school
vacations: Sun–Fri pms only.
**Closed** May 1. 🅿 ♿

🏛 **Musée Régional du Cidre
et du Calvados**
Rue du Petit-Versailles, Valognes.
**Tel** 02 33 40 11 55 (Office du
Tourisme). **Open** Apr–Sep: Wed–Sun
pms only (Jun–Aug: Mon–Sat & Sun
pm). 🅿

# ❷ Cherbourg

Manche. 🏙 44,000. ✈ 🚉 🚌 ⛴
🛈 2 quai Alexandre III (02 33 93 52 02).
🗓 Tue, Thu & Sat. Ⓦ **cherbourg
tourisme.com**

Cherbourg has been a strategic
port and naval base since the
mid-19th century. The French
Navy still uses its harbors, as do
transatlantic ships and ferries
from England and Ireland. For a

Cherbourg town center

good view of the port, drive to
the hilltop **Fort du Roule**, which
houses the **Musée de la
Libération**, recalling the D-Day
invasion and the subsequent
liberation of Cherbourg. Most
activity is centered on the flower-
filled market square, place
Général de Gaulle, and along
shopping streets such as rue
Tour-Carrée and rue de la Paix.
The fine art in the **Musée Thomas-
Henry** includes 17th-century
Flemish works, and portraits by
Jean François Millet, born in
Gréville-Hague. **Parc Emmanuel
Liais** has small botanical gardens
and a densely packed **Musée
d'Histoire Naturelle**.

The **Cité de la Mer**, a
bilingual center, has a deep-
sea aquarium, the world's
largest visitable submarine,
and other wonders.

🏛 **Musée de la Libération**
Fort du Roule. **Tel** 02 33 20 14 12.
**Open** Tue–Fri, Sat & Sun pms.
**Closed** public hols. 🅿

🏛 **Musée Thomas-Henry**
Espl. de la Laïcité. **Tel** 02 33 23 39 30.
**Open** Tue–Fri, Sat & Sun pms. ♿

🏛 **La Cité de la Mer**
Gare Maritime Transatlantique.
**Open** Feb & Apr–Oct: daily; Mar, Nov
& Dec: Tue–Sun. **Closed** Jan, Dec 25.
**Tel** 02 33 20 26 69. 🅿 🖉 📷 ♿
Ⓦ **citedelamer.com**

# ❸ Coutances

Manche. 🏙 12,000. 🚉 🚌 🛈 pl
Georges Leclerc (02 33 19 08 10).
🗓 Thu. Ⓦ **tourisme-coutances.fr**

From Roman times until the
Revolution, the hilltop town of
Coutances was the capital of
the Cotentin. The slender
**Cathédrale Notre-Dame**, a fine
example of Norman Gothic
architecture, has a soaring
217-ft (66-m) lantern
tower. Founded in the
1040s by Bishop
Geoffroi de Montbray,
it was financed by the
local de Hauteville
family using money
gained in Sicily, where
they had founded a
kingdom a few years
earlier. The town was
badly damaged during

World War II, but the cathedral, the churches of St. Nicholas and St. Peter, and the beautiful public gardens with their rare plants, all survived.

The back of Coutances Cathedral with its squat lantern tower

## ❹ Granville

Manche. 🗺 14,000. 🚃 🚌 🚢 ℹ 4 cours Jonville (02 33 91 30 03). 🗓 Sat. 🌐 ville-granville.fr

Ramparts enclose the upper town of Granville, which sits on a spur overlooking the Baie du Mont-St.-Michel. The walled town was developed from fortifications built by the English in 1439.

The chapel walls of the **Eglise de Notre-Dame** are lined with tributes from local fishermen to their patroness, Notre-Dame du Cap Lihou. The lower town is an old-fashioned beach resort with a casino, promenades, and public gardens. From the port there are boat trips to the Iles

Chausey, a scattering of low-lying granite islands.

The **Musée d'Art Moderne Richard Anacréon** houses a collection of early 20th-century art. Surrounded by a beautiful cliff garden, the **Musée Christian Dior** is housed in Villa Les Rhumbs, the fashion designer's fine childhood home.

🏛 **Musée d'Art Moderne Richard Anacréon**
pl de l'Isthme, la Haute-Ville. **Tel** 02 33 51 02 94. **Open** Feb–May, Oct & Nov: Fri–Sun pms; Jun–Sep: Tue–Sun. 🏛

🏛 **Musée Christian Dior**
Villa Les Rhumbs. **Tel** 02 33 61 48 21. **Open** Apr–Sep: daily; Oct–Apr: Wed–Sun pms. Gardens: open all year. 🏛

---

## D-Day Landings

In the early hours of June 6, 1944, Allied forces began landing on the shores of Normandy, the first step in a long-planned invasion of German-occupied France, known as Operation Overlord. Parachutists were dropped near Ste.-Mère-Eglise and Pegasus Bridge, and sea-borne assaults were made along a string of codenamed beaches. US troops landed on Utah and Omaha in the west, while British and Canadian troops, which included a contingent of Free French commandos, landed at Gold, Juno, and Sword. The beaches are still referred to by their code names. Pegasus

American troops coming ashore during the Allied invasion of France

Bridge, where the first French house was liberated, is a natural starting point for a tour around the sights and memorials. Farther west, evocative ruins of the artificial harbor towed across from England survive at Arromanches-les-Bains.

There are British, German, and American war cemeteries at La Cambe, Ranville, and St.-Laurent-sur-Mer. War museums at Bayeux, Caen, St.-Mère-Eglise, and Cherbourg provide background on D-Day and the ensuing Battle of Normandy.

### Allied Landings on June 6, 1944

*LA MANCHE*

Cherbourg
Douve
Ste-Mère-Eglise
UTAH
St-Laurent-sur-Mer
Carentan
La Cambe
OMAHA
GOLD JUNO SWORD
Arromanches-les-Bains
Bayeux
Pegasus Bridge
Ranville
Caen
Le Havre
Seine
Vire
Orne

**Key**
■ American troops
▪ British troops
■ Canadian troops
† War cemetery
🪂 Parachute drop

0 kilometers 25
0 miles 25

By the end of D-Day, over 135,000 men had been brought ashore, with losses totaling around 10,000

## ❺ Avranches

Manche. 🏔 9,500. 🚆 🚌 ℹ️ 2 rue
Général-de-Gaulle (02 33 58 00 22).
🛒 Sat. 🌐 **cc-avranchesmont
saintmichel.fr**

Avranches has been a religious
center since the 6th century and
is the final staging post for visitors
to the abbey on Mont-St.-Michel.
The origins of the famous abbey
lie in a vision experienced by
Aubert, the bishop of Avranches.
One night in 708 the Archangel
Michael instructed him to build
a church on the nearby island.
Aubert's skull, with the fingerhole
made in it by the angel, can be
seen in the treasury of **St.-Gervais**
in Avranches. The best views of
Mont-St.-Michel are from the
**Jardin des Plantes**. After the
Revolution, 203 illuminated
manuscripts were rescued from
Mont-St.-Michel's abbey. These
and many others are held in the
**Musée des Manuscrits du Mont-
St.-Michel**. Multimedia displays
show how monks copied and
illuminated the texts. The **Musée
d'Art et d'Histoire** highlights life
in the Cotentin during World War II.

🏛 **Musée des Manuscrits du
Mont-St.-Michel**
Pl d'Estouteville. **Tel** 02 33 79 57 00.
**Open** Tue–Sat pms (Apr–Sep: Tue–
Sun). **Closed** Jan, May 1, Nov 1, Dec 25.
🐾 🏛 ♿

🏛 **Musée d'Art et d'Histoire**
Place Jean de Saint-Avit. **Tel** 02 33 79
57 00. **Open** Wed–Sun. ♿

Remains of the Mulberry Harbor from World War II off the Côte de Nacre

## ❻ Mont-St.-Michel

*See pp260–65.*

## ❼ Côte de Nacre

Calvados. ✈ Caen. 🚆 🚌 Caen,
Bayeux. 🚌 Caen-Ouistreham.
ℹ️ pl St-Pierre, Caen (02 31 27 14 14).
🛒 Fri, Sun. 🌐 **caen-tourisme.fr**

The stretch of coast between
the mouths of the rivers Orne
and Vire was dubbed the Côte
de Nacre (Mother-of-Pearl
Coast) in the 19th century. More
recently it has become known
as the site of the D-Day
landings, when Allied troops
poured ashore at the start of
Operation Overlord *(see p255)*.
The associated cemeteries,
memorials, and museums, and
the remnants of the Mulberry
Harbor at Arromanches-les-
Bains, provide focal points for
a visit. However, the coastline
is equally popular as a summer
vacation destination, offering
long, sandy beaches backed
by resorts such as Courseulles-
sur-Mer and Luc-sur-Mer, which
are more relaxed than the
resorts of the Côte Fleurie
farther east.

## ❽ Bayeux

Calvados. 🏔 16,000. 🚆 🚌 ℹ️ Pont-
St-Jean (02 31 51 28 28). 🛒 Sat, Wed.
🌐 **bayeux-bessin-tourisme.com**

Bayeux was the first town to be
liberated by the Allies in 1944
and fortunate to escape war
damage. Today, an attractive
nucleus of 15th- to 19th-century
buildings remains around its
central high streets, rue St-Martin
and rue St.-Jean. The latter is lined
with stores and cafés.

### Bayeux Tapestry

A lively comic strip justifying William the Conqueror's invasion
of England, this 230-ft- (70-m-) long embroidered hanging
was commissioned by Bishop Odo of Bayeux. Offering insights
into 11th-century life, and an action-packed account of the
defeat of Harold, the King of England, at the Battle of Hastings,
the tapestry is valued as a work of art, a historical document,
an early example of spin, and an entertaining read.

**Harold's retinue** sets off for France
to inform William that he will succeed
to the English throne.

**Trees with** interlacing branches
are sometimes used to divide the
tapestry's 58 scenes.

Above the town rise the spires and domed lantern tower of the Gothic **Cathédrale Notre-Dame**. Beneath its interior is an 11th-century crypt decorated with restored 15th-century frescoes of angels playing musical instruments. The original Romanesque church that stood here was consecrated in 1077, and it is likely that Bayeux's famous tapestry was commissioned for this occasion by one of its key characters, Bishop Odo.

The tapestry is displayed in a renovated seminary, **Centre Guillaume-le-Conquérant-Tapisserie de Bayeux**, which gives a detailed audiovisual explanation of events leading up to the Norman conquest. On the southwest side of the town, the restored **Musée Mémorial de la Bataille de Normandie** traces the events of the Battle of Normandy in World War II, with an excellent film compilation made from contemporary newsreels.

🏛 **Centre Guillaume-le-Conquérant-Tapisserie de Bayeux**
Rue de Nesmond. **Tel** 02 31 51 25 50. **Open** daily. **Closed** 3 wks early Jan, Dec 25–26. 📷 ♿ 🌐 **tapisserie-bayeux.fr**

🏛 **Musée Mémorial de la Bataille de Normandie**
Bd Fabian-Ware. **Tel** 02 31 51 46 90. **Open** mid-Feb–Dec: daily. **Closed** Jan 1, Dec 25. 📷 ♿

The Abbaye aux Hommes in Caen

## 📍 Caen

Calvados. 🛆 115,000. ✈ 🚆 🚌 🚇 ℹ pl St-Pierre (02 31 27 14 14). 🗓 Fri & Sun. 🌐 caen-tourisme.fr

In the mid-11th century Caen became the favored residence of William the Conqueror and Queen Matilda, and despite the destruction of three-quarters of the city during World War II much remains of their creation. The monarchs built two great abbeys and a castle on the north bank of the River Orne, bequeathing Caen a core of historic interest that justifies penetrating its industrial areas and postwar housing. Much-loved by the citizens of Caen, the **Eglise St.-Pierre** was built on the south side of the castle in the 13th and 14th centuries, with an impressively ornate Renaissance east end added in the early 16th century. The frequently copied 14th-century bell tower was destroyed in 1944, but has now been restored. To the east, rue du Vaugueux is the central street in Caen's small Vieux Quartier (Old Quarter). Now traffic-free, the street still has some lovely half-timbered buildings. A walk west, along rue St-Pierre or boulevard du Maréchal Leclerc, leads to the city's main shopping district.

**The English** have a last meal on land before boarding with hunting dogs and falcons.

**Wide moustaches** distinguish the English characters from the clean-shaven Normans.

**The colored wool** used to embroider the linen has faded little since the 11th century.

**Latin inscriptions** caption each main scene in the work and embody the heroic ideals shared by all the participants.

**Borders provide** wry comment through fables and asides.

## Caen City Center

① Abbaye aux Hommes
② Eglise St.-Etienne
③ Château Ducal
④ Eglise St.-Pierre
⑤ La Trinité
⑥ Abbaye aux Dames

For keys to symbols *see back flap*

### ⛪ Abbaye-aux-Hommes

Esplanade Jean-Marie Louvel. **Tel** 02 31 30 42 81. **Open** for visits daily, except during services. **Closed** Jan 1, May 1, Dec 25. 🚶 guided tours. ♿ restr. 📷 (no tours Oct–Mar). ♿restr.

Work began on William's Abbey for Men in 1063 and was almost complete by his death 20 years later. The abbey church, **Eglise St.-Etienne**, is a masterpiece of Norman Romanesque, with a severe west front crowned with 13th-century spires. The sparingly decorated nave was roofed in the early 1100s with stone vaulting that anticipates the Gothic style.

### ⛪ Abbaye-aux-Dames

Pl de la Reine Mathilde. **Tel** 02 31 06 98 98. **Open** daily pms only. **Closed** Jan 1, May 1, Dec 25. 📷 obligatory. ♿

Like the Abbaye-aux- Hommes, Matilda's Abbey for Women also has a Norman Romanesque church, **La Trinité**, flanked by 18th-century buildings. Begun in 1060, it was consecrated six years later. Queen Matilda lies buried in the choir under a slab of black marble, and her restored abbey, with its creamy Caen stone, makes a serene, dignified mausoleum.

### 🏛 Château Ducal

Esplanade du Château. Musée des Beaux-Arts: **Tel** 02 31 30 47 70. **Open** daily (Nov–May: Wed–Mon). Musée de Normandie: **Tel** 02 31 30 47 60. **Open** Jun–Oct: daily: Nov–May: Wed–Mon. **Closed** Jan 1, Easter, May 1, Ascension, Nov 1, Dec 25 (both museums). 📷 ♿

The ruins of Caen's castle, one of the largest fortified enclosures in Europe, offer spacious lawns, museums, and rampart views. A fine art collection, strong on 17th-century French and Italian painting, is exhibited in the **Musée des Beaux-Arts**. The **Musée de Normandie** recalls traditional life in the region with utensils and displays on farming and lace.

### 🏛 Mémorial de Caen

Esplanade Dwight-Eisenhower. **Tel** 02 31 06 06 45. **Open** mid-Feb–Oct: daily; Nov–mid-Feb: Tue–Sun. **Closed** 3 weeks in Jan, Dec 25. 📷 ♿ 🌐 memorial-caen.fr

Northwest of Caen, close to the N13 beltway (exit 7), this museum is dedicated to peace, placing D-Day into the context of World War II using a host of interactive and audiovisual techniques, including stunning compilations of archive and fictional movies.

A modern extension gives a wider perspective on cultural, religious, border, and ecological conflicts in the second half of the 20th century.

Lush Orne Valley in the Suisse Normande

*For hotels and restaurants in this region see pp559–60 and pp583–5*

# ⑩ Suisse Normande

Calvados & Orne. ✈ Caen. 🚌
🚆 Caen, Argentan. ℹ 2 pl St-Sauveur, Thury-Harcourt (02 31 79 70 45).
🌐 **suisse-normande-tourisme.com**

Though hardly the mountains of Switzerland, the cliffs and valleys carved out by the River Orne as it winds north to Caen have become popular for walking, climbing, camping, and river sports. The area is also ideal for a rural drive. Its highest and most impressive point is the Oëtre Rock, off the D329, where you can look down over the dramatic gorges created by the River Rouvre.

# ⑪ Parc Naturel Régional de Normandie-Maine

Orne & Manche. ✈ Alençon. 🚌
🚆 Argentan. ℹ Carrouges (02 33 81 75 75). 🌐 **parc-naturel-normandie-maine.fr**

The southern fringes of central Normandy have been incorporated into France's largest regional park. Among the farmland and forests of oak and beech are several small towns. **Domfront** rests on a spur overlooking the River Varenne. The spa town **Bagnoles-de-l'Orne** offers a casino and sport amenities, while **Sées** has a Gothic cathedral. The **Maison du Parc** at Carrouges has information on walks, cycling, and canoeing.

Poster of Deauville, about 1930

### 🎋 Maison du Parc

Carrouges. **Tel** 02 33 81 13 33.
**Open** Apr–mid-Oct & Dec 6–21: daily.
**Closed** May 1.

### Environs

Just north of the park is the **Château d'O**, a Renaissance château with fine 17th-century frescoes. The **Haras du Pin** is France's national stud, called "a horses' Versailles" for its 17th-century architecture. Horse shows, dressage events, and various tours take place throughout the year.

# ⑫ Côte Fleurie

Calvados. ✈ 🚌 🚆 Deauville.
ℹ 112 rue Victor Hugo, Deauville (02 31 14 40 00). 🌐 **deauville.org**

The Côte Fleurie (Flowery Coast) between Villerville and Cabourg has been planted with chic resorts which, burst into bloom every summer. **Trouville** was once a humble fishing village, but in the mid-19th century caught the attention of writers Gustave Flaubert and Alexandre Dumas. By the 1870s Trouville had acquired grand hotels, a train station, and pseudo-Swiss villas along the beachfront. It has, however, long been outclassed by its neighbor, **Deauville**, created by the Duc de Morny in the 1860s. This resort boasts a casino, racetracks, marinas, and the famous beachside catwalk, Les Planches.

For something quieter, head west to smaller resorts such as Villers-sur-Mer or Houlgate. **Cabourg** farther west is dominated by the turn-of-the-century Grand Hôtel, where novelist Marcel Proust spent many summers. Proust used the resort as a model for the fictional Balbec in his novel *Remembrance of Things Past*.

# ⑬ Pays d'Auge

Calvados. ✈ Deauville. 🚌 🚆 Lisieux.
ℹ 11 rue d'Alençon, Lisieux (02 31 48 18 10). 🌐 **lisieux-tourisme.com**

Inland from the Côte Fleurie, the Pays d'Auge is classic Normandy countryside, lushly woven with fields, wooded valleys, cider orchards, dairy farms, and manor houses. Its capital is **Lisieux**, a cathedral town devoted to St. Thérèse of Lisieux, who was canonized in 1925 and still attracts hundreds of thousands of pilgrims each year. Lisieux is an obvious base for exploring the region, but nearby market towns, such as St.-Pierre-sur-Dives and Orbec, are smaller and more attractive.

The best way to enjoy the Pays d'Auge is to putter around its minor roads. There is a tourist route devoted to cider, and picturesque manor houses, farmhouses, and châteaux testify to the wealth of this fertile land. **St.-Germain-de-Livet** can be visited, as can **Crèvecoeur-en-Auge**, and the half-timbered village of **Beuvron-en-Auge** is charming.

## Apples and Cider

Apple orchards are a familiar feature of the Normandy countryside, and their fruit a fundamental ingredient in the region's gastronomic repertoire. No self-respecting patisserie would be without its *tarte normande* (apple tart), and every country lane seems to sport an *Ici Vente Cidre* (Cider Sold Here) sign. Much of the harvest forms the raw material for cider and Calvados, an apple brandy aged in oak barrels for at least two years. A local brew is also made from pears, and known as *poiré* (perry).

A crop ranging from sour cider apples to sweet eating varieties

# ❻ Mont-St.-Michel

Shrouded by mist, encircled by sea, soaring proudly above glistening sands – the silhouette of Mont-St.-Michel is one of the most enchanting sights in France. Now linked to the mainland by a causeway, the island of Mont-Tombe (Tomb on the Hill) stands at the mouth of the River Couesnon, crowned by a fortified abbey that almost doubles its height. Lying strategically on the frontier between Normandy and Brittany, Mont-St.-Michel grew from a humble 8th-century oratory to become a Benedictine monastery that had its greatest influence in the 12th and 13th centuries. Pilgrims known as *miquelots* journeyed from afar to honor the cult of St. Michael, and the monastery was a renowned center of medieval learning. Major engineering works to reverse the silting up of the sea around the island have been completed.

The 10th-century abbey

The 11th-century abbey

The mid-18th-century abbey

**St. Aubert's Chapel**
A small 15th-century chapel built on an outcrop of rock is dedicated to Aubert, the founder of Mont-St.-Michel.

★ **Gabriel Tower**
Three floors of cannons point in all directions from this imposing 16th-century tower.

Entrance

---

**966** Benedictine abbey founded by Duke Richard I

**1211–28** Construction of La Merveille

**1434** Last assault by English forces. Ramparts surround the town

**1789** French Revolution: abbey becomes a political prison

**1874** Abbey declared a national monument

**1922** Services again held in abbey church

| 700 | 1000 | 1300 | 1600 | 1900 |
|---|---|---|---|---|

**1017** Work on abbey church starts

**708** St. Aubert builds an oratory on Mont-Tombe

**1516** Abbey falls into decline

**1067–70** Mont-St.-Michel depicted in Bayeux Tapestry

*Bayeux Tapestry detail*

**1877–9** Causeway built

**1895–7** Belfry, spire, and statue of St. Michael added

**2007** Benedictine monks leave the abbey; they are replaced by the Fraternité de Jérusalem

**Tides of Mont-St.-Michel**
Extremely strong tides in the Baie du Mont-St.-Michel act as a natural defence. They rise and fall with the lunar calendar and can reach speeds of 6 mph (10 km/h).

**★ Abbey**
Protected by high walls, the abbey and its church occupy an impregnable position on the island.

**KEY**

① **Gautier's Leap**, the terrace at the top of the Inner Staircase, is named after a prisoner who leapt to his death.

② **Eglise St.-Pierre**

③ **Liberty Tower**

④ **The Arcade Tower** provided lodgings for the abbot's soldiers.

⑤ **King's Tower**

**★ Grande Rue**
Now crowded with restaurants, the pilgrims' route, followed since the 12th century, climbs up past Eglise St.-Pierre to the abbey gates.

# The Abbey of Mont-St.-Michel

The present buildings bear witness to the time when the abbey served both as a Benedictine monastery and, for 73 years after the Revolution, as a political prison. In 1017 work began on a Romanesque church at the island's highest point, building over its 10th-century predecessor, now the Chapel of Our Lady Underground. A monastery built on three levels, La Merveille (The Miracle) was added to the church's north side in the early 13th century.

**★ Church**
Four bays of the Romanesque nave survive. Three were pulled down in 1776, creating the West Terrace.

**★ La Merveille**
The Miracle is a Gothic masterpiece – a three-story monastic complex built in only 16 years.

**Refectory**
The monks took their meals in this long, narrow room, which is flooded with light through tall windows.

**Knights' Room**
The rib vaults and finely decorated capitals are typically Gothic.

CHURCH LEV

MIDDLE LEV

LOWER LEVE

**Crypt of the Thirty Candles** is one of two 11th-century crypts built to support the transepts of the main church.

**★ Cloisters**
The cloisters with their elegant columns in staggered rows are a beautiful example of early 13th-century Anglo-Norman style.

## Visiting the Abbey

*The three levels of the abbey reflect the monastic hierarchy. The monks lived at the highest level, in an enclosed world of church, cloister, and refectory. The abbot entertained his noble guests on the middle level. Soldiers and pilgrims farther down on the social scale were received at the lowest level. Guided tours begin at the West Terrace at the church level and end in the almonry, where alms were dispensed to the poor. The almonry is now a bookstore and souvenir hall.*

**CHURCH LEVEL**

Cloister
Refectory
Abbey church
West Terrace
Gautier's Leap
Great Inner Staircase

**MIDDLE LEVEL**

Knights' room
Guest room
Crypt of the Thirty Candles
Our Lady Underground
St. Etienne's Chapel
St. Martin's Crypt
Abbot's lodgings

**LOWER LEVEL**

Cellar
Almonry
Abbey gardens
Abbot's lodgings
Guard's room

**Church Interior**
A Flamboyant Gothic choir, built from 1446 to 1521, held up by crypts with massive supporting pillars.

**St. Martin's Crypt** is an 11th-century barrel-vaulted chapel that preserves the austere forms of the original Romanesque abbey.

**The abbot's lodgings** were close to the abbey entrance, and he received prestigious visitors in the guest room. Poorer pilgrims were received in the almonry.

**West Terrace**
Guided tours start here, at the West Terrace. The Fraternité de Jérusalem, a small monastic community, lives in the abbey and welcomes visitors.

Mont-St.-Michel by night ▶

# ⓮ Honfleur

Calvados. 🚉 8,500. 🚌 Deauville.
ℹ️ quai Lepaulmier (02 31 89 23 30).
🏴 Wed, Sat; Thu, Sun: fish market at
harbor. 🌐 ot-honfleur.fr

A major defensive port in the
15th century, Honfleur has
become one of Normandy's
most appealing harbors. At its
heart is the 17th-century **Vieux
Bassin** (Old Dock), with its
pretty, tall houses (6–7 stories).

Honfleur became a center
of artistic activity in the
19th century. Eugène Boudin,
the painter, was born here in
1824, as was the composer Erik
Satie in 1866. Courbet, Sisley,
Renoir, Pissarro, and Cézanne all
visited Honfleur, often meeting
at the Ferme St.-Siméon, now a
luxury hotel. Painters still work
from Honfleur's dockside, and
exhibit in the **Greniers à Sel**,
two salt warehouses built in
1670. These lie to the east of the
Vieux Bassin in an area known
as l'Enclos, which made up
the fortified heart of the town
in the 13th century.

The **Musée d'Ethnographie
et d'Art Populaire Normand**
displays mementos of Hon-
fleur's nautical past, with a
warren of Norman interiors next
door in the former prison. Place
Ste.-Catherine has an unusual
15th-century church built by
ship's carpenters. The **Musée
Eugène-Boudin** documents the
artistic appeal of Honfleur and
the Seine estuary, with works
from Boudin to Raoul Dufy. **Les
Maisons Satie** use extracts from
Satie's music to guide you round
reconstructions of the rooms.

🎫 **Greniers à Sel**
Rue de la Ville. ℹ️ 02 31 89 23 30.
**Open** for guided tours & exhibitions.
🕐 obligatory, except during summer
exhibitions (contact the tourist office
for details). 🅿️ ♿

🏛️ **Musée d'Ethnographie et
d'Art Populaire Normand**
Quai St.-Etienne. **Tel** 02 31 89 14 12.
**Open** mid-Feb–Mar, Oct–Nov: Tue–Fri
(pms only), Sat, Sun; Apr–Sep: Tue–
Sun. **Closed** May 1, Jul 14. 🅿️ ♿

🏛️ **Musée Eugène-Boudin**
Pl Erik Satie, rue de l'Homme de Bois.
**Tel** 02 31 89 54 00. **Open** mid-Mar–
Sep: Wed–Mon; Oct–mid-Mar: Tue–Fri
pms, Sat & Sun. 🅿️ ♿

🏛️ **Les Maisons Satie**
67 bd Charles V. **Tel** 02 31 89 11 11.
**Open** mid-Feb–Dec: Wed–Mon.
**Closed** public hols. 🅿️

Quai St-Etienne in Honfleur

# ⓯ Le Havre

Seine-Maritime. 🚉 195,000. ✈️ 🚆
🚌 🚢 ℹ️ 186 bd Clemenceau (02 32
74 04 04). 🏴 daily.
🌐 lehavretourisme.com

Strategically positioned on the
Seine estuary, Le Havre (The
Harbor) was created in 1517 by
François I after the nearby port
of Harfleur silted up. During
World War II it was virtually
obliterated by Allied bombing,
but despite a vast industrial
zone, which stands beside the
port, it still has appeal. It is an
important yachting center, and
its beach has a two blue flag
rating (very clean).

Much of the city center was
rebuilt in the 1950s–60s by
Auguste Perret, whose towering
**Eglise St.-Joseph** (a UNESCO
World Heritage Site) pierces the
skyline. On the seafront, the
**Musée Malraux** has works by,
amongst others, local artist Raoul
Dufy. France's biggest skateboard
park is also on the seafront.

🏛️ **Musée Malraux**
2 bd Clemenceau. **Tel** 02 35 19 62 62.
**Open** Tue–Sun. **Closed** public hols.
🅿️ 📷 🅿️ 🌐 muma-lehavre.fr

# ⓰ Côte d'Albâtre

Seine-Maritime. 🚆 🚌 🚢 ℹ️ Pont
Jehan Ango, Dieppe (02 32 14 40 60).
🌐 dieppetourisme.com

The Alabaster Coast gets its
name from the chalky cliffs and
milky waters that characterize
the Normandy coastline
between Le Havre and Le
Tréport. It is best known for the
**Falaise d'Aval**, west of Etretat,
eroded into an arch. The author
Guy de Maupassant, born near
Dieppe in 1850, compared
these cliffs to an elephant
dipping its trunk into the sea.
From Etretat, a chain of coastal
roads runs east across a switch-
back of breezy headlands and
wooded valleys to Dieppe.

**Fécamp** is the only major town
along this route. Its Benedictine
abbey was once an important
pilgrimage center after a tree
trunk said to contain drops of
Christ's blood was washed
ashore here in the 7th century.
This is enshrined in a reliquary at
the entrance to the Lady Chapel
of the abbey church, La Trinité.

The vast **Palais Bénédictine** is
a Neo-Gothic and Renaissance
homage to the ego of
Alexander Le Grand, a local wine
and spirits merchant who
rediscovered the monks' recipe
for Bénédictine, the famous
herbal liqueur. Built in 1882, it
incorporates a distillery and an

*Woman with Parasol* (1880) by Boudin in the Musée Eugène-Boudin

The cliffs at Falaise d'Aval, famously likened to an elephant dipping its trunk into the sea

eccentric museum packed with curios. The adjacent halls provide an aromatic account and tastings of the 27 herbs and spices that make up the elixir.

**🏛 Palais Bénédictine**

110 rue Alexandre Le Grand, Fécamp. **Tel** 02 35 10 26 10. **Open** daily. **Closed** Jan–mid-Feb, May 1, Dec 25. 🅿️ 🏛

View of Dieppe from the château and museum above the town

## ⓱ Dieppe

Seine-Maritime. 🏘 36,000. 🚃 🚌 🛳
ℹ️ Pont Jean Ango (02 32 14 40 60).
🛒 Tue, Thu & esp. Sat.
🌐 **dieppetourisme.com**

Dieppe exploits a break in the chalky cliffs bordering the Pays de Caux, and has won historical prestige as a Channel fort, port, and resort. Prosperity came during the 16th and 17th centuries, when local privateer Jehan Ango raided the Portuguese and English fleets, and a trading post called Petit Dieppe was founded on the West African coast. At that time, Dieppe's population was already 30,000, and included a 300-strong community of craftsmen carving imported ivory. This maritime past is celebrated in **Le Château-Musée**, the 15th-century castle crowning the headland to the west of the seafront. Here you can see historical maps and model ships, a collection of Dieppe ivories, and paintings that evoke the town's development as a fashionable beach resort during the 19th century. Dieppe had the nearest beach to Paris and quickly responded to the developing passion for promenading, seawater cures, and bathing.

Today Dieppe's broad seafront is given over to lawns, amusements, and parking lots, and its liveliest streets surround the battle-scarred **Eglise St.-Jacques** to the south. If the weather is poor, visit **L'Estran-La Cité de la Mer**, an exhibition center with models on maritime themes, and an aquarium.

**🏛 Le Château-Musée**

**Tel** 02 35 06 61 99. **Open** Wed–Mon. **Closed** Jan 1, May 1, Nov 1, Dec 25.

**🏛 L'Estran-La Cité de la Mer**

37 rue de l'Asile Thomas. **Tel** 02 35 06 93 20. **Open** daily. **Closed** Jan 1, Dec 25. 🅿️ ♿

## ⓲ Basse-Seine

Seine-Maritime & Eure. ✈️ Le Havre, Rouen. 🚃 🚌 Yvetot. 🛳 Le Havre.
ℹ️ Yvetot (02 32 70 99 96).

Meandering seaward from Rouen to Le Havre, the River Seine is crossed by three spectacular road bridges: the Pont de Brotonne, the Pont de Tancarville, and the Pont de Normandie (linking Le Havre and Honfleur). The grace and daring of these modern bridges echo the soaring aspirations of the abbeys founded on the river's banks in the 7th and 8th centuries. The abbeys now provide good stepping stones for a tour of the Lower Seine valley.

West of Rouen is the harmonious Eglise de St.-Georges at **St.-Martin-de-Boscherville**, which until the Revolution was the church of a small walled abbey. Its 12th-century chapter-house has remarkable biblical statues and carved capitals. From here the D67 runs south to the riverside village of La Bouille.

As you head northwest, an hourly car ferry at Mesnil-sous-Jumièges takes you over to the colossal ruins of the **Abbaye de Jumièges**. The abbey was founded in 654 and once housed 900 monks and 1,500 servants. The main abbey church dates from the 11th century; its consecration in 1067 was a major event, with William the Conqueror in attendance.

The D913 strikes through oak and beech woods in the Parc Régional de Brotonne to the Benedictine **Abbaye de St.-Wandrille**, founded in the 7th century. The Musée de la Marine de Seine at **Caudebec-en-Caux** gives an engrossing account of many aspects of life on this great river since the late 19th century.

**Monk from Abbaye de St.-Wandrille**

# ⑲ Rouen

Founded at the lowest point where the Seine could be bridged, Rouen has prospered through maritime trade and industrialization to become a rich and cultured city. Despite the severe damage of World War II, the city boasts a wealth of historic sights on its right bank, all within walking distance of the central Cathédrale Notre-Dame, frequently painted by Monet. In turn a Celtic trading post, Roman garrison, and Viking colony, Rouen became the capital of the Norman Duchy in 911. It was captured by Henry V in 1419 after a siege during the Hundred Years' War. In 1431 Joan of Arc was burned at the stake here in place du Vieux-Marché.

Rouen, a thriving port on the River Seine

| 0 meters | 250 |
| 0 yards | 250 |

### Exploring Rouen

From **place du Vieux Marché** and the 1979 **Eglise Ste.-Jeanne-d'Arc**, rue du **Gros Horloge** runs east under the city's Great Clock. Rue aux Juifs leads past the 15th-century Gothic **Palais de Justice**, once Normandy's parliament, to the smart stores and cafés around rue des Carmes. Farther east, between the St.-Maclou and St.-Ouen churches, are half-timbered houses in rue Damiette and rue Eau de Robec.

### 🏛 Cathédrale Notre-Dame

Jun–Sep: Sound and light show.
This Gothic masterpiece is dominated by the famous west facade (see p271), painted by Monet, and framed by two unequal towers – the northern

Cathédrale Notre-Dame, Rouen

Tour St.-Romain, and the later Tour du Beurre, supposedly paid for by a tax on butter consumption in Lent. Above the central lantern tower rises a Neo-Gothic cast iron spire, erected in 1876. Both the 14th-century northern Portail des Libraires and southern Portail de la Calende stand out for their precise sculpting and delicate tracery. Many of the cathedral's riches are accessible by guided tour only, including the tomb of Richard the Lionheart, whose heart was buried here, and the rare

11th-century semi-circular hall crypt, rediscovered in 1934.

### 🏛 Historial Jeanne d'Arc

7 rue Saint Romain. **Tel** 02 35 52 48 00. **Open** Tue–Sun. **Closed** public hols. 🅰 🅰 🆆 historial-jeannedarc.fr
Mulitimedia displays trace the story of Joan of Arc at this museum in the former archbishop's palace where she was sentenced.

## Sights at a Glance

① Place du Vieux Marché
② Gros Horloge
③ Palais de Justice
④ Cathédrale Notre-Dame
⑤ Historial Jeanne d'Arc
⑥ Eglise St.-Maclou
⑦ Aître St.-Maclou
⑧ Eglise St.-Ouen
⑨ Hôtel de Ville
⑩ Musée le Secq des Tournelles
⑪ Musée des Beaux-Arts
⑫ Musée de la Céramique
⑬ Musée d'Histoire Naturelle

surviving example of a medieval cemetery for the burial of plague victims. The timbers of its buildings, set around the quadrangle, are carved with a macabre array of grinning skulls, crossed bones, coffins, and gravediggers' implements.

### 🏠 Eglise St.-Ouen

Once part of a formadable Benedictine abbey, St.-Ouen is a solid Gothic church with a lofty, unadorned interior made all the more beautiful by its restored 14th-century stained glass. Next to the church is the 18th-century **Hôtel de Ville**.

### 🏛 Musée Le Secq des Tournelles

Rue Jacques-Villon. **Tel** 02 35 88 42 92. **Open** Wed–Mon pms. **Closed** public hols. 🚹 ground floor only.

Located in a 15th-century church, this wrought-ironwork museum exhibits antique ironmongery ranging from keys to corkscrews and Gallo-Roman spoons to mighty tavern signs.

### 🏛 Musée des Beaux-Arts

Square Verdrel. **Tel** 02 35 71 28 40. **Open** Wed–Mon. **Closed** some public hols. 🚹

The city's collection includes major art works: masterpieces by Caravaggio and Velázquez, and paintings by Normandy-born artists Théodore Géricault, Eugène Boudin, and Raoul Dufy. Also on display is Monet's *Rouen Cathedral, The Portal, Grey Weather*.

### 🏛 Musée de la Céramique

Hôtel d'Hocqueville, 1 rue Faucon. **Tel** 02 35 07 31 74. **Open** Wed–Mon pms. **Closed** public hols.

Exhibits of 1,000 pieces of Rouen faïence – colorful glazed earthenware – together with other pieces of French and foreign china are displayed in a 17th-century town house. The works trace the history of Rouen faïence to its zenith in the 18th century.

### 🏛 Musée d'Histoire Naturelle

198 rue Beauvoisine. **Tel** 02 35 71 41 50. **Open** Tue–Sun pms. **Closed** public hols.

The second-largest museum of its kind in France, this museum holds more than 800,000 objects.

### 🏛 Musée Flaubert

51 rue de Lecat. **Tel** 02 35 15 59 95. **Open** Tue & Wed–Sat pm. **Closed** public hols. 🚹

Flaubert's father was a surgeon at Rouen Hospital, and his family home combines memorabilia with an awesome – and occasionally gruesome – display of 17th- to 19th-century medical equipment.

### 🏠 Eglise St.-Maclou

This Flamboyant Gothic church has an intensively decorated west facade with a five-bay porch and carved wooden doors depicting biblical scenes. Behind the church, the **Aître St.-Maclou**, or ossuary, is a rare

## Gustave Flaubert

The novelist Gustave Flaubert (1821–80) was born and raised in Rouen, and the city provides the backdrop for some memorable scenes in his masterpiece, *Madame Bovary*. Published in 1856–7, this realistic study of a country doctor's wife driven to despair by her love affairs provoked a scandal that made Flaubert's name. His famous stuffed green parrot, which can be seen in the Musée Flaubert, was always perched on his writing desk.

Flaubert's stuffed parrot

Château Gaillard and the village of Les Andelys, in a loop of the River Seine

## ⑳ Haute-Seine

Eure. ✈ Rouen. 🚃 Vernon, Val de Reuil. 🚌 Gisors, Les Andelys. ℹ Les Andelys (02 32 54 41 93). 🌐 lesandelys-tourisme.fr

Southeast of Rouen, the river Seine follows a convoluted course, with most points of interest on its north bank. At the center of the Forêt de Lyons, once the hunting ground for the dukes of Normandy, is the country town of **Lyons-la-Forêt**, with half-timbered houses and an 18th-century covered market.

To the south the D313 follows the gracefully curving Seine to the town of **Les Andelys**. Above it tower the ruins of Château Gaillard, which Richard the Lionheart, as King of England and Duke of Normandy, built in 1197 to defend Rouen from the French. They eventually took the castle in 1204.

## ㉑ Giverny

Eure. 🏔 600. ℹ 80 rue Claude Monet, Giverny 27620 (02 32 64 45 01). 🌐 normandie-giverny.fr

In 1883 the Impressionist painter Claude Monet rented a house in the small village of Giverny, and worked here until his death. The house, known as the **Fondation Claude Monet**, and its garden are open to the public. The house is decorated in the color schemes that Monet admired; the glorious gardens are famous as the subject of some of the artist's studies. Only copies are on show, but there are outstanding original 19th- and 20th-century artworks in the **Musée des Impressionnismes** nearby.

🏛 **Fondation Claude Monet**
Giverny, Gasny. **Tel** 02 32 51 28 21. **Open** Apr–Oct: daily. 🚫 🖥 📷
🌐 fondation-monet.com

🏛 **Musée des Impressionnismes**
99 rue Claude Monet, Giverny. **Tel** 02 32 51 94 65. **Open** daily. 🚫 🖥 📷 ♿

## ㉒ Evreux

Eure. 🏔 55,000. 🚃 🚌
ℹ 1ter pl du Général de Gaulle (02 32 24 04 43). 🗓 Wed & Sat.
🌐 grandevreuxtourisme.fr

Though considerably damaged in the war, Evreux is a pleasant cathedral town set in wide, agricultural plains. At its heart, the **Cathédrale Notre-Dame** is renowned for its 14th- to 15th-century stained glass. The building is predominantly Gothic, though Romanesque arches survive in the nave, and Renaissance screens adorn its chapels. Next door, the former Bishop's Palace houses the **Musée de l'Ancien Evêché**, with Roman bronze statues of Jupiter and Apollo, and fine 18th-century furniture and decorative art.

Monet's garden at Giverny, restored to its original profuse glory

*For hotels and restaurants in this region see pp559–60 and pp583–5*

# Monet's Cathedral Series

In the 1890s Claude Monet made almost 30 paintings of Rouen's cathedral, several of which are now in the Musée d'Orsay in Paris *(see pp124–5)*. He studied the effects of changing light on its facades, and described both the surface detail and huge bulk, putting color before contour. The archetypal Impressionist, Monet said he conceived this series when he watched the effects of light on a country church, "as the sun's rays slowly dissolved the mists… that wrapped the golden stone in an ideally vaporous envelope."

### Harmony in Blue and Gold (1894)
Monet selected a close vantage point for the series and was keen on this southwest view. The sun would cast afternoon shadows across the carved west front, accentuating the cavernous portals and the large rose window.

**Monet's sketch**, one of many of Rouen, parallels the shimmering effect of the paintings.

**Harmony in Brown** (1894) is the only finished version of a frontal view of the west facade. Analysis has shown that it was begun as a southwest view like the others.

**Harmony in Blue** (1894), compared with Harmony in Blue and Gold, shows the stone of the west facade further softened by the diffuse light of a misty morning.

**The Portal, Gray Weather** (1894) was one of several canvases in the gray color group, which showed the cathedral facade in the soft light of an overcast day.

# BRITTANY

*Finistère · Côtes-d'Armor · Morbihan · Ille-et-Vilaine*

Jutting defiantly into the Atlantic, France's northwest corner has long been culturally and geographically distinct from the main bulk of the country. It was known to the Celts as Armorica, the land of the sea, and Brittany's past swirls with the legends of drowned cities and Arthurian forests. Prehistoric megaliths arise mysteriously from land and sea, and the medieval is never far from the modern.

A long, jagged coastline is the region's great attraction. Magnificent beaches line its northern shore, swept clean by huge tides and interspersed with well-established beach resorts, seasoned fishing ports, and abundant oysterbeds. The south coast is gentler, with wooded river valleys and a milder climate, while the west, being exposed to the Atlantic winds, has a drama that justifies the name Finistère – the End of the Earth.

Inland lies the Argoat – once the Land of the Forest, now a patchwork of undulating fields, woods, and rolling moorland. The Parc Naturel Régional d'Armorique occupies much of central Finistère, and it is in western Brittany that Breton culture remains most evident. In Quimper, and in the Pays Bigouden, crêpes and cider, traditional costumes, and Celtic music are still a genuine part of the Breton lifestyle. Eastern Brittany has a more conventional appeal. Vannes, Dinan, and Rennes, the Breton capital, have well-preserved medieval quarters, where half-timbered buildings shelter inviting markets, stores, crêperies, and restaurants. The walled port of St.-Malo on the Côte d'Emeraude recalls the region's maritime prowess, while the remarkably intact castles at Fougères and Vitré are reminders of the mighty border-fortresses that protected Brittany's eastern frontier before its final union with France in 1532.

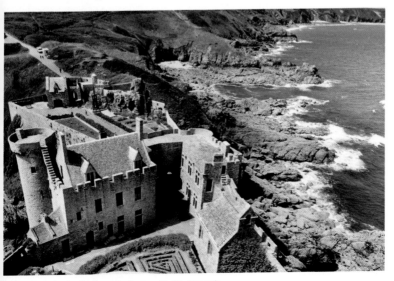

Fort la Latte, a medieval castle, offers spectacular views of the Côte d'Emeraude

◀ The sun sets over the dramatic coastline at the Pointe du Raz

# Exploring Brittany

Ideal for a beach holiday, Brittany offers enjoyable drives along the headlands and beaches of the northern Côte d'Emeraude and Côte de Granit Rose, while the south coast boasts wooded valleys and the prehistoric sites of Carnac and the Golfe du Morbihan. The parish closes (see pp280–81) provide intriguing insight into Breton culture, as does the cathedral town of Quimper. Be sure to visit the regional capital, Rennes, and the great castle at Fougères, and in summer take a boat trip to one of Brittany's islands.

## Sights at a Glance

1. Ile d'Ouessant
2. Brest
3. Parc Naturel Régional d'Armorique
4. Douarnenez
5. Locronan
6. Pointe du Raz
7. Pays Bigouden
8. Quimper
9. Concarneau
10. Pont-Aven
11. Le Pouldu
12. Roscoff
13. St.-Thégonnec
14. Guimiliau
15. Lampaul-Guimiliau
16. Côte de Granit Rose
17. Tréguier
18. Ile de Bréhat
19. Carnac
20. Presqu'île de Quiberon
21. Belle-Ile-en-Mer
22. Vannes
23. Golfe du Morbihan
24. Josselin
25. Forêt de Paimpont
26. Côte d'Emeraude
27. St.-Malo
28. Cancale
29. Dinan
30. Combourg
31. Rennes
32. Fougères
33. Vitré

**Key**

| | |
|---|---|
| ▬▬▬ | Freeway |
| ▬▬▬ | Highway |
| ▬▬▬ | Secondary road |
| ═══ | Minor road |
| ─── | Scenic route |
| ▬▪▬ | Main railroad |
| ──── | Minor railroad |
| ▬▬▬ | Regional border |

For keys to symbols see back flap

Lighthouse on the Île de Bréhat, Côte de Granit Rose

## Getting Around

Expressways N12/N165 encircle Brittany, giving easy access to coastal areas, while the N12 and N24 give direct access to Rennes, Brittany's capital. Brittany can be reached by air to Brest, Nantes, Rennes, and Dinard airports, by Channel ferries to St.-Malo and Roscoff, by *autoroutes* from Normandy, the Loire, and the A11 from Paris, or by TGV direct from Paris and Lille.

0 kilometers 25
0 miles 25

Half-timbered houses in the medieval part of Rennes

# ❶ Ile d'Ouessant

Finistère. ⚄ 900. ✈ Ouessant (via Brest). ☒ Brest, then boat. ⛴ Le Conquet, then boat. 🛈 pl de l'Eglise, Lampaul (02 98 48 85 83).
🅆 ot-ouessant.fr

A well-known Breton proverb declares "He who sees Ouessant sees his own blood." Also known as Ushant, the island is notorious among sailors for its fierce storms and strong currents. However, this westerly point of France has a pleasant climate in summer and, though often bleak and stormy, can be surprisingly mild in winter. Part of the Parc Naturel Régional d'Armorique, the windswept island supports migrating birds and a small seal population, which may be observed from the Pern and Pen-ar-Roc'h headlands.

Two museums shed light on the island's defiant history, dogged by shipwreck and tragedy. At Niou Uhella, the **Ecomusée du Niou** has furniture made from driftwood and wrecks, often painted blue and white in honor of the Virgin Mary. Nearby at Phare du Créac'h, the **Musée des Phares et Balises** explains the history of Brittany's many lighthouses and their keepers.

🏛 **Ecomusée du Niou**
Maison du Niou. **Tel** 02 98 48 86 37. **Open** Apr–Sep: daily; Oct–Mar: Tue–Sun pms. ▨ 🅗

🏛 **Musée des Phares et Balises**
Pointe de Créac'h. **Tel** 02 98 48 80 70. **Open** Apr–Sep: daily; Oct–Mar: Tue–Sun pms. ▨

# ❷ Brest

Finistère. ⚄ 155,000. ✈ ☒ ⛴ ⛴ to islands only. 🛈 8 av Georges Clemenceau (02 98 44 24 96). ⛴ daily.
🅆 brest-metropole-tourisme.fr

A natural harbor, protected by the Presqu'île de Crozon, Brest is France's premier Atlantic naval port, with a rich maritime history. Heavily bombed during World War II, it is now a modern commercial city, where cargo vessels, yachts, and fishing boats ply the waters. The Cours Dajot promenade has good views of the Rade de Brest (Bay

Windswept moorlands near Ménez-Meur, Parc Naturel Régional d'Armorique

of Brest). The **Château** houses a naval museum with historic maps, maritime paintings, model ships, carved wooden figure-heads, and nautical instruments.

Across the Penfeld river – reached by Europe's largest lifting bridge, Pont de Revouvrance – is the 14th-century **Tour de la Motte Tanguy**. By the Port de Plaisance, **Océanopolis** "sea center" has three vast pavilions simulating temperate, tropical and polar ecosystems.

🏰 **Château de Brest**
**Tel** 02 98 22 12 39. **Open** Feb–Mar & Oct–Dec: Wed–Mon pms only; Apr–Sep: daily. **Closed** May 1, Dec 25. ▨ 🏛

🗼 **Tour de la Motte Tanguy**
Sq Pierre Peron. **Tel** 02 98 00 87 93. **Open** Jun–Sep: daily; Oct–May: Mon, Wed–Thu pm, Sat–Sun pms. **Closed** Jan 1, May 1, Dec 25.

🐋 **Océanopolis**
Port de Plaisance du Moulin Blanc. **Tel** 02 98 34 40 40. **Open** Apr–mid-Sep: daily; mid-Sep–Mar: Tue–Sun. **Closed** 3 wks Jan, Dec 25. ▨ 🅗 🅒 🏛 🅆 oceanopolis.com

The 14th-century Tour de la Motte Tanguy, housing a museum on the history of Brest

# ❸ Parc Naturel Régional d'Armorique

Finistère. ✈ Brest. ☒ Chateaulin, Landernau. ⛴ Le Faou, Huelgoat, Carhaix. 🛈 Le Faou (02 98 81 90 08).
🅆 pnr-armorique.fr

The Armorican Regional Nature Park stretches from the moor-lands of the Monts d'Arrée to the Presqu'île de Crozon and Ile d'Ouessant. Within the protected area lies a mixture of farmland, heaths, remains of ancient oak forest, and wild, open spaces. The park is ideal for walking, horseback riding, and touring by bicycle or car.

**Huelgoat** is a good starting point for inland walks, while **Ménez-Hom** (1,082 ft/330 m), at the start of the Crozon Peninsula, has excellent views. The main park information center is at **Le Faou**. Nearby at **Ménez-Meur** is a wooded estate with wild and farm animals, and a Breton horse museum. Around the park are 16 small specialty museums, some paying tribute to country traditions such as hunting, fishing, and tanning. The **Musée de l'Ecole Rurale** (open Feb–Oct) at Trégarvan re-creates an early 20th-century rural school. Other museums cover subjects such as medieval monastic life, peddlers, and the lifestyle of a Breton country priest. The **Ferme d'Antéa** in Brasparts displays contemporary crafts and art.

## ❹ Douarnenez

Finistère. 🏠 17,000. 🚌 ℹ️ 2 rue du Docteur Mével (02 98 92 13 35). 🛒 Mon–Sat. 🔲 douarnenez-tourisme.com

At the start of the 20th century Douarnenez used to be France's leading sardine port; today it is still devoted to fishing, but is also a tourist resort with beaches on both sides of the Pouldavid estuary.

Nearby lies the tiny **Ile Tristan**, linked to the tragic love story of Tristan and Iseult. In the 16th century it was the stronghold of a notorious brigand, La Fontenelle.

The picturesque **Port du Rosmeur** offers cafés, fish restaurants, and boat trips around the bay, with a lively early morning *criée* (fish auction) held in the nearby Nouveau Port. The Port-Rhu has been turned into a floating museum, **Le Port Musée**, with over 100 boats and several shipyards. Some of the larger vessels can be visited.

🏛️ **Le Port Musée**
Pl de l'Enfer. **Tel** 02 98 92 65 20. **Open** Jul–Aug: daily; Feb–Jun & Sep–Oct: Tue–Sun. 🛒 🚻 🔲 port-musee.org

Locronan's 15th-century Eglise St.-Ronan, seen from the churchyard

## ❺ Locronan

Finistère. 🏠 1,000. ℹ️ pl de la Mairie (02 98 91 70 14). 🔲 locronan-tourisme.com

During the 15th–17th centuries Locronan grew wealthy from the manufacture of sailcloth. After Louis XIV ended the Breton monopoly on this trade, the town declined – leaving an

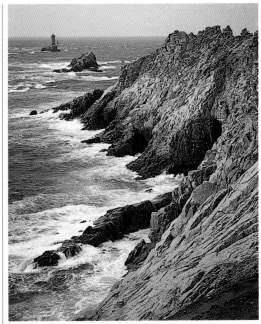
The awe-inspiring cliffs of Pointe du Raz

elegant ensemble of Renaissance buildings that attract many visitors. In the town's central cobblestone square is a late 15th-century church dedicated to the Irish missionary St.-Ronan. Down Rue Moal is the delightful **Chapelle Notre-Dame-de-Bonne-Nouvelle**, with a calvary and a fountain. Every July Locronan is the scene of a *Troménie*, a hilltop pilgrimage held in honor of St. Ronan. The more elaborate *Grande Troménie* takes place every six years.

## ❻ Pointe du Raz

Finistère. ✈️ Quimper. 🚌 Quimper, then bus. ℹ️ Audierne (02 98 70 12 20); Maison du Site (02 98 70 67 18). 🔲 pointeduraz.com

The dramatic Pointe du Raz, almost 262 ft (80 m) high, is a headland jutting into the Atlantic at the tip of Cap Sizun. The views of jagged rocks and pounding seas are breathtaking. Farther west is the flat Ile de Sein and beyond that the lighthouse of Ar Men. Despite being only 5 ft (1.5 m) above sea level, Ile de Sein is nevertheless

home to 260 inhabitants, and can be reached by boat from Audierne in an hour.

## ❼ Pays Bigouden

Finistère. 🚌 Pont l'Abbé. ℹ️ Pont l'Abbé (02 98 82 37 99). 🔲 ot-pontlabbe29.fr

Brittany's southwest tip is known as the Pays Bigouden, a windy peninsula with proud and ancient traditions. The region is famous for the women's tall *coiffes* still worn at festivals and *pardons (see p247)*, which can also be seen at the **Musée Bigouden**.

Along the Baie d'Audierne is a brooding landscape of hamlets and isolated chapels – the 15th-century calvary at **Notre-Dame-de-Tronoën** is the oldest in Brittany. There are invigorating sea views from **Pointe de la Torche** (a good surfing spot) and from the **Eckmühl lighthouse**.

🏛️ **Musée Bigouden**
Le Château, Pont l'Abbé. **Tel** 02 98 66 09 03. **Open** Apr–Jun & Sep & Oct: Tue–Sun pm only; Jul & Aug: daily. **Closed** May 1. 🛒

# ❽ Quimper

Finistère. 70,000. pl de la Résistance (02 98 53 04 05). Wed, Sat. quimper-tourisme.com

The ancient capital of Cornouaille, Quimper has a distinctly Breton character. Here you can find Breton language books and music on sale, buy a traditional costume, and tuck into some of the best *crêpes* and cider in Brittany. Quimper gets its name from *kemper*, a Breton word meaning "the confluence of two rivers," and the Steir and Odet still flow through this relaxed cathedral city.

West of the cathedral lies a traffic-free area known as **Vieux Quimper**, full of stores, *crêperies*, and half-timbered houses. Rue Kéréon is the main thoroughfare, with place au Beurre and the picturesque *hôtels particuliers* (mansions) of rue des Gentilshommes to the north.

Quimper has been producing faïence, elegant hand-painted pottery, since 1690. The design often features decorative flowers and animals framed by blue and yellow borders. Now mainly decorative, faïence is today exported to collectors all over the world. In the southwest of the city lies the oldest factory, **Faïenceries HB-Henriot**, which is open to visitors year round.

### ⌂ Cathédrale St.-Corentin

Quimper's cathedral is dedicated to the city's founder-bishop St. Corentin. Begun in 1240 – its colorfully painted interior now restored – it is the earliest Gothic building in Lower Brittany, and was bizarrely constructed with its choir at a slight angle to the nave, perhaps to fit in with some since-disappeared buildings. The two spires of the west facade were added in 1856. Between them rides a statue of King Gradlon, the

View of the Harbour of Quimper (1857) by Eugène Boudin at the Museé des Beaux-Arts, Quimper

mythical founder of the drowned city of Ys. After this deluge he chose Quimper as his new capital and St. Corentin as his spiritual guide.

### ▥ Musée des Beaux-Arts

40 pl St.-Corentin. **Tel** 02 98 95 45 20. **Open** Jul–Aug: daily; Sep–Jun: Wed–Mon. **Closed** most public hols; Nov–Mar: Sun am. mbaq.fr

Quimper's art museum is one of the best in the region. The collection is strong on late 19th- and early 20th-century artists, and their work – such as Jean-Eugène Buland's *Visite à Ste.-Marie de Bénodet*, offering a valuable insight into the way visiting painters perpetuated a romantic view of Brittany. Also on show are works by members of the Pont-Aven School and local artists such as J.-J. Lemordant and Max Jacob.

Typical faïence plate from Quimper

### ▥ Musée Départemental Breton

1 rue de Roi-Gradlon. **Tel** 02 98 95 21 60. **Open** mid-Jun–mid-Sep: daily; mid-Sep–mid-Jun: Tue–Sat; Sun pm.

The 16th-century Bishop's Palace has collections of Breton costumes, furniture, and faïence, including Cornouaille *coiffes*, ornately carved box-beds and closets, and turn-of-the-20th-century tourist posters for Brittany.

# ❾ Concarneau

Finistère. 20,000. only for islands. quai d'Aiguillon (02 98 97 01 44). Mon & Fri. tourismeconcarneau.fr

An important fishing port, Concarneau's principal attraction is its 14th-century **Ville Close** (walled town), built on an island in the harbor and encircled by massive lichen-covered granite ramparts. Access is by bridge from place Jean Jaurès. Parts of the ramparts can be toured, and the narrow streets are full of stores and restaurants. The **Musée de la Pêche**, housed in the port's ancient barracks, explains the local techniques and history of sea-fishing.

### ▥ Musée de la Pêche

3 rue Vauban. **Tel** 02 98 97 10 20. **Open** Feb, Mar, Nov & Dec: Tue–Sun pm; Apr–Jun & Sep–Oct: Tue–Sun; Jul & Aug: daily. **Closed** Jan, public hols.

Fishing boats in Concarneau's busy harbor

*For hotels and restaurants in this region see pp560–61 and pp585–6*

# ⑩ Pont-Aven

Finistère. ⚐ 3,000. 🚌 🛈 5 Pl Julia
(02 98 06 04 70). 🖦 Tue, Sat.
🌐 pontaven.com

Port-Aven was once a market town of "14 mills and 15 houses," but its picturesque location in the wooded Aven estuary made it attractive to many late 19th-century artists.

In 1888 Paul Gauguin, along with like-minded painters Emile Bernard and Paul Sérusier, developed a crude, colorful style of painting known as Synthetism. Drawing inspiration from the Breton landscape and its people, the Ecole de Pont-Aven (Pont-Aven School) worked here and in nearby Le Pouldu until 1896.

The town is devoted to art and has 50 private galleries, along with the informative **Musée de Pont-Aven**, which documents the achievements of the Pont-Aven School. The surrounding woods proved inspirational to many artists, and offer pleasant walks – one leads through the Bois d'Amour to the **Chapelle de Trémalo**, where the wooden Christ in Gauguin's *Le Christ Jaune* still hangs.

🏛 **Musée de Pont-Aven**
Place Julia. **Tel** 02 98 06 14 43. **Open** Feb, Mar, Nov & Dec: Tue–Sun pms; Apr–Jun, Sep & Oct: Tue–Sun; Jul & Aug: daily. **Closed** Jan 1, Dec 25. ♿ ⬛ 📷

Notre-Dame-de-Kroaz-Baz, Roscoff

# ⑪ Le Pouldu

Finistère. ⚐ 4,000. 🚌 🛈 Pl Ocean
Le Pouldu, Clohars (02 98 39 93 42).
🌐 quimperle-terreoceane.com

A quiet port at the mouth of the River Laïta, Le Pouldu has a small beach and good walks. Its main attraction is **Maison Musée du Pouldu**, a reconstruction of the inn where Paul Gauguin and other artists stayed between 1889 and 1893. They covered every inch of the dining room, including the window-panes, with self-portraits, caricatures, and still-lifes. These were discovered in 1924 beneath layers of wallpaper.

🏛 **Maison Musée du Pouldu**
10 rue des Grands Sables. **Tel** 02 98 39 98 51. **Open** Apr–mid-Jun & mid-Sep–Nov: Sat & Sun pm; mid-Jun–mid-Sep: Tue–Sun. ♿

# ⑫ Roscoff

Finistère. ⚐ 3,700. 🚢 🚌 🛳
🛈 Quai d'Auxerre (02 98 61 12 13).
🖦 Wed. 🌐 roscoff-tourisme.com

Roscoff is a thriving Channel port and beach resort. Signs of its wealthy sea-faring past can be found along rue Amiral Réveillère and in place Lacaze-Duthiers. The granite facades of the 16th- and 17th-century shipowners' mansions, and the weatherbeaten caravels and cannon on the **Eglise Notre-Dame-de-Kroaz-Baz**, testify to the days when Roscoff privateers were as notorious as those of St.-Malo *(see p286)*.

The famous French onion sellers (Johnnies) first crossed the Channel in 1828, selling plaited onions door to door. **Maison des Johnnies** tells their history.

To find out more about the manufacture and taste of products made with seaweed, visit **Algoplus**. From the harbor you can take a boat trip to the peaceful **Ile de Batz**. Near Pointe de Bloscon are tropical gardens.

🏛 **Maison des Johnnies**
48 rue Brizeux. **Tel** 02 98 61 25 48. **Open** mid-Apr–end Apr: Thu–Sat pm; May–mid-Jun & mid-Sep–Oct: Tue–Sat pm; mid-Jun–mid-Sep: Tue, Thu–Sat & Wed pm. **Closed** Nov–mid-Apr. ♿ ⬛ 📷 obligatory.

🏛 **Algoplus**
Zone de Bloscon. **Tel** 02 98 61 14 14. 📷 call ahead.

## Paul Gauguin in Brittany

Carving, Chapelle de Trémalo

Paul Gauguin's (1848–1903) story reads like a romantic novel. At the age of 35 he left his career as a stockbroker to become a full-time painter. From 1886 to 1894 he lived and worked in Brittany, at Pont-Aven and Le Pouldu, where he painted the landscape and its people. He chose to concentrate on the intense, almost "primitive" quality of the Breton Catholic faith, attempting to convey it in his work. This is evident in *Le Christ Jaune* (The Yellow Christ), inspired by a woodcarving in the Trémalo chapel. In Gauguin's painting, the Crucifixion is a reality in the midst of the contemporary Breton landscape, rather than a remote or symbolic event. This theme recurs in many of his paintings from the period, including *Jacob Wrestling with the Angel* (1888).

*Le Christ Jaune* (1889) by Paul Gauguin

## ⑬ St.-Thégonnec

Finistère. 🚉 **Open** daily. ♿

This is one of the most complete parish closes in Brittany. As you pass through its triumphal archway, the ossuary is to the left. The calvary, directly ahead, was built in 1610 and perfectly illustrates the extraordinary skills Breton sculptors developed as they worked with the local granite. Among the many animated figures surrounding the central cross, a small niche contains a statue of St. Thégonnec with a cart pulled by wolves.

## ⑭ Guimiliau

Finistère. **Open** daily. ♿

Almost 200 figures adorn Guimiliau's intensely decorated calvary (1581–8), many wearing 16th-century dress. Among them you can contemplate the legendary torment of Katell Gollet, a servant girl tortured by demons for stealing a consecrated wafer to please her lover. The church is dedicated to St. Miliau and has a richly decorated south porch. The baptistery's elaborate carved oak canopy dates from 1675.

**Font canopy from 1675, Guimiliau**

## ⑮ Lampaul-Guimiliau

Finistère. **Open** daily. ♿

Entering through the monumental gate, the chapel and ossuary lie to the left, while the calvary is to the right. Here, however, it is the church that demands most attention. The interior is zealously painted and carved, including some naive scenes from the Passion depicted along the 16th-century rood-beam dividing the nave and choir.

# Parish Closes

Reflecting the religious fervor of the Bretons, the Enclos Paroissiaux (parish closes) were built during the 15th–18th centuries. At that time Brittany had few urban centers but many wealthy rural settlements that profited from maritime trading and the manufacture of cloth. Grand religious monuments, some taking over 200 years to complete, were built by small villages inspired by spiritual zeal and the more earthly desire to rival their neighbors. Some of the finest parish closes lie in the Elorn Valley, linked by a well-signposted Circuit des Enclos Paroissiaux.

**The enclosure**, surrounded by a stone wall, is the hallowed area. By following the wall, visitors are drawn toward the triumphal arch, shown here in Pleyben.

**The small cemetery** reflects the size of the community that built these great churches.

### Guimiliau Parish Close

*The three essential features of a parish close are a triumphal gateway marking the entry into the hallowed enclosure, a calvary depicting scenes from the Passion and Crucifixion, and an ossuary beside the church porch.*

**The calvary** is unique to Brittany, and may have been inspired by the crosses set on top of menhirs (*see p283*) by the early Christians. They provide a walk-around Bible lesson, often with the characters in 17th-century costumes as in this example from St.-Thégonnec.

**Brittany's parish closes** are mostly in the Elorn Valley. As well as St.-Thégonnec, Lampaul-Guimiliau, and Guimiliau, other parish closes to visit include Bodilis, La Martyre, La Roche-Maurice, Ploudiry, Sizun, and Commana. Farther afield lie Plougastel-Daoulas and Pleyben, while Guéhenno is in the Morbihan region.
🛈 rue de Kerven, Landivisiau (02 98 68 33 33).

**Church interiors,** are usually adorned with depictions of local saints and scenes from their lives, along with ornately carved beams and furniture. This is the altarpiece in Guimiliau.

**In the ossuary** bones exhumed from the cemetery would be stored. Built close to the church entrance, the ossuary was considered a bridge between the living and the dead.

Church

South Porch

Calvary

Funeral Chapel

Field of the Dead

Triumphal Arch

**The triumphal arch** at St.-Thégonnec, a monumental entrance, heralds the worshiper's arrival on sacred ground, like the righteous entering Heaven.

**Carvings in stone** were created as biblical cartoons to instruct and inspire visitors. Their clear message is now often obscured by weather and lichen, but this one in St.-Thégonnec is well preserved.

The chapel of Notre-Dame, perched on the cliffs above the beach of Port-Blanc, Côte de Granit Rose

## ⑯ Côte de Granit Rose

Côtes d'Armor. ✈ 🚍 🚌 Lannion.
ℹ️ Lannion (02 96 05 60 70). 🛍️ Thu.
🌐 **bretagne-cotedegranitrose.com**

The coast between Paimpol and Trébeurden is known as the Côte de Granit Rose due to its pink cliffs. These are best between Trégastel and Trébeurden; their granite is also used in neighboring towns. The coast between Trébeurden and Perros-Guirec is one of Brittany's most popular family vacation areas.

Farther east there are quieter beaches and coves, as at **Trévou-Tréguignec** and **Port-Blanc**. Beyond Tréguier, **Paimpol** is a working fishing port that once sent huge cod and whaling fleets to fish off Iceland and Newfoundland.

## ⑰ Tréguier

Côtes d'Armor. 🔼 3,000. ℹ️ Port de Plaisance (02 96 92 22 33). 🛍️ Wed.
🌐 **tregor-cotedajoncstourisme.com**

Overlooking the estuary of the Jaundy and Guindy rivers, Tréguier stands apart from the resorts of the Côte de Granit Rose. It is a typically Breton market town, with one main attraction, the 14th to 15th-century **Cathédrale St.-Tugdual**. It has three towers: one Gothic, one Romanesque, and one 18th century. The last, financed by Louis XVI with winnings from the Paris Lottery, has holes in the shapes of playing-card suits.

### Environs

Chapelle St.-Gonery in Plougrescant has a leaning lead spire and a 15th-century painted wooden ceiling.

## ⑱ Ile de Bréhat

Côtes d'Armor. 🔼 420. 🚍
🚌 Paimpol, then bus to Pointe de l'Arcouest (Mon–Sat winter; daily summer), then boat. ℹ️ Office de tourisme de l'île de Breéhat (02 96 20 04 15). 🌐 **brehat-infos.fr**

A 15-minute crossing from the Pointe de l'Arcouest, the Île de Bréhat is actually two islands, joined by a bridge. Together they are only 2 miles (3.5 km) long. With motorized traffic banned, and a climate mild enough for mimosa and a variety of fruit trees to flourish, it has a relaxing atmosphere. Bicycle rentals and boat tours are available in the main town, **Port-Clos**, and you can walk to the island's highest point, the **Chapelle St.-Michel**.

Chapelle St.-Michel, a landmark on Île de Bréhat

## ⑲ Carnac

Morbihan. 🔼 4,600. 🚌 ℹ️ 74 avenue des Druides (02 97 52 13 52).
🌐 **ot-carnac.fr**

Carnac, a popular beach resort, is also one of the world's great prehistoric sites, with almost 3,000 menhirs in parallel rows, and an excellent **Musée de Préhistoire**.

The 17th-century **Eglise St.-Cornély** is dedicated to St. Cornelius, patron saint of horned animals. His life is depicted on its ceiling.

🏛️ **Maison des Megaliths**
**Tel** 02 97 52 29 81. **Open** daily.
**Closed** Jan 1, May 1, Dec 25. 🎫

🏛️ **Musée de Préhistoire**
10 pl de la Chapelle. **Tel** 02 97 52 22 04. **Open** Apr–Oct: Wed–Mon (Jul & Aug: daily); Mar & Nov: Wed–Mon pms only. **Closed** Jan, May 1, Dec. 🎫 ♿

## ⑳ Presqu'île de Quiberon

Morbihan. 🔼 5,000. ✈ Quiberon (via Lorient). 🚍 Jul–Aug. 🚌 Quiberon.
ℹ️ Quiberon (02 97 50 07 84).
🛍️ Sat, Wed (summer).
🌐 **quiberon.com**

Once an Island, the slender Quiberon peninsula has a bleak west coast with sea-punished cliffs, known as the Côte Sauvage. The east is more benign. At the peninsula's southern tip is the fishing port and resort of **Quiberon**, with a car ferry to Belle-Ile. In 1795, 10,000 Royalist troops were massacred here in an ill-fated attempt to reverse the French Revolution.

# Brittany's Prehistoric Monuments

At Carnac, thousands of ancient granite rocks were arranged in mysterious lines and patterns by Megalithic tribes as early as 4000 BC. Their original purpose remains obscure: the significance was probably religious, but the precise patterns also suggest an early astronomical calendar. Celts, Romans, and Christians have since adapted them to their own beliefs.

The Gavrinis Tumulus, Golfe du Morbihan

## Megaliths

*There are many different formations of megaliths, all with a particular purpose. Words from the Breton language, such as men (stone), dole (table) and hir (long), are still used to describe them.*

**Menhirs**, the most common megaliths, are upright stones, standing alone or arranged in lines. Those in circles are known as cromlechs.

**Dolmen**, two upright stones roofed by a third, were used as a burial chamber, such as the Merchant's Table at Locmariaquer.

***Allée couverte***, upright stones placed in a row and roofed to form a covered alley, can be seen at Carnac.

**A tumulus** is a dolmen covered with stones and soil to form a burial mound.

**Key**

- Megalithic sites
- Alignments

0 kilometers     10
0 miles     5

Carnac
Gavrinis
BAIE DE QUIBERON
Quiberon

Brittany's major megalithic sites

Alignment at Carnac

Menhirs of all shapes in a field near Carnac

## ❷❶ Belle-Ile-en-Mer

Morbihan. 🏠 5,000. 🚢 Quiberon (via Lorient). 🚢 from Quiberon. *i* quai Bonnelle, Le Palais (02 97 31 81 93). 🏪 daily. **w** belle-ile.com

Brittany's largest island lies 9 miles (14 km) south of Quiberon and can be reached in 45 minutes by car ferry from Quiberon. The coast has cliffs and good beaches; inland lie exposed highlands intersected by sheltered valleys. In the main town, Le Palais, stands the **Citadelle Vauban**, a 16th-century star-shaped fortress, and there are fine walks and views along the southern Côte Sauvage.

## ❷❷ Vannes

Morbihan. 🏠 58,000. 🚌 🚍 *i* 1 quai Tabarly (02 97 47 24 34). 🏪 Wed & Sat. **w** tourisme-vannes.com

Standing at the head of the Golfe du Morbihan, Vannes was the capital of the Veneti, a seafaring Armorican tribe defeated by Caesar in 56 BC. In the 9th century Nominoë, the first Duke of Brittany, made it his power base. The city remained influential up until the signing of the union with France in 1532, when Rennes became the Breton capital. Today it is a busy commercial city with a well-preserved medieval quarter, and a good base for exploring the Golfe du Morbihan.

The impressive eastern walls of old Vannes can be viewed from promenade de la Garenne. Two of the city's old gates survive at either end: Porte-Prison in the north, and the southern Porte-Poterne with a row of 17th-century washhouses close by.

Walking up from Porte St.-Vincent, you find the city's old market squares, still in use today. **Place des Lices** was once the scene of medieval tournaments and the streets around rue de la Monnaie are full of well-preserved 16th-century houses.

Begun in the 13th century, **Cathédrale St.-Pierre** has since been drastically remodeled and restored. The Chapel of the Holy Sacrament houses the

Cloisters of St.-Pierre in Vannes

revered tomb of Vincent Ferrier, a Spanish saint who died in Vannes in 1419.

Opposite the west front of the cathedral, the old covered market **La Cohue** (meaning "throng" or "hubbub") was once the city's central meeting place. Parts of the building date from the 13th century. A museum inside features works by contemporary artists such as Tal-Coat, Soulages, and Genevieve, plus a small collection related to seafaring.

Housed in the 15th-century Château Gaillard, the **Musée d'Histoire** is a rich assembly of finds from Morbihan's many prehistoric sites, including jewelry, pottery, and weapons. There is also a gallery of medieval and Renaissance objets d'art.

### 🏛 Musée d'Histoire

Château Gaillard, 2 rue Noé. **Tel** 02 97 01 63 00. **Open** Jun–Sep: pm only. **Closed** public hols. 🎟

### Environs

To the south of the city the **Parc du Golfe** is a beautiful leisure park with waterfront attractions, including a butterfly garden, a conservatory set in a tropical forest, and an aquarium that boasts over 400 species of fish. Northeast of Vannes, off the N166, lie the romantic ruins of the imposing 15th-century castle, **Tours d'Elven**. Very near Parc du Golfe is **Le Ker**, an educational theme park, which includes a museum and movie theater. It recounts the history of Brittany from prehistoric times to the arrival of the Romans through interactive exhibits and 4D movies.

### 🎡 Le Ker

1 rue Gilles Gahinet, Parc du Golfe, 56000 Vannes. **Tel** 02 97 47 60 22. **Open** 12:30–6pm Mon–Fri, 10am–6pm Sat & Sun. 🅿 🎟 ♿

## ❷❸ Golfe du Morbihan

Morbihan. 🚢 Lorient. 🚌 🚍 🚢 Vannes. *i* Vannes (02 97 47 24 34). **w** tourisme-vannes.com

Morbihan means "little sea" in Breton, an apt description for this landlocked expanse of tidal water. Only connected to the Atlantic by a small channel between the Locmariaquer and Rhuys peninsulas, the gulf is dotted with islands. Around 40 are inhabited, with the **Ile d'Arz** and the **Ile-aux-Moines** the largest. These are served by regular ferries from Conleau and Port-Blanc respectively.

Around the gulf several small harbors earn a living from fishing, oyster cultivation, and tourism. There is a wealth of

The picturesque fishing port of Le Bono in Golfe du Morbihan

The beach resort of Dinard, on the Côte d'Emeraude

megalithic sites, notably the island of **Gavrinis**, where stone carvings have been excavated (*see p283*). There are boat trips to Gavrinis from Larmor-Baden and around the gulf from Locmariaquer, Auray, Vannes, and Port-Navalo.

The medieval Château de Josselin on the banks of the River Oust

## ㉔ Josselin

Morbihan. 🏯 2,500. 🚌 🚺 21 rue Olivier de Clisson (02 97 22 36 43). 🛒 Sat. 🔲 **josselin-tourisme.fr**

Overlooking the River Oust, Josselin is dominated by a medieval **Château** owned by the de Rohan family since the end of the 15th century. Only four of its nine towers survive. The elaborate inner granite facade incorporates the letter "A" – a tribute to the much-loved Duchess Anne of Brittany (1477–1514), who presided over Brittany's "Golden Age." Tours are given of the 19th-century interior, and in the former stables there is a Musée des Poupées with 600 dolls. In the town, **Basilique**

**Notre-Dame-du-Roncier** contains the mausoleum of the castle's most famous owner and constable of France, Olivier de Clisson (1336–1407). West of Josselin at Kerguéhennec, the grounds of an 18th-century château have become a modern sculpture park.

🏠 **Château de Josselin**
**Tel** 02 97 22 36 45. **Open** Apr–Aug: daily (Apr–mid-Jul & Sep: pms only); Oct: Sat & Sun pms. 🎫 ♿
🔲 **chateaujosselin.com**

## ㉕ Forêt de Paimpont

Ille-et-Vilaine. ✈ Rennes. 🚌 Monfort-sur-Meu. 🚌 Rennes. 🚺 Pl du Roi St.-Judicael, Paimpont (02 99 07 84 23). 🔲 **tourisme-broceliande.bzh**

Also known as the Forêt de Brocéliande, this is a remnant of the dense primeval woods that once covered much of Armorica. It has long been associated with the legends of King Arthur, and

Legendary sorcerer Merlin and Viviane, the Lady of the Lake

visitors still search for the magical spring where the sorcerer Merlin first met the Lady of the Lake. The small village of **Paimpont** is a good base for exploring both the forest and its myths.

## ㉖ Côte d'Emeraude

Ille-et-Vilaine & Côtes d'Armor. ✈ 🚢 Dinard–St.-Malo. 🚌 🚌 🚢 🚺 Dinard (08 21 23 55 00). 🔲 **ot-dinard.com**

Between Le Val-André and the Pointe du Grouin, near Cancale, sandy beaches, rocky headlands, and classic beach resorts stretch along Brittany's northern shore. Known as the Emerald Coast, its self-proclaimed Queen is the aristocratic resort of **Dinard**, "discovered" in the 1850s and still playing host to the international rich.

To its west are resorts including St.-Jacut-de-la-Mer, St.-Cast-le-Guildo, Sables d'Or-les-Pins and Erquy, all with tempting beaches. In the Baie de la Frênaye, the medieval **Fort La Latte** provides good views from high in its ancient watchtower, while the lighthouse that dominates **Cap Fréhel** nearby offers even more extensive panoramas.

East of Dinard, the D186 runs across the **Barrage de la Rance** to St.-Malo. Built in 1966 it was the world's first dam to generate electricity by using tidal power. Beyond St.-Malo, coves and beaches surround La Guimorais, while around the Pointe du Grouin the seas are often truly emerald.

## Seafarers of St.-Malo

St.-Malo owes its wealth and reputation to the exploits of its mariners. In 1534 Jacques Cartier, born in nearby Rothéneuf, discovered the mouth of the St. Lawrence river in Canada and claimed the territory for France. It was Breton sailors who voyaged to South America in 1698 to colonize the Iles Malouines, known today as Las Malvinas or the Falklands. By the 17th century St.-Malo was the largest port in France and famous for its corsairs – privateers licensed by the king to prey on foreign ships. The most illustrious were the swashbuckling René Duguay-Trouin (1673–1736), who captured Rio de Janeiro from the Portuguese in 1711, and the intrepid Robert Surcouf (1773–1827), whose ships hounded vessels of the British East India Company. The riches won by trade and piracy enabled St.-Malo's shipowners to build great mansions known as *malouinières*.

Explorer Jacques Cartier (1491–1557)

# ⑳ St.-Malo

Ille-et-Vilaine. 🚗 53,000. ✈ 🚊 🚌 🚢 *i* Esplanade St.-Vincent (08 25 13 52 00). 🛍 Tue & Fri. 🌐 **saint-malo-tourisme.com**

Once a fortified island, St.-Malo stands in a commanding position at the mouth of the River Rance.

The city is named after Maclou, a Welsh monk who came here in the 6th century to spread the Christian message. During the 16th–19th centuries the port won prosperity and power through the exploits of its seafarers. St.-Malo was heavily bombed in 1944 but has since been scrupulously restored and is now a major port and ferry terminal as well as a resort.

The old city is encircled by ramparts that provide fine views of St.-Malo and its islands. Take the steps up by the **Porte St.-Vincent** and walk clockwise, passing the 15th-century **Grande Porte**.

Within the city is a web of cobblestone streets with tall 18th-century buildings housing stores, fish restaurants, and crêperies. Rue Porcon-de-la-Barbinais leads to **Cathédrale St.-Vincent**, with its somber 12th-century nave contrasting with the stained glass of the chancel. On cour La Houssaye, the 15th-century Maison de la Duchesse Anne has been carefully restored.

St.-Malo seen at low tide through the gate of Fort National

### 🏰 Château de St.-Malo

Pl Châteaubriand, near the Marina. **Tel** 02 99 40 71 57. **Open** Apr–Sep: daily; Oct–Mar: Tue–Sun. **Closed** Jan 1, May 1, Nov 1 & 11, Dec 25. 🖼

St.-Malo's castle dates from the 14th–15th centuries. The great keep contains a museum of the city's history, including the adventures of its state-sponsored corsairs. From its watchtowers there is an impressive view. Nearby, in place Vauban, a tropical aquarium has been built into the ramparts, while on the edge of town the Grand Aquarium has a shark tank and simulated submarine rides.

### 🏛 Fort National

**Open** Jun–Sep: daily at low tide. 🖼 Constructed in 1689 by Louis XIV's famous military architect, Vauban, this fort can be reached on foot at low tide and offers

good views of St.-Malo and its ramparts. At low tide you can also walk out to **Petit Bé Fort** (open Easter–mid-Nov) and **Grand Bé**, where St.-Malo-born writer François-René de Chateaubriand lies buried. From the top there are great views along the whole of Côte d'Emeraude (see p285).

### 🏛 Tour Solidor

St.-Servan. **Tel** 02 99 40 71 58. **Open** Apr–Sep: daily; Oct–Mar: Tue–Sun. **Closed** Jan 1, May 1, Nov 1 & 11, Dec 25. 🖼

To the west of St.-Malo in St.-Servan, the three-towered Tour Solidor was built in 1382. Formerly a toll house, it was also a prison under the Revolution, and now houses an intriguing museum devoted to the ships and sailors that rounded Cape Horn, with ship models, logs, and various nautical instruments.

### Environs

When the tide is out, good beaches are revealed around St.-Malo and in the nearby suburbs of St.-Servan and Paramé. A passenger ferry runs to Dinard in summer (see p285) and the Channel Islands and there are boat trips up the Rance to Dinan, and out to the Iles Chausey, Ile de Cézembre and Cap Fréhel.

At Rothéneuf you can visit the **Manoir Limoëlou**, home of the navigator Jacques Cartier. Nearby, on the coast, Les Rochers Sculptés is a beguiling array of

A stone sculpture at Les Rochers Sculptés created by the abbé Fouré near St.-Malo

granite faces and figures carved into the cliffs by a local priest, Abbé Fouré, at the end of the 19th century.

### 🏠 Manoir Limoëlou
Rue D. Macdonald-Stuart, Limoëlou-Rothéneuf. **Tel** 02 99 40 97 73. **Open** Jun–Sep: daily; Oct–May: Mon–Sat. **Closed** public hols. 🅿 🅲 oblig. 👤

## ㉘ Cancale
Ille-et-Vilaine. 🔼 5,500. 🚌 🛈 44 rue du Port (02 99 89 63 72). 🚢 Sun. 🌐 **cancale-tourisme.fr**

A small port with views across the Baie du Mont-St.-Michel, Cancale is entirely devoted to the cultivation and consumption of oysters. Prized by the Romans, the acclaimed flavor of Cancale's oysters is said to derive from the strong tides that wash over them daily. You can survey the beds from a *sentier des douaniers* (coastguards' footpath, the GR34) running along the cliffs.

There are plenty of opportunities for sampling the local specialty provided by a multitude of bars and restaurants along the busy docks of the Port de la Houle, where the fishing boats arrive at high tide. Devotees should pay a visit to the **Musée de l'Huître, du Coquillage et de la Mer.**

### 🏛 Musée de l'Huître, du Coquillage et de la Mer – La Ferme Marine
Aurore. **Tel** 02 99 89 69 99. **Open** mid-Feb–Jun & mid-Sep–Oct: Mon–Fri pms; Jul–mid-Sep: daily. 🅲 🅿

## ㉙ Dinan
Côtes d'Armor. 🔼 10,000. 🚌 🚍 🛈 9 rue du Château (02 96 87 69 76). 🚢 Thu. 🌐 **dinan-tourisme.com**

Set on a hill overlooking the wooded Rance Valley, Dinan is a modern market town with a medieval heart. Surrounded by ramparts, the half-timbered houses and cobblestone streets of its Vieille Ville have an impressive, unforced unity best appreciated by climbing to the top of its 15th-century **Tour d'Horloge**, in rue de l'Horloge. Nearby, **Basilique St.-Sauveur** contains the heart of Dinan's most famous son, the 14th-century warrior Bertrand du Guesclin.

Behind the church, Les Jardins Anglais offer good views of the River Rance and the viaduct spanning it. A couple of streets farther north, the steep, geranium-decorated rue du Jerzual winds down through the 14th-century town gate to the port. Once a busy harbor from which cloth was shipped, it is now a quiet backwater, where you can take a pleasure cruise, or walk along a towpath to the restored 17th-century **Abbaye St.-Magloire** at Léhon.

The **Château de Dinan** is flanked by the 14th-century Duc de Bretagne Jean IV keep and the 15th-century Tour de Coëtquen. In contrast to the military-style exterior, the inside comprises a kitchen, chapel, and residential rooms with monumental fireplaces.

### 🏠 Château de Dinan
rue du Château. **Tel** 02 96 87 58 72. **Open** Jun–Sep: daily; Easter–May & Oct–mid-Nov: daily pms only. **Closed** mid-Nov–Easter, public hols. 🅿

Author and diplomat François-René de Chateaubriand (1768–1848)

## ㉚ Combourg
Ille-et-Vilaine. 🔼 5,000. 🚌 🚍 🛈 9 rue Notre Dame (02 99 73 13 93). 🚢 Mon. 🌐 **tourisme.bretagneromantique.fr**

A small, sleepy town beside a lake, Combourg is completely overshadowed by the great, haunting **Château de Combourg**. The buildings seen today date from the 14th and 15th centuries. In 1761 the château was bought by the Comte de Chateaubriand, and the melancholic childhood spent there by his son, the author and diplomat François-René de Chateaubriand (1768–1848), is candidly described in his entertaining chronicle *Mémoires d'Outre-Tombe*.

Empty after the Revolution, the château was restored in the 19th century and is open for tours. One room has the belongings of François-René de Chateaubriand.

### 🏠 Château de Combourg
23 rue des Princes. **Tel** 02 99 73 22 95. **Open** Apr–Jun, Sep & Oct: Mon–Fri & Sun pm; Jul & Aug: daily. 🅲 🅿 🌐 **chateau-combourg.com**

Dinan and the Gothic bridge crossing the River Rance

## Rennes City Centre

① Portes Mordelaises
② Cathédrale St.-Pierre
③ Eglise St.-Sauveur
④ Hôtel de Ville
⑤ Opéra de Rennes
⑥ Eglise St.-Germain
⑦ Parc du Thabor
⑧ Palais du Parlement de Bretagne
⑨ Musée des Beaux-Arts

0 meters 250
0 yards 250

**For keys to symbols** *see back flap*

Gare Routière, Gare SNCF
300 m (330 yards)

# ① Rennes

Ille-et-Vilaine. 215,000. 11 rue St-Yves (02 99 67 11 11). Tue–Sat. **tourisme-rennes.com**

Founded by the Gauls and colonized by the Romans, Rennes is strategically located where the Vilaine and Ille rivers meet. After Brittany's union with France in 1532, the town became regional capital. In 1720 a fire lasting for six days devastated the city. Today a small part of the medieval city survives, together with the neat grid of 18th-century buildings that arose from the ashes.

The imposing Neoclassical façade of Cathédrale St.-Pierre

Around this historic core are the tower blocks and high-tech factories of modern Rennes – a confident provincial capital with two universities and a thriving cultural life.

Wandering through the streets that radiate from place des Lices and place Ste.-Anne, it is easy to imagine what Rennes was like before the Great Fire. Now mostly pedestrian-only, this area has become the city's youthful heart with plenty of bars, *crêperies*, and designer stores. At the western end of rue de la Monnaie is the 15th-century **Portes Mordelaises**, once part of the city's ramparts.

Close by, **Cathédrale St.-Pierre** was completed in 1844, the third on this site. Note the carved 16th-century Flemish altarpiece. Nearby is the 18th-century **Eglise St.-Sauveur**. In the place de la Mairie stands the early 18th-century **Hôtel de Ville** and the NeoClassical **Opéra de Rennes**. Just south of the attractive rue St.-George, **Eglise St.-Germain** has a typically Breton belfry and wooden vaulting. The **Parc du Thabor**, once part of a Benedictine monastery, is ideal for walks and picnics.

Half-timbered houses lining the narrow streets of old Rennes

### Palais du Parlement de Bretagne

Pl du Parlement. **Open** Tourist Office for guided tours (02 99 67 11 66). **tourisme-rennes.com**

Rennes' Law Courts, built in 1618–55, formed the seat of the region's governing body until the Revolution. Severely damaged by fire during riots over fish prices in 1994, the major restoration work is all but complete, including the unique coffered ceiling and gilded woodwork of the Grande Chambre. Today, the Salle des Pas Perdus, with its vaulted ceilings, can again be admired by the public.

### 🏛 Musée des Beaux-Arts

20 quai Zola. **Tel** 02 23 62 17 45.
**Open** Tue–Sun. **Closed** public hols.
🅿 w mbar.org.

The Musée des Beaux-Arts has a wide-ranging collection of art from the 14th century to the present, including a room of art on Breton themes. There are paintings by Gauguin, Bernard, and other members of the Pont-Aven School (see p279), and three works by Picasso, including the lively *Baigneuse* painted at Dinard in 1928.

### 🏛 Musée de Bretagne

10 cours des Alliés. **Tel** 02 23 40 66 00.
**Open** Tue–Sun pm only. **Closed** public hols. 🅿 ♿ w musee-bretagne.fr

Housed in the Rennes cultural center along with the Science Museum and Planetarium, the Musée de Bretagne includes examples of traditional Breton furniture and costume, and displays on Brittany's prehistoric megaliths, the growth of Rennes, rural crafts, and the fishing industry.

#### Environs

Just south of Rennes, the **Ecomusée du Pays de Rennes** traces the history of a local farm since the 17th century.

Some 10 miles (16 km) to the southeast of Rennes is **Châteaugiron**, a charming medieval village, with an imposing castle and houses preserving their wooden eaves.

### 🏛 Ecomusée du Pays de Rennes

Ferme de la Bintinais, rte de Châtillon-sur-Seiche. **Tel** 02 99 51 38 15.
**Open** Tue–Fri (Sat, Sun pm only).
**Closed** public hols. 🅿 ♿
w ecomusee-rennes-metropole.fr

### 🏠 Château de Châteaugiron

**Open** Jul & Aug: Mon–Sat & Sun pm;
call 02 99 37 89 02. 🅿 🅿

## ㉜ Fougères

Ille-et-Vilaine. 🗺 23,000. 🚍 🛈 2 rue Nationale (02 99 94 12 20). 🛒 Sat.
w ot-fougeres.fr

A fortress town close to the Breton border, Fougères rests on a hill overlooking the Nançon river. In the valley below, and still linked to the Haute Ville by a curtain of ancient ramparts, stands

The mighty fortifications of Château de Fougères

the mighty 11th- to 15th-century **Château de Fougères**. To get a good overview of the château, go to the gardens of place aux Arbres behind the 16th-century **Eglise St.-Léonard**. From here you can descend to the river and the medieval houses around place du Marchix. The Flamboyant Gothic **Eglise St.-Sulpice**, with its 18th-century wood-paneled interior and granite retables, is well worth visiting.

A walk around the castle's massive outer fortifications reveals the ambitious scale of its construction, with 13 towers and walls over 10 ft (3 m) thick. You can still climb the castle's ramparts to get a feel of what it was like to live within its staggered defenses. Much of the action in Balzac's novel *Les Chouans* (1829) takes place in and around Fougères and its castle.

### 🏠 Château de Fougères

Pl Pierre-Simon. **Tel** 02 99 99 79 59.
**Open** Jun–Sep: daily; Oct–May: Tue–Sun. **Closed** Jan, 25 Dec. 🅿
w chateau-fougeres.com

Overhanging timber-frame houses on rue Beaudrairie, Vitré

## ㉝ Vitré

Ille-et-Vilaine. 🗺 16,000. 🚆 🚍 🛈
pl Général de Gaulle (02 99 75 04 46).
🛒 Mon & Sat. w bretagne-vitre.com

The fortified town of Vitré is set high on a hill overlooking the Vilaine Valley. Its medieval **Château** is complete with pencil-point turrets and picturesque 15th- to 16th-century buildings in attendance. The castle was rebuilt in the 14th–15th centuries and follows a triangular plan, with some of its ramparts walkable. There is a museum in the Tour St.-Laurent.

To the east, rue Beaudrairie and rue d'Embas have overhanging timber-frame houses with remarkable patterning.

The 15th- to 16th-century **Cathédrale Notre-Dame**, built in Flamboyant Gothic style, has a south facade with an exterior stone pulpit. Farther along rue Notre-Dame, the promenade du Val skirts around the town's ramparts.

To the southeast of Vitré on the D88, the **Château des Rochers-Sévigné** was once the home of Mme de Sévigné (1626–96), famous letter-writer and chronicler of life at the court of Louis XIV. The park, chapel, and some of her rooms are open to the public.

### 🏠 Château de Vitré

**Tel** 02 99 75 04 54. **Open** Apr–Sep: daily; Mar & Oct: Wed–Mon; Nov–Feb: Mon, Wed–Fri & Sun pm. **Closed** Jan 1, Easter, Nov 1, Dec 25. 🅿

### 🏠 Château des Rochers-Sévigné

**Tel** 02 99 96 76 51. **Open** Mar & Oct: Wed–Mon; Apr–Sep: daily. **Closed** Nov–Feb. 🅿 obligatory. ♿ restricted.

# THE LOIRE VALLEY

*Loire-Atlantique · Vendée · Maine-et-Loire · Sarthe · Indre-et-Loire
Loir-et-Cher · Loiret · Eure-et-Loir · Cher*

Renowned for its sumptuous châteaux, the glorious valley of the Loire, now classified a UNESCO World Heritage Site, is rich both in history and architecture. Like the River Loire, this vast region runs through the heart of French life. Its sophisticated cities, luxuriant landscape, and magnificent food and wine add up to a bourgeois paradise.

The lush Loire Valley is supremely regal. Orléans was France's intellectual capital in the 13th century, attracting artists, poets, and troubadours to the royal court. But the medieval court never stayed in one place for long, which led to the building of magnificent châteaux all along the Loire. Chambord and Chenonceau, the two greatest Renaissance châteaux, remain prestigious symbols of royal rule, resplendent amid vast hunting forests and waterways.

Due to its central location, culture, and fine cuisine, Tours is the natural visitors' capital. Angers is a close second, but more authentic are the historic towns of Saumur, Amboise, Blois, and Beaugency, strung out like jewels along the river. This is the classic Loire Valley, a château trail that embraces the Renaissance gardens of Villandry and the fairy-tale turrets of Ussé. Venture northward, and the cathedral cities of Le Mans and Chartres reign supreme, their medieval centers bordered by Gallo-Roman walls. Nantes in the west is a breezy, forward-looking port and gateway to the Atlantic.

Southward, the windswept Vendée is edged by a wild, sandy coastline that is perfect for windsurfers and nature lovers alike. Inland, the Loire's more peaceful tributaries and the watery Sologne beg to be explored. Also ripe for discovery are troglodyte caves, sleepy hamlets, and small Romanesque churches decorated with frescoes. Inviting inns offer game, fish, and abundant fresh vegetables to be lingered over with a light white Vouvray wine or a fruity Bourgeuil. Overindulgence is no sin in this rich region.

he River Loire at Montsoreau, southeast of Saumur

◄ Formal gardens at the Château de Villandry

# Exploring the Loire Valley

The lush valley landscape, studded with France's greatest châteaux, is the main attraction. Numerous river cruises are available, while the sandy Atlantic coast offers beach vacations. Peaceful country vacations can be had in the Vendée, and in the Loir and Indre valleys. Wine tours focus on Bourgueil, Chinon, Muscadet, Saumur, and Vouvray vintages. The most charming bases are Amboise, Beaugency, Blois, and Saumur, but culture lovers are well provided for throughout the region.

Countryside around Vouvray

## Getting Around

The region is well-served by transportation links. Nantes and Tours airports have international flights; Tours airport also serves Marseille and Figari (Corsica). Chartres, Le Mans, Angers, and Nantes are reached from Paris by the A11, and the A10 links Orléans, Blois, and Tours. The TGV train travels from Paris to Le Mans (1 hr); Tours (1 hr); Angers (90 mins); and Nantes (2 hrs). There is also TGV access from Lille (Eurostar interchange). The smaller châteaux can be difficult to reach by public transportation, but there are tours from major tourist centers.

The Château de Chinon, on a rocky outcrop above the Vienne river

## Sights at a Glance

1. Nantes
2. The Vendée
3. Angers
4. Le Mans
5. Saumur
6. Montreuil-Bellay
7. Abbaye Royale de Fontevraud
8. Chinon
9. *Château d'Ussé*
10. Château de Langeais
11. Château d'Azay-le-Rideau
12. Château de Villandry
13. Tours
14. Vouvray
15. Loches
16. Montrésor
17. *Château de Chenonceau pp302–3*
18. Amboise
19. *Château de Chambord pp306–7*
20. Blois
21. Beaugency
22. Vendôme
23. The Loir
24. *Chartres pp311–15*
25. Orléans
26. St.-Benoît-sur-Loire
27. Bourges

### Key

— Freeway
— Highway
— Secondary road
— Minor road
— Scenic route
— Main railroad
— Minor railroad
— Regional border
△ Summit

A bridge over the River Loire pictured on a clear day

Tomb of François II and his wife, Marguerite de Foix, in Cathédrale St.-Pierre, Nantes

# ❶ Nantes

Loire-Atlantique. 270,000. 9 rue des Etats (08 92 46 40 44). Tue–Sun. nantes-tourisme.com

For centuries, Nantes disputed with Rennes the title of capital of Brittany. Yet links with the Plantagenets and Henri IV also bound it to the "royal" River Loire. Since the 1790s it has officially ceased to be part of Brittany, and, though still Breton at heart, it is today capital of the Pays de la Loire.

Visually, Nantes is a city of variety, with high-tech towers overlooking the port, canals, and Art Nouveau squares. Chic bars and restaurants cram the medieval nucleus, bounded by place St.-Croix and the château.

The **Cathédrale St.-Pierre et St.-Paul**, completed in 1893, is notable both for its sculpted Gothic portals and Renaissance tomb of François II, the last duke of Brittany.

More impressive is the **Château des Ducs de Bretagne**, where Anne of Brittany was born in 1477 and where the Edict of Nantes was signed by Henri IV in 1598, granting Protestants religious freedom. Following major restoration work the château now houses the lively, interactive **Musée d'Histoire**. It charts the history of Nantes through 32 rooms of exhibits, including Turner's painting of the Loire embankments in Nantes and a virtual visit of the city in 1757.

## 🏰 Château des Ducs de Bretagne

Pl Marc Elder. **Tel** 08 11 46 46 44. **Open** Jul & Aug: daily; Sep–Jun: Tue–Sun. **Closed** Jan 1, May 1, Nov 1, Dec 25.

## Environs

From Nantes, boats cruise the Erdre and Sèvre Nantaise rivers, passing châteaux and vineyards. Some 20 miles (32 km) southeast is **Clisson**, razed to the ground during the 1793 Vendée Uprising, and later rebuilt by sculptor François-Frédéric Lemot along Italian lines, with Neoclassical villas. On a spur overlooking the Sèvre Nantaise river is the ruined 13th-century **Château de Clisson**.

## 🏰 Château de Clisson

**Tel** 02 40 54 02 22. **Open** Feb–Apr & Oct–Dec: Wed–Mon pms; May–Jun & Sep: Wed–Mon; Jul & Aug: daily. **Closed** Jan 1, May 1, Christmas vacation.

# ❷ The Vendée

Vendée and Maine-et-Loire. Nantes. La Roche-sur-Yon. La Roche-sur-Yon (02 51 36 00 85). vendee-tourisme.com

The counter-revolutionary movement that swept western France between 1793 and 1799 began as a series of uprisings in the Vendée, still an evocative name to the French. As a bastion of the *ancien régime*, the region rebelled against urban Republican values. But a violent massacre in 1793 left 80,000 royalists dead in one day, as they tried to cross the Loire at St.-Florent-le-Vieil. The Vendée farmers were staunch royalists, and, although they ultimately lost, the region remains colored by conservatism and religious fervor to this day.

This local history is dramatically retraced at **Le Puy du Fou** in Les Epesses, south of Cholet, with its spectacular summer evening live show, *Cinéscénie*. More sober accounts are given at Logis de La Chabotterie, near St.-Sulpice-de-Verdon, and the Musée du Textile in Cholet, whose flax and hemp textiles provided the royalist heroes with their kerchiefs: originally white, then blood-red.

The tranquil Vendée offers green tourism inland, in the *bocage vendéen*, a wooded backwater with paths and nature trails. The Atlantic coast between the Loire and La Rochelle has beaches, yet the only sizable resort here is **Les Sables d'Olonne**, with boat trips to the salt-marshes, out to sea, or to the nearby **Ile d'Yeu**. To the north,

The harbor at Ile de Noirmoutier in the Vendée

*For hotels and restaurants in this region see pp561–2 and pp586–9*

the marshy **Ile de Noirmoutier** is connected to the mainland at low tide via the Gois causeway.

Inland lies the remote **Marais Poitevin** *(see pp412–13)*, its marshes home to bird sanctuaries and fine churches (Maillezais, Vix, Maillé) in hamlets bordered by canals. It is France's largest complex of manmade waterways, largely reclaimed for farming in the west, while farther east is a nature lover's paradise. Coulon is the main center for renting punts.

The Apocalypse tapestry in Angers

# ❸ Angers

Maine-et-Loire. ⛺ 155,000. ✈ 🚉 🚌 *i* 7 pl Kennedy (02 41 23 50 00). ✉ Tue–Sun. 🖥 **angersloiretourisme.com**

Angers is the historic capital of Anjou, home of the Plantagenets and gateway to the Loire Valley. The town has a formidable 13th-century **Château** *(see p246)*. Inside is the longest (338 ft/103 m) and one of the finest medieval tapestries in the world. It tells the story of the Apocalypse, with battles between hydras and angels.

A short walk from the castle is the **Cathédrale St.-Maurice**, noted for its facade and 13th-century stained-glass windows. Close by is Maison d'Adam, with carvings showing the tree of life. The nearby **Galerie David d'Angers**, housed in the glass-covered ruins of a 13th-century church, celebrates the sculptor born in Angers. Across the River Maine, the Hôpital St.-Jean, a hospital for the poor from 1174 to 1854, houses the **Musée Jean Lurçat**. Its prize exhibit is the exquisite *Chant du Monde* tapestry, which was created by Lurçat in 1957. In the same building is **Le Musée de la Tapisserie Contemporaine**, with displays of ceramics and paintings.

---

🏰 **Château d'Angers**
**Tel** 02 41 86 48 77. **Open** daily. **Closed** Jan 1, May 1, Nov 1 & 11, Dec 25. 🅿 🖥

🏛 **Galerie David d'Angers**
33bis rue Toussaint. **Tel** 02 41 05 38 90. **Open** Tue–Sun. **Closed** most public hols. 🅿

🏛 **Musée Jean Lurçat/Le Musée de la Tapisserie Contemporaine**
4 bd Arago. **Tel** 02 41 24 18 45. **Open** Tue–Sun. **Closed** most public vacations. 🅿 ♿

## Environs
Within a 13-mile (21-km) radius lie the Renaissance **Château de Serrant** and moated **Château du Plessis-Bourré**, a decorative pleasuredome in a feudal shell. Follow the Loire east along the sandbanks and dykes, enjoying the fish restaurants en route.

🏰 **Château de Serrant**
St.-Georges-sur-Loire. **Tel** 02 41 39 13 01. **Open** mid-Feb–mid-Jul & Sep–Oct: Wed–Sun; mid-Jul–Aug: daily. **Closed** Nov–mid-Feb. 🅿 🏯 obligatory. 🏯 🖥 **chateau-serrant.net**

🏰 **Château du Plessis-Bourré**
Écuillé. **Tel** 02 41 32 06 72. **Open** mid-Feb–Mar & Oct: Tue–Sun pms; Apr–Jun & Sep: Tue–Sun; Jul–Aug: daily; Nov: daily pms. 🅿 🖥 obligatory. 🖥 **plessis-bourre.com**

# ❹ Le Mans

Sarthe. ⛺ 150,000. ✈ 🚉 🚌 *i* 16 rue de l'Etoile (02 43 28 17 22). ✉ Tue–Sun. 🖥 **lemans-tourisme.com**

Ever since Monsieur Bollée became the first designer to place an engine under a car hood, Le Mans has been synonymous with the auto trade. Bollée's son created an embryonic Grand Prix, and the event

---

Stained-glass Ascension window in the Cathédrale St.-Julien, Le Mans

*(see p41)* and the associated **Musée des 24 Heures du Mans** have remained star attractions ever since. Cité Plantagenet, the ancient fortified center, is surrounded by the greatest Roman walls in France, best seen from the quai Louis Blanc. Once abandoned, the area has been restored, and is now used for filming epics such as *Cyrano de Bergerac*, set among Renaissance mansions, half-timbered houses, arcaded alleys, and tiny courtyards. The crown is the Gothic **Cathédrale St.-Julien**, borne aloft by flying buttresses, with its Romanesque portal rivaling that of Chartres. Inside, the Angevin nave opens into a Gothic choir, complemented by sculpted capitals and a 12th-century Ascension window.

🏛 **Musée des 24 Heures du Mans**
9 pl Luigi Chinetti. **Tel** 02 43 72 72 24. **Open** daily. 🅿 ♿

Le Mans racetrack: a 1933 print from the French magazine *Illustration*

# ❺ Saumur

Maine-et-Loire. 🚉 32,000. 🚉 🚌 ℹ️
8bis quai Carnot (02 41 40 20 60). 🗓️
Thu, Sat. 🅦 ot-saumur.fr

Saumur is celebrated for its fairytale château, cavalry school, mushrooms, and sparkling wines. Its stone mansions recall the city's 17th-century heyday, when it was a bastion of Protestantism and vied with Angers as the intellectual capital of Anjou.

High above both town and river is the turreted **Château de Saumur**. The present structure was started in the 14th century by Louis I of Anjou and remodeled later by his grandson, King René. Collections include medieval sculpture and equestrian exhibits.

The Military Cavalry School, established in Saumur in 1814, led to the creation of the **Musée des Blindés**, which exhibits 150 different armored vehicles, and of the prestigious Cadre Noir horseback-riding formation.

The Château de Saumur and spire of St.-Pierre seen from the Loire

King René's coat of arms

Morning training sessions and stable visits, along with occasional evening performances, can be seen at the **Ecole Nationale d'Equitation**. The nearby subterranean **Parc Pierre et Lumière** (sculptures in the tufa cave walls of prominent local tourist sites), is well worth a visit; as is Europe's largest dolmen, with its collection of prehistoric implements, in Bagneux.

Before you leave the area, be sure to sample the local *méthode champenoise* sparkling wine – the best in France outside Champagne – in one of the many wine cellars or at the Maison des Vins in town.

🏠 **Château de Saumur**
**Tel** 02 41 40 24 40. **Open** Apr–Oct: Tue–Sun (mid-Jun–mid-Sep: daily). 🅿️ 🚻

**Ecole Nationale d'Equitation**
St.-Hilaire-St.-Florent. **Tel** 02 41 53 50 60. **Open** Feb–mid-Nov for guided tours; Apr–Oct: call for performance times. **Closed** public hols. 🅿️ ♿ 🚻 oblig. 🖥️ 🅦 cadrenoir.fr

**Environs**
**Eglise Notre-Dame** at Cunault, an 11th-century Romanesque priory church, has a fine west door and carved capitals, while a subterranean fort and myriad caves and tunnels can be seen at **Château de Brézé**.

# ❻ Montreuil-Bellay

Maine-et-Loire. 🚉 4,500. 🚉 🚌
ℹ️ pl du Concorde (02 41 52 32 39).
🗓️ Tue (mid-Jun–mid-Sep: also Sun).
🅦 ville-montreuil-bellay.com

Set on the River Thouet 11 miles (17 km) south of Saumur, Montreuil-Bellay is one of the region's most gracious small towns and is an ideal base for touring Anjou. The towering roofline of the Gothic collegiate church overlooks walled mansions and surrounding vineyards (wine tasting recommended). The **Chapelle St.-Jean** was an ancient hospice and pilgrimage center.

The imposing **Château de Montreuil-Bellay**, established in 1025, is a veritable fortress with its 13 interlocking towers, barbican, and ramparts.

A 15th-century house lies beyond the fortified gateway, complete with vaulted medieval kitchen and an oratory decorated with 15th-century frescoes.

🏠 **Château de Montreuil-Bellay**
**Tel** 02 41 52 33 06. **Open** Apr–early Nov: Wed–Mon (Jul–Aug: daily). 🅿️ 🚻

---

## Troglodyte Dwellings

Some of the best troglodyte settlements in France have been carved out of the soft limestone (tufa) of the Loire Valley, especially around Saumur, Vouvray, and along the River Loir. The caves, cut out of cliff faces or dug underground, have been a source of cheap, secure accommodations for centuries. Today they are popular as *résidences secondaires*, or used for wine storage and mushroom growing. Some are now restaurants or hotels, and old quarries at Doué-la-Fontaine accommodate a zoo and a 15th-century amphitheater. At Rochemenier, near Saumur, is a well-preserved troglodyte village museum. A central pit is surrounded by a warren of caves, barns, wine cellars, dwellings, and even a simple underground chapel.

Heralded by chimneypots, the underground hamlet of La Fosse was inhabited until the late 20th century by three families, and is now a museum of family life underground.

A typical troglodyte dwelling

# Court Life in the Renaissance

François I's reign, from 1515 to 1547, witnessed the apogee of the French Renaissance, characterized by an intense period of château-building and an interest in humanism and the arts. The itinerant court traveled between the pleasure palaces of Amboise, Blois, and Chambord in the Loire. Days were devoted to hunting, falconry, *fêtes champêtres* (country festivals), or *jeu de paume*, a forerunner of tennis. Nights were given over to feasting, balls, poetry, and romantic assignations.

**Lute and mandolin** music were much in vogue, as were Italian recitals and masquerades. Musicians played at the twice-weekly balls, where the pavane and galliard were danced.

**The antics** of François I's fools, Triboulet and Caillette, amused the court. Yet they were often mistreated: courtiers regularly nailed Caillette's ears to a post for fun, daring him to remain silent.

## Renaissance Feasts

*Dinner usually took place before 7pm to the accompaniment of Italian music. Humanist texts were read aloud, and the king's fools amused the courtiers.*

**Courtiers** used their own knives at dinner. Forks were still rare, although their use was spreading from Italy.

**A typical royal dinner** comprised smoked eel, salted ham, veal *pâté*, egg and saffron soups, roast game, and boiled meats, as well as fish dishes in lemon or gooseberry sauce.

**The cost** of lavish damask, satin, and silk costumes often sent courtiers into debt.

**Diane de Poitiers** (1499–1566) became the mistress of the future Henri II when he was 12 years old. Two years later he married Catherine de' Medici, but Diane remained his favorite until his death.

**Artists symbolized love** in different ways during the Renaissance. Winged hearts charmingly perform the function here.

The Grand Moûtier cloisters

# ❼ Abbaye Royale de Fontevraud

Maine-et-Loire. 🚌 from Saumur.
**Tel** 02 41 51 73 52. **Open** daily.
**Closed** Jan, Dec 25. 🅿

The Abbaye Royale de Fontevraud is the largest and most remarkably intact medieval abbey in Europe. It was founded in the early 12th century by Robert d'Arbrissel, a visionary itinerant preacher, who set up a Benedictine community of monks,

**Tour Evraud**

**Pepper-pot chimneys** top the towers of the kitchen, restored in the 20th century.

**Fireplace alcoves** that look like side chapels housed the ovens.

## The Plantagenets

The legendary counts of Anjou were named after the *genêt*, the sprig of broom Geoffrey Plantagenet wore in his cap. He married Matilda, daughter of England's Henry I. In 1154, when their son Henry – who married Eleanor of Aquitaine *(see p55)* – acceded to the English throne, the Plantagenet dynasty of English kings was founded, fusing French and English destinies for 300 years.

Effigies of Henry II, Plantagenet King of England, and Eleanor of Aquitaine

nuns, nobles, lepers, and vagabonds. The radical founder entrusted the running of the abbey to an abbess, usually from a noble family, and the abbey became a favorite sanctuary for the female aristocracy, including Eleanor of Aquitaine.

From 1804 to 1963 the abbey was used as a prison, since when the buildings have been undergoing painstaking restoration by the French State. Wandering around the abbey buildings and gardens gives a fascinating insight into monastic life.

The focal point was the Romanesque abbey church, consecrated in 1119. It boasts beautifully carved capitals and an immense nave with four domes, one of the finest examples of a cupola nave in France. Inside are the painted effigies of the Plantagenets, dating from the early 13th century: Henry II of England, his redoubtable wife Queen Eleanor of Aquitaine, their crusading son Richard the Lionheart, and Isabelle d'Angoulême, widow of his infamous brother, King John of England.

The abbey's nuns lived around the Renaissance **Grand Moûtier cloisters**, forming one of the largest nunneries in France. The leper colony was once housed in the **St.-Lazare priory**, now a hotel and restaurant. The monastic quarters of **St.-Jean de l'Habit** no longer exist. Most impressive is the octagonal kitchen with its fireplaces and chimneys in the **Tour Evraud**, a rare example of secular Romanesque architecture. The abbey, now an important arts center, regularly hosts concerts and exhibitions.

# ❽ Chinon

Indre-et-Loire. 🏛 9,000. 🚉 🚌
ℹ 1 rue Rabelais (02 47 93 17 85).
🛍 Thu. 🌐 chinon-valdeloire.com

The Château de Chinon is an important shrine in Joan of Arc country and, as such, wheedles money from all passing pilgrims. It was here in 1429 that the saint first recognized the disguised dauphin (later Charles VII), and persuaded him to give

her an army to drive the English out of France. Before that, Chinon was the Plantagenet kings' favorite castle. Although the **château** is now mostly in ruins, the ramparts are an impressive sight from the opposite bank of the Vienne river. The town's bijou center is like a medieval movie set. **Rue**

Stallholder at Chinon's 1900s market

**Voltaire**, lined with 15th- and 16th-century houses and once enclosed by the castle walls, represents a cross-section of Chinonais history. At No. 12 is the **Musée Animé du Vin**, where animated figures tell the story of wine making. Nearby, at 44 rue Haute St.-Maurice is the Musée d'Art et d'Histoire, a stone

Vineyard in the Chinon wine region

mansion, where, in 1199, Richard the Lionheart is said to have died. The grandest mansion is the **Palais du Gouverneur,** with its double staircase and loggia. More charming is the **Maison Rouge** in the Grand Carroi, studded with a red-brick herringbone pattern.

The neighboring 15th-century **Château de Marçay,** built on an earlier 11th-century fortress *(see p561)* now offers luxurious rooms for a stay in the Loire Valley.

The 1900s market, with vendors in period costume, folk dancing, and music is a must (third Saturday of August).

**🏛 Musée Animé du Vin**
12 rue Voltaire. **Tel** 02 47 93 25 63. **Open** mid-Mar–mid-Oct: daily. 🌐 📷

**Environs**
Three miles (5 km) southwest of Chinon is **La Devinière,** birthplace of François Rabelais, the 16th-century writer, priest, doctor, and humanist scholar.

**🏛 La Devinière**
Seuilly. **Tel** 02 47 95 91 18. **Open** Apr–Sep: daily; Oct–Mar: Wed–Mon. **Closed** Jan 1, Dec 25. 🌐 📷

## 🄐 Château d'Ussé

Indre-et-Loire. 🚂 Chinon, then taxi. **Tel** 02 47 95 54 05. **Open** mid-Feb–mid-Nov: daily. 🌐 📷
**w** chateaudusse.fr

The fairytale Château d'Ussé enjoys a bucolic setting by the River Indre. Its romantic turrets, pointed towers, and chimneys inspired the writer Charles Perrault's *Sleeping Beauty*.

Constructed in the 15th century, the castle was gradually transformed into an aristocratic

château, which is still privately owned *(see p246)*. However, the sunless and musty interior is rather disappointing, and the *Sleeping Beauty* tableaux are clumsily presented.

The château's delightful Renaissance chapel, framed by the oak forest of Chinon, has lost its Aubusson tapestries, but retains a lovely della Robbia terracotta *Virgin*.

## 🄑 Château de Langeais

Indre-et-Loire. 🚂 Langeais. **Tel** 02 47 96 72 60. **Open** daily. **Closed** Jan 1, Dec 25. 🌐 📷 **w** chateau-de-langeais.com

Compared with neighboring towns, Langeais is distinctly untouristy and has a welcoming, unpretentious feel. Its château is fiercely feudal, built strictly for defence with a drawbridge, portcullis, and no concessions to the Renaissance. It was constructed by Louis XI in just four years, from 1465 to 1469, with hardly an alteration since then. The ruins of an impressive keep, built by Foulques Nerra in AD 994, stand in the small château courtyard.

A *son-et-lumière* display in the Salle de Mariage represents the marriage of Charles VIII and Anne of Brittany in 1491. Many of the rooms have intricate designs on the tiled floors, and all are hung with fine 15th- and 16th-century Flemish and Aubusson tapestries.

### François Rabelais

Rabelais, born in 1494, was a priest, doctor, diplomat, and humanist scholar noted for his wisdom and tolerance. He is best remembered for his many ribald satires (written as "medicine" for his patients), such as *Pantagruel* and *Gargantua*, set around his native Chinon.

Infant Pantagruel, depicted by Doré in 1854, was fed on the milk of 17,913 cows

## ⑪ Château d'Azay-le-Rideau

Indre-et-Loire. 🚉 🚌 Azay-le-Rideau.
**Tel** 02 47 45 42 04. **Open** daily; call
ahead for opening times. **Closed**
Jan 1, May 1, Dec 25. 🐾 🗐 🗐 🖺
**W** azay-le-rideau.fr

Balzac called Azay-le-Rideau "a
multifaceted diamond set in the
Indre." It is the most beguiling
and feminine of Loire châteaux,
created in the early 16th century
by Philippa Lesbahy, wife of
François I's corrupt finance
minister. Although Azay is
superficially Gothic (see pp60–61,
246), it clearly shows the
transition to the Renaissance:
the turrets are purely decorative
and the moats are picturesque
pools. Azay was a pleasure
palace, lived in during fine
weather and deserted in winter.

The interior is equally
delightful, an airy, creaking
mansion smelling faintly of
cedarwood and full of lovingly
re-created domestic detail. The
first floor is furnished in the
Renaissance style, with a fine
example of a portable Spanish
cabinet and exquisite tapestries.
The ground floor has 19th-
century furniture, dating from
the period of the château's
restoration. The four-storey
grand staircase is unusual for its
time, being straight as opposed
to spiral. In July and August, from
9pm until midnight, a sound and
light show takes place.

Wine-tasting opportunities
in the village are a welcome
reminder that vineyards are
all around.

The Château de Villandry's *jardin d'ornement*

## ⑫ Château de Villandry

Indre-et-Loire. 🚉 Tours, then taxi.
**Tel** 02 47 50 02 09. **Open** Château:
mid-Feb–mid-Nov & mid-Dec–early
Jan: daily. Gardens: daily. 🐾 🗐 🗐
Mar–Oct. **W** chateauvillandry.fr

Villandry was the last great Renaissance château built in the Loire
Valley, a perfect example of 16th-
century architecture. Its gardens
were restored to their original
splendor early in the last century
by Dr. Joachim Carvallo, whose
grandson continues his work.

The result is a patchwork of
sculpted shrubs and flowers on
three levels: the kitchen garden
(*jardin potager*), the ornamental
garden (*jardin d'ornement*), and,
on the highest level, the water
garden (*jardin d'eau*). There are
signs to explain the history and
meaning behind each plant:
the marrow, for instance, symbolized fertility; the cabbage,
sexual and spiritual corruption.
Plants were also prized for their
medicinal properties: cabbage
was thought to help cure

hangovers, while pimento
aided digestion.

The delicate roots of the
32 miles (51 km) of box hedge
that outline and highlight each
section mean that the whole
430,000 sq ft (40,000 sq m) of
gardens must be hand-weeded.

A *chocolatier* in Tours

## ⑬ Tours

Indre-et-Loire. 🚹 140,000. ✈ 🚉 🚌
🛈 78 rue Bernard Palissy (02 47 70 37
37). 🛒 Tue–Sun. **W** tours-tourisme.fr

Tours is the most appealing of
the major Loire cities, thanks
to bourgeois prosperity, an
intelligent restoration program
and its university population. It
is built on the site of a Roman
town, and was a center of
Christianity in the 4th century
under St. Martin, bishop of
Tours. In 1461 Louis XI made
the city the French capital.
However, during Henri IV's reign
the city lost favor with the
monarchy and the capital left
Tours for Paris.

Bombarded by the Prussians
in 1870, and bombed in World War II,
Tours suffered extensive damage.
By 1960, the middle classes had
abandoned the historic center
and it became a slum, full of
crumbling medieval masonry.

Château d'Azay-le-Rideau reflected in the River Indre

*For hotels and restaurants in this region see pp561–2 and pp586–9*

Regeneration of the city has succeeded due to the popular policies of Jean Royer, mayor of Tours from 1958 to 1996.

The traffic-free **place Plumereau** is Tours's most atmospheric quarter, set in the medieval heart of the city and full of cafés, boutiques, and galleries. Streets such as rue Briçonnet reveal half-timbered facades, hidden courtyards, and crooked towers. A gateway leads to place St.-Pierre-le-Puellier, a square with sunken Gallo-Roman remains and a Romanesque church converted into a café. A few streets away in place de Châteauneuf lies the Romanesque **Tour Charlemagne**, all that remains of St. Martin's first church. West of here is the highly upscale artisans' quarter, centered on rue du Petit St.-Martin.

On rue du Commerce lies the **Hôtel Goüin**, with its stunning facade. Just behind it is a contemporary art museum, **Centre de Création Contemporain Olivier Debré**, named after the 20th-century artist inspired by the Touraine region. It displays several of Olivier Debré's large-scale works and also hosts regular

Cathédrale St.-Gatien in Tours

temporary exhibitions of contemporary art throughout the year. A little farther west is the **Eglise St.-Julien**, whose Gothic monastic cells and chapterhouse contain a small wine museum. Next door, the **Musée du Compagnonnage** displays hundreds of finely crafted works by master craftsmen of the guilds.

The **Cathédrale St.-Gatien**, in the eastern sector of the city, was begun in the early 13th century and completed in the 16th. Its Flamboyant Gothic facade is

blackened and crumbling but still truly impressive, as are the medieval stained-glass windows.

The **Musée des Beaux-Arts**, set in the former archbishop's palace nearby, overlooks Classical gardens and a giant cedar of Lebanon. Its star exhibits are *Christ in the Garden of Olives* and *The Resurrection* by Mantegna.

**🏛 Centre de Création Contemporain Olivier Debré**
Jardin François 1er, Tours.
**Tel** 02 47 66 50 00. **Open** Winter: Wed–Sun; Summer: Tue–Sun. ♿ ♿

**🏛 Musée des Beaux-Arts**
18 pl François Sicard. **Tel** 02 47 05 68 73. **Open** Wed–Mon. **Closed** Jan 1, May 1, Jul 14, Nov 1 & 11, Dec 25. ♿

**🏛 Musée du Compagnonnage**
8 rue Nationale. **Tel** 02 47 21 62 20. **Open** mid-Jun–mid-Sep: daily; mid-Sep–mid-Jun: Wed–Mon. **Closed** Jan 1, May 1, Jul 14, Nov 1 & 11, Dec 25. ♿ ♿

**Environs**
Just outside Céré la Ronde, on the D764 from Montrichard to Loches, lies the 15th-century **Château de Montpoupon** and its excellent Musée du Veneur, which looks at the important role of horses in hunting.

## Tours Town Center

① Place Plumereau
② Tour Charlemagne
③ Hôtel Goüin
④ Centre de Création Contemporain Olivier Debré
⑤ Eglise St.-Julien
⑥ Cathédrale St.-Gatien
⑦ Musée des Beaux-Arts

0 meters    100
0 yards     100

For keys to symbols *see back flap*

# ⑭ Château de Chenonceau

A romantic pleasure palace, Chenonceau was created from the Renaissance onward by a series of aristocratic women. A magnificent avenue bordered by plane trees leads to symmetrical gardens and the serene vision that Flaubert praised as "floating on air and water." The château stretches across the River Cher with a 197-ft (60-m) gallery built over a series of arches, its elegant beauty reflected in the languid waters. The grandeur continues inside with splendidly furnished rooms, airy bedchambers, and fine paintings and tapestries.

**Turreted Pavilion**
This was built between 1513 and 1521 by Catherine Briçonnet and her husband, Thomas Bohier, over the foundations of an old water mill.

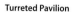

**Chapelle**
The chapel has a vaulted ceiling and pilasters sculpted with acanthus leaves and cockleshells. The stained glass, destroyed by a bomb in 1944, was replaced in 1953.

**Catherine de' Medici's Garden**
Lavish court receptions and transvestite balls were held under Catherine's auspices.

*Catherine de' Medici*

| 1500 | 1600 | 1700 | 1800 |
|---|---|---|---|

**1533** Marriage of Catherine de' Medici (1519–89) to Henri II (1519–59). Chenonceau becomes a Loire royal palace

**1559** On Henri's death, Catherine forces the disgraced Diane to accept the Château de Chaumont in exchange for Chenonceau

**1789** Chenonceau is spared in the French Revolution thanks to Madame Dupin

**1513** Thomas Bohier acquires medieval Chenonceau. His wife, Catherine Briçonnet, rebuilds it in Renaissance style

**1575** Louise de Lorraine (1554–1601) marries Henri III, Catherine's third and favorite son

**1547** Henri II offers Chenonceau to Diane de Poitiers, his lifelong mistress

**1863** Madame Pelouze restores château to its original

**1730–99** Madame Dupin, a "farmer-general's" wife, makes Chenonceau a salon for writers and philosophers

## VISITORS' CHECKLIST

**Practical Information**
Tel 08 20 20 90 90. **Open** daily.
gr. fl. only.
Promenades Nocturnes:
Jul–Aug (walks in the illuminated
grounds to the sound of classical
music). **chenonceau.com**

**Transportation**
Chenonceaux. from Tours.

**Grande Galerie**
The elegant gallery crowning
the bridge is Florentine in style,
and was created by Catherine de'
Medici between 1570 and 1576.

**1913** The château is
bought by the
Menier family, the
chocolatiers who still
own it today

**1900**

**1941** Chenonceau
chapel is damaged
in a bombing raid

*Diane de Poitiers*

# The Creation of Chenonceau

The women responsible for Chenonceau each left their mark.
Catherine Briçonnet, wife of the first owner, built the turreted
pavilion and one of the first straight staircases in France;
Henri II's mistress, Diane de Poitiers, added the formal gardens
and arched bridge over the river; Catherine de' Medici
transformed the bridge into an Italian-style gallery (having
evicted Diane following her husband's death in 1559); Louise
de Lorraine, bereaved wife of Henri III, inherited the château
in 1590 and painted the ceiling of her bedchamber black and
white (the color of royal mourning); Madame Dupin, a
cultured 18th-century châtelaine, saved the château from
destruction in the Revolution; and Madame Pelouze
undertook a complete restoration in 1863.

Ground floor

First floor

## Château Guide

The main living area was in the
square-shaped turreted pavilion
in the middle of the River Cher.
Four principal rooms open off the
Vestibule on the ground floor: the
Salle des Gardes and the Chambre
de Diane de Poitiers, both hung
with 16th-century Flemish
tapestries; the Chambre de
François I, with a Van Loo painting;
and the Salon Louis XIV. On the
first floor, reached via the
Italianate staircase, are other
sumptuous apartments
including the Chambre de
Catherine de' Médicis and the
Chambre de Vendôme.

1  Vestibule
2  Salle des Gardes
3  Chapelle
4  Terrasse
5  Librairie de Catherine
   de' Médicis
6  Cabinet Vert
7  Chambre de Diane de Poitiers
8  Grande Galerie
9  Chambre de François
10 Salon Louis XIV
11 Chambre des Cinq Reines
12 Cabinet des Estampes
13 Chambre de Catherine
   de' Médicis
14 Chambre de Vendôme
15 Chambre de Gabrielle d'Estrées

Chambre de Catherine de' Médicis

# ⓯ Vouvray

Indre-et-Loire. 🅼 3,500. 🅸 12 rue Rabelais (02 47 52 68 73). 🅴 Tue & Fri.
🅦 **tourismevouvray-valdeloire.com**

Just east of Tours is the village of Vouvray, home of the delicious white wine that Renaissance author Rabelais likened to taffeta.

The star vineyard is **Huet**, where, since 1990, grapes have been grown according to biodynamic methods: manual weeding, and natural fertilizers. In the preface to his novel *Quentin Durward,* Sir Walter Scott sang the praises of its dry white wines, which are still matured in chestnut barrels. Gaston Huet also hit the headlines in 1990 with his protests against the building of tracks for the TGV train over Vouvray vineyards. A compromise was reached and tunnels were built under the hilly vineyards.

The **Chateau de Montcontour**, where monks first planted vines in the 4th century, has its own winemaking museum in the 10th-century cellars hewn out of the tufa rock.

**Huet**
🏠 11–13 rue de la Croix-Buisée. **Tel** 02 47 52 78 87. **Open** Tue–Sat; wine

The medieval town of Loches

tastings and cellar visits by reservation only. **Closed** public hols. 🈯 for groups.

🏠 **Château de Moncontour**
Route de Rochecorbon. **Tel** 02 47 52 60 77. **Open** Apr–Sep: daily; Oct–Mar: Mon–Fri & Sat am. 🈯 🅲 Visits can be followed by wine tastings.
🅦 **moncontour.com**

# ⓰ Loches

Indre-et-Loire. 🅼 7,000. 🚌 🚃
🅸 pl de la Marne (02 47 91 82 82). 🅴 Wed & Sat. 🅦 **loches-tourainecotesud.com**

This picturesque, unspoiled medieval town is removed from the château trail in the Indre Valley. It is a backwater of late Gothic gateways and sculpted facades. Its keep boasts the deepest dungeons in the Loire. The **Logis Royal de Loches** is associated with Charles VII and his mistress Agnès Sorel. It is also where Joan of Arc pleaded with Charles to go to Reims and be crowned. Anne of Brittany's chapel is decorated with ermines, and contains an effigy of Agnès Sorel.

🏠 **Logis Royal de Loches**
**Tel** 02 47 59 01 32. **Open** daily. **Closed** Jan 1, Dec 25. 🈯 🅲 🅵

## The Heroine of France

Joan of Arc is the quintessential French national heroine, a virginal warrior, a woman martyr, a French figurehead. Her divinely led campaign to "drive the English out of France" during the Hundred Years' War has inspired plays, poetry, and films from Voltaire to Cecil B. de Mille. Responding to heavenly voices, she appeared on the scene as champion of the dauphin, the uncrowned Charles VII. He faced an Anglo-Burgundian alliance, which held most of northern France, and had escaped to the royal châteaux on the Loire. Joan convinced him of her mission, mustered the French troops and in May 1429 led them to victory over the English at Orléans. She then urged the dithering Charles to go to Reims to be crowned. However, in 1430 she was captured and handed over to the English. Accused of witchcraft, she was burned at the stake in Rouen in 1431 at the age of 19. Her legendary bravery and tragic martyrdom led to her canonization in 1920.

Earliest known drawing of Joan of Arc (1429)

**Portrait of Joan of Arc** in the Archives Nationales in Paris. She saved the city from the English on May 8, 1429, a date the Orléanais still celebrate annually *(see p316).*

# 🅱 Montrésor

Indre-et-Loire. 🄼 400. 🛈 43 grande rue (02 47 92 70 71). 🅦 tourisme-valdindrois-montresor.com

Classed as one of "the most beautiful villages in France," Montrésor does not disappoint. Set on the River Indrois, it became a Polish enclave in the 1840s. In 1849 a Polish nobleman, Count Branicki, bought the 15th-century **Château**, built on the site of one of Foulques Nerra's 11th-century fortifications. One of the most

Farm building and poppy fields near the village of Montrésor

charming castles in the Loire Valley, Château de Montrésor has remained in the family ever since, its interior unchanged since the mid-19th century.

🏠 **Château de Montrésor**
Tel 02 47 92 60 04. **Open** daily (mid-Nov–mid-Apr: Sat & Sun). 🕏 🗷

# 🅱 Amboise

Indre-et-Loire. 🄼 12,000. 🚇 🚌 🛈 quai du Général de Gaulle (02 47 57 09 28). 🖰 Fri & Sun am. 🅦 amboise-valdeloire.com

Few buildings are more historically important than the **Château d'Amboise**. Louis XI lived here; Charles VIII was born and died here; François I was brought up here, as were Catherine de'Medici's ten children. The château was also the setting for the 1560 Amboise Conspiracy, an ill-fated Huguenot plot against François II. Visitors are shown the metal lacework balcony that served as a gibbet for 12 of the 1,200 conspirators who were put to death. The **Tour des Minimes**, the château's original entrance, is famous for its huge spiral ramp, up which horsemen could ride to deliver provisions.

Amboise seen from the Loire

On the ramparts is the beautifully restored Gothic **Chapelle St.-Hubert**, Leonardo da Vinci's burial place. Under the patronage of François I, the artist lived in the nearby manor house of **Clos-Lucé** between 1516 and 1519. The Clos-Lucé contains a museum exhibiting models of Leonardo's inventions constructed from his sketches.

🏠 **Château d'Amboise**
Tel 02 47 57 00 98. **Open** daily. **Closed** Jan 1, Dec 25. 🕏 🗷 🅦 chateau-amboise.com

🏛 **Clos-Lucé**
2 rue de Clos-Lucé. **Tel** 02 47 57 00 73. **Open** daily. **Closed** Jan 1, Dec 25. 🕏 🕭 restricted. 🅦 vinci-closluce.com

**A romantic heroine**, Joan of Arc was a popular subject for artists. This painting of her is by François-Léon Benouville (1821–59).

**Burned at the stake** – a scene from *St. Joan*, Otto Preminger's 1957 epic movie, which starred Jean Seberg.

# ⑲ Château de Chambord

Henry James once said, "Chambord is truly royal – royal in its great scale, its grand air, and its indifference to common considerations." The Loire's largest residence, brainchild of the extravagant François I, began as a hunting lodge in the Forêt de Boulogne. In 1519 this was razed and the creation of present-day Chambord began, to a design probably initiated by Leonardo da Vinci. By 1537 the towers, keep, and terraces had been completed by 1,800 men and three master masons. At one point, François suggested diverting the Loire to flow in front of his château, but he settled for redirecting the nearby Cosson instead. His son Henry II continued his work, and Louis XIV completed the 440-roomed edifice in 1685.

The Château de Chambord with the River Cosson, a tributary of the Loire, in the foreground

**★ Roof Terraces**
This skyline of delicate cupolas has been likened to a miniature Oriental town. The roof terraces include a forest of elongated chimney pots, miniature spires, shell-shaped domes, and richly sculpted gables.

### KEY

① **The chapel** was begun by François I shortly before his death in 1547. Henri II added the second floor and Louis XIV the roof.

② **The central keep** (donjon), with its four circular towers, forms the nucleus of the château.

③ **The lantern tower** is 105 ft (32 m) high. Surmounting the terrace, it is supported by arched buttresses and crowned by a fleur-de-lis.

④ **François I's Bedchamber** is where the king, hurt by a failed romance, scratched a message on a pane of glass: "Souvent femme varie, bien fol est qui s'y fie." (Every woman is fickle, he who trusts one is a fool.)

**1547–59** Henri II adds the west wing and second story of the chapel

**1725–33** Inhabited by Stanislas Leczinski, exiled king of Poland who was made duke of Lorraine

**1748** The Maréchal de Saxe acquires Chambord. On his death, two years later, the château yet again falls into decline

**1840** Chambord declared a *Monument Historique*

| 1500 | 1600 | 1700 | 1800 | 1900 |
|------|------|------|------|------|

**1547** Death of François I

**1670** Molière's *Le Bourgeois Gentilhomme* staged at Chambord

**1970s** Chambord is restored and refurnished, and the moats re-dug.

**1519–47** The Count of Blois's hunting lodge demolished by François I, and the château created

**1669–85** Louis XIV completes the building, then abandons it

*Molière*

## ★ Vaulted Guardrooms

Arranged in the form of a Greek cross around the Grand Staircase, the vaulted guardrooms were once the setting for royal balls and plays. Their ceilings are decorated with François I's initials and salamander motif.

### The Salamander

François I chose the salamander as his enigmatic emblem. It appears over 800 times throughout the château.

## VISITORS' CHECKLIST

### Practical Information

**Tel** 02 54 50 40 00. **Open** Nov–Mar: 9am–5pm daily; Apr–Oct: 9am–6pm daily. **Closed** Jan 1, May 1, Dec 25. 🎫 🚫 📷 📹 📺 Apr–Sep: events include carriage rides, boat trips, and equestrian shows. 🔗 **chambord.org**

### Transportation

🚉 Blois, then taxi, bus (2, 4), or shuttle to Chambord (Apr–early Sep only). ℹ️ 02 54 90 41 41.

### Cabinet de François I

The king's barrel-vaulted study *(cabinet)* in the outer north tower was turned into an oratory in the 18th century by Queen Catherine Opalinska, wife of Stanislas Leczinski (Louis XV's father-in-law).

### ★ Grand Staircase

This innovative double-helix staircase was supposedly designed by Leonardo da Vinci. It ensures that the person going up and the person going down cannot meet.

### Louis XIV's Bedchamber

Within the Sun King's state apartments, the grandest quarters in the château, is Louis XIV's bedchamber.

Blois's Cathédrale St.-Louis and Hôtel de Ville seen from across the Loire

## ⑳ Blois

Loir-et-Cher. ⚊ 60,000. 🚊 🚌
ℹ️ 23 pl du château (02 54 90 41 41).
🛒 Wed, Sat. 🌐 bloischambord.com

Once a fief of the counts of Blois, the town rose to prominence as a royal domain in the 15th century, retaining its historic facades and refined atmosphere to this day. Architectural interest abounds in Vieux Blois, the hilly, partially pedestrianized quarter enclosed by the château, cathedral, and river. Four well-signposted walking tours act as a gentle introduction to the noble mansions and romantic courtyards that grace the Loire's most beguiling town.

Set back from the north bank of the river, the **Château Royal de Blois** was the principal royal residence until Henri IV moved the court to Paris in 1598 – Louis XIV's creation of Versailles (see pp178–81) was to mark the final eclipse of Blois. The château's four contrasting wings make a harmonious whole. The Salle des Etats Généraux, the only part of the building surviving from the 13th century, housed the council and court, and is the largest and best-preserved Gothic hall in France. The adjoining late 15th-century Louis XII wing, which houses the **Musée des Beaux Arts**, infuses Gothic design with Renaissance spirit, sealed with the king's porcupine symbol.

The 16th-century François I wing is a masterpiece of the French Renaissance containing a monumental spiral staircase in an octagonal tower. By contrast, the 17th-century Gaston d'Orléans wing is a model of Classical sobriety.

Blois is authentically furnished and hung with paintings interpreting its troubled past. These include a portrayal of the murder of the Duc de Guise in 1588. Suspected of heading a Catholic plot against Henri III, he was stabbed to death by guards in the king's chamber.

King Louis XII's porcupine symbol

The most intriguing room is Catherine de' Medici's study where, of the 237 carved wooden wall panels, four are secret cabinets said to have stored her poisons. Dominating the eastern

**François I Staircase**
Built between 1515 and 1524, this octagonal staircase is a masterpiece of the early French Renaissance.

**The gallery** provided an ideal setting for viewing jousts and receptions held in the inner courtyard.

**François I's salamander motif** adorns the openwork balustrades.

**The staircase** within the tower slopes appreciably more steeply than the balustrades.

Louis XII wing of the Château Royal de Blois

sector of the city, the **Cathédrale St.-Louis** is a 17th-century reconstruction of a Gothic church that was almost completely destroyed by a hurricane in 1678. Behind the cathedral the former bishop's palace, built in 1700, is the **Hôtel de Ville** (town hall). The surrounding terraced gardens have lovely views over the city and river. Opposite the cathedral is the **Maison des Acrobates**, carved with characters from medieval farces including acrobats and jugglers.

Place Louis-XII, the marketplace, is overlooked by splendid 17th-century facades. Rue Pierre de Blois, a quaint alley straddled by a Gothic passageway, winds downhill to the medieval Jewish ghetto. The rue des Juifs boasts several distinguished *hôtels particuliers* (mansions), including the galleried **Hôtel de Condé**, with its Renaissance archway and courtyard, and the **Hôtel Jassaud**, with magnificent 16th-century bas-reliefs above the main doorway. On the rue du Puits-Châtel, also rich in Renaissance mansions, is the galleried **Hôtel Sardini**.

Place Vauvert is the most charming square in Vieux Blois, with a fine example of a half-timbered house.

**🏠 Château Royal de Blois**
**Tel** 02 54 90 33 33. **Open** Jan–Mar & Nov–Dec: 10am–5pm daily; Apr–Jun & Sep–Oct: 9am–6:30pm daily; Jul–Aug: 9am–7pm daily. **Closed** Jan 1, Dec 25. 🎫 🎥 *Son y lumière* show: Apr–Sep nightly (with audioguides in English).

Covered Gothic passageway in rue Pierre de Blois

The nave of the abbey church of Notre-Dame in Beaugency

# ㉑ Beaugency

Loiret. 🗺 7,500. 🚉 🚌 🛈 3 pl de Docteur-Hyvernaud (02 38 44 54 42). 🛒 Sat. 🌐 **tourismebeaugency.fr**

Beaugency has long been the eastern gateway to the Loire. This compact medieval town makes a peaceful base for exploring the Orléanais region. Exceptionally for the Loire, it is possible to walk along the riverbanks and stone *levées*. At quai de l'Abbaye there is a good view of the 11th-century bridge which, until modern times, was the only crossing point between Blois and Orléans. An obvious target for enemy attack, it was captured four times by the English during the Hundred Years' War before being retaken by Joan of Arc in 1429.

The town center is dominated by a ruined 11th-century watchtower. It stands on **place St.-Firmin**, along with a 16th-century bell tower (the church was destroyed in the Revolution) and a statue of Joan of Arc. Period houses line the square.

Farther down is the **Château de Beaugency**, built on the site of the feudal castle by one of Joan of Arc's *compagnons d'armes*, Jean de Dunois. Highlights include the 16th-century seigneural lodgings and the kitchen. Facing the Château de Beaugency is **Notre-Dame**, a Romanesque abbey church that witnessed the annulment of the marriage between Eleanor of Aquitaine and Louis VII in 1152, leaving Eleanor free to marry the future Henry II of England.

Nearby is the medieval clock tower in rue du Change and the Renaissance **Hôtel de Ville**, its facade adorned with the town's arms. Equally lovely is the nearby ancient mill district around rue du Pont and rue du Ru, with its streams and riot of flowers.

**🏠 Château de Beaugency**
3 pl Dunois. **Tel** 02 38 44 36 47. **Open** mid-Feb–late-Feb: Tue–Sun pms; Mar: Sat & Sun pms; Apr–Jun & Sep–Oct: Tue–Sun; Jul–Aug: daily. **Closed** Nov–mid-Feb. 🎫 🎥

# Château Tour of the Sologne

The mysterious Sologne is a secretive landscape of woods and marshes edged by vineyards. Wine lovers can indulge in tastings of Loire Valley wines accompanied, in season, by a dinner of succulent wild game from the region's forests, popular hunting grounds for centuries. The Sologne is a hunter's paradise, and devotees of the sport can see today's hounds, as well as hunting trophies of the past.

This ambling rural route takes in some of the Loire's most varied châteaux. The five on this tour – for which a couple of days is required – represent a delightful encapsulation of regional architecture. All styles are here, from feudal might to Renaissance grace and Classical elegance. Several are inhabited but can still be visited.

② **Château de Beauregard**
Beauregard was built around 1520 as a hunting lodge for François I. It contains a gallery with 327 portraits of royalty.

① **Château de Chaumont**
Chaumont is a feudal castle with Renaissance embellishments and lofty views over the River Loire *(see p246)*.

0 kilometers 5
0 miles 5

**Key**
━━━ Tour route
═══ Other roads

Pontlevoy

## ㉒ Vendôme

Loir-et-Cher. 🚹 19,000. 🚉 🚌 🛈 47 rue Poterie (02 54 77 05 07). 🕐 Fri & Sun. 🌐 vendome-tourisme.fr

Once an important stop for pilgrims en route to Compostela in Spain, Vendôme is still popular with modern pilgrims, thanks to the TGV train service. Though a desirable address with Parisian commuters, the town still manages to retain its provincial charm. Vendôme's old stone buildings are encircled by the River Loir. Its lush gardens invite a relaxed exploration, especially Parc Ronsard. Reached by a footbridge across the Loir, this park boasts a plane tree planted in 1759 and a medieval *lavoir*.

The town's greatest monument is the abbey church of **La Trinité**, founded in 1034. Its Romanesque bell tower (all that remains of the original structure) is overshadowed by the church portal, a masterpiece

of Flamboyant Gothic tracery. The interior is embellished with Romanesque capitals and 15th-century choir stalls. Commanding a rocky spur high above the Loir is the ruined **château**, built by the counts of Vendôme in the 13th–14th centuries. The garden around the château is remarkable for its collection of hydrangeas.

Vendôme's native son Rochambeau, hero of the American Revolution

## ㉓ The Loir

Loir-et-Cher. ✈ Tours. 🚉 Vendôme. 🚌 Montoire-sur-le-Loir. 🛈 16 pl Clémenceau, Montoire-sur-le-Loir (02 54 85 23 30). 🌐 otsi.montoire.fr

Compared with the royal River Loire, the tranquil Loir to the north has a more rural charm. The stretch between Vendôme and Trôo is the most rewarding, offering troglodyte caves *(see p296)*, walking trails, wine tasting, fishing, and boat trips.

**Les Roches-l'Evêque** is a fortified village with cave dwellings visible in the cliff face. Just downstream is **Lavardin**, with its Romanesque church, half-timbered houses, Gothic bridge, and ruined château ringed by ramparts. In **Montoire-sur-le-Loir**, the Chapelle St.-Gilles, a former leper colony, has Romanesque frescoes. **Trôo**, the next major village, is known for its Romanesque Eglise de St.-Martin and a labyrinth of troglodyte

**③ Château de Cheverny**
Finished in 1634, this Classical château still belongs to a descendant of the original owner. His 70 hounds, used for stag-hunting, are fed at 5pm (summer) or 3pm (winter).

④ **Bracieux**

**Cellettes** ②

**D102** **D120**

**D765**

**D956** ③

**D102**

**Contres**

**D765**

**D20**

**D765**

**Mur-de-Sologne**

**④ Château de Villesavin**
This intriguing but dilapidated Renaissance château possesses an authentic dovecote, complete with revolving ladder and space for 3,000 birds.

**⑤ Château du Moulin**
The "pearl of the Sologne" (1490) was built by a knight of Charles VIII.

**D20**

⑤ *Romorantin-Lanthenay* ➝

**D765**

---

dwellings. **St.-Jacques-des-Guérets**, facing the village of Trôo, has a frescoed Romanesque chapel, as does **Poncé-sur-le-Loir**, farther downstream. On the slopes are vineyards producing Jasnières and Côteaux du Vendômois. Wine tastings enliven sleepy **Poncé** and **La Chartre-sur-le-Loir**. The cliffs on the opposite bank are studded with caves, commonly used as wine cellars.

Northward, the **Forêt de Bercé** abounds with paths and streams, while to the west the small town of **Le Lude** sits on the south bank of the Loir, dominated by its romantic 15th-century château. Some 12 miles (20 km) west of Le Lude lies the town of **La Flèche**, where the main attraction is the Prytanée Nationale Militaire, originally a Jesuit college founded by Henri IV in 1603. Philosopher René Descartes was one of the college's earliest and most illustrious pupils.

## ㉔ Chartres

Eure-et-Loir. 🏠 42,000. 🚆 🚍
🛈 8–10 rue de la Poissonnerie (02 37 18 26 26). 🛒 Tue, Thu, Sat.
🌐 **chartres-tourisme.com**

Chartres has the greatest Gothic cathedral in Europe *(see pp312–15)*, and its churches should not be ignored. The Benedictine abbey church of **St.-Pierre** has lovely medieval stained-glass windows, while **St.-Aignan** abuts 9th-century ramparts. By the river is the Romanesque **Eglise de St.-André**, a deconsecrated church used for art exhibitions and concerts.

Chartres is also one of the first urban conservation sites in France. Half-timbered houses abound along such cobblestone streets as rue des Ecuyers. Steep staircases known as *tertres* lead down to the River Eure, providing views of mills, humpback stone bridges, washhouses, and the cathedral.

One of the many washhouses along the Eure river

In the Grenier de Loens, next to the cathedral, is the **Centre International du Vitrail** (stained glass center). The building's 13th-century vaulted storerooms house a museum for temporary exhibitions of contemporary stained glass and the techniques of making it. There is a permanent exhibition of Renaissance stained glass panels. The center provides courses for beginners and experienced artists.

🏛 **Centre International du Vitrail**
5 rue du Cardinal Pie. **Tel** 02 37 21 65 72. **Open** Mon–Sat, & Sun pm. 🖼

# Chartres Cathedral

According to art historian Emile Mâle, "Chartres is the mind of the Middle Ages manifest." Begun in 1020, the Romanesque cathedral was destroyed by fire in 1194. Only the north and south towers, south steeple, west portal, and crypt remained; the sacred *Veil of the Virgin* relic was the sole treasure to survive. Peasant and lord alike helped to rebuild the church in just 25 years. Few alterations were made after 1250, and, fortunately, Chartres was unscathed by the Wars of Religion and the French Revolution. The result is a Gothic cathedral with a true "Bible in stone" reputation.

**Elongated Statues**
These statues on the Royal Portal represent Old Testament figures.

**Gothic Nave**
As wide as the Romanesque crypt below it, the nave reaches a lofty height of 121 ft (37 m).

**★ Royal Portal**
The central tympanum of the Royal Portal (1145–55) shows *Christ in Majesty*.

## KEY

① **The lower half** of the west front is a survivor of the original Romanesque church, with the portal and the three windows dating from the mid-12th century.

② **The taller** of the two spires dates from the start of the 16th century. Flamboyant Gothic in style, it contrasts sharply with the solemnity of its Romanesque counterpart.

③ **The vaulted ceiling** is supported by a network of ribs.

④ Labyrinth

## The Labyrinth

The 13th-century labyrinth, inlaid in the nave floor, was a feature of most medieval cathedrals. Pilgrims followed the tortuous route on their knees, echoing the way to Jerusalem and the complexity of life, in order to reach Christ. The journey – 851 ft (259 m) of broken concentric circles – took at least an hour.

### VISITORS' CHECKLIST

**Practical Information**
Pl de la Cathédrale. **Tel** 02 37 21 59 08. **Open** 8:30am–7:30pm daily. 9am Tue & Fri, 11:45am & 6:15pm Mon–Sat (6pm Sat), 9:15am (in Latin) & 11am Sun. for crypt and tower.
**w** cathedrale-chartres.org

**Our Lady of the Pillar**
Carved from dark pear wood, this 16th-century replica of a 13th-century statue is a striking shrine, which is often surrounded by candles.

★ **Stained-Glass Windows**
The windows cover a surface area of over 28,000 sq ft (2,600 sq m).

★ **South Porch**
Sculpture on the South Porch (1197–1209) reflects New Testament teaching.

**The Crypt**
This is the largest crypt in France, most of it dating from the early 11th century. It houses the *Veil of the Virgin* relic and comprises two galleries, a series of chapels, and the 9th-century St. Lubin's vault.

# The Stained Glass of Chartres

Donated by royalty, aristocracy, priests, and the merchant brotherhoods between 1210 and 1240, this glorious collection of stained glass is world renowned. Around 176 windows illustrate biblical stories and daily life in the 13th century. During both world wars the windows were dismantled piece by piece and removed for safety. There is an ongoing program, begun in the 1970s, to restore the windows in the cathedral.

Stained glass above the apse

**Redemption Window**
Six scenes illustrate *Christ's Passion* and death on the Cross (around 1210).

**★ Tree of Jesse**
This 12th-century stained glass shows Christ's genealogy. The tree rises up from Jesse, father of David, at the bottom, to Christ enthroned at the top.

**★ West Rose Window**
This window (1215), with Christ seated in the center, shows the *Last Judgment*.

## Key

| | | | | | | | |
|---|---|---|---|---|---|---|---|
| **1** | Tree of Jesse | **12** | Noah | **23** | Blue Virgin | **34** | St. Stephen |
| **2** | Incarnation | **13** | St. John the Evangelist | **24** | Life of the Virgin | **35** | St. Cheron |
| **3** | Passion and Resurrection | **14** | Mary Magdalene | **25** | Zodiac Window | **36** | St. Thomas |
| **4** | North Rose Window | **15** | Good Samaritan and Adam and Eve | **26** | St. Martin | **37** | Peace Window |
| **5** | West Rose Window | **16** | Assumption | **27** | St. Thomas Becket | **38** | Modern Window |
| **6** | South Rose Window | **17** | Vendôme Chapel Windows | **28** | St. Margaret and St. Catherine | **39** | Prodigal Son |
| **7** | Redemption Window | **18** | Miracles of Mary | **29** | St. Nicholas | **40** | Ezekiel and David |
| **8** | St. Nicholas | **19** | St. Apollinaris | **30** | St. Remy | **41** | Aaron |
| **9** | Joseph | **20** | Modern Window | **31** | St. James the Greater | **42** | Annunciation-Visitation |
| **10** | St. Eustache | **21** | St. Fulbert | **32** | Charlemagne | **43** | Isaiah and Moses |
| **11** | St. Lubin | **22** | St. Anthony and St. Paul | **33** | St. Theodore and St. Vincent | **44** | Daniel and Jeremiah |

**North Rose Window**
This depicts the *Glorification of the Virgin*, surrounded by the kings of Judah and the prophets (around 1230).

4

## Guide to Reading the Windows

Each window is divided into panels, usually read from left to right, bottom to top (Earth to Heaven). The number of figures or abstract shapes used is thought to be symbolic: three stands for divinity, while the number four symbolizes the material world or the four elements.

Mary and Child in the sacred mandorla (around 1150)

Two angels paying homage before the celestial throne

Christ's triumphal entry into Jerusalem on Palm Sunday

Upper panels of the Incarnation Window

37 36 35 34 33 32 31

40 41 42 43 44 30 29 28 27 26

22 23 24 25 21

6

**South Rose Window**
This illustrates the *Apocalypse*, with *Christ in Majesty* (around 1225).

★ **Blue Virgin Window**
The window's bottom panel depicts the conversion of water into wine by Christ at *The Wedding at Cana*.

Orléans's Cathédrale Sainte-Croix

# ㉕ Orléans

Loiret. 🚗 110,000. 🚉 🚌 ℹ️ 2 pl Etape (02 38 24 05 05). 🛒 Tue–Sun.
**w** tourisme-orleans.com

Orléans's dazzling contemporary bridge symbolizes the city's increasing importance at the geographic heart of both France and Europe. As a tourist, however, one is struck by the city's continued attachment to its past, most particularly to Joan of Arc. It was from here that the Maid of Orléans saved France

from the English in 1429 (see pp304–5). Since her martyrdom at Rouen in 1431, Joan remains a presence in Orléans. Every April 29 and May 1 and 7–8 her liberation of the city is re-enacted in a pageant and a blessing in the cathedral.

Orléans's historic center was badly damaged in World War II, but much has been reconstructed, and a faded grandeur lingers in Vieil Orléans, the quarter bounded by the cathedral, the River Loire, and **place du Martroi**. The latter, a Classical but rather windswept square, has an equestrian statue of the city's heroine. Nearby the half-timbered **Maison de Jeanne d'Arc**, rebuilt from period dwellings in 1961 on the site where Joan had lodgings in 1429, has multimedia displays telling her story.

From place du Martroi, rue d'Escures leads past Renaissance mansions to the cathedral. **Hôtel Groslot** is the grandest, a 16th-century red-brick mansion, where kings Charles IX, Henri III, and Henri IV all stayed. The 17-year-old François II died here in 1560 after attending a meeting of the Etats Généraux with his child bride, Mary, later Queen

of Scots. The building served as Orléans's town hall from 1790 to 1982, and the sumptuously decorated interior, with its Joan memorabilia, is still used for marriages and official ceremonies.

Virtually opposite the Hôtel Groslot and alongside the new town hall is the **Musée des Beaux-Arts**, displaying European works of art from the 16th to the 20th centuries.

The **Cathédrale Sainte-Croix** nearby is an imposing edifice begun in the late 13th century, destroyed by the Huguenots (Protestants) in 1568, and then rebuilt in supposedly Gothic style between the 17th and 19th centuries.

🏛 **Maison de Jeanne d'Arc**
3 pl du Général de Gaulle. **Tel** 02 38 68 32 63. **Open** Tue–Sun (Oct–Mar: pms only). 🎫 📷

🏛 **Hôtel Groslot**
Pl de l'Etape. **Tel** 02 38 79 22 30. **Open** Sun–Fri, Sat am. **Closed** sporadically.

🏛 **Musée des Beaux-Arts**
Pl Ste-Croix. **Tel** 02 38 79 21 55. **Open** Tue–Sun. **Closed** Jan 1, May 1 & 8, Jul 14, Nov 1 & 11, Dec 25. 🎫 free 1st Sun of month. ♿

## Orléans City Center

① Maison de Jeanne d'Arc
② Hôtel Groslot
③ Musée des Beaux-Arts
④ Cathédrale Sainte-Croix

Gare SNCF, Gare Routière
330 yards (300 m)

RUE DES FAUCHETS

RUE DU COLOMBIER

RUE BANNIER

RUE DE LA RÉPUBLIQUE

RUE STE-JEANNE

CRÉSPIN

RUE DE LA BRETONNERIE

CAMPO SANTO

Hôtel de Ville

CHAMPS

RUE DES GRANDS

D'ILLIERS

RUE A

RUE D'ESCURES

Hôtel Groslot ②

PL DE L'ÉTAPE

ℹ️

③ Musée des Beaux-Arts

RUE DU BOURDON BLANC

RUE DES CARMES

PLACE DU MARTROI

P

St-Pierre du Martroi

PLACE DU GÉNÉRAL DE GAULLE

RUE JEANNE D'ARC

PLACE STE-CROIX

④ Cathédrale Sainte-Croix

RUE DU TABOUR

① Maison de Jeanne d'Arc

RUE SANGLIER

Place de la République

RUE STE CATHERINE

RUE DE L'EMPEREUR

RUE ÉTIENNE DOLET

Salle des Thèses

DE

BOURGOGNE

RUE DE L'UNIVERSITE

PLACE DU VIEUX MARCHÉ

RUE TEMPLIER

Hôtel Cabu

RUE ROYALE

RUE THIERS

RUE

DE

RUE DU POIRIER

Préfecture

RUE DE LA POTERNE

PLACE DU CHÂTELET

RUE DE LA CHARPENTERIE

PLACE DE LA LOIRE

P

BLOIS, TOURS

QUAI DU CHÂTELET

GIEN, NEVERS

Pont George V

Loire

0 meters 250
0 yards 250

Joan of Arc stained-glass window in Orléans' Cathédrale Sainte-Croix

## ㉖ St.-Benoît-sur-Loire

Loiret. 2,000. 44 rue Orléanaise (02 38 35 79 00).
w tourisme-loire-foret.com

Located along the River Loire between Orléans and Gien, St.-Benoît-sur-Loire boasts one of the finest Romanesque abbey churches (1067–1108) in France. It is all that survives of an important monastery founded in AD 650 and named after St. Benedict, patron saint of Europe. His relics were brought from Italy at the end of the 7th century.

The church's belfry porch is graced with carved capitals depicting biblical scenes. The nave is tall and light, and the choir floor is an amazing patchwork of Italian marble. Daily services with Gregorian chant are open to the public.

## ㉗ Bourges

Cher. 80,000. 21 rue Victor Hugo (02 48 23 02 60). Tue–Sun. w bourges-tourisme.com

This Gallo-Roman city retains its original walls but is best known as the city of Jacques Coeur, financier and foreign minister to Charles VII. The greatest merchant of the Middle Ages and a self-made man *par excellence*, it was in his capacity as an arms dealer that he established a tradition maintained for four centuries, as Napoleon III had cannons manufactured here in 1862.

Built over part of the walls, the **Palais Jacques Coeur** is a Gothic gem and a lasting memorial to its first master. It was finished in 1453, and incorporates Coeur's two emblems, scallop shells and hearts, as well as his motto: *"A vaillan coeur, rien impossible"* – to the valiant heart, nothing is impossible. The guided tour reveals a barrel-vaulted gallery, a painted chapel, and a chamber that had Turkish baths.

Bourges also flourishes as a university town and cultural mecca, renowned for its spring festival of music.

Rue Bourbonnoux leads to **St.-Etienne**, a cathedral very similar to Paris's Notre-Dame. The west facade, the widest among France's Gothic cathedrals, has five sculpted portals, the central one depicting an enthralling Last Judgment. In the choir are

vivid 13th-century stained-glass windows presented by the guilds. The crypt holds the marble tomb of the 14th-century Duc de Berry, best known for commissioning the illuminated manuscript the *Très Riches Heures* (see pp208–9). From the top of the north tower stretch views of the beautifully restored medieval quarter and the marshes beyond. Beside the cathedral is a tithe barn and the remains of the Gallo-Roman ramparts. The **Jardin des Prés Fichaux**, set along the River Yèvre, contains pools and an open-air theater. To the north lie the **Marais de Bourges**, where gardeners transport their produce by boat.

Statue of Jacques Coeur

**🏛 Palais Jacques Coeur**
Rue Jacques Coeur. **Tel** 02 48 24 79 42. **Open** daily. **Closed** Jan 1, May 1, Nov 1 & 11, Dec 25. 🦽 📷

### Environs
About 22 miles (35 km) south of Bourges in the Berry region is the **Abbaye de Noirlac**. Founded in 1136, it is one of the best-preserved Cistercian abbeys in France.

Statue in the Jardin des Prés Fichaux

# CENTRAL FRANCE AND THE ALPS

Introducing Central France
and the Alps      **320–329**

Burgundy and
Franche-Comté      **330–355**

The Massif Central      **356–375**

The Rhône Valley and
French Alps      **376–395**

# Introducing Central France and the Alps

The geological contrasts of this region reflect its enormous variety, from the industrial and gastronomic metropolis of Lyon to the largely agricultural landscape of Burgundy. The mountains of the Massif Central and the Alps attract visitors for winter sports, superb walking, and other outdoor activities. The major sights of this richly rewarding area, both natural and architectural, are shown here.

Aux

**Basilique Ste.-Madeleine,** the famous pilgrimage church crowning the hilltop village of Vézelay, is a masterpiece of Burgundian Romanesque. It is renowned for its vividly decorated tympanum and capitals *(see pp340–41).*

Nevers

**The Abbaye de Ste.-Foy** in the village of Conques *(see pp372–3)* is one of the great pilgrimage churches of France, with a fabulous treasury of medieval and Renaissance gold reliquaries.

Monluçon

Bellac   Guéret

Saint-Avit

Limoges   THE MASSIF CENTRAL *(See pp356–75)*   Clermont-Ferrand

Tulle   Mauriac   Le Brioud

St-Flour

Aurillac

Conques

Villefranche-de-Rouergue   Rodez

Millau

**The Gorges du Tarn** have some of France's most spectacular natural scenery. The road that follows the plunging course of the River Tarn gives dramatic viewpoints along the canyon and across the limestone Causses *(see pp374–5).*

◄ The magnificent peak of Puy de Dôme, the tallest extinct volcano in the Monts Dôme range

**The Abbaye de Fontenay**, founded by St. Bernard in the early 12th century, is the oldest Cistercian monastery in France (see pp336–7). This well-preserved Romanesque abbey is a perfect testimony to the severe ideal of the Cistercian life.

Châtillon-sur-Seine

Belfort

Vesoul

Montbéliard

Dijon

Dijon (see pp344–6)

Besançon

**BURGUNDY AND FRANCHE-COMTÉ** (See pp330–55)

Beaune

Pontarlier

Théâtre Romain, Autun (see p343)

Chalon-sur-Saône

Lons-le-Saunier

Lac Léman

Brou Abbey Church, Bourg-en-Bresse (see p380)

Mâcon

Bourg-en-Bresse

Geneva

Les La Cluses

Nantua

Villefranche-sur-Saône

Annecy

Lac d'Annecy

Chamonix

Feurs

Lyon

Lac du Bourget

Mont Blanc (see pp326–7)

Vienne

Chambéry

Moûtiers

St-Étienne

Grenoble

Modane

Palais Idéal du Facteur Cheval, Hauterives (see p387)

Valence

La Mure

Briançon

**THE RHÔNE VALLEY AND FRENCH ALPS** (See pp376–95)

ubenas

Montélimar

Gap

Donzère

Le Puy (see pp368–9)

Temple d'Auguste et Livie, Vienne (see p386)

0 kilometers    50

0 miles    50

# The Flavors of Central France

The renowned gastronomic tradition of Lyon and the rich wine and food of Burgundy combine to make central France a gourmet paradise. The great chefs of the region have a wide choice of excellent local produce: fine Bresse chicken, Charolais beef, and Morvan ham; wildfowl and frogs from the marshes of the Dombe; fish from the Saône and the Rhône; and fat snails called "escargots de Bourgogne." Franche-Comté and the Jura contribute smoked sausages, farmhouse cheeses, walnut oil, and fish from glacier-fed lakes. In the Massif Central, sturdy regional fare features salted hams, pork, Cantal cheese, the celebrated green lentils of Le Puy, and wild mushrooms.

Chanterelle mushrooms

A mountain farmer shows off his fine salt-cured ham

## Burgundy and Franche-Comté

Burgundy is one of France's top wine regions, so, not surprisingly, wine plays a major role in the cuisine, such as in the signature dish, *boeuf bourguignon*, made from Charolais beef marinated and then stewed in good red wine, with baby onions, bacon, and mushrooms added. Other specialties include *coq au vin* and *oeufs en meurette*. Dijon's famous mustard appears most classically with steak and in *moutarde au lapin*, rabbit in a creamy mustard sauce. Burgundy and Franche-Comté produce some of the most celebrated French cheeses: Epoisses, a cow's-milk cheese washed with *marc de Bourgogne*; Cîteaux, made by monks; and the magnificent Vacherin-Mont d'Or, a winter treat to be scooped straight from its wooden box. Black currants are widely grown and contribute to many desserts as well as the famous Kir: white wine with cassis (black currant liqueur).

## The Massif Central

The peasant cuisine of the Auvergne is well-known in France due to the many cafés run by

Tomme de Savoie    Fourme d'Ambert    Raclette    Roquefort

St.-Nectaire    Emmenthal    Rebloc

Mouthwatering array of classic French cheeses

## Regional Dishes and Specialties

The cuisine of central France is rich with sauces using wine, butter, and cream, which enhance almost every dish: snails in butter and garlic; potatoes cooked with cheese and cream; and beef, lamb, and chicken stewed slowly in reduced wine sauces, often with cream or butter added at the end of cooking. Mushrooms are served in cream sauces, and fish is often baked in a creamy *gratin*. Most indulgent of all is the Alpine fondue, where cheeses are melted, together with Kirsch and wine, in a special earthenware fondue pot. This is placed on a burner on the table, and cubes of bread are speared onto special long forks and dipped into the cheese. Traditionally, anyone who loses their bread in the pot must kiss everyone else at the table.

String of onions

**Oeufs en meurette** This Burgundian dish is eggs poached in red wine with onions, mushrooms, and bacon.

Traditional *charcuterie* on sale in a Lyon market

and the most northerly outpost of the olive is at Nyons. The Bresse region is famous for its high-quality chickens.

The Dombes lakes and the Alps are good sources of fish, such as perch, trout, and lake salmon. Bony perch is most delicious eaten as *quenelles de brochet*, filleted fish blended, made into dumplings, and baked in a creamy sauce. From the Alps comes a wide range of cheeses. As well as being delicious to eat fresh, they will often be found melted in *raclettes* or fondues, or layered with sliced potato to make an unctuous *gratin dauphinois*.

### ON THE MENU

**Chou farci** Cabbage stuffed with pork and herbs.

**Gigot Brayaude** Leg of lamb baked over sliced potatoes and *lardons* of bacon.

**Gougère** Cheesy *choux* pastry baked in a ring shape.

**Jambon persillé** Ham and parsley in aspic jelly.

**Pochouse** Freshwater fish (carp, pike, eel, and trout) stewed in white wine.

**Potée savoyarde** Hotpot made with vegetables, chicken, ham, and sausage.

**Salade auvergnate** Cubes of Auvergne ham, Cantal cheese, and walnuts.

Auvergnats in Paris, where they serve local dishes such as pork stuffed with cabbage, or *aligot*. Puy lentils, grown in the fertile volcanic soils of the Puy-en-Velay basin, combine well with sausages or *petit salé*, or are served cold as a salad. Good beef comes from the Salers cattle of the Auvergne or from the Limousin, where there is also plentiful game. Wild mushrooms are eagerly sought in season. Cheeses include Cantal, one of the country's oldest, and similar in flavor to Cheddar, and the famous blue Roquefort, ripened in the limestone caves of the Lozère.

### The Rhône Valley and French Alps

Lyon is famous for its traditional bistros, *bouchons*, where the cooks are often women, known as *mères*, who

dish up substantial fare such as onion soup, *lyonnais* sausages, and *charcuterie*. The markets of Lyon are equally famous, stocked with the region's wide range of fruit, particularly apricots, peaches, and juicy berries. Vegetables include onions, chard, and cardoons,

Red currants and blackberries for sale by the punnet

**Petit salé** A specialty of the Auvergne region, salt pork is cooked in wine with tiny green Puy lentils.

**Aligot** Slivers of Cantal cheese are beaten into buttery, garlicky mashed potato, until the mixture forms long strands.

**Clafoutis** This is usually made with black cherries, baked in batter, and laced with Kirsch, a cherry liqueur.

# France's Wine Regions: Burgundy

Burgundy and its fine wines have inspired awe for centuries. The fame of the region's wines spread throughout Europe in the 14th century, under the Valois Dukes of Burgundy. The system of dividing wine areas into designated *appellations*, of which there are a bewildering number, came into effect in 1935. Even today, the classification system remains dauntingly complex. But, despite its impenetrable image, this is unmissable territory for the "serious" wine lover, with its rich vinous history and tradition and dazzling *grands crus*.

**Locator Map**
- Burgundy wine region

Clos de Vougeot on the Côte de Nuits

### Wine Regions

*Between Chablis in the north and the Côte Chalonnaise and Mâconnais in the south is the Côte d'Or, incorporating Côte de Nuits and Côte de Beaune. The Beaujolais region (see p381) lies below Mâcon.*

**Principal Wine Areas**

Châtillon-sur-Seine
Langres
Chablis
Auxerre
Avallon
Dijon
BOURGOGNE
Beaune
Dole
**Key**
- Chablis
- Côte de Nuits
- Côte de Beaune
- Côte Chalonnaise
- Mâconnais
- Beaujolais

Autun
Chalon-sur-Saône
Mâcon
Roanne
Villefranche-sur-Saône
Lyon

0 kilometers 50
0 miles 50

## Key Facts About Burgundy

**Location and Climate**
The continental climate (bleak winters and hot summers) can be very variable, making vintages a crucial quality factor. The best vineyards have chalky soil and face south or east.

**Grape Varieties**
Burgundy is at least relatively simple in its grape varieties. Red Burgundy is made from **Pinot Noir**, with its sweet flavors of raspberries, cherries, and strawberries, while the **Gamay** makes red Mâcon and Beaujolais. **Chardonnay** is the principal white variety for Chablis and white Burgundy, though small amounts of **Aligoté** and **Pinot Blanc** are grown and the **Sauvignon** is a specialty of St.-Bris.

**Good Producers**
*White Burgundy:* Jean-Marie Raveneau, René Dauvissat, La Chablisienne, Comtes Lafon, Guy Roulot, Etienne Sauzet, Pierre Morey, Louis Carillon, Jean-Marc Boillot, André Ramonet, Hubert Lamy, Jean-Marie Guffens-Heynen, Olivier Merlin, Louis Latour, Louis Jadot, Olivier Leflaive. *Red Burgundy:* Denis Bachelet, Daniel Rion, Domaine Dujac, Armand Rousseau, Joseph Roty, De Montille, Domaine de la Pousse d'Or, Domaine de l'Arlot, Jean-Jacques Confuron, Robert Chevillon, Georges Roumier, Leroy, Drouhin.

**Good Vintages**
*(Reds)* 2015, 2012, 2010, 2009, 2005.
*(Whites)* 2014, 2012, 2010, 2008, 2005.

**So elaborate** are Burgundy's *appellations* that individual vineyards, such as Clos la Roche, may have their own designation.

**Grand cru** vineyards are at the top of the quality pyramid; they also tend to occupy the upper slopes of the Côte d'Or.

0 kilometers 5
0 miles 5

**This "brotherhood"** of professionals distinguishes the area's best wines each year.

**Key**

◆ Village *appellations*
▢ Côte de Nuits-Villages
▢ Hautes-Côtes de Nuits
▢ Hautes-Côtes de Beaune
▢ Côte de Beaune-Villages

**Burgundian villages** have often appropriated the name of their most famous vineyard: all the village wines of Puligny, for example, can benefit from the fame of Le Montrachet.

## The Côte d'Or

*The Côte de Nuits and Côte de Beaune, together forming the "golden" Côte d'Or (see p348), meet at the historic town of Beaune, which hosts the most famous annual wine auction in the world (see p350). "Hautes-Côtes" and "Villages" wines, from a different terroir, are less sought after than wines from the starry individual appellations.*

Teams of grape-pickers at the vineyards of Nuits-St.-Georges

# The French Alps

In any season, the Alps are one of the most spectacular regions of France – a majestic mountain range stretching south from Lake Geneva almost to the Mediterranean, and climaxing in Europe's loftiest peak, the 15,770-ft (4,800-m) Mont Blanc. The area encompasses the old regions of Dauphiné and Savoie, once remote and independent (Savoie only became part of France in 1860). They have prospered since Alpine vacations and skiing became popular in the last century, but are still very conscious of their distinct identity.

Children in traditional Savoie costumes

The Alpine landscape in winter: chalets and skiers on the slopes at Courchevel

## Winter

The ski season usually starts just before Christmas, and finishes at the end of April. Most resorts offer both cross-country and downhill skiing, with many pistes linking two or more ski stations. The less energetic can still enjoy the landscape from some of the highest cable cars (*téléphériques*) in the world.

Of the 100 or more French Alpine resorts, the most popular include **Chamonix-Mont Blanc**, the historic capital of Alpine skiing and site of the first Winter Olympics in 1924; **Megève**, which boasts one of the best ski schools in Europe; **Morzine**, a year-round resort on the Swiss border, overlooked by the modern, car-free resort of **Avoriaz**; modern **Albertville**, site of the 1992 Winter Olympics; **Les Trois Vallées**, which include glamorous **Courchevel** and

A cable car at Courchevel, part of Les Trois Vallées complex

A downhill skier at Val d'Isère

**Méribel**, and the lesser-known **Val Thorens/Les Ménuires**; **Tignes**, a year-round resort; **Les Arcs** and **La Plagne**, both purpose-built; and **Val d'Isère**, a favorite among the rich and famous.

## Alpine Flowers

In spring and early summer the pastures of the French Alps are ablaze with flowers. These include blue-and-yellow gentians, bellflowers, lilies, saxifrages, and a variety of orchids. Steep mountain meadows cannot be farmed intensively, and the absence of fertilizers and weedkillers enables wildflowers to flourish.

Spring gentian (*Gentiana verna*)

Martagon lily (*Lilium martagon*)

The French Alps in summer: flower-filled meadows overlooked by brilliant white peaks

## Spring and Summer

The Alpine summer season starts in late June, extending to early September – most resorts close in October and November between the hiking and skiing seasons. After the spring thaw, flower-filled pastures, snow-fed mountain lakes, and a huge number of marked trails make this area a hiker's paradise. In the Chamonix area alone there are over 195 miles (310 km) of hiking trails. The best-known long-distance route is the **Tour du Mont Blanc**, a ten-day hike via France, Italy, and Switzerland. The **GR5** traverses the entire Alps, passing through the **Parc National de la Vanoise** and **Parc Régional du Queyras** (*see p391*) to the south. *Téléphériques* give access to the higher trails, where the views are even more awesome. Be sure to bring plenty of warm, waterproof clothing, as the weather can change very quickly.

Many resorts are now broadening their summer appeal – golf, tennis, mountain biking, horseback riding, paragliding, canoeing, whitewater rafting, glacier skiing, and mountain climbing are all widely available.

Bell-ringing dairy cows in an Alpine pasture

Mountain climbers scaling the heights around Mont Blanc

# Geology of the Massif Central

The Massif Central covers almost one-fifth of France and is over 250 million years old. Most of its peaks have been eroded to form a vast plateau split into deep valleys. The heart of the Massif consists of hard, igneous rocks such as granite, with softer rocks such as limestone at its margins. Different rock types are reflected in the landscape and buildings; in the eroded Gorges du Tarn, the houses are built of russet-colored limestone. Massive granite farmhouses are a feature of Limousin, and Le Puy-en-Velay is distinguished by its giant basalt pillars.

**Locator Map**
◼ Extent of the Massif Central

**This granite portal** is found in the Romanesque church at Moutier d'Ahun (see pp360–61). Granite underlies much of the Massif Central.

**Basalt** is a dark, fine-grained rock formed by volcanic lava. A common building stone in the Auvergne, it is often cut into blocks and bonded with lighter-colored mortar. In the medieval town of Salers (see p367), basalt was used for most of the buildings, including this one in the Grande Place.

**Schist tiling** is featured on these roofs at Argentat. Schist is a crystalline rock that splits readily into layers. It is particularly common on the edge of the Massif, and provides an effective roofing material.

**Limestone walls** can be seen on houses in Espalion (see p370). Of all the rocks in the Massif Central, it is among the most easily worked. It splits readily and is soft enough to be cut into blocks with a hand saw. As with granite, its color and consistency vary from area to area.

Montluç•

Moutier d'Ahun •

Limoges •

Clerm
Ferr

Dordogne

• Sale

• Argentat

Cère

Lot

M

Tarn

0 kilometers    50

0 miles         50

**Crystallized lava**, for example this dramatic curtain of columns at Prades, formed when liquid basalt seeped through the surrounding rock and solidified to form giant crystals.

**Key**

◾ Sedimentary rock
◾ Surface volcanic rock
◾ Granite
◽ Metamorphic rock

vers

Loire

Saône

Lyon •

•
St-Etienne

• Le-Puy-en-Velay

Rhône

**Limestone plateaux** *(causses)* are typical of this region. Gorges, where rivers have cut through layers of this slightly soluble rock, run deep into the Massif Central.

**This mature landscape** at Mont Aigoual is the highest point in the Cévennes *(see p375)*, dividing rivers flowing into the Atlantic and the Mediterranean. Its granite and schist rocks show erosion.

## Recognizing Rocks

Geologists divide rocks into three groups. Igneous rocks, such as granite, are formed by volcanic activity and either extruded on to the surface or intrude into other rocks below ground. Sedimentary rocks are produced by sediment build-up. Metamorphic rocks have been transformed by heat or pressure.

## Sedimentary Rock

**Oolitic limestone** often contains fossils and small amounts of quartz.

## Surface Volcanic Rock

**Basalt**, which can form very thick sheets, is the most common lava rock.

## Granite

**Pink granite**, a coarse-grained rock, is formed deep in the earth's crust.

## Metamorphic Rock

**Muscovite schist** is a medium-grained mud- or clay-based rock.

# BURGUNDY AND FRANCHE-COMTE

*Yonne · Niévre · Côte d'Or*
*Saône-et-Loire · Jura · Doubs · Haute-Saône*

Burgundy considers itself the heart of France, a prosperous region with world-renowned wine, earthy but excellent cuisine, and magnificent architecture. Franche-Comté, to the east, combines gentle farmland with lofty Alpine forests.

Under the dukes of Valois, Burgundy was France's most powerful rival, with territory extending well beyond its present boundaries. By the 16th century, however, the duchy was ruled by governors appointed by the French king, but it still retained its privileges and traditions. Once a part of Burgundy, Franche-Comté – the Free County – struggled to remain independent of the French crown, and was a province of the Holy Roman Empire until annexed by Louis XIV in 1674.

Burgundy, now as in the past, is a rich region, a center of medieval religious faith, which produced renowned Romanesque masterpieces at Vézelay, Fontenay, and Cluny. Dijon is a splendid city, filled with the great palaces of the old Burgundian nobility and a collection of great paintings and sculptures in the Musée des Beaux-Arts. The vineyards of the Côte d'Or, the Côte de Beaune, and Chablis yield some of the world's most venerated wines. Other varied landscapes – from the wild forests of the Morvan to the lush farmland of the Brionnais – produce snails, Bresse chickens, and Charolais beef.

Franche-Comté has none of this opulence, though its capital, Besançon, is a fine 17th-century city with a tradition of clockmaking. Topographically the Franche-Comté is divided into two, with gently rolling farmland in the Saône Valley and high Alpine scenery to the east. This forest country of Alpine torrents filled with trout is also the home of great cheeses, notably Vacherin and Comté, and of the characteristic yellow wine of Arbois.

The prehistoric site of the Roche de Solutré near Mâcon

◀ A view of Semur-en-Auxois, Burgundy, from the banks of the River Armançon

# Exploring Burgundy and Franche-Comté

Burgundy is arguably France's richest province – historically, culturally, gastronomically, and economically. This lush kernel of a once-great power possesses a concentration of unique Romanesque architecture in Fontenay and Vézelay, along with some of the world's most venerated wines. Dijon is a must for lovers of art, architecture, and food. Franche-Comté is better suited for outdoor vacations, such as trekking and canoeing in wild scenery and crystal-clear rivers.

Burgundian riverscape near Fontenay

Distinctive Burgundian glazed roof tiles, Hôtel Aubriot in Dijon

## Key

═══ Freeway

═ ═ Freeway under construction

─── Highway

─── Secondary road

═══ Minor road

─── Scenic route

┈┈┈ Main railroad

─── Minor railroad

─── Regional border

△ Summit

**For keys to symbols** *see back flap*

# Sights at a Glance

1 Sens
2 La Puisaye-Forterre
3 Auxerre
4 Chablis
5 Tonnerre
6 Château de Tanlay
7 *Abbaye de Fontenay pp336–7*
8 Château d'Ancy-le-Franc
9 Châtillon-sur-Seine
10 Alise-Ste.-Reine
11 Semur-en-Auxois
12 Avallon
13 *Vézelay pp340–41*
14 Morvan
15 Saulieu
16 Nevers
17 Autun
18 *Dijon pp344–6*
19 Côte d'Or
20 Beaune
21 Tournus
22 Cluny
23 Paray-le-Monial
24 Brionnais
25 Mâcon
26 Cascades du Hérisson
27 Arbois
28 Dole
29 Arc-et-Senans
30 Champlitte
31 Besançon
32 Ornans
33 Belfort
34 Ronchamp

Wine harvest in Nuits-St.-Georges, Côte d'Or

## Getting Around

Burgundy is well-served by the A6 *auto-route* from Paris to Lyon and Marseille, which is joined by the A31 from Nancy and Dijon (and the Channel ports via the A26), and the A36 from Besançon. An alternative route through the region from Dijon to Lyon is the A39. If you have time and a taste for quiet country roads, those in Burgundy and Franche-Comté are some of the most rewarding in France. The TGV links Dijon and Mâcon with Paris, Geneva, and Marseille. Dijon is a major railroad hub and connects other towns in the region. The TER network has regular connections to Dijon, Sens, Beaune, and Auxerre.

La Sainte Châsse, 11th-century reliquary in the Treasury in Sens

# ❶ Sens

Yonne. 🏠 30,000. 🚊 🚌 ℹ️ pl Jean-Jaurès (03 86 65 19 49). 🅿️ Mon, Wed, Fri, Sat & Sun. 🌐 office-de-tourisme-sens.com

The little town of Sens, at the confluence of the rivers Yonne and Vanne, was important before Caesar came to Gaul. It was the Senones whose attempt to sack the Roman Capitol in 390 BC was thwarted by a flock of geese.

The **Cathédrale St.-Etienne** is Sens' outstanding glory. Begun before 1140 it is the oldest of the great Gothic cathedrals and its noble simplicity influenced many other churches. Louis IX (see p57) did the town the honor of getting married here in 1234.

The exquisite stained-glass windows from the 12th–16th centuries show biblical scenes, including the Tree of Jesse, and a tribute to Thomas Becket who was exiled here. His liturgical robes are in the Treasury (part of the **Musées de Sens**), which has one of the finest collections in France, including a beautiful Byzantine reliquary.

🏛 **Les Musées de Sens**
Pl de la Cathédrale. **Tel** 03 86 64 46 22. **Open** Jun–Sep: Wed–Mon; Oct–May: Wed, Sat, Sun (Mon, Thu, Fri pm only). **Closed** Jan 1, May 1, Jul 14, Nov 1, Dec 25. 🚫 ♿ 📷

# ❷ La Puisaye-Forterre

Yonne, Nièvre. 🚍 Auxerre, Clamecy, Bonny-sur-Loire, Cosne-Cours-sur-Loire. 🚌 St.-Fargeau, St.-Sauveur-en-Puisaye. ℹ️ Charny (03 86 63 65 51).

The secret forest country of La Puisaye-Forterre was immortalized by Colette (1873–1954), who was born at **St.-Sauveur** in "a house that smiled only on its garden side…." This 17th-century château now houses the **Musée Colette**.

The best way to explore the region is on foot or by bicycle around its watery woodlands, orchards, and meadows. Or ride the *Transpoyaudin*, a 17 mile (27 km) train route from St.-Sauveur to Villiers St.-Benoît.

A hands-on visit can be made to **Château de Guédelon**, a 25-year project begun in 1997 to recreate a medieval castle, using only original building methods and local materials. Nearby, the genuine 13th-century **Château de Ratilly** features pottery, art exhibitions, concerts, and music workshops. More of this can be seen in **St.-Amand**, the center of Puisaye stoneware production, much of which was traditionally fired in the 18th-century horizontal kiln at Moutiers. Both the pottery and local frescoes (see the churches at **Moutiers**

Colette in the 1880s at St-Sauveur

and **La Ferté-Loupière**) made use of locally mined ocher, which was a major export in the 19th century. The pink brick **Château de St.-Fargeau** housed the exiled Grande Mademoiselle (p61).

🏛 **Musée Colette**
Château St.-Sauveur-en-Puisaye. **Tel** 03 86 45 61 95. **Open** Apr–Oct: Wed–Mon. 🚫

# ❸ Auxerre

Yonne. 🏠 40,000. 🚊 ℹ️ 1–2 quai de la République (03 86 52 06 19). 🅿️ Tue & Wed. 🌐 ot-auxerre.fr

Beautifully sited overlooking the Yonne river, Auxerre justly prides itself on a fine collection of churches along with a charming traffic-free main square, the place Charles-Surugue.

The Gothic **Cathédrale St.-Etienne** took over three centuries to build and was completed in about 1560. It is famous for its intricate 13th-century stained glass. The choir with its slender columns and colonettes is the epitome of Gothic elegance, while the western portals are decorated with beautiful flamboyant sculpture which has been sadly mutilated by war and weather. The Romanesque crypt is adorned by unique 11th–13th-century frescoes, including one depicting Christ on a white horse. The badly pillaged treasury is less impressive, but still has an interesting collection of illuminated manuscripts. St. Germanus, mentor of St. Patrick

Château de St.-Fargeau in the Puisaye-Forterre region

and bishop of Auxerre in the 5th century, was buried at the former abbey church of **St.-Germain**. The abbey was founded by Queen Clothilde, wife of Clovis *(see pp54–5)*, the first Christian king of France, and is an important shrine. The crypt is partly Carolingian, with tombs and 11th–13th century frescoes. The former abbey houses the **Musée St.-Germain** with local Gallo-Roman finds.

🏛 **Musée St.-Germain**
2 pl St.-Germain. **Tel** 03 86 18 05 50.
**Open** Wed–Sun. **Closed** May 1 & 8,
Nov 1 & 11, last week Dec. 📷

Medieval fresco in Cathédrale St-Etienne at Auxerre

## ❹ Chablis

Yonne. 🚹 2,700. 🚌 ℹ️ 1 rue du Maréchal de Lattre de Tassigny (03 86 42 80 80). 🛒 Sun.
🌐 **tourisme-chablis.fr**

There can be no question that Chablis tastes best in Chablis. Although this is one of the most famous wine villages on earth, its narrow stone streets still have an air of sleepy prosperity. February processions in nearby Fyé, attended by the wine brotherhood of Piliers Chablisiens, honor St. Vincent, patron saint of winegrowers.

## ❺ Tonnerre

Yonne. 🚹 6,200. 🚌 🚉 ℹ️ pl Marguerite de Bourgogne (03 86 55 14 48). 🛒 Sat & Wed. 🌐 **tourisme-tonnerre.fr**

The mystical cloudy-green spring of **Fosse Dionne** is a good reason to visit the small town of Tonnerre. An astonishing volume of water bursts up from the ground into an 18th-century washing-place. Due to its depth and strong currents it has never been thoroughly explored and local legend has it that a serpent lives on undisturbed.

The **Hôtel-Dieu** is 150 years older than the Hôtel-Dieu in Beaune *(see pp350–51)*. It was

The intriguing spring of Fosse Dionne in Tonnerre

founded by Margaret of Burgundy in 1293 to care for the poor. In the Revolution it lost its tiling but the barrel-vaulted oak ceiling survived.

🏛 **Hôtel-Dieu & Musée**
Rue du Prieuré. **Tel** 03 86 55 14 48.
**Open** daily (Oct–Mar: closed Wed, Sun).
**Closed** some public hols. 📷 ♿ 🎫

## ❻ Château de Tanlay

Tanlay. **Tel** 03 86 75 70 61. **Open** Apr–early-Nov: Wed–Mon. 📷 🎫 oblig.

The moated Château de Tanlay, built in the mid-16th century, is a beautiful example of French Renaissance. There is a *trompe l'oeil* in the Grande Galerie and, in the corner tower, an intriguing School of Fontainebleau painted ceiling. Its antique divinities represent famous Protestants and Catholics in the 16th century, such as Diane de Poitiers as Venus.

The Renaissance facade and *cour d'honneur* of Château de Tanlay

# ❼ Abbaye de Fontenay

The tranquil Abbey of Fontenay is the oldest surviving Cistercian foundation in France and offers a rare insight into the Cistercian way of life. It represents the spirit of the order in the sublime gravity of its Romanesque church and its plain but elegant chapterhouse, in early Gothic style. The abbey was founded in 1118 by St. Bernard. Located deep in the forest, it offered the peace and seclusion the Cistercians sought. Supported by the local aristocracy, the abbey began to thrive and remained in use until the Revolution, when it was sold and converted into a paper mill. In 1906 the abbey came under new ownership and was restored to its original appearance.

**Dovecote**
A magnificent circular dovecote, built in the 13th century, is located next to the kennel where the precious hunting dogs of the dukes of Burgundy were guarded by servants.

## KEY

① **In the forge** monks produced their own tools and hardware.

② **The visitors' hostel** is where weary wanderers and pilgrims were offered board and lodging.

③ **The bakehouse** is no longer intact, but the 13th-century oven and chimney have survived.

④ **The 17th-century** abbot's lodgings were built when the abbots were appointed by royal favor.

⑤ **Warming Room**

⑥ **The scriptorium** is where manuscripts were copied. The adjacent Warming Room was used to warm chilled hands.

⑦ **The herb garden** was skilfully cultivated by the monks in order to grow healing herbs for medicines and potions.

⑧ **Infirmary**

★ **Cloisters**
For a 12th-century monk, a walk through the cloisters was an opportunity for meditation, as well as providing shelter from the weather.

**Fontenay "Prison"**
It may be that this 15th-century building was actually used to lock up not local miscreants but important abbey archives, in order to protect them against damage by rats.

★ **Abbey Church**
Rich decoration has no place in this church from the 1140s. But the severe architectural forms, the warm color of the stone, and the diffused light convey a grandeur of their own.

**Dormitory**
Monks slept in long rows on straw mattresses in this large, unheated room. The timberwork roof is from the late 15th century.

⑦

**Chapterhouse**
Once a day, monks and abbot assembled in this room to discuss matters concerning the community. It derives much of its charm from the elegant 12th-century piers and the rib vaults.

## St. Bernard and the Cistercians

In 1112 Bernard, a young Burgundian nobleman, joined the Cistercians. At the time the order was still obscure, founded 14 years earlier by a group of monks who wanted to turn their back on the elaborate lifestyle of Cluny (*see pp54–5*), renounce the world, and espouse poverty and simplicity of life. During Bernard's lifetime the Cistercians became one of the largest and most famous orders of its time. Part of this success was clearly due to Bernard's powerful personality and his skills as a writer, theologian, and states-man. He reinforced the poverty rule, rejecting all forms of embellishment. In 1174, only 21 years after his death, he was canonized.

*The Virgin Protecting the Cistercian Order, by Jean Bellegambe*

## ❽ Château d'Ancy-le-Franc

Yonne. **Tel** 03 86 75 14 63. **Open** Apr–mid-Nov: Tue–Sun; July–Aug: Mon pm. 🏛 📷 **W** chateau-ancy.com

The Renaissance facade of the château may look austere, but its inner courtyard has rich ornamentation. The château was constructed during the 1540s by the Italian Sebastiano Serlio, for the Duke of Clermont-Tonnerre. Most of the interior decorations were carried out by Primaticcio and other members of the Fontainebleau School *(see pp184–5)*. Diane de Poitiers, the duke's sister-in-law and mistress of Henry II, is portrayed in the *Chambre de Judith et Holophernes*.

Diane's apartments, including her bedroom, decorated with murals, can also be visited.

Vase of Vix in the Musée du Pays du Châtillonnais, Châtillon-sur-Seine

## ❾ Châtillon-sur-Seine

Côte d'Or. 🏛 6,000. 🚆 🚌 **i** rue du Bourg (03 80 91 13 19). 🛒 Sat. **W** chatillonnais-tourisme.fr

World War II left Châtillon a ruin, hence the town's largely modern aspect. But the past is still present in the **Musée du Pays du Châtillonnais**, where the Vix treasure is displayed. In 1953, the tomb of a Gaulish princess, from the 6th century BC, was discovered near Vix at Mont Lassois. The trove of jewellery and artifacts of Greek origin includes a stunning bronze vase, an impressive 66 in (143 cm) high and weighing 459 lb (208 kg). Also of interest in the town is the

The staid facade of the Château d'Ancy-le-Franc

Romanesque **Eglise St-Vorles**, containing an *Entombment* with splendidly sculpted Christ and mourners (1527).

Nearby are the sources of the River Seine, between St.-Seine-l'Abbaye and Chanceau, and its tributory, the River Douix, each marked by a beautiful grotto.

🏛 **Musée du Pays du Châtillonnais**
Rue de la Libération. **Tel** 03 80 91 24 67. **Open** Jul–Aug: daily; Sep–Jun: Wed–Mon. **Closed** Jan 1, May 1, Dec 24–25 & 31. 🏛 📷
**W** musee-vix.fr

## ❿ Alise-Ste.-Reine

Côte d'Or. 🏛 3,300. **i** 1 av de la Gare, Venarey-Les Laumes 21150 (03 80 96 89 13). **W** alesia-tourisme.net

Mont Auxois, above the village of Alise-Ste.-Reine, was the site of Caesar's final victory over the heroic Gaulish chieftain Vercingétorix in 52 BC after a six-week siege *(see p52)*. The first excavations here were undertaken in the mid-19th century, and they uncovered the vestiges of a thriving Gallo-Roman town, with theater, forum, and well-laid-out street plan. The **Alésia MuséoParc** includes a historical discovery center with interactive media displays and lifesize reconstructions of siege engines.

Alise is dominated by Aimé Millet's gigantic moustachioed statue of Vercingétorix, which was placed here in 1865 to commemorate the first excavations. Cynics feel that it bears a more than passing resemblance to Napoleon III, who sponsored the dig.

🏛 **Alésia MuséoParc**
Rue de l'Hôpital. **Tel** 03 80 96 96 23. **Open** Feb–Nov: daily. 🏛 🅿 ♿
**W** alesia.com

**Environs**
In the vicinity lies **Château de Bussy-Rabutin**. The spiteful 17th-century soldier and wit

Excavations at the Roman site near Alise-Ste.-Reine

Roger de Bussy-Rabutin created its highly individualistic decor, while exiled from Louis XIV's court. One room is dedicated to portraits of his many mistresses, as well as a couple of imaginary ones.

🏠 **Château de Bussy-Rabutin**
Bussy-le-Grand. **Tel** 03 80 96 00 03.
**Open** daily. **Closed** Jan 1, May 1, Nov 1 & 11, Dec 25. 🎫 🏛

## ⑪ Semur-en-Auxois

Côte d'Or. 🚗 5,000. 🚌 ℹ️ 2 pl Gaveau (03 80 97 05 96). 🚍 Sun.
🌐 **tourisme-semur.fr**

Approached from the west, Semur-en-Auxois comes as a surprise on an otherwise uneventful road. Its massive round bastions built in the 14th century (one of them with an unnerving gash in it) suddenly appear, towering over the Pont Joly and the peaceful River Armançon.

The **Eglise Notre-Dame** dates from the 13th and 14th centuries, and was modeled on the cathedral of Auxerre. The fragile high walls had to be restored in the 15th and 19th centuries. The church houses significant artworks, from the tympanum showing the legend of Doubting Thomas on the north doorway, to the 15th-century *Entombment* by Antoine le Moiturier. The stained glass presents the legend of St Barbara, and the work of different guilds such as butchers and drapers.

**Environs**
The village of Epoisses is the site of the moated **Château d'Epoisses**, its 11th- to 18th-century construction blending medieval towers with fine Renaissance details, and a huge 15th-century dovecote.

Stained-glass window in Eglise Notre-Dame at Semur-en-Auxois

Semur-en-Auxois by the River Armançon

Epoisses is also the home of one of Burgundy's most revered cheeses, to be sampled at the local café or *fromagerie*.

🏠 **Château d'Epoisses**
Epoisses. **Tel** 01 42 27 73 11.
**Open** Jul–Aug: Wed–Mon (grounds: all year). 🎫 🏛
♿ ground floor only.

## ⑫ Avallon

Yonne. 🚗 9,000. 🚉 🚌 ℹ️ 6 rue Bocquillot (03 86 34 14 19). 🚍 Sat & Thu. 🌐 **avallon-morvan.com**

A fine old fortified town, Avallon is located on a granite spur between two ravines by the River Cousin. It suffered in the wars of Saracens, Normans, English, and French, which accounts for its defensive aspect. The town is quiet and full of charming details. The main monument is the 12th-century Romanesque **Eglise St.-Lazare**, with two carved doorways. The larger illustrates the signs of the zodiac, the labors of the month, and the horsemen of the Apocalypse. The nave is decorated with sophisticated acanthus capitals and polychrome statuary.

The **Musée de l'Avallonnais** features an intricate Venus mosaic from the 2nd century AD, and Georges Rouault's (1871–1958) series of Expressionist etchings, the *Miserere*.

🏛 **Musée de l'Avallonnais**
5 rue du College. **Tel** 03 86 34 03 19.
**Open** Apr–Sep: Wed–Mon pms; Oct–mid-Nov & mid-Feb–Mar: Sat–Sun pms. **Closed** mid-Nov–mid-Feb.
🎫 🏛 🏛

**Environs**
To the southwest of Avallon is the 12th-century **Château de Bazoches**, which was given to Maréchal de Vauban by Louis XIV in 1675, and transformed by him into a military garrison.

*Miserere* by Georges Rouault in the Musée d'Avallonnais, Avallon

# ⑬ Vézelay

The golden glow of the Basilique Ste.-Madeleine crowning Vézelay's hill is visible from afar. Tourists follow in the footsteps of medieval pilgrims, ascending the narrow street up to the former abbey church. In the 12th century, at the height of its glory, the abbey claimed to house relics of Mary Magdalene and was also an important meeting point for pilgrims en route to Santiago de Compostela in Spain *(see pp404–5)*. Today its attraction lies in the Romanesque church with its magnificent sculpture and Gothic choir.

**View of Vézelay**
The abbey dominates Vézelay's surroundings, as it once dominated the religious and worldly affairs of the area.

**Nave of Ste.-Madeleine**
The nave was rebuilt between 1120 and 1135, using alternate dark and light stone in the transverse arches.

## KEY

① **The narthex** used to be a gathering point for medieval processions.

② **The facade** dates from 1150 and has a large 13th-century window. It was about to collapse, when in 1840 Viollet-le-Duc was commissioned to restore it, according to old plans.

③ **Tour St.-Michel** was built from 1150 to 1250. It derives its name from the statue of the archangel in the tower's southwest corner.

④ **Nave of Ste.-Madeleine**

⑤ **Tour St.-Antoine** was built at the same time as the choir, in the late 12th century. Its counterpart on the north side was never finished.

⑥ **The chapterhouse** and cloister are the only parts remaining from the 12th-century monastic buildings. Viollet-le-Duc rebuilt part of the cloister and restored the rib-vaulted chapterhouse, once a graceful background for the monks' daily assemblies.

★ **Tympanum**
This masterpiece of sculpture (1120–35) shows Christ on his throne, stretching out his hands from which rays of light descend on to the apostles

### VISITORS' CHECKLIST

**Practical Information**
Basilique Ste.-Madeleine, Vézelay.
**Tel** 03 86 33 39 50 or 03 86 33 23
69 (tourist office). **Open** 7am–8pm
daily (7am–dusk winter). 🗓 ✝
6:30pm Mon–Fri; 12:30pm, 6pm
(winter), 7pm (summer) Sat; 11am
Sun. 🌐 basiliquedevezelay.org

**Transportation**
🚉 Sermizelles.

**Crypt of Ste.-Madeleine**
The Romanesque crypt houses relics once
thought to be Mary Magdalene's. The vault
was rebuilt in 1165.

**★ Capitals**
The capitals in the nave
and narthex are exquisitely
carved, and give a vivid
rendering of the stories of
classical antiquity and the Bible.
The master who created them
remains unknown.

**Choir of Ste.-Madeleine**
The choir was rebuilt in the last quarter of the
12th century in the then-modern Gothic style
of the Ile-de-France.

Morvan, a region of rivers and forests, well suited to fishing and other outdoor pursuits

## ⑭ Morvan

Yonne, Côte d'Or, Nièvre, Saône-et-Loire. ✈ Dijon. 🚌 Autun, Mombard. 🚆 Château-Chinon, Saulieu, Avallon. 𝒊 6 bd République, Château-Chinon (03 86 85 06 58); Maison du Parc, St-Brisson (03 86 78 79 57). W **tourisme.parcdumorvan.org**

Morvan is a Celtic word meaning "Black Mountain," which is a good description of this area seen from afar. The immense, sparsely inhabited plateau of granite and woodland appears suddenly in the center of the rich Burgundy hills and farmland. Stretching roughly north to south, it gains altitude as it proceeds southward, reaching a culminating point of 2,956 ft (901 m) at **Haut-Folin**.

The Morvan's two sources of natural wealth are abundant water and dense forests of oak, beech, and conifer. In the old days lumber used to be floated out of the area to Paris via a network of lakes and rivers. Today it travels by truck, and the Yonne, Cousin, and Cure rivers are instead used for recreation and the production of electricity.

The Morvan has always been a poor, remote area. Each of its largest towns, Château-Chinon in the center and Saulieu on the outskirts, has barely 3,000 inhabitants.

During World War II, the Morvan was a bastion of the French Resistance. Today a Regional Nature Park, its attraction is its wildness. Information on a variety of outdoor activities, including cycling, canoeing, skiing, and horseback trekking, is available at the **Maison du Parc** at St-Brisson, where there is also the very moving **Musée de la Resistance**. There are plenty of short walking trails, and two well-signed long-distance paths: the GR13 (Vézelay to Autun) and the Tour du Morvan par les Grands Lacs.

🏛 **Musée de la Résistance**
Maison du Parc, St.-Brisson. **Tel** 03 86 78 72 99. **Open** Easter–mid-Nov: Sat pm–Mon, Wed–Fri (Jul & Aug: daily). **Closed** Sat am. 🎦 📷 🏛 ♿

## ⑮ Saulieu

Côte d'Or. 🚹 3,000. 🚌 🚆 𝒊 24 rue d'Argentine (03 80 64 00 21). 🛒 Sat. W **saulieu.fr**

On the edge of the Morvan, Saulieu has been a shrine of Burgundian cooking since the 17th century. The town was then a staging post on the Paris to Lyon coach road. The stylized animal sculptures of François Pompon can be admired at the **Musée Pompon**, which also houses a collection of Gallo-Roman stelae on the ground floor.

The Romanesque **Basilique St.-Andoche**, built in the early 12th century, has decorated capitals with representations of the Flight into Egypt and a comical version of the story of Balaam and his donkey waylaid by the Angel.

## ⑯ Nevers

Nièvre. 🚹 41,000. 🚌 🚆 𝒊 Palais Ducal, rue Sabatier (03 86 68 46 00). 🛒 Sat. W **nevers-tourisme.com**

Like all Burgundian towns fronting the Loire, Nevers should be approached from the west side of the river for a full appreciation of its noble site. Though lacking historical importance, the town has much to show. Considered to be the earliest of the Loire châteaux, the **Palais Ducal** has a long Renaissance facade framed by polygonal towers and a broad esplanade. The Romanesque 11th-century **Eglise St.-Etienne** has graceful monolithic columns and a wreath of radiating chapels.

In the crypt of the Gothic **Cathédrale St.-Cyr** is a 16th-century sculpted *Entombment*, and the foundations of a 6th-century baptistery, discovered in 1944, after heavy bombing.

The contemporary stained-glass windows are also noteworthy. The overlordship of Nevers passed to the Gonzaga family in the 16th century. They brought with them an Italian school of artists skilled in faïence-making and glassblowing.

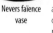

Nevers faïence vase

The industry has remained, and the modern pottery is still traditionally decorated in blue, white, yellow, and green, with its curious trademark, the little green arabesque knot, or *noeud vert*. The best place to view it is at the **Musée Municipal**. There are also several pottery workshops in the town center

🏛 **Musée Municipal Frédéric Blandin**
16 rue Saint-Genest. **Tel** 03 86 68 44 60. **Open** Tue–Sun (Oct–Apr: Tue–Fri pms only; Sat & Sun all day). 📷 📹

**Environs**
Just south of Nevers, the majestic 19th-century **Pont du Guetin** carries the Loire Canal across the Allier river. The church at **St.-Parize-le-Châtel** has a jolly Burgundian menagerie sculpted on the capitals of the crypt.

Autun's imposing Porte St.-André, once part of the Roman wall

The *Temptation of Eve* in Autun

⓱ **Autun**

Saône-et-Loire. 🚶 18,000. 🚍 🚉 ℹ 13 rue Général Demetz (03 85 86 80 38). 🚍 Wed & Fri, Journées Romaines d'Autun: 1st weekend of Aug. 🌐 autun-tourisme.com

Augustodunum, the town of Augustus, was founded in the late 1st century BC. It was a great center of learning, with a population four times what it is today. Its theater, built in the 1st century AD, could seat 20,000 people.

Today Autun is still a delight, deserving gastronomic as well as cultural investigation.

The magical **Cathédrale St.-Lazare** was built in the 12th century. It is notable for its sculptures, most of them by the mysterious 12th-century artist Gislebertus. He sculpted both the capitals inside and the glorious Last Judgment tympanum over the main portal. This masterpiece, called a "Romanesque Cézanne" by André Malraux, escaped notice and was saved from destruction during the Revolution because it had been plastered over in the 18th century. Inside, some of the capitals can be seen close-up in the Salle Capitulaire. Look also for the sculpture of Pierre

Jeannin and his wife. Jeannin was the president of the Dijon parliament that prevented the Massacre of St. Bartholomew *(see pp60–61)* spreading, with the perceptive remark, "the commands of very angry monarchs should be obeyed very slowly."

The collection of medieval art at the **Musée Rolin** includes the bas-relief *Temptation of Eve*, by Gislebertus, the 15th-century painted stone Virgin of Autun, and the *Nativity of Cardinal Rolin* by the Master of Moulins, from about 1480.

The **Porte St.-André** and **Porte d'Arroux**, and the ruins of the **Théâtre Romain** and the **Temple de Janus**, are reminders of Autun's glorious Roman past.

🏛 **Musée Rolin**
3 rue des Bancs. **Tel** 03 85 52 09 76. **Open** mid-Feb–Mar & mid-Oct–Nov: Wed–Sat, Sun pm; Apr–mid-Oct: Wed–Mon. **Closed** Dec–mid-Feb, public hols. 📷 📹

Remains of Autun's Roman theater, dating from the 1st century AD

# ⓲ Street by Street: Dijon

The center of Dijon is noted for its architectural splendor – a legacy from the dukes of Burgundy (see p347). Wealthy parliament members also had elegant *hôtels particuliers* built in the 17th–18th centuries. The capital of Burgundy, Dijon today has a rich cultural life and a renowned university. The city's great art treasures are housed in the Palais des Ducs. Dijon is also famous for its mustard (see p322) and *pain d'épices* (gingerbread), a reminder of the town's position on the spice route. It became a major railroad hub during the 19th century and now has a TGV link to Paris.

**Hôtel de Vogüé**
This elegant 17th-century mansion is decorated with Burgundian cabbages and fruit garlands by Hugues Sambin.

**★ Notre-Dame**
This magnificent 13th-century Gothic church has a facade with gargoyles, columns, and the popular Jacquemart clock. The *chouette* (owl) is reputed to bring good luck when touched.

**Musée des Beaux-Arts**
The collection of Flemish masters here includes this 14th-century triptych by Jacques de Baerze and Melchior Broederlam.

**Place de la Libération**
was created by Mansart in the 17th century.

**★ Palais des Ducs**
The dukes of Burgundy held court here, but the building seen today was mainly built in the 17th century for the parliament. It now houses the Musée des Beaux-Arts.

*For hotels and restaurants in this region see pp562–3 and pp589–91*

**Rue Verrerie**
This cobblestone street in the old merchants' quarter is lined by medieval half-timbered houses. Some have fine woodcarvings, such as Nos. 8, 10, and 12.

**VISITORS' CHECKLIST**

**Practical Information**
Côte d'Or. 🗺 155,000. 🛈 15 cour de la Gare & 11 rue des Forges (08 92 70 05 58). 🚍 Tue, Fri, Sat. 🎭 Florissimo (2020); Fêtes de la Vigne (2018); Festival International de Musique Mécanique (2018). Hôtel de Vogüé: inner courtyard open. Musée Magnin: (03 80 67 11 10). **Open** Tue–Sun. **Closed** Jan 1, Dec 25. 🌐
W destinationdijon.com

**Transportation**
🚆 🚌 cour de la Gare. 🚕

**★ St.-Michel**
Begun in the 15th century and completed in the 17th century, St.-Michel's facade combines Flamboyant Gothic with Renaissance details. On the richly carved porch, angels and biblical motifs mingle with mythological themes.

**Musée Magnin**
A collection of French and foreign 16th- to 19th-century paintings are displayed among period furniture in this 17th-century mansion.

RUE PROUDHON

RUE J J

R CHAUDRONNERIE

ROUSSEAU

RUE VANNERIE

RUE JEANNIN

RUE LA MONNOYE

PL STE CHAPELLE

PL DU THEATRE

R VAILLANT

PL ST MICHEL

RUE CHABOT CHARNY

RUE LE GOUZ GERLAND

RUE BUFFON

RUE DU VIEUX COLLEGE

**Eglise St.-Etienne** dates back to the 11th century but has been rebuilt many times. Its characteristic lantern was added in 1686.

**Key**

— Suggested route

| 0 meters | 100 |
| 0 yards | 100 |

*Well of Moses* by Claus Sluter, in the Chartreuse de Champmol

## Exploring Dijon

The center of Dijon is a warren of little streets that reward exploration. Rue des Forges, behind the Palais de Ducs, was the main street until the 18th century and is named after the jewelers and goldsmiths who had workshops there. Hôtel Chambellan at No. 34 is Flamboyant Gothic with a stone spiral staircase and wooden galleries. At No. 38 the Maison Maillard, built in 1560, has a stone facade decorated by Hugues Sambin.

Rue Chaudronnerie has several houses of note, notably Maison des Cariatides at No. 28, with fine stone carved caryatids framing the windows. Place Darcy is lined with hotels and restaurants; the Jardin Darcy, with its polar bear sculpture (*L'Ours Blanc*) by François Pompon, is delightful.

### 🏛 Musée des Beaux-Arts

Palais des Etats de Bourgogne, Cour de Bar. **Tel** 03 80 74 52 70. **Open** Wed–Mon. **Closed** Jan 1, May 1 & 8, Jul 14, Nov 1 & 11, Dec 25. 🚻 limited. 🗖

Dijon's prestigious art collection is housed in the former Palais des Ducs (*see p344*). The Salle des Gardes on the first floor is dominated by the giant mausoleums of the dukes, with tombs sculpted by Claus Sluter (around 1345–1405). Other exhibits include two gilded Flemish retables and a portrait of Philip the Good by Rogier van der Weyden.

The collection has Dutch and Flemish masters and sculpture by Sluter and Rude, as well as Swiss and German primitives, 16th- to 18th-century French paintings, the Donation Granville of 19th- and 20th-century French art, and sculptures by François Pompon. Note the ducal kitchens with six fireplaces, and the Tour Philippe le Bon, 150 ft (46 m) tall with a fine view of Burgundian tiled roof tops.

### ⛪ Cathédrale St.-Bénigne

Pl St.-Bénigne. **Tel** 03 80 30 39 33. **Open** daily. 🗖 🚻 🗖 for crypt.

Little remains of the 11th-century Benedictine abbey first founded in honor of St. Bénigne. Beneath the church is a Romanesque crypt with a fine rotunda ringed by three circles of columns.

### 🏛 Musée Archéologique

5 rue du Docteur Maret. **Tel** 03 80 48 83 70. **Open** Apr–Oct: Wed–Mon; Nov–Mar: Wed, Sat & Sun. **Closed** most public hols.

The museum is housed in the old dormitory of the Benedictine Abbey of St Bénigne. The 11th-century chapterhouse, its stocky columns supporting a barrel-vaulted roof, houses a fine collection of Gallo-Roman sculpture. The ground floor, with its lovely fan vaulting, houses the famous head of Christ by Claus Sluter, originally from the *Well of Moses*.

### 🏛 Chartreuse de Champmol

1 bd Chanoine Kir. **Open** daily (08 92 70 05 58). 🗖 🗖

This was originally the site of a family necropolis built by Philip the Bold, but destroyed during the Revolution. All that remains is a chapel doorway and the famous *Well of Moses* by Claus Sluter. It is now on the grounds of a psychiatric hospital east of Dijon train station – it is not very easy to find but worth the effort. The statue, representing Moses and five other prophets, is set on a hexagonal base above a basin. Sluter is renowned for his deeply cut carving and his work here is exquisitely lifelike.

The tomb of Philip the Bold by Claus Sluter, now in the Grande Salle of the Musée des Beaux-Arts

# The Golden Age of Burgundy

While the French Capetian dynasty fought in the Hundred Years' War *(see pp58–9)*, the dukes of Burgundy built up one of Europe's most powerful states, which included Flanders and parts of Holland. From the time of Philip the Bold (1342–1404), the ducal court became a cultural force, supporting many of Europe's finest artists, such as painters Rogier van der Weyden and the van Eyck brothers, and the sculptor Claus Sluter. The duchy's dominions were, however, broken up after the death of Duke Charles the Bold in 1477.

**The tomb of Philip the Bold** in Dijon was made by the Flemish sculptor Claus Sluter, who was among the most brilliant artists of the Burgundian Golden Age. The dramatic realism of the mourners is one of the most striking features of this spectacular tomb, begun while the duke was still alive.

**Burgundy In 1477**
Extent of the duchy at its peak

## The Marriage of Philip the Good

*Philip the Good, duke from 1419 to 1467, married Isabella of Portugal in 1430. This 17th-century copy of a painting by van Eyck shows the sumptuous wedding feast, when Philip also inaugurated the chivalric Order of the Golden Fleece.*

**The dukes** surrounded themselves with luxury, including fine gold and silverware.

Isabella of Portugal

The Duchess of Bedford, Philip's sister

**Greyhounds** were popular hunting animals at the Burgundian court.

**Philip the Good** is dressed in white ceremonial finery.

**Burgundian art**, such as this Franco-Flemish *Book of Hours*, reflected the Flemish origins of many of the dukes' favorite artists.

**Dijon's Palais des Ducs** was rebuilt in 1450 by Philip the Good to reflect the glory of the Burgundian court, a center of art, chivalry, and glorious feasts. Empty after Charles the Bold's death, it was reconstructed in the 17th century.

Wine harvest in the vineyards of Nuits-St.-Georges, part of the Côte d'Or district

## ⑲ Côte d'Or

Côte d'Or. ✈ Dijon. 🚗 🚌 Dijon, Nuits-St.-Georges, Beaune, Santenay. 𝒊 Dijon (08 92 70 05 58). 🆆 cotedor-tourisme.com

In winemaking terms, the Côte d'Or includes the Côte de Beaune and the Côte de Nuits in a nearly unbroken line of vines from Dijon to Santenay. Squeezed in between the flat plain of the Saône to the southeast and a plateau of woodland to the northwest, this narrow escarpment is about 30 miles (50 km) long. The grapes of the great Burgundy vineyards grow in the golden reddish soil of the slope (hence the area's name).

The classification of the characteristics of the land is fabulously technical and elaborate, but for the layman a rough rule of thumb might be that 95 percent of the best vines are on the uphill side of the

Narrow street in Beaune's historic center

D974 thoroughfare *(see pp324–5)*. The names on the signposts haunt the dreams of wine lovers the world over: Gevrey-Chambertin, Vougeot, Chambolle-Musigny, Vosne-Romanée, Nuits-St.-Georges, Aloxe-Corton, Meursault, and Chassagne Montrachet.

Typical grape basket in the Musée du Vin de Bourgogne at Beaune

## ⑳ Beaune

Côte d'Or. 🅐 23,000. 🚗 🚌 𝒊 6 bd Perpeuil (03 80 26 21 30). 🗓 Sat, Wed. 🎵 Baroque Music (Jul). 🆆 beaune-tourisme.fr

The old center of Beaune, snug within its ramparts and encircling boulevards, is easy to explore on foot. Its indisputable treasure is the **Hôtel-Dieu** *(see pp350–51)*. The Hôtel des Ducs de Bourgogne, built in the 14th–16th centuries, houses the **Musée du Vin de Bourgogne**. The building, with its flamboyant facade, is as interesting as its display of traditional winemaking equipment.

Farther to the north lies the **Collégiale Notre-Dame**, begun in the early 12th century. Inside this mainly Romanesque church hang five very fine 15th-century woollen and silk tapestries.

With hints of early Renaissance style, they delicately illustrate the life of the Virgin Mary in 19 scenes.

🏛 **Musée du Vin de Bourgogne**
Rue d'Enfer. **Tel** 03 80 22 08 19. **Open** Wed–Sun (Apr–Sep: Wed–Mon). **Closed** Dec–mid-Mar. 📷

## ㉑ Tournus

Saône-et-Loire. 🅐 6,500. 🚗 🚌 𝒊 pl de l'Abbaye (03 85 27 00 20). 🗓 Sat. 🆆 tournugeois.fr

The Abbaye de St.-Philibert is one of Burgundy's oldest and greatest Romanesque buildings. It was founded by a group of monks from Noirmoutier, who had been driven from their island by invading Normans in the 9th century, and brought with them relics of their patron saint, Philibert (still in the choir). Rebuilt in the 10th–12th centuries, the well-fortified abbey church is made from lovely

Dovecote in Cormatin château gardens, Mâconnais

Nave of St.-Philibert in Tournus

pale pink stone, with black-and-white vaulting inside.

The 17th-century Hôtel-Dieu has its original rooms intact with the furniture, equipment, and pharmacy on display. It also houses the **Musée Greuze** (open Apr–Oct) dedicated to Tournus's most famous son, the artist Jean-Baptiste Greuze (1725–1805).

### Environs

Southwest of Tournus lies the Mâconnais landscape of hills, vineyards, orchards, red-tiled farmhouses, and Romanesque churches. **Brancion** is a pretty hill village, **Chapaize** has an 11th-century church, and there is a sumptuous Renaissance château at **Cormatin**. The village of **Taizé** is the center of a world-famous ecumenical community. To the north, **Chalon-sur-Saône** features the Musée Niépce, dedicated to the inventor of photography.

## ㉒ Cluny

Saône-et-Loire. 🚹 4,800. 🚌 🚹 6 rue Mercière (03 85 59 05 34). 🛒 Sat.
🌐 cluny-tourisme.com

The little town of Cluny is overshadowed by the ruins of its great abbey, the **Ancienne Abbaye de Cluny**, once the most powerful monastic foundation in Europe (*see pp54–5*). It was founded by William the Pious, Duke of Aquitaine in 910. Within 200 years, Cluny had become the head of a major reforming order with monasteries all over Europe. Its abbots were considered to be

as powerful as monarchs or popes, and four are venerated as saints. But by the 14th century the system was in decline. The abbey was closed in 1790, and the church was later dismantled.

The guided tour presents the abbey remains, notably the Clocher de l'Eau Bénite (Holy Water Belltower); the remains of figured capitals, displayed in the 13th-century flour store; and the **Musée d'Art & Archéologie**, in the former abbot's palace. In the town, don't miss the 12th-century **Eglise St.-Marcel**.

Southwest of the town, the chapel in **Berzé-la-Ville** is decorated with superb 12th-century frescoes, similar to those once seen at Cluny.

🏛 **Ancienne Abbaye de Cluny**
Tel 03 85 59 15 93. **Open** daily.
**Closed** Jan 1, May 1, Nov 1 & 11, Dec 25. 🚫 ♿ 🅿 📷 ♿

🏛 **Musée d'Art & Archéologie**
Palais Jean de Bourbon. Tel 03 85 59 89 99. **Open** daily. **Closed** Jan 1, May 1, Nov 1 & 11, Dec 25. 🚫 ♿

## ㉓ Paray-le-Monial

Saône-et-Loire. 🚹 10,000. 🚌 🚃
🚹 25 av Jean-Paul II (03 85 81 10 92).
🛒 Fri. 🌐 **tourisme-paraylemonial.fr**

Dedicated to the cult of the Sacred Heart of Jesus, the **Basilique du Sacré-Coeur** has made Paray-le-Monial one of the most important sites of pilgrimage in modern France. Marguerite-Marie Alacoque, who was born here in 1647, had rather gory visions, from which the cult later developed, sweeping across France in the 19th century. The church is a small version of the now-lost abbey church of Cluny, with particularly harmonious and pure Romanesque architecture.

A visit to the **Musée du Hiéron** (open mid-Mar–Dec) provides an insight into industrial artistic tile production in the 19th and 20th centuries.

Located on place Guignaud is the ornate **Maison Jayet**, dating from the 16th century, which houses the town hall.

Basilique du Sacré-Coeur at Paray-le-Monial

# Hôtel-Dieu

After the Hundred Years' War, many of Beaune's inhabitants suffered the effects of poverty and famine. To remedy this, the chancellor, Nicolas Rolin, and his wife founded a hospice here in 1443, inspired by the architecture of northern French hospitals. The Rolins provided an annual grant and saltworks for income. Today the hospice is considered a medieval jewel, with its superb geometric, multicolored Burgundian roof tiles. It houses two religious masterpieces: the *Christ-de-Pitié* statue, carved from oak, and Rogier van der Weyden's *Last Judgment* polyptych.

★ **Great Hall of the Poor**
The hall, with its carved, painted roof, has 28 four-poster beds, each often used by two patients at a time. Meals were served at central tables.

**Tribute to Rolin's Wife**
A recurring motif features the entwined letters N and G, birds and stars, and the word *Seulle* referring to Rolin's wife Guigone, his "one and only."

Entrance

## KEY

① **St. Anne's Room** has a tableau of nuns working in what was once the linen room, and a colorful feast-day tapestry.

② **St. Hugues's Room** contains a painting of the saint curing two children. Frescoes by Isaac Moillon show the miracles of Christ.

③ **Glazed roof tiles**, in a colorful geometric pattern, are the most dramatic feature of the Hôtel-Dieu.

④ **St. Louis's Room**

## Annual Charity Wine Auction

On the third Sunday in November, an annual charity auction in Beaune is the centerpiece of three days of festivities known as *Les Trois Glorieuses*. Saturday sees the banquet of the Confrérie des Chevaliers du Tastevin at the Château Clos de Vougeot. On Sunday the auction of wine from vineyards owned by nearby hospitals takes place. Its prices are the benchmark for the entire vintage. On Monday, at La Paulée de Meursault, there is a party, where growers bring along bottles of their best vintages to enjoy.

Wine sold at the famous auction

### Kitchen
The centerpiece of the kitchen is a Gothic fireplace with a dual hearth and a mechanical spit, made in 1698 and is turned by a wooden "robot."

### Cour d'Honneur
The buildings of Hôtel-Dieu are arranged around a splendid central courtyard. This is flanked by a wooden gallery, above which rise high dormer windows topped by weather vanes. The courtyard well is a fine example of Gothic wrought-iron work.

### Pharmacy
Unusual potions with names such as woodlouse powder, shrimps' eyes, and vomit nut powder are stored in these earthenware pots. Nearby is a bronze mortar used to prepare the remedies.

### ★ Last Judgment Polyptych
The naked figures shown in Rogier van der Weyden's 15th-century polyptych were briefly given clothing in the 19th century. At the same time, the altarpiece was cut in half, so that the outer and inner panels could be seen together.

Château de Pierreclos in the Mâconnais region

## ❷❹ Brionnais

Saône-et-Loire. ✈ Mâcon. 🚍 Paray-le-Monial, Roanne. 🚌 Paray-le-Monial. 🛈 Marcigny (03 85 25 39 06).

The Brionnais is a small and peaceful rural district, squeezed between the River Loire and the Beaujolais foothills in the far south of Burgundy.

Its agricultural staple is the white Charolais cow, which can be seen grazing everywhere. For a closer look at this regional symbol, visit the lively cattle-market in **St.-Christophe** on Wednesdays.

The area has an abundance of Romanesque churches, most of which are built of the local ocher-colored stone. The 11th-century church of **Anzy-le-Duc** has a majestic three-tiered polygonal tower

Capital in St.-Julien-de-Jonzy

and exquisitely carved capitals. **Semur-en-Brionnais** was the birthplace of Cluny's famous abbot St. Hugues. Its church is inspired by his great monastery. The church at **St.-Julien-de-Jonzy** has a very finely carved tympanum.

A small town by the River Genette, **La Clayette** is graced by a château set in a lake (not open to the public). In nearby Curbigny, it is possible to visit the 18th-century Château de Drée, with its Louis XV and Louis XVI salons and its chapel.

Southeast of La Clayette the lonely **Montagne de Dun** rises just over 2,300 ft (700 m) and offers a panorama over the gentle, green Brionnais hills. This is some of the best picnic country in Burgundy, full of sleepy corners and quiet byways.

## ❷❺ Mâcon

Saône-et-Loire. 🚏 36,000. ✈ 🚍 🚌 🛈 1 pl Saint Pierre (03 85 21 07 07). 🗓 Sat. 🖳 macon-tourism.com

At the frontier between Burgundy and the south, Mâcon is an industrial town and wine center on the Saône.

The lack of churches is due to fervent anticlericalism during the Revolution, when 14 were destroyed. A 17th-century convent has been turned into the **Musée des Ursulines**. Its collections include French and Flemish painting and an exhibition on the prehistoric site of Solutré. On the charming place aux Herbes, where the market is held, the **Maison de Bois** is a 15th-century wooden house covered with bizarre carvings.

### 🏛 Musée des Ursulines

Allée de Matisco. **Tel** 03 85 39 90 38. **Open** Tue–Sat & Sun pm. **Closed** Jan 1, May 1, Jul 14, Nov 1, Dec 25. 🔲 🛍

### Environs

The great **Roche de Solutré** rises dramatically above the Pouilly-Fuissé vineyards in the Mâconnais district *(see p349)*. Below the rock, finds from the Stone Age have established it as a major archeological site.

Mâconnais is also the land of the Romantic poet Lamartine (1790–1869). Born in Mâcon, he spent his childhood at Milly Lamartine and later lived at Château de St.-Point. **Château de Pierreclos** is associated with his epic poem *Jocelyn*.

Charolais cattle grazing on the gentle hills of the Brionnais

# Franche-Comté

A region of woods and water, the Franche-Comté offers exceptional natural beauty combined with opportunities for canoeing, trekking, and skiing. Aside from towns well worth visiting, this is a region to explore in the wild. Glorious scenery with grottoes and cascading waterfalls can be found all along the Vallée du Doubs. Farther south are the spectacular sources of the rivers Lison and Loue. The Reculées is an area of extraordinary formations of ridges and waterfalls such as Baume-les-Messieurs. In Région des Lacs, the silent, peaceful lakes are surrounded by mountain peaks and virgin forests.

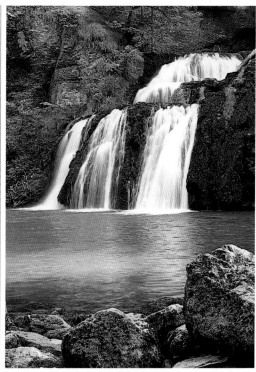

Nature at its purest at Source du Lison in the Franche-Comté

## 26 Cascades du Hérisson

Jura. *i* Clairvaux-les-Lacs (03 84 25 27 47). ⊖ Wed.

The village of Doucier, at the foot of the Pic de l'Aigle, is the starting point for the valley of the River Hérisson, one of the finest natural settings in the Jura. Leave the car at the park by the Moulin Jacquand and walk up the trail through the woods to a spectacular waterfall, the 213-ft (65-m) Cascade de L'Eventail, and beyond to the equally impressive Cascade du Grand Saut. The walk, which takes about 2 hours there and back, is steep at times and can be slippery, so suitable footwear is essential.

## 27 Arbois

Jura. 🚇 3,600. 🚉 *i* 17 rue de l'Hôtel de Ville (03 84 66 55 50). ⊖ Fri.
**w** tourisme.arbois.com

The jolly wine town of Arbois lies on the vine-covered banks of the River Cuisance. It is famous for the sherrylike *vin jaune* (yellow wine) of the district. On the north side of the town is **Maison de Pasteur**, the preserved house and laboratory of the great scientist Louis Pasteur (1822–95), the first to test vaccines on humans.

### Environs
Southeast of Dole is the 18th-century **Château d'Arlay**, with immaculately kept gardens.

## 28 Dole

Jura. 🚇 28,000. 🚉 🚌 *i* 6 pl Grévy (03 84 72 11 22). ⊖ Tue & Fri.
**w** tourisme-paysdedole.fr

The busy town of Dole lies where the Doubs meets the Rhine-Rhône canal. The former capital of the Comté was always a symbol of the region's resistance to the French. The region had become used to relative independence, first under the counts of Burgundy and then as part of the Holy Roman Empire. Though always French-speaking, its people did not appreciate the idea of the French absolute monarchy and in 1636 endured a very long siege. The town finally submitted to Louis XIV, first in 1668, and again in 1674.

There is a charming historic quarter in the center of town, full of winding alleys, houses dating back to the 15th century, and quiet inner courtyards. Place aux Fleurs offers an excellent view of this part of town and the mossy-roofed, 16th-century **Eglise Notre-Dame**.

Virgin and Child on the north portal of Eglise Notre-Dame, Dole

The Saline Royale at Arc-et-Senans

## ㉙ Arc-et-Senans

Doubs. 🅰 1,400. 🚉 🛈 3A rue de la Saline (03 81 57 43 21). 🌐 **destination louelison.com**

Designated a World Heritage Site since 1982, the **Saline Royale** (Royal Saltworks) at Arc-et-Senans were designed by the great French architect Claude-Nicolas Ledoux (1736–1806). He envisaged a development built in concentric circles around the main buildings. However, the only ones to be completed (in 1775) were the buildings used for salt production. Nevertheless, these show the staggering scale of Ledoux's idea: salt water was to be piped from Salins-les-Bains nearby, and fuel to reduce it was to come from the Chaux forest. The enterprise, which was never a success, was closed down in 1895, but the salt production buildings can be visited. The **Musée Ledoux Lieu du Sel** displays intriguing models of the grand projects imagined by the visionary architect.

🏛 **Musée Ledoux Lieu du Sel**
Saline Royale. **Tel** 03 81 54 45 45.
**Open** daily. **Closed** Jan 1, Dec 25.
📷 📹 🏛 ♿ ground floor.

## ㉚ Champlitte

Haute-Saône. 🅰 1,900. 🚌 🛈 2 allée du Sainfoin (03 84 67 67 19).
🌐 **ot-champlitte.fr**

In the small town of Champlitte, the **Musée des Arts et Traditions Populaires** was created by a local shepherd, who collected artifacts connected with disappearing local customs. One of the poignant displays housed in this Renaissance château recalls the emigration of 400 citizens to Mexico in the mid-19th century.

🏛 **Musée des Arts et Traditions Populaires**
Pl de l'Eglise. **Tel** 03 84 67 82 00.
**Open** Jul & Aug: daily (Sat & Sun pms only); Mar–Jun & Sep–Nov: Wed–Mon (Sat & Sun pm only). **Closed** Dec–Feb.
📷 📹 🏛

## ㉛ Besançon

Doubs. 🅰 120,000. 🚉 🚌 🛈 2 pl de la Première Armée Française (03 81 80 92 55). 🛒 Tue–Sat & Sun am.
🌐 **besancon-tourisme.com**

Besançon supplanted Dole as the capital of the Franche-Comté in the 17th century. It began as an ecclesiastical center and is now an industrial one, specializing in precision engineering. The stately architecture of the old town, with its elegant wrought-iron work, is a 17th-century legacy.

Behind the Renaissance facade of the Palais Granvelle, in the Grande Rue, is the **Musée du Temps**, a fine collection of timepieces of all ages – a tribute to Besançon's renown as a clock-and watchmaking center. An interactive exhibition on the third floor invites reflection on the relativity of the notion of time.

Farther along the same street are the birthplaces of novelist Victor Hugo (1802–85) at No. 140 and the Lumière brothers (see p67) at place Victor Hugo. Behind **Porte Noire**, a Roman arch, is the 12th-century Cathédrale St.-Jean. In its bell tower is the **Horloge Astronomique** with its automatons that pop out on the hour.

The stunning **Musée des Beaux-Arts et d'Archéologie**, in the old corn market, houses works by Fragonard, Cranach, Rubens, Ingres, Goya, Matisse, and Picasso.

Vauban's citadel, overlooking the River Doubs, has great views, plus three museums, including the **Musée Comtois**, with a collection of local artifacts, and a natural history museum with an insectarium and an aquarium.

🏛 **Musée du Temps**
Palais Granvelle, 96 Grande Rue. **Tel** 03 81 87 81 50. **Open** Tue–Sun. **Closed** Jan 1, May 1, Nov 1, Dec 25. 📷 📹 ♿

🕐 **Horloge Astronomique**
Rue de la Convention. **Tel** 03 81 81 12 76. **Open** Apr–Sep: Wed–Mon (winter: Thu–Mon). **Closed** Jan, May 1, Nov 1 & 11, Dec 25. 📷 📹

🏛 **Musée des Beaux-Arts et d'Archéologie**
1 pl de la Révolution. **Tel** 03 81 87 80 67. **Closed** for renovation until late 2018. 📷 free Sun. ♿

🏛 **Musée Comtois**
La Citadelle, rue des Fusillés de la Résistance. **Tel** 03 81 87 83 33. **Open** daily. **Closed** 3 wks Jan, Dec 25. 📷 📹 🏛

Besançon's astronomical clock, made in 1857–60

## ㉜ Ornans

Doubs. 🅰 4,300. 🚌 🛈 7 rue Pierre Vernier (03 81 62 21 50). 🛒 3rd Tue of month. 🌐 **destinationlouelison.com**

The great Realist painter Gustave Courbet was born at Ornans in 1819. He painted the town in every possible light. His *Enterrement à Ornans* proved to be one of the most influential

The striking Chapelle Notre-Dame-du-Haut by Le Corbusier at Ronchamp

paintings of the 19th century. Courbet's work is displayed in three historic buildings, including his childhood home, which make up the **Musée Courbet.**

### 🏛 Musée Courbet

Pl Robert Fernier. **Tel** 03 81 86 22 88. **Open** Wed–Mon. Closed Jan 1, May 1, Nov 1, Dec 25. 🛉 🗔 🖥 🎴
**W** doubs.fr

### Environs

A canoeist's paradise, the **Vallée de la Loue** is the loveliest in the Jura. The D67 follows the river from Ornans eastward to Ouhans, from where it is only a 15-minute walk to its magnificent source. Various belvederes offer splendid views over the area.

Southwest of Ornans, the spectacular **Source du Lison** (see p353) is a 20-minute walk from Nans-sous-Ste.-Anne.

### 🟤 Belfort

Territoire de Belfort. 🅰 52,000. 🚆 🚌
🛈 2 bis rue Clemenceau (03 84 55 90 90). 🛒 Wed–Sun. **W** belfort-tourisme.com

The symbol of Belfort is an enormous pink sandstone lion. It was built (rather than carved) by Frédéric-Auguste Bartholdi

(1834–1904), whose other major undertaking was the Statue of Liberty.

Belfort's immensely strong **citadel**, designed by Vauban under Louis XIV, withstood three sieges, in 1814, 1815, and 1870. Today this remarkable array of fortifications provides an interesting walk and extensive views of the surroundings. The **Musée d'Histoire** is housed in the citadel and displays models of the original fortifications as well as regional art and artifacts (closed Tue).

### 🟤 Ronchamp

Haute-Saône. 🅰 3,000. 🚌 🛈 25 rue Le Corbusier (03 84 63 50 82). 🛒 Sat.
**W** ot-ronchamp.fr

Le Corbusier's **Chapelle Notre-Dame-du-Haut** dominates this former miners' town. A sculpture rather than a building, its swelling concrete form was finalized in 1955. Inside, light, shape, and space form a unity.

There is also a **Musée de la Mine** evoking the industry and the life of local miners.

*Le Miroir d'Ornans* in the Musée Courbet, Ornans

# THE MASSIF CENTRAL

*Haute-Vienne · Creuse · Allier · Puy de Dôme · Corrèze · Cantal*
*Haute-Loire · Aveyron · Lozère ·*

The Massif Central is a region of strange, wild beauty – one of France's best-kept secrets. It is surprisingly little known beyond its sprinkling of spas and the major cities of Clermont-Ferrand, Vichy, and Limoges. However, the new *autoroutes* through the heart of its uplands have started to open up this previously remote region.

The huge central plateau of ancient granite and crystalline rock that makes up the Massif Central embraces the dramatic landscapes of the Auvergne, Limousin, Aveyron, and Lozère. Once a testing crossroads for pilgrims, and strung with giant volcanoes, it is a region of unsuspected richness, from the spectacular town of Le Puy-en-Velay, to the unique treasures at Conques.

With its crater lakes and hot springs, the Auvergne is the Massif Central's lush volcanic core, an outdoor paradise offering activities from hiking in summer to skiing in winter. It also has some of France's most beautiful Romanesque churches, medieval castles, and Renaissance palaces. To the east are the mountain ranges of Forez, Livardois, and Velay; to the west are the giant chains of extinct volcanoes, the Monts Dômes, Monts Dore, and the Monts du Cantal. The Limousin, on the northwestern edge of the Massif Central, is gentler country with green pastures and blissfully empty roads.

The Aveyron spreads into the south-west from the Aubrac mountains, carrying with it the rivers Lot, Aveyron, and Tarn through gorges and valleys with their cliff-hanging villages. To the east in the Lozère are the Grands Causses, the vast, isolated uplands of the Cévennes. These barren plateaus give farmers a poor living, but have been a favorite route with adventurous travelers across the centuries.

La Bourboule, a spa town in the Monts Dore

◄ The spectacular Gorges du Tarn

# Exploring the Massif Central

Nature is at its most magnificent in the volcanic mountain ranges and wild river gorges of the Massif Central. This is a vast and unspoiled territory, which offers spectacular sightseeing and every imaginable outdoor activity, with rafting, paragliding, canoeing, and hiking among the many choices. There are hundreds of churches, châteaux, and museums to nourish lovers of history, architecture, and art; and good, hearty regional cooking and interesting local wines for lovers of good living.

| 0 kilometers | 25 |
| 0 miles | 25 |

### Key

═══ Freeway

= = Freeway under construction

━━━ Highway

━━━ Secondary road

⋯⋯ Minor road

━━━ Scenic route

⋯⋯ Main railroad

---- Minor railroad

━━━ Regional border

△ Summit

Limestone cliffs of the Gorges du Tarn

### Getting Around

There are good air and train services connecting Paris with the major towns of Limoges and Clermont-Ferrand. Many of the most interesting towns and sights are easily accessible only by car, and AutoTrain from Paris to Brive is an effortless way of getting to the region with a car. Most minor roads are well-kept, but slow going in the mountains. A few roads are vertiginous, especially the road to the summit of Puy Mary, which is utterly breath-taking. The A71/A75 (toll-free) through the Auvergne is a magnificent road.

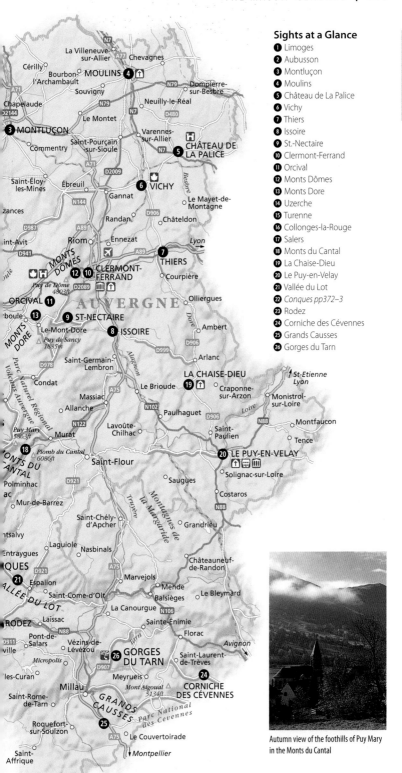

## Sights at a Glance

1. Limoges
2. Aubusson
3. Montluçon
4. Moulins
5. Château de La Palice
6. Vichy
7. Thiers
8. Issoire
9. St.-Nectaire
10. Clermont-Ferrand
11. Orcival
12. Monts Dômes
13. Monts Dore
14. Uzerche
15. Turenne
16. Collonges-la-Rouge
17. Salers
18. Monts du Cantal
19. La Chaise-Dieu
20. Le Puy-en-Velay
21. Vallée du Lot
22. *Conques pp372–3*
23. Rodez
24. Corniche des Cévennes
25. Grands Causses
26. Gorges du Tarn

Autumn view of the foothills of Puy Mary in the Monts du Cantal

A Limoges enamel plaque, *The Bad Shepherd*

# ❶ Limoges

Haute-Vienne. 🚶 200,000. ✈ 🚌 🚉
ℹ️ 12 bd de Fleurus (05 55 34 46 87).
🏪 daily. 🔲 **limoges-tourisme.com**

The capital of the Limousin has two hearts: the old Cité and the rival château, now the commercial center of the modern city. The Cité was ravaged by the Black Prince during the Hundred Years' War and today it is a quiet place of half-timbered houses and narrow streets.

It was not until the 1770s that Limoges became synonymous with porcelain. The legendary local ware is on display at the superb **Musée National Adrien-Dubouché**. More than 10,000 exhibits trace the history of ceramics. The **Musée des Beaux-Arts de Limoges** houses an Egyptian collection, archeological artifacts tracing the history of Limoges, over 600 Limousin enamels, and Impressionist paintings. This area was a center of Resistance operations in World War II; the **Musée de la Résistance et de la Déportation** has a collection of exhibits relating to Resistance activities.

🏛️ **Musée National Adrien-Dubouché**
Pl Winston Churchill. **Tel** 05 55 33 08 50. **Open** Wed–Mon. **Closed** Jan 1, Dec 25. 🅿️ ♿ 🅰️ 🔲 **musee-adriendebouche.fr**

🏛️ **Musée des Beaux-Arts de Limoges**
1 pl de l'Evêché. **Tel** 05 55 45 98 10. **Open** Wed–Mon. **Closed** Oct–Mar: Sun am, Jan 1, May 1, Nov 1 & 11, Dec 25. 🅿️ ♿ 🔲 **museebal.fr**

🏛️ **Musée de la Résistance et de la Déportation**
Rue Neuve Saint-Etienne. **Tel** 05 55 45 84 44. **Open** mid-Sep–mid-Jun: Wed–Sat, Sun pm & Mon; mid-Jun–mid-Sep: Wed–Mon. **Closed** Jan 1, May 1, Dec 25. 🅿️

## Environs
Resistance activity in Limousin led to severe reprisals. On June 10, 1944, at **Oradour-sur-Glane**, 16 miles (25 km) northwest of Limoges, SS troops shot the entire population. The ruins of the village are kept as a shrine, and a new village has been built nearby.

Close by, **St.-Junien**, a glove-making town since the Middle Ages, still supplies designers today with luxury leather items.

# ❷ Aubusson

Creuse. 🚶 5,000. 🚌 ℹ️ rue Vieille (05 55 66 32 12). 🏪 Sat. 🔲 **tourisme-aubusson.com**

Aubusson owes its renown to the exceptionally pure waters of the Creuse, perfect for making delicately colored dyes used for tapestries and rugs. Production was at its zenith in the 16th and 17th centuries, but by the end of the 18th century the Revolution and patterned wallpaper had swept away the clientele.

In the 1940s, Aubusson was revived, largely due to the artist Jean Lurçat, who persuaded other modern artists to design for tapestry. The **Cité Internationale de la Tapisserie** houses a museum with a permanent collection of these modern works. All 30 workshops welcome visitors – at the **Manufacture St.-Jean** you can watch tapestries and custom-made carpets being made by hand and restored.

🏛️ **Cité Internationale de la Tapisserie**
rue Williams-Dumazet. **Tel** 05 55 66 66 66. **Open** Feb–Dec: Wed–Mon. **Closed** Jan 🅿️ ♿ 🔲 **cite-tapisserie.fr**

🏛️ **Manufacture St.-Jean**
3 rue St.-Jean. **Tel** 05 55 66 10 08. **Open** Mon–Fri. 📷 🅿️

## Environs
A single street of 15th-century houses and a Roman bridge comprise **Moûtier-d'Ahun**, tucked into the lush Creuse

Tapestry restoration at the Manufacture St.-Jean in Aubusson

Church at Moûtier-d'Ahun, near Aubusson

Valley. Vestiges of a Benedictine abbey can still be detected in the half-Romanesque, half-Gothic church with its elaborate stone portal. The choir has wooden stalls, and it is worth paying a visit to the church just to see them. They are masterpieces of late 17th-century carving with fantastical and intricately worked motifs of flora and fauna representing the many different facets of Good and Evil in figurative form. Today, there is a garden where the nave once was.

# ❸ Montluçon

Allier. 🔝 45,000. 🚉 🚌 ℹ️ 67ter bd de Courtais (04 70 05 11 44). 🗓 Tue, Thu–Sun.
🌐 **montlucontourisme.com**

Montluçon is the economic center of the region, a small town with a medieval core. At its heart there is a Bourbon château, which now houses temporary exhibitions. **Jardin Wilson**, a pleasant *jardin à la française* in the medieval quarter, sits on the original ramparts of the town. Mostly destroyed in the 18th century, little remains of the ramparts now. The restored rose garden and spectacular flowerbeds are worth a visit. The 12th-century **Eglise de St.-Pierre** is a surprise, with giant stone columns and a huge barrel-vaulted ceiling.

# ❹ Moulins

Allier. 🔝 23,000. 🚉 🚌 ℹ️ rue François Péron (04 70 44 14 14). 🗓 Fri, Sun. 🌐 **moulins-tourisme.com**

Capital of the Bourbonnais and seat of the Bourbon Dukes since the 10th century, Moulins flourished during the early Renaissance. Its most celebrated sight is the Flamboyant Gothic **Cathédrale Notre-Dame**, where members of the Bourbon court appear amid the saints in the 15th- and 16th-century stained-glass windows. The treasury contains a luminous 15th-century Virgin and Child triptych by the "Master of Moulins." Benefactors Pierre II, Duke of Bourbon, and his wife Anne de Beaujeu, bedecked in embroidery and jewels, are shown being introduced to a less richly dressed Madonna.

The tower keep and the single remaining wing of the Bourbon **Vieux Château** house a superb collection of sculpture, painting, and decorative art from the 12th to the 16th centuries. Housed in the former cavalry barracks is a magnificent collection of 10,000 theatrical costumes.

🏛 **Cathédrale Notre-Dame**
Pl des Vosges. **Tel** 04 70 20 57 77.
Treasury: **Open** Tue–Sat & Sun pm.
**Closed** Dec 25. 🗝 📷 ♿

Stained-glass windows at the Cathédrale Notre-Dame in Moulins

## ❺ Château de La Palice

Allier. **Tel** 04 70 99 37 58. **Open** Apr–Oct: Wed–Mon. 🅿 🄫

In the early 16th century, the Marshal of France, Jacques II de Chabannes, hired Florentine architects to reconstruct the feudal château-fort at Lapalisse, creating a refined Renaissance castle, which has been inhabited ever since by his descendants. The *salon doré* (gilded room) has a beamed ceiling paneled in gold, and two huge 15th-century Flemish tapestries showing the Crusader Knight Godefroy de Bouillon and Greek hero Hector, two of the nine classic braves of chivalric legend.

### Environs

From Lapalisse, the D480 leads up through the beautiful Besbre Valley past a handful of other small, well-preserved châteaux, including **Château de Thoury** and **Château Beauvoir**. Though neither is open to the public, they can be admired from the outside.

Gilded ceiling, Château de La Palice

## ❻ Vichy

Allier. 🚗 27,000. 🚆 🚌 🅸 19 rue du Parc (08 25 77 10 10). 🄫 Wed.
🆆 vichy-destinations.fr

This small city on the River Allier has long been known for its hot and cold springs, and reputed cures for rheumatism, arthritis, and digestive complaints. The letter-writer Madame de Sévigné and the daughters of Louis XV visited in the late 17th and 18th centuries – the former compared the showers to "a rehearsal for Purgatory." The visits of Napoleon III in the 1860s

Interior of the original Thermal Establishment building in Vichy

put Vichy on the map and made taking the waters fashionable. The small town was spruced up and became a favorite among the French nobility and the world's wealthy middle classes. These days, the grand old **Thermal Establishment**, built in 1900 lies abandoned, but it is possible to walk in and admire the architecture. The modern baths are state-of-the-art and

An Art Nouveau travel poster from 1895 promoting Vichy

strictly for medical purposes. A doctor's prescription and a reservation 30 days in advance are required for all treatments.

Vichy's fortunes changed for the better once again in the 1960s with the damming of the Allier, creating a huge lake in the middle of town, which rapidly became a thriving center for watersports and international events. For a small fee, you can have a taste of sports from aikido to waterskiing or learn canoeing on the 2-mile- (3-km-) long artificial river.

The focal point of life in Vichy is the **Parc des Sources** in the center of town, with its turn-of-the-20th-century bandstand (afternoon concerts in season), *belle époque* glass-roofed shopping galleries, and the Grand Casino and Opera House. Here there is gambling every afternoon and musical performances in the evenings, and an atmosphere of gaiety pervades. Also open to the public are the beautiful bronze taps of the **Source Célestin**, in a riverside park containing vestiges of a convent bearing the same name. Only by making an effort to imagine the city in grainy black-and-white newsreel style is there the slightest reminder of the wartime Vichy government, which was based in the town from 1940 to 1944 (see p69).

**🏛 Source Célestin**
Bd du Président Kennedy. **Open** daily. **Closed** Dec–Jan. ♿

## ⑦ Thiers

Puy de Dôme. 🚉 13,500. 🚌 🚆
ℹ pl de Pirou (04 73 80 65 65).
🛍 Thu & Sat. 🅦 **thiers-tourisme.fr**

According to the writer La Bruyère, Thiers "seems painted on the slope of the hill," hanging dramatically as it does on a ravine over a sharp bend in the River Durolle. The city has been renowned for cutlery since the Middle Ages, when legend has it that Crusaders brought back techniques of metalwork from the Middle East. With grindstones powered by dozens of waterfalls on the opposite bank of the river, Thiers produced everything from table knives to guillotine blades, and cutlery remains its major industry today, much of it on display in the Cutlery Museum, the **Musée de la Coutellerie**.

The Old Town is filled with mysterious quarters including "the Corner of Chance" and "Hell's Hollow," honeycombed with tortuous streets and well-restored 14th- to 17th-century houses. Many have elaborately carved wooden facades, notably the Maison du Pirou in place

Pirou. The view to the west from the rampart terrace, toward Monts Dômes and Monts Dore, is particularly splendid at sunset.

**🏛 Musée de la Coutellerie**
58 rue de la Coutellerie. **Tel** 04 73 80 58 86. **Open** Jun–Sep: daily; mid-Feb–May & Oct: Tue–Sun; Nov–Christmas hols Tue–Sun pm. **Closed** Jan–mid-Feb.
📷 📹

## ⑧ Issoire

Puy de Dôme. 🚉 15,000. 🚌 🚆
ℹ 9 pl St-Paul (04 73 89 15 90).
🛍 Sat. 🅦 **issoire-tourisme.com**

Most of old Issoire was destroyed in the 16th-century Wars of Religion. The present-day town has been an important industrial center since the end of World War II.

Not only does Issoire have a thriving aeronautical tradition, it is also a mecca for glider pilots, who come from miles around to take advantage of the strong local air currents.

Issoire's colorful 12th-century abbey church of **St.-Austremoine** is one of the great Romanesque churches of the region. The capitals depict scenes from the Life of Christ (one of the Apostles at the Last Supper has fallen asleep at table), and imaginary demons and beasts. The 15th-century fresco of the Last Judgment shows Bosch-like figures of sinners being cast into the mouth of a dragon or carted off to hell. The nearby Tour de l'Horloge has scenes of Renaissance history.

### Pilgrimages and Ostensions

Parishes in the Auvergne and the Limousin are renowned for honoring their saints in outdoor processions. Ascension Day sees the Virgin of Orcival carried above the village by night, accompanied by gypsies and their children for baptism. Every seven years a score of villages in the Limousin hold Ostensions, when the saints' relics are paraded through the streets into the surrounding woods. The Ostension season begins the Sunday after Easter and runs until June. The next event in the seven-year cycle will be held in 2023.

The Saint-Martial reliquary parade during the Ostensions in Limoges

Viewed here from the south, Thiers spread over the slopes above the River Durolle

## ❾ St.-Nectaire

Puy de Dôme. 🚹 750. 🚌 ℹ️ Les
Grands Thermes (04 73 88 50 86).
🛒 Jul–Aug: Sun am. 🌐 **sancy.com**

The Auvergne is noted for
Romanesque churches. The
**Eglise St.-Nectaire** in the upper
village of St.-Nectaire-le Haut,
with its soaring, elegant
proportions, is one of the most
beautiful. The 103 stone capitals,
22 of them polychrome, are
vividly carved, and the treasury
includes a gold bust of St.
Baudime and a wooden Notre-
Dame-du-Mont-Cornadore,
both marvels of 12th-century
workmanship. The lower village,
St.-Nectaire-le-Bas, has more
than 40 hot and cold springs.

### Environs

The 12th-century citadel of
**Château de Murol**, partially in
ruins, offers costumed guides
demonstrating medieval life
and knightly pursuits. It is
wonderful for children.

🏰 **Château de Murol**
Murol. **Tel** 04 73 88 82 50. **Open**
Apr–Sep: daily; Oct–Mar: Sat & Sun.
**Closed** Jan 1, Jul 14, Dec 25.
📷 🎫 🌐 **murolchateau.com**

Fontaine d'Amboise (1515) in Clermont-Ferrand

## ❿ Clermont-Ferrand

Puy de Dôme. 🚹 140,000. ✈️ 🚆 🚌
ℹ️ pl de la Victoire (04 73 98 65 00).
🛒 Mon–Sat. 🌐 **clermont-fd.com**

Clermont-Ferrand began as two
distinct cities, united only in 1630.
Clermont is a lively commercial
center and student town, with
thriving cafés and restaurants.
It was a Celtic settlement before
the Roman era, had a cathedral
as early as the 5th century, and
by 1095 was significant enough
for the pope to announce the
First Crusade there. The counts of
Auvergne, challenging the episcopal power of Clermont, made
their base in what is now
old Montferrand, a short drive
from Clermont city center. Built
on a bastide pattern, it is a time
warp of quiet streets and
Renaissance houses.

Clermont's more ancient
origins are well illustrated at
the **Musée Bargoin** with its
remarkable collections of
locally found Roman domestic
artifacts (closed Mondays and
Sunday mornings).

**Place St.-Pierre** is Clermont's
principal marketplace, with a
daily food market – especially
good on Saturdays. Nearby,
the traffic-free rue du Port leads
steeply downhill from
the **Fontaine d'Amboise** (1515)
to the **Basilique Notre-Dame-
du-Port**. This is one of the
most important Romanesque
churches in the region and
has benefited from extensive
renovations. The stone interior
is beautifully proportioned, with
a magnificent raised choir and
vivid carved capitals showing
Charity battling Avarice, in the
form of two knights.

The contrast with the black
lava **Cathédrale Notre-Dame-
de-l'Assomption** is startling,
from austere 12th-century

Raised choir in the Basilique Notre-Dame-du-Port

## Clermont City Center

① Place St.-Pierre
② Fontaine d'Amboise
③ Basilique Notre-Dame-du-Port
④ Cathédrale Notre-Dame-de-l'Assomption

Romanesque to high-flying 13th-century Gothic. The graceful lines of the interior are due to the strong local stone used for construction, allowing pillars to be thinner and the whole structure to be lighter. The dark volcanic rock provides a foil for the jewel-like 12th- to 15th-century stained-glass windows, which are believed to be from the same workshop as Sainte-Chapelle's in Paris (see p88).

The old section of Montferrand thrived from the 13th to the 17th centuries, and many fine houses – known as hôtels particuliers – built by prosperous merchants –have survived. Some of the best of

Michelin man, around 1910

these, with Italianate loggias, mullioned windows, and intriguing courtyards, line the ancient **rue Kléber**. Between Clermont and old Montferrand lies a third minicity, the headquarters and factories of the Michelin rubber-and-tire company. Founded here in 1830, it dominates the town.

### Environs

Once the rival of Clermont-Ferrand for supremacy in Auvergne, **Riom** is a sombre provincial town of black stone houses and lava fountains. The 14th-century château of Duke Jean de Berry was razed in the 19th century to build the Palais de Justice; all that remains is the Sainte-Chapelle with its lovely 15th-century stained-glass windows.

Riom's greatest treasure is a graceful Madonna holding an infant with a small bird in his hand. The statue is housed in the Eglise de Notre-Dame-du-Marthuret, originally built in the 14th century, but greatly altered since then.

## ⑪ Orcival

Puy de Dôme. 🏠 300.
🚹 Le Bourg (04 73 65 89 77).
🌐 tourisme-sancy-artense.com

Crowded in summer, Orcival is nevertheless well worth visiting for its Romanesque church, the **Basilique d'Orcival**, which many would say is the best in the region. Completed at the beginning of the 12th century, and typically Auvergne Romanesque in style, the apse is multitiered, and the side walls are supported by powerful buttresses and strong arches. Inside, the ornate silver and vermilion *Virgin and Child* (in the forward-facing position known as "in majesty") is enigmatic, with an unusual, rigid, square chair. With an interior lit by 14 windows and a spacious crypt, the proportions of the building itself are the most graceful aspect.

*Virgin and Child* in the Basilique d'Orcival

Choir inside the Cathédrale Notre-Dame-de-l'Assomption, Clermont-Ferrand

Aerial view of Puy de Dôme in the Monts Dômes range

# ⑫ Monts Dômes

Puy de Dôme. ✈ 🚉 🚌 Clermont-Ferrand. 🛈 Aydat (04 73 65 64 26).
🅆 **parcdesvolcans.fr**

The youngest range of the Auvergne volcanos at 4,000 years old, the Monts Dômes, or Chaîne des Puys, encompass 112 extinct volcanos aligned over a 19-mile (30-km) stretch just west of Clermont-Ferrand. At the center, the **Puy de Dôme** towers above a high plateau. A mountain railroad spirals up the peak at a steady 12 percent gradient, taking 15 minutes to reach the top, while the steeper Roman path is still used by hikers. (No cars or buses ascend the Puy de Dôme; phone 08 26 39 96 15 for train information.)

At the summit are the vestiges of the Roman temple of Mercury and a meteorological/telecommunications tower. On a rare clear day, the view across the volcano will take away whatever breath you have left.

The volcanic Roche Tuilière below Col de Guéry in the Monts Dore

The controversial **Parc Européen du Volcanisme, Vulcania** uses the latest technology to simulate volcanic activity in its underground circuit.

In the southwest corner of the Monts Dômes region is the **Château de Cordès**, a small, privately owned 15th-century manor house with formal gardens designed by Le Nôtre *(see p183)*.

### 🗐 Vulcania
D941B, Saint-Ours-les-Roches. **Tel** 04 73 19 70 00. **Open** mid-Mar–mid-Nov; see website for times. 🏛 ♿ ✎ ▣ 🏛 Documentation center.
🅆 **vulcania.com**

### 🏠 Château de Cordès
Orcival. **Tel** 04 73 21 15 89. **Open** Jul & Aug: daily; Jun: Sun pm (gardens only). 🏛 ✎

# ⑬ Monts Dore

Puy de Dôme. ✈ Clermont-Ferrand. 🚉 🚌 Le Mont-Dore. 🛈 Montlosier, Aydat (04 73 65 64 26).

Three giant volcanos – the Puy de Sancy, the Banne d'Ordanche, and the Puy de l'Aiguiller – and their secondary cones make up the Monts Dore: dark green, heavily wooded mountains laced with rivers and lakes, and dotted with summer and winter resorts for skiing, hiking, paragliding, canoeing, and sailing.

The 6,185-ft (1,885-m) **Puy de Sancy** is the highest point in central France. It can be reached by taking a shuttle from the town of Le Mont-Dore to the cable car, which goes up to the peak, followed by a long hike

across open terrain. From Le Mont-Dore there is a scenic drive on the D36, which leads to the **Couze-Chambon Valley**, a beautiful stretch of high moorland threaded with waterfalls.

The area has two popular spa towns, **La Bourboule**, for children's ailments, with its casino, and Le Mont-Dore, with its grandiose turn-of-the-20th-century **Etablissement Thermal**.

Below the Col de Guéry on the D983, the eroded volcanic **Roche Sanadoire** and **Roche Tuilière** stand up like two gigantic gateposts. From their peaks are far-reaching views over the wooded Cirque de Chausse and beyond.

Church at La Bourboule in the Monts Dore

# ⑭ Uzerche

Corrèze. 🏔 3,000. 🚉 🚌 🛈 pl de la Libération (05 55 73 15 71). 🗓 Sat.
🅆 **uzerche-tourisme.com**

Uzerche is an impressive sight: gray slate roofs, turrets, and bell towers rising from a hill above the Vézère river. This prosperous town never capitulated during the conflicts of the Middle Ages, and earlier withstood a seven-year siege by Moorish forces in 732: the townspeople sent a feast out to their enemy – in fact, the last of their supplies. The Moors, thinking such lavish offerings meant the city had stores to spare, gave up.

The Romanesque **Eglise St.-Pierre** crests the hill above the town. Beyond Uzerche, the Vézère cuts through the green gorges of the Saillant.

## Cantal Cheese

Transhumance is still practiced in the Auvergne, with the local Salers cattle kept in barns in the valleys during winter and led up to mountain pastures for the summer. The robust grasses and flowers – gentian, myrtle, anemone – on which the cows graze produce a flavorsome milk that is the basis for the region's excellent cheese, Cantal. Curds were once turned and pressed through cheesecloth by hand, but now modern methods prevail. Cantal is the key ingredient in *aligot* – the potato-and-cheese purée flavored with garlic that is one of the region's most famous dishes.

Salers cattle enjoying rich pastures

## ⓵ Turenne

Corrèze. 🏔 750. 🚉 🚌 🛈 Brive-la-Gaillarde (05 55 24 08 80).

Turenne is one of the most appealing medieval towns in the Corrèze. Crescent-shaped and clustered on the cliffside, the town was the last independent feudal fiefdom in France, under the absolute rule of the La Tour d'Auvergne family until 1738. Henri de la Tour d'Auvergne, their most illustrious member, was a marshal of France under Louis XIV, and one of the greatest soldiers of modern times.

Now the sole remains of the **Château de Turenne** are the 13th-century Clock Tower and 11th-century Tower of Caesar, from which there is a quite stunning 360-degree view of the Cantal mountains across to the Dordogne Valley. Not far away is the 16th-century collegiate church and the **Chapelle des Capucins** dating from the 18th century.

🏠 **Château de Turenne**
**Tel** 05 55 85 90 66. **Open** Apr–Oct: daily; Nov–Mar: Sun pm. 🅿
🌐 **chateau-turenne.com**

## ⓶ Collonges-la-Rouge

Corrèze. 🏔 400. 🚉 Brive, then bus to Collonges. 🛈 13 rue de la République, Bellegarde-sur-Valserine 01200 (04 50 48 48 68). 🌐 **valle-dordogne.com**

There's something a little unsettling about Collonges' carmine sandstone architecture, quite beautiful in individual houses, though the overall effect is both austere and fairy-tale-like.

Founded in the 8th century, Collonges came under the rule of Turenne, whose burghers built the sturdy turreted houses in the surrounding vineyards. Look for the communal bread oven in the marketplace, and the 11th-century church, later fortified with a tower keep. The church's unusual carved white limestone tympanum shows a man driving a bear, and other lively figures.

## ⓷ Salers

Cantal. 🏔 400. 🚌 summer only. 🛈 pl Tyssandier d'Escous (04 71 40 58 08). 🗓 Wed. 🌐 **salers-tourisme.fr**

A handsome town of gray lava houses and 15th-century ramparts, Salers sits atop a steep escarpment at the edge of the Cantal mountains. It is one of few virtually intact Renaissance villages in the region. The church has an admirable polychrome *mise au tombeau* (entombment), dated 1495, and five 17th-century Aubusson tapestries.

From the fountain, streets lead up to the cliff edge, and allow views of the surrounding valleys, with the ever-present sound of cowbells in the distance. The town is very crowded in summer, but it makes a good starting point for excursions to the Puy Mary (*see p368*), the huge barrage at Bort-les-Orgues, the nearby Château de Val, and the Cère Valley to the south.

Medieval Château de Val at Bort-les-Orgues near Salers

Puy Mary peak in the volcanic Monts du Cantal

# ⑱ Monts du Cantal

Cantal. 🚉 Aurillac. 🚉 🚌 Lioran.
ℹ️ Aurillac (04 71 48 46 58).
🌐 iaurillac.com

The Cantal mountains were originally one enormous volcano – the oldest and the largest in Europe, dating from the Tertiary period. The highest peaks, the **Plomb du Cantal** at 6,086 ft (1,855 m) and the **Puy Mary** at 5,863 ft (1,787 m), are surrounded by crests and deep river valleys. Driving the narrow roads is a thrill, compounded by the views at every hairpin turn. Between peaks and gorges, rich mountain pastures provide summer grazing for red-gold Salers cows *(see p367)*. From the **Pas de Peyrol**, France's highest road pass at 5,191 ft (1,582 m), it's about a 25-minute journey on foot to the summit of the Puy Mary.

### Environs

One of the finest of the Auvergne châteaus, **Château d'Anjony** was built by Louis II d'Anjony, a supporter of Joan of Arc *(see p304)*. Highlights are the 16th-century frescoes: in the chapel, scenes from the Life and Passion of Christ, and, upstairs, in the *Salle des Preux* (Knights' Room), a dazzling series of the nine heroes of chivalry. To the south lies the small town of **Aurillac**, a good base for exploring the Cantal region.

🏠 **Château d'Anjony**
Tournemire. **Tel** 04 71 47 61 67.
**Open** mid-Feb–Jun & Sep–mid-Nov: daily pms; Jul & Aug: daily (closed Sun am). 🚫 🎫 obligatory.

# ⑲ La Chaise-Dieu

Haute-Loire. 🏔 700. 🚌 ℹ️ rue Saint-Esprit (04 71 00 01 16). 🛍 Thu.
🌐 la-chaise-dieu.info

Somber and massive, midway between Romanesque and Gothic, the 14th-century abbey church of St.-Robert is the prime reason to visit the small village of La Chaise-Dieu. The building is an amalgam of styles; the choir, however, is sensational: 144 oak stalls carved with figures of Vice and Virtue. Above them, entirely covering the walls, are some of the loveliest tapestries in France. Made in Brussels and Arras in the early 16th century and depicting scenes from the Old and New Testaments, they are rich in color and detail.

Statue of Notre-Dame-de-France at Le Puy

On the outer walls of the choir the 15th-century wall painting of the *Danse Macabre* shows Death in the form of skeletons leading rich and poor alike to their inevitable end. Beyond the cloister is the Echo room, in which two people whispering in opposite corners can hear one another perfectly. A Baroque Music Festival from mid-August to September makes the abbey crowded.

# ⑳ Le Puy-en-Velay

Haute-Loire. 🏔 21,000. 🚉 🚌
🚌 ℹ️ 2 pl de Clauzel (04 71 09 38 41). 🛍 Sat. 🎭 Sep.
🌐 ot-lepuyenvelay.fr

Located in the bowl of a volcanic cone, the town of Le Puy, a UNESCO World Heritage site, teeters on a series of rock outcrops and giant basalt pillars. The town has three peaks, each topped with a landmark church or statue. Seen from afar, this is one of the most impressive sights in France.

The town is now a commercial and tourist-oriented place, but its star attraction is its medieval **Holy City**. This became a pilgrimage center after the Bishop of Le Puy, Gotescalk, made one of the first pilgrimages to Santiago de Compostela in 962, and built the **Chapelle St.-Michel d'Aiguilhe**

Detail of *Danse Macabre* at St.-Robert, in La Chaise-Dieu

## The Auvergne's Black Madonnas

The cult of the Virgin Mary has always been strong in the Auvergne, and this is reflected in the concentration of her statues in the region. Carved in dark walnut or cedar, now blackened with age, the Madonnas are believed to originate from the Byzantine influence of the Crusaders. Perhaps the most famous Madonna is the one in Le-Puy-en-Velay, a 17th-century copy of one that belonged to Louis IX in the Middle Ages.

Louis IX's Black Virgin

on his return. Pilgrims from eastern France and Germany assembled at the **Cathédrale de Notre-Dame** with its famous Black Madonna and "fever stone" – a Druid ceremonial stone believed to have healing powers embedded in one of its walls – before setting off for Compostela.

Built on an early pagan site, the Cathédrale de Notre-Dame is a huge Romanesque structure. Multiform arches, carved palm and leaf designs, and a checkerboard facade show the influences of Moorish Spain, and indicate the considerable cultural exchange that took place with southern France in the 11th and 12th centuries. In the transept are Romanesque frescoes, notably an 11th- to 12th-century St. Michael; in the sacristy, the treasury includes the Bible of Theo-dolphus, a handwritten document from the era of Charlemagne. The cathedral is the center of the Holy City complex that dominates the upper town, encompassing a baptistery, cloister, Prior's house, and Penitents' chapel.

The colossal red statue of **Notre-Dame-de-France**, on the pinnacle of the Rocher Corneille, was erected in 1860, cast from 213 cannons captured at Sebas-topol during the Crimean War. The statue is reached by a steep pathway, and can be climbed by an iron ladder on the inside.

The **Chapelle St.-Michel d'Aiguilhe**, like the cathedral, shows Moorish influences in the trefoil decoration and colored mosaics on the rounded arch over the main entrance. It seems to grow out of a giant finger of lava rock and is reached by a steep climb. The church is thought to be located on the site of a Roman temple to Mercury, and its center dates from the 10th century, although most of the building was constructed a century later.

The floor has been constructed to follow the contours of the rock in places, and the interior is ornamented with faded 10th-century murals and 20th-century stained glass.

In the lower city, narrow streets of 15th- and 16th-century houses lead to the Vinay Garden and the **Musée Crozatier**, which has a collection of handmade lace from the 16th century to the present. The museum also has a good collection of archeological artifacts, medieval objets d'art, 15th-century paintings, and natural sciences exhibits.

In mid-September, Le Puy transforms itself entirely for a masked and costumed Renaissance carnival for The Bird King Festival, an ancient tradition celebrating the skill of the city's best archers (see p42).

**Notre-Dame-de-France**
Rocher Corneille. **Tel** 04 71 04 11 33. **Open** daily. **Closed** mid-Nov–Jan (except Christmas hols).

**Chapelle St-Michel d'Aiguilhe**
Aiguilhe. **Tel** 04 71 09 50 03. **Open** mid-Feb–mid-Dec: daily.

**Musée Crozatier**
Jardin Henri Vinay. **Tel** 04 71 06 62 40. **Open** call for up-to-date information.

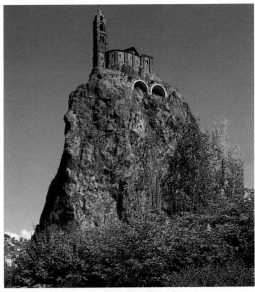

Chapelle St.-Michel d'Aiguilhe, standing on a finger of lava rock

Ruins of the Castle of Calmont d'Olt
at Espalion in the Lot Valley

## ㉑ Vallée du Lot

Aveyron. ✈ Aurillac, Rodez.
🚆 Rodez, Séverac-le-Château.
🚌 Espalion, Rodez. ℹ Espalion (05
65 44 10 63). 🌐 valleedulot.com

From Mende and the old River
port of La Canourgue all the
way to Conques, the River Lot
(or Olt in old usage) courses
through its fertile valley past
orchards, vineyards, and pine
forests. **Saint Côme d'Olt**, near
the Aubrac mountains, is an
unspoiled, fortified village
with a 15th-century church
surrounded by Medieval
and Renaissance houses.
At **Espalion**, the pastel
stone houses and a
turreted 16th-century
castle are reflected
in the river, which
runs beneath a
13th-century
arched stone bridge.
The town has one
of the best markets
in the region on Friday
mornings. Just outside town is
the 11th-century Perse Church,
with carved capitals portraying
battling knights and imaginary
birds sipping from a chalice.
**Estaing** was once the fiefdom
of one of the greatest families
of the Rouergue, dating back to
the 13th century. The village
nestles beneath its massive
château (open May–mid-Oct)
on the riverbank. The road
passes through the Lot Gorge
on the way to **Entraygues**
("between waters"), where the
old quarter and 13th-century
Gothic bridge are worth a visit.
Beyond Entraygues, the river
widens to join the Garonne.

## ㉒ Conques

*See pp372–3.*

## ㉓ Rodez

Aveyron. 🏔 26,000. ✈ 🚆 🚌
ℹ place de la Cité (05 65 75 76 77).
🏪 Wed, Sat. 🌐 tourisme.grand-
rodez.com

Like many medieval French cities,
Rodez was politically divided: the
store-lined **place du Bourg** on
one side of town and **place de la
Cité**, near the cathedral, on the
other, reflect conflicting secular
and ecclesiastical interests.
Rodez's commercial center is
the region's largest. The
13th-century huge pink stone
**Cathédrale Notre-Dame** is
worth a look, with its fortress-
like west facade, and its magnificent bell tower. The 15th-century
choir stalls show a panoply of
creatures, including a winged
lion and one naughty fellow
exposing his derrière.

The striking steel **Musée
Soulages** houses over 500
paintings and other works by
the artist Pierre Soulages,
who was born in Rodez
in 1919. It also hosts
temporary exhibitions
of modern and
contemporary art.

### Environs
Southeast (28 miles/
45km) lies Saint Léons,
birthplace of Jean-Henri
Fabre, the entymologist.
Here is **Micropolis**, part

*Entombment* in Rodez Cathedral

### Robert Louis Stevenson

Robert Louis Stevenson (1850–94),
best known for his novels *Treasure
Island, Kidnapped,* and *Strange Case
of Dr Jekyll and Mr Hyde,* was also an
accomplished travel writer. In 1878,
he set off across the remote Cévennes
mountain range with only
a small donkey, Modestine,
for company. His classic
account of this eventful
journey, *Travels with a
Donkey in the Cévennes,*
was published in the
following year.

Robert Louis Stevenson

interactive museum, part theme park, dedicated to the glory of insects (closed Nov–mid-Feb). Watch the breathtaking film of the same name, if nothing else.

### 🏛 Musée Soulages

Jardin du Foirail, av Victor Hugo. **Tel** 05 65 73 82 60. **Open** Tue–Sun (Jul–Aug: Mon pm). 🎨 ♿ 📷 🖊

## ㉔ Corniche des Cévennes

Lozère, Gard. ✈ Nîmes. 🚌 Alès. 🚍 St.-Jean-du-Gard. 🛈 Parc National de Cévennes, 6bis pl du Palais, Florac 48400 (04 66 49 53 00). 🌐 **cevennes-parcnational.fr**

The dramatic Corniche road from Florac on the Tarn to St.-Jean-du-Gard was cut in the early 18th century by the army of Louis XIV in pursuit of the Camisards, Protestant rebels who had no uniforms but fought in their ordinary shirts (*camiso* in the *langue d'oc*). The route of the D983 makes a spectacular drive. Fascination with the history of the Camisards was one of the reasons that Robert Louis Stevenson undertook his fabled trek in the Cévennes with Modestine, recounted in his *Travels with a Donkey in the Cévennes*.

At St.-Laurent-de-Trèves, where fossil remains suggest dinosaurs once roamed, there is a view of the Grands Causses, and the peaks of Lozère and Aigoual. The Corniche ends in St.-Jean-du-Gard.

Dramatic scenery in Corniche des Cévennes national park

## ㉕ Grands Causses

Aveyron. ✈ Rodez-Marcillac. 🚍 Millau. 🛈 Millau (05 65 60 02 42). 📅 Wed & Fri. 🌐 **millau-viaduc-tourisme.fr**

The Causses are vast, arid limestone plateaus, alternating with green, fertile canyon valleys. The only sign of life at times is a bird of prey wheeling in the sky, or an isolated stone farm or shepherd's hut. The whole area makes for some desolate hiking for those who like solitude.

The four Grands Causses – Sauveterre, Méjean, Noir, and Larzac – stretch out east of the city of Millau, which boasts the tallest vehicular bridge in the world. They extend from Mende in the north to the valley of the Vis river in the south.

Among the sights in the Causses are the *chaos* – bizarre rock formations reputed to resemble ruined cities, and named accordingly: there's the *chaos* of **Montpellier-le-Vieux**,

Nîmes-le-Vieux, and **Roquesaltes. Aven Armand** and the **Dargilan Grotto** are vast and deep natural underground grottoes.

A good place to head for in the Larzac Causse is the strange, rough-hewn stone village of **La Couvertoirade**, a fully enclosed citadel of the Knights Templar in the 12th century. The unpaved streets and medieval houses are an austere reminder of the dark side of the Middle Ages. Entry to the village is free, with a fee for the tour of the ramparts.

The Causse du Larzac's best-known village is probably **Roquefort-sur-Soulzon**, a small gray town terraced on the side of a crumbled lime-stone outcrop. It has one main street and one major product, Roquefort cheese. This is made from unpasteurized sheep's milk, seeded with a distinctive blue mould grown on loaves of bread, and aged in the warren of damp caves above the town.

View over Méjean, one of the four plateaus of the Grands Causses

# ㉒ Conques

The village of Conques clusters around the splendid Abbaye de Ste.-Foy, hemmed into a rugged site against the hillside. St. Foy was a young girl who became an early Christian martyr; her relics were first kept at a rival monastery in Agen. In the 9th century a monk from Conques stole the relics, thereby attracting pilgrims to this remote spot and firmly establishing Conques as a halt on the route to Santiago de Compostela *(see pp404–5)*. The treasury holds the most important collection of medieval and Renaissance gold work in Western Europe. Some of it was made in the abbey's own workshops as early as the 9th century. The Romanesque abbey church has beautiful stained-glass windows by Pierre Soulages (1994), and its tympanum is a triumph of medieval sculpture.

View of the church from the village

**Nave Interior**
Pure and elegantly austere, the Romanesque interior dates from 1050–1135. The short nave soars to a height of 72 ft (22 m), with three tiers of arches topped by 250 decorative carved capitals.

**KEY**

① **The broad transepts** were able to accommodate crowds of pilgrims.

② **The Cloister** consists of a reconstructed square: only two sections of the original early 12th-century arcades remain. However, 30 of the original carved capitals are displayed in the refectory and in the Musée Fau.

**Tympanum**
This sculpture from the early 12th century depicts the *Last Judgment*, with the Devil in Hell (shown) in the lower part of the sculpture and Christ in Heaven in the tympanum's central position.

## Conques' Treasures

The treasures date from the 9th to the 19th century, and are prized for both their beauty and their rarity. The gold-plated wood and silver reliquary of Ste.-Foy is studded with gems, rock crystal, and even an *intaglio* of the Roman Emperor Caracalla. The body is 9th century, but the face may be older, possibly 5th century. Other magnificent pieces include an "A"-shaped reliquary, said to be a gift from Charlemagne; the small but exquisite Pépin's shrine from AD 1000; and a late 16th-century processional cross.

The precious reliquary of Ste.-Foy

**VISITORS' CHECKLIST**

**Practical Information**
Aveyron. 🏘 1,600. 🛈 Pl de l'Eglise (05 65 72 85 00). Treasury/ museum: **Open** daily: Apr–Sep: 9:30am–12:30pm, 2–6:30pm; Oct– Mar: 10am–noon, 2–6pm. 🚗 🕆 8am Mon–Sat, 11am Sun. 🚻 restr. 📷 🌐 **tourisme-conques.fr**

**Transportation**
🚉 to St.-Christophe, then a bus. 🚌 from Rodez.

**Romanesque Chapels**
The east end is three-tiered, topped by the blind arcades of the choir and a central bell tower. Three chapels surround the eastern apse, built to accommodate extra altars for the celebration of Mass.

**Treasury**
The precious contents of the Treasury were hidden by the townspeople to prevent their destruction during the French Revolution. Perhaps surprisingly, all were returned.

Entrance to the Treasury

# ㉖ Gorges du Tarn

Near the beginning of its journey to meet the River Garonne, the Tarn flows through some of Europe's most spectacular gorges. For millions of years, the Tarn and its tributary the Jonte have eaten their way down through the limestone plateaus of the Cévennes, creating a sinuous forked canyon some 15 miles (24 km) long and nearly 1,300 ft (400 m) deep. The UNESCO-listed gorges are flanked by rocky bluffs and scaled by roads with dizzying bends and panoramic views, which are very popular in the high season. The surrounding plateaus, or *causses*, are eerily different, forming an open, austere landscape, dry in summer and snow-clad in winter, where wandering sheep and isolated farms are sometimes the only signs of life.

**Point Sublime**
From 2,600 ft (800 m) up, there are stunning views of a major bend in the Tarn gorge, with the Causse Méjean visible in the distance.

**Outdoor Activities**
The Tarn and Jonte gorges are popular for canoeing and river-rafting. Although the rivers are relatively placid in summer, melting snow can make them hazardous in spring.

0 kilometers 5
0 miles 3

**Pas de Souci**
Just upriver from Les Vignes, Pas de Souci flanks a narrow point in the gorge as the Tarn makes its way northward.

D46
D995
Gorges Du Tarn
D907
D907
le Rozier
D996
Gorges De La Jon
Tarn
CAUSSE NOIR
D110
N9
Millau

**Chaos de Montpellier-le-Vieux**
Located on the flank of the Causse Noir off the D110 is a remarkable geological site – bizarre rock formations created by limestone erosion.

**La Malène**
An old crossing-point between the Causse de Sauveterre and the Causse Méjean, this village, with its 16th-century fortified manor, is a good starting point for boat trips.

**CAUSSE DE SAUVETERRE**

Ste-Enimie

Ispagnac

D907

Malène

**CAUSSE MEJEAN**

D986

D996

Jonte

de an

D39 Meyrueis

**Aven Armand Caves**
On the Causse Méjean, many stalactites in the caves are tinted by minerals that are deposited by the slowly trickling water.

**Causse Méjean**
The high plateaus or *causses* are a botanist's paradise in spring and summer, with over 900 species of wildflowers, including orchids.

## The Wild Cévennes

One of the least populated parts of France, this area is well-known for its wildflowers and birds of prey, and griffon vultures were once common here. These giant but harmless scavengers nearly died out in the 20th century through being hunted, but now a reintroduction program has led to growing numbers breeding in the Gorges de la Jonte.

Yellow wort

Kidney vetch

Green-winged orchid

**Wildflowers** found in this thinly populated area include unusual Alpine plants.

**The griffon vulture**, which now breeds in the region, has a wingspan of over 8 ft (2.5 m).

# THE RHONE VALLEY AND FRENCH ALPS

*Ain · Rhône · Isère · Loire · Drôme · Ardèche*
*Hautes-Alpes · Savoie · Haute-Savoie*

Its two most important geographical features, the Alps and the River Rhône, give this region both its name and its dramatic character. The east is dominated by majestic snowcapped peaks, while the Rhône provides a vital conduit between north and south.

The Romans recognized this strategic route when they founded Lyon over 2,000 years ago. Today Lyon, with its great museums and fine Renaissance buildings, is the second city of France. It is one of the country's most vital commercial and cultural centers, as well as the undisputed capital of French gastronomy. To the north lie the flat marshlands of the Dombes and the rich agricultural Bresse plain. Here, too, are the famous Beaujolais vineyards, which, along with the Rhône ones, make the region such an important wine producer.

The French Alps are among the most popular year-round resort areas in the world, with internationally renowned ski stations such as Chamonix, Mégève,

and Courchevel, and historic cities including Chambéry, capital of Savoy before it joined France. Elegant spa towns line the shores of Lac Léman (Lake Geneva). Grenoble, a bustling university city and high-tech center, is flanked by two of the most spectacular nature preserves in France, the Chartreuse and the Vercors.

To the south, orchards and fields of sunflowers give way to brilliant rows of lavender interspersed with vineyards and olive groves. Châteaux and ancient towns dot the landscape. Mountains and pretty, old-fashioned spa towns characterize the rugged Ardèche, and the deeply scoured gorges along the River Ardèche offer some of the wildest scenery in France.

The restored Ferme de la Forêt at St.-Trivier-de-Courtes, north of Bourg-en-Bresse

◀ Chapelle Sainte-Marie-Madeleine set against the dramatic scenery of the Vallée de la Clarée, close to Briançon

# Exploring the Rhône Valley and French Alps

Lyon is the region's largest city, famed for its historic buildings and gastronomic tradition. Wine lovers can choose between the vineyards of the Beaujolais, Rhône Valley, and Drôme region to the south. To the west, the Ardèche offers rugged wilderness, canoeing, and climbing. Spa devotees from around the world flock to Evian-les-Bains and Aix-les-Bains, while the Alps are a favorite destination for sports enthusiasts (*see pp326–7*).

## Sights at a Glance

1. Bourg-en-Bresse
2. The Dombes
3. Pérouges
4. Lyon pp382–5
5. Vienne
6. St.-Romain-en-Gal
7. St.-Etienne
8. Palais Idéal du Facteur Cheval
9. Tournon-sur-Rhône
10. Valence
11. The Ardèche
12. Vals-les-Bains
13. Montélimar
14. Grignan
15. Nyons
16. Briançon
17. Le Bourg d'Oisans
18. Grenoble
19. The Vercors
20. The Chartreuse
21. Chambéry
22. Aix-les-Bains
23. Annecy
24. Lac Léman

The Pont des Amours in Annecy

**For keys to map symbols** *see back flap*

## Key

- Freeway
- Highway
- Secondary road
- Minor road
- Scenic route
- Main railroad
- Minor railroad
- International border
- Regional border
- △ Summit

Pont-en-Royans in the Vercors

## Getting Around

Lyon and Geneva are the main transit hubs of the region. For Lyon, change from Eurostar to TGV at Lille. Aside from the Alpine regions, local train and bus services tend to be slow and inconvenient. A car is essential if you wish to get off the most heavily traveled *autoroutes* – the most important ones being the A7, linking Lyon with Valence and the south; and the A40 and A43/A41, which run east to the Alps. The four international airports nearest the Alps are Geneva-Cointrin in Switzerland, St.-Exupéry near Lyon, Grenoble-Isère, and Chambéry. Note that high Alpine passes can be closed between November and June.

Farms around Le Poët Laval, near Montélimar

# ❶ Bourg-en-Bresse

Ain. 🚗 43,000. 🚉 🚌 ℹ️ Centre Culturel Albert Camus, 6 av Alsace-Lorraine (04 74 22 49 40). 🛒 Wed & Sat. 🌐 **bourgenbressetourisme.fr**

Bourg-en-Bresse is a busy market town, with some beautifully restored half-timbered buildings. It is best known for its tasty *poulet de Bresse* (chickens raised in the flat agricultural region of Bresse and designated *appellation d'origine protégée, or AOP*; and its abbey church of **Brou** on the southeast edge of town.

The latter, no longer a place of worship, has become one of the most visited sites in France. Flamboyant Gothic in style, it was built between 1505 and 1536 by Margaret of Austria after the death of her husband Philibert, Duke of Savoy, in 1504.

The couple's finely sculpted Carrara marble tombs can be seen in the choir, along with the tomb of Margaret of Bourbon, Philibert's mother, who died in 1483. Notice also the beautifully carved choir stalls, stained-glass windows, and rood screen with its elegant basket-handle arching.

The adjacent cloisters house a small museum with a good collection of 16th- and 17th-century Dutch and Flemish masters, as well as contemporary works by local artists.

### Environs

About 15 miles (24 km) north of Bourg-en-Bresse at St.-Trivier-de-Courtes, the restored **Ferme-Musée de la Forêt** offers a look at farm life in the region during the 17th century. The ancient house has what is known locally as a Saracen chimney, with a brick hood in the center of the room, similar to constructions in Sicily and Portugal, and a collection of antique farm implements.

🏛 **Ferme-Musée de la Forêt**
**Tel** 04 74 30 71 89. **Open** Apr–Oct: Sat & Sun (mid-Jun–Sep: Tue–Sun). 🅿 ♿

Tomb of Margaret of Austria in the abbey church of Brou at Bourg-en-Bresse

Bresse chickens

# ❷ The Dombes

Ain. ✈️ Lyon. 🚉 Lyon, Villars les Dombes, Bourg-en-Bresse. 🚌 Villars-les-Dombes (from Bourg-en-Bresse). ℹ️ 3 pl de Hôtel de Ville, Villars-les-Dombes (04 74 98 06 29).

This flat, glacier-gouged plateau south of Bourg-en-Bresse is dotted with small hills, ponds, and marshes, making it popular with anglers and birders. In the middle of the area at **Villars-les-Dombes** is an ornithological park, the **Parc des Oiseaux**. Over 400 species of native and exotic birds live here, including tufted herons, vultures, pink flamingos, emus, and ostriches.

🐦 **Parc des Oiseaux**
Route Nationale 83, Villars-les-Dombes.
**Tel** 04 74 98 05 54. **Open** daily.
**Closed** mid-Nov–Mar. 🅿 🚻 ♿

# ❸ Pérouges

Ain. 🚗 900. 🚉 Meximieux-Pérouges. 🚌 ℹ️ 09 67 12 70 84. 🌐 **perouges.org**

Originally the home of immigrants from Perugia, Pérouges is a fortified hilltop village of medieval houses and cobblestone streets. In the 13th century it was a center of linen-weaving, but with the mechanization of the industry in the 19th century, the local population fell from 1,500 to 90.

Restoration of its historic buildings and a new influx of artisans have breathed new life into Pérouges. Not surprisingly, the village has often been used as the setting for historical movies such as *The Three Musketeers* and *Monsieur Vincent*. The village's main square, place de la Halle, is shaded by a huge lime tree planted in 1792 to honor the Revolution.

# A Tour of Beaujolais

Beaujolais is an ideal area for wine tasting, offering delicious, affordable wine, and glorious countryside. The south of the region produces most of the Beaujolais Nouveau, released fresh from the cellars on the third Thursday of November each year. In the north are the ten superior quality *cru* wines – St.-Amour, Juliénas, Moulin-à-Vent, Chénas, Fleurie, Chiroubles, Morgon, Brouilly, Côte de Brouilly, and Regnié – most of which can be visited on a day's drive. The distinctive *maisons du pays* have living quarters built over the wine cellar. Almost every village has its *cave* (wine cellar), offering tastings and a glimpse of the wine culture that dominates local life.

② **Moulin-à-Vent**
This 17th-century windmill has lovely views of the Saône Valley. Tastings of *cru* wines from the region are held in the *caves* next door.

① **Juliénas**
Famous for coq au vin, this village stores and sells wine in its church, at the Château du Bois de la Salle, and at several private cellars.

Vineyard of Gamay grapes

⑦ **Chiroubles**
A bust on the village square honors Victor Pulliat, who saved the vines from the phylloxera blight in the 1880s by using American vine stocks.

③ **Fleurie**
The chapel of the Madonna (1875) stands guard over the vineyards, and village restaurants serve local *andouillettes au Fleurie*.

④ **Villié-Morgon**
Wine tasting takes place in the cellars of the 18th-century Château Fontcrenne in the village center.

**Key**

| | |
|---|---|
| ▬ | Tour route |
| ═ | Other roads |
| ✲ | Viewpoint |

0 kilometers 2
0 miles 1

⑥ **Beaujeu**
The town of Beaujeu was once the ancient capital of the region. There are displays on the process of making Beaujolais wines at the Renaissance-style Maison du Terroir Beaujolais on place de l'Hôtel de Ville.

⑤ **Brouilly**
The hill, with its tiny 19th-century chapel of Notre-Dame du Raisin, offers fine views and an annual Beaujolais wine festival.

Mâcon

Chénas

Romanèche-Thorins

Régnié-Durette

Cercié

Villefranche-sur-Saône

# ❹ Street by Street: Lyon

On the west bank of the River Saône, the restored old quarter of Vieux Lyon is an atmospheric warren of cobblestone streets, *traboules* (covered passageways), Renaissance palaces, first-class restaurants, lively *bouchons* (bistros), and bohemian stores. It is also the site of the Roman city of Lugdunum, the commercial and military capital of Gaul founded by Julius Caesar in 44 BC. Vestiges of this prosperous city can be seen in the superb Gallo-Roman museum at the top of Fourvière hill. Two excavated Roman theaters still stage performances, from opera to rock concerts. At the foot of the hill is the finest collection of Renaissance mansions in France. The Musée des Confluences sits in a spectacular structure of stainless steel and glass.

★ **Théâtres Romains**
There are two Roman amphitheaters here: the Grand Théâtre, the oldest theater in France, built in 15 BC to seat 30,000 spectators and still used for modern performances; and the smaller Odéon, with its geometric tiled flooring.

★ **Musée de la Civilisation Gallo-Romaine**
This underground museum contains a rich collection of statues, mosaics, coins, and inscriptions evoking Lyon's Roman past.

Entrance to funicular

**Cathédrale St.-Jean**
Begun in the late 12th century, the cathedral has a 14th-century astronomical clock that shows religious feast days till the year 2019.

0 meters 100
0 yards 100

*For hotels and restaurants in this region see pp564–5 and pp593–4*

★ **Basilique Notre-Dame de Fourvière**
This gaudy mock-Byzantine creation – a riot of turrets and crenellations, marble, and mosaic – was built in the late 19th century and has become one of the symbols of Lyon.

**The Chemin du Rosaire**
is a beautiful path leading down from Notre-Dame de Fourvière, with spectacular views of the sprawling metropolis below.

Entrance to funicular

PL DE FOURVIERE

ONTEE SAINT BERTHELEMY

MASSAC

RUE DU BOEUF

RUE JUIVERIE

RUE DE LA BOMBARDE

RUE SAINT JEAN

R DES TROIS MARIES

R DE LA BALEINE

ROLLAND

MAIN

**The Tour Métallique**
was erected in 1893 and is now used as a television transmitter.

**Rue Juiverie** boasts a number of splendid Renaissance mansions – look for the Hôtel Paterin at No. 4 and the Hôtel Bullioud at No. 8.

**Rue St.-Jean and rue du Boeuf** are lined with Renaissance mansions, the former homes of bankers and silk merchants.

**The 15th-century Hôtel Gadagne**
houses two museums: the **Musée Historique de Lyon** and the **Musée des Marionnettes du Monde**, which exhibits the famous Lyonnais puppets.

**Key**

— Suggested route

# Exploring Lyon

France's second city, dramatically sited on the banks of the Rhône and Saône rivers, has been a vital gateway between the north and south since ancient times. On arriving you immediately feel a *brin du sud*, or touch of the south. The crowds are not as quick-stepping as they are in Paris, and the sun is often shining here when it's rainy and cold in the north. Despite its importance as a banking, textile, and pharmaceutical center, most of the French immediately associate Lyon with their palates. The city is packed with restaurants, ranging from simple *bouchons* (bistros) to some of the most opulent tables in France.

Lyon's ornate 17th-century Hôtel de Ville

### The Presqu'île

The heart of Lyon is the Presqu'île, a narrow peninsula of land just north of the confluence of the Saône and Rhône rivers. Rue de la République, a traffic-free shopping street, links the twin poles of civic life: the vast place Bellecour, with its equestrian statue of Louis XIV in the middle, and **place des Terreaux**. The latter is overlooked by Lyon's ornate 17th-century **Hôtel de Ville** (town hall) and the Palais St.-Pierre, a former Benedictine convent and now home to the **Musée des Beaux-Arts**. In the square's center is a monumental 19th-century fountain by Bartholdi, sculptor of the Statue of Liberty.

Behind the town hall, architect Jean Nouvel's futuristic **Opéra de Lyon** – a black barrel vault of steel and glass in a Neoclassical shell – was remodeled to a controversial design in 1993.

A few blocks to the south, the **Musée de l'Imprimerie** illustrates Lyon's contribution to the early days of printing in the late 15th century. Three other museums worth visiting are the **Musée des Tissus**, which houses a collection of silks and tapestries dating from early Christian times to the present day; the **Musée des Arts Décoratifs**, which displays a range of tapestries, furniture, porcelain, and objets d'art; and the **Musée des Confluences**, a history and anthropology museum in a glass-and-steel structure.

Nearby, the **Abbaye St.-Martin d'Ainay** is a restored Carolingian church dating from 1107.

## Lyon City Centre

① Hôtel de Ville
② Musée des Beaux-Arts
③ Opéra de Lyon
④ Musée de l'Imprimerie
⑤ Musée des Tissus
⑥ Musée des Arts Décoratifs
⑦ Abbaye St.-Martin d'Ainay
⑧ Eglise St.-Polycarpe
⑨ Amphithéâtre des Trois Gaules

For keys to symbols *see back flap*

*For hotels and restaurants in this region see pp564–5 and pp593–4*

### La Croix-Rousse

This area north of Presqu'île became the center of the city's silk-weaving industry in the 15th century. It is traced with covered passages known as *traboules*, used by weavers to transport their finished fabrics. To get a sense of them, enter at No. 6 place des Terreaux and continue along till you reach the **Eglise St.-Polycarpe**. From here, it is a short walk to the ruins of the **Amphithéâtre des Trois Gaules**, built in AD 19, and the **Maison des Canuts**, with its traditional silk loom. A little north of here is **Musée Jean Couty**, which houses works by the Lyonnais 20th-century artist and modern and contemporary art exhibitions. Northeast is the **Musée d'Art Contemporain**.

### La Part-Dieu

This modern business area on the east bank of the Rhône has a huge shopping complex and the **Auditorium Maurice-Ravel** for cultural events.

🏛 **Musée de l'Imprimerie**
13 rue de la Poulaillerie. **Tel** 04 78 37 65 98. **Open** Wed–Sun. **Closed** public hols. 🖼 📷

🏛 **Musée des Tissus**
34 rue de la Charité. **Tel** 04 78 38 42 00. **Open** Tue–Sun. **Closed** public hols. 🖼

🏛 **Musée des Arts Décoratifs**
30 rue de la Charité. **Tel** 04 78 38 42 00. **Open** Tue–Sun. **Closed** pub hols. 🖼

🏛 **Musée des Confluences**
86 quai de Perrache. **Tel** 04 28 38 12 12. **Open** Tue–Sun. **Closed** Jan 1, May 1, Nov 1, Dec 25. 🖼 🅿 🏠 ♿

🏛 **Maison des Canuts**
10–12 rue d'Ivry. **Tel** 04 78 28 62 04. **Open** Mon–Sat. **Closed** public hols. 🖼 ♿ 📷

🏛 **Musée Jean Couty**
1 pl Henri Barbusse. **Tel** 04 72 42 20 00. **Open** 11am–6pm Wed–Sun. 🖼 ♿

🏛 **Musée d'Art Contemporain**
81 quai Charles de Gaulle. **Tel** 04 37 61 09. **Open** 11am–6pm Wed–Sun. 🖼 ♿

### Environs

Bourgoin-Jallieu, southeast of Lyon, still prints silk for fashion houses, and has a fine textile collection in its museum.

# Musée des Beaux-Arts

Lyon's Musée des Beaux-Arts showcases the country's largest and probably most important collection of art after the Louvre. The museum is housed in the 17th-century Palais St.-Pierre, a former Benedictine convent for the daughters of the nobility. The Musée d'Art Contemporain, formerly located in the Palais St.-Pierre, is now at 81 quai Charles de Gaulle, north of the Parc Tête d'Or. Housed in a building designed by Renzo Piano, it specializes in works dating from after the mid-20th century.

## Antiquities

Included in this wide-ranging collection on the first floor are Egyptian archaeological finds, Etruscan statuettes, and 4,000-year-old Cypriot ceramics. Temporary exhibits, with a separate entrance on 16 rue Edouard Herriott, are also on the ground and first floors.

## Sculpture and Objets d'Art

Occupying the old chapel on the ground floor, the sculpture department includes works from the French Romanesque period and Italian Renaissance, as well as late 19th- and early 20th-century pieces. Represented are Rodin and Bourdelle (whose statues also appear in the courtyard), Maillol, Despiau, and Pompon, among others. The huge objets d'art collection, on the first floor, comprises medieval ivories, bronzes and ceramics, coins, medals, weapons, jewelry, furniture, and tapestries.

*Odalisque* (1841) by James Pradier

## Paintings and Drawings

The museum's superb collection of paintings occupies the second floor. It covers all periods and includes works by Spanish and Dutch masters, the French schools of the 17th, 18th, and 19th centuries, Impressionist and modern paintings, as well as works

*Fleurs des Champs* (1845) by Louis Janmot of the Lyon School

by the Lyon School, whose exquisite flower paintings were used as sources of inspiration by the designers of silk fabrics through the ages. On the first floor, the Cabinet d'Arts Graphiques has over 4,000 drawings and etchings by such artists as Delacroix, Poussin, Géricault, Degas, and Rodin (by appointment only).

🏛 **Musée des Beaux-Arts**
Palais St.-Pierre, 20 pl des Terreaux. **Tel** 04 72 10 17 40. **Open** Wed–Mon. **Closed** public hols. 🖼 📷 ♿ 🏠

*La Méduse* (1923) by Alexeï von Jawlensky

*Châtiment de Lycurgue* in the Musée Archéologique, St.-Romain-en-Gal

## ❺ Vienne

Isère. 🚗 30,000. 🚆 🚌 *i* cours Brillier (04 74 53 70 10). 🛒 Tue–Sat. 🎷 International Jazz Festival (end Jun– mid-Jul). 🌐 vienne-tourisme.com

No other city in the Rhône Valley offers such a concentration of architectural history as Vienne. Located in a natural basin of land between the river and the hills, this site was recognized for both its strategic and aesthetic advantages by the Romans, who vastly expanded an existing village when they invaded the area in the 1st century BC.

The center of the Roman town was the **Temple d'Auguste et Livie** (10 BC) on place du Palais, a handsome structure

Vienne's Temple d'Auguste et Livie (1st century BC)

supported by Corinthian columns. Not far away off place de Miremont are the remains of the **Jardin Archéologique de Cybèle**, a temple dedicated to the goddess Cybele.

The **Théâtre Romain**, at the foot of Mont Pipet off rue du Cirque, was one of the largest amphitheaters in Roman France, capable of seating over 13,000 spectators. It was restored in 1938, and is now used for a variety of events, including an international jazz festival. From the very top seats the view of the town and river is spectacular.

Other interesting Roman vestiges include a fragment of Roman road in the public gardens and, on the southern edge of town, the **Pyramide du Cirque**, a curious structure about 65 ft (20 m) high that was once the centerpiece of the chariot racetrack. The **Musée des Beaux-Arts et d'Archéologie** also has a good collection of Gallo-Roman artifacts, as well as 18th-century French faïence.

The **Cathédrale de St.-Maurice** is the city's most important medieval monument. It was built between the 12th and 16th century and represents an unusual hybrid of Romanesque and Gothic styles. Two of Vienne's earliest Christian churches are the

12th-century **Eglise St.-André-le-Bas**, with richly carved capitals in its nave and cloister, and the **Eglise St.-Pierre**, parts of which date from the 5th and 6th centuries. The latter houses the **Musée Lapidaire**, a museum of stone-carving, with bas-reliefs and statues from Gallo-Roman buildings.

🏛 **Musée des Beaux-Arts et d'Archéologie**
Pl de Miremont. **Tel** 04 74 78 71 04.
**Open** Apr–Oct: Tue–Sun; Nov–Mar: Tue–Fri & Sat–Sun pm. **Closed** Jan 1, May 1, Nov 1 & 11, Dec25. 🖼

🏛 **Musée Lapidaire**
Pl St.-Pierre. **Tel** 04 74 85 20 35. **Open** Apr–Oct: Tue–Sun; Nov–Mar: Tue–Fri & Sat–Sun pm. **Closed** Jan 1, May 1, Nov 1 & 11, Dec. 25. 🖼 📷 📱

Ornate doorway of Cathédrale de St.-Maurice

## ❻ St.-Romain-en-Gal

Rhône. 🚗 1,300. 🚆 Vienne.
*i* Vienne (04 74 53 70 10).

In 1967, building work in this commercial town directly across the Rhône from Vienne revealed extensive remains of a significant Roman community dating from 100 BC to AD 300. It comprises the remnants of villas, public baths, stores, and warehouses. Of particular interest is the House of the Ocean Gods, with a magnificent mosaic floor depicting the bearded Neptune and other ocean images.

Much of what has been unearthed so far is housed in the **Musée Archéologique** near the ruins. The impressive collection includes household objects, murals and mosaics. The star exhibit is the *Châtiment de Lycurgue*, a mosaic discovered in 1907.

🏛 **Musée Archéologique**
**Tel** 04 74 53 74 01. **Open** Tue–Sun. **Closed** some public hols. 🗺 📷 ♿ restricted. 📷 ✎ 🌐 **musee-site. rhone.fr**

## ❼ St.-Etienne

Loire. 🗺 180,000. ✈ 🚆 🚌
ℹ 16 av de la Libération (04 77 49 39 00). 🛍 daily. 🎨 International Design Biennial (mid-Mar–mid-Apr, in odd-numbered years).
🌐 **saint-etiennetourisme.com**

The dour renown brought to this city by coal-mining and armaments is slowly being shaken off, with urban redevelopment well underway and an efficient street-car network. The downtown area around place du Peuple is lively. Nearby, Jean-Michel Wilmotte has overhauled the **Musée d'Art et d'Industrie**, which covers St.-Étienne's industrial history, including the development of the revolutionary Jacquard loom, and world-class collections of cycles and ribbon-making machines.
To the north of the city, the **Musée d'Art Moderne** has a collection of 20th-century art, including works by Andy Warhol and Frank Stella.

Detail of the bizarre Palais Idéal du Facteur Cheval at Hauterives

🏛 **Musée d'Art et d'Industrie**
2 pl Louis Comte. **Tel** 04 77 49 73 00. **Open** Wed–Mon. **Closed** some public hols. 🗺 ♿ 📷

🏛 **Musée d'Art Moderne**
Saint Priest en Jarez. **Tel** 04 77 79 52 52. **Open** Wed–Mon. **Closed** some public hols & when exhibitions change. 🗺 ♿ 📷 🌐 **mam-st-etienne.fr**

## ❽ Palais Idéal du Facteur Cheval

Hauterives, Drôme. 🚌 🚆 Romans-sur-Isère. **Tel** 04 75 68 81 19. **Open** daily. **Closed** Jan 1, 15–31, Dec 25. 🗺 📷 📷 ♿ restricted. 🌐 **facteurcheval.com**

At Hauterives, 24 km (15 miles) north of Romans-sur-Isère on the D538, is one of the greatest follies of France, an eccentric "palace" made of stones and evoking Egyptian, Roman, Aztec, and Siamese architecture. It was built by a local mailman, Ferdinand Cheval, who collected the stones during his daily rounds. His neighbors thought him mad, but the project attracted the admiring attention of Picasso, the Surrealist André Breton, and others.
The interior of the palace is inscribed with Cheval's numerous mottoes and exhortations, the most poignant of which refers to his assiduous efforts to realize his lifelong fantasy: "1879–1912: 10,000 days, 93,000 hours, 33 years of toil." Concerts are held here on summer evenings.

### The Bridges of the Rhône

The Rhône has played a crucial role in French history, transporting armies and commercial traffic between the north and south. It has always been dangerous, a challenge to boatmen and builders for centuries. In 1825 the brilliant engineer Marc Seguin built the first suspension bridge using steel-wire cables. This was followed by another 20 along the length of the Rhône, forever transforming communications between east and west.

Suspension bridge over the Rhône at Tournon-sur-Rhône *(see p388)*

Parc Jouvet in Valence

## ❾ Tournon-sur-Rhône

Ardèche. 🅰 10,000. 🚌 ℹ️ Hôtel de la Tourette (04 75 08 10 23). 🛒 Wed & Sat. 🎭 Festival de Shakespeare (Jul). 🌐 **hermitage-tournonais tourisme.com**

Located at the foot of impressive granite hills, Tournon is a lovely town with gracious tree-lined promenades and an imposing 11th- to 16th-century **château**. The latter houses a museum of local history, and has fine views of the town and river from its terraces.

The adjacent **Collégiale St.-Julien**, with its square bell tower and elaborate facade, is an interesting example of the Italian influence on architecture in the region during the 14th century. Inside is a powerful *Résurrection*, painted in 1576 by Capassin, a pupil of Raphael.

On quai Charles de Gaulle, the **Lycée Gabriel-Fauré** is the oldest high school in France, dating from 1536. Directly across the Rhône from Tournon, the village of **Tain l'Hermitage** is famous for its steep-climbing vineyards, which produce both red and white Hermitage, the finest of all Rhône wines.

### Environs

From Tournon's main square, place Jean Jaurès, a twisting road signposted **Route Panoramique** leads via the villages of Plats and St.-Romain-de-Lerps to St.-Péray. This route offers breathtaking views at every turn, and at St.-Romain you are rewarded with a superb panorama extending over 13 *départements*.

## ❿ Valence

Drôme. 🅰 67,000. ✈ 🚌 ℹ️ 11 bd Bancel (04 75 44 90 40). 🛒 Thu & Sat. 🎭 Summer Music (Jul). 🌐 **valence-romans-tourisme.com**

Valence is a large, thriving market town set on the east bank of the Rhône and looking across to the cliffs of the Ardèche. Its principal sight is the Romanesque **Cathédrale St.-Apollinaire** on place des Clercs, founded in 1095 and rebuilt in the 17th century.

Alongside the cathedral in the former bishop's palace, the small **Musée de Valence** contains a collection of late 18th-century chalk drawings of Rome by Hubert Robert.

A short walk from here are two Renaissance mansions. The **Maison des Têtes** at No. 57 Grande Rue was built in 1532 and is embellished with the sculpted heads of ancient Greeks including Aristotle, Homer, and Hippocrates. On rue Pérollerie, the **Maison Dupré-Latour** has a finely sculptured porch and staircase.

The **Parc Jouvet**, south of avenue Gambetta, offers lovely pools and gardens, with fine views across the river to the ruined **Château de Crussol**.

🏛 **Musée de Valence**
4 pl des Ormeaux. **Tel** 04 75 79 20 80. **Open** Tue pm & Wed–Sun. **Closed** some public hols. 🚫 ♿

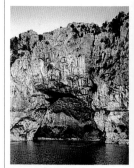

The limestone Pont d'Arc

## ⓫ The Ardèche

Ardèche. ✈ Avignon. 🚌 Montélimar. 🚌 Montélimar, Vallon Pont d'Arc. ℹ️ Vallon Pont d'Arc (04 28 91 24 10). 🌐 **vallon-pont-darc.com**

Over the course of thousands of years, wind and water have endowed this south-central region of France with such a

### Côtes du Rhône

Rising in the Swiss Alps and flowing south to the Mediterranean, the mighty Rhône is the common thread that links the many vineyards of the Rhône Valley. A hierarchy of *appellations* divides into three levels of quality: at the base, the regional Côtes du Rhône provides the bulk of the Rhône's wines; next, Côtes du Rhône-Villages comprises a plethora of picturesque villages; and, at the top, there are 13 individual *appellations*. The most famous are the steep slopes of Hermitage and Côte Rôtie in the northern Rhône, and historic Châteauneuf-du-Pape (*see pp506–7*) in the south. The lion's share of production is of red wine, which, based on the Syrah grape, is often spicy, full-bodied, and robust.

Harvest in a Côtes du Rhône vineyard

rugged landscape that it is more reminiscent of the American southwest than the verdure commonly associated with the French countryside. This visible drama is repeated underground as well, since the Ardèche is honeycombed with enormous stalagmite- and stalactite-ornamented caves. The most impressive are the **Grotte de la Madeleine**, reached via a signposted path from the D290, and the cave and museum **La Cité de la Préhistoire** (open Feb–mid-Nov) to the south of Vallon-Pont-d'Arc.

For those who prefer to stay above ground, the most arresting natural scenery in the region is the **Gorges de l'Ardèche**, best seen from the D290, a two-lane road that parallels the recessed river for 20 miles (32 km). Close to the head of the gorge, heading west, is the **Pont d'Arc**, a natural limestone "bridge" spanning the river, and created by erosion and the elements. Nearby is **Grotte Chauvet**, a replica of the oldest known decorated cave in the world, now closed to the public, and a UNESCO World Heritage site. Painted up to 36,000 years ago, the cave contains hundreds of animal paintings demonstrating astonishing technical ability.

Canoeing and whitewater rafting are the two most popular activities here. All the equipment necessary can be rented locally; operators at Vallon-Pont-d'Arc (among many other places) rent out two-person canoes and organize return transportation

The village of Vogüé on the banks of the River Ardèche

from St.-Martin d'Ardèche, 20 miles (32 km) downstream.

The softer side of the region is found in its ancient and picturesque villages, gracious spa towns, vineyards, and plantations of Spanish chestnuts (from which the delectable *marron glacé* is produced).

Some 8 miles (13 km) south of Aubenas, the 12th-century village of **Balazuc** is typical of the region, its stone houses built on a clifftop overlooking a secluded gorge of the River Ardèche. There are fine views as you approach on the D294.

Neighboring **Vogüé** is nestled between the Ardèche and a limestone cliff. A tiny but atmospheric village, its most commanding sight is the 12th-century **Château de Vogüé**, once the seat of the barons of Languedoc. Rebuilt in the 17th century, the building houses a museum featuring exhibitions about the region.

**🏠 Château de Vogüé**
**Tel** 04 75 37 01 95. **Open** Apr–Oct: Wed–Sun (Jul–Sep: daily). **Closed** 1 wk Jun. 🅰️ 🆆 chateaudevogue.net

## ⓬ Vals-les-Bains

Ardèche. 🅰️ 3,700. 🚍 Montélimar. 🛈 rue Jean Jaurès (04 75 89 02 03). 🛒 Thu & Sun (& Tue in summer). 🆆 aubenas-vals.com

This small spa town retains a hint of its past elegance. It is located in the valley of the Volane, where there are at least 150 springs, of which all but two are cold. The water, which contains bicarbonate of soda and other minerals, is said to help with digestive problems, rheumatism, and diabetes.

Discovered around 1600, Vals-les-Bains is one of the few spas in southern France to have been overlooked by the Romans. The town reached the height of its popularity in the late 19th century, and most of its parks and architecture retain something of the *belle époque*. Vals is a convenient first stop for an exploration of the Ardèche, with plenty of hotels and restaurants.

**Environs**
About 5 miles (8 km) east of Vals is the superb Romanesque church of **St.-Julien du Serre**.

The Gorges de l'Ardèche, between Vallon-Pont-d'Arc and Pont St.-Esprit

A farm near Le Poët Laval, east of Montélimar

# ⓭ Montélimar

Drôme. 🚏 33,000. 🚌 🚍 🛈 Montée St.-Martin, allées Provençales (04 75 01 00 20). 🚍 Wed–Sat. 🖵 **montelimar-tourisme.com**

Whether you choose to make a detour to Montélimar will largely depend on how sweet a tooth you might have. The main curiosity of this market town is its medieval center, chock-full of stores selling almond-studded nougat. This splendid confection has been made here since the start of the 17th century, when the almond tree was first introduced into France from Asia.

The **Château des Adhémar**, a mélange of 12th-, 14th-, and 16th- century architecture, surveys the town from a high hill to the east.

### 🏠 Château des Adhémar
**Tel** 04 75 91 83 50. **Open** May–Oct: daily. **Closed** Jan 1, Nov 11, Dec 25. 🖼️ ♿ 🎫

### Environs
The countryside east of Montélimar is full of picturesque medieval villages and scenic routes. **La Bégude-de-Mazenc** is a thriving little vacation center, with its fortified Old Town perched on a hilltop. Farther east is **Le Poët Laval**, a tiny medieval village set in the Alpine foothills. **Dieulefit**, the capital of this beautiful region, has several small hotels and restaurants, as well as amenities for tennis, swimming, and fishing. To the south, the fortified village of **Taulignan** is known for its truffles.

# ⓮ Grignan

Drôme. 🚏 1,500. 🚍 🛈 pl du Jeu de Ballon (04 75 46 56 75). 🚍 Tue. 🖵 **tourisme-paysdegrignan.com**

Attractively located on a rocky hill surrounded by fields of lavender, this charming little village owes its fame to Madame de Sévigné *(see p95)*, who wrote many of her celebrated letters while staying at the **Château de Grignan**.

Built during the 15th and 16th centuries, the château is one of the finest Renaissance structures in this part of France. Its interior contains a good collection of Louis XII furniture and Aubusson tapestries.

From the château's terrace, a panoramic view extends as far as the Vivarais mountains in the Ardèche. Directly below the terrace, the **Eglise de St.-Saveur** was built in the 1530s, and contains the tomb of Madame de Sévigné, who died here in 1696 at the age of 70.

### 🏠 Château de Grignan
**Tel** 04 75 91 83 55. **Open** Apr–Oct: daily; Nov–Mar: Wed–Mon. **Closed** Jan 1, Nov 11, Dec 25. 🖼️ 🎫

# ⓯ Nyons

Drôme. 🚏 7,000. 🚍 🛈 pl de la Libération (04 75 26 10 35). 🚍 Thu. 🖵 **paysdenyons.com**

As a major center of olive production, Nyons is synonymous with olives in France. All manner of olive products are on sale at the Thursday-morning market, from soap to *tapenade*, the olive paste so popular in the south.

The **Quartier des Forts** is Nyons' oldest quarter, a warren of narrow streets and stepped alleyways, the most rewarding of which is the covered rue des Grands Forts. Spanning the River Aygues is a graceful 13th-century bridge; on its town side are several old mills turned into stores, where you can see the enormous presses once used to extract olive oil. The **Espace Vignolis – Musée de l'Olivier** further explains the cultivation of the olive tree and the myriad local uses found for its fruit.

There is a fine view from the belvedere overlooking the town. Sheltered by mountains, Nyons enjoys an almost exotic climate, with all the trees and plants of the Riviera to be found here.

### 🏛 Espace Vignolis – Musée de l'Olivier
Pl Olivier de Serres. **Tel** 04 75 26 95 00. **Open** Mon–Fri. 🖼️ 🎫 ♿

### Environs
From Nyons, the D94 leads west to **Suze-la-Rousse**, a pleasant wine-producing village, which, during the Middle Ages, was the most important town in the area. Today, it is best known for its "university of wine," one of the most respected centers of oenology in the world. It is

The hilltop town of Grignan and its Renaissance château

Olive groves just outside Nyons

housed in the 14th-century **Château de Suze-la-Rousse**, the hunting lodge of the princes of Orange. The interior courtyard is a masterpiece of Renaissance architecture, and some rooms preserve original paint and stuccowork.

🏰 **Château de Suze-la-Rousse**
**Tel** 04 75 04 81 44. **Open** Apr–Oct: daily; Nov–Mar: Wed–Mon. **Closed** Jan 1, Nov 11, Dec 25. 🔲 🔲 🔲

Playing *boules* in Nyons

## ⑯ Briançon

Hautes-Alpes. 🚹 12,000. 🚌 🚍
🛈 1 pl du Temple (04 92 24 98 98). 
📅 Wed. 🎷 Altitude Jazz Festival (early Feb). 🌐 serre-chevalier.com

Briançon – the highest town in Europe at 4,330 ft (1,320 m) – has been an important stronghold since pre-Roman times, guarding as it does the road to the Col de Montgenèvre,

one of the oldest and most important passes into Italy. At the beginning of the 18th century, the town was fortified with ramparts and gates – still splendidly intact – by Louis XIV's military architect, Vauban. If driving, park at the Champs de Mars, and enter the traffic-free Old Town via the **Porte de Pignerol**.

This leads to the **grande rue**, a steep, narrow street with a stream running down the middle and bordered by lovely period houses. The nearby **Eglise de Notre-Dame** dates from 1718, and was also built by Vauban with an eye to defence. To visit Vauban's **citadel**, stop by the tourist office, which organizes guided tours.

Briançon is a major sports center, with skiing in winter, and rafting, cycling, and paragliding in summer *(see pp614–15)*.

### Environs
Just west of Briançon, the **Parc National des Ecrins** is the largest of the French national parks, offering lofty peaks and glaciers, and a magnificent variety of Alpine flowers.

The **Parc Régional du Queyras** is reached from Briançon over the rugged Col de l'Izoard. A wall of 9,850-ft (3,000-m) peaks separates this wild and beautiful national park from neighboring Italy.

## ⑰ Le Bourg d'Oisans

Isère. 🚹 3,000. 🚌 to Grenoble. 
🚌 to Le Bourg d'Oisans. 🛈 quai Docteur Girard (04 76 80 03 25). 🛒 Sat. 🌐 bourgdoisans.com

Le Bourg d'Oisans is an ideal base from which to explore the Romanche Valley, providing opportunities for cycling, rock-climbing, and skiing in the nearby resort of **L'Alpe d'Huez**.

Silver and other minerals have been mined here since the Middle Ages, and the town still has a reputation as a center for geology and mineralogy. Its **Musée des Minéraux et de la Faune des Alpes** is renowned for its collection of crystals and precious stones.

🏛 **Musée des Minéraux et de la Faune des Alpes**
Pl de l'Eglise. **Tel** 04 76 80 27 54. **Open** pm (days vary – check website). **Closed** Jan 1, mid-Nov–mid-Dec, Dec 25. 🔲 🌐 bourgdoisans.com

### Life on High

The Alpine ibex is one of the rarest inhabitants of the French Alps, living high above the tree line for all but the coldest part of the year. Until the creation of the Parc National de la Vanoise *(see p327)*, this sure-footed climber had become almost extinct in France, but after rigorous conservation there are now over 500. Both males and females have horns; in the oldest males they can be almost 3 ft (1 m) long.

An ibex in the Parc National de la Vanoise

## Grenoble Town Center

① Fort de la Bastille
② Musée Dauphinois
③ Ancien Palais du Parlement du Dauphiné
④ Collégiale St.-André
⑤ Musée Archéologique Grenoble Saint-Laurent
⑥ Musée de Grenoble
⑦ Musée de l'Ancien Evêché
⑧ Musée de la Résistance et de la Déportation

For keys to symbols *see back flap*

Fort de la Bastille on the Chartreuse mountain range, with views of Grenoble

## ⑱ Grenoble

Isère. 165,000.
14 rue de la République (04 76 42 41 41). Tue–Sun.
grenoble-tourisme.com

Ancient capital of the Dauphiné region and site of the 1968 Winter Olympics, Grenoble is a thriving city at the confluence of the Drac and Isère rivers, with the Vercors and Chartreuse massifs rising to the west and north. It is home to the science-oriented University of Grenoble, and is a center of chemical and electronics industries and nuclear research.

A cable car starting at quai Stéphane-Jay whisks you up to the 19th-century **Fort de la Bastille**, which has superb views of the city and surrounding mountains. Paths lead down through Parc Guy Pape and Jardin des Dauphins to the **Musée Dauphinois**, a regional museum in a 17th-century convent devoted to local history, arts, and crafts. Nearby, **Musée Archéologique Grenoble Saint-Laurent**, located in a former church with a 6th-century crypt, exhibits medieval artifacts and decorative and religious art.

On the left bank of the Isère, the focus of life is the traffic-free area around place Grenette. Nearby, place St.-André is the heart of the medieval city, overlooked by Grenoble's oldest buildings, including the 13th-century **Collégiale St.-André** and the 16th-century **Ancien Palais du Parlement du Dauphiné**.

The **Musée de Grenoble** exhibits works by Chagall, Picasso, and Matisse. The **Musée de l'Ancien Evêché** recounts the history of Isère, and includes the 4th-century baptistery. On rue Hébert, the **Musée de la Résistance et de la Déportation** has documents relating to the French Resistance. Displays of contemporary art can be seen at

**Le Magasin** (Centre National d'Art Contemporain) in a renovated warehouse. In the Quartier Malherbe, **MC2** (Maison de la Culture) hosts concerts, dance, and theater.

### 🏛 Musée Dauphinois
30 rue Maurice Gignoux. **Tel** 04 57 58 89 01. **Open** Wed–Mon. **Closed** Jan 1, May 1, Dec 25.

### 🏛 Musée Archéologique Grenoble Saint-Laurent
Pl St-Laurent. **Tel** 04 76 44 78 68. **Open** Wed–Mon. 🕹 🌐 musee-archeologique-grenoble.fr

### 🏛 Musée de Grenoble
5 pl de Lavalette. **Tel** 04 76 63 44 44. **Open** Wed–Mon. **Closed** Jan 1, May 1, Dec 25. 🎟 🕹 📷 🎥 📷 🖥

Grenoble's gondola cable car

*For hotels and restaurants in this region see pp564–5 and pp593–4*

🏛 **Musée de l'Ancien Evêché**
2 rue Très Cloîtres. **Tel** 04 76 03 15 25.
**Open** Thu–Tue. **Closed** Jan 1, May 1
& 8, Dec 25. ♿

🏛 **Musée de la Résistance et de la Déportation**
14 rue Hébert. **Tel** 04 76 42 38 53.
**Open** daily. **Closed** Tue am, Jan 1,
May 1, Dec 25. ♿

🏛 **Le Magasin (CNAC)**
8 esplanade Andry Farcy. **Tel** 04 76 21
95 84. **Open** times vary – call for
details. 📷 ♿ 🆆 **magasin-cnac.org**

🏛 **MC2**
4 rue Paul Claudel. **Tel** 04 76 00 79 00.
**Open** times vary – call for details. 📷
♿ 🆆 **mc2grenoble.fr**

# ⓳ The Vercors

Isère & Drôme. 🚄 Grenoble. 🚍
Romans-sur-Isère, St.-Marcellin, Grenoble. 🚌 Pont-en-Royans, Romans-
sur-Isère. 🛈 Pont-en-Royans (04 76
36 09 10). Maison du Parc: 255 chemin
des Fusillés, Lans-en-Vercors 38250 (04
76 94 38 26) 🆆 **parc-du-vercors.fr**

To the south and west of
Grenoble, the Vercors is one of
France's most magnificent
regional parks – a wilderness of
pine forests, mountains, waterfalls,
caves, and deep, narrow gorges.
   The D531 out of Grenoble
passes through **Villard-de-Lans** –
a good base for excursions – and
continues west to the dark
**Gorges de la Bournes**. About
5 miles (8 km) farther west, the
hamlet of **Pont-en-Royans** is
sited on a limestone gorge, its
stone houses built into the rocks
overlooking the River Bourne.
   South of Pont-en-Royans along
the D76, the **Route de Combe-
Laval** snakes along a sheer cliff
above the roaring river. The
**Grands Goulets**, 4 miles (7 km)
to the east, is a spectacularly
deep, narrow gorge overlooked
by sheer cliffs that virtually shut
out the sky above. The best-
known mountain in the park is
the **Mont Aiguille**, a soaring outcrop of 6,844 ft (2,086 m).
   The Vercors was a key base for
the French Resistance during
World War II. In July 1944 the
Germans launched an aerial
attack on the region, flattening
several of its villages. There are
Resistance museums at Vassieux
and Grenoble.

Cows grazing in the Chartreuse

# ⓴ The Chartreuse

Isère & Savoie. 🚄 Grenoble,
Chambéry. 🚍 Grenoble, Voiron.
🚌 St.-Pierre-de-Chartreuse. 🛈
St.-Pierre-de-Chartreuse (04 76 88 62
08). 🆆 **st-pierre-chartreuse.com**

From Grenoble, the D512 leads
north toward Chambéry into the
Chartreuse, a majestic region of
mountains and forests, where
hydroelectricity was invented in
the late 1800s. The **Monastère de
la Grande Chartreuse**, just west
of St.-Pierre-de-Chartreuse off
the D520-B, is the main sight.
   Founded by St. Bruno in 1084,
the monastery owes its fame
to the sticky green and yellow
Chartreuse liqueurs first produced
by the monks in 1605. The recipe,
based on a secret herbal elixir of
130 ingredients, is now produced
in the nearby town of Voiron.
   The monastery itself is inhabited by about 40 monks, who live
in silence and seclusion. It is not
open to visitors, but there is a
museum at the entrance, the
**Musée de la Correrie**, which
faithfully depicts the daily
routine of the Carthusian monks.

🏛 **Musée de la Correrie**
St.-Pierre-de-Chartreuse. **Tel** 04 76 88
60 45. **Open** Apr: daily pms; May–Sep:
daily; Oct–mid-Nov: Mon–Fri pm only,
Sat & Sun. 📷 ♿

A farm in the pine-clad mountains of the Chartreuse

# ❷❶ Chambéry

Savoie. 🅰 61,000. ✈ 🚆 🚌 ℹ 5bis
pl Palais de Justice (04 79 33 42 47). 🛒
Tue, Sat. 🆆 chambery-tourisme.com

Once the capital of Savoy, this
dignified city has aristocratic airs
and a distinctly Italianate feel.
Its best-loved monument is
the extravagant **Fontaine des
Eléphants** on rue de Boigne,
erected in 1838 to honor the
Comte de Boigne, who left to
his home town some of the
fortune he amassed in India.

The 14th-century **Château des
Ducs de Savoie**, at the opposite
end of rue de Boigne, is now
occupied by the Préfecture. Only
parts of the building, such as the
late Gothic Ste.-Chapelle, can be
visited, via guided tours arranged
with the tourist office.

On the southeast edge of
town is the 17th-century country house **Les Charmettes**,
where the philosopher
Rousseau lived with his
mistress, Madame de
Warens. It is worth a
visit for its gardens
and museum of
memorabilia.

### 🏠 Les Charmettes

892 chemin des
Charmettes. **Tel** 04 79 33
39 44. **Open** Wed–Mon
(Dec–late Mar: Sat & Sun).
**Closed** public hols.
📷 with fee.

The Lac du Bourget at Aix-les-Bains

# ❷❷ Aix-les-Bains

Savoie. 🅰 26,000. ✈ 🚌 ℹ pl
Maurice Mollard (04 79 88 68 00).
🛒 Wed & Sat am. 🎭 Festival Musilac
(Jul). 🆆 aixlesbains.com

The Romantic poet Lamartine
rhapsodized over the beauty
of Lac du Bourget, site of the
gracious spa town of Aix-les-
Bains. The heart of the
town is the 19th-century
**Thermes Nationaux**,
thermal baths, first
enjoyed by the
Romans over 2,000 years
ago – in the basement
are the remains of the
original Roman baths.
The ruins can be
visited on a guided
tour. Opposite the
baths, the 2nd-century
AD **Temple of Diana**

Roman statue in
the Temple of Diana

contains Gallo-Roman artifacts.
The tourist office runs guided
tours (Feb–Nov). The nearby
**Musée Faure** has some
stunning Impressionist
paintings by Degas and
Sisley, Rodin sculptures, and
Lamartine memorabilia.

### 🏛 Thermes Nationaux

Pl Maurice Mollard. 📷 📷
call 04 79 88 68 00 for guided tours.

### 🏛 Musée Faure

Villa des Chimères, 10 bd des Côtes.
**Tel** 04 79 61 06 57. **Open** Wed–Mon.
**Closed** Mon & Tue Nov–Mar, Dec 20–
Jan 5, public hols. 📷 ♿

#### Environs

Boats leave from Aix's Grand
Port and sail across Lac du
Bourget to the **Abbaye
d'Hautecombe**, a Benedictine
abbey containing the mausoleum of the Savoyard dynasty.

The small town of **Le Revard**,
just east of Aix on the D913, has
spectacular views of the lake
and Mont Blanc.

# ❷❸ Annecy

Haute-Savoie. 🅰 51,000. ✈ 🚌 🚌
ℹ 1 rue Jean Jaurès (04 50 45 00 33).
🛒 Tue, Fri–Sun. 🎆 Fête du Lac
(firework display; 1st Sat Aug).
🆆 lac-annecy.com

Annecy is one of the most
charming towns in the Alps,
set at the northern tip of Lac

Annecy's 12th-century Palais de l'Isle in the middle of Thiou canal

*For hotels and restaurants in this region see pp564–5 and pp593–4*

Cycling along the shores of Lac Léman (Lake Geneva)

d'Annecy and surrounded by snowcapped mountains. Its small medieval quarter is laced with canals, flower-covered bridges, and arcaded streets. Strolling around is the main attraction here, though there are a couple of specific sights worth having a look at more closely: the formidable **Palais de l'Isle**, a 12th-century prison in the middle of the Thiou canal; and the turreted **Château d'Annecy**, set high on a hill above the town with impressive views of Vieil Annecy and the crystal-clear lake beyond.

The best spot for swimming and watersports is at the eastern end of the avenue d'Albigny near the Imperial Palace hotel, while boat trips leave from quai Napoléon III.

### Environs

One of the best ways to enjoy the area's spectacular scenery is to take a boat from Annecy to **Talloires**, a tiny lakeside village celebrated for its hotels and restaurants. Facing Talloires across the lake is the 15th-century **Château de Duingt** (not open to visitors).

On the west bank of the lake, the Semnoz mountain and its summit, the **Crêt de Châtillon**, offer superb views of Mont Blanc and the Alps (*see pp326–7*).

## ㉔ Lac Léman

Haute-Savoie & Switzerland.
✈ Geneva. 🚉 🚌 Geneva, Thonon-les-Bains, Évian-les-Bains.
ℹ Thonon-les-Bains (04 50 71 55 55).
🌐 thononlesbains.com

The stirring scenery and gentle climate of the French shore of Lake Geneva (Lac Léman to the French) has made it a popular and fashionable resort area since the first spa buildings were erected at Évian-les-Bains in 1839.

**Yvoire** is a fine place to begin a visit to the area. This medieval port is guarded by a 14th-century castle, and its houses are bedecked with colorful flower boxes.

Farther east along Lake Geneva is **Thonon-les-Bains**, a prosperous, well-manicured little spa town perched on a cliff overlooking the lake. A funicular takes you down to Rives, the small harbor at the foot of the cliffs, where sailboats can be rented and excursion boats to the Swiss cities of Geneva and Lausanne call in. Just outside the town is the 15th-century **Château de Ripaille**, made famous by its one-time resident Duke Amadeus VIII, who later became antipope (Felix V).

Though it has been modernized and acquired an international reputation for its eponymous

spring water, **Evian-les-Bains** still exudes a polite *vie en rose* charm. The tree-lined lakefront promenade teems with leisurely strollers, while more energetic types can avail themselves of all kinds of sporting amenities including tennis, golf, horseback riding, sailing, and skiing in the winter. State-of-the-art spa treatments are available, and the exotic domed casino offers blackjack, roulette, and baccarat, among other games.

From Evian there are daily ferries across Lake Geneva to Lausanne in Switzerland, as well as bus excursions into the surrounding mountains.

The 14th-century castle at Yvoire, overlooking Lake Geneva (Lac Léman)

# SOUTHWEST FRANCE

Introducing Southwest
France      **398–407**

Poitou and Aquitaine      **408–429**

Périgord, Quercy,
and Gascony      **430–451**

The Pyrenees      **452–467**

# Introducing Southwest France

The southwest is farming France, a green and peaceful land nurturing produce from sunflowers to *foie gras*. Other key country products include Landes forest timber, Bordeaux wines, and Cognac. Major modern industries, including aerospace, are focused on the two chief cities, Bordeaux and Toulouse. Visitors are mainly drawn to the wide Atlantic beaches, the ski slopes of the Pyrenees, and the rural calm of the Dordogne. The major sights of this favored region are shown here and include some of France's most celebrated Romanesque buildings.

**La Rochelle's harbor** is today a haven for pleasure yachts as well as an important commercial port *(see p420)*. Tour de la Chaîne and Tour St.-Nicolas protect the entrance of the old port. The town's historic center is filled with cobblestone streets lined by merchants' houses.

**Bordeaux** is a town of grand 18th- and 19th-century buildings and monuments, including its theater and the Monument aux Girondins. A 21st-century addition is the Cité du Vin museum, which celebrates the region's wine production *(see pp424–6)*.

◀ Château de Castelnaud, overlooking the River Dordogne

Thoua
Bressu
Parthena
Niort
La Rochelle
St-Jean-d'Angé
Rochefort

Roman Ruins, Saintes
*(see p422)*

Saintes
La Palmyre
Pons
Soulac-sur-Mer
Barbezie
Mirambea
Pauillac
*Lac d'Hourtin-Carcans*
Cout
Bordeaux
Libou
Ares
Arcachon
Gujan-Mestras
Langon
Biscarrosse
Bazas

POITOU AND AQUITAINE
*(See pp408–29)*

Mimizan
Mont-de-Marsan
Léon
Dax
Aire-sur-l'Adour
Bayonne
Orthez
Biarritz
Saint Jean de Luz
Pau
Oloron-Ste-Marie
St-Jean-Pied-de-Port
Lourd

0 kilometers    50
0 miles    50

Cautere

Cirque de Gavarnie
*(see p463)*

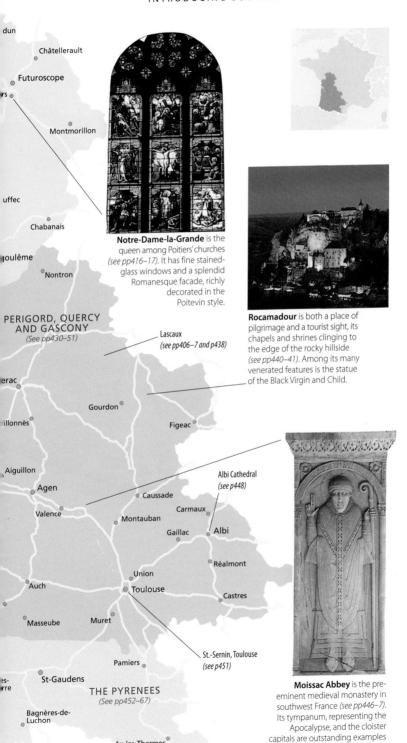

**Notre-Dame-la-Grande** is the queen among Poitiers' churches *(see pp416–17)*. It has fine stained-glass windows and a splendid Romanesque facade, richly decorated in the Poitevin style.

**Rocamadour** is both a place of pilgrimage and a tourist sight, its chapels and shrines clinging to the edge of the rocky hillside *(see pp440–41)*. Among its many venerated features is the statue of the Black Virgin and Child.

dun

Châtellerault

Futuroscope

rs

Montmorillon

uffec

Chabanais

goulême

Nontron

PERIGORD, QUERCY AND GASCONY
*(See pp430–51)*

Lascaux
*(see pp406–7 and p438)*

erac

Gourdon

Figeac

illonnès

Aiguillon

Agen

Caussade

Albi Cathedral
*(see p448)*

Carmaux

Valence

Montauban

Gaillac

Albi

Réalmont

Union

Auch

Toulouse

Castres

Masseube

Muret

St.-Sernin, Toulouse
*(see p451)*

Pamiers

es-
rre

St-Gaudens

THE PYRENEES
*(See pp452–67)*

Bagnères-de-
Luchon

Ax-les-Thermes

**Moissac Abbey** is the pre-eminent medieval monastery in southwest France *(see pp446–7)*. Its tympanum, representing the Apocalypse, and the cloister capitals are outstanding examples of Romanesque sculpture.

# The Flavors of Southwest France

"Great cooking and great wines make a paradise on earth," said Henri IV of his own region, Gascony. The southwest does indeed fulfill the requirements of the most demanding gourmet. The Atlantic coast supplies fine seafood; Bordeaux produces some of France's best wines to complement its rich cooking; geese and ducks provide the fat that is key to local cuisine; and regional produce includes delicacies such as *foie gras*, truffles, and wild mushrooms. The Pyrenees offer beef and lamb grazed on mountain pastures, cheese, and *charcuterie*, and the Basque country adds the spicy notes of red peppers and fine chocolate.

Espelette peppers

Walnuts, one of the southwest's most famous products

## Poitou and Aquitaine

The coast is famous for its seafood, and is the most important oyster-producing region of France – the oysters of Marennes-Oleron are of especially high quality. The species of blue algae on which they feed gives them a distinctive green coloring. Oysters are usually served simply with lemon or shallot vinegar, but in Bordeaux they like to eat them

with little sausages. Mussels are also raised here, and the sea yields a variety of fish. Eels, lamprey, and sturgeon are caught in the Gironde estuary.

Poitou-Charentes is one of France's main goat-rearing areas, producing cheeses such as *chabichou de Poitou*, a small, soft, cylindrical cheese of distinct flavor.

## Périgord, Quercy, and Gascony

High-quality ducks, geese, and poultry form the basis of the cuisine of this region, and their fat is a key ingredient of many dishes from simple *pommes sarladaises* (potatoes cooked in goose fat) to *confit*, where entire duck legs are preserved in their own fat. The ultimate

Wild boar ham    Chorizo    Garlic saucisson    Truffle saucisson    Wild boar saucisson    Bayonne ham    Blueberry saucisson

Selection of traditional southwestern *charcuterie*

## Regional Dishes and Specialties

Duck is one of the essential ingredients of southwestern cooking, and is served in a variety of ways. The *magret* is the breast – the best of all coming from a duck that has been bred for *foie gras*. Usually served pink *(rose)*, it may come with a variety of sauces but is most perfectly complemented by the smoky flavor of local cèpe mushrooms in season. Duck *confit* is usually made with the legs, but gizzards are also preserved in this way.

Pink garlic

*Foie gras* is the most expensive (and controversial) product, resulting from the process of *gavage*, when the duck or goose is force-fed maize to enlarge and enrich its liver. *Foie gras* can be eaten freshly cooked, served with sauce or fruit, or preserved and served with toast or brioche, ideally accompanied by a sweet white wine such as Sauternes.

**Omelette aux truffes** For this luxurious omelet the filling is local black truffles, with more sliced over the top.

Fattened Toulouse geese, the source of *foie gras*

southwestern dish has to be *cassoulet*, a stew of duck or goose, sausages, pork, and white beans topped with a crust of breadcrumbs; it arouses fierce competition among the dedicated chefs of the region.

Luxury ingredients enhance these basics: walnut oil is added to salads, and slivers of expensive truffles perfume sauces or omelettes. Wild mushrooms are eagerly sought in season, and are most delicious cooked simply with garlic, shallots, and parsley. The region is one of the main producers of garlic, which appears studded into meat or served as whole baked heads. The finest fruits include *reines-claudes* (green-gages) and the celebrated plums of Agen, which are dried as prunes or added to dishes of rabbit or hare.

## The Pyrenees

From the mountain pastures come beef and lamb of high quality, including Barèges mutton, as well as river trout and an array of excellent *charcuterie*. Strong cheeses of goat's or ewe's milk are sometimes served with jam made from the black cherries

Fishermen opening oysters at a local maritime festival

of Itxassou. One of the most popular dishes is *garbure*, a hearty stew of cabbage, bacon, and confit of duck or goose.

Basque cuisine has its own distinct identity, with the red Espelette pepper adding a touch of spice to chorizo, *piperade*, or *chipirones* (baby squid cooked in their own ink). Succulent Bayonne ham is made from pigs that forage for acorns and chestnuts. Bayonne was also home to the first chocolatiers in France – 17th-century Jewish refugees from the Inquisition – and the town still makes top-quality dark, bitter chocolate.

## ON THE MENU

**Cagouilles à la charentaise** Snails with sausage meat, herbs, and wine.

**Entrecôte à la bordelaise** Steak in sauce of red wine, shallots, and bone marrow.

**Farçi poitevin** Cabbage stuffed with bacon, pork, and sorrel.

**Gasconnade** Leg of lamb with garlic and anchovy.

**Mouclade** Mussels in curry sauce, from the spice port of La Rochelle.

**Salade landaise** Salad of *foie gras*, gizzards, and *confit*.

**Ttoro** Basque mixed fish and shellfish stew with potatoes, tomatoes, and onions.

**Cassoulet** This is a stew of white beans cooked with a variety of sausages and cuts of meat, such as pork or duck.

**Piperade** Eggs are added to a stew of peppers, onions, tomatoes, and garlic, with Bayonne ham laid on top.

**Croustade** Thin pastry is layered with melted butter and apples, perfumed with Armagnac and vanilla.

# France's Wine Regions: Bordeaux

Bordeaux is the world's largest fine wine region, and, for red wines, certainly the most familiar outside France. Following Henry II's marriage to Eleanor of Aquitaine, three centuries of courtly commerce with England ensured that claret was served at the finest foreign tables. In the 19th century, canny merchants capitalized on this fame and brought fantastic financial prosperity to the region and, with it, the famous 1855 Classification of the Médoc, a league table of châteaux that is still very much in force today.

**Locator Map**
◼ Bordeaux wine region

Picking red Merlot grapes at Château Palmer

## Wine Regions

*The great wine-producing areas of Bordeaux straddle two great rivers; the land between the rivers ("Entre-Deux-Mers") produces lesser, mainly white wines. The rivers, and the river port of Bordeaux itself, have been crucial to the trade in Bordeaux wines; some of the prettiest châteaux line the river banks, enabling easy transportation.*

0 kilometers    15
0 miles          15

## Key Facts About Bordeaux Wines

**Location and Climate**
Climatic conditions may vary not only from one year to another, but also within the region itself. The soils tend to be gravelly in the Médoc and Graves, and clayey on the right bank.

**Grape Varieties**
The five main red grape varieties are *Cabernet Franc*, *Cabernet Sauvignon*, *Merlot*, *Petit Verdot*, and *Malbec*. Cabernet Sauvignon is the dominant grape on the west side of the Gironde, Merlot to the east. Most Bordeaux reds are, however, a blend of grapes. *Sauvignon Blanc* and *Sémillon* are grown and often blended for both dry and sweet whites.

**Good Producers**
*(Reds)* Latour, Margaux, Haut-Brion, Cos d'Estournel, Léoville Las Cases, Léoville Barton, Lascombes, Pichon Longueville, Pichon Lalande, Lynch-Bages, Palmer, Rausan-Ségla, Duhart Milon, d'Angludet, Léoville Poyferré, Branaire Ducru, Ducru Beaucaillou, Malescot St.-Exupéry, Cantemerle, Phélan-Ségur, Chasse-Spleen, Poujeaux, Domaine de Chevalier, Pape Clément, Cheval Blanc, Canon, Pavie, l'Angelus, Troplong Mondot, La Conseillante, Lafleur, Trotanoy.

**Good Vintages**
*(Reds)* 2010, 2009, 2006, 2005, 2003, 2000, 1998, 1996.

**Key**
▢ Médoc
▢ Blaye
▢ Bourg
▢ Entre-Deux-Mers
▢ Graves
▢ Pessac-Léognan
▢ Cérons
▢ Barsac
▢ Sauternes
▢ Libournais District
▢ Pomerol
▢ Saint-Emilion

**Cos d'Estournel**, like all the châteaux included in the 1855 league of *crus classés* ("classed growths"), proudly proclaims the fact on its label.

One of many wine-producing properties in the Saint-Emilion district

**Entre-Deux-Mers,** largely undistinguished, has some good producers.

**Saint-Emilion** has its own *crus classés* league: Cheval Blanc shares top ranking.

rdon-
ler

St-Christoly-
Médoc

St-Seurin-
de-Cadourne

St-Estèphe

Pauillac

St-Laurent-
Médoc

Cussac-Fort Médoc

Listrac-Médoc

Castelnau-
de-Médoc        Margaux

Macau

Hélène

Blanquefort

St-Médard-en-Jalles

Martignas-
sur-Jalles

St-Jean-d'Illac

Bordeaux

Pessac

Cestas

Léognan

Castres-Gironde

Le Barp

Hostens

-Vivien
e-Médoc

Mirambeau

Montendre

Reignac

Montlieu-
la-Garde

Bedenac

Blaye

Berson

Moulis-en-Médoc        Pugnac

Bourg

Ambès

St-André-
de-Cubzac

Ambarès
et-Lagrave

Vayres

Pomerol
Libourne

Créon

Targon

Langoiran

Podensac        Cadillac

Cérons        Loupiac

Barsac

Landiras

Sauternes

Langon

Gironde

St-Savin

St-Emilion

Branne        Castillon-
la-Bataille

Ste-Foy-
la-Grande

La Dordogne

Ste-Croix-du-Mont        La Réole

St-Macaire

Le Drôpt

La Garonne

**Haut-Brion**, in the top division of Bordeaux's Classification, was and still is the single Graves château in this league of Médoc properties.

**The famous legend** that guarantees château-bottling originated in Bordeaux, as a check to unscrupulous merchants.

# The Road to Compostela

Throughout the Middle Ages millions of Christians visited Santiago de Compostela in Spain to pay homage at the shrine of St. James (Santiago). They traveled across France staying in monasteries or simple shelters and would return with a scallop shell, the symbol of St. James, as a souvenir. Most pilgrims went in hope of redemption and were often on the road for years. In 1140, a monk called Picaud wrote one of the world's first travel guides about the pilgrimage. Today, travelers can follow the same routes, passing through ancient towns and villages with their magnificent shrines and churches.

**Foreign pilgrims** joined at ports such as St.-Malo.

**The original cathedral** of Santiago de Compostela was built in 813 by Alfonso II over the tomb of St. James. In 1075, construction started on the grandiose Romanesque church seen today, which has, among other later additions, a resplendent 17th- to 18th-century Baroque facade.

**The routes** converged on Santiago de Compostela.

**Most pilgrims** crossed the Pyrenees at Roncesvalles.

**James the Greater**, an apostle, came to Spain to spread the Gospel, according to legend. On his return to Judaea, he was martyred by Herod. His remains were taken to Spain by boat and lay hidden for 800 years.

**The powerful Cluny monastery** in Burgundy *(see pp54–5)*, and its affiliated monasteries, played an important role in promoting the pilgrimage. They built shelters and set up churches and shrines housing precious relics, to encourage the pilgrims on their way.

# The Pilgrims' Way

*Paris, Vézelay (see pp340–41), Le Puy (see pp368–9), and Arles (see pp512–13) are the rallying points for the four "official" routes across France. They cross the Pyrenees at Roncesvalles and Somport, and merge at Puente la Reina to form one route, culminating at the shrine on the Galician coast*

## What to See Today

Huge Romanesque churches, including Ste.-Madeleine at Vézelay *(see p340)*, Ste.-Foy at Conques *(pp372–3)*, and St.-Sernin at Toulouse *(p451)*, along with many small chapels, were built to accommodate large numbers of pilgrims.

Basilique Ste.-Madeleine, Vézelay

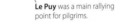

**Conques** purloined relics to boost its prestige.

**Le Puy** was a main rallying point for pilgrims.

**The first recorded pilgrim** was the bishop of Le Puy in 951. But pilgrims have probably been coming to Santiago since 814, soon after the saint's tomb was found.

**The reliquary** of Ste.-Foy, at Conques, is in one of many elaborate shrines that drew crowds of pilgrims on the way to Santiago de Compostela. A saint's relics were thought to have miraculous powers.

**The name** Santiago de Compostela is believed to originate from the Latin *Campus stellae* (field of stars). Legend has it that strange stars were seen hovering over a field in 814 and on July 25, now the feast of Santiago, the saint's remains were found. Subsequent evidence showed that St. James's remains were never in Compostela after all.

# Caves of the Southwest

Southwest France is well-known for its spectacular rock formations, created by the slow accumulation of dissolved mineral deposits. Caves and rock shelters exist throughout limestone country in France. But in the foothills of the Pyrenees and the Dordogne they also have something else to offer the visitor: a collection of extraordinary rock paintings, some dating back to the last Ice Age. These art forms were created when prehistoric peoples evolved and began engraving, painting, and carving. This unique artistic tradition lasted for more than 25,000 years, reaching its zenith around 17,000 years ago. Some very fine examples of cave painting are still visible today.

Ancient cave paintings at Lascaux

## Caves of the Dordogne

There are many different cave systems to visit in or near the Dordogne Valley. The entire Périgord region contains one of the densest concentrations of prehistoric sites anywhere in the world. In an uncertain climate, its rivers flanked by caves and rock shelters proved very attractive to prehistoric man.

## Cave Formation

Limestone is laid down in layers containing fissures that allow water to penetrate beneath the surface. Over thousands of years, the water slowly dissolves the rock, first forming potholes and then larger caverns. Stalactites develop where water drips from the cave roof; stalagmites grow upward from the floor.

Grotte du Grand Roc in the Vézère Valley, Périgord

**1** Water percolates through fissures, slowly dissolving the surrounding rock.

**2** The water produces potholes and loosens surrounding rocks, which gradually fall away.

**3** Dripping water containing dissolved limestone forms stalactites and stalagmites.

## Gouffre de Padirac

Chasm entrance — Elevators — Permeable limestone — Galerie de la Fontaine — Le Grand Cristal — Salle du Grand Dôme

Impermeable rock — Salle de la Fontaine — Rivière Plane (Smooth River) — Lac de la Pluie (Rain Lake) — Pas du Crocodile (Crocodile Track) — Lac des Grands Gours (Great Barrier Lake)

Underground river and chambers of the Gouffre de Padirac

Prehistoric caves at Les Eyzies

## Visiting the Caves

**Cougnac** contains chasms (gouffres) and galleries and its prehistoric paintings include human figures. Around **Les Eyzies** (see pp438–9) are the caves of **Les Combarelles**, and **Font de Gaume**, which have beautiful prehistoric paintings, drawings, and engravings, as does **Rouffignac** in its network of caves. **Grand Roc** has chambers containing a profusion of stalactites and stalagmites. Northeast of Les Eyzies is the rock shelter of **L'Abri du Cap Blanc**, with its rare frieze of horses and bison dating from around 14,000 years ago.

On the south bank of the Dordogne, an underground river and lake with extraordinary rock formations can be seen at **Lacave**. The gigantic chasm and caverns at **Gouffre de Padirac** (p442) are even more spectacular. The caves at **Lascaux** with the finest prehistoric paintings have been closed but the exceptional replica at **Lascaux IV** (p438) is well worth seeing. Farther south, **Pech-Merle's** caverns (pp442–3) have impressive rock formations. **Niaux**, in the foothills of the Pyrenees, can also be visited.

## The Story of Cave Art

The first prehistoric cave paintings in Europe were discovered in northwest Spain in 1879. Since then, over 200 decorated caves and rock shelters have been found in Spain and France, mainly in the Dordogne region. A wide range of clues, from stone lamps to miraculously preserved footprints, has helped prehistorians to work out the techniques the cave artists used. But their motives are still not clear. Nearly all the paintings are of animals, with few humans, and many of them are in inaccessible underground chambers. The paintings undoubtedly had a symbolic or magical significance; a new theory suggests they were the work of shamans.

**The techniques** used by Ice Age artists, who worked by lamplight, included cutting outlines into soft rock, using natural contours as part of the design. Black lines and shading were produced by charcoal, while color washes were applied with mineral pigments such as kaolin and haematite. Hand silhouettes were made by sucking up diluted pigment and blowing it through a plant stem to form a fine spray. When the hand was removed from the rock, its eerie shape was left behind.

Decorated stone lamp discovered in Lascaux cave

Kaolin

Charcoal

Haematite

The Great Bull from the Hall of Bulls frieze at Lascaux

# POITOU AND AQUITAINE

*Deux-Sèvres · Charente-Maritime · Vendée · Vienne · Charente*
*Gironde · Landes*

This vast area of southwest France spans a quarter of the country's windswept Atlantic coastline, a great expanse of fine sandy beaches. The region stretches from the marshes of the Marais Poitevin to the great pine forests of the Landes. Central to it is the celebrated wine region of Bordeaux and its great châteaux.

The turbulent history of Poitou and Aquitaine, fought over for centuries, has left a rich architectural and cultural heritage. The great arch and amphitheater at Saintes bear witness to Roman influence in the area. In the Middle Ages, the pilgrimage route to Santiago de Compostela *(see pp404–5)* created an impressive legacy of Romanesque churches, such as those at Poitiers and Parthenay, as well as tiny chapels and glowing frescoes. The Hundred Years' War *(see pp58–9)* caused great upheaval but also resulted in the construction of mighty defence keeps by the English Plantagenet kings. As a result of the Wars of Religion *(see pp60–61),* many towns, churches, and châteaux were destroyed and had to be rebuilt.

Present-day Poitiers is a big, thriving commercial center. To the west are the historic ports of La Rochelle and Rochefort. Farther south, the wine-producing district of Bordeaux combines with Cognac, famous for its brandy, to supply an important part of the region's income. The city of Bordeaux is as prosperous today as in Roman times, combining a lively cultural scene with elegant 18th-century architecture. Its wines complement the region's cuisine: lampreys, mussels, and oysters from the coast; and salty lamb and goat's cheeses from the inland pastures.

Shuttered houses in St.-Martin-de-Ré, on Ile de Ré, off the coast of La Rochelle

◄ Aerial view of Pointe de la Fumée, famous for its seafood restaurants, near Fouras, south of La Rochelle

# Exploring Poitou and Aquitaine

Blessed with a seemingly endless Atlantic coastline, abundant navigable waterways, excellent ports, and the finest wine and brandy in the world, the region is ideal for a relaxing vacation. Today most summer visitors head straight for the beaches with their thundering waves, but there is also a lush countryside inland with a lot to offer. Fine medieval architecture can be seen along the pilgrim's route to Santiago de Compostela *(see pp404–5)*, and châteaux of all shapes and sizes characterize the wine districts around Bordeaux. The only modern city of major importance in the region, Bordeaux is worth a visit for its elegant 18th-century architecture as well as for its rich cultural life. The vast manmade forest of Les Landes also adds to this greatly undervalued corner of France.

Beach life in Bassin d'Arcachon on the Côte d'Argent

## Getting Around

The region's main freeway is the A10 connecting Paris and Poitiers with Bordeaux and points east, such as Toulouse, west to Rochefort, and south to Bayonne and Spain. This road carries most of the area's heavy traffic, relieving the excellent smaller roads. Bordeaux can be reached by TGV direct from Lille (Eurostar interchange) and from Paris via the superfast TGV L'Océane, with a journey time of only 2 hours. Bordeaux, Poitiers, and La Rochelle have international airports (direct flights to UK), and Bordeaux also has coach services to most European capitals. Poitiers has buses to nearby towns.

**For keys to symbols** *see back flap*

Saum

Argenton-
Château
Mauléon

THO

N149

Bressuire

Airv

Moncoutant

PARTHENAY

Secondigny

Champdeniers

Ma
l'

D148

Coulon

**3**

NIORT

**4**

Ce

Marans

MARAIS POITEVIN

N11

*Île de Ré*
Saint-Martin-de-Ré

A10

MELL

LA ROCHELLE **16**

Surgères

POITO

Saint-Denis-
d'Oléron

*Île
d'Aix*
N137

**15**
Au

ÎLE-D'OLÉRON **18**

ROCHEFORT **17**

Saint-Je
d'Angél

BROUAGE **19**

D733

A837

Saint-Trojan

Marennes

SAINTES

La Tremblade

N150

**22**

*Pointe
de la Coubre*

Saujon

N141

COC

ROYAN **20**

Gémozac

Charente

**23**

Pons

*Pointe de Grave*
Soulac-sur-Mer

D730

**21**

TALMONT-
SUR-GIRONDE

Barbe

D137

Mirambeau

Montalivet-
les-Bains

D1215

Lesparre-
Médoc

PAUILLAC

Hourtin-Plage

Hourtin

**28**

A10

Saint-S

*Lac d'Hourtin-
Carcans*

Blaye

D101

D1215

Saint-André-
de-Cubzac

Co

Lacanau

Blanquefort

Libourne

Lacanau-
Océan

Mérignac

N89

Cenon

**26**

D'ARGENT

Ares

D106

BORDEAUX

BASSIN
D'ARCACHON **30**

**29**

*Parc Ornithologique
du Teich*

A62

D1

Arcachon

Gujan-
Mestras

D1010

A63

Langor

*Dune du Pilat*

D3

*Étang de Cazaux
et Sanguinet*

Sanguinet

Belin-Béliet

Biscarrosse

Moustey

Saint
Sympho

CÔTE

Labouheyre

Luxey

Mimizan-
Plage

Mimizan

*Marqueze*

Sabres

AQUITAIN

D38

Roquefort

LA

**31**

LANDES

Lévignacq

Morcenx

D834

Saint-Girons-Plage

LES

D93

*Étang de Léon*

Léon

Tartas

Midou

**32**

MONT-
MARSA

Vieux-Boucau-
les-Bains

Soustons

N10

D824

Mugron

D824

Aire-sur-
l'Adour

Capbreton

A63

**33**

DAX

Hagetmau

Pau

Bayonne
Biarritz

Adour

One of the Île de Ré's picturesque harbors

## Sights at a Glance

1. Thouars
2. Parthenay
3. Marais Poitevin
4. Niort
5. Melle
6. *Poitiers pp416–17*
7. Futuroscope
8. Abbaye de Nouaillé-Maupertuis
9. Chauvigny
10. Angles-sur-l'Anglin
11. St.-Savin
12. Montmorillon
13. Confolens
14. Charroux
15. Aulnay de Saintonge
16. La Rochelle
17. Rochefort
18. Ile d'Oléron
19. Brouage
20. Royan
21. Talmont-sur-Gironde
22. Saintes
23. Cognac
24. Angoulême
25. Aubeterre-sur-Dronne
26. *Bordeaux pp424–6*
27. Saint-Emilion
28. Pauillac
29. La Côte d'Argent
30. Bassin d'Arcachon
31. Les Landes
32. Mont-de-Marsan
33. Dax

0 kilometers  25

0 miles  25

## Key

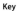

— Freeway

— Highway

— Secondary road

— Minor road

— Scenic route

— Main railroad

— Minor railroad

— Regional border

Boats moored at Coulon in the Marais Poitevin

Rose window of St.-Médard, Thouars

# ❶ Thouars

Deux-Sèvres. 🚊 10,000. 🚌 🚃
🛈 32 pl St.-Médard (05 49 66 17 65).
🛍 Tue & Fri. 🖥 **tourisme-pays-thouarsais.fr**

Thouars, on a rocky outcrop surrounded by the River Thouet, is on the border between Anjou and Poitou. There are as many roofs of northern slate as of southern red tiles.

In the center stands **Eglise St.-Médard**. Its Romanesque facade is a perfect example of the Poitevin style that is typical of the region *(see p416)*, although a splendid Gothic rose window has been added. Lined with half-timbered medieval houses, rue du Château leads up to the 17th-century château which houses a school and is open to the public April through September.

East of Thouars lies the moated **Château d'Oiron**, which now hosts contemporary art exhibitions. A masterpiece of Renaissance architecture, it was largely built from 1518 to 1549.

🏠 **Château d'Oiron**
10 rue du Château, 79100 Oiron. **Tel** 05 49 96 51 25. **Open** daily. **Closed** some public hols. 🅿️ 🏠 ♿ ground floor
🖥 **oiron.fr**

# ❷ Parthenay

Deux-Sèvres. 🚊 11,000. 🚌 🚃
🛈 8 rue de la Vau-St.-Jacques (05 49 64 24 24). 🛍 Wed. 🖥 **tourisme-gatine.com**

Parthenay is a sleepy provincial town, except on Wednesday mornings, when France's second-biggest livestock market is held here. In the Middle Ages, the town was an important halt on the route to Santiago de Compostela *(see pp404–5)*, and it is easy to imagine the processions of pilgrims in the medieval quarter. Steep, cobblestone rue de la Vau-St.-Jacques winds up to the 13th-century ramparts, leading on from the fortified Porte St.-Jacques, which guards a 13th-century bridge over the River Thouet.

West of Parthenay, the 12th-century church of **St.-Pierre de Parthenay-le-Vieux** has a splendid Poitevin facade, featuring Samson and the Lion and a cavalier with a falcon.

# ❸ Marais Poitevin

Charente-Maritime, Deux-Sèvres, Vendée. 🛫 La Rochelle. 🚊 Niort, La Rochelle. 🚌 Coulon, Arçais, Marans. 🛈 2 rue Brisson, Niort (05 49 24 18 79). 🖥 **niortmarais poitevin.com**

The Poitevin marshes, which have been slowly drained with canals, dikes, and sluices for a thousand years, cover about 309 sq miles (800 sq km) between Niort and the sea. The area is now a regional park, divided into two parts. To the north and south of the Sèvre estuary is the Marais Désséché (dry marsh), where cereal and other crops are grown. The huge swathe of the Marais Mouillé (wet marsh) is upstream toward Niort.

The wet marshes, known as the Venise Verte (Green Venice), are the most interesting. They are crisscrossed by a labyrinth of weed-choked canals, adorned by waterlilies and irises, shaded by poplars and beeches, and support a rich variety of birds and other wildlife. The *maraîchins* who live here stoutly maintain that much of the huge, water-logged forest is unexplored. The picturesque whitewashed villages hereabouts are all built on higher ground, and the customary means of trans-portation is a flat-bottomed boat, known as a *platte*.

Coulon, St.-Hilaire-la-Palud, La Garette, and Arçais, as well as Damvix and Maillezais in the Vendée, are all convenient

Medieval houses lining the cobblestone rue de la Vau-St.-Jacques in Parthenay

Flat-bottomed boats moored at Coulon in the Marais Poitevin

starting points for boat trips around the marshes. Boats can be rented with or without a guide. Be sure to bring plenty of insect repellent.

**Coulon** is the largest and best-equipped village, and a popular base for visiting the area. **La Maison du Marais Poitevin** presents an account of life in the marshes in times gone by, along with details of the wetlands' flora and fauna.

The Plantagenet donjon in Niort, now housing a local museum

## ❹ Niort

Deux-Sèvres. 🕮 60,000. 🚆 🚌 🅸 2 rue Brisson (05 49 24 18 79). 🅰 Thu & Sat. 🌐 niortmaraispoitevin.com

Once a medieval port by the green waters of the Sèvre, Niort is now a prosperous industrial town specializing in machine tools, electronics, chemicals, and insurance.

Its closeness to the marshes is evident in local specialties – eels, snails, and angelica. The last, a herb, has been cultivated in the wetlands for centuries and is used for anything from liqueur to ice cream.

The town's immediate attraction is the huge 12th-century donjon overlooking the Vieux Pont. Built by Henry II and Richard the Lion-Heart, it played an important role during the Hundred Years' War and was later used as a prison. One prisoner was the father of Madame de Maintenon (*see p62*), who spent her childhood in Niort. The donjon is

now a museum of local arts and crafts, and archeology. The **Musée d'Agesci** in avenue de Limoges exhibits ceramics, sculpture, and paintings from the 16th to 20th centuries.

### Environs
Halfway to Poitiers is the small town of **St.-Maixent-L'Ecole**. A marvel of light and space, its abbey church is a Flamboyant Gothic reconstruction by François Le Duc (1670) of a building destroyed during the Wars of Religion. Farther west, the **Tumulus de Bougon** consists of five tumuli (burial mounds), the oldest dating from 4500 BC.

## ❺ Melle

Deux-Sèvres. 🕮 4,000. 🚌 🅸 3 rue E. Traver (05 49 29 15 10). 🅰 Fri. 🌐 descouvertes. paysmellois.org

A Roman silver mine was the origin of Melle, which in the 9th century had the only mint in Aquitaine. Later its fame derived from the *baudet du Poitou*, an especially sturdy mule bred in the area. Now Melle is better known for its churches, of which the finest is **St.-Hilaire**. It has a 12th-century Poitevin facade with an equestrian statue of the Emperor Constantine above the north door.

### Environs
To the northwest, the abbey in **Celles-sur-Belle** has a great Moorish doorway, which contrasts strongly with the rest of the church, a 17th-century restoration in Gothic style.

Equestrian statue of Constantine on the facade of St.-Hilaire, Melle

A canal in the Marais Poitevin ▶

# ❻ Poitiers

Three of the greatest battles in French history were fought around Poitiers, the most famous in 732, when Charles Martel halted the Arab invasion. After two periods of English rule the town thrived during the reign of Jean de Berry (1369–1416), the great sponsor of the arts. Its university, founded in 1431, made Poitiers a major intellectual center and saw Rabelais among its students. The Wars of Religion left Poitiers in chaos, and not until the late 19th century did any major development take place. Today, however, the town is a modern and dynamic regional capital with a rich architectural heritage in its historic center.

Fresco in Eglise
St.-Hilaire-le-Grand

### 🏛 Notre-Dame-la-Grande

Despite its name, Notre-Dame-la-Grande is not a large church. One of Poitiers' great pilgrim churches, it is most celebrated as a masterpiece of lively 12th-century Poitevin sculpture, notably its richly detailed facade. In the choir is a Romanesque fresco of Christ and the Virgin. Most of the chapels were added in the Renaissance.

### 🏛 Palais de Justice

Pl Alphonse Lepetit. **Tel** 05 49 50 22 00. **Open** 8:30am–noon & 1:30–5pm Mon–Fri.

A bland Renaissance facade fronts the 12th-century great hall of the palace of Angevin kings, Henry II and Richard the Lionheart, thought to be the scene of Joan of Arc's examination by a council of theologians in 1429.

### 🏛 Cathédrale St.-Pierre

The 13th-century carved choir stalls in St.-Pierre are by far the oldest in France. Note the huge 12th-century east window

Pillars with colorful geometrical patterns in Notre-Dame-la-Grande

## Notre-Dame-la-Grande

Triangular gable

Cone-shaped pinnacles

**Christ** in Majesty is shown in the center of the gable, surrounded by symbols of the evangelists.

**Blind arcading** is a distinctive feature of the Poitevin facade.

**The portals** on the Poitevin facade are deep and richly sculpted, often showing a pronounced Moorish influence.

**The 12 apostles** are represented by statues in the arcatures, together with the first bishop St. Hilaire and his disciple St. Martin.

showing the Crucifixion. The tiny figures of the cathedral's patrons (Henry II and Eleanor of Aquitaine) are crouched at the foot of the window. Its organ (1787–91), made by François-Henri Cliquot, is one of the finest in Europe.

### 🏛 Espace Mendès France

1 pl de la Cathédrale. **Tel** 05 49 50 33 08. **Open** 9am–6:30pm Tue–Fri, 2–6:30pm Sat & Sun. **Closed** Jan 1, Sun in Jul–Aug. 🅿

A state-of-the-art planetarium here has laser shows to explain the mysteries of the universe, plus events and exhibitions.

### 🏛 Baptistère St.-Jean

Rue Jean Jaurès. **Open** Tue–Sun; mid-Jun–Sep: daily. 🅿

The polygonal 4th-century baptistery is one of France's oldest Christian buildings, where many of the earliest converts were baptized. Now a museum, it has Romanesque frescoes of Christ and Emperor Constantine, and some Merovingian sarcophagi.

### 🏛 Musée Sainte-Croix

3bis rue Jean Jaurès. **Tel** 05 49 41 07 53. **Open** Tue–Sun. **Closed** some public hols. 🅿 🔲

Musée Sainte-Croix exhibits prehistoric, Gallo-Roman, and

### VISITORS' CHECKLIST

**Practical Information**
Vienne. 🅼 91,000. 🅸 45 pl Charles de Gaulle (05 49 41 21 24). 🅐 Sat, Tue & Thu. 🅰 Les Expressifs (Oct). 🔲 ot-poitiers.fr

**Transport**
✈ 3 miles (5 km) W Poitiers. 🚆

medieval archeology, and a wide range of paintings and 19th-century sculpture. Seven bronzes by Camille Claudel are on show, including *La Valse*. There is also a collection of contemporary art.

### 🏛 Eglise St.-Hilaire-le-Grand

Fires and reconstructions have made St.-Hilaire a mosaic of different styles. With its origins in the 6th century, the church still displays an 11th-century bell tower and a 12th-century nave.

### 🏛 Médiathèque François Mitterrand

4 rue de l'Université. **Tel** 05 49 52 31 51. **Open** Tue–Sat. **Closed** public hols.

This modern building, located in the historic quarter, is home to the **Maison du Moyen Age**, which displays a collection of medieval manuscripts, maps, and engravings.

One of Futuroscope's most popular attractions: Europe's largest movie screen

## ❼ Futuroscope

Av René Monory, Chasseneuil-du-Poitou, Jaunay-Clan. 🅿 **Tel** 05 49 49 11 12. **Open** daily. **Closed** Jan–early Feb. 🅿 🔲 🔲 🔲 🔲 futuroscope.com

Futuroscope is a fantastic theme park 4 miles (7 km) north of Poitiers, exploring visual technology in a futuristic environment. Attractions evolve yearly and include simulators, 3-D and 360-degree screens, and the "magic carpet" movie theater, in which one of its screens is on the floor, creating the sensation of flying.

## Poitiers City Centre

① Notre-Dame-la-Grande
② Palais de Justice
③ Cathédrale St.-Pierre
④ Espace Mendès France
⑤ Baptistère St.-Jean
⑥ Musée Sainte-Croix
⑦ Eglise St.-Hilaire-le-Grand

For keys to symbols *see back flap*

The castle ruins of Angles-sur-l'Anglin, with the old watermill in the foreground

## ❽ Abbaye de Nouaillé-Maupertuis

Vienne. **Tel** 05 49 55 35 69. Church: **Open** 9am–6pm (7pm in summer). ♿ ◻ summer only.

On the banks of the River Miosson lies the Abbaye de Nouaillé-Maupertuis. First mentioned at the end of the 7th century, the abbey became independent in the late 700s and followed the Benedictine rule. The church was built at the start of the 12th century and reconstructed several times. Behind the altar is the 11th-century sarcophagus of St.-Junien, with three great eagles painted on the front.

More interesting is the nearby battlefield, scene of the great English victory at Poitiers Nouaillé by the Black Prince in 1356. The view has altered little since the 14th century. Drive down the small road to La Cardinerie (to the right off the D142), which leads to the river crossing at Gué de l'Omme, the epicenter of the battle. There is a monument commemorating the battle halfway up the hill, where the heaviest fighting took place and where the French king Jean le Bon was captured. He had put up a heroic resistance with only his battle-axe and his small son Philippe to tell him where the next English knight was coming from.

## ❾ Chauvigny

Vienne. 🚂 7,000. 🚌 ℹ 5 rue St.-Pierre (05 49 46 39 01). ♿ Tue, Thu, Sat. 🅦 **tourisme-chauvigny.com**

Chauvigny, on its steep promontory overlooking the broad River Vienne, displays the ruins of no fewer than four fortified medieval castles. Stone from the local quarry was so plentiful that nobody ever bothered to demolish earlier castles for building material.

Nevertheless, the best thing in this town is the 11th- to12th-century **Eglise St.-Pierre**, whose decorated capitals are a real treasure – particularly those in the choir stalls. The carvings represent biblical scenes along with monsters, sphinxes, and sirens. Look for the one that says

Monster capitals in the Eglise St.-Pierre in Chauvigny

*Gofridus me fecit* (Gofridus made me), with wonderfully natural scenes of the Epiphany.

### Environs

Nearby is the lovely **Château de Touffou**, a Renaissance dream on the banks of the Vienne, with terraces and hanging gardens.

🏰 **Château de Touffou** Bonnes. **Tel** 05 49 56 40 08. **Open** only by guided tour. Apr–Sep: 10am–noon, 2–6pm Sat & Sun; ♿ 🅦 **touffou.com**

## ❿ Angles-sur-l'Anglin

Vienne. 🚂 380. ℹ 2 rue du Four Banal (05 49 48 86 87). Roc-aux-Sorciers: 2 Les Certaux, 05 49 83 37 27. 🅦 **anglessuranglin.com**

The village of Angles lies in a stunning riverside setting, dominated by its castle ruins. Adding to the charm is an old watermill by the slow-running River Anglin, graced by waterlilies and swaying reeds.

Angles is famous for its tradition of fine needlework, the *jours d'Angles*, which is determinedly maintained by the local women today.

Located just outside the village is the Roc-aux-Sorciers, a sculpted rock shelter which dates back 15,000 years and is one of the world's most important Paleolithic cave art sites.

# ❶ St.-Savin

Vienne. 🗺 900. 🚍 🚹 20 pl de la
Libération (05 49 84 30 00). 🕙 Fri. 🔳
🌐 **saintsavin.com**

The glory of St.-Savin is its
11th-century abbey church
with its slender Gothic spire
and huge nave.

The abbey had enormous
influence until the Hundred Years'
War, when it was burned down.
It was later pillaged several times
during the Wars of Religion.
Despite restoration work by
monks in the 17th century and
again in the 19th century, the
church appears quite untouched.

Its interior contains the most
magnificent series of 12th-
century Romanesque frescoes
in Europe. These wallpaintings
were among the very first in
France to be classified as a
*monument historique* in 1836.
Some of the frescoes were
restored in 1967–74 and have
been protected by UNESCO
since 1983. A full-scale replica of
the St.-Savin murals can be seen
at the Palais de Chaillot in Paris
*(see pp114–15)*. The abbey-
museum explains the historical
context and techniques of
these murals.

The Gothic spire of St.-Savin

# ❷ Montmorillon

Vienne. 🗺 6,500. 🚍 🚹 2 pl du
Maréchal Leclerc (05 49 91 11 96).
🕙 Wed; la Foire des Hérolles: 29th
of each month (28th in Feb).
🌐 **tourisme-montmorillon.fr**

Montmorillon, built on the River
Gartempe, has its origins in the
11th century. Like most towns
in the region, it had a difficult
time during the Hundred Years'
War and the Wars of Religion.
Some buildings survived, such
as **Eglise Notre-Dame**, which
has beautiful frescoes in its

12th-century crypt (contact the
tourist office for key). These
include scenes from the life
of St. Catherine of Alexandria.

**Environs**
A short walk from the Pont de
Chez Ragon, south of Montmorillon, is the **Portes d'Enfer**,
a dramatically shaped rock above
the rapids of the Gartempe.
In nearby Coulonges, the animal
market **la Foire des Hérolles**
draws people from across France.

# ❸ Confolens

Charente. 🗺 2,900. 🚍 🚹 8 rue
Fontaine des Jardins (05 45 84 14 08).
🕙 Wed & Sat. 🌐 **mairie-confolens.fr**

On the border with Limousin,
Confolens was once an
important frontier town but now
suffers from rural exodus. Efforts
to prevent the town's isolation
include the annual international
folklore festival. Every August
the town is transformed by a
mix of music, costumes, and
crafts from all over the world.

Of historical interest is the
medieval bridge that runs across
the Vienne and was heavily
restored in the early 18th century.

# ❹ Charroux

Vienne. 🗺 1,200. 🚹 2 rte de
Chatain (05 49 87 60 12). 🕙 Thu.
🌐 **civraisiencharlois.com**

The 8th-century **Abbaye
St.-Sauveur** in Charroux was
once one of the richest abbeys
in the region. Today it is a ruin
open to the sky (call the tourist
office to arrange a visit).

Its chief contribution to history
was made in the 10th century,
when the Council of Charroux
declared the "Truce of God," the
earliest-known attempt to
regulate war in the manner of
the Geneva convention. Rules
included: "Christian soldiers may
not plunder churches, strike
priests, or steal peasants' livestock while campaigning."

A huge tower marks what was
once the center of the church,
and some superb sculpture from
the original abbey portal can be
seen in the small museum.

## St.-Savin Wall Paintings

The frescoes of St.-Savin represent Old Testament history from the
Creation to the Ten Commandments. The sequence starts to the
left of the entrance with the Creation of the stars and of Eve.
It continues with scenes from Noah's Ark to the Tower of Babel,
the story of Joseph and the parting of the Red Sea. It is believed
that all the frescoes were created by the same group of artists,
due to the similarity in style. Their harmonious colors – red, ocher,
green, black, and white – have been softened by time.

Noah's Ark, from a 12th-century wall painting in St.-Savin

## ⓭ Aulnay de Saintonge

Charente-Maritime. 🗺 1,500. 🛈 290 av de l'Eglise (05 46 32 60 71). 🛍 Thu & Sun. 🌐 saintongedoree-tourisme.com

Perhaps the most unusual fact about the lovely 12th-century **Eglise St.-Pierre** at Aulnay is that it was all built at once; there is no ill-fitting apse or transept added to an original nave. Surrounded by nothing but cypresses, it has remained the same since the time of the great pilgrimages.

The church is covered in glorious sculpture, particularly the outside of the south transept. It is a rare example of a complete Romanesque facade, with rank on rank of raucous monsters and graceful human figures. Look for the donkey with a harp. Inside the church there is a pillar decorated with elephants.

Facade of Eglise St.-Pierre at Aulnay

## ⓰ La Rochelle

Charente-Maritime. 🗺 78,000. ✈ 🚉 🚌 🛈 2 quai Georges Simenon, Le Gabut (05 46 41 14 68). 🛍 daily. 🌐 larochelle-tourisme.com

La Rochelle, a commercial center and busy port since the 11th century, has suffered much from a distressing tendency to back the wrong side – the English and the Calvinists, for example. This led to the ruthless siege of the city by Cardinal Richelieu in 1628, during which 23,000 people starved to death. The walls were destroyed and the city's privileges withdrawn.

Tour St.-Nicolas in La Rochelle

The glory of La Rochelle is the old harbor surrounded by stately buildings. The harbor is now the biggest yachting center on France's Atlantic coast. On either side of its entrance are **Tour de la Chaîne** and **Tour St.-Nicolas**. A huge chain used to be strung between them to ward off attack from the sea.

La Rochelle is easy to explore on foot, though its cobblestone streets and arcades can be congested in high summer. To get an overview, climb the 15th-century **Tour de la Lanterne**. Its inner walls were covered in graffiti by prisoners, mostly mariners, in the 17th–19th centuries. Ships are the most common motif.

The study of the 18th-century scientist Clément Lafaille is preserved in the renovated **Muséum d'Histoire Naturelle**, complete with shell collection and display cabinets. There are also stuffed animals and African masks. The town's relation to the New World is treated in the **Musée du Nouveau Monde**. Emigration, commerce, and the slave trade are explained through old maps, paintings, and artifacts.

The **Bunker of Rochelle** is well worth a visit. Constructed in secret for World War II submarine commanders, it has remained in its original condition for more than 70 years.

Next to the Vieux Port is the huge **Aquarium**. Transparent tunnels lead through tanks with different marine biotopes, including sharks and turtles.

🏛 **Tours de la Rochelle**
Rue des Murs, Le Port. **Tel** 05 46 41 74 13. **Open** daily. **Closed** Jan 1, May 1, Dec 25. 🗲 🏛 🌐 tours-la-rochelle.fr

🏛 **Muséum d'Histoire Naturelle**
28 rue Albert Premier. **Tel** 05 46 41 18 25. **Open** Tue–Sun. **Closed** Jan 1, May 1, Jul, 14 Nov 1 & 11, Dec 25. 🗲 🚹 🌐 museum-larochelle.fr

🏛 **Musée du Nouveau Monde**
10 rue Fleuriau. **Tel** 05 46 41 46 50. **Open** Wed–Mon. **Closed** Sat am (Oct–Mar), Sun am, 1 Jan, 1 May, 14 Jul, 1 & 11 Nov, 25 Dec. 🗲

🏛 **Bunker de la Rochelle**
8 rue des Dames. **Tel** 05 46 42 52 89. **Open** daily. **Closed** Dec 30–mid-Feb 🗲.

🐟 **Aquarium**
Bassin des Grands Yachts, quai Louis Prunier. **Tel** 05 46 34 00 00. **Open** daily. 🗲 🚹 📷 🏛 🌐 aquarium-larochelle.com

**Environs**
Ile de Ré is a long stretch of chalky cliffs and dunes, with a rich birdlife. It is linked to the mainland by a 2-mile (3-km) bridge. Its main town, **St.-Martin-de-Ré**, has many seafood restaurants serving local oysters.

A tank with an array of marine animals at La Rochelle Aquarium

## ⓱ Rochefort

Charente-Maritime. 🗺 25,000. 🚉 🚌 🛈 av Sadi-Carnot (05 46 99 08 60). 🛍 Tue, Thu, & Sat; flea market: 2nd Thu at Cour Roy Bry. 🌐 rochefort-ocean.com

The historic rival of La Rochelle, Rochefort was purpose-built by Colbert (*see pp62–3*) in the

Phare des Baleines on the eastern point of the Ile de Ré, opposite La Rochelle

17th century to be the greatest shipyard in France, producing over 300 sailing vessels per year.

This maritime heritage can be traced in the beautifully restored **Corderie Royale** from 1670. The building houses an exhibition on ropemaking. The **Musée National de la Marine** displays models of the ships built in the arsenal.

Rochefort is also the birthplace of the writer Pierre Loti (1850–1923). His extravagant **Maison de Pierre Loti** is filled with lush souvenirs in an Oriental decor.

Outside the town is **Pont Transbordeur**, France's last transporter bridge, built in 1897 to connect Rochefort with southern points.

Napoleon, who was detained at Île d'Aix in 1814

🏛 **La Corderie Royale**
Centre International de la Mer, rue Audebert. **Tel** 05 46 87 01 90. **Open** daily. **Closed** Jan 1, 7–25, Dec 25. 🔲 🌐 **corderie-royale.com**

🏛 **Musée National de la Marine**
Pl de la Gallissonnière. **Tel** 05 46 99 86 57. **Open** daily (Oct–Mar: Wed–Mon). **Closed** Jan, May 1, Dec 25. 🌐 **musee-marine.fr**

🏛 **Maison de Pierre Loti**
141 rue Pierre Loti. **Tel** 05 46 82 91 94. **Closed** for renovation; call for information. only. 🌐 **maisondepierreloti.fr**

🏛 **Pont Transbordeur**
3 av Maurice Chupin, Parc des Fourriers. **Tel** 05 46 83 30 86. **Open** Apr–mid-Nov: daily; call for opening times. 🌐 **pont-transbordeur.fr**

### Environs
**Île d'Aix** is served by a ferry from Fouras on the mainland. Napoleon was briefly kept here before being exiled to St.-Helena. There are Napoleonic mementos in the **Musée Napoléonien**. The camel he rode in the Egyptian campaign is in the **Musée Africain**.

🏛 **Musée Napoléonien**
30 rue Napoléon. **Tel** 05 46 84 66 40. **Open** Wed–Mon (Apr–Sep: daily). **Closed** May 1.

🏛 **Musée Africain**
Rue Napoléon. **Tel** 05 46 84 66 40. **Open** Wed–Mon (Apr–Sep: daily). **Closed** May 1.

## ⑱ Île d'Oléron

Charente-Maritime. 22,000. �ᴬ La Rochelle. 🚆 Rochefort, La Rochelle, Saintes, then bus. 🚌 from La Rochelle (in summer). 🛈 22 rue Dubois Meynardie, Marennes (05 46 85 65 23). 🌐 **oleron-island.com**

Accessible from the mainland by bridge, Oléron is the second-largest French island after Corsica, and a very popular vacation resort. Its south coast, the **Côte Sauvage**, is all dunes and pine forest, with excellent beaches at Vert Bois and Grande Plage, near La Cotinière, and a series of colorful ports. The north is used for farming, fishing, and winegrowing.

The train from **St-Trojan** makes a fine excursion through dunes and woodlands to the Pointe de Maumusson (Easter–October).

## ⑲ Brouage

Charente-Maritime. 600. 🛈 2 rue de l'Hospital (05 46 85 19 16). 🌐 **hiers-brouage-tourisme.fr**

Cardinal Richelieu's fortress at Brouage, his base during the Siege of La Rochelle (1627–8), once overlooked a thriving harbour, but its wealth and population declined in the 18th century, as the ocean receded. In 1659, Marie Mancini was sent into exile here by her uncle, Cardinal Mazarin, who did not approve of her liaison with Louis XIV. The king never forgot the beautiful Marie. Even on his way back from his wedding, he stayed alone at Brouage in the room once occupied by his first great love. Today the **ramparts** are a peaceful place to stroll and admire the view.

### Environs
There are two reasons to go to Marennes, southwest of Brouage: the famous green-tinged oysters and the view from the steeple of Eglise St.-Pierre-de-Sales. Nearby is the 18th-century **Château de la Gataudière** with an exhibition of horse-drawn vehicles.

Saintes' Roman amphitheater, with the Eglise St.-Eutrope in the background

# ❷⓿ Royan

Charente-Maritime. ⛰ 19,000. 🚊
🚌 ⛴ to Verdon only. 🛈 1 bd de la
Grandière (05 46 23 00 00). 📅 Tue–
Sun; daily in summer. 🌐 **royan-tourisme.com**

Badly damaged by Allied bombing in World War II, Royan is now thoroughly modern and different in tone from the rest of the towns on this weather-beaten coast. With five beaches of fine sand, here called *conches*, it becomes a heavily populated resort in the summer months.

Built between 1955 and 1958, **Eglise Notre-Dame** is a remarkable early example of reinforced concrete architecture. Its interior is flooded with color and light by the stained-glass windows.

The outstanding Renaissance **Phare de Cordouan**, visible in the distance from the coast, offers a change from all the modern architecture. Various lighthouses have been erected on the site since the 11th century. The present one was finished in 1611, with a chapel inside. The construction was later reinforced and heightened. Since 1789, nothing has changed but the lighting method. Boat trips in summer ferry visitors to Phare de Cordouan from Royan harbor.

# ❷❶ Talmont-sur-Gironde

Charente-Maritime. ⛰ 100. 🛈 rue de l'Église (05 46 90 16 25).
🌐 **talmont-sur-gironde.fr**

The tiny Romanesque **Eglise Ste.-Radegonde** is perched on a spit of land overlooking the Gironde. Built in 1094, the church's apse was designed to resemble the prow of a ship – which is apt, since the nave has already fallen into the estuary. A 15th-century facade closes off what's left. Inside are richly decorated capitals, including a tableau of St. George and the Dragon.

Talmont is a jewel of a village, packed full of little white houses and colorful hollyhocks in summer.

# ❷❷ Saintes

Charente-Maritime. ⛰ 27,000. 🚊 🚌
🛈 Pl Bassompierre (05 46 74 23 82).
📅 Tue–Sun. 🌐 **saintes-tourisme.fr**

Capital of the Saintonge region, Saintes has an extraordinarily rich architectural heritage. For centuries it boasted the only bridge over the lower Charente, well used by pilgrims on their way to Santiago de Compostela. The Roman bridge no longer exists, but you can still admire the magnificent **Arc de Germanicus** (AD 19), which used to mark its entrance.

On the same side of the river is the beautiful **Abbaye aux Dames**. Consecrated in 1047, it was modernized in the 12th century. During the 17th and 18th centuries noble ladies were educated here. Look for the decorated portal and the vigorous 12th-century head of Christ in the apse.

On the left bank is the 1st-century Roman **amphitheater**. Farther away lies the rather unknown gem, **Eglise St.-Eutrope**. In the 15th century, this church had the misfortune to effect a miraculous cure of the dropsy on Louis XI. In a paroxysm of gratitude, he did his best to wreck it with ill-considered Gothic additions. Luckily, its rare Romanesque capitals have survived.

Arc de Germanicus in Saintes

# ❷❸ Cognac

Charente. ⛰ 19,000. 🚊 🚌 🛈 16
rue du 14 Juillet (05 45 82 10 71). 📅
Tue–Sun. 🌐 **tourism-cognac.com**

Wherever you spot the black lichen stains from alcohol evaporation on the exterior of the buildings in this river port,

Necropolis in the monolithic Eglise St.-Jean in Aubeterre-sur-Dronne

you may be sure that you are looking at a storehouse of cognac.

All the great cognac houses do tours – a good one is at **Cognac Otard** in the 15th- to 16th-century château where François I was born. The distillery was established in 1795 by a Scot named Otard, who demolished an old chapel in the process. Luckily, much of the Renaissance architecture was saved and can be seen during the tour, which includes a cognac tasting.

*Cognac in traditional snifter*

The basic material for cognac is local white wine low in alcohol, which is then distilled. The resultant pale spirit is aged in oak barrels for 4–40 years before being bottled. The skill lies in the blending – therefore the only guide to quality is the name and the duration of ageing.

**Cognac Otard**
Château de Cognac, 127 bd Denfert-Rochereau. **Tel** 05 45 36 88 86. **Open** daily. **Closed** Jan, May 1 & public hols in winter. 🐾 🛈 obligatory.
W **baronotard.com**

## ❷❹ Angoulême

Charente. 🏠 45,000. 🚉 🚌 🛈 7 bis rue du Chat (05 45 95 16 84). 🛍 daily.
W **angouleme-tourisme.com**

The celebrated 12th-century **Cathédrale St.-Pierre**, which dominates this industrial center, is the fourth to be built on the site. One of its most interesting features is the Romanesque frieze on the facade. The cathedral's liturgical treasures are on show in a stunning display designed by contemporary artist Jean-Michel Othoniel. Some restoration work to the cathedral was carried out by the 19th-century architect Abadie. In his eagerness to wipe out all details added after the 12th century, he destroyed a 6th-century crypt. Unfortunately, he was also let loose on the old château, transforming it into a Neo-Gothic **Hôtel de Ville** (town hall). However, the 15th-century tower, where Marguerite d'Angoulême, sister of François I, was born in 1492, still stands. A statue of her can be seen in the garden. She spoke six languages, had a major role in foreign policy and wrote a popular work, *Heptaméron*. The ramparts offer a bracing walk with views over the Charente Valley.

Angoulême has become the capital of comic book *(bande dessinée)* art, hosting the prestigious Festival de la Bande Dessinée (Jan/Feb). The **Cité Internationale de la Bande-Dessinée et de l'Image** has a reference collection of French print and movie cartoons dating to 1946. From here, a footbridge leads to the Musée de la Bande Dessinée, where the art form's history, techniques, and aesthetics are explained.

**Cité Internationale de la Bande-Dessinée et de l'Image**
121 rue de Bordeaux. **Tel** 05 45 38 65 65. **Open** Tue–Sun (w/e pms only). **Closed** public hols. 🐾 🛈 🛈 🛈 🛈 📷 Cinema: W **citebd.org**

## ❷❺ Aubeterre-sur-Dronne

Charente. 🏠 420. 🚌 🛈 8 pl du Champ de Foine (05 45 98 57 18). 🛍 Sun. W **sudcharentetourisme.fr**

The chief ornament of this pretty white village is the staggering monolithic **Eglise St.-Jean**. Dug out of the white chalky cliff that gave the village its name (Alba Terra – White Earth), some parts of it date back to the 6th century. Between the Revolution and 1860, it served as the village's cemetery. It contains an early Christian baptismal font and an octagonal reliquary.

The Romanesque Eglise St.-Jacques is also of note for its fine sculpted facade.

Detail from the Romanesque facade of Cathédrale St.-Pierre in Angoulême

# ㉖ Street by Street: Bordeaux

Built on a curve of the River Garonne, Bordeaux has been a major port since pre-Roman times and for centuries a crossroads of European trade. Today Bordeaux shows little visible evidence of the Romans, Franks, English, or the Wars of Religion that have marked its past. This forward-looking town, the seventh largest in France and a UNESCO World Heritage site, is an industrial and maritime sprawl surrounding a noble 18th-century center.

Along the waterfront of this wealthy wine metropolis is a long sweep of elegant Classical facades, first built to mask the medieval slums behind. Adding to the magnificence are the Esplanade des Quinconces, the Grand Théâtre and the place de la Bourse.

Eglise Notre-Dame, built 1684–1707

RUE CONDILLA

COURS DE L'INTENDANCE

RUE MAUTREC

ALLEES DE T

RUE STE CATHERINE

PL DE LA COMEDIE

COURS DU 30 JUIL

RUE ST REMI

COURS DU CHAPEAU ROUGE

RUE ESPRIT DES LOIS

ALLEE D'ORLEA

PL DE LA BOURSE

LA GARONNE

**★ Grand Théâtre**
Built in 1773–80, the theater is a masterpiece of the Classical style, crowned by nine statues of the muses.

**Key**

— Suggested route

0 metres        100
0 yards        100

To Porte Cailhou

**The _quais_**, lined with graceful facades, make a beautiful walk along the Garonne.

**★ Place de la Bourse**
This elegant and harmonious square is flanked by two majestic 18th-century buildings, Palais de la Bourse and Hôtel des Douanes. In front of them, next to the river, is the Miroir d'Eau water feature.

*For hotels and restaurants in this region see pp565–6 and pp594–6*

★ **Esplanade des Quinconces**
Replacing the 15th-century Château de Trompette, this vast space of tree-lined esplanades with statues and fountains was created in 1827–58.

**Quartier des Chartrons**, the old merchants' quarter, has fine 18th-century buildings.

COURS DE TOURNON

RUE BOUDET

COURS DE GOURGUE

LE DES QUINCONCES

COURS DU MARECHAL FOCH

RUE VAUBAN

ESPLANADE DES QUINCONCES

ALLEE DE BRISTOL

ALLEE DE CHARTRES

RUE FOY

RUE FERRERE

UAI LOUIS XV111

**Terraces** provide good views over the river.

**The Monument aux Girondins** is a richly adorned monument (1804–1902). It commemorates the Girondists sent to the guillotine by Robespierre during the Terror (1793–4).

**CAPC Musée d'Art Contemporain**
This museum of contemporary art and cultural center is in an early 19th-century warehouse.

## The Bordeaux Wine Trade

Transporting wine barrels in 19th-century Aquitaine

After Marseille, Bordeaux is the oldest trading port in France. From Roman times the export of wine was the basis for a modest prosperity, but under English rule (1154–1453, *see pp56–9*), the merchants began making immense fortunes from their monopoly of wine sales to England. After the discovery of the New World, Bordeaux took advantage of its Atlantic position to diversify and extend its wine market. Today the Bordeaux region produces over 60 million cases of wine per year.

## Grand Théâtre de Bordeaux

Statues of the muses

Grand staircase

Concert hall

The facade's 12 Corinthian columns

Auditorium with paneling and gilded columns

Stage

### Exploring Bordeaux

Much of central Bordeaux is grand streets and 18th-century mansions. A triangle made by cours Clemenceau, cours de l'Intendance, and allées de Tourny has chic boutiques and cafés. Cathédrale St.-André is another focal point, with good museums nearby. Both the *quais* and the Chartrons district around the Jardin Public are worth exploring.

### 🎭 Grand Théâtre

Pl de la Comédie. **Tel** 05 56 00 85 95. **Open** by appointment only. 🅿️
Built by architect Victor Louis, the 18th-century Grand Théâtre is one of the finest Classical edifices of its type in France. The auditorium is renowned for its acoustics. The grand main stair-case was later imitated by Garnier for the Paris Opéra *(see p101).*

### 🏛 Cité du Vin

quai de Bacalan. **Tel** 05 56 16 20 20. **Open** daily. **Closed** Mon in winter, Jan 1 & Dec 25. 🅿️ 🅰️ 🅿️ 🅿️ 🅿️
🅦 laciteduvin.com
The City of Wine Museum offers the opportunity to discover the world of wine-making from its origins to the present day, and includes a tasting.

### ⛪ Basilique St.-Michel

Pl Canteloup et Meynard. **Open** daily. It took 200 years to build the Basilique St.-Michel, begun in 1350. This triple-naved edifice has a remarkable statue of St. Ursula. Its freestanding belfry, built in 1472–92, is the tallest in southern France (374 ft/114 m).

### 🏛 Musée des Beaux-Arts

20 cours d'Albret. **Tel** 05 56 10 20 56. **Open** Wed–Mon. **Closed** public hols. 🅿️ 🅰️ 🅦 musba-bordeaux.fr
Housed in two wings of the Hôtel de Ville, the excellent collection of paintings here ranges from the Renaissance to the present. Masterpieces include works by Titian, Veronese, Rubens, Delacroix, Corot, Renoir, Matisse, and Boudin.

### 🏛 Musée des Arts Décoratifs

39 rue Bouffard. **Tel** 05 56 10 14 00. **Open** Wed–Mon. **Closed** public hols. 🅿️ 🅿️
If you're interested in elegant fur-nishings and fine porcelain, stop off at this exceptional collection, housed in the suitably refined 18th-century Hôtel de Lalande.

### 🏛 Musée d'Aquitaine

20 cours Pasteur. **Tel** 05 56 01 51 00. **Open** Tue–Sun. **Closed** public hols. 🅰️
🅿️ 🅿️ 🅦 musee-aquitaine-bordeaux.fr
This important museum traces life in the region from prehistoric times to the present, through

The 15th-century Porte Cailhou, once the main gate to the city of Bordeaux

artifacts, furniture, and viticulture tools. Among its exhibits are the Tayac treasure from the 2nd century BC, and the Garonne treasure, a hoard of Roman coins.

### ⛪ Cathédrale St.-André

Pl Pey Berland. **Tel** 05 56 52 68 10.
The nave of this gigantic church was begun in the 11th century and modified 200 years later. The Gothic choir and transepts were added in the 14th and 15th centuries. The excellent medieval sculptures on the Porte Royale include scenes from the Last Judgement.

### 🏛 CAPC Musée d'Art Contemporain

Entrepôt Lainé, 7 rue Ferrère.
**Tel** 05 56 00 81 50. **Open** Tue–Sun. **Closed** public hols. 🅿️ 🅰️ 🅿️
🅦 capc-bordeaux.fr
This converted 19th-century warehouse merits a visit, whatever you make of its temporary exhi-bitions and permanent collection of contemporary art.

## ㉗ Saint-Emilion

Gironde. 🗺 2,000. 🚇 🚌 🅸 pl des Créneaux (05 57 55 28 28). 🚌 Sun. 🅦 saint-emilion-tourisme.com
This charming village in the middle of the red wine district to which it gives its name, dates back to an 8th-century hermit, Emilion, who dug out a cave for himself in the rock. A monastery followed, and by the Middle Ages Saint-Emilion had become a small town. Medieval houses still line the narrow streets, and parts of the 12th-century

ramparts remain. The interior of the church dug out of the chalky cliff by followers of St. Emilion after his death is somewhat ruined by concrete columns put up to prevent its collapse.

Famous châteaux in the district include the elegant **Figeac**, **Cheval Blanc,** and **Ausone**, all of them Saint-Emilion premiers grands crus classés.

Vineyard close to Margaux in the Médoc region west of Bordeaux

## ㉘ Pauillac

Gironde. ⛰ 5,000. 🚉 🚌
ℹ La Verrerie (05 56 59 03 08).
🛍 Sat. 🌐 pauillac-medoc.com

One of the most famous areas in the Médoc wine region *(see pp402–3)* is the commune of Pauillac. Three of its châteaux are Médoc premiers grands crus classés. The **Château Mouton Rothschild** uses leading artists to create its wine labels and has a small museum of paintings on wine themes from all over the world. The **Château Lafite Rothschild** is of medieval origin, and the **Château Latour** is recognizable by its distinctive stone turret. They can be visited by appointment (contact the tourist office well in advance of your visit). The town of Pauillac is located on the west bank of the Gironde. In the 19th century it was the bustling arrival point for transatlantic steamships, but now the sleepy port is mostly used by pleasure boats. There are picturesque river views from the *quais* and plenty of cafés serving the local wine.

### Bordeaux Wine Châteaux

The château is at the heart of the quality system in Bordeaux, the world's largest fine wine region. A château includes a vineyard and a building which can range from the most basic to the grandest, most historic as well as modern. But the château is also the symbol of a tradition and the philosophy that a wine's quality and character spring from the soil. Some châteaux welcome visitors for wine tasting as well as buying. Every major wine town has a Maison du Vin, which can provide information on visits to a château.

**Latour** in Pauillac is famous for its powerful wines and the medieval stone turret that appears on its label.

**Cheval Blanc**, a great château in the Saint-Emilion area, boasts a rich, spicy premier grand cru.

**Margaux**, built in 1802, produces a classic Margaux premier cru of the same elegant proportions as its Palladian facade.

**Palmer**, dating from 1856, is Neo-Renaissance in style and produces a very fine Margaux troisième cru.

**Gruaud-Larose** is a cream-colored château with a Classical facade, distinguished by its full-bodied St.-Julien deuxième cru classé.

**Vieux Château Certan** is Belgian-owned and one of the great historic properties of Pomerol. Its wines are consistently in the first rank in the district, challenged only by Pétrus.

The immense Dune du Pilat, stretching almost 2 miles (3 km) south of the inlet to Bassin d'Arcachon

## ❷ La Côte d'Argent

Gironde, Landes. ✈ Bordeaux, Biarritz. 🚉 Soulac-sur-Mer, Arcachon, Labenne, Dax. 🚌 Lacanau, Arcachon, Mimizan. 🛈 Lacanau (05 56 03 21 01), Mimizan-Plage (05 58 09 11 20), Capbreton (05 58 72 12 11).

The long stretch of coast between Pointe de Grave on the Gironde estuary and Bayonne (see p456) is called La Côte d'Argent – the Silver Coast. It is virtually one vast beach of shifting sand dunes. Treeplanting has now slowed down their progress.

The coast is dotted with surfing resorts such as **Soulac-sur-Mer** in the north, followed by the big **Lacanau-Océan**, and **Mimizan-Plage**. Down in the south is **Hossegor** with its salty lake, and **Capbreton**. Modern vacation resorts have been integrated with the old.

Inland are lakes popular for fishing and boating. They are connected to each other and the ocean by lively waterways, such as the **Courant d'Huchet** from Etang de Léon. Boat trips are available.

## ❸ Bassin d'Arcachon

Gironde. 🚶 12,000. 🚌 to Cap Ferret. 🚉 🚌 🛈 espl Georges Pompidou (05 57 52 97 97). 🚢 daily. 🌐 arcachon.com

In the middle of the Côte d'Argent the straight coastline suddenly forms a lagoon.

Famous for its natural beauty, fine beaches, and oysters, the Bassin d'Arcachon is a protected area, perfect for vacationers, sailing enthusiasts, and oyster-eaters.

The basin is dotted with smaller amorphous resorts, beaches, and fishing/oyster villages, all worth exploring. **Cap Ferret**, the northern headland that protects the basin from stiff Atlantic winds, is a preserve of the wealthy, whose luxurious villas stand among the pines. Look for the small road under the trees from Lège, which leads to the wild, magnificent beach of Grand-Crohot.

Between Cap Ferret and Arcachon, near Gujan-Mestras, the **Parc Ornithologique du Teich** provides care and shelter for damaged birds and endangered species. For the birdwatcher, there are two fascinating walks, each carefully marked: an introductory one,

and another of greater length. Both provide concealed observation points from which people can watch the wildfowl without disturbing them.

**Arcachon** was created as a beach resort in 1845. Its popularity grew, and in the late 19th and early 20th centuries the elegant villas in Ville d'Hiver were built. The livelier Ville d'Eté, facing the lagoon, has a casino and sport amenities.

The immense **Dune du Pilat** is the largest sand dune in Europe. It is nearly 2 miles (3 km) long, 340 ft (104 m) high, and 1,625 ft (500 m) wide. Aside from the view, the dune is a great vantage point in the fall for viewing flocks of migratory birds, as they pass overhead on their way to the sanctuary at Le Teich.

🗺 **Parc Ornithologique du Teich** Le Teich, rue du Port. **Tel** 05 56 22 80 93. **Open** daily. 🅿 ♿ 🖥 📷 🌐 **reserve-ornithologique-du-teich.com**

Parc Ornithologique du Teich, a bird sanctuary in Bassin d'Arcachon

## Landes Forest

The vast, totally artificial 19th-century forest of Les Landes was an ambitious project to make use of an area of sand and marshes. Pines and grasses were planted to anchor the coastal dunes, and inland dunes were stabilized with a mixture of pines, reeds, and broom. In 1855 the land was drained – it is now covered with pine groves and undergrowth, preserving a delicate ecological balance.

Pine trees in the Landes forest

# ❸ Les Landes

Gironde, Landes. ✈ Bordeaux, Biarritz. 🚊 Morcenx, Dax, Mont-de-Marsan. 🚌 Mont-de-Marsan. 🛈 Mont-de-Marsan (05 58 05 87 37).

Almost entirely covered by an immense pine forest, the Landes area extends over the two *départements* of Gironde and Landes. The soil here is uniformly sandy. Until the mid-19th century the whole region became a swamp in winter, because of a layer of tufa (porous rock) just under the surface which retained water from the brackish lakes. Any settlement or agriculture close to the sea was impossible due to the constantly shifting dunes. Furthermore, the mouth of the Adour river kept moving from Capbreton to Vieux-Boucau and back, a distance of 20 miles (32 km).

The Adour was fixed near Bayonne by a canal in the 16th century. This was the start of the slow conquest of the Landes. The planting of pine trees ultimately wiped out the migrant shepherds and their flocks. Today, the inner Landes is

still very underpopulated, but wealthy from its pinewood and pine derivatives. The coastal strip also has a large influx of vacationers.

In 1970, part of the forest was made into a nature park. At **Marquèze**, in the **Ecomusée Marquèze**, a typical 19th-century *airial* (clearing) has been restored. It commemorates the vanished world of Les Landes before the draining of the marshes, when shepherds still used stilts to get around. There are traditional *auberges landaises* (wooden houses with sloping roofs), as well as henhouses built on stilts because of foxes.

### 🏛 Ecomusée Marquèze
Rte de la Gare, 40630 Sabres. **Tel** 05 58 08 31 31. **Open** Apr–Oct: daily. 🎫 📷 ♿ 🖥 🌐 **marqueze.fr**.

# ❸ Mont-de-Marsan

Landes. 🏙 33,000. 🚊 🚌 🛈 1 pl Charles de Gaulle (05 58 05 87 37). 🛒 Tue & Sat. 🌐 **visitmontdemarsan.fr**

A bullfighting mecca, Mont-de-Marsan attracts all the great bullfighters of France and Spain in summer. A less-bloodthirsty local variant of the sport is the *course landaise*, in which the object is to vault over the horns and back of a charging bull.

The administrative capital of the Landes is also known for its hippodrome, poultry farming, and *foie gras* production.

Sculpture from the first half of the 20th century can be seen at **Musée Despiau-Wlérick**.

# ❸ Dax

Landes. 🏙 22,000. 🚊 🚌 🛈 11 cours Foch (05 58 56 86 86). 🛒 Tue–Sun am. 🌐 **dax-tourisme.com**

The thermal spa of Dax is second only to Aix-les-Bains *(see p394)* in importance. Its hot springs, with a constant temperature of 147° F (64° C) and tonic mud from the Adour, have been soothing aches and pains since the time of Emperor Augustus.

Aside from the 13th-century doorway of the otherwise 17th-century **Cathédrale Notre-Dame**, there isn't much of architectural interest in this peaceful town. But the promenade along the River Adour is charming and the bullring is world renowned.

*La Force* (1937) by Raoul Lamourdedieu, in the bullfighting capital of Mont-de-Marsan

# PERIGORD, QUERCY, AND GASCONY

*Dordogne · Lot · Haute-Garonne · Lot-et-Garonne
Gers · Tarn-et-Garonne · Tarn*

Southwest France is an archeologist's heaven, The region has been continuously inhabited by mankind for tens of thousands of years, longer than any other area in Europe. The landscape of these historic regions seems to have an ancient familiarity, derived from centuries of people living in harmony with the land.

The great cave sites around Les Eyzies and Lascaux harbor the earliest evidence we possess of primitive art. The castles, bastides *(see p449)*, and churches that grace the countryside from Périgueux to the Pyrenees, from the Bay of Biscay to Toulouse, and beyond to the Mediterranean, belong to a far more recent past. From the coming of Christianity until the late 18th century, this fine region was the battlefield for a string of conflicts. The English fought and lost the Hundred Years' War *(see pp58–9)* for Aquitaine (1345–1453); this was followed by intermittent Wars of Religion, in which Catholics fought Huguenots (French Protestants) in a series of massacres and guerrilla wars.

Today, nothing is left of these old struggles but crumbling ramparts, keeps, and bastides, which are part of the region's cultural and artistic heritage, attracting thousands of visitors every year. Yet it is as well to remember that all the great sights here, from the abbey church at Moissac, whose 12th-century portal is a masterpiece of Romanesque art, to the awesome clifftop site of Rocamadour, have suffered at one time or another from the attacks of marauding soldiers.

Since the mid-20th century, the rural southwest has gone through a radical demographic shift. There has been a continual decline in the old peasant way of life with fewer and fewer people cultivating the land. A steady migration by the young to the cities has been matched by an influx of downsizers and commuters looking for a more relaxed way of life.

Périgord geese, reared for the area's celebrated *foie gras*

◄ Limestone cliffs tower over the beautiful countryside of the Gorges de l'Aveyron

# Exploring Périgord, Quercy, and Gascony

The towns of Périgueux, Cahors, and Albi make good bases for exploring the region, and are quieter alternatives to Toulouse – the only major urban center. Elsewhere, the green hills and sleepy villages of Gascony and Périgord (also known as the Dordogne) are mainly for those who appreciate the slow pace of life in the countryside. But if you want more than peace and good food, this region offers some of France's finest medieval architecture, and Europe's most important prehistoric caves, notably Lascaux.

A narrow street in the medieval hilltop town of Cordes sur Ciel

## Key

- ══ Freeway
- ══ Highway
- ━━ Secondary road
- ═══ Minor road
- ━━ Scenic route
- ┄┄ Main railroad
- ---- Minor railroad
- ━━ Regional border

## Getting Around

The west–southeast Autoroute des Deux Mers (A62–A61) is the main road through the region, linking Bordeaux, the Atlantic coast, and the Mediterranean. The A20 from Montauban to Limoges provides access to the Dordogne and Quercy. Buses and main railroads, including a Bordeaux–Marseille TGV, pass along the same two axes. They meet at Toulouse, where an international airport has daily flights to and from most European destinations.

**For keys to symbols** *see back flap*

## Sights at a Glance

1. St.-Jean-de-Côle
2. Hautefort
3. Brantôme
4. Bourdeilles
5. Périgueux
6. St.-Amand-de-Coly
7. Lascaux IV
8. Bergerac
9. Les Eyzies
10. Dordogne Valley
11. *Sarlat pp436–7*
12. Domme
13. *Rocamadour pp440–41*
14. Gouffre de Padirac
15. Autoire
16. Cahors
17. Agen
18. Larressingle
19. Condom
20. Auch
21. Auvillar
22. *Moissac pp446–7*
23. Montauban
24. Gorges de l'Aveyron
25. Cordes-sur-Ciel
26. Albi
27. Castres
28. *Toulouse pp450–51*

Bourdeilles on the River Dronne

0 kilometers 25

0 miles 25

# ❶ St.-Jean-de-Côle

Dordogne. 🏔 360. 🛈 19 rue
du Château (05 53 62 14 15).
🎭 Floralies (Apr–May).
🌐 perigordgourmand.com

St.-Jean-de-Côle's medieval,
humpbacked bridge gives the
best view of this lovely Dordogne
village set in hilly countryside.
Stone and half-timbered houses,
roofed with the distinctive red-
brown tiles of the region, cram
the narrow streets around the
main square. Here stand a
covered marketplace, château,
and 12th-century church.

The cupola of the church
used to be the largest in the
region – too large, it seems, for
it fell down twice in the 18th
and 19th centuries. The second
time it happened, the builders
gave up, and there has been a
plank ceiling ever since.

Main square in the lovely village of
St.-Jean-de-Côle

# ❷ Hautefort

Dordogne. **Tel** 05 53 50 51 23.
Le Bourg: **Open** Apr–Sep: daily (Mar &
early Nov: Sat, Sun & hols, pm only;
Oct: daily, pm only). **Closed** mid-Nov–
Feb. 🗺 🎥 obligatory. ♿ limited.
🌐 chateau-hautefort.com

Hautefort clings to the sides of a
steep hill topped by a massive
17th-century château, one of
the finest in southwest France.
Partially fortified and built as a
pleasure palace in honor of
King Louis XIII's secret love, the
Marquis de Hautefort's sister
Marie, the castle sits among
French gardens on terraces with
superb views of the rolling
countryside of northeast Périgord.
In the village, the hospice, of a
similar date, has a museum of
early medical implements.

Brantôme Abbey

# ❸ Brantôme

Dordogne. 🏔 2,200. 🚌 🛈 Notre
Dame church (05 53 05 80 63). 🗓 Fri.
🌐 perigord-dronne-belle.fr

Surrounded by the River Dronne,
Brantôme is often called the
Venice of the Périgord Vert. Its
medieval abbey and 11th-
century belfry (reputedly the
oldest in France), together with
the verdant rockface behind,
provide a dramatic backdrop
for this picturesque town.

The poet Pierre de Bourdeille
(1540–1614) was appointed
abbot here in his youth. His lovers
allegedly included Mary, Queen
of Scots. After a crippling fall,
Bourdeille retired here in 1569 to
write his racy memoirs. It is possible to wander the stone staircases
and cloisters, and through the
main courtyard to the troglodyte
dwellings in the cliff behind. In one
are two scenes (the Last Judgment
and the Crucifixion) that were
cut into the stone between the
16th and 17th centuries.

Just 7 miles (12 km) northeast
lies the Renaissance **Château
de Puyguilhem** and **Grotte de
Villars**. As well as spectacular
rock formations, these caves
house some marvelous
19,000-year-old cave paintings.

🏰 **Château de Puyguilhem**
Villars. **Tel** 05 53 54 82 18. **Open**
Apr–Sep: daily; Oct–Mar: Wed–Sun.
**Closed** Jan 1, May 1, Nov 1 & 11,
Dec 25. 🗺 ♿ 🎥 🚫 🌐 chateau-
puyguilhem.fr

🏰 **Grotte de Villars**
Villars. **Tel** 05 53 54 82 36. **Open** Apr–
mid-Nov: daily. 🗺 🎥 obligatory.
🌐 grotte-villars.com

# ❹ Bourdeilles

Dordogne. 🏔 800. 🛈 63 place
Tilleuls (05 53 05 62 43). 🌐 perigord-
dronne-belle.fr

This town may be small, but it
has much to offer – a Gothic
bridge with cutwater piers, a
mill, and a medieval **château**.
The 16th-century additions
to the castle were designed
in a hurry by the châtelaine
Jacquette de Montbron, when
expecting a visit from Queen
Catherine de' Medici. After the
royal visit was called off, so
were the building works. The
highlight is the gilded salon,
decorated in the 1560s by
Ambroise le Noble, of the
Fontainebleau School.

🏰 **Château de Bourdeilles**
**Tel** 05 53 03 73 36. **Open** Feb–Mar &
Nov–mid-Dec: Tue–Sun; Apr–Oct:
daily. **Closed** Jan. 🗺 🎥 🏠 🖼
🌐 semitour.com

The impressive Château de Bourdeilles towering above the town

Périgueux's Cathédrale St.-Front, restored in the 19th century

## ❺ Périgueux

Dordogne. 🅼 32,000. 🚆 🚌 🅿
ℹ 26 pl Francheville (05 53 53 10 63).
📅 daily. 🆆 **tourisme-perigueux.fr**

The ancient and truly gastronomic city of Périgueux, like its neighbors Bergerac and Riberac, should be visited on market day, when stands in the lively squares in the medieval part of town offer the pick of local specialties, including truffles (Nov–Mar), *charcuterie*, and the succulent pies called *pâtés de Périgueux*.

Périgueux, now the busy regional capital, has long been the crossroads of Périgord. The earliest part remaining today is the quarter known as **La Cité**, once the important Gallo-Roman settlement of Vesunna. From Roman times to the Middle Ages, this was the focus of Périgueux. Most of the fabric of Vesunna was pulled down in the 3rd century, but some vestiges of a temple, a huge arena, and

a sumptuous villa remain. The **Eglise St.-Etienne** nearby dates to the 12th century. La Domus de Vesonne, a Gallo-Roman museum, is also in La Cité.

Walking up the hill to the city's dazzling white cathedral you pass through bustling streets and squares, each with its market activity. This is the medieval quarter of **Le Puy St.-Front**, which began to flourish as pilgrims on their way to Santiago de Compostela *(see pp404–5)* visited the cathedral. As they brought prestige and wealth to the quarter, it gradually eclipsed La Cité.

At the top stands the imposing **Cathédrale St.-Front**, the largest in southwestern France. The Romanesque construction was heavily restored in the 19th century, when architect Paul Abadie added the fancy domes and cones.

Elaborate 19th-century stained glass in Cathédrale St.-Front

He later used St.-Front as inspiration for the Sacré-Coeur in Paris *(see p138)*.

Other gems of medieval and Renaissance architecture include **Maison Estignard**, at No. 3 rue Limogeanne, with its unusual corkscrew staircase, and houses along rue Aubergerie and rue de la Constitution.

Also in the cathedral quarter is the **Musée d'Art et d'Archéologie du Périgord**, one of the most comprehensive prehistory museums in France, with remnants of burials dating back 70,000 years. Beautiful Roman glass, mosaics, earthenware, and other artifacts from Vesunna are in the Gallo-Roman museum.

🏛 **Musée d'Art et d'Archéologie du Périgord**
22 cours Tourny. **Tel** 05 53 06 40 70.
**Open** Wed–Mon. **Closed** public hols.
🅿 🆆 perigueux-maap.fr

## ❻ St.-Amand-de-Coly

Dordogne. **Tel** Maison du Patrimoine (09 64 01 46 39, summer only); La Mairie (05 53 51 47 85). **Open** daily.
🕐 Mon, Wed, Fri (call 05 53 50 74 32).
🆆 saint-amand-de-coly.org

This abbey church is an outstanding example of fortress architecture, built in the 12th to 13th centuries by Augustinian monks to protect their monastery. There are two lines of defence: a high stone rampart and, behind it, the arched tower of the church itself. The tower looks more like a castle keep, and was once pierced by arrow slits.

Inside, the church is beautifully simple, with pure lines, a flat ribbed vault, 12th-century cupola, a soaring nave, and a stone floor sloping up to the altar. Yet even this interior was arranged for defence, with a gallery from which enemies within the building could be attacked.

St.-Amand was damaged during the Hundred Years' War. In 1575, it survived a siege by Huguenot cavalry and a six-day bombardment by cannon. Religious life here ended after the Revolution.

# ⓫ Sarlat

Sarlat-la-Canéda possesses the highest concentration of medieval, Renaissance, and 17th-century facades of any town in France. Its prosperity was a reflection of the privileged status it was granted in return for loyalty to the French crown during the Hundred Years' War. Behind the nondescript rue de la République are narrow lanes and archways, and ancient, ocher-colored stone town houses rich in ornamental detail. Protected by law since 1962, Sarlat's buildings now form an open-air museum. The town is also famous for having one of the best markets in France.

**Place de la Liberté**
The Renaissance heart of Sarlat is now lined with luxury stores and cafés.

**Rue des Consuls** contains 15th-, 16th-, and 17th-century mansions, built for the town's middle-class merchants, magistrates, and church officials.

**Rue Jean-Jacques Rousseau** was the main street until rue de la République (known as "La Traverse") was built in the 19th century.

Walnuts, a key Périgord crop

## Sarlat Market

Every Wednesday, the great Sarlat food market is held on place de la Liberté; every Thursday organic markets meet at 5pm, and every Saturday there is a full-scale fair that attracts locals from all around. There is a daily indoor market at Eglise Sainte-Marie. Sarlat lies at the heart of the nation's *foie gras* and walnut trades. These typical Périgord products absorb much of the town's attention and supply a good proportion of its revenue, as they did during Sarlat's heyday in the 14th and 15th centuries. Other local specialties are black truffles, dug up in the woods in January, and wild mushrooms. Seek out the cheeses of every shape, age, and hue, and the huge range of pork delicacies: potted, fresh, smoked, dried, salted, fried, baked, or boiled.

Bulbs of pink garlic

Town walls

**Key**

— Suggested route

0 meters    50
0 yards     50

*(map labels: RUE PEYRAT, R DE LA CHARITE, R VICTOR H, RUE JEAN-JACQUES ROUSSEAU, RUE DE LA REPUBLIQUE, COTE DE TOULOUSE, RUE DE LA BOETIE, RUE DU SIEGE)*

**Rue de la Salamandre**
This lane was named after the salamander emblem of François I. It is seen on many of the town's 16th-century houses.

### VISITORS' CHECKLIST

**Practical Information**
Dordogne. 10,000. 3 rue Tourny (05 53 31 45 45). Wed & Sat. Theater (Jul–Aug); Film (Nov). sarlat-tourisme.com

**Transportation**
av de la Gare.

**Eglise Sainte-Marie**, built in 1365, now houses an indoor market offering local products. A panoramic elevator has been built up to the top of the church's steeple, providing a great view of Sarlat from above.

**Lanterne des Morts**
(Lantern of the Dead) The conical tower in the cemetery was built to commemorate the sermons of St. Bernard in Sarlat in August 1147.

**Cathédrale St.-Sacerdos**
Built largely in the 16th and 17th centuries, the cathedral is remarkable for its magnificent 18th-century organ.

RUE FENELON

RUE DE PRESIDIAL

RUE D'ALBUSSE

RUE MONTAIGNE

RUE TOURNY

**The Chapelle des Pénitents Bleus**, built in pure Romanesque style, is the last vestige of the 12th-century abbey.

**The former Bishop's Palace**, with remains of a 16th-century loggia and a Renaissance interior, is now a tourist office, which puts on excellent summer exhibitions.

**Cour des Fontaines**
A pure spring here attracted the monks who founded Sarlat's first abbey in the 9th century.

Replica of bulls and horses cave paintings at the Lascaux Centre International de l'Art Pariétal

## ❼ Lascaux IV

Lascaux Centre International de l'Art Pariétal, Dordogne. **Tel** 05 53 50 99 10. **Open** 9am–7pm daily. **Closed** Jan 1, Dec 25. 🅿️ 🚻 🏠 🖥️ 🛗
**W** lascaux.fr

Lascaux is the most famous of the prehistoric sites located on the River Vézère *(see pp406–7)*. Four boys came across the caves and their astonishing Palaeolithic paintings in 1940, and the importance of their discovery was swiftly recognized.

Lascaux has been closed to the public since 1963 because of deterioration, but the Centre International de l'Art Pariétal provides state-of the art replicas of the vivid cave paintings of bulls, high-antlered elk, bison, and horses. It includes an interactive exhibition using digital touchscreens that retraces the history of the discovery of Lascaux and a virtual reality tour of the caves. The on-site café serves excellent regional food.

## ❽ Bergerac

Dordogne. 🅰️ 29,000. 🚆 🚉 🚌
🛈 97 rue Neuve d'Argenson (05 53 57 03 11). 🔶 Wed & Sat; organic market: Tue. **W** bergerac-tourisme.com

This small port, a tobacco farming and commercial center, spreads itself over both sides of the Dordogne. Chief attractions are its extraordinary **Musée du Tabac** (tobacco museum), and its food and wine, which are invariably excellent. Bergerac's most celebrated wine is Monbazillac, a sweet white wine, often drunk on ceremonial occasions. On show in the small, lively museum are some Native American pipes.

🏛️ **Musée du Tabac**
Maison Peyrarède, pl du Feu.
**Tel** 05 53 63 04 13. **Open** Tue–Sun.
**Closed** Sun ams (Oct–Mar: Sun all day), public hols. 🚻 🛗

## ❾ Les Eyzies

Dordogne. 🅰️ 850. 🚉 🛈 19 av de la Préhistoire (05 53 06 97 05). 🔶 Mon (Apr–Oct). **W** lascaux-dordogne.com

Four major prehistoric sites and a group of smaller caves cluster around the unassuming village of Les Eyzies. Head first for the **Musée National de Préhistoire**, in a modern building at the foot of a 16th-century castle overlooking the village. The timelines and other exhibits are useful for putting the vast warren of prehistoric painting and sculpture into context.

The **Grotte de Font de Gaume** is the logical first stop after the museum. This cave, discovered in 1901, contains probably the finest prehistoric paintings still on public view in France.

Close by is the **Grotte des Combarelles**, with engravings of bison, reindeer, magic symbols, and human figures. Farther on, you reach the rock shelter of **Abri du Cap Blanc**, discovered in 1909,

Les Eyzies, a center for the area's concentration of prehistoric caves

with a rare, life-size frieze of horses and bison sculpted in the rock.

On the other side of Les Eyzies is the cave system at **Rouffignac**, a favorite place for excursions since the 15th century. There are 5 miles (8 km) of caves here, 1.5 miles (2.5 km) of which are served by electric train. The paintings include drawings of mammoths, and a frieze of two bison challenging each other to combat.

Tickets for the caves sell out fast, especially in summer, so arrive early or make an advance reservation. Note that tickets for Combarelles must be purchased at the Grotte de Font de Gaume.

Musée National de Préhistoire

🏛 **Musée National de Préhistoire**
Tel 05 53 06 45 65. **Open** Jul & Aug: daily; Sep–Jun: Wed–Mon. **Closed** Jan 1, Dec 25. ♿ 🅿 📷 🎧

🐾 **Grotte de Font de Gaume**
Tel 05 53 06 86 00. **Open** Sun–Fri by appt; book ahead. **Closed** some public hols.

🐾 **Grotte des Combarelles**
Tel 05 53 06 86 00. **Open** Sun–Fri (book ahead). **Closed** some public hols. ♿

🐾 **Abri du Cap Blanc**
Marquay, Les Eyzies. Tel 05 53 06 86 00. **Open** Sun–Fri. ♿ 🅿

🐾 **Grotte de Rouffignac**
Tel 05 53 05 41 71. **Open** Apr–Oct: daily (tickets at 9am and 2pm). ♿ 🅿 🎧 📷 W grotteroufignac.fr

🔟 **Dordogne Valley**

Dordogne. ✈ Bergerac. 🚂 Bergerac, Le Buisson de Cadouin. 🚌 Beynac. 🛈 Le Buisson de Cadouin (05 53 22 06 09).

Probably no river in France crosses so varied a landscape and such different geological

formations as the Dordogne. Starting in deep granite gorges in the Massif Central, it continues through fertile lowlands, then enters the limestone Causse country around Souillac. By the time the Dordogne has wound down to the Garonne, it is almost 2 miles (3 km) wide.

Don't be put off by the valley's touristy image. It is a beautiful area for wandering. Several villages make good stopping-off points, such as Limeuil, Beynac, and La Roque-Gageac, from where *gabarres* (riverboats) ferry visitors (Easter–Oct).

Perched high above the river, southwest of Sarlat, is the 17th-century **Château de Marqueyssac**. Its topiary park offers panoramic views from Domme to Beynac, and of the Château de Castelnaud on the opposite riverbank.

⓫ **Sarlat**

*See pp436–7.*

View of Domme from the medieval gateway of Porte de la Combe

⓬ **Domme**

Dordogne. 🏠 1,000. 🛈 pl de la Halle (05 53 31 71 00). 🗓 Thu. W perigord-noir-valleedordogne.com

Henry Miller wrote: "Just to glimpse the black, mysterious river at Domme from the beautiful bluff…is something to be grateful for all one's life." Domme itself is a neat bastide *(see p449)* of golden stone, with medieval gateways still standing. People come here to admire the view, which takes in the Dordogne Valley from Beynac in the west to Montfort in the east, and to wander the maze of old streets inside the walls. There is also a large cavern under the 17th-century covered market, where the inhabitants hid at perilous moments during the Hundred Years' War and the 16th-century Wars of Religion. Despite a seemingly impregnable position, 30 intrepid Huguenots managed to capture Domme by scaling the cliffs under cover of night and opening the gates.

A *cingle* (loop) of the River Dordogne, seen from the town of Domme

# ⑬ Rocamadour

Rocamadour became one of the most famous centers of pilgrimage following a spate of miracles heralded, it is claimed, by the bell above the Black Virgin and Child in the Chapel of Notre-Dame. This was followed by the discovery in 1166 of an ancient grave and sepulchre containing an undecayed body, said to be that of the early Christian hermit St. Amadour. Although the town suffered with the decline of pilgrimages in the 17th and 18th centuries, it was heavily restored in the 19th century. Still a holy shrine, as well as a popular tourist destination, Rocamadour enjoys a phenomenal site on a rocky plateau above the Alzou Valley. The best views are to be had from the ramparts of the château, reached from the hamlet of L'Hospitalet.

**General View**
Rocamadour is at its most breathtaking in the sunlight of early morning: the cluster of medieval houses, towers and battlements seems to sprout from the base of the cliff.

## KEY

① **The Tomb of St. Amadour** once held the body of the hermit called *roc amator* (lover of rock), from whom the town took its name.

② **St. Michael's Chapel** contains well-preserved 12th-century frescoes.

③ **The château** stands on the site of a fort that protected the sanctuary from the west.

④ **Ramparts**

⑤ **Cross of Jerusalem**

⑥ **The Basilica of St.-Sauveur,** a late 12th-century sanctuary, backs on to the bare rock face.

⑦ **The Chapel of St. John the Baptist** faces the fine Gothic portal of the Basilica of St.-Sauveur.

⑧ **St. Anne's Chapel** dates from the 13th century, and contains a 17th-century gilded altar screen.

⑨ **Chapel of St. Blaise** (13th century)

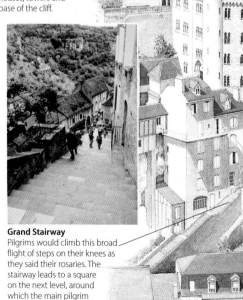

**Grand Stairway**
Pilgrims would climb this broad flight of steps on their knees as they said their rosaries. The stairway leads to a square on the next level, around which the main pilgrim chapels are grouped.

## VISITORS' CHECKLIST

**Practical Information**
Lot. 🗺 650. 🛈 L'Hospitalet,
Cour du Prieuré (05 65 33 22 00).
Chapel of Notre-Dame:
**Open** 9am–6:30pm daily
(to 9pm Jun–Sep).
Ⓦ vallee-dordogne.com

**Transportation**
🚌 3 miles (5 km) SW Rocamadour.

**Stations of the Cross**
Pilgrims encounter the Cross of
Jerusalem and 14 stations marking
Jesus's journey to the Cross on their
way up the hillside to the château.

**Rocamadour Town**
Now a traffic-free zone,
the main street is lined with
souvenir shops to tempt the
throngs of pilgrims.

**Chapel of Notre-Dame
(Miracles)**
St. Amadour's body was
found in the cliff, near
the Black Virgin Chapel.
A statue of the Black
Virgin, the supreme
object of veneration,
stands on the altar.

## ⓮ Gouffre de Padirac

Lot. **Tel** 05 65 33 64 56. **Open** Apr–mid-Nov: daily. 🅿 📷 🚻 ♿
**W** gouffre-de-padirac.com

Formed by the collapse of a cave, this huge crater measures 115 ft (35 m) wide and 337 ft (103 m) deep. The underground river and stunning succession of galleries (see pp406–7) were discovered in 1889. The immense Salle du Grand Dôme chamber dwarfs the tallest of cathedrals. Take a jacket; the cave is 55° F (13° C).

## ⓯ Autoire

Lot. 🖽 360. **i** Saint Céré (05 65 10 01 10). **W** vallee-dordogne.com

This is one of the loveliest places in Quercy, the fertile area east of Périgord. There are no grand monuments or dramatic history, just an unspoiled site at the mouth of the Autoire gorge. The **Château de Limarque** on the main square, and the **Château de Busqueille** overlooking it, are both built in characteristic Quercy style, with turrets and towers. Elsewhere, elaborate dovecotes stand in fields or are attached to houses.

Outside Autoire, past a 100-ft (30-m) waterfall, a path climbs to a rock amphitheater giving panoramic views of the region.

The picturesque village of Autoire, seen from across the gorge

## ⓰ Cahors

Lot. 🖽 21,000. 🚆 🚌 **i** pl François Mitterrand (05 65 53 20 65). 🛒 Wed & Sat am. **W** tourisme-cahors.fr

The capital of the Lot *département*, Cahors is renowned for its dark, heady wine, which was produced as far back as Roman times. It is also famous for being the birthplace of the statesman Léon Gambetta (1838–82), who led France to recovery after the war with Prussia in 1870. The main street of Cahors – like many towns in France – is named after him.

**Cathédrale de St.-Etienne**, entrenched behind the narrow streets of Cahors' Old Town, dates back to 1119. It has some fine medieval details: don't miss the lively figures of the Romanesque north door and tympanum, which depict the Ascension, or the huge cupola above the nave (said to be the

---

# A Tour of Two Rivers

Flanked by spectacular limestone cliffs, the beautiful Lot and Célé valleys feature ancient medieval villages and castles, narrow gorges, and rushing waterfalls along lazy stretches of river. An unhurried tour of both valleys, around 100 miles (160 km), is best spread over two days, to savor the gastronomic delights as well as the superb views.

From Cahors, the route follows the Lot, then meanders slowly up the peaceful and picturesque Célé Valley to reach Figeac, a handsome town full of charming stores, cafés, and restaurants. The return route is via the busier Lot Valley, which has more sights, including the spectacular village of St.-Cirq-Lapopie (allow time to park above or below the village and enter on foot).

① **Grotte de Pech-Merle**
This 29,000-year-old prehistoric site outside Cabrerets has huge chambers painted with mammoths, horses, bison, and human figures.

⑥ **St.-Cirq-Lapopie**
Perched high above the Lot, one of France's prettiest villages has a 15th-century church and timber-framed houses built into the cliffs.

largest in France). They are covered in 14th-century frescoes depicting the stoning of St. Stephen (St.-Etienne). The Renaissance cloisters are decorated with some intricate, though damaged, carvings.

Also worth seeking out in the cathedral quarter is the ornate 16th-century **Maison de Roaldès**, its north facade decorated with tree, sun, and rose of Quercy motifs. It was here that Henri of Navarre (who later became Henri IV) stayed for one night in 1580 after besieging and capturing Cahors.

The town's landmark monument is the **Pont Valentré**, a fortified bridge that spans the river. With seven pointed arches and three towers, it was built between 1308 and 1360, and has withstood many attacks since then. It is claimed that the bridge is one of the most photographed monuments in France. An alternative way to

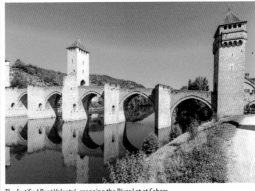

The fortified Pont Valentré, spanning the River Lot at Cahors

enjoy the scenery is to take a leisurely 90-minute boat trip through the lock from a wharf near the bridge (Apr–Oct).

**Environs**

Cahors makes a good base from which to explore the sights of the Lot. Visit the historic towns of Figeac – birthplace of Jean-

François Champollion, who first deciphered Egyptian hieroglyphics – and the **Grotte de Pech-Merle** with its extraordinary painted walls.

🏠 **Grotte de Pech-Merle**
Cabrerets. **Tel** 05 65 31 27 05.
**Open** Apr–Oct daily. 📷
🌐 **pechmerle.com**

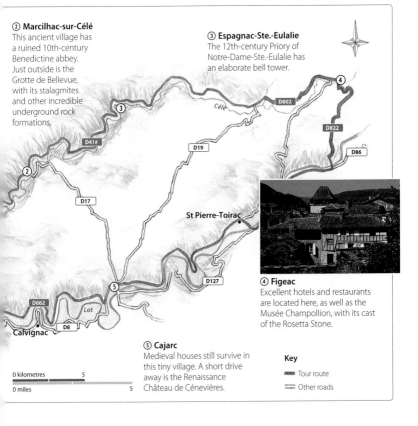

**② Marcilhac-sur-Célé**
This ancient village has a ruined 10th-century Benedictine abbey. Just outside is the Grotte de Bellevue, with its stalagmites and other incredible underground rock formations.

**③ Espagnac-Ste.-Eulalie**
The 12th-century Priory of Notre-Dame-Ste.-Eulalie has an elaborate bell tower.

Célé

D802

D822

D86

D41#

D19

D17

St Pierre-Toirac

D127

D662

Lot

D8

Calvignac

**⑤ Cajarc**
Medieval houses still survive in this tiny village. A short drive away is the Renaissance Château de Cénevières.

**④ Figeac**
Excellent hotels and restaurants are located here, as well as the Musée Champollion, with its cast of the Rosetta Stone.

**Key**
▬▬ Tour route
═══ Other roads

0 kilometres          5
0 miles               5

Orchards and vineyards outside Agen

# ⑰ Agen

Lot-et-Garonne. 35,000. ✈ 🚉
🚌 ℹ 38 rue Garonne (05 53 47 36
09. 🏛 Wed, Sat, & Sun.
🌐 **destination-agen.fr**

Vast orchards of regimented
plum trees – producing the
celebrated *pruneaux d'Agen* –
characterize the landscape
around this small provincial
city. Crusaders returning from
the Middle East brought the
fruit to France in the 11th
century, and monks in the
Lot Valley nearby were the
first to dry plums for prunes
in commercial quantities.

Agen's **Musée Municipal des
Beaux-Arts** contains paintings
by Goya, including a self-
portrait, Sisley's *September
Morning*, Corot's landscape
*L'Etang de Ville d'Avray*, and works
by Picabia. Undisputed jewel of
the collection is the *Vénus du
Mas*, a beautifully proportioned

marble statue dating from the
1st century BC, discovered
nearby in 1876.

### 🏛 Musée Municipal des Beaux-Arts

Pl du Docteur Esquirol. **Tel** 05 53 47 77
88. **Open** Wed–Mon. **Closed** Jan 1,
Easter Mon, May 1 & 8, Ascension Thu,
Nov 1 & 11, Dec 25. 🎫

### Environs

The fortified village of Moirax,
5 miles (8 km) south of Agen,
has a beautiful 12th-century
Romanesque church. Two of the
sculpted capitals depict biblical
accounts of Daniel in the lions'
den, and Original Sin.

The bastide town *(see p449)*
of Villeneuve-sur-Lot, 21 miles
(34 km) south of Agen stands
astride the River Lot. It has a tall
14th-century tower that once
formed a defensive gateway.
The red-brick Romano-Byzantine
church of Ste.-Catherine was

built in 1909 but contains
restored 15th-century stained-
glass windows. Just to the east of
Villeneuve is the pretty medieval
hilltop village of Penne D'Agenais.

# ⑱ Larressingle

Gers. 220. 🚌 to Condom.
ℹ Larressingle (05 62 68 22 49).
🌐 **tourisme-condom.com**

With its ramparts, ruined donjon
(defence tower), and fortress
gate, Larressingle is a tiny
fortified village in the middle
of the Gascon countryside. It
dates from the 13th century,
and is one of the last remaining
Gascon villages with its walls still
intact. The state of preservation
is unique, and gives an idea of
what life must have been like
for the small, embattled local
communities who had to live
for decades under conditions
of perpetual warfare.

# ⑲ Condom

Gers. 7,000. 🚌 ℹ 5 pl St-Pierre
(05 62 28 00 80). 🏛 Wed, Sat am &
Sun am. 🌐 **tourisme-condom.com**

Long a center for the Armagnac
trade, Condom is a market town
built around the late-Gothic
**Cathédrale St.-Pierre**. In 1569
during the Wars of Religion, the
Huguenot (French Protestant)
army threatened to demolish
the cathedral, but Condom's
citizens averted this by paying
a huge ransom.

The river Baïse skirts the
town center. Notable among
Condom's fine 17th- to 18th-
century mansions is the **Hôtel
de Cugnac** on rue Jean-Jaurès,
with its ancient *chai* (wine and
spirit storehouse) and distillery.
On the other side of the
town center, the **Musée de
l'Armagnac** is the place to find
out, finally, what the difference
between the brandy of
Armagnac and Cognac
really is.

### 🏛 Musée de l'Armagnac

2 rue Jules Ferry. **Tel** 05 62 28
47 17. **Open** Apr–Oct: Wed–
Mon; Nov–Mar: Wed–Sun pms.
**Closed** Jan, public hols. 🎫 📷 ♿

## Armagnac

Armagnac is one of the world's most
expensive brandies. It is also one of the
leading products of southwest France:
approximately 6.5 million bottles are produced
annually, 45 percent of which are exported to
132 countries. The vineyards of Armagnac
roughly straddle the border between
the Gers and the Lot-et-Garonne
regions, and the Landes. Similar in
style to Cognac, its more famous
neighbor, Armagnac's single
distillation leaves more individual
flavors in the spirit. The majority of
small, independent producers offer
direct sale to the public: look for
the battered, often half-hidden
farm signs advertising *Vente Directe*.

A Tenarèze Armagnac

## D'Artagnan

Gascons call their domain the "Pays d'Artagnan," after Alexandre Dumas' rollicking hero from *The Three Musketeers* (1844). The character of d'Artagnan was based on Charles de Batz, a typical Gascon, whose chivalry, passion, and impetuousness made him ideal as a musketeer, or royal bodyguard. De Batz's life was as fast and furious as that of the fictional hero, and he performed a feat of courtliness by arresting Louis XIV's most formidable minister without causing the slightest offense. The French have other opinions on the Gascon nature, too: a *promesse de Gascon,* for example, means an empty promise.

Statue of Dumas's musketeer d'Artagnan in Auch

prophets, patriarchs, and apostles, with 360 individually characterized figures and exceptional colors. Three depict the key biblical events of Creation, the Crucifixion, and the Resurrection.

Auch went through an urbanization program in the 18th century, when the allées d'Etigny, flanked by the grand Hôtel de Ville and Palais de Justice, were built. Some fine houses from this period line the traffic-free rue Dessoles. Auch's restaurants are known for their hearty dishes, including *foie gras de canard* (fattened duck liver).

## ⓴ Auch

Gers. 🚶 23,000. 🚉 🚌 🅸 1 rue Dessoles (05 62 05 22 89). 🛒 Tue am, Thu & Sat. 🆆 auch-tourisme.com

The ancient capital of the Gers department, Auch (pronounced "Ohsh") has long been a sleepy place that comes alive on market days. The new town by the train station is not a place that encourages you to linger. Head instead for the Old Town on the outcrop overlooking the River

Medallion from Cathédrale Ste.-Marie

Gers. If you climb the 234 stone steps from the river, you arrive directly in front of the restored late Gothic **Cathédrale Ste.-Marie**, begun in 1489. The furnishings of the cathedral are remarkable: highlights are the carved wooden choir stalls depicting more than 1,500 biblical, historical, and mythological characters, and the equally magnificent 15th-century stained glass, attributed to Arnaud de Moles. The windows show a mix of

## ⓴ Auvillar

Tarn-et-Garonne. 🚶 1,000. 🅸 pl de la Halle (05 63 39 89 82).

A perfect complement to the high emotion of Moissac *(see pp446–7),* Auvillar is one of the loveliest hilltop villages in France. It has a triangular marketplace lined with half-timbered arcades at its center, and extensive views from the promenade overlooking the River Garonne. There are picnic spots along this panoramic path plus an orientation map. This includes all but the chimneys visible in the distance, belonging to the nuclear facility at Golfech.

Sunflowers, a popular crop in southwest France grown for their seeds and oil

# ㉒ Moissac

At the core of this otherwise unremarkable riverside town is the abbey of St.-Pierre, one of the undisputed masterpieces of French Romanesque art. Founded in the 9th century by a Benedictine monk, the abbey was subsequently ransacked by Arabs, Normans, and Hungarians. In 1047, Moissac abbey was united with the rich foundation at Cluny and prospered under the direction of Abbot Durand de Bredon. By the 12th century it had become the preeminent monastery in southwest France. The superb south portal was created during this period.

**Abbey of St.-Pierre**
The church's exterior belongs to two periods: one part, in stone, is Romanesque; the other, in brick, is Gothic.

**Tympanum**
The lower register of the balanced, compact tympanum shows the expressive "24 Elders with crowns of gold" from St. John's vision.

**Christ in Majesty**
The figure of Christ sits in judgment at the center of the scene. He holds the Book of Life in his left hand and raises his right in benediction.

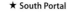

**★ South Portal**
The carved south portal (1100–1130) is a masterful translation into stone of St. John's dramatic vision of the Apocalypse (Book of Revelation, Chapters 4 and 5). The Evangelists Matthew, Mark, Luke, and John appear as "four beasts full of eyes." Moorish details on the door jambs reflect the contemporary cultural exchange between France and Spain.

★ **Cloister**
The late 11th-century cloister is
lined with alternate double and
single columns in white, pink,
green, and gray marble. In all, there
are 76 richly decorated arches.

## Floorplan: Church and Cloister

Ancienne Salle Capitulaire

Chapelle du St.-Sacrement

Musée Claustral

Sacristy

Choir

Cloister

Nave

Narthex

South Portal

**Cloister Capitals**
Flowers, beasts, and scenes from both the Old and New testaments
are featured in these superbly sculptured 11th-century
Romanesque capitals.

## ㉓ Montauban

Tarn-et-Garonne. 🏠 60,000. 🚉 🚌
ℹ️ 4 rue du Collège (05 63 63 60 60).
🛒 Wed & Sat; organic market: Thu pm.
🌐 montauban-tourisme.com

Toulouse's little pink-brick sister
and the capital of the 17th-
century "Protestant Republic" of
southern France, Montauban
was the birthplace of the painter
Jean-Auguste-Dominique Ingres
(1780–1867). The town's great
treasure is the **Musée Ingres**, a
17th-century palace with an
exceptional bequest of paintings
and 4,000 drawings, plus works
by Van Dyck, Tintoretto, Courbet,
and the sculptor Emile Bourdelle,
who was also born here.

Above all, Montauban has
a pleasant shopping area,
with a double-arcaded main
square (place Nationale) built in
the 17th and 18th centuries.
A few streets away, the stark
white **Cathédrale Notre-Dame**
was built on the orders of
Louis XIV in 1692, in the
backlash against Protestant
heresy, and houses *The Vow of
Louis XIII* by Ingres (1842).

🏛 **Musée Ingres**
Palais Episcopal, 19 rue de l'Hôtel de
Ville. **Tel** 05 63 22 12 91. **Closed** for
renovation unti 2019. 📷

## ㉔ Gorges de l'Aveyron

Tarn-et-Garonne. ✈️ Toulouse.
🚉 Montauban, Lexos. 🚌 Montauban.
ℹ️ 10 rue de la Pélisserie (05 63 30
63 47). 🌐 tourisme-saint-antonin-
noble-val.com

At the Gorges de l'Aveyron, the
sweltering plains of Montauban
change abruptly to cool, chestnut-
wooded hills. Here the villages are
of a different stamp from those
of Périgord and Quercy, displaying an obsession with defense.

The château at Bruniquel,
founded in the 6th century, is
built over the lip of a precipice.
Farther along the D115, the
village of Penne's position on
the tip of a giant rock fang is even
more extreme. The gorge narrows
and darkens; from St.-Antonin-
Noble-Val, beside the river, the
valley turns toward Cordes.

# ㉕ Cordes-sur-Ciel

Tarn. 🗺 1,000. 🚍 🚌 ℹ Maison Gaugiran, 38–42 rue Grand Raimond (05 63 56 00 52). 🛒 Sat. 🌐 **cordessurciel.fr**

Cordes-sur-Ciel is a fitting description as the town seems suspended against the skyline. During the 13th-century Cathar wars the entire town was excommunicated. Devastating epidemics of plague later sent it into decline, and the town was in an advanced state of decay at the beginning of the 20th century.

Restoration work began in the 1940s and the ramparts, and many of the gates built in 1222 have been well preserved. Also intact are Gothic houses such as the 14th-century **Maison du Grand Fauconnier**.

Today, Cordes still exudes a sense of loss. The town of which Albert Camus wrote "Everything is beautiful there, even regret," is now dependent on tourism. "Medieval" crafts aimed at visitors abound and a collection at the **Musée d'Art Moderne et Contemporain** evokes Cordes' former embroidery industry. The museum also houses works of modern art by such artists as Picasso and Miró. The **Jardin des Paradis** offers a corner of beauty and hope in which to reflect.

**🏛 Musée d'Art Moderne et Contemporain**
Maison du Grand Fauconnier.
**Tel** 05 63 56 14 79. **Open** mid-Mar–mid-Nov: Wed–Mon. 🖼 🏠

## Toulouse-Lautrec

Comte Henri de Toulouse-Lautrec was born in Albi in 1864. Crippled at 15 as a result of two falls, he moved to Paris in 1882, recording the life of the city's cabarets, brothels, racetracks, and circuses. He was a dedicated craftsman, and his bold, vivid posters did much to establish lithography as a major art form. Alcoholism and syphilis led to his early death at the age of 36.

Lautrec's *La Modiste* (1900)

Cathédrale Ste.-Cécile perched above the town of Albi

# ㉖ Albi

Tarn. 🗺 52,000. 🚍 🚌 ℹ Palais de la Berbie, pl Ste.-Cécile (05 63 36 36 00). 🛒 Tue–Sun. 🌐 **albi-tourisme.fr**

Like many large towns in this region, Albi is not only red, but also can become red hot, and not ideal for afternoon visits in summer. You need to get up in the cool early morning to walk the streets around the market and the cathedral.

Try to make for the **Musée Toulouse-Lautrec** in the Palais de la Berbie ahead of the crowds. The museum contains the most complete permanent collection of the artist's work in existence, including paintings, drawings, and his famous posters for the Moulin Rouge. There are also canvases by Matisse, Dufy, and Yves Brayer. After a stroll around the beautiful terraced gardens, step next door to the vast red-brick **Cathédrale Ste.-Cécile**, built in the aftermath of the Albigensian crusade in 1265. It was intended as a reminder to potential heretics that the Church meant business. From a distance, its semicircular towers and narrow windows give it the appearance more of a fortress than a place of worship. Every feature, from the huge bell tower to the apocalyptic fresco of the *Last Judgment*, is on a giant scale, built deliberately to dwarf the average person. The effect is breathtaking.

**🏛 Musée Toulouse-Lautrec**
Palais de la Berbie. **Tel** 05 63 49 48 70. **Open** Apr–Sep: daily; Oct–Mar: Wed–Mon. **Closed** Jan 1, May 1, Nov 1, Dec 25. 🖼 ♿ 🏠 📷
🌐 **museetoulouselautrec.net**

# ㉗ Castres

Tarn. 🗺 43,000. ✈ 🚍 🚌 ℹ 2 pl de la République (05 63 62 63 62). 🛒 Tue–Sun. 🌐 **tourisme-castres.fr**

A center for the cloth industry since the 14th century, today Castres is also the headquarters of one of France's biggest pharmaceutical companies. In the large collection of Spanish art in the **Musée Goya – Musée d'Art Hispanique**, the artist himself is well represented by a large, misty council scene and by a series of powerful prints, *Los Caprichos*. Outside, the formal gardens between the town hall and the River Agout were designed in the 17th century by André Le Nôtre *(see p183)*, the landscape architect of Vaux-le-Vicomte and Versailles.

**🏛 Musée Goya – Musée d'Art Hispanique**
Hôtel de Ville. **Tel** 05 63 71 59 30 or 05 63 71 59 27. **Open** Jul–Aug: daily; Sep–Jun: Tue–Sun. **Closed** Jan 1, May 1, Jul 14, Nov 1, Dec 25. 🖼

# Bastide Towns

Bastide towns were hurriedly built in the 13th century by both the English and the French to encourage settlement of empty areas before the Hundred Years' War. They are the medieval equivalent of modern residential developments, with planned grids of streets and fortified perimeters. Over 300 bastide towns and villages survive between Périgord and the Pyrenees.

**A broad arcaded marketplace** is the central feature of most bastides. Montauban's arcades still shelter a variety of stores.

**Lauzerte**, founded in 1241 by the Count of Toulouse, is a typical bastide town of gray stone houses. The town, long an English outpost, is perched for security on the brow of a hill.

**The church** could be used as a keep when the bastide's outer fortifications had been breached.

**The central square** is surrounded by a grid of interconnecting streets and alleys. This differs markedly from the usual jumble of medieval houses and lanes.

**Stone houses** protected the perimeter.

## Monflanquin

This military bastide town was built by the French in 1256 on a strategic north–south route. It changed hands several times during the Hundred Years' War.

**Today, the bastides** form a convenient network of market towns, known as the *route des bastides*. Enquire at the local tourist office about market days, the busiest but best time to visit.

**Porte de la Jane** in Cordes-sur-Ciel is a typical bastide feature. These narrow gateways were easily barred by portcullises.

# ❷⁸ Toulouse

Toulouse, the most important town in southwest France, is the country's fourth largest metropolis, and a major industrial and university city. The area is also famous for being the center of Europe's aerospace industry (both Concorde and Airbus originated here), as shown by the Cité de l'Espace, just outside the city.

Best seen on foot, Toulouse has fine cuisine, one of France's most striking churches, Basilique St.-Sernin, lively street life, and a rose-brick Old Town, which is described as "pink at dawn, red at noon, and mauve at dusk".

The River Garonne, crossed by the Pont Neuf

Houseboats at their moorings on the Canal du Midi

### Exploring Toulouse

This warm southern city has steadily expanded, crescent-like, from its original Roman site on the Garonne. First it was a flourishing Visigoth city, then a Renaissance town of towered brick palaces built with the wealth generated by the *pastel* (blue pigment) and grain trades. The grandest of these palaces still survive in the Old Town, centered around place du Capitole and the huge 18th-century **Hôtel de Ville**. Here, and in place St.-Georges and rue Alsace-Lorraine, is the main concentration of stores, bars, and cafés. The city's large student population keeps prices down in the numerous cafés, tapas bars, and bookstores, and in the flea market on Sundays in place St.-Aubin and allées Jules Guesde et Paul Fuegaplace.

A ring of 18th- and 19th-century boulevards encircles the city, surrounded in turn by

a tangle of *autoroutes*. The left bank of the Garonne is under development (St.-Cyprien) and is linked by Toulouse's driverless metro. The former abattoir has been superbly converted into a center for modern and contemporary art, **Les Abattoirs** (Wed–Sun), the highlight of which is Picasso's theater backdrop *Minotaur Disguised as Harlequin*.

### ⌂ Les Jacobins

Rue Lakanal. **Tel** 05 61 22 23 82.
**Open** Tue–Sun. **w** jacobins. toulouse.fr

This church was begun in 1229 and completed over the next two centuries. It was the first Dominican convent, founded to combat dissent. The Jacobins' convent became the founding institution of Toulouse University. Its church, a Gothic masterpiece, features a soaring, 22-branched palm tree vault in the apse. The delicate Chapelle St.-Antonin (1337) contains frescoes of the Apocalypse dating from 1341.

Palm vaulting in the apse of Les Jacobins

### 🏠 Fondation Bemberg

Hôtel d'Assézat, 7 pl d'Assézat.
**Tel** 05 61 12 06 89. **Open** Tue–Sun.
**Closed** Jan 1, Dec 25. 🖼 🛓 🏠 📷
🏠 **W** fondation-bemberg.fr

This 16th-century palace
houses the collection of local
art lover Georges Bemberg, and
covers Renaissance paintings,
19th- to 20th-century French
paintings and drawings,
including Impressionist, Post-
Impressionist, and Fauvist works,
objets d'art, and bronzes.

### 🏛 Musée des Augustins

21 rue de Metz. **Tel** 05 61 22 21 82. **Open**
Wed–Mon. **Closed** Jan 1, May 1, Dec 25.
🖼 🛓 📷 🏠 **W** augustins.org

Toulouse became a center of
Romanesque art due to its
position on the route to Santiago
de Compostela (see pp404–5). The
museum has sculpture from the
period and cloisters from a
14th-century Augustinian priory.
There are also 16th- to 19th-
century French, Italian, and
Flemish paintings, including
work by Ingres, Delacroix,
Constant, and Laurens.

### VISITORS' CHECKLIST

**Practical Information**
Haute-Garonne. 🗺 474,000.
🛈 Donjon du Capitole (08 92
180 180). 🏠 daily. 🎹 Piano aux
Jacobins (Sep). **W** toulouse-
tourisme.com

**Transportation**
✈ 4 miles (6 km) NW Toulouse.
🚉 🚌 bd Pierre Semard (trains:
Gare Matabiau). Guided minibus
tours: **W** citytour-toulouse.com

### 🏠 Basilique St.-Sernin

Pl St.-Sernin. **Tel** 05 61 21 80 45. **Open**
daily. **W** basilique-saint-sernin.fr

This is the largest Romanesque
basilica in Europe, built in the
11th–12th centuries to accommodate pilgrims. Highlights are the
octagonal brick belfry, with rows
of decorative brick arches topped
by an enormously tall spire. Beautiful 11th-century marble bas-
reliefs of Christ and the symbols
of the Evangelists, by Bernard
Gilduin, are in the ambulatory.

### 🏛 Cité de l'Espace

Av Jean Gonord. **Tel** 05 67 22 23 24.
**Open** Tue–Sun (daily Apr–Sep).
**Closed** Jan. 🖼 🛓 📷 🏠 🏠
**W** cite-espace.com

Southeast of the city center,
this vast "space park" includes
two planetariums, interactive
exhibits related to space
exploration, an IMAX movie
theater and a lifesize replica of
the Ariane 5 rocket. Visitors can
learn how, in theory at least, to
launch rockets and satellites.

The tiered, 12th-century tower of
Basilique St.-Sernin

## Sights at a Glance

① Les Jacobins
② Fondation Bemberg
③ Musée des Augustins
④ Basilique St.-Sernin

**For keys to symbols** see back flap

# THE PYRENEES

*Pyrénées-Atlantiques · Hautes-Pyrénées · Haute-Garonne · Ariège*

The mountains of the Pyrenees form a conspicuous frontier across southwestern France. Over centuries this remote terrain has fostered tenacious people, many descended from Spanish emigrants and refugees. Today it is the last remaining wilderness in southern Europe and a habitat for rare animal species.

Heading east from the Atlantic coast, the hills are wonderfully lush after the plains of Aquitaine. The deeper the Pyrenees are penetrated, the steeper the valley sides and the more gigantic the snow-clad peaks become. This is magnificent, empty, dangerous country, to be approached with caution and respect. In summer the region offers over 1,000 miles (1,600 km) of walking trails, as well as camping, fishing, and climbing. In winter there is both cross-country and downhill skiing at the busy resorts along the border, much livelier than their Spanish counterparts.

Historically, the Pyrenees are known as the birthplace of Henri IV, who put an end to the Wars of Religion in 1593 and united France, though the region has been characterized more often by independent fiefdoms. The region's oldest inhabitants, the Basque people *(see p459)*, have maintained their own language and culture, and their resorts of Bayonne, Biarritz, and St.-Jean-de-Luz reflect this, looking to the sea and to summer visitors for their livelihood.

Inland, Pau, Tarbes, and Foix rely on tourism and medium-scale industry, while Lourdes receives five million pilgrims every year. For the rest, life has been regulated by agriculture, though economic constraints today are causing an exodus from the land.

Countryside around St.-Lizier, in the heart of the Pyrenean countryside

◀ The Ariège river in Foix

# Exploring the Pyrenees

The towering Pyrenees cut across southwest France from the Mediterranean to the Atlantic coast, encompassing the craggy citadel of Montségur; the pilgrimage center of Lourdes; Pau, capital of the hilly Béarn country; and the Basque port of Bayonne. This formidable range, an un- spoiled paradise for walkers, anglers, and skiers, is as lush on its French side as it is arid in Spain, and contains the wild and beautiful Parc National des Pyrénées. Throughout the region, visitors can expect cool temperatures and grandiose scenery. Lovers of history and architecture will be richly rewarded by St.-Bertrand-de-Comminges and St.-Jean-de-Luz, among the region's important sights.

Marzipan sweets, a specialty
of southwest France

## Getting Around

Access to the Basque coast in the western Pyrenees is via the A63/N10 from Bordeaux. The length of the Pyrenees, including the mountain valleys, is served by the A64, which runs from Bayonne to Toulouse, via Orthez, Pau, Tarbes, and St.-Gaudens. Once you are high up, expect narrow, twisting roads and slow driving. The scenic but demanding D918/D618 road crosses 18 high passes between the Atlantic and the Mediterranean.

There are airports at Biarritz, Pau, and Lourdes. Both Pau and Lourdes, together with Orthez and Tarbes, are on the train route that loops south between Bordeaux and Toulouse.

The galleried church in the Basque village of Espelette

**For keys to symbols** see back flap

## Sights at a Glance

1. Bayonne
2. Biarritz
3. St.-Jean-de-Luz
4. Aïnhoa
5. Orthez
6. Sauveterre-de-Béarn
7. St.-Jean-Pied-de-Port
8. Forêt d'Iraty
9. Oloron-Ste-Marie
10. Pau
11. Tarbes
12. Lourdes
13. *Parc National des Pyrénées pp464–5*
14. Luz-St-Sauveur
15. Arreau
16. St.-Bertrand-de-Comminges
17. St.-Lizier
18. Foix
19. Montségur
20. Mirepoix

Wild *pottock* ponies on moorland in the Forêt d'Iraty

St.-Jean-de-Luz seen from Ciboure, across the Nivelle estuary

### Key

- ▬ Freeway
- ▬ Highway
- ▬ Secondary road
- ▭ Minor road
- ▬ Scenic route
- ▬ Main railroad
- --- Minor railroad
- ▨ International border
- ▬ Regional border
- △ Summit

## ❶ Bayonne

Pyrénées-Atlantiques. 🏔 49,500.
🚇 🚌 🚹 pl des Basques (05 59 46
09 900).). 🛍 daily. 🌐 **bayonne-tourisme.com**

Bayonne, capital of the French
Basque country, lies between
two rivers – the turbulent Nive,
which arrives straight from the
mountains, and the wide,
languid Adour. An important
town since Roman times
because of its command of one
of the few easily passable roads
to Spain, Bayonne prospered as
a free port under English rule
from 1154 to 1451. Since then it
has successfully withstood 14
sieges, including a particularly
bloody one directed by
Wellington in 1813.

Grand Bayonne, the district
around the cathedral, can be
easily explored on foot. The
13th-century **Cathédrale Ste.-
Marie** was begun under English
rule and is northern Gothic in
style. Look for the handsome
cloister and the 15th-century
knocker on the north door – if a
fugitive could put a hand to this,
he was entitled to sanctuary.
The traffic-free streets around
form a lively shopping area,
especially the arcaded rue Port
Neuf, with cafés serving hot
chocolate, a Bayonne specialty.
(Fine-quality chocolate-making
was introduced by the Jews
who fled Spain at the end of
the 15th century, and it has
remained a specialty of the

Grand Bayonne, clustered around the
twin-spired cathedral

Lighthouse at Biarritz

town.) Bayonne is also famous
for its ham.

Petit Bayonne lies on the
opposite side of the dock-lined
River Nive. The **Musée Basque**
gives an excellent introduction
to the customs and traditions
of the Basque nation, with
reconstructed house interiors
and exhibits on seafaring. Nearby,
the **Musée Bonnat-Helleu** has a
superb art gallery. The first floor
here is a must for art lovers, with
sketches by Leonardo, Van Dyck,
Rubens, and Rembrandt and
paintings by Goya, Corot, Ingres,
and Constable.

🏛 **Musée Basque**
37 quai des Corsaires. **Tel** 05 59 59 08
98. **Open** Tue–Sun (Jul–Aug: daily).
**Closed** public hols. 🎫 ♿ 📷
🌐 **musee-basque.com**

🏛 **Musée Bonnat-Helleu**
5 rue Jacques Lafitte. **Tel** 05 59 46 63
60. **Closed** for renovation. 🎫 ♿
🌐 **musee-bonnat.com**

## ❷ Biarritz

Pyrénées-Atlantiques. 🏔 26,000.
✈ 🚇 🚌 🚹 Javalquinto, square
d'Ixelles (05 59 22 37 00). 🛍 daily.
🌐 **tourisme.biarritz.fr**

Biarritz, west of Bayonne, has a
grandiose center, but has been
developed along the coast by
residential suburbs. The resort
began as a whaling town but was
transformed into a playground
for the European rich in the
19th century. Its popularity was
assured when Empress Eugénie
discovered its mild winter climate
during the reign of her husband,
Napoleon III. The town has three
good beaches, with some of the

best surfing in Europe, two
casinos, and one of the last great
luxury hotels in Europe, the Palais,
formerly the residence of Eugénie.

In the port des Pêcheurs, the
**Aquarium de Biarritz** is home
to specimens of some of the
marine life found in the Bay of
Biscay. Below it, a narrow
causeway leads across to the
Rocher de la Vierge, offering
far-reaching views along the
whole of the Basque coast. The
Planète Musée du Chocolat
is fine compensation for a
rainy day.

🏛 **Aquarium de Biarritz**
Esplanade du Rocher-de-la-Vierge,
14 plateau de l'Atalaye. **Tel** 05 59 22
75 40. **Open** daily. **Closed** Jan 1,
2nd–3rd wk Jan, Dec 25. 🎫 ♿ 📷
💻 🌐 **aquariumbiarritz.com**

Altar in Eglise St.-Jean-Baptiste

## ❸ St.-Jean-de-Luz

Pyrénées-Atlantiques. 🏔 14,000.
✈ Biarritz. 🚇 🚌 🚹 20 bd Victor
Hugo (05 59 26 03 16). 🛍 daily.
🌐 **saint-jean-de-luz.com**

St.-Jean is a quiet fishing town
out of season and a scorching
tourist resort in August, with
stores to rival the chic rue du
Faubourg St.-Honoré in Paris.
In the 11th century whale
carcasses were towed here
to feed the whole village.
The natural harbor protects the
shoreline, making it one of the
few beaches safe for swimming
along this stretch of coast.

An important historical event
took place in St.-Jean: the
wedding of Louis XIV and the
Infanta Maria Teresa of Spain in
1660, a union that had the

St.-Jean-de-Luz, a fishing village that explodes into life in summer

effect of sealing the long-awaited alliance between France and Spain, only to embroil the two countries ultimately in the War of the Spanish Succession. This wedding took place at the **Eglise St.-Jean-Baptiste**, still the biggest and best of the great Basque churches, a triple-galleried marvel with a glittering 17th-century altarpiece and an atmosphere of gaiety and fervor. The gate through which the Sun King led his bride was immediately walled up by masons: a plaque now marks the spot. The **Maison Louis XIV**, with its contemporary furnishings, is where the king stayed in 1660, and is worth a look.

The port is busy in summer, while the restaurants behind the covered markets serve sizzling bowls full of *chipirons* – squid cooked in their own ink – a local specialty. Place Louis XIV is a lovely place to sit and watch the world go by.

🏛 **Maison Louis XIV**
Place Louis XIV. **Tel** 05 59 26 27 58.
**Open** Apr–Oct: Wed–Mon. 📷 📋
🆆 maison-louis-xiv.fr

**Environs**
On the other side of the River Nivelle, Ciboure was the birthplace of composer Maurice Ravel. It is characterized by 18th-century merchants' houses, steep narrow streets, and seafood restaurants. A coastal walk of 1 hour leads to the neighboring village of **Socoa**, where the lighthouse on the clifftop offers a fine view of the coast all the way to Biarritz.

Basque men in traditional berets

## ❹ Aïnhoa

Pyrénées-Atlantiques. 🄰 700. 🚌
ℹ Maison du Patrimoine (05 59 29 93 99). 🆆 ainhoa-tourisme.com

A tiny township on the road to the Spanish border, Aïnhoa was founded in the 12th century as a waystation on the road to Santiago de Compostela *(see pp404–5)*. The main street of 17th-century whitewashed Basque houses and a galleried church from the same period survive.

**Environs**
There is a similar church in the village of Espelette nearby. Typically Basque in style, the galleries boosted the seating capacity and separated the men from the women and children. Espelette is the trading center for *pottocks*, an ancient local breed of pony, auctioned here at the end of January. It is also the shrine of the local crop, the red pimento pepper, especially in October when a pepper festival is held here.

At the foot of the St.-Ignace pass lies the mountain village of **Sare**. From the pass you can reach the summit of la Rhune by cog railroad. This provides the best vantage point in the entire Pays Basque. The descent on foot is worthwhile.

The 11th-century château, Espelette

Sauveterre-de-Béarn and the remains of the fortified bridge over the Gave d'Oloron, the Pont de la Légende

## ❺ Orthez

Pyrénées-Atlantiques. 🏛 12,000.
🚉 🚌 *i* 58 rue du Commerce,
Monein (05 59 12 30 40).
🛒 Tue; Nov–Mar: *foie gras* market Sat.
Ⓦ **coerdebearn.com**

Orthez is an important Béarn
market town, its 13th- to
14th-century fortified bridge a
vital river-crossing point over the
Gave de Pau in the Middle Ages.
It has a spectacular Saturday-
morning market held from
November to February, selling
*foie gras*, smoked and air-cured
Bayonne hams, and all kinds of
fresh produce. Fine buildings line
rue Bourg Vieux, especially the
house of Jeanne d'Albret, the
mother of Henry IV, on the corner
of rue Roarie. Jeanne's enthusiasm
for the Protestant faith alienated
both her own subjects and
Charles X, and ultimately caused
the Béarn region to be drawn into
the Wars of Religion (1562–98).

## ❻ Sauveterre-de- Béarn

Pyrénées-Atlantiques. 🏛 1,500. 🚌
*i* pl Royale (05 59 38 32 86). 🛒 Sat.
Ⓦ **tourisme-bearn-gaves.com**

An attractive market town,
Sauveterre is well worth a
night's stay. It has stunning
views southward over the Gave
d'Oloron, the graceful single

arch of the river's fortified
bridge, and the 16th-century
**Château de Nays**. Anglers
gather here for the annual
salmon-fishing championships,
in the fast-flowing Oloron
(April to July).

Be sure to visit the **Château
de Laàs**, 6 miles (9 km) along
the D27 from Sauveterre, which
has an excellent collection of
18th-century decorative art and
furniture – notably the bed
Napoleon slept in on the night
after his defeat at Waterloo.
There is also a pretty park with
romantic Italian gardens.

### 🏰 Château de Laàs
**Tel** 05 59 38 91 53. **Open** Apr–Oct:
2–6pm Tue–Fri, 10am–6pm Sat & Sun
(Jul–Aug: daily). 🖼

The Château de Nays at Sauveterre in the
Béarn region

## ❼ St.-Jean-Pied-de-Port

Pyrénées-Atlantiques. 🏛 1,800. 🚉
🚌 *i* 14 pl du Général de Gaulle
(05 59 37 03 57). 🛒 Mon.
Ⓦ **saintjeanpieddeport-
paysbasque-tourisme.com**

The old capital of Basse-Navarre,
St.-Jean-Pied-de-Port lies at the
foot of the Roncesvalles Pass.
Here the Basques crushed the
rear-guard of Charlemagne's
army in 778 and killed its
commander, Roland, later
glorified in the *Chanson
de Roland*.

Throughout the Middle Ages
this red sandstone fortress
town was famous as the last
rallying point before entering
Spain on the pilgrim road to
Santiago de Compostela *(see
pp404–5)*. Tall booths were
erected next to the gates for
additional security.

Visitors and pilgrims in all
seasons still provide St.-Jean with
its income. They enter the narrow
streets of the upper town on foot
from the Porte d'Espagne, and
pass cafés, hotels, and restaurants
on the way up. The ramparts are
worth the steep climb, as is the
citadel with panoramic views.

On Mondays the town hosts
a crafts market, Basque *pelota*
games, and, in summer,
shows with bulls.

# ❽ Forêt d'Iraty

Pyrénées-Atlantiques.. St.-Jean-Pied-de-Port. St.-Jean-Pied-de-Port (05 59 37 03 57), Larrau (05 59 28 62 80).

A plateau of beech woods and moorland, the Forêt d'Iraty is famous for its cross-country skiing and walking. Here the ancient breed of Basque ponies, the *pottocks*, run half-wild. These creatures have not changed since the prehistoric inhabitants of the region traced their silhouettes on the walls of local caves.

The tourist office at St.-Jean-Pied-de-Port publishes maps of local walks. The best begins at the Chalet Pedro parking lot, south of the lake on the Iraty plateau, and takes you along the GR10 to 3,000-year-old standing stones on the western side of the Sommet d'Occabé.

# ❾ Oloron-Ste.-Marie

Pyrénées-Atlantiques. 12,000. allées du Comte de Tréville (05 59 39 98 00). Fri & Sun. **tourisme-oloron.com**

Oloron, a small town at the junction of the Aspe and the Ossau valleys, has grown from a Celtiberian settlement. There are huge agricultural fairs here in May and September, and the town is famed for producing the famous classic French berets.

## Basque Culture

Most of Basque country is in Spain, but around 10 percent lies within France. The Basque people have their own complex language, isolated from other European tongues, and their music, games, and folklore are equally distinct. French Basques are less fiercely separatist than their Spanish counterparts, but both are still deeply attached to their unique way of life.

*Pelota*, the traditional Basque game

Cathédrale Ste.-Marie, Oloron

The town's great glory is the doorway of the Romanesque **Cathédrale Ste.-Marie**, with its biblical and Pyrenean scenes. Spain lies just on the other side of the Somport pass at the head of the mountainous Aspe Valley, and the influence of Spanish stonemasons is evident in Oloron's **Eglise Sainte-Croix** with its Moorish-style vaulting.

### Environs
Head up the Aspe Valley to try one of the area's famous ewe's cheeses, or mixed cow and goat's cheeses. A side road leads to Lescun, huddled around its church, beyond which is a spectacular range of saw-toothed peaks topped by the **Pic d'Anie** at 8,215 ft (2,504 m), one of the most beautiful sights in the Pyrenees. This is also one of the last refuges of the Pyrenean brown bear, whose numbers have been drastically diminished by human activity, particularly hunting and the building of roads and houses.

High moorland above the Forêt d'Iraty, long denuded of timber for use by the French and Spanish navies

Gobelins tapestry in the Château de Pau

## ⑩ Pau

Pyrénées-Atlantiques. 🏠 79,000. ✈️ 🚆 🚌 ℹ️ pl Royale (05 59 27 27 08). 🏛️ Mon–Sat. 🌐 **pau-pyrenees.com**

A lively university town, with elegant *belle époque* architecture and shady parks, Pau is the capital of the Béarn region, and the most interesting big town in the central Pyrenees. The weather in fall and winter is mild, so this has been a favorite resort of affluent foreigners, especially the English, since the early 19th century.

Pau is chiefly famous as the birthplace of Henry IV. His mother, Jeanne d'Albret, traveled for 19 days from Picardy, in the eighth month of her pregnancy, just to have her baby here. She sang during her labor, convinced that if she did so, Henry would grow up as tough as she was. As soon as the infant was born, his lips were smeared with garlic and local Jurançon wine, in keeping with the traditional custom.

The town's principal sight is the **Château de Pau**, first remodeled in the 14th century for the ruler of Béarn, Gaston Phoebus *(see p467)*. It was heavily restored 400 years later. Marguerite d'Angoulême, sister of the King of France, resided here in the late 16th century, and transformed the town into a center for the arts and free thinking. The château's

16th-century Gobelins tapestries, made by Flemish weavers working in Paris, are fabulous. (The Maison Carrée in Nay – 11 miles/18 km toward Lourdes – exhibits the former Musée Béarnais' collection of artifacts retracing the history, traditions, and culture of the Béarn.)

Outside, the boulevard des Pyrénées affords glorious views of some of the highest Pyrenean peaks, often snow-capped year round. Continue from here to the eclectic **Musée des Beaux-Arts**, where there is a splendid Degas, the *Cotton Exchange, New Orleans*, as well as two works by Rubens.

### 🏰 Château de Pau
Rue du Château. **Tel** 05 59 82 38 02. **Open** daily. **Closed** Jan 1, May 1, Dec 25. 🎫 🐾 📷 ♿ restricted. 🌐 **chateau-pau.fr**

Château de Pau, birthplace of Henry IV in 1553

### 🏛️ Musée des Beaux-Arts
Rue Mathieu Lalanne. **Tel** 05 59 27 33 02. **Open** Wed–Mon. **Closed** some public hols. 🐾 ♿ restricted. 🌐 **museedesbeauxartsdepau.com**

## ⑪ Tarbes

Hautes-Pyrénées. 🏠 42,500. 🚆 🚌 📮 ℹ️ 3 cours Gambetta (05 62 51 30 31). 🏛️ Thu. 🌐 **tarbes-tourisme.fr**

Tarbes is the capital of the Bigorre region and hosts a major agricultural fair. The **Jardin Massey** in the middle of town was designed at the turn of the 19th century and is one of the loveliest parks in the southwest, with many rare plants, including the North American sassafras, and a 14th-century cloister with finely carved capitals.

In the gardens is the **Musée Massey**, housing a unique collection on the history of French and international hussars and a fine arts collection.

### 🏛️ Musée Massey
Jardin Massey. **Tel** 05 62 44 36 95. **Open** Wed–Mon. **Closed** Jan 1, May 1, Dec 25. 🐾 ♿ 📷 📮 🌐 **musee-massey.com**

## ⑫ Lourdes

Hautes-Pyrénées. 🏠 15,000. 🚆 🚌 📮 ℹ️ pl Peyramale (05 62 42 77 40). 🏛️ daily. 🌐 **lourdes-infotourisme. com**

Lourdes, one of the great shrines of Europe, owes its celebrity to visions of the Virgin experienced by 14-year-old Bernadette Soubirous in 1858. Five million people annually

◀ The lush Forêt d'Iraty and surrounding moorland

visit **Grotte Massabielle**, where the visions occurred, and rue des Petits-Fossés where Bernadette lived, in search of a miracle cure. The **Musée du Petit Lourdes** gives information about Bernadette and the shrine.

Visit the **Grottes de Bétharram** for underground rides by boat and train, or the **Musée Pyrénéen**, about the pioneers who opened up these ranges.

**Musée du Petit Lourdes**
68 ave Peyramale. **Tel** 05 62 94 24 36. **Open** Apr–Oct: daily. **W** musee-lourdes.fr

**Grottes de Bétharram**
St.-Pé-de-Bigorre. **Tel** 05 62 41 80 04. **Open** Feb–late Mar: Mon–Fri pms; late Mar–Oct: daily. **W** betharram.com

Pilgrims participating in open-air Mass at Lourdes

Spectacular limestone formations at the Grottes de Bétharram

**Musée Pyrénéen**
rue du Fort. **Tel** 05 62 42 37 37. **Open** daily. **Closed** Jan 1, Nov 1 & 11, Dec 25. restricted. **W** lourdes-visite.fr

## ❸ Parc National des Pyrénées

*See pp464–5.*

## ❹ Luz-St.-Sauveur

Hautes-Pyrénées. 1,000. to Lourdes. pl du 8 mai 1945 (05 62 92 30 30). Mon am. **W** luz.org

Luz-St.-Sauveur is an attractive spa town, with an unusual church built in the 14th century by the Hospitaliers de Saint Jean de Jérusalem (later the Knights of Malta), an order established to protect pilgrims. The church is fortified with gun slits that provided protection for pilgrims on the way to Santiago de Compostela *(see pp404–5).*

**Environs**
The elegant spa town of **Cauterets** makes a good base for climbing, skiing, and walking in the rugged mountains of the Bigorre region.

**Gavarnie** is a former way-station on the Santiago de Compostela pilgrim route. A good track, accessible on foot or by donkey, leads from the village to the spectacular natural rock amphitheater known as the **Cirque de Gavarnie**. Here the longest waterfall in Europe, at 1,378 ft (420 m), cascades off the mountain into space, encircled by eleven 9,800-ft (3,000-m) peaks.

Tourists can now share much of the **Observatoire Pic du Midi de Bigorre** with scientists. It is even possible to spend the night here. Access is by cablecar from La Mongie. Alternatively there are a number of walks up to the Pic (4 hours minimum).

The French are justly proud of the Observatory, which has supplied some of the clearest images of Venus and other planets so far obtained from Earth. The 3.2-ft (1-m) telescope mapped out the moon for NASA's Apollo missions.

**Observatoire Pic du Midi de Bigorre**
**Tel** 08 25 00 28 77. **Open** daily. **Closed** Apr 18, May, Nov 6 & Dec. **W** picdumidi.com

### The Miracle of Lourdes

In 1858 a young girl named Bernadette Soubirous experienced 18 visions of the Virgin at the Grotte Massabielle near the town. Despite being told to keep away from the cave by her mother – and the local magistrate – she was guided to a spring with miraculous healing powers. The church endorsed the miracles in the 1860s, and since then many people claim to have been cured by the holy water. A religious city of shrines, churches, and hospices has since grown up around the spring, with a dynamic tourist industry to match.

Bernadette's vision

# ⑬ Parc National des Pyrénées

The Pyrenees National Park, designated in 1967, extends 100 km (62 miles) along the French and Spanish frontier. It boasts some of the most spectacular scenery in Europe, ranging from meadows glimmering with butterflies to high peaks, snowcapped even in summer. Variations in altitude and climate make the park rich in flora and fauna. One of the most enjoyable ways to see it is on foot: within the park are 217 miles (350 km) of well-marked footpaths.

**Vallée d'Aspe**
Jagged peaks tower above the Vallée d'Aspe and the Cirque de Lescun. An access road to Somport Tunnel has been built here.

**Pic d'Anie**
The limestone-flanked 8,215-ft (2,504-m) Pic d'Anie overlooks rich upland pastures watered by melting snow. In spring, the ground is ablaze with Pyrenean varieties of gentian and columbine, found nowhere else.

*Oloron-Ste-Marie*

**Pic d'Anie**
▲ 8,215 ft
(2,504 m)

VALLÉE D'ASPE

N134

VALLÉE D'OSSAU

D934

↑Pau

Larun

Pic
Sa
7,5
(2,

**Pic du Midi d'Ossau**
9,462 ft (2,884 m) ▲

## KEY

① **Col du Somport**, the Somport pass (5,354 ft/1,632 m), is a rugged route into Spain that is now bypassed by a tunnel.

② **The GR10 long-distance trail** is one of the great walks of France, linking the Atlantic with the Mediterranean.

③ **Brèche de Roland**

**Pic du Midi d'Ossau**
A tough trail leads from the Bious-Artigues lake at the base of the Pic du Midi d'Ossau and encircles the formidable, tooth-shaped summit (9,462 ft/2,884 m).

## Pyrenean Wildlife

The Pyrenees are home to a rich variety of wild creatures, many of them unique to the range. The ibex, a member of the antelope family, is still numerous in the valleys of Ossau and Cauterets. Birds of prey include the Egyptian, griffon and bearded vultures. Ground predators range from the pine marten to the stoat. The desman, a tiny aquatic mammal related to the mole, is found in many of the mountain streams.

**Pyrenean fritillary** flowers through late spring and early summer in mountain pastures.

**The Turk's Cap Lily** comes into flower June–August on rocky slopes at up to 7,218 ft (2,200 m).

**èche de Roland**
e famous breach in the sheer crest
the Cirque de Gavarnie forms a
teway for climbers between France
d Spain.

## Tips for Walkers

The park is crossed by a network of numbered trails. Each is well signposted and shows the length of time needed. Mountain huts offer a meal and a bed for the night. For maps and information, visit the Park Office at Cauterets (tel: 05 62 92 52 56) or at Luz-St.-Sauveur (tel: 05 62 92 38 38), both open year round, or visit www.parc-pyrenees.com.

Walking the trail in high summer

↑ *Lourdes*

Argelès-Gazost

Col du Soulor
l'Aubisque
Arrens
D918
D1054
D921

Pic du Midi de Bigorre
9,400 ft (2,865 m)
La Mongie

Col du Tourmalet
Bagnères-de-Bigorre

Cauterets

Luz-St-Sauveur
D918

MASSIF DE
NEOUVIELLE

Balaitous
10,322 ft (3,146 m)

Pont d'Espagne

Pic de Néouvielle
10,151 ft (3,094 m)

② 

0 kilometers 5

0 miles 5

Vignemale
10,814 ft (3,296 m)

D921
D922

Gavarnie

Cirque de Troumouse

Cirque de Gavarnie

③

### Key

— National park boundary

— French/Spanish border

— GR10 walking route

**e Egyptian vulture** is seen all
er the Pyrenees, especially on
ky cliff faces.

**Pyrenean bears** are close to extinction, but a few still live in this park, especially in the west.

Cleopatra

Scarce
Swallowtail

**These butterflies** are among several colorful species found at high altitudes.

## ⑮ Arreau

Hautes-Pyrénées. 🗺 850. 🚍 ℹ
Château des Nestes (05 62 98 63 15).
🛒 Thu. 🌐 **vallee-aure.com**

Arreau stands at the junction of
the rivers Aure and Louron. A
small, bustling half-timbered town
with good stores and restaurants,
this is the place to buy the basics
for hiking or fishing in the mountains. The town surrounds a
handsome town hall with a
covered marketplace beneath
it. Next door is a 16th-century
house, the Maison de Lys, which
has a facade ornamented with
the fleur-de-lys motifs.

### Environs

St.-Lary Soulan is a nearby ski
resort and a good base for
exploring the entire Massif du
Néouvielle. Head for the village
of Fabian and the smattering of
lakes above it, where the
GR10 (see pp464–5) and other
well-marked trails crisscross
the peaks. Here you may
see golden eagles or an
enormous lammergeier.

## ⑯ St.-Bertrand-de-Comminges

Haute-Garonne. 🗺 250. 🚊
Montrejeau, then taxi. 🚍 ℹ Les
Olivetains, parvis de la Cathédrale (05
61 95 44 44). 🎵 music festival (mid-
Jul–end Aug). 🌐 **tourisme-stgaudens.com**

The pretty hilltop town of
St.-Bertrand is the most remarkable artistic and historic site in
the Central Pyrenees and the
venue for an acclaimed music

Cloisters in the Cathédrale Ste.-Marie, St.-Bertrand-de-Comminges

festival in summer (see p41).
Some of the best sculpture in
the region adorns the portal of
the **Cathédrale Ste.-Marie**.
The adjoining Romanesque
and Gothic cloisters contain
sarcophagi, carved capitals, and
statues of the four Evangelists.

St.-Bertrand's origins lie on the
plain below, in the city founded
by the great Roman statesman
Pompey in 72 BC. At that time it
consisted of two thermal baths,
a theater, a temple, a market,
and a Christian basilica. All were
destroyed by Gontran, the
grandson of Clovis (see p54) in
585, and six centuries were to
pass before the Bishop of Comminges, Bertrand de l'Isle, saw
the site as a potential location for
a new cathedral and monastery.
The town, which was relatively
unimportant in political terms,
became a major religious center.

Inside the cathedral, look for
the 66 magnificent carved choir
stalls and the 16th-century
organ case. The tomb of
Bertrand de l'Isle is located at
the far end of the choir, with an

altar beside it; the beautiful
marble tomb in the Virgin's
chapel just off the nave is that
of Hugues de Châtillon, a
bishop who provided funds for
the completion of the cathedral
in the 14th century.

🏛 **Cathédrale Ste.-Marie**
**Tel** 05 61 95 44 44. **Open** daily.
**Closed** Sun am. 🚫 🔇.

Fresco in the Cathédrale St.-Lizier

## ⑰ St.-Lizier

Ariège. 🗺 1,500. 🚍 ℹ pl de l'Eglise
(05 61 96 77 77). 🌐 **tourisme-stgirons-stlizier.fr**

St.-Lizier is located in the Ariège,
a region famous for its steep-
sided valleys and wild mountain
scenery. The village dates back
to Roman times, and by the
Middle Ages was an important
religious center. St.-Lizier has
two cathedrals; the finer is the
12th- to 14th-century
**Cathédrale St.-Lizier** in the
lower town. The **Cathédrale de
la Sède** in the upper town has
the best view. Nearby is the
**Bishop's Palace**, which houses
a museum of local history.

The imposing 12th-century Cathédrale Ste.-Marie in St-Bertrand

St.-Lizier, with snowcapped mountains in the distance

## ⓲ Foix

Ariège. 🅜 11,000. 🚉 🚌 🅸 rue
Bayle (05 61 65 12 12). 🛒 Fri & 1st, 3rd
& 5th Mon of each month, also Tue,
Wed all day in Jul–Aug. 🆆 foix-
tourisme.com

With its battlements and towers,
Foix stands foursquare at the
junction of the rivers Arget and
Ariège. In the Middle Ages,
Foix's dynasty of counts ruled
the whole of the Béarn area.
Count Gaston Phoebus (1331–
91) was the most flamboyant,
a poet who wrote a famous
treatise on hunting. He was a
ruthless politician, who had his
brother and his son put to death.

Some of the pleasures of the
medieval court are recreated
in the local summer fair, the
largest in the southwest. At any
time, the 15th-century keep of
the **Château de Foix** is worth
climbing just for the view.
The restored 14th-century
**Eglise de St.-Volusien** is delightful in its simplicity and grace.

### 🅷 Château de Foix
**Tel** 05 61 05 10 10. **Open** daily.
**Closed** Jan 1, Dec 25. 🖉 🖱 🖼
🆆 sites-touristiques-ariege.fr

### Environs
The **Grotte de Niaux**, 9 miles
(15 km) south of Foix, features
some prehistoric cave paintings.

### 🅷 Grotte de Niaux
**Tel** 05 61 05 10 10. **Open** daily. 🖉 🖱
🖼 🆆 sites-touristiques-ariege.fr .

## ⓳ Montségur

Ariège. 🅜 130. 🅸 05 61 03 03 03.
**Open** Feb–Dec: daily. **Closed** Dec 25.
🖉 🖱 (May–Sep). 🆆 montsegur.fr

Montségur is famous as the last
stronghold of the Cathars *(see
p495)*. From the parking lot at the
foot of the mount, a path leads
up to the small castle above,
which was occupied in the 13th
century by *faidits* (dispossessed
aristocrats) and a Cathar community. The Cathars themselves lived
outside the fortress, in houses
clinging to the rock. Opposed to
Catholic authority, Cathar troops
marched on Avignonnet in
1243 and massacred members
of the Inquisitional tribunal. In
retaliation, an army of 10,000
laid siege to Montségur for ten
months. When captured,
205 Cathars refused to convert
and were burned alive.

## ⓴ Mirepoix

Ariège. 🅜 3,300. 🚌 🅸 pl du
Maréchal Leclerc (05 61 68 83 76).
🛒 Mon & Thu.
🆆 tourisme-mirepoix.com

Mirepoix is a solid country
bastide town *(see p449)* with
a huge main square – one of
the loveliest in the southwest –
surrounded by beamed 13th-
to 15th-century arcades and
half-timbered houses.

The **cathedral**, begun in 1317
with the last additions made in
1867, boasts the widest Gothic
nave (72 ft/22 m) in France.

The best times to visit the
town are on market days, when
stands on the square sell a mass
of local produce.

The arcaded main square at Mirepoix

# THE SOUTH
# OF FRANCE

Introducing the South
  of France                 470–479

Languedoc and Roussillon   480–501

Provence and
  the Côte d'Azur          502–535

Corsica                    536–547

# Introducing the South of France

The South is France's most popular holiday region, drawing millions of visitors each year to the Riviera resorts, and modern beach cities to the west. Agriculture is a mainstay of the economy, producing early fruits and an abundance of affordable wine. The new high-tech industries of Nice and Montpellier reflect the region's key role in the developing south coast sunbelt, while Corsica still preserves much of its natural beauty. The map shows the major sights of this sun-blessed region.

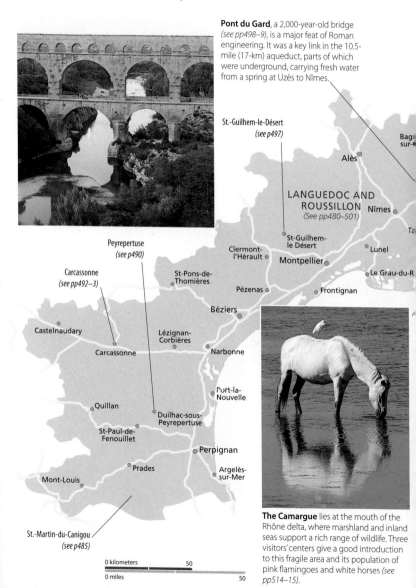

**Pont du Gard**, a 2,000-year-old bridge (*see pp498–9*), is a major feat of Roman engineering. It was a key link in the 10.5-mile (17-km) aqueduct, parts of which were underground, carrying fresh water from a spring at Uzès to Nîmes.

St.-Guilhem-le-Désert
(*see p497*)

Bag.
sur-.

Alès

LANGUEDOC AND
ROUSSILLON
(See pp480–501)

Nîmes

Ta.

Peyrepertuse
(*see p490*)

Clermont-
l'Hérault

St-Guilhem-
le Désert

Lunel

Carcassonne
(*see pp492–3*)

St-Pons-de-
Thomières

Montpellier

Le Grau-du-R.

Castelnaudary

Lézignan-
Corbières

Pézenas

Frontignan

Béziers

Carcassonne

Narbonne

Quillan

Duilhac-sous-
Peyrepertuse

Port-la-
Nouvelle

St-Paul-de-
Fenouillet

Perpignan

Prades

Argelès-
sur-Mer

Mont-Louis

St.-Martin-du-Canigou
(*see p485*)

**The Camargue** lies at the mouth of the Rhône delta, where marshland and inland seas support a rich range of wildlife. Three visitors' centers give a good introduction to this fragile area and its population of pink flamingoes and white horses (*see pp514–15*).

| 0 kilometers | 50 |
| 0 miles | 50 |

◀ A field of sunflowers in Languedoc

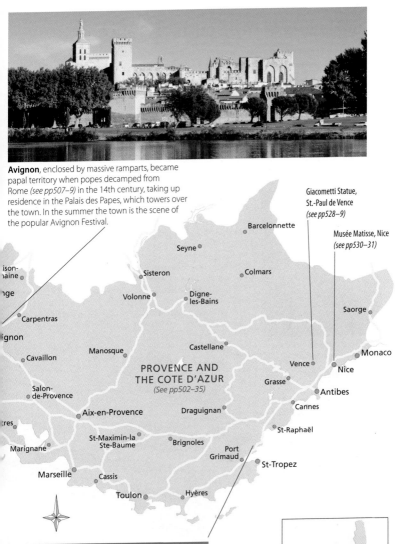

**Avignon**, enclosed by massive ramparts, became papal territory when popes decamped from Rome *(see pp507–9)* in the 14th century, taking up residence in the Palais des Papes, which towers over the town. In the summer the town is the scene of the popular Avignon Festival.

Giacometti Statue, St.-Paul de Vence *(see pp528–9)*

Musée Matisse, Nice *(see pp530–31)*

Barcelonnette

Seyne

Colmars

Sisteron

Digne-les-Bains

Volonne

Saorge

Carpentras

Cavaillon

Manosque

Castellane

Vence

Monaco

Nice

Salon-de-Provence

**PROVENCE AND THE COTE D'AZUR** *(See pp502–35)*

Grasse

Antibes

Aix-en-Provence

Draguignan

Cannes

Marignane

St-Maximin-la Ste-Baume

Brignoles

St-Raphaël

Marseille

Cassis

Port Grimaud

St-Tropez

Toulon

Hyères

**The Côte d'Azur** has attracted sun-worshippers and celebrities since the 1920s *(see pp478–9)*. The coast also offers some prize collections of 20th-century art *(pp476–7)* and yearly events such as the Cannes Film Festival and Jazz à Juan.

Statue of Napoleon, Ajaccio *(see p546)*

Bastia

Calvi

**CORSICA** *(See pp536–47)*

Ajaccio

Bonifacio

0 kilometers   50

0 miles   50

**For keys to symbols** *see back flap*

# The Flavors of the South of France

Mediterranean France has a fresh, sunny cuisine, with ripe and flavorful fruit and vegetables, fresh fish and seafood, and lean meat from mountain pastures. Good dishes are enhanced by key ingredients: olive oil, garlic, and aromatic herbs. Markets are a colorful feast of seasonal produce all year round. Whether you opt for a picnic choice of local hams, sausage, bread, and cheese to eat on the beach, share a simple lunch of tomato salad and grilled fish or lamb in a village bistro, or indulge in the sophisticated cuisine of one of France's top chefs, you can be sure of food that is not only authentic and delicious, but healthy too.

Local olives and olive oil

Preserving anchovies in seasoned olive oil in Languedoc and Roussillon

## Languedoc and Roussillon

There is a robust Catalan flavor to the food in this area bordering Spain. Spices and almonds add an exotic touch to the fruit and vegetables produced in abundance on the Roussillon plain, and the grass-fed beef and lamb of the Mediterranean Pyrenees. Fish is plentiful: Sète is the largest fishing port on the French Mediterranean, huge oyster and mussel beds thrive in the saltwater lagoons of the coast, and the little fishing port of Collioure is famous for its anchovies. Local dishes include *brandade de morue*, a specialty of Nîmes, squid stuffed with anchovies, and snails with garlic and ham. Roussillon is famous for its peaches and apricots, and the cherries of Ceret are always the first to be harvested in France. Goat's milk is the main source of cheese, with round, orange-rinded Pélardon the most common.

## Provence

This is the land of the olive and of rich green olive oil. These are evident in a wide range of dishes, such as *aioli*,

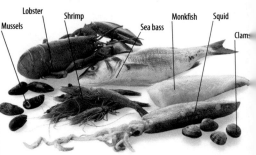

Lobster    Shrimp
Mussels                Monkfish    Squid
                Sea bass                Clams

Selection of Mediterranean seafood available in the south of France

### Regional Dishes and Specialties

The *cuisine du soleil*, "cuisine of the sun," has produced several classic dishes. *Bouillabaisse* is the most famous. The ingredients of this fish stew vary from place to place, though Marseille claims the original recipe. A variety of local seafood (always including *rascasse*, or scorpion fish) is cooked in stock with tomatoes and saffron. The fish stock is traditionally served first, with croûtons spread with *rouille*, a spicy mayonnaise, and the fish served afterward.

**Fresh figs**   Once a fisherman's supper, it is now a luxury item you may need to order 24 hours in advance. A simpler version is *bourride*, a garlicky fish soup. Rich red wine stews, known as *daubes*, are another specialty, usually made with beef, but sometimes with tuna or calamari. Other classics include *ratatouille* and *salade niçoise*.

**Artichauts à la barigoule** Small violet artichokes are stuffed with bacon and vegetables, cooked in wine.

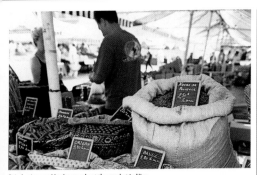

Dried spices and herbs on sale at the market in Nice

a rich mayonnaise of olive oil and garlic, served with vegetables or fish; *tapenade*, a purée of olives, anchovies, and capers; and *pissaladière*, a type of pizza made with onions, olives, and anchovies, with a distinct Italian accent. Vegetables play a leading role: zucchini or tomatoes stuffed in the Niçois style with meat, rice, and herbs; baby artichokes sautéed with bacon; or aromatic *pistou*, a bean and vegetable soup laced with a sauce of basil and garlic. Mediterranean fish is highly prized, and is often best appreciated simply grilled. Meat includes game and rabbit; Sisteron lamb, grazed on high mountain pastures; and the bull's meat stew of the Camargue, served with nutty local red rice. There is also ripe fruit aplenty, from juicy figs to fragrant Cavaillon melons to the vivid lemons of Menton.

## Corsica

The cuisine of Corsica is a robust version of the Mediterranean diet. Chestnuts were once the staple food of the island, and the flour is still widely used. There is a huge variety of *charcuterie*, including flavorsome hams and sausages,

Ripe chestnuts on the tree in a Corsican forest

smoked, cured or air-dried in the traditional way. Wild boar is a delicacy, stewed with chestnuts in red wine. Roast goat *(cabri roti)* is served as a festive meal, spiked with garlic and rosemary. Game, from rabbit to pigeon and partridge, is also very popular. On the coast there is locally caught fish and seafood, including monkfish, squid, sea urchins, and sardines, the latter most delicious stuffed with herbs and Brocciu, a ricotta-style soft cheese. Local honey is redolent of mountain herbs, and jams are made from a huge variety of ingredients.

### On the Menu

**Beignets des fleurs de courgette** Zucchini flower fritters.

**Estoficada** Salt cod stewed with tomatoes, potatoes, garlic, and olives.

**Fougasse** Flat olive oil bread often studded with olives.

**Ratatouille** Stew of garlic, onions, eggplant, tomatoes, zucchini, and peppers.

**Salade Niçoise** Lettuce with hard-boiled egg, olives, green beans, tomatoes, and anchovies.

**Socca** Garbanzo bean pancakes, a specialty of Nice.

**Tourte des blettes** Pie of chard, raisins, and pine nuts.

**Brandade de morue** Dried salted cod is cooked in water, then beaten with olive oil and milk to make a purée.

**Daube de Boeuf** Beef is marinated in red wine, onions, and garlic, then stewed with orange peel and tomato.

**Crème catalane** Originating in Spain, this dessert is an eggy custard topped with a flambéed sugar crust.

# France's Wine Regions: the South

A massive arc stretching from Banyuls, in the extreme southern corner of France, to Nice, close to the Italian border, encompasses the Mediterranean vineyards of Languedoc and Roussillon and Provence. This was for a century an area of mass-produced wine, and much is still of *vin de France* quality. Today, however, the more dynamic producers are applying new technology to traditional and classic grape varieties to revive southern France's nobler heritage of generous, warm, aromatic wines, redolent of sun-baked stone, the scent of wild herbs, and the shimmering waters of the Mediterranean.

**Locator Map**

■ Languedoc and Roussillon and Provence

**Coteaux du Languedoc** (since 2012, just "Languedoc") is a large and varied *appellation* stretching from Narbonne toward Nîmes.

**The quality** wines produced by Mass de Daumas Gassac have earned this vineyard its reputation as the *grand cru* of Languedoc.

**Stop here** to try the wines of Côtes du Roussillon – idiosyncratic yet characterful, dry white wines, dry rosés, and medium reds.

**Key**

■ Collioure & Banyuls
■ Côtes de Roussillon
■ Côtes de Roussillon Villages
■ Fitou
■ Corbières
■ Minervois
■ Coteaux du Languedoc/Languedoc
■ Costières du Gard
■ Coteaux d'Aix en Provence
■ Côtes de Provence
■ Bandol & Côtes de Provence
■ Coteaux Varois
■ Bellet

Rugged valley slopes in Corbières

Hand-picking grapes for Côtes de Provence red wine

## Wine Regions

*Both in the Provence wine region, east of Aix and Marseille, and in the larger Languedoc and Roussillon area to the west, new quality wine appellations, such as Cabardès (north of Carcassonne), are joining the more familiar names.*

**Bandol** is a small *appellation* that uses a traditional southern French red grape, the *Mourvèdre*, to produce its quality reds.

**La Courtade** reds, whites, and rosés are produced by the Domaine de la Courtade, one of three vineyards located on the Ile de Porquerolles off the coast of Provence.

## Key Facts About Wines of the South

### Location and Climate
A warm and sunny climate helps to create generously alcoholic wines. The flat coastal plains support acres of vines, but generally the best sites are on the schist and limestone hillsides.

### Grape Varieties
Mass-production grapes such as **Aramon** are giving way to quality varieties such as **Syrah**, **Mourvèdre** and **Grenache**. **Cabernet Sauvignon**, **Merlot** and **Syrah**, and the whites **Chardonnay**, **Sauvignon Blanc** and **Viognier**, are increasingly used for *IGPs* (see p30). Rich, sweet whites are made from the aromatic, honeyed **Muscat** grape.

### Good Producers
*Corbières & Minervois*: La Voulte Gasparets, Saint Auriol, Lastours, Villerambert-Julien. *Faugères*: Château des Estanilles, Château de la Liquiere. *St. Chinian*: Château Cazal-Viel, Domaine Navarre, Cave de Roquebrun. *Coteaux du Languedoc/Languedoc* and *IGPs*: Mas Jullien, Château de Capitoul, Domaine de la Garance, Mas de Daumas Gassac, Pech-Celeyran. *Roussillon*: Domaine Gauby, Domaine Sarda Malet. *Provence*: Domaine Tempier, Château Pibarnon, Domaine de Trévallon, Mas de la Dame, Domaine Richeaume, La Courtade, Château Simone, Château Pradeaux, Château de Bellet.

# Artists and Writers in the South of France

Artists and writers have helped to create our image of the South of France – the poet Stephen Liégeard even gave the Côte d'Azur its name in 1887. Many writers, French and foreign, found a haven in the warmth of the south. From Cézanne to van Gogh, Monet to Picasso, artists have been inspired by the special light and brilliant colors of this seductive region. Today, it is rich in art museums, some devoted to single artists including Matisse, Picasso, and Chagall, others with varied collections such as those in Céret *(see p486)*, Nîmes *(see pp500–1)*, Montpellier *(see pp498–9)*, St.-Tropez *(see p520)*, St.-Paul de Vence *(see pp528–9)*, and Nice *(see pp530–31)*.

Picasso and Françoise Gilot on the Golfe Juan, 1948

Paul Cézanne's studio in Aix-en-Provence *(see p515)*

## Festive Light

The Impressionists were fascinated by the effects of light, and Monet was entranced by "the glaring festive light" of the south, which made colors so intense he said no one would believe they were real if painted accurately. In 1883 Renoir came with him to the south, returning often to paint his voluptuous nudes in the filtered golden light. Bonnard too settled here, painting endless views of the red tiled roofs and palm trees.

Post-Impressionists van Gogh and Gauguin arrived in 1888, attracted by the region's rich colors. Cézanne, who was born in Aix in 1839, analysed and painted the structure of nature, above all the landscape of Provence and his beloved Mont-Ste.-Victoire. Pointillist Paul Signac came to St.-Tropez to paint sea and sky in a rainbow palette of dots.

## The Wild Beasts

The Fauves, dubbed "Wild Beasts" for their unnaturally bright and wild colors, led one of the first 20th-century avant-garde movements, founded by Matisse in Collioure in 1905 *(see p487)*. Other Fauves included Derain, Vlaminck, Marquet, Van Dongen, and Dufy. Matisse visited Corsica in 1898, and then St.-Tropez, and was inspired by the sensuality of Provence to paint the celebrated *Luxe, Calme et Volupté*. Eventually he settled in Nice, where he painted his great series of Odalisques. He wrote, "What made me stay are the great colored reflections of January, the luminosity of daylight." The exquisite blue-and-white chapel he designed in Vence is one of the most moving of his later works *(see p527)*.

Vincent van Gogh's *Sunflowers* (1888)

## Picasso Country

The South of France is, without question, Picasso country. His nymphs and sea urchins, his monumental women running on the beach, his shapes and colors, ceramics and sculpture are all derived from the hard shadows and bright colors of the south.

Pablo Picasso was born in Málaga in Spain in 1881, but he spent much of his life on the French Mediterranean, developing Cubism with Braque in Céret in 1911, and arriving in Juan-les-Pins in 1920. He was in Antibes, when war broke out in 1939, where he painted *Night Fishing at Antibes*, a luminous nocturnal seascape. He returned in 1946 and was given the Grimaldi Palace to use as a studio. It is now a Picasso Museum *(see p525)*. He also worked in Vallauris, producing ceramics and sculptures *(see p526)*.

*Deux Femmes Courant sur la Plage* (1922) by Pablo Picasso

## Lost Caviar Days

Just as F. Scott Fitzgerald wrote the Jazz Age into existence, he created the glittering image of life on the Riviera with *Tender is the Night*. He and Zelda arrived in 1924, attracted, like many expatriate writers, by the warm climate and the cheap, easy living. "One could get away with more on

*Scott and Zelda Fitzgerald with daughter Scottie*

the summer Riviera, and whatever happened seemed to have something to do with art," he wrote. They passed their villa on to another American, Ernest Hemingway. Many other writers flocked there including Katherine Mansfield, D. H. Lawrence, Aldous Huxley, Friedrich Nietzsche, Lawrence Durrell, and Graham Greene. Some, including Somerset Maugham, led glamorous lifestyles surrounded by exotic guests. Colette was an early visitor to St.-Tropez, and in 1954, Françoise Sagan captured the youthful hedonism of the time in her novel *Bonjour Tristesse*.

## New Realism

In the 1950s Nice produced its own school of artists, the Nouveaux Réalistes, including Yves Klein, Arman, Martial Raysse, Tinguely, César, Niki de Saint Phalle, and Daniel Spoerri *(see pp530–31)*. They explored the possibilities of everyday objects – Arman sliced violins, packaged and displayed trash; Tinguely exploded TV sets and cars. They had a lighthearted approach: "We live in a land of vacations, which gives us the spirit of nonsense," said Klein. He painted solid blue canvases of his personal color, International Klein Blue, taking the inspiration of the Mediterranean to its limit.

## Provençal Writers

The regions of Provence and Languedoc have always had a distinct literary identity, ever since the troubadours in the 12th–13th centuries composed their love poetry in the *langue d'oc* Provençal, a Latin-based language. In the 20th century, many regional writers have been inspired by the landscape and local traditions. They were influenced by the 19th-century Felibrige Movement to revive the language, led by Nobel Prize-winning poet Frédéric Mistral. Some, including Daudet and movie-maker-turned-writer Marcel Pagnol, celebrate the Provençal character; others, such as Jean Giono, explore the connection between nature and humanity.

*Frédéric Mistral in the* Petit Journal

# Beaches in the South of France

The glamorous Mediterranean coast is France's foremost vacation playground. To the east lie the Riviera's big, traditional resorts such as Menton, Nice, Cannes, and Monte-Carlo. To the west are smaller resorts in coves and bays including St.-Tropez and Cassis. Farther on is the Camargue Regional Nature Park at the mouth of the Rhône. West of the Rhône, making a majestic curve reaching almost to the Spanish border, is the long, sandy shore of Languedoc and Roussillon, where a string of purpose-built resorts range from modernistic beach cities to replicas of fishing villages.

The beaches are sandy west of Antibes; eastward, they are naturally shingly, so any sand is imported. Anti-pollution drives mean that most beaches are now clean, except in a few spots west of Marseille and around Nice. Private beaches are plentiful and pricey but are usually well equipped.

A railroad poster by David Dellepiane advertising the Côte d'Azur

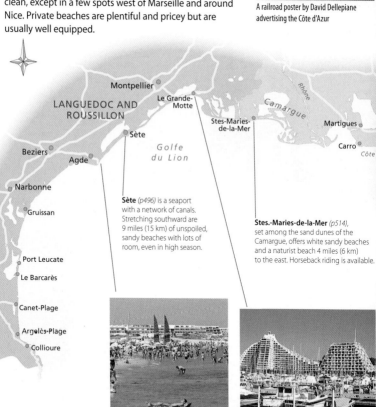

**Sète** *(p496)* is a seaport with a network of canals. Stretching southward are 9 miles (15 km) of unspoiled, sandy beaches with lots of room, even in high season.

**Stes.-Maries-de-la-Mer** *(p514),* set among the sand dunes of the Camargue, offers white sandy beaches and a naturist beach 4 miles (6 km) to the east. Horseback riding is available.

**Cap d'Agde** *(p491)* is a vast modern resort with long, golden sandy beaches and sport amenities of all kinds. It has Europe's largest naturist resort, accommodating 45,000 visitors.

**La Grande-Motte** *(p499)* is a huge purpose-built beach resort with excellent sport amenities, famous for its bizarre ziggurat architecture.

0 kilometers    25

0 miles    25

**In Victorian times** the Côte d'Azur, or Riviera, was the fashionable vacation venue of Europe's royalty and rich. They came to gamble and escape northern winters. Summer bathing did not come into vogue until the 1920s. Today the Riviera is busy year round, with the glamorous beaches and nightlife still a major attraction.

**PROVENCE AND THE COTE D'AZUR**

Menton
Monaco
Nice
Cap Ferrat
Antibes
Cannes
St-Raphaël
l'Esterel
Ste-Maxime
St-Tropez
Cavalaire-sur-Mer
Lavandou
La Ciotat
Toulon
Hyères
Cap Sicie
Iles d'Hyères

**Menton** *(p533)* has a warm climate in winter, giving beach weather all year. Its sheltered, shingly beaches are backed by beautiful villas.

**Cannes** *(pp524–5)* takes great pride in its golden beaches, keeping them scrupulously clean: most are private with entrance fees.

**Cassis** *(p517)* is a charming fishing village with a popular casino, white cliffs, and some lovely hidden creeks nearby.

**Cap Ferrat** *(p532)* is a wooded peninsula with a 6-mile (10-km) craggy cliff walk, offering glimpses of grand villas and private beaches.

**Nice** *(pp530–31)* has a visually dramatic waterfront with a wide, handsome promenade, but the beach itself is stony and has a busy highway alongside.

**St.-Tropez** *(p520)* is flanked by golden beaches, mostly occupied by stylish "clubs" offering amenities at a price.

# LANGUEDOC AND ROUSSILLON

*Pyrénées-Orientales · Aude · Gard · Hérault*

The southern area of Languedoc and Roussillon stretches from the foothills of the Pyrenees to the mouth of the Rhône. The flat beaches and lagoons of the coast form a popular sunbelt. In between is a dry, scorched land producing half of France's table wine and the season's first peaches and cherries.

Beyond such sensuous pleasures are many layers of history, not least the amalgamation of Languedoc and Roussillon within the new region of Occitanie, created in 2016. Languedoc is where Occitan, the tongue of the troubadours, was once spoken and the area still cherishes its linguistic and cultural identity. Roussillon was a Spanish possession until the treaty of the Pyrenees in 1659. Catalan heritage is displayed everywhere from the road signs to the Sardana dance, and the flavor of Spain is evident in the popularity of paella and gaudily painted facades.

This stretch of coastline was the first place in Gaul to be settled by the Romans, their enduring legacy evident in the great amphitheater at Nîmes and the magnificent engineering of the Pont du Gard. The abbeys of St.-Martin-du-Canigou, St.-Michel-de-Cuxa, and St.-Guilhem-le-Désert are superb examples of early Romanesque architecture, unaffected by Northern Gothic. The great craggy Cathar castles and the perfectly restored medieval city of Carcassonne bear witness to the bloody battles of the Middle Ages.

In parts, the area remains wild and untamed: from the high plateaus of the Cerdagne, to the wild hills of the Corbières, or the remote uplands of Haut Languedoc. But it also has the most youthful and progressive cities in France: Montpellier, the ancient university city and capital of the region, and Nîmes with its exuberant *feria*. The whole area is typified by an insouciant mixture of ancient and modern, from Roman temples and Postmodern architecture in its cities to solar power and ancient abbeys in the mountains.

The coastline at La Vieux Cap, Cap d'Agde

◀ The citadel of Carcassonne

# Exploring Languedoc and Roussillon

Languedoc and Roussillon combine miles of gentle coastline with a rugged hinterland. The clean, sandy beaches are perfect for family vacations, with resorts ranging from traditional fishing villages to new purpose-built resorts. Inland is quieter, with acres of vineyards in the Corbières and Minervois and mountain walks in the Haut Languedoc and Cerdagne. A rich architectural heritage ranges from Roman to Romanesque, contrasting with the modern, vibrant atmosphere of the main cities.

## Sights at a Glance

1. Cerdagne
2. Villefranche-de-Conflent
3. St.-Michel-de-Cuxa
4. St.-Martin-du-Canigou
5. Prieuré de Serrabone
6. Céret
7. Côte Vermeille
8. Collioure
9. Elne
10. Perpignan
11. Forteresse de Salses
12. Corbières
13. Narbonne
14. Golfe du Lion
15. *Carcassonne (pp492–3)*
16. Minerve
17. Béziers
18. Sète
19. Pézenas
20. Parc Naturel Régional du Haut Languedoc
21. St.-Guilhem-le-Désert
22. Montpellier
23. La Grande-Motte
24. Aigues-Mortes
25. *Nîmes (pp500–1)*
26. Pont du Gard

Jousting on the canal, a regular summer event in Sète

The ruined Barbarossa tower at Gruissan on the Golfe du Lion

## Getting Around

Montpellier's international airport serves the region; smaller airports at Béziers, Carcassonne, Perpignan, and Nîmes have direct flights to the UK. The TGV runs as far as Perpignan, and a good train and bus network connects the region's main towns. The A61 freeway provides access from the west and the A9 follows the coast. The A75 now enters from the north. Smaller roads, even in the mountains, are well maintained. Barges along the Canal du Midi are a leisurely alternative.

### Key

━━ Freeway

━━ Highway

━━ Secondary road

── Minor road

── Scenic route

╍╍ Main railroad

┄┄ Minor railroad

━━ International border

── Regional border

△ Summit

# ❶ Cerdagne

Pyrénées-Orientales. ✈ Perpignan.
🚉 🚌 Mont Louis, Bourg Madame,
Latour de Carol Enveitg. 🛈 1 pl de
Roser, Saillagouse (04 68 04 15 47);
Mont Louis (04 68 04 21 97).
🆆 pyrenees-cerdagne.com
🆆 mont-louis.net

Abbey cloisters of St.-Michel-de-Cuxa

The remote Cerdagne, an independent state in the Middle
Ages, is today divided between
Spain and France. Its high
plateaus offer skiing and walking
among clear mountain lakes and
pine and chestnut forests. The
Little Yellow Train (08 00 88 60 91,
www.ter-sncf.com) is an excellent
way to sample it in a day. Stops
include **Mont Louis**, a town
fortified by Vauban, Louis XIV's
military architect, and which
still accommodates French
troops; the huge ski resort
of **Font-Romeu**; **Latour-
de-Carol**; and the tiny
village of **Yravals** below.
Nearby **Odeillo** is the site
of a solar furnace, 150 ft (45 m)
tall and 165 ft (50 m) wide; its
giant curved mirrors create a
remarkable sight in the valley.

# ❷ Villefranche-
de-Conflent

Pyrénées-Orientales. 🚗 230. 🚉 🚌
🛈 33 rue Saint Jacques (04 68 96 22
96). 🆆 villefranchedeconflent.fr

In medieval times Villefranche's
position at the narrowest point
of the Têt Valley made it an
eminently defensible fortress
against Moorish invasion.
Fragments of 11th-century walls

remain, along with massive
ramparts, gates, and Fort Liberia
high above the gorge, and all
built by Vauban in the 17th
century. The 12th-century **Eglise
de St.-Jacques** has fine carved
capitals from the workshops of
St.-Michel-de-Cuxa and Catalan
painted wooden statues,
including a 14th-century Virgin
and Child. The 13th-century oak
door is embellished with intricate

Statue in St.-Jacques, Villefranche

local wrought ironwork, a craft
that still features on many of the
store signs in town. From the
streets of locally quarried pink
marble you can make the climb
up to the **Grottes des Canalettes**,
a superb underground setting for
concerts. The Little Yellow Train
will take you to the magnificent
mountain plain of the Cerdagne.

# ❸ St.-Michel-
de-Cuxa

Abbey of St.-Michel-de-Cuxa: Rte de
Tourinya Codalet, Prades, Pyrénées-
Orientales. **Tel** 04 68 96 15 35.
**Open** May–Sep: 9:30–11:50am &
2–6pm; Oct–Apr: 2–5pm. **Closed** Jan 1,
Easter Sunday, Dec 25. 🈸
🆆 abbaye-cuxa.com
🛈 10 pl de la République, Prades (04
68 05 41 02). 🆆 prades-tourisme.fr

Prades, a small, pink marble town
in the Têt Valley, is typical of the
local style. The **Eglise St.-Pierre**
has a southern Gothic wrought-
iron belfry and a Baroque Catalan
interior. But the town is distinguished by the pre-Romanesque
**abbey of St.-Michel-de-Cuxa**, 2
miles (3 km) farther up the valley,
and by the legacy of the Spanish
cellist Pablo Casals. Casals spent
many years here in exile from
Franco's Spain; every August the
abbey is the setting for Prades
music festival, held in his memory.
    St.-Michel-de-Cuxa abbey was
founded by Benedictine monks
in 878 and rapidly became
renowned throughout France
and Spain. Distinctive, Moorish-
influenced keyhole arches pierce
the massive walls of the abbey
church, which was consecrated
in 974. The mottled pink marble
cloisters, with their superbly
carved capitals, were added
in the 12th century.

## The Little Yellow Train

Arrive early for the best seats in the cars of *Le Petit Train Jaune*,
which winds its way on narrow-gauge tracks through gorges
and across towering viaducts up into the Cerdagne, stopping
at small mountain stations along the way. Built in 1910 to
improve access to the mountains, it now operates mainly
for tourists, beginning at Villefranche-de-Conflent and
terminating at Latour-de-Carol.

The Little Yellow Train, with open carriages for summer visitors

*For hotels and restaurants in this region see p569 and pp599–601*

After the Revolution the building was abandoned, and its famous carvings looted. From 1913, George Grey Bernard, a visiting American artist, began to discover some of the capitals incorporated in local buildings. In 1925 he sold the carvings to the Metropolitan Museum of Art in New York, where they formed the basis of the Cloisters Museum – a faithful re-creation of a Romanesque abbey in the unlikely setting of Manhattan.

## ❹ St.-Martin-du-Canigou

Casteil. **Tel** 04 68 05 50 03. **Open** (guided tours only: tours last an hour; times vary with seasons) Jun–Sep: daily; Oct–May: Tue–Sun. **Closed** Jan, Good Friday. 🌐 **W** stmartinducanigou.org

St.-Martin-du-Canigou is in a spectacular location a third of the way up Pic du Canigou, on a jagged spur of rock approached only by a 40-minute climb on foot from Casteil, a special shuttle (Jul–Aug: daily), or hired transportation. Built at the beginning of the 11th century, the abbey was financed by Guifred, Count of Cerdagne, who entered the monastery in 1035. He was buried there 14 years later in a tomb he carved from the rock himself, and which can still be seen. The early Romanesque church is based on a simple basilican plan. Two churches built quite literally one on top of the other make the lower church the crypt for the upper building.

The abbey complex is best viewed from above, by continuing up the path. From there, its irregular design clinging to the rock is framed by the dramatic mountain setting – the ensemble a tribute to the ingenuity and vitality of its early builders.

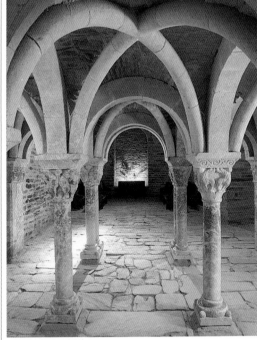

Serrabone priory's chapel tribune, with columns of local marble

## ❺ Prieuré de Serrabone

Boule d'Amont. **Tel** 04 68 84 09 30 (tourist office). **Open** 10am–6pm daily. **Closed** Jan 1, May 1, Nov 1, Dec 25. 🌐

Perched high up on the northern flanks of Pic du Canigou, the sacred mountain of the Catalans, is the priory of Serrabone. A final lap of hairpin bends on the approach road (the D618) reveals the simple square tower and round apse of this remote Romanesque abbey, surrounded by a botanical garden of local herbs and woodland plants clinging to the mountainside.

Inside the cool, austere 12th-century building is a surprisingly elaborate chapel tribune, its columns and arches glowing from the local red-veined marble, carved by the anonymous Master of Cuixà, whose work appears throughout the region. Note the strange beasts and verdant flora featured in the capital carvings, especially the rose of Roussillon.

The 11th-century cloister of St.-Martin-du-Canigou

# ❻ Céret

Pyrénées-Orientales. ⚠ 7,850. 🚌
ℹ 1 av Clémenceau (04 68 87 00 53).
🏪 Sat, Tue eve Jul–Aug. 🎪 Fête des
Cerises (May/Jun). 🖥 ot-ceret.fr

Surrounded by a cloud of pink
blossom in the early spring,
Céret produces the very first
cherries of the year. The annual
cherry festival is held in early
June. The tiled and painted
facades and loggias of the
buildings have a Spanish feel.
The town was popular with
Picasso, Braque, and Matisse, and
today the sophisticated **Musée
d'Art Moderne** houses a
remarkable collection, which
includes Catalan artists Tapiès
and Capdeville; 50 works
donated by Picasso, including a
series of bowls painted with
bullfighting scenes; and works
by Matisse, Chagall, Juan Gris,
and Salvador Dalí.

The town's Catalan heritage
is evident in regular bullfights
held in the arena, and in its
Sardana dance festivals in July.

🏛 **Musée d'Art Moderne**
8 bd Maréchal Joffre. **Tel** 04 68 87 27 76.
**Open** 10am–5:30pm Tue–Sun (Jul–
Sep: to 7pm daily. **Closed** Tue (Oct–
Jun), Jan 1, May 1, Nov 1, Dec 25. 🎫
♿ 📷 🖥 musee-ceret.com

## Environs
From Céret the D115 follows the
Tech Valley to the spa town of

Statue by Aristide Maillol, Banyuls

**Amélie-les-Bains**, where
fragments of Roman baths have
been discovered. Beyond, in
**Arles-sur-Tech**, the Eglise de
Ste.-Marie contains 12th-century
frescoes, and, beside
the church door,
a sarcophagus,
which, according
to local legend,
produces drops of
unaccountably pure
water every year.

Catalan flag

# ❼ Côte Vermeille

Pyrénées-Orientales. ✈ Perpignan.
🚉 Collioure, Cerbère. 🚌 Collioure,
Banyuls-sur-Mer. ℹ Collioure (04 68
82 15 47). 🖥 collioure.com

Here the Pyrenees meet the
Mediterranean, the coast road
twisting and turning around
secluded pebbly coves and
rocky outcrops. The *vermeille*

(vermilion-tinted) rock of the
headlands gives this stretch of
coast, the loveliest in the region,
its name.

The Côte Vermeille extends
all the way to the Costa Brava
in northern Spain. With its
Catalan character, it is as redolent of Spain as of France.
**Argelès-Plage** has three sandy
beaches and a palm-fringed
promenade, and is the largest
camping center in Europe.
The small resort of **Cerbère** is
the last French town before
the border, flying the red-and-
gold Catalan flag to signal its
true allegiance. All along the
coast, terraced vineyards cling
to the rocky hillsides, producing
strong, sweet wines
such as Banyuls and
Muscat. The difficult
terrain makes harvesting
a laborious process. Vines
were first cultivated
here by Greek settlers
in the 7th century BC,
and Banyuls itself has wine
cellars dating back to the
Middle Ages.

Banyuls is also famous as the
birthplace of Aristide Maillol,
the 19th-century sculptor,
whose work can be seen all
over the region. **Port Vendres**,
with fortifications built by the
indefatigable Vauban (architect
to Louis XIV), is a fishing port,
renowned for its anchovies
and sardines.

The spectacular Côte Vermeille, seen from the coast road south of Banyuls

Collioure harbor, with one of its beaches and the Eglise Notre-Dame-des-Anges

# ❽ Collioure

Pyrénées-Orientales. 🏠 3,000. 🚉 🚌 🅸 pl du 18 juin (04 68 82 15 47). 🛒 Wed & Sun. 🆆 collioure.com

The colors of Collioure first attracted Matisse here in 1905: brightly stuccoed houses sheltered by cypresses and gaily painted fishing boats, all bathed in the famous luminous light, and washed by a gentle sea. Other artists including André Derain worked here under Matisse's influence and were dubbed *fauves* (wild beasts) for their wild experiments with color. Art galleries and souvenir shops now fill the cobblestone streets, but this small fishing port has changed little since then, with anchovies still its main business. Two salting houses, which can be visited, are evidence of this tradition.

Three sheltered beaches, both pebble and sand, nestle round the harbor, dominated by the bulk of the **Château Royal**, which forms part of the harbor wall. It was first built by the Knights Templar in the 13th century, and Collioure became the main port of entry for Perpignan, remaining under the rule of Spanish Aragon until France took over in 1659. The outer fortifications were reinforced ten years later by Vauban, who demolished much of the original town in

the process. Today the château can be toured, or visited for its exhibitions of modern art.

The **Eglise Notre-Dame-des-Anges** on Collioure's dockside was rebuilt in the 17th century to replace the church that was destroyed by Vauban. A former lighthouse was incorporated as a bell tower. Inside the church are no fewer than five Baroque altarpieces by Joseph Sunyer and other Catalan masters of the genre.

Be warned that Collioure is extremely popular in July and August, with visitors cramming the tiny streets. Long lines of traffic are possible, too, though the building of another route, the D86, has helped to ease congestion.

**🏠 Château Royal**
**Tel** 04 68 82 06 43. **Open** daily. **Closed** Jan 1, May 1, Aug 15 & 16, Dec 25. 📷

# ❾ Elne

Pyrénées-Orientales. 🏠 8,400. 🚉 🚌 🅸 14 bd Voltaire (04 68 22 05 07). 🛒 Mon, Wed, Fri. 🆆 elne-tourisme.com

This ancient town accommodated Hannibal and his elephants in 218 BC on his epic journey to Rome, and was one of the most important towns in Roussillon until the 16th century. Today it is famed for the 11th-century **Cathédrale de Ste.-Eulalie et Ste.-Julie**, with its superb marble cloister. Its sculpted capitals are embellished with flowers, figures, and arabesques. The side nearest the cathedral dates from the 1100s; the remaining three date from the 13th and 14th centuries.

**🏠 Cathédrale de Ste.-Eulalie et Ste.-Julie**
**Tel** 04 68 22 70 90/05 07. **Open** Oct–Apr: Tue–Sun; May–Sep: daily. **Closed** Jan 1, May 1, Dec 25.

Carved capital at Elne, showing "The Dream of the Magi"

Entrance to the Palais des Rois de Majorque, Perpignan

# ⑩ Perpignan

Pyrénées-Orientales. 🚶 122,000.
✈ 🚉 🚌 *i* Place Arago (04 68 66 30 30). 🛒 daily.
🖥 perpignantourisme.com

Catalan Perpignan has a distinctly southern feel, with palm trees lining place Arago, house and store facades painted vibrant turquoise and pink, and the streets of the Arab quarter selling aromatic spices, couscous, and paella.

Today, Perpignan is the vibrant capital of Roussillon, and has an important position on the developing Mediterranean sunbelt. But it reached its zenith in the 13th and 14th centuries under the kings of Majorca and the kings of Aragón, who controlled great swathes of northern Spain and southern France. Their vast **Palais des Rois de Majorque** still straddles a substantial area in the southern part of the city.

Perpignan's strong Catalan identity is evident during the weekly summer celebrations when the Sardana – a key Catalan symbol – is danced. Arms raised, concentric circles of dancers keep step to the accompaniment of a Catalan woodwind band.

One of Perpignan's finest buildings, the **Loge de Mer**, lies at the head of the square. It was built in 1397 to house the Maritime Exchange, but only the eastern section retains the original Gothic design. The rest of the building was rebuilt in Renaissance style in 1540 with sumptuous carved wooden ceilings and sculpted window frames. The Loge de Mer has avoided becoming a hushed museum piece. Instead, it remains the center

Devout Christ in St.-Jean

of Perpignan life – elegant cafés cluster round it, producing a constant buzz of activity.

Next door is the **Hôtel de Ville** with its pebblestone facade and wrought-iron gates. Inside, parts of the arcaded courtyard date back to 1315; at the center is Aristide Maillol's allegorical sculpture, *The Mediterranean* (1950). To the east is the labyrinthine cathedral quarter of St.-Jean, made up of small streets and squares containing some fine 14th- and 15th-century buildings.

## 🏛 Cathédrale St.-Jean
Pl de Gambetta. **Tel** 04 68 51 33 72.
**Open** 8am–6pm Mon–Sat (7pm summer months); 2–6pm Sun.
🖥 cathedraleperpignan.fr

Topped by a wrought-iron belfry, this cathedral was begun in 1324 and was finally ready for use in 1509. It is constructed almost entirely from river pebbles layered with red brick, a style common throughout the region due to the scarcity of other building materials.

Inside the gloomy interior the nave is flanked by gilded altarpieces and painted wooden statues, with a massive pre-Romanesque marble font. A cloistered cemetery adjoins the church and the Chapel of the Devout Christ with its precious, poignantly realistic medieval wooden Crucifixion. The cathedral replaced the

## The Annual Procession de la Sanch

There is a very Catalan atmosphere in Perpignan during the annual Good Friday procession of the Confraternity of La Sanch (Brotherhood of the Holy Blood). Originally dedicated to the comfort of condemned prisoners in the 15th century, members of the brotherhood still wear macabre red or black robes as they carry sacred relics and the crucifix from the Chapel of the Devout Christ to the cathedral.

11th-century church of St.-Jean-le-Vieux, whose superb Romanesque doorway can be glimpsed to the left of the main entrance. Some areas may be restricted due to ongoing restoration work.

### ⊞ Palais des Rois de Majorque

2 rue des Archers. **Tel** 04 68 34 96 26. **Open** Oct–May: 9am–5pm; Jun–Sep: 10am–6pm. **Closed** Jan 1, May 1, Nov 1 & Dec 25. 🅿 📷

Access to the vast 13th-century fortified palace of the Kings of Majorca is as circuitous today as it was intended to be for invading soldiers. Flights of steps zigzag within the sheer red-brick ramparts, begun in the 15th century and added to successively over the next two centuries. Eventually, the elegant gardens and substantial castle within are revealed, entered by way of the Tour de l'Hommage, from the top of which is a panoramic view of city, mountains, and sea.

The palace itself is built around a central arcaded courtyard, flanked on one side by the Salle de Majorque, a great hall with a triple fireplace and giant Gothic arched windows. Adjacent, two royal chapels built one above the other show southern Gothic style at its best: pointed arches, patterned frescoes, and elaborate tilework demonstrating a distinct Moorish influence. The fine rose marble doorway of the upper King's Chapel is typical of the Roussillon Romanesque style, although the sculpted capitals are Gothic. Today the great courtyard is sometimes used for concerts.

Palais des Rois de Majorque

### 🏛 Musée des Arts et Traditions Populaires Catalans

pl de Verdun, Le Castillet. **Tel** 04 68 35 42 05. **Open** times vary with season. **Closed** public hols. 📷

The red-brick tower and pink belfry of the Castillet, built as the town gate in 1368, was at one time a prison and is all that remains of the town walls. It now houses a traditional Catalan kitchen with furniture, looms, and terracotta pots for storing water and oil.

### 🏛 Musée d'Art Hyacinthe Rigaud

21 rue Mailly. **Tel** 04 68 66 19 83. **Open** Oct–May: 11am–5:30pm Tue–Sun; Jun–Sep: 10:30am–7pm daily (Jul & Aug: till 9pm). **Closed** public hols. 📷 ♿ 🖥 musee-rigaud.fr

Two magnificient mansions dating from the 17th and 18th centuries house an eclectic permanent collection dominated by the work of Hyacinthe Rigaud (1659–1743), who was born in Perpignan and was the court painter to Louis XIV and Louis XV. This is complemented

by a display of the city's medieval art, whose *chef d'oeuvre* is the 15th-century *Retable de la Trinité* by the Master of the Loge de Mer. There is also a room dedicated to Aristide Maillol, whose work is on show alongside his contemporaries such as Alphonse Mucha and Picasso; the latter had several prolonged stays in the building and his studio on the second floor is open to the public.

Fortress tower and ramparts, Salses

### ⓫ Forteresse de Salses

Pyrénées-Orientales. 🚗 3,000. 🚌 🚆 ℹ Salses-le-Château 66600 (04 68 38 60 13). **Open** 10am–5:15pm daily. **Closed** Jan 1, May 1, Nov 1 & 11, Dec 25. 🚫 Wed. 📷 🎫 🖥 forteresse-salses.fr

Looking like a giant sandcastle against the ochre earth of the Corbières vineyards, the Forteresse de Salses stands at the old frontier of Spain and France. It guards the narrow defile between the Mediterranean lagoons and the mountains, and was built by King Ferdinand of Aragon between 1497 and 1506 to defend Spain's possession of Roussillon. Its massive walls and rounded towers are typical of Spanish military architecture, designed to deflect the new threat posed by gunpowder.

Inside were underground stables for 300 horses and a subterranean passageway.

The pebble and red-brick Cathédrale St.-Jean in Perpignan

Vineyards covering the hilly terrain of the Corbières

# ⓬ Corbières

Aude. ✈ Perpignan. 🚉 Narbonne, Carcassonne, Lézignan-Corbières. 🚌 Narbonne, Carcassonne, Lézignan-Corbières. 🛈 9 cours de la République, Lézignan-Corbières (04 68 27 05 42). 🆆 **tourisme-corbieres-minervois.com**

Still one of the wildest parts of France with few roads, let alone villages, the Corbières is best known for its wine and the great craggy hulks of the Cathar castles (see p495). Much of the land is untamed *garrigue* (scrubland), fragrant with honeysuckle and broom; south-facing slopes have been cleared and planted with vines.

To the south are the spectacular medieval castles of **Peyrepertuse** and **Quéribus**, the latter one of the last Cathar strongholds. The guided visits around the remarkable Cathar château at **Villerouge-Termenes** reveal some of its turbulent past. To the west is the barren, uninhabited Razès area in the upper Aude Valley. Its best-kept secret is the village of **Alet-les-Bains**, with beautifully preserved half-timbered houses and the remains of a Benedictine abbey, battle-scarred from the Wars of Religion.

# ⓭ Narbonne

Aude. ⌂ 54,000. 🚉 🚌 🛈 31 rue Jean Jaurès (04 68 65 15 60). 🗓 Thu & Sun. 🆆 **narbonne-tourisme.com**

Narbonne is a medium-sized, cheerful town profiting from the booming wine region that surrounds it. The town is bisected by the tree-shaded Canal de la Robine; to the north is the restored medieval quarter with many good stores and restaurants. Located here is one of Narbonne's most intriguing tourist attractions, the Roman **Horreum**. This underground warehouse dates back to the 1st century BC, when Narbonne was a major port and capital of the largest Roman province in Gaul.

The town prospered through the Middle Ages until the 15th century, when the harbor silted up and the course of the river Aude altered, taking Narbonne's fortunes with it. By then, an important bishopric had been established and an ambitious cathedral project, modeled on the great Gothic cathedrals of the north, was under way. However, the full grandiose design was abandoned, and just the chancel, begun in 1272, became the **Cathédrale St.-Just et St.-Pasteur** we see today.

It is still enormous, enhanced by 14th-century sculptures, fine stained-glass windows and an 18th-century carved organ. Aubusson and Gobelins tapestries adorn the walls, and above the Chapel of the Anonciade it is possible to visit a treasury of manuscripts, jeweled reliquaries, and tapestries.

The unfinished transept now forms a courtyard, and between the cathedral and the **Palais des Archevêques** (Archbishops' Palace) lies a cloister with four galleries of 14th-century vaulting.

This huge palace and cathedral complex dominates the center of Narbonne. Between the Palais des Archevêques' massive 14th-century towers is the town hall, with a 19th-century Neo-Gothic facade by Viollet-le-Duc (see p204), the architect who so determinedly restored medieval France. The palace itself is divided into

The vaulted chancel of Cathédrale St.-Just et St.-Pasteur in Narbonne

## Canal du Midi

From Sète to Toulouse the 149-mile (240-km) Canal du Midi flows between plane trees, vineyards, and villages. The complex system of locks, aqueducts, and bridges is a remarkable feat of engineering, built by the Béziers salt-tax baron Paul Riquet. Completed in 1681, it encouraged Languedoc trade and created a vital link, via the Garonne river, between the Atlantic and the Mediterranean. Today it is plied by vacation barges.

Tranquil waterway of the Canal du Midi

The Cistercian Abbaye de Fontfroide (1093), nestled amongst trees southwest of Narbonne

the Palais Vieux (Old Palace) and the Palais Neuf (New Palace). Narbonne's most important museums are in the Palais Neuf, on the left as you enter through the low medieval arches of the passage de l'Ancre. The **Musée d'Archéologie** collection includes fragments of Narbonne's Roman heritage, from remarkable Roman frescoes, milestones, and parts of the original walls to an assemblage of domestic objects, coins, tools, and glassware. Those with a head for heights shouldn't miss climbing to the top of the 138-ft (42-m) dungeon, Donjon Gilles Aycelin.

In the archbishops' former apartments is the **Musée d'Art et d'Histoire**, which is as interesting for its luxurious furnishings and richly decorated ceilings as for its art collection. This includes some fine paintings by Canaletto, Brueghel, Boucher, and Veronese as well as a large selection of local earthenware. In addition, the museum houses an outstanding collection of Orientalist paintings.

South of the Canal de la Robine are a number of fine mansions, including the Renaissance **Maison des Trois Nourrices** at rue des Trois-Nourrices and rue Edgard Quinet. Nearby is the

**Musée Lapidaire**, with architectural fragments from Gallo-Roman Narbonne, and the 13th-century Gothic **Basilique St.-Paul-Serge**. The collection will transfer to the new **Musée de la Romanité** when it opens in 2019.

### 🏠 Horreum
Rue Rouget-de-l'Isle. **Tel** 04 68 90 30 65. **Open** Jun–Sep: daily; Oct–May: Wed–Mon. **Closed** Jan 1, May 1, Nov 1 & 11, Dec 25.

### 🏛 Musée d'Archéologie/Musée d'Art et d'Histoire
Palais des Archevêques. **Tel** 04 68 90 30 65. **Open** Jun–Sep: daily; Oct–May: Wed–Mon. **Closed** Jan 1, May 1, Nov 1 & 11, Dec 25.

### 🏛 Musee Lapidaire
Eglise Notre-Dame de Lamourguier. **Tel** 04 68 90 30 65. **Open** Jun–Sep: daily; Oct–May: Wed–Mon. **Closed** Jan 1, May 1, Nov 1 & 11, Dec 25.

### Environs
Southwest (8 miles/13 km), the Cistercian **Abbaye de Fontfroide** has an elegant cloister. The abbey is tucked away in a quiet valley, surrounded by cypress trees.

## ⓮ Golfe du Lion

Aude, Hérault. 🚉 🚌 Montpellier. 🚌 Sète. ℹ️ 55 rue du Port, La Grande-Motte (04 67 56 42 00). 🌐 lagrandemotte.com

Languedoc and Roussillon's shoreline forms an almost unbroken sweep of sandy beach. Only at its southern limits does it break into the rocky inlets of the Côte Vermeille. Purpose-built resorts created since the 1960s emphasize eco-friendly, low-rise family accommodations, some in local styles, others with imaginative architecture.

**La Grande-Motte** marina has distinctive ziggurat-style buildings (*see p499*). **Cap d'Agde** has Europe's largest naturist quarter. Inland **Agde**, founded by ancient Greek traders, is built of black basalt and has a fortified cathedral. **Port Leucate** and **Port Bacarès** are ideal for watersports. An older town is **Sète** (*see p496*). A feature of the flat Languedoc coast is its *étangs* – large shallow lagoons. Those nearest the Camargue are the haunt of thousands of wading birds.

A wide, sandy beach on the Cap d'Agde

# ⑮ Carcassonne

The citadel of Carcassonne is a perfectly restored medieval town, and protected by UNESCO. It crowns a steep bank above the River Aude, a fairytale sight of turrets and ramparts overlooking the Basse Ville below. The strategic position of the citadel between the Atlantic and the Mediterranean and on the corridor between the Iberian peninsula and the rest of Europe led to its original settlement, consolidated by the Romans in the 2nd century BC. It became a key element in medieval military conflicts. At its zenith in the 12th century, it was ruled by the Trencavels, who built the château and cathedral. Military advances and the Treaty of the Pyrenees in 1659, which relocated the French–Spanish border, hastened its decline. The attentions of architectural historian Viollet-le-Duc *(see p204)* led to its restoration in the 19th century.

**The Restored Citadel**
Restoration of La Cité has always been controversial. Critics complain that it looks too new, favoring a more romantic ruin.

★ **Basilique St.-Nazaire**
Within the Romanesque and Gothic cathedral is the famous Siege Stone, said to depict the 1209 Siege of Carcassonne by crusaders.

**KEY**

① **The ramparts** were built by Kings Louis VIII, Louis IX, and Philip the Bold, in the 13th century.

② **Bishop's Tower**

③ **Porte d'Aude**

④ **Gallo-Roman walls**

⑤ **The Great Well**

⑥ **The *lices***, the easily defended spaces between the inner and outer ramparts, were also used for jousting, for crossbow practice, and for storage of lumber and other materials.

★ **Le Château**
A fortress within a fortress, the château has a moat, five towers, and defensive wooden galleries on the walls.

## Religious Persecution

Carcassonne's strategic position meant it was often at the center of religious conflict. The Cathars *(see p495)* were given sanctuary here in 1209 by Raymond-Roger Trencavel when besieged by Simon de Montfort in his crusade against heresy. In the 14th century the Inquisition continued to root out the Cathars. This painting depicts intended victims in the Inquisition Tower.

*Les Emmurés de Carcassonne*, J. P. Laurens

### VISITORS' CHECKLIST

**Practical Information**
Aude. 47,000. 28 rue de Verdun (04 68 10 24 30). Tue, Thu & Sat. Festival de Carcassonne (Jul–Aug); l'Embrasement de la Cité (Jul 14). Le Château: **Open** 9:30am–5pm daily (Apr–Sep: to 6.30pm). **Closed** Jan 1, May 1, July 14, Nov 1 & 11, Dec 25.
**tourisme-carcassonne.fr**

**Transportation**
2 miles (4 km) W Carcassonne. Port du Canal du Midi. 30 rue Georges Brassens.

**Musée Lapidaire**
The collection includes Roman amphorae and terracotta, Romanesque murals and fragments from the cathedral, a set of Gothic windows, and these medieval stone missiles.

**Porte Narbonnaise**
Flanked by two sandstone towers, built in 1280, the defenses included two portcullises, two iron doors, a moat, and a drawbridge.

Main entrance to La Cité

**Old City Entrance**
Entering La Cité is still a step back in time, although it is one of France's top tourist destinations, filled with souvenir shops.

**Key**
— Suggested route

Béziers with its medieval cathedral, seen from Pont Vieux in the southwest

## ⑯ Minerve

Hérault. 🚗 130. 🛈 Rue des Martyrs (04 68 91 81 43). 🖳 **minervois-tourisme.fr**

In the parched, arid hills of the Minervois, surrounded by vines and not much else, Minerve appears defiant on its rocky outcrop at the confluence of the rivers Cesse and Briant. It is defended by what the Minervois call the "Candela" (Candle), an octagonal tower that is all that remains of the medieval château. In 1210, the small town resisted the vengeful Simon de Montfort, scourge of the Cathars, in a siege lasting seven weeks. This culminated in the execution of 140 Cathars, who were burned at the stake.

Today visitors enter Minerve by a high bridge spanning the gorge. Turn right and follow the route of the Cathars past the Romanesque arch of the Porte des Templiers to the 12th-century **Eglise St.-Etienne**. Outside the church is a crudely carved dove, symbol of the Cathars, and within is a 5th-century white marble altar table, one of the oldest artifacts in the region.

A rocky path follows the riverbed below the town, where the water has cut out caves and two bridges – the Grand Pont and the Petit Pont – from the soft limestone.

## ⑰ Béziers

Hérault. 🚗 77,000. ✈ 🚆 🚌 🛈 pl du Forum (04 99 41 36 36). 🖳 Fri. 🖳 **beziers-mediteranee.com**

Famous for its bullfights and rugby, and the wine of the surrounding region, Béziers has several other points of interest. The town seems turned in on itself, its roads leading up to the massive 14th-century **Cathédrale St.-Nazaire**, with its fine sculpture, stained glass, and frescoes. In 1209, several thousand citizens were massacred in the crusade against the Cathars. The papal legate's troops were ordered not to discriminate between Catholics and Cathars, but to "Kill them all. God will recognize his own!" The **Musée du Biterrois**

Statue of the engineer Paul Riquet in the allées Paul Riquet, Béziers

holds exhibitions (in French only) on local history, wine, and the Canal du Midi, engineered in the late 17th century by Paul Riquet, Béziers' most famous son (see p490). His statue presides over the Allées Paul Riquet, which is lined by rows of plane trees and large canopied restaurants, a civilized focus to this otherwise businesslike town.

**🏛 Musée du Biterrois**
Ramp du 96ème, Caserne St.-Jacques. **Tel** 04 67 36 81 60. **Open** 10am–6pm Tue–Sun (Oct–May: to 5pm Tue–Fri). **Closed** Jan 1, Easter, May 1, Dec 25. 🚫 ♿

### Environs
Overlooking the Béziers plain and the mountains to the north is Oppidum d'Ensérune, a superb Roman site. The **Musée de l'Oppidum d'Ensérune** has a good archeological collection, from Celtic, Greek, and Roman vases to jewelry and weapons.

The **Château de Raissac** (between Béziers and Lignan) houses an unusual 19th-century faïence museum in its stables.

**🏛 Musée de l'Oppidum d'Ensérune**
Nissan-lez-Ensérune. **Tel** 04 67 37 01 23. **Open** daily (Sep–Apr: Tue–Sun). **Closed** public hols. 🚫 📷 ♿ limited. 🖳 **enserune.fr**

**🏛 Château de Raissac**
Rte de Lignan sur Orr. **Tel** 04 67 49 17 60. **Open** by appt. 🖳 **raissac.com**

# The Cathars

The Cathars (from Greek *katharos*, meaning "pure") were a 12th- to 14th-century Christian sect critical of corruption in the established Catholic Church. Cathar dissent flourished in independent Languedoc as an expression of separatism, but the rebellion was rapidly exploited for political purposes. Peter II of Aragon was keen to annex Languedoc, and Philippe II of France joined forces with the pope to crush the Cathar heretics in a crusade led by Simon de Montfort in 1209. This began over two centuries of ruthless killing and torture.

**Cathar Castles**
The Cathars took refuge in the defensive castles of the Corbières and Ariège. Peyrepertuse is one of the most remote and difficult to get to even today: a long, narrow stone citadel hacked from a high, craggy peak over 2,000 ft (609 m) high.

**Cathars** (also known as Albigensians) believed in the duality of good and evil. They considered the material world entirely evil. To be truly pure they had to renounce the world, and be nonviolent, vegetarian, and sexually abstinent.

**The crusade** against the Cathars was vicious. Heretics' land was promised to the crusaders by the pope, who assured forgiveness in advance of their crimes. In 1209, 20,000 citizens were massacred in Béziers, and, in 1210 some 140 were burned to death in Minerve. In 1244, another 225 Cathars died defending one of their last fortresses at Montségur.

## Cathar Country
Castles and towns with a Cathar association, some of them spectacular sites, are concentrated in Languedoc, the center of Catharism in the Middle Ages.

The impressive Grand Hôtel *(see p569)* with the Canal Royal in the foreground

## ⑱ Sète

Hérault. 🗺 45,000. 🚊 🚌 ⛴ 🛈 60 grand' rue Mario Roustan (04 99 04 71 71). ⛴ daily. 🌐 **tourisme-sete.com**

Sète is a major fishing and industrial port. It has a gutsier, more raffish air than much of the leisure-oriented Mediterranean, with its stores selling ships' lamps and propellers, and its dockside restaurants full of hungry sailors demolishing vast platters of mussels, oysters, and sea snails straight off the boat. Most of Sète's restaurants can be found on a stroll along the Grand Canal, with its Italianate houses painted in pastel colors and with wrought-iron balconies overlooking Sète's network of canals and bridges. Boisterous water jousting

tournaments on Canal Royal, dating back to 1666, form part of the patron saint's festival in August *(see p42)*.

To the west of the town, next to the open-air Théâtre de la Mer, is the **Musée de la Mer**, which explores Sète's maritime and water jousting history from the 18th century to the present day.

Nearby is the **Cimetière Marin**, where Sète's most famous son, poet Paul Valéry (1871–1945), is buried. There is a small art museum and breathtaking views of the coast and the mountains from the lookout on Mont St.-Clair.

### 🏛 Musée de la Mer

1 rue Jean Vilar. **Tel** 04 99 04 71 55. **Open** Tue–Sun. **Closed** Jan 1, May 1, Dec 25. 🎫 ♿

## ⑲ Pézenas

Hérault. 🗺 8,500. 🚌 🛈 Pl des Etats de Languedoc (04 67 98 36 40). ⛴ Sat. 🌐 **pezenas-tourisme.fr**

Pézenas is a charming little town, easily appreciated in a gentle stroll of its main sights, and abounding in revealing details, fragmentary evidence of its past brilliance as the seat of local government in the 16th–17th centuries. Then the town also played host to many troupes of musicians and actors, including Molière.

The narrow streets in the old town are beautifully preserved. Best of all are the glimpses of fine houses through courtyard doorways, such as the **Hôtel des Barons de Lacoste**, at 8 rue François-Oustrin, with its beautiful stone staircase, and the **Maison des Pauvres** at 12 rue Alfred Sabatier, with its three galleries and staircase.

Look for the medieval store window on rue Triperie-Vieille, and just within the 14th-century **Porte Faugères**, the streets of the Jewish quarter (rue Juiverie and rue des Litanies), with their chilling feeling of enclosure. Stores selling antiques, secondhand goods and books abound. All around the town, vines stretch as far as the eye can see.

The stone lobby of the Hôtel des Barons de Lacoste in Pézenas

Cimetière Marin in Sète, burial place of the poet Paul Valéry

*For hotels and restaurants in this region see p569 and pp599–601*

# ⑳ Parc Naturel Régional du Haut Languedoc

Hérault, Tarn. 🚄 Béziers. 🚌 Béziers, Bédarieux. 🚌 St.-Pons-de-Thomières. 🛈 St.-Pons-de-Thomières (04 67 38 22). 🔲 **parc-haut-languedoc.fr**

The high limestone plateaus and wooded slopes of upper Languedoc are a world away from the coast. From the Montagne Noire, a mountainous region between Béziers and Castres, up into the Cévennes is a landscape of remote sheep farms, eroded rock formations, and deep river gorges. Much of this area has been designated the Parc Naturel Régional du Haut Languedoc, one of the largest of the French regional parks.

You can enter the park at **St.-Pons-de-Thomières**, with access to forest and mountain trails for walking and horseback riding, plus a wildlife research center, where one can glimpse the mouflons (wild mountain sheep), eagles, and wild boar, that were once a common sight in the region. You can also enter the park at Revel, Castres, St.-Chinian, and Lodéve.

If you take the D908 from St.-Pons through the park, you pass the village of **Olargues** with its 12th-century bridge over the River Jaur. **Lamalou-les-Bains**, on the park's eastern edge, is a small spa town with a restored *belle époque* spa building and theater, and a soporifically slow pace.

Outside the park boundaries to the northeast there are spectacular natural phenomena. At the **Cirque de Navacelles**, the River Vis has joined up with itself cutting out an entire island. On it sits the peaceful village of Navacelles, visible from the road higher up. The **Grotte des Demoiselles** is one of the most magnificent in an area full of caves, where you walk through a calcified world. A funicular takes visitors from the foot of the mountain to the top.

The **Grotte de Clamouse** is also an extraordinary experience, the reflections from underground rivers and pools flickering on the cavern roofs. The Spéléopark offers caving activities.

🎫 **Grotte des Demoiselles**
St.-Bauzille-de-Putois, Ganges. **Tel** 04 67 73 70 02. **Open** daily. **Closed** Jan, Dec 25. 🎫 📷 💻 🔲 **demoiselles.com**

🎫 **Grotte de Clamouse**
Rte de St.-Guilhem-le-Désert, St.-Jean-de-Fos. **Tel** 04 67 57 71 05. **Open** daily. 🎫 📷 💻 🔲 **clamouse.com**

Grotte des Demoiselles

# ㉑ St.-Guilhem-le-Désert

Hérault. 🏘 270. 🚌 🛈 2 pl de la Liberté (04 67 56 41 97). 🔲 **saint guilhem-valleeherault.fr**

Tucked away in the Celette mountains, St.-Guilhem-le-Désert is no longer as remote as when Guillaume of Aquitaine retired here as a hermit in the 9th century. After a lifetime as a soldier, Guillaume received a fragment of the True Cross from Emperor Charlemagne and established a monastery in this ravine above the River Hérault.

Vestiges of the first 10th-century church have been discovered, but most of the building is a superb example of 11th- to 12th-century Romanesque architecture. Its lovely apsidal chapels dominate the heights of the village, behind which the carved doorway opens on to a central square.

Within the church is a sombre barrel-vaulted central aisle leading to the sunlit central apse. Only two galleries of the cloisters remain: the rest are in New York, along with carvings from St.-Michel-de-Cuxa (*see p484–5*).

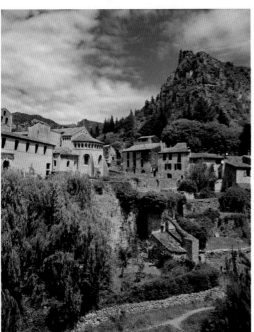

The picturesque village of St.-Guilhem-le-Désert

## Montpellier City Center

① Place de la Comédie
② CORUM
③ Tour de la Babote
④ Tours des Pins
⑤ Cathédrale St.-Pierre
⑥ Notre-Dame des Tables
⑦ Hôtel de Manse
⑧ Hôtel de Mirman
⑨ Hôtel des Trésoriers de la Bourse
⑩ Musée Fabre
⑪ Promenade de Peyrou
⑫ Château d'Eau
⑬ Jardin des Plantes

0 meters 250
0 yards 250

**For keys to symbols** see back flap

Open-air café in place de la Comédie, in the heart of Montpellier

## ㉒ Montpellier

Hérault. 🅜 279,000. ✈ 🚉 🚌
🛈 30 allée Jean de Lattré de Tassigny (04 67 60 60 60). 🏬 daily. 🎭 Festival International Montpellier Danse (Jun–Jul). 🖥 **montpellier-france.com**

Montpellier is one of the liveliest and most forward-looking cities in the south, with a quarter of its population under 25. Sometimes on an evening in university term time it resembles a rock festival more than the second-largest city in Occitanie. Center of the action is the egg-shaped

place de la Comédie, known as "l'Oeuf" ("the egg"), with its 19th-century opera house fronted by the Fontaine des Trois Graces and surrounded by buzzing cafés. An esplanade of plane trees and fountains leads to the **CORUM**, an opera and conference center typical of the city's brave new architectural projects. The best of these is Ricardo Bofill's Postmodern housing complex, known as Antigone, and modelled on St. Peter's in Rome, Jean Nouvel and François Fortes's city hall, and La Nuage, a Philippe-Starck-designed sports and wellness center.

Montpellier was founded relatively late, developing in the 10th century as a result of the spice trade with the Middle East. The city's medical school was founded in 1220, partly as a result of this cross-fertilization of knowledge between the two cultures, and remains one of the most respected in France.

Most of Montpellier was ravaged by the Wars of Religion in the 16th century. Only the **Tour de la Babote** and the **Tours des Pins** remain of the 12th-century fortifications.

There are few fine churches, the exceptions being the **Cathédrale St.-Pierre** and the 18th-century **Notre-Dame des Tables**.

The 1600s saw the building of mansions with elegant court-yards, stone staircases, and balconies. Examples open to the public include **Hôtel de Manse** on rue Embouque-d'Or, **Hôtel de Mirman** near place des Martyrs de la Resistance, and **Hôtel des Trésoriers de la Bourse**.

Another 17th-century building houses the **Musée Fabre**, with its collection of mainly French art. Highlights include Courbet's *Bonjour M. Courbet*, Berthe Morisot's *L'Eté*, and some evocative paintings of the region by Raoul Dufy. Look for

## Pont du Gard

← To Uzès

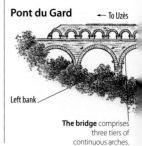

Left bank

**The bridge** comprises three tiers of continuous arches.

paintings by a local Impressionist artist, Frédéric Bazille, who died tragically young at the age of 29.

To view the city's position between mountains and sea, go to the **Promenade de Peyrou**, a grand 18th-century square dominated by the **Château d'Eau** and the aqueduct that used to serve the city. North of here is the **Jardin des Plantes**, France's oldest botanical gardens (1593). Not to be missed is **Mare Nostrum**, the aquarium in the Odysseum leisure zone, which has over 300 marine species.

**🏛 Musée Fabre**
39 bd Bonne Nouvelle. **Tel** 04 67 14 83 00. **Open** Tue–Sun. 🦽 📷 🚫 📷 ♿
**W** museefabre.montpellier3m.fr

**🐠 Mare Nostrum**
Allée Ulysse, Odysseum. **Tel** 04 67 13 05 50. **Open** daily. **Closed** Jan 1, Dec 25. 🦽 ♿ 📷 📷
**W** aquariummarenostrum.fr

Château d'Eau, Montpellier

## ㉓ La Grande-Motte

Hérault. 🔼 8,700. 🚌 **ℹ** 55 rue du Port (04 67 56 42 00). 🛍 Sun (& Thu: mid-Jun–mid-Sep). **W** lagrandemotte.fr

The bizarre white ziggurats of this modern marina exemplify the development of France's

La Grande-Motte

southwest coast. One of several on the lagoons south of Montpellier, there are marinas and amenities for every kind of sport, from tennis and golf to watersports, all flanked by golden beaches and pine forests. To the east are Le Grau-du-Roi, once a tiny fishing village, and Port-Camargue, with its big marina.

## ㉔ Aigues-Mortes

Gard. 🔼 8,500. 🚇 🚌 **ℹ** pl St. Louis (04 66 53 73 00). 🛍 Wed & Sun.
**W** ot-aiguesmortes.fr

The best approach to this perfectly preserved walled town is across the salt marshes of the Camargue Gardoise. Now marooned 3 miles (5 km) from the sea, the imposing defenses of this once-important port have become a tourist experience, worth visiting more for the effect of the ensemble than the touristy stores within. Aigues-Mortes ("Place of Dead Waters") was established by Louis XI in the 13th century to consolidate his power on the Mediterranean, and built according to a strict

grid pattern. By climbing up the **Tour de Constance** you can walk out onto the rectangular walls, which afford a superb view over the Camargue.

**Environs**
To the northeast is **St.-Gilles-du-Gard**, also once an important medieval port. Today it is worth a detour to see the superbly sculpted 12th-century facade of its abbey church. This was originally established by the monks of Cluny abbey as a shrine to St. Gilles, and a resting place on the famous pilgrimage route to Santiago de Compostela (see pp404–5).

## ㉕ Nîmes

See pp500–1.

## ㉖ Pont du Gard

400 rte du Pont du Gard-La Bégud, Gard. 🚌 from Nîmes. **ℹ** 04 66 37 50 99. **Open** daily. 🦽 ♿ 📷 📷 📷
**W** pontdugard.fr

No amount of fame can diminish the first sight of the 2,000-year-old Pont du Gard, a UNESCO World Heritage site. The Romans considered it the best testimony to the greatness of their empire, and at 160 ft (49 m) it was the highest bridge they ever built.

It is made from blocks of stone, hauled into place by slaves using an ingenious system of pulleys. The huge build-up of calcium in the water channels suggests the aqueduct was in continuous use for 400 to 500 years, carrying water to Nîmes along a 31-mile (50-km) route from the springs at **Uzès**. This charming town has an arcaded marketplace and several fine medieval towers.

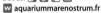

Water channel ———

To Nîmes →

Right bank

**Roman inscriptions** include a damaged phallus carving as a good luck symbol.

**Some stones** weighed up to six tonnes.

# ㉕ Nîmes

One of the most popular sites in Nîmes is the bus stop designed by Philippe Starck, who is also credited with reworking the city's traffic-free zone. Such innovations are part of the city's design renaissance. Architectural projects range from imaginative housing to a glittering arts complex, under the guidance of a dynamic mayor. An important crossroads in the ancient world, Nîmes is equally well known for its Roman antiquities such as the amphitheater, the best preserved of its kind. The city is also famous for its festivals and bullfights (*ferias*). These are good times to see the rest of Nîmes with its museums, archaeological collections, and Old Town of narrow streets and intimate squares.

Arches of the Roman amphitheater

## Historic Nîmes

Nîmes has had a turbulent history, suffering particularly during the 16th-century Wars of Religion, when the Romanesque **Cathédrale Notre-Dame et St.-Castor** was badly damaged. During the 17th and 18th centuries the town prospered from textile manufacturing, one of the most enduring products being denim, or "de Nîmes." Many of the fine houses of this period have been restored – elegant examples can be seen on rue de l'Aspic, rue des Marchands, and rue du Chapitre in the Old Town. Just outside the town center is a futuristic apartment building, **Nemausus I**.

The Roman gate, the **Porte Auguste** was once part of one of the longest city walls in Gaul.

Jug from Musée Archéologique

Of the original arches still standing, two (large ones) were for chariots and carts, and two (smaller ones) for pedestrians. The other major Roman remnant is the **Castellum**. Water used to arrive here from the Pont du Gard (see pp498–9) to be distributed around the city.

## Les Jardins de la Fontaine (Tour Magne)

Quai de la Fontaine. **Tel** 04 66 21 82 56. **Open** 7:30am–6:30pm daily (Mar & Sep: to 8pm; Apr–Aug: to 10pm). reserve at tourist office.

When the Romans arrived in Nîmes, they found a town established by the Gauls,

---

0 meters 250
0 yards 250

Tour Magne ⑥
Mont Cavalier ⑤
Temple de Diane
Les Jardins de la Fontaine ④

ALÈS

RUE ROUGÉ
RUE DE LA TOUR MAGNE
BÉNÉDICTINS
RUE PASTEUR
RUE TRAJAN
QUAI DE LA FONTAINE
QUAI DE LA FONTAINE
RUE BOISSIE
RUE GRETRY  d'Art J Bous
RUE DES CHASSAINTES
PLACE J. GUESTE
RUE FERNAND PELLOUTIER
BOULEVARD JEAN-JAURÈS
RUE MARESCHAL
RUE EMILE JAMA
RUE DÉLON SOUBEYRAN
RUE BEC DE L
RUE DE L'HOTE
RUE RENAN
RUE LO
RUE

---

## Sights at a Glance

① Cathédrale Notre-Dame et St.-Castor
② Porte Auguste
③ Castellum
④ Les Jardins de la Fontaine
⑤ Mont Cavalier
⑥ Tour Magne
⑦ Les Arènes
⑧ Maison Carrée
⑨ Musée des Beaux-Arts
⑩ Carré d'Art Jean Bousquet/ Musée d'Art Contemporain

Les Jardins de la Fontaine, with a view over the city

centered on the source of a spring. They named the town Nemausus, after their river god. In the 18th century, formal gardens were constructed, and a network of limpid pools and cool stone terraces remains. High above the garden on **Mont Cavalier** is the octagonal **Tour Magne**, once a key part of the Roman walls, offering a great view of the city.

Arms of the city in a sculpture by Martial Raysse

up to 20,000 spectators. Today it is a perfect venue for concerts, sport events, and bullfights.

Les Grands Jeux Romains, a three-day reenactment of traditional Roman games at the end of April, are a sight to behold. Facing Les Arènes, the Musée de la Romanité houses ancient Roman statues, ceramics, coins, glass, and mosaics.

### 🏛 Maison Carrée

Pl de la Maison Carrée. **Tel** 04 66 21 82 56. **Open** daily.

This elegant Roman temple built around AD 2 is one of the best preserved in the world. Inside, a multimedia experience, "Nemausus," illustrates the birth of the city.

### 🏛 Musée des Beaux-Arts

Rue Cité Foulc. **Tel** 04 66 28 18 32. **Open** 10am–6pm Tue–Sun. **Closed** Jan 1, May 1, Nov 1, Dec 25. 🎫 ♿

This fine arts museum houses an eclectic collection of 16th–19th-century Dutch, French, Italian, and Flemish works, notably Jacopo Bassano's *Susanna and the Elders* and the *Mystic Marriage of St. Catherine* by Michele Giambono. The Gallo-Roman mosaic of *The Marriage of Admetus*, discovered in 1882, is on the main floor.

### 🏛 Les Arènes (L'Amphithéâtre)

10 bd des Arènes. **Tel** 04 66 21 82 56. **Open** daily. **Closed** Feria des Vendanges, Feria de Pentecôte, performance days. 🎫 ♿ 🏛 🎧 📶 **arenes.nimes.fr**

All roads lead to the amphitheater, Les Arènes. Built at the end of the 1st century AD, the design of the oval arena and tiers of stone seats accommodated huge crowds of

The Maison Carrée

### 🏛 Carré d'Art Jean Bousquet/Musée d'Art Contemporain

Pl de la Maison Carrée. **Tel** 04 66 76 35 70 (Mon–Fri), 04 66 76 35 35 (Sat & Sun). **Open** 10am–6pm Tue–Sun. **Closed** Jan 1, May 1, Nov 1, Dec 25. 🎫 📶 🖥 ♿ **carreartmusee.com**

Nîmes' glass-and-steel arts complex, designed by the British architect Sir Norman Foster, was built in tribute to the Maison Carrée opposite. Five of its floors lie underground. The complex has a library, a roof-terrace restaurant around a huge glass atrium, and the Musée d'Art Contemporain. The collection covers the main European art movements from the 1960s on, and includes works by French artists Raysse, Boltanski, and Lavier.

*Virgil, Horace, and Varius in Mecene's home* (1846) by Charles Jalabert at the Musée des Beaux-Arts

For keys to symbols *see back flap*

# PROVENCE AND THE COTE D'AZUR

*Vaucluse · Bouches-du-Rhône · Var*
*Alpes-de-Haute-Provence · Alpes-Maritimes*

No other region of France fires the imagination as strongly as Provence, from its herb-scented hills to its yacht-filled harbors. The vivid landscape and luminous light have inspired artists and writers from van Gogh to Picasso, and F. Scott Fitzgerald to Pagnol.

The borders of Provence are defined by nature: to the west, the Rhône; south, the Mediterranean; and north, where the olive trees end. To the east are the Alps and a border that has shifted over the centuries between France and Italy. Within is a contrasting terrain of plummeting gorges, Camargue salt flats, lavender fields, and sun-drenched beaches.

Past visitors have left their mark. In Orange and Arles, the buildings of Roman Provincia are still in use. Fortified villages such as Eze were built to withstand the Saracen pirates who plagued the coast in the 6th century.

In the 19th century, rich Europeans sought winter warmth on the Riviera; by the 1920s, high society was in residence year round, and their elegant villas remain. The warm sunlight nurtures intense flavors and colors. Peppers, garlic, and olives transform a netful of Mediterranean fish into that vibrant epitome of Provençal cuisine, *bouillabaisse.*

The image of Provence bathed in sunshine is marred only when the bitter Mistral wind scours the land. It has shaped a people as hardy as the olive tree, yet quick to embrace life to the full the moment the sun returns.

Cap Martin, seen from the village of Roquebrune

◀ Boats moored in the harbor at Nice

# Exploring Provence

This sun-drenched southeastern region is France's most popular holiday destination. Sunworshippers cram the beaches in the summer months, and entertainment includes opera, dance, and jazz festivals, bullfights, casinos, and *boules* games. Inland is a paradise for walkers and nature lovers, with remote mountain plateaus, perched villages, and dramatic river gorges.

Visitors at a souvenir shop in St.-Paul de Vence

## Sights at a Glance

1. Mont Ventoux
2. Vaison-la-Romaine
3. Orange
4. Châteauneuf-du-Pape
5. *Avignon (pp507–9)*
6. Carpentras
7. Fontaine-de-Vaucluse
8. Gordes
9. Luberon
10. St.-Rémy-de-Provence
11. Les Baux-de-Provence
12. Tarascon
13. *Arles (pp512–13)*
14. *The Camargue (pp514–15)*
15. Aix-en-Provence
16. Marseille
17. Cassis
18. Toulon
19. Hyères
20. Îles d'Hyères
21. Massif des Maures
22. St.-Tropez
23. Digne-les-Bains
24. Fréjus
25. St.-Raphaël
26. Grasse
27. Cannes
28. Cap d'Antibes
29. Antibes
30. Vallauris
31. Biot
32. Cagnes-sur-Mer
33. Gorges du Loup
34. Vence
35. *St.-Paul de Vence (pp528–9)*
36. *Nice (pp530–31)*
37. Villefranche-sur-Mer
38. St.-Jean-Cap-Ferrat
39. Eze
40. Roquebrune-Cap-Martin
41. Alpes-Maritimes
42. Menton
43. *Monaco (pp534–5)*

For keys to symbols *see back flap*

## Getting Around

The largest airport in the region, and second busiest in France, is Nice. Fly-drive packages are popular, although mainly recommended for touring inland. Traffic jams on coastal roads in high season can usually be avoided by using the *autoroutes*. Main coastal towns have good bus and train links, and bicycles can be rented at most train stations. The Chemin de Fer de Provence railroad track runs from Nice to Digne-les-Bains through spectacular mountain scenery. Mountain roads, though tortuous, are good.

**Key**

- ▬▬ Freeway
- ▬▬ Highway
- ▬▬ Secondary road
- ▬▬ Minor road
- ▬ Scenic route
- ▬ Main railroad
- ▬ Minor railroad
- ▬▬ International border
- ▬▬ Regional border
- △ Summit

Spectacular scenery near the quiet market town of Forcalquier

# ❶ Mont Ventoux

Vaucluse. ✈ Avignon. 🚃 Avignon.
🚌 Carpentras. ℹ️ av de la Promenade,
Sault-en-Provence (04 90 64 01 21).
🅦 ventoux-en-provence.com

The name means "Windy
Mountain" in Provençal. A variety
of flora and fauna may be found
on the lower slopes but only moss
survives at the peak, where the
temperature can drop to –17° F
(–27°C). The bare white scree at
the summit makes it look snowcapped even during summer.

The legendary British cyclist
Tommy Simpson died during
1967's Tour de France on Mont
Ventoux. Today, a road leads up
to the radio beacon pinnacle, but
the trip should not be attempted
in bad weather. At other times,
spectacular views from the top
make the effort worthwhile.

Roman mosaic from the Villa du Paon
in Vaison-la-Romaine

# ❷ Vaison-la-Romaine

Vaucluse. 🚹 6,200. 🚌 ℹ️ pl du
Chanoine Sautel (04 90 36 02 11).
🏛 Tue. 🅦 vaison-ventoux-
tourisme.com

This site has been settled since
the Bronze Age, but its name
stems from five centuries as a
Roman town. Although the
upper town, dominated by the
ruins of a 12th-century castle, has
some charming narrow streets,
stone houses, and fountains,
Vaison's main attractions lie on
the opposite side of the river.

The **Roman City** is split into two
districts: Puymin and La Villasse.
At Puymin, an opulent mansion,
the Villa du Paon, and a Roman
theater have been uncovered.

In 1992, the River Ouvèze burst
its banks, taking many lives in
Vaison and the nearby area.

Damage to some ruins, such as
the Roman bridge, has since
been repaired. Also at Vaison is
the fine Romanesque **Cathédrale
Notre-Dame-de-Nazareth**, with
medieval cloisters.

## 🏛 Roman City
Fouilles de Puymin & Musée Théo
Desplans, pl du Chanoine Sautel. **Tel** 04
90 36 50 48. **Open** daily. **Closed** Jan–
mid-Feb, Dec 25. 🚻 🖼 🛗 🏛 📷

# ❸ Orange

Vaucluse. 🚹 30,000. 🚌 🚌 ℹ️ 5
cours Aristide Briand (04 90 34 70 88).
🏛 Thu. 🅦 orange-tourisme.fr

Orange is a thriving regional
center in the Rhône Valley, an
important marketplace for
produce such as grapes, olives,
honey, and truffles. Visitors
should explore the area around
the 17th-century Hôtel de Ville,
where attractive streets open on
to quiet, shady squares. Orange
also has two of the greatest
Roman monuments in Europe:
the **Théâtre Antique** and the
**Arc de Triomphe**.

## 🏛 Roman Theater
(Théâtre Antique)
1 rue Madeleine-Roch. **Tel** 04 90 51
17 60. **Open** daily. 🖼 also valid for
Musée d'Orange. 🖼 🛗 🏛 📷
💻 🅦 theatre-antique.com

Dating from the 1st-century-AD
reign of Augustus, the well-
preserved theater, a UNESCO
World Heritage Site, has perfect
acoustics. It is still used for theater
performances and concerts. The
back wall rises to a height of 120
ft (37 m) and is 338 ft (103 m)
wide. In 2006 an immense glass
roof, built high above the
theater so as not to affect the
acoustics, replaced the original
roof, destroyed in a fire.

Statue of Augustus Caesar in the Roman
Theater at Orange

## 🏛 Arc de Triomphe
Av de l'Arc de Triomphe.
The triple-arched monument,
built about AD 20, is decorated
with battle scenes, trophies
and inscriptions to the honor of
Tiberius and the conquest of
Rome after the Battle of Actium.

## 🏛 Musée d'Art et d'Histoire
d'Orange
1 rue Madeleine-Roch. **Tel** 04 90 51
17 60. **Open** daily. 🖼
Relics here reflect the Roman
presence in Orange, including
400 marble fragments, some of
which date to Emperor Vespasian's
reign in the 1st century BC.

# ❹ Châteauneuf-du-Pape

Vaucluse. 🚹 2,200. 🚌 Sorgues, then
taxi. 🚌 from Avignon or Orange.
ℹ️ 3 rue de la République (04 90 83
71 08). 🏛 Fri. 🅦 chateauneuf-du-
pape-tourisme.fr

Here, in the 14th century, the
popes of Avignon chose to build
a new castle (château neuf) and

View across the vineyards of Châteauneuf-du-Pape

*For hotels and restaurants in this region see pp569–71 and pp601–3*

plant the vineyards from which one of the finest wines of the Côtes du Rhône is produced. Now almost every doorway in this attractive little town seems to open into a *vigneron*'s cellar.

After the Wars of Religion *(see pp60–61)*, all that remained of the papal fortress were a few fragments of walls and tower, but the ruins look spectacular and offer magnificent views across to Avignon and the Vaucluse uplands beyond.

Wine festivals punctuate the year, including the Fête de la Véraison in August *(see p42)*, when the grapes start to ripen, and the Châteauneuf-du-Pape Spring Wine Fair, hosted by local growers.

# ❺ Avignon

Vaucluse. 🅰 94,000. 🚄 🚉 🚌 ℹ️
41 cours Jean Jaurès (04 32 74 32 74).
🍴 Tue–Sun. 🎭 Festival d'Avignon (3 wks Jul). 🌐 **avignon-tourisme.com**

Massive ramparts enclose one of the most fascinating towns in southern France. The **Palais des Papes** *(see pp508–9)* dominates, but there are also other riches, including the nearby Carré du Palais, a showcase for Rhône valley wines and comprising a wine school, bar, and restaurant. North of the Palais is the 13th-century **Musée du Petit Palais**, once the Archbishop of Avignon's residence. Now a museum, it displays Romanesque and Gothic sculpture and medieval paintings, with works by Botticelli and Carpaccio.

Rue Joseph-Vernet and rue du Roi-René are lined with 17th- and 18th-century houses. There are also fine churches, such as the **Cathédrale de Notre-Dame-des-Doms** and the 14th-century **Eglise St.-Didier**. The **Musée Lapidaire** contains statues, mosaics and carvings from pre-Roman Provence. The **Musée Calvet** features a superb array of exhibits, including wrought-iron works and Roman finds. It also gives an overview of French art during the past 500 years, with works by Rodin, Utrillo, and Dufy.

Two major modern and contemporary art collections, the **Musée Angladon** and the

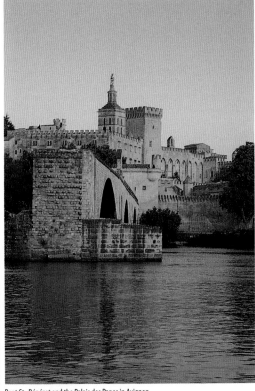
Pont St.-Bénézet and the Palais des Papes in Avignon

**Collection Lambert**, have been added to the city's cultural repertoire. The former has works by Degas, van Gogh, Cézanne, Picasso, and Modigliani, while the latter features minimalist and conceptual art.

Place de l'Horloge is the social center of Avignon, with pavement cafés and a 1900 merry-go-round. One of the prettiest streets is rue des Teinturiers.

Actors in historical costume at the Avignon Theater Festival

Avignon's renowned 12th-century bridge, the **Pont St.-Bénézet**, was largely destroyed by floods in 1668. People danced on an island below the bridge but over the years, as the famous song testifies, *sous* has become *sur*.

Avignon hosts France's largest festival, which includes ballet, drama, and classical concerts. The "Off" festival features 600 companies from all areas of show business.

🏛 **Musée du Petit Palais**
Pl du Palais. **Tel** 04 90 86 44 58.
**Open** Wed–Mon. **Closed** Jan 1, May 1, Dec 25. 🅿️ 🖥 🌐 petit-palais.org

🏛 **Musée Lapidaire**
27 rue de la République. **Tel** 04 90 85 75 38. **Open** Tue–Sun. **Closed** Jan 1, May 1, Dec 25. 🅿️ 📷 ♿ restricted.
🌐 **musee-lapidaire.org**

🏛 **Musée Calvet**
65 rue Joseph Vernet. **Tel** 04 90 86 33 84. **Open** Wed–Mon. **Closed** Jan 1, May 1, Dec 25. 🅿️ 📷 ♿
🌐 **musee-calvet-avignon.org**

# Palais des Papes

Confronted with factional strife in Rome and encouraged by the scheming of Philippe IV of France, Pope Clement V moved the papal court to Avignon in 1309. Here it remained until 1377, during which time his successors transformed the modest episcopal building into the present magnificent palace. Its heavy fortification was vital to defend against rogue bands of mercenaries. Today, it is empty of the luxurious trappings of 14th-century court life, as virtually all the furnishings and works of art were destroyed or looted in the course of the centuries.

**★ Consistory Hall**
Simone Martini's frescoes (1340) were taken from the cathedral to replace works destroyed by fire in the papal reception hall in 1413.

**Military Architecture**
The palace and its ten towers were designed as an impregnable fortress. It eventually covered an area of 161,500 sq ft (15,000 sq m).

## KEY

① **Champeaux gate**

② **Corner tower**

③ **Bell tower**

④ **Trouillas tower**

⑤ **Benedict XII's cloister** incorporates the guest and staff wings, and the Benedictine chapel.

⑥ **La Gache tower**

⑦ **Angels' tower**

⑧ **Pope's chamber**

⑨ **Great courtyard**

⑩ **The Great Chapel** is 66 ft (20 m) high and covers an area of 8,400 sq ft (780 sq m).

⑪ **The Great Audience Hall** is divided into two naves by five columns with bestiary sculpture on their capitals.

## The Avignon Popes

Seven "official" popes reigned in Avignon until 1376. They were followed by two "anti-popes," the last of whom, Benedict XIII, fled in 1403. Popes or anti-popes, few were known for their sanctity. Clement V died eating powdered emeralds, prescribed as an indigestion cure; Clement VI (1342–52) thought that the best way to honor God was through luxury. Petrarch was shocked by "the filth of the universe" at court. In 1367, Urban V tried to return the Curia (papal court) to Rome, a move that became permanent in 1377.

Benedict XII (1334–42)

**Papal Power**
More like a warlord's citadel than a papal palace, the building's heavy fortification reflects the insecure climate of 14th-century religious life.

## VISITORS' CHECKLIST

**Practical Information**
Pl du Palais, Avignon. **Tel** 04 90 27 50 00. **Open** Apr–Jun: 9am–7pm; Jul: 9am–8pm; Aug: 9am–8:30pm; Sep–Oct: 9am–7pm; Nov–Mar: 9:30am–6:30pm (Mar: from 9am). Last adm: 1 hr before closing. 🔊 in 11 languages. 🛒 🚻 💻 📷
**W** palais-des-papes.com

**★ Stag Room**
Fourteenth-century hunting frescoes and ceramic tiles adorn Clement VI's study, making it the palace's most lovely room.

## Building the Palace

The palace comprises Pope Benedict XII's simple Palais Vieux (1334–42) and Clement VI's flamboyant Palais Neuf (1342–52). Ten towers, some of which are more than 164 ft (50 m) high, are set in the walls to protect its four wings.

**Key**

☐ By Benedict XII (1334–42)
☐ By Clement VI (1342–52)

# ❻ Carpentras

Vaucluse. 30,000. ℹ️ Maison de Pays, 97 pl du 25 Août 1944 (04 90 63 00 78). Fri. **carpentras-ventoux.com**

In 1320, Carpentras became capital of the papal county of Venaissin, and remained so until 1791. Modern boulevards trace the former ramparts, with one original gate, the Porte d'Orange, surviving.

In the Middle Ages the town was home to a large Jewish community. The 1367 **Synagogue** is the oldest in France. The Sanctuary has been restored. While not openly persecuted under papal rule, many Jews changed faith, entering **Cathédrale St.-Siffrein** by the Porte Juive (Jews' Door).

The Law Courts were built in 1640 as the episcopal palace. The Criminal Court has 17th-century carved tablets of the local towns. In the pharmacy of the Hôtel-Dieu, the 18th-century cupboards are painted with quaint figures of monkey "doctors." More regional art and history is on show at the **Musée Sobirats**.

### ✡️ Synagogue
15 pl Maurice Charretier. **Tel** 04 90 63 39 97. **Open** Mon–Fri. **Closed** Jewish feast days. **synagoguecarpentras.fr**

### 🏛️ Musée Sobirats
112 rue du Collège. **Tel** 04 90 63 04 92. **Open** Wed–Mon. **Closed** Oct–Mar & public hols.

Riverfront and watermill at Fontaine-de-Vaucluse

# ❼ Fontaine-de-Vaucluse

Vaucluse. 650. Avignon. ℹ️ Av Robert Garcin, Residence Jean Garcin (04 90 20 32 22). **oti-delasorgue.fr**

The main attraction here is the source of the River Sorgue. It is the most powerful spring in France, gushing at up to 19,800 gallons (90,000 liters) per second from the foot of a cliff. It powers the Moulin à Papier Vallis Clausa (papermill), which produces handmade paper using the same methods as in the 15th century, and now sells maps, prints, and lampshades. There are also several museums. One is devoted to the poet Petrarch, who lived and wrote here, and another to the French Resistance of World War II.

# ❽ Gordes

Vaucluse. 2,000. ℹ️ pl du Château (04 90 72 02 75). Tue. **gordes-village.com**

Dominated by a 16th-century **château**, the perched village of Gordes forms such a harmonious whole that it might have been designed by an architect. The arcaded medieval lanes add to the attractive hilltop position.

Just south lies the **Village des Bories**, a primitive habitat of tiny beehive-shaped huts built of overlapping dry stones. The construction techniques are thought to date back to Neolithic times. This group was inhabited from the 16th to the early 20th century.

The **Abbaye de Sénanque**, to the north, is a fine Romanesque Cistercian monastery.

### 🏰 Château de Gordes
Pl du Château. **Tel** 04 90 72 98 64. **Open** Apr–Sep: Tue–Sun. **Closed** Jan 1, Dec 25 & 31.

### 🏘️ Village des Bories
Rte de Gorde. **Tel** 04 90 72 03 48. **Open** daily. **Closed** Jan 1, Dec 25 & 31. **levillagedesbories.com**

# ❾ Luberon

Vaucluse. Avignon. Cavaillon, Avignon. Apt. ℹ️ pl François Tourel, Cavaillon (04 90 71 32 01). **luberoncoeurdeprovence.com**

A huge limestone range, the Montagne du Luberon is one of the most appealing areas of Provence. Rising to 3,690 ft (1,125 m), it combines wild

Perched village of Gordes

areas with picturesque villages. Almost the entire area is designated a regional nature park. Within it are more than 1,000 plant species and cedar and oak forests. The wildlife is varied, and includes eagles, vultures, snakes, beavers, wild boar, and the largest lizards in Europe. The park headquarters is in **Apt**, the capital of the Luberon.

Once notorious as the haunt of highwaymen, the Luberon hills now hide sumptuous vacation homes. The major village is **Bonnieux**, with its 12th-century church and 13th-century walls. Also popular are **Roussillon**, with red ocher buildings, **Lacoste**, the site of the ruins of the Marquis de Sade's castle, and **Ansouis**, with its 14th-century Eglise St.-Martin and 17th-century castle. **Ménerbes** drew to it the writer Peter Mayle, whose tales of life here brought this quiet region a worldwide audience.

Herb stall at St.-Rémy-de-Provence

# ❿ St.-Rémy-de-Provence

Bouches-du-Rhône. 🗺 10,000. 🚋 Avignon. ℹ️ pl Jean Jaurès (04 90 92 05 22). 🗓 Wed. 🌐 **saintremy-de-provence.com**

For centuries St.-Rémy, with its boulevards, fountains, and narrow streets, had two claims to fame. One was that Vincent van Gogh spent a year here, in 1889–90, at the St.-Paul-de-Mausole hospital. *Wheat Field with Cypress* and *Ravine* are among the 150 works he produced here. St.-Rémy-de-Provence was also, in 1503, the birthplace of Nostradamus,

known for his prophecies. But, in 1921, it found new fame when archeologists unearthed the Roman ruins at the **Site Archéologique de Glanum**. Little remains of the ancient city, sacked in AD 480 by the Goths, but the site impresses. Around the ruins of a Roman arch is a mausoleum, decorated with scenes such as the death of Adonis.

🏛 **Site Archéologique de Glanum** **Tel** 04 90 92 23 79. **Open** Apr–Aug: daily; Sep–Mar: Tue–Sun. **Closed** Jan 1, May 1, Nov 1 & 11, Dec 25. 🎫 ♿ 🖥 🌐 **site-glanum.fr**

# ⓫ Les Baux-de-Provence

Bouches-du-Rhône. 🗺 470. 🚌 Arles. ℹ️ La Maison du Roy (04 90 54 34 39). 🌐 **lesbauxdeprovence.com**

One of the strangest places in Provence, the deserted citadel of Les Baux stands like a natural extension of a huge rocky plateau. The ruined castle and old houses overlook the Val d'Enfer (Infernal Valley), with its weird rocks.

In the Middle Ages Les Baux was home to powerful feudal lords, who claimed descent from the Magus Balthazar. It was the most famous of the Provençal Cours d'Amour, at which troubadours sang the praises of high-born ladies. The ideal of ever-lasting but unrequited courtly love contrasts with the warlike nature of the citadel's lords.

The glory of Les Baux ended in 1632. It had become a Protestant stronghold, and Louis XIII ordered its destruction. The ruins of **Château de Baux de Provence** are a reminder of a turbulent past and offer spectacular views. The living

Deserted medieval citadel of Les Baux-de-Provence

village below has a pleasant little square, the 12th-century **Eglise St.-Vincent** and the **Chapelle des Pénitents Blancs**, decorated by local artist Yves Brayer, whose work can be seen in the **Musée Yves Brayer**.

In 1821 bauxite, a deep-red mineral, was discovered here and named after the town. Deposits were intensely exploited until they ran out at the end of the 20th century.

To the southwest are the ruins of the **Abbaye de Montmajour** with its fine 12th-century Romanesque church.

Parading the Tarasque, 1850

# ⓬ Tarascon

Bouches-du-Rhône. 🗺 14,000. 🚉 🚌 ℹ️ Les Panoramiques, av de la République (04 90 91 03 52). 🗓 Tue & Fri. 🌐 **tarascon.org**

According to legend, the town takes its name from the Tarasque, a monster, half-animal and half-fish, which terrorized the countryside. It was tamed by Ste. Marthe, who is buried in the church here. An effigy of the Tarasque is still paraded through the streets each June (see p41).

The striking 15th-century **Château Royal de Provence** on the banks of the Rhône is one of the finest examples of Gothic military architecture in Provence. Its somber exterior gives no hint of the beauties within: the Flemish-Gothic courtyard; the spiral staircase; and the painted ceilings of the banqueting hall.

Opposite is Beaucaire, a ruined castle and gardens.

🏛 **Château Royal de Provence (Tarascon)** Bd du Roi René. **Tel** 04 90 91 01 93. **Open** daily. **Closed** some public hols. 🎫 🖼 🌐 **chateau.tarascon.fr**

# ⓲ Arles

Few other towns in Provence combine all the region's charms as well as Arles. Its position on the Rhône makes it a natural, historic gateway to the Camargue *(see pp514–15)*. Its Roman remains, such as the arena and Constantine's baths, are complemented by the ocher walls and Roman-tiled roofs of later buildings. A bastion of Provençal tradition and culture, it has museums that are among the best in the region. Van Gogh spent time here in 1888–9, but Arles is no longer the industrial town he painted. Visitors are now its main business, and entertainment ranges from the Arles Festival to bullfights.

**Palais Constantine** was once a grand imperial palace. Now only its vast Roman baths remain, dating from the 4th century AD. They are remarkably well preserved and give an idea of the luxury that bathers enjoyed.

**Musée Réattu**
This museum, in the old Commandery of the Knights of Malta, houses witty Picasso sketches, paintings by the local artist Jacques Réattu (1760–1833), and sculptures by Ossip Zadkine, including *La Grande Odalisque* (1932), above.

Hôtel de Ville and entrance to Cryptoportiques

**Museon Arlaten**
In 1904 the poet Frédéric Mistral used his Nobel Prize money to establish this museum devoted to his beloved native Provence. Parts of the collection are arranged in room settings, and even the museum attendants wear traditional Arles costume. (Note that the museum is closed for renovation until 2019.)

**Espace Van Gogh**, in a former hospital where the artist was treated in 1889, is a cultural center devoted to his life and work.

★ **Eglise St.-Trophime**
This church combines a noble 12th-century Romanesque exterior with superb Romanesque and Gothic cloisters. The ornate main portal is carved with saints and apostles.

Tourist information

*Les Alyscamps* by Paul Gauguin

## Les Alyscamps

A tree-lined avenue of broken medieval tombs is the focal point of these "Elysian Fields" to the southeast of Arles. It became Christian in the 4th century and was a prestigious burial ground until the 12th century. Some sarcophagi were sold to museums; others have been neglected. Mentioned in Dante's *Inferno*, painted by van Gogh and Gauguin, it is a place for thought and inspiration.

### VISITORS' CHECKLIST

**Practical Information**
Bouches-du-Rhône. 53,000.
arlestourisme.com
bd des Lices (04 90 18 41 20).
Wed, Sat. Arles Festival (Jul); Prémice du Riz (Sep). Musée Réattu: **Open** Tue–Sun. **Closed** Jan 1, May 1, Nov 1, Dec 25. Museon Arlaten: **Closed** until 2019. museonarlaten.fr

**Transportation**
16 miles (25 km) NW Arles.
av Paulin Talabot.

To train and bus stations

RUE DE GRILLE
RUE BARBES
R ARISTIDE BRIAND
R DE LA
RUE DIDEROT
BASTILLE
RALADE
ROND-POINT DES ARENES
R TARDIEU
R DE LA MADELEINE
RUE DU GRAND COUVENT
R PORTE DE LAURE
DU CLOITRE
MONTEE VAUBAN
BOULEVARD DES LICES

★ **Roman Amphitheater**
This is one of the best-preserved monuments of Roman Provence. Each arch is supported by Doric and Corinthian columns. In summer there are bull contests in the 21,000-seat arena. The top tier provides a panoramic view of Arles.

**Eglise Notre-Dame-de-la-Major** is the church in which the *gardians* (cowboys) of the Camargue celebrate the feast day of their patron saint, St. George. Although the building dates from the 12th to 17th centuries, a Roman temple existed on this spot hundreds of years earlier.

★ **Roman Theater**
Once a fortress, the theater's stones were later used for other buildings. Today, it hosts the Arles Festival. Its remaining columns are called the "two widows."

**Key**
— Suggested route

0 meters          100
0 yards           100

# ⓮ The Camargue

The Rhône delta was responsible for the formation of more than 432 sq miles (1,120 sq km) of wetlands, pastures, dunes, and salt flats that make up the Camargue, but human efforts are needed to preserve it. The region now maintains a fragile ecological balance, in which a unique collection of flora flourishes, including tamarisk and narcissi, and fauna such as egrets and ibises. The pastures provide grazing for sheep, cattle, and small white Arab-type horses, ridden by the *gardians* or cowboys, a hardy community who traditionally lived in thatched huts *(cabanes)* and still play their part in keeping Camargue traditions alive.

Sunset over the Camargue

Mas du Pont de R

D572

D570

D570

Méjanes ●

D37

Le Petit Rhône

PLAINE DE LA CAMARGUE

Etang de V

PARC REGIONAL DE CAMARG

Centre de Ginès

CAMARGUE GARDOISE

Stes-Maries-de-la-Mer

MEDITERRANEE

**Black Bulls**
In a Provençal bull contest (known as a *course*), the animals are not killed. Instead, red rosettes are plucked from between their horns with a small hook.

0 kilometers      5
0 miles           5

**Les Saintes-Maries-de-la-Mer**
The May gypsy pilgrimage to this fortified church marks the legendary arrival by boat in AD 18 of Mary Magdalene, St. Martha, and the sister of the Virgin Mary. Statues in the church depict the event.

**Flamingoes**
These striking birds are always associated with the Camargue, but the region supports many other breeds, including herons, kingfishers, owls, and birds of prey. The area around Ginès is the best place to see them.

*For hotels and restaurants in this region see pp569–71 and pp601–3*

## Key

— Nature preserve boundary

– – Walking routes

– – Walking and cycling routes

*'illeneuve*

*La Capelière*

**PLAINE DE LA CAMARGUE**

D36

La Grande Rhône

D36C

Salin de Giraud

### White Horses

These small, sturdy horses, which are never stabled, were once used to thresh grain. The foal's dark coat turns white after about five years.

### Gardians' Cabin

Traditionally, *gardians* lived in thatched cabins, as seen here. Today, members of the *gardian* brotherhood show off their horsemanship in the Arles arena each April.

### Mountains of Salt

Sea salt is by far the largest "harvest" of the Camargue. Throughout the summer, water collected in vast brine pans evaporate and the crystals are heaped into shimmering *camelles* up to 26 ft (8 m) high.

---

## VISITORS' CHECKLIST

### Practical Information

Bouches-du-Rhône. **i** Mas du Pont de Rousty. **Tel** 04 90 97 10 40. Les Pèlerinages (end May, end Oct), Festival du Cheval (Jul 14). Musée de la Camargue, Pont de Rousty: **Tel** 04 90 97 10 82. **Open** daily. **Closed** Jan 1, May 1, Dec 25. **w** saintes maries.com; parc-camargue.fr

### Transportation

Montpellier-Méditerranée, 56 miles (90 km) east. av Paulin Talabot, Arles.

---

## ⑮ Aix-en-Provence

Bouches-du-Rhône. 145,000. **i** Les allées provençales, 300 ave Giuseppe Verdi (04 42 16 11 61). daily. **w** aixenprovencetourism.com

Founded by the Romans in 103 BC, Aix was frequently attacked, first by the Visigoths in AD 477, later by Lombards, Franks, and Saracens. Despite this, the city prospered. By the end of the 12th century it was capital of Provence. A center of art and learning, it reached its peak in the 15th century during the reign of "Good King" René. He is shown in Nicolas Froment's *Triptych of the Burning Bush* in the 13th- century Gothic **Cathédrale St.-Sauveur**, also noted for its 16th-century walnut doors, Merovingian baptistery and Romanesque cloisters.

Aix is still a center of art and learning, and its many museums include the **Musée Granet** of fine arts and archaeology in the Palais de l'Archevêché.

Aix has been called "the city of a thousand fountains." Three of the best are on cours Mirabeau. On one side are 17th- and 18th-buildings with wrought-iron balconies; on the other are cafés. The Old Town centers on place de l'Hôtel de Ville, with its colorful flower market. The **Caumont Centre d'Art**, located in one of the city's most stunning mansions, is an art gallery and cultural center.

Aix's most famous son is Paul Cézanne (1839–1906). The **Atelier de Cézanne** is kept as it was when he died. Montagne Ste.-Victoire, inspiration for many of his paintings, is 9 miles (15 km) east of Aix.

**Musée Granet**
pl St.-Jean de Malte. **Tel** 04 42 52 88 32. **Open** Tue–Sun. **Closed** Jan 1, May 1, Dec 25. **w** museegranet-aixenprovence.fr

**Caumont Centre d'Art**
3 rue Joseph Cabassol. **Tel** 04 42 20 70 01. **Open** daily.

**Atelier de Cézanne**
9 av Paul Cézanne. **Tel** 04 42 21 06 53. **Open** daily. **Closed** Dec–Feb: Sun; Jan 1–10, May 1, Dec 25. **w** atelier-cezanne.com

*For keys to symbols see back flap*

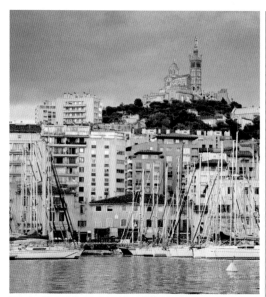
Old harbor of Marseille, looking toward the quai de Rive Neuve

# ⑯ Marseille

Bouches-du-Rhône. 🚗 866,000. ✈
🚉 🚌 🚢 ℹ 11 La Canebière (0826 500 500). 🚢 Mon–Sat. 🔲 **marseilletourisme.com**

A Greek settlement, founded in the 7th century BC, then called Massilia, Marseille was seized by the Romans in 49 BC. It became the "Gateway to the West" for most Oriental trade. France's largest port and lively second-largest city has close links with the Middle East and North Africa. Designated a European Capital of Culture in 2013, Marseille has renovated its old harbor and port terminal.

Narrow stepped streets, quiet squares and fine 18th-century facades contrast with the bustle of boulevard Canebière and the Cité Radieuse, Le Corbusier's post-war radical housing complex.

The old harbor now only handles small boats, but its daily fish market is renowned.

Marseille has many excellent museums. Those in the old harbor area include the **Musée des Docks Romains**, the **Musée d'Histoire de Marseille**, and the upbeat **Musée de Savon**.

The **Musée Cantini**, to the south, houses the 20th-century art collection of sculptor Jules Cantini.

It includes Surrealist, Cubist, and Fauve paintings. On the other side of the city is the **Château Borély**, home to the Musée des Arts Décoratifs and the Musée de la Mode. Marseille has an extensive streetcar system and has introduced a bicycle-rental scheme that allows people to rent a bicycle in one part of town and deposit it in another.

## 🏛 Musée des Beaux-Arts

Palais Longchamp, pl Aile Gauche (left wing). **Tel** 04 91 14 59 30. **Open** Tue–Sun. **Closed** Jan 1, May 1, Nov 1, Dec 25, 26. 🚫 ♿

This museum is housed in the handsome 19th-century Palais Longchamp. Works include Michel Serre's graphic views of Marseille's plague of 1721, Pierre Puget's town plans for the city, and murals depicting it in Greek and Roman times.

## 🏰 Château d'If

Vieux Port. **Tel** 06 03 06 25 26. **Open** Apr–Sep: daily; Oct–Mar: Tue–Sun. 🚫 📷 🏛 💻 🔲 **chateau-if.fr**

The Château d'If (Castle of Yew) stands on a tiny island 1 mile (2 km) southwest of the port. A formidable fortress, it was built in 1529 to house artillery, but never put to military use and later became a prison. Alexandre Dumas'

fictional Count of Monte Cristo was supposed to have been imprisoned here, and visitors can see a special cell, complete with escape hole. Most real-life inmates were either common criminals or political prisoners.

## 🏰 Basilique de Notre-Dame-de-la-Garde

Built between 1853 and 1864, this Neo-Byzantine basilica dominates the city. Its belfry, 151 ft (46 m) high, is capped by a huge gilded statue of the Virgin. The lavishly decorated interior has colored marble and mosaic facings.

## 🏰 Abbaye de St.-Victor

Similar to a fortress in appearance, the abbey was rebuilt in the 11th century after destruction by the Saracens. In the French Revolution, the rebels used it as a barracks and prison. There is an intriguing crypt in the abbey's church, with an original catacomb chapel and a number of pagan and Christian sarcophagi.

On February 2 each year, St.-Victor becomes a place of pilgrimage. Boat-shaped cakes are sold to commemorate the legendary arrival of St. Mary Magdalene, Lazarus, and St. Martha nearly 2,000 years ago.

## 🏰 Cathédrale de la Major

Built in Neo-Byzantine style, this is the largest 19th-century church in France, 463 ft (141 m) long and 230 ft (70 m) high. In the crypt are the tombs of the bishops of Marseille. The small and beautiful Ancienne Cathédrale de la Major is close by.

## 🏛 La Vieille Charité

2 rue de la Charité. **Tel** 04 91 14 58 11. **Open** Tue–Sun. **Closed** public hols. 🚫 ♿ 🔲 **vieille-charite-marseille.com**

In 1640, construction of a shelter "for the poor and beggars" of Marseille was begun by royal decree. A hundred years later, Pierre Puget's hospital and church opened. The restored building houses the Musée d'Archéologie Méditerranéenne; the Musée des Arts Africains, Océaniens et Amérindiens (MAAOA) is on the second floor.

Vendor at the fish market in Marseille

### 🏛 Musée des Civilisations de l'Europe et de la Méditerranée (MuCEM)

1 esplanade de J4, 201 quai du Port (VJ4 and Fort Saint-Jean). **Tel** 04 84 35 13 00. **Open** Wed–Mon. 🅿 ♿ 🔍 📷 🚫 **W** mucem.org

Linking Marseille's harbor, a former port terminal, and the 17th-century Fort St.-Jean, this cultural center facing the Mediterranean Sea focuses on the history of civilization in the European and Mediterranean region. Its ethnographical collection includes over 500,000 items, some dating back to 1884, plus drawings, paintings, photographs, and books.

# 🟠 Cassis

Bouches-du-Rhône. 👥 8,000. 🚉 🚌
ℹ quai des Moulins, Le Port (08 92 39 01 03). 🚢 Wed & Fri. **W** ot-cassis.com

Many villages along this coast have been built up and have all but lost their original charm, but Cassis is still much the same little fishing port that attracted artists such as Dufy, Signac, and Derain. This is a place in which to relax at a waterside café, watching the fishermen or street performers, while enjoying the seafood and a bottle of the local dry white wine for which Cassis is noted.

From Marseille to Cassis the coastline forms narrow inlets, the **Calanques**, their jagged white cliffs (some as high as 1,312 ft/400 m) reflected in dazzling turquoise water. Wildlife abounds here, with countless seabirds, foxes, stone martens, bats, large snakes, and lizards. The flora is no less impressive, with more than 900 plant species, of which 50 are classified as rare. The En-Vau and Sormiou Calanques are especially lovely. The Massif de Calanque and Cap Canaille are designated national parks.

# 🟠 Toulon

Var. 👥 167,000. ✈ 🚉 🚌 ⛴
ℹ 12 pl Louis-Blanc (04 94 18 53 00). 🚢 Tue–Sun. **W** toulontourisme.com

In 1793 this naval base was captured by an Anglo-Spanish fleet, but was retaken by the young Napoleon Bonaparte. The impressive collection of the **Musée National de la Marine** explores maritime history. The **Musée d'Art de Toulon**, housed in an Italian Renaissance building, has a collection representing Fauvism, Minimalism, and Realism. The war-damaged Old Town has a few original buildings, and the fish market is worth a visit. For lovely views, the boat trip around the bay and the cablecar ride up to Mont Faron are highly recommended.

### 🏛 Musée National de la Marine

Pl Monsenergue. **Tel** 04 22 42 02 01. **Open** daily. **Closed** Tue (Sep–Jun), May 1, Dec 25. 🅿 ♿ restr. 📷 **W** musee-marine.fr

### 🏛 Musée d'Art de Toulon

113 bd Mar Leclerc. **Tel** 04 94 36 81 01. **Open** Tue–Sun pms only. **Closed** public hols.

Paul Signac's *Cap Canaille*, painted at Cassis in 1889

# Tour of the Gorges du Verdon

The Verdon Gorges constitute one of the most dramatic natural sights in Europe. The dark green River Verdon flows through a deeply cut valley with twisted rocks and cone-shaped peaks. In places, the Gorges reach depths of 2,297 ft (700 m), passing through largely uninhabited country between the vast natural amphitheater of Moustiers-Ste.-Marie and the narrow streets of Castellane. Dramatic viewpoints include the Balcons de la Mescla, beyond the Pont de l'Artuby, and the Point Sublime. A detour southwest of Moutiers to Quinson's Musée de Préhistoire is worthwhile.

Verdon Gorges from the Castellane road

**③ Aiguines**
This village has an atttractive 17th-century château with four pepper-pot towers. There is a fine view of the artificial Lac de Sainte-Croix from here.

# ⑲ Hyères

Var. 🗺 57,000. 🚆 🚌 🚐 🚢
ℹ Rotonde du Park Hotel, av de Belgique (04 94 01 84 50). 🛒 Tue, Thu & Sat. 🌐 hyeres-tourisme.com

Toward the end of the 18th century, Hyères became one of the first health resorts of the Côte d'Azur. Among its subsequent visitors were Queen Victoria and writers Robert Louis Stevenson (1850–94) and Edith Wharton (1862–1937).

The main sights are found in the Vieille Ville's medieval streets, which lead past the spacious, flagstoned place Massillon to a ruined castle and views over the coast.

Modern Hyères is imbued with a lingering *belle époque* charm, which has become popular with experimental movie-makers. It attracts a health-conscious crowd and is a major center for aquatic sports.

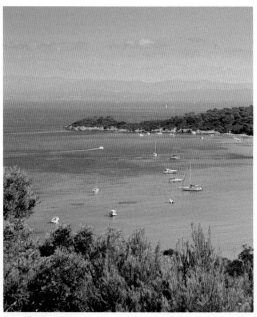

Porquerolles island marina

*For hotels and restaurants in this region see pp569–71 and pp601–3*

④ **Moustiers-Ste.-Marie**
Set in a deep ravine, this village is famous for pottery. Suspended across the twin peaks above it is an iron chain with a star, first placed there after the Crusades.

⑥ **Point Sublime**
From this superb viewpoint 591 ft (180 m) high, two walking routes lead to the bottom.

⑤ **La Palud-sur-Verdon**
This village is on the Route des Crêtes, one of the most wild and beautiful walks.

**Rougon**

① **Castellane**
This town has a 14th-century clock tower and a lion fountain. On a cliff high above it, once used as a look-out, is the tiny chapel of Notre-Dame du Roc.

**Trigance**

**Key**

━━ Tour route
═══ Other roads
🌟 Viewpoint

② **Pont de l'Artuby**
From this boldly curved bridge there is a breathtaking view of the gorge 820 ft (250 m) below.

0 kilometers 2
0 miles 2

## ⑳ Iles d'Hyères

Var. ✈ Toulon-Hyères. 🚃 🚌 🛥
Hyères. ℹ Hyères (Porquerolles office: 04 94 58 33 76). 🌐 **hyeres-tourisme. com** 🌐 **porquerolles.com**

Locally known as the Iles d'Or ("Golden Islands"), after the gold color of their cliffs, this lovely trio of islands can be reached by boat from Hyères, Tour Fondue, Le Lavandou, Cavalaire, La Croix Valmer, and St. Tropez.

**Porquerolles**, the largest of the three, measures 4 miles (7 km) by 1.5 miles (2.5 km). It is covered in rich vegetation, much of which, for instance the Mexican bellombra tree, was introduced from a variety of exotic foreign climes.

The island's main town, also known as Porquerolles, looks more like a North African colonial settlement than a Provençal village. It was established in 1820 as a retirement town for Napoleon's most honored

troops. All the island's beaches lie along the northern coastline. The best, the long, sandy Plage Notre-Dame, one of the finest beaches in Provence, sits in a sheltered bay about an hour's walk from Porquerolles village.

A stroll around lush **Port-Cros**, covering 1 sq mile (2.5 sq km), takes the best part of a day. It rises to 640 ft (195 m), the highest point on any of the islands.

Both Porquerolles and Port-Cros are national parks. Unique reserves of flora and fauna, their waters are also protected. There is even a 984-ft (300-m) scenic swimming route. You can buy a waterproof guide to the underwater wildlife.

The wild, virtually treeless **Ile du Levant** is reached by boat from Port-Cros. Its main draw is the oldest naturist resort in France, Héliopolis, founded in 1931. The eastern half of the island, controlled by the French navy, is permanently closed to the public.

## ㉑ Massif des Maures

Var. ✈ Toulon-Hyères. 🚃 Hyères, Toulon or Fréjus. 🚌 Bormes-les-Mimosas. 🛥 Toulon. ℹ 1 pl Gambetta, Bormes-les-Mimosas (04 94 01 38 38).
🌐 **bormeslesmimosas.com**

The dense wilderness of pine, oak and chestnut covering the Maures mountains probably gave rise to its name, meaning "dark" or "gloomy." It extends nearly 40 miles (65 km) between Hyères and Fréjus. The D558 north of Cogolin leads to the heart of the Maures. Along the way is La Garde-Freinet, well-known for its bottle-cork industry.

Northwest of Cannet-des-Maures lies the Abbaye de Thoronet. With the abbeys at Sénanque, in Vaucluse, and Silvacane, in the Bouches-du-Rhône, it is known as one of the "Three Sisters" of Provence.

Harborside at St.-Tropez

## ❷ St.-Tropez

Var. 🚗 4,500. 🚌 ℹ quai Jean Jaurès
(08 92 68 48 28 or, from abroad,
04 94 97 45 21). 🚢 Tue & Sat.
🌐 sainttropeztourisme.com

The geography of St.-Tropez kept it untouched by the earliest development of the Côte d'Azur. Tucked away at the tip of a peninsula, it is the only north-facing town on the coast and so did not appeal to those seeking a warm and sheltered winter resort. In 1892 the painter Paul Signac was among the first outsiders to respond to its unspoiled charm, encouraging friends, such as the painters Matisse and Bonnard, to join him. In the 1920s the Parisian writer Colette also made her home here. St.-Tropez also began to attract star-spotters, hoping for a glimpse of celebrities such as the Prince of Wales.

During World War II the beaches around St.-Tropez were the scene of Allied landings, and part of the town was heavily bombed. Then, in the 1950s, young Parisians began to arrive, and the Bardot-Vadim movie helped to create the reputation of modern St.-Tropez as a play-ground for gilded youth. The wild public behavior and turbulent love affairs of Roger Vadim, Brigitte Bardot, Sacha Distel, and others left fiction far behind. Mass tourism followed, with visitors again more keen to spot a celebrity than visit the **Musée de l'Annonciade** with its outstanding collection of works by Signac, Derain, Rouault, Bonnard, and others.

Today, there are far more luxury yachts than fishing boats moored in St.-Tropez harbor. Its cafés make ideal bases for people- and yacht-watching. Another center of the action is place des Lices, both for the Harley-Davidson set and the morning market. The **Musée de l'Histoire Maritime**, located in the tower of the citadel from where there are great views, recounts the village's impressive seafaring past.

The best beaches are found outside the town, including the golden curve of Pampelonne, with its beach clubs and restaurants. This is the beach on which to see and be seen. St.-Tropez has no train station, so driving and parking can be a nightmare in summer – it is best to get the boat from St.-Raphaël or St.-Maxime.

It is said that St.-Tropez takes its name from a Roman soldier martyred as a Christian by the

Emperor Nero. Each May a *bravade* in his honor takes place, whereby an effigy of the saint is carried through the town to the accompaniment of musket fire.

Nearby are two small towns of differing character but equal charm. **Port-Grimaud** was only built in 1966, but the sensitive use of traditional architecture makes it seem older. Most of its "streets" are canals. Up in the hills, the winding streets of **Ramatuelle** have been restored to perfection by the largely celebrity population.

🏛 **Musée de l'Annonciade**
2 rue l'Annonciade, pl Grammont.
**Tel** 04 94 17 84 10. **Open** Wed–Mon.
**Closed** Jan 1, Ascension, May 1 & 17,
Nov 1, Dec 25. 🦽 🖼 📷

🏛 **Musée de l'Histoire Maritime**
Citadelle de St.-Tropez. **Tel** 04 94 97
59 43. **Open** daily. **Closed** Jan 1,
May 1 & 17, Nov 11, Dec 25. 🦽 ♿

Scooters, a stylish solution to the traffic problems in St.-Tropez

### Brigitte Bardot

In 1956, Brigitte Bardot's film *And God Created Woman* was shot in St.-Tropez by her new husband, Roger Vadim. By settling in St.-Tropez, "BB" the sex goddess (b.1934) changed the fortunes of the sleepy little fishing village and ultimately the Côte d'Azur, making it the center of her then-hedonistic lifestyle. In 1974, on her 40th birthday, she celebrated her retirement from movies at Club 55 on Pampelonne Beach. She now devotes her time to her animal sanctuary.

Brigitte Bardot in 1956

## ㉓ Digne-les-Bains

Alpes-de-Haute-Provence. 🚊 17,000.
🚉 🚌 ℹ Le Rond Point (04 92
36 62 62). 🛒 Wed, Sat.
🌐 ot-dignelesbains.fr

This charming spa town in the
foothills of the Alps features in
Victor Hugo's *Les Misérables*. A
trip on the Train des Pignes
from Nice offers superb views.
Aside from the spa, Digne-les-
Bains also offers a lavender
festival *(see p42)* and **Le Jardin
des Papillons**, France's only
butterfly garden.

🦋 **Le Jardin des Papillons**
St. Benoît. **Tel** 04 92 36 70 70. **Open**
Apr–Sep. 🎫 🅿 📷 in summer. 📷

## ㉔ Fréjus

Var. 🚊 54,000. 🚉 🚌 ℹ 249 rue
Jean Jaurès (04 94 51 83 83). 🛒 Wed,
Fri–Sun. 🌐 frejus.fr

The modern town of Fréjus is
dwarfed in importance by
two impressive historic sites.
The remains of the Roman
**Amphithéâtre** (founded by
Julius Caesar in 49 BC) may not
be as complete as those at
Orange or Arles but they are
of exceptional variety. A great
amphitheater, fragments of an
aqueduct, a theater, and part
of a rampart gateway remain.
The sea has receded over the
centuries and there are few
traces of the original harbor.
   The cathedral on rue de Fleury
marks the entrance to the **Groupe
Episcopal**. The fortified enclave
includes a 5th-century baptistery,
one of the oldest in France, and
the cathedral cloister, its coffered
medieval roof decorated with a
spectacular bestiary.
   In 1959 Fréjus was hit by a
wall of water, as the Malpasset
Barrage burst. To the north, the
ruined dam can still be seen.

🏛 **Amphithéâtre**
Rue Henri Vadon. **Tel** 04 94 51 34 31.
**Open** Tue–Sun (Oct–Mar: Tue–Sat). **Closed**
Jan 1, May 1, Dec 25. 🎫 🅿 📷 ♿

🏛 **Groupe Episcopal**
48–58 rue de Fleury. **Tel** 04 94 51 26 30.
**Open** Tue–Sun (Jun–Sep: daily). **Closed**
Jan 1, May 1, Nov 1 & 11, Dec 25. 📷
cloisters. 📷 🎫 🌐 cloitre-frejus.fr

---

### The Creation of a Perfume

The best perfumes begin as a formula of essential
oils extracted from natural sources. The blend of
aromas is created by a perfumer called a "nose"
because of his or her exceptional sense of smell.
A perfume may use as many as 300 essences,
all painstakingly extracted from plants by
various methods: steam distillation, extraction
by volatile solvents, and *enfleurage à froid* (for
costly or potent essences). With this process,
pungent blossoms are placed onto layers of
fats for several days
until the fats are
saturated. The oils are then
"washed" out with alcohol,
and, when this evaporates,
it leaves the "pure" perfume
essence behind.

Lavender water

Grasse flowers

## ㉕ St.-Raphaël

Var. 🚊 35,000. 🚉 🚌 ℹ 99 quai
Albert 1er (04 94 19 52 52).
🌐 saint-raphael.com

Delightfully located, St.-Raphaël
is a charming, old-style Côte
d'Azur resort with *belle époque*
architecture and a palm-
fronded promenade. Aside from
its beaches, it offers a marina, a
casino, a Neo-Byzantine basilica,
a 12th-century church, and an
archaeology museum with
treasures from prehistoric
underwater wrecks.
   It was here that Napoleon
Bonaparte landed in 1799 on
his return from Egypt.

## ㉖ Grasse

Alpes-Maritimes. 🚊 52,000. 🚌
ℹ pl de la Buanderie (04 93 36 66 66).
🌐 grassetourisme.fr

Cradled by hills, with views
out to sea, Grasse is
surrounded by fields of
lavender, mimosa,
jasmine, and roses.
Grasse has been the
center of the world's
perfume industry since
the 16th century, when
Catherine de' Medici set
the fashion for scented
leather gloves. At that
time, Grasse was also
known as the center
for leather tanning.
The tanneries have
gone, but the
perfume houses

founded in the 18th and
19th centuries are still in
business, although today Grasse
perfumes are made from
imported flowers or chemicals.
Fragonard and Molinard have
museums, but the best place to
learn the history of perfume is
at the **Musée Internationale de
la Parfumerie**, which has a
garden of fragrant plants.
   Grasse was the birthplace
of the artist Jean-Honoré
Fragonard (1732–1806). The
late 17th-century **Villa-Musée
Fragonard** is decorated with
murals by his son. Fragonard's
only religious work is in the
**Cathédrale de Notre-Dame-
du-Puy** in the Old Town, which
also has three paintings by
Rubens. Place aux Aires and
place du Cours typify Grasse's
charm, surrounded by streets
with Renaissance staircases
and balconies.

🏛 **Musée International
de la Parfumerie**
2 bd de Jeu du Ballon. **Tel** 04 97
05 58 00. **Open** daily.
**Closed** Jan 1, May 1,
Dec 25. 🎫 🅿 📷
🌐 museesde
grasse.com

🏛 **Villa-Musée
Fragonard**
23 bd Fragonard. **Tel** 04
93 36 52 98. **Open** Jul–
Sep daily. 🎫 📷

Statue honoring
Jean-Honoré Fragonard
in Grasse

Menton at dusk ▶

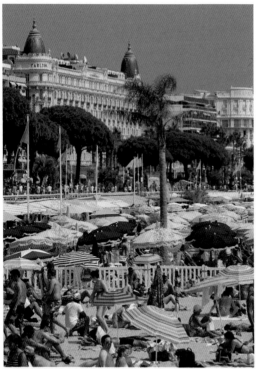

High summer on the beach at Cannes, overlooked by the Carlton Hotel

## ㉗ Cannes

Alpes-Maritimes. ⚠ 75,000. 🚄 🚌
🚢 ℹ Palais des Festivals, 1 bd de la
Croisette (04 92 99 84 22). 🏛 Tue–
Sun. 🔲 cannes-destination.com

Just as Grasse is synonymous
with the perfume industry, the
first thing that most people
associate with Cannes is its
many festivals, especially the
Film Festival. There is much
more to the city than these
glittering events. It was Lord
Brougham, the British Lord
Chancellor, who put Cannes
on the map, although Prosper
Mérimée, Inspector of Historic
Monuments, allegedly visited
Cannes two months before him.
Lord Brougham stopped here in
1834, unable to reach Nice due
to a cholera outbreak there.
Struck by the beauty and mild
climate of what was then just a
small fishing port, he built a villa
here. Other foreigners followed
and Cannes became established
as a top Mediterranean resort.

The Old Town that Lord
Brougham knew is centered in
the district of Le Suquet, on the
slopes of Mont Chevalier. Part of
the old city wall can still be seen
on place de la Castre, which is
dominated by the **Notre-Dame
de l'Espérance**, built in the
16th and 17th centuries in the
Provençal Gothic style. An 11th-
century watchtower is another
attractive feature of the quarter,
and the castle keep houses the
**Musée de la Castre**, the eclectic
finds of a 19th-century Dutch
explorer, Baron Lycklama.

The famed **boulevard de la
Croisette** is lined with gardens
and palm trees. One side is
occupied by luxury boutiques
and hotels such as the Carlton,
built in *belle époque* style, with
twin cupolas modeled on the
breasts of La Belle Otero, a
famous member of the
19th-century *demi-monde*.
Opposite are some of the finest
sandy beaches on this coast.
The glamour of the Croisette,
once one of the world's grandest
thoroughfares, seems faded in
the noise and fumes of summer.

### 🚢 Iles de Lérins

🚢 depart from: le Quai des Iles.
ℹ Horizon (04 92 98 71 36 for Ile Ste.-
Marguerite), Planaria (04 92 98 71 38
for Ile St.-Honorat).

Just off the coast from Cannes
are the Iles de Lérins. The fort on
**Ile Sainte-Marguerite** is where
the mysterious Man in the Iron
Mask was imprisoned in the late
17th century. A popular theory

### Cannes Film Festival

The first Cannes Film Festival took place in 1946 and,
for almost 20 years, it remained a small and exclusive
affair, attended by the artists and celebrities who lived
or were staying on the coast. The arrival of the "starlet,"
especially Brigitte Bardot, in the mid-1950s marked the
change from artistic event to media circus, but Cannes
remains the international marketplace for movie-makers
and distributors, with the *Palme d'Or* award conferring high
status on its winner. The annual film festival is held in May
in the huge Palais des Festivals et des Congrés, opened in
1982. It has 13 auditoriums, two exhibition halls, conference
rooms, a casino, and a nightclub.

The red carpet at the Cannes Film Festival

*For hotels and restaurants in this region see pp569–71 and pp601–3*

is that his face had to be hidden because he resembled someone very important indeed – possibly even Louis XIV. Visitors can see the tiny cell that held him for over ten years.

**Ile Saint-Honorat** has an 11th-century tower in which the resident monks took refuge during raids by the Saracens. There are also five ancient chapels. Both islands offer peaceful woodland walks, fine views, and quiet coves for swimming.

Beside the boulevard de la Croisette

## ❷❽ Cap d'Antibes

Alpes-Maritimes. 🛫 Nice. 🚌 🚐 Antibes. 🚢 Nice. 𝒊 42 av Robert Soleau, Antibes (04 22 10 60 10). 🆆 antibesjuanlespins.com

With its sumptuous villas, this rocky peninsula, also known as "the Cap," has been a symbol of luxury life on the Riviera since it was frequented by F. Scott Fitzgerald and the rich American set in the 1920s. The magnate Frank Jay Gould invested in the resort of Juan-les-Pins, and it became the focus of high life on the Cap. Today, memories of the Jazz Age live on at the Jazz Festival held here and in Antibes, when international stars perform *(see p41)*.

At the highest point of the peninsula, the sailors' chapel of **La Garoupe** has a collection of votive offerings and a 14th-century Russian icon. Nearby is the **Jardin Botanique de la Villa Thuret**, created in 1856 to acclimatize tropical plants. Much of the exotic flora of the region began its naturalization here.

🌳 **Jardin Botanique de la Villa Thuret**
90 chemin Raymond, Antibes Juan-les-Pins. **Tel** 04 97 21 25 00. **Open** Mon–Fri. **Closed** public hols.

## ❷❾ Antibes

Alpes-Maritimes. 🏔 77,000. 🚌 🚐 🚢 𝒊 42 av Robert Soleau (04 22 10 60 10). 🚢 Tue–Sun (Jul–Aug: daily). 🆆 antibesjuanlespins.com

The lively town of Antibes was founded by the Greeks as Antipolis and settled by the Romans. In the 14th century, Savoy's possession of the town was contended by France until it fell to them in 1481, after which **Fort Carré** was built and the port, now the base of many luxury superyachts, was remodeled by Vauban.

The Château Grimaldi, formerly a residence of Monaco's ruling family, was built in the 12th century. It now houses the **Musée Picasso**. In 1946 the artist used part of the castle as a studio and, in gratitude, donated 23 paintings and 44 drawings, including *The Goat*. Most are inspired by his love of the Mediterranean, including *La Joie de Vivre*.

*The Goat* (1946) by Pablo Picasso

Over the years, the collection has grown to include more than 150 works.

The pottery in the **Musée d'Archéologie** includes objects salvaged from shipwrecks from the Middle Ages to the 18th century.

🏛 **Musée Picasso**
Château Grimaldi. **Tel** 04 92 90 54 20/26. **Open** Tue–Sun. **Closed** Jan 1, May 1, Nov 1, Dec 25. 🚫 ♿ 📷

🏛 **Musée d'Archéologie**
Bastion St.-André. **Tel** 04 93 95 85 98. **Open** Tue–Sun. **Closed** public hols. 🚫 ♿ 📷

Yachts in the harbor at Antibes

# ⓪ Vallauris

Alpes-Maritimes. 🏛 26,000. 🚊 🚌
ℹ 4 av Georges Clémenceau (04 93
63 18 38); Golfe Juan Vieux Port (04 93
63 73 12). 🏛 Tue–Sun. **w** vallauris-
golfe-juan.fr

Vallauris owes its fame to Pablo
Picasso, who rescued the town's
pottery industry. In 1951, the
village authorities commissioned
Picasso to paint a mural in the
deconsecrated chapel next to
the castle, and his *War and Peace*
(1952) is the chief exhibit of the
**Musée National Picasso**. On the
main square is a bronze statue,
*Man with a Sheep* (1943),
donated by Picasso.

🏛 **Musée National Picasso**
Place de la Libération. **Tel** 04 93 64 71
83. **Open** Wed–Mon (Jul & Aug: daily).
**Closed** Jan 1, May 1, Nov 1 & 11, Dec
25. 🔊 🏠 **w** musees-nationaux-
alpesmaritimes.fr

# ㉛ Biot

Alpes-Maritimes. 🏛 11,000. 🚊 🚌
ℹ 4 Chemin Neuf (04 93 65 78 00).
🏛 Tue. **w** biot-tourisme.com

A typical hill village, charming
Biot has always attracted artists
and artisans. The best known is
Fernand Léger, who made his
first ceramics here in 1949. Some
of these and other works by him
are in the **Musée National
Fernand Léger** outside town.
　The town is also famous for
its bubble-flecked glassware.
The craft of the glassblowers
can be seen (and purchased)
at the **Verrerie de Biot**.

🏛 **Musée National Fernand Léger**
316 chemin du Val-de-Pome. **Tel** 04 92
91 50 30. **Open** Wed–Mon. **Closed**
Jan 1, May 1, Dec 25. 🔊 ♿ 🏠 🏠
📷 **w** musee-fernandleger.fr

🏠 **La Verrerie de Biot**
5 chemin des Combes. **Tel** 04 93 65 03
00. **Open** daily. **Closed** Jan 1 & 15–27.
♿ 🏠 ✏ **w** verreriebiot.com

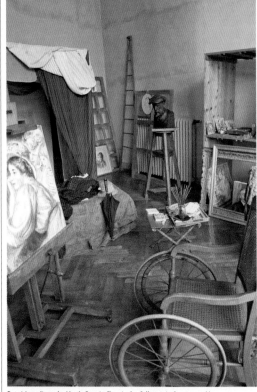
Renoir's studio at the Musée Renoir, Chemin des Collettes, in Cagnes-sur-Mer

# ㉜ Cagnes-sur-Mer

Alpes-Maritimes. 🏛 48,000. 🚊 🚌
ℹ 6 bd Maréchal Juin (04 93 20 61
64). 🏛 Tue–Sun. **w** cagnes-
tourisme.com

Cagnes-sur-Mer is divided into
three districts. The oldest and
most interesting is Haut-de-
Cagnes, with its steep streets,
covered passageways, and
ancient buildings, including a
number of Renaissance arcaded
houses. The other districts are
Cagnes-Ville, the modern town
where hotels and stores are
concentrated, and Cros-de-
Cagnes, a seaside fishing
resort and yachting harbor.

The **Château Grimaldi** in Haut-
de-Cagnes was built in the 14th
century and reworked in the
17th by Henri Grimaldi. Behind
the fortress walls is a shady
courtyard. The surrounding
marble columns conceal a
museum devoted to the olive
tree and a small collection of
modern Mediterranean art.
There is also a group of
paintings bequeathed by
*chanteuse* Suzy Solidor. The 40
works, all portraits of her, are by
artists such as Lolita Lempicka
and Kees van Dongen. On the
ceiling of the banqueting hall is
a vast illusionistic fresco of the
*Fall of Phaeton*, attributed to
Carlone in the 1620s.
　The last 12 years of Pierre-
Auguste Renoir's life were spent
in Cagnes, at the **Musée Renoir**.
The house has been kept almost
exactly as it was when he died
in 1919 and contains 14 of his
paintings as well as 17 plaster

Exterior of the Musée National Fernand Léger in Biot, with a mural by the artist

sculptures. The views from the garden across the countryside down to the sea are simply stunning.

🏠 **Château Grimaldi**
pl du Château. **Tel** 04 92 02 47 30.
**Open** mid-Dec–mid-Nov: Wed–Mon.
**Closed** Jan 1, Dec 25. 🖼

🏛 **Musée Renoir**
**Tel** 04 93 20 61 07. **Open** Wed–Mon
(call to confirm opening hours).
**Closed** May 1, Jan 1, Dec 25. 🖼 📷
♿ 📷

## 🟤 Gorges du Loup

Alpes-Maritimes. ✈ Nice.
🚆 Cagnes-sur-Mer. 🚌 Grasse.
🚌 Nice. ℹ 2 pl de la Libération,
Tourrettes-sur-Loup (04 93 24 18 93).
🌐 **tourrettessurloup.com**

The River Loup rises in the Pre-Alps behind Grasse and cuts a deep path down to the sea. Along its route are dramatic cascades and spectacular views. The superb countryside is crowned by the perched villages for which the region is famous.

**Gourdon** owes much of its appeal to its ancient houses, grouped round a 12th-century **château** built on the site of a Saracen stronghold and perched high on the cliffside. Its terraced gardens were laid out by André Le Nôtre *(see p183)*.

**Tourrettes-sur-Loup** is a fortified village, in which the ramparts are formed by the outer houses. It is famous for its fields of violets, grown for use in perfume and candied sweets. The **Bastide aux Violettes** museum explores the role of the flower in the village's history and economy.

**La Bastide aux Violettes**
quartier de La Ferrage. **Tel** 04 93 59 06 97. **Open** Tue–Sat (Jul & Aug: daily).
📷 ♿ 📷 🌐 **tourrettessurloup.com**

## 🟤 Vence

Alpes-Maritimes. 🚆 19,000. 🚌
ℹ pl du Grand Jardin (04 93 58 06 38).
🗓 Tue & Fri. 🌐 **vence-tourisme.fr**

Vence's gentle climate has always been its main attraction; today it is surrounded by vacation villas. It was an important religious center in the Middle Ages. The **Cathédrale** was restored by Vence's most famous bishop, Antoine Godeau. A 5th-century Roman sarcophagus serves as its altar and there are Carolingian wall carvings. Note, too, the 15th-century carved choir stalls and Godeau's tomb.

Within the ramparts of the Old Town, which retains its 13th- to 14th-century town gates, is place du Peyra, once a

Domed roof in Vence

Roman forum. Its fountain, built in 1822, still provides fresh water. Found on the edge of town, the **Chapelle du Rosaire**, built in 1947 to 1951, was decorated by Henri Matisse, in gratitude to the nuns who nursed him during an illness. On its white walls, biblical scenes are reduced to simple black lines tinted by splashes of light from the blue and yellow stained-glass windows.

🏠 **Chapelle du Rosaire**
466 av Henri Matisse. **Tel** 04 93 58 03 26. **Open** Tue, Thu & Fri am and pm, Wed & Sat pm. **Closed** public hols. 🖼 📷 🏠 Sun 10am.

Chapelle du Rosaire in Vence, whose architecture and interior were designed and decorated by Matisse

# ⏣ Street by Street: St.-Paul de Vence

One of the most famous and frequently visited hill villages of the Nice hinterland, St.-Paul de Vence was once a French frontier post facing Savoy. Its 16th-century ramparts offer views over a landscape of cypress trees and red-roofed villas with palm trees and swimming pools. The village has been heavily restored, but its winding streets and medieval buildings are authentic. It has proved a magnet for artists, both established and aspiring, throughout the 20th century. Today galleries and studios dominate the village.

**Painting of St.-Paul de Vence**
The local landscape is a favorite subject for artists. Neo-Impressionist Paul Signac (1863–1935) painted this view of St.-Paul.

**The Chapelle des Pénitents Blancs** is 16th century.

**The Musée d'Histoire Locale and Folon Chapel** has local waxwork scenes from the town's past.

To Fondation Maeght

RDE A POURTOUNE

RUE DES DORIERS

RUE DES BAUQUES

MONTEE DE L'EGLISE

DES

Auberge de la Colombe d'Or

**The Boules court** and adjacent café are the village social center.

RUE GRANDE

**Ramparts** provide a walk that encircles the village.

COURTINE ST PAUL

BASTION ST REMY

**Le Donjon**, a grim medieval building, was used as a prison until the 19th century.

## Fondation Maeght

Built in 1964 by Paris art dealers Aimé and Marguerite Maeght, this is one of Europe's finest museums of modern art. The striking pink and white building, set outside St.-Paul, was designed by Catalan architect José-Luis Sert, who worked on it directly with artists such as Miró and Chagall. Inside are paintings by Bonnard, Braque, Kandinsky, Chagall, and others. There are also summer concerts, exhibitions, a library, and lectures. In the terraced gardens, sculptures, mobiles, and mosaics by Arp, Calder, Miró, Giacometti, and Hepworth are set amid the pine trees.

*L'Homme qui Marche* by Giacometti

**The Colombe d'Or**
This famous auberge includes a Léger mural (above) on the terrace; a Braque dove by the pool; and a Picasso and a Matisse in the dining room.

**Eglise Collégiale**
Begun in the 12th century, the church has treasures including a painting of St. Catherine, attributed to Claudio Coello.

### VISITORS' CHECKLIST

**Practical Information**
Alpes-Maritimes. 3,500.
2 rue Grande (04 93 32 86 95).
saint-pauldevence.com
Fondation Maeght: 623 chemin Gardettes (04 93 32 81 63). **Open** 10am–6pm (Jul–Sep: to 7pm).

**Transportation**
840 av Emile Hugues, Vence (04 93 58 37 60).

**Grand Fountain**
This charming cobblestone *place* has a pretty urn-shaped fountain.

**Rue Grande**
The doors of the 16th- and 17th-century houses bear coats of arms.

R DU HAUT FOUR
R DU PONTIS
R DU PLUS BAS FOUR
RUE GRANDE
RUE GRANDE
PLACE DE L'HOSPICE
REMPARTS OUEST

### Celebrity Village

The Colombe d'Or (Golden Dove) auberge *(see p602)* was popular with many of the artists and writers who flocked to the Riviera in the 1920s. Early patrons included Picasso, Soutine, Modigliani, Signac, Colette, and Cocteau. Thanks to a friendship with the owners, these artists often paid for their rooms and meals with paintings, resulting in the priceless collection that can be seen by diners today. The rich and famous have continued to come to St.-Paul de Vence: Zelda and F. Scott Fitzgerald had a dramatic fight over Isadora Duncan at dinner here one night, and Yves Montand married Simone Signoret on the terrace. Modern-day fans include Elton John, Michael Caine, Roger Moore, and Hugh Grant.

Artist Marc Chagall (1887–1985), who moved to St.-Paul de Vence in 1950

# ㊱ Nice

The largest resort on the Mediterranean coast and the fifth biggest city in France, with its second busiest airport, Nice was founded by the Greeks and colonized by the Romans. Its temperate winter climate and verdant subtropical vegetation have long attracted visitors. Until World War II it was favored by aristocrats, including Tsar Nicholas I's widow, who visited in 1856, and Queen Victoria, who stayed in 1895. This glittering past has contributed to Nice becoming capital of the Côte d'Azur, and today it is also a center for business conferences and package vacations. Nice has worthy museums, good beaches, and an atmospheric street life. Best of all is Carnival: 18 days of celebrations finishing on Shrove Tuesday in a fireworks display and the Battle of the Flowers (see p43).

Nice's Old Quarter

Yachts at anchor in Nice harbor

## Exploring Nice

The promenade des Anglais, along the seafront, was built in the 1830s with funds raised by the English colony. Today it is an eight-lane, 5-mile (8-km) highway, with galleries, stores, and grand hotels such as the 1913 **Negresco**, reflecting Nice's prosperity.

Nice was Italian until 1860, and the pastel facades and balconies of the Old Town have a distinctly Italianate feel. It lies at the foot of a hill still known as the Château for the castle that once stood there. The district's tall, narrow buildings house artists and galleries, boutiques, and restaurants. The daily flower market in cours Saleya should not be missed. The **Cimiez** district, on the hills overlooking the town, is the fashionable quarter of Nice. The old monastery of Notre-Dame-de-Cimiez is well worth a visit. Lower down the hillside are Les Arènes, remains of a Roman settlement with vestiges of the great baths and an amphitheater. Excavated artifacts are on show at the archaeological museum, next to the Musée Matisse. At the foot of the Cimiez hill is the **Musée National Marc Chagall**. The promenade du Paillon, a strip of park with a central waterway, runs from the Old Town through the center to the promenade des Anglais.

As well as guided tours on foot or by bicycle, it is possible to explore the foodie side of the city on a culinary tour.

### 🏛 Musée National Marc Chagall

36 av du Docteur Ménard. **Tel** 04 93 53 87 20. **Open** Nov–Apr: 10am–5pm Wed–Mon (May–Oct: to 6pm). **Closed** Jan 1, May 1, Dec 25. 🅿 🎨 🏠 🔲 📷 🆆 musee-chagall.fr

The largest collection of works by Marc Chagall, includes paintings, drawings, sculpture, and 17 canvases of the artist's Biblical Message.

### 🏛 Villa Masséna

65 rue de France. **Tel** 04 93 91 19 10. **Open** Wed–Mon. 🎨 🅿 🏠

Housed in a 19th-century Italianate mansion, the Villa Masséna exhibits trace the history of Nice.

### ⛪ Cathédrale Ste.-Réparate

3 pl Rossetti. **Tel** 08 92 70 74 07 or 04 93 92 01 35 for guided tours. **Open** daily.

This 17th-century Baroque building has a handsome tiled dome and is lavishly decorated with marble and original paneling.

### 🏛 Palais Lascaris

15 rue Droite. **Tel** 04 93 62 72 40. **Open** Wed–Mon. **Closed** Jan 1, Easter, May 1, Dec 25. 🎨 🏠

Ornate woodwork, Flemish tapestries and illusionistic

An azure view – relaxing on the promenade des Anglais

ceilings thought to be by Carlone adorn this stuccoed 17th-century palace. Its small but delightful collection includes a reconstruction of an 18th-century apothecary's shop.

### 🏛 Musée d'Art Moderne et d'Art Contemporain (MAMAC)

pl Yves Klein. **Tel** 04 97 13 42 01. **Open** Tue–Sun. **Closed** Jan 1, Easter, May 1, Dec 25. 🖼 ♿ 📷
**W** mamac-nice.org

The museum occupies a strikingly original complex of four marble-faced towers linked by glass passageways. The collection is particularly strong in Neo-Realism and Pop Art, with works by Andy Warhol, Jean Tinguely, and Niki de Saint Phalle. Also well-represented are such Ecole de Nice artists as César, Arman, and Yves Klein.

### 🏛 Musée Matisse

164 av des Arènes de Cimiez. **Tel** 04 93 81 08 08. **Open** Wed–Mon. **Closed** some public hols. 🖼 ♿ 📷
**W** musee-matisse-nice.org

Inspired by the Mediterranean light, Matisse spent many years

*Blue Nude IV* (1952) by Henri Matisse

in Nice. The museum, housed in and below the 17th-century Arena Villa, displays drawings, paintings, bronzes, fabrics, and artifacts. Highlights include *Still Life With Pomegranates* and Matisse's last completed work, *Flowers and Fruits*.

### 🏛 Musée National du Sport

Stade Allianz Riviera, bd des Jardiniers. **Tel** 04 89 22 44 00. **Open** Tue–Sun. 🖼 📷 ♿ **W** museedusport.fr

With its superb collection of memorabilia and photographs, this museum gives an interactive view of France's sporting history.

### 🏛 Musée des Beaux-Arts

33 av des Baumettes. **Tel** 04 92 15 28 28. **Open** Tue–Sun. **Closed** Jan 1, Easter, May 1, Dec 25. 🖼 ♿ restr. 📷
**W** musee-beaux-arts-nice.org

The 19th-century home of a Ukrainian princess displays works sent to Nice by Napoleon III after Italy ceded the city to France.

### 🏛 Musée des Arts Asiatiques

405 prom des Anglais. **Tel** 04 92 29 37 00. **Open** May–mid-Oct: 10am–6pm Wed–Mon (mid-Oct–Apr: to 5pm). **Closed** Jan 1, May 1, Dec 25. ♿ 💻
📷 ♿ **W** arts-asiatiques.com

Ancient and contemporary Asian art is displayed in Kenzo Tange's white marble and glass setting.

# Nice

① Musée National Marc Chagall
② Villa Masséna
③ Cathédrale Ste.-Réparate
④ Palais Lascaris
⑤ Musée d'Art Moderne et d'Art Contemporain

Chapelle de St.-Pierre, Villefranche

# ❸ Villefranche-sur-Mer

Alpes-Maritimes. 🚠 5,000. 🚌 🚇
🛈 Jardin François Binon (04 93 01 73 68). 🛒 Wed, Sat, Sun. 🖥 tourisme-villefranche-sur-mer.com

One of the most perfectly located towns on the coast, Villefranche lies at the foot of hills forming a sheltered amphitheater. The town overlooks a beautiful natural harbor, which is deep enough to be a naval port of call.

The bright and animated waterfront is lined by Italianate facades, with cafés and bars from which to watch the fishermen. Here, too, is the **Chapelle de St.-Pierre**, which, after years of service storing fishing nets, was restored in 1957 and decorated by Jean Cocteau. His frescoes depict non-religious images and the life of St. Peter.

Also worth a visit is the 16th-century **Citadelle St.-Elme**, incorporating three museums, an exhibition room, a congress room, and a garden.

Behind the harbor, the streets are narrow, winding and often stepped. Walking through them, you get the odd glimpse of the harbor. The vaulted 14th-century rue Obscure has always provided shelter from bombardment, right up to World War II.

🏛 **Chapelle de St.-Pierre**
Quai Amiral Courbet. **Tel** 04 93 76 90 70. **Open** Wed–Mon. **Closed** mid-Nov–mid-Dec, Dec 25. 🖼

# ❸ St.-Jean-Cap-Ferrat

Alpes-Maritimes. 🚠 1,600. ✈ Nice. 🚌 Nice. 🚉 Beaulieu-sur-Mer. 🚇 🛈 5/59 av Denis Semeria (04 93 76 08 90). 🖥 saintjeancapferrat-tourisme.fr

This peninsula boasts some of the most sumptuous villas on the Riviera. From 1926 until the author's death, the best-known was Somerset Maugham's Villa Mauresque, where he received celebrities from Noël Coward to Winston Churchill.

High walls shield most of the exclusive villas, but possibly the best one is open to the public. The **Villa Ephrussi de Rothschild** is a terracotta and marble mansion set in themed gardens on the crest of the cape. It belonged to the Baroness Ephrussi de Rothschild, who bequeathed it to the Institut de France in 1934. It is furnished as she left it, with her collections of priceless porcelain, items that belonged to Marie Antoinette, and a unique collection of drawings by Fragonard.

The town of **Beaulieu-sur-Mer** lies where the cape joins the mainland. A pleasant marina with an exceptionally mild climate and very fine hotels, it is the site of another unique house, the extraordinary **Villa Grecque Kérylos**. Built between 1902 and 1908 for archaeologist Theodore Reinach in imitation of an ancient Greek residence, it contains lovingly reproduced mosaics, frescoes, and furniture.

🏛 **Villa Ephrussi de Rothschild**
1 av Ephrussi de Rothschild, Cap Ferrat. **Tel** 04 93 01 45 90. **Open** Mar–Oct: 10am–6pm daily (Jul & Aug: to 7pm); Nov–Feb: pms daily (10am–6pm w/e & school hols). 🖼 🖻 🏛 🖥 🏛 🖛 restricted. 🖥 villa-ephrussi.com

🏛 **Villa Grecque Kérylos**
Imp Gustave Eiffel, Beaulieu. **Tel** 04 93 01 01 44. **Open** as above. 🖼 🖻 🏛 🖥 villakerylos.fr

Greek-style Villa Grecque Kérylos at Beaulieu-sur-Mer

Louis XV salon at the Villa Ephrussi de Rothschild, St.-Jean-Cap-Ferrat

## ❸❾ Eze

Alpes-Maritimes. ⛰ 2,500. 🚉 🚌
🛈 pl Général de Gaulle (04 93 41
26 00). 🌐 **eze-tourisme.com**

For many, Eze is the ultimate
perched village, balancing on a
rocky pinnacle high above the
Mediterranean. Every summer,
thousands of visitors stream
through the 14th-century
fortified gate. The flower-decked
buildings are almost all stores,
galleries, and craft workshops. At
the top of the village, the château
is surrounded by the lush tropical
plants of the **Jardin Exotique**.
The view from here is superb.
 Farther along the Upper
Corniche is the Roman Alpine
**Trophée d'Auguste à La Turbie**
*(see pp52–3)*. This vast 6 BC
structure dominates the
surrounding village, with fine
views toward Monaco and Italy.

### 🟦 Jardin Exotique
Rue du Château. **Tel** 04 93 41 10 30.
**Open** daily. **Closed** Christmas wk. 🈁

### 🟥 Trophée d'Auguste à La Turbie
**Open** Tue–Sun. **Closed** public hols.
🈁 📷 🈁 🌐 **trophee-auguste.fr**

## ❹⓪ Roquebrune-Cap-Martin

Alpes-Maritimes. ⛰ 13,000. 🛫 Nice.
🚉 🚌 🛈 218 av Aristide Briand
(04 93 35 62 87). 🅰 Wed. 🌐 **rcm-tourisme.com**

The medieval village of Roquebrune overlooks the wooded
cape where the villas of the rich
and famous still stand. Residents
have included Coco Chanel and
Empress Eugenie. The cape has
not always been kind – poet
W. B. Yeats died here in 1939 and
architect Le Corbusier was
drowned off the coast in 1965.
 In 1467 Roquebrune believed
that by performing scenes from
the Passion it escaped the
plague, and every August it
continues this tradition.

## ❹❶ Alpes-Maritimes

Alpes-Maritimes. 🛫 Nice. 🚉 Nice.
🚌 Peille. 🅰 Nice. 🛈 15 rue
Centrale, Peille (04 93 82 14 40).
🌐 **peille.fr**

In the hinterland of the Côte
d'Azur, it is still possible to find
quiet, unspoiled villages off the
tourist track. The tiny twin villages
of **Peille** and **Peillon** are typical.
Both have changed little since
the Middle Ages, perched on
outcrops over the Paillon river,
their streets a mass of steps and
arches. Peille, the more remote,
even has its own dialect. The
Alpes-Maritimes countryside is
also unspoiled, its craggy gorges,
tumbling rivers and windswept
plateaus just a few hours from
the coast. Of note are the ancient
rock carvings of the **Vallée des
Merveilles** and rare wildlife in
the **Parc National du Mercantour**.

## ❹❷ Menton

Alpes-Maritimes. ⛰ 30,000. 🚉 🚌
🛈 Palais de l'Europe, 8 av Boyer (04
92 41 76 76). 🅰 Tue–Sun.
🌐 **tourisme-menton.fr**

Menton's beaches, with the Alps
and the golden buildings and
*belle époque* villas of the Old Town
as a backdrop, would be enough
to lure most visitors. Tropical
gardens and citrus fruits thrive
in the town's glorious climate,
mild even in February for the
lemon festival *(see p43)*.
 The **Basilica St.-Michel** is a
superb example of Baroque
architecture. The square before it
is paved with a mosaic of the
Grimaldi coat of arms. The **Salle
des Mariages** in the Hôtel de
Ville was decorated in 1957 by
Jean Cocteau. Drawings, paintings, ceramics, and stage designs
by the renowned artist are
displayed in the **Musée Jean
Cocteau Collection Séverin
Wunderman**, housed in a striking
modern building. Inside the Palais
Carnolès, the **Musée des Beaux-
Arts** features works from the
Middle Ages to the 20th century.

### 🚪 Salle des Mariages
Hôtel de Ville, pl Ardoino. **Tel** 04 92 10
50 00. **Open** Mon–Fri. **Closed** public
hols. 🈁

### 🏛 Musée Jean Cocteau Collection Séverin Wunderman
2 quai de Monléon. **Tel** 04 89 81 52 50.
**Open** Wed–Mon. **Closed** pub hols. 🈁
🈁 🈁 🈁 🌐 **museecocteaumenton.fr**

### 🏛 Musée des Beaux-Arts
Palais Carnolès, 3 av de la Madone.
**Tel** 04 93 35 49 71. **Open** Wed–Mon.
**Closed** public hols.

The facade of the Musée Jean Cocteau Collection Séverin Wunderman

# ㊸ Monaco

Travelers to Monaco by car would do well to take the Moyenne Corniche, one of the most beautiful highways in the world, with incomparable views of the Mediterranean coastline. Arriving among the skyscrapers of Monaco today, it is hard to envisage the turbulence of its history. At first a Greek settlement, later taken by the Romans, it was bought from the Genoese in 1297 by the Grimaldis, who, in spite of bitter family feuds and at least one political assassination, are still the world's oldest ruling dynasty. Monaco covers 0.74 sq miles (1.9 sq km) and, although its size has increased by one-third in the form of landfills, it still occupies an area smaller than that of New York's Central Park.

Skyscrapers and apartment buildings of modern Monte Carlo

Casino de Monte Carlo

## Exploring Monaco

Monaco owes its renown principally to its casino. Source of countless legends, it was instituted in 1878 by Charles III to save himself from bankruptcy. The first casino was opened in 1865 on a barren promontory (later named Monte Carlo in his honor) across the harbor from ancient Monaco-Ville. So successful was Charles's money-making venture that, by 1870, he was able to abolish taxation for his people. Today, Monaco is a tax haven for thousands, and its residents have the highest per capita income in the world.

Visitors come from all over the world for the Grand Prix de Monaco in May (see p40) and the Monte Carlo Rally in January (see p43). Many of the greatest singers perform in the opera season. There is a fireworks festival (July–August), and an international circus festival at the end of January as well as world-class ballet and concerts. Amenities exist for every sort of leisure activity, and there is much else to enjoy without breaking the bank, including **Fort Antoine** and the Neo-Romanesque **Cathédrale**.

### 🎰 Casino de Monte Carlo
Place du Casino. **Tel** 00 377 98 06 21 21. **Open** daily, from 2pm (for players). ♿ 📷 ✏ 🆆 **casinomontecarlo.com**

Renovated in 1878 by Charles Garnier, architect of the Paris Opéra (see p101), and set in formal gardens, the Casino de Monte Carlo gives a splendid view over Monaco. The lavish interior is still decorated in belle époque style, recalling an era when this was the rendezvous of Russian Grand Dukes. Anyone can play the odds on the slots of the Salon Blanc or the roulette wheels of the Salons Européens. Tours run daily from 9am to noon. Check the website for rules, regulations, and dress code.

### 🏰 Palais Princier
Place du Palais. **Tel** 00 377 93 25 18 31. **Open** Apr–Oct: daily. 📷 🆆 **palais.mc**

Monaco-Ville, the seat of government, is the site of the 13th-century Palais Princier. The interior, with its priceless furniture and carpets and its magnificent frescoes of

Aerial view of Monaco

## Monaco's Royal Family

Prince Albert II assumed the Monaco throne in July 2005, three months after his father Prince Rainier III died, aged 81, ending a reign of over 55 years. Rainier was descended from a Grimaldi who entered the Monaco fortress in 1297. His wife, former movie star Grace Kelly, died tragically in 1982. In 2011 Prince Albert married the South African Charlene Wittstuck; they welcomed their twin children in December 2014.

The wedding of Prince Albert and Princess Charlene

---

mythological figures, is only open to the public in the summer. The Changing of the Guard takes place at 11:55am.

### 🏛 Musée du Vieux Monaco

2 rue Emile de Loth. **Tel** 00 377 93 50 57 28. **Open** Jun–Sep: Wed & Fri. 🌐 **traditions-monaco.com**

This museum aims to preserve and promote Monaco's historic national identity through a collection of paintings, ceramics, furniture, traditional costumes and reconstructed interiors typical of the area.

Guard outside the Palais Princier

### 🌊 Musée Océanographique

Av Saint-Martin. **Tel** 00 377 93 15 36 00. **Open** daily. **Closed** Jan 1, Grand Prix, Dec 25. 🅿 ♿ 🖊 🎥 🌐 **oceano.mc**

This museum was founded in 1910 by Prince Albert I. Its aquarium, fed with seawater, holds rare species of marine plants and animals. The museum houses an important scientific collection, diving equipment, and model ships. Marine explorer Jacques Cousteau established his research center here.

### 🌿 Jardin Exotique

62 bd du Jardin Exotique. **Tel** 00 377 93 15 29 80. **Open** daily. **Closed** Nov 19, Dec 25. 🅿 🎥 🌐 **jardin-exotique.mc**

These gardens are considered to be the finest in Europe, with a huge range of tropical and sub-tropical plants. A museum of anthropology offers evidence that mammoths once lived on the coast here.

### 🏛 Nouveau Musée National de Monaco

Villa Sauber, 17 av Princesse Grace. **Tel** 00 377 98 98 91 26. **Open** daily. **Closed** Grand Prix and public hols. 🅿 🎥

Villa Sauber and Villa Paloma are the two magnificent *belle époque* villas that make up this museum, which hosts temporary exhibitions on themes of art and performance.

---

## Monaco

① Jardin Exotique
② Musée du Vieux Monaco
③ Palais Princier
④ Cathédrale
⑤ Musée Océanographique
⑥ Casino de Monte Carlo

**Key**

— Grand Prix route

For keys to symbols *see back flap*

# CORSICA

*Haute-Corse · Corse-du-Sud*

Corsica, where the people speak their own language, has all the attributes of a mini-continent. There are tropical palm trees, vineyards, olive and orange groves, forests of chestnut and indigenous pine, alpine lakes and cool mountain torrents filled with trout. Most distinctive of all is the parched maquis (scrub), heavy with the scent of myrtle, which Napoleon swore he could smell from Elba.

The fourth largest island in the Mediterranean after Sicily, Sardinia, and Cyprus, Corsica has been a problem and a bafflement to mainland France ever since 1769, when it was "sold" to Louis XV by the Genoese for 40 million francs. Before that, following years of struggle, the Corsican people had enjoyed 14 years of independence under the revered leadership of Pasquale Paoli. They understandably felt cheated by the deal with the French, and have resented them ever since. To vacationers visiting the island – in July and August tourists outnumber the inhabitants six to one – the Corsican–French relationship may be a matter of indifference. However, there is a strong (and sometimes quite violent)

separatist movement, which does deter some tourists. As a result, Corsica's wild beauty has been preserved to an extent not seen in the rest of the Mediterranean.

For 200 years, from the 11th to the 13th century, Corsica was a colony of the old Tuscan republic of Pisa, whose builders founded beautifully proportioned Romanesque churches. These buildings are, along with the megalithic stone warriors in Filitosa, the noblest monuments to be seen here. For the rest, the birthplace of Napoleon is a place of wild seacoasts and mountain peaks, one of the last unspoiled corners of the Mediterranean: poor, depopulated, beautiful, old-fashioned, and doggedly aloof.

The village of Oletta in the Nebbio region around St.-Florent

◀ Dramatic limestone cliffs at Bonifacio

# Exploring Corsica

Corsica's main appeal is its scenery: a wildly beautiful landscape of mountains, forests, myrtle-scented maquis, and countless miles of sandy beaches. Late spring (when the wildflowers are in bloom) and early autumn are the best times to visit – the temperature is moderate and there aren't too many visitors. The island is renowned for its superb hiking trails, some of which become cross-country skiing trails during the winter. Downhill skiing is also possible in February and March.

Calvi's port and 15th-century citadel

## Key

- ▬▬ Highway
- ▬▬ Secondary road
- ⋯⋯ Minor road
- ▬▬ Scenic route
- △ Summit

## Winds of Corsica

The island is affected by winds from every direction. The two not shown here are the Mezzogiorno, which blows at noon, and the Terrana, which is strongest at midnight.

**Tramontane** (cold wind blowing from the north)

**Maestrale** (can be very strong)

**Grecale** (bringing rain in autumn and spring)

**Ponente** (milder west wind)

**Levante** (warm)

**Sirocco** (dusty wind from Africa)

**Libeccio** (dry in summer and bringing rain in winter)

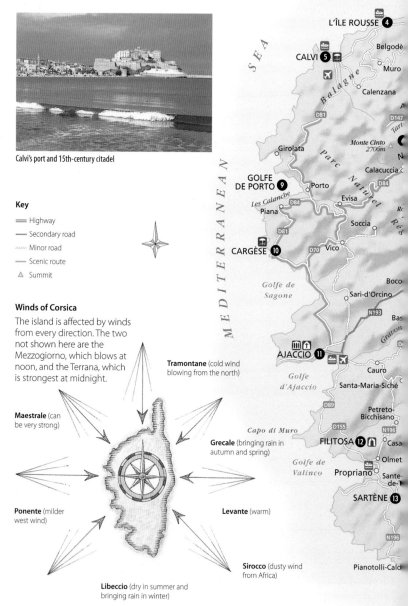

*Ligurian Sea*

L'ÎLE ROUSSE 4

Belgodè

CALVI 5

Muro

Calenzana

*Balagne*

D81

D147

Girolata

*Monte Cinto 2706m*

Calacuccia

*Parc Naturel*

GOLFE DE PORTO 9

Porto

D84

*Les Calanche*

Evisa

Piana

D84

Soccia

D81

Vico

CARGÈSE 10

D70

Boco

*Golfe de Sagone*

Sari-d'Orcino

N193

Bas

*Gravon*

AJACCIO 11

Cauro

*Golfe d'Ajaccio*

Santa-Maria-Siché

D89

Petreto-Bicchisano

*Capo di Muro*

D155

N196

FILITOSA 12

Casa

*Golfe de Valinco*

Olmet

Propriano

Sante-de-

SARTÈNE 13

N196

Pianotolli-Calo

## Sights at a Glance

**1** Cap Corse
**2** Bastia
**3** St.-Florent
**4** L'Ile Rousse
**5** Calvi
**6** The Niolo
**7** Corte
**8** The Castagniccia

**9** Golfe de Porto
**10** Cargèse
**11** Ajaccio
**12** Filitosa
**13** Sartène
**14** Bonifacio
**15** Côte Orientale

The Calanche cliffs in the Golfe de Porto

## Getting Around

Car ferries (which should be reserved well in advance) depart from Marseille, Nice, and Toulon, arriving at Bastia, L'Ile Rousse, Calvi, Ajaccio, Propriano, and Porto-Vecchio. There are also ferries from Sardinia to Bonifacio and Propriano, and from several Italian ports. There are small airports at Ajaccio, Bastia, Calvi, and Figari. Corsica's roads are narrow, twisting, and often tortuously slow, though breathtaking views reward the effort. A car is a must for exploring the island, as public transportation is limited. Carry spare gas – filling stations are few and far between.

0 kilometers 20
0 miles 10

Corte's Old Town, with its citadel high up on a rocky outcrop

# ❶ Cap Corse

Haute-Corse. ✈ Bastia. 🚌 Bastia.
🚢 Bastia. *i* Port de Plaisance,
Macinaggio (04 95 35 40 34);
Port Toga, Pietrabugna (04 95 31 02 32).
w macinaggiorogliano-capcorse.fr

Cap Corse is the northern tip of
Corsica, 25 miles (40 km) in length
but seldom more than 7 miles (12
km) wide, pointing like an accus-
atory finger toward Genoa.

There are two roads out of
Bastia to the cape: the D81
leading west across the mountains and joining up with the
D80 after the wine village of
Patrimonio; and the D80 traveling north along the eastern
shore to **Erbalunga** and
**Macinaggio**. The road is narrow
and twisting, a taste of what
awaits you in Corsica.

From the coastal village of
**Lavasina**, the D54 leads left off
the D80 to Pozzo; from here it is
a 5-hour round trip on foot to
the 4,288-ft (1,307-m) summit of
**Monte Stello**, the highest peak
on the cape. The 360-degree
view from the top takes in
St.-Florent to the west, the
massif of central Corsica to the
south, and the Italian island of
Elba to the east.

Farther up the coast, the
restored **Tour de Losse** is one of
many 16th-century Genoese
towers along the coast – part
of an elaborate system that
enabled all Corsican towns to
be warned within 2 hours of
impending barbarian raids.

The charming 18th-century
fishing port of **Centuri**, near
the tip of the peninsula on the
west coast, is an ideal spot for
a delicious seafood feast. **Pino**,

The village of Erbalunga on the east coast of Cap Corse

a pretty little village straggling
down the green mountainside
farther to the south, has no
hotel, only a lovely little
church dedicated to the
Virgin, full of model ships
placed there by mariners
grateful for her protection.

On the way south along the
vertiginous lower corniche, be
sure to turn left up the hill to
**Canari**. One of the larger
villages in this area, Canari has
a jewel of a 12th-century Pisan
church, Santa Maria Assunta,
a magnificent view across the
sea, and a thoroughly convivial
hotel-restaurant. All the byroads
in this thickly wooded area
seem to lead somewhere
interesting. There are dozens
of picturesque hamlets in the
vicinity, and it should be borne
in mind that from this point
onward the landscape becomes
steadily less attractive as the
road winds on past the old
asbestos workings and beaches
of black sand below the village
of **Nonza**.

# ❷ Bastia

Haute-Corse. 🅿 44,000. ✈ 🚆 🚌
🚢 *i* north end of pl St.-Nicolas
(04 95 54 20 40). 🗓 Tue–Sun.
w bastia-tourisme.com

A thriving port and the
administrative capital of Upper
Corsica, Bastia is utterly different
in style from its sedate west
coast rival, Ajaccio. The
Genoese citadel and colorful
19th-century Italianate buildings around the old port are for
many people their first taste of
the authentic Mediterranean –
as it was half a century ago,
and as it stubbornly remains
in our imagination.

The center of Bastia's life is
**place St.-Nicolas**, facing the
wharf where ferries from
the mainland and Italy arrive.
Heading south along the
waterfront, you come to **place
de l'Hôtel de Ville**, site of a daily
food market. Bordering the
square are the early 17th-century
**Chapelle de l'Immaculée
Conception**, with its ornate
18th-century interior, and the
mid-17th-century **Eglise de
St.-Jean-Baptiste**, whose facade
dominates the Vieux Port.

From here it is a short walk
up to the 16th-century **citadel**,
housing the **Musée de Bastia**,
which recounts the town's
history from its medieval origins
in an impressive setting.

🏛 **Musée de Bastia**
Pl du Dujon. **Tel** 04 95 31 09 12.
**Open** Oct–Apr: Tue–Sat; May, Jun &
Sep: Tue–Sun; Jul–Aug: daily. 🅰
w musee-bastia.com

Bastia's Vieux Port seen from the Jetée du Dragon

*For hotels and restaurants in this region see p571 and p603*

## ❸ St.-Florent

Haute-Corse. 🗺 1,700. 🚌
ℹ️ Bâtiment Administratif, BP 53 (04 95 37 06 04). 🕐 first Wed of month.
🅦 corsica-saintflorent.com

St.-Florent is almost a Corsican St.-Tropez – chic, affluent, and packed with yachts. Its citadel, which showcases photography exhibitions, dates from 1439, and is a fine example of Genoese military architecture. The town itself is pleasant to wander around; its main attraction, the 12th-century Pisan **Cathédrale de Santa Maria Assunta**, lies just inland on the road to Poggio-d'Oletta.

### Environs

A leisurely 4-hour circuit by car of the **Nebbio** region, which extends in an amphitheater around St.-Florent, might take in the following: **Santo-Pietro-di-Tenda**; **Murato**, famous for its magnificent **Eglise de San Michele de Murato**, a 12th-century Pisan Romanesque construction built of white and green stone; the **San Stefano** pass, with the sea on either side; **Oletta**, which produces a special blue cheese made from ewe's milk; the **Teghime** pass; and finally the wine village of **Patrimonio**, where there is a strange, big-eared menhir dating from 900–800 BC.
    Along the coast to the west of St.-Florent lies the barren, un-inhabited **Désert des Agriates**. If you can face the 6-mile (10-km) haul to the sea – on foot, by bicycle, or by motorbike – the Saleccia beach is the most beautiful on the island.

San Michele de Murato

## ❹ L'Ile Rousse

Haute-Corse. 🗺 3,400. 🚌 🚍 🛳
ℹ️ av Calizi (04 95 60 04 35).
🕐 summer: daily; winter: Tue & Fri.
🅦 ot-ile-rousse.fr

Founded in 1758 by Pasquale Paoli, leader of independent Corsica, L'Ile Rousse is today a major resort and ferry terminal. The center of town is dominated by a marble statue of Corsica's national hero, Paoli. On the north side of the square is the covered market, with the Old Town located just beyond.
    In summer, L'Ile Rousse becomes overcrowded, its beaches a mass of bodies. It is worth traveling 6 miles (10 km) up the coast to **Lozari**, which offers a magnificent, virtually unspoiled stretch of sand.

### Environs

One very pleasant way to discover the **Balagne** region is to take the trolley-train from L'Ile Rousse to Calvi and back. This odd little service runs year-round (more frequent in summer), roughly keeping to the coastline and stopping at Algajola, Lumio, and various villages along the way.

## ❺ Calvi

Haute-Corse. 🗺 5,500. 🚌 🚍 🛳
ℹ️ 97 Port de Plaisance, chemin de la Plage (04 95 65 16 67). 🕐 daily.
🅦 balagne-corsica.com;
🅦 calvi-tourisme.com

Calvi, where Nelson lost his eye in an "explosion of stones" in 1794, is today half military town, half budget vacation resort. Its 15th-century Genoese citadel sitting high above Calvi port, from where it towers over the sea, is one of the most beautiful sights on the island. The town makes a half-hearted case for being the birthplace of Christopher Columbus, but there is no evidence to support this. A much better claim to fame is the food, which is very good and reasonably priced. There is also a respectable jazz festival toward the end of June. Outside of town, the 19th-century **Chapelle de Notre-Dame de la Serra** is gloriously located on a hilltop commanding extensive views in all directions.

French foreign legionnaire

The Chapelle de Notre-Dame de la Serra, 3 miles (6 km) southwest of Calvi

Corte's 15th-century citadel perched on a rocky outcrop above the town

## ❻ The Niolo (Niolu)

Haute-Corse. 🚌 Corte. 🛈 rte de Cuccia, Calacuccia (04 95 48 05 22). 🌐 office-tourisme-niolu.com

The Niolo, west of Corte, extends westward to the Vergio pass and the upper Golo basin, and to the east as far as the Scala di Santa Regina. It includes Corsica's highest mountain, the 8,878-ft (2,706-m) **Monte Cinto**, and its biggest river, the **Golo**, which meets the sea south of Bastia.

Of the various regions of Corsica, the Niolo is the only one to persist in the cultivation of livestock for its economic mainstay.

The main town, **Calacuccia**, is suitable for excursions to Monte Cinto. The nearby ski resort of **Haut Asco** is best reached by the D147 from **Asco**, but enthusiasts can walk from Calacuccia (8–9 hours). To the south is the huge forest of **Valdu Niello**.

## ❼ Corte

Haute-Corse. 🔼 7,500. 🚌 🚏 🛈 La Citadelle (04 95 46 26 70). 🏪 Fri. 🌐 corte-tourisme.com

In the geographical center of Corsica, Corte was the chosen capital of the independence leader Pasquale Paoli from 1755 to 1769, and today is the seat of the island's university. In the Old Town is the 15th-century citadel, housing the **Musée de la Corse**. Its exhibits relate to traditional Corsican life and anthropology.

Corte is the best base for exploring nearby mountain areas, especially as it stands exactly halfway along the GR20, the legendary 137-mile (220-k) trail from Calenzana to Conca.

### 🏛 Musée de la Corse

La Citadelle. **Tel** 04 95 45 25 45. **Open** Tue–Sun (mid-Jun–mid-Sep: daily; Nov–Mar: Tue–Sat). **Closed** public hols. 🖼 ♿ 🎧 📷 🖼 🌐 musee-corse.com

### Environs

Don't miss the beautiful **Gorges de la Restonica**, about 7 miles (12 km) out of town via the D623. Above these gorges adventurous walkers may wish to make the well-marked climb to the snow-fed **Lac de Melo** (allow 60–90 minutes); or the **Lac de Capitello**, 30 minutes farther on, where the snow stays as late as early June. The path – in winter a cross-country skiing trail – follows the river.

South of Corte, the **Forêt de Vizzavona** features beech and pine woodland crisscrossed by trout-filled streams and walking trails (notably the GR20). It is a fine refuge from the summer heat and is also an excuse to take the small-gauge train up from Ajaccio or Bastia, stopping at Vizzavona.

## ❽ The Castagniccia

Haute-Corse. ✈ Bastia. 🚌 Corte, Ponte Leccia. 🚌 Piedicroce, La Porta, Valle-d'Alesani. 🛈 Maison des Enterprises, Folelli, Piedicroce (04 95 35 82 54 or 04 95 33 38 21). 🌐 castagniccia.fr

East of Corte is the hilly, chestnut-covered region of Castagniccia (literally "small chestnut grove"), which most Corsicans agree is the very heart and kernel of the island. It was here that independence leader Pasquale Paoli was born in 1725, and where the revolts against Genoa and later France began in earnest in 1729. Alas, many of the villages in this beautiful, remote area are nearly empty, their inhabitants having joined the 800,000 or so Corsicans (almost three times the present population) who live and work in mainland France or Italy. It seems hard to believe that in the 17th century, when the great chestnut forests introduced here by the Genoese were at the height of their production, this was the most prosperous and populated region in Corsica.

The D71 from Ponte Leccia (north of Corte) to the east coast winds through the center of the Castagniccia region, and to see it at a leisurely pace will take the best part of a week. Stock up on groceries before you start, as there is little to be had in the way of supplies en route.

◀ One of the Genoese towers on the beautiful Iles Sanguinaires

# ⑨ Golfe de Porto

Corse-du-Sud. ✈ 🚗 ⛴ Ajaccio.
🚌 Porto. 🛈 Quartier la Marine (04 95
26 10 55). 🆆 **porto-tourisme.com**

Porto is sited at the head of
the Golfe de Porto, one of the
most beautiful bays in the
Mediterranean, which for the
sake of its fauna and flora has
been included among UNESCO's
World's Heritage sites. The town
has a magnificent Genoese
watchtower – the perfect spot
for admiring the sunset – and
regular boat excursions (Apr–
Oct) to the Calanche, Scandola,
and Girolata.

The **Calanche** begin 5 miles
(8 km) out of Porto, on the road
to Piana. These 1,000-ft (300-m)
red-granite cliffs plunge sheer
to the sea, and are quite simply
breathtaking. They are
accessible by boat or on foot:
well-defined trails start from the
Tête du Chien and the Pont de
Mezanu, while boat tickets are
available at Porto's Hôtel Le
Cyrnée and a few other places
in the marina.

East of Porto are the Gorges
de la Spelunca, accessed by a
mule route punctuated by
Genoese bridges.

Just south of Porto, along
a spectacular corniche drive
passing under granite
archways, lies the pretty
village of **Piana**, a good base
for visiting this whole area,
with information about
recommended walks. One
worthwhile destination is the
cove at **Ficajola** just below
Piana – a truly delightful beach.

Genoese watchtower at Golfe de Porto

## Environs

The road over the mountains
from Porto to Calvi offers no
more than a taste of this
grandiose corner of Corsica
– you have to take to the
sea to view it properly
(ferries from Porto and
Galéria). **Girolata**, a tiny
hamlet north of Porto, can be
reached only by sea or via a
mule track (4 hours round trip
on foot) from a clearly marked
point 14 miles (23 km) north
of Porto on the D81.

At the mouth of the Golfe
de Girolata, the **Réserve
Naturelle de Scandola**,
instituted in 1975, is the first
land and sea preserve in France,
covering over 4 sq miles
(10 sq km) of sea, and a similar
area of cliffs, caves, and maquis.
Marine life is abundant in these
clear, protected waters; the
birds include ospreys, puffins
and falcons.

## Corsican Flowers

For people who love
wildflowers, Corsica
is a Mediterranean
jewel. Much of the
island is covered
with maquis, a
tangle of aromatic
shrubs and low
trees that flowers
from late winter
onward. Among its
dense variety are
showy rockroses,
which shower the
ground with short-
lived pink or white
petals, and brilliant yellow
broom. Grassy and rocky
slopes are good places to
spot the widespread tassel
hyacinth and the Illyrian sea
lily, which grows only in
Corsica and Sardinia.

Rock-
rose

Spanish
broom

Illyrian sea lily

Tassel hyacinth

The town of Piana with the Calanche in the background

*For hotels and restaurants in this region see p571 and p603*

Cargèse's Greek rite church

## ⑩ Cargèse

Corse-du-Sud. 🅰 1,300. 🚌 *i* rue du Docteur Dragacci (04 95 26 41 31). 🖥 **cargese.net**; 🖥 **ouestcorsica.com**

Cargèse overlooks the sea from a promontory between the bays of Sagone and Pero. It is a small town with an odd history: many of the people who live here are the descendants of 17th-century Greek refugees from Turkish rule, and given asylum in Corsica.

A few Cargésiens still speak Greek, and their icon-filled Eastern (Greek) rite church faces its Catholic counterpart in an attitude that must once have seemed confrontational. Today the old rivalries have vanished, and the Orthodox priest and Catholic *curé* often stand in for one another.

There are many splendid beaches in the vicinity, notably at **Pero** and **Chiuni** just to the north, and at **Ménasina** and **Stagnoli** to the south.

## ⑪ Ajaccio

Corse-du-Sud. 🅰 69,000. ✈ 🚌 🚌 🚌 *i* 3 bd du Roi Jérôme (04 95 51 53 03). 🖥 Tue–Sun. 🖥 **ajaccio-tourisme.com**

Ajaccio, a noisy, busy town by Corsican standards, was the birthplace of Napoleon Bonaparte in 1769. Napoleon never returned to Corsica after crowning himself emperor of the French in 1804, but the town – modern capital of nationalist Corsica – celebrates his birthday every August 15.

The 16th-century **Cathédrale Notre-Dame de la Miséricorde**, where Napoleon was baptized in 1771, houses Delacroix's painting *Vierge du Sacré-Coeur*.

A few streets away, the **Musée National de la Maison Bonaparte**, where Napoleon was born and spent his childhood, contains family portraits, period furniture, and assorted memorabilia.

Much more extraordinary is the art collection assembled by Napoleon's unscrupulous uncle, Cardinal Fesch, who merrily looted churches, palaces, and museums during the Italian campaign and brought the swag home to Ajaccio. Housed in the 19th-century **Palais Fesch**, the **Musée des Beaux-Arts** contains the finest collection of Italian primitive art in France after the Louvre. Among its masterpieces are works by Bellini, Botticelli, Titian, Veronese, Bernini, and Poussin. Next to the Palais Fesch stands the **Chapelle Impériale**, built in 1855 by Napoleon III to accommodate the tombs of the Bonapartes. From here, walk back along the dock to the Jetée de la Citadelle, which offers superb views of the town, the marina, and the Golfe d'Ajaccio. The adjacent 16th-century **citadel** is occupied by the army.

🏛 **Musée National de la Maison Bonaparte**
Rue St.-Charles. **Tel** 04 95 21 43 89. **Open** Tue–Sun. 🖥 🖥
🖥 **musee-maisonbonaparte.fr**

🏛 **Palais Fesch, Musée des Beaux-Arts**
50–52 rue Cardinal Fesch. **Tel** 04 95 26 26 26. **Open** Wed–Mon. 🖥 🖥 🖥
🖥 **musee-fesch.com**

**Environs**
From the Quai de la Citadelle there are daily excursions to the **Îles Sanguinaires** at the mouth of the Golfe d'Ajaccio.

At Vero, 13 miles (21 km) northeast on the N193, is an unusual park, **A Cupulatta**, with over 170 species of tortoises and turtles (Apr–Oct).

A statue-menhir at Filitosa

## ⑫ Filitosa

Station Préhistorique de Filitosa, Sollacaro, Corse-du-Sud. **Tel** 04 95 74 00 91. **Open** Apr–Oct: daily. 🖥 🖥 🖥 🖥 **filitosa.fr**

The 4,000-year-old, life-size stone warriors of Filitosa are the most spectacular relics of megalithic man in Corsica. Discovered in 1946, these phallus-like granite menhirs represent an interesting progression from mere silhouettes to detailed sculpture etched with human features.

The five most recent and most sophisticated figures (about 1500 BC) stand around

Statue of Napoleon by Laboureur in place Maréchal Foch, Ajaccio

*For hotels and restaurants in this region see p571 and p603*

The fortified Old Town of Bonifacio, with the harbor in the foreground

a 1,000-year-old olive tree, in the field below a tumulus. Other finds, which include a heavily armed warrior with shield, helmet, and sword, can be seen in the site's archaeological museum.

## ⓭ Sartène

Corse-du-Sud. 🏠 3,500. 🚌
🛈 14 cours Soeur Amélie (04 95 77 15 40). 🛍 summer: daily; winter: Sat. 🌐 lacoursedesorigines.com

Sartène is a medieval fortified town of narrow cobblestone streets and grey granite houses rising above the Rizzanese Valley. Founded by the Genoese in the early 16th century, it has survived attacks by Barbary pirates and centuries of bloody feuding among the town's leading families.

Despite all this, Sartène has a reputation for deep piety, reinforced each year by the oldest and most intense Christian ceremony in Corsica, the Good Friday Catenacciu (literally, the "chained one"). A red-hooded penitent, barefoot and in chains, drags a wooden cross through the Old Town in a re-enactment of Christ's ascent to Golgotha.

### Environs
In the town center, the **Musée Départemental de la Préhistoire et d'Archéologie** has a collection of Neolithic, Bronze- and Iron-Age artifacts.

🏛 **Musée Départemental de la Préhistoire et d'Archéologie**
Bd Jacques Nicolaï. **Tel** 04 95 77 01 09.
**Open** Jun–Sep: daily; Oct–May: Mon–Fri. 🌐 prehistoire-corse.org

## ⓮ Bonifacio

Corse-du-Sud. 🏠 3,000. 🚌 🚢
🛈 2 rue Fred Scamaroni (04 95 73 11 88). 🛍 Wed. 🌐 bonifacio.fr

Bonifacio is the southernmost town in Corsica, dramatically sited on a limestone and granite cliff peninsula with stunning views *(see p536)*. Its handsome harbor at the foot of the cliffs is the focus of life: cafés, restaurants, and boutiques abound and boats depart regularly for neighboring Sardinia and the uninhabited island of Lavezzi.

From the harbor, steps lead up to Bonifacio's fortified Old Town. The citadel, which was built by the conquering Genoese at the end of the 12th century, has long been the town's main defensive post, and from 1963 to 1983 was the headquarters of the French foreign legion. From here, wander down to the tip of the promontory to see the three old windmills and the ruins of a Franciscan monastery.

## ⓯ Côte Orientale

Haute-Corse & Corse-du-Sud. ✈ Bastia. 🛈 80 av St.-Alexandra, Aléria (04 95 57 01 51); rue Maréchal Leclerc, BP 92, Porto-Vecchio (04 95 70 09 58). 🚢 Bastia, Porto-Vecchio. 🌐 **oriente-corsica.com**; 🌐 **ot-portovecchio.com**.

The flat, rather dreary alluvial plain stretching from Bastia to Solenzara has been rich farmland since 1945, the year it was finally drained and rid of malaria. More recently, seaside resorts and even high-rise hotels have mushroomed along the coast, cashing in on its long, sandy beaches.

The best sight in **Mariana**, which is otherwise uncomfortably close to the Bastia-Poretta airport, is the early 12th-century cathedral of Mariana known as **La Canonica**. A short distance away is the slightly older **Eglise de San Perteo**, surrounded by meadows.

About halfway down the coast, the port of **Aléria**, originally a Greek colony and the base for Rome's conquest of Corsica in 259 BC, is interesting for its rich archaeological heritage. Just outside town, a museum housed in the 15th-century Fort de Matra chronicles daily life in Roman Aléria.

Toward the southern tip of the island, the fortified town of **Porto-Vecchio**, built by Corsica's Genoese conquerors, is now an extremely popular resort. The setting is perfect for the conventional beach holiday, with umbrella pines, cork oak forests, and glorious white sandy beaches within easy reach of the town, especially at **Palombaggia** and **Pinarello**.

The Golfe de Porto-Vecchio

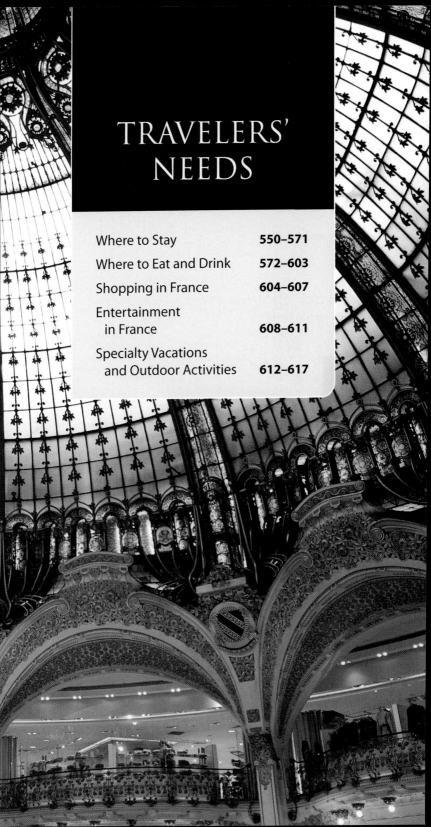

# TRAVELERS' NEEDS

Where to Stay      **550–571**

Where to Eat and Drink      **572–603**

Shopping in France      **604–607**

Entertainment
  in France      **608–611**

Specialty Vacations
  and Outdoor Activities      **612–617**

# WHERE TO STAY

France has thousands of registered hotels that range from some of the most glamorous establishments in the world to charming and idiosyncratic little inns tucked away in the countryside. On these four pages, the types of hotels on offer are summarized with tips on what to expect. The hotel listings pages *(see pp554–71)* describe some of the best hotels around the country in every price category and style. Alternatively, you can choose from the increasingly popular *chambres d'hôtes* (bed-and-breakfasts), which range from simple farms to grandiose châteaux. As France is one of the most popular countries in the world for vacation rentals, there is also information on finding a rural home or *gîte*, and also how to get the most out of a camping holiday.

Entrance to the Hôtel-Restaurant Euzkadi at Espelette in the Pyrenees *(see p568)*

## Gradings

French hotels are graded from one star to five stars, based on the range of amenities they offer. Hotels with two or more stars must have an elevator, where appropriate. Three-star hotels must have 80 percent of rooms with private bathrooms. Four- and five-star hotels must have air conditioning and room service, and all rooms with private bath. The top five-star hotels are called palace hotels.

## Meals and Amenities

In high season, many resort hotels insist on *demi-pension* (a rate per person for the room, dinner and breakfast). There is also *pension*, which covers lunch too. While it is cost-effective to opt for inclusive rates, set or limited-choice menus often omit the more interesting dishes. And if you do not have *pension* or *demi-pension* accommodations, breakfast is often charged as an extra. Go instead to the local café, as it tends to be cheaper and more filling. Many hotels do not provide meals on Sunday evenings and often stop serving dinner as early as 9pm on other days.

Rooms usually have double beds; twin or single beds must be requested when booking. All mid-range hotels, with a few historic exceptions, mostly in Paris, have private bathrooms. Elsewhere, there are still a handful of budget options with separate bathrooms down the corridor, but most now offer private in-room amenities. A bathroom with a *bain* (bath) is usually more expensive than one with a *douche* (shower).

## Prices

Rates, including tax and service, are quoted per room (aside from *pension* and *demi-pension* arrangements). There is usually a small surcharge for a third person in a room for two, and little reduction for lone travelers.

As a rule, the higher the star rating, the more you pay. Rates for a double room start from about €50 in a budget chain hotel on the outskirts of town, €70–€80 per night for a one-star downtown hotel, and upward of €160 for a four-star hotel. The best palace hotels charge as much as €1,000 per night. Costs also vary geographically, with remote rural areas like Brittany being the cheapest. For equivalent accommodations in fashionable areas such as Dordogne and Provence, expect to pay 20 percent more, plus another 20 percent for Paris and the Côte d'Azur. Prices vary seasonally too, with coastal and Alpine areas increasing their tariffs by up to 50 percent during peak periods.

## Reservations

Advance booking is always wise, especially for Paris and hotels in popular tourist areas over the vacation months of July and August. Places where you think hotels should be easy

Imposing white exteriors of Le Negresco in Nice, Côte d'Azur *(see p570)*

◀ Interior of the Galeries Lafayette department store in Paris

The comfortable lounge area in the lobby at the Jeu du Paume, Paris *(see p554)*

to find can suddenly fill up, thanks to a sporting event or concert. Even the chain hotels by the freeways tend to be full out of season. Choice can also be limited, because many hotels are seasonal: many beach resorts shut down from October through March, and ski resort hotels often close in April.

These days most people book their accommodations in France online, either through a hotel booking site or directly via the hotel's own website, paying for at least one night's stay to hold the reservation – although there may be web discounts for paying all in advance. It is advisable to read the small print carefully about cancellations and refunds. Those who want to book on arrival can do so from tourist offices in all main cities and towns – they offer reservations up to eight days in advance.

## Hotel Chains

France's hotel chains vary from basic pit stops, located on the outskirts of towns by freeways or main roads, to sleek and upscale four-star business hotels and hospitality suites in city centers. Almost all of them offer the usual conveniences and free Wi-Fi access.

Among the cheapest options are one-star, no-frills **Formule 1** motels, offering bedrooms with

two single beds or a double and single bed but no private bathroom. **Hotels Première Classe** fall under the two-star category – they offer rooms with private bathrooms and charge the same low rates for up to three people sharing. Other options in this category include **Ibis**, which also offers reasonably good deals, and **Campanile**. Three-star chains include **Novotel** and **Mercure** – both offer rooms with private bathroom and usually allow one child with no additional charge, provided the whole family sleeps in one room. Novotel allows two under-16s. **Adagio** offers downtown apartments sleeping up to six for a minimum of four nights. The top spots in the

Stone steps leading to the charmingly rustic Hôtel de l'Abbaye in Longpont *(see p556)*

hotel chain accommodations list undoubtedly belong to the boutique-style **MGallery** hotels and the international luxury chain **Sofitel**. Most of these chains are now part of the vast **Accor** hotel empire.

## Vacation Rentals

A *gîte* is a rural vacation home, often a converted farmhouse or its outbuildings. *Gîte* vacations are a popular and relatively inexpensive way to see France, particularly out of season, but you should book many months in advance in order to secure the best properties in summer or for skiing vacations in winter.

**Gîtes de France** registers some 60,000 *gîtes*, all inspected and graded to indicate the level of amenities. Book directly on their website by region or by theme – country, charm, children, hiking, extreme sports, wellbeing, and many others. They also list city-break rentals, B&Bs, campgrounds and cottages.

**Clévacances**, another reliable national organization, also lists good-quality *gîtes* through-out France.

France has numerous other rental options such as historic south-coast villas, stunning ski-resort chalets, and modern city and coastal apartments. **Allo Vacances** provides a rental booking service throughout the different regions.

Lovely dining area at the Hôtel de la Cité, Carcassonne *(see p569)*

## Camping

There are 11,000 official campgrounds spread around France's diverse countryside. The **Fédération Française de Camping et de Caravaning (FFCC)** publishes a detailed list, which is updated every year. There is a wide range of campgrounds listed on the Gîtes de France website too. **Bienvenue à la Ferme** offers a number of campgrounds as well as *gîtes* and B&Bs, on farms.

Campgrounds are graded from one to four stars. Three- and four-stars usually means impressively spacious with plenty of amenities and electricity connections for a percentage of tents and trailers. One- and two-star choices always have toilets, a public phone and running water, although some one-star places may have only cold water. However, what they lack in amenities, they often make up for with peaceful surroundings and rural charm. Glamping (glamorous camping) is also popular. Luxury campgrounds offer a range of unusual accommodations: **Belrepayre Trailer Park** has a range of 1950s trailers; **La Cabane en l'Air** offers treehouses; and **Carre d'Etoiles** has wood cabins with glass roofs for star-gazing.

**Camping Card International (CCI)**, available through various national camping clubs, offers campers, especially in France, numerous discounts and third party liability insurance.

## Hostels

Hostels are a money-saving option for single travelers, though cheap hostels don't remain as inexpensive for those traveling with a partner.

The IYHF's hostelling guide details the 220 hostels around France offered by the **Fédération Unie des Auberges de Jeunesse (FUAJ)**, open to all ages and providing decent dormitory accommodations. Those who are not members of the **Youth Hostel Association (YHA)** in their home country will have to pay a small surcharge each time they stay in a French youth hostel. **Ethic Etapes** has 50 centers with a cultural bent scattered all over France. All have a restaurant and single, shared, and dormitory accommodations for groups, individuals, and families. *Gîtes d'étape* are usually large farmhouses with dormitories close to walking, cycling and horseback-riding routes.

## Disabled Travelers

A number of associations publish information on accommodations throughout France with wheelchair access, notably the **Association des Paralysés de France (APF)** and the Gîtes de France's guide *Accessibles*. **Les Compagnons du Voyage** can organize escorted door-to-door transportation on all public transportation networks throughout France. **Guide Accessible** (in French) is a useful website that lists, region by region, transportation companies and lodgings adapted for wheelchair users.

## Further Information

The French tourism development agency, **Atout France**, offers a wide range of useful brochures, and most can be downloaded for easy reference. The first option for all non-hotel accommodations in the French countryside, however, should be **Gîtes de France**.

## Recommended Hotels

The accommodations featured in this guide – listed by area and then by price – have been selected across a wide price range for their excellent amenities and unique appeal. They cover categories such as family, value for money, romantic, luxury, boutique, rooms with views, and B&Bs.

**Family** hotels are especially suited for visitors traveling with children, offering either rooms with multiple beds or interconnected rooms. Both independent and chain hotels have rooms and amenities geared to families.

Vacationers enjoying the pool at a campground in high season

**Value for money** hotels offer great rates for their amenities, location, or service. Select from a range of independent establishments of character offering excellent deals in cities and the countryside. A large proportion of these hotels are part of the **Logis de France** organization.

**Romantic** hotels are aimed at couples. Hotels this category may either have special decor, or four-poster beds, or perhaps a romantic spa.

Many of France's châteaux and historic mansions have been converted into hotels – from Renaissance piles with sweeping lawns to medieval castles with battlements. Lots of these **historic** hotels belong to the **Relais et Châteaux** group, which guarantees beautifully designed rooms and top-notch fine dining. From glamorous hotels in Paris to swanky beach resorts, the **luxury** category features all the plush places to splurge on.

Chic **boutique** hotels are springing up in many French cities – these are generally small but

A deluxe room at the Mandarin Oriental Hotel Paris *(see p554)*

full of character with smart designs and all modern conveniences. They tend to be pricey, but the experience is usually worth it.

**Rooms with views** are hotels set in scenic locations – high in the mountains, on the coast, or in some of France's most beautiful landscapes.

**Bed and breakfasts (B&Bs)**, or *chambres d'hôtes*, have increased by a huge margin all over the country, primarily due to strict EU regulations that have led to

the closing of lots of the old family-run hotels, with many B&Bs springing up in their place. Most of these establishments are full of character and range from tiny cottages to elaborate châteaux full of family portraits and antiques, to boutique suites for couples in historic town houses. B&Bs located on farms are called *fermes-auberges* (farm inns). Besides breakfast, many B&Bs offer dinner on request. Over 10,000 B&Bs are inspected and registered by Gîtes de France. Many others are not registered, but information on these is available from local tourist offices or online.

For choosing the very best in hospitality and lodging, look for the hotels marked **DK Choice** – highlighted in recognition of a superlative feature. It may have beautiful surroundings, be a historically important building, have a noteworthy sustainable outlook, or just be incredibly charming. Whatever the reason, it is a guarantee of an especially memorable stay.

# DIRECTORY

## Hotels

**Accor (Formule 1, Ibis, MGallery, Mercure, Novotel, Adagio, Sofitel)**
Tel 844 382 2267 (US).
Tel 0825 012 011 (France).
W accorhotels.com

**Campanile**
08 92 23 48 12 (France).
W campanile.com

**Hotels Première Classe**
Tel 08 92 23 48 14 (France).
W premiereclasse.com

**Logis de France**
Tel 01 45 84 83 84 (France).
W logishotels.com

**Relais et Châteaux**
Tel 01 76 49 39 39 (France).
W relaischateaux.com

## B&B & Vacation Rentals

**Allo Vacances**
W allovacances.com

**Clévacances**
Tel 05 32 10 82 30.
W clevacances.com

**Gîtes de France**
W gites-de-france.com

## Camping

**Belrepayre Trailer Park**
W airstreameurope.com

**Bienvenue à la Ferme**
Tel 01 53 57 11 50.
W bienvenue-a-la-ferme.com

**La Cabane en l'Air**
W lacabaneenlair.com

**Camping Card International (CCI)**
W campingcard international.com

**Carre d'Etoiles**
W carre-detoiles.com

**Fédération Française de Camping et de Caravaning (FFCC)**
78 rue de Rivoli, 75004 Paris.
Tel 01 42 72 84 08.
W ffcc.fr

## Hostels

**Ethic Etapes**
27 rue de Turbigo, 75002 Paris. Tel 01 40 26 57 64.
W ethic-etapes.fr

**FUAJ (Fédération Unie des Auberges de Jeunesse)**
27 rue Pajol, 75018 Paris.
Tel 01 44 89 87 27.
W fuaj.org

**YHA (Youth Hostel Association)**
Trevelyan House, Matlock, Derbyshire DE4 3YH.
Tel 01629 592 600.
W yha.org.uk

## Disabled Travelers

**Association des Paralysés de France (APF)**
13 pl de Rungis, 75013 Paris.
Tel 01 53 80 92 97.
W apf.asso.fr

**Les Compagnons du Voyage**
34 rue Championnet, LAC CG25, 75018 Paris.
Tel 01 58 76 08 33.
W compagnons.com

**Guide Accessible**
W guide-accessible.com

## Further Information

**Atout France**
Lincoln House, 300 High Holborn, London W1V 7JH.
Tel 020 7061 6600 (within UK only).
W us.france.fr

# Where to Stay

## Paris

### Ile de la Cité, Marais and Beaubourg

**Britannique** €€
B&B **Map** 9 A3
*20 av Victoria, 75001*
**Tel** *01 42 33 74 59*
W hotel-britannique.fr
British seascapes and other details
adorn this hotel on a tree-lined
street. Personalized romantic
weekend packages are available.

**Caron de Beaumarchais** €€
Boutique **Map** 9 C3
*12 rue Vieille-du-Temple, 75004*
**Tel** *01 42 72 34 12*
W carondebeaumarchais.com
This elegant hotel is gracefully
decorated with colors, fabrics,
and upholstered furniture from
the 18th century.

**Hospitel** €€
B&B **Map** 9 A4
*1 pl du Parvis Notre-Dame, 75004*
**Tel** *01 44 32 01 00*
W hotel-hospitel.fr
Bright, comfortable accommo-
dations can be found at this
central hotel above a hospital.
Welcoming staff and free Wi-Fi.

**Hôtel de la Bretonnerie** €€
Historic **Map** 9 C3
*22 rue Ste.-Croix de la Bretonnerie,
75004*
**Tel** *01 48 87 77 63*
W hotelbretonnerie.com
Exposed beams, stone vaulting,
canopy beds, and rich fabrics give
this hotel a medieval ambience.

**St.-Louis en l'Isle** €€
Romantic **Map** 9 C4
*75 rue St.-Louis en l'Ile, 75004*
**Tel** *01 46 34 04 80*
W saintlouisenlisle.com
Enjoy great service in this stylish
hotel with peaceful rooms in
neutral shades. Excellent location.

---

### DK Choice

**Jeu du Paume** €€€
Historic **Map** 9 C4
*54 rue St.-Louis en l'Ile, 75004*
**Tel** *01 43 26 14 18*
W jeudepaumehotel.com
What were the Royal Tennis
Courts under Louis XIII now
house a rustic-chic hotel
with exposed wooden beams,
grand ceilings and well-
appointed rooms. Equipped
with all modern comforts.

---

**Le Pavillon de la Reine** €€€
Luxury **Map** 10 D3
*28 pl des Vosges, 75003*
**Tel** *01 40 29 19 19*
W pavillon-de-la-reine.com
Overlooking the city's most
beautiful square, this hotel has
an unrivaled setting. The 17th-
century mansion has been
refurbished in elegant country-
house style, and it offers romantic
bedrooms and a lovely spa.

---

### DK Choice

**Le Petit Moulin** €€€
Boutique **Map** 10 D2
*29–31 rue de Poitou, 75003*
**Tel** *01 42 74 10 10*
W paris-hotel-petitmoulin.com
The oldest *boulangerie* (bakery)
in Paris now houses this petite,
quirky hotel. All the individually
decorated rooms reflect
Christian Lacroix's love for color
and opulence, and they are
wildly romantic, with audacious
murals. There is wheelchair
access, free Wi-Fi, and private
parking for guests.

---

## Tuileries & Opéra

**Citadines Prestige Opéra
Vendôme** €€
Family **Map** 4 D5
*2 rue Edouard VII, 75009*
**Tel** *01 40 15 14 00*
W citadines.com
The well-equipped vacation
rental apartments on offer here
are a practical option and perfect
for families. Friendly and
accommodating staff.

Entrance to the gorgeous Caron de
Beaumarchais hotel

---

**Price Guide**
Prices are based on one night's stay in
high season for a standard double room,
inclusive of service charges and taxes.

| | |
|---|---|
| € | up to €100 |
| €€ | €100 to €250 |
| €€€ | over €250 |

---

**Brighton** €€€
Luxury **Map** 8 D1
*218 rue de Rivoli, 75001*
**Tel** *01 47 03 61 61*
W paris-hotel-brighton.com
Enjoy breathtaking views of the
Tuileries amid antique furnishings,
glittering chandeliers, and faux-
marble columns. Family-friendly.

**Mandarin Oriental** €€€
Luxury **Map** 8 D1
*251 rue St.-Honoré, 75001*
**Tel** *01 70 98 78 88*
W mandarinoriental.com
Oriental charm meets Parisian
style at this luxurious world-class
establishment. Spacious rooms
have Art Deco details.

**Le Meurice** €€€
Luxury **Map** 8 D1
*228 rue de Rivoli, 75001*
**Tel** *01 44 58 10 10*
W lemeurice.com
This celebrated plush palace
offers glittering rooms, glorious
views, and great service. There is
also a luxurious spa.

### Champs-Elysées and Invalides

**Mayet** €€
Boutique **Map** 11 B1
*3 rue Mayet, 75006*
**Tel** *01 47 83 21 35*
W mayet.com
Bright, jazzy murals decorate
this well-run, small hotel with
chic urban design.

**Le Bristol** €€€
Luxury **Map** 3 A4
*112 rue de Faubourg-St.-Honoré, 75008*
**Tel** *01 53 43 43 00*
W lebristolparis.com
Admire the antiques, chandeliers,
and tapestries at this elegant
hotel. A children's club and pool
will keep the little ones happy.

**Four Seasons George V** €€€
Luxury **Map** 2 E5
*31 av George V, 75008*
**Tel** *01 49 52 70 00*
W fourseasons.com/paris
Guests at this iconic
establishment enjoy modern
comforts in a luxurious setting.
A Parisian symbol of opulence.

**Hôtel Daniel** €€€
Romantic Map 2 F4
*8 rue Frédéric Bastiat, 75008*
**Tel** *01 42 56 17 00*
W hoteldanielparis.com
Located near the Champs-Elysées, this flamboyant hotel has Oriental fabrics, wallpaper, and carpets.

**Hôtel de la Tour Maubourg** €€€
Romantic Map 7 B3
*150 rue de Grenelle, 75007*
**Tel** *01 47 05 16 16*
W hoteltourmaubourgparis.com
Boasting a great location, this charming boutique hotel has eclectic and delightful decor.

**The Peninsula Paris** €€€
Historic
*19 av Kléber, 75016*
**Tel** *01 58 12 28 88*
W paris.peninsula.com
This opulent hotel set in a 1908 building has 200 elegant rooms and suites. The rooftop restaurant has great skyline views.

**Shangri La** €€€
Romantic Map 6 D1
*10 av d'Iéna, 75116*
**Tel** *01 53 67 19 98*
W shangri-la.com/paris/shangrila
Housed in a *belle époque* palace, the Shangri La has parquet floors, chandeliers, and two luxe eateries.

## The Left Bank

**Les Degrés de Notre Dame** €€
B&B Map 9 B4
*10 rue des Grands Degrés, 75005*
**Tel** *01 55 42 88 88*
This vintage charmer offers attractive beamed bedrooms leading off a frescoed stairway.

**Hôtel des Grandes Ecoles** €€
Family Map 9 B5
*75 rue Cardinal Lemoine, 75005*
**Tel** *01 43 26 79 23*
W hotel-grandes-ecoles.com
The charming breakfast room and flowery bedrooms at this hotel are reminiscent of a Provençal villa.

**Hôtel des Grands Hommes** €€
Romantic Map 13 A1
*17 pl du Panthéon, 75005*
**Tel** *01 46 34 19 60*
W hoteldesgrandshommes.com
Enjoy views of the Panthéon from this Empire-style hotel. The deluxe rooms have quaint terraces.

**Hôtel de Buci** €€€
Romantic Map 8 E4
*22 rue de Buci, 75006*
**Tel** *01 55 42 74 74*
W buci-hotel.com
Antiques, rich colors, four-poster beds and plush fabrics lend this hotel a distinctly 18th-century feel.

**Relais Christine** €€€
Historic Map 8 F4
*3 rue Christine, 75006*
**Tel** *01 40 51 60 80*
W relais-christine.com
Built on the remains of a 13th-century abbey, this is a luxurious and impressive haven of calm.

**Relais St.-Germain** €€€
Romantic Map 8 F4
*9 Carrefour de l'Odéon, 75006*
**Tel** *01 44 27 07 97*
W hotel-paris-relais-saint-germain.com
This 17th-century conversion is irresistibly Parisian and has plush, soundproofed bedrooms.

**Résidence Le Prince Regent** €€€
Boutique Map 8 F5
*28 rue Monsieur le Prince, 75006*
**Tel** *01 56 24 19 21*
W leprinceregent.com
These modern apartments offer great services, from babysitting to spa relaxation and housekeeping.

## Farther Afield

**Loft Paris** €
B&B
*7 cité Véron, 75018*
**Tel** *06 14 48 47 48*
W loft-paris.fr
Four neat apartments have quirky decor and lots of character. The one on the fourth floor has a view of the Moulin Rouge windmill.

## DK Choice

**Arvor St.-Georges** €€
B&B
*8 rue Laferrière, 75009*
**Tel** *01 48 78 60 92*
W hotelarvor.com
This family-friendly B&B with charming rooms and suites has been refurbished in smart retro-contemporary style. The open-plan reception, which includes a bar and breakfast area, is decorated with conceptual artist Daniel Buren's striped posters.

**L'Ermitage** €€
B&B
*24 rue Lamarck, 75018*
**Tel** *01 42 64 79 22*
Light, floral-themed bedrooms offer hilltop views over the city. There is also a lovely garden.

**Mama Shelter** €€
Boutique
*109 rue de Bagnolet, 75020*
**Tel** *01 43 48 48 48*
W mamashelter.com/en/paris
Super-trendy, Philippe Starck-designed rooms have iMacs, microwaves, and mood lighting.

The classic exterior of the Terrass hotel, located in the Montmartre district, Paris

**Le Relais Montmartre** €€
Romantic
*6 rue Constance, 75018*
**Tel** *01 70 64 25 25*
W hotel-relais-montmartre.com
Rooms here have pretty fabrics, exposed beams and dainty period furniture. Attactive courtyard, too.

## DK Choice

**Terrass** €€
Romantic
*12–14 rue Joseph de Maistre, 75018*
**Tel** *01 46 06 72 85*
W terrass-hotel.com
This relaxed four-star hotel with elegant rooms is perfect in any season. In winter, guests enjoy the piano bar, with its open fire and cozy armchairs. In summer, sofas dot the roof, allowing visitors to take in the views.

**La Villa Paris** €€
B&B
*33 rue de la Fontaine à Mulard, 75013*
**Tel** *01 43 47 15 66*
W la-villa-paris.com
Enjoy all the comforts of home at this lovely 1920s B&B with parquet floors and refined decor.

## Ile-de-France

**CERNAY LA VILLE:**
**Abbaye des Vaux de Cernay** €€
Rooms with views
*Domaine des Vaux de Cernay, 78720*
**Tel** *01 34 85 23 00*
W abbayedecernay.com
Beautifully restored, this 12th-century abbey has large vaulted rooms and stunning grounds.

**ST.-GERMAIN-EN-LAYE:**
**Pavillon Henri IV** €€
Historic
*19–21 rue Thiers, 78100*
**Tel** *01 39 10 15 15*
W pavillonhenri4.fr
The birthplace of Louis XIV, this beautiful château near a pleasant park has fine views of Paris.

**For more information on types of hotels** *see pp552–3*

**VERSAILLES: Hôtel des Roys** €€
Value for money
*14 av de Paris, 78000*
**Tel** *01 39 50 56 00*
W hotel-roys-versailles.com
In a great location, this elegant
town house provides its guests
with simple and neat rooms.

## DK Choice

**VILLIERS LE MAHIEU:**
**Château de Villiers**
**le Mahieu** €€
Luxury
*rue du Centre, 78770*
**Tel** *01 34 87 44 25*
W chateauvilliers.com
Set within a moated fortress,
this 17th-century château
strikes a balance between
conservation and comfort.
Superb courtyard and grounds.

# Le Nord and Picardy

**AMIENS: Victor Hugo** €
Value for money
*2 rue de l'Oratoire, 80000*
**Tel** *03 22 91 57 91*
W hotel-a-amiens.com
Stay in basic but pleasant rooms
at this cheerful family-run hotel
next to the cathedral.

**AMIENS: Hôtel Marotte** €€
Boutique
*3 rue Marotte, 80000*
**Tel** *03 60 12 50 00*
W hotel-marotte.com
Housed in a beautifully restored
building, this family-run hotel
has gracefully decorated rooms.

## DK Choice

**BUSNES:**
**Château de Beaulieu** €€
Luxury
*1098 rue de Lillers, 62350*
**Tel** *03 21 68 88 88*
W lechateaudebeaulieu.fr
Seamlessly converted into a
contemporary hotel, this 18th-
century château is surrounded
by sprawling elegant gardens.
Herbs from the grounds are
used in the luxury Michelin-
starred restaurant.

**CALAIS: Les Dunes** €
Family
*48 rte Nationale, Blériot Plage, 62231*
**Tel** *03 21 34 54 30*
W les-dunes.com
Rooms have no frills at this small
hotel with a beach location, just
a 5-minute drive from the city
center. Good restaurant on site.

Elegant, well-appointed rooms at the
Hôtel Marotte in Amiens

**FERE EN TARDENOIS:**
**Château de Fère** €€€
Historic
*Rte de Fismes, 02130*
**Tel** *03 23 82 21 13*
W chateaudefere.com
There are stylish rooms and a
well-stocked wine cellar at this
stunning 16th-century château
hotel just 1 hour from Paris.

**GOSNAY: La Chartreuse**
**du Val St-Esprit** €€
Luxury
*1 rue de Fouquières, 62199*
**Tel** *03 21 62 80 00*
W lachartreuse.com
This 18th-century château built
on medieval ruins offers large
delightful rooms, a lovely park,
and three restaurants.

**GOUVIEUX:**
**Château de la Tour** €€
Luxury
*Chemin de la Chaussée, 60270*
**Tel** *03 44 62 38 38*
W lechateaudelatour.fr
The pretty rooms at this hotel
not far from Chantilly have views
over the expansive garden or
the forest. Guests also enjoy a
restaurant, tennis courts, and
an outdoor heated pool, plus
impeccable service.

**LAON:**
**La Maison des Trois Rois** €€
Value for money
*17 rue St.-Martin, 02000*
**Tel** *03 23 20 74 24*
W lamaisondes3rois.com
Friendly and very comfortable,
this B&B is set in a beautiful
14th-century mansion with five
excellently restored rooms.

**LE TOUQUET:**
**Le Castel – Victoria** €
Value for money
*11 rue de Paris, 62520*
**Tel** *03 21 90 01 00*
W castelvictoria.com
Close to the beach and town
center, this sleek hotel has tasteful
rooms and a great roof terrace.

**LILLE: Alliance Couvent**
**des Minimes** €€
City centre
*17 quai du Wault, 59000*
**Tel** *03 20 30 62 62*
W alliance-lille.com
This converted monastery has
stylish rooms, lovely cloisters
and a spectacular atrium with
a trendy bar and restaurant.

**LILLE: Hermitage Gantois** €€
Luxury
*224 rue de Paris, 59000*
**Tel** *03 20 85 30 30*
W hotelhermitagegantois.com
The rooms at this 14th-century
hospice are set around an indoor
patio. Some have authentic
fireplaces; others boast Louis XV-
style wood paneling.

**LONGPONT: Hôtel de l'Abbaye** €
Value for money
*8 rue des Tourelles, 02600*
**Tel** *03 23 96 02 44*
W hotel-abbaye-longpont.fr
Stay in old-fashioned and
comfortable rooms at this hotel
opposite a 12th-century abbey.

**LUMBRES:**
**Moulin de Mombreux** €
Family
*70 rue Mombreux, 62380*
**Tel** *03 21 98 68 72*
W moulindemombreux.com
The rooms at this attractive
18th-century mill on the banks
of the River Bléquin are in an
annexe building, some with
pleasant river views.

**MONTREUIL SUR MER:**
**Château de Montreuil** €€€
Luxury
*4 chaussée des Capucins, 62170*
**Tel** *03 21 81 53 04*
W chateaudemontreuil.com
There is a restaurant, plus lovely
gardens, at this stylish manor house
within the ramparts of the town.

**REUILLY-SAUVIGNY:**
**L'Auberge le Relais** €€
Value for money
*2 rue de Paris, 02850*
**Tel** *03 23 70 35 36*
W relaisreuilly.com
In a scenic location, with views of
Champagne's vine-covered hills,
this hotel has cosy rooms, a good
restaurant, and fine service.

**SAINTE-PREUVE:**
**Château de Barive** €€
Rooms with views
*Domaine du Château de Barive, 02350*
**Tel** *03 23 22 15 15*
w domainedebarive.com
Guests here stay in large rooms
in beautifully converted 18th-
century stables. There is also
a gourmet restaurant.

**ST.-QUENTIN:**
**Hôtel des Cannoniers** €
Value for money
*15 rue des Cannoniers, 02100*
**Tel** *03 23 62 87 87*
w hotel-cannoniers.com
The rooms at this period town
house with a courtyard for
summer breakfasts have vibrant
color schemes and floral fabrics.
Opt for a suite, at little extra cost.

**WIMEREUX: Hôtel St.-Jean** €
Family
*1 rue Georges Romain, 62930*
**Tel** *03 21 83 57 40*
w hotel-saint-jean.fr
Located very close to the beach,
this hotel offers brightly colored
but stylishly decorated rooms.
Spa amenities are also available.

# Champagne

**AUBERIVE:**
**Auberge du Palais Abbatial** €€
Historic
*Pl de l'Abbaye, 52160*
**Tel** *03 25 84 33 66*
w auberge-abbatiale.com
The stately rooms at this
medieval auberge feature
stone floors and fireplaces,
canopy beds, and timbered
ceilings. There is also a pleasant
garden, plus a restaurant with
exposed-brick walls hung
with tapestries.

**AY: Le Castel Jeanson** €€
Family
*24 rue Jeanson, 51560*
**Tel** *03 26 54 21 75*
w casteljeanson.fr
Guests at this neat 18th-century
converted château can relax in
the Art Deco veranda by the
indoor pool or with a book
from the hotel library.

**CHALONS-EN-CHAMPAGNE:**
**Hôtel d'Angleterre** €€
City center
*19 pl Monseigneur Tissier, 51000*
**Tel** *03 26 68 21 51*
w hotel-dangleterre.fr
The spacious, individually
decorated guest rooms at the
Hôtel d'Angleterre boast sleek
marble bathrooms.

**DK Choice**

**CHARLEVILLE MEZIERES:**
**Le Dormeur du Val** €€
Boutique
*32 bis rue de la Gravière, 08000*
**Tel** *03 24 42 04 30*
w hotel-dormeur-du-val.com
This remarkable hotel has zany
modern interiors and vibrant,
well-appointed rooms. Enjoy
a drink at the lively bar or sit
down with a book in the well-
stocked hotel library. Le
Dormeur du Val also has a gym,
plus saunas and Turkish baths.

**COLOMBEY-LES-DEUX-EGLISES:**
**La Grange du Relais** €
Family
*26 rte Nationale 19, 52330*
**Tel** *03 25 02 03 89*
w lagrangedurelais.fr
The rooms at this simple hotel
with an excellent restaurant open
out on to a flower-filled terrace.

**COURCELLES-SUR-VESLE:**
**Château de Courcelles** €€€
Luxury
*8 rue du Château, 02220*
**Tel** *03 23 74 13 53*
w chateau-de-courcelles.fr
Sumptuous bedrooms and a
stately reading room await at
this magnificent château.

**EPERNAY: Hôtel de la Cloche** €
Value for money
*3 pl Mendès-France, 51200*
**Tel** *03 26 55 15 15*
w hotel-la-cloche.com
A practical base from which to
explore neighboring areas, this
cheerful establishment offers
simple but immaculate rooms.

**ETOGES: Château d'Etoges** €€
Luxury
*4 rue Richebourg, 51270*
**Tel** *03 26 59 30 08*
w etoges.com
This fairytale castle offers period
rooms, large grounds, a moat,
and an excellent restaurant.

Rustic setting of the grand Château de
Barive, Sainte-Preuve

**MESNIL-SAINT-PERE :**
**Auberge du Lac** €
Value for money
*5–7 rue du 28 Août 1944, 10140*
**Tel** *03 25 41 27 16*
w auberge-du-lac.fr
Located in the Lac et Forêt
d'Orient Natural Park, this family
hotel has nicely restored half-
timbered buildings.

**MOUSSEY: Domaine de
la Creuse** €€
Family
*Domaine de la Creuse, 10800*
**Tel** *03 25 41 74 01*
w domainedelacreuse.fr
The five ground-floor rooms at
this charming B&B in an old farm
with a courtyard are decorated
in soothing natural tones, aside
from the bright-pink Peony Room.

**PEIGNEY: Auberge des
Voiliers** €
Value for money
*1 chemin du bord de Lac de la Liez,
52200*
**Tel** *03 25 87 05 74*
w hotel-voiliers.com
The rooms at this hotel-
restaurant alongside the Lac
de la Liez are basic, but some
have lakeside views.

**REIMS: Hôtel de la Paix** €€
City center
*9 rue de Buirette, 51100*
**Tel** *03 26 40 04 08*
w bestwestern-lapaix-reims.com
Guest rooms here are housed
within contemporary buildings
with an elegant central courtyard.

**REIMS: Château
Les Crayères** €€€
Luxury
*64 bd Henry Vasnier, 51100*
**Tel** *03 26 24 90 00*
w lescrayeres.com
There is an excellent restaurant
at this splendid château on lovely
grounds with a wooded park.

**SEDAN: Le Château Fort** €
Value for money
*Port des Princes, 08200*
**Tel** *03 24 26 11 00*
w chateaufort-sedan.fr
Some rooms have wheelchair
access at this exceptional hotel
in Europe's largest fortress.

**TROYES: Champs des
Oiseaux** €€
City center
*20 rue Linard Gonthier, 10000*
**Tel** *03 25 80 58 50*
w champdesoiseaux.com
The stunningly restored 15th-
and 16th-century half-timbered
buildings housing this hotel
also offer delightful courtyards.

**For more information on types of hotels** *see pp552–3*

**VIENNE-LE-CHATEAU:**
**Le Tulipier** €€
Family
*Rue St.-Jacques, 51800*
**Tel** *03 26 60 69 90*
W letulipier.com
Deep in the forests of the
Argonne, this modern hotel
has a heated indoor pool and a
well-stocked bar. Free bicycles.

**VILLIERS SUR MARNE:**
**La Source Bleue** €
Value for money
*La Papeterie, 52320 Gudmont*
**Tel** *03 25 94 70 35*
W hotelsourcebleue.com
Smartly designed rooms and
suites, some with balconies,
can be found at this old mill
in the countryside.

**VINAY:**
**Hostellerie La Briqueterie** €€
Luxury
*4 rte de Sézanne, 51530*
**Tel** *03 26 59 99 99*
W labriqueterie.fr
Guests at this hotel located
among the vineyards of
Champagne enjoy spacious
rooms and an excellent gourmet
restaurant. There is also a spa
offering treatments and a pool.

## Alsace and Lorraine

**AMNEVILLE: Diane** €
Family
*rue de la Source, 57360*
**Tel** *03 87 70 16 33*
W acceuil-amneville.com
Located at the edge of the forest,
close to the Amneville's famous
leisure park, this hotel offers
affordable, sleek, and elegant
rooms decorated in brown
and beige tones.

**COLMAR:**
**Hostellerie Le Marechal** €€
City center
*4–6 pl des Six Montagnes Noires,
Petite Venise, 68000*
**Tel** *03 89 41 60 32*
W hotel-le-marechal.com
Rooms at this romantic
riverside hotel in the heart
of the Petite Venise area are
extravagantly decorated.

**DIEVE: Hostellerie du Château
des Monthairons** €€
Family
*26 rte de Verdun, Les Monthairons,
55320*
**Tel** *03 29 87 78 55*
W chateaudesmonthairons.com
This palatial château has two
chapels, extensive grounds and
a private beach on the Meuse.

**DRACHENBRONN: Auberge
du Moulin des 7 Fontaines** €
Family
*1 Sept Fontaines, 67160*
**Tel** *03 88 94 50 90*
W 7fontaines.fr
Set on a working farm, this 18th-
century house offers simple
rooms and an on-site restaurant
serving great food.

**KAYSERSBERG:**
**Hôtel Constantin** €
Value for money
*10 rue Père Kohlman, 68240*
**Tel** *03 89 47 19 90*
W hotel-constantin.com
An old winemaker's house, this
is now a pleasant, quiet hotel
with unpretentious rooms and
a warm Alsatian welcome.

**LAPOUTROIE: Les Alisiers** €
Rooms with views
*5 rue du Faudé, 68650*
**Tel** *03 89 47 52 82*
W alisiers.com
This farmhouse hotel offers
no-frills chalet-style rooms and
a terrace with scenic views of
the Vosges mountains.

**METZ: La Cathédrale** €€
Historic
*25 pl de Chambre, 57000*
**Tel** *03 87 75 00 02*
W hotelcathedrale-metz.fr
Located in the historic center,
facing the cathedral of St.-
Etienne, this hotel is made up
of two elegant 17th-century
buildings. It is worth paying a
little extra to stay in a room
with a view of the cathedral.

**MULHOUSE:**
**Hôtel du Parc** €€
City center
*26 rue de la Sinne, 68100*
**Tel** *03 89 66 12 22*
W hotelduparc-mulhouse.com
The comfortable, Art Deco-style
rooms at this hotel feature white
marble bathrooms.

**NANCY: Grand Hôtel
de la Reine** €€
Luxury
*2 pl Stanislas, 54000*
**Tel** *03 83 35 03 01*
W hoteldelareine.com
Stay in a refurbished Neoclassical
building on one of Europe's finest
18th-century squares.

**OBERNAI: Hôtel du Parc** €€
Family
*169 rte de Otrott, 67210*
**Tel** *03 88 95 50 08*
W hotel-du-parc.com
A historic Alsatian exterior
contrasts with modern interiors
at this hotel. Excellent amenities.

Elegant bedroom at Le Bouclier d'Or
in Strasbourg

**RIQUEWIHR: L'Oriel** €
Value for money
*3 rue Ecuries Seigneuriales, 68340*
**Tel** *03 89 86 03 13*
W hotel-oriel.com
In a picturesque village, this hotel
has a half-timbered facade and
vibrant interiors. Lovely courtyard.

**SELESTAT: Hôtel Illwald** €€
Value for money
*Le Schnellenbuhl, 67600*
**Tel** *03 90 56 11 40*
W illwald.fr
On the edge of the Illwald forest,
this auberge has a pleasant mix
of traditional and contemporary
styles, plus a good restaurant.

**STRASBOURG:**
**Le Bouclier d'Or** €€
Luxury
*1 rue du Bouclier, 67000*
**Tel** *03 88 13 73 55*
W lebouclierdor.com
Comprising three restored
Renaissance buildings, this
hotel is furnished with Alsatian
antiques. It also has a fully
equipped spa.

**STRASBOURG: Le Chut** €€
Value for money
*4 rue du Bain aux Plantes, 67000*
**Tel** *03 88 32 05 06*
Located in the center of old
Strasbourg, this hotel has sleek,
modern rooms. Great restaurant.

### DK Choice

**STRASBOURG: Les Haras** €€
Luxury
*23 rue des Glacières, 67000*
**Tel** *03 90 20 50 00*
W les-haras-hotel.com
A former Louis XV stud farm
is now a chic, minimalist hotel
featuring elegantly furnished
rooms. Materials such as wood
and saddle leather hint to the
equestrian history. An upscale
brasserie is in the ex-stables.

# Normandy

**AGNEAUX:**
**Château d'Agneaux** €€
Value for money
*Av Ste.-Marie, 50180*
**Tel** *02 33 56 19 21*
W chateau-agneaux.com
This 13th-century hotel features
period furniture, parquet floors,
and wood paneling.

## DK Choice

**BAGNOLES DE L'ORME:**
**Le Manoir de Lys** €€
Family
*Rte de Juvigny, 61140*
**Tel** *02 33 37 80 69*
W manoir-du-lys.fr
Surrounded by a lush deer-filled
forest, this charming family
hotel offers cozy, up-to-date
rooms. Seven family suites,
called "The Wood Pavilions",
are dotted along the forest's
edge – ideal for those seeking
solitude. Lots of fun activities
on offer for guests.

**BAYEUX: Hôtel Bellefontaine** €€
Family
*49 rue de Bellefontaine, 14400*
**Tel** *02 31 22 00 10*
W hotel-bellefontaine.com
The best rooms at this 18th-
century château have Louis XV-
style furniture and views of either
the cathedral or the park.

**CAEN: Best Western**
**Le Dauphin** €€
City center
*29 rue Gémare, 14000*
**Tel** *02 31 86 22 26*
W bestwestern.fr
Top-notch amenities at this
tastefully renovated 15th-century
priory with comfortable rooms
include a spa with *hammam* and
sauna. On-site restaurant, too.

**CHERBOURG: Le Louvre** €
City center
*2 rue Henri Dunant, 50100*
**Tel** *02 33 53 02 28*
W hotel-le-louvre-cherbourg.com
Stay in neat, bright, and modern
rooms at this no-frills hotel. Good
breakfast buffet.

**CREPON: La Ferme de**
**la Rançonnière** €€
Value for money
*Rte d'Arromanches, 14480*
**Tel** *02 31 22 21 73*
W ranconniere.fr
This 13th-century farmhouse
offers large rooms with exposed
beams, stone walls, and Louis XV-
style furnishings.

**DEAUVILLE: Hôtel**
**Normandy Barrière** €€€
Luxury
*38 rue Jean Mermoz, 14800*
**Tel** *02 31 98 66 22*
W lucienbarriere.com
This Anglo-Normandy manor
house has lavishly decorated
rooms with 1920s charm.

**DIEPPE: Hôtel La Présidence** €€
Rooms with views
*1 bd de Verdun, 76200*
**Tel** *02 35 84 31 31*
W mercure.com
Behind the drab exterior, this
hotel has smart, modern rooms,
some with sea views.

**ETRETAT: Domaine St.-Clair** €€€
Rooms with views
*Chemin de St.-Clair, 76790*
**Tel** *02 35 27 08 23*
W hoteletretat.com
This 19th-century Anglo-Norman
château has panoramic views of
the village and the cliffs of Etretat.

**FECAMP: Le Grand Pavois** €€
Rooms with views
*15 quai Vicomté, 76400*
**Tel** *02 35 10 01 01*
W hotel-grand-pavois.com
Some of the bright rooms at this
dockside hotel, with an attractive
marine-themed decor, have
balconies overlooking the port.

**GRANVILLE: Brit Hotel Essential**
**de Granville** €
Family
*57 av des Matignon, 50400*
**Tel** *02 33 50 05 05*
W brithotel.fr
This modern chain hotel has good-
value, functional rooms, including
some for groups of three or four.
Buffet breakfast and cheerful staff.

Open courtyard leading up to the stately
Hôtel Normandy Barrière in Deauville

**HONFLEUR: La Ferme**
**Saint Siméon** €€€
Luxury
*rue Adolphe Marais, 14600*
**Tel** *02 31 81 78 00*
W fermesaintsimeon.fr
Rooms are sumptuous at this
19th-century farmhouse
mansion, once the haunt of
Impressionist artists.

**MACE: Hôtel l'Ile de Sées** €
Value for money
*Le Tour de Vandel, 61500*
**Tel** *02 33 27 98 65*
W ile-sees.fr
Stay in pleasant, cozy rooms
in an ivy-clad converted dairy.
Good restaurant and fine service.

**MESNIL-VAL: Hostellerie**
**de la Vieille Ferme** €€
Value for money
*23 rue de la Mer, 76910*
**Tel** *02 35 86 72 18*
W vieille-ferme.net
This hotel, close to the beach,
is made up of Anglo-Norman-
style buildings dating from the
18th to 20th centuries. Pretty
garden terrace.

**MONT-ST.-MICHEL:**
**Terrasses Poulard** €€
Rooms with views
*BP 18, 50170*
**Tel** *02 33 89 02 02*
W terrasses-poulard.fr
Located in the heart of Mont-
St.-Michel, this hotel has stunning
views of the bay and the abbey.

**PONT DE L'ARCHE:**
**Hôtel de la Tour** €
Value for money
*41 quai Foch, 27340*
**Tel** *02 35 23 00 99*
W hoteldelatour.org
Next to the town's 13th-century
ramparts, this place has stunning
18th-century Norman architecture.
Rooms are spacious, with cozy, if
a little time-worn, furnishings.

**PONT AUDEMER:**
**Belle Ile sur Risle** €€
Luxury
*112 rte de Rouen, 27500*
**Tel** *02 32 56 96 22*
W bellile.com
Superb cuisine is served in the
19th-century rotunda at this
elegant hotel on its own island.
Classic-style rooms.

**ROUEN: Inter Hôtel Notre Dame** €
City center
*4 rue de la Savonnerie, 76000*
**Tel** *02 35 71 87 73*
W hotelnotredame.com
This centrally located hotel
offers guest rooms decorated
in a chic contemporary style.

**For more information on types of hotels** *see pp552–3*

**ROUEN: Hôtel de Bourgtheroulde** €€
Luxury
*15 pl de la Pucelle d'Orléans, 76000*
**Tel** *02 35 14 50 50*
w hotelsparouen.com
The ornate Renaissance facade belies all the modern comforts of this boutique hotel. Great spa.

**ST.-PATERNE: Château de St.-Paterne** €€€
Historic
*Le Château, 72610*
**Tel** *02 33 27 54 71*
w chateau-saintpaterne.com
Henry IV's 15th-century love nest offers magnificent, stately rooms and dinner by candlelight.

**ST.-VAAST: Hôtel de France et Fuchsias** €
Value for money
*20 rue de Maréchal Foch, 50550*
**Tel** *02 33 54 40 41*
w france-fuchsias.com
This country-house hotel has warm, snug rooms, most of them overlooking the garden.

# Brittany

**BENODET: Domaine de Kereven** €
Value for money
*Bénodet, 29950*
**Tel** *02 98 57 02 46*
w kereven.fr
Beautifully decorated rooms overlook the expansive grounds of an 18th-century farm.

**BREST: Hôtel de la Corniche** €
Family
*1 rue Amiral-Nicol, 29200*
**Tel** *02 98 45 12 42*
w hotel-la-corniche.com
Set in a peaceful neighborhood near the scenic coastline, this hotel offers pretty pastel-hued rooms.

**CARNAC: Hôtel Tumulus** €€
Rooms with views
*Rte du Tumulus, 56340*
**Tel** *02 97 52 08 21*
w hotel-tumulus.com
Enjoy fine views of Quiberon Bay from this 1920s villa with elegant, large rooms, some with private terraces. Lovely spa and pool.

**COURNON: La Grée des Landes** €€
Rooms with views
*La Gacilly, 56200*
**Tel** *02 99 08 50 50*
w lagreedeslandes.com
This eco-friendly hotel features minimalist rooms with terraces overlooking the lush countryside. It has an organic restaurant.

**DINAN: L'Avaugour** €€
Family
*1 pl du Champ Clos, 22100*
**Tel** *02 96 39 07 49*
w avaugourhotel.com
The best rooms overlook the garden at this family-run hotel in a traditional granite building near the ramparts. They are simply furnished, but spacious.

**DINARD: Villa Reine Hortense** €€
Rooms with views
*19 rue Malouine, 35800*
**Tel** *02 99 46 54 31*
w villa-reine-hortense.com
Relive the splendor of the *belle époque* at this romantic hotel in a clifftop setting. Rooms have garden or sea views, and three have private balconies.

**DOL DE BRETAGNE: Domaine des Ormes** €€
Family
*35120*
**Tel** *02 99 73 53 00*
w lesormes.com
These charming guest rooms are in a resort with great amenities, including a golf course, horseback riding, and aquapark.

**FOUESNANT: Hôtel l'Orée du Bois** €
Value for money
*4 rue Kergoadig, 29170*
**Tel** *02 98 56 00 06*
w hotel-oreedubois.com
Some of the simply furnished guest rooms here have sea views. Lovely outdoor terrace.

**LANDEDA: Hôtel La Baie des Anges** €€
Family
*350 rte des Anges, 29870*
**Tel** *02 98 04 90 04*
w baie-des-anges.com
Stay in smartly decorated rooms at this family-friendly hotel with a pool, *hammam,* and sauna.

**LOCQUIREC: Le Grand Hôtel des Bains** €€
Luxury
*15 rue de l'Eglise, 29241*
**Tel** *02 98 67 41 02*
w grand-hotel-des-bains.com
There are stylish rooms, most of them with balconies, at this *belle époque* hotel with direct access to the beach.

**MORLAIX: Hôtel de l'Europe** €€
City center
*1 rue d'Aiguillon, 29600*
**Tel** *02 98 62 11 99*
w hoteleurope-morlaix.com
Boasting a great location and a good-value brasserie, this Second Empire hotel has an elegant, richly decorated interior.

Neat, well-kept room at the Manoir du Vaumadeuc, Pleven

**PLEVEN: Manoir du Vaumadeuc** €
Historic
*Le Vaumadeuc, 22130*
**Tel** *02 96 84 46 17*
w vaumadeuc.com
This authentic 15th-century granite manor house has a pretty Renaissance garden and a lake.

**PLOUBAZLANEC: Les Agapanthes** €€
Rooms with views
*1 rue Adrien Rebours, 22620*
**Tel** *02 96 55 89 06*
w hotel-les-agapanthes.com
Most of the beautiful rooms in this stone house on the village square have views of Paimpol Bay.

**QUIBERON: Ker Noyal** €
Value for money
*43 chemin des Dunes, 56170*
**Tel** *02 97 50 33 31*
w ker-noyal.com
Stay in spacious, modern rooms in a typical resort hotel on a quiet street near the casino.

**QUIMPER: Hôtel Gradlon** €€
City center
*30 rue de Brest, 29000*
**Tel** *02 98 95 04 39*
w hotel-gradlon.com
Rooms here are charming and quiet. Some overlook the hotel's flower garden and fountain.

**RENNES: The Magic Hall Hotel** €€
City center
*17 rue de la Quintaine, 35000*
**Tel** *02 99 66 21 83*
w lemagichall.com
Choose from movie-, theater-, dance- and music-themed rooms at this quirky, theatrical-style hotel.

**ROSCOFF: La Résidence** €
Family
*14 rue des Johnnies, 29680*
**Tel** *02 98 69 74 85*
w hotelroscoff-laresidence.fr
Located close to the port, this hotel is smartly decorated and has a great family room.

### ST.-MALO: La Maison des Armateurs €€
City center
*6 Grand Rue, 35400*
**Tel** *02 99 40 87 70*
🆆 maisondesarmateurs.com
This former shipowner's house in the old town is now a chic hotel with bright and modern rooms.

### DK Choice

#### TREBOUL: Ty Mad €€
Boutique
*Plage St.-Jean, 29100*
**Tel** *02 98 74 00 53*
🆆 hoteltymad.com
Frequented in the 1920s by local artists such as Max Jacob, the eco-friendly Ty Mad has 15 individually decorated rooms with garden or sea views. Closed mid-Nov–Mar.

### VANNES: Villa Kerasy €€
City center
*20 av Favrel et Lincy, 56000*
**Tel** *02 97 68 36 83*
🆆 villakerasy.com
Near the medieval town center, this hotel features exotic decor inspired by the Spice Route.

## The Loire Valley

### AMBOISE: Le Choiseul €€
Rooms with views
*36 quai Charles-Guinot, 37400*
**Tel** *02 47 30 45 45*
🆆 choiseul-hotelrestaurant.com
This 18th-century ivy-clad manor house is set on flower-filled grounds with views of the Loire.

### ANGERS: Hôtel Mail €€
City center
*8 rue des Ursules, 49100*
**Tel** *02 41 25 05 25*
🆆 hoteldumail.fr
Charming and family-run, this hotel in a 17th-century building was once part of a convent.

### AZAY-LE-RIDEAU: Manoir de la Rémonière €€
Value for money
*La Chapelle Ste.-Blaise, 37190*
**Tel** *02 47 45 24 88*
🆆 manoirdelaremoniere.com
The stately rooms at this hotel built on the site of a Roman villa have an old-world feel.

### BOURGES: Le Bourbon €€
City center
*Bd République, 18000*
**Tel** *02 48 70 70 00*
🆆 hoteldebourbon.fr
Guests stay in elegant, spacious rooms in this renovated 17th-century abbey. Great restaurant.

### CHAMPIGNE: Château des Briottières €€
Luxury
*Rte Marigné, 49330*
**Tel** *02 41 42 00 02*
🆆 briottieres.com
This family-run 18th-century château has stately rooms with luxurious furnishings.

### CHARTRES: Le Grand Monarque €€
Family
*22 pl des Epars, 28005*
**Tel** *02 37 18 15 15*
🆆 bw-grand-monarque.com
A converted 16th-century staging post with modern rooms, this place has a bistro and a fine-dining restaurant.

### CHENONCEAUX: Hôtel du Bon Laboureur €€
Luxury
*6 rue de Dr Bretonneau, 37150*
**Tel** *02 47 23 90 02*
🆆 bonlaboureur.com
Located very close to the Château de Chenonceau, this picturesque 18th-century inn has lovely gardens.

### CHINON: Hôtel Diderot €
Value for money
*4 rue Buffon, 37500*
**Tel** *02 47 93 18 87*
🆆 hoteldiderot.com
On a quiet street near the city center, this tuffeau stone building dating from the 1600s has elegant rooms.

### CHINON: Château de Marçay €€
Historic
*Le Château, 37500*
**Tel** *02 47 93 03 47*
🆆 chateaudemarcay.com
Rooms in this restored 15th-century fortified château have a refined, aristocratic atmosphere. Views over the park and vineyards.

### LA CHARTRE SUR LE LOIR: Hôtel de France €€
Value for money
*20 pl de la République, 72340*
**Tel** *02 43 44 40 16*
🆆 lhoteldefrance.fr
Fully renovated, this ivy-clad hotel has smartly furnished, comfortable rooms that mix old and modern styles. Pretty terrace.

### LE CROISIC: Fort de l'Océan €€
Rooms with views
*Pointe du Croisic, 44490*
**Tel** *02 40 15 77 77*
🆆 hotelfortocean.com
This Vauban fortress facing the sea now houses a delightful hotel. Rooms are stylish and comfortable, and no traces remain of harsh military life.

### LE MANS: Le Charleston €
City center
*18 rue Gastelier, 72000*
**Tel** *02 43 24 87 46*
🆆 lecharlestonhotel.com
Rooms at this pleasant and friendly hotel are attractive, and there is a small patio for breakfast in good weather.

### LOCHES: Hôtel de France €
Value for money
*6 rue Picois, 37600*
**Tel** *02 47 59 00 32*
🆆 hoteldefrance-loches.com
Modest but comfortable rooms are offered at this former staging post with a restaurant serving good regional food.

### LOUE: Hôtel Ricordeau €
Family
*13 rue de la Libération, 72540*
**Tel** *02 43 88 40 03*
🆆 hotel-ricordeau.fr
Some of the individually decorated rooms at this former coaching inn overlook the garden.

### MONTLOUIS SUR LOIRE: Château de la Bourdaisière €€
Luxury
*25 rue de la Bourdaisière, 37270*
**Tel** *02 47 45 16 31*
🆆 labourdaisiere.com
This luxury hotel is set within a magnificent château. Some of the guest rooms are furnished with antiques.

### MUIDES SUR LOIRE: Château de Colliers €€
Rooms with views
*Rte Départementale 951, 41500*
**Tel** *02 54 87 50 75*
🆆 chateau-colliers.com
Back in the 18th century, this château belonged to the governor of Louisiana. It is a rustic but grand building, with a number of delightfully romantic rooms.

Exquisitely decorated room at the Château des Briottières, Champigné

**For more information on types of hotels** *see pp552–3*

**NANTES: Amiral** €
City center
*26 bis rue Scribe, 44000*
**Tel** *02 40 69 20 21*
w amiralhotelnantes.com
In addition to a central location, this hotel boasts comfortable, modern and soundproofed rooms.

**NANTES: Hôtel La Pérouse** €€
Boutique
*3 allée Duquesne, 44000*
**Tel** *02 40 89 75 00*
w hotel-laperouse.fr
Named after a French navigator, this chic hotel has rooms with designer furniture. Fine service.

**NOIRMOITIER EN L'ILE:**
**Hôtel Fleur de Sel** €€
Family
*Rue des Saulniers, 85330*
**Tel** *02 51 39 09 07*
w fleurdesel.fr
Some guest rooms have a private terrace at this comfortable hotel with a vast garden and a pool.

**DK Choice**

**ONZAIN: Domaine des**
**Hauts de Loire** €€€
Luxury
*Rte d'Herbault, 41150*
**Tel** *02 54 20 72 57*
w domainehautsloire.com
This turreted, ivy-clad hunting lodge with large grounds boasts lavishly furnished interiors. Rooms in the old coach house are the most opulent. The chef prepares cutting-edge food, served with superb local wines.

**ORLEANS: Hôtel de l'Abeille** €€
City center
*64 rue Alsace Lorraine, 45000*
**Tel** *02 38 53 54 87*
w hoteldelabeille.com
This grand Neoclassical building offers well-decorated, old-style rooms. Rooftop terrace.

**ROMORANTIN-LANTHENAY:**
**Grand Hôtel du Lion d'Or** €€
Luxury
*69 rue Georges Clémenceau, 41200*
**Tel** *02 54 94 15 15*
w hotel-liondor-romorantin.fr
Stay in well-furnished rooms at this Renaissance mansion with authentic Empire-style decor.

**ST.-MARC-SUR-MER:**
**Hôtel de la Plage** €
Rooms with views
*Plage de M. Hulot, 44600*
**Tel** *02 40 91 99 01*
w hotel-delaplage.fr
This lovely beach hotel featured in the movie *Les Vacances de Monsieur Hulot*. Modern rooms.

**SAUMUR: Hôtel Anne d'Anjou** €
Rooms with views
*32–34 quai Mayaud, 49400*
**Tel** *02 41 67 30 30*
w hotel-anneanjou.com
Some of the rooms at this elegant building on the banks of the Loire are decorated in Empire style. There is also a grand staircase.

**SILLE-LE-GUILLAUME:**
**Relais des Etangs de Guibert** €
Value for money
*Neufchâtel-en-Saosnois, 72600*
**Tel** *02 43 97 15 38*
w lesetangsdeguibert.com
Overlooking a lake, this rustic farmhouse is in a romantic setting deep in the forest.

**TOURS: Hôtel l'Adresse** €
City center
*12 rue de la Rôtisserie, 37000*
**Tel** *02 47 20 85 76*
w hotel-ladresse.com
In the historic Plumereau district, this modern hotel is set within an elegant 18th-century town house.

# Burgundy and Franche-Comté

**ARC-ET-SENANS:**
**La Saline Royale** €€
Historic
*Arc-et-Senans, 25610*
**Tel** *03 81 54 45 32*
w salineroyale.com
A World Heritage site, this hotel features sleek, contemporary rooms. Good service.

**AUXERRE: Le Parc**
**des Maréchaux** €€
City center
*6 av Foch, 89000*
**Tel** *03 86 51 43 77*
w leparcdesmarechaux.com
The Empire-style rooms here are named after French marshals. The best ones overlook the park.

Extensive gardens and inviting pool at Hôtel Fleur de Sel, Noirmoitier en L'Ile

**BEAUNE: Hôtel Grillon** €
Value for money
*21 rte de Seurre, 21200*
**Tel** *03 80 22 44 25*
w hotel-grillon.fr
This charming hotel is set within a walled garden. Rooms in the addition are more spacious.

**BEAUNE: Hôtel Le Cep** €€
Romantic
*27 rue Maufoux, 21200*
**Tel** *03 80 22 35 48*
w hotel-cep-beaune.com
In the old town, this hotel has rooms named after local wines and furnished with antiques.

**BESANCON: Hôtel Le Sauvage** €€
City center
*6 rue du Chapitre, 25000*
**Tel** *03 81 82 00 21*
w hotel-lesauvage.com
Some of the stylish rooms in this former monastery have a view of the citadel.

**CHABLIS: Hostellerie**
**des Clos** €€
Value for money
*Rue Jules-Rathier, 89800*
**Tel** *03 86 42 10 63*
w hostellerie-des-clos.fr
Enjoy delightful rooms and top-notch dining in this restored medieval convent.

**DK Choice**

**CHAGNY: Lameloise** €€
Luxury
*36 pl d'Armes, 71150*
**Tel** *03 85 87 65 65*
w lameloise.fr
Lameloise is a beautifully restored old house with classic decor that includes oak-beamed ceilings and period furniture. Large rooms and impeccable bathrooms. It is also home to one of Burgundy's best restaurants.

**DIJON: Le Jacquemart** €
Value for money
*32 rue Verrerie, 21000*
**Tel** *03 80 60 09 60*
w hotel-lejacquemart.fr
This rambling 17th-century building in the historic center has rooms with rustic furniture.

**DIJON: Hostellerie du**
**Chapeau Rouge** €€
Romantic
*5 rue Michelet, 21000*
**Tel** *03 80 50 88 88*
w chapeau-rouge.fr
In the heart of the city, this smart 16th-century hotel offers slick, contemporary rooms and an impressive dining space.

The vibrant exterior of Le Relais Bernard Loiseau, Saulieu

**DOLE: La Chaumière** €€
Family
*346 av du Maréchal-Juin, 39100*
**Tel** *03 84 70 72 40*
W lachaumiere-dole.fr
Run by one of the region's top chefs, this ancient farmhouse has a chic ambience. Rooms are floral, Zen, or color-themed.

**JOIGNY: La Côte St.-Jacques** €€€
Luxury
*14 faubourg de Paris, 89300*
**Tel** *03 86 62 09 70*
W cotesaintjacques.com
This classy hotel overlooking the Yonne river has a pretty garden leading to the water's edge.

**LEVERNOIS:**
**Hostellerie de Levernois** €€€
Romantic
*Rue du Golf, 21200*
**Tel** *03 80 24 73 58*
W levernois.com
Near Beaune, in the Burgundian countryside, this 17th-century manor-house hotel features a large park and gardens.

**MALBUISSON: Le Bon Accueil** €
Value for money
*Rue de la Source, 25160*
**Tel** *03 81 69 30 58*
W le-bon-accueil.fr
Rooms have simple pine furniture and patterned fabrics at this friendly hotel. Good restaurant.

**MARTAILLY-LES-BRANCION:**
**La Montagne de Brancion** €€
Rooms with views
*Col de Brancion, 71700*
**Tel** *03 85 51 12 40*
W lamontagnedebrancion.com
This modern hotel on a hillside overlooks vineyards and lush countryside. Impressive cuisine.

**NEVERS: Clos Ste.-Marie** €
Value for money
*25 rue du Petit-Mouësse, 58000*
**Tel** *03 86 71 94 50*
W clos-sainte-marie.fr
Some of the rooms at this serene hotel have antique furniture and quaint decor, others are modern.

**NITRY: Auberge de
la Beursaudière** €
Value for money
*5 & 7 rue Hyacinthe-Gautherin, 89310*
**Tel** *03 86 33 69 70*
W beursaudiere.com
The attractive rooms in this 12th-century former priory have been named after ancient trades. Breakfast is served in a wine cellar.

**RULLY: Le Vendangerot** €
Value for money
*6 pl Sainte-Marie, 71150*
**Tel** *03 85 87 20 09*
W vendangerot.fr
This welcoming hotel has neat and unpretentious rooms, and a popular restaurant serving local delicacies.

**SAULIEU: Le Relais
Bernard Loiseau** €€€
Luxury
*2 rue d'Argentine, 21210*
**Tel** *03 80 90 53 53*
W bernard-loiseau.com
Enjoy refined rooms and Michelin-starred dining at this upscale hotel with impeccable service and authentic Burgundy charm.

**VALLEE DE COUSIN: Hostellerie
du Moulin des Ruats** €€
Romantic
*9 rue des Isles Labaumes, 89200*
**Tel** *03 86 34 97 00*
W moulindesruats.com
A former flour mill has been turned into a hotel-restaurant with beautifully furnished rooms.

**VONNAS: Georges Blanc** €€€
Luxury
*Pl Marché, 01540*
**Tel** *04 74 50 90 90*
W georgesblanc.com
Plush hotel-restaurant with a glitzy spa and sauna, and one of the region's top restaurants.

# The Massif Central

**BEAULIEU-SUR-DORDOGNE:**
**Manoir de Beaulieu** €
Family
*4 pl Champ de Mars, 19120*
**Tel** *05 55 91 01 34*
W hotelbeaulieudordogne.com
This traditional hotel offers nicely renovated rooms – some rustic, some modern.

**BELCASTEL: Du Vieux Pont** €€
Family
*Le Bourg, 12390*
**Tel** *05 65 64 52 29*
W hotelbelcastel.com
All the rooms at this modest hotel by the Aveyron river have

wonderful views. The owners run a superb restaurant just across the bridge.

**CANTAL: Instants d'Absolu
Ecolodge & Spa** €€
Rooms with view
*Le Lac du Pêcher, Fons Nostre 15300*
**Tel** *04 71 20 83 09*
W ecolodge-france.com
This 17th-century lava-stone farmhouse has been converted into an eco-friendly hotel. Complete the detox experience with a spa and hot basalt stone massage.

## DK Choice

**CHAMALIERES:**
**Hôtel Radio** €€
Rooms with views
*43 av Pierre et Marie Curie, 63400*
**Tel** *04 73 30 87 83*
W hotel-radio.fr
Fans of Art Deco will love this 1930s gem located on a hill overlooking Clermont Ferrand. Original floor mosaics, mirrors and wrought-iron decor sit side-by-side with radio memorabilia. The spacious rooms have period furnishings. Opt for a room with a balcony.

**CONQUES: Hôtel Ste.-Foy** €€
Romantic
*Le Bourg, 12320*
**Tel** *05 65 69 84 03*
W hotelsaintefoy.com
This 17th-century Aveyron inn features stone walls, low-beamed ceilings, and modern amenities.

**LE BOURG: Auberge
des Montagnes** €
Value for money
*Pailherols, 15800*
**Tel** *04 71 47 57 01*
W auberge-des-montagnes.com
On the flanks of the Monts du Cantal, this auberge has snug chalet-style rooms and a good restaurant serving regional fare.

**LIMOGES: Hôtel Jeanne d'Arc** €
City center
*17 av du Général-de-Gaulle, 87000*
**Tel** *05 55 77 67 77*
W hoteljeannedarc.fr
Behind the facade of a 19th-century coaching inn is a tastefully renovated hotel with stylish, well-equipped rooms.

**MENDE: Hôtel de France** €€
Family
*9 bd Lucien-Arnault, 48000*
**Tel** *04 66 65 00 04*
W hoteldefrance-mende.com
A renovated 1856 staging post, this hotel has comfortable, chic rooms and a fabulous terrace.

**For more information on types of hotels** see pp552–3

Pleasant, simply furnished room at Château d'Ygrande, Ygrande

**MILLAU: Château de Creissels** €€
Romantic
Rte de St.-Afrique, 12100
**Tel** 05 65 60 16 59
🌐 chateau-de-creissels.com
This atmospheric 12th-century château has fine views of the Tarn Valley and the Millau viaduct. Rooms in the 1970s extension are comfortable and quiet.

**ORCIVAL: Hôtel Notre Dame** €
Value for money
Pl de la Basilique, 63210
**Tel** 04 73 65 82 02
🌐 hotelnotredame-orcival.com
Opposite the basilica, this cosy, family-run hotel has cheerful rooms. It serves hearty breakfasts.

**PEYRELEAU: Grand Hôtel de la Muse et du Rozier** €€
Rooms with views
Rue des Gorges du Tarn, 12720
**Tel** 05 65 62 60 01
🌐 hotel-delamuse.fr
In an idyllic setting overlooking the Tarn river, this historic country inn has a quaint exterior that contrasts with its contemporary interior features.

**RODEZ: La Ferme de Bourran** €€
Rooms with views
Quartier de Bourran, 12000
**Tel** 05 65 73 62 62
🌐 fermedebourran.com
On a secluded hillock, this renovated farmhouse has bright, contemporary rooms in soothing tones of white, grey, and ivory.

**SALERS: Le Bailliage** €
Value for money
Rue Notre-Dame, 15410
**Tel** 04 71 40 71 95
🌐 salers-hotel-bailliage.com
Rooms at this grand old house with a delightful garden are simple and well kept. Some have mountain views.

**SALERS: Hôtel Saluces** €
Family
Rue de la Martille, 15140
**Tel** 04 71 40 70 82
🌐 hotel-salers.fr
Relax in stylish rooms with wooden floors in this gorgeous family-run 16th-century mansion.

**ST.-ALBAN-SUR-LIMAGNOLE: Relais St.-Roch** €€
Luxury
Château de la Chastre, chemin du Carreirou, 48120
**Tel** 04 66 31 55 48
🌐 relais-saint-roch.fr
There is a well-stocked lounge bar with over 300 whiskies at this 18th-century mansion with elegant rooms and classy decor.

**ST.-BONNET-LE-FROID: Le Clos des Cimes** €€€
Luxury
Le Bourg, 43290
**Tel** 04 71 59 93 72
🌐 regismarcon.fr
Luxurious rooms, original works of art, and wonderful valley views can all be found at this fabulous country auberge for gourmands.

**ST.-GERVAIS D'AUVERGNE: Castel-Hôtel 1904** €
Value for money
rue de Castel, 63390
**Tel** 04 73 85 70 42
🌐 castel-hotel-1904.com
This turreted château features oak beams, classy wooden floors, and period furniture.

**ST.-MARTIN-VALMEROUX: Hostellerie de la Maronne** €€
Romantic
Le Theil, 15140
**Tel** 04 71 69 20 33
🌐 maronne.com
Tastefully renovated, this 19th-century manor house offers beautifully decorated rooms and a great restaurant.

**VICHY: Aletti Palace Hôtel** €€
City center
3 pl Joseph-Aletti, 03200
**Tel** 04 70 30 20 20
🌐 hotel-aletti.fr
This hotel oozes belle époque grandeur, from its stately reception hall to the crystal chandeliers. Fine restaurant and a terraced pool. Good service.

**YGRANDE: Château d'Ygrande** €€
Luxury
Le Mont, 03160
**Tel** 04 70 66 33 11
🌐 chateauygrande.fr
Meticulously renovated, this 19th-century château located on vast grounds offers a number of bright and elegant rooms.

# The Rhône Valley and French Alps

**ANNECY: Hôtel Palais de l'Isle** €€
City center
13 rue Perrière, 74000
**Tel** 04 50 45 86 87
🌐 palaisannecy.com
On the Thouin canal, this renovated 18th-century house has comfortable rooms and modern decor.

**BRIANCON: Hôtel Cristol** €
Value for money
6 rte d'Italie, 05100
**Tel** 04 92 20 20 11
🌐 hotel-cristol-briancon.fr
Ideal for families, this unpretentious hotel has bright, airy, contemporary rooms.

**CHAMBERY: Hôtel des Princes** €€
City center
4 rue de Boigne, 73000
**Tel** 04 79 33 45 36
🌐 hoteldesprinces.com
Quiet and comfortable rooms can be found at this lovely hotel near the Fontaine des Eléphants.

**CHAMONIX-MONT BLANC: Le Hameau Albert 1er** €€€
Luxury
119 impasse du Montenvers, 74402
**Tel** 04 50 53 05 09
🌐 hameaualbert.fr
This chic hotel complex has various accommodations options and stunning views of Mont Blanc.

**CHANTEMERLE-LES-GRIGNAN: Le Parfum Bleu** €€
Value for money
615b rte de Valaurie, 26230
**Tel** 04 75 98 54 21
🌐 parfum-bleu.com
Take in the sound of cicadas and the smell of lavender at this stylish, restored farmhouse.

**CLIOUSCLAT: La Treille Muscate** €
Value for money
Le Village, 26270
**Tel** 04 75 63 13 10
🌐 hotelrestaurant-latreille muscate.com
A pleasant inn with tasteful, individually decorated rooms, La Treille Muscate also has a vaulted dining room serving local cuisine.

**GRENOBLE: Splendid Hôtel** €
Value for money
22 rue Thiers, 38000
**Tel** 04 76 46 33 12
🌐 splendid-hotel.com
Centrally located in an oasis of tranquility, the Splendid has a walled garden and brightly decorated rooms.

**GRENOBLE: Le Grand Hôtel** €€
City center
*5 rue de la République, 38000*
**Tel** *04 76 51 22 59*
W grand-hotel-grenoble.com
This high-end hotel is in a central location, but the triple glazing ensures a peaceful night's sleep. Rooms are decorated in black, white, and grey tones.

**LE POET-LAVAL:**
**Les Hospitaliers** €
Romantic
*Vieux Village, 26160*
**Tel** *04 75 46 22 32*
W hotel-les-hospitaliers.com
In a dreamy hilltop medieval hamlet, this classy hotel offers spacious rooms and a top-notch restaurant.

**LYON: Hôtel des Artistes** €€
City center
*8 rue Gaspard-André, 69002*
**Tel** *04 78 42 04 88*
W hotel-des-artistes.fr
This cosy hotel featuring bright rooms is a popular haunt for the actors performing at the famous theater opposite.

**LYON: Cour des Loges** €€€
Luxury
*6 rue du Boeuf, 69005*
**Tel** *04 72 77 44 44*
W courdesloges.com
The elegant rooms at this hotel blend Renaissance-period features and contemporary decor.

**MANIGOD: Hôtel-Chalets**
**de la Croix-Fry** €€€
Luxury
*Rte du Col de la Croix-Fry, 74230*
**Tel** *04 50 44 90 16*
W hotelchaletcroixfry.com
Alpine rustic chic meets self-indulgent comfort at this classy chalet-style hotel with great log-cabin-style rooms.

**MEGEVE: Les Fermes**
**de Marie** €€€
Luxury
*163 chemin de Riante Colline, 74120*
**Tel** *04 50 93 03 10*
W fermesdemarie.com
The chic Savoyard country-style chalets here have an air of relaxed sophistication. Guests can pamper themselves at the onsite spa, featuring a sauna, *hammam*, Jacuzzi, and hair salon.

**MONTELIMAR: Le Sphinx** €
Value for money
*19 bd Desmarais, 26200*
**Tel** *04 75 01 86 64*
W sphinx-hotel.fr
Old-school charm greets visitors to this 17th-century townhouse mansion with a delightful terrace.

## DK Choice

**PEROUGES: Hostellerie**
**du Vieux Pérouges** €€
Historic
*Pl du Tilleuil, 01800*
**Tel** *04 74 61 00 88*
W hostelleriedeperouges.com
Set in a medieval hilltop village, this historic inn has rooms in four 13th-century timbered houses clustered around the cobblestone square – the decor is different in each house. The on-site restaurant serves authentic traditional dishes with flair. A truly unique place.

**ROMANS-SUR-ISERE:**
**Hôtel l'Orée du Parc** €€
Family
*6 av Gambetta, 26100*
**Tel** *04 75 70 26 12*
W hotel-oreeparc.com
An elegant bolthole, this hotel is perfect for exploring the Drôme region. Impeccably maintained rooms.

**ST.-CYR-AU-MONT-D'OR:**
**L'Ermitage Hôtel** €€
Rooms with views
*Chemin de l'Ermitage Mont Cindre, 69450*
**Tel** *04 72 19 69 69*
W ermitage-college-hotel.com
Rooms are bright, with quirky accessories and views of Fourvière, at this sleek, ultramodern hotel.

**TALLOIRES: Hôtel l'Abbaye** €€€
Luxury
*Chemin des Moines, 74290*
**Tel** *04 50 60 77 33*
W abbaye-talloires.com
Relax in the wonderful rooms in this 17th-century Benedictine abbey on the shores of Lake Annecy. Cézanne was a fan.

**VAL D'ISERE: Christiania** €€€
Rooms with views
*Chef Lieu, 73152*
**Tel** *04 79 06 08 25*
W hotel-christiania.com
Deluxe Alpine-style rooms come with balconies and magnificent views at this modern chalet hotel.

**VALLON-PONT D'ARC:**
**Le Clos des Bruyères** €€
Family
*Rte des Gorges, 07150*
**Tel** *04 75 37 18 85*
W closdesbruyeres.fr
At this modern Provençal-style hotel, rooms open onto the pool area via a balcony or terrace. The breakfast buffet has plenty of variety and the restaurant is excellent. Enjoy a treatment at the pleasant onsite spa.

## Poitou and Aquitaine

**ARCACHON: Hôtel Le Dauphin** €€
Family
*7 av Gounod, 33120*
**Tel** *05 56 83 02 89*
W dauphin-arcachon.com
Leo Tolstoy spent a year at this attractive hotel that is just a short walk from Arcachon's beaches. Bright rooms and a nice pool.

**BORDEAUX: La Maison**
**du Lierre** €€
B&B
*57 rue Huguerie, 33000*
**Tel** *05 56 51 92 71*
W hotel-maisondulierre-bordeaux.com
This charming hotel in central Bordeaux is set in a historic house with a pretty garden. Breakfast is served in a lovely inner courtyard.

**BORDEAUX: Grand Hôtel**
**de Bordeaux** €€€
Luxury
*2–5 pl de la Comédie, 33000*
**Tel** *05 57 30 44 44*
W ghbordeaux.com
An outstanding spa and two restaurants run by Gordon Ramsay are on offer at this magnificent hotel in a great location. Guests can sign up for wine tours.

**CAP-FERRET: La Maison**
**du Bassin** €€
Romantic
*5 rue des Pionniers, 33950*
**Tel** *05 56 60 60 63*
W lamaisondubassin.com
With the charm of a family home, this chic hotel has colonial decor in the rooms, a bar and restaurant.

**COGNAC: Les Pigeons Blancs** €
Historic
*110 rue Jules Brisson, 16100*
**Tel** *05 45 82 16 36*
W pigeons-blancs.com
Welcoming guests since the time of François I, this old coaching inn near the vineyards has lovely gardens and a famous restaurant.

Outdoor seating area at L'Ermitage Hôtel, St.-Cyr-au-Mont-d'Or

**COULON: Hôtel Le Central** €
Boutique
*4 rue d'Autremont, 79510*
**Tel** *05 49 35 90 20*
[w] hotel-lecentral-coulon.com
This hotel combines romantic boutique style with comfort. Good location, along the "Venice Vert," and great food.

**EUGENIE-LES-BAINS:**
**Les Prés d'Eugénie** €€€
Luxury
*Pl de l'Impératrice, 40320*
**Tel** *05 58 05 06 07*
[w] michelguerard.com
Run by chef Michel Guérard, this colonial-style hotel has a fabulous spa and gorgeous gardens.

**HOSSEGOR:**
**Les Hortensias du Lac** €€
Romantic
*1578 av du Tour du Lac, 40150*
**Tel** *05 58 43 99 00*
[w] hortensias-du-lac.com
Located near France's best surfing beaches, this sprawling villa overlooks gardens and a lake. Delightful rooms.

**ILE DE RE: Hôtel Le Sénéchal** €€
Boutique
*6 rue Gambetta, 17590 Ars-en-Ré*
**Tel** *05 46 29 40 42*
[w] hotel-le-senechal.com
Rooms are distinctive at this laidback village hotel on a pretty island, with exposed brick, wood beams, and rural-chic decor.

**LA ROCHELLE: Hôtel**
**Les Brises** €€
Rooms with views
*Chemin de la Digue Richelieu, 17000*
**Tel** *05 46 43 89 37*
[w] hotellesbrises.eu
Offering stunning views of the harbor, this popular hotel is close to several beaches. Ideal location, a short walk to town.

**MAGESQ: Relais de la Poste** €€€
Boutique
*24 av de Maremne, 40140*
**Tel** *05 58 47 70 25*
[w] relaisposte.com
This peaceful, family-owned hotel is set in beautiful gardens with a large pool. There is also a spa and a Michelin-starred restaurant.

**PAUILLAC: Château**
**Cordeillan-Bages** €€
Historic
*Rte des Châteaux, 33250*
**Tel** *05 56 59 24 24*
[w] cordeillanbages.com
Amid the Médoc vineyards, this magnificent 17th century, château offers splendid gardens, Michelin-starred dining, and elegant rooms. Closed Dec–Feb.

**POITIERS: Château du Clos de la Ribaudière** €€
Romantic
*10 rue du Champ de Foire, 86360 Chasseneuil du Poitou*
**Tel** *05 49 52 86 66*
[w] ribaudiere.com
This delightful hotel offers elegantly modernized rooms and excellent service. The grounds comprise large gardens, a pool, and a relaxing spa.

**POITIERS: Les Cours du Clain** €€
Family
*117 chemin de la Grotte à Calvin, 86000*
**Tel** *06 10 16 09 55*
[w] lescoursduclain-poitiers.com
Set in a historic 1830 house with gardens, this is a beautiful, quiet B&B near central Poitiers. A generous breakfast is served on a terrace overlooking the swimming pool. Closed Nov–Mar.

**ROYAN: Domaine de Saint-Palais** €€
Value for money
*50 rue du Logis, 17420 Saint-Palais-sur-Mer*
**Tel** *05 46 39 85 26*
[w] domainedesaintpalais.eu
Close to both woods and beaches, this charming former hunting lodge dating to the 17th century offers bright, elegant rooms. There is also a Cognac-tasting facility.

**SAINT-EMILION:**
**Au Logis des Remparts** €€
Rooms with views
*18 rue Guadet, 33330*
**Tel** *05 57 24 70 43*
[w] logisdesremparts.com
This boutique hotel is ideal for wine touring and exploring the medieval town. Some rooms have views of the gardens and swimming pool.

Communal area looking out to the gardens at Les Prés d'Eugénie, Eugénie-les-Bains

**DK Choice**

**ST.-LOUP-SUR-THOUET:**
**Château de Saint-Loup** €€
Historic
*79600 St.-Loup-sur-Thouet*
**Tel** *05 49 64 81 73*
[w] chateaudesaint-loup.com
A magical experience is guaranteed at this moated medieval château in the countryside north of Poitiers. Choose from several exquisite rooms in the 17th-century main house – the most fascinating ones are in a medieval keep and round tower.

**SEIGNOSSE:**
**Villa de l'Etang Blanc** €€
Romantic
*2265 route de l'Etang Blanc, 40510*
**Tel** *05 58 72 80 15*
[w] villaetangblanc.fr
Stay in beautifully stylish rooms at this calm country house by a lake. An excellent restaurant and cooking classes are also available.

# Périgord, Quercy, and Gascony

**AGEN: Hôtel Château des Jacobins** €€
Historic
*2 rue Jacob, 47000*
**Tel** *05 53 47 03 31*
[w] chateau-des-jacobins.com
Housed in a 19th-century mansion near the old town, this hotel is opposite a 13th-century church.

**ALBI: L'Autre Rives** €
B&B
*60 rue Cantepau, 81000*
**Tel** *06 75 47 01 51*
[w] lautrerives.com
In a 1930s house, this stylish B&B has five large rooms furnished with designer accessories.

**BERGERAC: Le Clos d'Argenson** €€
B&B
*99 rue Neuve d'Argenson, 24100*
**Tel** *06 12 90 59 58*
[w] leclosdargenson.com
This beautiful B&B offers four ultra-comfortable suites, plus a pool in the garden.

**BOURDEILLES:**
**Hostellerie Les Griffons** €€
Rooms with views
*24310 Bourdeilles*
**Tel** *05 53 45 45 35*
[w] griffons.fr
Most of the characterful rooms at this lovely 16th-century house in a gorgeous village have river views. Closed Nov–Apr.

**BRANTOME: Le Chatenet**  €€
B&B
*24310 Brantôme*
**Tel** *05 53 05 81 08*
**W** lechatenet.com
Housed in a Périgord stone manor house, this B&B offers a pool and gardens. Closed mid-Oct–Mar.

**BRANTOME: Le Moulin de l'Abbaye**  €€
Family
*1 rte de Bourdeilles, 24310*
**Tel** *05 53 05 80 22*
**W** moulinabbaye.com
Stay in sumptuous rooms at this beautiful riverside mill with delightful garden terraces. The Michelin-starred restaurant uses locally sourced produce.

**CHANCELADE: Château des Reynats**  €€
Romantic
*15 av des Reynats, 24650*
**Tel** *05 53 03 53 59*
**W** chateau-hotel-perigord.com
Rooms are divided between the main house and the orangerie at this grand Périgord château-hotel with a pool and tennis courts.

**CORDES-SUR-CIEL: Hostellerie du Vieux Cordes**  €
Historic
*Haut de la Cité, 21 rue St-Michel, 81170*
**Tel** *05 63 53 79 20*
**W** hostelleriehvc.com
In a superb hill-town, this medieval mansion offers great views and charming rooms. The restaurant has a good regional menu. Ask for a table on the terrace.

**CORDES-SUR-CIEL: Le Secret du Chat**  €€
B&B
*Haut de la Cité, Le Planol, 81170*
**Tel** *06 95 48 18 10*
**W** chambres-cordes-tarn-charme-lesecretduchat.com
This gorgeous B&B and *gîte* set in an old townhouse affords amazing views. Closed Nov–Mar.

---

**DK Choice**

**CUQ-TOULZA: Hôtel Cuq en Terrasses**  €€
Rooms with views
*Cuq le Château, 81470*
**Tel** *05 63 82 54 00*
**W** cuqenterrasses.com
Rising up on a hilltop east of Toulouse, this renovated 18th-century manor house feels a part of the Languedoc landscape. The pool is set in lush, picturesque gardens, and the views from the terrace restaurant are glorious. Closed mid-Oct–mid-Apr.

---

Bright, well-furnished room at the Le Pont de l'Ouysse, Lacave

**DOMME: L'Esplanade**  €
Rooms with views
*2 rue Pontcarral, 24250*
**Tel** *05 53 28 31 41*
**W** esplanade-perigord.com
Enjoy the warm welcome from the mother-and-daughter team running this clifftop hotel. Superb views from most rooms and an excellent restaurant. Closed Nov–Feb.

**LACAVE: Le Pont de l'Ouysse**  €€
Luxury
*Lacave, 46200*
**Tel** *05 65 37 87 04*
**W** lepontdelouysse.com
Rooms are bright and sunny, with hardwood floors, at this indulgent retreat with a spa, a terrace pool, and a Michelin-starred restaurant.

**LASCABANES: Le Domaine de Saint-Géry**  €€
Historic
*Le Bourg, 46800*
**Tel** *05 65 31 82 51*
**W** saint-gery.com
Tall ceilings and parquet floors add to the luxurious ambience at this palatial B&B set in a historic manor. Magnificent grounds.

**LECTOURE: Hôtel de Bastard**  €€
Value for money
*Rue Lagrange, 32700*
**Tel** *05 62 68 82 44*
**W** hotel-de-bastard.com
A beautiful wooden staircase leads to the sleeping quarters at this comfortable small-town hotel with a garden pool and a good restaurant.

**LES EYZIES-DE-TAYAC: Les Glycines**  €€
Boutique
*4 av de Laugerie, 24620*
**Tel** *05 53 06 97 07*
**W** les-glycines-dordogne.com
This small and mellow hotel combines a country location with boutique style. Especially lovely restaurant, pool, and garden on site.

**MAUROUX: Hostellerie Le Vert**  €€
Historic
*Lieu dit "Le Vert", 46700 Mauroux*
**Tel** *05 65 36 51 36*
**W** hotellevert.com
Rooms have heaps of character at this family-friendly, 17th-century house in the Cahors wine country. Closed Nov–Mar.

**ROCAMADOUR: Domaine de la Rhue**  €
Boutique
*La Rue, 46500*
**Tel** *05 65 33 71 50*
**W** domainedelarhue.com
This hotel is an ideal base for exploring the countryside and has spacious rooms and a pool. Closed mid-Oct–Mar.

**ST.-EUTROPE-DE-BORN: Le Moulin de Labique**  €€
Romantic
*47210 St.-Eutrope-de-Born*
**Tel** *05 53 01 63 90*
**W** moulin-de-labique.net
Rooms at this good-value B&B in a 13th-century manor house are decorated with antiques.

**SARLAT: Le Moulin Pointu**  €
Value for money
*Ste.-Nathalène, 24200*
**Tel** *05 53 28 15 54*
**W** moulinpointu.com
Start the day with an organic breakfast at this B&B with charming rooms, large gardens, and a pool.

**SARLAT: La Villa des Consuls**  €€
Family
*3 rue Jean-Jacques Rousseau, 24200*
**Tel** *05 53 31 90 05*
**W** villaconsuls.fr
These modern vacation rental rooms and apartments are in historic buildings in the old town.

**TOULOUSE: Hotel Saint-Sernin**  €
Value for money
*2 rue St.-Bernard, 31000*
**Tel** *05 61 21 73 08*
**W** hotelstsernin.com
There are 17 bright, stylish rooms in this 19th-century townhouse near the Saint-Sernin basilica.

**For more information on types of hotels** *see pp552–3*

**TOULOUSE: La Cour
des Consuls** €€
Luxury
*46 rue des Couteliers, 31000*
**Tel** *05 67 16 19 99*
W sofitel.com
Housed in two former lords'
mansions, this stunning five-star
hotel features contemporary
design, a gourmet restaurant,
and an elegant spa.

**TOULOUSE:
Hôtel des Beaux Arts** €€
City center
*1 pl du Pont-Neuf, 31000*
**Tel** *05 34 45 42 42*
W hoteldesbeauxarts.com
Smartly modernized rooms,
some with great views of the
Garonne river, can be found in
this *belle époque* building.
Friendly, helpful staff.

# The Pyrenees

**AINHOA: Hôtel Ithurria** €€
Family
*Place de Fronton, 64250*
**Tel** *05 59 29 92 11*
W ithurria.com
Housed in a giant Basque-style
chalet at the foot of the Pyrenees,
this charming hotel features an
excellent pool and a *hammam*.
The restaurant serves generous
portions and makes use of the
eggs laid daily by the resident
hens. Closed Nov–Mar.

**ANGLET: Château
de Brindos** €€
Luxury
*1 allée du Château, 64600*
**Tel** *05 59 23 89 80*
W chateaudebrindos.com
Exquisite attention to detail
rules at this spacious country-
house hotel located by the Etang
de Brindos lake near Biarritz. Visit
the sauna or the steam room,
then grab a cocktail at their
lakeside pub.

**ARREAU: Hôtel d'Angleterre** €
Family
*Rte de Luchon, 65240*
**Tel** *05 62 98 63 30*
W hotel-angleterre-saint-lary.com
Stay in an 18th-century coaching
inn in a stunning mountain
location. Pretty garden and a pool.

**BIARRITZ: Villa le Goëland** €€
Historic
*12 rue Grande Atalaye, 64200*
**Tel** *05 59 24 25 76*
W villagoeland-biarritz.com
There are views of the ocean from
the high-ceilinged rooms at this
19th-century villa on the cliffs.

**BIARRITZ: Hôtel du Palais** €€€
Luxury
*1 av de l'Impératrice, 64200*
**Tel** *05 59 41 64 00*
W hotel-du-palais.com
Enjoy the opulent spa, pool, and
other amenities at this hotel in a
superb location. The building's
history adds to the romantic vibe.

**CAMON: L'Abbaye-Château
de Camon** €€
B&B
*3 place Philippe de Lévis, 09500*
**Tel** *05 61 60 31 23*
W chateaudecamon.com
A restored 10th-century monastery,
this hotel is located in a historic
village. Gracefully decorated
rooms. Closed Nov–Mar.

## DK Choice

**ESPELETTE:
Hôtel-Restaurant Euzkadi** €
Rooms with views
*285 Karrika Nagusia, 64250*
**Tel** *05 59 93 91 88*
W hotel-restaurant-euzkadi.com
The family-run Euzkadi offers
well-appointed rooms, lovely
terrace views, and a large
swimming pool. An ideal place
for sampling Basque-influenced
dishes. Impeccable service.
Closed mid-Feb–mid-Mar.

**FOIX: Hôtel-Restaurant Lons** €
Value for money
*6 pl Georges Dutilh, 09000*
**Tel** *05 34 09 28 00*
W hotel-lons-foix.com
Close to the historic Château de
Foix, this traditional hotel has
old-fashioned but comfortable
rooms. The courtyard overlooks
the town square.

**LOURDES: Grand Hôtel
Belfry** €€
B&B
*66 rue de la Grotte, 65100*
**Tel** *05 62 94 58 87*
W belfry.fr
Large, black-and-white hued
rooms combine modern features
with traditional style.

**MIREPOIX: Maison
des Consuls** €€
Historic
*6 pl du Maréchal Leclerc, 09500*
**Tel** *05 61 68 81 81*
W maisondesconsuls.com
Enjoy pleasant views across the
cathedral square from the rooms
at this hotel housed in a 13th-
century building.

**ORTHEZ: Hôtel Reine Jeanne** €
Romantic
*44 rue Bourg Vieux, 64300*
**Tel** *05 59 67 00 76*
W reinejeanne.com
This 18th-century building has
chic, modern rooms set around a
courtyard, plus a fine restaurant.

**PAU: Hôtel Bristol** €
Family
*3 rue Gambetta, 64000*
**Tel** *05 59 27 72 98*
W hotelbristol-pau.com
Some rooms at this pleasant
hotel in the center of Pau have
balconies with great views
of the Pyrenees.

**ST.-ETIENNE-DE-BAIGORRY:
Hôtel-Restaurant Arcé** €€
Romantic
*St.-Etienne-de-Baïgorry, 64430*
**Tel** *05 59 37 40 14*
W hotel-arce.com
This hotel blends boutique style
and Basque architecture. Pool
and gardens, plus a restaurant.
Closed mid-Nov–mid-Apr.

**ST.-JEAN-DE-LUZ:
Hôtel La Devinière** €€
Romantic
*5 rue Louis-Fortuné Loquin, 64500*
**Tel** *05 59 26 05 51*
W hotel-la-deviniere.com
The former home of the author
Rabelais, this hotel has antique
furnishings and modern comforts.
Terraces of the rooms overlook
the Eglise St.-Jean-Baptiste.

Elegant, gracefully decorated room at the Hôtel du Palais, Biarritz

**ST.-JEAN-PIED-DE-PORT:**
**Hôtel Les Pyrénées** €€
Luxury
*19 pl Charles de Gaulle, 64220*
**Tel** *05 59 37 01 01*
[w] hotel-les-pyrenees.com
Enjoy breakfast around the pool at this prestigious hotel with elegant rooms and gardens.

**ST.-LIZIER: Villa Belisama** €€
Rooms with views
*3 rue Notre Dame, 09190*
**Tel** *05 61 65 65 65*
[w] lecarredelange.com
Take in the views of the Salat river valley from this charming B&B in a historic hilltop village. Meal-deal accommodations only.

**SARE: Ttakoinenborda** €
Value for money
*Rte de Lizarrieta, 64310*
**Tel** *05 59 47 51 42*
[w] chambredhotebasque.fr
Built in 1680, this B&B in a Basque farmhouse amid rolling fields is excellent for exploring the area.

# Languedoc and Roussillon

**BEZIERS: Hôtel des Poètes** €
B&B
*80 allées Paul Riquet, 34500*
**Tel** *04 67 76 38 66*
[w] hoteldespoetes.net
Free bicycles for touring the Canal du Midi are available at this hotel overlooking the Parc des Poètes.

**CARCASSONNE: Hôtel du Pont Vieux** €
Value for money
*32 rue Trivalle, 11000*
**Tel** *04 68 25 24 99*
[w] hotelpontvieux.com
This attractively furnished hotel has 19 rooms, an inner courtyard, and views of the citadel.

**CARCASSONNE: Hôtel de la Cité** €€€
Luxury
*Pl August-Pierre Pont, 11000*
**Tel** *04 68 71 98 71*
[w] hoteldelacite.com
Expect impeccable service and period rooms at this hotel with gardens, a pool, and a restaurant.

**CERET: Le Mas Trilles** €€
Historic
*Av du Vallespir, Le Pont de Reynes, 66400*
**Tel** *04 68 87 38 37*
[w] le-mas-trilles.com
This stone-built 14th-century farmhouse has charming rooms and a pleasant rooftop terrace. Closed mid-Oct–mid-Apr.

Comfortable room at Le Mas Trilles in a 14th-century farmhouse in Ceret

**COLLIOURE: Relais des Trois Mas** €€
Boutique
*Rte de Port-Vendres, 66190*
**Tel** *04 68 82 05 07*
[w] relaisdestroismas.com
A calm retreat in pine-shaded gardens, this hotel boasts great bay views. Michelin-starred restaurant.

## DK Choice

**MOLITG-LES-BAINS: Château de Riell** €€
Rooms with views
*66500*
**Tel** *04 68 05 04 40*
[w] chateauderiell.com
This Baroque-style château offers fabulous views over forests and Mount Canigou. The interiors are enhanced with antiques and exotic furniture.

**MONTPELLIER: Hôtel du Palais** €
City center
*3 rue Palais des Guilhem, 34000*
**Tel** *04 67 60 47 38*
[w] hoteldupalais-montpellier.fr
Located in the old town, just steps away from the Peyrou Gardens, this historic building has cozy, classic rooms and a relaxed atmosphere.

**NARBONNE: Hotel La Résidence** €€
City center
*6 rue du 1er Mai, 11100*
**Tel** *04 68 32 19 41*
[w] hotel-laresidence-narbonne.fr
Rooms are spacious, with high ceilings, and there is a good wine bar at this hotel with friendly, knowledgeable hosts.

**NIMES: Hotel de l'Amphithéâtre** €
Boutique
*4 rue des Arènes, 30000*
**Tel** *04 66 67 28 51*
[w] hoteldelamphitheatre.com
This small hotel located near the historic amphitheater features rooms decorated in Provençal style. Delicious breakfast.

**PERPIGNAN: Hôtel de la Loge** €
Value for money
*1 rue des Fabriques d'en Nabot, 66000*
**Tel** *04 68 34 41 02*
[w] hoteldelaloge.fr
In the city center, but close to the beaches and mountains, this 16th-century Catalan mansion has lots of character, including a wrought-iron staircase.

**PERPIGNAN: Villa Duflot** €€
Boutique
*7 Rond Point Albert Donnezan, 66000*
**Tel** *04 68 56 67 67*
[w] villa-duflot.com
This Italian-style villa features stylish decor and striking modern sculptures. Guests enjoy fine dining next to the exquisite gardens and pool.

**PEZENAS: Aire de Vacances** €
Historic
*1 rue Calquières Basses, 34120*
**Tel** *09 50 58 99 11*
[w] air-de-vacances.com
Tuck into a breakfast made with local organic products at this delightful 19th-century house near the town center.

**SETE: Grand Hôtel** €€
Rooms with views
*17 Quai de Tassigny, 34200*
**Tel** *04 67 74 71 77*
[w] legrandhotelsete.com
Overlooking Sète's grand canal, this traditional 19th-century hotel has an excellent conservatory-restaurant.

**UZES: Hostellerie Provençale** €€
City center
*1–3 rue de la Grande Bourgade, 30700*
**Tel** *04 66 22 11 06*
[w] hostellerieprovencale.com
This small, friendly hotel in an 18th-century building features terracotta tiled floors, rustic furniture, and up-to-date amenities. Plentiful breakfast.

# Provence and the Côte d'Azur

**AIX-EN-PROVENCE: Hôtel Cézanne** €€
Boutique
*40 av Victor Hugo, 13100*
**Tel** *04 42 91 11 11*
[w] hotelaix.com
The decor at this hotel is artsy and chic. The individually styled rooms ensure a comfortable stay. Breakfast is served until noon on the terrace, and there is an attractive outdoor bar.

For more information on types of hotels *see pp552–3*

**ANTIBES: Mas Djoliba** €€
B&B
*29 av Provence, 06600*
**Tel** *04 93 34 02 48*
w hotel-djoliba.com
Some rooms have views of the gardens at this farmhouse with palm trees around its pool.

## DK Choice

**ARLES: L'Hôtel
Particulier à Arles** €€€
Historic
*4 rue de la Monnaie, 13200*
**Tel** *04 90 52 51 40*
w hotel-particulier.com
Step into a world of rich elegance and opulent living at this historic hotel. A walled garden, a pool, and an ultra-sophisticated spa and *hammam* all make for a dreamy stay.

**AVIGNON: Hôtel Bristol** €€
Family
*44 cours Jean Jaurès, 84000*
**Tel** *04 90 16 48 48*
w bristol-avignon.com
Classy and conveniently located, this pet-friendly hotel has several family rooms and refined decor.

**AVIGNON: La Mirande** €€€
Luxury
*4 pl de la Mirande, 84000*
**Tel** *04 90 14 20 20*
w la-mirande.fr
Renovated in 18th-century style, this hotel is in a splendid cardinal's mansion by the Palais des Papes.

**BORMES-LES-MIMOSAS:
Domaine du Mirage** €€
Family
*38 rue de la Vue des Îles, 83230*
**Tel** *04 94 05 32 60*
w domainedumirage.com
The service is impeccable at this Victorian-style hotel with family rooms, sea views, and a pool.

**CANNES: Hotel de Provence** €€
City center
*9 rue Molière, 06400*
**Tel** *04 93 38 44 35*
w hotel-de-provence.com
This lovely three-star hotel in the shopping district features contemporary rooms and studios and a lovely garden.

**CASTELLANE:
Nouvel Hôtel du Commerce** €€
Value for money
*Pl Marcel Sauvaire, 04120*
**Tel** *04 92 83 61 00*
w hotel-du-commerce-verdon.com
An excellent stopover option, this place has clean, simple rooms, a fine garden restaurant and a pool. Closed Nov–mid-Mar.

Lush trees shading the charming La Bastide de Voulonne in Gordes

## DK Choice

**CHATEAU-ARNOUX:
La Bonne Etape** €€
Romantic
*Chemin du Lac, 04160*
**Tel** *04 92 64 00 09*
w bonneetape.com
At this 18th-century posthouse inherited by current owner and master chef Jany Gleize, rooms are stunningly done up with antiques. Excellent heated pool amid the olive groves.

**EZE: La Chèvre d'Or** €€€
Luxury
*Rue du Barri, 06360*
**Tel** *04 92 10 66 66*
w chevredor.com
Romantic, individually decorated rooms and suites have Jacuzzis and private gardens. The pool and terrace have views of the Mediterranean Sea.

**FAYENCE: Moulin de la
Camandoule** €
Historic
*159 chemin de Notre-Dame des Cyprès, 83440*
**Tel** *04 94 76 00 84*
w camandoule.com
Rooms are decorated in rustic Provençal style at this hotel in a converted 15th-century olive mill with beautiful grounds and a pool.

## DK Choice

**GORDES:
La Bastide de Voulonne** €€
Family
*Cabrières d'Avignon, 84220*
**Tel** *04 90 76 77 55*
w bastide-voulonne.com
This guesthouse in a Provençal farmhouse is an idyllic spot for a family break – the heated pool and terrace have spectacular views over the Luberon. Family suites and lush gardens.

**ILE DE PORT-CROS:
Le Manoir** €€€
Romantic
*Port-Cros, 83400*
**Tel** *04 94 05 90 52*
w hotel-lemanoirportcros.com
Surrounded by palm trees, this historic mansion has balconies overlooking the sea.

**JUAN-LES-PINS:
Hôtel des Mimosas** €€
Value for money
*Rue Pauline, 06160*
**Tel** *04 93 61 04 16*
w hotelmimosas.com
This elegant hotel is surrounded by a park full of exotic flowers. Simple rooms decorated with splashes of color.

**MARSEILLE: Hotel La Résidence
du Vieux Port** €€
Family
*18 quai du Port, 13002*
**Tel** *04 91 91 91 22*
w hotel-residence-marseille.com
Most rooms overlook the Old Port and the Basilica at this hotel with colorful 1950s-style decor.

**MONACO: Columbus
Monte-Carlo** €€
Boutique
*23 av des Papalins, 98000*
**Tel** *00 377 92 05 92 22*
w columbushotels.com
The sleek rooms at this hotel are decorated in dark stone and polished metal. Good restaurant and cigar bar with sea views.

**MOUSTIERS-STE.-MARIE:
La Bastide de Moustiers** €€€
Boutique
*Chemin de Quinson, 04360*
**Tel** *04 92 70 47 47*
w bastide-moustiers.com
Created by Alain Ducasse in a 17th-century building, La Bastide has a superb restaurant, gorgeous gardens, and mountain views. Closed Nov–Mar.

**NICE: Hôtel Windsor** €€
Romantic
*11 rue Dalpozzo, 06000*
**Tel** *04 93 88 59 35*
w hotelwindsornice.com
Art-filled rooms and a pool inside an exotic garden await here. Dine alfresco in summer or next to the fireplace in winter.

**NICE: Le Negresco** €€€
Luxury
*37 promenade des Anglais, 06000*
**Tel** *04 93 16 64 00*
w hotel-negresco-nice.com
Designed by Henri Négresco, this vintage hotel has superb works of art and top-notch amenities. Private beach on La Promenade.

**ST.-PAUL DE VENCE:**
**Hostellerie des Remparts** €
Value for money
*72 rue Grande, 06570*
**Tel** *04 93 24 10 47*
w hostellerielesremparts.com
Modern comforts, antiques-filled
rooms, and marvelous views
of the Mediterranean can all be
found at this medieval building.
Gracious, warm hosts.

**ST.-REMY DE PROVENCE:**
**Hôtel du Soleil** €
Boutique
*35 av Pasteur, 13210*
**Tel** *04 90 92 00 63*
w hotelsoleil.com
Featuring contemporary rooms
with minimalist decor, this stylish
three-star hotel and spa is located
in an old farmhouse on the edge
of the town. It has a heated pool.

**ST.-TROPEZ: Lou Cagnard** €
B&B
*18 av Paul Roussel, 83990*
**Tel** *04 94 97 04 24*
w hotel-lou-cagnard.com
Conveniently located a few
minutes walk from the port and
town center, this elegant Provençal
townhouse has airy rooms and
a lush garden. Closed Oct–Feb.

**DK Choice**

**ST.-TROPEZ: Pastis Hôtel**
**St.-Tropez** €€€
Boutique
*6 av du Général Leclerc, 83990*
**Tel** *04 98 12 56 50*
w pastis-st-tropez.com
This intimate hideaway, filled
with 20th-century art, has
stylish rooms that are all
beautifully furnished and have
lovely garden or sea views.
The pool, surrounded by palm
trees, is the perfect spot for
breakfast. The hotel is a 10 min-
ute walk from the port and
main attractions. Attentive
and welcoming staff.

**SAINTES-MARIES-DE-LA-MER:**
**Mas de la Fouque** €€€
Boutique
*rte du Petit Rhône, 13460*
**Tel** *04 90 97 81 02*
w masdelafouque.com
Overlooking a lagoon and with
views of the Camargue Nature
Park, this chic hotel and spa
features a fine restaurant, pool,
tennis, and horseback riding.

**SEILLANS VAR: Hôtel des**
**Deux Rocs** €
Historic
*1 pl Font d'Amont, 83440*
**Tel** *04 94 76 87 32*
w hoteldeuxrocs.com
An 18th-century mansion with
graceful decor, this is great for
families. Closed mid-Nov–mid-Mar.

**VAISON LA ROMAINE:**
**Les Tilleuls d'Elisée** €
B&B
*1 av J. Mazen, chemin Bon Ange, 84110*
**Tel** *04 90 35 63 04*
w vaisonchambres.info
In an idyllic rural setting, this
charming B&B is set in a 19th-
century Provençal farmhouse.

**VILLEFRANCHE-SUR-MER:**
**Hôtel Welcome** €€
Boutique
*1 quai Amiral Courbet, 06230*
**Tel** *04 93 76 27 62*
w welcomehotel.com
Artist Jean Cocteau's favorite
hotel is full of artsy, period charm.
A sailboat is available to rent.

# Corsica

**AJACCIO: Les Mouettes** €€
Boutique
*9 cours Lucien Bonaparte, 20000*
**Tel** *04 95 50 40 40*
w hotellesmouettes.fr
Enjoy airy Riviera-style rooms in
a 19th-century seafront mansion
with stunning views of the bay.
Closed Nov–Mar.

**BASTIA: Hôtel Pietracap** €
Boutique
*20 rte San Martino, San Martino*
*di Lota, 20200*
**Tel** *04 95 31 64 63*
w pietracap.com
In a beautiful seafront park, this
hotel offers views of the island
of Elba. Closed Nov–Mar.

**BONIFACIO: Hôtel des Etrangers** €
Value for money
*Av Sylvère Bohn, 20169*
**Tel** *04 95 73 01 09*
w hoteldesetrangers.fr
Beautifully furnished rooms have
private bathrooms at this family-
owned hotel. Closed Nov–Mar.

**CALVI: Château Hôtel**
**La Signoria** €€€
Luxury
*Rte de la Forêt de Bonifato, 20260*
**Tel** *04 95 65 93 00*
w hotel-la-signoria.com
There are chic rooms and villas, a
*hammam*, and a private beach at
this hotel. Closed Nov–Mar.

**CORTE: Hôtel Dominique**
**Colonna** €€
B&B
*Vallée de la Restonica, BP 83, 20250*
**Tel** *04 95 45 25 65*
w dominique-colonna.com
In the midst of a nature preserve,
this smart hotel has stylish decor
and a lovely pool. Closed Nov–Mar.

**DK Choice**

**ERBALUNGA: Hôtel**
**Demeure Castel Brando** €€
Historic
*Erbalunga, Brando, 20222*
**Tel** *04 95 30 10 30*
w castelbrando.com
Built in 1853, Castel Brando is set
in a park of ancient olive trees
and exotic palms. Rooms are
spacious and elegant. There are
two pools, a breakfast patio and
top-notch staff. Closed Nov–Mar.

**PIANA: Les Roches Rouges** €€
Romantic
*Rte de Porto, 20115*
**Tel** *04 95 27 81 81*
w lesrochesrouges.com
Dating from 1912, this hotel
boasts a magical location, with a
view of the gulf. Closed Nov–Mar.

**PORTO-VECCHIO:**
**E Casette Private Hotel** €€
Boutique
*Rte de Palombaggia, 20137*
**Tel** *04 95 70 13 66*
w private-hotel-corsica.com
This romantic hotel has views
across the gulf. All rooms have a
private Jacuzzi. Closed Oct–Apr.

Colorful decor in the lobby at Château Hôtel La Signoria in Calvi

**For more information on types of hotels** *see pp552–3*

# WHERE TO EAT AND DRINK

The French consider eating well an essential part of their national birthright. Restaurant reviews, as well as cooking and food shows on television, are avidly followed, and the general quality of both fresh food and restaurant offerings is excellent. This introduction to the restaurant listings, which are arranged by region and town *(see pp576–603),* looks at the different types of restaurants in France. Find practical tips on eating out, reading menus, ordering, and service – everything you need to know to enjoy your meal. At the front of the book is a guide to a typical menu and an introduction to French wine *(see pp28–31).* The main food and wine features are at the beginning of each of the five regional sections.

## French Eating Habits

The traditional main meal at noon survives mainly in rural regions. In cities, French families get together for Sunday lunches that can last 3 hours or more. However, a weekday city lunch is increasingly likely to consist of a sandwich, salad, or steak in a café, while dinner is the main meal of the day. Usually, lunch is from noon to 2pm and dinner from 8 to 10pm, with last orders taken 30 minutes before closing time.

Some family-owned places and downtown restaurants, catering mainly to workers, close on the weekends. A large proportion of French restaurants, even the ones in hotels, are closed on Sunday night, so be sure to check in advance – though there is likely to be a pizzeria open somewhere. Off the beaten path and in resort towns, restaurants, and hotels are often closed out of season or open only on Friday and Saturday nights. It is always advisable to call ahead.

Over the past few decades, French eating habits have changed dramatically, becoming much more international in outlook. The growing popularity of foods from former French colonies and beyond means that North African and Vietnamese establishments are easy to find, as are Chinese and Italian restaurants. Burger and Tex-Mex joints are also popular with young people.

## Brasseries

The brasserie has its origins in the region of Alsace and they were originally attached to breweries; the name *brasserie*

Customers tuck into Lyonnais specialties at the Benoît restaurant, Paris *(see p576)*

actually means "brewery." Usually found in larger cities and towns, they are big, bustling places, many with fresh shellfish stands outside. They serve beer on tap as well as a *vin de la maison* (house wine) and a variety of regional wines. Menus usually include simple fish and grilled meat dishes along with Alsatian specialties such as *choucroute garnie* (sauerkraut with sausage and pork). Prices are very much on par with those at bistros. Like cafés, brasseries usually serve food from morning until night.

## Ferme-Auberges

In the country, a simple "farm inn," or *ferme-auberge,* serves good, inexpensive meals prepared with fresh farm produce. *Ferme-auberges* can be dining rooms attached to a working farm, offering in many cases – as in parts of Corsica – an accurate reflection of authentic regional cuisine. Other *ferme-auberges* may be part of a farm's lodgings, where meals are taken with the host's family as part of the room and board.

The *belle époque* interior of La Cigale, a brasserie in Nantes *(see p588)*

## Cafés

The soul of France, cafés serve drinks, coffee, tea, simple meals, and snacks such as salads, omelets, and sandwiches throughout the day, and usually provide a cheaper breakfast than most hotels. In addition to serving refreshments, cafés are a good source of information and provide the traveler with endless opportunities to people-watch at leisure.

In villages, almost the entire population may drift in and out of a single café during the course of the day, while large cities have cafés that cater to a specific clientele such as workers or students. Paris's most famous cafés were traditional meeting places for intellectuals and artists to exchange ideas (*see p156*).

## Bistro Annexes, Salons du Thé, and Wine Bars

Since the 1990s, bistro annexes have appeared in many cities. They are lower-priced sister eateries of famous – and much more expensive – restaurants run by well-known chefs. Many of them offer *formule* or *prix-fixe* (fixed-price) menus and the chance to sample the cooking of a celebrated chef.

*Salons du thé* (tearooms) are also good-value options for light meals, generally offering a choice of salads, savory tarts, and sandwiches. Wine bars offer light suppers in the evenings, with a choice of Spanish-style tapas, *charcuterie* (cured meats), breads, and cheeses on the menu.

## Reservations

In cities, larger towns, and major resorts, it is always best to make a reservation, especially May through September, and for evening meals or a Sunday lunch. But this rarely applies to cafés or in the country, where one can walk into most places. However, when traveling in remote rural and resort areas off season, it is advisable to check whether the restaurant is open year round.

The bar at La Ferme aux Grives in Eugénie-les-Bains *(see p595)*

If you have a reservation, and your plans change, then call and cancel – smaller restaurants, in particular, must fill all their tables to make a profit.

## Reading the Menu and Ordering

When the menu is presented, it is common practice for guests to be asked their choice of apéritif, which could be Kir (white wine mixed with a dash of black-currant liqueur), vermouth, light port – drunk in France as a cocktail – or, as many French people do not drink spirits before a meal, a soda.

The menu opens with *les entrées* (appetizers) and is followed by *les plats* (entrées); most restaurants will also offer a *plat du jour*, or daily special, for lunch. A selection of dishes from a classic French menu is given on pages 28–9.

Cheese is served as a separate course between the main course and dessert. Coffee is always black, unless one specifies "*crème*," and served after dessert. Alternatively, one can ask for a *tisane* (herbal tea).

Many restaurants offer a choice of fixed-price menus for lunch or dinner. These usually comprise several *entrées, plats,* and desserts to choose from in each price category – which generally works out to be cheaper than ordering à la carte. Many chefs in upscale restaurants also offer a *menu dégustation* (tasting menu) that has numerous courses of small portions, allowing diners to try a variety of the chef's dishes.

Because tasting menus are complex for both the chef and wait staff, the whole table is often required to order the same menu.

## Wine

As restaurants put a large mark-up on wine, it is more affordable to further your connoisseurship with bottles purchased in stores. Local or house wine, however, is often served in carafes, and is generally quite acceptable. If in doubt, ordering a small carafe is a cheaper way to test it out; ask for a *demi* (50 cl) or *quart* (25 cl).

French law divides the country's wines into three classes, in ascending order of quality: *Vin de France, Indication Géographique Protégée* (IGP), and *Appellation d'Origine Protégée* (AOP). The Vin de France wines are rarely found in restaurants. For help in choosing a regional wine (IGP upward), refer to the wine features in the regional sections of this book. For an introduction to French wine, see pages 30–31.

Classic wood interiors at Auberge du XIIème Siècle, Saché *(see p588)*

The well-kept grounds and attractive facade of Les Ursulines, Autun *(see p589)*

## Water

A carafe of *eau du robinet* (tap water) is supplied on request free of charge and is perfectly safe to drink. The French also pride themselves on their wide range of mineral waters. Favorite mealtime brands include Evian and the slightly fizzy Badoit.

## Prices

Prices for restaurants of the same rating are more or less consistent throughout France, except in large cities and the more fashionable resort areas, where they can be significantly more expensive. The quality of food and service is the most decisive price factor, and one can easily spend over €150 per head to eat at one of the top establishments – much more if you choose a prestigious wine.

## How to Pay

Visa/Carte Bleue (V) is the most widely accepted credit card in France. MasterCard (MC) is also commonly accepted, while American Express (AE) and Diners Club (DC) tend to be accepted only in upscale establishments. However, it is best to always carry plenty of cash, especially when touring the countryside, as small family-run restaurants and *ferme-auberges* may not take any credit cards. If in doubt, ask when making the reservation.

## Service and Tipping

French meals are generally enjoyed at a leisurely pace. People think nothing of spending 4 hours at the table, so, if pressed for time, it is better to go to a café, bistro, or brasserie.

A service charge of 12.5 to 15 percent is almost always included in the price of the meal, but most French people leave a few euro cents behind in a café, and an additional 5 percent or so of the total check in other restaurants. In the grander restaurants, which pride themselves on their service, an additional tip of 5 to 10 percent is expected. Around €0.50 to €0.70 is appropriate for coat-check staff, and €0.30 is sufficient for restroom attendants.

## Dress Code

Even when dressed casually, the French are generally well turned out; visitors should aim for the same level of presentable comfort. Sneakers, shorts, beach clothes, or active sportswear are unacceptable everywhere except in cafés or beachside places.

## Children

French children are introduced from an early age to restaurants and as a rule are very well behaved. Some restaurants provide equipment such as highchairs or baby seats. There is often not much room for strollers.

A plate of delicious oysters, a popular dish on the menu of many seafood restaurants

## Pets

Dogs are usually accepted at all but the most elegant restaurants. The French are great dog lovers, so do not be surprised to see your neighbor's lapdog sitting on the adjacent *banquette*.

## Smoking

The French now adhere to government regulations that prohibit smoking inside restaurants and cafés. However, smoking is generally permitted at outdoor tables.

## Wheelchair Access

Though newer restaurants usually provide wheelchair access, it is often restricted elsewhere. A word when booking should ensure that you are given a conveniently located table and assistance, if needed, upon arrival.

## Vegetarian Food

France remains difficult for vegetarians, although some progress has been made in recent years. In most restaurants

Bright, spacious sitting area at La Tour d'Argent, Paris *(see p578)*

the main courses are firmly orientated toward meat and fish. However, you can often fare well by ordering from the *entrées* and should not shy away from asking for a dish to be served without its meat content. Provided you make the request in advance, most smart restaurants will prepare a special vegetarian dish.

Only larger cities and university towns are likely to have fully fledged vegetarian restaurants. Otherwise cafés, pizzerias, creperies, and Oriental restaurants are good places to find vegetarian meals.

## Picnics

Picnicking is the best way to enjoy France's wonderful fresh produce while taking in the delights of the French countryside. Select local bread, cheeses, and *charcuterie* from markets and enticing stores.

Picnic areas along highways are well marked and furnished with tables and chairs, but country lanes are better still.

## Recommended Restaurants

The restaurants in this guide have been carefully selected to reflect the wide range that France offers when it comes to eating out – suitable for every budget. The listings are organized by area, then by price.

At the top of the list are the country's **fine dining** restaurants, including some of the torch-bearers for the nation's world-renowned culinary art. Some of them, however, still serve classic, sauce-based haute cuisine.

Most top chefs take great pride in their individual styles and recipes, adapting haute cuisine techniques to modern tastes. Their restaurants are invariably expensive, but often make for an unforgettable dining experience. Many of these establishments are located inside elegant hotels, but are open to nonguests as well.

**Traditional French** restaurants concentrate on the country's classic dishes such as *escargots* (snails), pâté, *foie gras*,

A beautifully presented plate of food at Le Jardin Gourmand, Auxerre *(see p589)*

*steak au poivre* (pepper steak), *sole meunière* (sole pan-fried with brown butter sauce and lemon), *crème brûlée* (rich creamy custard topped with hard caramel), and chocolate mousse. Then there are **modern French** restaurants, generally with a casual-chic atmosphere – the heirs of the nouvelle cuisine movement that began in the 1960s, emphasizing fresh, top-quality ingredients and inventive food pairings that are beautifully presented and consider modern dietary needs. Contemporary chefs also tend to be more open to inspiration from across a wide spectrum of culinary styles, notably Mediterranean, Asian, North African, and North American.

For a foodie, the best aspect of traveling across France has to be the country's many restaurants that specialize in authentic **regional** cuisine – eateries that lay genuine emphasis on local ingredients and traditional recipes. Many such dishes have

Wine is served by the glass at Le Baron Rouge, Paris *(see p578)*

now attained popularity around the world, such as the cheese fondues of the Alps, the rich seafood *bouillabaisse* of Marseille in Provence, the *cassoulet* – duck and bean stew – of southwest France, and the crêpes and cider of Brittany.

Although Paris may have the country's most famous restaurants, Lyon as a whole is acknowledged as France's gastronomic capital, known for its fabulous array of hearty meat dishes, such as sausages, duck pâté, and roast pork.

**Bistros**, varying widely in size and services offered, are often informal and affordable, and stay open later than the average restaurant. Generally they offer a good, moderately priced meal from a traditional menu of an *entrée* or *hors d'oeuvre* (appetizer), *plats mijotés* (simmered dishes), and *grillades* (grilled fish and meats), followed by cheese and dessert. They may also have a reasonably priced three- or four-course meal, usually featuring comfort dishes such as onion soup and *boeuf bourguignon* (beef stewed in red wine).

The establishments labeled **DK Choice** are places that have been highlighted in recognition of a special feature – a celebrity chef, exquisite food, an inviting ambience, or simply great value for money. Most of these eateries are popular among locals and visitors, so be sure to inquire regarding reservations well in advance to avoid waiting in long lines. Entries with the DK Choice label provide not only a delicious meal, but also a superb dining experience.

# Where to Eat and Drink

## Paris
### Ile de la Cité, Marais, and Beaubourg

### DK Choice

**L'As du Fallafel**                        €
Israeli                          Map 9 C3
*34 rue des Rosiers, 75004*
**Tel** *01 48 87 63 60*        **Closed** *Sat*
The falafels here are arguably the best in town, perhaps even in France, so expect to find very long lines, snaking down the street at lunchtime, for the famous sandwiches. The hummus is a velvety delight.

**Chez H'Anna**                        €
Israeli                          Map 9 C3
*54 rue des Rosiers, 75004*
**Tel** *01 42 74 74 99*        **Closed** *Mon*
Sample creamy homemade hummus and exquisite falafels at this delightful Israeli eatery.

**L'Ambassade d'Auvergne**      €€
Auvergnat                        Map 9 B2
*22 rue du Grenier St.-Lazare, 75003*
**Tel** *01 42 72 31 22*        **Closed** *Sat*
Typical Auvergne dishes such as *aligot* (mashed potatoes with cheese and garlic) are served at this rustic, dark-beamed inn.

**Frenchie**                        €€
Bistro                          Map 9 A1
*5–6 rue du Nil, 75002*
**Tel** *01 40 39 96 19*   **Closed** *Sat & Sun*
Book months ahead for a chance to dine at one of Paris's hottest bistros. Try the exquisite dishes on the fixed-price menus.

**Le Garde Robe**                  €€
Tapas                           Map 8 F2
*41 rue de l'Arbre Sec, 75001*
**Tel** *01 49 26 90 60*        **Closed** *Sun*
Charcuterie, cheese, and oysters are served as tasty accompaniments to an outstanding wine menu.

**Le Hangar**                        €€
Traditional French              Map 9 B2
*12 impasse Berthaud, 75003*
**Tel** *01 42 74 55 44*   **Closed** *Sun & Mon*
Cheerful staffers serve delicious food in this modest setting. Savor pan-fried *foie gras* on puréed potatoes.

**Les Philosophes**                  €€
Traditional French              Map 9 C3
*28 rue Vieille du Temple, 75004*
**Tel** *01 48 87 49 64*
Visit this delightful all-day café for first-rate onion soup, *steak*

*frites*, and the house specialty, tomato *tarte Tatin*. There is a good fixed-price menu.

**Benoît**                        €€€
Bistro                          Map 9 B3
*20 rue St.-Martin, 75004*
**Tel** *01 58 00 22 05*
Enjoy hearty food in this Michelin-starred Alain Ducasse bistro. Don't miss the veal sweetbreads and *cassoulet*.

**Spring**                        €€€
Modern French                   Map 8 F2
*6 rue Bailleul, 75001*
**Tel** *01 45 96 05 72*        **Closed** *Sun & Mon*
Creative versions of French classics are paired with outstanding wines at Spring. Excellent fixed-price tasting menu.

**Yam'Tcha**                        €€€
Asian                           Map 8 F2
*121 rue St.-Honoré, 75001*
**Tel** *01 40 26 06 06*   **Closed** *Sun–Tue*
The name means "drink tea." Try different brews to complement the mouthwatering Chinese-influenced dishes. A tea boutique is nearby, at 4 rue Sauval.

### Tuileries and Opéra

**Bouillon Chartier**                  €
Brasserie                        Map 4 F4
*7 rue du Faubourg Montmartre, 75009*
**Tel** *01 47 70 86 29*
Enjoy great food in glorious *belle époque* surroundings. Try the house pâté, snails, or the tender meat stew.

**Bistrot Victoires**                  €€
Traditional French              Map 8 F1
*6 rue la Vrillière, 75001*
**Tel** *01 42 61 43 78*
*Confit*, *steak frites* and other tasty dishes are served in impeccable surroundings. Great value.

Le Grand Véfour, which has retained much of its original 18th-century decoration

**Chez Georges**                        €€
Traditional French              Map 8 F1
*1 rue du Mail, 75002*
**Tel** *01 42 60 07 11*   **Closed** *Sat & Sun*
Try the exceptional *steak au poivre* at this vintage treasure, beloved of cookery writer Julia Child.

**Pascade**                        €€
Auvergnat                        Map 4 D5
*14 rue Daunou, 75002*
**Tel** *01 42 60 11 00*   **Closed** *Sun & Mon*
Come here for *pascade* – a crispy, thick savory or sweet *crêpe* filled with gourmet ingredients.

### DK Choice

**Racines**                        €€
Wine bar                        Map 4 F5
*8 passage des Panoramas, 75002*
**Tel** *01 40 13 06 41*   **Closed** *Sat & Sun*
Racines has a short menu that combines French and Italian dishes. Choose from a selection of very good wines, and try the excellent *charcuterie*, *ratatouille*, lamb, and pork. Save room for the seriously seductive desserts.

**Caviar Kaspia**                        €€€
Russian                          Map 3 C5
*17 pl de la Madeleine, 75008*
**Tel** *01 42 65 33 32*        **Closed** *Sun*
Sample caviar, smoked salmon, and chilled vodka in the plush surroundings of an early 20th-century Russian aristocrat's salon.

**Le Grand Véfour**                  €€€
Fine dining                      Map 8 F1
*17 rue de Beaujolais, 75001*
**Tel** *01 42 96 56 27*   **Closed** *Sat & Sun*
The decor in this 18th-century room has barely altered since Napoleon brought Josephine here to dine. Innovative cuisine.

### Champs-Elysées and Invalides

**Korean Barbecue Champs-Elysées**                        €
Korean                          Map 3 A5
*7 rue de Ponthieu, 75008*
**Tel** *01 42 25 35 41*        **Closed** *Sun*
Tuck into unbelievably tender, paper-thin beef teamed with crisp greens. Great gyoza and sushi.

Gorgeous dining space with a retractable roof at Lasserre

**Bistrot de Paris** €€
Bistro Map 8 D3
*33 rue de Lille, 75007*
**Tel** *01 42 61 16 83* **Closed** *Sun & Mon*
This delightful Art Nouveau gem rustles up tasty bistro classics for a busy crowd of loyal customers.

**Café Constant** €€
Bistro Map 6 E3
*139 rue St.-Dominique, 75007*
**Tel** *01 47 53 73 34*
Arrive early to get a seat at this popular bistro where comfort food takes center stage. Try the veal *cordon bleu*.

**Le Florimond** €€
Traditional French Map 6 F3
*19 av de la Motte-Picquet, 75007*
**Tel** *01 45 55 40 38* **Closed** *Sun & first Sat of every month*
Hearty food such as tasty lobster ravioli is served in a bright locale. End with the vanilla *millefeuille*.

**La Fontaine de Mars** €€
Southwest French Map 6 E3
*129 rue St.-Dominique, 75007*
**Tel** *01 47 05 46 44*
Duck *cassoulet* is the flagship dish at this family-friendly bistro with beautiful interiors. Great service.

**Huîtrier** €€
Seafood Map 2 D2
*16 rue Saussier-Leroy, 75017*
**Tel** *01 40 54 83 44*
The oysters steal the show at this modern, minimalist restaurant that also serves classic French fare.

**Minipalais** €€
Fine dining Map 7 A1
*Grand Palais, 3 av Winston Churchill, 75008*
**Tel** *01 42 56 42 42*
Diners are in for a gastronomic treat in a trendy setting with floor-to-ceiling windows, a fabulous terrace, and a grand cocktail bar.

**DK Choice**

**Relais de l'Entrecôte** €€
Steakhouse Map 2 F5
*15 rue Marbeuf, 75008*
**Tel** *01 49 52 07 17*
This place is a true carnivore's paradise. The high-quality beef is cut thin, the *frites* are cooked to perfection and the secret-recipe sauce is really something to write home about.

**DK Choice**

**Antoine** €€€
Seafood Map 6 E1
*10 av de New York, 75116*
**Tel** *01 40 70 19 28* **Closed** *Sun & Mon*
Enjoy sensational seafood and spectacular views across the Seine to the Eiffel Tower. Try the signature sea bass for two, grilled on fennel wood and served with steamed vegetables.

**L'Arpège** €€€
Fine dining Map 7 B3
*84 rue de Varenne, 75007*
**Tel** *01 45 05 09 06* **Closed** *Sat & Sun*
Home-grown organic vegetables take pride of place in this establishment run by Michelin-starred chef Alain Passard.

**L'Astrance** €€€
Modern French Map 5 C3
*4 rue Beethoven, 75016*
**Tel** *01 40 50 84 40* **Closed** *Sat–Mon*
Book months in advance to secure a table at this intimate, globally celebrated restaurant. Sample the inspired tasting menu.

**Hiramatsu** €€€
Modern French Map 5 C1
*52 rue de Longchamp, 75116*
**Tel** *01 56 81 08 80* **Closed** *Sat & Sun*
Diners are treated to a flawless blend of French cuisine with Japanese influences in elegant surroundings. Great service.

**Le Jules Verne** €€€
Fine dining Map 6 D3
*5 av Gustave Eiffel, 75007*
**Tel** *01 45 55 61 44*
Alain Ducasse's restaurant on the Eiffel Tower's second platform offers stylish dining to complement the 360-degree view over Paris.

**Lasserre** €€€
Fine dining Map 7 A1
*17 av Franklin Delano Roosevelt, 75008*
**Tel** *01 43 59 02 13* **Closed** *Sun & Mon*
Linger over deliciously refined cooking in an elegantly decorated

dining room. The retractable roof opens to the stars, and the service is impeccable.

**Prunier** €€€
Seafood Map 2 D4
*16 av Victor-Hugo, 75116*
**Tel** *01 44 17 35 85* **Closed** *Sun*
Enjoy a seasonal menu of inventive fish dishes, plus an impressive variety of caviars, at this beautiful Art Deco gem.

## Left Bank

**Breakfast in America** €
American Map 9 A5
*17 rue des Ecoles, 75005*
**Tel** *01 43 54 50 28*
All-day breakfasts and other US staples – bacon, pancakes, burgers, and more – are served at this classic diner. There is another branch on the Right Bank.

**Le Loubnane** €
Lebanese Map 9 A4
*29 rue Gallande, 75005*
**Tel** *01 43 26 70 60* **Closed** *Mon*
Delicious meze is dished up at this family-run establishment. Don't miss the exceptional pistachio-stuffed *crêpes*.

**L'Agrume** €€
Bistro Map 13 C3
*15 rue des Fossés St.-Marcel, 75005*
**Tel** *01 43 31 86 48* **Closed** *Sun & Mon*
Foodies line up to sample Franck Marchesi-Grandi's delicious five-course tasting menu.

**DK Choice**

**Brasserie Balzar** €€
Brasserie Map 9 A5
*49 rue des Ecoles, 75005*
**Tel** *01 43 54 13 67*
Skilled waiters in long aprons serve typical brasserie fare, such as onion soup, at this venerable institution, the former haunt of many great artists and literary figures. There is a separate café and bar section.

**L'Epigramme** €€
Bistro Map 8 F4
*9 rue de l'Eperon, 75006*
**Tel** *01 44 41 00 09* **Closed** *Sun & Mon*
Enjoy bistro classics such as Basque pork with turnip *choucroute* and traditional *escargots*.

**Kitchen Galerie Bis** €€
Modern French Map 8 F4
*25 rue des Grands Augustins, 75006*
**Tel** *01 46 33 00 85* **Closed** *Sun & Mon*
This place, the younger sibling to the celebrated original, offers contemporary French cuisine with an Asian twist. Great appetizers.

**For more information on types of restaurants** *see p575*

**Mavrommatis** €€
Greek **Map** 13 B2
*42 rue Daubenton, 75005*
**Tel** *01 43 31 17 17* **Closed** *Mon*
Beautifully presented dishes and
stylish decor are teamed with
friendly service at Mavrommatis.
Be sure to try the *moussaka*.

**Les Papilles** €€
Bistro **Map** 12 F1
*30 rue Gay Lussac, 75005*
**Tel** *01 43 25 20 79* **Closed** *Sun & Mon*
There are daily changing menus
at this deli, coffee bar, wine store,
and bistro all rolled into one.

**Le Procope** €€
Traditional French **Map** 8 F4
*13 rue de l'Ancienne Comédie, 75006*
**Tel** *01 40 46 79 00*
Opened in 1686, the city's oldest
restaurant is delightfully nostalgic.
Great selection of desserts.

**Shu** €€
Japanese **Map** 8 F4
*8 rue Suger, 75006*
**Tel** *01 46 34 25 88* **Closed** *Sun*
There's no menu in this *omakase*-
style restaurant. The traditional
dishes look and taste stunning.

**Terroir Parisien** €€
Traditional French **Map** 9 B5
*20 rue St.-Victor, 75005*
**Tel** *01 44 31 54 54*
This beautifully designed space
serves delicious, locally sourced
food cooked by an award-
winning chef.

**Le Timbre** €€
Bistro **Map** 12 D1
*3 rue Ste.-Beuve, 75006*
**Tel** *01 45 49 10 40* **Closed** *Sun & Mon*
All the dishes here are prepared
using only the finest, freshest
ingredients. Delicious *millefeuille*.

**Le Comptoir du Relais** €€€
Bistro **Map** 8 F4
*9 carrefour de l'Odéon, 75006*
**Tel** *01 44 27 07 97*
Try the lobster bisque at this
much celebrated temple to
French bistro cuisine. No
reservations, so get there early.

### DK Choice

**La Tour d'Argent** €€€
Fine dining **Map** 9 B5
*15 quai de la Tournelle, 75005*
**Tel** *01 43 54 23 31* **Closed** *Sun
& Mon*
This family-run Paris institution,
with its romantic sixth-floor
dining room and panoramic
views, is world-famous. The
ground-floor bar doubles
as a gastronomic museum.

Lovely *belle époque* interior of popular
Bofinger brasserie

# Farther Afield

**Amici Miei** €
Italian
*44 rue St.-Sabin, 75011*
**Tel** *01 42 71 82 62* **Closed** *Sun & Mon*
This popular, unpretentious
*trattoria* rolls out some of the
best thin-crust pizzas in Paris.
Try the authentic Sardinian
specialties, too. Arrive early to
avoid the line.

**Arbre de Sel** €
Korean
*138 rue de Vaugirard, 75015*
**Tel** *01 47 83 29 52* **Closed** *Sun*
The beautifully presented dishes
here range from spicy to very
spicy. Vegetarian options are
also available. Friendly and
efficient service.

### DK Choice

**Le Baron Rouge** €
Wine bar
*1 rue Théophile Roussel, 75012*
**Tel** *01 43 43 14 32*
Fresh, succulent oysters brought
directly from the Atlantic coast
can be eaten inside the tiny
bustling bar or on the pavement,
standing around large barrels.
They also have a great selection
of cheese, *charcuterie*, and wine
by the glass. Great, fun vibe.

**Chez Gladines** €
Basque
*30 rue des Cinq Diamants, 75013*
**Tel** *01 45 80 70 10*
Huge salads, smothered with
sautéed potatoes, are served
in earthenware bowls at this
no-frills eatery.

**Chez Toinette** €
Traditional French
*20 rue Germain Pilon, 75018*
**Tel** *01 42 54 44 36* **Closed** *Sun & Mon*
Enjoy delectable duck *foie gras*,
snails, lamb shank, and sea bass
at this unassuming restaurant
with a cozy interior.

**Rose Bakery** €
Vegetarian
*46 rue des Martyrs, 75009*
**Tel** *01 42 82 12 80*
This is the haunt of British
expatriates homesick for scones.
The homemade carrot cake is
legendary. Fabulous coffee and
Neal's Yard cheeses, plus a
selection of healthy brunches.

**La Balançoire** €€
Traditional French
*6 rue Aristide Bruant, 75018*
**Tel** *01 42 23 70 83* **Closed** *Sun & Mon*
Filled with jars of candy, this
child-friendly restaurant has
a menu that features lots of
classics. The steak and *foie gras*
are particularly noteworthy.
Helpful and friendly staff.

**Le Bistrot Paul Bert** €€
Bistro
*18 rue Paul Bert, 75011*
**Tel** *01 43 72 24 01* **Closed** *Sun & Mon*
Generous portions of top-notch
food, a serious wine list and
lovely prewar decor await at this
ever-popular bistro. The fixed-
priced lunch menu is great value.
Reservations are recommended.

**Bofinger** €€
Brasserie
*5–7 rue de la Bastille, 75004*
**Tel** *01 42 72 87 82*
The city's most beautiful brasserie
has a perfectly preserved *belle
époque* interior. On the menu
are classic Alsatian dishes, plus
beer on tap.

**La Cantine du Troquet** €€
Basque
*101 rue de l'Ouest, 75014*
**Tel** *01 45 40 04 98* **Closed** *Sun & Mon*
This is a popular restaurant
where mouthwatering regional
food is served with a unique
touch at canteen-style tables.
The desserts are excellent, too.

**La Coupole** €€
Brasserie
*102 bd du Montparnasse, 75014*
**Tel** *01 43 20 14 20*
Seafood platters draw the
crowds at this historic 600-seat
brasserie with authentic Art
Deco interiors. A veritable
Parisian landmark.

**Marty** €€
Brasserie
*20 av des Gobelins, 75005*
**Tel** *01 43 31 39 51*
Robust cooking is served in
original 1913 interiors. Sample
the roast duck or the seafood
platters. For a truly unique
experience, reserve a seat at
the chef's table.

**Le Miroir** €€
Bistro
*94 rue des Martyrs, 75018*
**Tel** *01 46 06 50 73* **Closed** *Mon*
Comfort food and lovely desserts (try the lemon pie) are cooked by haute cuisine-trained chefs.

**La Villa Corse** €€
Corsican
*164 bd de Grenelle, 75015*
**Tel** *01 53 86 70 81* **Closed** *Sun*
An inventive Corsican menu is delivered in a hospitable setting, with a cosy bar and a library.

**DK Choice**

**La Closerie des Lilas** €€€
Traditional French
*171 bd du Montparnasse, 75006*
**Tel** *01 40 51 34 50*
Splash out on classic dishes, such as *boeuf bourguignon*, in the restaurant proper, or head for the brasserie and bar, where a pianist plays every evening. Hemingway was a regular at this historic establishment.

## Ile-de-France

**BRAY SUR SEINE:**
**Au Bon Laboureur** €
Seafood
*2 rue Grande, 77480*
**Tel** *01 60 67 10 81* **Closed** *Wed & Sun eve*
An unassuming exterior belies the award-winning fare on offer at this great-value hotel restaurant.

**DAMPIERRE:**
**Auberge Saint-Pierre** €
Traditional French
*1 rue de Chevreuse, 78720*
**Tel** *01 30 52 53 53* **Closed** *Sun eve, Mon & Tue*
This 17th-century half-timbered house offers a welcoming dining room and very good food.

**FONTAINEBLEAU: L'Axel** €€
Modern French
*43 rue de France, 77300*
**Tel** *01 64 22 01 57* **Closed** *Mon & Tue, Wed lunch*
Rising star Kunihisa Goto and his team run this Michelin-starred kitchen with Japanese creativity. Try the chef's tasting menu.

**LE PERREUX SUR MARNE:**
**Les Magnolias** €€
Fine dining
*48 av de Bry, 94170*
**Tel** *01 48 72 47 43* **Closed** *Sat lunch, Sun & Mon*
For an avant-garde take on classic dishes, try the lobster ravioli or one of the delicious desserts.

**NEUILLY-SUR-SEINE:**
**Le Zinc Zinc** €
Bistro
*209 ter av du Général-de-Gaulle, 92200*
**Tel** *01 40 88 36 06*
Offering great food and wines from all over France, this lively bistro is also open for breakfast.

**PROVINS: Aux Vieux Remparts** €€
Bistro
*3 rue Couverte, 77160*
**Tel** *01 64 08 94 00*
In a half-timbered building, this eatery offers dishes such as mascarpone, white radish with shiso, and smoked salmon. Alfresco dining in the summer.

**RAMBOUILLET:**
**Le Cheval Rouge** €€
Traditional French
*78 rue du Général de Gaulle, 78120*
**Tel** *01 30 88 80 61* **Closed** *Tue & Wed*
This is the place for top-notch French cuisine. Try *foie gras* and *morilles* mushrooms, and roast lamb with thyme.

**ST.-GERMAIN-EN-LAYE:**
**Le Saint Exupéry** €€
Traditional French
*11 av des Loges, 78100*
**Tel** *01 39 21 50 90* **Closed** *Sat & Sun*
Diners choose this pleasant restaurant for specialties such as shellfish and grilled meat.

**DK Choice**

**VERSAILLES: Ramsay Trianon Palace** €€€
Fine dining
*1 bd de la Reine, 78000*
**Tel** *01 30 84 50 18* **Closed** *Sun*
Gordon Ramsay's restaurant is the jewel in the crown of this superb royal château hotel. Expect a culinary extravaganza in majestic surroundings, but be prepared to feel considerably lighter in the pockets after the meal. Dinner only.

The façade of L'Axel, a Michelin-starred restaurant in Fontainebleau

## Le Nord and Picardy

**AIRE-SUR-LA-LYS: Hostellerie des Trois Mousquetaires** €€
Traditional French
*Château de la Redoute, rte de Béthune, 62120*
**Tel** *03 21 39 01 11* **Closed** *Sun eve*
Good old-fashioned cooking such as turbot with Saint Omer cauliflower and Rossini steak can be sampled here.

**AMIENS: L'Aubergade** €€€
Regional
*78 rte Nationale*
**Tel** *03 22 89 51 41* **Closed** *Sun & Mon*
Located just outside Amiens, this prestigious restaurant has lovely decor and excellent regional fare.

**ARRAS: La Faisanderie** €€
Traditional French
*45 Grand Place, 62000*
**Tel** *03 21 48 20 76* **Closed** *Sun eve, Mon, Thu lunch*
This superb restaurant with a Baroque brick-vaulted dining room offers a traditional menu.

**BEAUVAIS: Le Palais d'Antan** €€
Traditional French
*75 rue St.-Pierre, 60000*
**Tel** *03 44 45 06 52* **Closed** *Tue*
Enjoy inventive cuisine with a great view of the impressive cathedral. Try grilled monkfish with vegetables, potatoes, and Camembert sauce.

**BELLE-EGLISE:**
**La Grange de la Belle Eglise** €€€
Traditional French
*28 bd René-Aimé-la-Gabrielle, 60540*
**Tel** *03 44 08 49 00* **Closed** *Sun eve, Mon & Tue lunch*
Specialties at this luxury restaurant include lobster and scallops with Sauternes sauce.

**BOULOGNE-SUR-MER:**
**La Plage** €€
Seafood
*124 bd Sainte-Beuve, 62200*
**Tel** *03 21 99 90 90* **Closed** *Wed eve*
Located on the waterfront, La Plage is the place for modern takes on classic seafood dishes. Try the tartare of beef with fresh oysters and wasabi, or roast monkfish with parsnip purée and grilled hazelnuts.

**CALAIS: Histoire Ancienne** €€
Traditional French
*20 rue Royale, 62100*
**Tel** *03 21 34 11 20* **Closed** *Sun & Mon eves; Jul–Aug: Mon & Sun*
Come to the Histoire Ancienne for old-world bistro-style cooking: marrowbones, snails in garlic butter and pepper steak.

The rustic interior decor of Estaminet T'Kasteel Hof, in Cassel

**CALAIS: La Sole Meunière** €€
Seafood
*1 bd de la Résistance  62100*
**Tel** *03 21 34 43 01*   **Closed** *Sun eve, Mon*
The fish served here comes straight from the harbor. Do not miss the seafood platter.

**CAMBRAI: L'Escargot** €€
Bistro
*10 rue du Général de Gaulle, 59400*
**Tel** *03 27 81 24 54*   **Closed** *Wed & Fri eve*
Savor simple dishes such as lamb chops, veal kidneys, trout, and bream at this cozy, rustic eatery.

**CASSEL: Estaminet T'Kasteel Hof** €€
Traditional French
*Rue St.-Nicolas, 59670*
**Tel** *03 28 40 59 29* **Closed** *Mon–Wed*
This no-frills Flanders café has fantastic views and a store selling local produce. Booking advised.

**COMPIEGNE: Bistrot de Flandre** €€
Traditional French
*2 rue d'Amiens, 60200*
**Tel** *03 44 83 26 35*   **Closed** *Sun eve*
Try the roast fillet steak with peppers at this classic bistro with hearty meals and a good wine list.

**DOUAI: La Terrasse** €€
Seafood
*36 Terrasse St.-Pierre, 59500*
**Tel** *03 27 88 70 04*
Hidden on a sidestreet, this restaurant dishes up fantastic fresh fish and delectable *fois gras*.

**DUNKERQUE: L'Auberge de Jules** €€
Seafood
*9 rue de la Poudrière, 59140*
**Tel** *03 28 63 68 80* **Closed** *Sat & Sun; 2 weeks in Aug*
Fresh fish and shellfish dishes are prepared at this popular bistro near the port. Cheery atmosphere.

**FAVIERES: La Clé des Champs** €€
Traditional French
*13 pl Frères Caudron, 80120*
**Tel** *03 22 27 88 00*   **Closed** *Mon & Tue*
Specialties at this great-value eatery include Saint Vaast oysters and pigeon with cabbage and chicory-flavored sauce.

**LAON: Zorn-La Petite Auberge** €€
Modern French
*45 bd Brossolette, 02000*
**Tel** *03 23 23 02 38*   **Closed** *Sat lunch, Sun, Mon eve*
Enjoy creative cooking with an emphasis on fish. Stylish decor and an excellent wine list.

**LENS: L'Atelier de Marc Meurin** €€
Regional
*Parc du Musée du Louvre-Lens, 97 rue Paul Bert, 62300*
**Tel** *03 21 18 24 90*    **Closed** *Tue & Sun eves*
Just steps from the Louvre-Lens museum, Marc Meurin creates great dishes from local produce.

**LILLE: Au Vieux de la Vieille** €€
Regional
*2–4 rue des Vieux-Murs, 59800*
**Tel** *03 20 13 81 64*
This café specializes in Flemish cuisine. Try the chicken in *Maroilles* cheese.

**LILLE: Le Compostelle** €€
Traditional French
*4 rue Saint-Etienne, 59800*
**Tel** *03 28 38 08 30*    **Closed** *Sun eve*
Great food and delicious desserts are served in a fine 16th-century Renaissance interior.

**LILLE: N'Autre Monde** €€
Bistro
*1 bis rue du Cure Saint-Etienne, 59000*
**Tel** *03 20 15 01 31*    **Closed** *Mon*
The menu changes seasonally at this bijou bistro, and it includes innovative dishes with an exotic touch, such as bream served with potato and coconut cream.

**DK Choice**

**MONTREUIL SUR MER: Auberge de la Grenouillère** €€€
Traditional French
*19 rue de la Grenouillère, La Madeleine sous Montreuil, 62170*
**Tel** *03 21 06 07 22*   **Closed** *Mon lunch, Tue & Wed*
Diners come to enjoy the creative 11-course tasting menu at this riverside farm restaurant with traditional interiors. Located in a tranquil setting by a stream.

**POIX-DE-PICARDIE: L'Auberge de la Forge** €€
Traditional French
*14 rue du 49ème Régiment BCA Caulières, 80290*
**Tel** *03 22 38 00 91*   **Closed** *Sun eve*
There are great-value meals to be had at this half-timbered Picardy coaching inn, plus a brasserie for those who just want to grab a quick bite to eat.

**ROYE: La Flamiche** €€
Traditional French
*20 pl de l'Hôtel de Ville, 80700*
**Tel** *03 22 87 00 56*   **Closed** *Sun eve, Mon & Tue*
Seasonal dishes are prepared with great originality at this top-notch restaurant. Try the scallops and oysters wrapped in spinach and served with a Japanese seaweed sauce.

**STEENVOORDE: Auberge du Noord Meulen** €
Traditional French
*rte du Whormhout, 59112*
**Tel** *03 28 48 11 18*
Delicious food is served in wonderfully quaint surroundings. Try the *ficelle picarde* (baked pancake with ham, mushrooms, and cream).

## Champagne

**CHALONS-EN-CHAMPAGNE: Au Carillon Gourmand** €€
Traditional French
*15 pl Monseigneur Tissier, 51000*
**Tel** *03 26 64 45 07*   **Closed** *Sun eve, Mon & Wed eve*
This welcoming restaurant offers a traditional menu that features dishes such as saddle of rabbit served with mustard sauce, and beef fillet in bread crust with chorizo.

**CHALONS-EN-CHAMPAGNE: Le Petit Pasteur** €€
Bistro
*42 rue Pasteur, 51000*
**Tel** *03 26 68 24 78*    **Closed** *Sun & Wed eves, Mon*
Diners can choose from bistro, regional, and traditional menus at this unpretentious restaurant with simple decor. There is terrace seating on sunny days.

**CHARLEVILLE-MEZIERES: Au Cochon Qui Louche** €€
Traditional French
*31 rue Victoire Cousin 08000*
**Tel** *03 24 35 49 05* **Closed** *Sun & Mon*
Enjoy a bistro menu and home-style cooking at this fun eatery. The desserts are delicious –don't miss the chocolate mousse.

**COLOMBEY-LES-DEUX-EGLISES:
Hostellerie La Montagne** €€
Traditional French
*10 rue Pisseloup, 52330*
**Tel** *03 25 01 51 69* **Closed** *Mon & Tue*
Don't miss the Ile d'Yeu sole with
parsnip gnocchi at this elegant
restaurant with friendly service.

**CUMIERES: Le Caveau** €€
Traditional French
*44 rue de la Coopérative, 51480*
**Tel** *03 26 54 83 23* **Closed** *Sun &
Tue eves, Mon*
Dine on excellent *foie gras* salad
and duck breast in red wine inside
a rustic old vaulted cellar.

**EPERNAY: La Cave à
Champagne** €€
Traditional French
*16 rue Gambetta, 51200*
**Tel** *03 26 55 50 70* **Closed** *Tue & Wed*
Try the steak with Pinot Noir
sauce or the cod in Chardonnay
at this cosy restaurant that
reinvents classic French dishes
using local wines.

**EPERNAY: Les Berceaux** €€€
Regional
*13 rue des Berceaux, 51200*
**Tel** *03 26 55 28 84* **Closed** *Mon & Tue*
This centrally located hotel houses
both an upscale restaurant and
an informal bistro. They both
serve classic local cuisine, which
includes game dishes in season.

**GIFFAUMONT-CHAMPAUBERT:
La Grange aux Abeilles** €
Creperie
*4 rue du Grand Der, 51290*
**Tel** *03 26 72 61 97* **Closed** *Mon &
Tue, Wed eve*
An ancient beekeepers' barn has
been converted into a restaurant
and creperie. It is possible to buy
pots of honey, too. Good service.

**LANGRES: Restaurant
Diderot** €€
Traditional French
*4 rue de l'Estres, 52200*
**Tel** *03 25 87 07 00* **Closed** *Wed
lunch*
This elegant, beamed restaurant
specializes in putting creative
twists on classic French dishes. Try
the loin of lamb with fig juice, or
haddock in a bacon crust with
red wine. Hearty portions.

**MAGNANT: Le Val Moret** €€
Modern French
*Rue du Maréchal Leclerc, 10110*
**Tel** *03 25 29 85 12*
Chef Julien Lasserre offers
original takes on classic dishes.
Meat is sourced from the
adjacent farm owned by the
restaurant. The creative menu
changes seasonally.

**MAISONS LES CHAOURCE:
Aux Maisons** €€
Regional
*11 rue Anciens Combattants d'AFN,
10210*
**Tel** *03 25 70 07 19* **Closed** *Sun eve*
Authentic local fare with creative
variations is served in a converted
barn. The guinea fowl breast with
Marc de Champagne sauce is a
menu highlight.

**NOGENT-SUR-SEINE:
Le Beau Rivage** €€
Traditional French
*20 rue Villiers-aux-Choux, 10400*
**Tel** *03 25 39 84 22* **Closed** *Sun eve
& Mon*
Expect delicious food, old-school
service, and fabulous views of
the Seine at this restaurant.
The desserts are superb.

**PONT-SAINTE-MARIE:
Bistrot DuPont** €€
Traditional French
*5 pl Charles de Gaulle, 10150*
**Tel** *03 25 80 90 99* **Closed** *Mon,
Thu & Sun eves*
Staple bistro choices are on the
menu at this lively eatery. House
specials include homemade
*foie gras, coq au vin,* grilled
steak, and *andouillette de Troyes*
(pork sausages).

**REIMS: Brasserie du
Boulingrin** €€
Traditional French
*48 rue de Mars, 51100*
**Tel** *03 26 40 96 22* **Closed** *Sun*
A very popular meeting place for
locals, this eatery serves excellent
oysters and steak tartare.

> ## DK Choice
>
> **REIMS: Café du Palais** €€
> Traditional French
> *14 pl Myron Herrick, 51100*
> **Tel** *03 26 47 52 54* **Closed** *Sun,
> Mon; Tue–Fri dinner*
> Enter an Aladdin's cave of
> theatrical memorabilia under
> a heritage-listed stained-glass
> roof. A much-loved family-run
> brasserie, the Café du Palais
> offers excellent main dishes,
> great desserts, and a fine
> selection of Champagne.

**SERMIERS: Lys du Roy** €
Traditional French
*1 rte de Damery, 51500*
**Tel** *03 26 97 66 11* **Closed** *Mon & Tue
eves, Wed*
Quaint old-world exteriors and a
menu of classic choices with a
refined twist await here. The
specialties include homemade
*foie gras* and the entrecote steak
with Chaource cheese sauce.

**SEZANNE: Le Relais
Champenois** €€
Traditional French
*157 rue Notre Dame, 51120*
**Tel** *03 26 80 58 03* **Closed** *Sun &
Fri eves*
Eat among rustic beams and
copper saucepans. The chef
showcases local products in
dishes such as red mullet fillets
with Ratafia sauce, and duck
breast with Griotte cherries.

**TINQUEUX:
Assiette Champenoise** €€€
Traditional French
*40 av Paul Vaillant-Couturier, 51430*
**Tel** *03 26 84 64 64* **Closed** *Tue & Wed*
Enjoy exquisitely prepared
dishes of lobster, scallops,
turbot, and venison at this
delightful restaurant with
stylish modern interiors. There
is a choice of menus – the
lunchtime taster menu is
particularly recommended.

**TROYES: Aux Crieurs de Vin** €€
Bistro
*4 pl Jean Jaurès, 10000*
**Tel** *03 25 40 01 01* **Closed** *Sun & Mon*
The homemade cooking at
this lively wine store and bistro
with an informal atmosphere
and wooden tables and chairs
attracts both families and local
businesspeople. Try the local
specialty – *andouillette* sausage –
and wash it down with their
good choice of natural wines.

**TROYES: Le Valentino** €€
Regional
*35 rue Paillot de Montabert, 10000*
**Tel** *03 25 73 14 14* **Closed** *Sun & Mon*
The innovative menu at this
picturesque half-timbered
house with a courtyard for
outdoor dining features dishes
such as turbot with morel
mushroom sauce.

Exquisite fare laid out at the brasserie Café
du Palais, Reims

For more information on types of restaurants *see p575*

Gracefully laid table at the refined
L'Arnsbourg in Baerenthal

**VILLIERS-SUR-SUIZE:**
**Auberge de la Fontaine** €€
Traditional French
*2 pl de la Fontaine, 52210*
**Tel** *03 25 31 22 22* **Closed** *Sat lunch & Sun eve*
The menu offers lots of choice, the food is good and prices are fairly low. Great rustic setting.

**VINAY: La Briqueterie** €€€
Modern French
*4 rte de Sézanne, 51530*
**Tel** *03 26 59 99 99* **Closed** *Sat lunch*
Sitting pretty amid Champagne vineyards, this plush restaurant prepares creative dishes. The wine list showcases local champagnes.

## Alsace and Lorraine

**BAERENTHAL: L'Arnsbourg** €€€
Traditional French
*18 Untermuhlthal, 57230*
**Tel** *03 87 06 50 85* **Closed** *Mon & Tue*
Enjoy an outstanding dining experience at one of France's finest restaurants, tucked away in the countryside.

**BITCHE: Le Strasbourg** €€
Traditional French
*24 rue Col. Teyssier, 57230*
**Tel** *03 87 96 00 44* **Closed** *Sun eve, Mon, Tue lunch*
Try a wide range of fish dishes – Guilvinec sole, lobster, pike-perch – at this first-class restaurant with a big dining room. The home-made *foie gras* is also delicious.

**COLMAR: Wistub Brenner** €€
Regional
*1 rue de Turenne, 68000*
**Tel** *03 89 41 42 33*
Wistub Brenner is famous for its Alsatian dishes and cheery, unpretentious atmosphere. The salad with potent Munster cheese is particularly popular.

**COLMAR: JY's** €€€
Modern French
*17 rue de la Poissonerie 68000*
**Tel** *03 89 21 53 60* **Closed** *Sun & Mon*
Contemporary dining based on an audacious fusion of flavors can be sampled in this 17th-century building. Excellent wine list. Reasonable prices.

**ILLHAEUSERN:**
**L'Auberge de l'Ill** €€€
Regional
*2 rue de Collonges, 68970*
**Tel** *03 89 71 89 00* **Closed** *Mon & Tue*
This Michelin-starred establishment offers a varied selection of Alsatian dishes. Try the truffle wrapped in *fois gras*.

**KAYSERSBERG:**
**Restaurant Saint Alexis** €
Traditional French
*Lieu-dit Saint Alexis, 68240*
**Tel** *03 89 73 90 38* **Closed** *Fri*
This eatery in the mountains offers excellent traditional cooking, including delicious soups and omelets, plus game dishes and sauerkraut.

**LEMBACH: Gimbelhof** €€
Traditional French
*Rte Forestière, 67510*
**Tel** *03 88 94 43 58* **Closed** *Mon & Tue*
Surrounded by a forest and ruined medieval castles, Gimbelhof is a successful family-run hotel-restaurant.

**LES THONS: Le Couvent des Cordeliers** €
Regional
*Les Thons, 88410*
**Tel** *03 29 07 90 84* **Closed** *Mon & Tue–Fri eves*
The owner roasts slices of gammon on an open fire at this popular, friendly eatery. The steak with fried mushrooms is also recommended.

**MARLENHEIM: Le Cerf** €€€
Traditional French
*30 rue Général de Gaulle, 67520*
**Tel** *03 88 87 73 73* **Closed** *Tue & Wed*
At this half-timbered coaching inn with a cobblestone courtyard, dine on delicious dishes such as fillet of beef cooked in Licorne Black Beer served with seasonal vegetables.

**METZ: Le Bistro des Sommeliers** €€
Bistro
*10 rue Pasteur, 57000*
**Tel** *03 87 63 40 20* **Closed** *Sat lunch, Sun*
Sample excellent food and a wide range of wines in a brasserie setting. The fixed-price menu is great value.

**METZ: Le Magasin aux Vivres** €€
Traditional French
*5 av Ney, 57000*
**Tel** *03 87 17 17 17* **Closed** *Sat lunch, Sun eve & Mon*
This is a great place to enjoy good food in elegant historic surroundings. The dessert menu is outstanding. Cookery lessons are also offered.

**NANCY: Au Grand Serieux** €
Brasserie
*27 rue Raugraff, 54000*
**Tel** *03 83 36 68 87* **Closed** *Sun & Mon, Tue–Sat lunch, Fri eve*
A popular institution since 1870, this eatery serves a daily changing menu based on fresh market produce. Good local wine list. Friendly service.

**NANCY: La Poule'Ange** €€
Modern French
*74 rue Saint-Julien, 54000*
**Tel** *03 83 34 19 62* **Closed** *Sun eve, Mon*
Rustic-chic decor with comfortable chairs sets the scene at this landmark restaurant just five minutes' walk from Place Stanislas. The menu offers beautifully presented dishes such as seared prawns with carrot mousse and *langoustine bisque*.

**NIEDERSTEINBACH:**
**Au Wasigenstein** €€
Regional
*32 rue Principale Wengelsbach, 67510*
**Tel** *03 88 09 50 54* **Closed** *Mon & Tue; Nov–Feb: Sun–Thu*
This excellent village auberge in a stunning location boasts a lovely terrace for outdoor dining. On the menu is superb wild game.

**OBERNAI: La Fourchette des Ducs** €€€
Traditional French
*6 rue de la Gare, 67210*
**Tel** *03 88 48 33 38* **Closed** *Sun eve, Mon, Tue–Sat lunch*
A sophisticated dining experience based on authentic local flavors is guaranteed at this luxury restaurant, founded in the 1920s by local motoring genius Ettore Bugatti.

**RIBEAUVILLE: Zum Pfifferhüs** €€
Regional
*14 Grand'Rue, 68150*
**Tel** *03 89 73 62 28* **Closed** *Wed & Thu*
An authentic *winstub* on the main street, this charming wine bar and restaurant serves dishes such as ham hock, *choucroute*, and Mirabelle plum tart. There's a good selection of wine by the glass.

**RIQUEWIHR: Le Sarment d'Or** €€
Traditional French
*4 rue du Cerf, 68340*
**Tel** *03 89 86 02 86* **Closed** *Sun eve,*
*Mon, Tue lunch*
Fabulous food is served in this
17th-century house in a quiet
corner of this pretty village. The
elegantly decorated beamed
dining room adds to the charm.
Great attention to detail.

**SAVERNE: Taverne Katz** €€
Regional
*80 Grand Rue, 67700*
**Tel** *03 88 71 16 56* **Closed** *Mon*
*& Thu eves*
The braised hock in beer is the
highlight of the menu at this
restaurant with stunning exterior
and beautifully paneled interiors.

**STRASBOURG: Winstub**
**Zuem Strissel** €
Regional
*5 pl de la Grande Boucherie, 67000*
**Tel** *03 88 32 14 73*
Good-value brasserie-style food
is served at this restaurant dating
from the 1300s. Try the *bibelekäse*
(cream cheese and fries).

---

**DK Choice**

**STRASBOURG: Buerehiesel** €€€
Traditional French
*4 Parc de Orangerie, 67000*
**Tel** *038 84 56 65* **Closed** *Sun &*
*Mon*
Buerehiesel is a unique Michelin-
starred restaurant that gave up
its three Rosettes to give clients
a better deal. Now it serves great
food without all the bells and
whistles that go with such star-
rated establishments.

---

**WISSEMBOURG:**
**Daniel Rebert** €
Bistro
*7 pl du Marché aux Choux, 67100*
**Tel** *03 88 94 01 66* **Closed** *Mon*
This lovely patisserie has a
discreet tearoom at the back
serving light lunches and coffee,
plus exquisite cakes.

---

# Normandy

**ACQUIGNY:**
**Hostellerie d'Acquigny** €€
Traditional French
*1 rue Evreux, 27400*
**Tel** *02 32 50 20 05* **Closed** *Sun eve,*
*Mon & Tue*
This former coaching inn houses
a smart restaurant with good-
value set menus, which include
vegetarian options, great service
and an eclectic wine list.

**ALENCON: Le Bistro** €€
Bistro
*21 rue de Sarthe, 61000*
**Tel** *02 33 26 51 69* **Closed** *Sun & Mon*
Featuring a well-stocked wine
list, this classic French bistro
also has a distinctive green-
painted facade, red-chequered
tablecloths, and old movie posters.

**AUMALE: La Villa des Houx** €€
Regional
*6 av Général de Gaulle, 76390*
**Tel** *02 35 93 93 30* **Closed** *Oct–Mar:*
*Sun eve*
Housed in a former police
station, this restaurant offers a
taste of real Normandy cuisine.
Try the apricot *foie gras* starter.

**BARNEVILLE-CARTERET:**
**Marine** €€
Traditional French
*11 rue de Paris, 50270*
**Tel** *02 33 53 83 31* **Closed** *Nov–*
*mid-Mar*
The wine list matches the
exquisite food at this modern,
stylish dining room with a
panoramic view of the port.
Excellent service.

**BAYEUX: Le Lion d'Or** €€
Traditional French
*71 rue St-Jean, 14400*
**Tel** *02 31 92 06 90* **Closed** *Tue*
*& Sat lunch; mid-Nov–mid-Mar:*
*Mon eve*
Le Lion d'Or serves a range
of well-prepared, traditional
Normandy dishes in a converted
18th-century post office. The
desserts are a highlight.
Reservations are recommended.

**BEUVRON-EN-AUGE:**
**Le Pavé Auge** €€
Regional
*Les Halles, 14430*
**Tel** *02 31 79 26 71* **Closed** *Mon & Tue*
Once a village market hall, this
restaurant uses locally sourced
produce. The focus is on fish.

Beautiful glass-covered dining area at
Buerehiesel in Strasbourg

**BLAINVILLE-SUR-MER:**
**Le Mascaret** €€
Modern French
*1 rue de Bas, 50560*
**Tel** *02 33 45 86 09* **Closed** *Sep–mid-*
*Jul: Sun & Mon*
Experience top experimental
cuisine, made with fresh, home-
grown produce. The five-course
tasting menu is great value.

**BRICQUEVILLE-SUR-MER:**
**Couleurs Saveurs** €€
Modern French
*2 rte de Bretonnière, 50290*
**Tel** *02 33 61 65 62* **Closed** *Wed;*
*Mon & Sun eves*
The modern dining room of this
coastal restaurant sets the stage
for a menu where regional
produce meets Oriental spices.

**CAEN: Le Pressoir –**
**Ivan Vautier** €€€
Fine dining
*3 av Henry-Chéron, 14000*
**Tel** *02 31 73 32 71* **Closed** *Mon &*
*Sun eve*
Award-winning chef Ivan Vautier
creates delectable dishes for
discerning guests, with emphasis
on using the best local produce.

**CHERBOURG: Le Faitout** €€
Bistro
*25 rue Tour-Carrée, 50100*
**Tel** *02 33 04 25 04* **Closed** *Sun;*
*Mon–Wed lunch*
A bastion of culinary tradition,
Le Faitout is an animated
bistro-style restaurant serving
wholesome dishes.

**DEAUVILLE: Le Spinnaker** €€
Seafood
*52 rue Mirabeau, 14800*
**Tel** *02 31 88 24 40* **Closed** *Mon*
*& Tue*
One of Normandy's finest fish
restaurants, Le Spinnaker has an
attractive modern dining room.
It also offers grilled meat dishes.

**DIEPPE: Bistrot du Pollet** €€
Bistro
*23 rue Tête de Boeuf, 76200*
**Tel** *02 35 84 68 57* **Closed** *Sun*
*& Mon*
Reservations are strongly
recommended at this small,
friendly eatery with a simple
but wholesome menu. Try the
haddock salad or grilled sardines.

**FALAISE: L'Attache** €€
Traditional French
*Rte de Caen, 14700*
**Tel** *02 31 90 05 38* **Closed** *Tue*
*& Wed*
The chef uses unusual plants
and aromatic herbs to flavor
his cooking at this beautifully
renovated former staging post.

For more information on types of restaurants *see p575*

**FECAMP: La Marée** €€
Seafood
*77 quai Bérigny, 76400*
**Tel** *02 35 29 39 15* **Closed** *Mon, Thu & Sun eves*
This very popular and lively first-floor restaurant offers huge seafood platters and views of the fishing port.

**GISORS: Le Cappeville** €€
Regional
*17 rue Cappeville, 27410*
**Tel** *02 32 55 11 08* **Closed** *Wed & Thu*
Sample the refined dishes at this elegantly furbished converted townhouse. Impressive cheeseboard on offer.

**GRANVILLE: La Citadelle** €€
Seafood
*34 rue du Port, 50406*
**Tel** *02 33 50 34 10* **Closed** *Wed; Oct–Mar: Tue*
Overlooking the bay of St.-Michel, this charming restaurant is said to serve the biggest portions of sole in town. There are various fixed menus to choose from.

**HONFLEUR:**
**La Ferme St.-Siméon** €€€
Fine dining
*Rue A. Marais, 14600*
**Tel** *02 31 81 78 00*
There is an excellent wine list to go with the delectable fish on offer at this luxurious spa-hotel restaurant.

**JUVIGNY-SOUS-ANDAINE:**
**Au Bon Accueil** €€
Traditional French
*23 pl St.-Michel, 61140*
**Tel** *02 33 38 10 04* **Closed** *Sun eve, Mon*
Good menus are prepared from fresh local produce at this stylish restaurant offering creative French cuisine.

**LA CROIX ST.-LEUFROY:**
**Le Cheval Blanc** €€
Traditional French
*27 rue de Louviers, 27490*
**Tel** *02 32 34 82 86* **Closed** *Sun & Tue eves, Wed*
Drive out to a quiet village in the Eure Valley for a taste of top-notch cuisine. Excellent cheese selection and good-value fixed-price menu.

**LA FERRIERE AUX ETANGS:**
**Auberge de la Mine** €€
Regional
*Le Gué-Plat, 61450*
**Tel** *02 33 66 91 10* **Closed** *Sun eve, Mon & Tue*
Authentic Norman dishes are prepared with refreshing originality at this auberge. The desserts are to die for.

Entrance to the ever-popular brasserie La Mère Poulard, Mont-St.-Michel

**LE BREUIL-EN-AUGE:**
**Le Dauphin** €€
Traditional French
*2 rue de l'Eglise, 14130*
**Tel** *02 31 65 08 11* **Closed** *Sun eve, Mon*
The chef at this restaurant in a half-timbered Normandy house reinvents classic dishes using the best local produce.

**LE HAVRE: Jean-Luc**
**Tartarin** €€€
Fine dining
*73 av Foch, 76600*
**Tel** *02 35 45 46 20* **Closed** *Sun & Mon*
Diners come to this restaurant for the imaginative dishes based on produce sourced from local farms and fishing harbors, accompanied by fine service.

**LES ANDELYS: La Chaine d'Or** €€
Traditional French
*27 rue Grande, 27700*
**Tel** *02 32 54 00 31* **Closed** *Sun eve, Tue*
Exquisite culinary classics, perfectly prepared, can be enjoyed in a romantic setting on the banks of the Seine.

**LYONS-LA-FORET:**
**Le Grand Cerf** €€
Bistro
*20 pl Isaac Benserade, 27480*
**Tel** *02 32 49 50 50* **Closed** *Mon & Tue*
Hearty homemade fare is complemented by the rustic setting at Le Grand Cerf. Oak beams and bare red-brick walls add to the charm.

**MONT-ST.-MICHEL:**
**La Mère Poulard** €€€
Brasserie
*Grande Rue, 50170*
**Tel** *02 33 89 68 68*
Visitors from across the world stop at this historic restaurant for omelets cooked in a long-handled pan over a fire.

**PONT L'EVEQUE:**
**Auberge des Deux Tonneaux** €€
Bistro
*Pierrefitte en Auge, 14130*
**Tel** *02 31 64 09 31* **Closed** *Mon eve, Tue*
Robust dishes and local ciders are served at this thatched cottage. The shady terrace has valley views.

**PONT SAINT-PIERRE:**
**Auberge de l'Andelle** €€
Traditional French
*27 Grande Rue, 27360*
**Tel** *02 32 49 70 18* **Closed** *Oct–mid-Mar: Tue eve*
Pick a live lobster from the tank and have it cooked to perfection at this rustic dining room.

**ROUEN: Le 37** €€
Bistro
*37 rue St.-Etienne-des-Tonneliers, 76000*
**Tel** *02 35 70 56 65* **Closed** *Sun & Mon*
This attractive downtown bistro serves modern cuisine. Find the daily specials on the chalkboard.

> **DK Choice**
>
> **ROUEN: Restaurant Gill** €€€
> Fine dining
> *8–9 quai de la Bourse, 76000*
> **Tel** *02 35 71 16 14* **Closed** *Sun & Mon*
> This highly recommended restaurant is located on the banks of the Seine and has an elegant dining room. Try the roast turbot. There is also a tasting menu.

**STE.-CECILE:**
**Le Manoir de l'Archerie** €€
Traditional French
*37 rue Michel de l'Epinay, 50800*
**Tel** *02 33 51 13 87* **Closed** *Mon; Oct–Mar: Sun eve*
Fresh Normandy produce is served in a beautiful manor house. Also on the menu is a good selection of local cheeses.

**TROUVILLE-SUR-MER:**
**La Régence** €€
Seafood
*132 bd Fernand Moureaux, 14360*
**Tel** *02 31 88 10 71* **Closed** *Winter: Wed & Thu*
The shellfish is a house specialty at La Régence, a beautiful restaurant featuring mirrors and 19th-century wood paneling.

**VEULES LES ROSES: Les Galets** €€
Seafood
*3 rue Victor Hugo, 76980*
**Tel** *02 35 97 61 33* **Closed** *Wed (except Aug) & Tue*
Close to the pebbly beach, this traditional restaurant has a comfortable dining area.

**VILLERS BOCAGE:**
**Les Trois Rois** €€
Traditional French
*2 pl Jeanne d'Arc, 14310*
**Tel** *02 31 77 00 32* **Closed** *Winter: Sun eve & Mon lunch*
Located on a vast square surrounded by gardens, this restaurant serves generous portions of classic local dishes.

# Brittany

**ARRADON:**
**Les Logoden** €
Creperie
*24 rue Albert-Danet, 56610*
**Tel** *02 97 46 79 03* **Closed** *Sun lunch, Mon & Tue*
The authentic and delicious *crêpes* prepared here feature a different filling each week. The produce is sourced from neighboring farms.

**AUDIERNE: Le Goyen** €€
Seafood
*Pl Jean-Simon, 29770*
**Tel** *02 98 70 08 88* **Closed** *Jan–Mar*
Sample fresh oysters and excellent seafood platters at this hotel-restaurant by the sea. Try the scrumptious pan-fried scallops.

**BELLE ILE EN MER:**
**La Désirade** €€
Seafood
*Le Petit Cosquet, 56360*
**Tel** *02 97 31 70 70* **Closed** *Mon–Fri lunch*
This farmhouse restaurant offers a great breakfast menu in addition to fantastic seafood.

**BREST: Le M** €€€
Fine dining
*22 rue du Commandant Drogou, 29200*
**Tel** *02 98 47 90 00*
A typical granite-built manor house with a contemporary dining room, Le M serves a range of inventive dishes. Pretty garden terrace with outdoor tables for alfresco dining in good weather.

**CARANTEC:**
**Restaurant Patrick Jeoffroy** €€€
Fine dining
*20 rue Kélénn, 29660*
**Tel** *02 98 67 00 47* **Closed** *Sun eve, Mon & Tue*
Classic food with a modern twist is served in this sleek restaurant with views over Kélénn beach. Try the line-caught sea bass.

**CARNAC: Le Calypso** €€
Seafood
*158 rte du Pô, 56340*
**Tel** *02 97 52 06 14* **Closed** *Sun eve, Mon*
This popular seafood restaurant overlooks the oyster beds of Anse du Pô. Great service.

**CONCARNEAU:**
**Le Petit Chaperon Rouge** €
Creperie
*7 pl Duguesclin, 29900*
**Tel** *02 98 60 53 32* **Closed** *Sun eve, Mon*
Near the harbor, this lovely creperie has decor inspired by "Little Red Riding Hood".

**DINAN: Ma Mère Pourcel** €€
Traditional French
*3 pl des Merciers, 22100*
**Tel** *02 96 39 03 80* **Closed** *Sun & Tue eves, Wed*
Enjoy locally reared lamb and a variety of innovative fish dishes at this restaurant inside a medieval half-timbered building.

**DOUARNENEZ: Insolite** €€
Modern French
*4 rue Jean Jaurès, 29100*
**Tel** *02 98 92 00 02* **Closed** *Sun eve, Mon*
Original dishes blended with regional produce and Eastern spices at this stylish restaurant.

**FOUESNANT CAP COZ: Restaurant de la Pointe du Cap Coz** €€
Traditional French
*153 av de la Pointe, 29170*
**Tel** *02 98 56 01 63* **Closed** *Mon & Wed; Sep–Jun: Sun & Tue eves*
Top-notch cuisine is served in a dining room decorated to complement the coastal setting.

**FOUGERES: Haute Sève** €€
Regional
*37 bd Jean Jaurès, 35300*
**Tel** *02 99 94 23 39* **Closed** *Sun eve, Mon*
The timbered facade belies the vibrant modern interior that acts as a backdrop for a range of regional classics with a twist.

**GUIMILIAU: Ar Chupen** €
Creperie
*43 rue de Calvaire, 29400*
**Tel** *02 98 68 73 63* **Closed** *Winter: Fri eve & Sat lunch*
Traditional galettes and *crêpes* made to order ensure that this renovated Breton farmhouse is a budget winner.

**GUINGAMP:**
**Le Clos de la Fontaine** €€
Traditional French
*9 rue du Général de Gaulle, 22200*
**Tel** *02 96 21 33 63* **Closed** *Sun eve, Mon; Sep–Jun: Tue eve*
Wonderful fish dishes are served with delicate sauces at this eatery. The chef uses only the best local produce.

**HEDE: L'Hostellerie du Vieux Moulin** €€
Traditional French
*Ancienne rte de St.-Malo, 35630*
**Tel** *02 99 45 45 70* **Closed** *Mon, Sun & Thu lunch*
There are good-value lunchtime menus to be had at this place overlooking Hédé Castle. The menu changes seasonally.

**ILE DE NOIRMOUTIER:**
**Le Grand Four** €€
Seafood
*1 rue de la Cure, 85330*
**Tel** *02 51 39 61 97* **Closed** *Jan & Dec; Winter: Sun eve, Thu lunch; Jul–Aug: Mon*
Dine in a 17th-century house with pink shutters and cloaked in green ivy. Also on offer is a decent selection of Loire wines.

**LORIENT: Le Neptune** €€
Seafood
*15 av de la Perrière, 56100*
**Tel** *02 97 37 04 56* **Closed** *Sun*
The haul at the nearby Keroman fishing port determines the dish of the day at Le Neptune. Trendy modern decor.

**LORIENT: L'Amphitryon** €€€
Fine dining
*127 rue du Colonel Jean Müller, 56100*
**Tel** *02 97 83 34 04* **Closed** *Sun & Mon*
Inspirational cuisine is prepared with simplicity in the stylish surroundings of L'Amphitryon. There is a good choice of wines by the glass.

Spacious dining area at Restaurant Patrick Jeoffroy, Carantec

**For more information on types of restaurants** *see p575*

**PAIMPOL: L'Islandais** €
Creperie
*19 quai Morand, 22500*
**Tel** *02 96 20 93 80*
A dockside restaurant with an aquatic theme, L'Islandais serves a wide range of tasty sweet and savory galettes.

### DK Choice

**PLOMODIERN:**
**Auberge des Glazicks** €€€
Fine dining
*7 rue de la Plage, 29550*
**Tel** *02 98 81 52 32* **Closed** *Mon & Tue*
Headed by Olivier Bellin, this award-winning restaurant has stunning views over the Bay of Douarnenez. The celebrated chef uses Breton produce to create sublime and original food.

**PLOUBALAY: La Gare** €€
Regional
*4 rue des Ormelets, 22650*
**Tel** *02 96 27 25 16* **Closed** *Jul & Aug: Mon & Tue; Sep–Jun: Mon & Tue eves, Wed*
Market-driven dishes are given a modern twist in this restaurant with two dining rooms, one of which opens out on to a terrace.

**QUIMPER: L'Ambroisie** €€
Modern French
*49 rue Elie Fréron, 29000*
**Tel** *02 98 95 00 02* **Closed** *Sun eve, Mon*
Located close to the cathedral, this atmospheric restaurant offers both modern and classical fare.

**RENNES: Essential** €€
Modern French
*11 rue Armand Rébillon, 35000*
**Tel** *02 99 14 25 14* **Closed** *Sat lunch & Sun*
Dine on contemporary bistro-style cuisine in a distinctive glass cube-shaped restaurant.

**RENNES:**
**La Fontaine aux Perles** €€€
Fine dining
*96 rue de la Poterie, 35000*
**Tel** *02 99 53 90 90* **Closed** *Sun eve, Mon; Aug: Sun–Tue*
This manor house provides the perfect setting for delights such as John Dory flavored with sweet spices and pineapple.

**ROSCOFF: L'Ecume des Jours** €€
Traditional French
*Quai d'Auxerre, 29680*
**Tel** *02 98 61 22 83* **Closed** *Sep–Jul: Tue & Wed*
An authentic 16th-century ship-owner's house offers a wide range of local coastal produce.

**ST.-BRIEUC: Air du Temps** €€
Bistro
*4 rue du Gouët, 22000*
**Tel** *02 96 68 58 40* **Closed** *Sun & Mon*
Try the pork casserole at this pleasant eatery, where the modern decor offsets the historic stone walls.

**ST.-MALO: Le Chalut** €€
Seafood
*8 rue de la Corne de Cerf, 35400*
**Tel** *02 99 56 71 58* **Closed** *Mon & Tue*
Fishing nets, buoys, and an aquarium provide the perfect ambience to this seafood eatery.

**TREGUIER: Aigue Marine** €€€
Seafood
*5 rue Marcelin Berthelot, 22220*
**Tel** *02 96 92 97 00* **Closed** *Sun eve, Mon, Sat lunch; Jan & Feb*
This fine restaurant in a harbor-front hotel serves sublime fish. Fixed-price menus available.

**VANNES: Dan Ewen** €
Creperie
*3 pl Général de Gaulle, 56000*
**Tel** *02 97 42 44 34* **Closed** *Sun*
The decor may be a little worn and rustic, but this creperie serves the best buckwheat pancakes in town.

**VANNES: L'Eden** €€
Modern French
*3 rue Pasteur, 56000*
**Tel** *02 97 46 42 62* **Closed** *Sun & Mon*
A local favorite, this restaurant prepares contemporary dishes with originality.

# The Loire Valley

**AMBOISE: Le 36** €€€
Fine dining
*36 quai C. Guinot, 37400*
**Tel** *02 47 30 63 36* **Closed** *Nov–Mar: Tue & Wed*
Serving seasonal food, Le 36 also offers a pretty garden and Loire views from the dining room.

Exquisitely decorated dining space at Le 36, Amboise

**ANCENIS:**
**Les Terrasses de Bel Air** €€
Traditional French
*Rte d'Angers, 44150*
**Tel** *02 40 83 02 87* **Closed** *Sun eve, Mon*
Classic cuisine is prepared creatively in this 18th-century manor house with a garden.

**ANGERS: Ma Campagne** €€
Traditional French
*14 promenade de la Reculée, 49000*
**Tel** *02 41 48 38 06* **Closed** *Sun eve, Mon*
Select one of the chef's famous chocolate creations for dessert at this country-style auberge very close to the town center.

**BEAUGENCY: Le Petit Bateau** €€
Modern French
*54 rue du Pont, 45190*
**Tel** *02 38 44 56 38* **Closed** *Mon & Tue*
This appealing restaurant reinvents classic dishes. Specialties include fresh fish and wild mushrooms.

**BLOIS: Côté Loire** €€
Traditional French
*2 pl de la Grève, 41000*
**Tel** *02 54 78 07 86* **Closed** *Sun & Mon*
Enjoy the simple but delicious menu at this old-fashioned hotel-restaurant overlooking the River Loire.

**BLOIS: Orangerie du Château** €€€
Fine dining
*1 av Jean Laigret, 41000*
**Tel** *02 54 78 05 36* **Closed** *Sun & Mon*
Excellent regional food and wines are served in the beautiful winter gardens of this château.

**BOURGES: Le Cercle** €€
Modern French
*44 bd Lahitolle, 18000*
**Tel** *02 48 70 33 27* **Closed** *Sun & Mon*
In a lovely manor house, this contemporary restaurant offers modern, inventive cuisine.

**BOURGES: Le Louis XI** €€
Bistro
*11 rue Porte Jaune, 11000*
**Tel** *02 48 70 92 14* **Closed** *Sep–Jun: Sun & Mon*
Enjoy large portions of classic, no-frills bistro fare and a convivial ambience. Good service.

**BOURGUEIL: Le Moulin Bleu** €€
Traditional French
*7 rue du Moulin Bleu, 37140*
**Tel** *02 47 97 73 13* **Closed** *Wed & Sun–Tue eves; off-season: Sun–Thu, Fri lunch & Sat lunch*
Traditional dishes are served in two vaulted dining rooms at Le Moulin Bleu. Great location and friendly service.

**BRACIEUX: Le Rendez-vous des Gourmets** €€
Regional
*20 rue Roger Brun, 41250*
**Tel** *02 54 46 03 87* **Closed** *Wed, Sat lunch; mid-Aug & mid-Jul: Sun eve, Mon lunch*
Be sure to make a reservation at this very popular auberge serving traditional regional food.

**CHARTRES: Le Grand Monarque – Le Georges** €€€
Fine dining
*22 pl des Epars, 28000*
**Tel** *02 37 18 15 15* **Closed** *Sun & Mon*
*Grands crus* wines accompany the very best of classic French cuisine at this gourmet restaurant.

**CHINON: Les Années 30** €€
Modern French
*78 rue Haute St-Maurice, 37500*
**Tel** *02 47 93 37 18* **Closed** *Wed; Sep–Jun: Tue*
Interesting dishes such as fillet of veal with a tajine of dried fruit and sweet potato gnocchi feature on the menu at this elegant eatery.

**CLISSON: La Bonne Auberge** €€
Traditional French
*1 rue Olivier de Clisson, 44190*
**Tel** *02 40 54 01 90* **Closed** *Sun eve, Mon, Tue lunch, Wed eve*
This auberge has three dining rooms. Specialties include seafood and game (in season).

**CONTRES: La Botte d'Asperges** €
Traditional French
*52 rue Pierre-Henri Mauger, 41700*
**Tel** *02 54 79 50 49* **Closed** *Sun eve, Mon*
Locally grown asparagus features prominently on the menu, when in season. Delicious food served in a contemporary setting.

**DOUE LA FONTAINE: Auberge Bienvenue** €€
Traditional French
*104 rte de Cholet, 49700*
**Tel** *02 41 59 22 44* **Closed** *Sun eve, Mon*
Hearty meals made with local produce, often doused in regional wines, are on the menu at this pretty inn. Opt for the roast turbot with a creamy Savennieres sauce.

**FONTEVRAUD ABBAYE: La Licorne** €€
Traditional French
*allée Sainte-Catherine, 49590*
**Tel** *02 41 51 72 49* **Closed** *Mon, Sun & Wed eves; Oct–Easter*
Next to the splendid abbey, this popular restaurant has a lovely courtyard terrace and an elegant dining room. It serves delicately flavored dishes. Reserve.

Entrance to Le Georges, the restaurant of Le Grand Monarque, Chartres

**GENNES: Auberge du Moulin de Sarré** €
Traditional French
*Rte de Louerre, 49350*
**Tel** *02 41 51 81 32* **Closed** *Mon–Fri (but will open for parties of at least 12 people)*
Sample robust cuisine in a 16th-century watermill. Ask for the local specialty, *fouées* (warm bread puffs cooked in a wood-fired oven).

**GENNES: L'Aubergade** €€€
Fine dining
*7 av des Cadets de Saumur, 49350*
**Tel** *02 41 51 81 07* **Closed** *Tue & Wed*
Two elegantly laid-out dining rooms serve up a variety of dishes with exotic flavors.

**ILE D'YEU: Les Bafouettes** €€
Seafood
*8 rue Gabriel-Guist'Hau, 84350*
**Tel** *02 51 59 38 38* **Closed** *Mon; Sep–Mar: Sun*
Traditional fish dishes and *foie gras* feature prominently on the menu of this unpretentious restaurant. The small dining room fills up quickly, so reserve ahead.

**LA FERTE IMBAULT: La Tête de Lard** €€
Traditional French
*13 pl des Tilleuls, 41300*
**Tel** *02 54 96 22 32* **Closed** *Sun eve, Mon, Tue lunch*
Housed in a refurbished country hotel, La Tête de Lard has a great menu that offers seasonal choices. It features a lovely summer terrace.

**LAMOTTE BEUVRON: Hôtel Tatin** €€
Traditional French
*5 av de Vierzon, 41600*
**Tel** *02 54 88 00 03* **Closed** *Sun eve, Mon, Tue lunch*
Serving fresh local produce, *foie gras* and homemade *pâté*, this hotel-restaurant is also a great place to try a typical *tarte Tatin*.

**LANGEAIS: Au Coin des Halles** €€
Bistro
*9 rue Gambetta, 37120*
**Tel** *02 47 96 37 25* **Closed** *Wed & Thu*
Combining chic interiors with excellent cuisine, Au Coin des Halles is a top-notch bistro. In summer, ask for a table in the garden. Reservations essential.

**LE MANS: Auberge des 7 Plats** €€
Traditional French
*79 Grande Rue*
**Tel** *02 43 24 57 77* **Closed** *Sun & Mon*
Select from the seven starters, seven mains, and 14 desserts on the menu at this unique eatery located in the old town.

**LE MANS: Le Beaulieu** €€
Fine dining
*34 bis place de la République, 72000*
**Tel** *02 43 87 78 37* **Closed** *Sat & Sun*
This sophisticated downtown restaurant offers superb seasonal menus accompanied by fine service.

**MALICORNE-SUR-SARTHE: La Petite Auberge** €€
Traditional French
*5 pl du Guesclin, 72270*
**Tel** *02 43 94 80 52* **Closed** *Sun–Thu eves; Mon*
Gourmet food can be enjoyed in a charming setting at La Petite Auberge. In summer, it is possible to dine on the lovely terrace; in winter, diners take refuge around the huge fireplace.

**MONTBAZON: La Chancelière** €€
Modern French
*1 pl des Marronniers, 37250*
**Tel** *02 47 26 00 67* **Closed** *Sun & Mon*
Modern, sophisticated cuisine is prepared with great precision and attention to detail at this chic and elegant restaurant.

For more information on types of restaurants *see p575*

**MONTSOREAU: Diane de Méridor** €€
Fine dining
*12 quai Philippe de Commines, 49730*
**Tel** *02 41 51 71 76* **Closed** *Tue & Wed*
Carved out of tuffeau rock, this restaurant has exposed beams and an open fireplace. Specializes in freshwater fish dishes.

**NANTES: La Cigale** €€
Brasserie
*4 pl Graslin, 44000*
**Tel** *02 51 84 94 94*
This ornate *belle époque* brasserie dates from 1895. The quality of food perfectly matches the exceptional interiors.

**NANTES: L'Océanide** €€
Seafood
*2 rue Paul Bellamy, 44000*
**Tel** *02 40 20 32 28* **Closed** *Sun, Mon lunch*
A first-class seafood restaurant, this place was designed during World War II to resemble the interior of an ocean liner.

### DK Choice

**NANTES: L'U.Ni** €€
Modern French
*36 rue Fouré*
**Tel** *02 40 75 53 05* **Closed** *Mon & Tue*
Serving creative food in a modern setting, L'U.Ni has made a name for itself in gourmet circles. Good-value lunch menus include dishes such as monkfish with yellow carrot purée flavored with citrus fruit, followed by hazelnut dacquoise.

**ONZAIN: Domaine des Hauts de Loire** €€€
Fine dining
*Rte de Herbault, 41150*
**Tel** *02 54 20 72 57* **Closed** *Wed–Fri lunch; Oct–Apr: Mon & Tue*
Award-winning cuisine is served in a former hunting lodge set within its own park.

**ORLEANS: La Dariole** €€
Traditional French
*25 rue Etienne Dolet, 45000*
**Tel** *02 38 77 26 67* **Closed** *Sat & Sun; Mon, Wed & Thu eves*
A 15th-century half-timbered building houses this little restaurant and tearoom. Great cakes.

**ORLEANS: Le Lièvre Gourmand** €€
Modern French
*28 quai de Chatelet, 45000*
**Tel** *02 38 53 66 14* **Closed** *Tue*
The all-white decor belies the exciting menu at this restaurant. Original dishes include mullet with seaweed and coriander.

**ROCHECORBON: Les Hautes Roches** €€€
Fine dining
*86 quai Loire, 37210*
**Tel** *02 47 52 88 88* **Closed** *Sun eve, Mon*
This château dining room with an elegant and contemporary interior serves meticulously prepared classic cuisine.

**SACHE: Auberge du XIIème Siècle** €€
Traditional French
*1 rue du Château, 37190*
**Tel** *02 47 26 88 77* **Closed** *Sun eve, Mon, Tue lunch*
A good choice of fixed-price menus built around classic dishes is served in historic surrounds.

**ST.-OUEN LES VIGNES: L'Aubinière** €€
Traditional French
*29 rue Jules Gautier, 37530*
**Tel** *02 47 30 15 29* **Closed** *Mon; Oct–May: Tue lunch*
L'Aubinière is a small but lovely restaurant that produces outstanding dishes. It features a pretty garden leading down to the river.

**SANCERRE: Auberge La Pomme d'Or** €€
Traditional French
*Pl de la Mairie, 18300*
**Tel** *02 48 54 13 30* **Closed** *Tue & Wed; Oct–Mar: Sun eve*
Enjoy Chavignol goat's cheese and other flavorsome dishes based on seasonal, regional produce with a glass of Sancerre wine.

**SANCERRE: La Tour** €€
Modern French
*31 Nouvelle Place, 18300*
**Tel** *02 48 54 00 81* **Closed** *Sun eve, Mon*
With views over the Sancerre vineyards, this elegant restaurant

The exterior of Domaine des Hauts de Loire, a popular restaurant in Onzain

serves contemporary cuisine using the best local produce. Fine selection of red and white wines from Sancerre.

**SAUMUR: L'Escargot** €€
Traditional French
*30 rue du Maréchal Leclerc, 49400*
**Tel** *02 41 51 20 88* **Closed** *Tue, Wed, Sat lunch*
Unpretentious eatery serving good, simple dishes, including turbot and slow-braised lamb.

**TOURS: L'Atelier Gourmand** €€
Traditional French
*37 rue Etienne Marcel, 37000*
**Tel** *02 47 38 59 87* **Closed** *Sat lunch–Mon*
This charming restaurant in the old part of Tours offers an interesting menu at competitive prices. The dishes are beautifully presented. Good wine list.

**TOURS: L'Odéon** €€
Brasserie
*10 pl du Général Leclerc, 37000*
**Tel** *02 47 20 12 65* **Closed** *Mon & Sat lunch; Sun*
A quality Art Deco-style restaurant, L'Odéon creatively reinvents traditional French regional dishes.

**TOURS: Les Saveurs** €€
Bistro
*1 pl Gaston Paillhou, 37000*
**Tel** *02 47 37 03 13* **Closed** *Sun & Mon*
The tasty dishes at this chic, modern city-center bistro are based around seasonal produce sourced from the daily market.

**TOURS: La Roche Le Roy** €€€
Fine dining
*55 rte de St.-Avertin, 37000*
**Tel** *02 47 27 22 00* **Closed** *Sun & Mon*
Fine Loire and Bordeaux wines accompany the classic top-notch French cuisine at this Michelin-starred restaurant.

**VALAIRE: L'Herbe Rouge** €
Bistro
*Le Bourg, 41120*
**Tel** *02 54 44 98 14* **Closed** *Mon & Tue; winter*
At this excellent country bistro nestled in tiny Valaire, the focus is firmly on organic vegetables, farm-reared meat, and natural wines.

**VENDOME: La Vallée** €€
Traditional French
*34 rue Barré-de-St.-Venant, 41100*
**Tel** *02 54 77 29 93* **Closed** *Sun eve, Mon & Tue*
Diners flock here to enjoy well-prepared traditional dishes in a rustic dining room. Good choice of regional wines.

The elegant, minimalist lines of Le Jardin Gourmand, Auxerre

**VIGNOUX-SUR-BARANGEON:**
**Le Prieuré** €€
Traditional French
*2 rte de St.-Laurent, 18500*
**Tel** *02 48 51 58 80* **Closed** *Oct–May: Tue & Wed*
Meals for the discerning diner are served in the elegant dining room or on the covered terrace.

**VOUVRAY: Les Geules Noires** €€
Traditional French
*66 vallée Coquette, 37210*
**Tel** *02 47 52 62 18* **Closed** *Sun eve, Mon; Sep–May: Tue*
Carved into a cave, this place is ideal for wine lovers. Be sure to try sweet Vouvray with your dessert. Daily changing menu.

# Burgundy and Franche-Comté

**ARBOIS: Jean-Paul Jeunet** €€€
Fine dining
*9 rue de l'Hôtel de Ville, 39600*
**Tel** *03 84 66 05 67* **Closed** *Jul–Aug: lunch; Sep–Jun*
The famous chef creates dishes such as Bresse chicken gently poached in Jura wine, or guinea fowl cooked with Danané pepper and served with Trousseau jelly. In a lovely location, the restaurant has a pretty terrace and attentive staff.

**ARNAY LE DUC:**
**Chez Camille** €€
Traditional French
*1 pl Edouard Herriot, 21230*
**Tel** *03 80 90 01 38*
Come to Chez Camille's stone-walled dining room to savor hearty dishes such as rabbit *pâté* and game.

**AUTUN: Les Ursulines** €€
Fine dining
*14 rue de Rivault, 71400*
**Tel** *03 85 86 58 58* **Closed** *Mon–Fri lunch*
The turbot and duck fillet are superb at this elegant restaurant serving gourmet fare.

**AUXERRE: Le Jardin Gourmand** €€
Modern French
*56 bd Vauban, 89000*
**Tel** *03 86 51 53 52* **Closed** *Mon & Tue; Sep–Jun: Sun eve*
Inventive dishes and a legendary veal are served in an attractive room. The chef grows his own herbs and vegetables.

**AVALLON: Relais des**
**Gourmets** €€
Traditional French
*45–47 rue de Paris, 89200*
**Tel** *03 86 34 18 90* **Closed** *Sun eve, Mon*
Choose from unpretentious fixed-priced menus at this traditional auberge with two dining rooms.

**BEAUNE: Le Bistro de L'Hôtel** €€
Bistro
*3 rue Samuel Legay, 21200*
**Tel** *03 80 25 94 10* **Closed** *Sun & lunch*
This chic bistro uses high-quality ingredients sourced from local suppliers. It also has an excellent selection of wines.

**BEAUNE: La Ciboulette** €€
Bistro
*69 rue Lorraine, 21200*
**Tel** *03 80 24 70 72* **Closed** *Mon & Tue*
The simple decor belies the high culinary standards here. Expect Burgundian classics, such as Charolais steak with Epoisses cheese sauce and pear poached in red wine.

**BEAUNE: L'Ecusson** €€
Modern French
*Pl Malmedy, 21200*
**Tel** *03 80 24 03 82* **Closed** *Wed & Sun*
Daring, inventive cuisine can be enjoyed in L'Ecusson's pleasant interior of wooden floors and oak beams.

**BELFORT: Le Pot au Feu** €€
Traditional French
*27 bis Grand'Rue, 90000*
**Tel** *03 84 28 57 84* **Closed** *Sat & Mon lunch, Sun*
A 17th-century vaulted cellar is the setting for home-style dishes,

such as the *pot au feu* (braised beef-and-vegetable stew). An extensive selection of wines.

**BONLIEU: La Poutre** €€
Regional
*25 Grande Rue, 39130*
**Tel** *03 84 25 57 77* **Closed** *Nov–Apr; May–Oct: Mon lunch*
Enjoy hearty home-cooked food in an 18th-century farmhouse with stone walls and oak beams. Try the tasting menu.

**CHABLIS: La Cuisine au Vin** €€
Regional
*16 rue Auxerroise, 89800*
**Tel** *03 86 18 98 52* **Closed** *Mon & Tue; Sun–Thu eves*
Diners can expect innovative takes on classics such as Burgundy snails and *boeuf bourguignon* at this place atmospherically located in an old wine cellar. Friendly staff.

**CHAGNY: Lameloise** €€€
Fine dining
*36 pl Armes, 71150*
**Tel** *03 85 87 65 65* **Closed** *Jul–Sep: Tue–Thu lunch; Oct–Jun: Tue & Wed*
This is the place for fine Burgundian cooking prepared with only the best ingredients Everything is cooked to perfection.

**CHAINTRE: La Table**
**de Chaintré** €€
Regional
*Le Bourg, 71570*
**Tel** *03 85 32 90 95* **Closed** *Sun eve–Tue*
La Table de Chaintré is a well-established restaurant with a menu that changes weekly.

**CHALON-SUR-SAONE:**
**Le Bistrot** €€
Bistro
*31 rue de Strasbourg*
**Tel** *03 85 93 22 01* **Closed** *Sat & Sun*
Try the seafood risotto or the Bresse chicken at this friendly bistro-style restaurant.

**CHAROLLES: Restaurant**
**Frédéric Doucet** €€€
Modern French
*2 av de la Libération, 71120*
**Tel** *03 85 24 11 32* **Closed** *Sun eve, Mon, Tue lunch*
For a modern spin on traditional dishes, try this chic restaurant serving sizzling Charolais steak.

**DIJON: La Dame d'Aquitaine** €€
Traditional French
*23 pl Bossuet, 21000*
**Tel** *03 80 30 45 65* **Closed** *Mon–Wed lunch, Sun*
This eatery in an 18th-century stone-walled crypt offers regional specialties using local produce.

**For more information on types of restaurants** *see p575*

**DIJON: DZ'Envies** €€
Modern French
*12 rue Odebert, 21000*
**Tel** *03 80 50 09 26* **Closed** *Sun*
Facing the marketplace, this
eatery has a minimalist decor
that provides the ideal backdrop
to its simple gourmet dishes.

**DIJON: Hostellerie du
Chapeau Rouge** €€€
Modern French
*5 rue Michelet, 21000*
**Tel** *03 80 50 88 88* **Closed** *Sun & Mon*
Try scallops and *foie gras* ravioli
with truffle and creamy soy sauce
and other creative dishes in a
sleek setting.

**DOLE: La Chaumière** €€€
Modern French
*346 av du Maréchal Juin, 39100*
**Tel** *03 84 70 72 40* **Closed** *Sat &
Mon lunch, Sun*
Come to this delightful eatery
for dishes such as chicken with
mushrooms cooked in *vin jaune*,
and carrots flavored with ginger.

**FONTANGY: Ferme-Auberge
de la Morvandelle** €
Traditional French
*Précy-sous-Thil, 21390*
**Tel** *06 78 80 88 68* **Open** *Apr–mid-
Nov: Sat eve & Sun lunch; groups of
minimum 10 people on weekdays*
Many ingredients used in the
dishes are grown at this farm with
a dining area in a converted barn.

**GEVREY-CHAMBERTIN:
Chez Guy** €€
Regional
*3 pl de la Mairie, 21220*
**Tel** *03 80 58 51 51* **Closed** *Nov–Mar:
Sun*
At this chic restaurant with
exposed beams and a terrace,
you can try simple cuisine such
as *coq au vin* and rabbit *fricassée*.

**IGUERANDE: La Colline du
Colombier** €€
Modern French
*Colombier, 71340*
**Tel** *03 85 84 07 24* **Closed** *Tue & Wed
(Jul & Aug: Wed only)*
At this ancient farmhouse
renovated by legendary chefs
Michel and Marie-Pierre Troigros,
the cuisine focuses on local meat
and organic produce.

**LONS-LE-SAUNIER:
La Comédie** €€
Modern French
*65 pl de la Comédie, 39000*
**Tel** *03 84 24 20 66* **Closed** *Sun &
Mon*
The fixed-price menus change
daily at this contemporary restau-
rant, while the desserts and the
à la carte choices are seasonal.

**MAGNY-COURS:
Absolue Renaissance** €€
Modern French
*2 rue de Paris, 58470*
**Tel** *03 86 58 10 40* **Closed** *Sun,
Mon eve*
Set in a vast garden with its own
vegetable patch, this restaurant
puts a new spin on classic dishes.

**MALBUISSON:
Le Bon Acceuil** €€
Modern French
*Rue de la Source, 25160*
**Tel** *03 81 69 30 58* **Closed** *Sun eve,
Mon, Tue lunch*
Sample Lake Geneva *féra* trout
with a watercress sauce and
other creative seasonal dishes
in a converted farmhouse.

**MONTFAUCON: La Cheminée** €€
Regional
*3 rue de la Vue des Alpes, 25660*
**Tel** *03 81 81 17 48* **Closed** *Sun & Wed
eves, Mon*
Enjoy spectacular Alpine scenery
from this rustic eatery serving
dishes based on local produce.

**NEVERS: Jean-Michel Couron** €€
Modern French
*21 rue St.-Etienne, 58000*
**Tel** *03 86 61 19 28* **Closed** *Sun eve–
Tue*
The chef at this intimate restaurant
selects top produce to create
perfectly balanced flavors.

**NITRY: Auberge de la
Beursaudière** €€
Traditional French
*Chemin de Ronde, 89310*
**Tel** *03 86 33 69 69*
Hearty local dishes such as
braised steak are served up by
staff in regional dress.

**NUITS-ST.-GEORGES:
L'Alambic** €€
Regional
*Rue de Général de Gaulle, 21700*
**Tel** *03 80 61 35 00* **Closed** *Mon,
Tue lunch; Nov–Mar: Sun eve*
There is a vast selection of wines
to go with the classic dishes on
offer in this Cistercian dining room.

**PORT LESNEY: Le Bistro
Pontarlier** €€
Bistro
*Port Lesney, 39600*
**Tel** *03 84 37 83 27* **Closed** *Mon & Tue
eves, Wed & Thu (except Jul & Aug)*
This much-loved bistro is in
the old schoolhouse of a
pretty wine-producing village
near Arbois.

**PULIGNY-MONTRACHET:
La Table d'Olivier Leflaive** €€€
Regional
*Pl du Monument, 21190*
**Tel** *03 80 21 95 27* **Closed** *Sun*
Try the specialty wine-tasting
lunches at this rustic spot with a
background in wine production.
The seasonal menu uses locally
grown produce.

**QUARRE LES TOMBES:
Auberge de Atre** €€
Traditional French
*Les Lavaults, 89630*
**Tel** *03 86 32 20 79* **Closed** *Tue & Wed*
Classic dishes such as roast duck
with pepper sauce are served in
a cosy dining room.

## DK Choice

**ST.-AMOUR BELLEVUE:
L'Auberge du Paradis** €€€
Modern French
*Le Plâtre Durand, 71570*
**Tel** *03 85 37 10 26* **Closed** *Mon,
Tue, Wed–Sat lunch*
The monthly changing menu
at this exciting restaurant may
include Iberian black pig served
with a mousse of Brie de Meaux,
flavored with grainy mustard.
The dining room is modern
and quirky, with forks hanging
from lampshades.

**ST.-ROMAIN: Les Roches** €€
Regional
*Pl de la Mairie, 21190*
**Tel** *03 80 21 21 63* **Closed** *Tue
& Wed*
Simple, no-frills cooking is served
at this small hotel-restaurant. Try
the four-course set menu.

Smart, modern dining space at La Table d'Olivier Leflaive, Puligny-Montrachet

**SAULIEU:**
**Le Relais Bernard Loiseau** €€€
Fine dining
*2 rue d'Argentine, 21210*
**Tel** *03 80 90 53 53* **Closed** *Tue & Wed; Feb*
Renowned across France, this restaurant creates masterful interpretations of traditional dishes.

**SENS: La Madeleine** €€€
Fine dining
*1 rue Alsace-Lorraine, 89100*
**Tel** *03 86 65 09 31* **Closed** *Sun, Mon, Tue lunch*
The seasonal menus at this smart establishment offer dishes such as scallop *carpaccio*.

**TOURNUS:**
**Le Restaurant Greuze** €€€
Traditional French
*1 rue A. Thibaudet, 71700*
**Tel** *03 85 51 13 52* **Closed** *Wed; Nov–Mar*
Enjoy classic cuisine in simple but charming surroundings. Try the Bresse chicken and pair with a good Mâcon or Beaujolais wine.

**VENOY: Le Moulin de la Coudre** €€
Traditional French
*2 rue des Gravottes, La Coudre, 89290*
**Tel** *03 86 40 23 79* **Closed** *Sun eve, Mon lunch*
The menu changes weekly here, according to the seasonal produce available. Creatively prepared classic cuisine.

**VERDUN-SUR-LE-DOUBS:**
**L'Hostellerie Bourguignonne –**
**Didier Denis** €€
Traditional French
*2 av Pdt-Borgeot, 71350*
**Tel** *03 85 91 51 45* **Closed** *Tue & Wed lunch; winter: Sun eve*
This rustic venue specializes in honest, straightforward cooking made with local ingredients. Enjoy the superb Charolais beef fillet and the excellent wines.

**VEZELAY: Le Bougainville** €€
Regional
*28 rue Saint-Étienne, 89450*
**Tel** *03 86 33 27 57* **Closed** *Tue & Wed; mid-Nov–mid-Mar*
Expect Burgundy favorites such as homemade terrine, *jambon persillé*, hare stew and snails.

**VILLENEUVE SUR YONNE:**
**Auberge La Lucarne**
**aux Chouettes** €€
Regional
*7 quai Bretoche, 89500*
**Tel** *03 86 87 18 26* **Closed** *Sun eve, Mon*
The menu at this 17th-century inn by the River Yonne features dishes such as eggs poached in red wine, snails, and more.

Rustic exteriors of the Georges Blanc restaurant in Vonnas

**VILLERS-LE-LAC: Le France** €€
Modern French
*8 pl Cupillard, 25130*
**Tel** *03 81 68 00 06* **Closed** *Sun eve, Mon*
The delicious dishes served at this hotel-restaurant are infused with herbs from the hotel garden. Try the Bresse chicken with morel mushrooms. Great service.

**VINCELOTTES:**
**Auberge des Tilleuls** €€
Traditional French
*12 quai de l'Yonne, 82290*
**Tel** *03 86 42 22 13* **Closed** *Tue & Wed*
Enjoy mouthwatering cuisine in this attractive riverside auberge. Fish specialties include oyster soup, scallops, and langoustines.

**VONNAS: Georges Blanc** €€€
Fine dining
*Pl Marché, 01540*
**Tel** *04 74 50 90 90* **Closed** *Mon & Tue, Wed & Thu lunch*
A gourmet shrine, Georges Blanc offers such inventive cuisine as lobster cooked in *vin jaune* and served with morel mushroom ravioli. Excellent wines.

# The Massif Central

## DK Choice

**ALLEYRAS: Le Haut Allier** €€
Modern French
*Pont d'Alleyras, 43580*
**Tel** *04 71 57 57 63* **Closed** *Mon & Tue; mid-Nov–Mar*
Nestled in the Allier gorge, this hotel-restaurant believes in local produce. Enjoy traditional dishes such as saddle of Saugues lamb, or more imaginative ones such as pigeon breast in a cep mushroom crumble with corn flour gnocchi. The set menus are great value.

**BELCASTEL: Vieux Pont** €€€
Modern French
*Le Bourg, 12390*
**Tel** *05 65 64 52 29* **Closed** *Jan–mid-Mar; Sun & Mon (except Jul & Aug)*
Straddling a medieval bridge, this place produces creative dishes with flair. Try Ségela veal cooked with kaffir lime, and mashed potatoes with almond, lemon, and ginger oil.

**BOUDES: La Vigne** €€
Modern French
*Pl de la Mairie, 63340*
**Tel** *04 73 96 55 66* **Closed** *Sun eve, Mon & Tue*
The chef constantly seeks out new ideas for his changing menu at this creative restaurant on the main square of this wine village. Great set menus.

**BRIVE-LA-GAILLARDE:**
**Chez Francis** €€
Bistro
*61 av de Paris, 19100*
**Tel** *05 55 74 41 72* **Closed** *Sun & Mon*
This Paris-style bistro serves well-prepared reworkings of regional favorites. Good selection of southern French wines.

**CLERMONT-FERRAND:**
**Amphitryon Capucine** €€
Traditional French
*50 rue Fontgiève, 63000*
**Tel** *04 73 31 38 39* **Closed** *Sun & Mon*
Try the roast turbot basted with cep mushroom sauce at this stately dining room complete with a fireplace and oak beams. Excellent wine list.

**CLERMONT-FERRAND:**
**Le Caveau** €€
Regional
*1 rue Tour de la Monnaie, 63000*
**Tel** *04 73 14 07 03* **Closed** *Sun*
Rustic and traditional, Le Caveau is a meat eater's paradise serving huge chunks of Salers or Aubrac beef and *coq au vin*.

**For more information on types of restaurants** *see p575*

**CLERMONT-FERRAND:**
**Goûts et Couleurs** €€
Modern French
*6 pl Champgil, 63000*
**Tel** *04 73 19 37 82* **Closed** *Sat lunch, Sun & Mon lunch*
The geometric decor is softened by an ancient vaulted ceiling in this former mirror workshop serving modern, inventive cuisine.

**LAGUIOLE: Michel Bras** €€€
Fine dining
*rte de l'Aubrac, 12210*
**Tel** *05 65 51 18 20* **Closed** *Mon & Tue, Wed lunch*
A wall of glass overlooks the beautiful Aubrac countryside from this hilltop restaurant renowned for its cutting-edge cuisine.

**LE PUY-EN-VELAY: Tournayre** €€
Regional
*12 rue Chênebouterie, 43000*
**Tel** *04 71 09 58 94* **Closed** *Sun & Wed eves, Mon*
Vaulted ceilings and stone walls distinguish this 12th-century townhouse. Try typical Auvergnat dishes such as lentils or Velay veal.

**LE ROUGET: Hôtel des Voyageurs** €
Traditional French
*20 av de 15 Septembre 1945, 15290*
**Tel** *04 71 46 10 14* **Closed** *Sep–May: Sun lunch*
This stone-built Cantal hotel-restaurant serves well-prepared traditional dishes. Go for the *menu du terroir*. The fish with chorizo is especially good.

**LES ESTABLES: Auberge des Fermiers du Mézenc** €€
Regional
*Le Bourg, 43150*
**Tel** *04 71 08 34 30*
A restored 18th-century stone farmhouse, this place serves local produce, such as Mézenc beef, *crique* (fried potato galette), and regional cheeses.

**LIMOGES: Chez Alphonse** €€
Bistro
*5 pl de la Motte, 87000*
**Tel** *05 55 34 34 14* **Closed** *Sun*
There are good *prix-fixe* menus at this lively bistro serving regional cuisine. The chef sources all the ingredients from the local market.

**LIMOGES: L'Amphitryon** €€€
Modern French
*26 rue de la Boucherie, 87000*
**Tel** *05 55 33 36 39* **Closed** *Sun & Mon*
The food is sophisticated and the flavors are delicate at this contemporary dining space. The Limousin beef is a perennial favorite.

Striking, contemporary interiors of the refined Michel Bras restaurant, Laguiole

**MILLAU: La Braconne** €€
Traditional French
*7 pl Maréchal Foch, 12100*
**Tel** *05 65 60 30 93* **Closed** *Sun eve, Mon*
Specialties at this 13th-century vaulted restaurant on an arcaded square include flambéed leg of lamb. Classic cuisine.

**MONTLUCON:**
**Le Grenier à Sel** €€
Traditional French
*10 rue Ste.-Anne, 03100*
**Tel** *04 70 05 53 79* **Closed** *Sun eve, Mon*
Dine in an elegant pastel-hued room set in an impressive ivy-clad 18th-century mansion with massive fireplaces.

**MONTSALVY: L'Auberge Fleurie** €€
Traditional French
*Pl du Barry, 15120*
**Tel** *04 71 49 20 02* **Closed** *Sun eve; Sep–Jun: Mon; mid-Nov–mid-Mar*
This charming auberge has oak beams, an open fireplace and a rustic feel. The roast hen with chestnut charlotte is a must.

**MOULINS: Le Trait d'Union** €€
Bistro
*16 rue Gambetta, 3000*
**Tel** *04 70 34 24 61* **Closed** *Sun & Mon*
Sizzling dishes such as Monts du Forez veal and steak Rossini can be found on the menu at this upscale bistro.

**MURAT: Le Jarrousset** €€
Modern French
*Rte de Clermont-Ferrand, 15300*
**Tel** *04 71 20 10 69* **Closed** *Sun, Tue & Wed eves; Sep–Jun: Mon*
The emphasis here is on using top-quality seasonal ingredients, most of them sourced locally.

**RODEZ: Goûts en Couleurs** €€
Modern French
*38 rue Bonald, 12000*
**Tel** *05 65 42 75 10* **Closed** *Sun & Mon*
At this charming eatery with a garden terrace in the old town, the chef prepares imaginative

fare such as line-caught whiting served with a mussel and vervain tart.

**ST.-BONNET-LE-FROID:**
**Auberge des Cimes** €€€
Fine dining
*Le Bourg, 43290*
**Tel** *04 71 59 93 72* **Closed** *Tue & Wed*
The delicious, seasonally determined dishes on the menu at the rustically decorated Auberge des Cimes include roast quail with caramelized pear, and monkfish served with assorted pumpkins.

**ST.-JULIEN-CHAPTEUIL: Vidal** €€
Traditional French
*Pl du Marché, 43260*
**Tel** *04 71 08 70 50* **Closed** *Sun & Mon*
Opt for the juicy stuffed fillet of beef or the Velay lamb at this family-run restaurant serving authentic cuisine in a quaint village. There's an excellent dessert menu, too.

**UZERCHE: Restaurant Jean Teyssier** €€
Mediterranean
*Rue du Pont-Turgot, 19140*
**Tel** *05 55 73 10 05* **Closed** *Sep–Jun: Tue & Wed*
The chef at Jean Teyssier serves Mediterranean dishes such as grilled red mullet fillets on parmesan shortbread and *tapenade (see p473)* in an elegant dining room with a chandelier and great views of the Vezère.

**VICHY: Brasserie du Casino** €€
Brasserie
*4 rue du Casino, 03200*
**Tel** *04 70 98 23 06* **Closed** *Tue & Wed*
Housed in a stylish Art Deco salon decked out with wood and mirrors, the Brasserie du Casino is a veritable institution on the Vichy restaurant scene. The excellent menu features classic upscale brasserie fare. Impeccable service.

**VICHY: Jacques Decoret** €€€
Modern French
*15 rue du Parc, 3200*
**Tel** *04 70 97 65 06* **Closed** *Tue & Wed*
The finest regional produce is used in refined dishes that are prepared with great skill. The setting is also lovely – in a huge conservatory.

## The Rhône Valley and French Alps

**ANNECY: Le Belvédère** €€€
Modern French
*7 chemin Belvédère, 74000*
**Tel** *04 50 45 04 90* **Closed** *Sun eve, Wed; Oct–May: Tue eve*
Enjoy lake views and appetizing contemporary food – *foie gras* perfumed with vanilla, and desserts such as the chocolate cigar filled with coffee mousse.

**ARGENTIERE: Le Chêne Vert** €€
Regional
*Rocher, 7110 Tel*
**Tel** *04 75 88 34 02*
This traditional Ardèchois hotel and restaurant offers a number of regional classics. Try the *foie gras* served with a fig *confit*.

**CHAMBERY: Château de Candie – Orangerie** €€
Modern French
*Rue de Bois de Candie, Chambéry le Vieux, 73000*
**Tel** *04 79 96 63 00*
At this elegant restaurant you can choose such experimental dishes as fera fish fillet served with olives and chorizo, accompanied by carrot, orange, and fennel sauce.

### DK Choice

**CHAMONIX: La Calèche** €€
Traditional French
*Rue Dr. Paccard, 74400*
**Tel** *04 50 55 94 68*
This mountain restaurant serves typical Savoyard cuisine, including *tartiflette* (a gratin made with *lardons*, cheese, potatoes, and onions), fondue, and grilled meats. The dining room is crammed with Swiss clocks, copper pans and a bobsled from the 1924 Winter Olympics.

**CHAMONIX: Les Jardins du Mont Blanc** €€€
Modern French
*62 allée du Majestic, 74400*
**Tel** *04 50 53 05 64*
Housed in a charming mountain hotel, this smart restaurant offers modern Alpine cuisine prepared with the best regional produce.

**COLLONGES MONT D'OR: Paul Bocuse** €€€
Fine dining
*40 quai de la Plage, 69660*
**Tel** *04 72 42 90 90*
National treasure Paul Bocuse makes dishes such as black truffle soup topped with pastry, or his legendary gratin of crayfish. The restaurant is decorated with chandeliers and gilded mirrors.

**COURCHEVEL: Le Chabichou** €€€
Modern French
*Quartier des Chenus, 73120*
**Tel** *04 79 08 00 55* **Closed** *Summer: Tue*
Experience creative cuisine while enjoying breathtaking mountain views. Old-school favorites on offer include pork from the Cantal region.

**COURCHEVEL: Le Genépi** €€€
Traditional French
*Courchevel 1850, 73120*
**Tel** *04 79 08 08 63* **Closed** *Sep–Nov: Sat & Sun*
Savor traditional mountain fare at this excellent dining establishment, located within a luxury ski resort. Good wine and cocktail list.

**GRENOBLE: A Ma Table** €€
Traditional French
*92 cours Jean-Jaurès, 38000*
**Tel** *04 76 96 77 04* **Closed** *Sat–Mon, Tue, Wed & Fri eves*
This beautiful restaurant serves tasty dishes such as breast of farm-reared guinea fowl cooked in cider, duck *foie gras* with cocoa, and roast squid with truffle cream.

**GRENOBLE: Badine** €€
Modern French
*168 cours Berriat, 38000*
**Tel** *04 76 21 95 33* **Closed** *Sat & Sun*
The dishes at Badine reflect the creativity of the young chef. The seasonal menu uses local produce. In summer, tables are set up outside, under the ancient wisteria.

**LE BOURGET-LAC: Beaurivage** €€
Regional
*Bd du Lac, 73370*
**Tel** *04 79 25 00 38* **Closed** *Sun eve, Wed (except Jul & Aug) & Thu*
Diners flock here to sample classic Savoyard cuisine. This lakeside auberge features a lovely terrace overhung with plantain trees.

**LE CLUSAZ: La Scierie** €€
Modern French
*321–331 rte du Col des Aravis, 74220*
**Tel** *04 50 63 34 68*
Dishes at this restaurant in a former sawmill range from local mountain *charcuterie* to

John Dory fillet with Mondeuse wine sauce and creamy risotto, served in a friendly ambience.

**LYON: 33 Cité** €€
Brasserie
*33 quai Charles de Gaulle, 69006*
**Tel** *04 37 45 45 45* **Closed** *Sun*
A modern brasserie in the heart of downtown Lyon, 33 Cité offers carefully prepared classic and contemporary cuisine in a stylish dining room. The extensive wine list is excellent.

**LYON: Brasserie Georges** €€
Bistro
*30 cours Verdun, 69002*
**Tel** *04 72 56 54 54*
Dating to 1836, Brasserie Georges is a huge, bustling downtown bistro with Art Deco interiors. The menu covers Lyonnais specialties, seafood dishes, and sauerkraut.

**LYON: La Gargotte** €€
Modern French
*15 rue Royale, 69001*
**Tel** *04 78 28 79 20* **Closed** *Sat, Sun, Mon lunch & Tue*
Classic dishes are reworked with originality at this friendly restaurant in an old pastry store with retro decor and mirrored walls.

**LYON: L'Alexandrin** €€€
Regional
*83 rue Moncey, 69003*
**Tel** *04 72 61 15 69* **Closed** *Sun & Mon*
L'Alexandrin specializes in exquisite gourmet reinventions of typical Lyonnais dishes, including roast turbot on a *carpaccio* of mango, and lobster ravioli with celery tagliatelle, served in a warm and elegant interior or on the outside terrace.

Brightly lit, vibrant dining room at Le Chabichou in Courchevel

**For more information on types of restaurants** *see p575*

The charming dining room at La Taverne du Mont d'Arbois in Megeve

## MEGEVE: La Petite Ravine €€
Traditional French
*743 chemin de la Ravine, Demi Quartier Combloux, 74120*
**Tel** *04 50 21 38 67*
The limited selection of dishes at this alpine chalet restaurant with a warm ambience includes cheese-based regional classics.

## MEGEVE: La Taverne du Mont d'Arbois €€
Modern French
*3001 rte Edmond de Rothschild, 74120*
**Tel** *04 50 21 03 53*
This authentic chalet attracts a chic Megève crowd with its modern reworkings of traditional recipes. Old favorites such as *raclette* and fondue also on offer.

## MORZINE: La Chamade €€
Traditional French
*La Crusaz, 90 rte de la Plagne, 74110*
**Tel** *04 50 79 13 91*
Choose from a wide-ranging menu that features wood-oven pizzas and regional fare such as *charcuterie*. Alternatively, try the warm Reblochon salad.

## OUCHES: Troisgros €€€
Fine dining
*728 rte de Villerest, 42155*
**Tel** *04 77 71 66 97* **Closed** *Mon lunch; Tue & Wed*
One of the country's top restaurants, Troisgros features striking contemporary decor, pure lines, and a Zen atmosphere, plus an exceptionally high caliber of cooking.

## ST.-AGREVE: Domaine de Rilhac €€
Modern French
*Rilhac, 07320*
**Tel** *04 75 30 20 20* **Closed** *Tue eve, Wed & Thu lunch; mid-Dec–mid-Mar*
Chef Ludovic Sinz reinvents classic fare in this smartly renovated farmhouse. Try the pumpkin soup with snails or the pan-fried chicory.

## ST.-ETIENNE: Le Bistrot de Paris €€
Bistro
*7 pl Jean Jaurès, 42000*
**Tel** *04 77 21 56 74* **Closed** *Sun eve*
This jovial bistro has a simple menu that changes in accordance with what is in season.

## ST.-MARTIN-DE-BELLEVILLE: La Bouitte €€€
Modern French
*St.-Marcel, 73440*
**Tel** *04 79 08 96 77*
Order the farm-reared chicken with truffles at this Alpine chalet restaurant. Inventive dishes.

## TAIN L'HERMITAGE: Lycée Hotelier de l'Hermitage €
Traditional French
*Rue Jean Monnet, 26600*
**Tel** *04 75 07 57 14* **Closed** *Sat, Sun, Mon–Wed eve & Fri eve, and school vacations*
Students training to become chefs run two restaurants serving classic gourmet dishes..

## TALLOIRES: La Villa des Fleurs €€
Regional
*Rte du Port, 74290*
**Tel** *04 50 60 71 14* **Closed** *Sun eve, Mon*
Fish caught in Lake Annecy features prominently on the seasonal menu at this lovely waterside villa.

## TOURNON: Le Tournesol €€
Modern French
*44 av Maréchal Foch, 07300*
**Tel** *04 75 07 08 26* **Closed** *Sun eve, Tue & Wed*
Sample the homemade duck and pistachio terrine at this smart restaurant with views of the Hermitage vineyards.

## URIAGE-LES-BAINS: Les Terrasses d'Uriage €€€
Modern French
*Pl de la Déesse-Hygie, 38410*
**Tel** *04 76 89 10 80* **Closed** *Sun eve, Mon, Tue–Thu lunch; late Dec–Jan*
Les Terrasses is an upscale restaurant in a Napoleon III

building that opens out onto a lovely park. The place for creative, beautifully presented dishes.

## VALENCE: Restaurant Pic €€€
Fine dining
*285 av Victor Hugo, 26000*
**Tel** *04 75 44 15 32* **Closed** *Sun eve & Mon*
A chic restaurant in a luxury hotel, Pic features a constantly evolving menu. Excellent Rhône wines.

### DK Choice

## VIENNE: La Pyramide €€€
Fine dining
*14 bd Fernand Point, 38200*
**Tel** *04 74 53 01 96* **Closed** *Tue & Wed*
Beautifully presented, the gastronomic creations at La Pyramide are based on regional produce – try the saddle of lamb cooked in a bread crust and served with a leek *tarte tatin*. Excellent wine list. A classic Michelin-starred establishment.

# Poitou and Aquitaine

## ANGOULEME: Le Terminus €
Bistro
*3 pl de la Gare, 16000*
**Tel** *05 45 95 27 13* **Closed** *Sun*
Stylish and modern, Le Terminus has a lovely summer terrace. On the menu is a great selection of seafood purchased from the local market.

## ARCACHON: La Cabane de L'Aiguillon €
Seafood
*Bd Pierre Loti, 33120*
**Tel** *05 56 54 88 20* **Closed** *Oct–Easter*
Enjoy a platter of oysters on the terrace of this family-run eatery on the beach.

## ARCACHON: Chez Yvette €€
Seafood
*59 bd du Général Leclerc, 33120*
**Tel** *05 56 83 05 11*
Set on the waterfront, this lively and atmospheric local institution has been serving plates of fish and oysters since 1962. There is a good wine list to complement the dishes.

## ARCINS: Le Lion d'Or €€
Regional
*11 rte de Pauillac, 33460*
**Tel** *05 56 58 96 79* **Closed** *Sun & Mon*
An intimate restaurant in a Médoc wine village, Le Lion d'Or is renowned for great local cuisine and superb wines.

**BORDEAUX: Tante Charlotte**  €
Traditional French
*7 rue des Bahutiers, 33000*
**Tel** *09 82 60 13 12* **Closed** *Sun & Mon*
Traditional cuisine made with
seasonal, organic produce is on
offer at this cosy, modern bistro.

**BORDEAUX: Le Chapon Fin**  €€€
Fine dining
*5 rue Montesquieu, 33000*
**Tel** *05 56 79 10 10* **Closed** *Sun & Mon*
Exquisite creative fare is on the
menu at this historic restaurant
with glorious *belle époque* decor.
Impressive selection of wines.

**COGNAC: Les Pigeons
Blancs**  €€
Regional
*110 rue Jules Brisson, 16100*
**Tel** *05 45 82 16 36*
This traditional restaurant serves
locally based cuisine. Highlights
on the menu include the
succulent beef and duck dishes.

**COULON: Le Central**  €
Regional
*4 rue d'Autremont, 79510*
**Tel** *05 49 35 90 20* **Closed** *Mon*
For innovative regional cuisine
and an excellent range of fruit
desserts, head to Le Central.
The dining room and terrace
overlook the Poitevin marshes.

**EUGENIE-LES-BAINS:
La Ferme aux Grives**  €€
Fine dining
*11 rue des Thermes, 40320*
**Tel** *05 58 05 05 06* **Closed** *Tue & Wed*
Chef Michel Guérard's upscale
restaurant serves sublime French
fare with a modern twist. Try the
suckling pig or chicken cooked
on the spit in their fireplace.

**ILE D'OLERON: Ecailler**  €
Seafood
*65 rue du Port, 17310 St.-Pierre-d'Oléron*
**Tel** *05 46 47 10 31* **Closed** *mid-Dec–
Feb*
Great local oysters, crab and
other seafood specialties are
served at this harborside eatery
that sources its ingredients from
the market at the end of the pier.

Guests dining alfresco at La Ferme aux Grives in Eugènie-les-Bains

**ILE DE RE: La Baleine Bleue**  €€
Brasserie
*Quai Launay Razilly, 17410
St.-Martin-de-Ré*
**Tel** *05 46 09 03 30* **Closed** *Mon eve,
Tue (except Jul & Aug)*
In a great harborside location,
this stylish bar and brasserie sells
fish, seafood, and fine wines.

**JARNAC: Restaurant
du Château**  €€
Fine dining
*15 pl du Château, 16200*
**Tel** *05 45 81 07 17* **Closed** *Mon, Wed
& Sun eves*
This elegant restaurant provides
refined dishes such as roast
pheasant in cognac sauce.

**LA ROCHELLE: Le Boute en Train**  €
Bistro
*7 rue des Bonnes Femmes, 17000*
**Tel** *05 46 41 73 74* **Closed** *Sun & Mon*
Enjoy hearty classic fare made
with market-fresh ingredients
at this eatery. Great service, too.

**LA ROCHELLE: Coquillages
et Crustacés**  €
Seafood
*Port du Plomb (côté l'Houmeau), 17000*
**Tel** *05 46 45 32 52* **Closed** *Mon, Sun
eve*
This waterside restaurant offers
all types of seafood, including
platters of lobsters, crustaceans,
and fish. Some dishes have an
Asian touch

**LA ROCHELLE: L'Entracte**  €€
Brasserie
*35 rue St.-Jean-du-Pérot, 17000*
**Tel** *05 46 52 26 69*
The friendly staffers at L'Entracte
plate up inventive takes on simple
regional cuisine in a stylish interior
with an open kitchen.

**LANGON: Restaurant
Claude Darroze**  €€
Fine dining
*95 cours du Général Leclerc, 33210*
**Tel** *05 56 63 00 48*
Enjoy excellent Southwestern
French cooking and Bordeaux
wines in this intimate restaurant
with striking decor.

Stone facade with red awnings of
Restaurant du Château, Jarnac

**MARGAUX: Le Pavillon
de Margaux**  €
Traditional French
*3 rue Georges Mandel, 33460*
**Tel** *05 57 88 77 54* **Closed** *Jun–Sep:
Tue; Oct–May: Tue & Wed*
Set in a villa hotel, this mellow
dining room serves a great
selection of light lunches.

**MONTMORILLON: Le Lucullus**  €
Regional
*4 bd de Strasbourg, 86500*
**Tel** *05 49 84 09 09* **Closed** *Mon & Tue,
Sun eve*
Refined regional cuisine and an
excellent wine list await at this
bar-bistro. Casual dining.

**NIORT: Bloom Restaurant**  €€
Bistro
*9 rue de l'Hotel de Ville, 79000*
**Tel** *05 49 77 44 35* **Closed** *Sun*
Chic, airy modern bistro where
local fish is the highlight of the
varied menus.

**PAUILLAC: Château
Cordeillan-Bages**  €€
Fine dining
*Rte des Châteaux, 33250*
**Tel** *05 56 59 24 24* **Closed** *Mon & Tue;
Dec–Mar*
Gourmet cuisine is offered at this
lavish Médoc château-hotel.
Excellent Bordeaux wines.

**POITIERS: Les Bons Enfants**  €
Regional
*11bis rue Cloche Perse, 86000*
**Tel** *05 49 41 49 82* **Closed** *Sun & Mon*
Snug and tightly packed, this
eatery serves generous portions
of duck and other local specialties.

**POITIERS: Le Pince Oreille**  €€
Bistro
*11 rue des Trois Rois, 86000*
**Tel** *05 49 60 25 99* **Closed** *Sun & Mon*
At this laid-back bar-restaurant
with live music there is a good
selection of wholesome meals.

For more information on types of restaurants *see p575*

**ROCHEFORT: La Belle Poule**  €€
Regional
*102 av du 11 Novembre, 17300*
**Tel** *05 46 99 71 87*     **Closed** *Fri*
Sample regionally inspired cooking at this lovely restaurant with a terrace by the River Charente.

**SABRES: Auberge des Pins**  €€
Fine dining
*Rte de la Piscine, 40630*
**Tel** *05 58 08 30 00*  **Closed** *Sep–Jun: Mon*
Enjoy delicate cuisine in serene environs. The menu features pigeon, langoustines, and ice-cream cannelloni. Convivial host.

**SAINT-EMILION: L'Envers du Décor**  €€
Bistro
*11 rue du Clocher, 33330*
**Tel** *05 57 74 48 31*
This award-winning bistro and wine bar serves healthy salads and snacks as well as intricate dishes.

---

**DK Choice**

**SAINT-EMILION:**
**Restaurant Le Tertre**  €€
Fine dining
*5 rue du Tertre de la Tente, 33330*
**Tel** *05 57 74 46 33*   **Closed** *Feb–Mar: Wed & Thu; Apr–Nov: Wed; mid-Jul–Jan*
Le Tertre has won many fans with its outstanding food, warm service, and superb wines. Choose from classic local dishes such as duck, *foie gras* or line-caught *maigre* fish – all prepared with great flair.

---

**SAUTERNES: Le Saprien**  €
Regional
*14 rue Principale, 33210*
**Tel** *05 56 76 60 87*  **Closed** *Sun eve & Mon*
In a converted farmhouse this smart restaurant serves good-value, traditional French dishes

Cooking wood pigeon over coals, Auberge des Pins, Sabres

**Key to Price Guide** *see p576*

**TALMONT-SUR-GIRONDE:**
**Hôtel-Restaurant L'Estuaire**  €
Seafood
*1 av de l'Estuaire, 17120*
**Tel** *05 46 90 43 85*  **Closed** *Oct–Mar: Mon & Tue*
A selection of local fish and seafood can be enjoyed in a lovely, remote location beside the Gironde estuary.

---

# Périgord, Quercy, and Gascony

**AGEN: Mariottat**  €€
Fine dining
*25 rue Louis Vivent, 47000*
**Tel** *05 53 77 99 77*  **Closed** *Mon, Sat lunch & Sun eve; Nov–May: Wed lunch*
Refined food made with fresh produce is served in a beautiful 19th-century town mansion furnished with antiques.

**ALBI: L'Épicurien**  €
Bistro
*42 pl Jean Jaurès, 81000*
**Tel** *05 63 53 10 70*  **Closed** *Sun & Mon*
This smart, contemporary bistro offers creative takes on classic French dishes. Great local wines.

**ALBI: Le Jardin des Quatre Saisons**  €
Regional
*5 rue de la Pompe, 81000*
**Tel** *05 63 60 77 76*   **Closed** *Mon; Thu & Sun eves*
In the heart of historic Albi, this lovely eatery serves great local favorites. Truffle and mushroom dishes are highly recommended.

**AUCH: Le Papillon**  €
Regional
*rte d'Agen (RN 21), 32810 Montaut-les-Créneaux*
**Tel** *05 62 65 51 29*  **Closed** *Sun eve & Mon*
Gascon specialties such as *cassoulet* and lamb are served in a tranquil room beside a lovely garden. Perfect for big groups.

**BERGERAC: La Flambée**  €€
Regional
*49 av Marceau Feyry, 24100*
**Tel** *05 53 57 52 33*
In addition to an excellent wine list, this place offers great local fare such as duck, *foie gras* and goat's cheese.

**BRANTOME: Au Fil du Temps**  €
Bistro
*1 chemin du Vert Galant, 24310*
**Tel** *05 53 05 24 12*   **Closed** *Sun eve*
This popular bistro with a lively atmosphere and nostalgic decor specializes in dishes prepared on a traditional *rôtissoire*.

**BRANTOME: Les Frères Charbonnel**  €€
Regional
*Rue Gambetta, 24310*
**Tel** *05 53 05 70 15*
Duck and truffles are the house specialties at this renowned hotel-restaurant located beside the River Dronne.

**CAHORS: Auberge du Vieux Cahors**  €
Regional
*144 rue St.-Urcisse, 46000*
**Tel** *05 65 35 06 05*
Hearty local dishes can be enjoyed at this atmospheric 15th-century inn with friendly service.

**CAHORS: Le Balandre**  €€
Fine dining
*Hôtel Terminus, 5 av Charles de Freycinet, 46000*
**Tel** *05 65 53 32 00*  **Closed** *Sun & Mon*
Cahors' most elegant restaurant presents an entire truffle-based tasting menu – and more. It also offers a range of cooking classes.

**CASTRES: La Lanterne des Salvages**  €€
Bistro
*1 av du Sidobre, Les Salvages, 81100 Burlats*
**Tel** *05 63 35 08 21*
An eatery with a riverside terrace in a village north of Castres, La Lanterne provides fresh, seasonal menus and an inviting bar.

**CHAMPAGNAC-DE-BELAIR:**
**Le Moulin du Roc**  €€€
Fine dining
*Av Eugene Leroy, 24530 Champagnac-de-Bélair*
**Tel** *05 53 02 86 00*     **Closed** *Tue; mid-Nov–mid-Mar*
The Michelin-starred Moulin du Roc offers beautifully presented Périgord cuisine in the romantic setting of a converted 1670s mill.

**CONDOM: La Table des Cordeliers**  €
Traditional French
*1 rue des Cordeliers, 32100*
**Tel** *05 62 68 43 82*   **Closed** *Sun & Mon*
Enjoy impeccable service and creative cuisine in this bistro housed in a 13th-century convent. Exceptional value for money.

**CORDES-SUR-CIEL:**
**Bistrot Tonin'ty**  €€
Regional
*Hostellerie du Vieux Cordes, Haut de la Cité, 81170*
**Tel** *05 63 53 79 20*  **Closed** *Sun eve, Mon & Tue lunch*
Bistrot Tonin'ty is renowned for the irresistible desserts

created by Yves Thuries, master chocolatier and owner. Dine in the courtyard in good weather.

**DOMME: L'Esplanade** €€
Regional
*2 rue Pontcarral, 24250*
**Tel** *05 53 28 31 41* **Closed** *Mon; mid-Jan–mid-Feb; mid-Nov–mid-Dec*
There is a terrace overlooking the Dordogne Valley at this popular eatery with duck, *foie gras* and truffles as menu highlights.

**FIGEAC: La Cuisine du Marché** €€
Bistro
*15 rue Clermont, 46100*
**Tel** *05 65 50 18 55* **Closed** *Sun & Mon lunch*
The seasonal menus at this attractively converted stone wine cellar in medieval Figeac mix local favorites with Spanish dishes.

**FRANCESCAS: Le Relais de la Hire** €€
Regional
*11 rue Porteneuve, 47600*
**Tel** *05 53 65 41 59* **Closed** *Sun*
Fresh herbs from the chef's garden add bold flavors to the cuisine in this charming historic building.

**ISSIGEAC: La Brucelière** €€
Regional
*Pl de la Capelle, 24560*
**Tel** *05 53 73 89 61* **Closed** *May–Oct: Tue eve & Wed; Nov–Apr: Tue & Wed*
This rugged inn outside Bergerac serves lighter variations of local cuisine. Charming terrace.

**LACAVE: Le Pont de l'Ouysse** €€
Fine dining
*Le Pont de l'Ouysse, 46200*
**Tel** *05 65 37 87 04* **Closed** *Nov–Mar; weekly closing days vary*
This gorgeous restaurant has fabulous terrace views. Truffles are from the hotel's own grounds.

**LES EYZIES-DE-TAYAC: Au Vieux Moulin** €
Regional
*2 rue du Moulin Bas, 24620*
**Tel** *05 53 06 94 33* **Closed** *Tue, Wed & Sat lunch; Nov–Mar*
Classic local dishes are served in a very pretty old mill that overlooks a stream near the Lascaux caves.

**MANCIET: La Bonne Auberge** €
Regional
*Pl du Pesquèrot, 32370*
**Tel** *05 62 08 50 04* **Closed** *Mon*
Diners come to this family-run restaurant for the rich Gascon fare and the fine Armagnacs.

One of the many gastronomic creations at Le Pont de l'Ouysse, Lacave

**MONBAZILLAC: La Tour des Vents** €€
Traditional French
*Moulin de Malfourat, 24240*
**Tel** *05 53 58 30 10* **Closed** *Sun eve, Mon & Tue lunch*
There are stunning views of the Dordogne countryside from this Michelin-starred hilltop restaurant. Creative menus.

**MONTAUBAN: Au Fil de l'Eau** €
Bistro
*14 quai du Dr Lafforgue, 82000*
**Tel** *05 63 66 11 85* **Closed** *Sun & Mon*
A sizzling *cassoulet* heads the list of local specialties at this smart restaurant in the heart of old Montauban.

**PERIGUEUX: Restaurant L'Essentiel** €€
Regional
*8 rue de la Clarté, 24000*
**Tel** *05 53 35 15 15* **Closed** *Mon & Sun*
Sample subtle combinations of classic Périgord food and modern innovation at this local Michelin-starred favorite. The decor is warm and charming.

**PUJAUDRAN: Le Puits Saint-Jacques** €€€
Fine dining
*Av Victor Capoul, 32600*
**Tel** *05 62 07 41 11* **Closed** *Sun eve, Mon & Tue*
Exquisite cuisine and excellent wines are showcased at this prestigious restaurant in a historic farmhouse setting.

**PUJOLS: La Toque Blanche** €€
Regional
*47300, Pujols*
**Tel** *05 53 49 00 30* **Closed** *Sun & Mon*
Book in advance at this long-established restaurant with lovely views and an inventive chef.

**ROCAMADOUR: Le Roc du Berger** €
Regional
*Bois de Belveyre, rte de Padirac, 46500*
**Tel** *05 65 33 19 99* **Closed** *Oct: Mon–Fri; Nov–mid-Mar*
Local lamb and trout feature on the menu at this rustic eatery with tables inside wood cabins or under trees.

**ST.-MEDARD: Le Gindreau** €€€
Fine dining
*Le Bourg, 46150*
**Tel** *05 65 36 22 27* **Closed** *Mon & Tue*
Savor gourmet meals in a converted village school. Delicious truffles and an exemplary wine cellar.

**SARLAT: La Couleuvrine** €
Regional
*1 pl de la Bouquerie, 24200*
**Tel** *05 53 59 27 80*
Enjoy hearty bistro-style food by the medieval fireplace in a tower in Sarlat's grand ramparts.

**DK Choice**

**SORGES: Auberge de la Truffe** €
Regional
*Le Bourg, 24420*
**Tel** *05 53 05 02 05*
Truffles figure prominently in Périgord cuisine, and Sorges proclaims itself the "world truffle capital." This inn is the ideal place to sample truffles in all their variety – *consommé*, omelets, with scallops, and in desserts.

**TOULOUSE: Brasserie Flo – Les Beaux Arts** €€
Brasserie
*1 quai de la Daurade, 31000*
**Tel** *05 61 21 12 12*
A local institution, Brasserie Flo has grand 1900s decor, a bustling atmosphere, and a huge menu.

**TOULOUSE: Le Louchebem** €€
Traditional French
*Marché Victor Hugo, 31000*
**Tel** *05 67 00 51 75* **Closed** *Mon, dinner*
Carnivores will love this meat haven on the first floor of the Victor Hugo market. Try the Toulouse sausage or *cassoulet*.

**TOULOUSE: Michel Sarran** €€€
Fine dining
*21 bd Armand Duportal, 31000*
**Tel** *05 61 12 32 32* **Closed** *Wed lunch, Sat & Sun; Aug*
A real gourmet experience awaits at this elegant Michelin-starred restaurant. Try the creative and delicious chef's tasting menu.

**For more information on types of restaurants** *see p575*

**TURSAC: La Source**     €
Regional
*Le Bourg, 24620*
**Tel** *05 53 06 98 00* **Closed** *Tue & Wed*
This friendly restaurant serves local dishes featuring herbs and mushrooms from the onsite garden.

# The Pyrenees

**AINHOA: La Maison Oppoca**     €€
Regional
*Le Bourg, 64250*
**Tel** *05 59 29 90 72*     **Closed** *Thu, Fri lunch, Sun eve*
Serving Basque cuisine, this stylish establishment specializes in crab dishes and inventive cooking.

**ARGELES-GAZOST: Au Fond du Gosier**     €
Bistro
*7 rue du Capitaine Digoy, 65400*
**Tel** *05 62 90 13 40*     **Closed** *Sat lunch, Sun & Mon*
Local dishes are prepared with fresh produce and culinary flair at this place. Original wine list.

**ASCAIN: L'Atelier Gourmand Basque**     €
Regional
*Pl du Fronton, 64310*
**Tel** *05 59 54 46 82*     **Closed** *Sun; Jul & Aug; Mon*
This lively bar-restaurant offers great local cuisine, plus a range of tapas dishes.

**AX-LES-THERMES: Le Chalet**     €€
Regional
*4 av Durandeau, 09110*
**Tel** *05 61 64 24 31*     **Closed** *Sun & Mon*
One of the best restaurants in the Ariège serves dishes such as local trout and deer in creative ways.

**BAGNERES-DE-LUCHON: Les Caprices Etigny**     €
Regional
*30 bis allées d'Etigny, 31110*
**Tel** *05 61 94 31 05*     **Closed** *Mon*
Try local lamb, organic trout or pork grilled over an open fire at this eatery with mountain views.

---

## DK Choice

**BAREGES: Auberge du Lienz Chez Louisette**     €
Regional
*Rte de Lienz, 65120*
**Tel** *05 62 92 67 17*     **Closed** *mid-Apr–mid-May & Nov*
Few restaurants boast such a spectacular location, in the High Pyrenees. In winter, skiers warm up with *garbure* (thick soup); for summer hikers, there are dishes with wildflowers and fruits.

---

Chic, comfortable dining space at Le Sin restaurant, Biarritz

**BAYONNE: Le Bayonnais**     €
Bistro
*38 quai des Corsaires, 64100*
**Tel** *05 59 25 61 19*     **Closed** *Sun & Mon; 3 wks in Jun & 2 wks in Dec*
Enjoy Basque fare, including great squid, at this pleasant place with a terrace on a riverside dock.

**BAYONNE: Auberge du Cheval Blanc**     €€
Fine dining
*68 rue Bourgneuf, 64100*
**Tel** *05 59 59 01 33*     **Closed** *Mon, Sat lunch, Sun eve*
Family-run and Michelin-starred, this inn offers particularly good ham and Atlantic seafood.

**BIARRITZ: Chez Albert**     €€
Seafood
*51 bis allée Port des Pêcheurs, 64200*
**Tel** *05 59 24 43 84*     **Closed** *Feb–Jun & Sep–Nov; Wed; Dec–Jan*
Great sea views come as a bonus at this seafood brasserie located right on the port. The seafood platter is immense.

**BIARRITZ: Le Sin**     €€
Fine dining
*Cité de Océan, 1 av de la Plage, 64200*
**Tel** *05 59 47 82 89*     **Closed** *Sep–Jun: Mon, Sun eve*
Enjoy creative Basque cuisine based on local fish at this modern restaurant that comes with fabulous views.

**ESPELETTE: Hôtel-Restaurant Euzkadi**     €
Regional
*285 Karrika Nagusia, 64250*
**Tel** *05 59 93 91 88* **Closed** *Mon & Tue; mid-Feb–mid-Mar*
This charming eatery serves classic Basque fare, and the dishes often feature the village's famous fiery peppers.

**FOIX: Le Phoebus**     €
Regional
*3 cours Irénée Cros, 09000*
**Tel** *05 61 65 10 42*     **Closed** *Mon, Sat lunch, Sun eve; late July–mid-Aug*
Specialties here include duck, *foie gras* and chocolate fondant, but there are also vegetarian options. There are great views of the Ariège river and the château.

**LARRAU: Etchemaïte**     €
Regional
*Le Bourg, 64560*
**Tel** *05 59 28 61 45*     **Closed** *Jan–mid-Feb*
In the Pic d'Orhy, this family-run establishment boasts a gorgeous location. Lamb cooked in several ways is the star dish.

**LOURDES: Le Magret**     €
Bistro
*10 rue des 4 Frères Soulas, 65100*
**Tel** *05 62 94 20 55*     **Closed** *Wed*
Known for regional specialties from black pig, to *foie gras* and lamb, this small, relaxed bistro has good-value seasonal menus and wines.

**MIREPOIX: Les Remparts**     €
Bistro
*6 cours Louis Pons Tande, 09500*
**Tel** *05 61 60 80 22*
Global touches are given to local produce and traditions at this historic inn. Great surf 'n' turf.

**MONTSEGUR: La Patate Qui Fume**     €
Regional
*118 rue du Village, 09300*
**Tel** *05 61 02 65 07* **Closed** *Wed; Jul & Aug: Thu; Nov–Mar*
Set in a village house, this cosy restaurant serves hearty dishes made with local produce.

**PAU: Restaurant Pierre**     €€
Bistro
*14–16 rue Louis Barthou, 64000*
**Tel** *05 59 27 76 86*     **Closed** *Sat & Sun*
There are monthly menus at this snug spot with old-fashioned decor and an attached pub.

**ST.-GAUDENS: La Connivence**     €€
Fine dining
*Chemin Ample, Valentine, 31800*
**Tel** *05 61 95 29 31*     **Closed** *Mon*
Sophisticated and family-owned, this restaurant offers excellent wines and regional specialties.

**ST.-JEAN-DE-LUZ: Chez Pablo**     €€
Regional
*5 rue Mlle Etcheto, 64500*
**Tel** *05 59 26 37 81*     **Closed** *Wed*
Family-owned for three generations, this friendly eatery has a copious menu and specializes in Basque seafood.

**ST.-JEAN-DE-LUZ: Le Kaïku** €€€
Fine Dining
*17 rue de la République, 64500*
**Tel** *05 59 26 13 20* **Closed** *Tue & Wed*
Enjoy inventive Basque cuisine and
superb fish in a lovely old stone
house. Good-value lunch menu.

**ST.-JEAN-PIED-DE-PORT:**
**Relais de la Nive** €
Brasserie
*4 pl Charles de Gaulle, 64220*
**Tel** *05 59 37 04 22*
This spacious brasserie with fine
views over the River Nive makes
great salads and light meals.

**ST.-LARY-SOULAN:**
**Restaurant La Grange** €
Regional
*13 rte d'Autun, 65170*
**Tel** *05 62 40 07 14* **Closed** *Sep–Jun:*
*Tue & Wed; Nov*
Enjoy local bean stews and
grilled meats at this large stone
farmhouse in the High Pyrenees.

**SAINT-GIRONS: L'Auberge**
**d'Antan** €€
Regional
*Av de la Résistance, 09200*
**Tel** *05 61 64 11 02* **Closed** *Mon, Sat*
*lunch, Sun eve*
Savor spit-roast suckling pig – the
house specialty – at this restaurant set in a renovated barn.

**SARE: Baratxartea** €
Regional
*Ihalar, 64310*
**Tel** *05 59 54 20 48* **Closed** *mid-Nov–*
*mid-Mar*
The chef plates fine food made
with vegetables from the hotel's
garden at this large Basque chalet.

**TARBES: L'Agora** €
Fine dining
*48 rue Abbé Torné, 65000*
**Tel** *05 62 93 09 34* **Closed** *Mon*
Tarbes' top restaurant features
fresh produce and fish. Excellent
wines and a charming terrace.

Pretty shaded eating area at the popular
La Marquière, Carcassonne

# Languedoc and Roussillon

**AIGUES-MORTES: Le Duendé** €
Regional
*13 rue Amiral Courbet, 30220*
**Tel** *04 66 51 79 28*
This simple restaurant in an old
townhouse is a good place to
sample the local flavors of
traditional Camargue cuisine
in a warm ambience.

**AIGUES-MORTES: Le Café**
**des Bouzigues** €€
Regional
*7 rue Pasteur, 30220*
**Tel** *04 66 53 93 95* **Closed** *most of*
*Jan, late Nov–early Dec*
This cheerful restaurant with a
terrace supplies a creative and
hearty fixed-price menu.

**ANDUZE: Auberge**
**Les Trois Barbus** €€
Fine dining
*Rte de Mialet, Camaou et Roucan,*
*Générargues, 30140*
**Tel** *04 66 61 72 12* **Closed** *Mon & Tue;*
*Nov–late Mar*
This elegant restaurant in a rustic
setting has plenty of dishes
featuring *foie gras* and wild
mushrooms. Rich desserts, too.

**ARGELLIERS: Auberge**
**de Saugras** €€
Traditional French
*Domaine de Saugras, 34380*
**Tel** *04 67 55 08 71* **Closed** *Tue & Wed*
There is an impressive cellar at
this traditional farmhouse serving
lots of duck and mountain trout.

**BEZIERS: Octopus** €€€
Fine dining
*12 rue Boiledieu, 34500*
**Tel** *04 67 49 90 00* **Closed** *Sun & Mon*
Béziers' best restaurant is a
Michelin-starred affair with lots
of truffles, a touch of Asia, and a
great wine selection.

**BIZE MINERVOIS: La Bastide**
**Cabezac** €
Traditional French
*18–20 Hameau de Cabezac, 11120,*
**Tel** *04 68 46 66 10* **Closed** *Sun eve,*
*Mon*
Come to this atttractive 18th-
century staging post with
refined creative fare such
as Cathar chicken *fricassée*.

**CAP D'AGDE: La Manade** €
Regional
*15 pl Saint-Clair, 34300*
**Tel** *04 67 21 23 38* **Closed** *winter:*
*Tue & Wed*
This is the place for affordable,
tasty seafood and succulent
steaks from the Camargue.

**CARCASSONNE: L'Escargot** €
Regional
*7 rue Viollet le Duc, 11000*
**Tel** *04 68 47 12 55* **Closed** *Wed*
A popular tapas and wine bar,
L'Escargot offers a range of dishes
with international influences
made with local produce.

## DK Choice

**CARCASSONNE:**
**La Marquière** €€
Regional
*13 rue St.-Jean, 11000*
**Tel** *04 68 71 52 00* **Closed** *Wed &*
*Thu; Jan 10–Feb 10*
Located up in the Cité, La
Marquière is a popular family-
run local favorite. The food is
authentic Southwestern – duck
breasts and *confits, foie gras* and
*cassoulet.* Oysters and other
seafood are available too.

**CARCASSONNE:**
**Le Parc Franck Putelat** €€€
Fine dining
*80 chemin des Anglais, 11000*
**Tel** *04 68 71 80 80* **Closed** *Sun*
*& Mon; 3 weeks in Jan*
Sample radically creative cuisine
at this two-star restaurant with a
good-value lunch menu.

**CERET: Alcatalà** €
Catalan
*15 av Georges Clémenceau, 66400*
**Tel** *04 68 87 07 91* **Closed** *Mon*
Creative cooking, exotic flavors,
and a dash of Catalan style can
be enjoyed on a chic bamboo-
shaded terrace.

**CLARA: Les Loges du Jardin**
**d'Aymeric** €€
Traditional French
*7 rue du Canigou, 66500*
**Tel** *04 68 96 08 72* **Closed** *Sun eve &*
*Mon; Jan*
Classic dishes with a
contemporary twist are served
in a tranquil garden setting.

**COLLIOURE: Le 5e Péché** €€
Regional
*18 rue Fraternité, 66190*
**Tel** *04 68 98 09 76* **Closed** *Sun &*
*Mon*
A Japanese chef creates his own
remarkable Languedoc-Asian
fusion cuisine from a choice of
fresh, local ingredients.

**COLLIOURE: La Balette** €€
Fine dining
*114 rte de Port-Vendres, 66190*
**Tel** *04 68 82 05 07* **Closed** *Mon (also*
*Tue in low season); late Nov–early Feb*
Dine on elaborate creations in a
beautiful setting with magical
views of Collioure over the bay.

**For more information on types of restaurants** *see p575*

**CUCUGNAN: Auberge
du Vigneron** €
Regional
*2 rue Achille Mir, 11350*
**Tel** *04 68 45 03 00* **Closed** *Mon;
late Nov–early Mar*
The hearty Languedoc fare here
uses produce from the kitchen
garden. Good Corbières wines.

**FONTJONCOUSE:
Gilles Goujon** €€€
Fine dining
*5 av St.-Victor, 11360*
**Tel** *04 68 44 07 37* **Closed** *Mon;
Dec–late Mar*
Culinary masterpieces are
served at this Michelin-starred
restaurant. Try the "truffle eggs".

**LE BOULOU: Hostalet de Vivès** €
Catalan
*Le Village, Vivès, 66490*
**Tel** *04 68 83 05 52* **Closed** *Mon &
Tue; Jul & Aug: Mon*
Grilled snails, rabbit cooked on an
open fire, and all things Catalan
are on offer at this rustic eatery.

**MARAUSSAN: Le Parfum
des Garrigues** €€
Regional
*37 rue de l'Ancienne Poste, 34370*
**Tel** *09 70 35 53 34* **Closed** *Mon & Tue*
Fresh seafood, grilled meat, and
game dishes are delivered on a
pretty courtyard.

**MINERVE: Relais Chantovent** €
Bistro
*17 Grande Rue, 34210*
**Tel** *04 68 91 14 18* **Closed** *Sun &
Wed, Tue eve; mid-Dec–mid-Mar*
Terrace views over the Gorges du
Brian accompany the creative
cooking. Home-made ice cream.

**MONTPELLIER: Au Bonheur
des Tartes** €
Bistro
*4 rue des Trésoriers de la Bourse, 34000*
**Tel** *04 67 02 77 38* **Closed** *Sun, Wed
eve*
Enjoy perfect cooking and
excellent *plats du jour* in this cosy
eatery with a tearoom attached.

**MONTPELLIER: La Diligence** €€
Traditional French
*2 pl Pétrarque, 34000*
**Tel** *04 67 66 12 21* **Closed** *Sun,
Mon & Sat lunch*
Set in a vaulted medieval hall,
this downtown restaurant serves
grilled dishes, wines, and desserts.

**MONTPELLIER: Le Petit Jardin** €€
Fine dining
*20 rue Jean-Jacques Rousseau, 34000*
**Tel** *04 67 60 78 78* **Closed** *winter:
Sun & Mon*
Enjoy old-world elegance and
refined cuisine at this eatery that

boasts a lovely garden setting.
The seasonally changing menu
takes inspiration from cuisines
across the world.

**NARBONNE: Chez Bebelle** €
Bistro
*Halles de Narbonne, 1 bd Dr. Ferroul,
11100*
**Tel** *06 85 40 09 01* **Closed** *Sun & Mon*
At this inexpensive, cheerful
family-run steakhouse in the
covered market, the meat is
sourced daily from the
neighboring butcher.

**NARBONNE: Le Table
de St.-Crescent** €€
Fine dining
*Rond pt de la Liberté, 68 av Général
Leclerc, 11100*
**Tel** *04 68 41 37 37* **Closed** *Mon
& Tue (Jul–Sep: Mon only)*
An old medieval chapel provides
the perfect setting for a special
evening. A creative, seasonal
menu is on offer.

**NIMES: Aux Plaisirs des Halles** €
Traditional French
*4 rue Littré, 30000*
**Tel** *04 66 36 01 02* **Closed** *Sun & Mon*
Classic dishes made from locally
sourced ingredients, including
lamb and olives, is served in a
pleasant wood-paneled interior.

**NIMES: Le Cheval Blanc** €
Wine bar
*1 pl des Arènes, 30000*
**Tel** *04 66 76 19 59* **Closed** *Sun*
Facing the arena, this lively
brasserie has a great cellar and
Pyrenean *charcuterie* and cheeses.

**PERPIGNAN: Le Grain de Folie** €
Bistro
*71 av Général Leclerc, 66000*
**Tel** *04 68 51 00 50* **Closed** *Sun eve*
The dining room here may be
austere, but the cooking is first
rate. It provides good-value
meals and great desserts.

The well-stocked Le Cheval Blanc wine
bar in Nîmes

**PERPIGNAN: La Galinette** €€
Fine dining
*23 rue Jean Payra, 66000*
**Tel** *04 68 35 00 90* **Closed** *Sun & Mon*
Boasting a huge wine list, this is
also the place for creative, critically
acclaimed Catalan cuisine.

**PEZENAS: L'Entre-Pots** €€
Modern French
*8 av Louis-Montagne, 34120*
**Tel** *04 67 39 00 00* **Closed** *Jul & Aug:
Mon; Sep–Jun: Sun & Mon*
In an old warehouse, this
restaurant serves inventive food
and boasts a large wine cellar.

**PORT CAMARGUE:
Le Spinaker** €€
Traditional French
*Pointe du Môle, Le Grau du Roi, 30240*
**Tel** *04 66 53 36 37* **Closed** *Mon–
Wed (out of season); Jan; Jul & Aug:
Mon & Tue*
Seafood, grilled beef, and duck are
served on a terrace overlooking
the marina. Decadent desserts.

**PORT-VENDRES:
La Cote Vermeille** €€
Seafood
*Quai Fanal, 66660*
**Tel** *04 68 82 05 71* **Closed** *Mon*
Enjoying a dockside location, this
famous seafood restaurant has
delicious lobster and oysters.

**SAILLAGOUSE: La Vieille
Maison Cerdane** €
Catalan
*Pl de Cerdagne, 66800*
**Tel** *04 68 04 72 08* **Closed** *Mon;
mid-Nov–mid-Apr*
This old family-run coach inn
specializes in venison and other
game dishes.

**SETE: Terre et Mer** €€
Regional
*Pl de Souras Bas, 34200*
**Tel** *04 67 74 49 43* **Closed** *Tue & Wed*
Come here for fresh seafood,
meat, and *charcuterie* from the
Aveyron. Great desserts, too.

**SOURNIA: Auberge de Sournia** €
Traditional French
*4 rte de Prades, 66730*
**Tel** *04 68 97 72 82* **Closed** *Wed &
Sun eves; 2 weeks in Feb & Nov*
The hearty mountain cooking at
this popular village inn includes
steak, duck, and a range of
game dishes.

**UZES: Au Petit Jardin** €€
Bistro
*4 bd Gambetta, 30700*
**Tel** *04 66 81 56 88* **Closed** *Oct–Jun:
Sun*
Enjoy good bistro food in a lovely
garden setting. There is live jazz
on Saturday evenings.

**VILLEFRANCHE-DE-CONFLENT:**
**Auberge St-Paul** €€
Bistro
*7 pl de Eglise, 66500*
**Tel** *04 68 96 30 95* **Closed** *Mon*
Sample creative dishes with
a Spanish touch, including a
mushroom-themed "land and
sea" menu.

# Provence and the Côte d'Azur

**AIX-EN-PROVENCE: Le Formal** €€
Fine dining
*32 rue Espariat, 13100*
**Tel** *04 42 27 08 31* **Closed** *Sat lunch,
Sun & Mon; late Aug–early Sep*
Choose from a range of truffle
dishes at Le Formal. The lunch
menus are a good value.

**ANTIBES: Aubergine** €
Regional
*7 rue Sade, 06600*
**Tel** *04 93 34 55 93* **Closed** *Wed*
This popular restaurant is the
place to visit for excellent
Provençal dishes. Book ahead.

**ARLES: La Grignotte** €
Regional
*6 rue Favorin, 13200*
**Tel** *04 90 93 10 43* **Closed** *Sun & Mon*
Try the fish soup and beef stew
with Camargue rice at this simple
eatery. Good house wines.

**ARLES: Lou Marques** €€
Fine dining
*9 bd Lices, 13200*
**Tel** *04 90 52 52 52*
This elegant restaurant offers a
garden terrace and beautifully
presented classic Provençal dishes.

**AVIGNON: La Fourchette** €€
Regional
*17 rue Racine, 84000*
**Tel** *04 90 85 20 93* **Closed** *Sat & Sun*
Putting an innovative spin on
Provençal classics, this quirky place
offers tasty seafood and cheeses.

**AVIGNON: Christian Etienne** €€€
Fine dining
*10 rue Mons, 84000*
**Tel** *04 90 86 16 50* **Closed** *Wed & Thu*
This restaurant serves superb
seasonal fare and an elaborate
truffle menu in a stunning 14th-
century dining room.

**BIOT: Les Terrailiers** €€€
Fine dining
*11 rte Chemin Neuf, 06410*
**Tel** *04 93 65 01 59* **Closed** *Wed & Thu;
mid-Oct–Nov*
Lobster, truffles, and *foie gras*
await here, along with an
excellent list of Provençal wines.

Dining area at Les Terrailiers in Biot, in a 16th-century stone house

**BONNIEUX: Edouard**
**Loubet** €€€
Fine dining
*Les Claparèdes,
chemin des Cabanes, 84480*
**Tel** *04 90 75 89 78* **Closed** *Wed;
winter (except hols)*
Diners can enjoy ravishing dishes
from one of France's top chefs at
this gourmet restaurant in a great
location with views of the
Provençal countryside.

**CAGNES-SUR-MER:**
**Fleur de Sel** €€
Traditional French
*85 montée de la Bourgade, 06800*
**Tel** *04 93 20 33 33* **Closed** *Wed & Thu*
The lofty Haut de Cagnes makes
a lovely setting for some refined
cooking. There are great-value
set menus.

**CANNES: Angolo Italiano** €
Italian
*18 rue du Commandant André,
06400*
**Tel** *04 93 39 82 57* **Closed** *Mon*
This Neapolitan-run restaurant
serves *charcuterie*, cheeses,
grilled meat and seafood, as well
as lots of pasta dishes.

**CANNES: La Palme d'Or** €€€
Fine dining
*73 la Croisette, 06400*
**Tel** *04 92 98 74 14* **Closed** *Sun–Tue;
Jan & Feb*
Part of the famous Hôtel Martinez,
this fashionable Michellin-starred
restaurant has a terrace with
stunning views of the Bay of
Cannes. The exquisite food,
wonderful atmosphere, and
great service make this a
memorable experience.

**CARPENTRAS: Chez Serge** €
Bistro
*90 rue Cottier, 84200*
**Tel** *04 90 63 21 24*
Striking modern decor and
imaginative food featuring fish
and wild mushrooms can be found
here. There is a huge wine list.

**CASTELLANE: Auberge**
**du Teillon** €
Traditional French
*Rte Napoléon le Garde, 04120*
**Tel** *04 92 83 60 88* **Closed** *Mon;
Nov–Mar*
This country inn is famed for fine
dishes such as hand-smoked
salmon and *foie gras millefeuille*.

**CHATEAUNEUF-DU-PAPE:**
**La Mère Germaine** €€
Regional
*3 rue Commandant Lemaitre, 84230*
**Tel** *04 90 22 78 34* **Closed** *mid-Sep–
mid-Mar: Wed*
The wide range of classic
Provençal dishes is accompanied
by an excellent list of wines.

**EZE: Café La Gascogne** €
Bistro
*151 av de Verdun, 06360*
**Tel** *04 93 41 18 50*
Enjoy no-frills wholesome fare in
the Hotel du Golf – everything
from *foie gras* to pizza. Fantastic
selection of wines.

**EZE: Château Eza** €€€
Fine dining
*Rue de la Pise, 06360*
**Tel** *04 93 41 12 24* **Closed** *Mon & Tue;
Jan–Mar*
Château Eza offers stunning
terrace views and high-quality
Michelin-star cooking.

**DK Choice**

**FAYENCE: L'Escourtin** €€
Bistro
*159 chemin de Notre Dame des
Cyprès, 83440*
**Tel** *04 94 76 00 84* **Closed** *Wed*
Filled with antiques and flowers,
L'Escourtin has an idyllic location
inside an ancient olive mill with
a delightful garden courtyard.
The cuisine is authentic, with an
emphasis on game dishes, *foie
gras*, and fish in subtle sauces –
all flavored with the best garden
produce and herbs.

**For more information on types of restaurants** *see p575*

## ILE DE PORQUEROLLES:
**L'Olivier** €€€
Seafood
*Ile de Porquerolles Ouest, 83400*
**Tel** *04 94 58 34 83* **Closed** *Mon &*
*Tue (except Jul & Aug); Oct–Apr*
This isolated, semi-tropical island
retreat offers a delightful culinary
experience. Mostly seafood.

## L'ISLE-SUR-LE SORGUE:
**Le Vivier** €€
Regional
*800 cours Fernande Peyre, 84800*
**Tel** *04 90 38 52 80* **Closed** *Mon,*
*Fri & Sat lunch*
Ask for the famous pigeon pie with
porcini mushrooms and enjoy it
on the magical riverside terrace.

## LA TURBIE: Hostellerie Jérôme €€€
Fine dining
*20 rue Comte de Cessole, 06320*
**Tel** *04 92 41 51 51* **Closed** *Sep–Jun:*
*Mon & Tue*
All dishes are prepared daily using
market produce at this Michelin-
starred establishment. Dinner only.

## LES-BAUX-DE-PROVENCE:
**L'Oustau de Baumanière** €€€
Fine dining
*Rte Départementale 27,*
*Le Val d'Enfer 13520*
**Tel** *04 90 54 33 07* **Closed** *Jan & Feb*
Great for celebrity-spotting, this
Michelin-starred gem has a great
setting and inventive menus.

## LES-SAINTES-MARIES-DE-LA-
**MER: El Campo** €
Spanish
*13 rue Victor Hugo, 13460*
**Tel** *04 90 97 84 11* **Closed** *Sep–Jun:*
*Wed*
Enjoy an evening with live
flamenco and Gypsy-Kings-style
guitar music. Paella is a specialty

## MARSEILLE: Toinou €
Seafood
*3 cours Saint-Louis, 13001*
**Tel** *04 91 33 14 94*
Fresh oysters, mussels, and shrimp
are served with crusty bread and
white wine. Ideal seafood place.

## DK Choice

### MARSEILLE: L'Epuisette €€€
Seafood
*158 rue du Vallon des Auffes, 13007*
**Tel** *04 91 52 17 82* **Closed** *Sun*
*& Mon; 1 week in Mar*
Heavenly *bouillabaisse*, lobster
tajine and other seafood
delicacies are accompanied by
fine wines and followed by great
desserts. Attentive staff ensure a
memorable dining experience in
a spectacular glass dining room
overlooking the turquoise sea.

Refined and graceful dining room at the renowned Le Louis XV in Monaco

## MENTON: Le Mirazur €€€
Fine dining
*30 ave Aristide Briand, 06500*
**Tel** *04 92 41 86 86* **Closed** *Mon & Tue;*
*Nov–mid-Feb*
With magnificent sea and old
town views, the Michelin-starred
Le Mirazur offers colorful dishes
made with fresh seafood, local
lamb, and vegetables from the
chef's own garden.

## MONACO: Le Louis XV €€€
Fine dining
*Hotel de Paris, pl du Casino, Monte*
*Carlo, 98000*
**Tel** *00 377 98 06 88 64* **Closed** *Tue &*
*Wed*
Capital of Alain Ducasse's culinary
empire since 1987, Le Louis XV
is all about contemporary haute
cuisine in a supremely elegant
setting. It has a huge wine cellar.
Dinner only.

## DK Choice

### MOUSTIERS-STE.-MARIE:
**La Treille Muscate** €
Regional
*Pl de l'Eglise, 04360*
**Tel** *04 92 74 64 31* **Closed** *Wed*
*eve, Thu*
Near a waterfall, under the
crags, this restaurant has a
shady terrace under an ancient
plane tree on which to savor
Provençal and Mediterranean
dishes such as *pieds et paquets*
(sheeps' feet and stuffed sheep
tripe) with baby vegetables.

## NICE: Les Amoureux €
Italian
*46 bd Stalingrad, 06300*
**Tel** *04 93 07 59 73* **Closed** *Sun & Mon*
Visit Les Amoureux for some of
the best Neapolitan pizzas on the
Riviera, with the perfect crust,
served in a convivial atmosphere.

## NICE: Jan €€€
Fine dining
*12 rue Lascaris, 06000*
**Tel** *04 97 19 32 23* **Closed** *Sun & Mon*
Enjoy Michelin-starred cuisine from
South African chef Jan Hendrik,
who mixes French and South
African flavors in his creative,
contemporary dishes.

## ROQUEBRUNE-CAP-MARTIN:
**Au Grand Inquisiteur** €€
Traditional French
*15–18 rue du Château, 06190*
**Tel** *04 93 35 05 37* **Closed** *Mon*
This intimate, family-run
restaurant rustles up authentic
traditional dishes, including
snails. Dinner only.

## ST.-JEAN-CAP-FERRAT:
**La Cabane de L'Écailler** €€
Seafood **Map** F3
*Nouveau Port, 06230*
**Tel** *04 93 87 39 31* **Closed** *Nov–Mar*
Be sure to try the grilled fish,
*bouillabaisse* and roast lobster
at this delightful place on a
picturesque port.

## ST.-PAUL DE VENCE:
**La Colombe d'Or** €€
Regional
*Pl du Général de Gaulle, 06570*
**Tel** *04 93 32 80 02* **Closed** *Nov–*
*mid-Dec*
A legendary artists' retreat, La
Colombe d'Or offers simple but
excellent Provençal cooking.
Guests can eat alfresco on the
garden terrace.

## ST.-REMY DE PROVENCE:
**La Cantina** €
Italian
*18 bd Victor Hugo, 13210*
**Tel** *04 90 90 90 60* **Closed** *Mon*
There is an excellent selection
of Italian wines at this informal
restaurant specializing in thin-
crust pizzas and pasta dishes.

### ST.-TROPEZ: Vague d'Or   €€€
Fine dining
*Plage de la Bouillabaisse, 83990*
**Tel** *04 94 55 91 00*   **Closed** *Early Oct–late Apr*
Sample a range of imaginative Mediterranean dishes using local ingredients in a romantic setting. Excellent service and fine wines. Dinner only.

### STE.-AGNES: Le Righi   €
Regional
*1 pl du Fort, 06500*
**Tel** *04 92 10 90 88*   **Closed** *Wed*
Enjoy food such as ravioli, gnocchi, and lamb cooked in hay, while admiring the amazing views of the surrounding landscape.

### VENCE: La Litote   €€
Bistro
*5 rue de l'Evêché, 06140*
**Tel** *04 93 24 27 82*   **Closed** *Sun eve, Mon*
On a little square, with tables under the trees, this laid-back restaurant offers inventive fare.

### VILLEFRANCHE-SUR-MER: La Mère Germaine   €€
Seafood
*9 quai Courbet, 06230*
**Tel** *04 93 01 71 39*   **Closed** *mid-Nov–25 Dec*
A long-established favorite on the port since 1938, this place serves an excellent *bouillabaisse*.

### VILLENEUVE-LES-AVIGNON: Guinguette du Vieux Moulin   €€
Seafood
*5 rue du Vieux Moulin, 30400*
**Tel** *04 90 94 50 72*
This lively riverside restaurant specializes in grilled sardines and other fish. Live music.

## Corsica

### AJACCIO: A Nepita   €
Bistro
*4 rue St. Lazaro, 20000*
**Tel** *04 95 26 75 68*   **Closed** *Sat lunch, Sun, Mon–Wed eves*
The chef here bases his daily-changing menu on produce fresh from the market.

### DK Choice

#### AJACCIO: Le Week End   €€
Regional
*Rte des Sanguinaires, 20000*
**Tel** *04 95 52 01 39*   **Closed** *Winter*
This smart beach restaurant offers a mix of seafood and regional produce. Finish off with *limoncello* ice cream or a platter of Corsican cheeses.

Exterior of the popular restaurant La Mère Germaine in Villefranche-Sur-Mer

### BASTIA: Chez Huguette   €€
Seafood
*Vieux Port, rue de la Marine, 20200*
**Tel** *04 95 31 37 60*   **Closed** *2 weeks at Christmas*
A favorite on the Vieux Port, Chez Huguette is ideal for oysters and grilled fish. Excellent wine cellar.

### BONIFACIO: The Kissing Pigs   €
Regional
*15 quai Banda del Ferro, 20169*
**Tel** *04 95 73 56 09*
This portside eatery and wine bar serves *charcuterie*, omelets, grills, and a good range of wines.

### BONIFACIO: Le Voilier   €€
Fine dining
*81 quai Jérôme Comparetti, 20169*
**Tel** *04 95 73 07 06*   **Closed** *Wed; mid-Jan–mid-Feb*
In summer this chic restaurant has a mozzarella bar that is perfect for a light lunch. Lovely tapas.

### CALVI: A Casetta   €
Regional
*16 rue Clémenceau, 20280*
**Tel** *04 95 65 32 15*
This deli stocking regional products has a "tasting terrace" that offers great views. Try a platter of local hams and cheeses.

### CARGESE: Bel'Mare   €
Mediterranean
*Rte d'Ajaccio, 20130*
**Tel** *04 95 26 40 13*   **Closed** *Nov–Feb*
Enjoy the views from the terrace and choose from a range of pizzas, pasta dishes, steaks, and salads. Evenings only.

### CORTE: Osteria di l'Orta   €€
Bistro
*Casa Guelfucci, Pont de l'Orta, 20250*
**Tel** *04 95 61 06 41*   **Closed** *Sat & Sun; mid-Nov–Mar*
Meals here feature homegrown produce, plus meat raised and cured by the owners.

### ERBALUNGA: Le Pirate   €€€
Fine dining
*Port, 20222*
**Tel** *04 95 33 24 20*   **Closed** *Jan–Feb; Sep–Jun: Mon & Tue*
Diners can sample organic lamb and veal, plus wonderful desserts, in a romantic, Michelin-starred spot on the water.

### LEVIE: A Pignata   €€
Regional
*Rte du Pianu, 20170*
**Tel** *04 95 78 41 90*   **Closed** *Winter*
Book ahead to dine at A Pignata, a beautiful *ferme-auberge* that guarantees first-rate cooking.

### PORTO-VECCHIO: Casa del Mare   €€€
Fine dining
*Rte de Palombaggia, 20137*
**Tel** *04 95 72 34 34*   **Closed** *Sun; mid-Nov–mid-Apr*
A modern seafront pavilion is the setting for sumptuous, Italian-influenced meals. Dinner only.

### SAINT-FLORENT: Le Petit Caporal   €€
Brasserie
*Port de Plaisance, 20217*
**Tel** *04 95 37 20 26*   **Closed** *Wed & Thu*
As well as excellent pizzas, pasta, mussels, and *frites*, the menu here includes steaks and seafood.

Sea views and a refined dining area at the waterside restaurant Le Pirate, Erbalunga

**For more information on types of restaurants** *see p575*

# Shopping in France

Shopping in France is a delight. Whether you go to the hypermarkets and department stores, or seek out the small specialty stores and markets, you will be tempted by stylish French presentation and the quality of goods on offer. Renowned for its food and wine, France also offers world-famous fashion, perfume, pottery, porcelain, and crystal. This section provides guidelines on opening hours and the range of goods stocked by the different types of stores. There are also details of quintessentially French products that are worth hunting down and a size conversion chart to aid clothes shopping.

Fresh nectarines and melons on sale at a market stall

## Opening Hours

Food stores open anytime between 7 and 8am and close around noon for lunch. In the north, the lunch break generally lasts for 2 hours; in the south, it is 3–4 hours (except in resorts, where it is shorter). After lunch, most food stores reopen until 7pm or later.

Bakeries open early and many stay open until early evening, to catch the late baguette buyers. They also serve a range of lunchtime snacks.

Supermarkets, department stores, and most hypermarkets remain open all day, with no lunchtime closure.

General opening hours for non-food stores are 9am–6pm Monday through Saturday, often with a break for lunch. Many of these stores are closed on Monday mornings, and the smaller stores may be closed all day. In the tourist regions, however, stores usually open every day in high season.

Sunday is by far the quietest shopping day, although most food stores (and newsstands) open (usually for the morning), as do many stores in the main tourist areas of large cities.

## Hypermarkets and Department Stores

Hypermarkets (*hypermarchés* or *grandes surfaces*) can be found on the outskirts of every sizable town: look for signs indicating *centre commercial*. Much bigger than supermarkets, they sell mainly groceries, but their other lines include clothing, home accessories, and electronic equipment. They also sell discount gasoline. **Carrefour**, **Casino**, **Auchan**, **Leclerc**, and **Intermarché** are the biggest.

Supermarkets and retail chains, such as **Monoprix** and **Franprix**, are usually found downtown, as are the more upscale *(grands magasins)* **Printemps** and **Galeries Lafayette**.

A local bakery, which often sells pastries as well as bread

## Specialty Stores

One of the pleasures of shopping in France is that specialty food stores continue to flourish, despite the influx of supermarkets and hypermarkets. The *boulangerie* (bakery) is frequently combined with a *pâtisserie* selling cakes and pastries. The *traiteur* sells prepared foods. *Fromagers* (cheese stores) and other stores specializing in dairy products *(produits laitiers)* may be combined, but the *boucherie* (butcher) and *charcuterie* (pork butcher-delicatessen) are often separate stores. For general groceries go to an *épicerie* or *alimentation*, but don't confuse this with an *épicerie fine* – a delicatessen.

Cleaning and household products are available from a *droguerie*, while hardware is bought from a *quincaillerie*. The term *papeterie* (stationer) covers both the expensive, specialty retailers and their hypermarket equivalents.

## Markets

This guide lists the market day for most towns featured in the *Area by Area* section. To find out where the market is, ask a passerby for *le marché*. Markets are open in the morning and usually finish promptly at noon.

Look for local producers, including those with only one or two special items to sell, as their goods are often more reasonably priced and of better quality than stands with multiple items. By law (but not always in practice) price tags include the origin of all produce: *pays* means "local." Chickens from Bresse are marketed featuring a red, white, and blue badge with the name of the producer.

If you are visiting markets over several weeks, look for items just coming into season, such as fresh walnuts, the first wild asparagus, early artichokes, or wild strawberries. At the market, you can also buy spices and herbs, some offbeat peculiarities (such as decorative cabbages), shoes, and clothing.

The year is full of seasonal regional markets in France, specializing in such things as truffles, hams, garlic, *foie gras*, and livestock. *Foires artisanales* may be held at the same time as the seasonal markets, selling local produce and crafts.

Sausages and cheeses, regional specialties on offer in a Lyon market

## Regional Produce

French regional specialties are available outside their area of origin, but it is more interesting to buy them locally as their creation and flavor reflect the traditions, tastes, and climate of the region.

Provence, in the south, prides itself on the quality of its olive oil, the best of which is made from the first cold pressing, lovingly decanted every day for a week. If you cannot get to a niche olive oil producer in Provence, head to **Oliviers et Co**, which has branches throughout the country, and sells an excellent selection of oils. Be sure to indulge in a tasting session to sample the flavors. In the temperate north, delicious Camembert cheese is the product of fresh Normandy milk that has been cured for at least 3 weeks.

Popular drinks are also associated with particular regions. Pastis, flavored with aniseed, is popular in the south. Calvados, made in Normandy from apples, is popular in the

Provençal dried herbs for culinary use and for making teas

**Pastis 51, a popular *apéritif***

north. Fruit liqueur, the secret ingredient to many a good cocktail or dessert, comes in many flavors (from peach to wild strawberry) in addition to the well-known blackcurrant – **Crème de Cassis**. Visit local producers to buy good versions of this thick, alcoholic syrup.

To a large extent, location determines the quality of regional produce. For example, the culinary tradition of Lyon *(see pp382–5)*, France's premier gastronomic city, stems from the proximity of Charolais cattle, Bresse chickens and pork, wild game from La Dombes, and the finest Rhône Valley wines.

Alongside sachets of dried herbs from Provence and plaited strings of garlic and onions, be sure to buy the seasoning loved by all self-respecting francophile cooks – salt from the Ile de Ré *(see p420)* or Guérande. If you happen to be visiting the area, check out the salt flats and pick up the crumbly coarse grains at a local market. The Fleur de Sel is a delicate, fine-grained variety and the Sel Marin is a gray, coarser type of salt.

## Beauty Products

French women are renowned for their grooming, and there is a plethora of good beauty products in France. The major French labels, such as **Chanel** and **Guerlain**, are available overseas, but die-hard cosmetics fans should scour the local beauty counters to find special products that are only on sale in France.

While in Paris, beauty junkies must visit the Chanel store on rue Cambon and the Guerlain store on the Champs-Elysées to buy special scent that is only available in those particular stores.

Throughout the rest of the country, brands such as Evian, Eau Thermale d'Avene, and Barbara Gould, available at many supermarkets, are popular. A visit to any branch of Monoprix or especially to one of their Monop'Beauty outposts, will reveal a large selection of quality products that can mostly only be found in department stores in other countries. The cosmetics chain Sephora has several hundred brands of skincare, fragrances, and cosmetics. Likewise, pharmacies in every town also carry a range of high-end healthcare and beauty items not found in supermarkets. If you are looking for standard sunscreen or hair products, don't expect to find too many low-end brands in pharmacies.

A more traditional approach to French grooming can be found by buying *savon de Marseille* – good-quality traditional soap made with plenty of olive oil.

True scent aficionados should head for Grasse *(see p521)*, the perfume capital of the world. Be sure to visit the three largest scent factories, **Fragonard**, **Molinard**, and **Galimard**, all of which have scent available for purchase.

## Accessories

French fashion is rightfully famous, but aside from the main couture labels and stores (see pp146–8), the best way to get the French look is to accessorize à la française. In keeping with the French tradition of specialty local trades, there are certain regions that excel in producing accessories.

For a start, a handmade umbrella from Aurillac (see p368) is guaranteed to chase away rainy-day blues in style. The best-known umbrella manufacturers are **L'Ondée au Parapluie d'Aurillac**, **Piganiol**, and **Delos**, who will customize one for you with a photograph of whomever you choose to protect you from the storms.

Beautiful hands are easily available courtesy of the glove trade in Millau. Visit **L'Atelier Gantier** (the Glove Workshop) to pick up a stunning pair of expertly hand-stitched leather gloves in one of a seemingly endless array of colors.

More casual chic can be found with brightly colored wicker baskets from local markets and hardware stores. These quickly turn a casual ensemble into a boho-chic outfit. Beachside boutiques are great places for picking up stylish sarongs, beads, and bracelets for any trip to la plage

(the beach). **K Jacques** sandals from St.-Tropez have long been must-have items among the fashion set.

When it is time to hit the slopes rather than the beach, French ski-wear labels such as Rossignol can be a good buy, but only at the end of the season. At the height of piste time, ski resort stores are expensive. Once the snow starts to melt, however, ex-rental gear including skis and boots can be picked up relatively cheaply, while ski jackets, hats, and après-ski-wear tends to be gloriously cut-price.

## Household Goods

If you are in the market for housewares, the best stores are **Conforama**, **Alinea**, and **Habitat**. **Truffaut** sells garden furniture, and **Leroy Merlin** is the hypermarket of the home-improvement world.

It is surprisingly rare to see the whole range of kitchen goods in a specialty store. Instead, try the kitchen section of department stores. General hardware stores stock cast-iron cooking equipment. White china is sold in specialty stores.

Traveling through Normandy provides the perfect excuse for sampling many wonderful products, not least the crème Chantilly, but for tableware

fans or lingerie lovers the lace industry here is also guaranteed to please. While **Alençon** lace is extremely expensive and mainly finds its way onto couture sold in top Parisian stores, hitting the stores in Argentan, Chantilly (see pp208–9), and Bayeux (see pp256–7) is likely to yield exquisite yet affordable lace. For those who want to keep costs to a minimum, it is worth hunting around for small lace pieces that can be used to liven up an outfit, such as a delicate lace flower that can be added to a bag or blouse.

Lace curtains are easy to come by, as are lovely table-cloths. The best way to be sure to see or buy good lace is to take "the lace road" and visit the **Alençon Lace Museum** and the lace boutiques in Alençon, Argentan, Caen (see pp257–8), Courseulles, Villedieu-les-Poêles, and La Perrière.

With a beautiful tablecloth in place, you can proceed to pick up stunning crystal from which to sniff, swirl, and sip great French wine. The most famous crystal maker in France, **Baccarat**, has a museum where you can take in some of their amazing creations and a store where you can buy a little Baccarat bauble to take home with you. A cheaper French crystal that is still elegant for every-day use is **Cristal d'Arques**. You can tour the small museum in the factory and buy stemware at discount prices in the factory store.

Pottery is available at reasonable prices, especially near centers of production, such as Quimper (see p278) in Brittany, Aubagne near Marseille, and Vallauris (see p526) near Grasse.

Porcelain from Limoges (see p360) sets off any meal beautifully: a dinner set from the **Royal Limoges** factory store can be a great investment.

Similarly, stunning **Aubusson** tapestries are seriously expensive and unlikely to be an impulse vacation buy. However, interior design fanatics could do worse than plan their tapestry or rug

## Size Chart

**Women's dresses, coats, and skirts**

| | | | | | | | |
|---|---|---|---|---|---|---|---|
| French | 36 | 38 | 40 | 42 | 44 | 46 | 48 |
| British | 8 | 10 | 12 | 14 | 16 | 18 | 20 |
| American | 4 | 6 | 8 | 10 | 12 | 14 | 16 |

**Women's shoes**

| | | | | | | |
|---|---|---|---|---|---|---|
| French | 36 | 37 | 38 | 39 | 40 | 41 |
| British | 3 | 4 | 5 | 6 | 7 | 8 |
| American | 5 | 6 | 7 | 8 | 9 | 10 |

**Men's suits**

| | | | | | | | |
|---|---|---|---|---|---|---|---|
| French | 44 | 46 | 48 | 50 | 52 | 54 | 56 | 58 |
| British | 34 | 36 | 38 | 40 | 42 | 44 | 46 | 48 |
| American | 34 | 36 | 38 | 40 | 42 | 44 | 46 | 48 |

**Men's shirts**

| | | | | | | | |
|---|---|---|---|---|---|---|---|
| French | 36 | 38 | 39 | 41 | 42 | 43 | 44 | 45 |
| British | 14 | 15 | 15½ | 16 | 16½ | 17 | 17½ | 18 |
| American | 14 | 15 | 15½ | 16 | 16½ | 17 | 17½ | 18 |

**Men's shoes**

| | | | | | | | |
|---|---|---|---|---|---|---|---|
| French | 39 | 40 | 41 | 42 | 43 | 44 | 45 | 46 |
| British | 6 | 7 | 7½ | 8 | 9 | 10 | 11 | 12 |
| American | 7 | 7½ | 8 | 8½ | 9½ | 10½ | 11 | 11½ |

purchase around a trip to the home of weaving in Aubusson (see pp360–61).

Finishing touches are fun to shop for and can certainly be more frivolous. Be sure to visit the local markets for gingham cotton napkins, linen cleaning cloths, and seafood accoutrements (such as lobster crackers and oyster forks). In Provence, be sure to stock up on cheap, brightly colored cookware – tagines, terracotta bowls, and painted plates are all in abundance.

## Wine

To buy wine straight from the vineyards (domaines) and wine cooperatives, follow the tasting (dégustation) signs. You may be expected to buy at least one bottle, except where a small fee is charged for wine tasting. Wine cooperatives make and sell the wine of small producers. Here you can buy wine in 5- and 10-liter containers (en tonneau), as well as in bottles. Wine sold en tonneau, once opened, needs to be consumed fairly quickly, as it will deteriorate within a few days. Wine sold in bottles travels better.

**Nicolas** is France's main liquor store, with many branches.

## Factory Outlets

The French sales system is very rigid (see p144), but true bargain hunters know that factory outlets have some items on sale all year round. The biggest factory outlets in France can be found in and around Troyes in outlet malls called **Marques Avenue** (Brands Avenue), **Marques City** (Brands City), and **McArthurGlen**, a large American outlet. They sell everything from Yves Saint Laurent suits to Black and Decker drills, Cristofle silverware, and Bonpoint baby clothes. As different an experience as you can get from browsing around French markets and local specialty stores, what factory outlets lack in charm they make up for in bargains. If a whole new wardrobe is in order, it is definitely worth a trip.

# DIRECTORY

## Hypermarkets and Department Stores

For details of addresses, visit the following websites:

**Auchan**
w auchan.fr

**Carrefour**
w carrefour.fr

**Casino**
w supercasino.fr

**Franprix**
w franprix.fr

**Galeries Lafayette**
w galerieslafayette.com

**Intermarché**
w intermarche.com

**Leclerc**
w e-leclerc.com

**Monoprix**
w monoprix.fr

**Printemps**
w printemps.com

## Regional Produce

**Crème de Cassis**
Gabriel Boudier, 14 rue de Cluj, 21007 Dijon.
Tel 03 80 74 33 33.

**Oliviers et Co**
For details of addresses, visit w oliviers-co.com

## Beauty Products

**Chanel**
31 rue Cambon, 75008 Paris.Tel 01 44 50 66 00.
w chanel.com

**Fragonard**
20 bd Fragonard, 06130 Grasse. Tel 04 93 36 44 65.
w fragonard.com

**Galimard**
73 route de Cannes, 06130 Grasse. Tel 04 93 09 20 00.w galimard.com

**Guerlain**
68 av des Champs-Elysées, 75008 Paris.
Tel 01 45 62 52 57.
w guerlain.com

**Molinard**
60 bd Victor Hugo, 06130 Grasse. Tel 04 93 36 01 62.
w molinard.com

## Accessories

**L'Atelier Gantier**
21 rue Droite, 12100 Millau. Tel 05 65 60 81 50.
w atelierdugantier.fr

**Delos**
14 rue Rocher, 15000 Aurillac. Tel 04 71 48 86 85. w delos-france.com

**K Jacques**
32 rte Plages, 83990 St.-Tropez. Tel 04 94 97 41 50. w kjacques.fr

## L'Ondée au Parapluie d'Aurillac
27 rue Victor Hugo, 15000 Aurillac.
Tel 04 71 48 29 53.

**Piganiol**
9 rue Ampère 15000 Aurillac. Tel 04 71 63 42 60.

## Household Goods

**Alençon Lace Museum**
Cour carrée de la Dentelle, 61000 Alençon.
Tel 02 33 32 40 07.

**Alinea**
w alinea.fr

**Aubusson**
Manufacture Saint-Jean 3 rue Saint-Jean, 23200 Aubusson. Tel 05 55 66 10 08. w manufacture-saint-jean.fr

**Baccarat**
20 rue des Cristalleries, 54120 Baccarat.
Tel 03 83 76 60 06.
w baccarat.com

**Conforama**
w conforama.fr

**Cristal d'Arques**
132 av Gén de Gaulle, 62510 Arques.
Tel 03 21 95 46 96.
w arcdecoration.com

**Habitat**
w habitat.net

**Leroy Merlin**
w leroymerlin.fr

**Royal Limoges**
28 rue Donzelot Accès par le quai du Port du Naveix, 87000 Limoges.
Tel 05 55 33 27 37.
w royal-limoges.fr

**Truffaut**
w truffaut.com

## Wine

**Nicolas**
w nicolas.com

## Factory Outlets

**Marques Avenue**
Av de la Maille, 10800 Saint-Julien-les-Villas.
Tel 03 25 82 80 80.
w marquesavenue.com

**Marques City**
21 rue Marc Verdier, 10150 Pont Sainte Marie.
Tel 09 71 27 02 66.
w marquescity.fr

**McArthurGlen**
McArthurGlen Troyes, Voie du Bois, 10150 Pont-Sainte-Marie.
Tel 03 25 70 47 10.
w mcarthurglen.com

# Entertainment in France

Paris is one of the world's great entertainment cities, but France's reputation as a center of excellence in the arts extends well beyond the capital. Whether you prefer to attend theater or catch a movie, listen to jazz or techno, or watch modern dance, the country has a wide array of choices. The regional chapters in this guide will give you an insight into local gems, while these pages provide an overview of entertainment trends and events. Major festivals, such as Avignon and Cannes, occupy an important place in French hearts, so book well ahead if you plan to attend. For small festivals and local happenings, tourist office websites have up-to-the-minute listings.

The spectacular setting of Avignon Theater at night

## Theater

Going to the theater in France can be as formal or intimate as you choose. A trip to a major theater can involve dressing up, making special *souper* (late dinner) reservations at a nearby restaurant specializing in theater suppers, and quaffing Champagne during the interval. On the other hand, a trip to a small-scale theater can be about casual dress, cheap tickets, and an intimate experience.

Whatever the genre, the French love an evening *au théâtre*, be it a French farce or a festival of street theater.

France's biggest theater event is at **Avignon** *(see p507)*. It is held during three weeks in July and is mainly open-air. It also includes ballets, drama, and classical concerts. Many outdoor theaters operate in summer and are often free – contact the town's tourist office

for a program. The **Off Festival** is also worth a look.

Circus is also popular with the French. In small towns, summertime is often heralded by the circus loudspeaker strapped to the top of a car cruising the streets and inviting adults and children alike to flock to the big top. For larger circus events, head to Monaco for the Festival International du Cirque de Monte-Carlo or visit the colorful Festival International du Cirque de Bayeux, or the Cirque d'Hiver Bouglione in Paris.

Large-scale *spectacles* or shows are another popular form of theater, be they massive musicals or *son et lumière* performances. Marionettes are also given due respect in France, where engaging shows go beyond traditional puppet territory.

## Movies

*Le Septième Art*, as the French refer to film, reveals the respect with which the genre is held. From the Lumière brothers and their innovative technology to contemporary critical smashes, such as *The Chorus*, *Amélie*, *The Artist*, and *The Intouchables*, France's influence on film is undeniable. The French are supportive of local, independent movie theaters, and small towns are often fiercely protective of their screening center. So, when visiting the movies, don't be restricted to the behemoths of UGC and Gaumont, and instead head to a tiny *salle de cinéma*. If your language skills won't stretch to seeing a French film

while in France, be sure to catch the VO *(Version Originale)* of any other language movies, which will be screened in the original language. VF *(Version Française)* denotes a dubbed screening in French. As any expatriate in France knows, hearing a strange French voice coming out of a Hollywood A-lister's mouth is likely to dull any enjoyment of a major blockbuster movie.

Another thing to bear in mind is the French attitude to snacking. Essentially, it is only acceptable for children, and even then only at a designated time after school. While French movie theaters do have concession stands selling popcorn and candy, it is only the foreigners who can be heard munching throughout the tense parts of the movie. On the other hand, some French movie theaters have bars and restaurants attached, so that movie-goers can dissect the movie over a meal.

Many movie theaters run mini directors' festivals with several movies shown back to back, attracting serious film buffs, and those curious to learn more.

As the fame of **Cannes** *(see pp524–5)* reflects, film festivals are taken seriously by the French. Cannes itself is a maelstrom of media hype, old-school glamor, and shiny new cash. It is an amazing experience, if you can get tickets to any of the movies or parties, but these are notoriously difficult to get, as they are by invitation only. An easier way to experience the

Poster promoting La Rochelle international film festival

Red carpet and razzmatazz at the Cannes Film Festival

fabulous side of film is to attend the lower-key American film festival in **Deauville** *(see p259)*. The former is seen as a major launch pad for US independent movies looking for European release, and attracts big stars and cult directors alike. The competition section of the festival has ten movies in the running each year. The chic town of Deauville is small and accessible, and, while the chance of bumping into a huge star is slim, it feels possible.

The film festival in **La Rochelle** *(see p420)*, the second largest in France, does not attract big-name actors, but movie fans will not be disappointed with the broad selection.

A truly great way to catch a movie in France is at an open-air festival. There are many such events throughout the country; check local listings. The Festival International du Film de la Rochelle and Toulouse's **Cinéma en Plein Air** both feature outdoor screenings in summer, while **Cinéma en Plein Air à La Villette** in Paris attracts tourists and locals at the end of summer with a series of themed movies.

## Dance

Dancing is a way of life in France. From formal lessons to spontaneous outbreaks of grooving on the village square, moving to music is central to all types of celebration. Most foreigners' first experience with French dancers occurs in a nightclub and, more often than not, is accompanied by an expression of surprise. In even

the most upscale nightclub, it is not unusual to see trendy twentysomethings jiving away to *le rock*, a formal form of rock-and-roll dancing. French teens are taught *le rock* before being unleashed on the party scene, and a basic understanding of its signature twirls and twists is considered vital to being a good dancer.

The love affair with formal dance sessions starts young, but lasts until late in life: tea dances are a major fixture of most older people's social calendars. Community centers, sports halls, restaurants, and chic nightclubs often host *thé dansants* (tea dances), normally in the late afternoon or early evening.

Another way to experience French dance culture is to head to a *guingette*, a moored party boat with a convivial, old-fashioned atmosphere. People here dance the *quadrille* or the *musette* to accordion music, spinning around on the banks

of the river. While the *guingettes* were traditionally clustered around the Marne river, they have now spread throughout France and are definitely worth seeking out if your travels take you close to a major tributary.

In general, lots of dancing takes place near to water in France. Those looking to get into the groove in the south should take their dancing shoes to the docks in Bordeaux and Marseille.

Once a year, on July 13 and 14, a most unusual impromptu dancing venue springs up around the country with the *Bals des Pompiers*. The "Firemen's Balls" are a national institution, when the French of all ages head down to their local fire department to celebrate Bastille day by dancing to everything from Edith Piaf to hip hop until the early hours of the morning.

If you would prefer to watch rather than participate, there are several major dance festivals that celebrate the dance traditions of different regions. The **Gannat festival** held in the Auvergne *(see p357)* is a fine example of a regional dance extravaganza, as is the **Festival Interceltique de Lorient** *(see p274)*, which celebrates Celtic music and dance. The main international dance festivals are held in **Montpellier** *(see pp498–9)* and **Lyon** *(see pp382–5)*. These provide a wonderful opportunity to enjoy major contemporary dance talent from around the world.

Wonderful costumes and choreography at the Montpellier dance festival

## Music

The French music scene is about far more than Johnny Hallyday, although it must be said that the aging rocker still manages to sell stacks of records, concert tickets, and gossip magazines. It should also be pointed out that he is actually Belgian, but the French have taken him to their hearts anyway. Acts such as Bob Sinclar, Daft Punk, David Guetta, and Christine and the Queens are big international names catering to English-speaking audiences.

*Chanson* is ever popular, as the success of the movement's poster boy Benjamin Biolay reveals. The new French *nouvelle chanson* scene is dominated by Biolay, although other well-known artists in this genre include Vincent Delerm, Benabar, Olivia Ruiz, and French-Canadian Coeur de Pirate.

"Le French Touch," a genre of house music originating in the 1990s, has been made popular by acts such as Daft Punk, Modjo, and Cassius.

Well-known female singers include Lara Fabian and reality-TV pop star Chimène Badi.

France is the world's second-biggest market for hip-hop after the USA. The success of artists such as MC Solaar, IAM, and Assassin have ensured international recognition for the country's thriving urban scene.

The event that best symbolizes this musical cornucopia is the **Fête de la Musique**. Every year, on June 21, France resonates to the sound of this national music festival. Amateur and professional musicians alike set up their stages throughout villages and towns and perform. The best way to enjoy this is to walk around and try and take in as many different "concerts" as possible, but be aware that for some wannabe rock stars this is their only chance to shine, regardless of whether or not they can sing. Musical quality aside, what is most impressive about the Fête de la Musique is the sheer number of genres that one can hear in a few streets. Ranging from full orchestras to one-man rap artists, you can expect to hear everything from accordion music to panpipes, *chanson*, hip-hop, and electro.

If you prefer your festivals a little more specialized, visit one of the events focusing on the very best of a particular genre, from chamber music to jazz. The July **Festival of Francofolies** in La Rochelle *(see p420)* brings together French music enthusiasts from around the world, just as **Jazz in Antibes** draws top performers to this chic seaside town *(see p525)*. The **Chorégies d'Orange**, France's oldest opera festival, takes place throughout July and August in the well-preserved Roman amphitheater, which retains perfect acoustics. The organ festival in **Aubusson** *(see pp360–61)* focuses around the glorious organ in the Sainte-Croix church, and **La Roque d'Anthéron** continues to pull in piano-loving crowds. The **Colmar international festival** *(see p231)* is a major draw for classical music buffs, and the **Aix festival** *(see p515)* is a must for any serious fan of classical music and opera, while the **Radio France Occitanie Montpellier Festival** has a wide-ranging appeal with symphony concerts, chamber music, jazz, and world music.

## Clubs

Cool clubs and artful partying most definitely exist outside the capital city, despite what Parisians may believe. There are, of course, bars and clubs throughout the country, and night owls looking to dance are unlikely to be disappointed by the range of options on offer. Small local venues can be great fun, and community events such as open-air parties and festivals are almost always worth a peek.

In general, nightclubs open late and even in small towns, don't really get going until after midnight. The French are more likely to nurse a few drinks rather than dash around buying multiple rounds, and shots are almost unheard of over here. It is considered uncouth to drink wine outside of mealtimes, although Champagne is always a good thing! The prevailing custom is to club together with friends and buy a bottle of spirits between you. The nightclub will present you with plenty of mixers, and – the big benefit of going for this option – you will usually get a table all to yourselves. Tables are generally reserved for those in possession of a full bottle of spirits; a single gin and tonic does not warrant a seat. As extravagant as this may seem, it is generally cheaper than buying individual drinks for four or more people.

In terms of dress code, sneakers are almost always forbidden in clubs, and the smarter the better could be seen as the rule. In house or hip-hop clubs strict dress codes tend to be relaxed. However, in more traditional *boîtes de nuit* (nightclubs) getting glammed up is the way to go. Clubs with difficult door policies can often be outfoxed by dining late. If you are worried about getting in, call ahead and make a dinner reservation. Alternatively flaunt designer labels at the doormen.

To experience one of France's most glamorous clubs head to **Les Planches** – an uber-chic spot outside Deauville *(see p259)*. Aside from its swimming pool, in which starlets frolic at 3am, Les Planches is surprisingly inclusive, offering a friendly and fun vibe. Vintage cars tear around town rounding up partygoers to keep the night going.

Up in the mountains **Le Privilege** in Chamonix *(see p326)* is a jumping Alpine party place.

The Côte d'Azur *(see pp502–35)* is, of course, renowned for its hedonistic nightlife. **Les Caves du Roy** in the Hotel Byblos and **Nikki Beach** in St.-Tropez *(see p520)* are perfect for the jet set, while **Jimmy'z** in Monaco *(see pp534–5)* is the place to hang out with highrollers.

## Spectator Sports

Sports enthusiasts are spoiled for choice in France, with myriad opportunities to indulge in spectator sport throughout the country. If you don't want to wait to see the *grande finale* of the **Tour de France** in Paris, taking in the spectacle from a tiny village en route is a great experience (drivers beware: the Tour takes precedence, and the traffic will be stopped for an extremely long time).

If soccer is more your thing, then head to the Olympic stadiums to catch huge teams, such as **Lyon** and **Marseille**, in action.

Surfing fans should make for Biarritz *(see p456)*, Lacanau *(see p428)*, and Hossegor *(see p428)* to watch the tournaments there, while ski aficionados might want to watch the European Cup in Les Trois Vallées *(see p326)*.

Golfers flock to the **PGA Open** held outside Paris and to the **LPGA in Evian**, which is the world's second most valuable tournament after the US Open.

Equestrians will be drawn to one of France's national studs at the **Haras National de Pompadour** for dressage, showjumping and other competitions throughout the year. Similarly, equine enthusiasts should not miss out on exciting horseracing at the renowned **Chantilly Racetrack**.

The **Le Mans** 24-hour car race is an institution, as is the famous **Grand Prix** in Monaco *(see pp534–5)*. The **French Grand Prix** at Magny Cours, south of Nevers *(see pp342–3)*, is also well worth a visit.

No visitor to France in the summer should miss out on one of the greatest spectator sports of them all: head to the village square and take in a game of *pétanque* (also known as *boules*).

# DIRECTORY

## Theater

**Avignon Theater Festival**
**Tel** 04 90 27 66 50.
W festival-avignon.com

**Off Festival**
W avignonleoff.com

## Movies

**Cannes Film Festival**
W festival-cannes.fr

**Cinéma en Plein Air Toulouse**
W lacinecinemathequedetoulouse.com

**Cinéma en Plein Air La Villette**
W lavillette.com

**Deauville Film Festival**
W festival-deauville.com

**La Rochelle Film Festival**
W festival-larochelle.org

## Dance

**Festival Interceltique de Lorient**
**Tel** 02 97 21 24 29.
W festival-interceltique.bzh

**Gannat Festival**
**Tel** 04 70 90 12 67.
W cultures-traditions.org

**Lyon Festival**
**Tel** 04 27 46 65 60.
W labiennaledelyon.com

**Montpellier Festival**
W montpellierdanse.fr

## Music

**Aix Festival**
**Tel** 04 42 17 34 00.
W festival-aix.com

**Aubusson Festival**
**Tel** 05 55 66 18 36.
W orgue-aubusson.org

**Chorégies d'Orange**
**Tel** 04 90 34 24 24.
W choregies.fr

**Colmar International Festival**
**Tel** 03 89 20 68 97.
W festival-colmar.com

**Festival of Francofolies**
**Tel** 05 46 50 55 77.
W francofolies.fr

**Jazz in Antibes**
W jazzjuan.com

**Radio France Occitanie Montpellier Festival**
**Tel** 04 67 02 02 01.
W festivalradiofrancemontpellier.com

**La Roque d'Anthéron**
**Tel** 04 42 50 51 15.
W festival-piano.com

## Clubs

**Les Caves du Roy**
Av Paul Signac, 83990 St.-Tropez.
**Tel** 04 94 56 68 00.

**Jimmy'z**
Le Sporting Club
Av Princesse Grace,
Monte Carlo.
**Tel** 00 377 98 06 70 68.
W loft-club.fr

**Nikki Beach**
Route de l'Epi,
83350 Ramatuelle.
**Tel** 04 94 79 82 04.
W nikkibeach.com

**Les Planches**
Les Longs Champs,
14910 Blonville sur Mer.
**Tel** 06 67 59 72 75.
W lesplanches.com

**Le Privilège**
52 rue des Moulins,
74400 Chamonix.
**Tel** 06 72 43 92 83.

## Spectator Sports

**Chantilly Racetrack**
Rue Plaine des Aigles,
Chantilly, Oise.
**Tel** 03 44 62 44 00.
W france-galop.com

**French Grand Prix**
58170 Magny Cours.
**Tel** 03 86 21 80 00.
W circuitmagnycours.com

**Grand Prix**
Automobile Club de Monaco.
**Tel** 01 82 88 27 34.
W monaco-grand-prix.com

**Haras National de Pompadour**
**Tel** 08 11 90 21 31.
W ifce.fr/haras-nationaux

**LPGA in Evian**
W lgpa.com

**Le Mans**
**Tel** 02 43 40 24 00.
W lemans.org

**Olympique Lyon**
350 av Jean Jaurès,
69007 Lyon.
W olweb.fr

**Olympique de Marseille**
3 bd Michelet,
13008 Marseille.
W om.net

**PGA Open**
W pgafrance.net

**Tour de France**
W letour.fr

# Specialty Vacations and Outdoor Activities

France offers an amazing variety of leisure and sport activities, making it a wonderful choice for a specialty vacation. The French take great pride in the *art de vivre*, which entails not only eating and drinking well, but also pursuing special interests and hobbies. For the best in entertainment and spectator sports, festivals, and annual events, see *France Through the Year* on pages 40–43. Information on leisure and sporting activities in a particular region is available from the tourist offices listed for each town in this guide. The suggestions below cover the most popular, and also some more unusual, pursuits.

Students honing their culinary skills on a Hostellerie Bérard cookery course

## Specialty Vacations

French government tourist offices *(see p623)* have a wide range of information on travel companies that offer special-interest vacations. The official website for tourism in France is www.rendezvousenfrance.com, and it is an excellent source of information.

If you want to improve your French, many language courses are available. These are very often combined with other activities, such as cooking or painting. For more information, request *cours de français pour étudiants étrangers* (French courses for foreign students) from the **French Institute** in London.

Young people can enjoy a French-speaking vacation by working part time on restoration of historic sites with **Union REMPART** (Union pour la Réhabilitation et Entretien des Monuments et du Patrimoine Artistique).

A tantalizing array of gastronomic courses is on offer, to introduce you to classical French cuisine or the cooking of a particular region. For experienced cooks, advanced and specialty courses are available too. Wine-appreciation courses can also be found and are always very popular.

There are numerous art and crafts courses throughout the country, catering to everyone from the absolute beginner to the most accomplished artist.

Nature lovers can enjoy the national parks *(parcs nationaux)* and join organized birdwatching and botanical trips in many areas, including the Camargue, the Cévennes, and Corsica. *Le Guide des Jardins en France*, published by Actes Sud, is a useful reference guide when visiting France's many beautiful gardens.

Painting the picturesque French landscape

## Golf

There are golf courses all over France, especially along the north and south coasts and in Aquitaine. Players have to reach a minimum standard and obtain a license in order to play, so be sure to take your handicap certificate with you. Top courses offer weekend or longer tutored breaks geared to all levels of experience. The **Fédération Française de Golf** will provide a list of all the courses throughout France.

Specialty golf packages, including deluxe hotel accommodations, can be ideal for serious golfers and any non-golfing partners alike. The spectacular Evian Resort and its renowned **Evian Championship** golf course is a very exclusive, pampering option. The 18-hole course is guaranteed to appeal to fans. There is also a spa and five swimming pools, perfect for lazing. The climbing wall, squash, and tennis courts will appeal to more active visitors.

In the south, the **American Golf Academy** offers a team of golf pros who are adept at coaching children, beginners, and also experts through their eight different courses and private lessons. Their summer schools and masterclasses are highly sought after.

The **Hotel de Mougins**, with a lovely address on the "avenue du Golf," is located near to ten prestigious golf courses, including the Golf Country Club Cannes, the Royal Mougins Golf Club, and the Golf d'Opio-Valbonne. The hotel can arrange rounds at the different clubs, and offers packages that include extras, such as lunch in the clubhouse.

The **Golf Hotel Grenoble Charmeil** can organize green fees for three courses, including the Grenoble International course. In Brittany, the **St.-Malo Golf and Country Club** has a 19th-century manor-house interior and an impressive 27-hole golf course, surrounded by the Mesnil forest.

## Tennis

Tennis is a very popular sport in France, and courts for hourly rental can be found in almost every town. It is a good idea to bring your own equipment with you, as rental amenities may not be available.

## Hiking

In France, more than 38,000 miles (60,000 km) of long-distance tracks, known as *Grandes Randonnées* (GR), are clearly marked. There are also 50,000 miles (80,000 km) of the shorter *Petites Randonnées* (PR).

The routes vary in difficulty and include long pilgrim routes, Alpine crossings, and tracks through national parks. Some *Grandes* and *Petites Randonnées* are open for mountain biking as well as horseback riding.

*Topo Guides*, published by **Féderation Française de la Randonnée Pédestre**, describe the tracks, providing details of transportation, places for overnight stops, and food stores. A useful book series geared specifically toward families is *Les 200 Plus Belles Balades en France en Famille*, which can be ordered online.

## Cycling

For advice on cycling in France, contact the British **CTC** (Cyclists' Touring Club) or the **Fédération Française de Cyclisme**.

Serious cyclists could live their dreams by joining up for a Tour

Mountain biking – a great way to explore

Escaping into the forest at Fontainebleau *(see pp184–5)*

de France stage vacation with the **Velo Echappe** *Etape du Tour* team. The company organizes two types of adventure – a fully guided program or self-guided option. They handle all the registration forms and paperwork, and on the guided option they will arrange hotel accommodations a block away from the end of the stage. Applications to the tour company must be received by the end of March every year to have a chance to ride along with the Tour de France professionals.

At the other end of the scale, people who enjoy a gentle bicycle ride could opt for a wine cycling tour through the vineyards of France. Free-wheeling down the Route des Grands Crus in Burgundy may be more than enough vacation exercise for some.

**Duvine Adventures** organize tours that take in famed vineyards such as La Tache, Romanée-Conti, and Nuit-St.-Georges. The riding includes flat spells and hills, and there are excellent lunches.

Local tourist offices provide details about riding amenities in their areas. **Voies Vertes** offers information on "greenways," easy rides through some of France's loveliest countryside. *Gîtes de France (see p551)* offer dormitory accommodations in the vicinity of well-known tracks.

## Horseback Riding

There are many reputable companies that offer horseback riding breaks, from 1-hour treks to long weekends or vacations of a week or more. The best way to choose is to decide which type of countryside you would prefer to see from the saddle. If the Mont-St.-Michel *(see pp260–63)* and the beaches of Brittany appeal, then **A La Carte Sportive** offer stables with horses trained in trekking for beginners and intermediates. For more experienced riders, riding a Camargue mount through the countryside of Provence *(see pp514–15)* is a wonderful treat. **Ride in France** organizes rides through beautiful scenery, vineyards, and picturesque villages, allowing riders to experience the flora and fauna of the area. Horse lovers with a taste for the historical, or those hankering after a little luxury, could do worse than to sign up for a break with the **Cheval et Châteaux** company, which organizes horseback-riding tours around châteaux in the Loire. Not only do riders get to take in the majesty of the châteaux of the region, the overnight accommodations come courtesy of a castle. It's an ideal way to play lord or lady of the manor, while indulging in a passion for horses.

Hiking along the Gorges du Verdon in Provence *(see pp518–19)*

## Mountain Sports

The French mountains, especially the Alps and the Pyrenees, provide a wide range of sports opportunities. In addition to winter downhill skiing and *ski de fond* (cross-country skiing), the mountains are enjoyed in the summer by rock-climbers and mountaineers, and by those skiers who can't wait for winter and so indulge in some of Europe's best glacier skiing.

Mountain climbing is possible not just in summer, but year round, although some high routes will be snowbound until quite late in the year and require special equipment such as ice axes. These should not be attempted without experience or a local guide. Climbers should contact the **Fédération Française de la Montagne et de l'Escalade** for more information on the best climbing locations and other useful tips.

Winter sports fans should join the serious skiers and snowboarders who head to the French hills in droves every season. The mountains here have terrain to satisfy all levels of expertise from toddlers in the kids' club through to death-defying off-piste athletes, adrenalin-junkie snowboarders, kitesurfers, and middle-of-the-road snow fans who are happiest cruising blue runs and eating in slope-side restaurants.

## Skiing

Undoubtedly, France has some of the best ski resorts anywhere in the world. The sheer scale of some of the larger areas can be quite daunting if you're on a week-long trip – especially to those who insist on covering all the trails on the map. The Trois Vallées ski area *(see p326)*, for example, is made up of three valleys, which include the resorts of Courchevel, Méribel, Val Thorens, and Les Ménuires. Added together, they comprise a staggering 375 miles (600 km) worth of pistes.

The Trois Vallées is an excellent example of how

French ski resorts differ wildly in style. Super-chic stations such as Courchevel and Méribel draw skiers from around the world, often dressed in cutting-edge ski fashion and using the latest high-tech equipment. In these resorts the hotels – especially those dubbed to be "in" – are expensive, and eating and drinking in the "see and be seen spots" here puts a significant dent in the most generous of vacation budgets. On the other hand, resorts that are considered less glamorous, such as Vals Thorens and Les Menuires, can be enjoyed without designer labels and huge credit card limits.

The main consideration when choosing a resort should be the percentage of terrain to suit your ability. For example, a beginner might be miserable in a resort aimed at experts and offering only a few green runs. Similarly, a more confident intermediate who is looking to improve will be frustrated by a ski area full of easy cruising slopes that are overrun with beginners.

It is also important to think about whether or not it matters to you if the village is picturesque. Die-hard ski fans can overlook ugly concrete architecture in towns such as Flaine, while those looking for the bigger picture would be best off heading to somewhere pretty, such as La Clusaz or Megève *(see p326)*.

The proximity of accommodation to piste is also very important; most people find it is worth paying a premium for accommodations near the slopes and ski lifts, rather than having to stagger back in heavy boots carrying your skis after a long day's schussing.

Aside from obvious concerns such as nightlife, children's day-care, and the efficiency of lift networks, it can also be useful to look at historic snow reports for the last few years for the time you are planning your trip. The weather can be unpredictable, though, so be sure to also check the resorts' snow-making

capabilities. Armed with these details, you should be in a good position to pick the right resort for you, but, remember, while the Alps get most of the attention, the Pyrenees can offer some seriously good skiing, too.

## Aeronautical Sports

Learning to fly in France can be relatively inexpensive. Information on the different flying schools is available from the **Fédération Nationale Aéronautique**. There are also plenty of opportunities to learn the exhilarating skills of gliding, paragliding, and hang-gliding, popular in the Alps of Provence, in the Pyrenees, and Corsica. For more information, contact the **Fédération Française de Vol Libre**.

If piloting a plane is a little too much, you can opt for ballooning instead. France has an illustrious ballooning history, being the birthplace of the Montgolfier brothers, who pioneered the art in 1783. **Ballon de Paris** provide a tethered taste of adventure in Paris with a trip into the air in the Parc André-Citroën, but floating unfettered over the countryside can be arranged by several companies around the country. **France Montgolfières** can organize trips over Fontainebleau *(see pp184–5)* outside Paris or over the Burgundian vineyards. Alternatively, they offer the opportunity to appreciate the spectacular châteaux of the Loire from a balloon. In Provence the same company can float you over the picturesque villages, cornfields, and vines of the Luberon *(see pp510–11)*.

## Watersports

Whitewater rafting, kayaking, and canoeing all take place on many French rivers, especially in the Massif Central and the Southwest. More information on these sports and the best places to take part can be obtained from the **Fédération Française de Canoë-Kayak**.

The Atlantic coast around Biarritz *(see p456)* offers some

of the best surfing and wind-surfing in Europe. Excellent windsurfing can also be found in Brittany, with **Wissant** in particular being a big draw. A charming small fishing village, Wissant is considered a decent stop on any windsurf tour. The western Mediterranean is also popular with windsurfers

Surfers who prefer to do it without the sail head to **Hossegor** outside Biarritz (see p456) for spectacular waves. The surfing here is world-class and perhaps not ideal for beginners, but the after-surf scene is great fun for anyone who is more interested in lying on the beach or paddling at the shore than carving up the water.

Similarly the town of **Lacanau** (see p428) plays host to international surf competitions, drawing wave fans from all over the world.

Sailing and waterskiing are also very popular in France. Contact the **Fédération Française de Voile** for more details. Training schools and equipment rentals are found at numerous places along the coast and on lakes. In particular, the coastal towns of Brittany have a good choice of sailing schools

If cruising on a boat is your kind of thing, there are many outfitters that can help. One of the swankier options is to take a **Sunsail** bareboat tour around the Côte d'Azur, although this option is only available to those who have reached a certain level of boatmanship. The company also offers a range of skippered tours around the beautiful coastline.

Swimming amenities throughout the country are generally good, although swimming on the Atlantic coast can be dangerous and may be forbidden outside patrolled areas. The beaches in the South of France can be very crowded in high season (see pp478–9).

For diving enthusiasts, the Côte d'Azur, which has a number of World War II wrecks, offers good opportunities, as does Corsica. More information is available from **Fédération Française d'Études et de Sports Sous-Marins**.

## Naturism

There are nearly 90 naturism centers in France. These are mostly located in the south and southwest of the country, as well as in Corsica. Information in English can be obtained from French Government Tourist Offices (see p620), or from the **Fédération Française de Naturisme**.

## Public Events

To join the French as they enjoy their spare time, look for local soccer and rugby games, cycling races, or other sporting events suited to spectators.

Special seasonal markets and local *fêtes* often combine antiques fairs and *boules* tournaments with rock and pop concerts, making an enjoyable day out.

## Spa Breaks

France is renowned for its seawater-based thalassotherapy spa techniques, with many centers, salons, and hotels offering "thalasso" treatments. The seaside towns and resorts seem to be the most logical place to head for ocean-based treatments, and, not surprisingly, there are some excellent spots dotted around the coastline.

The Chic coastal town of Deauville (see p259) plays host to upscale spa seekers in the **Algotherm Thalassotherapy Spa**. Similarly the **Hôtel Thalasso Sofitel** in Quiberon (see p282) offers top-class water therapy. More water therapy can be found near the springs at Vichy (see pp362–3) at the **Les Celestins** spa, and at **Evian-les-Bains** (see p395).

Wine in France is considered to be almost as important as water, so it is not surprising that a spa specializing in "vinotherapy" or wine therapy has hordes of loyal fans. Head to **Les Sources de Caudalie** spa among the vines near Bordeaux and indulge in a vinosource grape facial and cabernet scrub.

If big-name treatments are your thing, you should head to **Le Mas Candille**, which hosts the first Shiseido spa in continental Europe. The products used are as exceptional as one would expect from such a swanky brand, and the techniques are Oriental-inspired.

Finally, if a thoroughly indulgent approach to a spa session is your idea of vacation heaven, then splurge at the **Terre Blanche Hôtel Spa Golf Resort** in Provence. The half-day retreat of total indulgence involves an aromatherapy massage, a Provençal body wrap, and relaxing in the sauna, spa, *hammam*, or laconium. If you want to go à la carte, you can choose from a wide range of delights, such as an eye-lifting facial, a body-toning massage, or an Oshadi clay wrap.

If you can't escape from the city, the Valmont spa at the **Hotel Meurice** and the **Four Seasons** spa at the George V can provide the ultimate escape and spa break right in the center of Paris.

## Yoga

The beautiful countryside in France provides the perfect backdrop for a restorative yoga retreat vacation. The **Manolaya Yoga Center** offers relaxing and fun hatha yoga vacations throughout Provence and at its Avignon-based center. For the more relaxing style of hatha yoga, try **Silvananda Ashram Yoga** retreats held near Orléans in the beautiful Loire.

Another excellent option is a break at the **Domaine de la Grausse** in the foothills of the Pyrenees, where walking and visiting local waterfalls, châteaux, medieval villages, and even taking in some cave paintings are all on the agenda. Those with any energy left over can take up options to go mountain biking, horseback riding, playing golf, and fishing.

Beginners and experienced yoga fans alike are welcome at **Les Passeroses**, near Angoulême, which specializes in hatha and vinyasa yoga. Boutique accommodations with private bathrooms and a vegetarian menu are part of the package here.

## Gourmet

For gourmets looking to learn how to recreate some of the stunning meals enjoyed in French restaurants, or wine buffs seeking to increase their knowledge and cellar at the same time, there are many excellent options. The sheer number of cookery classes available throughout the country may seem overwhelming, so the first step in choosing an activity holiday of this kind is to consider your initial skill level and what you wish to achieve from the break. From die-hard kitchen disasters to budding restaurateurs, there is a gourmet break in France that will suit.

The **Go Learn To** cookery courses offer short breaks or week-long holidays to suit your taste in Provence, Bordeaux, Lyon, Gascony, La Rochelle, Brittany, and the Loire Valley. They provide cookery courses in stunning château settings, as well as more specialized courses in Paris, such as cheese and wine pairing and wine tasting.

**Petra Carter**, chef and food writer, shows food lovers how to rustle up a menu based on whatever looks great in the market that day, as well as how to prepare foolproof fish recipes and duck confit. These cookery courses, which take place near Nîmes in the Languedoc area, combine fun with practical tips, and include waterside picnics and visits to saltpans, olive presses, beekeepers, and local markets. There are also tutored wine tastings.

Budding culinary stars might want to head to Paris and Alain Ducasse's **Ecole de Cuisine**, which organizes both cooking and wine courses. It offers day and evening courses, held in an ultra-modern, professionally equipped kitchen. Also in Paris is the **Ecole Ritz Escoffier**, which holds workshops, for both adults and children, at the Ritz Hotel. Lessons last from an hour to half a day and cover themes such as chocolate or making the perfect pastry.

Oenophiles, on the other hand, might like to join the **French Wine Explorers**, who offer tours around vineyards. Alternatively, arranging wine classes via the French tourist office can be an excellent idea. **French Wine Adventures** offers a range of wine tours – day courses, walking tours, play winemaker for a day – in the Bordeaux wine regions of Saint-Emilion, Bergerac, and Médoc.

## Arts and Crafts

France is a top choice for creative people looking to get away from it all and to express themselves in beautiful surroundings. Whether you prefer to doodle in a notebook alone on the banks of a river, or perfect your pastel technique in an art masterclass, there is an outlet for you somewhere in France.

**Adam Cope Painting Holidays** offers painting courses in several historic sites in the Dordogne, including a 17th-century abbey and an 18th-century château. Adam Cope provides personal instruction and caters to all levels of ability. It is possible to rent paints on the courses.

Martine Vaugel, winner of the International Rodin prize, is the founder of the Loire Valley's **Vaugel Sculpture Studio**, which offers foundation and advanced portrait, standing, and reclining figure courses ranging from one week to two months.

Those with a passion for seeing life through a lens are well catered to with photography courses by **Graham and Belinda Berry** at their farmhouse in the Lot, southwest France. Courses suitable for all ages and abilities are offered here.

## DIRECTORY

### Specialty Vacations

**French Institute**
17 Queensberry Place,
London SW7 2DT,
United Kingdom.
**Tel** 020 7871 3515.
W institut-
francais.org.uk

**Union REMPART**
1 rue des Guillemites,
75004 Paris.
**Tel** 01 42 71 96 55.
W rempart.com

### Golf

**American Golf Academy**
**Tel** 06 81 54 96 42.
W american-golf-
academy.com

**Evian Championship Golf Course**
South Shore Lake Geneva,
74500 Evian.
**Tel** 04 50 26 85 00.
W evianresort.com

**Fédération Française de Golf**
68 rue Anatole France,
92300 Levallois Perret.
**Tel** 01 41 49 77 00.
W ffgolf.org

**Golf Hotel Grenoble Charmeil**
38210 Saint Quentin sur
Isère. **Tel** 04 76 93 67 28.
W golfhotel
charmeil.com

**Hotel de Mougins**
205 av du Golf, 06250
Mougins. **Tel** 04 92 92 17
07. W hotel-de-
mougins.com

**St.-Malo Golf and Country Club**
Domaine de St.-Yvieux,
35540 Le Tronchet.
**Tel** 02 99 58 96 69.
W saintmalogolf.com

### Hiking

**Fédération Française de Randonnée Pédestre**
64 rue du Dessous des
Berges, 75013 Paris.
**Tel** 01 44 89 93 90.
W ffrandonnee.fr

### Cycling

**CTC**
Parklands, Railton Road,
Guildford, Surrey GU2 9JX,
United Kingdom. **Tel** 0148
3238 301. W ctc.org.uk

**Duvine Adventures**
W duvine.com

**Fédération Française de Cyclisme**
1 rue Laurent Fignon, CS
40 100, 78180 Montigny
le Bretonneux. W ffc.fr

**Velo Echappe**
W veloechappe.com

**Voies Vertes**
W voiesvertes.com

### Horseback Riding

**A La Carte Sportive**
W carte-sportive-com.
iowners.net

**Cheval et Châteaux**
W cheval-et-chateaux.
com

**Ride in France**
W rideinfrance.com

# DIRECTORY

## Mountain Sports

**Fédération Française de la Montagne et de l'Escalade**
8–10 quai de la Marne, 75019 Paris.
**Tel** 01 40 18 75 50.
W ffme.fr

## Skiing

For information on the different resorts, visit the following websites:

**La Clusaz**
W laclusaz.com

**Courchevel**
W courchevel.com

**Flaine**
W flaine.com

**Megève**
W megeve.com

**Les Menuires**
W lesmenuires.com

**Méribel**
W meribel.net

**Les Trois Vallées**
W les3vallees.com

**Val Thorens**
W valthorens.com

## Aeronautical Sports

**Ballon de Paris**
Parc André-Citroën, 75015 Paris.
**Tel** 01 44 26 20 00.
W ballondeparis.com

**Fédération Française de Vol Libre**
4 rue de Suisse, 06000 Nice. **Tel** 04 97 03 82 82.
W federation.ffvl.fr

**Fédération Nationale Aéronautique**
155 av Wagram, 75017 Paris.
**Tel** 01 44 29 92 00.
W ff-aero.fr

**France Montgolfières**
**Tel** 03 80 97 38 61.
W franceballoons.com

## Watersports

**Fédération Française de Canoë-Kayak**
87 quai de la Marne, 94340 Joinville-le-Pont.
**Tel** 01 45 11 08 50.
W ffck.org

**Fédération Française d'Etudes et de Sports Sous-Marins**
W ffessm.fr

**Fédération Française de Voile**
17 rue Henri Bocquillon, 75015 Paris. **Tel** 01 45 58 75 75. W ffcv.org

**Hossegor Tourist Office**
166 av de la Gare BP 6, 40150 Hossegor.
**Tel** 05 58 41 79 00.
W hossegor.fr

**Lacanau Tourist Office**
Pl de l'Europe, 33680 Lacanau. **Tel** 05 56 03 21 01. W medoc-atlantique.com

**Sunsail**
W sunsail.com

**Wissant Tourist Office**
Pl de la Mairie, 62179 Wissant. **Tel** 03 21 82 48 00. W terredes2caps.fr

## Naturism

**Fédération Française de Naturisme**
W ffn-naturisme.com

## Spa Vacations

**Algotherm Thalassotherapy Spa**
3 rue Sem, 14800 Deauville. **Tel** 02 31 87 72 00. W algotherm.fr

**Les Celestins Vichy**
111 bd des Etats-Unis, 03200 Vichy. **Tel** 04 70 30 82 82. W vichy-spa-hotel.fr

**Evian-les-Bains**
Rive Sud du Lac de Génève, 74501 Evian-les-Bains. **Tel** 04 50 26 85 00. W evianresort.com

## Hotel Four Seasons George V
31 av George V, 75008 Paris. **Tel** 01 49 52 70 00.
W fourseasons.com

**Hotel Meurice**
228 rue de Rivoli, 75001 Paris.
**Tel** 01 44 58 10 10.
W lemeurice.com

**Hôtel Thalasso Sofitel (Quiberon)**
Pointe de Goulvars, BP 10802 Quiberon Cedex, 56178 Quiberon.
**Tel** 02 97 50 20 00.
W sofitel-quiberon-thalassa.com

**Le Mas Candille**
Bd Clément Rebuffel, 06250 Mougins.
**Tel** 04 92 28 43 43.
W lemascandille.com

**Les Sources de Caudalie**
Chemin de Smith Haut Lafitte, 33650 Bordeaux–Martillac.
**Tel** 05 57 83 83 83.
W sources-caudalie.com

**Terre Blanche Hôtel Spa Golf Resort**
Domaine de Terre Blanche, 83440 Tourrettes, Var.
**Tel** 04 94 39 90 00.
W terre-blanche.com

## Yoga

**Domaine de la Grausse**
09420 Clermont la Grausse, Ariège.
**Tel** 05 61 66 30 53.
W yogafrance.com

**Manolaya Yoga Centre**
FFPY 39 rue de la Bonneterie, 84000 Avignon. **Tel** 04 90 82 10 52. W manolaya.org

**Les Passeroses**
Le Bas Metraud, 16190 Nonac. **Tel** 05 45 21 51 74.
W passeroses.com

## Sivananda Ashram Yoga Group
Neuville aux Bois, Loiret 45170.
**Tel** 02 38 91 88 82.
W sivananda.org

## Gourmet

**Ecole de Cuisine**
64 rue du Ranelagh, 75016 Paris.
**Tel** 01 44 90 91 00.
W ecolecuisine-alainducasse.com

**Ecole Ritz Escoffier**
**Tel** 01 44 16 30 50.
W ritzescoffier.com

**French Wine Adventures**
**Tel** 05 53 22 72 71.
W frenchwineadventures.com

**French Wine Explorers**
W wine-tours-france.com

**Go Learn To**
**Tel** 020 8144 5990 (UK).
W http://euro.golearnto.com

**Petra Carter**
Place Albert 1er, 30700 Uzès.
**Tel** 07 77 23 41 57.
W petracarter.com

## Arts and Crafts

**Adam Cope Painting Holidays**
**Tel** 05 53 01 22 91.
W artists-atelier.com

**Graham and Belinda Berry**
46800 Montcuq.
**Tel** 05 65 31 49 72.
W imagefrance.co.uk

**Vaugel Sculpture Studio**
2 rue Petit Anjou, Les Cerqueux Sous Passavant, 49310 Vihiers.
**Tel** 02 41 59 54 14.
W vaugelsculpture.com

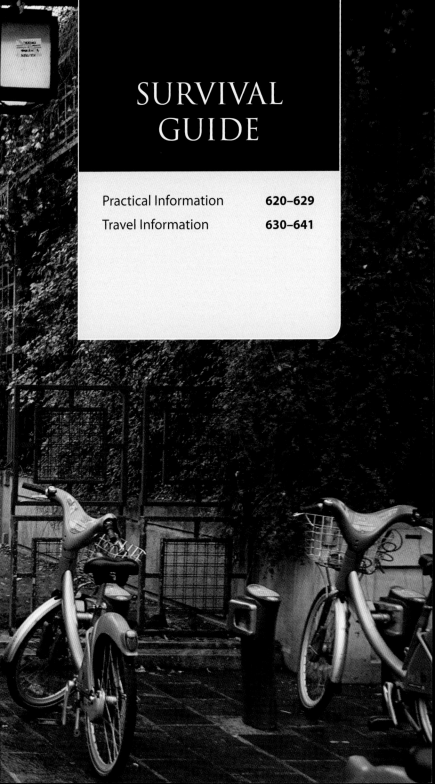

# SURVIVAL GUIDE

Practical Information      **620–629**

Travel Information      **630–641**

# PRACTICAL INFORMATION

France is justifiably proud of its many attractions, for which it has excellent tourist information services. Both in France and abroad, French government tourist offices are an invaluable source of reference for practical aspects of your stay. Most towns and large villages have a tourist information office; the relevant address, telephone number, and website (if available) are provided for each town and area listed in this guide. Domestic tourism in France creates peak vacation migration periods, especially between July 14 and August 31. Consequently, the hotel and restaurant trades are seasonal. A little forward planning will allow you to avoid the pitfalls of seasonal closure.

## Visas and Passports

Citizens of EU countries, aside from the UK and Ireland, can enter France with a national identity card. Visitors from the UK, Ireland, the US, Canada, Australia, and New Zealand need a full passport. Tourist trips may last up to 3 months; after this a *carte de séjour* (residency permit) is required. Like most EU countries (but not the UK and Ireland), France is part of the Schengen agreement for shared border controls. If you enter the Schengen area through a member country, you are free to cross into all member countries within your 90-day stay.

Non-EU nationals who wish to work or study in France, or stay longer than three months, should obtain a visa from a French consulate in their home country. For more information, check the website of your French embassy and your own country's state department.

## Travel Safety Advice

Visitors can get up-to-date travel safety information from the **State Department** in the US, the **Foreign and Commonwealth Office** in the UK, and the **Department of Foreign Affairs and Trade** in Australia.

## Customs Information

EU residents are allowed to carry any amount of goods between EU countries without paying customs duties, as long as the goods are for personal use. Among the limits generally accepted as being for personal use are 800 cigarettes, 90 litres of wine and 110 litres of beer.

Visitors from outside the EU can reclaim sales tax *(TVA)* on many French goods, if more than €175 is spent in one store in one day. To claim the tax back you must get a *détaxe* form from the store and take your goods out of the EU within three months. Present the receipt at customs when leaving the country, and mail the stamped receipt as instructed. The refund will then be sent to you or credited to your bank card. There are *détaxe* desks at all main airports and in big stores. Full information is available from the **Centre des Renseignements des Douanes**.

Tourist office in Bagnoles de l'Orne in Normandy

## Tourist Information

All cities, towns, and many villages have *offices de tourisme*, which provide invaluable free maps and information on local attractions and accommodations. Tourist offices often produce useful guides covering walking and cycling routes, bicycle rental, local gastronomy, traditional farm produce and more. Some regional and *département* offices also offer well-priced hotel and tour packages, and many city offices have organized imaginative guided tours and themed routes.

Before traveling to France, you can get basic orientation information and advice from France's official tourist website **Atout France** or from the French government tourist office in your country. For in-depth regional planning, it is best to use the websites of the relevant Regional Tourist Boards *(Comité Régional du Tourisme)* or those of the many *départements (Comités Départementaux du Tourisme)*. The latter provide a valuable range of detailed information. Nearly all websites are available in English. Links to these sites can be found on the Atout France website.

## Admission Charges

Most museums and monuments in France charge an entry fee, usually from €2 to €10. There are often family discounts, and those under 26 years old with an EU passport have free access to permanent exhibitions at state-owned sights.

Several multi-entry schemes are available that reduce costs if you plan to visit a number of sights. Foremost, the Paris Museum Pass gives unlimited entry to over 60 museums and monuments in and around Paris for either 2, 4, or 6 days. It can be bought in advance online (www.parismuseumpass.com). In other places, local schemes, often include unlimited use of local transportation. Check local tourism websites to see what is available.

The Arc de Triomphe du Carrousel and the Musée du Louvre in Paris

## Opening Hours

This guide lists which days of the week sights are open. National museums and sights normally close on Tuesdays, with a few exceptions that close on Mondays. Generally, the larger museums and sights are open from 9am or 10am to 6pm, sometimes with one late evening a week, often Thursday. Note that smaller museums and churches may close from 12:30pm to 2pm.

Opening times can also vary considerably by season, especially for country châteaux, estates, and gardens. Many are open daily in the peak July to August holiday season and then close completely from November to March, or are only open on weekends. Most sights are closed on Christmas Day and New Year's Day.

See page 604 for details on opening hours for stores; page 626 for banks; and pages 572–3 for restaurants.

## Taxes and Tipping

A service charge of 10 to 20 percent is included on all restaurant bills, and it is customary to round up the bill by a few euros in a restaurant, or a few cents in a café, especially if the service has been good. In grander restaurants, an extra tip of 5–10 percent is the norm.

For taxi drivers, the usual tipping rate is around 10 percent. For hotel bellhops, it is common to tip around €1–€2.

## Travelers with Special Needs

France is working hard to improve access to all its services. There are designated parking spaces on many streets and in all public parking lots. These can be used free of charge with a European Blue Badge. SNCF (French railroads) has the *Accès Plus* scheme, through which wheelchair users and others with mobility problems can book ahead to guarantee a space and free assistance. For information, go to the "Everyday Life" *(Vie Pratique)* section on the SNCF website and look under *Services + (see p634).*

In Paris, some buses, some RER lines, and one Métro line (no. 14) are wheelchair-accessible *(see pp640–41)*. By law, all taxis must carry wheelchair users for no extra charge *(see p640)*.

Much has been done to improve access to attractions, but access to smaller historic houses and country châteaux can be difficult at times. The blue *Tourisme & Handicap* label indicates attractions, hotels, restaurants, and other amenities that meet full disabled access criteria. Many hotels and *chambres d'hôtes* (bed-and-breakfasts) have adapted rooms, and major booking agencies such as Logis de France or Gîtes de France indicate this on their websites.

For information on disabled amenities in France, the best resource is the **Association des Paralysés de France** (APF), which produces an annual *Guide Vacances* booklet. The **Infomobi** website also has comprehensive information on transportation services for the disabled in and around Paris. Both these resources are in French and in English. Further information in English can be found on the Atout France website.

## Traveling with Children

Families traveling in France benefit from a range of cost-cutting discounts, including reduced or free admission to attractions for children. Those under 4 travel free on most public transportation, and youngsters aged 4 to 11 (4 to 9 in Paris) travel half-price.

Some of the big French hotel chains (notably Novotel) specialize in catering to families, while many small country hotels and *chambres d'hôtes* have cost-efficient family rooms *(chambres familiales)*. If you base yourself in one area for two days or more, a self-contained *gîte*, with several rooms and a kitchen, can offer exceptional value for money *(see p551)*.

Virtually all French restaurants welcome children, and many have a children's menu *(menu d'enfants)* for €8–€12.

The Atout France website has information on attractions throughout France, while local tourism websites list regional-specific family attractions and activities. For more ideas, consult websites such as **France for Families** and **Kids in Tow**.

The Château de Versailles has excellent access for those with mobility issues

## Senior Travelers

Senior visitors to France do not enjoy reduced admission fees at national museums and monuments, although some privately owned châteaux and attractions do offer lower prices for older people. Discounted travel on public transportation is only available with multi-journey passes issued by some cities, and the SNCF *Carte Senior* for the over-60s *(see p634)*. However, these cards are not much use for short visits, as you'll only notice the discount if you make several journeys on each system. Train passes *(see p634)* bought in advance outside France can be better value.

## Student Information

Students aged under 26 with a valid **International Student Identity Card** (ISIC) benefit from many discounts, as well as those available to everyone in France aged 25 or under. The Centre d'Information et de Documentation Jeunesse will provide you with further information (www.cidj.com).

## Gay and Lesbian Travelers

France has prominent gay and lesbian communities that are becoming ever more part of the cultural mainstream. The Marais district of Paris is the country's foremost "gay village," but there are gay clubs and services all over the capital. There are gay communities in many other cities, especially in Toulouse, Nantes, Montpellier, and Nice. Tune into Radio FG (98.2 MHz) or consult listings in *Têtu* magazine for a wide range of gay-friendly information. For further help, contact **Centre LGBT** in Paris.

## Traveling on a Budget

How much you spend on a vacation in France will vary enormously depending on what you do. However, in general, two people staying at a basic hotel (an average of €60 for a double room), eating both lunch and dinner in restaurants, visiting a few attractions, and using public transportation can roughly expect to spend €160 per day in most parts of France, or €80 each.

Staying in Paris, the Côte d'Azur and other fashionable resorts is expensive, but less-visited rural regions such as Normandy, inland Brittany and Lorraine can be more affordable. Traveling in peak season (July–mid-September) will also be costly with high hotel rates, particularly in the most popular regions. December through to March, the winter sports season, can also be pricey, particularly in the Alps. If you want to keep costs down it is best to travel during the low season, when hotel prices are much lower. City hotels, however, can be more reasonable between July and August, when most French

International Student Identity Card

people head for the country.

Staying in a *chambre d'hôte* (bed-and-breakfast) is a good alternative to costly hotels. Traditionally, these are located in the countryside but they are now popping up in towns and the average price for a comfortable double room is around €40 including breakfast. Another option is a vacation-rental *gîte,* though these usually require a minimum stay of a weekend or a week.

When dining, opt for a set menu – ordering from the à la carte menu will be far more expensive. Taking your main meal at midday rather than in the evening will mean you can make the most of the best-value set menus or *formules*. To keep costs down when sightseeing, obtain a City Pass that gives unlimited travel on local transportation as well as entry to local monuments *(see p641)*. If you intend to rent a car, reserve in advance through an internet rental agency for the best rates.

## French Time

France is one hour ahead of Greenwich Mean Time (GMT) or British Summer Time (BST).

Waiting to travel at Marseille Gare St.-Charles train station

## Electrical Adaptors

The voltage in France is 220 volts. Plugs are the standard type used in most of Europe with two round pins, or three for applications that need to be earthed. Many hotels offer built-in adaptors for shavers.

## Conversion Chart

**Imperial to metric**
1 inch = 2.54 centimetres
1 foot = 30 centimetres
1 mile = 1.6 kilometres
1 ounce = 28 grams
1 pound = 454 grams
1 pint = 0.6 litre
1 gallon = 4.6 litres

**Metric to imperial**
1 millimetre = 0.04 inch
1 centimetre = 0.4 inch
1 metre = 3 feet 3 inches
1 kilometre = 0.6 mile
1 gram = 0.04 ounce
1 kilogram = 2.2 pounds
1 litre = 1.8 pints

The line for the Eiffel Tower

## Responsible Travel

In France, as in many other countries, there has been a rapid growth in environmental awareness. **Echoway** and the **Association Française d'Eco-tourisme** are two leading French ecotourism organizations, encouraging heightened awareness of responsible travel. **Mountain Riders** promotes sustainable winter tourism in the Alps, providing information on how to get to the mountains by public transportation and arranging group walks to clean up mountain pistes each spring.

France has a long-running rural tourism network, with farmhouse accommodations available through the central Gîtes de France agency (*see p551*). There are also smaller organizations with a more defined ecological stance, such as **Accueil Paysan**, which is a network of small-scale farmers practising low-impact, sustainable agriculture. Another alternative to staying in a hotel is camping, and there are over 11,000 fully equipped campgrounds across the country to choose from (*see p552*).

Information on local green tourism (*tourisme vert* or *eco*) initiatives and activities can be found through local tourist offices. Many towns have weekly markets selling only organic and traditional produce (usually called a *marché bio*), which allow visitors to give back to the local community. Market days have been provided throughout the guide.

# DIRECTORY

## Embassies

**Australia**
4 rue Jean Rey, 75015 Paris. **Map** 6 D3. **Tel** 01 40 59 33 00. W france.embassy.gov.au

**Canada**
35 av Montaigne, 75008 Paris. **Map** 6 F1. **Tel** 01 44 43 29 00. W canada international.gc.ca/france

**United Kingdom**
35 rue du Faubourg-St.-Honoré, 75383 Paris. **Map** 3 C5. **Tel** 01 44 51 31 00. W ukinfrance.fco.gov.uk

**United States**
2 av Gabriel, 75008 Paris. **Map** 3 A5. **Tel** 01 43 12 22 22. W france.usembassy.gov

## Travel Safety Advice

**Australia**
Department of Foreign Affairs and Trade
W dfat.gov.au
W smartraveller.gov.au

**United Kingdom**
Foreign and Commonwealth Office
W gov.uk/foreign-travel-advice

**United States**
Department of State
W travel.state.gov

## Tourist Offices

**Atout France**
W atout-france.fr

**Australia**
Level 13, 25 Bligh St, Sydney NSW 2000.
**Tel** (2) 9210 5400.
W au.france.fr

**Paris Convention and Visitors Bureau**
25 rue des Pyramides, 75001 Paris.
**Tel** 01 49 52 42 63.
W parisinfo.com

**United Kingdom**
Lincoln House, 300 High Holborn, London WC1V 7JH.
**Tel** 020 7061 6600.
W uk.france.fr

**United States**
825 Third Ave, 29th Floor, NY 10022.
**Tel** (1) 212 838 7800.
W us.france.fr

## Customs Information

**Centre des Renseignements des Douanes**
**Tel** 08 11 20 44 44.
W douane.gouv.fr

## Gay and Lesbian Travelers

**Centre LGBT**
63 rue Beaubourg, 75003 Paris.
**Tel** 01 43 57 21 47.

*Têtu*
W tetu.com

## Special Needs

**APF**
W apf.asso.fr

**Infomobi**
W infomobi.com

**Tourisme et Handicaps**
W tourisme-handicaps.org

## Families and Students

**France for Families**
W francefor families.com

**International Student Identity Card (ISIC)**
W isic.org
W isiccard.com

**Kids in Tow**
W kidsintow.co.uk

## Responsible Travel

**Accueil Paysan**
**Tel** 04 76 43 44 83.
W accueil-paysan.com

**Association Française d'Ecotourisme**
W ecotourisme.info

**Echoway**
W echoway.org

**Mountain Riders**
W mountain-riders.org

# Personal Security and Health

On the whole France is a safe place for visitors, but it is always a good idea to take the normal precautions of looking after your possessions and avoiding unfamiliar or unfrequented residential urban areas after dark. If you fall ill during your stay, pharmacies generally offer good advice, while the emergency services can be contacted for any serious medical problems. Consulates and consular departments *(see p623)* at your embassy can also provide assistance in an emergency.

*Gendarmes*

## Police

Violent crime is not a major problem in France, but, as in any country, it is advisable to be on your guard against petty theft, especially in cities. If you are robbed, lose any property, or are the victim of any other type of crime, report the incident as soon as possible at the nearest *commissariat de police* (police station). In an emergency, dialing 17 will also connect you to the police department, but you will still have to go to a station to make a statement. In small towns and villages, crime is reported to the *gendarmerie*, the force mainly responsible for rural policing. The *mairie* (town hall) is also a good place to go for help, but this will only be open during office hours.

At all police stations you will be required to make a statement, called a *PV* or *procès verbal*, listing any lost or stolen items. You will need your passport and, if relevant, your vehicle papers. It is important to keep a copy of your police statement for your insurance claim.

## Lost and Stolen Property

The likelihood, and impact, of street theft can be considerably reduced by a few simple precautions. In the first instance, ensure that all possessions are covered by comprehensive travel insurance before arrival. Once in France, avoid risky city neighborhoods, and beware of pickpockets, especially on the Paris Métro during rush hour (particularly just as the carriage doors are closing). When you sit at a sidewalk café table, always keep your bag within reach and in sight, preferably on your lap or on the table, and never leave it on the ground or hanging on the back of a chair. Keep bags zipped up and held close to you when walking along, and never leave luggage unattended at train stations or other travel centers. Keep valuables securely concealed and only carry with you as much cash as you think you will need for the day.

For lost or stolen property, it may be worth returning to the station where you reported the incident to check if the police have retrieved some of the items. In addition, all French town halls have a *Bureau d'Objets Trouvés* (lost property office), although they are often inefficient, and finding items can take time. Lost property offices can also be found at larger train stations, which will be open during office hours.

If your passport is lost or stolen, notify your consulate immediately *(see p623)*. The loss of credit or debit cards should also be reported as soon as possible to your bank to avoid fraudulent use.

## What to Be Aware Of

Isolated terrorist incidents over the past few years have led to an increased police presence. Be sure to carry a photo ID, avoid carrying large bags and suitcases to public buildings, and be prepared for your bags to be searched upon entering museums, theaters, large stores, and public buildings.

## Travel Insurance

All travelers in France should have comprehensive travel insurance providing adequate cover for any eventuality, including medical and legal expenses, theft, lost luggage, and other personal property, accidents, travel delays, and the option of immediate repatriation by air in the event of a major medical emergency. Winter sports are not covered by standard travel insurance, so if you plan to ski or to undertake other adventure sports in France, you should pay an additional premium to ensure you are protected. All insurance should come with a 24-hour emergency number in case of need.

## In an Emergency

The phone number for all emergency services is 112, but in practice it is often quicker to call the relevant authority direct on their traditional two-digit numbers. In a medical emergency, for an **ambulance**, call the **Service d'Aide Médicale Urgence** (SAMU), who will send an ambulance. However, it can sometimes be faster to call the **fire service –Sapeurs**

---

### DIRECTORY

#### Emergency Numbers

**All Emergency Services**
Tel 112.

**Ambulance (SAMU)**
Tel 15.

**Fire (Sapeurs Pompiers)**
Tel 18.

**Police and Gendarmerie**
Tel 17.

**Pompiers**, who also offer first aid and can take you to the nearest hospital. This is particularly true in rural areas, where the fire department is likely to be much closer than the ambulance service based in town. The paramedics are called *secouristes*.

## Hospitals and Pharmacies

All European Union nationals holding a European Health Insurance Card (EHIC) are entitled to use the French national health service. However, under the French system patients must pay for all treatments and then reclaim most of the cost from the health authorities. Therefore, non-French EU nationals who use health services in France will need to ensure they keep the statement of costs (*feuille de soins*) that is provided by the doctor or hospital. This should include stickers for any prescription drugs, which must be stuck onto the statement by the pharmacist once you have made your purchase. Around 80 percent of the cost can be claimed back by following the instructions provided with your EHIC card. This can be a time-consuming process, and it can often be simpler to use private travel insurance. Non-EU nationals must have full private medical insurance while in France and pay for services in the same way, claiming their costs back in full from their insurance company.

Well-equipped public hospitals can be found throughout France. In all towns and cities there are hospitals with general emergency rooms (called *urgences* or *service des urgences*) that can deal with immediate medical problems. If your hotel cannot direct you to one, call the SAMU or fire department. Should you require an English-speaking doctor, your consulate should be able to recommend one in the area, and in Paris and some other cities in France, there are both American and British

private hospitals (these do not have emergency or *urgences* rooms). Pharmacies, identified by an illuminated green cross sign, are plentiful and easy to find. French pharmacists are highly trained and can diagnose minor health problems and suggest appropriate treatments. When one is closed, a card in the window will give details of the nearest *pharmacie de garde* that is open on Sundays or during the night.

## Natural Hazards

Forest fires are a major risk in many parts of France. High winds can mean fires spread rapidly in winter as well as in summer, so be vigilant about putting out all campfires and cigarette butts. Keep well away from any area where there is a fire, as its direction can change quickly.

Before exploring any of the country's seven national parks or its regional nature parks (*parcs naturels*), visit the relevant park information center to check the regulations and recommendations that apply within the area, and be sure to observe them. When walking in mountains or sailing, inform the relevant authority – such as a park information center or a harbor-master – of your intended route

Police car

Fire engine

Ambulance

and when you expect to return. Never try to walk in remote mountain areas or across tidal marshes without an experienced guide, or against local advice.

During the hunting season (Sep–Feb and especially Sundays) dress in visible colors when out walking and avoid areas where hunters are staked out in hides (see p615).

## Safety on Beaches

Throughout France, there are many good family beaches where bathing is rarely dangerous. Many beaches are guarded in summer by lifeguards (*sauveteurs*) – always heed their instructions and only swim in supervised areas. Also be aware of the system of colored flags, indicating whether it is safe to swim. Green flags mean bathing is safe; orange flags warn that bathing may be dangerous and that only the part of the beach marked out by flags is guarded. Swimming outside this area is therefore not recommended. Red flags indicate dangerous conditions (high waves, shifting sands, strong undercurrents), so all bathing is forbidden. Many beaches also display blue flags, which are used throughout the European Union as a sign of cleanliness.

**ATTENTION** AU **FEU**

Fire hazard poster

# Banking and Local Currency

Banks usually offer the best rates of exchange. Cash can be changed at banks and main post offices. The easiest method for obtaining local currency is by using a debit card or credit card to withdraw cash from an ATM. Bureaux de change can be found at airports, large train stations, in some international hotels and stores, and in the center of large cities, but they have variable rates and charges, and often charge a high commission for transactions.

ATM in Paris

## Using Banks

Currencies other than euros are generally not accepted in France. Most banks will exchange foreign currency, but the commission rates vary, so it is worth looking around to make sure you get the best deal. Virtually all bank branches have ATMs (called *distributeurs* or *points argent* in French), which accept major credit and debit cards. Most ATMs give instructions in several European languages.

## Banking Hours

In Paris, and many other cities, banks are generally open from 9 or 10am to 5pm Monday to Friday, with some branches open on Saturdays. Outside large cities banks are usually closed on Mondays and generally open from 8 or 9am to 12:30pm and 2–5pm Tuesday to Friday and 8am or 9am to 12:30pm on Saturday. There are, however, many variations between banks, and individual branches. All banks close on Sundays and public holidays, and many also close at noon on the working day before a holiday.

Credit and debit card reader requiring you to enter your PIN

## Credit and Debit Cards

Major credit cards such as **Visa** (called Carte Bleue in France) and **MasterCard** and debit cards such as Switch, Maestro, or Cirrus are widely used. American Express credit cards are less widely accepted in France. Some smaller establishments do not take cards, or will do so only if you spend a certain amount of money. Many credit card companies charge a sizeable fee for every transaction.

A convenient way to access local currency is to withdraw it from an ATM with a debit card. There is a transaction fee, so it costs less to take out a sizeable sum each time, rather than make many small withdrawals. If an ATM is not working, you can also withdraw cash on major credit cards at the foreign counter of a bank. The bank may need to obtain telephone authorization for such withdrawals first.

## Pre-Paid Currency Cards

Pre-paid currency cards, such as those offered by **FairFX**, are more economical than credit and debit cards and are widely accepted in France. You can use them to withdraw cash at an ATM and pay for goods and services. You can load up your card with credit ahead of your trip, and top it up online or by phone while in France. Currency cards are often linked to Visa or MasterCard so you can use them anywhere you would normally use a credit or debit card. Some currency card providers charge a fee to top up your card and for ATM cash withdrawals, but this is much lower than for a standard credit card.

# DIRECTORY

## Foreign Banks

**Barclays**
24bis av de l'Opéra, 75001 Paris.
**Map** 8 E1. **Tel** 08 10 06 06 60 or
01 44 86 00 00.
W barclays.fr

**HSBC**
103 av des Champs-Elysées,
75008 Paris. **Map** 2 E4.
**Tel** 08 10 24 68 10
or 08 10 83 84 85.
W hsbc.fr

## Bureaux de Change

**Travelex**

**Paris**
125 av des Champs-Elysées,
75008. **Map** 2 E4.
**Tel** 01 47 20 25 14.
W travelex.fr

**Lille**
69 rue Faidherbe, 59000.

**Lyon**
Gare de Lyon-Part-Dieu,
bd Marius Vivier Merle, 69003.

**Nice**
13 av Thiers, 06000.

## Lost Credit Cards

**MasterCard**
**Tel** 08 00 90 13 87.

**Visa**
**Tel** 08 00 90 11 79.

## Pre-Paid Currency Cards

**FairFX**
**Tel** 020 7107 1206.
W fairfx.com

## The Euro

France was one of the 12 countries taking the euro (€) in 2002, with the original currency, the franc, phased out on February 17, 2002.

EU members using the euro as sole official currency are known as the Eurozone.

Several EU members have either opted out or have not met the conditions for adopting the single currency.

Euro bills are identical throughout the Eurozone countries, each one including designs of fictional monuments and architectural structures, and the 12 stars of the EU. The coins, however, have one side identical (the value side), and one side with an image unique to each country. Both bills and coins are exchangeable in any of the participating Eurozone countries.

## Bank bills

*Euro bills have seven denominations. The €5 bill (gray in color) is the smallest, followed by the €10 bill (pink), €20 bill (blue), €50 bill (orange), €100 bill (green), €200 bill (yellow), and €500 bill (purple). All notes show the stars of the European Union.*

5 euros

10 euros

20 euros

50 euros

100 euros

200 euros

500 euros

2 euros    1 euro    50 cents    20 cents    10 cents

## Coins

*The euro has eight coin denominations: €1 and €2; 50 cents, 20 cents, 10 cents, 5 cents, 2 cents, and 1 cent. The €2 and €1 coins are both silver and gold in color. The 50-, 20-, and 10-cent coins are gold. The 5-, 2-, and 1-cent coins are bronze.*

5 cents    2 cents    1 cent

# Communications and Media

France has world-class telecommunications. Many cities and venues offer free public Wi-Fi. Phone booths have given way to affordable prepaid SIM cards, with 3G and 4G coverage available even in the Paris Metro. With many competing providers, prices for internet and phone services are competitive. Post offices (bureaux des postes), identified by the blue-on-yellow La Poste sign, are your best bet for sending items nationally or worldwide. The French generally speak more English than they let on, but the service industry is better than ever at communicating with English-speakers. Publications, TV, and radio in foreign languages can be found easily in major towns.

A distinctive yellow French mailbox

## Local and International Phone Calls

All French telephone numbers have ten digits, and you must key in all the digits, even if you are in the same area. In landline numbers the first two digits indicate the region: 01 is for Paris and the Ile-de-France; 02, the northwest; 03, the northeast; 04, the southeast; and 05, the southwest. French cell phone numbers begin with 06, and 08 indicates a special rate number. All 0800 numbers are free. For landline numbers, low rates operate on evenings, weekends, and public holidays. It is best to avoid making calls from hotels, as most add hefty surcharges.

To call France from abroad, dial 00 33 and omit the initial zero from the 10-digit French number. You cannot call French 08 numbers from outside France.

To call abroad from France, dial 00 and then the country code (Australia 61, USA and Canada 1, Irish Republic 353, New Zealand 64, and UK 44).

## Cell Phones

Cell phone coverage is generally good throughout France, although signals may be weak in some mountain areas. French cells use the European-standard 900 and 1900 MHz frequencies, so UK cell phones work if they have a roaming facility enabled. North American cell phones will only operate in France if they are tri- or quad-band. Always check roaming charges with your service provider before traveling, as making and receiving calls can be very expensive. Some companies offer "packages" for foreign calls and these can work out cheaper.

If you expect to use your phone frequently, it can be more economical to buy a pay-as-you-go French cell phone from one of the main local providers such as **Orange France**, **Bouygues Télécom, SFR,** and **Free**. All four companies have stores in most towns. You can also insert a local SIM card into your own phone,

but this will only work if your phone has not been blocked by your service provider.

## Public Telephones

With the rise in the use of cell phones, there are now very few pay phones (cabines téléphoniques), and few of these accept coins. Many phones now accept credit cards (with a PIN), but for some you will need to use a phone card (télécarte). Sold in tabacs, post offices, train stations, and some newsstands, cards are available for 50 or 120 telephone units, and are simple to use. For calls abroad, international code cards are available at the Travelex bureaux de change (see p626).

The cheapest way to phone abroad is to connect to Wi-Fi (for free) and use an internet calling app such as WhatsApp or Skype.

## Internet Access

The internet is widely used in France, but internet cafés have diminished in number. There are usually a few Taxiphone internet cafés offering computers with cheap Wi-Fi in most cities and resorts, but in small towns and rural areas they can be hard to find. For cell phone, tablet, and laptop users, there are free Wi-Fi hotspots in many Métro stations, public libraries, and other locations in Paris and other major cities. Many hotels and even chambres d'hôtes now offer Wi-Fi connections, but check that these are free. Most

Tourists using smartphones at the Colonnes de Buren, Palais Royal in Paris

hotels use one of several subscription services such as Orange France and **Meteor**, with which you buy a certain amount of time-credit and are then given an access code. Any time-credit remaining can be used anywhere that uses the same service.

French Wi-Fi servers often use different frequencies to those in the UK and North America, so you may need to manually search for the network (for more details, see the Orange Wi-Fi website). If you need to use a cable connection, note that the French modem socket is incompatible with US and UK plugs. Adaptors are available, but it is often cheaper and easier to buy a French modem cable.

## Postal Services

The postal service in France is fast and usually reliable. There are post offices in most towns, and there are large main offices in all cities. Postage stamps *(timbres)* can be bought at post offices individually or in a *carnet* of seven or ten, although the most convenient place to buy stamps is often at a *tabac*, where phone cards can also be purchased.

Post offices usually open 9am–5pm Mon–Fri, often with a break for lunch, and 9am–noon on Saturday. Post offices in towns and cities are best avoided when they first open, as this is when they are at their busiest.

Letters are posted in yellow mailboxes, which often have separate slots for post within the town such as in, within the *département,* and for other destinations *(autres destinations)*. There are eight different price zones for international mail. Information on mail services is provided on the **La Poste** website.

## Newspapers and Magazines

Newspapers and magazines can be bought at newsagents *(maisons de la presse)* or news-stands *(kiosques)*. Regional newspapers tend to be more popular than the Paris-based national papers, such as the conservative *Le Figaro*, weighty *Le Monde* or leftist *Libération*. The daily *International Herald Tribune* can be found in Paris and throughout France. Other foreign newspapers are also often available on the day of publication in resorts and large cities.

The weekly listings magazines *Pariscope* (Thursday) and *L'Officiel des Spectacles* (Wednesday) give the latest on entertainment news in Paris. *Les Inrockuptibles* has information on current music, movies, and the other arts from all over France. Many smaller cities have their own listings magazines, usually in French and often free, which can generally be found at tourist offices.

## TV and Radio

All French television networks use Digital Video Broadcasting (DVB). There are 18 free channels, including the major national channels TF1 and France 2. Canal Plus (or Canal +), a subscription-only channel, offers a broad mix of programs including live sport and movies in English with French subtitles. A movie shown in its original language is listed as *VO (Version Originale)*; a film dubbed into French is indicated as *VF (Version Française)*. Most hotels subscribe to Canal +, and many also have cable and satellite TV, including English-language stations such as CNN, MTV, Sky, BBC World, and the English version of the round-the-clock French news service France24.

It is easy to pick up UK radio stations in France, including Radio 4 (198 long wave). BBC World Service broadcasts through the night on the same wavelength. Voice of America can be found at 90.5, 98.8 and 102.4 FM. Radio France International (738 AM) gives daily news in English from 3–4pm.

Newspapers sold in France

## DIRECTORY

### Telephone and Internet Services

**Bouygues Télécom**
Tel 1064 (from a landline).
🌐 bouyguestelecom.fr

**Free**
🌐 free.fr

**Meteor**
🌐 meteornetworks.com

**Orange France**
Tel 0810 555 421.
🌐 orange.fr
🌐 orange-wifi.com

**SFR**
Tel 1026 (from a landline phone in France).
🌐 sfr.fr

### Postal Services

**La Poste**
🌐 laposte.fr

### Useful Telephone Numbers and Codes

- **Information**
  118 712.
- **International information** 118 700.
- **France Telecom/Orange**
  0800 36 47 75; 0969 363 900 (for English).
- **Free, reduced, and premium numbers** 0800; 0810, 0820, 0825 (free and reduced rate); 0890, 0891, 0892 (premium rate).
- **In case of emergencies** 17.

LA POSTE

La Poste road sign

# TRAVEL INFORMATION

France enjoys sophisticated air, road, and train travel. Direct flights from all over the world serve Paris and some regional airports. Paris is the hub of a vast internal railroad network and of Europe's high-speed train network, with the Eurostar to London, Thalys to Brussels, and TGVs to Geneva and other destinations. Highways cross into all surrounding countries including, via the Eurotunnel, the UK. France is also served by frequent Channel and Mediterranean ferries.

Getting to or from France on the national carrier, Air France

## Arriving by Air

France is served by nearly all international airlines. Most long-haul flights arrive at Paris Charles de Gaulle airport, but there are flights from Europe and North Africa to many other airports around the country.

Airlines with regular flights between the UK and France include **British Airways**, **Air France**, and low-cost airlines such as **Flybe**, **Jet2**, **Ryanair**, and **easyJet**. From North America there are direct flights to Paris from about 20 cities, mainly on **Air Canada**, **American Airlines**, **Delta**, **United**, and **Air France**. **Qantas** provides connecting flights from Australia and New Zealand.

## Paris Airports

Paris's Charles de Gaulle airport (CDG), about 19 miles (30 km) from the city, is the main hub airport in France. Access to central Paris is by RER line B from CDG2, which takes 40 minutes to Gare du Nord and 45 minutes to Châtelet-Les Halles. Regular bus services run from the airport to different parts of Paris, and to Disneyland® Paris theme park. Air France buses run to the Arc de Triomphe and western Paris, and to Montparnasse; each journey

takes about 45 minutes. RATP buses (Roissybus) depart every 20 minutes for L'Opéra and take about 50 minutes. Taxi fares are fixed from CDG to the Right Bank (€50) and Left Bank (€55) for up to four people.

Paris's other main airport, Orly, in the south of the city, serves primarily domestic and short-haul international flights. Shuttle buses link the airport with RER line C at Pont de Rungis and an automatic train, Orlyval, links the airport with RER line B at Antony, from where trains run to Châtelet-Les Halles in 35 minutes. Air France buses for central Paris depart every 30 minutes; RATP Orlybus runs to Denfert-Rochereau Métro; and the Jetbus connects Orly to Châtelet-Les Halles, departing every 15–20

minutes. Taxis fares from Orly to the Left Bank are €30 and €35 to the Right Bank.

## Arriving by Sea

Several regular ferry services operate between the UK and Ireland and France. Dover–Calais is the fastest route: **P&O Ferries** has up to 25 crossings daily, with a journey time of 90 minutes or less. **DFDS Seaways** runs from Dover to Dunkerque in about 2 hours and has some of the lowest fares. It also has crossings between Newhaven and Dieppe (about 4 hrs), and between Dover and Calais or Dunkerque. The biggest operator in the western Channel is **Brittany Ferries**, which sails from Portsmouth to Caen (7 hrs overnight), Poole to Cherbourg (6 hrs overnight), Portsmouth to St.-Malo (10 hrs overnight), Plymouth to Roscoff (8 hrs overnight), and between Cork and Roscoff (14 hrs). From April/May to September/October, Brittany Ferries also runs high-speed services on the Poole–Cherbourg and Portsmouth–Cherbourg routes (4 hrs 30 mins). **Condor Ferries** sail from Portsmouth to Cherbourg in 5 hours (July–September only) and from Poole and Weymouth

Plying the Mediterranean with SNCM Ferryterranée

to St-Malo via Jersey or Guernsey (May–September only).

**Irish Ferries** run between Rosslare and Cherbourg (17 hrs overnight) from January to December, and to Roscoff (15 hrs 30 mins overnight) from mid-May to September. **Maritima Ferries** run from a range of European ports (*see p635*).

## Arriving by Train

There are at least 20 **Eurostar** trains daily between London St. Pancras and the Gare du Nord in Paris. The journey via the Channel Tunnel takes 2 hrs 15 mins. Several trains also stop at Ebbsfleet or Ashford in Kent, Calais–Frethun, Lille (1 hr 30 mins from London), and Disneyland® Paris.

Paris and its six main stations are the great hub of the French railroad network. Traveling from Belgium, Holland, and north Germany, you arrive at the Gare du Nord; from other parts of Germany you come into the Gare de l'Est. Trains from Switzerland and Italy arrive at

the Gare de Lyon. From Spain you come into the Gare d'Austerlitz. Outside Paris, other major rail hubs include Lille, Tours, Bordeaux, and Lyon. For more information on French train services and traveling to France by train, see pp632–4.

Eurotunnel logo

## Arriving by Road

Passengers from the UK can travel to France with their vehicle either by ferry or on the **Eurotunnel** shuttle through the Channel Tunnel. Eurotunnel runs at least four trains an hour during the day, and the trip takes about 35 minutes. Fares compete with those of the ferry companies, and similarly vary by season, day, and time of travel. For Eurotunnel crossings, it is possible to turn up and wait for the next available space.

Bus travel is a good-value alternative, and **Eurolines** runs three to five departures daily from Victoria Coach Station in London to Bagnolet in eastern Paris. Buses also run from London and other parts of

the UK to Lille, Lyon, Marseille, and several other French towns and cities. The SNCF-run **Ouigo** bus service offers low-cost bus travel within France and to cities in other countries.

## Green Travel

Traveling in France without flying or driving is easier than in many countries thanks to the high quality of public transportation, particularly the SNCF railroad network. There are daily train services from across Europe, ferries to the UK, Ireland, and Mediterranean destinations, and the Eurostar connection with London.

The French government has introduced an "Ecomobility" program, which aims to make it easier to transfer from trains to local buses, bicycles, or other non-car forms of transportation. This includes public bicycle schemes such as the *Vélib'* in Paris and similar bike-share initiatives in other cities (*see p641*). Many regions have also developed **Voies Vertes**, long-distance paths for cycling or walking, such as the one along the Loire from Orléans to St.-Nazaire.

# DIRECTORY

## Arriving by Air

**Air Canada**
Tel 01 888 247 2262 (Canada), 0825 880 881 (France).
w aircanada.com

**Air France**
Tel 01 800 667 2747 (France).
w airfrance.com

**American Airlines**
Tel 01 800 433 7300 (USA), 0821 980 999 (France).
w aa.com

**British Airways**
Tel 0844 493 0787 (UK), 0825 825 400 (France).
w britishairways.com

**Delta**
Tel 01 800 221 1212 (USA), 08 11 64 00 05 (France).
w delta.com

**easyJet**
Tel 0330 3655 0000 (UK), 0820 420 315 (France).
w easyjet.com

**Flybe**
w flybe.com

**Jet2**
Tel 0333 300 0404 (UK), 0821 230 203 (France).
w jet2.com

**Qantas**
Tel 13 13 13 (Australia), 01 57 32 92 83 (France).
w qantas.com

**Ryanair**
Tel 0871 246 000 (UK), 0892 562 150 (France).
w ryanair.com

**United**
Tel 01 800 864 8331 (USA), 01 71 23 03 35 (France).
w united.com

## Arriving by Sea

**Brittany Ferries**
w brittany-ferries.com

**Condor Ferries**
w condorferries.co.uk

**DFDS Seaways**
w dfdsseaways.co.uk

**Irish Ferries**
w irishferries.com

**P&O Ferries**
w poferries.com

**Maritima Ferries**
w ferries.co.uk/maritima_ferries.html

## Arriving by Train

*See also pp632–4*

**Eurostar**
Tel 08705 186 186 (UK), 0892 35 35 39 (France).
w eurostar.com

## Arriving by Road

**Eurolines**
Tel 0871 781 8181 (UK), 0892 899 091 (France).
w eurolines.co.uk

**Eurotunnel**
Tel 08443 35 35 35 (UK), 0810 630 304 (France).
w eurotunnel.com

**Ouigo**
w ouigo.com

## Green Travel

**Train+Bicycle Travel**
w velo.sncf.com

**Voies Vertes**
w voiesvertes.com

# Traveling by Train

The French state railroad, the Société Nationale des Chemins de Fer (**SNCF**), runs Europe's most comprehensive national train network. Its services include high-speed, long-distance TGVs and mainline expresses, overnight sleepers, AutoTrain, and rural branch lines that reach every corner of the country. Lines closed for economic reasons are replaced by SNCF's modern buses, which are free to Rail Pass holders. Travel off the main lines can be slow, though some cross-country journeys are quicker, if you change trains in Paris.

## Traveling around France by Train

France has always been known for the punctuality of its trains, and has maintained a high level of investment in the state-owned train system, SNCF. The pride of the SNCF is its TGV high-speed train, with journey times such as Lille–Lyon or Paris–Marseille in just 3 hours. In addition, frequent, fast, and comfortable mainline express trains provide a comprehensive city-to-city service, while regional lines provide connections to smaller towns and villages. SNCF is also the largest bus operator in France, filling in the gaps where railroad routes have closed.

Sleeper trains are a convenient way to travel long distances at night, and motorists can travel with their cars on **AutoTrain** trains. Most (but not all) long-distance trains have restaurant cars.

Further information on French railroads is provided on the main SNCF website (*see p634*), where reservations can also be made. To book a long-distance train from abroad, visit the **Voyages SNCF** website. **Rail Europe** also offers a comprehensive information and booking service for travel throughout Europe. For useful links and an invaluable guide to every aspect of using French and other European railroads, visit **The Man in Seat 61** website.

## Local and Scenic Railroads

Alongside the national train network, there are several special railroads that operate around France. On Corsica, the **Chemins de Fer de la Corse** has narrow-gauge routes between Calvi, Bastia, and Ajaccio. Particularly spectacular is the train trip along the north-west coast between L'Ile-Rousse and Calvi. In summer, old-style *trains touristiques* run on this and other lines. In Provence, the privately run **Chemins de Fer de Provence** runs the *Train des Pignes* over a magnificent 90-mile (150-km) mountain route from Nice to Digne-les-Bains. SNCF also runs many more *trains touristiques* on particularly scenic sections of its regional network. These are usually in mountainous areas during the winter months and in summer on the coast and in the countryside. *Gentiane Bleu* trains run from Dijon to the winter snows in the Jura, and the *Train des Merveilles* runs from Nice into the Alps at Tende. For a guide to all these routes, visit www.sncf.com/fr/trains/trains-touristiques.

Several privately or locally owned rail routes around France are kept going by enthusiasts, who offer excursions for part of the year, often using steam trains. The *Chemin de Fer de la Baie de la Somme* travels around the Somme Bay in Picardy and the *Chemin de Fer Touristique du Tarn* operates in the Tarn hills near Albi. Nearly all of these companies are members of the **UNECTO** association.

**RER**

Symbol for Paris suburban trains

## Types of Train

SNCF trains are divided into several types. TGV (*Train à Grande Vitesse*) trains are the flagships of the network, traveling on specially built track at around 186 mph (300 kph). There are four main TGV route networks; to the north, west, east, and southeast from Paris, with additional hubs at Lille, Lyon, Bordeaux, and Marseille. In some places, TGVs have separate stations built outside town centers. The trains have first- and second-class cars, and some of them offer internet access. Seat reservations are obligatory for all TGV trains: tickets can be bought at stations until shortly before departure time, or booked ahead online.

Within the TGV network there are several international

The train to Le Montenvers is a particularly scenic route

services, including Eurostar, linking France with the UK; Thalys, which links stations in France with Belgium, Holland, and Germany; Lyria, serving Switzerland; and TGV and ITALO, which run TGV services to the main cities in Italy, and a conventional train from Paris to Rome. Non-TGV international trains also operate, notably the nightly Elipsos from Paris to Madrid and Barcelona.

Intercités and Transilien trains are conventional long-distance express trains with modern cars. Reservations are obligatory for all long-distance trains and can be made through Rail Europe or SNCF.

The AutoTrain allows drivers to cut out long distances by traveling overnight with their vehicle on the same train. Those using the service from the UK

The TGV, with its distinctive-looking "nose"

should take the Eurostar to reach Paris first. The AutoTrain runs to 12 destinations in the south of France including Nice, Narbonne, Avignon, Lyon, and Bordeaux.

**TER** trains are regional services that usually stop at every station. Reservations are not required, although tickets

can be purchased in advance. Route maps and information (in French only) for each region are available at stations and on the TER website (see p634). Transilien is the TER network for the Ile-de-France around Paris, and is integrated with the RER suburban trains and the Métro.

## TGV Rail Service

*Trains à Grande Vitesse*, or high-speed trains, travel at speeds up to 186 mph (300 kph). There are four routes: TGV Nord from Paris Gare du Nord, TGV Atlantique from Paris Gare Montparnasse, TGV Sud-Est from Paris Gare de Lyon, and TGV Est from Paris Gare de l'Est.

### Key

━━ High-speed routes

── Other routes

The automatic ticket machines at the Gare de Lyon in Paris

## Fares and Passes

Fare rates vary according to the type of train. For all trains that can be booked online (TGV, Transilien, Eurostar), there are two or three basic fare rates for each class. The cheapest tickets are called Prems, which must be booked well in advance and cannot be altered after payment. On most TER and some Transilien trains fares are cheaper at off-peak times (*périodes bleus*); peak times (*périodes blanches*) are 5–10am Monday and 3–8pm Friday and Sunday.

SNCF sells several travel cards that give fare reductions. Examples are *Carte Weekend* giving 25 percent off weekend travel, *Carte Jeune* for those ages 12–27, *Carte Senior* for over-60s, *Carte Escapades* for frequent travelers, and *Carte Enfant +* for parents with children under age 12. Further details are available on the SNCF website.

For visitors intending to make several train journeys around France, it is worth investing in a multijourney rail pass, which can only be bought outside the country. The **Interrail** pass, for UK and other European residents, is valid for several European countries, giving unlimited travel for 3, 4, 6, or 8 days (not necessarily consecutively) within one month. Visitors from outside Europe can buy a France Rail Pass, permitting 3 to 9 days of unlimited travel within one month, or a **Eurail** Select Pass that covers France and neighboring countries. Be aware that some trains, including the TGV, charge additional supplements, which are not included in the price. For more information, visit the Rail Europe website.

## Booking Tickets

Train tickets can be bought at any SNCF station and by phone or online through SNCF's free app. At most stations, there are both staffed counters and automatic ticket machines (*billetteries automatiques*), which accept cash or credit cards and have instructions in English. Tickets for trains that require a reservation (TGV) can be bought up to 90 days in advance and up until 5 minutes before departure. Tickets bought in advance can be collected from the station, or sent to your address.

From outside France, you can book TGV and Intercité tickets through www.voyages-sncf.com, (the website is in multiple languages), although it can be easier to use Rail Europe. Travelers with mobility problems can arrange assistance through the *Accès Plus* program; more information is available online or from Atout France (*see pp620–23*).

Note that before any train journey in France, you must validate your ticket in a *composteur* machine (*below*).

## Timetables

French train timetables change twice a year, in May and September, and all of them can be consulted on the SNCF website. Stations have free regional TER timetables available and information on the TGV network. Other free leaflets provide information on topics such as traveling with children, reduced fares, and travel for the disabled.

## DIRECTORY

### Rail Information

**AutoTrain**
⊞ autotrain.voyages-sncf.com

**Eurail**
⊞ eurail.com

**Interrail**
⊞ rail.cc

**The Man in Seat 61**
⊞ seat61.com

**Rail Europe**
⊞ raileurope.com

**SNCF**
⊞ sncf.com

**TER**
⊞ sncf.com/en/trains/ter

**Voyages SNCF**
⊞ voyages-sncf.com

### Local and Scenic Railroads

**Chemins de Fer de la Corse**
⊞ train-corse.com

**Chemins de Fer de Provence**
⊞ trainprovence.com

**UNECTO**
⊞ unecto.fr

## Composteur Machine

Yellow *composteur* machines (left) are located in station halls and at the head of each platform. You must validate passes by inserting tickets and reservations separately, with the printed side up. The *composteur* will punch your ticket and print the time and date on the back. A penalty may be imposed by the inspector on the train, if you fail to do this.

# Traveling by Boat

With both Mediterranean and Atlantic coastlines, France offers excellent opportunities for sailing and has very good amenities. Inland, there is an extensive network of rivers, canals, and other waterways. Cruising through them is an ideal way to discover some of the country's most charming countryside. Frequent scheduled ferries also connect mainland France to Corsica and other parts of the Mediterranean as well as to the British Channel Islands off Normandy.

Boats moored along the Canal du Midi, Roussillon

## Traveling by Ferry

Car ferries sail to Corsica from Marseille, Nice, and Toulon, the main operators being **Maritima Ferries** and **Corsica Ferries**. **La Méridionale** sails between Corsica and Sardinia, and **Moby Lines** also connects Corsica with Livorno and Genoa in mainland Italy. Regular ferries also connect France and North Africa; Maritima Ferries runs to Algeria and Tunisia, while **Aferry** goes to Morocco and Italy; it also has a luxury service from Sète to Morocco.

In the Atlantic, **Manche-Iles Express** and **Compagnie Corsaire** sail from St.-Malo and the Normandy ports of Granville, Barneville-Carteret, and Diélette to the British Channel Islands. For a guide to all European ferry services, visit www.ferrylines.com.

## Sailing in France

France has excellent sailing amenities, with marinas all around its coast. On the Atlantic, well-equipped ports include Honfleur and St.-Vaast-la-Hougue in Normandy, St.-Malo and Pleneuf-St.-André in Brittany, and La Rochelle and Arcachon on the west coast. Among the best on the Mediterranean are St.-Cyprien near the Spanish border, Antibes on the Côte d'Azur, and the small harbors of Corsica. Charters or short-term rentals are available at most marinas, and information on rules and permits is available from the **Ministère de l'Ecologie**. The **Fédération Française de Voile** provides updates on sailing conditions.

## Canal and River Trips

There are many options for exploring French waterways, from short boat trips to cruises of several days. The official guide to the system is provided by **Voies Navigables de France**. Many companies offer cruises around France, among the best of which are **En Péniche**, which uses traditional barges or *peniches*; **Locaboat**; and **En-Bateau Tourisme Fluvial**. For narrowboats on the Canal du Midi, try **Minervois Cruisers**.

Short excursions are popular around the Marais Poitevin wetlands between La Rochelle and Poitiers, and along the Canal de Bourgogne from Dijon. **Best of Perigord** runs trips on the Dordogne in traditional *gabarre* boats. For rides on the River Seine in Paris see p641.

For rides on the River Seine in Paris see p641.

## DIRECTORY

### Traveling by Ferry

**Aferry**
Tel 09 70 80 90 18. W aferry.fr

**Compagnie Corsaire**
Tel 0825 138 100.
W compagniecorsaire.com

**Corsica Ferries**
Tel 0825 095 095.
W corsica-ferries.fr

**Manche-Iles Express**
Tel 0825 133 050 (in France),
015 34 88 07 56 (in Jersey).
W manche-iles-express.com

**Maritima Ferries**
Tel 0844 815 7785
W ferries.co.uk/maritima_ferries.html

**La Méridionale**
Tel 0970 83 20 20.
W lameridionale.fr

**Moby Lines**
Tel 00 49 (0)611 14020.
W mobylines.fr

### Sailing in France

**Fédération Française de Voile**
W ffvoile.fr

**Ministère de l'Ecologie**
W developpement-durable.gouv.fr

### Canal and River Trips

**Best of Perigord**
Tel 06 44 06 83 48.
W best-of-perigord.tm.fr

**En-Bateau Tourisme Fluvial**
Tel 04 67 13 19 62.
W en-bateau.com

**En Péniche**
Tel 04 67 13 19 62.
W en-peniche.com

**Locaboat**
Tel 03 86 91 72 72.
W locaboat.com

**Minervois Cruisers**
Tel 01926 811 842 (in UK).
W minervoiscruisers.com

**Voies Navigables de France**
W vnf.fr

# On the Road

France's network of modern freeways (*autoroutes*) allows quick and easy access to all parts of the country. However, you can save money on tolls and explore France in a more leisurely way by using some of the other high-quality highways that dissect the country. This section outlines both alternatives and gives instructions on how to use freeway tollbooths (*péage*) and French parking meters (*horodateurs*), as well as some of the rules governing driving in France. There are also tips on how to get weather and traffic forecasts, where to rent a car, and how to get the best road maps.

Freeway and highway signs

## What to Take

Effective insurance is essential when taking a car to France. All car insurance in the EU automatically includes minimum third-party insurance cover, which is valid in any EU country. However, the extent of cover provided beyond the legal minimum varies between insurance companies, so it is best to check your details before you travel, and, if necessary, procure additional coverage. For holders of full car insurance, most companies provide full European cover for a small extra fee; some do not charge for this, but still require you to notify them before traveling. It is also advisable to have breakdown cover with one of the Europe-wide networks with English-speaking phone lines.

While driving in France you must carry in the car your driver's license, passport, the vehicle registration document, and a certificate of insurance. You must also have a set of spare light bulbs, at least one red warning triangle, and a luminous reflecting jacket to be worn if you ever have to stop on a highway because of a breakdown or other emergency. You can be fined if you are stopped by the police and do not have this equipment. The car's country of registration

should be displayed on a sticker or as part of the registration plate, and right-hand-drive cars need headlamp deflectors for driving on the right – kits are available at most ports.

## Buying Gas

All gas stations have unleaded gas and diesel fuel (*gazole* or *gas-oil*, or a high-grade *gas-oil +*). Many stations also have LPG (*GPL*). The cheapest places are attached to big supermarkets, and many major service stations have 24-hour pumps, with payment by credit card.

## Rules of the Road

Wearing seatbelts, in the front and back of the car, is compulsory in France, as is the use of booster seats for children under 10. It is illegal to use a cell phone while driving, even if it's on hands-free mode. Dipped headlights must be used in poor visibility, and motorcyclists must have dipped headlights lit at all times. Unless road signs indicate otherwise, *Priorité à droite* means

that you must give way to any vehicle joining the road from the right except on traffic circles. Flashing headlights mean that the driver is claiming the right of way. For further details, consult **AA** or **RAC** websites (*see p639*).

## Speed Limits and Fines

Speed limits in France are as follows:
• On freeways (*autoroutes*): 80 mph (130 kph); 68 mph (110 kph) when it rains.
• On divided highways: 68 mph (110 kph); 56–62 mph (90–100 kph) when it rains.
• On other roads: 56 mph (90 kph); 49 mph (80 kph) when it rains.
• In towns and villages: 31 mph (50 kph).

There are also lower speed limits on all roads for vehicles towing a trailer.

On-the-spot fines are levied for speeding, not stopping at a Stop sign, for overtaking where forbidden and exceeding the speed limit by over 25 mph (40 kph). Driving with over 0.05 percent alcohol in the blood is illegal.

## Freeways

Most freeways in France are toll roads (*autoroutes à péage*). The **Societé d'Autoroutes** website (*see p639*) lists the rates charged for each journey. There are also toll-free autoroutes, notably those around big cities such as Paris (A3 and A86) and Lille, and some cross-country stretches such as the A84 from Caen to Rennes, and the A75 south of Clermont-Ferrand.

A sign at a gas pump points to *GPL* (LPG) or *gazole* (gasoline)

The scenic route around Mont Cenis lake

Much of the *autoroute* network includes rest areas, gas stations every 25 miles (40 km) and emergency phones every 1 mile (2 km).

## Other Roads

RN (*Route Nationale*) highways are the main alternative to freeways for long-distance trips. They are often far more scenic, but can be more congested. To get really off the beaten path, travel by D (*départementale*) roads, which snake around the countryside. Look for the **Bis/Bison Futé** signs, which indicate quieter, alternative routes.

Try to avoid traveling at the French vacation rush periods, known as *grands départs*. The worst times are weekends in mid-July, and the beginning and end of August.

Certain signs are particularly useful to know when driving in and out of towns. Follow *Centre Ville* signs for downtown and *Toutes Directions* (all routes) to take you out of the center to where you can find ongoing routes. If your destination is not signposted, follow *Autres Directions* (other directions).

## Scenic Routes

France's dense web of *Routes Nationales* and D roads weave through some of the country's most gorgeous scenery. The most celebrated roads are in mountain regions, such as the Col du Galibier road over the Alps east of Grenoble (N91, then D902) but there are many others throughout the country. Some hug the coast, such as the roads along the Côte d'Azur or the rugged coasts of Brittany and Normandy. Information on these *routes touristiques* is available from tourist offices (*see p620*).

## Highway Conditions

The French Highway Authorities' *Bison Futé* website (*see p639*) provides essential information for driving in France, with details of weather conditions, winter driving requirements, and roadworks. Check also www.autoroutes.fr for highway driving.

Motoring organizations such as the AA and RAC sell tailor-made route-planning services, giving scenic options and road conditions (*see p639*).

---

## Using the Autoroute Toll

Collect a ticket from the tollbooth and keep it safe until you reach an exit toll, where you will be charged according to the distance traveled and type of vehicle used. To pay at small tolls, just throw your coins into the large receptacle.

### Highway Sign

These signs (left) indicate the name and distance to the next tollbooth. They are usually blue and white; some show the tariff rates for cars, motorbikes, trucks, and trailers.

### Tollbooth with Attendant

When you hand in your ticket at a manned tollbooth, the attendant will tell you the cost of your journey on the *autoroute*, and the price will be displayed. You can pay with coins, bills, credit cards, or with a check in euros. A receipt can be issued on request.

### Automatic Machine

On reaching the exit toll, insert your ticket into the machine, and the price of your journey will be displayed in euros. You can pay either with coins or by credit card. The machine will give change and can issue a receipt.

## Parking

Parking regulations vary from town to town, but most cities have street pay-and-display machines *(horodateurs)*, with spaces marked out in blue. Some machines accept a parking payment card, sold at *tabacs*. Parking is normally limited to 2 hours. Charges are relatively low, and in most provincial towns parking is free between noon and 1:30pm. In narrow streets, parking may be confined to one side of the street and this can alternate at different times of the month.

Finding a parking space in larger cities, especially in Paris, can be difficult and it is often easier to use a parking lot or garage. These are well indicated by a large "P" sign, accompanied by the word *libre* to indicate that there are spaces available.

## Car Rental

All the main international car-rental companies operate in France, as well as local French-based companies such as **ADA** and **Rentacar**, which often have very competitive prices. You will nearly always get the best rates by reserving in advance through one of the internet car-rental booking services including **Auto Europe** or **Autos Abroad**.

Requirements for car rental vary, but in general you must be over 21 and have held a drivers' license for at least a year. You will need your license, passport, and a credit card for a deposit.

The price quoted should include all taxes and unlimited mileage. All rental contracts include basic third-party insurance, and some companies also include comprehensive insurance. Extras such as child car seats, snow chains or automatic transmission should be indicated when booking. Most rentals offer GPS devices, which help in navigating the French roads.

Before you drive away, check the general condition of the car and also ensure it has a set of spare bulbs, a warning triangle, and a luminous jacket, which are all legal requirements in France *(see p636)*.

## Maps

Each chapter in this guide begins with a map of the region showing all the sights and information on getting around. As additional maps, the excellent **Michelin** Tourist and Motoring Atlas at a scale of 1:200,000 is the most comprehensive driving map available. The red-cover Michelin maps of the whole of France (scale 1:1,000,000) are useful for

planning trips, as are the regional maps with orange covers (scale 1:200,000). Larger-scale Michelin maps with green covers are only for certain parts of France such as Paris and the Côte d'Azur.

The **Institut Géographique National** (IGN), the equivalent of the British Ordnance Survey and the USGS, produces high-quality maps in different scales. Particularly useful are their *Cartes de Randonnée* (scale 1:25,000), an excellent series of walking maps covering all of France. Also recommended, are the **Blay Foldex** town maps.

In France, all newsstands and gas stations stock maps and most tourist offices provide good free maps. In the UK, **Stanfords** is one of the best places to look for a full selection of French maps.

## Traveling by Bus

The French railroad is so fast and reliable that there is not much demand for long-distance buses and they tend to only operate in areas with poor train services.

**Eurolines** offers a wide range of low-priced international services, many of which make stops within France. These services are centered on the Porte de Bagnolet bus station in Paris (Métro Galliéni).

**Transdev** runs an extensive network of buses that cover the Ile-de-France, and **Lignes d'Azur** provides a good service along the Côte d'Azur. **OuiGo** is the SNCF's low-cost bus service providing trips for as little as €10.

Local buses are an important means of transportation, particularly in rural areas. These run in and out of villages from the *gare routière* (bus station), which is often located next to the SNCF train station of the main town of each *département* or area. Buses run mostly at peak times to take people to and from work and school.

## Taxis

There are taxi services in every part of France, although in rural areas you will normally have to book a cab by phone.

Eurolines buses at Porte Bagnolet bus station in Paris

Mountain bikers in the Alps

Hotels, bars, and restaurants will have the numbers of local taxis. Otherwise, in towns look for a taxi stand (station de taxi) outside train stations, airports, or downtown.

All taxis must use meters (compteurs), but prices do vary from one region to another. In general, the pick-up charge should be about €2 plus 50 cents or more per kilometre (half mile). It is often possible to agree a fixed price for a long journey. For city taxis, see pp640–41.

## Cycling

Cycling is extremely popular in France and amenities are steadily improving as part of the government-backed "Eco-mobility" scheme (see p631). Several long-distance **Voies Vertes** footpaths and cycle tracks have been created, and more are being established. Every local tourist office has a leaflet on nearby véloroutes, and many have developed their own schemes, such as the network of cycle routes

around the main Loire Valley châteaux (La Loire à Vélo). Details are available from local tourist offices and département websites.

Bicycles can be taken on nearly all **SNCF** trains, and on some routes you can reserve a rental bike at your destination station when booking a train ticket. There are also cycle rental stores in nearly every town, with standard and mountain bikes (VTT) for rent at reasonable prices. Tourist offices can advise on local companies.

More information on cycling in France can be found on the Atout France website and through the **Fédération Française de Cyclisme** (in French only). Most cities offer rental cycling schemes (see p641).

## Hitchhiking

It is not easy to get around France by hitchhiking, and it is not advisable to try either. There is, however, a safe car-sharing (co-voiturage) scheme called BlaBlaCar (www.blablacar.fr), which has branches in many towns and through which you can set up rides at reasonable rates.

# DIRECTORY

## General Motoring Information

**AA**
Tel 08 00 88 77 55 (from abroad).
w theaa.com

**Bison Futé**
w bison-fute.gouv.fr

**RAC**
Tel 0330 159 1111.
w rac.co.uk

**Societé d'Autoroutes**
w autoroutes.fr

**Zagaz**
w zagaz.com (for fuel price guide in French).

## Car Rental

**ADA**
Tel 08 99 46 46 36.
w ada.fr

**Autos Abroad**
Tel 0844 826 6536 (UK).
w autosabroad.com

**Auto Europe**
Tel 1 888 223 5555 (USA & Canada). w autoeurope.com

**Avis**
Tel 0821 230 760 (France), 0808 284 0014 (UK).
w avis.co.uk

**Budget**
Tel 0825 003 564 (France), 0844 544 3455 (UK).
w budget.com

**Europcar**
Tel 0825 358 358 (France), 0871 384 0235 (UK).
w europcar.co.uk

**Hertz**
Tel 01 41 91 95 25 (France), 020 7026 0077 (UK).
w hertz.com

**National/Citer**
Tel 0800 131 211 (France), 0800 121 8303 (UK).
w nationalcar.com

**Rentacar**
Tel 0891 700 200.
w rentacar.fr

## Maps

**Blay Foldex**
w blayfoldex.com

**Institut Géographique National**
w ign.fr

**Michelin**
w viamichelin.fr

**Stanfords**
12–14 Long Acre, London WC2E 9LP.
Tel 020 7836 1321.
w stanfords.co.uk

## Bus Travel

**Eurolines**
Tel 0892 899 091.
w eurolines.fr

**Lignes d'Azur**
w lignesdazur.com

**OuiGo**
w ouigo.com

**Transdev**
w transdev.com

## Cycling

**Fédération Française de Cyclisme**
Tel 08 11 04 05 55.
w ffc.fr

**SNCF**
w velo.sncf.com (for train and bicycle travel).

**Voies Vertes**
w voiesvertes.com

# Traveling within Cities

The charming centers of France's cities are best enjoyed on foot. If, however, you need to cover a fair amount of ground in a day, it is best to use the excellent range of public transportation available. Paris and many other cities have trolley and subway networks, often integrated with local train and bus services, and efforts have been made to create user-friendly ticketing systems. France has led the world in encouraging urban bicycle use as an alternative to the car, with easy-access bicycle-rental schemes. In each city, tourist offices will provide full information on services, including free maps.

Marseille streetcar traveling along boulevard Longchamp

### Paris Subway, RER, and Streetcar

The **RATP** operates 14 Métro subway lines. The Métro is the most convenient way to get around the city, and you are never far away from a station in central Paris. Each line can be identified by its color and number. The direction the train is traveling in is indicated by the name of the station on the front of the train – this is always the last station on the route, so it's worth checking the Métro map before boarding. Trains run frequently on each line from 5:20am to 1:20am Monday to Thursday and till 2am on Friday and Saturday.

The RER commuter trains complement the Métro and run across Paris and the suburbs. There are five lines (A–E). The most useful for visitors are B3 from Charles de Gaulle airport; A4 to Disneyland® Paris Resort; and C5 to Versailles.

The streetcar lines most useful for visitors are from Gare de St.-Denis to Noisy-le-Sec; La Défense to Porte de Versailles; and Pont du Gariglinano to Porte d'Ivry.

### Other Subway and Streetcar Systems

The cities of Lyon, Marseille, Toulouse, Lille, and Rennes all have subway systems. The Lille Métro serves the whole conurbation known as Lille-Métropole, including towns such as Roubaix and Tourcoing. All Métros connect with SNCF railroads at main train stations.

Rouen's two-line Métro is actually made up of overground streetcars (light train lines) that connect the city to the outer suburbs. Some 22 other cities around France use streetcars as well as local buses, and Paris too has some suburban streetcar lines that connect the Métro and RER.

### Buses

Every city has local buses. In Paris, RATP buses provide cheap opportunities for sightseeing. Throughout France, most routes operate from around 6am to midnight; routes and times are indicated at bus stops. Most French cities also have several night bus routes, and in Paris and the Ile-de-France, 42 Noctilien bus routes operate throughout the night, passing the main train stations. A fast-growing number of buses in Paris and other cities have wheelchair ramps. On all French city buses, you must board at the front of the bus, and get off through the middle or rear doors. Tickets can be bought from the driver or in advance from a range of outlets, which saves time when boarding.

### Local Trains

Regional TER lines *(see p633)* are operated by the SNCF and are well integrated with local transportation around cities. Tickets may be interchangeable. Around Paris, the SNCF Transilien routes form a third level of train services with the Métro and RER.

### Taxi Cabs

In Paris and most other cities cabs have a light on top, which is white when the cab is free, and orange (or just switched off) when it is taken. Paris cab fares are more expensive between 5pm and 10am, Monday to Saturday, and all day Sunday and holidays, and cost more for any journey outside central Paris (limited by, but including, the boulevard Périphérique). Many cabs take credit cards, but often only for fares over €15. At busy times the best places to find cabs in Paris are taxi cab stands *(stations de taxis)* marked with a blue "T" sign. Stands are found at major road intersections and train stations. Though cabs are operated by several companies, **Paris Taxis** provides a single number to call for them in Paris. All cabs in France are required to carry wheelchair users for no extra charge, but in the Paris region **Taxis G7** provide a specialized service for passengers with mobility problems.

In other cities cabs are similarly operated by several companies. Stands are found at airports, most train stations, and around city centers. Otherwise, tourist offices and hotels can provide you with local company numbers.

Taking a bicycle from one of the Vélib' stands in Paris

## Cycling

Great efforts are underway in French cities to encourage town cycling. On Sundays, some major streets are closed to traffic to make way for cyclists and roller-bladers. Paris city council has a world-leading pro-cycling program, and there are now over 435 miles (700 km) of cycle routes. The centerpiece of the program is the **Vélib'** scheme, where you can pick up a basic bicycle at any one of hundreds of Vélib' stations around Paris and leave it at another. To do this you must purchase a Vélib' card, which is available for a day or a week and can be bought from machines at the bike racks, or by annual subscription. Other cities run similar bike-sharing schemes under different names (**Vélo'V** in Lyon, **Le Vélo** in Marseille, **Vélobleu** in Nice, and **Vélopop** in Avignon). Tourist offices will have full information on them.

## Tickets

In Paris, RATP T-tickets are valid for city buses, the Métro, the streetcar, and the RER. Tickets are available singly or for lower prices in carnets (books) of 10 and can be bought at Métro and RER stations, the airports, tourist offices, and *tabacs*. Single tickets can also be bought on board buses but these are not valid for other forms of transportation. Don't forget to validate the ticket.

An alternative aimed at tourists is the ParisVisite card, which gives unlimited travel on all systems for 1, 2, 3, or 5 days, as well as discounted admission fees to sights. The card is sold at Métro, RER, and train stations, as well as at tourist offices or online.

Nearly all larger cities offer some kind of city pass for visitors, giving unlimited travel and other advantages for one or more days. Inquire at tourist offices for local schemes.

## Seine Cruises

A boat trip on the Seine is one of the classic ways to see Paris. The long-running **Bateaux-Mouches**, **Bateaux Parisiens**, and **Vedettes du Pont-Neuf** offer traditional cruises along the river with multilingual commentary. The **Batobus** is a more flexible alternative, allowing you to hop on and off as many times as you want during the day. Another option is to see a more intimate side of Paris with a cruise along the St.-Martin canal. Full information is available from tourist offices.

Cruise boats plying the River Seine

## DIRECTORY

### Transportation Authorities

**Lille – Transpole**
W transpole.fr

**Lyon – TCL**
Tel 04 26 10 12 12. W tcl.fr

**Marseille – Le Pilote/RTM**
Tel 08 10 00 13 26.
W lepilote.com

**Paris – RATP**
Tel 3246. W ratp.fr

**Rennes – STAR**
Tel 08 11 55 55 35
or 09 70 82 18 00. W star.fr

**Rouen – TCAR**
Tel 02 35 52 52 52. W tcar.fr

**Toulouse – Tisséo**
Tel 05 61 41 70 70. W tisseo.fr

### Taxi Cabs

**Paris Taxis**
W taxis-paris.fr

**Taxis G7**
Tel 3607. W taxisg7.fr

### Cycling Schemes

**Vélib' (Paris)**
Tel 01 30 79 79 30.
W velib.paris.fr

**Le Vélo (Marseille)**
Tel 01 30 79 29 13.
W levelo-mpm.fr

**Vélobleu (Nice)**
Tel 04 93 72 06 06.
W velobleu.org

**Vélopop (Avignon)**
Tel 08 10 45 64 56.
W velopop.fr

**Velo'V (Lyon)**
Tel 01 30 79 33 40.
W velov.grandlyon.com

### Seine Cruises

**Bateaux-Mouches**
Tel 01 42 25 96 10.
W bateaux-mouches.fr

**Bateaux Parisiens**
Tel 08 25 01 01 01.
W bateauxparisiens.com

**Batobus**
Tel 01 76 64 79 12.
W batobus.com

**Vedettes du Pont-Neuf**
Tel 01 46 33 98 38.
W vedettesdupontneuf.com

# General Index

Page numbers in **bold** refer to main entries.

## A

A Cupulatta 546
Abadie, Paul 138, 423, 435
Abbeys
    Abbaye-aux-Dames (Caen) **258**
    Abbaye de Fontenay
        321, 331, **336–7**
    Abbaye de Fontfroide 491
    Abbaye d'Hautecombe 394
    Abbaye-aux-Hommes (Caen) **258**
    Abbaye de Jumièges 251, 267
    Abbaye de Montmajour 511
    Abbaye de Noirlac 317
    Abbaye de Nouaillé-Maupertuis **418**
    Abbaye Royale de Fontevraud 13, **298**
    Abbaye de Royaumont **176**
    Abbaye de Ste-Foy (Conques) 320, **372–3**
    Abbaye de St-Victor (Marseille) **516**
    Abbaye de St-Wandrille 267
    Abbaye de Sénanque 510
    Anciene Abbaye de Cluny 16, 54–5, 349
    Marmoutier 37, 237
    Moissac 399, 431, **446–7**
    Mont-St-Michel **262–3**
Abelard, Peter 56
L'Abri du Cap Blanc 407, 438–9
Académie Française 62
Accessories stores **147**, 148, **606**, 607
Accommodations **550–71**
Acquigny
    restaurants 583
Adhémar, Château des 390
Admission charges 620
Aeronautical sports **614**, 617
Agde 491
Agen **444**
    hotels 566
    restaurants 596
Agincourt, Battle of (1415) 59
Agneaux
    hotels 559
Aigues-Mortes **499**
    restaurants 599
Aiguines 518
Aïnhoa **457**
    hotels 568
    restaurants 598
Air France 70
Air travel **630**, 631
Aire-sur-la-Lys
    restaurants 579
Aix-les-Bains **394**
Aix-en-Provence **515**
    festivals 41
    hotels 569
    restaurants 601
Ajaccio **546**
    hotels 571
    restaurants 603
Alabaster Coast see Côte d'Albâtre
Alacoque, Marguerite-Marie 349
Alain-Fournier 34
Albert (Somme) 194
Albert I, Prince of Monaco 535
Albert II, Prince of Monaco 73, 535
Albertville 326
Albi **448**
    hotels 566
    restaurants 596

Albigensians see Cathars
Albret, Jeanne d' 458, 462
Alençon
    restaurants 583
Aléria 547
Alésia MuséoParc (Alise-Ste.-Reine)
    338
Alet-les-Bains 490
Alexander II, Tsar 135
Alexander III, Tsar 113
Algoplus (Roscoff) 279
Alise-Ste.-Reine **338–9**
All Saints' Day 43
Alleyras
    restaurants 591
Alpais 56
Alpes-Maritimes **533**
Alphand, Adolphe 139, 142
Alps **326–7**
    see also Rhône Valley and
        French Alps
Alsace and Lorraine **223–37**
    Alsace wine **237**
    climate 45
    food and drink **191**
    hotels 558
    map 224
    restaurants 582–3
    Route des Vins **236**
    travel 225
Les Alyscamps (Arles) 513
Les Alyscamps (Gauguin) 513
Amadour, St. 440, 441
Amboise 291
    Château d' 13, 14, **305**
    hotels 561
    restaurants 586
Amboise family 246
Amélie-les-Bains 486
Amiens 13, **204**
    Cathedral 36, 188, 197, **206–7**
    hotels 556
    restaurants 579
Amiens, Treaty of (1802) 66
Amneville
    hotels 558
Ancenis
    restaurants 586
Ancy-le-Franc, Château d' **338**
Androuet du Cerceau, Jean 184
Anduze
    restaurants 599
Angelico, Fra 106
Angers 291, **295**
    Château 246, 295
    hotels 561
    restaurants 586
Angevin Empire 56, 57
Angles-sur-l'Anglin **418**
Anglet
    hotels 568
Ango, Jehan 267
Angoulême 36, **423**
    festivals 43, 423
    restaurants 594
Anjony, Château d' 368
Anne of Austria 63, 95, 131
Anne de Beaujeu 361
Anne of Brittany (Anne de Bretagne)
    Basilique St.-Denis 177
    Josselin 285
    Loches 304
    marriage 299
    Nantes 294

Annecy 378, **394–5**
    hotels 564
    restaurants 593
Anouilh, Jean 35
Ansouis 511
Antibes **525**
    festivals 41
    hotels 570
    restaurants 601
Antiques shops **152**
Anzy-le-Duc 352
Apollinaire, Guillaume 136
Apples and cider **259**
Apt 511
Aquariums
    Biarritz 456
    Cinéaqua (Paris) 114
    Cité de la Mer (Cherbourg) 254
    La Rochelle 420
    Mare Nostrum (Montpellier) 499
    Musée Océanographique (Monaco) 535
    Nausicaa (Boulogne) 200
    Océanopolis (Brest) 276
    St.-Malo 286
Aquitaine see Poitou and Aquitaine
Arbois **353**
    restaurants 589
Arbrissel, Robert d' 298
Arc-et-Senans **354**
    hotels 562
Arc de Triomphe (Orange) **506**
Arc de Triomphe (Paris)
    12, 66, **111**
Arc de Triomphe du Carrousel (Paris)
    **103**, 104
Arcachon 428
    hotels 565
    restaurants 594
Architecture 26
    A one-week tour of great
        architectural sites 10, 13
    Romanesque and Gothic architecture
        **36–7**
    rural architecture **38–9**
Arcins
    restaurants 594
The Ardèche 15, 377, **388–9**
    festivals 42
Ardèche, River 377
Ardennes 211
Areas of natural beauty **28–9**
Les Arènes (Nîmes) **501**
Argeles-Gazost
    restaurants 598
Argelès-Plage 486
Argelliers
    restaurants 599
Argentat 328
Argentière
    restaurants 593
Argoat 273
Argonne **219**
Ariège river 452
Arlay, Château d' 353
Arles 15, 503, **512–13**
    festivals 40
    hotels 570
    map 512–13
    restaurants 601
Arles-sur-Tech 486
Armagnac **444**
Arman 477, 531
Arnay le Duc
    restaurants 589

Arp, Jean 528
Arradon
    restaurants 585
Arras 197, 198, **203**
    restaurants 579
Arreau **466**
    hotels 568
Art 26
    artists in France **32–3**
    artists in the South of France
        **476–7**
    shopping **152**
    specialty vacations **616**, 617
    see also Museums and galleries
Art Deco 70
Art Nouveau 68, 69
    No. 29 Avenue Rapp (Paris) **116**
    Rue la Fontaine (Paris) **134–5**
Arthur, King 285
Artois, Comte de 134
Ascain
    restaurants 598
Ascension Day 43
Asco 544
Asparagus harvest 40
Assemblée Nationale Palais-Bourbon
    (Paris) 81
Assumption Day 43
ATMs 626
Au Lapin Agile (Paris) 136
Auberive
    hotels 557
Aubert, Jean 209
Aubert, St., Bishop of Avranches 256,
    260
Aubeterre-sur-Dronne **423**
Aubrac mountains 357
Aubry, Martine 24
Aubusson **360–61**
Auch 445
    restaurants 596
Auction houses 152
Audierne
    restaurants 585
Augustus, Emperor 52–3
Aulnay de Saintonge **420**
Aumale
    restaurants 583
Aumale, Duke of 209
Aurillac 368
Ausone 427
Austerlitz, Battle of (1805)
    103, 111
Autoire **442**
Autoroute tolls **637**
Autumn in France **42**
Autun **343**
    restaurants 589
Auvergne 29, 357
    Black Madonnas **369**
    pilgrimages and ostensions **363**
Auvergne, Counts of 364
Auvillar **445**
Auxerre 13, 16, **334–5**
    hotels 562
    restaurants 589
Avallon **339**
    restaurants 589
Avant-Garde France **70–71**
Aven Armand 371, 375
Avenue des Champs-Elysées (Paris)
    110, **112**
Avenue Rapp (Paris), No. 29 **116**
Aveyron 357
Aveyron, River 357

Avignon 15, 471, **507–9**
    hotels 570
    Popes **508**
    restaurants 601
Avignon Theatre Festival 41
Avoriaz 326
Avranches **256**
Avril, Jane 138
Ax-les-Thermes
    restaurants 598
Ay
    hotels 557
Azay-le-Rideau 60–61
    Château d' 246, **300**
    hotels 561
Azéma, Léon 114

**B**

Babel Med Music (Marseilles) 40
Badiou, Alain 35
Baerenthal
    restaurants 582
Baerze, Jacques de 344
Bagnères-de-Luchon
    restaurants 598
Bagnoles-de-l'Orne 259
    hotels 559
Bags, shopping **147**, 148
Baker, Josephine 71
Balagne 541
Balazuc 389
Balenciaga, Cristóbal 114
Ballet
    Ballets Russes 71
    Les Ballets Suédois 71
    Paris **155**, 157
Balmain, Pierre 114
Balzac, Honoré de 34, 289, 300
    grave 139
Bandol 532
Banking **626**
Bank bills 627
Banlieues Bleues Jazz Festival
    (St.-Denis) 40
Banyuls 486
Baptistère St.-Jean (Poitiers) **417**
Barbarians 52, 53
Barbie, Klaus 72
Barbizon School
    33, 111, 113, **185**
Bardot, Brigitte 17, **520**, 524
Barèges
    restaurants 598
Barillet-Deschamps, Jean-Pierre 139
Barneville-Carteret
    restaurants 583
Barrage de la Rance 285
Bart, Jean 201
Barthes, Roland 35
Bartholdi, Frédéric-Auguste 355, 384
    Musée Bartholdi (Colmar) 231
Basilique Notre-Dame de Fourvière
    (Lyon) 383
Basilique de Notre-Dame-de-la-Garde
    (Marseille) **516**
Basilique St.-Denis **176–7**
Basilique Ste.-Madeleine (Vézelay) 320,
    **340–41**
Basilique St.-Michel (Bordeaux) **426**
Basilique St.-Remi (Reims) **214**
Basilique St.-Sernin (Toulouse) **451**
Basque culture 453, **459**
Bassano, Jacopo 501
Basse-Seine **267**
Bassin d'Arcachon 410, **428**

Bastia **540**
    hotels 571
    restaurants 603
Bastide towns **449**
Bastille (Paris) 65, 95
Bastille Day 43
Batobus cruises (Paris) 82
Batz, Charles de 445
Baudelaire, Charles 35, 67
    grave 143
Bayeux 14, **256–7**
    hotels 559
    restaurants 583
Bayeux Tapestry 14, 55, 241, 251,
    **256–7**
Bayonne 453, **456**
    restaurants 598
Bazille, Frédéric 499
Bazoches, Château de 339
Beach, Sylvia 35, 126
Beaches
    safety 625
    South of France **478–9**
Beaubourg (Paris) see Ile de la Cité,
    Marais and Beaubourg
Beaugency 291, **309**
    restaurants 586
Beaujeu 381
Beaujolais 16, 377
    A tour of Beaujolais **381**
Beaulieu-en-Argonne 219
Beaulieu-sur-Dordogne
    hotels 563
Beaulieu-sur-Mer 532
Beaumarchais, Pierre Augustin Caron
    de 35
Beaumont Hamel Memorial Park 194
Beaune 14, 16, **348**
    festivals 42
    Hôtel-Dieu **350–51**
    hotels 562
    restaurants 589
Beauregard, Château de 310
Beauty products, shopping **605**, 607
Beauvais **204–5**
    Cathedral 36, 37, 188, 197, 204
    restaurants 579
Beauvoir, Château 362
Beauvoir, Simone de 35, 122
    grave 143
Bechet, Sidney 70
Becket, Thomas 184, 334
Beckett, Samuel 35
Belcastel
    hotels 563
    restaurants 591
Belfort **355**
    restaurants 589
The Belfry of Douai (Corot) 33
Belle-Eglise
    restaurants 579
Belle Epoque **68–9**
Belle-Ile-en-Mer **284**
    restaurants 585
Bellegambe, Jean
    The Virgin Protecting the Cistercian
    Order 337
Bellini, Giovanni 546
Bemberg, Georges 451
Benedict, St 54, 317
Benedict XII, Pope 508, 509
Benedict XIII, Pope 508
Bénigne, St. 346
Benodet
    hotels 560

Benouville, François-Léon 305
Bercy **139**
Bergerac **438**
  hotels 566
  restaurants 596
Berges de Seine (Paris) 79
Berlioz, Hector 94, **119**
  grave 138
Bernanos, Georges 34
Bernard, St. 57, **337**
  Abbaye de Fontenay 336
  Abbaye de Royaumont 176
  Clairvaux 56
  Sarlat 437
Bernard, Emile 279
  *La Ronde Bretonne* 32
Bernard, George Grey 485
Bernhardt, Sarah 69
Bernini, Gian Lorenzo 546
Béroud, Louis 69
Berry, Jean, Duke de
  317, 365, 416
Berthelot, Gilles 246
Berzé-la-Ville 349
Besançon 14, 331, **354**
  hotels 562
Betschdorf **237**
Beuvron-en-Auge 251, 259
  restaurants 583
Béziers **494**, 495
  hotels 569
  restaurants 599
Biarritz 15, 453, **456**
  hotels 568
  restaurants 598
Bibliothèque d'Agglomération
  (St.-Omer) 201
Bibliothèque Humaniste (Sélestat)
  233
Bibliothèque and Musée de l'Opéra
  (Paris) 101
Bibliothèque Nationale de France
  (Paris) **142**
Bicycles *see* Cycling
Biennale de Lyon 42
Biot **526**
  restaurants 601
Birds
  The Camargue 514
  Cévennes 375
  Cotentin Peninsula 254
  Parc des Oiseaux (Villars-les-Dombes)
    380
  Parc Ornithologique du Teich
    428
  Réserve Naturelle de Scandola
    545
  Vallée de la Somme 203
  white storks **227**
Bistro annexes **573**
Bitche
  restaurants 582
Bize Minervois
  restaurants 599
Black Death 47, 58
Black Madonnas, Auvergne **369**
Blainville-sur-Mer
  restaurants 583
Blanchard, Jean-Pierre 201
Blanche de Castille 176
Blanche de France 177
Blandine, St. 53
Blasset, Nicolas 206
Blériot, Louis 69, 201
Blois 13, 291, **308–9**
  restaurants 586
Blois, Count of 306
*Blue Nude IV* (Matisse) 531

*Blue Waterlilies* (Monet) 125
Boats **635**
  Batobus cruises (Paris) 82
  canal and river trips **635**
  ferries **630–31, 635**
  Musée National de la Marine (Paris)
    115
  sailing **635**
  seafarers of St.-Malo **286**
  Seine cruises 83, **641**
  water sports **614–15**, 617
Bofill, Ricardo 498
Bohier, Thomas 302
Boigne, Comte de 394
Boileau, Louis-Auguste 114
Bois de Boulogne (Paris) **134**
Bois Préau, Château 177
Boltanski, Christian 501
Bonifacio 536, **547**
  hotels 571
  restaurants 603
Bonlieu
  restaurants 589
Bonnard, Pierre 476, 520, 528
Bonnieux 511
  restaurants 601
Bookstores **149**
Bordeaux 16, 65, 398, 409, **424–6**
  France's wine regions: Bordeaux
    **402–3**
  hotels 565
  restaurants 595
  Street by Street map 424–5
  A wine and food tour of Burgundy,
    Périgord and Bordeaux 11, 16
  wine châteaux **427**
  wine trade **425**
Bordeilles
  hotels 566
*Bories* 510
Bormes-les-Mimosas
  festivals 43
  hotels 570
Bosch, Hieronymus 106
Botticelli, Sandro 507, 546
Boucher, François 491
Boudes
  restaurants 591
Boudin, Eugène 266, 269
  Musée Eugène Boudin (Honfleur)
    266
  *Woman with Parasol* 266
Bouillon, Godefroy de 362
Boulevard des Capucines (Paris)
  100
Boulevard St.-Germain (Paris)
  122, **123**
Boulevard St.-Michel (Paris) 128
Boulle, André-Charles 107
Boulogne-sur-Mer 197, **200**
  restaurants 579
Les Bouquinistes (Paris) 79
Bourbon, Prince Louis-Henri de 208
Bourbon dynasty 48, 49, 66
Bourdeilles 433, **434**
Bourdeille, Pierre de 434
Bourdelle, Antoine 80, 385
  bust of Gustave Eiffel 117
Bourdelle, Emile 447
Bourg-en-Bresse **380**
Bourges 13, **317**
  hotels 561
  restaurants 586
Bourges Spring Festival 40
Bourgueil
  restaurants 586
Bouts, Dirk 202
Bouvines, Battle of (1214) 57

Bracieux
  restaurants 587
Brancion 349
Brancusi, Constantin **97**
Brandy
  Armagnac **444**
  Cognac 422–3
Branicki, Count 305
Brantôme **434**
  hotels 567
  restaurants 596
Braque, Georges
  114, 477, 486, 528
  *Le Duo* 97
Brasserie Lipp (Paris) 122
Brasseries **572**
La Bravade (St.-Tropez) 41
Bray sur Seine
  restaurants 579
Brayer, Yves 448, 511
Bread stores **150**, 151
Brèche de Roland 465
Bresse 377
Brest **276**
  hotels 560
  restaurants 585
Breton, André 70, 387
Breton traditions **247**
Brézé, Château de 296
Briançon **391**
  hotels 564
Briçonnet, Catherine 302, 303
Bricqueville-sur-Mer
  restaurants 583
The Bridges of the Rhône
  **387**
Brionnais 331, **352**
British Tank Memorial 194
Brittany **273–89**
  Breton traditions **247**
  climate 44
  coastal wildlife **248–9**
  The flavors of Western France
    **242–3**
  hotels 560–61
  map 274–5
  Parish closes **280–81**
  Prehistoric monuments **283**
  restaurants 585–6
  travel 275
Brive-la-Gaillarde
  restaurants 591
Broederlam, Melchior 344
Bronze Age 51
Brosse, Salomon de 131
Brou 380
Brouage **421**
Brougham, Lord 524
Bruand, Libéral 118, 119
Brueghel, Pieter 491
Brunet, P
  *Virgin Mary and Child* 137
Bruno, St 393
Budget travel 622
Bué
  festivals 42
Buell, Jean de 246
Buffon, Comte de 142
Buland, Jean-Eugène 278
Bullfighting 41, 42, 429
Bunker of Rochelle (La Rochelle)
  420
Buñuel, Luis 70
Bureaux de change 626
*The Burghers of Calais* (Rodin)
  200–201
Burgundy, Dukes of
  324, 344

Burgundy and Franche-Comté 29,
   **331–55**
   climate 45
   food and drink **322**
   France's wine regions: Burgundy
      **324–5**
   Franche-Comté **353–5**
   The Golden Age of Burgundy **347**
   hotels 562–3
   map 332–3
   restaurants 589–91
   travel 333
   A wine and food tour of Burgundy,
      Périgord and Bordeaux 11, 16
Buses **640**
Busnes
   hotels 556
Bussy-Rabutin, Château de 338–9
Butte de Vauquois 219

## C

Cabaret
   Paris **155**, 157
Cabourg 259
Caen 14, 251, **257–8**
   hotels 559
   map 258
   restaurants 583
Caesar, Julius 47, 52
   Alise-Ste.-Reine 338
   Fréjus 521
   Lyon 382
   Vannes 284
Café de Flore (Paris) 122
Café le Procope (Paris) 64
Cafés **573**
   The celebrated cafés of Paris **156**
Cagnes-sur-Mer **526–7**
   restaurants 601
Cahors **442–3**
   restaurants 596
Caillette 297
Cajarc 443
Cake stores **150**, 151
Calacuccia 544
Calais 197, **200–201**
   hotels 556
   restaurants 579–80
Calanche 539, 545
Calanques 17, 29, 517
Calder, Alexander 528
   Mobile on Two Planes 96
Calvi 538, **541**
   hotels 571
   restaurants 603
Calvin, Jean 60, 205
The Camargue 15, 29, 470, 503,
   **514–15**
   map 514–15
Cambrai
   restaurants 580
Camon
   hotels 568
Camping **552**, 553
Camus, Albert 35, 448
Canal du Midi 450, **490**, 494
Canal St.-Martin (Paris) **139**
Canal trips **635**
Canaletto 491
Canari 540
Cancale 14, **287**
Cannes 17, 479, **524–5**
   hotels 570
   restaurants 601
Cannes Film Festival 41, 71, **524**
Cantal 16
   hotels 563
Cantal cheese **367**

Cantini, Jules 516
Cap d'Agde 17, 478, 481, 491
   restaurants 599
Cap d'Antibes 17, **525**
Cap Blanc-Nez 200
Cap Canaille (Signac) 517
Cap Corse **540**
Cap Ferrat 17, 479
Cap Ferret 428
   hotels 565
Cap Fréhel 285
Cap Gris-Nez 200
Cap Martin 503
Capassin, Jean 388
Capbreton 428
CAPC Musée d'Art Contemporain
   (Bordeaux) 425, **426**
Capdeville, Jean 486
Capet, Hugh 48
Capetian dynasty 47, 48, 347
Carantec
   restaurants 585
Caravaggio 269
Carcassonne 15, 480, 481, **492–3**
   hotels 569
   restaurants 599
Cargèse **546**
   restaurants 603
Caribert, King 48
Carloman II, King 48
Carlone, Carlo Innocenzo 526, 531
Carlu, Jacques 114
Carmontele, Louis 135
Carnac **282**, 283
   hotels 560
   megaliths 50, 240
   restaurants 585
Carné, Marcel 139
Carolingian dynasty 48, 54, 55
Carpaccio, Vittore 507
Carpeaux, Jean-Baptiste
   The Dance 124, 125
   Fontaine de l'Observatoire (Paris)
      120, **131**
   Four Quarters of the World 76
Carpentras **510**
   restaurants 601
Carré d'Art Jean Bousquet/Musée d'Art
   Contemporain (Nîmes) **501**
Cars
   Cité de l'Automobile (Mulhouse)
      229
   driving in France **636–8**
   driving to France **631**
   Le Mans 295
   racing 41, 43
   see also Tours by car
Cartier, Jacques 61, 286
Carvalho, Dr. Joachim 300
Casals, Pablo 41, 484
Cascades du Hérisson **353**
Casino de Monte Carlo (Monaco)
   **534**
Cassel 202
   restaurants 580
Cassis 17, 479, **517**
Les Castagnades (Ardèche) 42
The Castagniccia **544**
Castellane 519
   hotels 570
   restaurants 601
Castelnaud, Château de 396–7
Castles see Châteaux
Castres **448**
   restaurants 596
Catacombes (Paris) **143**
Cateau-Cambrésis, Treaty of (1559)
   61

Cathars 481, **495**
   Béziers 494
   Carcassonne 493
   Corbières 490
   Minerve 494
   Montségur 467
Cathedrals
   Aix-en-Provence 515
   Ajaccio 546
   Albi 448
   Amiens 13, 36, 188, 197, 204, **206–7**
   Angers 295
   Angoulême 36, 423
   Auch 445
   Autun 343
   Auxerre 13, 334–5
   Avignon 507
   Bayeux 257
   Bayonne 456
   Beauvais 36, 37, 188, 197, 204
   Béziers 494
   Blois 309
   Bordeaux **426**
   Bourges 13, 317
   Cahors 442–3
   Carcassonne 492
   Carpentras 510
   Châlons-en-Champagne 220
   Chartres 13, 14, 311, **312–15**
   Clermont-Ferrand 364–5
   Condom 444
   Coutances 254
   Dax 429
   Dijon **346**
   Elne 487
   Evreux 270
   Fréjus 521
   Grasse 521
   Langres 221
   Laon 13, 37, 197, 209
   Le Mans 295
   Le Puy-en-Velay 36, 369
   Lyon 382
   Mariana 547
   Marseille **516**
   Metz 227
   Mirepoix 467
   Monaco 534
   Montauban 447
   Montpellier 498
   Moulins 361
   Nantes 294
   Narbonne 15, 490
   Nevers 37, 342
   Nice **530**
   Nîmes 500
   Notre-Dame (Paris) 12, 77, 83, 87,
      **90–91**
   Noyon 13, 197, 205
   Oloron-Ste.-Marie 459
   Orléans 316
   Périgueux 435
   Perpignan **488–9**
   Poitiers **416–17**
   Quimper **278**
   Reims 13, 14, 36, 210, 211, 214,
      **216–17**
   Rennes 288
   Rodez 370
   Rouen 14, **268**
   St.-Bertrand-de-Comminges 466
   St.-Florent 541
   St.-Lizier 466
   St.-Malo 286
   St.-Omer 201
   Santiago de Compostela 404
   Sarlat 437
   Senlis 197, 208

Cathedrals (cont.)
Sens 334
Strasbourg **234**
Toul 226
Tours 14, 301
Tréguier 282
Troyes 14, 220
Vaison-la-Romaine 506
Valence 388
Vannes 284
Vence 527
Verdun 226
Vienne 386
Vitré 289
*see also* Churches
Catherine de' Medici 60, 297
Bourdeilles 434
Château d'Amboise 305
Château de Blois 308
Château de Chenonceau 302, 303
Grasse 521
Catherine Opalinska, Queen 307
Catholic Church 24
Caudebec-en-Caux 267
Caumont Centre d'Art (Aix-en-Provence) 515
Causse Méjean 375
Cauterets 463
Cave paintings 406, **407**
Grotte de Niaux 467
Lascaux IV **438**
Les Eyzies **438–9**
Caves
Grands Causses 371, 375
Grottes des Canalettes 484
Grotte Chauvet 389
Grotte de Clamouse 497
Grotte des Demoiselles 497
Grotte de la Madeleine 389
Grotte Massabielle (Lourdes) 463
Grotte de Pech-Merle 442, 443
Grotte de Villars 434
Southwest France **406–7**
troglodyte dwellings **296**
Célé Valley
A tour of two rivers **442–3**
Celles-sur-Belle 413
Cellini, Benvenuto 60, 107
Cell phones **628**, 629
Celts 51
Cemeteries
Aître St.-Maclou (Rouen) 269
Cimetière de Montmartre (Paris) **138**
Cimetière du Montparnasse (Paris) **143**
Cimetière du Père-Lachaise (Paris) **139**
Douaumont Memorial 189, 226
Central France and the Alps **319–95**
Burgundy and Franche-Comté **331–55**
The flavors of Central France **322–3**
France's wine regions: Burgundy **324–5**
The French Alps **326–7**
geology of the Massif Central **328–9**
map 320–21
The Massif Central **357–75**
Rhône Valley and French Alps **377–95**
Centre de Création Contemporain Olivier Debré (Tours) 301
Centre Guillaume-le-Conquérant-Tapisserie de Bayeux 257
Centre International du Vitrail (Chartres) 311

Centre Pompidou (Paris) 12, 72, 77, 84, **96–7**
Centre Pompidou Metz **227**
Centuri 540
Ceramics
Betschdorf 237
Musée de la Céramique (Rouen) **269**
Quimper 278
Sèvres: Cité de la Céramique **182**
Soufflenheim 237
Cerbère 486
Cerdagne 481, **484**
Céret **486**
hotels 569
restaurants 599
Cernay la Ville
hotels 555
César 477, 531
Cévennes 329, 357
Gorges du Tarn **374–5**
wildlife **375**
Cézanne, Paul 476, 507
Atelier de Cézanne (Aix-en-Provence) 515
Honfleur 266
Musée de l'Orangerie (Paris) 102
Chabannes, Jacques II de 362
Chablis 16, 331, **335**
hotels 562
restaurants 589
Chagall, Marc 476, 486, 529
Fondation Maeght (St-Paul de Vence) 528
Metz Cathedral windows 227
Musée National Marc Chagall (Nice) **530**
Opéra National de Paris Garnier 101
Reims Cathedral 217
Chagny
hotels 562
restaurants 589
Chaintre
restaurants 589
Chalgrin, Jean 111
Chalon-sur-Saône 349
restaurants 589
Châlons-en-Champagne 211, **220**
hotels 557
restaurants 580
Chalus, Pierre de 127
Chamalières
hotels 563
Chambéry 377, **394**
hotels 564
restaurants 593
Chambord, Château de 13, 14, 241, 291, **306–7**
Chamonix 326, 377
hotels 564
restaurants 593
Champagnac-de-Belair
restaurants 596
Champagne **211–21**
climate 45
food and drink **190–91**
hotels 557–8
map 212–13
*méthode champenoise* **214–15**
restaurants 580–82
timber churches **219**
travel 212
Champigné
hotels 561
Champlitte **354**
Champollion, Jean-François 443

Champs-Elysées and Invalides (Paris) 12, **109–19**
area map 109
hotels 554–5
restaurants 576–7
Street by Street map: Champs-Elysées 110–11
Chancelade
hotels 567
Chanel, Coco 71, 533
Channel crossings **201**
Channel Tunnel 72, 73
*Chanson de Roland* 56
Chantemerle-les-Grignan
hotels 564
Chantilly 13, 197, **208–9**
horse racing **208**
Chaos de Montpellier-le-Vieux 371, 374
Chapaize 349
Charlemagne, Emperor 48, 54, 55, 247
Conques reliquary 373
St.-Guilhem-le-Désert 497
St.-Jean-Pied-de-Port 458
Charlene, Princess of Monaco 535
Charles I the Bald, King 48
Charles II the Fat, King 48
Charles III, Prince of Monaco 534
Charles III the Simple, King 48
Charles IV the Fair, King 49
Charles V, Emperor 107
Charles V the Wise, King 49
Basilique St.-Denis 176
Louvre (Paris) 92, 105
Palais de Justice (Paris) 88
sceptre 107
Charles VI the Beloved, King 49, 59
Charles VII the Victorious, King 49, 59, 298
coronation 216
and Joan of Arc 304
Loches 304
Charles VIII, King 49
Amboise 305
Château du Moulin 311
marriage 299
Charles IX, King 49, 60, 316
Charles X, King 49, 67, 216, 458
Charles the Bold, Duke of Burgundy 347
Charles Martel 54, 416
Charleville-Mézières **218**
hotels 557
restaurants 580
*Charlie Hebdo* 73
Charolles
restaurants 589
Charroux **419**
Chartres 13, 14, 291, **311**
Cathedral 311, **312–15**
hotels 561
restaurants 587
Chartres, Duc de 135
The Chartreuse 377, **393**
Chartreuse de Champmol (Dijon) **346**
Châteaux
Adhémar 390
Amboise 13, 14, **305**
Ancy-le-Franc **338**
Angers 246, 295
Anjony 368
Annecy 395
Antibes 525
Arlay 353
Ausone 427
Azay-le-Rideau 60–61, 246, **300**
Bazoches 339

Châteaux (cont.)
Beaugency 309
Beauregard 310
Beauvoir 362
Blois 13, 308, 309
Bois Préau 177
Boulogne-sur-Mer 200
Bourdeilles 434
Brest 276
Brézé 296
Busqueille 442
Bussy-Rabutin 338–9
Cagnes-sur-Mer 526, 527
Carcassonne 492
Castelnaud 396–7
Chambéry 394
Chambord 13, 14, 241, 291, **306–7**
Chantilly 13, 197, 208–9
Château Ducal (Caen) **258**
Le Château-Musée (Dieppe) 267
Chaumont 246, 310
Chenonceau 13, 14, 61, 291, **302–3**
Cheval Blanc 427
Cheverny 311
Chinon 292, 298
Clisson 294
Collioure 487
Combourg 287
Compiègne 13, 197, 205
Cordès 366
Crussol 388
Dinan 287
Drée 352
Duingt 395
d'Eau (Montpellier) 499
Ecouen 176
Epoisses 339
Figeac 427
Foix 467
Fontainebleau 13, 174, **184–5**
Fougères 289
Gataudière 421
Gordes 510
Gourdon 527
Grignan 390
Gruaud-Larose 427
Guédelon 334
Haut-Barr 237
Haut-Koenigsbourg
189, 223, **232–3**
Hautefort 434
d'If 516
Josselin 285
La Palice **362**
Laàs 458
Lafite Rothschild 427
Langeais **299**
Latour 427
Les Baux-de-Provence 511
Limarque 442
Malmaison **177**
Marçay 299
Margaux 427
Marqueyssac 439
Marseille 516
Montcontour 304
Montpoupon 301
Montrésor 13, 305
Montreuil-Bellay 296
du Moulin 311
Moulins 361
Mouton Rothschild 427
Murol 364
Nantes 294
Nays 458
d'O 259
Oiron 412
Palmer 427

Châteaux (cont.)
Pau 462
Peyrepertuse 490, 495
Pierreclos 492
Pierrefonds 13, 196, **205**
Plessis-Bourré 295
Puyguilhem 434
Quéribus 490
Raissac 494
Rambouillet **182**
Ratilly 334
Ripaille 395
Rochers-Sévigné 289
Royaumont 176
St.-Fargeau 334
St.-Malo **286**
St.-Sauveur 334
Saumur 23, 296
Sceaux **182**
Sedan 218–19
Serrant 295
Sologne tour **310–11**
Suze-la-Rousse 391
Tanlay **335**
Tarascon 511
Thoiry 182
Thoury 362
Touffou 418
Tournon-sur-Rhône 388
Tours d'Elven (Vannes) 284
Turenne 427
Ussé 246, 291, **299**
Vaux-le-Vicomte 13, **182–3**
Vendôme 310
Versailles 13, **178–81**
Vieux Château Certan 427
Villandry 13, 290, 291, **300**
Villesavin 311
Vincennes **142**
Vitré 289
Vogüé 389
Château-Arnoux
hotels 570
Chateaubriand, François-René de
287
grave 286
Châteaugiron 289
Châteauneuf-du-Pape 15, **506–7**
festivals 42
restaurants 601
Châtillon-sur-Seine **338**
Chaumont **221**
Chaumont sur Loire, Château de 246,
310
festivals 41
Chauvigny **418**
Cheese
Cantal cheese **367**
shopping **150**, 151
Chemetov, Paul 139
Chemin du Rosaire (Lyon) 383
Chenonceau
Château de 13, 14, 61, 291, **302–3**
hotels 561
Cherbourg 251, **254**
hotels 559
restaurants 583
Cheval, Ferdinand 387
Cheval Blanc 427
Cheverny, Château de 311
Childebert I, King 48
Childebert II, King 48
Childéric I, King 48
Childéric II, King 48
Childéric III, King 48
Children **621**
clothes stores **146**, 148
in restaurants 574

Chilpéric I, King 48
Chilpéric II, King 48
Chinon 13, 244, **298–9**
Château de 13, 292, 298
hotels 561
restaurants 587
Chirac, Jacques 25, 72, 73
Chiroubles 381
Chiuni 546
Chocolate stores **150**, 151
Chopin, Frédéric 102
grave 139
Le Christ Jaune (Gauguin) 279
Christmas 43
The Church at Auvers (Van Gogh)
32
The Church of St. Bernard, Ain, in
Summer (Utrillo) 33
Churches
Basilique St.-Denis **176–7**
Basilique Ste.-Madeleine (Vézelay)
320, **340–41**
Basilique St.-Remi (Reims) **214**
Cathedral of St.-Louis-des-Invalides
(Paris) **119**
Champagne timber churches **219**
Eglise du Dôme (Paris) 81, 118, **119**
La Madeleine (Paris) 100, **101**
Sacré-Coeur (Paris) 137, **138**
St.-Alexandre-Nevsky (Paris) **135**
Sainte-Chapelle (Paris) 12, 86, **88–9**
Sainte-Clotilde (Paris) **119**
St.-Etienne-du-Mont (Paris) **127**
St.-Eustache (Paris) **94**
St.-Germain-des-Prés (Paris) 12, 122,
**126**
St.-Gervais-St-Protais (Paris) **89**
St.-Julien-le-Pauvre (Paris) **127**, 129
St.-Michel (Dijon) 345
St.-Pierre de Montmartre (Paris) 137
St.-Roch (Paris) **103**
St.-Séverin (Paris) **126**, 128
St.-Sulpice (Paris) 130, **131**
Val-de-Grâce (Paris) **131**
see also Cathedrals and individual
towns and cities
Churchill, Winston 532
Ciboure 457
Cider **259**
Musée Régional du Cidre et du
Calvados (Valognes) 254
Cimabue 106
Cimetière de Montmartre (Paris)
**138**
Cimetière du Montparnasse (Paris)
**143**
Cimetière du Père-Lachaise (Paris)
**139**
Cinema 26, 72, **608–9**, 611
Cannes Film Festival **524**
Cinémathèque Française (Paris)
139
festivals 41, 42
Paris **156**, 157
Cirque de Gavarnie 28, 463
Cirque de Navacelles 497
Cistercian order 55, 57
Abbaye de Fontenay **336–7**
Abbaye de Noirlac 317
Abbaye de Royaumont **176**
Citadelle Souterraine (Verdun) 226
Citadelle Vauban (Belle-Ile-en-Mer)
284
Citadelle de Verdun 226
Cité de l'Architecture et du Patrimoine
(Paris) 115
Cité de l'Automobile (Mulhouse)
229

Cité de la Dentelle et de la Mode (Calais) 201
Cité de l'Espace (Toulouse) **451**
Cité Internationale de la Bande Dessinée (Angoulême) 43, 423
Cité Internationale de la Tapisserie (Aubusson) 360
Cité de la Mer (Cherbourg) 254
Cité Nationale de l'Histoire de l'Immigration (Paris) **142**
La Cité de la Préhistoire 389
Cité des Sciences et de l'Industrie (Paris) **140–41**
Cité du Vin (Bordeaux) **426**
Cité du Vitrail (Troyes) **220**
Citroën 70
Clara
    restaurants 599
Claude Lorrain 228
Claudel, Camille 417
Claudius, Emperor 53
Clement V, Pope 508
Clement VI, Pope 508, 509
Clermont-Ferrand **364–5**
    map 365
    restaurants 591–2
Clermont-Tonnerre, Duke of 338
*The Cliffs at Etretat after a Storm* (Courbet) 32
Climate **44–5**
Climbing **614**, 617
Cliousclat
    hotels 564
Cliquot, François-Henri 417
Clisson 294
    restaurants 587
Clisson, Olivier de
    tomb 285
Clos-Lucé (Amboise) 305
Clos Montmartre (Paris) 136
Clothaire I, King 48
Clothaire II, King 48
Clothaire III, King 48
Clothes
    Breton costumes 247
    fashion shows (Paris) 43
    Musée Galliera (Paris) **114**
    in restaurants 574
    shopping **146–8**
    size chart 606
Clothilde, Queen 335
Clouet brothers 209
Clovis, King of the Franks 48, 54, 55
    baptism 214, 216, 217
Clovis II, King 48
Clovis III, King 48
Clubs **610**, 611
    Paris **155**, 157
Cluny 331, **349**, 404
    Abbey 16, 54–5, 349
Coach travel **638**, 639
Cocteau, Jean 71, 103
    Colombe d'Or (St.-Paul de Vence) 529
    Menton 533
    Montparnasse (Paris) 143
    Villefranche-sur-Mer 532
Coello, Claudio 529
Coeur, Jacques 13, 317
Cognac 16, 409, **422–3**
    hotels 565
    restaurants 595
Coins 627
Col du Somport 464
Colbert, Jean Baptiste 62, 63
    Château de Sceaux 182
    Rochefort 420–21
    St.-Eustache (Paris) 94

Colette 34, 103, 477
    Colombe d'Or (St.-Paul de Vence) 529
    Musée Colette (La Puisaye-Forterre) 334
    St.-Tropez 520
Collection Lambert (Avignon) 507
Collioure 17, **487**
    hotels 569
    restaurants 599
Collonges Mont d'Or
    restaurants 593
Collonges-la-Rouge **367**
Colmar 186–7, 222, **231**
    hotels 558
    restaurants 582
Colombanus, St. 54
Colombey-les-Deux-Eglises 221
    hotels 557
    restaurants 581
Columbus, Christopher 541
Combourg **287**
Comédie Française (Paris) 62, 63, 103
Comminges Music Festival 41
Communications **628–9**
Communist Party 70
Compiègne **205**
    Château 13, 197, 205
    restaurants 580
Compostela
    The road to Compostela **404–5**
*Composteur* machines, trains 634
Concarneau **278**
    restaurants 585
Conciergerie (Paris) 83, 86, **87**
Condé, Great Prince of 208
Condom **444**
    restaurants 596
Confolens **419**
Conques 357, **372–3**, 405
    hotels 563
Constable, John 456
Constantine, Emperor 53, 413
Contres
    restaurants 587
Conversion chart 623
Corbières 481, **490**
Corday, Charlotte 87, 102
Cordès, Château de 366
Cordes-sur-Ciel 432, **448**, 449
    hotels 567
    restaurants 596–7
Corentin, St 278
Cormatin 349
Corneille, Pierre 35
    tomb 103
Cornelius, St 282
Corniche des Cévennes **371**
Corot, Jean-Baptiste-Camille 456
    *The Belfry of Douai* 33
    Montmartre (Paris) 136
    Musée des Beaux-Arts (Reims) 214
    Musée Municipal des Beaux-Arts (Agen) 444
Corot, J. P. 111
Corsica 17, 29, **537–47**
    climate 45
    flowers **545**
    food and drink **473**
    hotels 571
    map 21, 471, 538–9
    restaurants 603
    travel 539
    winds 538
Corte 539, **544**
    hotels 571
    restaurants 603

Cos d'Estournel 403
Côte d'Albâtre 251, 252, **266–7**
La Côte d'Argent **428**
Côte d'Azur *see* Provence and the Côte d'Azur
Côte de Beaune 331
Côte d'Emeraude 273, **285**
Côte Fleurie 14, 251, **259**
Côte de Granit Rose 28, 275, **282**
Côte de Nacre 251, **256**
Côte d'Opale 197
Côte d'Or 14, 16, 325, 331, **348**
Côte Orientale **547**
Côte Sauvage 421
Côte Vermeille **486**, 491
Coteaux du Languedoc 474
Cotentin Peninsula 251, **254**
Côtes du Rhône **388**
Cotte, Robert de 234
Cougnac 407
Coulon 411, 413
    hotels 566
    restaurants 595
Couperin, François 89
La Coupole (St.-Omer) 201
Courant d'Huchet 428
Courbet, Gustave
    *The Cliffs at Etretat after a Storm* 32
    Honfleur 266
    *Le Miroir d'Ornans* 355
    Musée Fabre (Montpellier) 498
    Musée d'Orsay (Paris) 125
    Ornans 354–5
    Palais des Beaux-Arts (Lille) 202
    Petit Palais (Paris) 113
    *Young Ladies of the Village Giving Alms to a Cow Girl in a Valley near Ornans* 33
Courcelles-sur-Vesle
    hotels 557
Courchevel 326, 377
    restaurants 593
Cournon
    hotels 560
Court life in the Renaissance **297**
Cousteau, Jacques 535
Coustou, Guillaume
    *Marly Horses* 104, 107
Coutances **254–5**
Couture, Thomas 125
Couty, Jean 385
Couze-Chambon Valley 366
Coward, Noël 532
Coysevox, Antoine 181
Cranach, Lucas 106
*La Création du Monde* (ballet) 70–71
Crécy, Battle of (1346) 58
Credit cards 626
    in restaurants 574
    shopping 144
Crepon
    hotels 559
Cresson, Edith 24, 73
Crêt de Châtillon 395
Crèvecoeur-en-Auge 259
Crime 624
Critérium International de la Première Neige (Val d'Isère) 43
Crusades 57
Crussol, Château de 388
Crypte Archéologique (Paris) 86, **88**
Cubism 96, 97

Cucugnan
restaurants 600
Culture and the arts **26**
Cumières
restaurants 581
Cuq-Toulza
hotels 567
Curie, Marie 69, 129
Curie, Pierre 69, 129
Currency exchange 626
Cusset, Catherine 34
Customs information 620, 623
Cycling **613**, 616, **639**
in cities **641**
Tour de France 41

**D**

D-Day landings (1944)
14, 71, 251, **255**
Mémorial de Caen **258**
Dada 70
Dagobert I, King 48, 54, 176
Dagobert III, King 48
Daguerre, Louis 67
Dalí, Salvador 70, 486
Espace Dalí Paris 136
Dambach-la-Ville 233, 236
Dames de la Meuse 218
Dampierre
restaurants 579
Dance **609**, 611
Paris **155**, 157
*The Dance* (Carpeaux) 124, 125
*Dance at the Moulin de la Galette*
(Renoir) 124, 125
Dante Alighieri 513
Danton, Georges Jacques 102
Darcel 139
Dargilan Grotto 371
D'Artagnan **445**
Daudet, Alphonse 477
Daum 228
Daumier, Honoré 125
David, Jacques-Louis 67
portraits of Napoleon 177, 180
Musée des Beaux-Arts (Reims) 214
David d'Angers 295
Dax **429**
festivals 42
De Gaulle, Charles 25, 47, 72
Colombey-les-Deux-Eglises 221
Free French movement 71
grave 221
Musée de l'Ordre de la Libération
(Paris) 118
De Mille, Cecil B 304
Deauville 259
festivals 40, 42
hotels 559
restaurants 583
Debit cards 626
Debré, Olivier 301
La Défense (Paris) **134**
Degas, Edgar 394, 462, 507
Musée d'Orsay (Paris) 125
Musée Marmottan Monet (Paris) 135
*Le Déjeuner sur l'Herbe* (Manet) 125
Delacroix, Eugène 202, 546
*Jacob Wrestling with the Angel* 126,
131
Musée Eugène Delacroix (Paris) 123,
**126**
Musée d'Orsay (Paris) 125
Petit Palais (Paris) 113
St.-Sulpice (Paris) 130, 131
Delaunay, Robert
*Eiffel Tower* 32
Delaunay, Sonia 32, 71

Deleuze, Gilles 35
Delville Wood 195
Denis, St. 176
Department stores **604**, 607
Paris **145**
Derain, André 102, 476, 487, 517
Derrida, Jacques 35
Des Rives et Des Notes (Oloron-Ste-
Marie) 41
Descartes, René 35, 62, 311
tomb 122, 126
Désert des Agriates 541
Despiau, Charles 385
*Les Détours de Babel* (Grenoble)
40
*Deux Femmes Courant sur la Plage*
(Picasso) 477
Les Deux Magots (Paris) 122
Diaghilev, Sergei 71
Diane de Poitiers 106, 297, 335
Château d'Ancy-le-Franc 338
Chenonceau 302, 303
Diderot, Denis 64, 107, 221
tomb 103
Dieppe **267**
hotels 559
restaurants 583
Dieulefit 390
Dieve
hotels 558
Digne-les-Bains **521**
festivals 42
Dijon 14, 16, 331, **344–6**
Cathedral St-Bénigne **346**
hotels 562
restaurants 589–90
Street by Street map 344–5
Dijon International Food and Wine
Festival 42
Dinan 273, **287**
hotels 560
restaurants 585
Dinard 14, 285
hotels 560
Dinard British Film Festival 42
Dior, Christian
Musée Christian Dior (Granville)
255
Disabled travelers **621**, 623
in hotels **552**, 553
in restaurants 574
Disneyland® Resort Paris **182**
Distel, Sacha 520
Dix, Otto
*Portrait of the Journalist Sylvia von
Harden* 97
*Doctor Paul Gachet* (Van Gogh) 125
Doctors 625
Dogs, in restaurants 574
Dol de Bretagne
hotels 560
Dole **353**
hotels 563
restaurants 590
The Dombes 377, **380**
Domfront 259
Domme 16, **439**
hotels 567
restaurants 597
Dongen, Kees van 526
Dordogne Valley **439**
caves 406
Doré, Gustave 299
Douai
restaurants 580
Douarnenez **277**
restaurants 585
Douaumont Memorial 189, 226

Doue la Fontaine
restaurants 587
Drachenbronn
hotels 558
Dramatists **35**
Drée, Château de 352
Dreyfus Affair 68, 69, 94
Drinks *see* Food and drink; Wines
Du Barry, Madame 102
Duban, Félix 88
Dufy, Raoul 448, 476, 517
Musée d'Art Moderne de la Ville de
Paris 114
Musée des Beaux-Arts (Rouen) 269
Musée Calvet (Avignon) 507
Musée Eugène Boudin (Honfleur)
266
Musée Fabre (Montpellier) 498
Musée Malraux (Le Havre) 266
*The Pier and Promenade at Nice* 33
Duguay-Trouin, René 286
Duingt, Château de 395
Dumas, Alexandre 259, 445, 516
Duncan, Isadora 529
Dune du Pilat 428
Dunerque 197, **201**
restaurants 580
Dunois, Jean de 309
*Le Duo* (Braque) 97
Dupin, Madame 302, 303
Dupuis, Nicolas 95
Dürer, Albrecht 106, 214
Durrell, Lawrence 477

**E**

Easter 43
Ebersmunster 233
Ebhardt, Bodo 232
Eckmühl lighthouse 277
Ecole Militaire (Paris) **116**
Ecole Nationale Supérieure des
Beaux-Arts (Paris) **126**
Ecomusée d'Alsace (Ungersheim)
229
Ecomusée Marquèze 429
Ecomusée du Niou (Niou Uhella)
276
Ecomusée du Pays de Rennes
289
Edward, Black Prince 360, 418
Edward III, King of England
200–201
Eglise et Couvent des Cordeliers
(Nancy) **228**
Eglise du Dôme (Paris)
81, 118, **119**
Eglise Notre-Dame (Cunault) 296
Eglise St.-Hilaire-le-Grand (Poitiers)
**417**
Les Égouts (Paris) **116**
Eguisheim **231**, 236
Eiffel, Gustave 68, 117
Eiffel Tower (Paris)
12, 71, 74–5, 76, **117**
*Eiffel Tower* (Delaunay) 32
Eisenhower, Dwight D. 214
Eleanor of Aquitaine
**57**, 298, 309, 417
Electrical adaptors 623
Elne **487**
Embassies 623
Emerald Coast *see* Côte d'Emeraude
Emergencies **624–5**
Emilion, St 427
*Les Emmurés de Carcassonne* (Laurens)
493

Enlightenment 34, 47, **64–5**
Entertainment **608–11**
　booking tickets **154**, 157
　cabaret **155**, 157
　The celebrated cafés of Paris **156**
　classical music **154–5**, 157
　clubs **155**, 157, **610**, 611
　dance **155**, 157, **609**, 611
　listings magazines **154**
　movies **156**, 157, **608–9**, 611
　music **610**, 611
　Paris **154–7**
　rock, jazz, and world music **155**, 157
　spectator sports **611**
　sport **156**, 157
　theater **154**, 157, **608**, 611
*Entrance to the Port at La Rochelle*
　(Signac) 32
Entraygues 370
Entre-Deux-Mers 403
Epernay 13, 14, 211, **215**
　festivals 43
　hotels 557
　restaurants 581
Ephrussi de Rothschild, Baroness 532
Epinal
　festivals 40
Epoisses, Château d' 339
Erasmus 233
Erbalunga 540
　hotels 571
　restaurants 603
Erhard, Gregor 106
Espace Dalí Paris 136
Espace Mendès France (Poitiers)
　**417**
Espace Van Gogh (Arles) 512
Espace Vignolis – Musée de l'Olivier
　(Nyons) 390
Espagnac-Ste.-Eulalie 443
Espalion 328, 370
Espelette 454, 457
　hotels 568
　restaurants 598
Espelette Pepper Festival 42
Espinay family 246
Esplanade des Quinconces (Bordeaux)
　425
Estaing 370
L'Estran-La Cité de la Mer (Dieppe)
　267
Etoges
　hotels 557
Etretat 28
　hotels 559
Eugénie, Empress 205, 456, 533
Eugénie-les-Bains
　hotels 566
　restaurants 595
Euro 627
Europa Jazz Festival (Le Mans) 40
European Constitution 25
European Union 25, 47, 73, 234
Evian-les-Bains 395
Evreux **270**
Exporting arts and antiques 152
Eze 17, 503, **533**
　hotels 570
　restaurants 601

**F**

Fabre, Jean-Henri 370
Factory outlets **607**
Fainsilber, Adrien 140, 235
Falaise
　restaurants 583
Falaise d'Aval 266
Farmhouses **38–9**

Fauves 33, 96, **476**, 487
Favières
　restaurants 580
Fayence
　hotels 570
　restaurants 601
Feast of St. Nicolas (Nancy) 43
Fécamp 266
　hotels 559
　restaurants 584
Feleggakis, S 137
Felibrige Movement 477
Felix V, antipope 395
Feminism 24
Ferdinand, King of Aragon 489
Fère en Tardenois
　hotels 556
Feria – Bullfight (Dax) 42
Feria Pascale (Arles) 40
Ferme d'Antéa (Brasparts) 276
*Ferme-auberges* **572**
Ferme-Musée de la Forêt (Bourg-en-
　Bresse) 380
Ferrari Galliera, Duchesse Maria de 114
Ferrier, Vincent
　tomb 284
Ferries **630–31**, **635**
Ferry, Jules 68
Fesch, Cardinal 546
Festival d'Art Lyrique (Aix-en-Provence)
　41
Festival du Cirque (Monaco) 43
Festival de Lanvellec and Trégor 42
Festival of Lights (Lyon) 43
Festival de Pâquex (Deauville) 40
Festivals **40–43**
　*pardons* 247
Fête du Jasmin (Grasse) 42
Fête de Mimosa (Bormes-les-Mimosas)
　43
Fête de la Musique 41
Fête de St. Jean 41
Fête de St.-Louis (Sète) 42
Fête de la Transhumance 41
Fête de la Véraison (Châteauneuf-du-
　Pape) 42
Ficajola 545
Figeac 16, 427, 443
　restaurants 597
Filibert, Canon 56
Filitosa 537, **546–7**
Film *see* Cinema
Finistère 273
Fire services 624–5
Firmin, St 206
Fitzgerald, F. Scott 70, 477, 503, 525,
　529
Fitzgerald, Zelda 477, 529
Flandre Maritime **202**
Flaubert, Gustave 34, 67, 68, **269**
　Château de Chenonceau 302
　Musée Flaubert (Rouen) **269**
　Trouville 259
Flea markets, Paris **153**
Fleurie 381
*Fleurs des Champs* (Janmot) 385
Floréal Musical d'Epinal 40
Flowers
　Alpine flowers **327**
　Corsica **545**
Flying schools 614, 617
Foire aux Sorciers (Bué) 42
La Foire des Hérolles 419
Foix 452, 453, **467**
　hotels 568
　restaurants 598
Fondation Bemberg (Toulouse)
　**451**

Fondation Claude Monet (Giverny)
　270
Fondation Le Corbusier (Paris)
　**134**
Fondation Louis Vuitton (Paris) 72–3,
　**134**
Fondation Maeght (St.-Paul de Vence)
　**528**
Font de Gaume 407
Font-Romeu 484
Fontagny
　restaurants 590
Fontaine Médicis (Paris) 131
Fontaine de l'Observatoire (Paris) 120,
　**131**
Fontaine-de-Vaucluse **510**
Fontainebleau, Château de 13, 174,
　**184–5**
　restaurants 579
Fontainebleau School 60, 176, 338
Fontenay, Abbaye de 331, **336–7**
Fontenay, Aubert de 95
Fontevraud, Abbaye Royale de 13, **298**
　restaurants 587
Fontjoncouse
　restaurants 600
Food and drink 27
　apples and cider **259**
　Armagnac **444**
　Cantal cheese **367**
　Cognac 422–3
　festivals 42
　The flavors of Central France
　**322–3**
　The flavors of the South of France
　**472–3**
　The flavors of Southwest France
　**400–401**
　The flavors of Western France **242–3**
　gourmet food **616**, 617
　markets **153**
　Northeast France **190–91**
　picnics 575
　shopping **150–51**, **604–5**
　A wine and food tour of Burgundy,
　　Périgord and Bordeaux 11, 16
　*see also* Restaurants; Wines
Football *see* Soccer
Forcalquier 505
*La Force* (Lamourdedieu) 429
Forêt de Bercé 311
Forêt d'Iraty 455, **459**, 460–61
Forêt de Paimpont **285**
Forêt de Vizzavona 544
Forez 357
Fort la Latte 273, 285
Fort National (St.-Malo) **286**
Fort de la Pompelle (Reims) **215**
Fort de Villy-la-Ferté 219
Forteresse de Salses **489**
Fortes, François 498
Forum des Halles (Paris) **94**
Foster, Sir Norman 501
Foucault, Michel 35
Fouesnant
　hotels 560
　restaurants 585
Fougères 273, **289**
　restaurants 585
Fouquet, Jean 106
Fouquet, Nicolas 183
*Four Quarters of the World* (Carpeaux)
　76
Fouré, Abbé 287
Foy, St. 372–3, 405
Fragonard, Jean-Honoré 106, 521
Francescas
　restaurants 597

Franche-Comté *see* Burgundy and Franche-Comté
Franchini, Gianfranco 96
Franck, César 119
Franco-Prussian War (1870–71) 68
Francofolies (La Rochelle) 41
François I, King 49, 60–61
  Amboise 305
  Beauregard 310
  Château de Chambord 241, 306, 307
  Cognac 423
  Court life in the Renaissance 297
  Fontainebleau 184, 185
  Le Havre 266
  Louvre (Paris) 104
  St.-Germain-en-Laye 177
  salamander emblem 60, 241, 246, 307, 308, 437
François II, Duke of Brittany tomb 294
François II, King 49, 60, 316
Franks 47
Frederick of Hohenstaufen 232
Frederick Barbarossa, Emperor 57
Free French movement 71
Fréjus 17, **521**
French Alps **326–7**
  *see also* Rhône Valley and French Alps
French Revolution (1789) 47, 48, **64–5**
  Bicentennial 72
  Place de la Concorde (Paris) 102
French Tennis Open 41
Froment, Nicolas 515
The Fronde 62
Front National 25
Futuroscope **417**

**G**

Gabriel, Jacques-Ange 102, 116
Gainsbourg, Serge grave 143
Galerie David d'Angers (Angers) 295
Galerie Nationale du Jeu de Paume (Paris) **102**
Gallé, Emile 228
Galleries *see* Museums and galleries
Gallic Wars (58–51 BC) 52
Gambetta, Léon 442
Gardens *see* Parks and gardens
Garnier, Charles 69, 101, 426, 534
Garonne, River 450
Gascony *see* Périgord, Quercy, and Gascony
Gataudière, Château de la 421
*The Gates of Hell* (Rodin) 124, 125
Gau, Franz Christian 119
Gauguin, Paul 247, **279**, 476
  *Les Alyscamps* 513
  *Le Christ Jaune* 279
  Maison Musée du Pouldu (Le Pouldu) 279
  Musée Marmottan Monet (Paris) 135
  Musée d'Orsay (Paris) 125
  Pont-Aven 279
Gavarnie 463
Gavrinis 285
Gay and lesbian travelers **622**, 623
Gehry, Frank 134, 139
Genet, Jean 35
Geneva, Lake *see* Léman, Lac
Geneviève, St 127, 129
  statue of 131
Genghis Khan 195
Gennes
  restaurants 587

La Géode (Paris) 140
Geology
  caves of the Southwest **406–7**
  Massif Central **328–9**
George, St 513
Gérardmer **229**
Géricault, Théodore 136, 269
  *The Raft of the Medusa* 106
Germanus, St. 334–5
Gevrey-Chambertin
  restaurants 590
Giacometti, Alberto 143
  *L'Homme qui Marche* 528
Giambono, Michele 501
Gide, André 34
Giffaumont-Champaubert
  restaurants 581
Gift shops **149**
Gilduin, Bernard 451
Gilles, St. 499
Gillespie, Dizzy 70
Gilot, Françoise 476
Giono, Jean 34, 477
Giotto 106
Girault, Charles 110, 112
Girolata 545
Giscard d'Estaing, Valéry 72
Gislebertus 343
Gisors
  restaurants 584
*Gîtes* 551
Giverny 14, 72, **270**
*The Goat* (Picasso) 525
Godeau, Antoine 527
Goethe, Johann Wolfgang von 35, 234
Golden Age of Burgundy **347**
Golf **612**, 616
Golfe du Lion **491**
Golfe du Morbihan **284–5**
Golfe de Porto 539, **545**
Golo river 544
Gontran 487
Gonzaga family 342
Gordes **510**
  hotels 570
Gorges de l'Ardèche 389
Gorges de l'Aveyron 430, **447**
Gorges de la Bournes 393
Gorges du Loup **527**
Gorges de la Restonica 544
Gorges du Tarn 320, 356, **374–5**
Gorges du Verdon 29, **518–19**
Gosnay
  hotels 556
Gotescalk, Bishop of Le Puy 368
Gothic France **56–7**
  architecture **36–7**
Gouffre de Padirac 407, **442**
Goujon, Jean 104
Gould, Frank Jay 525
Gourdon 527
Gourmet food **616**, 617
Gouvieux
  hotels 556
Goya, Francisco José de 202, 444, 448, 456
Goyen, Jan van 202
Grace, Princess of Monaco 114, 535
Grand Palais (Paris) 81, 110, **112–13**
Grand Roc 407
Grand Siècle **62–3**
Grand Théâtre (Bordeaux) 16, 424, **426**
La Grande Arche (Paris) 132, 134
Grande Mademoiselle 63, 334
Grande Mosquée de Paris **143**

La Grande-Motte 478, 491, **499**
*La Grande Odalisque* (Zadkine) 512
Grandes Eaux Musicales (Versailles) 41
Grands Causses 357, **371**
Grands Goulets 393
Granville **255**
  hotels 559
  restaurants 584
Grasse 17, **521**
  festivals 42
Greater Paris
  map 19
Greco, Juliette 122
Green travel **631**
Greene, Graham 35, 477
Greniers à Sel (Honfleur) 266
Grenoble 377, **392–3**
  festivals 40
  hotels 564–5
  map 392
  restaurants 593
Greuze, Jean-Baptiste
  Musée Greuze (Tournus) 349
Grignan **390**
Grimaldi, Henri 526
Grimaldi family 533, 534
Gris, Juan 486
Grotte Chauvet 389
Grotte de Clamouse 497
Grotte des Combareles 438, 439
Grotte des Demoiselles 497
Grotte de Font de Gaume 438, 439
Grotte de la Madeleine 389
Grotte Massabielle (Lourdes) 463
Grotte de Niaux 467
Grotte de Pech-Merle 442, 443
Grotte de Villars 434
Grottes de Bétharram (Lourdes) 463
Grottes des Canalettes 484
Gruaud-Larose, Château 427
Gruissan 483
Grünewald, Matthias
  Issenheim Altarpiece 231
Guebwiller **230**, 236
Guédelon, Château de 334
Guesclin, Bertrand du 287
Guifred, Count of Cerdagne 485
Guillaume d'Aquitaine 497
Guimard, Hector 69, 125, 135
Guimiliau **280–81**
  restaurants 585
Guingamp
  restaurants 585
Guise, Duc de 308
Gumery, Charles 100
Guyot, Georges Lucien 114
Gypsy Pilgrimage (Stes.-Maries-de-la-Mer) 41

**H**

Habits de Lumière (Epernay) 43
Les Halles (Paris) **94**
Hannibal 487
Haras du Pin 259
Hardouin-Mansart, Jules
  Cathedral of St.-Louis-des-Invalides (Paris) 119
  Château de Sceaux 182
  Eglise du Dôme (Paris) 119
  Hôtel des Invalides (Paris) 118
  Palais du Tau (Reims) 217
  Place Vendôme (Paris) 102
  Versailles 178
*Harmony in Blue and Gold* (Monet) 271
Harold II, King of England 256

Haussmann, Baron Georges-Eugène 67, 99, **112**
Bois de Boulogne (Paris) 134
Boulevard St.-Germain (Paris) 123
Les Égouts (Paris) 116
Parc des Buttes-Chaumont (Paris) 139
Place de l'Opéra (Paris) 101
Haut Asco 544
Haut-Barr, Château du 237
Haut-Brion 403
Haut-Koenigsbourg, Château du 189, 223, **232–3**
Haut Languedoc 481
Haute couture 144, **146**
Haute-Seine **270**
Hautefort **434**
Hauteville family 254
Health care **625**
Hede
restaurants 585
Héloïse 56
Hemingway, Ernest 35, 70, 126, 143, 477
Henri I, King 48
Henri II, King 49
Château de Chambord 306
Chenonceau 302
and Diane de Poitiers 297, 302
Fontainebleau 184, 185
Louvre (Paris) 104
Rocroi 218
St.-Germain-en-Laye 177
Henri III, King 49, 60, 61, 308
Angers 246
marriage 302
Orléans 316
Pont Neuf (Paris) 87
Henri IV, King 49, 61, 73
Cahors 443
Châlons-en-Champagne 220
Edict of Nantes 294
Fontainebleau 184
La Flèche 311
Nantes 294
Orléans 316
Pau 462
Place des Vosges (Paris) 95
Pont Neuf (Paris) 87
Pyrenees 453
St.-Germain-en-Laye 177
Tours 300
Henri of Navarre see Henri IV
Henry II, King of England 56
Abbaye Royale de Fontevraud 298
Chinon 13
marriage 309, 402
Niort 413
Poitiers 416, 417
tomb 57, 298
Henry V, King of England 59
Hepworth, Barbara 528
Hérouard, Jean 142
Hidalgo, Anne 24
Hiking see Walking
Hiring cars **638**, 639
Historial de la Grande Guerre (Péronne) 203
Historial Jeanne d'Arc (Rouen) **268**
History **47–73**
Hitchhiking **639**
Hitler, Adolf 205
Hittorff, Jacques 110
Holbein, Hans 106
Holidays, public 45
Hollande, François 25, 73
L'Homme qui Marche (Giacometti) 528

Honfleur 10, 14, 250, 251, **266**
hotels 559
restaurants 584
Horses
The Camargue 515
Ecole Nationale d'Equitation (Saumur) 296
Haras du Pin 259
horseback riding **613**, 616
Musée du Cheval (Chantilly) 209
racing 42, **208**
Hospitals **625**
Hossegor 428
hotels 566
Hostels **552**, 553
Hôtel des Archeveques de Sens (Paris) **89**
Hôtel-Dieu (Beaune) **350–51**
Hôtel Dieu (Paris) 87
Hôtel des Invalides (Paris) **118**
Hôtel de Lamoignon (Paris) 92
Hôtel du Petit Louvre (Troyes) **220**
Hôtel Sandelin (St.-Omer) 201
Hôtel de Soubise (Paris) **94**
Hôtel de Sully (Paris) 93
Hôtel de Vergeur Museum (Reims) **214**
Hôtel de Ville (Arras) 203
Hôtel de Ville (Paris) **93**
Hotels **550–71**
Alsace and Lorraine 558
Brittany 560–61
Burgundy and Franche-Comté 562–3
chain hotels 551
Champagne 557–8
Corsica 571
gradings 550
Ile-de-France 555–6
Languedoc and Roussillon 569
Loire Valley 561–2
Massif Central 563–4
meals and amenities 550
Le Nord and Picardy 556–7
Normandy 559–60
Paris 554–5
Périgord, Quercy, and Gascony 566–8
Poitou and Aquitaine 565–6
prices 550
Provence and the Côte d'Azur 569–71
The Pyrenees 568–9
reservations 550–51
Rhône Valley and French Alps 564–5
Houdon, Jean-Antoine 107
Houllebecq, Michel 34
Household goods
shopping **149**, **606–7**
Huelgoat 276
Huet, Gaston 304
Hugo, Victor 34, 35
Besançon 354
Digne-les-Bains 521
Maison de Victor Hugo (Paris) 93, **95**
Sainte-Clotilde (Paris) 119
Huguenots 431
Hugues, St 352
Hundred Years' War (1337–1453) 47, **58–9**, 304, 409, 431
Hunspach 223
Hurtault, Maximilien-Joseph 184
Huxley, Aldous 477
Hyères 17, **518**
Hypermarkets **604**, 607

**I**

Ibex **391**
Iguerande
restaurants 590
Ile d'Aix 421
Ile d'Arz 284
Ile de Batz 279
Ile de Bréhat 248, 275, **282**
Ile de la Cité, Marais and Beaubourg (Paris) 12, 83, **85–97**
area map 85
hotels 554
restaurants 576
Street by Street map: Ile de la Cité 86–7
Street by Street map: The Marais 86–7
Ile-de-France **175–85**
area map 175
climate 44
hotels 555–6
map 77
restaurants 579
Ile du Levant 519
Ile-aux-Moines 284
Ile de Noirmoutier 295
restaurants 585
Ile d'Oléron 16, **421**
restaurants 595
Ile d'Ouessant **276**
Ile de Porquerolles
restaurants 602
Ile de Port-Cros
hotels 570
Ile de Ré 411, 420
hotels 566
restaurants 595
L'Ile Rousse **541**
Ile Saint-Honorat 525
Ile St.-Louis (Paris) 12, 83, **89**
Ile Sainte-Marguerite 524–5
Ile Tristan 277
Ile d'Yeu 294
restaurants 587
Iles d'Hyères 17, **519**
Iles de Lérins **524–5**
Iles Sanguinaires 542–3, 546
Illhaeusern
restaurants 582
Impressionists 68, 251, **476**
Ingres, Jean-Auguste
Montauban 447
Musée Bonnat-Helleu (Bayonne) 456
Musée d'Orsay (Paris) 125
Petit Palais (Paris) 113
Institut du Monde Arabe (Paris) **143**
Insurance 624
Interceltic Festival (Lorient) 42
International Exhibition, Paris (1925) 70
International Garden Festival (Chaumont sur Loire) 41
International Grand Prix de Monaco 40
International Jazz Festival (Antibes) 41
International Sailing Week (La Rochelle) 41
Internet access **628–9**
Ionesco, Eugène 35
Iron Age 51
Isabella of Portugal 347
Isabelle d'Angoulême 298
Islam
Grande Mosquée de Paris **143**

Issenheim Altarpiece (Grünewald) 231
Issigeac
  restaurants 597
Issoire **363**

## J

Jacob, Max 278
*Jacob Wrestling with the Angel* (Delacroix) 126, 131
Les Jacobins (Toulouse) **450**
Jacquerie peasant uprising (1358) 58
Jalabert, Charles
  *Virgile, Horace and Varius in Mecene's Home* 501
James, Henry 306
James, St. 404
James the Greater, St 404
Janmot, Louis
  *Fleurs des Champs* 385
Jardin Botanique de la Villa Thuret (Antibes) 525
Jardin du Carrousel (Paris) 104
Jardin Exotique (Eze) 533
Jardin Exotique (Monaco) **535**
Jardin du Luxembourg (Paris) 130
Jardin Massey (Pau) 462
Jardin des Plantes (Avranches) 256
Jardin des Plantes (Montpellier) 499
Jardin des Plantes (Paris) **142**
Jardin des Prés Fichaux (Bourges) 317
Jardin des Tuileries (Paris) 12, 82, **102–3**
Jardin Wilson (Montluçon) 361
Jardins des Champs-Elysées (Paris) 111
Les Jardins de la Fontaine (Nîmes) **500–501**
Jardins du Trocadéro (Paris) **114**
Jarnac
  restaurants 595
Jaussely, Léon 142
Jawlensky, Alexei von
  *La Méduse* 385
Jazz 70
  festivals 40, 41, 42
  Paris **155**, 157
Jazz Pulsations (Nancy) 42
Jazz Vienne 41
Jean II the Good, King 49, 418
Jeannin, Pierre 343
Jewellery stores **147**, 148
Jews
  Carpentras 510
  Musée d'Art et d'Histoire du Judaïsme (Paris) **94**
  Rue des Rosiers (Paris) 92
Joan of Arc 58, 59, **304–5**
  Beaugency 309
  birthplace 226–7
  Château de Chinon 298
  Compiègne 205
  Historial Jeanne d'Arc (Rouen) **268**
  Orléans 316–17
  Poitiers 416
  Reims 216
Joan of Arc Festival (Orléans) 40
John, King of England 298
John the Baptist, St. 206
Joigny
  hotels 563
Josephine, Empress 66
  Château de Malmaison 177
  Palais de l'Elysée (Paris) 112
Jospin, Lionel 25

Josselin **285**
Journées du Patrimoine 42
Joyce, James 35, 126
Juan-les-Pins
  festivals 41
  hotels 570
Julian, Emperor 53
Juliénas 381
July Monarchy (1830) 66, 67
Jumièges, Abbaye de 251, 267
Juvigny-sous-Andaine
  restaurants 584

## K

Kandinsky, Wassily 528
  *With the Black Arc* 97
Kaysersberg
  hotels 558
  restaurants 582
Le Ker (Vannes) 284
Kings and emperors **48–9**
Klein, Yves 477, 531
Knights of Malta 463
Knights Templar 227, 371, 487
Kraft, Hugues 214
Kristeva, Julia 35

## L

La Bégude-de-Mazenc 390
La Bourboule 357, 366
La Brosse, Guy de 142
La Bruyère, Jean de 363
La Chaise, Père de 139
La Chaise-Dieu **368**
La Chartre-sur-le-Loir 311
  hotels 561
La Clayette 352
La Courtade 475
La Couvertoirade 371
La Croix St.-Leufroy
  restaurants 584
La Devinière 299
La Ferrière aux Etangs
  restaurants 584
La Ferte Imbault
  restaurants 587
La Ferté-Loupière 334
La Flèche 311
La Fontaine 94
La Malène 375
La Palice, Château de **362**
La Palud-sur-Verdon 519
La Plagne 326
La Puisaye-Forterre **334**
La Rochelle 16, 398, 409, **420**
  festivals 41
  hotels 566
  restaurants 595
La Tour, Georges de 228
La Tour d'Auvergne, Henri de 367
La Turbie 52–3
  restaurants 602
Labor Day 43
Laboureur, Jean-Emile 546
Labyrinth, Chartres Cathedral **313**
Lac de Capitello 544
Lac et Forêt d'Orient 221
Lac de Melo 544
Lacanau-Océan 428
Lacave 407
  hotels 567
  restaurants 597
Lacoste 511
*Lady with the Unicorn* tapestries **127**
Lafaille, Clément 420

Lafite Rothschild, Château 427
Lagarde, Christine 24
Laguiole
  restaurants 592
Lalique, René 125
Laloux, Victor 124
L'Alpe d'Huez 391
Lamalou-les-Bains 497
Lamartine, Alphonse de 35, 352, 394
Lamotte Beuvron
  restaurants 587
Lamourdedieu, Raoul
  *La Force* 429
Lampaul-Guimiliau **280**
Landeda
  hotels 560
Landelle, Charles
  *La République* 46
Les Landes **429**
  forest **429**
Langeais, Château de **299**
  restaurants 587
Langon
  restaurants 595
Langres **221**
  restaurants 581
Language, phrase book 671–2
Languedoc and Roussillon **481–501**, 511
  climate 45
  food and drink **472**
  hotels 569
  map 482–3
  Provençal writers **477**
  restaurants 599–601
  travel 483
  A week in the Rhône Valley and Languedoc 15
Lanvin, Jeanne 103
Laon 13, **209**
  Cathedral 13, 37, 197, 209
  hotels 556
  restaurants 580
Lapoutroie
  hotels 558
Laprade, Albert 142
Larrau
  restaurants 598
Larressingle **444**
Lascabanes
  hotels 567
Lascaux 50, 51, 407, 431
Lascaux IV **438**
Lassus, Jean-Baptiste 88
*The Last Judgment* (van der Weyden) 58–9, 350, 351
Latin Quarter (Paris) 12, **128–9**
Latour, Château 427
Latour-de-Carol 484
Laurens, J. P.
  *Les Emmurés de Carcassonne* 493
Lautenbach 230
Lauzerte 449
Laval, Pierre 71
Lavardin 310
Lavasina 540
Lavier, Bertrand 501
Lavirotte, Jules 116
Lawrence, D. H. 477
Le Boulou
  restaurants 600
Le Bourg
  hotels 563

Le Bourg d'Oisans **391**
Le Bourget-Lac
  restaurants 593
Le Breton, Gilles 185
Le Breuil-en-Auge
  restaurants 584
Le Brun, Charles 95
  Notre-Dame (Paris) 91
  Vaux-le-Vicomte 183
  Versailles 180, 181
Le Clézio, Jean-Marie Gustave 73
Le Clusaz
  restaurants 593
Le Corbusier 533
  Cité Radieuse (Marseille) 516
  Fondation Le Corbusier (Paris) **134**
  Ronchamp 355
Le Croisic
  hotels 561
Le Duc, François 413
Le Faou 276
Le Grand, Alexander 266
Le Havre **266**
  restaurants 584
Le Lude 311
Le Mans 14, 291, **295**
  festivals 40
  hotels 561
  restaurants 587
Le Mans 24-Hour Automobile Race
  41
Le Moiturier, Antoine 339
  tomb of Philippe Pot 106
Le Noble, Ambroise 434
Le Nôtre, André **183**
  Avenue des Champs-Elysées (Paris)
    112
  Castres 448
  Château de Chantilly
    197, 208
  Château de Sceaux 182
  Château de Vaux-le-Vicomte 183
  Cordès de Château 366
  Gourdon 527
  Jardin des Tuileries (Paris) 103
  St.-Germain-en-Laye 177
  tomb 103
  Versailles 178
Le Perreux sur Marne
  restaurants 579
Le Poët Laval 390
  hotels 565
Le Pouldu **279**
Le Puy du Fou 294
Le Puy "Roi de l'Oiseau" 42
Le Puy-en-Velay
  36, 357, **368–9**, 405
  restaurants 592
Le Revard 394
Le Rouget
  restaurants 592
Le Sueur, Eustache 91
Le Touquet 197, **200**
  hotels 556
Le Vau, Louis
  Château de Vaux-le-Vicomte 183
  Louvre (Paris) 105
  St.-Louis-en-l'Ile (Paris) 89
  Versailles 178, 181
Lectoure
  hotels 567
Ledoux, Claude-Nicolas 354
The Left Bank (Paris) **121–31**
  area map 121
  hotels 555
  restaurants 577–8
  Street by Street map: Latin Quarter
    128–9

The Left Bank (Paris) (cont.)
  Street by Street map: Luxembourg
    Quarter 130–31
  Street by Street map: St.-Germain-
    des-Prés 122–3
Legentil, Alexandre 138
Léger, Fernand 70, 71, 526, 528
Légion d'Honneur 66
Léman, Lac 377, **395**
Lembach
  restaurants 582
Lemercier, Jacques 103
Lemon Festival (Menton) 43
Lemordant, J.-J. 278
Lemot, François-Frédéric 294
Lempicka, Lolita 526
Lens
  restaurants 580
Lentilles 219
Léon IX, Pope 231
Leonardo da Vinci 13, 60, 61, 456
  Château de Chambord 306, 307
  *Mona Lisa* 106
  tomb 305
L'Epine **219**
Les Andelys 253, 270
  restaurants 584
Les Arcs 326
Les Baux-de-Provence **511**
  restaurants 602
Les Combarelles 407
Les Estables
  restaurants 592
Les Eyzies 407, 431, **438–9**
  hotels 567
  restaurants 597
Les Islettes 219
Les Ménuires 326
Les Roches-l'Evêque 310
Les Saintes-Maries-de-la-Mer
  478, 514
  festivals 41
  hotels 571
  restaurants 602
Les Thons
  restaurants 582
Lesbahy, Philippa 246, 300
Lesseps, Ferdinand de 68
Levernois
  hotels 563
Levie
  restaurants 603
Levy, Mark 34
Liberty Flame (Paris) 81
Libraries
  Bibliothèque d'Agglomération
    (St.-Omer) 201
  Bibliothèque Humaniste (Sélestat)
    233
  Bibliothèque Nationale de France
    (Paris) **142**
Liégeard, Stephen 476
Lieu d'Art et d'Action Contemporaine
  (Dunkerque) 201
Lighthouses
  Eckmühl 277
  Musée des Phares et Balises (Phare
    du Créac'h) 276
  Phare de Cordouan (Royan) 422
Lille 197, **202**
  hotels 556
  restaurants 580
Limbourg, Paul and Jean de 59
Limoges **360**
  hotels 563
  restaurants 592
Limousin 357
  pilgrimages and *ostensions* **363**

Limoux Carnival 43
Lingerie stores **147**, 148
Lisieux 259
L'Isle, Bertrand de 466
L'Isle-sur-la-Sorgue
  restaurants 602
Listings magazines **154**
Literature 26
Little Yellow Train **484**
Livardois 357
Loches 13, **304**
  hotels 561
Lochnager Mine Crater 194
Locquirec
  hotels 560
Locronan **277**
  festivals 41
Loir, River **310–11**
Loire Valley 14, 28, **291–317**
  Châteaux **246**
  Châteaux tour of the Sologne
    **310–11**
  climate 44
  Court life in the Renaissance **297**
  The flavors of Western France
    **243**
  France's wine regions: The Loire
    **244–5**
  hotels 561–2
  map 292–3
  restaurants 586–9
  travel 292
  troglodyte dwellings **296**
Longchamps (Paris) 42
Longpont
  hotels 556
Lons-le-Saunier
  restaurants 590
Lorient
  festivals 42
  restaurants 585
Lorraine *see* Alsace and Lorraine
Lorraine, Dukes of 228
Lost property 624
Lot, River 357, 370
  A tour of two rivers **442–3**
Lothaire, King 48
Loti, Pierre 421
Loue
  hotels 561
Louis I of Anjou 296
Louis I the Pious, King 48
Louis II the Stammerer, King 48
Louis III, King 48
Louis IV the Foreigner, King 48
Louis V, King 48
Louis VI the Fat, King 48, 177
Louis VII, King 48, 57
  Château de Fontainebleau 184
  marriage 309
Louis VIII, King 49, 492
Louis IX (St. Louis), King 49, 57, 89
  Abbaye de Royaumont 176
  Carcassonne 492
  Sainte-Chapelle (Paris) 88
  Sens 334
Louis X, King 49
Louis XI the Spider 49
  Aigues-Mortes 499
  Amboise 305
  Château de Langeais 299
  Saintes 422
  Tours 300
Louis XII, King 49, 177
Louis XIII, King 49, 62, 63
  Charleville-Mézières 218
  Château de Fontainebleau 184
  Les Baux-de-Provence 511

Louis XIII, King (cont.)
  Place des Vosges (Paris) 95
  Versailles 178
Louis XIV, King
  47, 49, 62–3, 64
  Brouage 421
  Château de Bazoches 339
  Château de Chambord
    241, 306, 307
  Château de Vaux-le-Vicomte 183
  Comédie Française (Paris) 103
  Dole 353
  Église du Dôme (Paris) 119
  Franche-Comté 331
  Hôtel des Invalides (Paris) 116, 118
  Montauban 447
  Palais Royal (Paris) 103
  St.-Germain-en-Laye 177
  St.-Roch (Paris) 103
  Val-de-Grâce (Paris) 131
  Versailles 178–9, 181, 308
  wedding 456–7
Louis XV, King 49, 64
  Compiègne 197, 205
  coronation 107
  Corsica 537
  Ecole Militaire (Paris) 116
  Neuf-Brisach 231
  Panthéon (Paris) 129
  Sèvres 182
  Versailles 178, 179, 181
Louis XVI, King 49, 65
  Château de Rambouillet 182
  Compiègne 205
  execution 64, 65, 102, 181
  Parc du Champs-de-Mars (Paris) 116
  statue of 176
  Tréguier 282
  Versailles 181
Louis XVII, King 49
Louis XVIII, King 49, 130, 178
Louis, Victor 426
Louis d'Orléans 205
Louis-Philippe, King
  49, 67, 102
Louise de Lorraine 302, 303
Lourdes 453, **462–3**
  hotels 568
  The miracle of Lourdes **463**
  pilgrimages 40
  restaurants 598
Louvre (Paris) see Musée du Louvre
Lozari 541
Lozère 357
Luberon **510–11**
Lully, Giovanni Battista 62
Lumbres
  hotels 556
Lumière brothers 69, 100, 354
Lurçat, Jean 295, 360
Lutyens, Sir Edwin 194
Luxembourg Quarter (Paris)
  12, 130–31
Luz-St.-Sauveur **463**
Lycklama, Baron 524
Lyon 14, 15, 16, 377, **382–5**
  festivals 42, 43
  hotels 565
  map 384
  restaurants 593
  Street by Street map 382–3
Lyons-la-Forêt 270
  restaurants 584
Lyotard, Jean-François 35

**M**

Mace
  hotels 559

Macinaggio 540
Maclou 286
Mâcon **352**
Macron, Emmanuel 25, 73
La Madeleine (Paris) 100, **101**
Maeght, Aimé and Marguerite
  528
Le Magasin (Grenoble) 392, 393
Magazines **629**
Magesq
  hotels 566
Maginot Line 211, 219
Magnant
  restaurants 581
Magny-Cours
  restaurants 590
Maillol, Aristide 385, 486, 488, 489
  Musée Maillol (Paris) **119**
Maintenon, Madame de
  62, 179, 413
Maison des Canuts (Lyon) 385
Maison Carrée (Nîmes) **501**
Maison de Jeanne d'Arc (Orléans)
  316
Maison des Johnnies (Roscoff) 279
Maison Musée du Pouldu (Le Pouldu)
  279
Maison de Radio France (Paris) 80
Maison de Victor Hugo (Paris)
  93, **95**
Maisons les Chaource
  restaurants 581
Malbuisson
  hotels 563
  restaurants 590
Male, Emile 312
Malicorne-sur-Sarthe
  restaurants 587
Malmaison, Château **177**
Malraux, André 129, 343
Man in the Iron Mask 524–5
Manciet
  restaurants 597
Mancini, Marie 421
Manet, Edouard
  Le Déjeuner sur l'Herbe 125
Manigod
  hotels 565
Manoir Limoëlou (Rothéneuf) 286–7
Mansfield, Katherine 35, 477
Mantegna, Andrea 301
Manufacture Nationale de la Tapisserie
  (Beauvais) 205
Maps
  Alsace and Lorraine 224
  Alsace Route des Vins 236
  areas of natural beauty 28–9
  Arles 512–13
  artists in France 32–3
  The Battle of the Somme 194–5
  beaches in the South of France 478–
    9
  Beaujolais tour 381
  Bordeaux 424–5
  Brittany 274–5
  Burgundy and Franche-Comté 332–3
  Caen 258
  The Camargue 514–15
  Cathar country 495
  caves of the Dordogne 406
  Central France and the Alps 320–21
  Champagne 212–13
  Clermont-Ferrand 365
  climate of France 44–5
  Corsica 21, 471, 538–9
  D-Day landings 255
  Dijon 344–5
  driving maps **638**, 639

Maps (cont.)
  Europe 19
  France 10–11, 18–19
  geology of the Massif Central 328–9
  Gorges du Tarn 374–5
  Gorges du Verdon 518–19
  Grenoble 392
  Ile-de-France 77, 175
  Languedoc and Roussillon
    482–3
  Loire Valley 292–3
  Lyon 382–3, 384
  Massif Central 358–9
  Monaco 535
  Montmartre (Paris) 136–7
  Montpellier 498
  Neuf-Brisach 230
  Nice 531
  Nîmes 500–501
  Le Nord and Picardy 198–9
  Normandy 252–3
  Northeast France 188–9
  Orléans 316
  Parc National des Pyrénées 464–5
  Paris 76–7
  Paris: Champs-Elysées and Invalides
    109, 110–11
  Paris: Farther afield 133
  Paris: Greater Paris 19
  Paris: Ile de la Cité, Marais and
    Beaubourg 85, 86–7
  Paris: Latin Quarter 128–9
  Paris: The Left Bank 121
  Paris: Luxembourg Quarter 130–31
  Paris: The Marais 92–3
  Paris: Opéra Quarter 100–101
  Paris: A river view of Paris 79–83
  Paris: St.-Germain-des-Prés 122–3
  Paris: Tuileries and Opéra 99
  Paris couture 144
  Paris Street Finder 158–73
  Parish closes 281
  Périgord, Quercy and Gascony
    432–3
  Poitiers 417
  Poitou and Aquitaine 410–11
  Provence and the Côte d'Azur
    504–5
  The Pyrenees 454–5
  regional France 20–21
  Rennes 288
  Rhône Valley and the French Alps
    378–9
  The road to Compostela 404–5
  Rouen 268–9
  St.-Paul de Vence 528–9
  Sarlat 436–7
  Sologne châteaux tour 310–11
  South of France 470–71
  Southwest France 398–9
  Strasbourg 234–5
  TGV rail service 633
  Toulouse 450–51
  A tour of two rivers 442–3
  Tours 301
  Western France 240–41
  wines of Bordeaux 402–3
  wines of Burgundy 324–5
  wines of Champagne 192–3
  wines of France 30
  wines of the Loire 244–5
  wines of the South 474–5
Marais (Paris) see Ile de la Cité, Marais
  and Beaubourg
Marais Poitevin 28, 295, **412–13**,
  414–15
Marat, Jean Paul 87
Marathons, Paris 40

Maraussan
  restaurants 600
Marçay, Château de 299
Marcel, Etienne 58
Marché d'Aligre (Paris) **153**
Marché aux Fleurs et Oiseaux (Paris) 86
Marché aux Puces de Montreuil (Paris) **153**
Marché aux Puces de la Porte de Vanves (Paris) **153**
Marché aux Puces de St.-Ouen (Paris) **138**, **153**
Marché Couvert Saint Quentin (Paris) **153**
Marché des Enfants Rouges (Paris) **153**
La Marche des Fièrtes Lesbiennes, Gaies, Bi et Trans (Paris) 41
Marché Raspail (Paris) **153**
Marché St.-Germain (Paris) **153**
Marcilhac-sur-Célé 443
Mare Nostrum (Montpellier) 499
Margaret of Austria 380
Margaret of Bourbon 380
Margaret of Burgundy 335
Margaux, Château 427
  restaurants 595
Marguerite d'Angoulême 423, 462
Maria Teresa, Queen 456–7
Mariana 547
Marie Antoinette, Queen 532
  Bois de Boulogne (Paris) 134
  execution 65, 87, 102, 181
  Rambouillet 182
  Versailles 13, 179, 181
Marie de Hautefort 434
Marie-Louis, Queen 205
Marie de' Medici 62, 131
Marie-Thérèse, Queen 62, 63, 181
Marivaux, Pierre Carlet de 35
Markets **604–5**
  Marché aux Puces de St.-Ouen (Paris) **138**
  Paris **153**
  Sarlat **436**
Marlenheim
  restaurants 582
*Marly Horses* (Coustou) 104, 107
Marmottan, Paul 135
Marmoutier Abbey 37, 237
Marquet, Albert 476
Marqueyssac, Château de 439
Marquèze 429
Marseille 17, **516–17**
  festivals 40
  history 51
  hotels 570
  restaurants 602
Marsy, Balthazar 178
Martailly-Brancion
  hotels 563
Marthe, Ste. 511
Martin, St., Bishop of Tours 300, 301
Martini, Simone 508
Mary, Queen of Scots 316, 434
Mary, Virgin
  The Auvergne's Black Madonnas **369**
Massif Central **357–75**
  climate 45
  food and drink **322–3**
  geology **328–9**

Massif Central (cont.)
  hotels 563–4
  map 358–9
  restaurants 591–3
  travel 358
Massif des Maures **519**
Master of Cuixà 485
Master of the Loge de Mer 489
Master of Moulins 343, 361
Matilda, Queen 251, 257
  tomb 258
Matisse, Henri 70, 476
  *Blue Nude IV* 531
  Centre Pompidou (Paris) 77, 96
  Céret 486
  Chapelle du Rosaire (Vence) 527
  Collioure 487
  *Landscape at Collioure* 33
  Montparnasse (Paris) 143
  Musée d'Art Moderne de la Ville de Paris 114
  Musée Matisse (Nice) **531**
  Musée de l'Orangerie (Paris) 102
  Musée d'Orsay (Paris) 125
  St.-Tropez 520
  *Sorrow of the King* 96
Maugham, Somerset 35, 477, 532
Maupassant, Guy de 266
  grave 143
Mauriac, François 34
Mauroux
  hotels 567
Mayle, Peter 511
Mazarin, Cardinal 62, 63, 421
Media **628–9**
Médiathèque François Mitterrand (Poitiers) **417**
Mediterranean
  beaches in the South of France **478–9**
  A week in the Mediterranean 11, 17
*La Méduse* (Jawlensky) 385
Megaliths
  Brittany 283
Mégève 326, 377
  hotels 565
  restaurants 594
Melle **413**
Le Mémorial de l'Alsace-Moselle 233
Mémorial de Caen **258**
Le Mémorial du Souvenir (Dunkerque) 201
Ménasina 546
Mende
  hotels 563
Ménerbes 511
Ménez-Hom 276
Ménez-Meur 276
Menier family 303
Men's clothes stores **146**, 148
Menton 479, 522–3, **533**
  festivals 43
  restaurants 602
La Mère Catherine (Paris) 137
Mérimée, Prosper 524
Merovich, King 48
Merovingian dynasty 48, 54
Merson, Luc Olivier 138
Mesnil
  hotels 559
Mesnil-Saint-Père
  hotels 559
*Méthode champenoise* **214–15**
Métro systems 69, **640**
Metz 223, **227**
  hotels 558
  restaurants 582

Meuse River 211, 218
Michelangelo 61, 107
Micropolis (Saint Léons) 370–71
Mignard, Pierre 131
Milhaud, Darius 71
Millau
  hotels 564
  restaurants 592
Miller, Henry 439
Millet, Aimé 68, 338
Millet, Jean François 254
  *Spring at Barbizon* 185
Mimizan-Plage 428
Mimos (Périgueux) 42
Minerve **494**, 495
  restaurants 600
Mirabeau, Comte de 94
Mirepoix **467**
  hotels 568
  restaurants 598
Miró, Joan 77, 96, 118, 528
*Le Miroir d'Ornans* (Courbet) 355
*Miserere* (Rouault) 339
Mistinguett 79
Mistral, Frédéric 35, 477, 512
Mitterrand, François 25, 72
MM Park Museum (Strasbourg) 235
*Mobile on Two Planes* (Calder) 96
Modern France **72–3**
Modigliani, Amedeo 102, 143, 507, 529
  *Portrait of a Woman* 136
*La Modiste* (Toulouse-Lautrec) 448
Moillon, Isaac 350
Moirax 444
Moissac Abbey 399, 431, **446–7**
Moles, Arnaud de 445
Molière 35, 62, 94, 306, 496
Molitg-les-Bains
  hotels 569
Molsheim 233, 236
*Mona Lisa* (Leonardo da Vinci) 106
Monaco **534–5**
  festivals 40, 43
  hotels 570
  map 535
  restaurants 602
  royal family **535**
Monastère de la Grande Chartreuse 393
Monastic Realm **54–5**
  see also Abbeys
Monbazillac
  restaurants 597
Monet, Claude 476
  *Blue Waterlilies* 125
  Cathedral series 268, 269, **271**
  Giverny 14, 72, **270**
  *Harmony in Blue and Gold* 271
  Musée Marmottan Monet (Paris) **135**
  Musée de l'Orangerie (Paris) 102
  *Waterlilies* (*Nymphéas*) 102
Money **626–7**
Monflanquin 449
Monnaie de Paris 82
Mont Aigoual 329
Mont Aiguille 393
Mont Blanc 326, 327
Mont Louis 484
Mont Malgré Tout 218
Mont-de-Marsan 16, **429**
Mont-de-Marsan Feria 41
Mont-St.-Michel 14, 240, 251, **260–65**
  hotels 559
  restaurants 584
Mont Sainte-Odile 233
Mont Ventoux **506**

Montagne de Dun 352
Montaigne, Michel Eyquem de 35
Montand, Yves 529
  grave 139
Montauban **447**
  restaurants 597
Montbazon
  restaurants 587
Montbray, Bishop Geoffroi de 254
Montbron, Jacquette de 434
Montcontour, Château de 304
Monte-Carlo see Monaco
Monte-Carlo Rally 43
Monte Cinto 544
Monte Stello 540
Montélimar **390**
  hotels 565
Montfaucon
  restaurants 590
Montfort, Simon de 493, 494, 495
Monthermé 213, 218
Montier-en-Der 212
Montlouis sur Loire
  hotels 561
Montluçon **361**
  restaurants 592
Montmartre (Paris) **136–7**
Montmorency, Anne de 176, 208
Montmorillon **419**
  restaurants 595
Montoire-sur-le-Loir 310
Montparnasse (Paris) **143**
Montpellier 481, **498–9**
  hotels 569
  map 498
  restaurants 600
Montpellier-le-Vieux 371, 374
Montpoupon, Château de 301
Montrésor 13, **305**
Montreuil-Bellay **296**
Montreuil sur Mer 200
  hotels 556
  restaurants 580
Monts du Cantal 357, 359, **368**
Monts Dômes 357, **366**
Monts Dore 16, 357, **366**
Montsalvy
  restaurants 592
Montségur **467**, 495
  restaurants 598
Montsoreau
  restaurants 588
Monument aux Girondins (Bordeaux)
  425
Moore, Henry 118
Moreau, Gustave
  Musée Gustave Moreau (Paris) **135**
Morisot, Berthe 498
Morlaix
  hotels 560
Morny, Duc de 259
Morrison, Jim
  grave 139
Morvan 331, **342**
Morzine 326
  restaurants 594
Mosques
  Grande Mosquée de Paris **143**
Motorways **636–7**
Moulin, Château du 311
Moulin, Jean 71
Moulin Rouge (Paris) **138**
Moulin-à-Vent 381
Moulins **361**
  restaurants 592
Mountain sports **614**, 617
Moussey
  hotels 557

Moustiers-Ste.-Marie 519
  hotels 570
  restaurants 602
Moûtier-d'Ahun 328, 360–61
Moutiers 334
Mouton Rothschild, Château 427
Mucha, Alphonse 69, 489
Le MUDO – Musée de l'Oise (Beauvais)
  204–5
Muides sur Loire
  hotels 561
Mulhouse **229**
  hotels 558
Munich Conference (1938) 70
Murat
  restaurants 592
Murat, Caroline 112
Murato 541
Murol, Château de 364
Museums and galleries (general)
  admission charges 620
  opening hours 621
Museums and galleries (individual)
  Les Abattoirs (Toulouse) 450
  Alésia MuséoParc (Alise-Ste.-Reine)
    338
  Algoplus (Roscoff) 279
  Baptistère St.-Jean (Poitiers) **417**
  Bastide aux Violettes (Tourrettes-
    sur-Loup) 527
  La Boisserie (Colombey-les-Deux-
    Eglises) 221
  Bunker of Rochelle (La Rochelle) 420
  CAPC Musée d'Art Contemporain
    (Bordeaux) 425, **426**
  Caumont Centre d'Art (Aix-en-
    Provence) 515
  Centre de Création Contemporain
    Olivier Debré (Tours) 301
  Centre Guillaume-le-Conquérant-
    Tapisserie de Bayeux 257
  Centre International du Vitrail
    (Chartres) 311
  Centre Pompidou (Paris) 12, 72, 77,
    84, **96–7**
  Centre Pompidou Metz **227**
  Le Château-Musée (Dieppe) 267
  Château de Pierrefonds 205
  Cinémathèque Française (Paris) 139
  Citadelle Souterraine (Verdun) 226
  Cité de l'Architecture et du
    Patrimoine (Paris) 115
  Cité de l'Automobile (Mulhouse) 229
  Cité de la Dentelle et de la Mode
    (Calais) 201
  Cité Internationale de la Tapisserie
    (Aubusson) 360
  Cité Nationale de l'Histoire de
    l'Immigration (Paris) **142**
  La Cité de la Préhistoire (The
    Ardèche) 389
  Cité des Sciences et de l'Industrie
    (Paris) **140–41**
  Cité du Vin (Bordeaux) **426**
  Cité du Vitrail (Troyes) **220**
  Clos-Lucé (Amboise) 305
  Collection Lambert (Avignon) 507
  La Coupole (St.-Omer) 201
  Ecomusée d'Alsace (Ungersheim) 229
  Ecomusée Marquèze 429
  Ecomusée du Niou (Niou Uhella) 276
  Ecomusée du Pays de Rennes 289
  Espace Dalí Paris 136
  Espace Mendès France (Poitiers) **417**
  Espace Vignolis – Musée de l'Olivier
    (Nyons) 390
  L'Estran-La Cité de la Mer (Dieppe)
    267

Museums and galleries (individual)
  (cont.)
  Ferme d'Antéa (Brasparts) 276
  Ferme-Musée du Cotentin (Ste.-
    Mère-Eglise) 254
  Ferme-Musée de la Forêt (Bourg-en-
    Bresse) 380
  Fondation Bemberg (Toulouse) **451**
  Fondation Claude Monet (Giverny)
    270
  Fondation Louis Vuitton (Paris) 72–3,
    **134**
  Fondation Maeght (St.-Paul de Vence)
    **528**
  Galerie David d'Angers (Angers) 295
  Galerie Nationale du Jeu de Paume
    (Paris) **102**
  Grand Palais (Paris) 81, 110, **112–13**
  Greniers à Sel (Honfleur) 266
  Historial Jeanne d'Arc (Rouen) **268**
  Hôtel Sandelin (St.-Omer) 201
  Hôtel de Soubise (Paris) **94**
  Hôtel de Vergeur Museum (Reims)
    **214**
  Institut du Monde Arabe (Paris) **143**
  Lieu d'Art et d'Action Contemporaine
    (Dunkerque) 201
  Le Magasin (Grenoble) 392, 393
  Maison des Canuts (Lyon) 385
  Maison de Jeanne d'Arc (Orléans) 316
  Maison des Johnnies (Roscoff) 279
  Maison de Jules Verne (Amiens) 204
  Maison Musée du Pouldu (Le Pouldu)
    279
  Maison de Pierre Loti (Rochefort) 421
  Maison de Radio France (Paris) 80
  Maison de Victor Hugo (Paris) 93, **95**
  Les Maisons Satie (Honfleur) 266
  Manufacture Nationale de la
    Tapisserie (Beauvais) 205
  Mémorial de Caen **258**
  Mémorial Charles de Gaulle
    (Colombey-les-Deux-Eglises) 221
  Le Mémorial du Souvenir
    (Dunkerque) 201
  Micropolis (Saint Léons) 370–71
  MM Park Museum (Strasbourg) 235
  Le MUDO – Musée de l'Oise
    (Beauvais) 204–5
  Musée des 24 Heures du Mans (Le
    Mans) 295
  Musée Africain (Ile d'Aix) 421
  Musée d'Agesci (Niort) 413
  Musée Airborne (Ste-Mère-Eglise)
    254
  Musée Alsacien (Strasbourg) **235**
  Musée de l'Ancien Evêché (Evreux)
    270
  Musée de l'Ancien Evêché (Grenoble)
    392, 393
  Musée Angladon (Avignon) 507
  Musée Animé du Vin (Chinon) 298,
    299
  Musée de l'Annonciade (St.-Tropez)
    520
  Musée d'Aquitaine (Bordeaux) **426**
  Musée d'Archéologie (Antibes) 525
  Musée d'Archéologie (Narbonne)
    491
  Musée d'Archéologie Nationale
    (St.-Germain-en-Laye) 177
  Musée Archéologique (Dijon) **346**
  Musée Archéologique (St.-Romain-
    en-Gal) 386–7
  Musée Archéologique Grenoble
    Saint-Laurent (Grenoble) 392
  Musée de l'Armagnac (Condom) 444
  Musée de l'Armée (Paris) **118**

Museums and galleries (individual) (cont.)

Musée d'Art & Archéologie (Cluny) 349

Musée d'Art et d'Archéologie (Senlis) 208

Musée d'Art et d'Archéologie du Périgord (Périgueux) 435

Musée d'Art Contemporain (Lyon) 385

Musée d'Art et d'Histoire (Avranches) 256

Musée d'Art et d'Histoire (Narbonne) 491

Musée d'Art et d'Histoire du Judaïsme (Paris) **94**

Musée d'Art et d'Histoire d'Orange **506**

Musée d'Art Hyacinthe Rigaud (Perpignan) **489**

Musée d'Art et d'Industrie (St.-Étienne) 387

Musée d'Art Moderne (Céret) 486

Musée d'Art Moderne (St.-Étienne) 387

Musée d'Art Moderne (Troyes) **220**

Musée d'Art Moderne et d'Art Contemporain (Nice) **531**

Musée d'Art Moderne, d'Art Contemporain et d'Art Brut (Lille) **202**

Musée d'Art Moderne et Contemporain (Cordes-sur-Ciel) 448

Musée d'Art Moderne et Contemporain (Strasbourg) **235**

Musée d'Art Moderne Richard Anacréon (Granville) 255

Musée d'Art Moderne de la Ville de Paris **114**

Musée d'Art de Toulon 517

Musée des Arts Asiatiques (Nice) **531**

Musée des Arts Décoratifs (Bordeaux) **426**

Musée des Arts Décoratifs (Lyon) 384, 385

Musée des Arts Décoratifs (Paris) **103**

Musée des Arts et Traditions Populaires (Champlitte) 354

Musée des Arts et Traditions Populaires Catalans (Perpignan) **489**

Musée des Augustins (Toulouse) **451**

Musée de l'Avallonnais (Avallon) 339

Musée Bargoin (Clermont-Ferrand) 364

Musée Bartholdi (Colmar) 231

Musée Basque (Bayonne) 456

Musée de Bastia 540

Musée des Beaux-Arts (Ajaccio) 546

Musée des Beaux-Arts (Arras) 203

Musée des Beaux-Arts (Blois) 308

Musée des Beaux-Arts (Bordeaux) **426**

Musée des Beaux-Arts (Caen) 258

Musée des Beaux-Arts (Calais) 200

Musée des Beaux-Arts (Dijon) 331, 344, **346**

Musée des Beaux-Arts (Lyon) 384, **385**

Musée des Beaux-Arts (Marseille) **516**

Musée des Beaux-Arts (Menton) 533

Musée des Beaux-Arts (Nancy) **228**

Musée des Beaux-Arts (Nice) **531**

Musée des Beaux-Arts (Nîmes) **501**

Musée des Beaux-Arts (Orléans) 316

Musée des Beaux-Arts (Pau) 462

Musée des Beaux-Arts (Quimper) **278**

Musée des Beaux-Arts (Reims) 214

Musée des Beaux-Arts (Rennes) **289**

Museums and galleries (individual) (cont.)

Musée des Beaux-Arts (Rouen) **269**

Musée des Beaux-Arts (Tours) 301

Musée des Beaux-Arts et d'Archéologie (Besançon) 354

Musée des Beaux-Arts et d'Archéologie (Vienne) 386

Musée des Beaux-Arts de Limoges 360

Musée des Beaux-Arts de la Ville de Paris 112–13

Musée Bigouden (Pont l'Abbé) 277

Musée du Biterrois (Béziers) 494

Musée des Blindés (Saumur) 296

Musée Bonnat-Helleu (Bayonne) 456

Musée de Bretagne (Rennes) **289**

Musée Calvet (Avignon) 507

Musée Cantini (Marseille) 516

Musée Carnavalet (Paris) 92, **95**

Musée de la Castre (Cannes) 524

Musée de la Céramique (Rouen) **269**

Musée du Château (Sedan) 219

Musée du Château de Rohan-Pontivy (Saverne) 237

Musée du Cheval (Chantilly) 209

Musée Christian Dior (Granville) 255

Musée de la Civilisation Gallo-Romaine (Lyon) 382

Musée des Civilisations de l'Europe et de la Méditerranée (Marseille) **517**

Musée du Cloître de Notre-Dame-en-Vaux (Châlons-en-Champagne) 220

Musée de Cluny (Paris) 12, **126–7**, 128

Musée Cognacq-Jay (Paris) 92

Musée Colette (St.-Sauveur) 334

Musée du Compagnonnage (Tours) 301

Musée Comtois (Besançon) 354

Musée Condé (Chantilly) 209

Musée des Confluences (Lyon) 384, 385

Musée de la Correrie (St.-Pierre-de-Chartreuse) 393

Musée de la Corse (Corte) 544

Musée de la Cour d'Or (Metz) **227**

Musée Courbet (Ornans) 355

Musée de la Coutellerie (Thiers) 363

Musée Crozatier (Le Puy-en-Velay) 369

Musée Dapper (Paris) **114**

Musée Dauphinois (Grenoble) 392

Musée Départemental Breton (Quimper) **278**

Musée Départemental de la Préhistoire et d'Archéologie (Sartène) 547

Musée Despiau-Wlérick (Mont-de-Marsan) 429

Musée des Docks Romains (Marseille) 516

Musée de l'Ecole de Nancy **228**

Musée de l'Ecole Rurale (Trégarvan) 276

Musée d'Ethnographie et d'Art Populaire Normand (Honfleur) 266

Musée Eugène Boudin (Honfleur) 266

Musée Eugène Delacroix (Paris) 123, **126**

Musée Fabre (Montpellier) 498

Musée Fauré (Aix-les-Bains) 394

Musée Flaubert (Rouen) **269**

Musée Français du Chemin de Fer (Mulhouse) 229

Musée Galliera (Paris) **114**

Musée Goya – Musée d'Art Hispanique (Castres) 448

Musée Granet (Aix-en-Provence) 515

Museums and galleries (individual) (cont.)

Musée de Grenoble 392

Musée Greuze (Tournus) 349

Musée Grevin (Paris) **101**

Musée Gustave Moreau (Paris) **135**

Musée de la Halle Saint Pierre (Paris) 137

Musée du Hiéron (Paray-le-Monial) 349

Musée d'Histoire (Belfort) 355

Musée d'Histoire (Nantes) 294

Musée d'Histoire (Vannes) 284

Musée d'Histoire Locale (St.-Paul de Vence) 528

Musée de l'Histoire Maritime (St.-Tropez) 520

Musée d'Histoire de Marseille 516

Musée d'Histoire Naturelle (Cherbourg) 254

Musée d'Histoire Naturelle (Rouen) **269**

Musée Historique (Mulhouse) 229

Musée Historique (Strasbourg) **235**

Musée Historique Lorraine (Nancy) **228**

Musée Historique de Lyon 383

Musée de l'Homme (Paris) 115

Musée de l'Hospice Comtesse (Lille) **202**

Musée de l'Huître, du Coquillage et de la Mer (Cancale) 287

Musée de l'Impression sur Etoffes (Mulhouse) 229

Musée des Impressionismes (Giverny) 270

Musée de l'Imprimerie (Lyon) 384, 385

Musée Ingres (Montauban) 447

Musée Internationale de la Parfumerie (Grasse) 521

Musée Jean Calvin (Noyon) 205

Musée Jean Cocteau Collection Séverin Wunderman (Menton) 533

Musée Jean Couty (Lyon) 385

Musée Jean Lurçat (Angers) 295

Musée Lapidaire (Avignon) 507

Musée Lapidaire (Carcassonne) 493

Musée Lapidaire (Narbonne) 491

Musée Lapidaire (Vienne) 386

Musée Ledoux Lieu du Sel (Arc-et-Senans) 354

Musée de la Libération (Cherbourg) 254

Musée du Louvre (Paris) 12, 22, 66, 82, **104–7**

Musée Magnin (Dijon) 345

Musée Maillol (Paris) **119**

Musée Malraux (Le Havre) 266

Musée des Manuscrits du Mont-St.-Michel (Avranches) 256

Musée des Marionettes du Monde (Lyon) 383

Musée Marmottan Monet (Paris) **135**

Musée Massey (Pau) 462

Musée Matisse (Nice) **531**

Musée Mémoire 1939–1945 (Calais) 201

Musée Mémorial de la Bataille de Normandie (Bayeux) 257

Musée-Mémorial de Fleury 226

Musée de la Mer (Sète) 496

Musée de la Mine (Ronchamp) 355

Musée des Minéraux et de la Faune des Alpes (Le Bourg d'Oisans) 391

Musée de Montmartre (Paris) 136

Musée Municipal (Bergues) 202

Museums and galleries (individual) (cont.)
Musée Municipal des Beaux-Arts (Agen) 444
Musée Municipal Frédéric Blandin (Nevers) 343
Musée Napoleonién (Ile d'Aix ) 421
Musée National Adrien-Dubouché (Limoges) 360
Musée National Fernand Léger (Biot) 526
Musée National d'Histoire Naturelle (Paris) **142**
Musée National de la Maison Bonaparte (Ajaccio) 546
Musée National Marc Chagall (Nice) **530**
Musée National de la Marine (Paris) 115
Musée National de la Marine (Rochefort) 421
Musée National de la Marine (Toulon) 517
Musée National Picasso (Vallauris) 526
Musée National de Préhistoire (Les Eyzies) 438, 439
Musée National de la Renaissance **176**
Musée National du Sport (Nice) **531**
Musée de Normandie (Caen) 258
Musée du Nouveau Monde (La Rochelle) 420
Musée du Noyonnais (Noyon) 205
Musée Océanographique (Monaco) **535**
Musée de l'Oeuvre Notre-Dame (Strasbourg) **235**
Musée de l'Opéra (Paris) 101
Musée de l'Oppidum d'Ensérune 494
Musée de l'Orangerie (Paris) 82, **102**
Musée d'Orsay (Paris) 12, 76, 82, **124–5**
Musée du Pays du Châtillonnais (Châtillon-sur-Seine) 338
Musée de la Pêche (Concarneau) 278
Musée du Petit Lourdes (Lourdes) 463
Musée du Petit Palais (Avignon) 507
Musée des Phares et Balises (Phare du Créac'h) 276
Musée de Picardie (Amiens) 204
Musée Picasso (Antibes) 525
Musée Picasso (Paris) 92, **94–5**
Musée Pompon (Saulieu) 342
Musée de Pont-Aven 279
Musée Portuaire (Dunkerque) 201
Musée de Préhistoire (Carnac) 282
Musée Pyrénéen (Lourdes) 463
Musée du Quai Branly (Paris) **116**
Musée Réattu (Arles) 512
Musée de la Reddition (Reims) **214**
Musée Régional des Arts et Traditions Populaires (Nancy) **228**
Musée Régional du Cidre et du Calvados (Valognes) 254
Musée Renoir (Cagnes-sur-Mer) 526–7
Musée de la Résistance (Morvan) 342
Musée de la Résistance et de la Déportation (Grenoble) 392, 393
Musée de la Résistance et de la Déportation (Limoges) 360
Musée Rimbaud (Charleville-Mézières) 218
Musée Rodin (Paris) **119**
Musée Rolin (Autun) 343
Musée de la Romanité (Narbonne) 491
Musée Sainte-Croix (Poitiers) **417**

Museums and galleries (individual) (cont.)
Musée St.-Germain (Auxerre) 335
Musée St.-Remi (Reims) **215**
Musée de Savon (Marseille) 516
Musée Le Secq des Tournelles (Rouen) **269**
Musée Sobirats (Carpentras) 510
Musée Soulages (Rodez) 370, 371
Musée du Tabac (Bergerac) 438
Le Musée de la Tapisserie Contemporaine (Angers) 295
Musée du Temps (Besançon) 354
Musée Thomas-Henry (Cherbourg) 254
Musée des Tissus (Lyon) 384, 385
Musée Toulouse-Lautrec (Albi) 448
Musée d'Unterlinden (Colmar) 231
Musée des Ursulines (Mâcon) 352
Musée de Valence 388
Musée Vauban (Neuf-Brisach) 231
Musée de la Vénerie (Senlis) 208
Musée du Vieux Monaco **535**
Musée du Vin de Bourgogne (Beaune) 348
Musée Wagon de l'Armistice (Compiègne) 205
Musée Yves Brayer (Les Baux-de-Provence) 511
Les Musées de Sens 334
Museon Arlaten (Arles) 512
Muséum d'Histoire Naturelle (La Rochelle) 420
Nouveau Musée National de Monaco **535**
Palais des Beaux-Arts (Lille) **202**
Palais Bénédictine (Fécamp) 266–7
Palais de Chaillot (Paris) 80
Palais de la Découverte (Paris) 113
Petit Palais (Paris) 81, 111, **112–13**
Le Port Musée (Port du Rosmeur) 277
Samara 203
Sèvres: Cité de la Céramique **182**
Villa Ephrussi de Rothschild (St-Jean-Cap-Ferrat) 532
Villa Masséna (Nice) **530**
Villa-Musée Fragonard (Grasse) 521
Music **610**, 611
Breton 247
classical music **154–5**, 157
festivals 40–43
rock, jazz and world music **155**, 157
Musica (Strasbourg) 42
Muslims
Grande Mosquée de Paris **143**

## N

Nancy 223, **228**
festivals 42, 43
hotels 558
restaurants 582
Nantes 291, **294**
festivals 41, 42
hotels 562
restaurants 588
Nantes, Edict of (1598) 61, 63, 294
Napoleon I, Emperor 47, 49, **66–7**, 421, 458
Ajaccio 546
Arc de Triomphe (Paris) 111
Arc de Triomphe du Carrousel (Paris) 103, 104
Château de Malmaison 177
Château de Pierrefonds 205
Cimetière du Père-Lachaise (Paris) 139
Colonne de la Grande Armée 200

Napoleon I, Emperor (cont.)
Compiègne 205
coronation 90, 107
Corsica 537
Ecole Militaire (Paris) 116
Fontainebleau 184
Hôtel de Soubise (Paris) 94
Ile d'Aix 421
Musée de l'Armée (Paris) 118
Musée du Château (Sedan) 219
Panthéon (Paris) 129
St.-Raphaël 521
La Sorbonne (Paris) 127
tomb 81, 119
Toulon 517
Versailles 180
Napoleon II 67
Napoleon III, Emperor 49, 66, 67, 338
Ajaccio 546
Bois de Boulogne (Paris) 134
Bourges 317
Château de Pierrefonds 13, 205
Château de Sedan 218
Compiègne 197, 205
Jeu de Paume (Paris) 102
Musée d'Archéologie Nationale (St.-Germain-en-Laye) 177
Nice 531
Opéra National de Paris Garnier (Paris) 69, 101
Vichy 362
Narbonne 15, **490–91**
hotels 569
restaurants 600
National Front 73
National parks 625
des Ecrins 391
Mercantour 533
Pyrenees **464–5**
Vanoise 327
NATO 71
Natoire, Charles-Joseph 94
Natural hazards 625
Naturism **615**, 617
Nausicaa (Boulogne) 200
Nebbio 541
Nelson, Admiral Lord 541
Neo-Impressionism 32
Nero, Emperor 89, 520
Nerra, Foulques 299, 305
Neuf-Brisach **230–31**
map 230
Neuilly-sur-Seine
restaurants 579
Nevers 37, **342–3**
hotels 563
restaurants 590
New Realism **477**
New Year's Day 43
Newspapers **629**
Niaux 407
Nice 17, 479, 502, **530–31**
hotels 570
map 531
restaurants 602
Nice Carnival and the Battle of Flowers 43
Nice Jazz Festival 41
Niedersteinbach
restaurants 582
Nietzsche, Friedrich 477
Nijinsky, Vaslav 101
grave 138
Nîmes 15, 53, 481, **500–501**
hotels 569
map 500–501
restaurants 600
Nîmes Feria 41

Nîmes-le-Vieux 371
The Niolo (Niolu) **544**
Niort **413**
  restaurants 595
Nitry
  hotels 563
  restaurants 590
Nocret, Jean
  *The Sun King and his Family* 62–3
Nogent-sur-Seine
  restaurants 581
Noguchi, Isamu 118
Noirmoitier en l'Ile
  hotels 562
Nominoë, Duke of Brittany 284
Nonza 540
Le Nord and Picardy **197–209**
  climate 45
  hotels 556–7
  food and drink **190**
  map 198–9
  restaurants 579–80
  travel 199
Normandy **251–71**
  apples and cider **259**
  climate 44
  D-Day landings 14, **255**
  The flavors of Western France **242**
  hotels 559–60
  map 252–3
  restaurants 583–5
  travel 253
Normans 55
Northeast France **187–237**
  Alsace and Lorraine **223–37**
  The Battle of the Somme **194–5**
  Champagne **211–21**
  food and drink **190–91**
  France's wine regions: Champagne
    **192–3**
  map 188–9
  Le Nord and Picardy **197–209**
  Northern France, a week in 10, 14
Nostradamus 511
Notre-Dame (Paris) 12, 77, 83, 87, **90–91**
Notre-Dame-la-Grande (Poitiers) 399,
  **416**
Nouveau Musée National de Monaco
  **535**
Nouveaux Réalistes **477**
Nouvel, Jean
  Institut du Monde Arabe (Paris) 143
  Montpellier 498
  Musée du Quai Branly (Paris) 116
  Opéra de Lyon 384
  Philharmonie de Paris 139
Novelists **34**
Noyon 13, 197, **205**
Nuits-St.-Georges
  restaurants 590
Nyons **390–91**

**O**

O, Château d' 259
Obernai **233**, 236
  hotels 558
  restaurants 582
Observatoire Pic du Midi de Bigorre
  463
Océanopolis (Brest) 276
Odeillo 484
Odile, St 233
Odo, Bishop of Bayeux 257
Odo, Count of Paris 48
Offenbach, Jacques
  grave 138
Oiron, Château d' 412
Olargues 497

Oletta 537, 541
Oloron-Ste.-Marie **459**
  festivals 41
Olympic Games, Paris (1924) 70
Omaha Beach 14, 255
Onzain
  hotels 562
  restaurants 588
Opening hours 621
  banks 626
  stores 144, 604
Opéra National de Paris Bastille (Paris)
  95
Opéra National de Paris Garnier (Paris)
  68–9, 98, 100, **101**
Opéra Quarter (Paris) 100–101
Operation Overlord **255**, 256
Oradour-sur-Glane 360
Orange 15, 503, **506**
Orcival **365**
  hotels 564
Orléans 291, **316–17**
  festivals 40
  hotels 562
  map 316
  restaurants 588
Orléans, Dukes of 103
Ornans **354–5**
Orthez **458**
  hotels 568
Ossuaire de Douaumont 226
Otéro, La Belle 524
Othoniel, Jean-Michel 423
Ouches
  restaurants 594
Outdoor activities **612–17**
Oysters
  Cancale 287

**P**

Pablo Casals Festival (Prades) 41
Pagnol, Marcel 477, 503
Paimpol 282
  restaurants 586
Paimpont 285
Palais Abbatial de St.-Germain-des-Prés
  (Paris) 123
Palais des Archevêques (Narbonne)
  490–91
Palais des Beaux-Arts (Lille) **202**
Palais Bénédictine (Fécamp) 266–7
Palais de Chaillot (Paris) 80, **114–15**
Palais de la Découverte (Paris) 113
Palais des Ducs (Dijon) 344, 347
Palais de l'Elysée (Paris) **112**
Palais Idéal du Facteur Cheval **387**
Palais de Justice (Paris) 86, **88**
Palais de Justice (Poitiers) **416**
Palais Lascaris (Nice) **530–31**
Palais du Luxembourg (Paris) 130, **131**
Palais des Papes (Avignon) 15, 507,
  **508–9**
Palais du Parlement de Bretagne
  (Rennes) **288**
Palais Princier (Monaco) **534–5**
Palais Rohan (Strasbourg) **234**
Palais des Rois de Majorque
  (Perpignan) 488, **489**
Palais Royal (Paris) 64, **103**
Palais du Tau (Reims) **217**
Palais de Tokyo (Paris) 80
Palmer, Château 427
Palombaggia 547
Panthéon (Paris) 12, **129**
Paoli, Pasquale 537, 541, 544
Parade of Lavender Floats (Digne) 42
Paray-le-Monial **349**
Parc Astérix **209**

Parc Européen du Volcanisme 366
Parc National des Ecrins 391
Parc National des Pyrénées **464–5**
Parc National du Mercantour 533
Parc National de la Vanoise 327
Parc Naturel de la Montagne de Reims
  212
Parc Naturel Régional d'Armorique 273,
  **276**
Parc Naturel Régional du Haut
  Languedoc **497**
Parc Naturel Régional de Normandie-
  Maine **259**
Parc des Oiseaux (Villars-les-Dombes)
  380
Parc Ornithologique du Teich 428
Parc Pierre et Lumière (Saumur) 296
Parc Régional de Lorraine 227
Parc Régional du Queyras 327, 391
*Pardons* 247
Paris **75–173**
  airports **630**
  Champs-Elysées and Invalides
    **109–19**
  climate 44
  entertainment **154–7**
  festivals 40–43
  French Revolution 64–5
  Farther afield **133–43**
  hotels 554–5
  Ile de la Cité, Marais and Beaubourg
    **85–97**
  The Left Bank **121–31**
  restaurants 576–9
  A river view of Paris **79–83**
  stores and markets **144–53**
  Street Finder 158–73
  travel in **640–41**
  Tuileries and Opéra **99–107**
  Two days in Paris 12
Paris Carnaval 43
Paris Commune 68
Paris-Plage 41
Parish closes **280–81**
Parking **638**
Parks and gardens
  Bois de Boulogne (Paris) **134**
  Château de Chantilly 208
  Château de Fontainebleau 184
  Château de Sceaux 182
  Château de Vaux-le-Vicomte 183
  Château de Villandry 13, **300**
  Giverny 14, 72, **270**
  Jardin Botanique de la Villa Thuret
    (Antibes) 525
  Jardin du Carrousel (Paris) 104
  Jardin Exotique (Eze) 533
  Jardin Exotique (Monaco) **535**
  Jardin du Luxembourg (Paris) 130
  Jardin Massey (Pau) 462
  Jardin des Plantes (Avranches) 256
  Jardin des Plantes (Montpellier) 499
  Jardin des Plantes (Paris) **142**
  Jardin des Prés Fichaux (Bourges) 317
  Jardin des Tuileries (Paris) 12, 82,
    **102–3**
  Jardin Wilson (Montluçon) 361
  Jardins des Champs-Elysées (Paris) 111
  Les Jardins de la Fontaine (Nîmes)
    **500–501**
  Jardins du Trocadéro (Paris) **114**
  Parc André Citroën (Paris) **143**
  Parc des Buttes-Chaumont (Paris) **139**
  Parc du Champ-de-Mars (Paris) 108,
    **116**
  Parc Emmanuel Llais (Cherbourg) 254
  Parc du Golfe (Vannes) 284
  Parc Monceau (Paris) **135**

Parks and gardens (cont.)
Parc Montsouris (Paris) **142**
Parc des Sources (Vichy) 362
Parc de la Villette (Paris) **138–9**
Versailles 178
Parthenay 409, **412**
Pas de Peyrol 368
Pas de Souci 374
Pascal, Blaise 35, 93
tomb 127
Les Passages (Paris) **101**
Passerelle des Arts (Paris) 82
Passports 620
Pasteur, Louis 68, 353
Patrimonio 541
Pau 15, 453, **462**
hotels 568
restaurants 598
Pauillac 16, **427**
hotels 566
restaurants 595
Pays d'Auge 14, 251, 252, **259**
Pays Bigouden 273, **277**
Pech-Merle 407
Pei, I M 105
Peigney
hotels 557
Peille 533
Peillon 533
Pellevé, Cardinal de 89
Pelouze, Madame 302, 303
Pepin, King 54
Pépin the Short, King of the Franks
48
Perfume **521**, **605**, 607
shopping **149**
Pérignon, Dom 192
Périgord, Quercy, and Gascony
**431–51**
climate 44
food and drink **400–401**
hotels 566–8
map 432–3
restaurants 596–8
travel 432
A wine and food tour of Burgundy,
Périgord and Bordeaux 11, 16
Périgueux 16, **435**
festivals 42
restaurants 597
Pero 546
Pérouges **380**
hotels 565
Perpignan **488–9**
hotels 569
restaurants 600
Perrault, Charles 299
Perrault, Claude 105
Perret, Auguste 266
Personal security **624–5**
Pétain, Marshal 69, 71
Peter II, King of Aragon 495
Petit Palais (Paris) 81, 111,
**112–13**
Petrarch 35, 508, 510
Petrol **636**
Peugeot 68
Peyreleau
hotels 564
Peyrepertuse 490, 495
Pézenas **496**
hotels 569
restaurants 600
Phare de Cordouan (Royan) 422
Pharmacies **625**
Philibert, Duke of Savoy 380
Philibert, St 348
Philip Augustus, King 49, 56, 57

Philip the Bold, Duke of Burgundy 346,
347, 492
tomb 347
Philip the Fair, King 57
Philip the Good, Duke of Burgundy 347
Philippe I, King 48
Philippe II, King 495
Philippe III, King 49
Philippe IV the Fair, King 49, 508
Philippe V, King 49
Philippe VI, King 49, 58
Philippe-Auguste, King 104, 105
Philosophers **35**
Phoebus, Gaston 462, 467
Phrase book 671–2
Piaf, Edith 71
Piana 545
hotels 571
Piano, Renzo 96, 97, 385
Pic d'Anie 459, 464
Pic du Midi d'Ossau 464
Picabia, Francis 71, 444
Picardy see Le Nord and Picardy
Picasso, Pablo 70, 136
Les Abattoirs (Toulouse) 450
Centre Pompidou (Paris) 77, 96
*Deux Femmes Courant sur la Plage* 477
*The Goat* 525
Montparnasse (Paris) 143
Musée d'Art Hyacinthe Rigaud
(Perpignan) 489
Musée d'Art Moderne (Céret) 486
Musée des Beaux-Arts (Rennes) 289
Musée de l'Orangerie (Paris) 102
Musée Picasso (Antibes) 525
Musée Picasso (Paris) 92, **94–5**
Musée Réattu (Arles) 512
St.-Paul de Vence 528, 529
South of France 476, **477**
UNESCO (Paris) 118
Vallauris 526
*Woman Reading* 94
Picaud (monk) 404
Picnics 575
*The Pier and Promenade at Nice* (Dufy)
33
Pierre II, Duke of Bourbon 361
Pierreclos, Château de 352
Pierrefonds, Château de 13, 196,
**205**
Pilgrimages
Lourdes 462–3
*ostensions* **363**
The road to Compostela **404–5**
Rocamadour **440–41**
St.-Jean-Pied-de-Port 458
Pinarello 547
Pino 540
Pissarro, Camille 135, 266
Place de la Bastille (Paris) **95**
Place de la Bourse (Bordeaux) 424
Place de la Concorde (Paris) 12, **102**
Place de l'Opéra (Paris) 101
Place St.-Sulpice (Paris) 130
Place du Tertre (Paris) 136
Place Vendôme (Paris) **102**
Place des Vosges (Paris) 12, 93, **95**
Planetariums
Cité des Sciences et de l'Industrie
(Paris) 140
Plantagenet, Geoffrey 298
Plantagenets **298**, 409
Plessis-Bourré, Château du 295
Pleven
hotels 560
Plomb du Cantal 368
Plomodiern
restaurants 586

Ploubalay
restaurants 586
Ploubazlanec
hotels 560
Poets **35**
Point Sublime 374, 519
Point Zéro (Paris) 86
Pointe de la Fumée 408
Pointe du Raz 248, 272, **277**
Pointe de la Torche 277
Poitiers 409, **416–17**
hotels 566
map 417
restaurants 595
Poitiers, Battle of (732) 54
Poitiers, Battle of (1356) 58, 418
Poitou and Aquitaine **409–29**
climate 44
food and drink **400**
hotels 565–6
map 410–11
restaurants 594–6
travel 410
Poix-de-Picardie
restaurants 580
Police **624**
Politics **25**
Pollock, Jackson 96
Pompadour, Madame de 64
baptism 94
Ecole Militaire (Paris) 116
Palais de l'Elysée (Paris) 112
Sèvres 182
Pompey 466
Pompidou, Georges 72
Pompon, François 342, 385
Poncé 311
Poncé-sur-le-Loir 311
Pont Alexandre III (Paris) 81, 111, **113**
Pont d'Arc 389
Pont de l'Arche
hotels 559
Pont de l'Artuby 519
Pont Audemer
hotels 559
Pont-Aven **279**
Pont-Aven School 278, 279, 289
Pont Bir-Hakeim (Paris) 80
Pont de la Concorde (Paris) 80, 82
Pont l'Eveque
restaurants 584
Pont du Gard 15, 470, 481, **498–9**
Pont de Grenelle (Paris) 80
Pont du Guetin 343
Pont Neuf (Paris) 12, **87**
Pont-en-Royans 379, 393
Pont-Sainte-Marie
restaurants 581
Pont Saint-Pierre
restaurants 584
Pont de Sully (Paris) 82
Pont Valentré 443
Popes, Avignon **508**
Popular Front 70
Porquerolles 519
Port Bacarès 491
Port-Blanc 282
Port Camargue
restaurants 600
Port-Clos 282
Port-Cros 519
Port-Grimaud 520
Port Lesney
restaurants 590
Port Leucate 491
Le Port Musée (Port du Rosmeur)
277
Port du Rosmeur 277

Port Vendres 486
  restaurants 600
Portes d'Enfer 419
Porto-Vecchio 547
  hotels 571
  restaurants 603
*Portrait of the Journalist Sylvia von Harden* (Dix) 97
*Portrait of a Woman* (Modigliani) 136
Postal services **629**
Pot, Philippe
  tomb 106
Pottery *see* Ceramics
Pound, Ezra 126
Poussin, Nicolas 546
Prades 329
  festivals 41
Pradier, James 119
Prehistoric France **50–51**
  Angles-sur-l'Anglin 418
  Bagneux 296
  Brittany's Prehistoric monuments **283**
  Carnac 50, 240, **282**, 283
  cave art 406, **407**
  Filitosa **546–7**
  Grotte de Niaux 467
  Grotte de Pech-Merle 442, 443
  Lascaux 50, 51, **438**
  Les Eyzies **438–9**
  Roquepertuse 51
  Tumulus de Bougon 413
Preminger, Otto 305
Presqu'île de Quiberon **282**
Prieuré de Serrabone **485**
Primaticcio 338
Le Printemp des Arts (Nantes) 41
Prix de l'Arc de Triomphe (Longchamps) 42
Procession de la Sanch (Perpignan) **488**
Propaganda, World War I 195
Proust, Marcel 34, 69, 259
Provençal writers **477**
Provence and the Côte d'Azur 471, 478–9, **503–35**
  climate 45
  food and drink **472–3**
  hotels 569–71
  map 504–5
  restaurants 601–3
  travel 505
Provins **183**
  restaurants 579
Public events **615**
Public holidays 43
Puget, Pierre 107, 516
Pujaudan
  restaurants 597
Pujols
  restaurants 597
Puligny-Montrachet
  restaurants 590
Pulliat, Victor 381
Puy de Dôme 366
Puy du Fou Pageant 41
Puy Mary 359, 368
Puy de Sancy 366
Puyguilhem, Château de 434
The Pyrenees 28, **453–67**
  climate 44
  food and drink **401**
  hotels 568–9
  map 454–5
  Parc National des Pyrénées **464–5**
  restaurants 598–9
  travel 454
  wildlife **464–5**

Q
Quai Voltaire (Paris) **123**
Quarre les Tombes
  restaurants 590
Quercy *see* Périgord, Quercy and Gascony
Quéribus 490
Quiberon **282**
  hotels 560
Quimper 273, **278**
  hotels 560
  restaurants 586

R
Rabelais, François 34, 60, **299**
  birthplace 299
  Poitiers 416
  Vouvray 304
Racine, Jean 35, 62, 63
  tomb 127
Radio **629**
*The Raft of the Medusa* (Géricault) 106
Railroads *see* Trains
Rainfall 44–5
Rainier III, King of Monaco 73, 535
Ramatuelle 520
Rambouillet, Château de **182**
  restaurants 579
Raphael 61, 106, 388
Ratilly, Château de 334
Ravaillac, François 87
Ravel, Maurice 457
Ravy, Jean 91
Raysse, Martial 477, 501
Réattu, Jacques 512
Récamier, Madame 67
Reichelt (stuntman) 117
Reims 13, 14, 211, **214–17**
  Cathedral 13, 14, 36, 210, 211, 214, **216–17**
  hotels 557
  restaurants 581
Reinach, Theodore 532
Religion
  The Auvergne's Black Madonnas **369**
  The Avignon Popes **508**
  Cathars **495**
  *pardons* 247
  pilgrimages and *ostensions* **363**
  religious persecution **493**
Rembrandt 106, 456
Remembrance Day 43
Remi, St. 214, 215
Renaissance France 47, **60–61**
  Court life in the Renaissance **297**
Les Rendezvous de l'Erdre (Nantes) 42
René of Anjou 296, 515
Rennes 14, 273, 275, **288–9**
  festivals 41
  hotels 560
  map 288
  restaurants 586
Renoir, Jean 70
Renoir, Pierre Auguste 136, 476
  *Dance at the Moulin de la Galette* 124, 125
  Honfleur 266
  Musée Marmottan Monet (Paris) 135
  Musée de l'Orangerie (Paris) 102
  Musée Renoir (Cagnes-sur-Mer) 526–7
*La République* (Landelle) 46
RER trains 640
Réserve Naturelle de Scandola 545
Resistance 71

Responsible travel **623**
Restaurants **572–603**
  Alsace and Lorraine 582–3
  bistro annexes **573**
  brasseries **572**
  Brittany 585–6
  Burgundy and Franche-Comté 589–91
  Champagne 580–82
  children in 574
  Corsica 603
  dress code 574
  *ferme-auberges* **572**
  French eating habits 572
  how to pay 574
  Ile-de-France 579
  Langedoc-Roussillon 599–601
  Loire Valley 586–9
  Massif Central 591–3
  menus and ordering 574
  Le Nord and Picardy 579–80
  Normandy 583–5
  Paris 576–9
  Périgord, Quercy and Gascony 596–8
  pets in 574
  Poitou and Aquitaine 594–6
  prices 574
  Provence and the Côte d'Azur 601–3
  Pyrenees 598–9
  reservations 573
  Rhône Valley and French Alps 593–4
  service and tipping 574, 621
  smoking in 574
  vegetarian food 574–5
  water 574
  wheelchair access 574
  wine in 573
  *see also* Food and drink
Reuilly-Sauvigny
  hotels 556
Revin 218
Rhenanus, Beatus 233
Rhône delta 514
Rhône Valley and French Alps **377–95**
  The bridges of the Rhône **387**
  climate 45
  food and drink **323**
  hotels 564–5
  map 378–9
  restaurants 593–4
  travel 379
  A week in the Rhône Valley and Languedoc 11, 15
Ribeauvillé **232**, 236
  restaurants 582
Richard I, Duke of Normandy 260
Richard the Lionheart, King of England 57, 298
  Chinon 299
  Les Andelys 270
  Niort 413
  Poitiers 416
  tomb 268
Richelieu, Cardinal 62
  baptism 94
  Brouage 421
  Palais Royal (Paris) 103
  siege of La Rochelle 420
Riemenschneider, Tilman 106
Rigaud, Hyacinthe 181
  Musée d'Art Hyacinthe Rigaud (Perpignan) **489**
Rimbaud, Arthur 35
  Musée Rimbaud (Charleville-Mézières) 218
Riom 365
Ripaille, Château de 395
Riquet, Paul 490, 494

Riquewihr 225, **232**, 236
  hotels 558
  restaurants 583
Ritz, César 102
River trips **635**
Riviera 479, 503
  artists 33
Road transportation **636–9**
Robbe-Grillet, Alain 34
Robert, Hubert 388
Robert II the Pious, King 48
Robespierre, Maximilien de 65, 102, 475
Rocamadour 399, 431, **440–41**
  hotels 567
  restaurants 597
Roche Sanadoire 366
Roche à Sept Heures 218
Roche de Solutré 331, 352
Roche Tuilière 366
Rochecorbon
  restaurants 588
Rochefort 409, **420–21**
  restaurants 596
Rocher des Quatre Fils d'Aymon 218
Rock music **155**, 157
Rocks
  Massif Central **329**
Rocroi 211, **218**
Rodez **370**
  hotels 564
  restaurants 592
Rodin, Auguste
  The Burghers of Calais 200–201
  bust of Victor Hugo 95
  The Gates of Hell 124, 125
  Musée d'Art Moderne (Troyes) 220
  Musée des Beaux-Arts (Lyon) 385
  Musée Calvet (Avignon) 507
  Musée Rodin (Paris) **119**
  statue of Claude Lorrain 228
  The Thinker 119
  Verdun 226
Rogers, Richard 96
Rohan, Princesse de 94
Rohault de Fleury, Hubert 138
Roland 458
Rolin, Nicolas 350
Roman Gaul 47, **52–3**
  Aix-les-Bains 394
  Aix-en-Provence 515
  Alise-Ste.-Reine 338
  Arles 512–13
  Autun 343
  Corsica 547
  Eze 533
  Fréjus 521
  Languedoc and Roussillon 481
  Lyon 377, 382
  Musée de l'Oppidum d'Ensérune 494
  Nîmes 500–501
  Orange 506
  Pont du Gard 15, 470, **498–9**
  St.-Bertrand-de-Comminges 466
  St.-Romain-en-Gal **386–7**
  Saintes 422
  Site Archéologique de Glanum (St.-Rémy-de-Provence) 511
  La Turbie 52–3
  Vaison-la-Romaine **506**
  Vienne 386
Roman Theatre (Orange) **506**
Romanesque architecture **36–7**
Romans-sur-Isère
  hotels 565
Romorantin-Lanthenay
  hotels 562
Ronchamp **355**

La Ronde Bretonne (Bernard) 32
Rondelet, Guillaume 129
Ronsard, Pierre de 35
Roquebrune-Cap-Martin 503, **533**
  restaurants 602
Roquefort-sur-Soulzon 371
Roquepertuse 51
Roquesaltes 371
Roscoff **279**
  hotels 560
  restaurants 586
Rosso Fiorentino 185
Rothschild, Baronne Hélène de 114
Rouault, Georges 520
  Miserere 339
Rouen 14, 251, **268–9**
  Cathedral 14, **268**
  hotels 559–60
  map 268–9
  Monet's Cathedral series 268, **271**
  restaurants 584
Rouffignac 407, 439
Rousseau, Henri "Le Douanier" 102
Rousseau, Jean-Jacques 35, 64, 65, 394
  tomb 129
Rousseau, Théodore 185
  Sunset, Auvergne 33
Roussillon see Languedoc and Roussillon
Route de Combe Laval 393
Route des Crêtes **228**, 229
Route des Vins (Alsace) 223, **236**
Royal, Ségolène 24
Royan **422**
  hotels 566
Roye
  restaurants 580
Royer, Jean 301
Rubens, Peter Paul 202, 456, 462, 521
Rude, François 346
Rue de Buci (Paris) 123
Rue la Fontaine (Paris) **134–5**
Rue des Francs-Bourgeois (Paris) 92
Rue Montorgueil (Paris) **153**
Rue Mouffetard (Paris) **153**
Rue de l'Odéon (Paris) **126**
Rue Poncelet (Paris) **153**
Rue des Rosiers (Paris) 92
Rugby 40
Rules of the road **636**
Rully
  hotels 563
Rural architecture **38–9**
Ruskin, John 206
Russian Orthodox Church
  St.-Alexandre-Nevsky (Paris) **135**

## S

Les Sables d'Olonne 294
Sabres
  restaurants 596
Sache
  restaurants 588
Sacré-Coeur (Paris) 137, **138**
Sade, Marquis de 511
Safety 620, 623, **624–5**
Sagan, Françoise 477
Sailing 615, **635**
Saillagouse
  restaurants 600
Ste.-Agnes
  restaurants 603
St.-Agreve
  restaurants 594
St.-Alban-sur-Limagnole
  hotels 564
St.-Alexandre-Nevsky (Paris) **135**
St.-Amand 334
St.-Amand-de-Coly **435**

St.-Amour Bellevue
  restaurants 590
St. Bartholomew's Day Massacre (1572) 61, 343
St.-Benoît-sur-Loire **317**
St.-Bertrand-de-Comminges **466**
St.-Bonnet-le-Froid
  hotels 564
  restaurants 592
St.-Brieuc
  restaurants 586
Ste.-Cecile
  restaurants 584
Sainte-Chapelle (Paris) 12, 86, **88–9**
St.-Christophe 352
St.-Cirq-Lapopie 442
Sainte-Clotilde (Paris) **119**
St. Côme d'Olt 370
St.-Cyr-au-Mont-d'Or
  hotels 565
St.-Denis, Basilique 56, **176–7**
  festivals 40
St. Denis Preaching to the Gauls (Vien) 103
Saint-Emilion 16, 403, **426–7**
  hotels 566
  restaurants 596
St.-Etienne **387**
  restaurants 594
St.-Etienne-de-Baigorry
  hotels 568
St.-Etienne-du-Mont (Paris) **127**
St.-Eustache (Paris) **94**
St.-Eutrope-de-Born
  hotels 567
St.-Fargeau, Château de 334
St.-Florent **541**
  restaurants 603
St.-Gaudens
  restaurants 598
St.-Germain-en-Laye **177**
  hotels 555
  restaurants 579
St.-Germain-de-Livet 259
St.-Germain-des-Prés (Paris) 12, 122, **126**
St.-Germain-des-Prés Quarter (Paris) 122–3
St.-Gervais d'Auvergne
  hotels 564
St.-Gervais-St.-Protais (Paris) **89**
St.-Gilles-du-Gard 499
Saint-Girons
  restaurants 599
St.-Guilhem-le-Désert 481, **497**
St.-Jacques-des-Guérets 311
St.-Jean-Cap-Ferrat **532**
  restaurants 602
St.-Jean-de-Côle **434**
St.-Jean-de-Luz 453, 455, **456–7**
  hotels 568
  restaurants 598–9
St.-Jean-Pied-de-Port **458**
  hotels 569
  restaurants 599
St.-Jean-Pied-de-Port Basque Fête 42
St.-Julien-Chapteuil
  restaurants 592
St.-Julien-de-Jonzy 352
St.-Julien-le-Pauvre (Paris) **127**, 129
St.-Junien 360
St.-Lary-Soulan
  restaurants 599
Saint Laurent, Yves 73
St.-Lizier 453, **466**
  hotels 569
St.-Louis-des-Invalides (Paris) **119**

St.-Loup-sur-Thouet
  hotels 566
St.-Maixent-L'Ecole 413
St.-Malo 14, 273, **286–7**
  hotels 561
  restaurants 586
  seafarers of St.-Malo **286**
St.-Marc-sur-Mer
  hotels 562
St.-Martin-de-Belleville
  restaurants 594
St.-Martin-de-Boscherville 267
St.-Martin-du-Canigou 481, **485**
St.-Martin-de-Ré 409, 420
St.-Martin-Valmeroux
  hotels 564
St.-Medard
  restaurants 597
St.-Michel (Dijon) 345
St.-Michel-de-Cuxa 481, **484–5**
St.-Nectaire 16, **364**
St.-Omer **201**
St.-Ouen les Vignes
  restaurants 588
St.-Parize-le-Châtel 343
St.-Paterne
  hotels 560
St.-Paul de Vence 17, 504, **528–9**
  hotels 571
  restaurants 602
Saint Phalle, Niki de 477, 531
  Stravinsky Fountain 97
St.-Pierre de Montmartre (Paris)
  137
St.-Pons-de-Thomières 497
Sainte-Preuve
  hotels 557
St.-Quentin
  hotels 557
St.-Raphaël 17, **521**
St.-Rémy-de-Provence 15, **511**
  hotels 571
  restaurants 602
St.-Roch (Paris) **103**
St.-Romain
  restaurants 590
St.-Romain-en-Gal **386–7**
St.-Sauveur 334
St.-Savin **419**
St.-Séverin (Paris) **126**, 128
St.-Sulpice (Paris) 130, **131**
St.-Thégonnec **280**, 281
St.-Trivier-de-Courtes 377
St.-Trojan 421
St.-Tropez 17, 479, **520**
  festivals 41
  hotels 571
  restaurants 603
St.-Vaast
  hotels 560
St.-Wandrille 251
Saintes 409, **422**
Salers 328, **367**
  hotels 564
Sales tax 620
Salons du thé **573**
Salt
  The Camargue 515
Samara 203
Sambin, Hugues 344, 346
San Stefano pass 541
Sancerre
  restaurants 588
Sand, George 34, 126
Santiago de Compostela 409
  The road to Compostela **404–5**
Santo-Pietro-di-Tenda 541
Saône Valley 331

Sare 457
  hotels 569
  restaurants 599
Sarkozy, Nicolas 25, 73
Sarlat 16, **436–7**
  hotels 567
  map 436–7
  restaurants 597
Sartène **547**
Sartre, Jean-Paul 35, 71, 122
  grave 143
Satie, Erik 71
  Les Maisons Satie (Honfleur) 266
Saulieu **342**
  hotels 563
  restaurants 591
Saumur 23, 291, **296**
  hotels 562
  restaurants 588
Sauternes
  restaurants 596
Sauveterre-de-Béarn **458**
Saverne 223, **237**
  restaurants 583
Saxe, Maréchal de 306
Scandola Nature Reserve (Corsica) 29
Sceaux, Château de **182**
Scenic routes **637**
Schongauer, Martin 231
Scott, Sir Walter 304
Secondhand clothes stores
  **146**, 148
Sedan 211, **218–19**
  hotels 557
Sées 259
Seguin, Marc 387
Seignosse
  hotels 566
Seillans Var
  hotels 571
Seine, River 251, 267
  cruises on 83, **641**
  A river view of Paris **79–83**
Sélestat **233**
  hotels 558
Semur-en-Auxois 56, 330, **339**
Semur-en-Brionnais 352
Senior travelers **622**
Senlis 197, **208**
Sens **334**
  restaurants 591
Serlio, Sebastiano 338
Sermiers
  restaurants 581
Serrant, Château de 295
Serre, Michel 516
Sert, José-Luis 528
Sérusier, Paul 279
Service charges, in restaurants
  574
Sète 15, 17, 478, 482, 491, **496**
  festivals 42
  hotels 569
  restaurants 600
Seurat, Georges 125
Seven Years' War (1756–63) 64
Sévigné, Madame de
  95, 289, 362
  tomb 390
Sèvres: Cité de la Céramique **182**
Sewers
  Les Égouts (Paris) **116**
Sezanne
  restaurants 581
Shoe stores **147**, 148
Shopping 144–53, **604–7**
  accessories **606**, 607
  arts and antiques **152**

Shopping (cont.)
  beauty products **605**, 607
  clothes and accessories **146–8**
  department stores **145**, 604, 607
  factory outlets **607**
  food and drink **150–51**
  gifts and souvenirs **149**
  household goods **606–7**
  hypermarkets **604**, 607
  opening hours 144, 604
  payment and VAT 144, 620
  regional produce **605**, 607
  specialty stores **604**
  wine **607**
Sibelius, Jean 123
Signac, Paul 476, 520, 529
  Cap Canaille 517
  Entrance to the Port at La Rochelle 32
  View of St.-Paul de Vence 528
Signoret, Simone 529
  grave 139
Sille-le-Guillaume
  hotels 562
Silver Coast see La Côte d'Argent
Simpson, Tommy 506
Sisley, Alfred 135, 266, 394, 444
Site Archéologique de Glanum
  (St.-Rémy-de-Provence) 511
Skiing **614**, 617
  Cerdagne 484
  in the French Alps **326**
Sluter, Claus 346, 347
  Well of Moses 346
Smoking, in restaurants 574
Soccer 41
Social customs **24–5**
Socoa 457
Solidor, Suzy 526
Sologne 291
  Châteaux tour of the Sologne **310–11**
Somme, Battle of the (1916) **194–5**
Somme estuary 197
Somme Valley see Vallée de la Somme
Sorbon, Robert de 127
La Sorbonne (Paris) 12, **127**
Sorel, Agnès 304
Sorges
  restaurants 597
Sorrow of the King (Matisse) 96
Soubirous, Bernadette 462–3
Soufflenheim 237
Soufflot, Jacques-Germain 129
Soulac-sur-Mer 428
Soulages, Pierre 370, 372
Source du Lison 355
Sournia
  restaurants 600
South of France **469–547**
  artists and writers in the South of
    France **476–7**
  beaches **478–9**
  Corsica **537–47**
  The flavors of the South of France
    **472–3**
  France's wine regions: the South
    **474–5**
  Languedoc and Roussillon **481–501**
  map 470–71
  Provence and the Côte d'Azur **503–35**
Southwest France **397–467**
  caves of the Southwest **406–7**
  The flavors of Southwest France
    **400–401**
  France's wine regions: Bordeaux
    **402–3**
  map 398–9
  Périgord, Quercy, and Gascony
    **431–51**

Southwest France (cont.)
Poitou and Aquitaine 409–29
The Pyrenees 453–67
The road to Compostela 404–5
Soutine, Chaim 102, 529
Souvenirs, shopping 149
Spas 615, 617
Aix-les-Bains 394
Amélie-les-Bains 486
Dax 429
Digne-les-Bains 521
Luz-St.-Sauveur 463
Monts Dore 366
Vals-les-Bains 389
Vichy 362
Specialty vacations 612, 616
Specialty stores 149
Speed limits 636
Spielberg, Steven 34
Spoerri, Daniel 477
Sport 611, 612–17
Paris 156, 157
Sprecklesen, Otto von 134
Spring at Barbizon (Millet) 185
Spring in France 40–41
Spring in the French Alps 327
Square Jean-XXIII (Paris) 87
Square Willette (Paris) 137
Stagnoli 546
Stained glass of Chartres 314–15
Stanislas Leczinski, King of Poland 228, 306, 307
Starck, Philippe 498, 500
Statue of Liberty (Paris) 80
Steenvoorde
restaurants 580
Stella, Frank 387
Stendhal 34
Stevenson, Robert Louis 370, 371, 518
Storks, white 227
Strasbourg 189, 223, 234–5
festivals 42
hotels 558
map 234–5
restaurants 583
Stravinsky Fountain (Tinguely and Saint Phalle) 97
Streetcars 640
Student travelers 622, 623
subway systems 69, 640
Suger, Abbot of St.-Denis 107
Suisse Normande 259
Sully, Bishop de 90
Summer in France 41–2
Summer in the French Alps 327
The Sun King and his Family (Nocret) 62–3
Sunflowers (Van Gogh) 476
Sunset, Auvergne (Rousseau) 33
Sunshine 44–5
Sunyer, Joseph 487
Surcouf, Robert 286
Surfing 614–15
Surrealism 70, 96
Suze-la-Rousse 390–91
Swimming 615, 625

**T**

Tain l'Hermitage 388
restaurants 594
Taizé 349
Talloires 395
hotels 565
restaurants 594
Talmont-sur-Gironde 422
restaurants 596
Tange, Kenzo 531
Tanlay, Château de 335
Tapiès, Antoni 486

Tarascon 511
festivals 41
Tarasque Festival 41
Tarbes 453, 462
restaurants 599
Tarn, River 320, 357, 374–5
Taulignan 390
Taxes 621
sales tax 144, 620
Taxis 638–9, 640, 641
tipping 621
Teghime pass 541
Telephones 628, 629
Television 629
Temperatures 44–5
Tennis 41, 613, 616
TGV (Train à Grande Vitesse) 73
Thatcher, Margaret 72
Theater 35, 608, 611
Comédie Française (Paris) 62, 63, 103
festivals 41
Grand Théâtre (Bordeaux) 424
Opéra National de Paris Garnier 100, 101
Paris 154, 157
Théâtre National de Chaillot (Paris) 115
Théâtre du Rond Point (Paris) 110
Théâtres Romains (Lyon) 382
Theft 624
Theme parks
Disneyland® Resort Paris 182
Futuroscope 417
Le Ker (Vannes) 284
Parc Astérix 209
Thérèse of Lisieux , St 259
Thiepval Memorial 194
Thierry III, King 48
Thierry IV, King 48
Thiers 363
The Thinker (Rodin) 119
Thirty Years' War (1618–48) 62
Thoiry, Château 182
Thonon-les-Bains 395
Thouars 412
Thoury, Château de 362
Tiberius, Emperor 506
Tickets
for entertainments 154, 157
for trains 634
traveling in cities 641
Tignes 326
Time zone 622
Timetables, trains 634
Tinguely, Jean 477, 531
Stravinsky Fountain 97
Tinqueux
restaurants 581
Tinta' Mars 40
Tipping 621
in restaurants 574
Titian 61, 546
Tolls, autoroute 637
Tombées de la Nuit (Rennes) 41
Tonnerre 335
Touffou, Château de 418
Toul 223, 226–7
Toulon 517
Toulouse 15, 431, 450–51
hotels 567–8
map 450–51
restaurants 597
Toulouse, Count of 449
Toulouse-Lautrec, Henri de 448
La Modiste 448
Moulin Rouge (Paris) 138
Musée d'Orsay (Paris) 125
Musée Toulouse-Lautrec (Albi) 448

Tour de France 41
Tour de Losse 540
Tour Métallique (Lyon) 383
Tour Montparnasse (Paris) 143
Tour de la Motte Tanguy (Brest) 276
Tour St.-Jacques (Paris) 93
Tour Solidor (St.-Malo) 286
Tourist information 620, 623
Tournon-sur-Rhône 15, 388
restaurants 594
Tournus 348–9
restaurants 591
Tourrettes-sur-Loup 527
Tours 14, 300–305
hotels 562
map 301
restaurants 588
Tours by car
Beaujolais 381
Gorges du Verdon 518–19
Sologne châteaux tour 310–11
A tour of two rivers 442–3
Tours d'Elven (Vannes) 284
Towns, bastide 449
Traditions, Breton 247
Trains 631, 632–4
Little Yellow Train 484
local trains 640
Musée Français du Chemin de Fer (Mulhouse) 229
TGV (Train à Grande Vitesse) 73, 632–3
Travel 630–41
air 630, 631
Alsace and Lorraine 225
boats 635
Brittany 275
Burgundy and Franche-Comté 333
buses 640
cars 631, 636–8
Champagne 212
in cities 640–41
coaches 638, 639
Corsica 539
ferries 630–31, 635
Languedoc and Roussillon 483
Loire Valley 292
Massif Central 358
Le Nord and Picardy 199
Normandy 253
Périgord, Quercy, and Gascony 432
Poitou and Aquitaine 410
Provence and the Côte d'Azur 505
The Pyrenees 454
Rhône Valley and French Alps 379
streetcars 640
taxis 638–9, 640, 641
trains 631, 632–4, 640
Travel insurance 624
Travel safety advice 620, 623
Treboul
hotels 561
Tréguier 282
restaurants 586
Trencavel family 492, 493
Trévou-Tréguignec 282
Triboulet 297
Troglodyte dwellings 296
Les Trois Vallées 29, 326
Troménie (Locronan) 41
Trôo 310–11
Trouville 259
restaurants 584
Troyes 13, 14, 188, 220–21
hotels 557
restaurants 581
Troyes, School of 211, 219
Truffaut, François
grave 138

Truffles 42
Tuileries and Opéra (Paris) **99–107**
  area map 99
  hotels 554
  restaurants 576
  Street by Street map: Opéra Quarter
    100–101
Tumulus de Bougon 413
Turckheim 224, 236
Turenne **367**
Turner, J. M. W. 294
Tursac
  restaurants 598
Tzara, Tristan 70

# U

UNESCO (Paris) **118**
Universal Exhibition, Paris (1889) 68,
  117
Universal Exhibition, Paris (1900) 110
Universities
  La Sorbonne (Paris) 12, **127**
Urban V, Pope 508
Uriage-les-Bains
  restaurants 594
Ussé, Château d' 246, 291, **299**
Utrillo, Maurice 102, 136, 507
  *The Church of St. Bernard, Ain, in
    Summer* 33
  grave 138
Uzerche **366**
  restaurants 592
Uzès 499
  hotels 569
  restaurants 600

# V

Vacation rental accommodations
  **551**, 553
Vadim, Roger 520
Vaison-la-Romaine **506**
  hotels 571
Val-de-Grâce (Paris) **131**
Val d'Isère 326
  festivals 43
  hotels 565
Val Thorens 326
Valaire
  restaurants 588
Valdu Niello 544
Valence 15, **388**
  restaurants 594
Valéry, Paul 35, 114
  grave 496
Vallauris **526**
Vallée d'Aspe 464
Vallée de la Clarée 376
Vallée de Cousin
  hotels 563
Vallée du Lot **370**
Vallée de la Loue 355
Vallée des Merveilles 533
Valléee de la Meuse **218**
Vallée de la Somme 197, 199, **203**
Vallon-Pont-d'Arc
  hotels 565
Valois dynasty 49
Vals-les-Bains **389**
Van Dongen, Kees 476
Van Dyck, Sir Anthony 202, 456
Van Eyck, Jan 106, 347
Van Gogh, Vincent 476, 503, 507
  Arles 15, 512, 513
  *The Church at Auvers* 32
  *Doctor Paul Gachet* 125
  St.-Rémy-de-Provence 15, 511
  *Sunflowers* 476
Van Loo 303

Vannes 273, **284**
  hotels 561
  restaurants 586
VAT, in stores 144, 620
Vauban, Maréchal de
  Belfort 355
  Besançon 354
  Briançon 391
  Château de Bazoches 339
  Collioure 487
  Fort National (St.-Malo) 286
  Lille 202
  Mont Louis 484
  Neuf-Brisach 230–31
  Port Vendres 486
  Rocroi 218
  Toul 226
  Verdun 226
Vaux-le-Vicomte, Château 13, **182–3**
VE Day 43
Vegetarian food 574–5
Velay 357
Velázquez, Diego de Silva y 269
Vence **527**
  restaurants 603
The Vendée 291, **294–5**
Vendôme **310**
  restaurants 588
Venoy
  restaurants 591
Vercingetorix 52, 338
The Vercors 377, **393**
Verdon Gorges *see* Gorges du Verdon
Verdon River 29
Verdun 223, **226**
Verdun, Battle of (1916) 69, 226
Verdun-sur-le-Doubs
  restaurants 591
Verlaine, Paul 136
Verne, Jules
  Maison de Jules Verne (Amiens) 204
Veronese, Paolo 491, 546
Versailles, Château de 11, 13, 62, 63,
  **178–81**
  festivals 41
  hotels 556
  restaurants 579
Versailles, Treaty of (1919) 69, 181
Veules les Roses
  restaurants 584
Vézelay 331, **340–41**
  restaurants 591
Vichy **362–3**
  hotels 564
  restaurants 592–3
Vichy government 47, 71
Victor, Michel-Louis 131
Victoria, Queen of England
  518, 530
La Vieille Charité (Marseille) **516**
Vien, Comte Joseph-Marie
  *St. Denis Preaching to the Gauls* 103
Vienne 15, **386**
  festivals 41
  restaurants 594
Vienne-le-Château
  hotels 558
Vierny, Dina 119
La Vieux Cap 481
Vieux Château Certan 427
*View of St.-Paul de Vence* (Signac) 528
Vignoux-sur-Barangeon
  restaurants 589
Vikings, in Normandy 251
Villa Masséna (Nice) **530**
Village des Bories 510
Villandry, Château de
  13, 290, 291, **300**

Villard-de-Lans 393
Villars-les-Dombes 380
Villefranche-de-Conflent **484**
  restaurants 601
Villefranche-sur-Mer **532**
  hotels 571
  restaurants 603
Villeneuve-les-Avignon
  restaurants 603
Villeneuve-sur-Lot 444
Villeneuve sur Yonne
  restaurants 591
Villerouge-Termenes 490
Villers Bocage
  restaurants 585
Villers Cotterets, Edict of (1539) 61
Villers-le-Lac
  restaurants 591
Villers-sur-Suize
  restaurants 582
Villesavin, Château de 311
Villié-Morgon 381
Villiers le Mahieu
  hotels 556
Villiers sur Marne
  hotels 558
Vinay
  hotels 558
  restaurants 582
Vincelottes
  restaurants 591
Vincennes, Château de **142**
Vineyards *see* Wines
Vintage clothes stores **146**, 148
Viollet-le-Duc, Eugène **204**
  Amiens Cathedral 206
  Basilique Ste.-Madeleine (Vézelay)
    340
  Carcassonne 492
  Château de Pierrefonds 205
  Narbonne 490
  Notre-Dame (Paris) 77, 90
*Virgile, Horace and Varius in Mecene's
  Home* (Jalabert) 501
*Virgin Mary and Child* (Brunet)
  137
*The Virgin Protecting the Cistercian Order*
  (Bellegambe) 337
Visas 620
Vitré 14, 273, **289**
Vlaminck, Maurice de 476
Vogüé 389
Volcanoes 366
Voltaire 35, 64, 107, 304
  Quai Voltaire (Paris) 123
  tomb 129
Vonnas
  hotels 563
  restaurants 591
Vosges 223
  Route des Crêtes **228**, 229
Vouvray 245, **304**
  restaurants 589
Vries, Adrian de 106
Vulcania 366

# W

Wagner, Richard 123
Walking **613**, 616
  hitchhiking **639**
  Pyrenees 465
  Tour du Mont Blanc 327
Warens, Madame de 394
Warhol, Andy 387, 531
Wars of Religion (1562–93) 48, 60, 61,
  62, 409, 416, 431
Water, drinking 574
Watersports **614–15**, 617

Waterfalls
  Cascades du Hérisson **353**
  Cirque de Gavarnie 28, 463
*Waterlilies (Nymphéas)* (Monet) 102
Waterskiing 615
Watteau, J. A. 106
Weather **44–5**
Webb, Captain M. 201
Wedekinch 80
*Well of Moses* (Sluter) 346
Wellington, Duke of 456
Western France **239–317**
  Breton traditions **247**
  Brittany **273–89**
  Brittany's coastal wildlife **248–9**
  Châteaux of the Loire Valley **246**
  The flavors of Western France
    **242–3**
  map 240–41
  Normandy **251–71**
Weyden, Rogier van der 346, 347
  *The Last Judgment* 58–9, 350, 351
Wharton, Edith 518
Wheelchair access *see* Disabled
  travelers
Whit Monday 43
Wilde, Oscar 123
Wildlife
  A Cupulatta 546
  Brittany's coastal wildlife **248–9**
  Calanques 517
  Cévennes **375**
  ibex **391**
  Le Jardin des Papillons (Digne-les-
    Bains) 521
  Luberon 511
  Parc Naturel Régional du Haut
    Languedoc 497
  Pyrenees **464–5**
  *see also* Aquariums; Birds; National
    parks
Wilhelm II, Kaiser 189, 232
William the Conqueror, King of
  England 55, 203
  Abbaye de Jumièges 267

William the Conqueror, King of
  England (cont.)
  Bayeux Tapestry
    14, 241, 251, **256–7**
  Caen 14, 251, 257
William the Pious, Duke of Aquitaine
  349
Wilmotte, Jean-Michel 387
Wimereux
  hotels 557
Winds, Corsica 538
Wines **30–31**
  Alsace **237**
  Beaune wine auction **350**
  Bordeaux **402–3**
  Bordeaux wine châteaux **427**
  Bordeaux wine trade **425**
  Burgundy **324–5**
  Champagne **192–3**
  Cité du Vin (Bordeaux) **426**
  Côte d'Or **348**
  Côte Vermeille 486
  Côtes du Rhône **388**
  festivals 42
  grape harvest 42
  The Loire **244–5**
  *méthode champenoise* **214–15**
  Musée Animé du Vin (Chinon) 298,
    299
  in restaurants 573
  Route des Vins 223, **236**
  shopping **151, 607**
  The South **474–5**
  wine bars **573**
  A wine and food tour of Burgundy,
    Périgord, and Bordeaux 11, 16
  wine labels **30**
  wine-making **31**
Winter in France **43**
Winter in the French Alps **326**
Wissembourg 237
  restaurants 583
*With the Black Arc* (Kandinsky) 97
*Woman Reading* (Picasso) 94
*Woman with Parasol* (Boudin) 266

World Fair, Paris (1855) 110
World music
  Paris **155**, 157
World War I 47, 69
  The Battle of the Somme **194–5**
  Compiègne 205
  Douaumont Memorial 189
  Mémorial de Caen **258**
  Vallée de la Somme **203**
  Verdun 226
World War II 47, **71**
  Bunker of Rochelle (La Rochelle)
    420
  D-Day landings 14, 251, **255**
  Maginot Line 211
  Le Mémorial de l'Alsace-Moselle
    233
  MM Park Museum (Strasbourg)
    235
  Musée de la Libération (Cherbourg)
    254
  Musée Mémoire 1939–1945 (Calais)
    201
  Musée de la Reddition (Reims) **214**
  The Vercors 393
Writers **34–5**
  South of France **476–7**

## Y

Yeats, W. B. 533
Ygrande
  hotels 564
Yoga **615**, 617
*Young Ladies of the Village Giving Alms
  to a Cow Girl in a Valley near Ornans*
  (Courbet) 33
Yravals 484
Yvoire 395

## Z

Zadkine, Ossip
  *La Grande Odalisque* 512
Zola, Emile 34, 68, 69
  tomb 129
The Zouave (Paris) 81

# Acknowledgments

Dorling Kindersley would like to thank the following people, whose contributions and assistance have made the preparation of this book possible.

**Main Contributors**
John Ardagh, Rosemary Bailey, Judith Fayard, Lisa Gerard-Sharp, Robert Harneis, Alister Kershaw, Alec Lobrano, Anthony Roberts, Alan Tillier, Nigel Tisdall.

**Contributors and Consultants**
John Ardagh is a writer and broadcaster, and author of many books on France, among them *France Today* and *Writers' France*.

Rosemary Bailey has written and edited several guides to regional France, including *Burgundy*, the *Loire Valley*, and the *Côte d'Azur*.

Alexandra Boyle is a writer and editor based in England and France.

Elsie Burch Donald, editor and writer, is the author of *The French Farmhouse*.

David Burnie B.Sc. has written over 30 books on natural sciences, including *How Nature Works*.

Judith Fayard, an American based in Paris, was Paris bureau chief for *Life* magazine for 10 years, and is now European editor of *Town & Country*. She contributes to various publications, including the *Wall Street Journal*.

Lisa Gerard-Sharp is a broadcaster and author of several regional guides to France and Italy.

Robert Harneis is editorial correspondent for the English-language newspaper *French News*.

Colin Jones is Professor of History at Exeter University. His books include *The Longman Companion to the French Revolution* and *The Cambridge Illustrated History of France*.

Alister Kershaw is an Australian writer and broadcaster who lives in the Loire Valley.

Alec Lobrano is an American writer, based in Paris. He is the European editor of *Departures* magazine and contributes to *International Herald Tribune, Los Angeles Times*, and *The Independent*.

Anthony Roberts is a writer and translator who lives in Gascony and contributes to various publications including *The Times, World of Interiors*, and *Architectural Digest*.

Anthony Rose is the wine correspondent of *The Independent* and co-author of the *Grapevine*.

Jane Sigal is the author of two books on French food, *Normandy Gastronomique* and *Backroom Bistros, Farmhouse Fare*.

The late Alan Tillier was the main contributor to the *Eyewitness Guide to Paris*. He lived in Paris from the 1960s until 2004 and was correspondent for the *International Herald Tribune, Newsweek*, and *The Times*.

Nigel Tisdall is a travel writer and author of guides to Brittany and Normandy.

Patricia Wells is food critic of the *International Herald Tribune* and author of the *Food Lovers' Guide to Paris* and the *Food Lovers' Guide to France*.

**Additional Contributors**
Nathalie Boyer, Caroline Bugler, Ann Cremin, Jan Dodd, Bill Echikson, Robin Gauldie, Adrian Gilbert, Peter Graham, Marion Kaplan, Jim Keeble, Alexandra Kennedy, Rolli Lucarotti, Fred Mawer, Lyn Parry, Andrew Sanger, Katherine Spenley, Clive Unger-Hamilton, Roger Williams.

**Additional Photography**
Jo Craig, Andy Crawford, Michael Crockett, Mike Dunning, Philip Enticknap, Lydia Evans, Philippe Giraud, Steve Gorton, Alison Harris, John Heseltine, Roger Hilton, Andrew Holligan, Paul Kenwood, Oliver Knight, Eric Meacher, Neil Mersh, Roger Moss, Robert O'Dea, Ian O'Leary, Rough Guides: Marc Dubin, Jules Selmes, Tony Souter, Alan Williams, Peter Wilson.

**Additional Illustrations**
Dinwiddie Maclaren, John Fox, Nick Gibbard, Paul Guest, Stephen Gyapay, Kevin Jones Associates, Chris Orr, Robbie Polley, Sue Sharples.

**Additional Cartography**
Colourmap Scanning Limited; Contour Publishing; Cosmographics; European Map Graphics; Meteo-France. Street Finder maps: ERAMaptec Ltd (Dublin), adapted with permission from original survey and mapping by Shobunsha (Japan).

**Cartographic Research**
Rachel Hawtin (Lovell Johns); James Mills-Hicks, Jennifer Skelley, Peter Winfield, Claudine Zarte (Dorling Kindersley Cartography).

**Revisions Team**
Peter Adams, Azeem Alam, Michelle Arness Frederic, Elizabeth Ayre, Laetitia Benloulou, Steve Bere, Kate Berens, Sonal Bhatt, Uma Bhattacharya, Hilary Bird, Anna Brooke, Arwen Burnett, Cate Craker, Maggie Crowley, Alison Culliford, Lisa Davidson, Simon Davis, Emer FitzGerald, Helen Foulkes, Fay Franklin, Tom Fraser, Kyra Freestar, Anna Freiberger, Rhiannon Furbear, Catherine Gauthier, Camilla Gersh, Eric Gibory, Emily Green, Vinod Harish, Robert Harneis, Elaine Harries, Victoria Heyworth-Dunne, Paul Hines, Nicholas Inman, Rosa Jackson, Sarah Jackson-Lambert, Stuart James, Laura Jones, Nancy Jones, Bharti Karakoti, Sumita Khatwani, Kim Laidlaw Adrey, Cécile Landau, Kathryn Lane, Maite Lantaron, Delphine Lawrance, Jude Ledger, Colette Levitt, Jason Little, Siri Lowe, Francesca Machiavelli, Carly Madden, Hayley Maher, Nicola Malone, Lesley McCave, Alison McGill, Ella Milroy, Jason Mitchell, Casper Morris, Claire Naylor, George Nimmo, Malcolm Parchment, Lyn Parry, Helen Partington, Shirin Patel, Susie Peachey, Alice Peebles, Clare Peel, Alice Pennington-Mellor, Marianne Petrou, Bryan Pirolli, Pollyanna Poulter, Pete Quinlan, Salim Qurashi, Rada Radojicic, Akshay Rana, Marisa Renzullo, Philippa Richmond, Nick Rider, Ellen Root, Sands Publishing Solutions, Baishakhee Sengupta, Shailesh Sharma, Kunal Singh, Rituraj Singh, Shruti Singhi, Cathy Skipper, Jaynan Spengler, Niamh Smith, Joanna Stenlake, Andrew Szudek, Hollie Teague, Priyanka Thakur, Helen Townsend, Victoria Trott, Nikky Twyman, Conrad van Dyck, Vinita Venugopal, Dora Whitaker, Fiona Wild, Nicholas Wood, Sophie Wright, Irina Zarb.

**Special Assistance**
Mme Jassinger, French Embassy Press Department; Peter Mills, Christine Lagardère, French Railways Ltd.

**Photographic Reference**
Altitude, Paris; Sea and See; Editions Combier, Maçon; Thomas d'Hoste, Paris.

**Photography Permissions**
Dorling Kindersley would like to thank the following for their assistance and kind permission to photograph at their establishments: The Caisse Nationale des Monuments Historiques et des Sites; M. A. Leonetti, the Abbey of Mont St.-Michel; Chartres Cathedral; M. Voisin, Château de Chenonceau; M. P. Mistral, Cité de Carcassonne; M. D. Vingtain, Palais des Papes, Avignon; Château de Fontainebleau; Amiens Cathedral; Conques Abbey; Fontenay Abbey; Moissac Abbey; Vézelay Abbey; Reims Cathedral and all the other churches, museums, hotels, restaurants, stores, galleries, and sights too numerous to thank individually.

## Picture Credits

a = above; b = below/bottom; c = center; f = far;
l = left; r = right; t = top.

Works of art have been reproduced with the permission of the following copyright holders; ©ADAGP, Paris and DACS, London 2011: 33ca, 33crb, 67tl, 68–9, 69tl (d), 94tc, 97cra, 97cb, 97bl, 97br, 103tr, 217bc, 355t, 339bl, 486tc, 512ca, 526b, 528bc, 528br; ©ARS, NY and DACS, London 2011: 96c; ©DACS, London 2011: 97tc, 385br, 426t; Artwork and photograph © Succession H. Matisse/DACS 2015: 33bl, 96bl, 530br; © Succession Picasso/DACS, London 2011: 92cl, 94br, 477t, 525tr.

Photos achieved with the assistance of the EPPV and the CSI: 140–41; Photo of Euro Disneyland® Park and the Euro Disneyland Paris® 182crb; The characters, architectural works, and trademarks are the property of The Walt Disney Company. All rights reserved; Courtesy of the Maison Victor Hugo, Ville de Paris: 95cra; Musée National des Châteaux de Malmaison et Bois-Préau: 177br; Musée de Montmartre, Paris: 136cb.

The publisher would like to thank the following individuals, companies, and picture libraries for permission to reproduce their photographs.

**123RF.com** Philippe Halle 620c, Ostill 108, Pedro Antonio Salaverría Calahorra 464tr, Wallace Weeks 386cr.

**Le 36, Amboise:** 586bc.

**Alamy Stock Photo:** AF archive 72clb; age fotostock 422tl, 553tc; amana images inc. 468–9; Jon Arnold Images Ltd 272; Arterra Picture Library 439cl; Andy Arthur 424bc; Martin Bache 98; Sébastien Baussais 626tr; Tibor Bognar 213tr; Josse Christophel 501br; Chronicle 247bl; Directphoto.org 621br; dpa picture alliance 438tl; David R. Frazier Photolibrary, Inc 624cla; FORGET Patrick/SAGAPHOTO.COM 587tr; David Giral 137tc; Bjorn Grotting 440cb; guichaoua 205cl; Cris Haigh 481b; Philippe Hays 627cb; Chris Hellier 533br; Hemis 53tl, 79cr, 122clb, 139br, 183b, 196, 273bc, 278tr, 374br, 408, 420cr, 520cr, 594tl, 600bc; Iconotec 285tc; imageBROKER 545tr; Images & Stories 22; inkemarstock 250; INTERFOTO 405br; Eric James 437br; Brian Jannsen 222; Joy 174; Neil Juggins 634tl; Michael Juno 243c; Justin Kase Zfivez 625tr; Valerijs Kostreckis 120; LOOK Die Bildagentur der Fotografen GmbH 536; London Entertainment 524br; mauritius images GmbH 496t; mcx images 376; George Munday 497bl; nagelstock.com 502; nobleIMAGES 460–61; North Wind Picture Archives 285bc; Peter Noyce FRA 595tr; James Osmond Photography 452; a la poste 628tr, 622b; Prisma Bildagentur AG 133; SFL Choice 430; robertharding 436tr; Craig Roberts 276bc; SAGAPHOTO.COM/FORGET Patrick 603tc; Shawshots 325ca, 325cb; SOTK2011 68clb; Antony SOUTER 571bl; Jack Sullivan 625cra; travelbild.com 527b; F. Vrouenraths (Spain) 664cla; **Alpine Garden Society/Christopher Grey-Wilson:** 464bc, 464br; **Agence Photo Aquitaine:** D Lelann 425tc; **Ancient Art and Architecture Collection:** 51crb, 54ca, 54cb, 61clb, 256–7b, 339bl, 386tl, 442crb; **Photo AKG, Berlin:** 49cra, 50bl, 59crb, 406tr, 407br; **Archives Photographiques, Paris/DACS:** 426t; by kind permission of www.artinswfrance.com: 612bc; **L'Arnsbourg:** 582tl; **Atelier Brancusi/Centre Georges Pompidou, Paris:** Bernard Prerost 97br; **Atelier du Regard/A Allemand:** 446cl, 446cr, 446br; **L'Axel:** 579bc. **La Bastide de Voulonne:** 570tc; **Hostellerie Berard:** 612cla; **Bibliothèque Nationale, Dijon:** 53cb; **F Blackburn:** 465bl; **Le Bouclier d'Or:** 558tl; **Gerard Boullay/Photola:** 91bl, 91cra; **Brasserie Bofinger:** 578tc; **Bridgeman Art Library:** Albright Knox Art Gallery, Buffalo, New York 279br; Anthony Crane Collection 215br; Bibliothèque Nationale, Paris 54cr–55cl, 57crb, 73bl; British Library, London 56bl, 72br, 296c, 297br, 297tl; Bonhams, London 33ca; Château de Versailles, France 73tr; Christie's, London 33ca, 517b; Giraudon 33tl, 32cla, 60cr–61cl, 61tl, 63tl, 73bc, 185br, 338cl,

347c, 369tl; Guildhall Library, Corporation of London 421c; Index 476br; Kress Collection, Washington D C 297bl; Lauros-Giraudon 73br; Musée des Beaux-Arts, Quimper 247cr; Musée Condé, Chantilly 61tr, 72bl, 73tc, 73tl, 73cb, 208tr, 297c; Musée d'Orsay, Paris 32bl; Musée du Quai Branly, Paris 116cb; Paul Bremen Collection 259tc; Sotheby's New York 59tl; V&A Museum, London 342crb; Walters Art Gallery, Baltimore, Maryland 360tl; **Buerehiesel:** 583bc; **Bureau Alain Ducasse:** 602tr. **Cafe du Palais:** 581br; **Campagne, Campagne:** 354tl; C. Guy 329t; Lara 195cr; B. Lichtstein 221br, 328clb; Pyszel 194bl; **CNMHS, Paris/DACS:** Longchamps Delehaye 217cla; **Hôtel Caron de Beaumarchais:** 554bc; **Centre Georges Pompidou:** Cephas: 42crb; Stuart Boreham 264–5; Hervé Champollion 326tr, 338tr, 354crb; Mick Rock 402cla, 475t, 522–3; **Le Chabichou:** 593br; **Hostellerie du Chapeau Rouge:** 589tc; **Champagne Billecart-Salmon:** 193cr; **Jean Loup Charmet:** 51cb, 54br, 56clb, 66cl, 66clb, 67tl, 67ca, 68bl, 68br, 69crb, 218br, 269crb, 347br, 365c, 405cr, 479t, 511cr, **Château de Barive:** 557tc; **Château des Brottières:** 561br; **Château de La Lquière:** 474ca; **Château d'Ygrande:** 564tl; **Château Margaux:** 30crb, 30br; **Cité des Sciences et l'Industrie:** Michel Lamoureux 140ca; NASA/ESA 140tr, 141br; Sylvain Sonnet 140clb; **Collection CDT Gard:** 329bl; **CDT Lot:** 443br; **Corbis:** Stuart Black/Robert Harding World Imagery 13bl; Guillaume Bonn 26tl; Gary Braasch 473c; Joel Damase/Photononstop 318–19; Leroy Francis/Hemis 414–15; Owen Franken 16bc; Frumm John/Hemis 238–9; Ray Juno 12cla, Patrice Latron 240cla, 636br; Leemage 8–9; Douglas Pearson 396–7; People Avenue/Pool 535tc; Reuters 609tl; Robert Harding World Imagery/Charles Bowman 637tl; Jean-Daniel Sudres/Hemis 597tc; Russel Wong 40cr; Jim Zuckerman 186–7; **Depositphotos Inc:** Picturereflex 398cl; **E. Donard:** 39c, 39clb, 39bc; **Editions D'Art Daniel Derveaux:** 404cr–405cl; **Photo Daspet, Avignon:** 508bl; **Doherty:** 249tc; **Domaine de la Courtade:** 475cr; **Domaine des Hauts de Loire:** 588bc; **Domaine Sarda Malet:** 474ca; **Domaine Tempier:** 475cl; **Dreamstime.com:** Adeliepenguin 15bc; Sibel Aisha 179bl; Steve Allen 509tl, 517tl; Americanspirit 526tr; Auris 189cr; Ihar Balaikin 78; Bargotiphotography 525br; Michal Bednarek 516tl; Philip Bird 398bl; Bjulien03 432cl; Lesley De Boelpaep 388tl; Flaviu Boerescu 330; Ryhor Bruyeu 534tr; Olga Buiacova 525cl; Bunyos 520tl; Julia Burlachenko 394b; Byelikova 489tc; Musat Christian 327tc; Ciolca 476cl; Claudio Giovanni Colombo 13tr, 356; Demid 497cr; Dennis Dolkens 11tc; Pierre Jean Durieu 491tl; Elenaphotos 327c; Elena Elisseeva 240bl, 263br; Erdalakan 72cl; Steve Estvanik 441crb; Eugenesergeev 547tl; Eyewave 29tl; Henri Faure 391br; Prochasson Frederic 4cb; Janos Gaspar 29bc; Radu Razvan Gheorghe 15tc, 41bl; Rostislav Glinsky 530tr; Gynane 290; Hornet83 384cl; Ifeelstock 73crb; Sergey Kelin 84; Veniamin Kraskov 534cl; Mihai-bogdan Lazar 10bc; Rozenn Leard 434tc; Rainer Lesniewski 26b; Neil Letson 471t; Lev Levin 292br; Elisa Locci 28clb; Frank Lukasseck 542–3; Madrabothair 471bl; Denis Makarenko 526br; Tomas Marek 4c; Marekusz 463tr; Zdeněk Matyáš 29c, 479bl; Milosk50 426bc; Minacarson 79bl, 628bl; Oleg Mitiukhin 392cl; Radovan Mlatec 182c; Martin Molcan 16tl, 522–3; Enrico Morando 327tr; Moskwa 134tr; Roland Nagy 12bc; Nexus7 132; Fabio Nodari 2–3; Odrachenko 29crb; Olegmit 355t; Olgacov 638bl; Andrey Omelyanchuk 143bl; Palaine 17cl; Patrickwang 1c; Petr 122cl; Photoprofi30 507bc; Photowitch 29cr; Patrick Poendl 287tl; Beatrice Preve 327bl; 480; Ondřej Prosický 375br; Richair 630cla; Ricok 28cla; Rndmst 544tc; Guy Rouget 28tr; Sam74100 518brl; Richard Semik 29tr, 29bl, 210; Jose I. Soto 264–5; Stevanzz 534br; Timothy Stirling 548–9; Takepicsforfun 234cl; Tehnik83 524tl; Anibal Trejo 443tr; Tupungato 74–5; Vlastas 234tr; Viachaslau Zhukau 43b; **Alain Ducasse Entreprise:** 572cra.**Editions Tallandier:** 46, 48cb, 51tl, 52br, 52br–53bl, 55tl, 55cb, 56cl, 57tr, 58br, 62clb, 62bl, 62cr–63cl,

63crb, 63bc, 65tr, 65crb, 65br, 67bl, 67bc, 68cla, 68crb, 69tc, 69cra; **L'Ermitage Hotel:** 565bc; **Estaminet T'Kasteel Hof:** 580tl; **ET Archive:** 304bl; Cathedral Treasury, Aachen 4tr; 52cla; Musée Carnavalet, Paris 65tl; Museum of Fine Arts, Lausanne 59br; Musée d'Orsay, Paris 65cra; Musée de Versailles 60bl; 303bl; National Gallery, Scotland 62br; V&A Museum, London 57tl; 347bl; **European Commission:** 679; **Mary Evans Picture Library:** 50br, 54bl, 55c, 57br, 60cla, 62c, 66bc, 67cr, 67br, 69br, 117clb, 181cb, 187c, 195tc, 201bc, 295br, 297tr, 305bl, 370b, 459tr, 477br; Explorer 35br; **La Ferme aux Grives:** 595bc; Xavier Boymond 573tr; **Festival d'Avignon:** Marc Chaumeil 608cl; **Festival International du Film de la Rochelle:** 608br; **Fleur de Sel:** 562bc; **Foundation Royaumont:** J Johnson 176tl; **Fotolia:** Paula Kirsch 14bl.**Georges Blanc:** 591tr; **Getty Images:** AFP/Jean Ayissi 641tl; De Agostini Picture Library 488t; Andia 363cr; Christophel Fine Art 56bc, 304br; Soltan Frédéric 72-73c; Historical Picture Archive 69tl; Hulton Archive 195br; Glenn Van Der Knijff 529cr; Leemage / Photo Josse 69c; MIGUEL MEDINA 73ca; Manfred Mehlig 632bl; National Geographic/Ed George 635cla; Panoramic Images 155br; Sergio Pitamitz 641bl; David Pollack 70bc, 362bc; Pascal Preti 618–19; Peter Scholey 621tl; Stringer 72bc; Stringer/John Chillingworth 520bc; Stringer/London Express 70crb; Stringer/Thurston Hopkins 305br; swim ink 2 llc 478tr; UniversalImagesGroup 58clb; WireImage/Tony Barson 71bc; **Giraudon, Paris:** 32cla, 21cb, 33cra, 33crb, 50cla, 52clb, 53tl, 54cl, 56cr–57cl, 60clb, 62cl, 64cl, 64cr–65cl, 337br, 351br, 373br, 495cb MS Nero Ell pt.2 fol. 20V0; Lauros-Giraudon 48bc, 49tc, 49crb, 49cb, 49br, 51ca, 53tr, 55crb, 59cr, 64clb, 64br–65bl, 495cl; Musée d'Art Moderne, Paris 32cb; Musée de Beaux-Arts, Quimper 32cl; **Le Grand Véfour:** 576bl; **Ronald Grant Archive:** 70clb. **La Halle Saint Pierre:** *Untitled* Stavroula Feleggakis 137br; **Sonia Halliday Photographs:** Laura Lushington 313cla; **Robert Harding Picture Library:** 34bl, 41tr, 43tr, 43clb, 47cb, 116br, 247tr, 326bl, 326br, 327br, 353tr, 404cla, 441cr, 465tr, 493bc; C Bowman 456tc; Explorer, Paris 71br; 105bl, 366tl, 375cra, 464cb, 465tl, 488bl, 613bl, 639tl; Robert Francis 28bl; D Hughes 396–7; Peter Langer 419tc; W Rawlings 53br, 71tl, 241tl, 260bc; A.Wolfitt 30tr; **Hemispheres Images:** Hervé Hughes 263br; **John Heseltine:** 143c; Honfleur, Musée Boudin: 266bl; **Hotel le Mas Trilles:** *596tc;* Stavroula Feleggakis 137br; **David Hughes:** 371t, 371b; **L'Huitrière:** 574tr; **Hôtel Imperator:** 569br; **Jacana:** JM Labat 465bc; **Le Jardin Gourmand:** 575tr, 589tl; **Restaurant Patrick Jeffroy:** 585bl; **Trevor Jones:** 208bl; **Louis XV Monaco:** Bernard Touillon 602br; **Magnum Photos ltd:** 25c; Bruno Barbey 24br, 35tr, 40bl; R Capa 476tr; P Halsman 529bl; **La Maison d'Olivier Leflaive:** 590bl; **Manoir du Vaumadeuc:** 560tr; **The Mansell Collection:** 35tl, 286t, 299br, 463bc; **Hotel Marotte:** 556bl; **Le Marquière:** 599bx; **Mas Daumas Gassac:** 474cr; **Michel Bras:** Aragorn agence de communication 592tr; **John Miller:** 228bl, 340tr, 411br; **Montpellier Danse Festival:** 609br; Musée de l'Annonciade, St-Tropez: 528tr; Musée d'Art Moderne et Contemporain de Strasbourg: Edith Rodeghiero 235bl; Musée des Beaux-Arts, Carcassonne: 493tl; Musée des Beaux-Arts, Dijon: 347tl; Musée des

Beaux-Arts de Lyon: 385cra, 385c, 385br; Musée de la Civilisation Gallo-Romaine, Lyon: 51cr, 382clb; Musée Courbet: Pierre Guénat 355br; Musée Departmental Breton, Quimper: 278clb; Musée Flaubert, Rouen: 269bl; Museum National d'Histoire Naturelle, Paris: 142c; Musée National d'Art Moderne, Paris: 96clb, 97tc, 97cra, 97cb, 339br; Musée Réattu, Arles: M Lacanaud 512ca; Cliché Musée de Sens/J P Elie: 334tl; Musée Toulouse-Lautrec, Albi: 448bc; **Network Photographers:** Barry Lewis 342t; Rapho/Mark Buscail 613tc; Rapho/De Sazo 613br; **Hôtel Normandy Barrière:** 559bc; **Office de Tourisme de Dijon:** Musée Magnin 345fcr; **Orient-Express Hotels Trains & Cruises:** 552tl; Hotel du Palais 568tl; **OTC Marseille:** 638tl, 640cla; **Photos Editions Combier, Mâcon:** 207tc; **Photolibrary:** Jean-Marc Romain 625cr, Widmann Widmann/F1 Online 626bl; **Pictures Colour Library:** 406clb, 430, 670–71; **Le Pirate:** 603br; **Michel le Poer Trench:** 34br; Bernard Prerost 97b; **Le Pont de l'Ouysse:** 567tc; **Popperfoto:** 255cr; **La Poste:** 629bl; **Les Pres d'Eugenie:** Tim Clinch 566bc; **Pyrenees Magazine/DR:** 404bl. **Reims Tourisme:** Carmen Moya 214tl, 214cr; **Rennes Tourisme:** Jose Mouret 288bl; **Restaurant de La Tour d'Argent:** 574br; **Réunion des Musées Nationaux:** Musée des Antiquités Nationales 407cr; Musée Guimet 115tl; Musée du Louvre 61ca, 105bl, 106cla, 106bl, 106br, 107tl, 107c, 107bc; Musée Picasso 92cl, 94br, 477tr; Musée de Versailles 183tl; **RF Reynolds:** 248tl; **M Reynard:** 674b; **Rocamadour:** 441tr; **Roger-Viollet:** 117cla; **Réunion des Musées Nationaux:** *Le Duo* (1937) by Georges Braque, Collections du Centre Pompidou, Musée National d'Art Moderne, 97cra; **Le Sin:** 598tc; **Sipa Press:** 136bl; **Photo SNCM/Southern Ferries:** 630br; **SNCF – Société National des Chemins de Fer:** 634bc, Fabbro & Levesque 633tr; **Spectrum Colour Library:** P Thompson 253br; **Frank Spooner Pictures:** Simon 71ca; 71crb; **STA Travel Group:** 674tr; **Tony Stone Images:** 326c; **SuperStock:** age fotostock/ J.D. Dallet 425bl; Hemis.fr 596bl; Hemis.fr/SUDRES Jean-Daniel 441bc; **Sygma:** 535t; C de Bare 40cr; L'Illustration 112tl; T Prat 440cl; L de Raemy 70br. **Telarci:** 53cr; **Les Terraillers:** 601tl; **Tourist Office Semur-en-Auxois:** 339tr; **Les Ursulines Hotel:** Gourmet restaurant 574tl. **Jean Vertut:** 48br–49bl; **La Villa:** U Callelu 603tl; **Visual Arts Library:** 33cr; **O. Zimmerman/Musée d'Unterlinden 6800 Colmar:** 231tl.

Front Endpaper: **Alamy Images:** Jon Arnold Images Ltd Ltl; Hemis Rtl, Lcl; incamerastock Ltc; Brian Jannsen Rtr; LOOK Die Bildagentur der Fotografen GmbH Rbr; mcx images Rcrb; nagelstock.com Rcb; James Osmond Photography Lbl; SFL Choice Lbc; **Dreamstime.com:** Flaviu Boerescu Rca; Claudio Giovanni Colombo Rcr; Gynane Lc; Beatrice Preve Rbl; Joern Rynio Rcra; Richard Semik Rtc.

Back Endpaper: **Alamy Images:** Martin Bache Rtc; Valerijis Kostreckis Lbc; **Dreamstimecom:** Sergey Kelin Rtr; Luciano Mortula Lclb.

Cover: Front and spine – **4Corners:** Olimpio Fantuz; Back – **Dreamstime.com:** Elena Duvernay.

All other images © Dorling Kindersley. For more information see www.dkimages.com

# Phrase Book

## In Emergency

| | | |
|---|---|---|
| Help! | **Au secours!** | oh se**koor** |
| Stop! | **Arrêtez!** | aret-**ay** |
| Call a doctor! | **Appelez un médecin!** | apuh-**lay** uñ medsañ |
| Call an ambulance! | **Appelez une ambulance!** | apuh-**lay** oon oñboo-**loñs** |
| Call the police! | **Appelez la police!** | apuh-**lay** lah poh-**lees** |
| Call the fire department! | **Appelez les pompiers!** | apuh-**lay** leh poñ-**peeyay** |
| Where is the nearest telephone? | **Où est le téléphone le plus proche?** | oo ay luh tehleh**fon** luh ploo prosh |
| Where is the nearest hospital? | **Où est l'hôpital le plus proche?** | oo ay l'**o**peetal luh ploo **prosh** |

## Communication Essentials

| | | |
|---|---|---|
| Yes | **Oui** | wee |
| No | **Non** | noñ |
| Please | **S'il vous plaît** | seel voo play |
| Thank you | **Merci** | mer-**see** |
| Excuse me | **Excusez-moi** | exkoo-**zay** mwah |
| Hello | **Bonjour** | boñzhoor |
| Goodbye | **Au revoir** | oh ruh-**vwar** |
| Good night | **Bonsoir** | boñ-**swar** |
| Morning | **Le matin** | matañ |
| Afternoon | **L'après-midi** | l'apreh-**meedee** |
| Evening | **Le soir** | swar |
| Yesterday | **Hier** | eeyehr |
| Today | **Aujourd'hui** | oh-zhoor-**dwee** |
| Tomorrow | **Demain** | duhmañ |
| Here | **Ici** | ee-**see** |
| There | **Là** | lah |
| What? | **Quel, quelle?** | kel, kel |
| When? | **Quand?** | koñ |
| Why? | **Pourquoi?** | poor-**kwah** |
| Where? | **Où?** | oo |

## Useful Phrases

| | | |
|---|---|---|
| How are you? | **Comment allez-vous?** | kom-moñ tal**ay voo** |
| Very well, thank you. | **Très bien, merci.** | treh byañ, mer-**see** |
| Pleased to meet you. | **Enchanté de faire votre connaissance.** | oñshoñ-**tay** duh fehr votr kon-ay-**sans** |
| See you soon. | **A bientôt.** | byañ-**toh** |
| That's fine | **Voilà qui est parfait** | vwalah kee ay par**fay** |
| Where is/are…? | **Où est/sont…?** | oo ay/soñ |
| How far is it to…? | **Combien de kilomètres d'ici à…?** | kom-**byañ** duh keelo-metr d'ee-**see** ah |
| Which way to…? | **Quelle est la direction pour…?** | kel ay lah deer-ek-**syoñ** poor |
| Do you speak English? | **Parlez-vous anglais?** | par-lay voo oñg-**lay** |
| I don't understand. | **Je ne comprends pas.** | zhuh nuh kom-proñ pah |
| Could you speak slowly, please? | **Pouvez-vous parler moins vite, s'il vous plaît.** | poo-**vay** voo par-**lay** mwañ veet seel voo play |
| I'm sorry. | **Excusez-moi.** | exkoo-**zay** mwah |

## Useful Words

| | | |
|---|---|---|
| big | **grand** | groñ |
| small | **petit** | puh-**tee** |
| hot | **chaud** | show |
| cold | **froid** | frwah |
| good | **bon** | boñ |
| bad | **mauvais** | moh-**veh** |
| enough | **assez** | as**say** |
| well | **bien** | byañ |
| open | **ouvert** | oo-**ver** |
| closed | **fermé** | fer-**meh** |
| left | **gauche** | gohsh |
| right | **droit** | drwah |
| straight ahead | **tout droit** | too drwah |
| near | **près** | preh |
| far | **loin** | lwañ |
| up | **en haut** | oñ oh |
| down | **en bas** | oñ bah |
| early | **de bonne heure** | duh bon urr |
| late | **en retard** | oñ ruh-**tar** |
| entrance | **l'entrée** | l'on-**tray** |
| exit | **la sortie** | sor-**tee** |
| restroom | **les toilettes, les WC** | twah-let, vay-**see** |
| free, unoccupied | **libre** | leebr |
| free, no charge | **gratuit** | grah-**twee** |

## Making a Telephone Call

| | | |
|---|---|---|
| I'd like to make a long-distance call. | **Je voudrais faire un interurbain.** | zhuh **voo**-dreh fehr uñ añter-**oor**bañ |
| I'd like to make a collect call. | **Je voudrais faire une communication PCV.** | zhuh voo**dreh** fehr oon ko**moo**nikah-**syoñ** peh-seh-veh |
| I'll try again later. | **Je rappelerai plus tard.** | zhuh rapel-**eray** ploo tar |
| Can I leave a message? | **Est-ce que je peux laisser un message?** | es-**keh** zhuh puh leh-**say** uñ mehsazh |
| Hold on. | **Ne quittez pas, s'il vous plaît.** | nuh kee-**tay** pah seel voo play |
| Could you speak up a little, please? | **Pouvez-vous parler un peu plus fort?** | poo-**vay** voo par-**lay** uñ puh ploo for |
| local call | **la communication locale** | komoonikah-**syoñ** low-kal |

## Shopping

| | | |
|---|---|---|
| How much does this cost? | **C'est combien s'il vous plaît?** | say kom-**byañ** seel voo play |
| I would like… | **Je voudrais…** | zhuh voo-**dray** |
| Do you have? | **Est-ce que vous avez?** | es-**kuh** voo zavay |
| I'm just looking. | **Je regarde seulement.** | zhuh ruh**gar** suhl**moñ** |
| Do you take credit cards? | **Est-ce que vous acceptez les cartes de crédit?** | es-**kuh** voo zaksept-**ay** leh kart duh kreh-**dee** |
| Do you take travelers' checks? | **Est-ce que vous acceptez les chèques de voyage?** | es-**kuh** voo zaksept-**ay** leh shek duh vway**azh** |
| What time do you open? | **A quelle heure vous êtes ouvert?** | ah kel urr voo zet oo-**ver** |
| What time do you close? | **A quelle heure vous êtes fermé?** | ah kel urr voo zet fer-**may** |
| This one. | **Celui-ci.** | suhl-wee-**see** |
| That one. | **Celui-là.** | suhl-wee-**lah** |
| expensive | **cher** | shehr |
| cheap | **pas cher, bon marché** | pah shehr, boñ mar-**shay** |
| size, clothes | **la taille** | tye |
| size, shoes | **la pointure** | pwañ-**tur** |
| white | **blanc** | bloñ |
| black | **noir** | nwahr |
| red | **rouge** | roozh |
| yellow | **jaune** | zhohwn |
| green | **vert** | vehr |
| blue | **bleu** | bluh |

## Types of Stores

| | | |
|---|---|---|
| antiques shop | **le magasin d'antiquités** | maga-**zañ** d'oñteekee-**tay** |
| bakery | **la boulangerie** | booloñ-**zhuree** |
| bank | **la banque** | boñk |
| bookstore | **la librairie** | lee-**brehree** |
| butcher | **la boucherie** | boo-**shehree** |
| cake store | **la pâtisserie** | patee-**sree** |
| cheese store | **la fromagerie** | fromazh-**ree** |
| dairy | **la crémerie** | krem-**ree** |
| department store | **le grand magasin** | groñ maga-**zañ** |
| delicatessen | **la charcuterie** | sharkoot-**ree** |
| fish seller | **la poissonnerie** | pwasson-**ree** |
| gift shop | **le magasin de cadeaux** | maga-**zañ** duh ka**doh** |
| greengrocer | **le marchand de légumes** | mar-**shoñ** duh lay-**goom** |
| grocery store | **l'alimentation** | alee-moñta-**syoñ** |
| hair salon | **le coiffeur** | kwa**fuhr** |
| market | **le marché** | marsh-**ay** |
| newsstand | **le magasin de journaux** | maga-**zañ** duh zhoor-**no** |
| pharmacy | **la pharmacie** | farmah-**see** |
| post office | **la poste, le bureau de poste, le PTT** | pohst, booroh duh pohst, peh-teh-teh |
| shoe store | **le magasin de chaussures** | maga-**zañ** duh show-**soor** |
| supermarket | **le supermarché** | soo pehr-**marshay** |
| tobacconist | **le tabac** | tabah |
| travel agent | **l'agence de voyages** | l'**azh**oñs duh vway**azh** |

## Sightseeing

| | | |
|---|---|---|
| abbey | **l'abbaye** | l'abay-**ee** |
| art gallery | **la galerie d'art** | galer-**ree** dart |
| bus station | **la gare routière** | gahr roo-tee-**yehr** |

| cathedral | la cathédrale | katay-**dral** |
| church | l'église | ayg**leez** |
| garden | le jardin | zhar-**dañ** |
| library | la bibliothèque | beeb**leeo**-tek |
| museum | le musée | moo-**zay** |
| tourist information office | les renseignements touristiques, le syndicat d'initiative | roñsayn-**moñ** too-rees-**teek**, sandee-ka d'eenee-sya**teev** |
| town hall | l'hôtel de ville | oh**tel** duh veel |
| train station | la gare (SNCF) | gahr (es-en-say-ef) |
| private mansion | l'hôtel particulier | ohtel partikoo-**lyay** |
| closed for public holiday | fermeture jour fériée | fehrmeh-**tur** zhoor fehree-**ay** |

## Staying in a Hotel

| Do you have a vacant room? | Est-ce que vous avez une chambre? | es-kuh voo-**zavay** oon shambr |
| double room, with double bed | la chambre à deux personnes, avec un grand lit | shambr ah duh pehr-**son**, avek un gronñ lee |
| twin room | la chambre à deux lits | shambr ah duh lee |
| single room | la chambre à une personne | shambr ah oon pehr-**son** |
| room with a bathtub, shower | la chambre avec salle de bains, une douche | shambr avek sal duh bañ, oon doosh |
| bell-hop | le garçon | gar-**soñ** |
| key | la clef | klay |
| I have a reservation. | J'ai fait une réservation. | zhay fay oon rayzehrva-**syoñ** |

## Eating Out

| Have you got a table? | Avez-vous une table libre? | avay-**voo** oon tahbl leebr |
| I want to reserve a table. | Je voudrais réserver une table. | zhuh voo-**dray** rayzehr-**vay** oon tahb |
| The check, please. | L'addition, s'il vous plaît. | l'adee-**syoñ** seel voo **play** |
| I am a vegetarian. | Je suis végétarien. | zhuh swee vezhay-**tehryañ** |
| Waitress/ waiter | Madame, Mademoiselle/ Monsieur | mah-**dam**, mah-demwah**zel**/ muh-**syuh** |
| menu | le menu, la carte | men-**oo**, kart |
| fixed-price menu | le menu à prix fixe | men-**oo** ah pree feeks |
| cover charge | le couvert | koo-**vehr** |
| wine list | la carte des vins | **kart**-deh vañ |
| glass | le verre | vehr |
| bottle | la bouteille | boo-**tay** |
| knife | le couteau | koo-**toh** |
| fork | la fourchette | for-**shet** |
| spoon | la cuillère | kwee-**yehr** |
| breakfast | le petit déjeuner | puh-**tee** deh-**zhuh-nay** |
| lunch | le déjeuner | deh-**zhuh-nay** |
| dinner | le dîner | dee-**nay** |
| main course | le plat principal | plah prañsee-**pal** |
| appetizer, first course | l'entrée, le hors d'oeuvre | oñ-**tray**, or-**duhvr** |
| dish of the day | le plat du jour | plah doo zhoor |
| wine bar | le bar à vin | bar ah vañ |
| café | le café | ka-**fay** |
| rare | saignant | say-**noñ** |
| medium | à point | ah **pwañ** |
| well done | bien cuit | byañ **kwee** |

## Menu Decoder

| l'agneau | an**yoh** | lamb |
| l'ail | eye | garlic |
| la banane | ba**nan** | banana |
| le beurre | burr | butter |
| la bière, bière à la pression | bee-**yehr**, bee-**yehr** ah lah pres-**syoñ** | beer draught beer |
| le bifteck, le steack | beef-**tek**, stek | steak |
| le boeuf | buhf | beef |
| bouilli | boo-**yee** | boiled |
| le café | kah-**fay** | coffee |
| le canard | kanar | duck |
| le chocolat | shoko-lah | chocolate |
| le citron | see-**troñ** | lemon |
| le citron pressé | see-**troñ** press-**eh** | fresh lemon juice |
| les crevettes | kruh-**vet** | shrimp |
| les crustacés | kroos-ta-**say** | shellfish |
| cuit au four | kweet oh foor | baked |

| le dessert | deh-**ser** | dessert |
| l'eau minérale | oh **meeney**-ral | mineral water |
| les escargots | zes-kar-**goh** | snails |
| les frites | freet | fries |
| le fromage | from-**azh** | cheese |
| le fruit frais | frwee freh | fresh fruit |
| les fruits de mer | frwee duh mer | seafood |
| le gâteau | gah-**toh** | cake |
| la glace | glas | ice, ice cream |
| grillé | gree-**yay** | grilled |
| le homard | omahr | lobster |
| l'huile | weel | oil |
| le jambon | zhoñ-**boñ** | ham |
| le lait | leh | milk |
| les légumes | lay-**goom** | vegetables |
| la moutarde | moo-**tard** | mustard |
| l'oeuf | uf | egg |
| les oignons | zonyoñ | onions |
| les olives | zo**leev** | olives |
| l'orange | oroñzh | orange |
| l'orange pressée | oroñzh press-**eh** | fresh orange juice |
| le pain | pan | bread |
| le petit pain | puh-**tee** pañ | roll |
| poché | posh-**ay** | poached |
| le poisson | pwah-**ssoñ** | fish |
| le poivre | pwavr | pepper |
| la pomme | pom | apple |
| les pommes de terre | pom-duh **tehr** | potatoes |
| le porc | por | pork |
| le potage | poh-**tazh** | soup |
| le poulet | poo-**lay** | chicken |
| le riz | ree | rice |
| rôti | row-**tee** | roast |
| la sauce | sohs | sauce |
| la saucisse | soh**sees** | sausage, fresh |
| sec | sek | dry |
| le sel | sel | salt |
| la soupe | soop | soup |
| le sucre | sookr | sugar |
| le thé | tay | tea |
| la viande | vee-**yand** | meat |
| le vin blanc | vañ **bloñ** | white wine |
| le vin rouge | vañ **roozh** | red wine |
| le vinaigre | vee**naygr** | vinegar |

## Numbers

| 0 | zéro | zeh-**roh** |
| 1 | un, une | uñ, oon |
| 2 | deux | duh |
| 3 | trois | trwah |
| 4 | quatre | katr |
| 5 | cinq | sañk |
| 6 | six | sees |
| 7 | sept | set |
| 8 | huit | weet |
| 9 | neuf | nerf |
| 10 | dix | dees |
| 11 | onze | oñz |
| 12 | douze | dooz |
| 13 | treize | trehz |
| 14 | quatorze | ka**torz** |
| 15 | quinze | kañz |
| 16 | seize | sehz |
| 17 | dix-sept | dees-**set** |
| 18 | dix-huit | dees-**weet** |
| 19 | dix-neuf | dees-**nerf** |
| 20 | vingt | vañ |
| 30 | trente | tront |
| 40 | quarante | karoñt |
| 50 | cinquante | sañkoñt |
| 60 | soixante | swasoñt |
| 70 | soixante-dix | swasoñt-**dees** |
| 80 | quatre-vingts | katr-**vañ** |
| 90 | quatre-vingt-dix | katr-vañ-**dees** |
| 100 | cent | soñ |
| 1,000 | mille | meel |

## Time

| one minute | une minute | oon mee-**noot** |
| one hour | une heure | oon urr |
| half an hour | une demi-heure | oon **duh-mee** urr |
| Monday | lundi | luñ-**dee** |
| Tuesday | mardi | mar-**dee** |
| Wednesday | mercredi | mehrkruh-**dee** |
| Thursday | jeudi | zhuh-**dee** |
| Friday | vendredi | voñdruh-**dee** |
| Saturday | samedi | sam-**dee** |
| Sunday | dimanche | dee-**moñsh** |

# Central Paris

La Seine

QUAI D'ORSAY

INVALIDES

Arc de Triomphe

CHAILLOT

Tour Eiffel

PARC DU CHAMP DE MARS

JARDINS DU TROCADERO

PLACE DE LA CONCORDE

JARDIN DES TUILERIES

Musée d'Orsay

Hôtel des Invalides

**Champs-Elysées and Invalides**
Pages 108–119
Street Finder maps 1–3, 5–8

**The Left Bank**
Pages 120–131
Street Finder maps 7–9, 12, 13

**Key**

- ▨ Major sight
- Ⓜ Métro station
- RER RER station
- ⛴ Riverboat boarding point

0 meters   500
0 yards    500